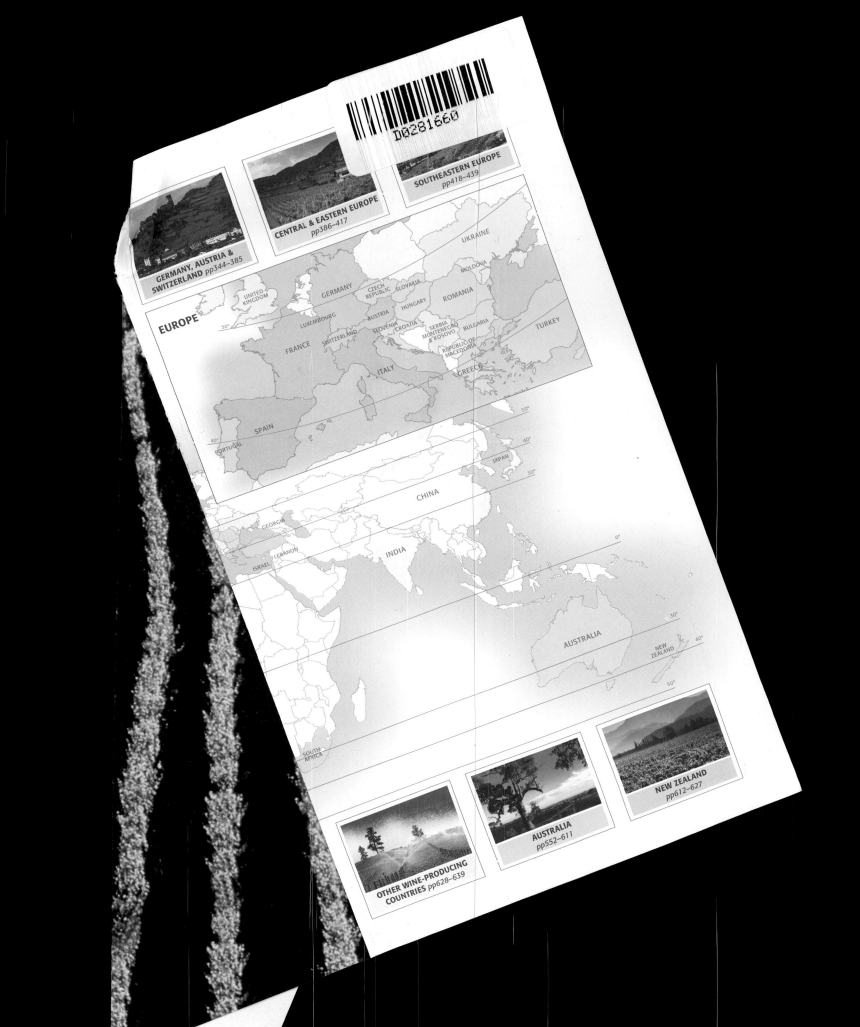

EUROPE

GERMANY, AUSTRIA &
SWITZERLAND pp344–385

CENTRAL & EASTERN EUROPE
pp386–417

SOUTHEASTERN EUROPE
pp418–439

OTHER WINE-PRODUCING
COUNTRIES pp628–639

AUSTRALIA
pp552–611

NEW ZEALAND
pp612–627

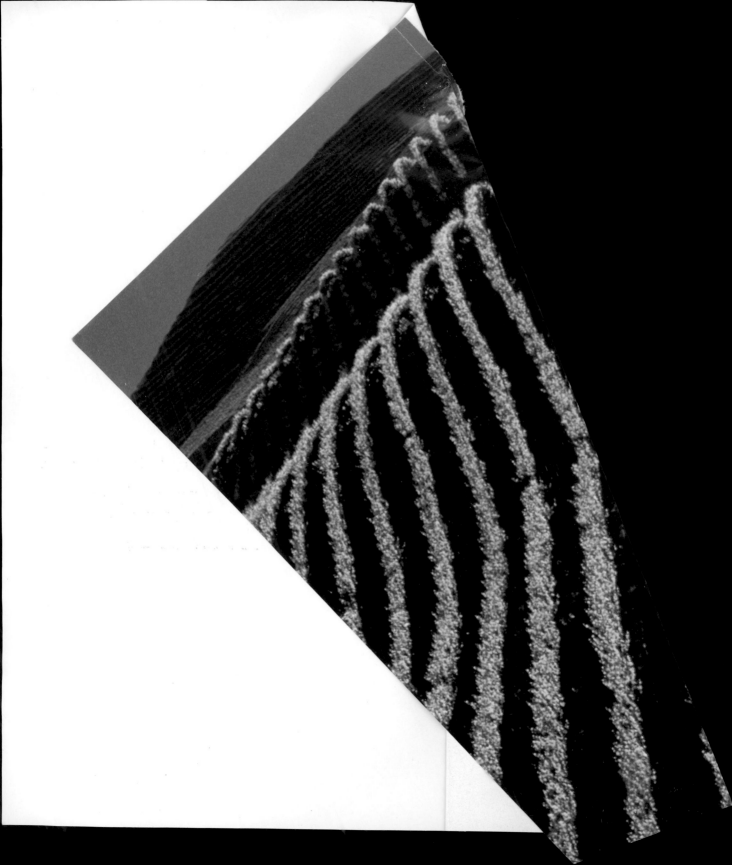

Wines
of the World

Consultant: SUSAN KEEVIL

Contributors: GEOFF ADAMS, CHRISTINE AUSTIN,
RICHARD BAUDAINS, JULIE BESONEN, KATHLEEN BUCKLEY,
STEPHEN BROOK, GILES FALLOWFIELD, DR CAROLINE GILBY MW,
RICHARD JONES, SUSAN KEEVIL, JAMES LAWTHER MW,
KONSTANTINOS LAZARAKIS, ANGELA LLOYD, GILES MacDONOGH,
RICHARD MAYSON, MICHAEL PALIJ MW, STUART PESKETT,
JENI PORT, JOHN RADFORD, ROGER VOSS, GARY WERNER,
DR PAUL WHITE, DAVID WILLIAMS

LONDON, NEW YORK, MUNICH,
MELBOURNE, DELHI

Produced for Dorling Kindersley
by Departure Lounge
Editorial Georgina Matthews, Ella Milroy,
Kelly Thompson, Debbie Woska,Caroline Blake
Design Lisa Kosky, Juliane Otterbach,
Lee Redmond, Clare Tomlinson
Maps Draughtsman Ltd

Revised edition produced
by Sands Publishing Solutions
Editorial David & Sylvia Tombesi-Walton
Design Simon Murrell

This revised edition published in 2009
by Dorling Kindersley Limited,
80 Strand, London WC2R 0RL

A Penguin Company

2 4 6 8 10 9 7 5 3 1

Copyright©2004, 2006, 2009
Dorling Kindersley Limited
Text copyright©2004, 2006, 2009
Dorling Kindersley Limited

A CIP catalogue record for this book
is available from the British Library
ISBN: 978-1-4053-4183-7
Reproduced by Colourscan, Singapore
Printed in China by South China Printing Company Ltd

Discover more at
www.dk.com

◁ **Napa Valley Vineyard, California, USA**

Contents

500ml PRODUCT OF SOUTH AFRICA Alc 13,5% Vol.

de Trafford

VIN DE PAILLE
Wine from naturally dried grapes
WINE OF ORIGIN STELLENBOSCH
1999

MONT FLEUR · PO BOX 495 · STELLENBOSCH · FAX 021 8801611

HOW TO USE THIS GUIDE

THIS GUIDE ENSURES YOU WILL GET maximum enjoyment from the world's myriad wine offerings. The first chapter sets wine in its historical and cultural context and gives an overview of grape varieties, wine styles, and production practices in the vineyard and in the winery. The following 13 country chapters provide insight into the world's most important winegrowing countries with an exploration of the key regions alongside expert recommendations of

top producers and individual wines. Specially-commissioned maps illustrate the key viticultural areas for each major wine region or country, while features and story boxes throughout the book focus on significant aspects of the wine industry, such as wine law and production methods. Finally, the last chapter gives essential reference information on everything from how to read a wine label to tips on tasting, buying, and storing wine, plus an essential glossary of wine terms.

Top Winegrowing Countries

There are 13 colour-coded country chapters, each focusing on a significant winegrowing country – or a group of two or more neighbouring countries. Each sub-section breaks down into the following elements: a general introduction; a wine map of the area; a round up of key winegrowing areas; and profiles of top producers. In addition, there are wine tours, story boxes, and thematic features within each chapter.

Chapter introduction

A map illustrates the key winegrowing regions or countries.

1 Country & Regional Introductions

The historical context of wine-making in each region, country, or group of countries is explored here, along with a snapshot of the wine industry today, and an overview of the dominant grape varieties and wine styles.

2 Wine Map

These maps show the main winegrowing regions or districts of a particular area or country.

Sub-section introduction

Each country can be easily identified by its colour coding.

A box gives an overview of climate, topography, and other factors relating to the *terroir* of the area.

Each main winegrowing area is colour-coded on the map.

A key gives all the colour-coded areas and the producers within each area, providing an easy reference for the content of the pages to follow.

3 Winegrowing Areas
These pages feature individual profiles on the key winegrowing areas and districts, giving an overview of the terroir, viticulture, winemaking, and wine characteristics.

Detailed information is given on the dominant soil types, red and white grapes grown, and wine styles for each key area.

Story boxes focus on important aspects of winegrowing.

4 Leading Producers
Top producers have been selected, with information on winemakers, house styles, and individual wines.

The Perfect Case lists 12 recommended wines. Symbols indicate the wine styles and £ signs the price range. (£ is the cheapest; ££££ the most expensive.)

Detailed information is given on the dominant wine styles, the best vintages, and recommended wines.

The region or district indicates where the producer's main winery is located. This is followed by contact details.

A Visitors' Tips box gives essential practical information including distance covered and general information on opening hours.

5 Regional Wine Tour
Wine tours feature a map and itinerary covering wine-related attractions in some of the world's most famous wine regions.

Each attraction covered is numbered on the map.

KEY TO SYMBOLS

R	Red	**⬛**	Soil type	**◻**	Winery open to public
W	White	**🏛**	White grape variety	**●**	Winery closed to public
r	Rose	**🏛**	Red grape variety	**📷**	Best vintages
S	Sparkling	**🏛**	Wine styles	**★**	Recommended wines
D	Dessert	**📞**	Telephone number	**☰**	Key producers
F	Fortified	**w**	Website	**◫**	Area under cultivation

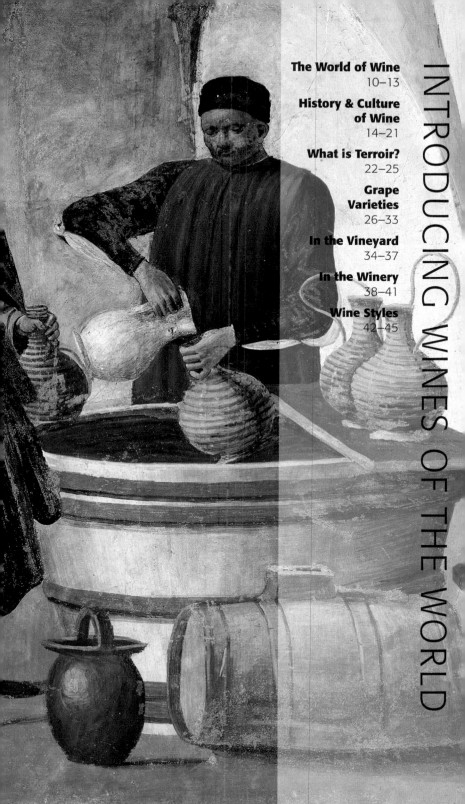

INTRODUCING WINES OF THE WORLD

THE WORLD OF WINE

WINE IS A PURE REFLECTION *of its* terroir (see pp22–5) *and no other single product sums up its cultural, geographical, and historical origins in quite the same way. Each harvest yields wines that are the culmination of different climatic and human processes, so no two wines are ever identical. Wine is as simple or as complex as you wish: on one level it can be an immediate sensory pleasure, or, at a deeper level, the embodiment of a piece of land and a moment in time.*

ORIGINS & CULTURAL SIGNIFICANCE OF WINE

WINE IS THOUGHT to have originated in the Caucasus mountains of Georgia and it has been part of world culture since historical records began. A feature of ancient Greek and Roman civilizations the god Dionysus (or Bacchus) invited celebration with wine, bringing it firmly into the Mediterranean way of life. Subsequently, it became an important part of Christian religion, with European monasteries in the Middle Ages doing much to advance the quality of wine, improving vinegrowing techniques and winemaking operations in the cellar.

In the 16th century, as Europeans ventured into the New World, their religion and their vines went with them. Being clean and safer to drink than water, wine became as much a part of daily life for slaking thirst as it was an important element of religious tradition. Meanwhile, wine trading in

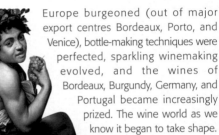

Bacchus painting by Caravaggio (1598)

Europe burgeoned (out of major export centres Bordeaux, Porto, and Venice), bottle-making techniques were perfected, sparkling winemaking evolved, and the wines of Bordeaux, Burgundy, Germany, and Portugal became increasingly prized. The wine world as we know it began to take shape.

Today, more than ever, wine is a part of everyday life throughout the world, both as a celebratory drink and a versatile partner to food. That it has become so intrinsic to world culture is hardly surprising. Aside from the relaxing effects of alcohol, wine continues to fascinate with its ever-changing character, so inextricably linked to the land, people, and culture that created it.

THE EXPANDING WORLD OF WINE

AT THE END OF THE 20TH CENTURY the world had over 8 million hectares under vine and was producing nearly 300 million hectolitres of wine. It is now made virtually all over the world

◁ **Detail of a fresco from San Martino dei Buonomini, Florence, by Ghirlandaio**

from Chile to South Africa to New Zealand and China. The world map of wine *(see front endpaper)* shows that vineyards are concentrated between 32° and 51° in the northern hemisphere, and between 28° and 42° in the southern.

Mediterranean Europe is the heartland of viticulture; here there are around 240 hours of sunshine a month, temperatures averaging 17°C in the growing season, an annual rainfall of around 600mm, and a crisp coldness to the winters, which allows the vines a period of dormancy. The classic regions of Bordeaux, Burgundy, the Rhône Valley, Rioja, and Tuscany benefit from these ideal conditions, and their wines have consequently developed as global benchmarks. It is in these Old World regions that *terroir* is all important. Find the right *terroir* and the resulting wines will have the most harmonious composition with acidity, sweetness, fruit flavours, and tannins, all poised to perfection. With the wrong *terroir*, the harvest will all too often fail.

It is the pursuit of new *terroir* that has led winegrowers to venture into viticulturally unexplored corners of Europe and into the New World. Many of the new-found lands have proved easy vineyard territory, growing grapes prolifically in the heat with little apparent effort. But more and more, producers have found that the best wines have come from vineyards where heat is tempered by the soothing effects of

Enjoying wine at Voyager Estate, Australia

water – a lake, river or coastline – or the cooling influence of altitude. When the vines have to work that bit harder to survive, grapes tend to develop more refined flavours.

OLD WORLD VERSUS NEW

TODAY WINE IS SAID TO come from the Old World or the New. The Old World is the heartland of vinegrowing, where viticulture has evolved since 7000 BC. The classic regions of France, Italy, and Spain are at the core, and sum up all that is traditional about making wine the time-honoured way. The New World comprises the pioneering vineyards of the southern hemisphere and North America, which were established by explorers and missionaries from the 14th century onwards. Chile, Argentina, Australia, New Zealand, California, and South Africa all fall into the New World category.

Tending the vines in spring at Panther Creek in Oregon, USA

Until recently it was relatively easy to pick up a glass of wine and identify, with a sniff and a sip, whether it was from the New World or the Old. A New World wine would have all the rich fruit flavours and aromas that reflect warm-climate vineyards. An Old World example would be more subtle, with delicate, complex aromas and leaner, multi-dimensional flavours. Today, this difference is no longer as marked as it once was. Improved grape-growing and winemaking techniques mean that an Old World wine can taste as luscious as a New World version. New World winemakers are learning much from the traditional winemaking countries, and the Old World is learning a thing or two from the New as well. In hotter countries, viticulturalists are seeking out cooler pockets of vineyard to grow grapes with more subtle flavours. In the winery, Old World techniques such as barrel-fermenting, use of wild yeasts, and lees-stirring are all being adopted to generate more complexity in the wine. All of this means that the flavour boundaries between Old and New World wines are becoming increasingly blurred.

New World winery of Haras de Pirque, Chile

create virtually whatever he or she chooses. A few bottles of carefully crafted 'prestige' wine can be made from top-quality vineyards to reflect the *terroir,* or wine may be skilfully blended from many vineyards in greater, more commercial quantities. Each of these wines has its own advantages. The blended wines have the potential to become world 'brands'. The art with branded wines is to make each batch and each vintage the same as the last. These are wines in which reliability comes first. As they are made in bulk, they are also infinitely more affordable and widely available. Purists, however, argue that it is the estate wines that show the real diversity of wine. These wines are a true reflection of their land. Made on a smaller scale, they are more difficult to obtain, and can be significantly more expensive. These are the wines that evoke fervent opinions, passionate discussion, and genuine loyalty. They are also the wines that undergo near-miraculous flavour transformations when laid down to age for a few years. They have flavours and aromas that linger on the palate and memory. They are what real wine is all about.

ESTATE VERSUS BRANDED WINES

WINE IS MADE in many different styles and at many different quality levels. Techniques in the winery are now so advanced that, with recourse to appropriate grapes, a winemaker can

Old World château and vineyard, Burgundy

TRENDS IN WINE CONSUMPTION

IN THE TRADITIONAL wine-drinking countries – France, Italy, Spain – where production is high, there has been a considerable slump in consumption over the last 40 years. Firstly, water quality has improved, so wine is no longer needed as a general beverage; secondly, wine is no longer perceived as a nutritional source but as an impediment to work performance; and thirdly, there has been a decline in café drinking. Additionally, in an effort to combat overproduction and an unwanted European 'wine lake', wine is being produced in smaller quantities and to a higher standard. Quality (and the price that goes with it) means it is no longer used for quaffing, but for sipping and enjoying.

In the English-speaking world, however, the picture is quite different; wine consumption in the UK for example has risen by over 500 per cent since 1970. The surge in wine's popularity is a direct result of the huge quantities of affordable ripe-fruited New World wines flooding onto the market and the advent of 'branded' wines. Wine has become widely available to everyone via traditional merchants, easy-access supermarkets, and the internet and is no longer the preserve of a wealthy elite. With increased opportunities for cheaper foreign travel, potential wine drinkers are also now being introduced to a greater variety of wines.

There is also a general belief that wine and healthy living go hand in hand. Wine's benefits as a sociable beverage, a health-giver, and an all-round focus of interest suggest that it will be part of culture for many years to come.

Wine Production (1,000s hectolitres) 2006

Italy	52,000
France	51,700
Spain	39,300
USA	19,700
Argentina	15,400
Australia	13,900
South Africa	9,200
Germany	9,000
Chile	8,400
Portugal	7,400
Greece	3,910
Hungary	3,000
Austria	2,260
New Zealand	1,300
Switzerland	1,010
UK	25
Canada	not available

Wine Consumption (litres per capita/pa) 2005

France	55.85
Italy	48.16
Portugal	46.67
Switzerland	39.87
Spain	34.66
Hungary	33.06
Argentina	28.81
Austria	28.81
Australia	24.67
Germany	24.51
Greece	22.92
UK	18.97
New Zealand	16.68
Chile	15.50
Canada	10.48
USA	8.69
South Africa	8.37

Harvesting grapes in Australia for the Jacob's Creek brand

THE ANCIENT WORLD

WINE HAS BEEN FIRMLY *established at the heart of civilization since ancient times. The first evidence of domesticated agriculture reveals the vine among the crops cultivated. From the 'cradle of viticulture' (Armenia, Georgia, and the shores of the Black Sea), through Egypt, Greece, and into other parts of Europe, the vine burgeoned as a crop, and thrived as a dietary, social, economic, and cultural necessity.*

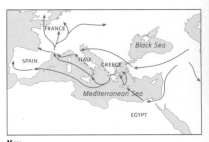

KEY

→ Spread of viticulture up to 1st century AD

Dionysus, Original Wine God ◁

The Greeks drank to the god Dionysus (featured on bowl left) in order to banish their worries, a tradition inherited by the Romans, who called their god Bacchus.

Greek Amphora ▷

Used for fermenting, ageing, storing, and transporting wine, amphorae came in varying shapes, sizes, and designs reflecting their origins and the aspirations of the producer. This one is from Cyprus, c540 BC.

Transporting Wine by River ◁

The Rhône and Mosel rivers were important trading routes for wine in Germany and France. Wooden barrels, like these carved on this wine merchant's tomb in Neumagen, began to be used around the 2nd century AD.

TIMELINE

7,000 BC First evidence of intentionally cultivated grapes in Georgia	**3,150 BC** Wine jars buried with the early Egyptian king Scorpion I; jars contain traces of wine	**1,600 BC** Evidence of wine press at Palaikastro on Crete. Mycenaean rulers of Crete introduced viticulture to mainland Greece	**300 BC** Greece begins to dominate the Mediterranean wine 'industry', instigating its spread to Italy, southern France, and the Iberian Peninsula

Roman amphora

6,000 BC   **2,000 BC**   **1000 BC**

5,000 BC Earliest evidence of stored wine in the Zagros mountains of western Iran	**2,750 BC** Wine mentioned in texts written on clay tablets in the city of Ur, Mesopotamia	**1,750 BC** Code of Babylonian King Hammurabi set laws regulating the retail trade of wine	**1,500 BC** First hollow glass drinking vessels made in Egypt; these were later widely made and used by the Romans	**186 BC** Cult of god Bacchus banned as too debauched for Rome

Bacchus at Vesuvius

◁ *When Mount Vesuvius erupted in AD 79, destroying Pompeii and its surrounding vineyards, the Romans had to urgently find new sources of wine and prices sky-rocketed. Preserved evidence, such as this 1st century Pompeii wall painting, shows how important the cult of Bacchus was to the Romans.*

Vines were trained on high pergolas on the fertile Nile Delta and the grapes collected in wicker baskets.

Red grapes and dark juice were shown on most paintings, suggesting red grapes were trodden in troughs to extract colour.

WINE & CHRISTIANITY

The tradition of the Christian Eucharist (wine symbolizing Christ's blood, bread his body) has complex roots. The representation of wine as blood has Greek origins, pre-dating Christianity. Wine as a blessing is also part of the Jewish ritual. Christ's miracle of turning water into wine (at the wedding at Cana) echoes Roman feasts at which Bacchus was believed to have done the same. The Christian Eucharist had evolved into its current form by the 4th century AD, although images of the Eucharist date from earlier.

EGYPTIAN WINE HARVEST △

Detailed records of the Egyptian way of harvesting, making, and transporting wine are set down in paintings such as this, on the tomb of Nakht (1,500 BC), from ancient Thebes. Many of the techniques illustrated here are still used today.

Pliny's *Natural History* △

Roman writer, Pliny the Elder (AD 23–79), carefully catalogued the wines of his time by quality, variety, and country of origin, providing invaluable insights into the winemaking practices of the day.

1st century AD Romans introduce viticulture to Bordeaux area		**AD 92–280** Roman Emperor Domitian forbids planting of any more vines in Italy to protect against a significant shortfall in grain. Edict repealed in 280 AD and vineyards then expanded in France		**AD 300** Barrels supersede amphorae as vessels of transport	**AD 350** Vines now well-established around Trier and Mosel Valley in Germany
AD 100		**AD 200**		**AD 300**	
AD 65 Spaniard Columella sets down principles of viticulture in his work *De Re Rustica*	**Mount Vesuvius erupting**	**AD 79** Eruption of Mount Vesuvius destroys wine-shipping port of Pompeii	**Emperor Domitian**	**AD 300** Wine has become well established as part of Christian Eucharist	

THE MIDDLE AGES & THE RENAISSANCE

B Y THE EARLY MIDDLE AGES, *the production of wine had become so established within the Church that the future of Europe's vineyards was assured. From the late Middle Ages, wine became increasingly important: viticultural techniques were honed, favoured grape varieties cultivated, and pressing techniques in the winery improved. By this time wine also benefitted from a few years' ageing. With the increase in quality, transport and trade of wine in Europe boomed.*

KEY

→ Wine trade routes in Europe, 1500s

Making Medieval Wine ◁

In the early Middle Ages red winemaking was risky: treading fermenting grapes (as left) exposed workers to carbon dioxide, and therefore suffocation. In the late Middle Ages, as wine's durability became more important, grape presses became popular, since they extracted better-quality juice.

Harvesting dates were decided not only by the ripeness of the grapes but by the positioning of the moon and stars.

Burgundy's Wines ▽

Burgundy's vineyards, as seen in this medieval tapestry, thrived under Emperor Charlemagne and then the Cistercian monks, but were later neglected as the bubonic plague and years of warfare took their toll.

Renaissance Wine Flask ◁

In the 15th and 16th centuries, Venice was a wine trading hub. An enamelled wine flask such as this would have been precious, but not unusual given the wealth generated by wine.

CHÂTEAU SAUMUR IN THE LOIRE ▷

The September grape harvest is depicted here at Château Saumur in the Loire Valley (early 1400s). Loire wines were popular in the later Middle Ages. It would take 20 pickers one day to harvest 1ha of vines, and skilled vineyard workers became increasingly important as the demand for quality grew.

TIMELINE

c500 Collapse of Rome disrupts patterns of trade and has adverse effect on wine production; the Church, however, keeps viticulture alive	**816** Charlemagne's son, Louis, is crowned at Reims, securing the Carolingian Empire and establishing a royal connection for the local wines – champagne		**1000** Leif Ericsson reaches northern coast of Newfoundland where the number of wild vines inspires him to call it Vinland (or Wineland)
500	**750**		**1000**
632 On death of Mohammed, wine ceases to become part of daily life in Arabia	**750** Emperor Charlemagne is credited with organizing and setting down viticultural law in northern France and Germany	**c900** Caliph Ozman orders destruction of two thirds of the vineyards in Valencia, Spain **Leif Ericsson**	**c1050** French landowners clear land to extend vineyards; expansion also occurs in Germany and later Hungary

Charlemagne's Viticultural Laws ▷

Emperor Charlemagne's passion for wine and his detailed rules covering the planting of vines and winemaking helped many French and German vineyards out of the Dark Ages. Legend has it that he ordered white grapes to be planted in a red wine vineyard (Corton-Charlemagne) because the red wine stained his beard.

Monasteries & Wine △

Monastic vineyards contributed to the development of quality wine, but, since these wines were non-commercial, secular producers became increasingly important for general wine supply.

Records of grape names began in the 1300s. Many vineyards would have grown a mixture of varieties.

Wealth of the Merchants ▷

Edward I assured Bordeaux's vintners power and wealth in order to secure their loyalty. He granted them the freedom of the city of London and gave them the right to establish their own guild, the Vintners' Company.

THE RISE & FALL OF BORDEAUX

The marriage in 1152 of Eléanor Duchess of Aquitaine and Henry II *(below)* brought Bordeaux under the English crown for 300 years. Eléanor's favourite son, Richard (the Lion Heart), used Bordeaux as his base, making its wine his own. The trade between Bordeaux and England subsequently boomed. The preferred wine style changed from thin and white to increasingly desirable light red *clairet*. In 1453, the French won Bordeaux back. The trade restrictions that followed meant exports to England dwindled.

1200	c1300	1350		1453
Spain's vineyards make a full recovery as Muslim power ebbs	Cistercian monks extend vineyards in Burgundy and the Rhineland	Britain is absorbing roughly half of Bordeaux's total export of wine; by 1390 this has risen to 80 per cent		Bordeaux reverts back to French ownership. Sweeter wines from the Mediterranean and Spanish 'sack' (forerunner of sherry) become fashionable

1200		**1400**		**1500**

Vintners' seal

1152	1335	1420	1437	1550s
Marriage of Henry II and Eléanor of Aquitaine brings wine region of Bordeaux under the English crown for 300 years	Two thirds of municipal revenues in Bruges, Flanders are from taxes on imported wine	Portugal settles island of Madeira and begins vine cultivation for a new fortified wine	Vintners' Company established in London to regulate the city's retail and wholesale trade	Wine decreed to be better for general health than water (often tainted)

THE GOLDEN AGE

THE 1500–1800s WERE A PERIOD OF development and adventure in the history of wine. The Americas, South Africa, and Australia opened up for vine growing, while in Europe skills were being perfected for making sweet, sparkling, and fortified wines. The discovery of stronger glass for bottles and subsequently cork to seal them revolutionized how wine was stored. The classic wines of Europe could now be aged to perfection.

KEY

→ Spread of viticulture to 1900

Thomas Jefferson Champions Wine ◁
Following his time as US ambassador to France (1784–9), Jefferson brought many vines back to the United States. As president, he reduced wine taxes and spared no effort in promoting winegrowing in his own country.

On his Constantia estate Simon van der Stel experimented with grape varieties, brought in modern equipment, and ensured grapes were only harvested when properly ripe.

French Ships Arrive in Florida ◁
Refugee French Huguenots arrived in Florida in 1562 and settled in by cultivating vines. They were later expelled by Spanish settlers who almost certainly also grew vines and made wine here.

TIMELINE

c1520
Vines established in Mexico

1557
Argentinian vineyards are established

1568
Spanish settlers are probably first to make wine in North America

1660s
Sauternes area of Bordeaux begins producing sweet wines

1680s
English merchants reach the upper Douro Valley of Portugal and discover the forerunner of modern port

1500

1600

c1540
Vineyards planted in Chile

King Philip II

1597
Don Lorenzo Garcia establishes a winery in Mexico by direction of Spanish King Philip II – Parras de la Fuente winery still operates today

1630s
First modern wine bottles are created in Newcastle, England

1655
First shipment of vines arrives in Cape Town, South Africa

1679
English parliament bans French wines; Portuguese wine exports to England skyrocket

Bordeaux Château ◁

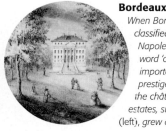

When Bordeaux wines were classified in 1855 (under Napoleon's instruction), the word 'château' bore little importance. Thereafter, the prestige and grandeur of the château buildings and estates, such as Margaux (left), grew and grew.

PHYLLOXERA VASTATRIX

Despite innocent appearances, *Phylloxera vastatrix* is the insect that caused wholesale devastation of the wine industry in the late 19th century. By attacking vine roots it wiped out swathes of vineyards at a time, first in England and southern France, then the Rhône Valley and Bordeaux, until in the 1880s yields in France had almost halved. From France it swept through Spain, Italy, Portugal, and Greece, where, due to expense, many vineyards were never replanted. Even today, the only method of addressing phylloxera is to graft European vines onto resistant American vine rootstock (see pp510–11).

Origins of Sparkling Wine ▷

The father of champagne, Dom Pérignon spent much of his life trying to avoid making sparkling wines (since he perceived the sparkle to be a flaw) but he knew how the fizz got there. By the time sparkling wine became fashionable (he was 60), his knowledge had become invaluable.

SOUTH AFRICA'S FIRST VINEYARDS △

Jan van Riebeeck, a Dutch doctor, first brought vines to South Africa's Cape in 1655; he rightly felt that the climate and landscape would be as suitable as Europe. After a shaky start, Dutch commander, Simon van der Stel revolutionized wine production with vine trials at his estate in Constantia (above), which was established in 1685.

Bottles for Every Wine ▷

By the early 1700s glass was strong enough to be used for transporting, storing, and ageing wine. Factories sprang up everywhere and bottles became widely available.

1769	1788	1820		1850s	1863
Monastic vineyards established at San Diego, USA	Captain Arthur Phillip brings vines to New South Wales, Australia	Viticulture reaches northern California	**Dom Pérignon**	Outbreak of powdery mildew reduces yields in French vineyards	First reports of infestation of phylloxera; effects on European vines are devastating.

1700 — **1800**

1703		Tasting wine at London docks 1821	1821	1840	1881
Methuen Treaty between England and Portugal ensures lower taxes on Portuguese wine (port) than French			Dom Pérignon credited with the invention of champagne	Two fifths of English imports are of sweet sherry	Programme of grafting French vines onto American rootstock discovered as effective defence against phylloxera

20TH CENTURY & THE NEW MILLENNIUM

THE 20TH CENTURY *has seen major technical advances in both winery and vineyard. The 1970s witnessed the discovery that the New World could compete with the 'classic' European regions in producing top quality wine. At the same time, bulk production forced a drop in quality, but the 1980s and 1990s brought technical advances. The new millennium heralded better quality and reliability than ever before.*

KEY

◼ *Winegrowing countries today*

Promoting Wines ▷

Ever-more elaborate advertising has been used to promote wine since this 1930s poster for champagne. Effective tools for generating sales have included the addition of a back label to describe the wine, and the use of grape names on the front label.

Prohibition in the USA △

Bottles of wine were systematically destroyed at the start of Prohibition in 1920; over the next 13 years the US wine industry virtually ground to a halt and did not recover until the 1960s.

Over-the-Row Vine Tractor △

Vineyard technology hit its stride in the 1960s with the introduction of machines able to straddle vines in order to spray, prune, and harvest. This made night harvesting and bulk vine-growing possible.

MODERN SUPER-WINERY △

With an even climate and extensive space the New World saw the advent of the super-wineries such as New Zealand's Montana *(above)*, which churn out millions of bottles per day. These factories offer wines that are affordable to all.

TIMELINE

1900				1950		1960
1914–18 World War I and subsequent depression has dampening effect on the wine industry	**1935** First AOC legislation passed in France, controlling yields, origin, minimum alcohol, methods of growing grapes, and winemaking	**Soldiers harvesting grapes, World War II**		**1950s** Technological advance hits vineyards: tractors for tending vines; sprays for more effective disease control, and more sophisticated clonal selection		**1957** Max Schubert makes 'the first great Australian wine: Grange Hermitage'
1920 Prohibition in the USA forbids the use of wine except for religious and medicinal purposes; industry slow to bounce back on repeal in 1933	**1940–45** World War II increased pressure on wine industry			**1950s** Improvement in quality of tap water across Europe sees wine becoming even less of an everyday item		**1960s** Varietal revolution begins to bring accessibility to wine – labelling wine with its grape variety pulls down smokescree

The Rise of the Boutique Winery △

Small-scale winemaking enables growers to concentrate on an individual vineyard and create wines that are terroir-focused. They have become important for quality wine production.

Paris Tasting, 1976 ▽

In a blind tasting that included cru classé bordeaux and Californian Cabernet-based wines, judges surprised themselves, and the world, by placing an American wine top. A huge boom of confidence in New World wines followed.

1973
Cabernet Sauvignon
Napa Valley
Stag's Leap Vineyard

STAG'S LEAP WINE CELLARS

WINE CRITICS

Commentators on wine are a modern phenomenon. Not only do they aid the public's understanding of a complex and changing subject, but the most influential (such as US writer Robert Parker, below) receive such an avid following that even the lightest praise can send prices of a wine sky-rocketing. Opponents argue that wine is a matter of taste as everybody's perception of aroma and flavour differs. Reliance on one critic's view severely limits the potential to enjoy wine and discover new flavours. Better to take an unbiased approach.

Progress in the Vineyard ▽

In the 1990s came a realization that fine wines are not only a result of good winemaking but also from care in the vineyard. Pruning to ensure low yields, keeping the vine in balance with its environment, and organic/biodynamic viticulture encourage quality results.

Stainless steel vats can moderate temperature, so wines now undergo a controlled fermentation even in the hottest regions.

Wine made in bulk has the advantage of being consistent and reliable – one bottle is much like another.

1964	1970s	1980s	1980s/90s
Big business wine begins in USA with the birth of the Gallo Brothers' empire *(right)* making wine for the mass market	Bag-in-box wine in Australia set to rival beer; thus begins the advent of bulk-made Australian wine	Government-sponsored vine-pull schemes see poor bulk-producing vinestock ripped out in favour of high-quality vines	Small boutique wineries in the New World increase push toward quality winemaking

1970   **1980**   **2000**

1963	1966	1976	1981	2000
Italy perfects its own appellation system (DOC/DOCG): Goria's Law	Napa Valley becomes the first American prestige appellation, with the founding of Robert Mondavi Winery	Paris tasting establishes quality of New World wine when Californian wine beats a French one	Émile Peynaud revolutionizes winemaking with his book setting out the importance of temperature-controlled fermentation	Top-class vintage in Bordeaux heralds the prime of the 'marketing' era of wine

WHAT IS TERROIR ?

IN EVERY VINEYARD, a unique combination of climate, topography, and soil type shapes the character of the vines that grow there and the grapes that they yield. The choices man makes for their cultivation, and for the subsequent transformation of the grapes into wine, reflect aspects of this distinct place. The French word *terroir*, literally meaning 'soil', is used to describe the entire environment in which the vine grows.

Maritime region of Provence, France

The dominant topographic feature is proximity to a large body of water.

Lack of natural landscape features may leave vineyards exposed to the elements, including strong winds.

Rows of trees can be planted to act as a windbreak.

Maritime settings are often located at low altitude.

High humidity can lead to fungal problems among leaves and grapes.

Maritime Climate

Proximity to a large body of water, such as an ocean, defines a maritime climate. The illustration below represents the key climatic factors associated with a maritime climate and their impact on growing vines.

Maritime regions are often subject to higher rainfall throughout the year.

Water absorbs and re-radiates the heat of the sun to moderate daily and seasonal temperature variation in nearby vineyards.

Flat terrain may make good soil drainage difficult.

Shoot positioning may be used to promote the circulation of air and minimize rot.

THE SIGNIFICANCE OF CLIMATE

Climate is the major factor determining the character of vines and grapes. Wine-producing areas are divided broadly into two climatic types: maritime (below) and continental (overleaf). The chart below compares them according to several atmospheric factors:

AVERAGE JULY FIGURES FOR TYPICAL MARITIME & CONTINENTAL CLIMATES

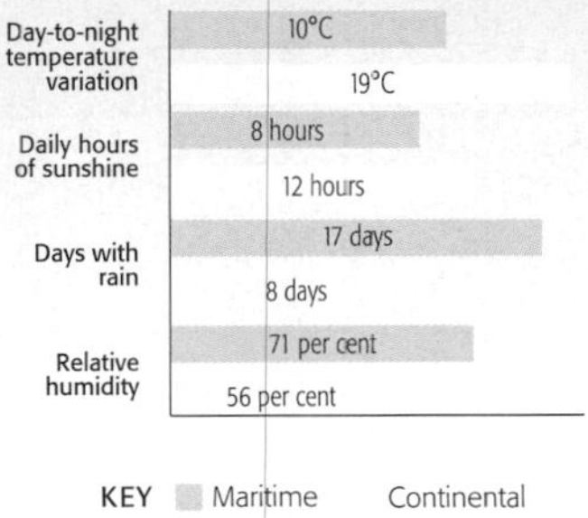

	Maritime	Continental
Day-to-night temperature variation	10°C	19°C
Daily hours of sunshine	8 hours	12 hours
Days with rain	17 days	8 days
Relative humidity	71 per cent	56 per cent

KEY Maritime   Continental

CLIMATIC SCALES

Wine-related discussions of climate often refer to three terms of scale:
• **Macroclimate** closely approximates what is meant colloquially by the word 'climate'. It refers to hundreds of square kilometres;
• **Mesoclimate** refers to hundreds of square metres, often the size of a vineyard;
• **Microclimate** concerns a tiny area, such as that between the rows of vines or even within the vine leaf canopy. (The term microclimate may be used when the area under consideration is actually large enough to be a mesoclimate.)

Continental Climate

Continental areas generally lack the influence of a large body of water, making the climate in these locations drier and sometimes sunnier. Continental regions experience wide temperature variation, both from day to night and from season to season. These extremes can be beneficial in that cooler nights slow grape development, and a longer growing season often yields riper and more flavourful fruit. Frost, however, is a significant danger in continental settings.

Continental region of Alto Adige, Italy

Slopes promote air circulation – warm air rises and cold air descends along the face of a hillside. This air movement helps prevent frost.

Bodies of water play a minor climatic role in continental areas.

Excessive leaf growth inhibits grape ripening.

Slopes facilitate soil drainage, which helps control vine vigour or leaf growth.

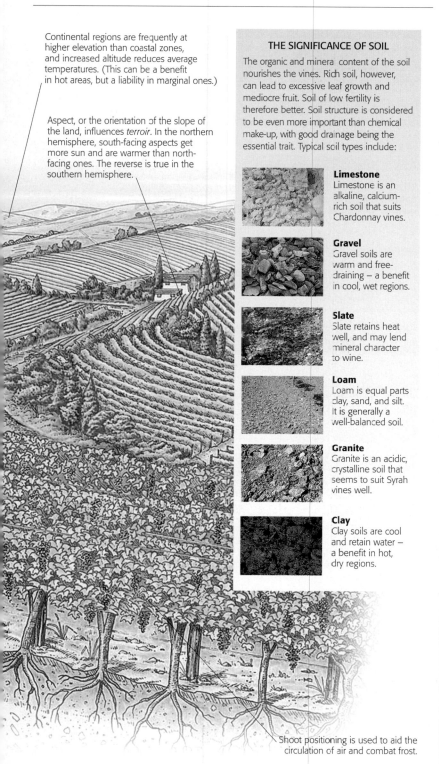

Continental regions are frequently at higher elevation than coastal zones, and increased altitude reduces average temperatures. (This can be a benefit in hot areas, but a liability in marginal ones.)

Aspect, or the orientation of the slope of the land, influences *terroir*. In the northern hemisphere, south-facing aspects get more sun and are warmer than north-facing ones. The reverse is true in the southern hemisphere.

THE SIGNIFICANCE OF SOIL

The organic and mineral content of the soil nourishes the vines. Rich soil, however, can lead to excessive leaf growth and mediocre fruit. Soil of low fertility is therefore better. Soil structure is considered to be even more important than chemical make-up, with good drainage being the essential trait. Typical soil types include:

Limestone
Limestone is an alkaline, calcium-rich soil that suits Chardonnay vines.

Gravel
Gravel soils are warm and free-draining – a benefit in cool, wet regions.

Slate
Slate retains heat well, and may lend mineral character to wine.

Loam
Loam is equal parts clay, sand, and silt. It is generally a well-balanced soil.

Granite
Granite is an acidic, crystalline soil that seems to suit Syrah vines well.

Clay
Clay soils are cool and retain water – a benefit in hot, dry regions.

Shoot positioning is used to aid the circulation of air and combat frost.

GRAPE VARIETIES

Athough terrain and winemaking techniques *play an important role, it is the individual grape variety or blend of grapes that is most influential in determining the taste of a wine. Familiarity with some of the most exceptional grape varieties is one of the best ways to appreciate the plethora of styles and flavours of the world's wines.*

LEADING RED GRAPE VARIETIES

These four red varieties are the most important in terms of quality and distribution.

Cabernet Sauvignon

More quality wines are made from Cabernet Sauvignon than any other red variety. The grape originated on Bordeaux's Left Bank, where it achieves its ultimate expression in full-bodied, elegant, and age-worthy wines. In these classic reds, it is blended with Merlot and Cabernet Franc. The grape has also been successful in Napa Valley, California, where it produces approachable wines bursting with ripe fruit. 614,800ha *France: Bordeaux (Pauillac, Margaux, Pessac-Léognan); California; South Africa; Australia; Chile Bidure, Petite Vidure (France)*

Big & Bold
Full-bodied, deep-coloured wines with blackcurrant, mint, and green pepper flavours. If matured in oak, aromas of vanilla or cedar emerge.

FRUIT FLAVOUR INTENSITY						
DELICATE						PRONOUNCED
BULGARIA	BORDEAUX	SOUTH AFRICA	NEW ZEALAND	CHILE	AUSTRALIA	CALIFORNIA

Pinot Noir

Pinot Noir makes some of the world's greatest wines – medium-bodied reds with perfumed aromas that can also evolve with age. It is, however, a fickle grape which demands a cool climate, low yields, and great care in the vineyard. Its spiritual home is Burgundy but it is also successfully grown in Oregon, USA and New Zealand. These New World wines tend to be more reliable than their French counterparts, although they rarely reach the same heights. Pinot Noir is also used in champagne and other sparkling wines. 207,300ha *France: Burgundy (Gevrey-Chambertin, Volnay, Vosne-Romanée); New Zealand: Central Otago, Martinborough; USA: Oregon, California (Sonoma); Australia Spätburgunder or Blauburgunder (Germany); Blauer Spätburgunder (Austria); Pineau, Noirien (France); Pinot Nero (Italy)*

Soft & Silky
Displays summer fruit flavours when young. Oak maturation adds a creamy, vanilla dimension. With age, aromas of game and truffles develop.

FRUIT FLAVOUR INTENSITY					
DELICATE					PRONOUNCED
BURGUNDY	CHILE	OREGON	NEW ZEALAND	AUSTRALIA	CALIFORNIA

Syrah/Shiraz

In France the grape is known as Syrah, and it yields the full-bodied, perfumed, and age-worthy red wines of the Northern Rhône. Syrah is also increasingly grown in the South of France, where it is usually found in blends. Known mostly as Shiraz in the New World, this same grape is responsible for some of the most profound and desirable wines in Australia, particularly from the Barossa and Hunter valleys and McLaren Vale. Here, the warmer climate makes for an altogether riper and more powerful, blockbuster-style wine. Shiraz is also blended with Cabernet Sauvignon in more everyday wines across Australia. Outside France and Australia, both 'Syrah' and 'Shiraz' can be seen on labels – the choice of grape name giving an indication of style. 🍇 *309,700ha*
🚜 *France: Rhône Valley (Côte-Rotie, Hermitage, Cornas), South of France; Australia* 🏷 *Petite Syrah (Northern Rhône)*

Powerful & Spicy
French Syrah is deep-coloured and full-bodied with flavours of black fruits, pepper, and burnt rubber. Australian Shiraz is a riper and more intense style of wine.

FRUIT FLAVOUR INTENSITY				
DELICATE				PRONOUNCED
NORTHERN RHÔNE VALLEY	CALIFORNIA	SOUTHERN RHÔNE VALLEY	SOUTH OF FRANCE	AUSTRALIA

Merlot

Merlot comes from Bordeaux, where it is usually blended with Cabernet Sauvignon and Franc. It is in the wines of Pomerol and St-Émilion on Bordeaux's Right Bank that Merlot achieves its greatest triumph. Here, as the dominant variety in the mix, it produces silky smooth, plummy reds that last for decades. In other parts of the world Merlot is popular as a varietal wine. Soft tannins and juicy flavours are characteristic of Californian Merlot, although some of the better examples are also capable of ageing. Chile has adopted this grape variety as its own, producing wines in a light, easy-drinking style.
🍇 *598,000ha* 🚜 *France: Bordeaux (St-Émilion, Pomerol); California; Chile* 🏷 *Merlot Noir; Médoc Noir (Hungary)*

Soft & Juicy
Produces medium-bodied, soft tasting wine with flavours of plum, black berries and, in bordeaux, an earthy character. If oaked it may have creamy, vanilla notes.

FRUIT FLAVOUR INTENSITY			
DELICATE			PRONOUNCED
CHILE	BORDEAUX	AUSTRALIA	CALIFORNIA

Continued overleaf ▷

OTHER TOP RED GRAPE VARIETIES

Barbera
Popular in northern Italy and Argentina, Barbera makes medium- to full-bodied, easy-to-drink wines, which are light in tannin and have sweet fruit flavours of red berries and spice. 🍇 *Italy (Alba, Asti)*

Cabernet Franc
A Cabernet Sauvignon relation, this grape produces reds in a lighter, softer style with flavours of blackberries, redcurrants, and herbs. Used for blending in Bordeaux and for varietals in the Loire Valley. 🍇 *France: Bordeaux, Loire Valley* 🥂 *Breton (Loire)*

Carignan
A tannic, rustic grape variety found in the South of France, Spain, and parts of California, Carignan produces wine with robust deep colour and simple red berry flavours. 🍇 *France: South of France; Spain; California* 🥂 *Cariñena (Spain); Mazuelo (Rioja); Carignane (USA)*

Cinsaut
This perfumed, spicy variety with a pale colour is widely grown in the South of France and Corsica. Normally used in blends, it also makes an interesting varietal rosé. 🍇 *France: South of France, Corsica* 🥂 *Cinsault*

Dolcetto
This grape produces deliciously drinkable wines with a deep, vivid colour and vibrant, attractive cherry, almond, and red-fruit flavours. It is normally made for early drinking but more concentrated examples are also found. 🍇 *Italy: North (Piemonte)*

Gamay
The grape of Beaujolais, this variety is also found elsewhere in France and Europe. Best known for its bright, cherry-fruit flavours, vivid pink-purple colour, and easy-drinking, low tannin style. 🍇 *France: Beaujolais, Loire Valley*

Grenache
Producer of juicy, high-alcohol, cherry- and pepper-flavoured wines, the world's most planted red variety is normally used in blends. 🍇 *France: Rhône Valley (Châteauneuf-du-Pape); Spain (Rioja, Priorato)* 🥂 *Garnacha Tinta (Spain)*

Malbec
This gutsy red variety, full of spicy red berry flavours, is found in France and widely grown in Argentina, where it makes deep coloured wines with powerful tannins. 🍇 *France: Cahors, Bordeaux; Argentina* 🥂 *Côt (southwest France, Loire Valley); Auxerrois (Cahors)*

Mourvèdre
A deep-coloured, powerfully flavoured variety used in blends in the southern France and Spain, this grape is now gaining popularity for its opaque colour and intense liquorice character. 🍇 *France: southern France; Spain* 🥂 *Monastrell (Spain), Mataro (California)*

Nebbiolo
This variety makes a full-bodied, intensely powerful, classic wine in Barolo and Barbaresco in Piemonte, with a bouquet of red berries, violet, and rose and, with age, tar and truffles. 🍇 *Italy: Piemonte (Barbaresco, Barolo)* 🍇 *Spanna (Piemonte)*

Pinotage
A variety created in the early 20th century by crossing Pinot Noir and Cinsaut, this grape possesses the berry and sweet flavours of Pinot, and the fruity spiciness of Cinsaut. Widely planted in South Africa, it has not yet found fame elsewhere. 🍇 *South Africa*

Sangiovese
Italy's most widely planted variety produces medium- to full-bodied reds with lively acidity and sour cherry, plum, and dried herb flavours. 🍇 *Italy: Tuscany (Chianti, Brunello di Montalcino, Vino Nobile di Montepulciano)* 🍇 *Brunello (Montalcino)*

Tempranillo
This top quality Spanish grape is at its finest in the wines of Rioja and Ribera del Duero. It produces medium- to full-bodied wines with powerful tannins and flavours of raspberry and spice. 🍇 *Spain (Rioja, Ribera del Duero)* 🍇 *Tinto Fino (Ribera del Duero)*

Touriga Nacional
One of the finest grapes used in port and conventional Portuguese wines, Touriga Nacional offsets its concentration and tannic structure with masses of velvety smoothness and charm. 🍇 *Portugal (Porto, Douro, Dão)*

Zinfandel/Primitivo
Zinfandel in California, Primitivo in South Italy, this versatile grape produces wines that vary from light pink rosés to powerful, alcoholic reds, with juicy berry flavours and soft tannins. 🍇 *California; Italy: South*

THE HEART OF THE GRAPE

The wine industry today exists only because of the unique properties of the humble grape berry. Ripe grapes contain high levels of natural sugar that can be fermented into alcohol. Berries also possess essential acids that help counteract this sweetness, keeping a wine fresh-tasting and balanced. The most important decision a grower has to make during the year is deciding on the optimal moment to harvest. As the grapes ripen, sugar, tannin, colour, and flavouring compounds increase, but acidity falls. Pick too early and the wine will taste green and acidic; too late and it will lack the essential structure and acidity of a good wine.

The skin is the source of colouring agents, tannins, and flavouring compounds, which give the wine its character.

Stalks contain bitter tannins and are only rarely used for winemaking.

Bloom, or waxy coating on the outside of the skin, contains natural yeasts.

The pips contain bitter tannins and will generally be removed during winemaking.

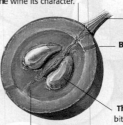

The pulp makes up most of the grape and comprises water, sugar, acids plus flavour compounds.

Continued overleaf ▷

LEADING WHITE GRAPE VARIETIES

OTHER GRAPE VARIETIES might be more widely planted, but in terms of quality these are the four leading white varieties.

Chardonnay

Grown in many different countries, Chardonnay is the world's most popular white variety and arguably the best in terms of the quality of wine produced. It is the main white grape in burgundy and it plays a crucial role in champagne. This variety generally makes a full-bodied, dry white wine, but its flavour varies dramatically from crisp and steely to intense and tropical depending on where it is planted and the winemaking techniques used. The most intensely flavoured examples come from California, Chile, and Australia. 🔵 *411,100ha*
🔺 *France: Burgundy (Meursault, Chablis, Pouilly-Fuissé), Champagne; California; Australia* 🔳 *Morillon (Austria)*

Full & Flavoursome
Flavours of green fruits are found in cooler climates, moving through to tropical fruits in warmer regions. Oak is often used.

FRUIT FLAVOUR INTENSITY					
DELICATE				**PRONOUNCED**	
CHABLIS	BURGUNDY	NEW ZEALAND	CHILE	AUSTRALIA	CALIFORNIA

Riesling

Riesling is credited by many to be the world's best white grape variety. It typically produces a light, fragrant wine with lively acidity, gloriously aromatic flavours, and relatively low alcohol levels. Riesling comes in a range of styles from bone dry and minerally through to lusciously sweet and overly fruity, and it is rarely vinified with oak. Germany grows more Riesling than any other country and is responsible for many of the most impressive examples. The grape is also key in neighbouring Alsace and is gaining ground in Australia, New Zealand, and the USA.
🔵 *136,900ha* 🔺 *Germany; France: Alsace; Australia; New Zealand; USA* 🔳 *Johannisberger Riesling, Rhine Riesling, White Riesling; Riesling Renano (Italy)*

Rich & Zesty
Young Riesling tastes of lime, apricot, and apples. With age, aromas of diesel and spice can develop. Sweet examples display delicious honey and marmalade nuances.

FRUIT FLAVOUR INTENSITY			
DELICATE			**PRONOUNCED**
GERMANY	NEW ZEALAND	ALSACE	AUSTRALIA

Sauvignon Blanc

A dry, crisp, and intensely aromatic variety with a firm streak of acidity, Sauvignon Blanc has recently enjoyed a surge in popularity. The Loire Valley is the heartland of this grape, where it produces medium-bodied, incredibly zesty white wines. Widely planted in Bordeaux, it is increasingly released as a varietal wine, but is also blended with Sémillon in both the dry and sweet white wines of the region. Marlborough in New Zealand is home to the most powerful and aromatic expressions of Sauvignon Blanc, with vibrant gooseberry and exotic fruit flavours. The grape is sometimes aged in oak barrels in Bordeaux and California (when it is often called Fumé Blanc). 178,000ha

France: Loire Valley (Sancerre, Pouilly-Fumé), Bordeaux; New Zealand: Marlborough, Chile Fumé Blanc (Loire Valley); Muskat-Sylvaner (Germany, Austria)

Aromatic & Crisp

Gooseberries are the signature flavour of Sauvignon Blanc, alongside green peppers, nettles, and even cat's pee. In New Zealand, tropical fruit flavours are also typical. Oak tends to subdue these distinctive aromas.

FRUIT FLAVOUR INTENSITY

DELICATE ———————————————————— PRONOUNCED

BORDEAUX · LOIRE VALLEY · CHILE · CALIFORNIA · NEW ZEALAND

Sémillon

Sémillon is not the most widely known variety, but its role should not be underestimated. It features as the main grape in the legendary sweet wines of Sauternes in Bordeaux, where its rich, concentrated, and lusciously sweet flavours are blended with the acidic charms of Sauvignon Blanc. Sémillon is paired with the same grape and often fermented in oak in the increasingly popular dry white wines of Bordeaux. This variety also makes remarkable dry whites in Australia's Hunter Valley. Made without the use of oak, these wines are light and zesty when young, but then develop delicious toasted aromas with age. approx 23,000ha France: Bordeaux (Sauternes, Barsac); Australia: Hunter and Barossa valleys Boal (Portugal)

Versatile & Varied

Sémillon comes in a number of different styles but common flavours include wax, honey, orange marmalade, and burnt toast.

FRUIT FLAVOUR INTENSITY

DELICATE ———————————————————— PRONOUNCED

HUNTER VALLEY · BORDEAUX (DRY) · WESTERN AUSTRALIA · BAROSSA VALLEY · BORDEAUX (SWEET)

Continued overleaf ▷

OTHER TOP WHITE GRAPE VARIETIES

Albariño
At its most impressive, this slightly peachy grape variety produces good-quality dry whites. Spanish examples tend to have more weight and intensity than those from Portugal. ⟁ *Spain (Rías Baixas); Portugal (Vinho Verde)* 🍷 *Alvarinho (Portugal)*

Chasselas
Grown in France and Germany but most prized in Switzerland where it is dry, crisp, and delicately flavoured. In the best sites, Chasselas can have a distinctive minerally concentration. ⟁ *France; Switzerland* 🍷 *Fendant, Dorin (Switzerland)*

Chenin Blanc
This versatile grape is at its best in the Loire Valley where it produces a range of styles, from dry through to rich and sweet with flavours such as honey, lime, and vanilla. ⟁ *France: Loire Valley (Savennières, Bonnezeaux); South Africa*

Furmint
Hungary's most important variety, Furmint is largely responsible for the legendary sweet wine Tokaji. Renowned for its lively acidity and powerful alcohol, the grape's thin skins make it ideal for the production of dessert wine. ⟁ *Hungary*

Gewürztraminer
Unmistakable aromas of lychee, rose, Turkish delight, and sometimes smoky bacon make this one of the world's easiest varieties to recognize. Alsace provides the most intense examples. ⟁ *France: Alsace*

Grüner Veltliner
A potentially top quality variety, it is widely planted in Austria. At its finest in the Wachau region, this grape produces full-bodied, dry whites with a distinctive spicy flavour. The wines age superbly. ⟁ *Austria: Wachau, Vienna (Wien)*

Marsanne
With flavours of marzipan and almonds, this grape is grown widely in the Southern Rhône, where it is often blended with Roussanne. Wines are full-bodied with low acidity and plenty of character. ⟁ *France: Rhône Valley; Australia*

Muscat
This complicated family of grapes has three distinct varieties (Blanc à Petits Grains, of Alexandria, and Ottonel). It is best as a dry white in Alsace and the Australian dessert wine Liqueur Muscat. ⟁ *France: Alsace, South of France; Australia; Italy* 🍷 *Moscato (Italy); Muscatel (Spain)*

Palomino
A quality grape, it is used to make sherry in Andalucía, southern Spain. Low in acidity and fermentable sugars, which suits sherry production, it is unremarkable when grown elsewhere. ⟁ *Spain (Jerez)* 🍷 *Palomino Fino (Spain)*

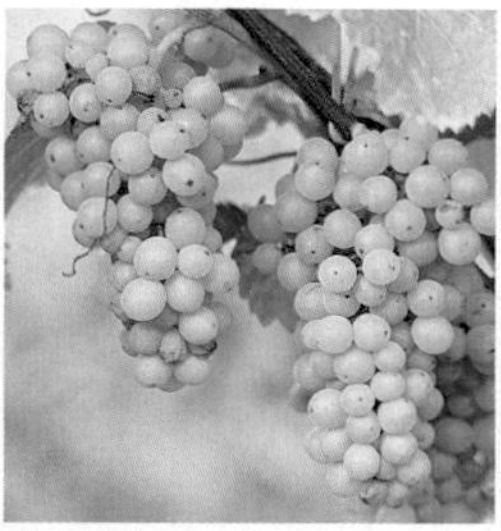

Pinot Blanc
A relatively neutral grape, Pinot Blanc usually makes dry and full-bodied wines with subtle smoky flavours. It is of particular note in Alsace and Austria.
France: Alsace; Italy; Austria
Pinot Bianco (Italy); Weissburgunder (Germany, Austria)

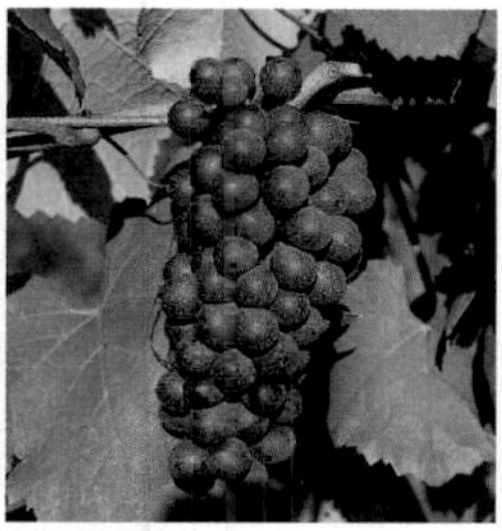

Pinot Gris
A full-bodied, deep-coloured white grape, Pinot Gris has fairly subtle flavours of honey, smoke, and spice. The Italian wines are lighter than those from Alsace.
France: Alsace, Italy *Tokay Pinot Gris (Alsace), Pinot Grigio (Italy), Grauburgunder (Germany)*

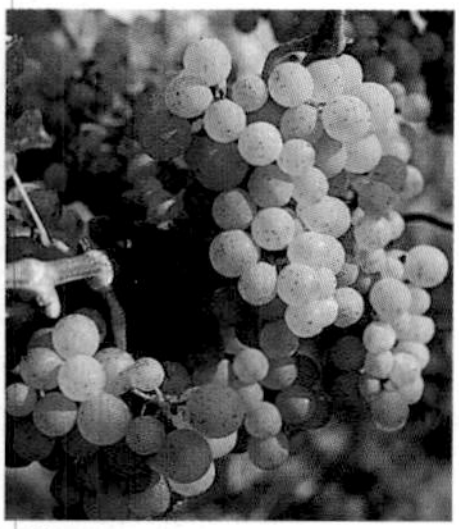

Silvaner
This variety is widely grown in both Germany and neighbouring Alsace. Silvaner is a relatively neutral grape with lively acidity, that can produce distinctive dry whites. *Germany; France: Alsace* *Sylvaner (Alsace)*

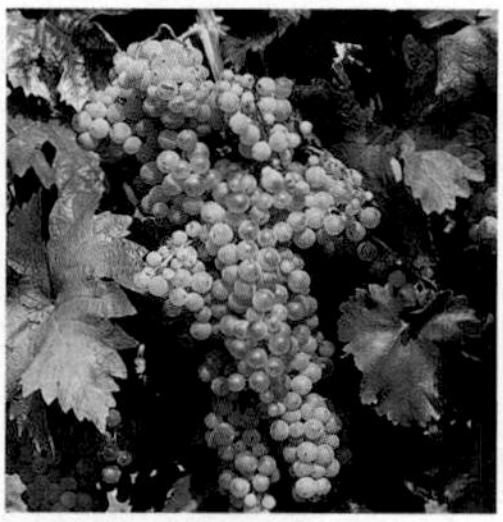

Trebbiano/Ugni Blanc
Trebbiano, the same grape as France's Ugni Blanc, is the most widely planted white variety in Italy. Generally the source of bland, dry white wines, normally found in blends. *Italy; France*

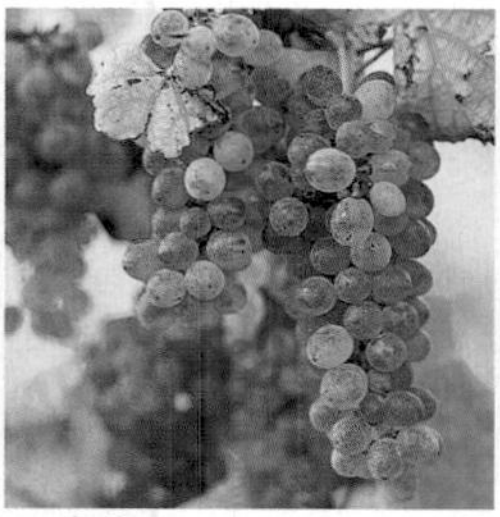

Verdelho
A Portuguese variety notable for its acidity, Verdelho is used in madeira and white ports. Australia makes a distinctive, full-bodied, and zesty still wine. *Portugal (Madeira, Douro); Australia* *Gouveio (Douro)*

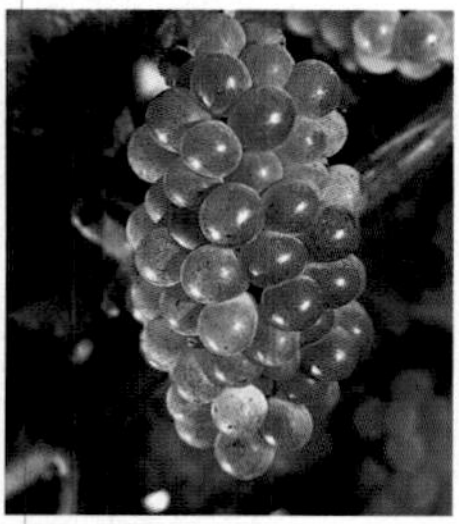

Viognier
This top-quality grape variety produces full-bodied, dry whites with aromas of apricots and musk. At its peak in the Northern Rhône.
France: Rhône Valley (Condrieu), South of France; California; Chile

THE VINE FAMILY TREE

The grapevine belongs to the *Vitaceae* family of plants. Within this, the genus *Vitis* is the only important one for wine production. There are a number of *Vitis* species but the most significant is *Vitis vinifera*, which accounts for the majority of wines. Popular varieties such as Chardonnay and Cabernet Sauvignon belong to *Vitis vinifera*. Other species do produce wine in certain parts of the world – like *Vitis labrusca* in New York State – but the major role of these other species is as rootstocks. Following the devastation of European vines by the phylloxera louse (which attacks vine roots) in the 19th century, virtually all *Vitis vinifera* vines are now grafted onto the rootstocks of resistant species such as *Vitis berlandieri*, *Vitis riparia*, and *Vitis rupestris*. This allows the *Vitis vinifera* varieties to produce their distinctive flavours, while also protecting them from attack.

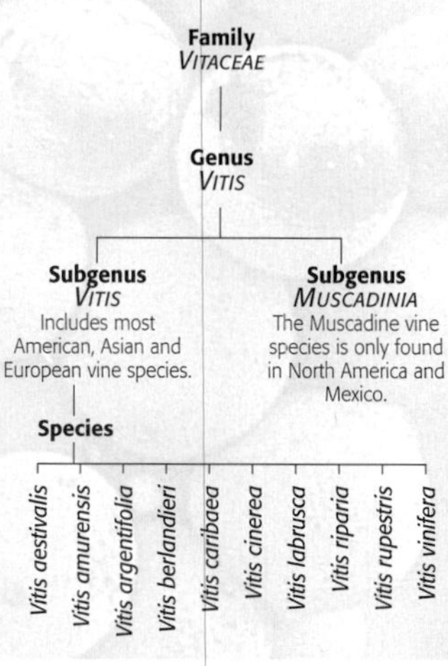
Family
VITACEAE
Genus
VITIS
Subgenus
VITIS
Includes most American, Asian and European vine species.
Subgenus
MUSCADINIA
The Muscadine vine species is only found in North America and Mexico.
Species
Vitis aestivalis
Vitis amurensis
Vitis argentifolia
Vitis berlandieri
Vitis caribaea
Vitis cinerea
Vitis labrusca
Vitis riparia
Vitis rupestris
Vitis vinifera

IN THE VINEYARD

PRODUCERS CAN influence the quality and style of the wine they make through their choice of vineyard location, planting methods, and decisions made during the year, but they are still largely at the mercy of nature. When the grapes are harvested, they bear the hallmark of the conditions in that particular vineyard in that year. Each of the seasons, therefore, has a significant role to play in the winemaking process.

Northern hemisphere in Sonoma, California, USA

JANUARY TO JUNE

In the northern hemisphere the warm spring weather brings the vineyards to life. In the south the grapes go through their final ripening stages and harvest begins.

Pruning & Vine Training
Pruning starts in January as seen here in Campania, southern Italy. It is the process where the previous year's growth is removed from the vine, reducing the number of potential buds and thus the quantity of grapes. It is one of the main ways of controlling yields and producing more concentrated fruit. There are a number of different pruning systems available to growers, with cane (one or two canes with more buds) and spur (more canes but fewer buds on each) being the most important. The system used depends on the climate, grape variety, method of harvest and, in European wine appellations, local legislation.

Ploughing
The soil between the vines is ploughed in March/April to aerate it *(right)*. Banked up earth is also removed from around the base of the vines.

NORTHERN HEMISPHERE

JANUARY	FEBRUARY	MARCH

SOUTHERN HEMISPHERE

Summer Pruning
If flowering and fruit set are successful, growers may remove some grape bunches to create the optimum yield. Hotter southern hemisphere vineyards can often riper higher crops of good quality than their northern counterparts.

Spraying
Spraying against fungal diseases, pests, and weeds, as shown here in South Island, New Zealand, starts in January and only stops four weeks before harvest.

Preparation for Harvest
Harvest equipment is generally prepared from February onwards, but growers must be ready to harvest hotter vineyards in January, or even before this. Grapes are checked for ripeness using scientific equipment, and with taste tests.

GROWTH STAGES OF THE VINE

1. Budbreak
Budbreak is the first sign of the annual growth of the vine. This is when the buds swell and open, allowing green shoot tips to break through.

2. First Foliage
Once the buds have opened, foliage develops. The shoots grow rapidly and leaves appear. Tiny embryo bunches of flowers are found on the young shoots.

3. Flowering
The embryo bunches enlarge and small green flowers bloom. Over the next 10 days, pollination and fertilization take place.

4. Fruit Set
Most of the 'set' or fertilized flowers (about 70 per cent) now develop into berries; the others fail to grow and eventually fall off.

5. Veraison
The first sign of ripening is when the berries increase in size and change colour (to red in red grapes and green/yellow in white).

6. Leaf Fall
The leaves fall naturally from the vine some time after the grapes have ripened. This marks the end of its productive cycle.

New Plantings
In April/May fragile new vines are taken out of the nursery and planted in the vineyard.

Frost Danger
In frost-prone areas, growers bring heaters, wind machines, and even sprinklers into the vineyards to protect the fragile buds.

Spraying
Spraying the vines with pesticides begins in May/June to protect against insects and fungal diseases. Cooler and more humid areas require more frequent spraying.

Training
Following flowering, the shoots are tied to their training wires. In Europe, training systems are often dictated by regional tradition.

APRIL	MAY	JUNE

Vineyard Maintenance
After harvest comes a quiet time in the vineyard. Mending the machinery and trellis systems becomes a priority. Dead wood is pruned from the vines, and unproductive plants are removed. Vineyards are also ploughed to break up the soil.

Banking Up
Following leaf fall, the vine moves into a period of dormancy when it can survive extremely cold temperatures. Even so, growers tend to earth up the bases of the vines in May/June to protect against low temperatures during the winter.

Harvest
The busiest time of year is the harvest, which takes place in March/April. Teams of pickers (such as those at Fabre Montmayou in Mendoza, Chile; *above*) or machines (as seen in Victoria, Australia, *right*) harvest the grapes as carefully and rapidly as possible.

Continued overleaf ▷

JULY TO DECEMBER

While the northern hemisphere vineyards warm up for their most important annual event, the harvest, the southern hemisphere spends time concentrating on preparation and nurturing new growth.

Summer Pruning

If flowering and fruit set are successful, come July time quality-conscious growers remove some grape bunches to reduce their yield. Summer pruning takes place here in Côte Blonde vineyards in the Northern Rhône, France.

Yarra Valley vineyard in the southern hemisphere, Victoria, Australia

Preparation for Harvest

Equipment is prepared during August and September and, as harvest approaches, the grapes are regularly tested for ripeness with a refractometer, as here in the Mosel, Germany.

Spraying

Spraying, now mostly done mechanically, against fungal diseases, pests, and weeds continues and stops four weeks before harvest.

NORTHERN HEMISPHERE		
JULY	AUGUST	SEPTEMBER
SOUTHERN HEMISPHERE		

Pruning & Vine Training

Pruning generally takes place in July/August and is one of the most skilled jobs in the vineyard, although it can now be done by machine.

Ploughing

The soil between the vines is ploughed to aerate it. Where frost is a problem, protective earth is moved from the base of the vines.

DISEASES, PESTS & HAZARDS

During the course of a year, vines face a number of potential dangers. The weather is the most obvious hazard, ranging from spring frosts which can kill young buds, through to hailstorms capable of quickly devastating a vineyard. In humid conditions rot can be equally problematic (although *Botrytis cinerea* or noble rot is welcomed by producers of sweet white wines). Phylloxera *(see pp510–11)* is an insect that nearly destroyed the European wine industry in the 19th century by attacking vine roots, and today most vineyards use resistant American rootstocks as protection. Other pests range from caterpillars and spiders, which can damage the vine, through to birds *(top right)*, deer, wild boar and kangaroos in Australia *(bottom right)*, who all like to feast on ripe grapes.

Harvest

The September/October harvest is the culmination of the year's work in the vineyard. Good weather conditions and decisions by the grower at this time can make or break a vintage. As the grapes ripen, sugar levels rise while acidity falls, and the harvest is timed to achieve a perfect balance between these elements. Weather conditions play a vital role: rainfall at the wrong time leaves the grapes vulnerable to rot, and water on the bunches at picking dilutes the juice. In European viticultural areas, the earliest harvest date is set by local authorities. Manual harvesting (as in the Lavaux, Switzerland; *left*) is generally considered to be gentler on the grapes and vines; however machine-harvesting (as in Paso Robles, California; *below*) is significantly cheaper and in warmer climates allows the picking to take place in the cool of night.

Late Harvest

For sweet wines, grapes are often left to hang on the vine longer, they are harvested late, and pressed to release sweeter juice. Where winter temperatures fall below freezing as here in Ontario, Canada, concentrated juice from frozen grapes is used to make ice wine.

Vineyard Maintenance

In October some of the old wood is removed from the vines and any unproductive, older vines are dug up. The vineyard is then ploughed.

Banking Up

After the harvest, the vine begins to build up reserves of energy for the months ahead. The bases of the vines are earthed up in November to protect against low temperatures during the winter.

OCTOBER	NOVEMBER	DECEMBER

New Plantings

In October/November, new vines (*above*) are taken out of the nursery and planted. New World vineyards often plant vines further apart than northern hemisphere European vineyards to allow mechanized pruning and harvesting.

Spraying

Where necessary, spraying the vines with pesticides begins in November/December to protect against insects and fungal diseases. Hotter vineyards can be less disease-prone.

Training

Following flowering, the shoots are tied to their training wires. Mechanical pruning and harvesting are made easier if all shoots are encouraged to grow in the same direction.

Frost Danger

In frost-prone areas, growers are ready to implement measures – such as this anti-frost smudge pot in Central Otago, New Zealand (*left*) – to protect the fragile buds during October and November. Helicopters can also successfully prevent frost by mixing higher warmer air with colder lower layers.

IN THE WINERY

A WINERY CAN RANGE IN SIZE from a small shed or cellar with a single winemaker, through to a vast, industrial operation with a team of workers and state-of-the-art equipment. Whatever the scale, the success of a winery largely depends on the quality of its grapes; it is simply impossible to turn poor raw materials into fine wine. A skilled winemaker and modern techno-logy will, however, play a vital role in assuring quality.

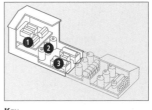

KEY
— Upper winery (see p40 for lower winery)

THE RED WINEMAKING PROCESS

The initial stages of the winemaking process, as illustrated here, transform harvested grapes into juice. Technically this is already wine but it needs to go through several stages before it can be released.

Receiving hopper

Crusher/ destemmer

❶ Crushing & Destemming Grapes

On arrival, bunches of grapes are transported via a receiving hopper *(above)* which feeds into a crusher/destemmer where the grapes are crushed between rollers to expose the sugar-rich grape juice to the yeast and stalks. Stems are then removed and sieved away from the juice (must) using a rotating perforated cylinder.

Adding yeast to must: The yeasts needed for fermentation are found naturally on the grape skins. If cultured yeasts are preferred they are made up and added to the must at this stage to initiate fermentation.

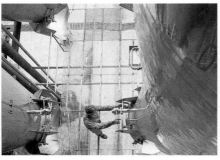

Upright fermentation vessel

❷ Fermentation

Yeasts convert the sugar in the grapes into alcohol and carbon dioxide gas. A large amount of heat is produced during fermentation, so temperatures must be carefully controlled to avoid boiling off flavours. Red wine fermentation is generally complete within four to seven days, but the grapes remain in the vats *(left)* for maceration.

THE WHITE WINEMAKING PROCESS

The major difference between red and white winemaking is the timing of the pressing and fermentation stages. The white wine process is as follows:

1. Crushing and destemming: This stage is optional.

2. Pressing: Skins are not required for colour in white wine and grapes are pressed before fermentation.

3. Treating the must: The must is usually allowed to 'settle' for around 24 hours to remove any other solid elements (skin, pips etc).

4. Fermentation: Temperatures are kept lower during fermentation to enhance the delicate fruit flavour and the process generally lasts

longer. Fermentation for white wine can take place in sealed oak barrels.

5. Stirring the lees: The yeast deposit left after fermentation can be stirred to encourage additional flavours.

6. Malolactic fermentation: This can be employed, but it is not as common as in red wine production.

7. Maturing, fining, filtering, blending, and bottling *(left):* These stages are carried out in basically the same way as red wine *(see pp40–41).*

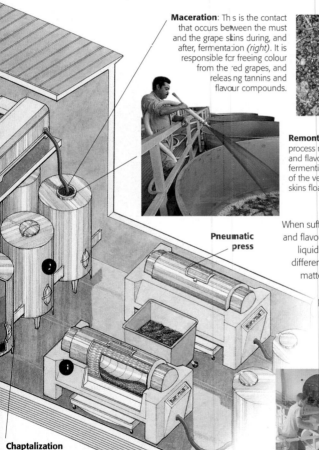

Maceration: This is the contact that occurs between the must and the grape skins during, and after, fermentation *(right).* It is responsible for freeing colour from the red grapes, and releasing tannins and flavour compounds.

Remontage: Part of maceration, this process maximizes extraction of colour and flavour. It can involve drawing fermenting red wine from the bottom of the vessel and pumping it over the skins floating at the top *(left).*

❸ Pressing

When sufficient alcohol, colour, tannins, and flavours have been extracted, the liquid (free-run juice) is run into a different container. The largely solid matter that remains in the tank is then pressed *(below),* producing a thick, dark liquid known as press wine. Press wine may be added to the free-run juice at blending to increase tannin and colour.

Pneumatic press

Chaptalization & Acidification:
If the grapes are insufficiently ripe, sugar may be added to the fermenting must to raise alcohol levels in the chaptalization process. If grapes lack acidity, acid may be added (acidification).

Continued overleaf ▷

THE MATURATION PROCESS

The second half of the winemaking process shapes and prepares the wine for release. Malolactic fermentation and maturation are essential for many wines, especially reds, helping to soften and enhance the flavours, while filtration and fining ensure the wine is clear and stable when it is bottled.

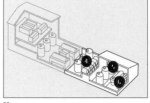

KEY

— *Lower winery*

❹ Maturing

Maturation generally applies to ageing in oak barrels *(above)*. Normally reserved for high quality wines of both colours, it can take many years. The porous nature of oak barrels encourages a gentle oxidation, which helps to soften tannins and increase complexity of flavours.

Malolactic Fermentation: A process which occurs after the first alcoholic fermentation. Winemakers create the right conditions for certain bacteria to convert malic acids (also found in apples) into lactic acids (as in milk), softening the taste or mouth feel of the wine. It can occur in oak barrels or fermentation vats and is encouraged in virtually all red wines.

Upright vats

Racking: As a wine matures, sediment will naturally form in the liquid and contact with these particles can create undesirable flavours in the wine. In racking (which can follow fining), the wine is drained or pumped away *(above)* from the sediment into a clean vessel where it continues to mature.

Oak barrels for maturation

THE USE OF STEEL VERSUS OAK

Oak is the traditional material for barrels, tanks, and other equipment in the winery, but the vast majority of wines produced today are partly or entirely made in stainless steel vats. Airtight, inert, and easy to clean, stainless steel is extremely simple to work with. Modern fermentation vats have inbuilt cooling mechanisms, allowing temperatures to be carefully controlled. Stainless steel tends to emphasize

the bright, fruity characteristics of a wine, particularly if the tanks are sealed to exclude oxygen. Because oak is porous a certain amount of oxidation is inevitable, and this tends to subdue primary fruits, although it can allow more complex flavours to develop. New oak can also impart spicy or vanilla overtones in a wine, and oak chips or staves are sometimes placed in stainless steel tanks to achieve similar characteristics. *See pp158–9.*

⑤ Fining & Filtering

The techniques of fining *(above)* and filtering are known as clarification and they help to produce a wine that is clear in appearance and stable in the bottle. Fining removes tiny proteins using an 'agent' such as egg whites or bentonite clay to bind with the suspended particles and cause them to fall to the bottom of the cask. Filtration focuses on removing solid deposits from the liquid.

THE ART OF BLENDING

The majority of wines today are made up of a blend from a number of different casks or vats of wine. A blend may range from a mixture of two barrels containing the free-run juice and the press wine through to multi-regional blends from many individual components *(below)*. The fundamental rule of blending is that the final wine should be greater than the sum of its constituent parts. The parts could consist of: wines from different grape varieties, different vineyards, or distinct plots within the same vineyard; wines matured with and without oak barrels; different vintages; and other permutations. Blending is an extremely skilled job requiring experience, a fine palate, and the ability to anticipate how different flavours will work in combination.

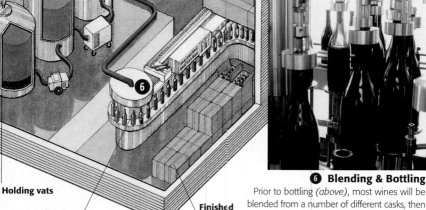

Holding vats

Bottling line

Finished cases

Bottle Ageing: Many top quality wines will be moved to the producer's cellars to mature further before release. In some European appellations this is a legal requirement, but many quality-conscious estates elsewhere voluntarily undertake this expensive commitment.

⑥ Blending & Bottling

Prior to bottling *(above)*, most wines will be blended from a number of different casks, then allowed to settle in a tank (they might also be filtered at this stage). Automated bottling equipment is expensive and many small producers will use contract mobile bottlers. The aim is to preserve the wine's inherent character, using a slow, careful fill protected from oxygen by nitrogen or carbon dioxide.

WINE STYLES

THERE ARE MYRIAD *wine styles made the world over. No two wines are ever exactly alike due to the influence of climate, geology, grape blends, and the makers' approach in the vineyard and winery – all the factors that combine together to make what the French call terroir. They can broadly be categorized as follows:*

SPARKLING

Sparkling wines run the style gamut from light-as-air Italian *prosecco* and elegant, steely French champagnes which mellow with age, to rich, heart-warming toasty bubblies from warmer New World vineyards and ripe-fruit red sparkling Shiraz from Australia. The classic blend of grapes for sparkling wine (champagne in particular) is Chardonnay, Pinot Noir, and Pinot Meunier. This combination develops fruitiness with firmness and fragrance. Top sparkling wines also gain biscuity complex characters from the second fermentation in bottle and contact with the finished fermentation yeasts. Good champagne should have complex **toast**, **nut**, **butter**, and **biscuit** flavours, and the bubbles should give a tingling sensation to balance the flavour.

★ *champagne (France); Cava (Spain); Sekt (Germany); Prosecco, Franciacorta (Italy); 'traditional method' sparkling wines (France, Australia, New Zealand, and California)*

TANGY OR STEELY, MEDIUM-BODIED WHITES

Less flamboyant on the nose, but more assertive on the palate than aromatic wines, tangy/steely styles are some of the best to pair with food. Expect creamier, smoother aromas and allow time for these to open out in the glass as the wine warms up, and as it ages. Grippy firm-fruited flavours tend to mellow and mature as the wine gets older. Tangy wines often contain flavours of **hazelnuts** (Chardonnay), **damp stones** (Chenin Blanc), and **beeswax** (Sémillon); steely ones lean towards **flint** and **gooseberries** (Sauvignon Blanc), and **limes** (Riesling). In general tangy wines respond better to oak-ageing than steely ones, but not for long: oaky vanilla flavours can easily overpower these wines.

★ *Chablis Premier and Grand Cru, white burgundy, white bordeaux, Sancerre and Pouilly-Fumé (France); Sauvignon Blanc (New Zealand); Sémillon (Hunter Valley, Australia); Chenin Blanc (South Africa); Riesling, Verdelho (Australia)*

FULL-BODIED, RICH-FLAVOURED WHITES

Full-on, bold, and golden in the glass, these wines look as luscious as they taste. Expect a waft of **buttery**, **honeyed aromas**, along with **tropical fruit**, **peaches**, **nectarines**, even **pineapple**. There will be a similar barrage of rich, mouth-filling creamy flavour on the palate. Full-bodied wines often have higher alcohol too – being from sunnier climes – but the best of them still have a twang of acidity to keep them balanced. Although they all benefit from additional **vanilla oak** characters, these wines should never be overwhelmed by them. Full-bodied whites mainly hail from warmer New World countries, but pockets of the Northern Rhône, Languedoc-Roussillon, and central Spain produce some powerful whites too. Many of these wines gain complexity with age.

★ *Chardonnay (California, Chile, and Australia); Marsanne and Viognier (Australia); white Rioja (Spain); Condrieu and white Rhône (France)*

CRISP, DRY, LIGHT-BODIED WHITES

Expect pale, white, even green-tinged colours in the glass, and **green apple**, **fresh-mown grass**, **wet stones**, and sometimes **gooseberry** on the nose. These wines will be light, with neutral aromas backed up by crisp acidity and tangy, refreshing fruit on the palate – with flavours of **apples**, **pears**, **citrus fruits**. Grapes to watch out for are Pinot Blanc, Sauvignon Blanc, Riesling, and lighter versions of Chardonnay. These wines are not widely found in the New World (except the coolest parts of New Zealand); many classic examples come from the Old World including Vinho Verde from Portugal and Chablis and Muscadet from France. Oak-ageing does a crisp, dry white no favours, and a good producer will not weigh his wines down in this way. Best drunk young and fresh, these wines should be refreshing on the palate rather than limp, bland, and lifeless.

★ *Chablis and Muscadet (France); Pinot Grigio (Italy); Kabinett Riesling (Germany); Vinho Verde (Portugal)*

AROMATIC OR FLOWERY, DRY TO MEDIUM-SWEET WHITES

Aromatic wines may have a strong colour, but it is on the nose that they really make their mark. Expect anything from **honey**, **diesel**, and **hay** (Riesling), to **smoky citrus** notes (Pinot Gris), **peaches** (Viognier), to **pure grape** flavours (Muscat) and even **roses**, **lychees**, and **Turkish delight** from the most aromatic grape of all, Gewürztraminer. Most of these aromas will be backed up on the palate with similar flavours, but the wine can vary from light and delicate (Germany, Greece) to robustly perfumed and weighty (Alsace, Australia). The powerful aromatic character of these wines can often integrate well with a touch of sugar, so they can be made in an 'off-dry' or medium-sweet style. No sensible producer will smother the lively character with oak.

★ *Alsace Gewürztraminer, Pinot Gris, and Riesling (France); Spätlese Riesling (Germany); Grüner Veltliner (Austria); Albariño (Spain); Assyrtiko, Moschofilero (Greece); Riesling (New Zealand)*

ROSÉ

Made from red grapes, but left only for a limited time with the colour-giving grape skins, rosé can vary from palest powderpuff pink (California Zinfandel), to deep opaque red (Australian Grenache), depending on how long the grapes macerate. Many have the weight of a white wine on the palate, but the aromas of **red fruits** and **hedgerow berries** nearly always give away their red grape origins. Lighter wines generally from Old World countries (Loire Valley and Provence in France, and Navarra in Spain) will be delicate, thirst-quenching, and tangy with a hint of red fruits. Heavier examples (from the Rhône Valley, and Australia) have richer, deeper, almost red wine flavours, not forgetting a touch of grippy tannin. Grenache is one of the most popular rosé grapes.

★ *Tavel, Lirac, Provence, Languedoc-Roussillon, and Anjou rosé (France); Grenache (Navarra, Spain); Zinfandel (California, USA); Grenache (Australia)*

THE BUILDING BLOCKS OF WINE

The basic elements that make up a glass of wine – those that the wine experts analyse when they are assessing the wine's quality – are sugar, acidity, tannin, and alcohol. **Grape sugar** is fermented into alcohol, and gives the wine its richness and its fruitiness. The riper the grapes, the better the fruit/sugar quality. **Acidity** is what keeps this fruit lively on the palate, especially in a white wine. Without it, white wines become limp and bland, while reds not only seem flabby and unexciting, they also lack the structure to age well. **Tannin** comes from the grape skins and pips, and is rarely noticeable in whites (although it is there), but it is what gives a red wine its all-important structure, helping it to last and mature with age. Finally, **alcohol** gives a wine weight on the palate – a German wine with 7 per cent alcohol will taste light, while a chunky Californian Zinfandel with 17 per cent will be more than a mouthful. In a good wine, alcohol should never leave a burning sensation.

Continued overleaf ▷

TANNIC VERSUS NON-TANNIC

That mouth-puckering, tongue-coating sensation you get from a strong cup of cold tea is not a pleasant one, and drinking a particularly tannic red wine is a similar experience. Young wines, especially the good quality ones, can be very tannic. Just because they are a difficult mouthful in their youth, however, does not mean that they will not charm drinkers after a few years in the cellar. Off-putting though it may seem, it is tannin that gives a red wine its 'backbone' – it supports the fruit characters and keeps a good wine lingering on the palate. The important factor is that when the wine ages, the tannin softens so that it becomes barely noticeable. If a wine has lots of ripe fruit, in the quantities typical of hot New World countries like Australia and Chile, this will often overtake the tannin in weight, making the wine seem softer and easier to drink even when it is newly bottled. Non-tannic wines, while refreshingly fruity in their youth (think juicy Beaujolais, and easy-drinking Grenache), will not have the structure to last more than a couple of years in bottle.

FRESH, FRUITY, LOW TANNIN REDS

This style is red wine at its simplest, freshest, and most juicy. These pinky reds are for drinking as young as possible, as they will greet you with pure, primary fruit aromas of **raspberry**, **red apple**, and **cherry**, backed up with cheery red-fruit characters which fill the palate. There will be no chalky tannins getting in the way of their satiny smoothness, and any acidity will be soft and supple. Fresh, fruity reds are just as likely to come from the Old World as the New, from grapes like Gamay, Grenache, and Barbera, which are naturally low in tannin. From hotter countries where grapes get riper in the sun, tannins are often overtaken by full fruity flavours, so a usually robust grape like Merlot can exchange its tannin for plummy fruit. These reds trade on their fruity freshness, so are best without ageing in oak.

★ *Beaujolais (France); Barbera d'Asti and d'Alba (Italy); Grenache (Spain, Australia); lighter Merlots (California, Australia, Chile, Argentina)*

SWEET/DESSERT

Sweet wines vary from light, grapey versions from the Muscat grape, which press the palate delicately with soft fruiti-ness, to full-on Australian liqueur wines (again Muscats), which display all the golden sunshine of their origins. The former are subtle aperitifs, the latter are too powerful and concentrated for drinking with a meal. In between are a host of sweet wines with richly honeyed aromas and buttery-smooth flavours (**apricots**, **peaches**, **apple pie**, **spice**) that become ever-more luscious the warmer their origin. All sweet wines should have a crisp acidity to balance their sweet fruit or they become lifeless. Those from the Riesling grape are some of the zestiest; but Tokaji from Hungary has the tangiest, most lingering sweetness of all.

★ *Moscato d'Asti (Italy); Alsace vendange tardive, Sauternes, Vouvray (France); Spätlese, Auslese, Beeren-auslese, Eiswein (Germany, Austria); Tokaji (Hungary); late-harvest sweet wines (California, Australia); ice wine (Canada); Liqueur Muscat (Australia)*

TANGY, DRY, FORTIFIED

Deceptively pale in the glass, these wines are extraordinarily powerful on the nose and palate. Expect a strong whiff of **salt**, **almonds**, **cut-grass**, and even **cheese** aromas when you take a sniff. Then, to follow, dry, tangy, almondy flavours that grip the palate and linger for ages. *Fino* and *manzanilla* sherries are bone-dry with no acidity at all. A heady, salty character almost reminiscent of the sea develops from ageing in barrels in the presence of a special yeast called *flor* (see p322). *Sercial* and *Verdelho* madeiras are crisper and more appley than their Spanish counterparts, but they are just as tangy and long-lasting. No other wine in the world approaches this unusual style and no other makes as refreshing an aperitif, or as good a match for snacks such as salty crisps and peanuts.

★ *fino, manzanilla, amontillado sherry (Spain); Sercial and Verdelho madeira (Portugal)*

MEDIUM- TO FULL-BODIED REDS

This group includes the world's classic red wines, which first and foremost have a firm structure and plenty of backbone. In medium- to full-bodied Old World wines – such as burgundy, bordeaux and Barolo – aromas and flavours might not be very expressive at first, but with a year or two's age, the wines will open up to reveal wafts of **bramble fruit**, **mulberry**, **plum**, and **violet**. They develop in a similar way on the palate too: youthful hard tannins will soften, and as the wines mature, their range of fruit flavours will evolve to include **cranberries**, **spice**, **truffles**, and **chocolate**. Medium- and full-bodied reds call out for oak, which adds both structure and a touch of vanilla aroma. These wines match perfectly with meat dishes.

★ *burgundy, bordeaux (France); Chianti, Barolo, Barbaresco (Italy); Rioja (Spain); Pinot Noir (Chile, New Zealand, Oregon USA, and Australia); Cabernet Sauvignon-Merlot blends (California, Australia)*

FULL, POWERFUL, OFTEN SPICY REDS

These are the most mouth-filling wines of them all. Grapes such as Cabernet Sauvignon (**blackcurranty black fruit**), Shiraz (**spicy plum** and **liquorice**), and Zinfandel (**leather** and **strawberries**) dominate this category. The wines will look inky-black in the glass, show intense sweet black fruit on the nose, then dense, velvety-smooth inky fruit on the palate. The key here is ripeness: these wines are mainly from grapes tough enough to survive in hot vineyards (Napa Valley in California, Barossa Valley in Australia). Many will evolve in the cellar but their overwhelming ripeness also makes them fruity enough to drink young. They all need oak to balance their powerful fruit flavours. Many come from the New World, but parts of Europe create these wines too.

★ *Rhône Valley Syrah (France); Shiraz and Mourvèdre (Australia); Cabernet Sauvignon (California, Australia); Zinfandel (California); Primitivo (Italy); Toro (Spain)*

DARK, SWEET, FORTIFIED

A hedonistic bunch, these wines range from tawny coloured, walnutty ports to amber *oloroso* sherry and red-black, **plum-,** and **violet**-flavoured vintage ports. In general the browner colours reflect time spent in wood – and these wines will typically gain nutty, caramelly aromas. The deep red wines, on the other hand, gain colour and flavours almost solely from the grape, and tend to be pure fruited in youth, evolving (in the best wines) into complex **berry**, **tar**, and **dark chocolate** flavours with age – for vintage port this can mean 40 years plus storage time. Fortification, with grape spirit, occurs half way through fermentation, so all of these wines retain a distinguishing sweetness from their natural grape sugars.

★ *oloroso sherry, Málaga (Spain); tawny port, late-bottled vintage (LBV), vintage port, Malmsey and Bual madeira (Portugal); New World fortifieds (California, Australia)*

OLD VERSUS YOUNG WINES

The most impressive characteristic of a fresh young wine is its obvious vibrancy of fruit. Its welcoming primary aromas and flavours of pure **green apple** (Sauvignon Blanc or Riesling) and **blackcurrant** (Cabernet Sauvignon) make it easy to understand and refreshing to drink. In most better quality young wines, however, there will also be some rough edges – grippy tannins, crisp, even stern acidity – that need time to soften. Given a few years to mature (in bottle or in oak barrels) both white and red wines change dramatically. Their upfront fruitiness mellows, and complex characters emerge like **spice**, **dried fruit**, and **honey** in white wines, and **leather**, **truffles**, **Christmas cake**, and **earthiness** in red wines. Not only this but harsh tannins, heavy oak flavours, and pointed acidity will soften and integrate with the fruit flavours, creating a fuller, more complex, and longer-lasting, mouthfilling palate. Although this transformation works less well for wines of modest quality, for the better ones, it is worth waiting for.

FRANCE

FRANCE

FRANCE *is still the envy of the wine-producing world, and its global influence is far-reaching. Other nations have made great strides in winemaking but no other has the natural conditions to produce such an array of great and varied wines. Geographical diversity, a range of noble grape varieties linked to specific sites, and historical pride and tradition are what keeps France firmly in the limelight.*

THE EARLY YEARS

THE VINE WAS INTRODUCED to Mediterranean France by Greeks from Phocaea around 600 BC. The Romans then spread the knowledge of wine further afield. From their early settlement at Narbonne there were two important trading routes: west through Garonne to Bordeaux and north via the Rhône Valley. Viticulture developed along these axes, eventually extending as far north as the Loire Valley and Champagne. With the fall of the Roman Empire in the 5th century AD, the Church became the most important influence in the spread of viticulture in France. Monastic land holdings became extensive,

Manuscript detail depicting Benedictine monk in a cellar

and wine for the sacrament provided a source of revenue. By the Middle Ages the Benedictine and Cistercian orders alone owned significant vineyards in Burgundy, the Loire Valley, and Champagne.

Trade in wine also became well established during the Middle Ages. Bordeaux, under the jurisdiction of the English crown, had a ready market for its wines and later developed links with cities in northern Europe. The Atlantic port of La Rochelle exported wines from the Loire and the neighbouring province of Poitou. The Dukes of Burgundy, with concessions in Flanders, meanwhile, helped advance trade with the Benelux countries.

The expansion of French vineyards continued through the 17th to the mid-19th century. The French Revolution at the end of the 18th century had little effect on wine production. The religious orders, however, were stripped of their land, resulting in a significant change of ownership in regions like Burgundy. Bordeaux entered a period of extraordinary wealth and expansion thanks to lucrative foreign trade, particularly with the French West Indies. This was reflected in the rising reputation of individual wine estates, the construction of many of the prestigious châteaux that can still be seen today, and the establishment of the famous 1855 classification system.

15th-century illustration of workers in a vineyard

◁ **Château de Corton-André and its vineyards in Aloxe-Corton, Côte de Beaune, Burgundy**

WINEGROWING REGIONS

France has a range of climatic and topographical conditions suitable to a diversity of grape varieties and wine styles. The country's key winegrowing regions fall into three climatic zones. Along the Atlantic seaboard Bordeaux, the Southwest, and the Loire Valley experience maritime influence. In the south a Mediterranean regime prevails, influencing the wines of the South of France and the Southern Rhône. In the east, in Alsace, Champagne, Burgundy, and the Northern Rhône (as well as Central Loire), a continental climate is apparent.

MODERN HISTORY

FRANCE'S PERIOD OF PROSPERITY came to a dramatic end in the 1850s with the arrival of a triumvirate of viticultural afflictions imported from North America. The fungal diseases oidium and mildew and then the vine louse phylloxera *(see pp510–11)* brought about a series of catastrophes, completely devastating vineyards throughout the country.

Economic decline in the early 20th century, exacerbated by two world wars, meant that French viticulture fell into a poor state. Quality dropped and Languedoc-Roussillon, in particular, became the source of an unlimited supply of inferior table wine. Standards and authenticity were threatened by cheap imports and imitations, and as a means of combating this problem the *Appellation d'Origine Contrôlée* system *(see p52)* was introduced in the 1930s. Ready investment and the interest of a new generation came to the fore in the 1970s, accelerating the industry in the 1980s and ushering in the high standards found today.

THEATRE OF FOOD & WINE

Wine and food are inextricably inter-linked in France, both forming part of a strong cultural and gastronomic inheritance. Wine is nearly always consumed with an appropriate food accompaniment, which invariably means that regional food is served with wine from the same region. Having evolved alongside each other over the centuries, local dishes and wines are tailored to suit one another. Classic pairings include the rich, textured cuisine of Bordeaux and its tannic, digestible reds, river fish in a buttery sauce with flavoursome white burgundy, crisp, tangy Muscadet with local seafood, and unctuous sweet Sauternes with rich *foie gras*.

THE WINE INDUSTRY TODAY

FRANCE VIES WITH ITALY for the place as the world's number one wine producer in terms of volume. In recent decades, however, production has fallen from 69 million hectolitres in 1985 to 52 million in 2005. The total vineyard area is around 894,000ha, AOC vineyards accounting for 55 per cent, *vin de pays* 31 per cent, and *vin de table* 14 per cent.

In terms of internal consumption, France again leads the way, consuming 33.5 million hectolitres of wine a year, at an average of 55 litres per person. In export markets around the world, France has been losing ground to the growing competition but remains second to Italy in volume with around 15 million hectolitres per year.

The fabric of the industry is maintained by some 145,000 grape growers. These either produce and bottle their own wines under the banner of a domaine, château, or estate; deliver their grapes to a co-operative; or sell their grapes or wines to a *négociant*.

VITICULTURE & VINIFICATION

RECENT ADVANCES in wine production have been focussed mainly on the vineyards, where the hours of work have multiplied in an attempt to improve standards. Much work is carried out mechanically, but at the top estates labour is much in demand for tasks such as hand-pruning and harvesting.

Harvesting at Clos de Vougeot in Burgundy

There has also been a general move away from the wholesale use of chemical fertilizers and sprays (as seen in the 1960s and 70s) to a more pragmatic approach. Treatment for disease is linked to local weather reports and adjustments to the soil made after analysis. Those seeking a more comprehensive organic approach have gone as far as adopting the biodynamic system of cultivation *(see p105)*. Over the past 20 years, programmes of vine-pulling and replanting have altered the proportions of land allocated to each grape variety. In 2008, the EU approved proposals for a voluntary vine-pull scheme covering 175,000ha in a bid to improve quality; it also agreed to phase out subsidies for crisis distillation.

The 1980s saw huge improvements in technology in the cellars. Current developments continue to concentrate on improvements in hygiene and safety controls and investment in equipment such as systems of temperature regulation and new oak barrels.

RED GRAPE VARIETIES
& WINE STYLES

IN BORDEAUX'S MILD CLIMATE, Merlot, Cabernet Sauvignon, and Cabernet Franc are used in a variable blend to produce more top-quality wine than any other region. Styles vary from grassy and fruity to firm, full, and long-ageing. The same three varieties are also vinified individually as varietal *vin de*

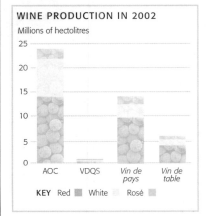

WINE PRODUCTION IN 2002

Millions of hectolitres

	AOC	VDQS	Vin de pays	Vin de table

KEY Red ■ White Rosé ■

pays, chiefly in Languedoc-Roussillon. In Provence, Cabernet Sauvignon is used to add complexity and tannic structure to some blends, while cousin Cabernet Franc takes ascendancy in the Loire Valley, where it makes a fresh, fruity, invigorating wine.

Pinot Noir appears in the cooler north as Burgundy's red grape, giving vibrant, perfumed, and potentially long-lived wines. It also produces the only red wine in Alsace and is used as part of the blend in champagne. The inherent fruitiness of Beaujolais stems from Gamay, which also appears in the Loire Valley.

Bordelais harvester

Syrah holds sway in the Northern Rhône, where the wines are deep coloured with a spicy, dark-fruit intensity. This grape is also increasingly used in blends in the Southern Rhône and Languedoc-Roussillon. The major variety in both these regions, though, is warm, generous Grenache. Mourvèdre is the other noble grape found in southern blends.

WHITE GRAPE VARIETIES & WINE STYLES

CHARDONNAY IS THE most widely planted white variety in France. In Burgundy it reaches its apogee, producing a range of styles from rich, buttery, barrel-aged Meursault to intense, minerally wines in the more extreme climate of Chablis. It is also one of the principal components of champagne, where it can appear as a single variety *blanc de blancs*. Elsewhere Chardonnay is cultivated in the Loire Valley and has had great success as a fruity varietal *vin de pays* in Languedoc-Roussillon.

Crisp, tangy Sauvignon Blanc is found in the cool to mild climes of the Loire Valley and Bordeaux. In the latter, it is often blended with Sémillon for both dry and sweet wine styles. The Loire's other major white grape variety is Chenin Blanc, which produces everything from dry to luscious sweet wines.

The distinctive wines of Alsace showcase a range of white grapes, the principal varieties being dry, fragrant Riesling, perfumed Gewürztraminer, and full-bodied Pinot Gris. Further south in the Rhône Valley and the South of France, a host of white varieties generally have less acidity due to the warmer climate. The most characterful are the grapey Muscat and the opulently fragrant Viognier of Condrieu.

Château Pichon-Longueville in Pauillac on Bordeaux's Left Bank

FRENCH WINE LAW

FRANCE HAS ONE OF THE *most extensive and widely imitated systems of wine legislation in the world today*. Founded in the 1930s, the Appellation d'Origine Contrôlée (AOC or AC) regulations today provide the model for all the wine industries in the European Union. The AOC system is founded on the principle that distinct geographical locations (rather than grape varieties in isolation) are responsible for the unique flavour and character of individual French wines. The boundaries of each AOC region are clearly defined, and within these areas producers must follow strict rules. An AOC designation on a label guarantees that a wine originates from the specified appellation and is produced according to local legislation. With the exception of wines from Alsace, the name of the grape is rarely found on AOC wine labels, thus placing considerable demands on the knowledge of the drinker.

AOC sits at the top of the French classification hierarchy with the virtually extinct VDQS directly beneath it; both apply to so-called quality wine. Beneath these there is vin de pays or country wine which comes from a broad region (and can be high quality) and the distinctly inferior vin de table or basic table wine, which can originate from anywhere in France.

AOC Chassagne-Montrachet Premier Cru label, Burgundy

French Wine Classification

There are four different categories of French wine, two within the quality division and two ranked as 'table' wine.

Appellation d'Origine Contrôlée (AOC or AC): The highest level of French wine acts as a guarantee that a wine has been produced in a designated area in accordance with local laws and regulations. Rules cover factors such as the boundaries of the appellation, permitted grape varieties, the style of wine, vine training, yield, harvest dates, minimum levels of alcohol, and other winemaking specifications. AOCs are sometimes categorized further by classifying individual estates or vineyards (see right).

Vin Délimité de Qualité Supérieure (VDQS): This is a relatively unimportant category that is in the process of being phased out.

Vin de pays (VdP): Country wine originates from a broad, designated area. Regulations are not as strict as those for AOC, and certain producers adopt the category in order to make wine from grape varieties prohibited under AOC laws. A vintage and one or two grape varieties can be stated on the label. Six new large-scale *Vin de Pays* zones have been added to the category, covering all major French regions.

Vin de table (VdT): This is the most basic, least regulated category and neither the vintage, the region, or the names of individual grape varieties are permitted on the label.

Classification within an AOC: A number of

AOC Châteauneuf-du-Pape label, Rhône Valley

AOC regions in France further rank and categorize estates or vineyards. Bordeaux has the most famous – and most complex – system of classification (see p62). Its prestigious Médoc châteaux on the Left Bank are divided among five levels from *premier* to *cinquième cru*. Across the Gironde Estuary on the Right Bank, St-Émilion has its own hierarchy, with *premier grand cru classé* for the most highly regarded châteaux. In Burgundy, individual vineyards, rather than estates, are classified; *grands crus* are the most celebrated, followed by *premiers crus*. Champagne villages are also classified with *grand cru* at the top, then *premier cru*. There is no *premier cru* rating in Alsace, but the best vineyards are entitled to the designation *grand cru*.

Altenberg de Bergheim Grand Cru label, AOC Alsace

READING A FRENCH WINE LABEL

When faced with an unfamiliar French wine label, first consider the appellation or other classification. This will provide an idea of the style of the wine and the main grape varieties used. Terms such as *grand cru* or *grand cru classé* may indicate the potential quality, but the name of the producer tends to be the most important factor. A good producer's basic wine, for example, might be superior to another's *grand cru*. Finally, vintages are crucial in French wine, so use the vintage chart *(see back endpaper)* to ensure a good year is selected. The label illustrated here is from Château Margaux, one of Bordeaux's most prestigious first growths.

Château Margaux is the name of the producer. This could be a château, domaine, maison or simply a brand name.

Grand vin literally means 'great wine', but is generally used to indicate the top wine of the estate.

Mis en bouteille au château indicates the wine was bottled at the estate, generally a sign of a quality-conscious producer.

Appellation Margaux Contrôlée confirms that the wine comes from and conforms to the regulations of the AOC Margaux.

2000 indicates the vintage, the year the grapes were harvested.

Premier Grand Cru Classé indicates that Margaux attained first growth status in the Bordeaux 1855 Classification.

Glossary of Label Terms

blanc: white.
cave: cellar.
château: an estate, a common term in Bordeaux.
coopérative: a collective organization that makes wine for a number of growers.
côte/coteaux: hillside/hillsides.
crémant: indicates a sparkling wine made using the traditional method – eg Crémant d'Alsace.
cru: literally 'growth', usually used to mean vineyard.
cru classé: classified vineyard.
demi-sec: medium-dry.
domaine: estate.
doux: sweet.
grand cru: great growth.
méthode classique/méthode traditionnelle: a sparkling wine made using the same techniques as those used for making champagne.
mis (en bouteille) au château/domaine/à la propriété: estate bottled.

négociant: a merchant who buys grapes, must, or wine from growers and then sells wine under its own individual label.
premier cru: first growth.
propriétaire: the estate or vineyard owner.
récoltant: the person who harvests the grapes.
récolte: vintage or harvest.
rouge: red.
sec: dry.
sélection de grains nobles: the sweetest style of wine in Alsace, made from grapes affected by botrytis.
supérieur: a wine with a higher level of alcohol.
vendange tardive: late harvest.

AOC Condrieu label, Rhône Valley

In Alsace this is an AOC in its own right, for sweet wine made from ultra-ripe grapes.
vieilles vignes: old vines.
vigneron/viticulteur: vinegrower.
vignoble: vineyard.
vin: wine.

ICONIC FRENCH WINES

FRENCH WINES *are marketed under regional names, rather than individual grape names, since time has shown the location of a vineyard to be as important as the vines grown within it. Today AOC laws protect the many regional styles in France, which have generated unique wines famed the world over. The regional name on the label proclaims this individuality.*

① Champagne
The world's most famous sparkling wine is produced in France's northernmost viticultural district. Chardonnay, Pinot Noir, and Pinot Meunier struggle for ripeness here, producing base wines of high acidity and nuanced flavour, ideal for making the sleekest and subtlest of sparkling wines. *See pp170–75.*

② Sweet Wines of the Loire
In exceptional years, when botrytis strikes the Loire Valley, the sweet white wines made from Chenin Blanc – Coteaux du Layon among them – can be world ranking. These unctuous wines with well-balanced acidity are full of fruit and floral aromas in youth, and honey and dried fruits when mature. *See pp154–163.*

③ Pauillac
Powerful and long-lived with a steely mineral quality and the fragrance of blackcurrant, cedar, and cigar box, Pauillac is the perfect example of a red wine from Bordeaux's Left Bank. Deep gravelly soils and a dominance of Cabernet Sauvignon (blended with a little Merlot and Cabernet Franc) help forge this character. *See pp64 & 68–9.*

④ St-Émilion
St-Émilion is one of the classic reds from Bordeaux's Right Bank. Merlot and Cabernet Franc grown on the limestone-and-clay soils (often combined with a touch of Cabernet Sauvignon) offer round, full-bodied wines that have a cool freshness and fine tannic structure. There is also a modern wave of ripe-fruited wines with more concentration. *See pp76 & 80–82.*

⑤ Sauternes
Rich, luscious, exotic Sauternes really is a miracle of nature. In the south of Bordeaux, misty, humid conditions provoke the onset of botrytis, which naturally concentrates the Sémillon, Sauvignon Blanc, and Muscadelle grapes. The result is this opulent, sweet white elixir. *See pp66 & 74–5.*

⑥ Côte Rôtie
Côte Rôtie, along with Hermitage, is one of the stars of the Northern Rhône. Syrah, granite soils, and a continental climate combine to produce this dark-fruited, spicy but elegant, long-ageing red wine. With only 200ha under production there is, unfortunately, very little to go around. *See pp122 & 130.*

English Channel
50°
Seine
PARIS
48°
LOIRE VALLEY ②
Nantes
Orléan
Loire
Atlantic Ocean
46°
PAUILLAC ③ ④ ST-ÉMILION
Bordeaux
BORDEAUX
44°
⑤ SAUTERNES
Garonne
Pyrénées

⑦ Red Burgundy
Red burgundy is produced from the fickle but perfumed Pinot Noir and varies in nuance and flavour according to the mosaic of Burgundian *terroirs*. Forming Burgundy's heartland are the Côte de Nuits and Côte de Beaune, home to great reds like the firm, intense Chambertin and refined, elegant Volnay. *See pp96–107.*

⑧ White Burgundy
White burgundy is deemed to be the ultimate expression of Chardonnay. The greatest wines come from the Côte de Beaune and include rich, nutty, honeyed but dry wines such as Corton-Charlemagne and floral and intense wines like Le Montrachet. All are long-lived. The designation also includes wines from Chablis and Mâconnais. *See pp96–107.*

⑨ Alsace Riesling
Riesling is king of Alsace wines. Clean and vital with a floral-citrus bouquet moving to a mineral-petrol nuance with age, it is more powerful and full-bodied than its German cousins, but being from a borderland, is a totally different style from any other French wine. The finest examples are the *grands crus* and the sweeter *vendanges tardives*. *See pp180–83.*

⑩ Beaujolais
At the southern tip of Burgundy, the red Gamay grape cultivated on clay-limestone-and-granite soils produces fresh, fruity, quaffable Beaujolais. A fair percentage is sold as sprightly, youthful Beaujolais Nouveau. More serious Beaujolais comes from *crus* like Moulin-à-Vent. *See pp114–17.*

⑪ Chablis
Crisp, dry, and minerally, Chablis comes from northern Burgundy. Chardonnay cultivated on clay-and-limestone soils in a continental climate gives an austerity to the wine. The *premiers* and *grands crus* improve with eight years' bottle age. *See pp92–5.*

⑫ Châteauneuf-du-Pape
Warm, generous, powerful, and packed with red fruits, this celebrated red from the Southern Rhône reflects the Mediterranean climate of this extensive district. An astonishing 13 different grape varieties are permitted in the blend, but in reality Grenache provides the mainstay, supported by Syrah and Mourvèdre. *See pp128 &133–4.*

Reims · CHAMPAGNE · Strasbourg · ALSACE ⑨ · Rhine · CHABLIS ⑪ · Dijon · CÔTE DE NUITS ⑦ · CÔTE DE BEAUNE ⑧ · BURGUNDY · BEAUJOLAIS ⑩ · Lyon · CÔTE RÔTIE ⑥ · RHÔNE VALLEY · ALPS · Rhône · ⑫ CHÂTEAUNEUF-DU-PAPE · Marseille · Mediterranean Sea

GREAT VINEYARDS OF FRANCE

IMPRESSIVE EXAMPLES OF *the all-important concept of terroir are manifest in France. These seven renowned French vineyards,* each from a key winegrowing region, give greater meaning to this intrinsically French notion. They show the influence of the local environment on classic grape varieties and – with man's complicity – the resulting wines, which each reveal a unique sense of location.

Chardonnay vines in kimmeridgian limestone, Grand Cru Les Clos, Chablis

Clos du Mesnil, Champagne

The unpredictable nature of Champagne's climate usually means that wines are blended from different vineyards (and harvests), but the Clos du Mesnil single vineyard champagne by Krug (*see p174*) is a rare exception. The 1.85-ha walled vineyard is surrounded by the village of Le Mesnil-sur-Oger, which protects it from the extremes of wind, rain, and frost. A favourable south, southeasterly exposure and Champagne's well-drained chalky soils help bring the Chardonnay grapes to steady ripeness. Thereafter, vinification in small (205-litre) oak barrels and ageing on lees for up to 12 years develops vivacity, balance, and flavour in this champagne.

Château Pétrus plaque

Château Pétrus, Pomerol, Bordeaux

The early ripening grape variety Merlot, combined with Bordeaux's mild but humid climate, and a unique soil structure provide the recipe for success in the wines of Château Pétrus (*see p83*). The heart of the 11-ha vineyard, an area known as the Pétrus 'buttonhole', is composed of heavy, blue clay. Merlot grown on these water-retaining clays provides the concentration needed to produce the colour, power, and volume associated with the wines of this world-famous château. The availability of a large team of pickers to harvest the grapes at optimum ripeness in little over a day is also an important factor.

Les Clos, Chablis Grand Cru, Burgundy

Les Clos is the quintessential example of great Chablis (*see p93*): full, intense, minerally, and long-ageing. The largest of Chablis' seven *grands crus* with 26ha, Les Clos' steep slope faces south to southwest, giving optimum sunlight exposure to the Chardonnay grapes – a distinct advantage given this region's precarious continental climate. A bedrock of kimmeridgian

Krug's walled Clos du Mesnil vineyard enclosed by the village of Le Mesnil-sur-Oger, Champagne

limestone, formed from fossilized sea shells, creates an outcrop near the surface and gives a firm mineral quality to the wines. The 1.7ha of Les Clos owned by Domaine René and Vincent Dauvissat (see p95) yields one of its purest expressions; the vines are cultivated by hand and then vinified to extract the true character of the wine.

Côte Blonde, Côte Rôtie, Rhône Valley

Marcel Guigal's Côte Rôtie La Mouline (see p130) is produced from a small parcel of vines in the Côte Blonde (see p122). The steep, southeast-facing, schistous slopes give maximum exposure to the sun, ripening the Syrah grapes to a good, rather than heady, degree and encouraging a restrained expression of dark fruits, violet, and spice. The light, sandy top soils of the Côte Blonde produce an elegant wine, as does the 11 per cent Viognier that Guigal has co-planted with the Syrah. Guigal's method of vinification, with rich extraction and lengthy ageing in new oak casks, adds further suavity and weight.

Slopes of La Mouline, Côte Rôtie, Rhône Valley

Coulée de Serrant, Savennières, Loire Valley

Chenin Blanc, a maritime climate, and schistous soils combine to produce the dry, minerally, apple and quince-scented wines of Savennières (see p154). The 7-ha grand cru Coulée de Serrant (see p160) is the supreme vineyard in the appellation. Located in a valley at right angles to the Loire River, it has greater protection from the rain-bearing westerly winds, a southerly aspect, and stony schistous slopes, which combined with low yields help to accentuate the intensity, flavour, and minerally aspect of the wine. Sole owner Nicolas Joly cultivates the vineyard biodynamically, which further complements the influence of terroir.

Altenberg de Bergheim, Alsace Grand Cru

This 36-ha grand cru vineyard has what producer Jean-Michel Deiss (see p182) describes as a dominating terroir, capable of overwhelming the characteristics of grape varieties. A steep slope (220–320m), southerly aspect, and protection from rain-bearing westerly winds favours a warm, temperate mesoclimate. The soils, a mix of limestone, marl, and sandstone, allow the vine roots to penetrate deep. Deiss produces a Gewürztraminer and a Riesling here, but in defence of his notion of terroir he also has (against AOC regulations) a parcel of mixed Alsatian grape varieties, which he harvests and vinifies together to produce a powerful, yet elegant, wine devoid of specific varietal character. This he identifies as the true expression of Altenberg de Bergheim.

Marcel Deiss Altenberg de Bergheim label

La Coume, Banyuls, Languedoc-Roussillon

Facing the Mediterranean, Banyuls (see p143) is almost permanently bathed in sunshine, and produces wines of rich fruit concentration. The La Coume vineyard of Domaine du Mas Blanc (see p145) benefits from this climate, but is also affected by more localized influences. The altitude, at 300m, and the tramontane wind reduce temperatures, imparting a certain freshness to the Grenache-based wines. Steep, schistous slopes with a thin top soil help to ensure low yields, enhancing the quality of extract and tannins. Vinification includes mutage to stop fermentation at five to six days and then 18 months' ageing in tank before bottling.

BORDEAUX

BORDEAUX IS MORE THAN *just a world-famous wine region. It is a vinous empire, with just over 120,000ha of vineyards producing 5.7 million hectolitres of wine a year, including many of the world's most prestigious and expensive examples. Châteaux Margaux, Lafite, Haut-Brion, and Cheval Blanc, to name but a few, are the gilt-edged image of Bordeaux, but they are just the icing on a very large cake.*

The Romans were probably the first to cultivate the vine in Bordeaux, but it was not until the 12th century, under English rule, that wine trading started. The marriage of Eléanor, Duchess of Aquitaine, to Henry Plantagenet (later Henry II of England) in 1152 effectively ceded the region to the English crown and opened the gateway to trade with Britain *(see p15)*. This political tie was broken in 1453, but trading links remained, and Bordeaux's other overseas markets steadily developed.

Cabernet Sauvignon grapes

Today, wine is Bordeaux's lifeblood: there are 57 appellations in the region, with some 12,500 winegrowers, 44 co-operatives, 400 *négociants,* and 100 brokers. The producers consist of grape growers – the majority members of co-ops – and 'châteaux', which are individual estates, not necessarily grandiose residences. Generic appellation Bordeaux accounts for half the annual production, then there are the *petites appellations* like the Côtes de Bourg, the larger Côtes de Bordeaux appellation (introduced in 2008), and finally illustrious appellations such as Pomerol and Margaux.

For most oenophiles, Bordeaux is about red wine, which accounts for 85 per cent of production and is made from a blend of three principal varieties: Cabernet Sauvignon, Merlot, and Cabernet Franc. Dry and sweet white wines, although dwindling in production, still have an important place in Bordeaux. Sweet Sauternes is one of the world's great wines, while Bordeaux's crisp, fresh, dry whites have improved immeasurably. Both are blends of Sémillon, Sauvignon Blanc, and occasionally a little Muscadelle.

Typical Bordeaux *barriques*, used for maturing wine prior to bottling

◁ **Vineyard at Château Mouton-Rothschild in Pauillac**

WINE MAP OF BORDEAUX

THE GARONNE AND DORDOGNE rivers carve their way northwest through Bordeaux towards the Atlantic. They divide the region into three segments: west of the Garonne are the Left Bank vineyards of the Médoc, Graves, and Sauternes; east of the Dordogne is the Right Bank area including St-Émilion, Pomerol, and Fronsac. In between is the wedge of land known as Entre-Deux-Mers, literally 'between the two seas'.

KEY

Bordeaux

Harvesting Merlot grapes at Château Margaux's vineyards, Margaux, Left Bank

LEFT BANK: AREAS & TOP PRODUCERS

MÉDOC *p63*

HAUT-MÉDOC *p63*

ST-ESTÈPHE *p63*
Château Cos d'Estournel *p68*
Château Montrose *p68*

PAUILLAC *p64*
Château Lafite-Rothschild *p68*
Château Latour *p68*
Château Lynch-Bages *p69*
Château Mouton-Rothschild *p69*
Château Pichon-Longueville *p69*
Château Pichon-Longueville Comtesse de Lalande *p69*

ST-JULIEN *p64*
Château Ducru-Beaucaillou *p72*
Château Gruaud-Larose *p72*
Château Léoville-Barton *p72*
Château Léoville Las Cases *p72*

LISTRAC-MÉDOC *p64*

MOULIS *p64*

MARGAUX *p65*
Château Margaux *p72*
Château Palmer *p73*
Château Rauzan-Ségla *p73*

PESSAC-LÉOGNAN *p65*
Château Haut-Brion *p73*
Château La Mission Haut-Brion *p73*
Château Pape Clément *p74*
Château Smith-Haut-Lafitte *p74*
Domaine de Chevalier *p74*

GRAVES *p66*

SAUTERNES *p66*
Château Climens *p74*
Château d'Yquem *p75*
Château Lafaurie-Peyraguey *p75*
Château Rieussec *p75*
Château Suduiraut *p75*

Soulac-sur-Mer

Gironde

MÉDOC

MÉDOC

ST-ESTÈPHE
HAUT-MÉDOC
Pauillac
PAUILLAC
ST-JULIEN
Blaye

BLAYE, CÔTES DE BLAYE & PREMIÈRES CÔTES DE BLAYE

LISTRAC-MÉDOC

CÔTES DE BOURG

MOULIS
MARGAUX

FRONSAC
CANON FRONSA

Dordogne

HAUT-MÉDOC

LEFT BANK

BORDEAUX

PESSAC-LÉOGNAN

PREMIÈRES CÔTES DE BORDEAUX

Garonne

GRAVES

0 — km — 20

Château Pichon-Longueville in Pauillac, Left Bank

TERROIR AT A GLANCE

Latitude: 44.5–45.5°N.

Altitude: 0–10Cm.

Topography: Land form has little impact on winegrowing in this relatively flat region. Aspect, exposure, and proximity to the thermal warmth of the Gironde Estuary help ripening and protect against frost.

Soil: Varied; the best, notably St-Émilion's limestone plateau and the gravelly soils of the Médoc and Graves, help regulate the water supply to the vine.

Climate: Bordeaux's climate is temperate and maritime. Differences in temperature and rainfall patterns from one year to the next mean that quality varies from vintage to vintage. Overall, winters are mild and summers are hot.

Temperature: July average is 20.5°C.

Rainfall: Annual average is 900mm.

Viticultural hazards: Harvest rain; spring frost; water stress; grey rot.

RIGHT BANK
Coutras •
LALANDE-DE-
POMEROL
POMEROL
CÔTES DE
CASTILLON
& BORDEAUX-
CÔTES DE FRANCS
ST-ÉMILION
SATELLITES
• Libourne
ST-ÉMILION
& ST-ÉMILION
GRAND CRU
GRAVES
VAYRES
ENTRE-DEUX-MERS
& HAUT-BENAUGE
ENTRE-
DEUX-MERS
CADILLAC,
LOUPIAC &
STE-CROIX-
DU-MONT
• Langon
SAUTERNES

Red wines from Bordeaux

BORDEAUX CLASSIFICATIONS

THE PEOPLE OF BORDEAUX *like to know where they stand – hence the need to rank their wines in a table of merit. However, there is not just one system of classification in place; several different hierarchies have been introduced at various times over the past two centuries, each with its own history and intricate set of rules.*

1855 Classification
THE MOST FAMOUS Bordeaux classification relates to the red wines of the Médoc peninsula and the sweet white wines of Sauternes. The system was drawn up at the demand of Emperor Napoleon III for the wines that were being exhibited at the Universal Exhibition in Paris in 1855. The Bordeaux Syndicat des Courtiers ranked the wines based on decades of trading statistics. Sixty châteaux from the Médoc and one (Château Haut-Brion) from Graves were ordered in five different grades (*premier cru* to *cinquième cru* or first to fifth growth) according to commercial value. Likewise 26 châteaux in Sauternes and Barsac were ranked as either first or second growths, with Château d'Yquem singled out as *premier cru supérieur*. The list has changed only once: in 1973, Château Mouton-Rothschild was upgraded from second to first growth. The classification is still a fair indication of quality today, although some châteaux are more deserving of their status than others, and this is generally indicated by the price of the wines.

Graves *cru classé* label

Médoc that had missed out on classification in 1855. The 2003 decision to reclassify the category led to 78 châteaux being excluded, prompting heated legal battles. In 2007, the term *cru bourgeois* was officially annulled and deemed illegal by the French fraud office (DGCCRF). In 2008, however, the decision was taken to revive the category. It will be reintroduced in 2009, but the three-tiered ranking system (which included categories such as *cru bourgeois supérieur* and *cru bourgeois exceptionnel*) will not form part of the new classification.

1959 Graves Classification
THE GRAVES CLASSIFICATION was first compiled by the Institut National des Appellations d'Origine (INAO) in 1953 and updated in 1959. There is only one category, Graves *cru classé*, and châteaux are classified for either red wines or white wines, or both. The 16 châteaux selected are all located in AOC Pessac-Léognan.

Classification of the Médoc Crus Bourgeois
IN 1932, the *cru bourgeois* category was set up for estates located in one of the eight appellations in the

Classification of St-Émilion
ST-EMILION'S CLASSIFICATION is revised every 10 years, although the most recent one has caused no end of legal wrangles after four out of eight demoted châteaux protested. All were temporarily reinstated, but the French government council dismissed the move. There are two categories: *premier grand cru classé* and *grand cru classé*. Châteaux Ausone and Cheval Blanc are *premier grand cru classé* 'A'; a further 13 have 'B' status. The *grands crus classés* number 53.

St-Émilion *premier grand cru classé* label

Château Cos d'Estournel in St-Estèphe on the Left Bank

WINEGROWING AREAS OF THE LEFT BANK

THE LEFT BANK is the favoured zone for Cabernet Sauvignon, as the gravel soils of St-Estèphe, Pauillac, St-Julien, and Margaux on the Médoc peninsula, and Graves further south, are well suited to this late-ripening variety. Wines are usually firm and complex, and those of the top châteaux have great ageing potential. The Left Bank is also home to Sauternes, one of the world's finest sweet whites.

Château detail

ideal for the principal grape variety, Cabernet Sauvignon. With the requisite investment and skill, the area has the capacity to produce wines of a high standard with concentration, structure, and ageing potential. Five estates included in the 1855 classification – Belgrave, Camensac, Cantemerle, La Lagune, and La Tour Carnet – are located here, but most producers make the often good value *crus bourgeois*.

🏔 *gravel, limestone-and-clay* 🏵 *Cabernet Sauvignon, Merlot, Cabernet Franc, Petit Verdot* 🍷 *red*

Médoc

THE AOC MÉDOC is located, confusingly, only in the northern tip of 'the Médoc', the peninsula to the north of Bordeaux city. Formerly known as the Bas-Médoc, this area now has 5,000ha under vine. The land is flat with marshy areas, pasture, and generally heavy soils interspersed with the occasional gravelly outcrop. Médoc wines can be earthy, rustic, and even a little lean, but a recent increase in Merlot plantings and better winemaking have added more flesh and finesse. Much of the production is handled by co-operatives, but there are a growing number of good-value wines from individual châteaux.

🏔 *limestone-and-clay, sand, gravel* 🏵 *Cabernet Sauvignon, Merlot, Cabernet Franc, Petit Verdot* 🍷 *red*

Haut-Médoc

IN THE SOUTHERN half of the Médoc, the 4,500ha of viticultural land not covered by the six communal appellations (St-Estèphe, Pauillac, St-Julien, Listrac, Moulis, Margaux) is designated AOC Haut-Médoc. The mainly gravel soils are

St-Estèphe

THE MOST NORTHERLY of the Médoc's four pre-eminent communal appellations, AOC St-Estèphe has more of a rural feel than its neighbours. Large corporations are less evident here than further south, and estates remain primarily family owned. St-Estèphe has its share of gravel soils near the estuary, but there are also outcrops of limestone known as *calcaire de St-Estèphe*, and deposits of sand and clay to the west and north. Cabernet Sauvignon, grown on the cooler limestone soils, gives a slightly austere character to the wines, hence the move to plant the rounder, fleshier Merlot. In general, the wines are mouth-filling, firm, and long ageing. The *crus bourgeois* account for 54 per cent of production, the five classed growths 20 per cent, and the area's single co-op a further 17 per cent.

🏔 *gravel, limestone-and-clay, sand* 🏵 *Cabernet Sauvignon, Merlot, Cabernet Franc, Petit Verdot* 🍷 *red*

Pauillac

FOR MANY, PAUILLAC IS THE PERFECT example of a Médoc wine – powerful, concentrated, and long-lived with an almost pencil-lead mineral quality and the aroma of blackcurrants, cedar, and cigar box. It comes as no surprise, therefore, that three of the five 1855 first growths are located in AOC Pauillac (châteaux Lafite-Rothschild, Latour, and Mouton-Rothschild), as well as 15 other classified estates. Separated by a tiny stream from St-Estèphe, which lies to the north, Pauillac's deep, gravelly soils and close proximity to the warmth of the Gironde Estuary are the secrets behind its distinctive character. The *terroir* proves ideal for Cabernet Sauvignon, Pauillac's principal grape variety.

gravel *Cabernet Sauvignon, Merlot, Cabernet Franc, Petit Verdot* *red*

St-Julien

ONE REASON FOR St-Julien's unrivalled consistency in recent years is that 80 per cent of its 900ha is owned by 11 high-profile classified châteaux, five of them second growths, and all of them committed to a high level of quality. The other reason is location. A compact appellation on the Médoc, AOC St-Julien comprises two well-exposed and well-drained gravelly plateaux giving on to the Gironde Estuary. Cabernet Sauvignon is the dominant grape variety, but unlike the powerfully concentrated reds of neighbouring Pauillac, St-Julien's offerings show restraint, with a more mellow fruit character; 'balance' is their defining feature. They are, however, equally long-lived.

gravel *Cabernet Sauvignon, Merlot, Cabernet Franc, Petit Verdot* *red*

Listrac-Médoc

PLANTINGS OF MERLOT in AOC Listrac-Médoc now exceed those of Cabernet Sauvignon. The cool limestone-and-clay soils and greater distance from the warming Gironde Estuary mean the ripening cycle begins slightly later here than in the other Médoc appellations, making it harder to ripen Cabernet Sauvignon fully. In the past this meant tougher wines, but the use of more Merlot has added flesh and helped to soften tannins. The Listrac co-op is an important producer in this communal appellation, but the best wines come from the 20 individual *cru bourgeois* châteaux.

limestone-and-clay, gravel, sand *Merlot, Cabernet Sauvignon, Cabernet Franc, Petit Verdot* *red*

Moulis

THE SMALLEST of the Médoc's communal appellations, with 630ha, AOC Moulis shares its northern border with Listrac-Médoc and similarly has a percentage of limestone and clay soils. However, it also has a ridge of

Workers at Château Lafite-Rothschild, Pauillac

Turreted 19th-century residence of Château Palmer in Margaux

gravel to the east where Cabernet Sauvignon ripens fully. A handful of châteaux here produce wines of a quality and style similar to good Haut-Médoc, occasionally even of classed growth standard. Further inland on the cooler soils there is a greater percentage of Merlot and the wines are fruitier and less intense. As in Listrac-Médoc, the best wines come from the *crus bourgeois*.

gravel, limestone-and-clay Cabernet Sauvignon, Merlot, Cabernet Franc, Petit Verdot red

Margaux

THE LARGEST of the Médoc's communal appellations, world-famous Margaux has 1,500ha under vine, distributed through the villages of Arsac, Labarde, Cantenac, Soussans, and Margaux itself. The gravelly soils here, with low clay content and scant fertility, are suitable for little other than the vine. Ideal for Cabernet Sauvignon in particular, they result in wines of delicate weight, fragrant aroma, and fine tannic structure. 'Feminine' is often the adjective used to describe them, although modern winemaking techniques have slightly distorted this ideal, and some wines are now more concentrated. With 21 classified châteaux (1855), including first growth Château Margaux, standards should be high, but until the mid-1990s producers were complacent and Margaux underachieved. Now, with a younger generation at the helm, this AOC has gained considerably in quality

Château Margaux label, Margaux

and consistency, and is still improving.

gravel Cabernet Sauvignon, Merlot, Cabernet Franc, Petit Verdot red

Pessac-Léognan

THIS IS PROBABLY Bordeaux's oldest viticultural district, and the vine was cultivated here as far back as the Middle Ages. In 1987 the northern part of Graves became the separate appellation of Pessac-Léognan, taking its name from the two principal communes located to the west and south of the city of Bordeaux. Some of the vineyards are even enveloped in the city's urban sprawl. With its gravel soils, this is a district of great potential – as demonstrated by prestigious names such as châteaux Haut-Brion and Pape Clément – and has benefited from considerable investment in recent years. Both red and dry white wines are produced, but the region has always been noted for its reds – now accounting for 80 per cent of the total 1,450ha under vine. The red wines are similar in style to those of the Médoc – firm, structured, long-lived – but perhaps a little fuller on the palate, with a smoky, mineral nuance. The tiny production of dry white is the best seen in Bordeaux: fine, full, and persistent with the aroma and flavour of citrus fruits and an ability to age.

gravel Cabernet Sauvignon, Merlot, Cabernet Franc, Petit Verdot Sauvignon Blanc, Sémillon, Muscadelle red, white

BOTRYTIS CINEREA

Noble rot (*pourriture noble*), *Botrytis cinerea*, or botrytis is a fungal spore common in Sauternes. It reduces the water content of the grape, effectively increasing its sugar levels, acidity, viscosity, and flavour to give sweet, unctuous, and succulently aromatic wine. The humidity born of misty autumnal mornings followed by sunshine is ideal for the development of botrytis *(right)*, enabling it to perforate the fruit's skin but leave the pulp un-touched. The rot first appears as a brown spot, which then extends to cover the grape until it eventually shrivels. As the onset of noble rot is always irregular, the grapes are harvested selectively, often with several passages, or *tris*, through the vines. This explains the relatively small quantities of wine and the high production costs. The requisite nature of the climate means that a good Sauternes vintage does not necessarily correspond with a good vintage for red bordeaux.

Graves

THIS IS A REGION of small, family-owned estates that lack the level of investment of their northern neighbours in Pessac-Léognan. Good-value wines can be found, though, and increasingly so. As the name suggests, gravel soils exist, but there is also limestone-and-clay and sand. Reds from AOC Graves, produced from 2,750ha, have an increasing percentage of Merlot in the blend. These are fruity and should be drunk at four to five years. Dry white Graves, from a further 800ha, comes in two styles: crisp, fresh, aromatic, and bone dry, or rich and barrel-aged. There is also a small production of sweet Graves Supérieur made from late-harvested grapes.

🗺 *gravel, limestone-and-clay, sand* 🍇 *Cabernet Sauvignon, Merlot, Cabernet Franc* 🍇 *Sauvignon Blanc, Sémillon, Muscadelle* 🍷 *red, white, dessert*

Sauternes

THIS IS HOME TO SOME of the most luxuriously sweet, unctuous, aromatic wines in the world. The region of Sauternes, for white wines made only from botrytized grapes, is located 40km upstream from the city of Bordeaux on the left bank of the Garonne, surrounded by the vineyards of Graves. The AOC totals some 2,200ha dispersed through the five communes of Bommes, Fargues, Sauternes, Preignac, and Barsac. Producers in Barsac are permitted to label their wines as either Sauternes or Barsac, the rest are labelled as Sauternes. The top châteaux were classified in 1855, the most famous being Château d'Yquem. These rich, opulent wines are very representative of their *terroir*. The grapes, a majority Sémillon, ripen naturally at first, but in the autumn, if all goes well, the influence of the cool waters of the Ciron stream running into the warmer Garonne gives rise to the mists and humidity that provoke the onset of *Botrytis cinerea*. The grapes thus concentrated are selectively hand-picked, sometimes through to December. Yields are very low, officially no more than 25hl/ha. The variability of climate means there is considerable vintage variation, to the extent that top châteaux occasionally forego a vintage. The lower-lying land and higher limestone content in the soils make Barsac a generally lighter, less powerful wine than Sauternes. A tiny quantity of sweet wine of a less sumptuous nature than both Sauternes and Barsac is also produced in neighbouring AOC Cérons.

🗺 *gravel, limestone, sand* 🍇 *Sémillon, Sauvignon Blanc, Muscadelle* 🍷 *white, dessert*

Vineyards and ruined château in Sauternes

THE AUTHENTIC SOUTHWEST

THE SOUTHWEST IS *more a convenient grouping than a homogenous wine region, with vineyards dispersed over a wide and varying terrain. It encompasses some 30 AOCs in the southwest corner of France, from the edge of Bordeaux south to the Pyrenees and east to the city of Toulouse. The common denominator is wine of strong character produced from an eclectic selection of grape varieties.*

Located upstream from Bordeaux, the appellations of **Bergerac**, **Monbazillac** (known for sweet white wines), **Buzet**, **Côtes de Duras**, **Cahors**, and **Gaillac** were considered serious rivals to Bordeaux in the Middle Ages. The climate here is temperate, with winters a little colder further inland. The co-ops in these areas play an important role, supplying a large percentage of the wines. Bordeaux varieties – Cabernet Sauvignon, Merlot, and Cabernet Franc for reds and Sémillon, Sauvignon Blanc, and Muscadelle for whites – are usually cultivated in these AOCs, and the wines are comparable in style to those of Bordeaux. In Cahors, Malbec (known locally as Auxerrois) produces dark, minerally, tannic red wines. Gaillac, meanwhile, has an array of local grape varieties, including the white Mauzac and Len de l'El, resulting in a range of styles. The Négrette grape appears in the AOC **Côtes de Frontonnais**, producing spicy, aromatic reds.

Further south towards the Spanish border in Gascony and the Basque country are the appellations of **Madiran**, **Jurançon**, and **Irouléguy**. A revival in quality winemaking has taken place here over the past 15 years, led by a number of individual producers. The climate is again maritime, but with the influence of altitude in Jurançon and Irouléguy, where the vine is grown at 300 to 400m. The Tannat grape in Madiran produces firm, tannic reds softened by modern winemaking practices. The same variety blended with Cabernet Franc and Cabernet Sauvignon is found in Irouléguy. Tangy Jurançon comes in sweet and dry white versions made from Petit and Gros Manseng and Petit Courbu.

Château Montus label

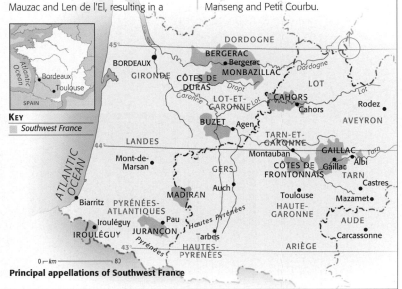

KEY

Southwest France

Principal appellations of Southwest France

TOP PRODUCERS OF THE LEFT BANK

Château Cos d'Estournel label

Château Cos d'Estournel
St-Estèphe

St-Estèphe **C** *05 56 73 15 50*
W *www.cosestournel.com* ☐ *by appt*

COS D'ESTOURNEL WAS founded in 1811 by Louis Gaspard d'Estournel, and it was his fascination with Asia that led to the construction of the eye-catching pagoda-like cellars that are still in use today. One of two second growths in St-Estèphe, Cos makes a distinctively rich, dense, and finely textured *grand vin*, with an uncharacteristically high percentage of Merlot in the blend, which adds extra body. The noteworthy second wine, Les Pagodes de Cos, was introduced in 1994. The property is currently owned by a French businessman and managed by Jean-Guillaume Prats – whose family were previous owners.
🍷 *red* 📆 *2005, 2001, 2000, 1998, 1996, 1995, 1994, 1990*

Château Montrose
St-Estèphe

St-Estèphe **C** *05 56 59 30 12*
☐ *by appt*

OWNED BY THE Charmolüe family since 1896, St-Estèphe's other second growth has a profile similar to that of Château Latour in Pauillac. Montrose's deep, gravelly vineyard lies in close proximity to the Gironde Estuary with a southeasterly exposure, and the Cabernet Sauvignon-dominated wines are firm, steely, and made for long ageing. In recent vintages, a heightened level of maturity in the wine has helped to soften the sometimes tough exterior.
🍷 *red* 📆 *2005, 2001, 2000, 1999, 1998, 1996, 1995, 1994, 1990*

Château Lafite-Rothschild
Pauillac

Pauillac **C** *05 56 73 18 18*
W *www.lafite.com* ☐ *by appt*

THE HISTORY OF Château Lafite can be traced back to the 14th century. Its name stems from the Gascon term *la hite* – meaning 'the hillock' – and indeed the 100-ha vineyard is planted on a gravelly knoll facing the Gironde Estuary. The estate was ranked first of the first growths in 1855, and Lafite's wines have always been noted for their elegance and capacity for ageing. Thanks to changes in the selection and in the winemaking processes, vintages since 1995 have been sublime with added weight, volume, and texture. The estate has been owned by the Rothschild family since 1868. Its second label is called Carruades de Lafite, a wine that has also much improved since 1995.
🍷 *red* 📆 *2005, 2001, 2000, 1999, 1998, 1997, 1996, 1995, 1994, 1990*

Château Latour
Pauillac

Pauillac **C** *05 56 73 19 80*
W *www.chateau-latour.com* ☐ *by appt*

CHÂTEAU LATOUR HAS the classic profile of a Pauillac. Produced mainly from Cabernet Sauvignon grown on deep gravel soils, the wine has a subdued power, cool, steely frame, and scents of blackcurrant and cedar. The heart of the estate

Cellar designed by Ricardo Bofill at Château Lafite-Rothschild

Château Lynch-Bages label

is the Enclos vineyard, which surrounds the château and recently renovated cellars (2002); this is the mainstay of the wine, while other parcels of land are used for the excellent second label wine, Les Forts de Latour. Following 30 years of British ownership, Château Latour was purchased by French businessman François Pinault in 1993.

🍷 red 🔖 2005, 2001, 2000, 1999, 1998, 1996, 1995, 1994, 1990

Château Lynch-Bages
Pauillac

Pauillac 📞 05 56 73 24 00
🖥 www.lynchbages.com 🔲 by appt

CHÂTEAU LYNCH-BAGES has the most distinctive of wine styles. Dominated by Cabernet Sauvignon, opulence and exuberance distinguish the wine here from other more steely and reserved Pauillacs. Its popularity is evident: Lynch-Bages has for a number of years sold well above the price of its fifth growth status. Located on the Bages plateau, the estate was at one time owned by the Lynch family from Galway in Ireland, but is now in the hands of the Cazes. A tiny amount of white wine, Blanc de Lynch-Bages, is also made – from Sémillon, Sauvignon Blanc, and Muscadelle. Something of a rarity for the Médoc, it is similar in style to white Graves.

🍷 red, white 🔖 red: 2005, 2001, 2000, 1999, 1998, 1996, 1995, 1990

Château Mouton-Rothschild
Pauillac

Pauillac 📞 05 56 73 21 29
🖥 www.bphr.com 🔲 by appt

ORIGINALLY KNOWN AS Château Brane-Mouton, the name was changed in 1853 when Baron Nathaniel de Rothschild bought the property. Classified as a second growth in 1855, Château Mouton-Rothschild was upgraded to first growth status in 1973. This was largely due to the persistence of Baron Philippe de Rothschild, who took over in 1922. Among other things, he initiated the idea of artist-designed labels *(see pp70–71)*. Since 1945, every vintage has had a label created by one of a host of illustrious names including Marc Chagall, Salvador Dalí, Joan Miró, and Andy Warhol. Mouton is a rich, dense, and opulent wine, and there is also a second label, Le Petit Mouton, and a small amount of white, called L'Aile d'Argent.

🍷 red, white 🔖 red: 2005, 2001, 2000, 1999, 1998, 1996, 1995, 1994, 1990

Château Pichon-Longueville
Pauillac

Pauillac 📞 05 56 73 17 17
🖥 www.pichonlongueville.com
🔲 by appt

IN 1850 Baron Joseph de Pichon-Longueville divided the family property equally between his five children. Second growth Château Pichon-Longueville (Baron) was the part inherited by his two sons. Its Cabernet Sauvignon-dominated wine is more classically powerful than the wine from the other division across the road. The

Château Mouton-Rothschild

CHÂTEAU LABELS

Each of Bordeaux's châteaux has a main wine, or grand vin, which is identified simply by the name of the château. The names of second label wines are usually also derived from the names of their estates. Some estates additionally have third labels.

estate has been owned since 1987 by insurance company AXA-Millésimes, who restored the château and built a modern winery designed by two international architects.

🍷 red 🔖 2005, 2001, 2000, 1999, 1998, 1996, 1995, 1990

Château Pichon-Longueville Comtesse de Lalande
Pauillac

Pauillac 📞 05 56 59 19 40 🖥 www.pichon-lalande.com 🔲 by appt

THIS PROPERTY IS made up of the three fifths of the original Pichon-Longueville estate *(see left)* belonging to Baron de Pichon-Longueville's daughters. As all three parts were managed by one daughter, Virginie, they came to be known by her married name, Comtesse de Lalande. Another indomitable lady, May-Eliane de Lencquesaing has owned and administered the estate since 1978, maintaining its status as a top second growth. The wine, with a slightly higher percentage of Merlot in the blend than is normal in Pauillac, is round and suave, and seductive from an early age.

🍷 red 🔖 2005, 2001, 2000, 1999, 1998, 1996, 1995, 1994, 1990

MOUTON-ROTHSCHILD WINE LABELS

Baron Philippe (right)

IN 1945, BARON PHILIPPE DE ROTHSCHILD celebrated the end of World War II by commissioning an illustrated label for Château Mouton-Rothschild. It was the beginning of a tradition. For each vintage since the war, the estate has called on a contemporary artist to create an original work for the new wine. Two exceptions are 1953, celebrating the estate's centenary, and 1977, in honour of a visit from Britain's late Queen Mother.

FAMOUS CONTRIBUTORS

Illustrations by many celebrated artists have graced the labels of Mouton-Rothschild. Each contributor was asked to interpret the themes of the vine, the joy of drinking, and the symbol of the estate – the Augsburg Ram, a 16th-century drinking vessel in the Rothschild estate museum. Each artist received cases of the estate's wine as payment for their work. The artists include:

1955 Georges Braque
1957 André Masson
1958 Salvador Dali
1964 Henry Moore
1959 Joan Miró
1970 Marc Chagall
1971 Wassily Kandinsky
1972 Serge Poliakoff
1973 Pablo Picasso
1974 Robert Motherwell
1975 Andy Warhol
1980 Hans Hartung
1990 Francis Bacon

2000 vintage
The 2000 Mouton-Rothschild has no paper label. The bottle was decorated with an enamel reproduction of the Augsburg Ram.

Statues at the estate museum

1987 vintage
Swiss painter Hans Erni (born 1909) created the label for the 1987 vintage. It symbolizes Baron Philippe de Rothschild resplendent with the Augsburg Ram's grape-laden horns. Erni's label proved a final tribute to Baron Philippe, who died in January 1988.

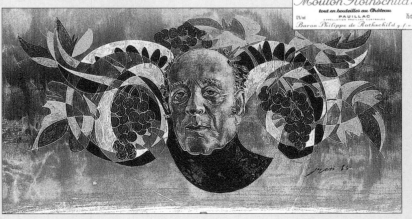

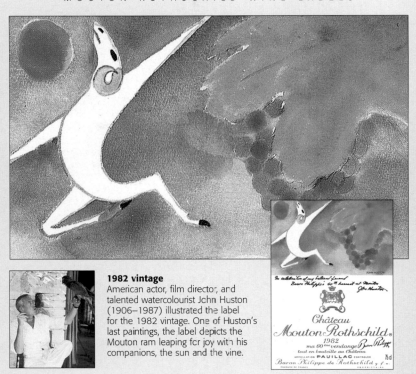

1982 vintage

American actor, film director, and talented watercolourist John Huston (1906–1987) illustrated the label for the 1982 vintage. One of Huston's last paintings, the label depicts the Mouton ram leaping for joy with his companions, the sun and the vine.

1947 vintage

French poet, film director, and designer Jean Cocteau (1889–1963) inspired the illustration for the 1947 vintage. Cocteau's line-drawing was a profile of the actor and painter Jean Marais. The original was lost, but Marais created a copy for the 1947 Mouton label.

Château Ducru-Beaucaillou
St-Julien

St-Julien Beychevelle
☎ 05 56 73 16 73 ☐ *by appt*

THIS 19TH-CENTURY château, with its long central building and twin square towers, is prominently positioned close to the Gironde Estuary at the southern end of St-Julien. Set discreetly behind it is a new, hi-tech barrel cellar built in 1999. The pebbles of quartz, flint, and other rocks, or *beaux cailloux*, which gave the château its 'Beaucaillou' name, are visible in the vineyard. Wood contamination in the old barrel cellars caused some irregularity with vintages in the late 1980s, but the estate is now back on top form. The wines of this second growth château are ripe and elegant, but need at least 10 years to fully develop.
🍷 *red* 🔖 *2005, 2001, 2000, 1999, 1998, 1996, 1995*

Château Ducru-Beaucaillou

Château Gruaud-Larose
St-Julien

St-Julien Beychevelle
☎ 05 56 73 15 20 ☐ *by appt*

CHÂTEAU GRUAUD-LAROSE overlooks a tiny stream to the south of the appellation St-Julien. The well-exposed vineyard is located in one single plot on deep gravel soils with a high percentage of clay. This partly accounts for the rich, full nature of the wine. The estate has changed hands several times in the last 20 years, but between 1993 and 1997 it benefited from a massive programme of investment under owner Alcatel-Alstom, the industrial

conglomerate. The Merlaut family is the present owner of this second growth estate.
🍷 *red* 🔖 *2005, 2001, 2000, 1999, 1998, 1996, 1995, 1990*

Château Léoville-Barton
St-Julien

St-Julien Beychevelle ☎ 05 56 59 06 05 🌐 *www.leoville-barton.com* ☐ *by appt*

HAVING PURCHASED Château Léoville-Barton in 1826, the originally Irish Barton family has the longest-standing ownership of a classified estate in the Médoc. The present guardian, Anthony Barton, has been managing this second growth property since 1982 and has confirmed it as one of the most consistent in the Médoc. Traditionally made in wooden vats, the wine is classically long-lived with balance and reserve. Winemaking facilities are shared with third growth Château Langoa-Barton, which is also owned by the Barton family.
🍷 *red* 🔖 *2005, 2001, 2000, 1999, 1998, 1996, 1995, 1994, 1990*

Château Léoville Las Cases
St-Julien

St-Julien Beychevelle
☎ 05 56 73 25 26 ☐ *by appt*

ALTHOUGH SITUATED IN St-Julien, the heart of the Léoville Las Cases vineyard – the Grand Enclos – lies adjacent to Château Latour, and not surprisingly the wine has more than a hint of Pauillac steel. A draconian system of selection sees only 40 per cent of the production destined

for the *grand vin*, the rest going to the very good second label, Clos du Marquis, or sold on in bulk to *négociants*. Although classified as a second growth, Las Cases now merits comparison with the first growths.
🍷 *red* 🔖 *2005, 2001, 2000, 1999, 1998, 1996, 1995, 1994, 1990*

Château Margaux
Margaux

Margaux ☎ 05 57 88 83 83 🌐 *www.chateau-margaux.com* ☐ *by appt*

THIS FIRST GROWTH château, with its imposing colonnaded residence, has rarely put a foot wrong since its purchase by the Mentzelopoulos family in 1978. The estate has a total of 90ha under production, and the wine, a mainly Cabernet Sauvignon blend with an often rather interesting 'seasoning' of Petit Verdot, combines natural power with elegance. The excellent second label wine is called Pavillon Rouge, and there is also a top quality white, Pavillon Blanc, which is made solely from Sauvignon Blanc and designated, as the appellation rules demand, as a generic bordeaux.
🍷 *red, white* 🔖 *red: 2005, 2001, 2000, 1999, 1998, 1996, 1995, 1994, 1993, 1990*

Château Léoville Barton label

Château Palmer
Margaux

Cantenac ☎ 05 57 88 72 72
ⓦ www.chateau-palmer.com
☐ by appt

THIS ESTATE WAS established in
the 19th century by Major-
General Charles Palmer, an
English officer in Wellington's
army. It is now owned by a
consortium of Dutch, English,
and French families. For many
years Palmer's reputation has
exceeded its third growth
ranking, and in the 1960s
and 70s the wines were
superior even to Château
Margaux. A healthy percentage
of Merlot contributes to
Château Palmer's legendary
velvety texture, while recent
investment (1995) in new
winemaking facilities has
helped to maintain quality.
The second wine, Alter Ego
de Palmer, is also excellent.
🟥 red 🔺 2005, 2001, 2000,
1999, 1998, 1996, 1995, 1990

Château Rauzan-Ségla
Margaux

Margaux ☎ 05 57 88 82 10
☐ by appt

DEEMED THE appellation's
second wine after
Château Margaux in
the 1855 ranking,
Château Rauzan-Ségla had a
chequered reputation in the
late 1900s. Fine vintages were
produced in 1983, 1986, and
1988 but it is only since the
property was bought by the
Wertheimer family, owners
of Chanel, in 1994 that the
estate has regained its former
glory and consistency. A
massive programme of investment has transformed this
second growth property,
and the wine now expresses
true distinction and elegance.
🟥 red 🔺 2005, 2001, 2000, 1999,
1998, 1996, 1995

Château La Mission Haut-Brion

Château Palmer

Château Haut-Brion
Pessac-Léognan

Pessac Cedex ☎ 05 56 00 29 30
ⓦ www.haut-brion.com ☐ by appt

OWNED BY THE American
Dillon family since 1935,
Château Haut-Brion was first
established in the 16th
century. It was the only
estate outside the Médoc
to be classified as a first
growth in 1855. The
45-ha vineyard is
now surrounded by
Bordeaux's urban
sprawl and grapes
grown here are some
of the earliest in the
region to ripen, bringing
a reliable maturity.
This and a generous
helping of Merlot
in the blend make
Haut-Brion less
austere than its Médoc peers.
A tiny quantity of lush, rich,
dry white is also produced.
🟥 red, white 🔺 red: 2005, 2001,
2000, 1999, 1998, 1996, 1995,
1994, 1993, 1990

Château La Mission Haut-Brion
Pessac-Léognan

Pessac Cedex ☎ 05 56 00 29 30
ⓦ www.haut-brion.com ☐ by appt

CHÂTEAU LA MISSION Haut-Brion
was acquired by the Dillon
family in 1993 and is now
part of the same stable as
neighbouring Château
Haut-Brion. Despite sharing
the same winemaking team
and using similar technical
facilities, each wine
maintains a distinctive style.
While Haut-Brion is fine and
elegant with a certain
subtlety, La Mission is rich
and fleshy with a powerful,
open character. Haut-Brion
is usually the superior wine.
🟥 red 🔺 2005, 2001, 2000, 1999,
1998, 1996, 1995, 1994, 1990

PERFECT CASE: LEFT BANK SECOND LABELS

Ⓡ Château Palmer Alter Ego ££

Ⓡ Château Lafite-Rothschild Carruades de Lafite £££

Ⓡ Château Bahans Haut-Brion £££

Ⓡ Château Léoville Las Cases Clos du Marquis £££

Ⓡ Château Montrose La Dame ££

Ⓡ Château Léoville-Barton La Réserve ££

Ⓡ Château Mouton-Roth- schild Le Petit Mouton £

Ⓡ Château Pape Clément Le Clémentin £££

Ⓡ Château Latour Les Forts £££

Ⓡ Château Cos d'Estournel Les Pagodes de Cos ££

Ⓡ Château Margaux Pavillon Rouge £££

Ⓡ Château Pichon-Longue- ville Comtesse Réserve ££

Château Pape Clément label

Château Pape Clément
Pessac-Léognan

216 ave du Docteur Nancel Pénard, Pessac 📞 *05 57 26 38 38* 🖥 *www.pape-clement.com* ⬜ *by appt*

PAPE CLÉMENT'S history can be traced back to the 14th century, but its modern renaissance began in 1985. A new vinification cellar was built, a second wine, Le Clémentin, introduced to improve selection, and the vineyards were steadily over-hauled. A further revolution came in 2001, when an army of 120 people was brought in to destem the grapes by hand. Already deeply coloured, rich, and full, Pape Clément has gained even more in concentration and texture since this vintage. A tiny quantity of white Pape Clément is also produced.
🟥 *red, white* ➡ *red: 2005, 2001, 2000, 1999, 1998, 1996, 1995, 1990*

Château Smith-Haut-Lafitte
Pessac-Léognan

Martillac 📞 *05 57 83 11 22* 🖥 *www.smith-haut-lafitte.com* ⬜ *by appt*

THERE HAS BEEN no expense spared to improve this ancient estate since it was purchased by Florence and Daniel Cathiard in 1990. The vineyard has been entirely restructured, yields reduced, and organic methods applied. The cellars have been renovated, new wooden fermenting tanks introduced, and a cooperage, which provides 50 per cent of the barrels, launched. The château's aromatic Sauvignon Blanc was the first to benefit, but since 1994 the red, made from the usual blend of Cabernet Sauvignon, Cabernet Franc, and Merlot, has gained in density, body, and finesse.
🟥 *red, white* ➡ *red: 2005, 2001, 2000, 1999, 1998, 1996, 1995, 1994, 1990*

Domaine de Chevalier
Pessac-Léognan

102 chemin de Mignoy, Léognan 📞 *05 56 64 16 16* 🖥 *www.domainedechevalier.com* ⬜ *by appt*

THE LONG-LIVED, Sauvignon Blanc-based white wine is the star of this property, but quantities are extremely limited. The red, mainly Cabernet Sauvignon, has improved in recent years and is now a classic Graves wine, complex and minerally with balance and great length. Domaine de Chevalier has been immaculately run by Olivier Bernard since 1983. New winemaking facilities have been built, the vineyard revamped, and four large wind machines introduced to counter the spring frosts.
🟥 *red, white* ➡ *red: 2005, 2001, 2000, 1999, 1998, 1996, 1995, 1990*

Château Climens
Sauternes

Barsac 📞 *05 56 27 15 33* ⬜ *by appt*

FIRST GROWTH Château Climens is the leading estate in Barsac, producing archetypal sweet white wine from this region, rich and concentrated but with a delicate edge of acidity. Usually discreet at first, Climens needs at least 10 years to develop a complex panoply of honeyed aromas, and then continues to evolve for a number of years. The

NO ORDINARY OENOLOGISTS

Bordeaux University's Faculté d'Oenologie has had a vital influence on winemaking around the world. Its *raison d'être* is to facilitate research, introduce new production methods, and educate oenologists. Since its foundation in 1880, the faculty's work has been continued by a number of dedicated directors, including three members of the same family – Ulysse Gayon (who studied and worked with Louis Pasteur), Jean Ribéreau-Gayon, and his son Pascal – and the present incumbent Yves Glories.

Consultant oenologists connected with the faculty have also had an impact on modern winemaking. One of the best known is Émile Peynaud, who established many existing winemaking practices, including the control of malolactic fermentation and the importance of mastering fermentation temperatures. Also of international fame is Bordelais Michel Rolland *(right)*, an advocate of super ripeness in grapes, who works worldwide.

Harvesting in the vineyard of Château Suduiraut with Château d'Yquem in the distance

property was bought by Lucien Lurton in 1971 and is now owned and run by his daughter Bérénice.

🖼 *white, dessert*
📂 *2007, 2005, 2003, 2001*

Château d'Yquem
Sauternes

Sauternes 📞 *05 57 98 07 07*
🌐 *www.chateau-yquem.fr* ⬤

CHÂTEAU D'YQUEM has been in a league of its own for many years. Classified *premier cru supérieur* in 1855 *(see p62)*, it enjoyed the continuity of single ownership under the Lur-Saluces family from 1785 until its sale to the luxury goods group LVMH in 1996. The commitment stays the same. The grapes, mainly Sémillon with a little Sauvignon Blanc, are selectively harvested in the extensive 100-ha vineyard, sometimes berry by berry. Yields are tiny – the equivalent of a glass of wine per vine – and if the vintage is not up to scratch (as in 1992), no Yquem is made. Fermentation and ageing take place in new oak barrels, where the wine

Château d'Yquem

remains for three and a half years. The result is a rich, powerful, exotic elixir.

🖼 *white, dessert*
📂 *2007, 2005, 2003, 2001*

Château Lafaurie-Peyraguey
Sauternes

Bommes 📞 *05 57 19 57 77*
⬛ *by appt*

THE MAGNIFICENT 1983 vintage re-launched the reputation of this first growth château. Since then its sweet white wines have been rich and fragrant with a wonderful concentration of fruit. The property comprises a château, which dates from the 13th century, and a well-exposed vineyard situated on a hillock in the commune of Bommes.

🖼 *white, dessert*
📂 *2007, 2005, 2003, 2001*

Château Rieussec
Sauternes

Fargues de Langon 📞 *05 57 98 14 14* 🌐 *www.lafite.com* ⬛ *by appt*

IF EVER CHÂTEAU D'YQUEM had a rival for the power and concentration of its Sauternes, it would have to

be neighbouring Château Rieussec. Purchased by the Rothschild family of Château Lafite in 1985, this first growth estate has since developed greater continuity and purity of fruit. The selective harvesting is more precise, fermentation takes place in barrel (since 1996), and the period of ageing has been lengthened from 15 months to two and a half years.

🖼 *white, dessert*
📂 *2007, 2005, 2003, 2001*

Château Suduiraut
Sauternes

Preignac 📞 *05 56 63 61 92*
🌐 *www.chateausuduiraut.com*
⬛ *by appt*

INSURANCE COMPANY owners AXA-Millésimes have completely renovated the magnificent 18th-century château of this first growth estate, with its gardens designed by Le Nôtre. The wine, too, has benefited from greater investment both in the extensive 90-ha vineyard and in the cellars. Recent vintages have all been a great success, producing unctuous Sauternes that is finely balanced and has considerable ageing potential.

🖼 *white, dessert*
📂 *2007, 2005, 2003, 2001*

Harvest time at the world-famous Château Pétrus in Pomerol

WINEGROWING AREAS OF THE RIGHT BANK

THE LIMESTONE AND CLAY soils of the Right Bank make earlier ripening Merlot the king in this part of Bordeaux. St-Émilion and Pomerol are the key appellations, producing round, sappy, full-bodied wines. There is also good value from Fronsac and the numerous 'Côtes'.

St-Émilion & St-Émilion Grand Cru

THE VINE WAS CULTIVATED in St-Émilion as far back as Gallo-Roman times. Today, the appellation encompasses exactly the same area that was set out in the original administrative charter of 1289: nine parishes, including the medieval town of St-Émilion. In 1999, the whole district was declared a

Detail of Château Pavie, a *premier grand cru classé* in St-Émilion

World Heritage site by UNESCO. In contrast to the Médoc on the Left Bank, the mainly limestone-and-clay soils are better adapted to Merlot than the later ripening Cabernet Sauvignon. Cabernet Franc, known locally as Bouchet, used to be more widely planted and is an important second element in most blends. St-Émilion wines as a whole offer soft fruit and a cool freshness, the best with a fine tannic structure and the ability to age. Modern styles are darker, riper, and more concentrated. In all, St-Émilion has 5,500ha under production, declared as either AOC St-Émilion or AOC St-Émilion Grand Cru. Both have the same geographical delimitations, but

the latter requires a higher minimum alcohol content, lower yields, and the approval of two tasting panels. The superior designation accounts for 65 per cent of production and includes all the classified châteaux.

 *limestone-and-clay, gravel, sand*
Merlot, Cabernet Franc, Cabernet Sauvignon *red*

St-Émilion Satellites

THE SO-CALLED St-Émilion Satellites are really the northern extension of the St-Émilion hillslopes, separated from these by the tiny Barbanne stream. Four AOC communes – Lussac, Montagne, Puisseguin, and St-Georges – have the authorization to append St-Émilion to their communal names. The same limestone-and-clay soils can be found as well as silty sand, but the ripening cycle is just that bit later, meaning the autumn weather is critical for the harvest. Merlot is the dominant grape variety, and the wines are similar in style to St-Émilion, although perhaps a touch more rustic. The level of investment is not as high, but this is reflected in the prices – these wines remain in the value-for-money bracket. There are numerous small producers, but the co-operative, Les Producteurs Réunis, accounts for 40 per cent of AOC Lussac-St-Émilion's production and 20 per cent of AOC Puisseguin-St-Émilion's. All told, there are

3,900ha under production in the area; AOC Montagne-St-Émilion is the largest division.
limestone-and-clay, sand Merlot, Cabernet Franc, Cabernet Sauvignon red

Pomerol

AT ITS VERY BEST, Pomerol is the ultimate in wine seduction. Rich and unctuous, it has a velvety texture and sumptuous bouquet as well as a firm inner core, which allows it to age well. There are nearly 800ha in production. The average holding is only 6.5ha, so quantities of wine are limited. Accordingly, there is a rarity value and the prices are high. Strangely, these wines were relatively unknown outside of France and the Benelux countries until the 1950s. Unlike neighbouring St-Émilion, there is no limestone in Pomerol, but gravel, sand, and clay make this an early ripening zone in which mainly Merlot (80 per cent) is cultivated with positive results. Located on a gently sloping plateau northeast of the town of Libourne, the richest wines come from the clay and gravel soils of the central plateau. It is here that all the top châteaux, including Pétrus, Lafleur, and Le Pin, can be found. On the lower terraces to the west and south, the soils are sandier and the wines lighter and less powerful in style. AOC Pomerol is the only major wine district in Bordeaux to have no official classification system.
gravel, clay, sand Merlot, Cabernet Franc, Cabernet Sauvignon red

Château Angélus entrance, St-Émilion Grand Cru

THE SOILS OF ST-ÉMILION

Hillslope vineyard of Château Ausone

Six principal soil zones can be identified in the large St-Émilion region, each with its own effect on the quality and style of the wine. The best restrict the water supply to the vine, thus helping to concentrate tannins, colour, and extract in the grapes.

Limestone plateau
In the centre of the district lies a bedrock of limestone formed from an accumulation of fossilized marine life. The porous limestone rations the uptake of water to the vine, giving the wines fine tannins, a cool freshness, and the ability to age. A good percentage of St-Émilion's *premiers grands crus classés* (châteaux Belair, Canon, Magdelaine, and Clos Fourtet) have vineyards here.

Hillslopes
The hillslopes or *côtes* around the limestone plateau are composed of a deeper clay-and-limestone mix. The wines are more tannic and equally long-lived. St-Émilion's classified estates (châteaux Ausone, Pavie, l'Arrosée, La Clotte, Larcis-Ducasse) are much in evidence here.

Footslopes
The footslopes, or *pieds de côtes*, have a mixture of sand and clay soils. These are not as favourable as those of the plateau and *côtes*, but can produce interesting results.

Quaternary gravel
At the northwest limit, bordering Pomerol, lies a band of gravelly soils identical to those in the Médoc. Two *premiers grands crus classés*, Cheval Blanc and Figeac, are the principal beneficiaries of these warmer soils. Wines are complex and age well.

Ancient sands
These wind-blown sands cover a large percentage of the northwest corner of St-Émilion. Water control is less efficient and the wines have a lighter weight and frame, are attractively fruity, and are best drunk at two to five years.

Dordogne plain
The fertile alluvial plain between the footslopes and the Dordogne River is less conducive to producing top-quality wines. Wines are generally fruity and for early drinking.

Vineyards around Canon-Fronsac

Lalande-de-Pomerol

THERE HAS RECENTLY been an undercurrent of activity in this satellite district, with new investment and a younger generation coming to the helm. Located directly north of its more prestigious neighbour Pomerol, across the tiny Barbanne stream, AOC Lalande-de-Pomerol has 1,150ha under vine. As in Pomerol, the properties are small, the price of the wines is on the high side (although not in the same league as Pomerol), and Merlot is the dominant variety, with 75 per cent of vineyard space. The soils vary, but it is the areas of gravel and clay that have the potential to produce wines of a similar type to Pomerol, if not with the same weight and ability to age. The further west one goes in the appellation, the sandier the soils, and the lighter the wines.

 gravel, clay, sand Merlot, Cabernet Franc, Cabernet Sauvignon, Malbec red

Fronsac & Canon-Fronsac

WEST OF THE TOWN of Libourne, AOC Fronsac and the tiny 300-ha enclave of AOC Canon-Fronsac form a triangular area bounded to the east by the Isle River and to the south by the Dordogne River. In the 18th and 19th centuries, wines from this area were as highly regarded as those of St-Émilion. Towards the end of the 19th century, however, phylloxera destroyed the vineyards, and it was not until the 1970s that a renaissance got under way. Investment in the 1980s and 90s has given new life to these appellations, and the top wines are now back on a par with those of

St-Émilion. The soils on this hilly terrain are mostly clay and limestone on a bedrock of loamy-clay known as *fronsadais molasse*. The main grape variety, as in most Right Bank AOCs, is Merlot (78 per cent). The wines have a natural power and concentration, but there is a tendency towards astringency and rusticity if not carefully produced. Later harvests and investment in new barrels and winemaking equipment have gone some way to eradicating this problem. The generally south-facing exposure and higher limestone content of Canon-Fronsac gives it the potential to produce finer wines then Fronsac. In reality, however, this potential is rarely fulfilled; the quality of the wines is often variable.

limestone-and-clay, sandstone Merlot, Cabernet Franc, Cabernet Sauvignon, Malbec red

Côtes de Castillon & Bordeaux-Côtes de Francs

THE CÔTES DE CASTILLON has 3,000ha under vine and a similar profile to St-Émilion. The limestone plateau and hillslopes are planted with a majority of Merlot vines and some Cabernet Franc, which make full-bodied red wines with a firm, fresh finish. The key difference is that the Côtes de Castillon has a slightly cooler climate, and therefore the harvest is later, as good fruit ripeness is needed to prevent the wines from becoming too acidic. The area had been held back by limited investment, but this AOC is now making some of the most interesting wines on the Right Bank. The AOC Côtes de Castillon takes its name from the town of Castillon-la-Bataille, where in 1453 the French army defeated the English, ending 300 years of English rule in Aquitaine *(see p17)*.

Located northeast of the Côtes de Castillon, AOC Bordeaux-Côtes de Francs is a much smaller district producing red and a limited quantity of white wines. Standards for both tend to be high. Cabernet Sauvignon and Cabernet Franc play a greater role in the reds

THE BORDEAUX BARRIQUE

The famous Bordeaux barrels, or *barriques (right)*, are used throughout France and all over the world. The *barrique* classically holds 225l of wine, measures 95cm in height, and is made from oak staves that are 20 to 22mm thick. The *barrique* is used for fermenting, maturing, or conditioning wine prior to bottling, and fine wines can spend up to two years in barrel. The slow absorption of tiny amounts of oxygen through the wood helps to soften tannins, stabilize colour, and increase the wine's aromatic complexity. Many top Bordeaux estates use new oak barrels, which are micro-biologically more stable than old ones, and give additional aroma and flavour.

here, yielding wines that are less aromatic but with a firm presence on the palate and good ageing potential. The whites are full, rich, and fragrant, with good acidity. In 2009 the first wines will be made under the new Côtes de Bordeaux appellation. It will run alongside the *premières côtes* appellations and comprise Côtes de Bordeaux Blaye, Côtes de Bordeaux Castillon, Côtes de Bordeaux Francs, and Côtes de Bordeaux Cadillac.

🗺 *limestone-and-clay, sand, gravel* 🍇 *Merlot, Cabernet Franc, Cabernet Sauvignon* 🍇 *Sémillon, Sauvignon Blanc, Muscadelle* 🍷 *red, white*

Côtes de Bourg

THE AOC CÔTES DE BOURG is known locally as the Gironde's little Switzerland because of the hilly limestone-and-clay terrain. Located at the confluence of the Dordogne river and the Gironde estuary, this area has a slightly warmer climate than other parts of Bordeaux, which helps to ward off frost. Average rainfall is also one of the lowest in the region. The Romans were the first to discover the viticultural potential of this compact district, and wines have been made here ever since. Merlot is the main red variety cultivated in the area's 3,900ha, but wines are still very much a blend, occasionally including Malbec, which represents six per cent of the vineyard area.

Wines are usually full-bodied and firm, with an earthy fruitiness that has become more refined in recent years. A very small quantity of white is also produced. There are a few good individual producers, and the co-operatives are becoming increasingly quality-conscious, in particular the Cave de Bourg-Tauriac.

🗺 *limestone-and-clay* 🍇 *Merlot, Cabernet Franc, Cabernet Sauvignon, Malbec* 🍇 *Sauvignon Blanc, Sémillon, Colombard, Muscadelle* 🍷 *red, white*

Blaye, Côtes de Blaye & Premières Côtes de Blaye

THE DISTRICT OF BLAYE surrounds that of Bourg, but the vineyards are more spread out and the terrain varied. There are three main poles of production: around the port of Blaye to the west, north near the little town of St-Ciers, and south at St-Savin. Nearly 6,000ha are planted in these zones with mixed agriculture in between. Over 90 per cent of the production is red, labelled AOC Premières Côtes de Blaye. Merlot is still the dominant variety, but the wines are crisper in style than those of the Côtes de Bourg, with less weight and structure. Since 2000 there has been a superior designation for red wines, AOC Blaye. These are essentially richer and more concentrated wines, requiring lower yields, and verification by a second tasting panel at 18 months. White Premières Côtes de Blaye is Sauvignon Blanc-dominated and often good value. It can be fresh and fruity, as well as generous in style.

🗺 *limestone-and-clay, sand, gravel* 🍇 *Merlot, Cabernet Sauvignon, Cabernet Franc, Malbec* 🍇 *Sauvignon Blanc, Sémillon, Muscadelle* 🍷 *red, white*

Detail on château, Premières Côtes de Blaye

TOP PRODUCERS OF THE RIGHT BANK

Château Angélus
St-Émilion Grand Cru

St-Émilion ☎ 05 57 24 71 39
Ⓦ *www.chateau-angelus.com*
Ⓞ *b/ appt*

CHÂTEAU ANGÉLUS has been a catalyst for improvement in St-Émilion since the mid-1980s, and it was justly promoted to *premier grand cru classé* in 1996. Better management, strict grape selection, and skilled cellar techniques have been the stamp of owner Hubert de Boüard. The wines, a blend of Merlot and Cabernet Franc, display a contemporary style of St-Émilion: deep in colour, aromatic, rich, and concentrated, with an overlay of new oak.
🍷 *red* ⯃ *2005, 2001, 2000, 1999, 1998, 1997, 1996, 1995, 1994, 1990*

Château Ausone
St-Émilion Grand Cru

St-Émilion ☎ 05 57 24 68 88 ◉

ALTHOUGH ONE OF two A status St-Émilion *premiers grands crus classés*, there is still an air of exclusivity about Ausone due to its limited production – only 2,000 cases per year from the 7-ha vineyard. Those who have the privilege of tasting the wines find a freshness and elegance that persists with time. Under the aegis of owner Alain Vauthier,

vintages since 1995 have been exemplary, with great aromatic complexity and a polished texture.
🍷 *red* ⯃ *2005, 2001, 2000, 1999, 1998, 1997, 1996, 1995, 1990*

Château Beau-Séjour Bécot
St-Émilion Grand Cru

St-Émilion ☎ 05 57 74 46 87
Ⓦ *www.beausejour-becot.com*
Ⓞ *by appt*

CHÂTEAU BEAU-SÉJOUR Bécot suffered the ignominy of being demoted from *premier grand cru classé* in 1986, but was reinstated 10 years later. Brothers Gérard and Dominique Bécot worked hard to regain the status and now maintain a high-level estate. The vineyard is on St-Émilion limestone plateau and *côtes*. The wines have structure and balance for long ageing, complemented by a rich, ripe texture. The Bécots also produce tiny amounts of hand-tailored garage wine *(see p83)* La Gomerie.
🍷 *red* ⯃ *2005, 2000, 1999, 1998, 1996, 1995, 1990*

Château Belair
St-Émilion Grand Cru

St-Émilion ☎ 05 57 24 70 94
Ⓦ *www.chateaubelair.com* Ⓞ *by appt*

The style of Château Belair's wine is elegant, even delicate, and respectful of the limestone *terroir* from which it hails. It will never be a hit with those who like big, concentrated wines, but its track record shows that it ages gracefully. Owner and winemaker Pascal Delbeck pursues his own philosophy

at this *premier grand cru classé* estate regardless of changing trends. In 1998, he converted the 12-ha vineyard to the biodynamic system of cultivation.
🍷 *red* ⯃ *2005, 2000, 1999, 1998, 1996, 1995, 1994, 1990*

Château Cheval Blanc
St-Émilion Grand Cru

St-Émilion ☎ 05 57 55 55 55
Ⓦ *www.chateau-chevalblanc.com* ◉

AS AN A STATUS *premier grand cru classé*, Château Cheval Blanc has the deceptive quality of being both flatteringly alluring when young and also capable of long ageing. There is more than a hint of neighbouring district Pomerol's unctuous character, but Merlot is not the main variety at this 37-ha estate. The wine's originality is achieved by 60 per cent Cabernet Franc, which gives aromatic complexity and balance. The second wine, Le Petit Cheval, is also good.
🍷 *red* ⯃ *2005, 2000, 1999, 1998, 1996, 1995, 1994, 1990*

Château Beau-Séjour Bécot

Château de Valandraud
St-Émilion Grand Cru

St-Émilion ☎ 05 57 55 09 13
Ⓦ *www.thunevin.com* ◉

JEAN-LUC THUNEVIN is the father of the garage movement *(see p83)*, and Château de Valandraud is his *pièce de résistance*. Originally produced in 1991 from three small parcels of vines located predominantly on the less favoured Dordogne plain, Valandraud has always been made in a fastidious fashion – low yields, strict selection, the best equipment, only new

Château de Valandraud label

Château Figeac label

oak barrels. The wines are big, dark, spicy, and richly concentrated. The prices attained have enabled Thunevin to buy other plots, so the composition of the wine has changed from the early days.

🔴 *red* 📈 *2005, 2000, 1999, 1998, 1997, 1996, 1995, 1994*

Château Figeac
St-Émilion Grand Cru

St-Émilion ☎ 05 57 24 72 26
🖥 www.chateau-figeac.com ⬜ by appt

IN THE 18TH CENTURY, Figeac comprised 200ha including what is now Château Cheval Blanc. Reduced to 40ha, it is still one of the largest *premiers grands crus classés*. The gravel soils in this area have led to a vineyard planting of one third each Cabernet Franc, Merlot, and Cabernet Sauvignon. The wine is fragrant, well structured, and almost Médoc in style, with a deceptive ability to age.

🔴 *red* 📈 *2005, 2000, 1999, 1998, 1996, 1995, 1990*

Château Le Tertre Roteboeuf
St-Émilion Grand Cru

St-Émilion ☎ 05 57 74 42 11 ●

SINCE TAKING OVER this 6-ha estate in 1977, François Mitjavile has propelled it to the top of the appellation. The wines are not classified – a personal choice – but sell at the same price as the *premiers grands crus classés*. They are ripe in style, even exotic, and the warmer vintages have a southern, Mediterranean character. Very ripe grapes and astute barrel-ageing are part of the secret of this estate's success.

🔴 *red* 📈 *2005. 2000, 1999, 1998, 1997, 1996, 1995, 1994, 1990*

Château Pavie Macquin
St-Émilion Grand Cru

St-Émilion ☎ 05 57 24 74 23
⬜ by appt

ONE OF THE TOP *grands crus classés*, Château Pavie Macquin will clearly be a favourite for promotion to *premier grand cru classé* in the next classification. The vineyard is superbly located in a single parcel on St-Émilion's limestone plateau and the property is astutely managed by Nicolas Thienpont and winemaker Stéphane Derenoncourt. The wines are deep, dark, and firmly structured with a minerally core, and they need at least seven or eight years' bottle age.

🔴 *red* 📈 *2005, 2001, 2000, 1999, 1998, 1997, 1996, 1995, 1994, 1990*

Château Pavie
St-Émilion Grand Cru

St-Émilion ☎ 05 57 55 43 43
🖥 www.vignoblesperse.com ●

THIS MAGNIFICENT *premier grand cru classé* situated on St-Émilion's clay-and-limestone *côtes* has been revitalized since its purchase by Gérard Perse in 1998. The yields have been dramatically reduced, a programme of replanting introduced, and a new winery and barrel cellars built. The wines now have enormous weight, power, and concentration, but are just a little too excessive for some. Only time will tell.

🔴 *red* 📈 *2005, 2000, 1999, 1998, 1996, 1995, 1990*

Clos Fourtet
St-Émilion Grand Cru

St-Émilion ☎ 05 57 24 70 90
🖥 www.closfourtet.com ⬜ by appt

IDEALLY SITUATED on the limestone plateau just outside St-Émilion, Clos Fourtet is the best value of the *premiers grands crus classés*. The wines are perhaps less fashionable than those from other top estates, but they are well defined, fresh, and structured for ageing. They have also maintained a remarkable consistency in the past 10 years. The property was recently sold to French businessman Philippe Cuvelier, whose ambition is to maintain Clos Fourtet's high level of winemaking.

Clos Fourtet

🔴 *red* 📈 *2005, 2000, 1999, 1998, 1996. 1995, 1990*

La Mondotte
St-Émilion Grand Cru

St-Émilion 🔲 *05 57 24 71 33*
Ⓦ *www.neipperg.com* ☐ *by appt*

LA MONDOTTE WAS created in 1996 from a 4.5-ha parcel of vines located on St-Émilion's limestone plateau. Owner Stephan von Neipperg's request to have them integrated into his *grand cru classé* Château Canon-la-Gaffelière was refused by the authorities, so he created this garage wine *(see right)*. The Merlot-dominated blend shows expressive, succulent fruit, a density of extract, and powerful tannic structure. Every vintage has been a success from the outset.
🟥 *red* 🔼 *2005, 2001, 2000, 1999, 1998, 1997, 1996*

Château La Conseillante
Pomerol

Pomerol 🔲 *05 57 51 15 32* 🔳

THE 12-HA VINEYARD of La Conseillante is situated just opposite that of Château Cheval Blanc on a mix of clay, gravel, and sand soils. As with those of its close neighbour, the wines of this château have a smooth, velvety texture making them appealing when young but belying the fact that they age

splendidly. A more rigorous approach in the vineyard and better grape selection would add even greater lustre.
🟥 *red* 🔼 *2005, 1999, 1998, 1996, 1995, 1994, 1990*

Château Lafleur
Pomerol

Grand Village, Mouillac
🔲 *05 57 84 44 03* 🔳

THIS TINY JEWEL of a property is located on the Pomerol plateau next to Château Pétrus and Vieux Château Certan. The small vineyard is tended like a garden. The wine, a 50/50 blend of Cabernet Franc and Merlot, is the most elegant in Pomerol, with voluptuous texture, rich fruit, fine tannins, and a minerally complexity. The second wine, Pensées de Lafleur, is also very fine and excellent value, given the price of the *grand vin*.
🟥 *red* 🔼 *2005, 2001, 2000, 1999, 1998, 1996, 1995, 1990*

Château Le Pin
Pomerol

Pomerol 🔲 *05 57 51 33 99* 🔳

THIS SMALL 2-HA PROPERTY came to prominence with the 1979 vintage. It has since become

Château L'Église-Clinet label

one of Pomerol's major sensations, the wines occasionally surpassing Château Pétrus in price and quality. Rich, fragrant, velvety, and with the allure of a top class burgundy, Château Le Pin has instant appeal but also the structure to age. Production of this Merlot-dominated wine is low – another reason for the high price. Much to the (classically minded) owner's chagrin, Le Pin is also often considered the precursor of the garage movement *(see right)*.
🟥 *red* 🔼 *2005, 2000, 1999, 1998, 1996, 1995, 1994, 1990*

Château L'Église-Clinet
Pomerol

Pomerol 🔲 *05 57 25 96 59*
Ⓦ *www.eglise-clinet.com* 🔳

ANOTHER TINY PROPERTY on the Pomerol plateau, Château L'Église-Clinet has achieved star status over the past decade. The recipe for success has been a large portion of old vines (some dating back to the 1930s), an interesting proportion of Cabernet Franc (up to 30 per cent) in the blend, and the winemaking skills of owner Denis Durantou. The results

Barrel storage in the wine cellar at La Mondotte

GARAGE WINES

The so-called garage or cult wines of the Right Bank originally evolved as a way of bucking Bordeaux's strict historical, hierarchical structure. How could producers make a top quality wine, and have a decent return, when the Bordeaux market was reluctant to register their existence? Technically proficient, handcrafted wines of rich concentration made in tiny quantities from super-ripe grapes provided the formula.

A positive mention from American wine critic Robert Parker *(see p21)* was all it took for rapid recognition on the world stage. The scarcity of the wine and the egos of wealthy collectors around the world have caused prices to rocket. Château Le Pin in Pomerol is often named as the catalyst for the movement, but the real instigator was Jean-Luc Thunevin with Château de Valandraud in St-Émilion. Thunevin made his first vintage, 1991, in his garage, hence the name. Among the best garage wines are: *Le Dôme (www.teyssier.fr); Château Gracia (05 57 24 70 35); La Gomerie (www. beausejour-becot.com); Magrez Fombrauge (www.fombrauge.com); La Mondotte; Château Péby Faugères (www.chateau-faugeres.com); Château de Valandraud (see p80).*

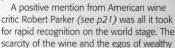

Le Dôme label

---

are rich and concentrated wines, with distinctive balance and refinement.
🍷 red 📅 *2005, 2001, 2000, 1999, 1998, 1997, 1996, 1995, 1994, 1990*

Château L'Évangile
Pomerol

Pomerol 📞 *05 57 55 45 55*
🌐 *www.lafite.com* ⏰ *by appt*

THE ROTHSCHILDS of Lafite-Rothschild *(see p68)* have been co-owners of L'Évangile since 1989 but only took on sole ownership in 1999. Since then a heavy pro-gramme of investment has been under way, including replanting vines and the construction of new cellars. The vineyard is located on the Pomerol plateau, with châteaux Pétrus and Cheval Blanc as neighbours. The wines – rich, powerful, and already impressive – can only improve further.
🍷 red 📅 *2005, 1999, 1998, 1997, 1995, 1994, 1990*

Château Pétrus
Pomerol

Pomerol 📞 *05 57 51 78 96* 🔴

ALTHOUGH VIRTUALLY unknown in Britain and the USA before the 1960s, Pétrus is one of Bordeaux's legendary wines. Almost 100 per cent Merlot is grown on a unique soil of heavy, blue clay that is known as the Pétrus 'button-hole', producing wines of power, volume, and rich extract with firm but fine tannins. The technical expertise of *négociant* owner Jean-Pierre Moueix, and his ability to harvest at optimum ripeness in little more than a day, also court for a lot.
🍷 red 📅 *2005, 2000, 1999, 1998, 1997, 1996, 1995, 1994, 1990*

Château Trotanoy
Pomerol

Pomerol 📞 *05 57 51 78 96* 🔴

PURCHASED IN 1953, Château Trotanoy, like Château Pétrus, is now part of *négociant* Jean-Pierre Moueix's stable. It benefits from the same highly skilled technical team and its vineyards, too, have a high percentage of Merlot, grown on clay-gravel soils. The red wines come closest to Pétrus in terms of their power and weight. Replanting of vines during the 1980s caused a slight dip in quality, but it is now back on top form.
🍷 red 📅 *2005, 2000, 1999, 1998, 1995, 1994, 1990*

Vieux Château Certan
Pomerol

Pomerol 📞 *05 57 51 17 33*
🌐 *www.vieux-chateau-certan.com*
⏰ *by appt*

ALTHOUGH A CLOSE neighbour of Château Pétrus, this estate makes a style of wine that is anything but similar. Vieux Château Certan is more svelte than fleshy, and its aromatic charm and firm, taut structure make it more charac-teristic of the Médoc than of Pomerol. The presence of Cabernet Franc (30 per cent) and Cabernet Sauvignon (10 per cent) explain why. The property has been owned by the Belgian Thienpont family since 1924.
🍷 red 📅 *2005, 2001, 2000, 1999, 1998, 1996, 1995, 1990*

Vieux Château Certan

Vineyards around an old church in Entre-Deux-Mers

WINEGROWING AREAS OF ENTRE-DEUX-MERS

ENTRE-DEUX-MERS IS both a geographical region, between the Garonne and Dordogne rivers, and an appellation for dry, white wines. This is also Bordeaux's production engine room, turning out huge quantities of red bordeaux and bordeaux supérieur *(see right)*, in addition to a little sweet white.

Entre-Deux-Mers & Haut-Benauge

WITHIN THE GREATER Entre-Deux-Mers region lies the appellation Entre-Deux-Mers, known for dry, white wines made from a blend of classic white Bordeaux varieties Sauvignon Blanc, Sémillon, and Muscadelle. These are crisp, fresh, fruity wines to be drunk young, normally representing good value. The production area covers around 1,600ha. AOC Haut-Benauge is a delimited zone in the south of Entre-Deux-Mers. The wines are similar, and production is negligible, most producers preferring the more marketable Entre-Deux-Mers or Bordeaux labels.

🌾 *silt, sand, gravel, limestone-and-clay*
🍇 *Sauvignon Blanc, Sémillon, Muscadelle* 🍷 *white*

Graves de Vayres

THIS SMALL AOC has nothing to do with the Graves region but is a small enclave in the north of Entre-Deux-Mers, centred on the town of Vayres. As the name suggests, the soils are mainly gravel. Light, fruity reds are the main product, with a limited amount of dry white.

🌾 *gravel, sand* 🍇 *Merlot, Cabernet Sauvignon, Cabernet Franc, Malbec* 🍇 *Sauvignon Blanc, Sémillon, Muscadelle* 🍷 *red, white*

Premières Côtes de Bordeaux

THIS AOC FORMS A LONG, narrow strip of land in the south of Entre-Deux-Mers. It consists of a limestone scarp that follows the meandering path of the Garonne River, with a tumble of hills behind. The area was once known for its semi-sweet and sweet whites, however the main staple today is red wine. The dominant variety is Merlot, but these are blended wines, with both Cabernet Sauvignon and

CLAIRET

Clairet is a Bordeaux speciality which is steadily growing in popularity. It pays homage to the style of wine that was probably exported to Britain in the Middle Ages and was the inspiration for the English term 'claret', which was used to describe red bordeaux. Basically, clairet is more characterful and vigorous than rosé, but less tannic than a red wine. It is a dark pink colour, and is fruity and easy to drink. It is ideal as an apéritif or with certain grills and starters. The wine is made by macerating the grape skins with the juice for up to two days, rather than the short four or five hours that rosé is given. Merlot is the favoured grape variety, but both Cabernets are also used. Occasionally the wine is aged for a short spell in oak barrels *(barriques)*. Clairet is best drunk young and chilled, in the year following the harvest.

Cabernet Franc playing an important role.
These lively, fruity, medium-bodied wines are
intended for drinking over three to five years.
Some special *cuvées* will age longer.

limestone-and-clay, gravel Merlot, Cabernet
Sauvignon, Cabernet Franc, Malbec Sauvignon
Blanc, Sémillon, Muscadelle red, white

Cadillac, Loupiac & Ste-Croix-du-Mont

THESE THREE SWEET white wine AOCs face
Sauternes and Barsac across the Garonne
River. Like their illustrious cousins, they have
the propensity to produce botrytized grapes
(see p66); autumnal morning mists provoking
the onset of this fungus that helps concentrate
the juice. The wines are less powerful and
concentrated than Sauternes but represent
excellent value for money, particularly with the
recent spate of top vintages (2005, 2003,
2001, 1999). Ste-Croix-du-Mont (425ha) is
historically the most important of the three
AOCs, and considered capable of producing
wines that rival all but the very best Sauternes.
Loupiac (400ha) is a little fresher, with more
apparent acidity, while the smaller Cadillac
varies from the rich and exotic to semi-sweet
styles. The human factor also plays an
important role with regard to style and quality.

limestone-and-clay, gravel Sémillon,
Sauvignon Blanc, Muscadelle white, dessert

**View of mill seen across rows of vines
in Haut-Benauge**

BORDEAUX

Bottles of Bordeaux

The generic AOC Bordeaux encompasses
over 50,000ha and accounts for 50 per cent
of production in the Bordeaux area. Generic
bordeaux is produced throughout the
Gironde *département*, but Entre-Deux-Mers
provides 75 per cent of it. Two thirds of generic
bordeaux is red, with white, rosé, clairet, and
sparkling making up the rest. Given the extent
and volume of the appellation, quality and
style can vary, with everything from low-yielding
garage-style wines to high-volume 'plonk'.
Seventy-five per cent of bordeaux AOC *rouge*
is bulk-commercialized, feeding brand names
like Mouton Cadet *(below)* and own-label
supermarket wines. At its best, red bordeaux
has a grassy fruitiness; the white is crisp, dry,
and refreshing. Ste-
Foy-Bordeaux is a
delimited zone in the
east of Entre-Deux-
Mers, where producers
may bottle their wines
using the Ste-Foy label,
but most prefer
appellation Bordeaux.

BORDEAUX SUPÉRIEUR

The AOC Bordeaux Supérieur is predominantly for red wines, although there is
also a tiny amount of sweet white. The
appellation covers the same geographical
area as generic bordeaux (and a similar
amount of its wine comes from Entre-Deux-
Mers), but demands higher minimum
alcohol (10 per cent instead of 9.5) and a
slight reduction in maximum yield. More
importantly, the wines are not allowed on
the market until the September following
the harvest, eliciting a longer period of
maturation. The implication is that these
wines have a little more structure and depth
than regular bordeaux. Just over 10,000ha
of red bordeaux supérieur are declared each
year, with 75 per cent of the wine bottled at
the property – the opposite of appellation
Bordeaux. Again, standards vary, but
generally these wines are more reliable.

TOP PRODUCERS OF ENTRE-DEUX-MERS

Château Ste-Marie
Entre-Deux-Mers

51 rte de Bordeaux, Targon
☎ 05 56 23 64 30 ☐ *by appt*

CHÂTEAU STE-MARIE is a white wine specialist; the Entre-Deux-Mers Vieilles Vignes (vines over 25 years old) and barrel-fermented Madlys are Sauvignon Blanc-dominated, but both have a percentage of grapes from 100-year-old Sémillon vines. The former is classically fresh and fruity; the latter a little rounder and fuller. There is also a red Bordeaux Supérieur and a Premières Côtes de Bordeaux Alios, which are both soft and fruity.
🍷 *red, white* 🍾 *red: 2005*
★ *Entre-Deux-Mers Vieilles Vignes*

Château Reynon
Premières Côtes de Bordeaux

21 rte de Cardan, Beguey
☎ 05 56 62 96 51 🖾 *www.denis dubourdieu.com* ☐ *by appt*

CHÂTEAU REYNON belongs to Denis Dubourdieu, a professor of oenology at Bordeaux University. Although better

Château Reynon label

known for his work on white wines, he has put considerable effort into upgrading the Reynon red – and it shows. The wine is beautifully balanced with an elegant expression of red fruits, gentle use of oak, and a long, fresh finish. It is best drunk at two to five years old. The white Bordeaux Vieilles Vignes has a citrusy aroma and flavour, and lovely depth of fruit. There is also a little sweet white Cadillac.
🍷 *red, white, dessert* 🍾 *red: 2005, 2000, 1999, 1998* ★ *Premières Côtes de Bordeaux, Vieilles Vignes Bordeaux Blanc*

Château Suau
Premières Côtes de Bordeaux

Capian ☎ 05 56 72 19 06
🖾 *www.chateausuau.com*
☐ *by appt*

MONIQUE BONNET is one of the leading producers in the Premières Côtes de Bordeaux. Her 60-ha vineyard has been restructured over the past 10 years, and there has also been considerable investment in this château's winery and cellars. She makes two *cuvées*, each with red and white versions: Tradition and Cuvée Prestige. Of most interest is the sturdy, ripe red Cuvée Prestige made from a blend of Merlot, Cabernet Sauvignon, and Cabernet Franc aged in 30 per cent new oak barrels.
🍷 *red, white, rosé* 🍾 *red: 2005, 2000, 1998* ★ *Cuvée Prestige*

Château Bonnet
Bordeaux

Grézillac ☎ 05 57 25 58 58
🖾 *www.andrelurton.com* ☐

ANDRÉ LURTON has led the field in upgrading the quality of Bordeaux's generic wines, and Château Bonnet has set the standard. There is always a good level of ripeness and extraction of fruit. The red Réserve is aged in *barriques* for 12 months and has a little more volume and definition than the Cuvée Classique. The white Entre-Deux-Mers is always crisp, clean, and fruity. A recent addition is the garage-style Divinius.
🍷 *red, white, rosé* 🍾 *red: 2005, 2000, 1999, 1998* ★ *Réserve, Entre-Deux-Mers*

BORDEAUX BRANDS

A large proportion of generic bordeaux is used to produce *négociant* brand name wines. The wines and sometimes grapes for these are sourced from across the whole of Bordeaux, from individual producers, growers, and co-operatives, and then blended to order at the *négociants'* cellars. The undisputed leader in this field, with yearly sales of 15 million bottles, is Baron Philippe de Rothschild's Mouton Cadet. William Pitter's Malesan and Castel's Baron de Lestac are next in line. The big *négociants* tend to produce fairly average wine at fairly average prices, but the brand loyalty they command results in success. Produced in more limited volume but of qualitative interest are Yvon Mau's Premius and Exigence, Sichel's Sirius, Bordeaux Vins Sélection's Epicure, and Dourthe Numéro 1 Blanc.

Château de Fontenille
Bordeaux

La Sauve 📞 05 56 23 03 26
🌐 *www.chateau-fontenille.com*
⏱ *by appt*

THE THREE WINES that Stéphane Defraine produces at the 36-ha Château de Fontenille are all of a regular and consistent quality. The red bordeaux is round, soft, fruity, and drinkable early on. The white Entre-Deux-Mers is lighter-bodied than some but wonderfully aromatic with an almost exotic, New World character. The Cabernet Franc-led clairet is fruity and fun.

🍷 *red, white, clairet* 📕 *red: 2005, 2000, 1999, 1998 ★ Bordeaux, Entre-Deux-Mers, Bordeaux Clairet*

Château Thieuley
Bordeaux

La Sauve-Majeure 📞 05 56 23 00 01
⏱ *by appt*

FORMER OENOLOGY teacher Francis Courselle has spent the past 30 years placing this family-owned château at the top of its class. The vineyard is immaculately run, and technically the estate is on a par with many a *grand cru*. The standard red and white *cuvées* are regularly good, while the barrel-aged Cuvée Francis Courselle (which appears in both red and white) has more depth and ageability.

🍷 *red, white, clairet* 📕 *red: 2005, 2000, 1999, 1998 ★ Cuvée Francis Courselle*

Château Tour de Mirambeau
Bordeaux

Naujan et Postiac 📞 05 57 84 55 08
⏱ *by appt*

JEAN-LOUIS DESPAGNE owns six properties in the Bordeaux area, with a total of 300ha. Château Tour de Mirambeau is the flagship estate, which produces a range of wines including a consistently good Entre-Deux-Mers and a wholesome Bordeaux Supérieur. The Cuvée Passion is a special oak-aged selection in both red and white.

Château Tour de Mirambeau

🍷 *red, white, rosé* 📕 *red: 2005, 2000, 1998 ★ Entre-Deux-Mers, Cuvée Passion*

Château de Reignac
Bordeaux Supérieur

St-Loubès 📞 05 56 20 41 05
⏱ *by appt*

CHÂTEAU DE REIGNAC, with its park and majestic château, has the allure of a stately home. The wines have benefited from the massive investment and technical expertise of owner Yves Vatelot since 1990. Château de Reignac is the second label, an easy-drinking, fresh, aromatic wine. The top wine, Reignac, is rich, concentrated, and chocolaty, aged 100 per cent in new oak barrels. There is also a limited edition micro-*cuvée*, Balthus, and a little barrel-fermented white Reignac.

🍷 *red, white* 📕 *red: 2005, 2000, 1999, 1998 ★ Bordeaux Supérieur*

Château Penin
Bordeaux Supérieur

Génissac 📞 05 57 24 46 98
🌐 *www.chateaupenin.com* ⏱

OWNER PATRICK CARTEYRON has made Château Penin one of the safe bets of generic bordeaux. The wines are good without exception. There are three red *cuvées* – Tradition, Grande Sélection, and Les Cailloux – all made from a high proportion of Merlot and with the accent on the fruit. The latter is produced from a parcel of vines grown on clay-and-gravel soils and is aged for 12 months in new oak barrels. It is as good as, if not better than, many St-Émilions. Also exceptional is the clairet.

🍷 *red, white, rosé, clairet* 📕 *red: 2005, 2000, 1999, 1998, 1995 ★ Grande Sélection, Les Cailloux, Clairet*

Domaine de Courteillac
Bordeaux Supérieur

Ruch 📞 05 57 40 79 48 ⏱ *by appt*

TALENTED WINEMAKER Stéphane Asseo, now making a name for himself in California, set up Domaine de Courteillac in the 1980s. Although now owned by *négociant* Dominique Meneret, the estate still sets high standards. The red Domaine de Courteillac is a classic, elegant bordeaux, with well-integrated oak and a firm but fine structure for ageing up to 10 years. The tiny volume of white is aromatic and finely textured.

🍷 *red, white* 📕 *red: 2005, 2000, 1999, 1998 ★ Domaine de Courteillac*

Château de Reignac label

BURGUNDY

MORE THAN ANY *other wine region in France, Burgundy has distilled the wisdom and experience of its history into winegrowing. Established by powerful monasteries from the 7th century onwards, the vineyards have been cultivated by men who came to understand every nuance of the soil. Burgundian wine, patronized by royalty through the ages, is celebrated for its elegance and subtlety.*

The vineyards of Burgundy *(Bourgogne)* lie mostly in a narrow strip running south from Chablis to the suburbs of Lyon. Over the years they have been placed in a hierarchy, beginning with those that produce simple *bourgogne* wines from the most basic soils, ascending to *village* sites whose wines bear the names of the many villages or communes, and continuing to the *premiers* and *grands crus* that invariably deliver Burgundy's finest, most long-lived wines.

Chardonnay grapes

It is not always easy to see why one vineyard should be designated *grand cru* while its neighbour may be a mere *village*, but these distinctions have stood the test of time. It comes down to *terroir*, a somewhat baffling combination of soil type, microclimate, exposure, susceptibility to frost, and countless other factors, each of which affects the performance of any given patch of earth.

Complex inheritance laws, determined by the Napoleonic code, require estates to be divided equally among the children of the deceased. As a result, properties have been broken up among numerous heirs and vineyards have been split into tiny parcels of land, often with no more than a row or two of vines in the *grand cru* sites. Burgundian estates therefore tend to be small (just 5 to 15ha) and fragmented, and most producers vinify and sell wines from a dozen or more appellations. Some of the largest vineyard holdings are in the hands of *négociants (see p97)*, who supplement their own harvests by purchasing from small growers in order to create sizeable volumes of sought-after wines.

In all these respects viticulture in Burgundy is infinitely complicated, but in one it is simple to grasp. Just three grape varieties are cultivated: Chardonnay accounts for virtually all of the whites; Pinot Noir is the red grape to be found in most vineyards, and the juicy, if less refined, red Gamay thrives in Beaujolais.

Harvesting grapes in Nuit-St-Georges, Côte de Nuits

◁ **Patchwork of tiny parcels of Burgundian vines**

WINE MAP OF BURGUNDY

Burgundy covers some 175km from Chablis in the north to Beaujolais in the south. With the exception of Chablis, which is isolated from the rest of the region, the vineyards are virtually continuous and fall into six AOCs, each with its own distinctive character. The most prestigious sites lie in the Côte de Nuits and the Côte de Beaune, which together form the Côte d'Or, Burgundy's famous 'Golden Slope' between Dijon and Chagny.

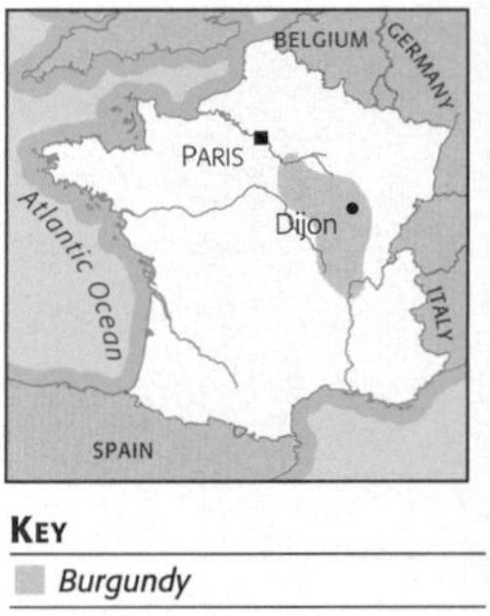

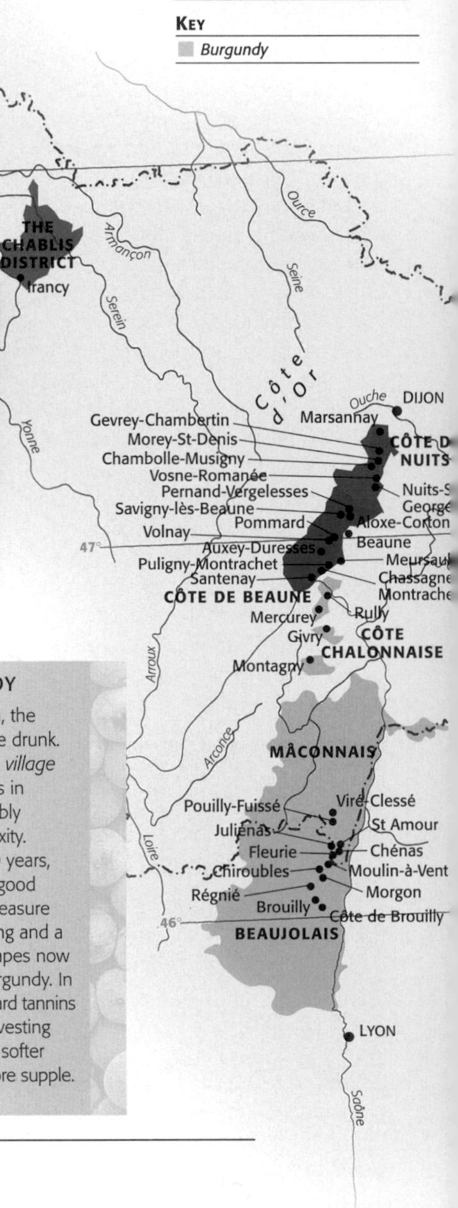

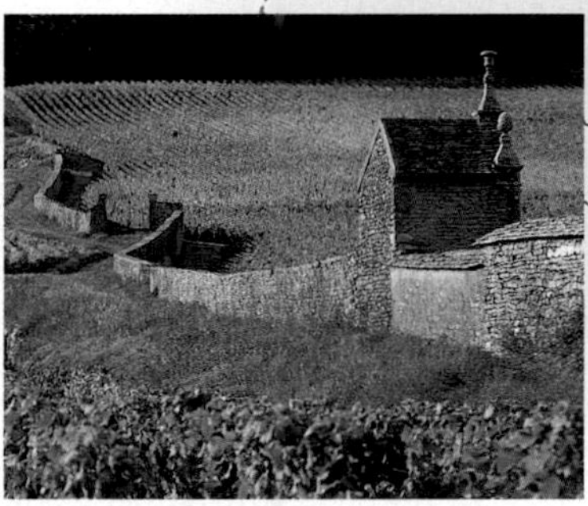

Key

Burgundy

Walled vineyard of Clos-St-Jacques, Gevrey-Chambertin, Côte de Nuits

WHEN TO DRINK BURGUNDY

As a general rule, the simpler the appellation, the younger the wine can, and usually should, be drunk. A basic *bourgogne* can be drunk on release; *village* wines usually benefit from two or three years in bottle; and *premiers* and *grands crus* invariably benefit from ageing to give aromatic complexity. A top red burgundy can be kept for up to 30 years, although 10 years is a more reliable limit. A good white burgundy can usually be drunk with pleasure at five years old. The effects of global warming and a greater emphasis on picking fully-ripened grapes now mean that it is no longer essential to age burgundy. In the past, grapes that were not fully ripe gave hard tannins which needed years to soften; now later harvesting and modern winemaking techniques deliver softer tannins, leaving the wine tasting richer and more supple.

Map labels:

Auxerre
THE CHABLIS DISTRICT
Irancy

Gevrey-Chambertin — Marsannay — DIJON
Morey-St-Denis
Chambolle-Musigny
Vosne-Romanée
Pernand-Vergelesses
Savigny-lès-Beaune
Volnay
Pommard
Auxey-Duresses
Puligny-Montrachet
Santenay
CÔTE DE BEAUNE
Mercurey
Givry
Montagny

CÔTE DE NUITS
Nuits-St-George
Aloxe-Corton
Beaune
Meursault
Chassagne
Montrachet
Rully
CÔTE CHALONNAISE

MÂCONNAIS

Pouilly-Fuissé — Viré-Clessé
Juliénas — St Amour
Fleurie — Chénas
Chiroubles — Moulin-à-Vent
Régnié — Morgon
Brouilly — Côte de Brouilly
BEAUJOLAIS

LYON

Detail of Bacchus from *négociant*
Louis Jadot, Côte de Nuits

TERROIR AT A GLANCE

Latitude: 45.5–48°N.

Altitude: 175–500m.

Topography: The most famous vineyards line the 50km stretch of the Côte d'Or. The escarpment is broken up by streams which run down the hills to join the Saône River. The exposure and angle of the slope are critical in this region.

Soil: Limestone soils dominate, with some clay, granite, and sand.

Climate: Moderate continental, with cold, dry winters and warm summers. Balmy Septembers help to bring grapes to full ripeness.

Temperature: July average is 20°C.

Rainfall: Annual average is 690mm. Heavy rainfall in May, June, and October.

Viticultural hazards: Frost; mildew; hail; harvest rain.

Château de la Maltroye, Chassagne-
Montrachet, Côte de Beaune

0 — km ————— 50

Wines from the Côte D'Or

Grape pickers harvesting Chardonnay grapes in the Chablis district

WINEGROWING AREAS OF THE CHABLIS DISTRICT

IN THE FAR NORTH OF BURGUNDY lies Chablis, which produces exclusively white wine. Chablis has been an important wine region for at least 1,400 years, initially supplying thirsty consumers in Paris. By the late 19th century there were over 40,000ha under vine here. However, phylloxera, disease, and competition from other regions then caused a dramatic decline. This has been turned around in recent decades; but even so, the total vineyard area today is still only around 4,600ha.

The name Chablis has been much misused, having been adopted in California and elsewhere as a synonym for dryish white wine. This is a back-handed compliment that has not gone down well in Chablis itself, where the growers are proud of the unique character of their wine. Made only from Chardonnay, Chablis should be bone-dry but not harsh; steely but not austere; rich but not heavy. Its blend of ripe fruit and mineral nuances is what makes Chablis so sublime with seafood and grilled fish. It derives its characteristics both from the northerly climate, which encourages high acidity, and from the chalky limestone soils on which the best grapes are grown.

Like the rest of Burgundy, Chablis is divided into a hierarchy of vineyards, beginning with AOC Petit Chablis and generic AOC Chablis, and rising through to AOC Premier Cru Chablis and AOC Grand Cru Chablis.

 *Kimmeridgian limestone* 🍇 *Chardonnay* 🍷 *white*

Petit Chablis

THIS IS, IN THE EYES OF MANY Burgundy fanciers, a slightly suspect category, since the soils on which Petit Chablis grapes are grown often lack the strong limestone content found elsewhere in the region. But even Petit Chablis is pure Chardonnay and can offer good value, though it rarely reaches great heights. It should be drunk young and fresh.

Chablis

GENERIC CHABLIS is produced from more than 3,000ha of vineyards, making it by far Burgundy's most important appellation in terms of quantity. Although the zone has been extended considerably in recent decades, quality does not seem to have deteriorated as a consequence.

La Chablisienne label

Premier Cru Chablis

CHABLIS BECOMES INTERESTING at *premier cru* level. It also becomes complicated, since there are no fewer than 40 qualifying vineyards dispersed throughout Chablis, varying considerably in exposure and gradient. The number is high because small sections within *premier cru* vineyards are recognized as *premier cru* appellations, or *lieux-dits*, in their own right. For example, growers with vines in Fourchaume, a well-known *premier cru*, are permitted to choose whether to give the name of the whole vineyard, or the name of their section (either Vaupulent, Côte de Fontenay, Vaulorent, or

L'Homme Mort) on the label. In practice, most growers, conscious of the marketing implications, opt to use the bigger name.

A Chablis *premier cru* will usually show more mineral complexity – tanginess, bracing acidity, flintiness, and almost a stoniness – than a simple Chablis or Petit Chablis, and it may need two or three years in bottle to bring out its aromatic complexity. From a top producer in a top vintage, these wines can age well for a decade, becoming golden in colour and more mellow in flavour.

The other *premiers crus* are Montée de Tonnerre (including Chapelot and Pied d'Aloup); Mont de Milieu (including Morein, Fourneaux, and Côte des Prés Girots); Vaucoupin, Beaurcy (including Troesmes); Côte de Léchet; Vaillons (including Châtains, Sécher, Beugnons, Les Lys, Mélinots, Roncières, and Les Épinottes); Montmains (including La Forest and Butteaux); Vosgros (including Vaugiraut); Vau Ligneau; Vau-de-Vey (including Vaux Ragons); and a handful of others rarely identified on the labels.

Grand Cru Chablis

GRAND CRU CHABLIS SHOWS similar characteristics to those of *premier cru*, but to an even greater degree. These are the boldest, richest, most complex wines of the region, and they repay keeping – ideally for 10 years. Yields are lower for *grands crus* than for other Chablis sites, and with only 109ha of vineyard – accounting for just three per cent of Chablis' total production – the wines are relatively scarce and therefore command high prices. Chablis' northerly position means that getting the grapes to ripen

can be problematic. While the *premier cru* vineyards are dispersed, the *grands crus* are in a single band, along a southwest-facing slope where the mesoclimate encourages the grapes to ripen relatively early. There are only seven *grands crus:* Les Clos is the largest and best known; the others are Bougros, Les Preuses, Vaudésir, Grenouilles, Valmur, and Blanchot.

Irancy & Sauvignon de St-Bris

OFFICIALLY OUTSIDE THE CHABLIS AOC, between Chablis and the town of Auxerre to the southwest, is a small region of Pinot Noir vineyards. The best known of these is Irancy, which has its own AOC; wines made elsewhere are sold as *bourgogne rouge* or vinified as sparklings and labelled Crémant de Bourgogne. The wines can be charming and delicate in good years, but distinctly lean in cooler vintages. There is also a local anomaly: Sauvignon de St-Bris. As the name suggests, the grape here is Sauvignon Blanc, not Chardonnay, and the wines are zesty and good value.

Jean-Marc Brocard's winery and the church of Préhy, Chablis

TOP PRODUCERS OF THE CHABLIS DISTRICT

Domaine Billaud-Simon
Chablis

1 quai de Reugny 🔳 *03 86 42 10 33* 🟦 *www.billaud-simon.com* ⬜

THIS 20-HA ESTATE is blessed with one of the most extensive and complete ranges of *premiers* and *grands crus* in Chablis. Today it is run by Bernard Billaud and his nephew Samuel, who have created one of the most technically up-to-date wineries in the region. Almost all the wines are aged in stainless steel, although one or two *crus*, including Mont de Milieu and Blanchot, receive some oak-ageing. These are wines marked by purity and mineral complexity.

🖼 *white* 🔼 *2006, 2005, 2002, 2000, 1998* ★ *Vaillons, Blanchot*

Domaine Billaud-Simon

Domaine Jean-Paul & Benoît Droin
Chablis

14 bis rue Jean-Jaurès 🔳 *03 86 42 16 78* 🟦 *www.jeanpaul-droin.fr* ⬜

JEAN-PAUL DROIN is one of the region's most thoughtful winemakers, and the fortunate possessor of plots in four *grands crus*: Blanchot, Les Clos, Valmur, and Vaudésir. For many years he was a believer in fermentation and ageing in new oak, but in the 1990s, he took heed from critics, who found the woody aromas in his wines too dominant. Today the wines are much better balanced, with oak as a nuance rather than a flavour component. Today the wines are made by Jean-Paul's son Benoît.

🖼 *white* 🔼 *2006, 2005, 2002, 2000, 1998* ★ *Vaucoupin, Les Clos*

Domaine Laroche
Chablis

22 rue Louis Bro 🔳 *03 86 42 89 00* 🟦 *www.larochewines.com* ⬜

MICHEL LAROCHE is a man of prodigious energy and ambition. He owns around 100ha in Chablis and successfully combines sound commercial sense with top quality at all levels – from his generic Chablis brand (St-Martin) to the parade of sumptuous *grands crus*. Laroche has been ageing his top wines in old oak for over 20 years and since 1991 has made Réserve de l'Obédience, which is vinified with scrupulous care from some of Blanchot's oldest vines and released at a high price.

🖼 *white* 🔼 *2006, 2005, 2002, 2000, 1998* ★ *St Martin, Fourchaume, Réserve de l'Obédience*

Domaine Louis Michel
Chablis

9 blvd de Ferrières 🔳 *03 86 42 88 55* 🟦 *www.louismicheletfils.com* ⬜

THE LATE LOUIS MICHEL and his son Jean-Loup owned 25ha in Chablis, mostly in the *premiers crus* of Montmains and Montée de Tonnerre. All wines are aged solely in stainless steel, which helps preserve the primary fruit and vigour. The absence of oak ageing also helps retain the individuality of each *cru*. All the wines are fairly priced.

🖼 *white* 🔼 *2006, 2005, 2002, 2000, 1998* ★ *Montmains, Vaudésir*

Domaine Raveneau
Chablis

9 rue de Chichée 🔳 *03 86 42 17 46* ◼

RAVENEAU ONLY OWNS 8HA of vineyards, but they are all outstanding sites, and everything is *premier* or *grand cru*. The wines are fermented in tanks but partly aged in older wood. Before bottling, different lots of the same wine are blended to ensure that the balance is consistent. The result is classic Chablis: mineral and even austere in its youth, but flowering with age into a rich, nutty complexity. Les Clos is usually the finest and most long-lived of the wines, but production is limited and demand is high.

🖼 *white* 🔼 *2006, 2005, 2002, 2000, 1998* ★ *Butteaux, Les Clos, Blanchot*

PRODUCT OF FRANCE

2002   2002

Chablis Grand Cru
Les Clos
APPELLATION CHABLIS GRAND CRU CONTRÔLÉE

750 ml

Mise en bouteilles à la Propriété par
Jean-Paul & Benoît DROIN
Propriétaires-Viticulteurs à Chablis - Yonne - France

Alc. 13% vol.

Domaine Jean-Paul & Benoît Droin *grand cru* label

Domaine Vincent Dauvissat
Chablis

8 rue Émile Zola
☎ 03 86 42 11 58 ◉

THE ENTHUSIASTIC Vincent Dauvissat has inherited his father René's winemaking skills, and this remains one of the region's finest and most traditional producers. Dauvissat believes that a long maturation period accentuates mineral nuances and all his wines are fermented and aged in older oak. Consequently there is a loss of overt grapey fruitiness, but these are wines for ageing, and after five years they reveal their immaculate balance and complexity.
🏵 *white* 🔖 *2006, 2005, 2002, 2000, 1998* ★ *La Forest, Vaillons, Les Clos*

Domaine William Fèvre
Chablis

21 ave d'Oberwesel ☎ *03 86 98 98 98* ⓦ *www.williamfevre.com* ◻

WITH 16HA, William Fèvre owned more *grand cru* vines than any other grower in Chablis. In 1998, he sold his holdings to Bouchard Père & Fils *(see p104)*, who within a few years transformed the wines into some of the most exuberant in the region, richly fruity and wonderfully varied from *cru* to *cru*. Fèvre's wines had been over-oaked, but the new team uses the technique with more moderation and skill.
🏵 *white* 🔖 *2006, 2005, 2002, 2000, 1998* ★ *Montée de Tonnerre, Blanchots*

Jean-Marc Brocard
Chablis

3 rte de Chablis, Préhy ☎ *03 86 41 49 00* ⓦ *www.brocard.fr* ◻

THE EBULLIENT Jean-Marc Brocard is a rarity in Chablis, a self-made man who

Stainless steel tank at Jean-Marc Brocard

inherited 2ha and has astutely built up a substantial 80-ha estate. The wines are aged entirely in stainless steel, not oak, since he feels it is the soil rather than the wood that gives Chablis its character. As well as Chablis of very reliable quality, Brocard produces some fascinating and good-value *bourgogne blanc* from outside the Chablis zone. The large production allows Brocard to maintain fair prices.
🏵 *white* 🔖 *2006, 2005, 2002, 2000, 1998* ★ *Montée de Tonnerre, Beauregard*

La Chablisienne
Chablis

8 blvd Pasteur ☎ *03 86 42 89 89* ⓦ *www.chablisienne.com* ◻

WITH A PRODUCTION of some 500,000 cases, this co-op is a major player in the region and quality has always been consistently high. Prices, although not low, offer good value. In addition to a wide range of *premiers* and *grands crus*, La Chablisienne produces blends such as the Vieilles Vignes (from old vines), which is given some oak-ageing and is released ready to drink.
🏵 *white* 🔖 *2006, 2005, 2002, 2000, 1998* ★ *Vieilles Vignes, Beauroy*

Maison Pascal Bouchard
Chablis

Parc des Lys ☎ *03 86 42 18 64* ⓦ *www.pascalbouchard.com* ◻

THIS IS ONE of Chablis' largest estates, with ownership of (or contracts with) more than 100ha of vines. The firm opened a modern winery here in 1995. The wines are true to type, and only some of the *grands crus* are treated to a touch of barrel-fermentation and oak ageing. They are enjoyable young for their rich fruit and firm minerality, but the finest *crus* are best kept for a few years.
🏵 *white* 🔖 *2006, 2005, 2002, 2000, 1998* ★ *Fourchaume Vieilles Vignes, Les Clos*

PERFECT CASE: CHABLIS

Ⓦ Domaine Billaud-Simon Chablis Blanchot Vieilles Vignes £££

Ⓦ Domaine Jean-Paul & Benoît Droin Chablis Vaudésir ££

Ⓦ Domaine Laroche Chablis Réserve de l'Obédience ££££

Ⓦ Domaine Laroche Chablis St Martin ££

Ⓦ Domaine Louis Michel Chablis £

Ⓦ Domaine Raveneau Chablis Les Clos ££

Ⓦ Domaine Vincent Dauvissat Chablis Vaillons ££

Ⓦ Domaine William Fèvre Chablis Montée de Tonnerre ££

Ⓦ Jean-Marc Brocard Chablis ££

Ⓦ La Chablisienne Chablis Beauroy ££

Ⓦ La Chablisienne Chablis Vieilles Vignes ££

Ⓦ Maison Pascal Bouchard Chablis Fourchaume Vieilles Vignes ££

Clos de Vougeot's *grand cru* vineyard and château, Vougeot

WINEGROWING VILLAGES OF THE CÔTE DE NUITS

FOR MANY BURGUNDY LOVERS, the Côte de Nuits produces the area's finest red wines. Almost all the red *grands crus* lie here in Burgundy's heartland, tucked among the mighty monastic estates that once dominated the east-facing slopes. Nowhere else in the world does Pinot Noir attain such heart-stopping complexity and elegance. Its delicate red-fruit aromas are married to a firmness of structure that allows a well-made example to age for decades, developing ever more subtle aromas and flavours. Burgundians insist that the greatness of their wines comes from the soil rather than the grape, that Pinot Noir is merely a vehicle through which the mineral limestone soils of the Côte de Nuits express themselves most brilliantly.

The vineyards begin just south of Dijon, rising from the plains onto east-facing slopes, and continue in a sweep of vines until a few miles south of Nuits-St-Georges. There the vineyards continue, but the name changes to Côte de Beaune *(see pp102–103)*. The AOC Côte de Nuits Villages is used mostly for villages high up on the plateau behind the renowned slopes; a cooler mesoclimate and higher altitude make it more difficult for the grapes to ripen, so the wines are less highly esteemed than those from the Côte de Nuits itself. The region breaks down into numerous AOCs including the following key ones.

🞕 *limestone* 🞕 *Pinot Noir* 🞕 *Chardonnay*
🞕 *red, white, rosé*

Domaine des Lambrays

Marsannay

UNTIL THE 1980s, Marsannay was mostly known for its rosés. These rosés – made, like the red, from Pinot Noir – can be delicious, but are really thought to be a waste of good *terroir*. Bruno Clair is probably the best known producer, but others, such as Charlopin, also take their winemaking seriously, and produce rich, enjoyable, and quite inexpensive wines, of which the reds are most worthwhile.

Fixin

THIS SOMEWHAT OBSCURE VILLAGE dines out on its authentic connections with Napoleon: one of his closest associates came from here, and returned from accompanying the emperor into exile to name a vineyard after him, erect a statue, and open a small museum. The best site is the Clos du Chapître, on the slopes behind the village. The wines here are solid in style rather than elegant, but can be good value.

Gevrey-Chambertin

THE LARGEST wine-producing village in the Côte de Nuits, Gevrey-Chambertin is richly endowed with nine *grands crus*, of which the best known (and usually the finest) is Le Chambertin. Vineyard status is by no means an infallible guide to quality: some producers of *grand cru* wines are consistently disappointing, while top growers like Denis Bachelet make wonderful wines from mere *village* sites.

Among the *premiers crus* here, Clos-St-Jacques reigns supreme. Everyone agrees it delivers wine of *grand cru* quality, which explains why its five co-owners charge *grand cru* prices. The wines of Gevrey-Chambertin tend to be muscular and very long-lived, yet the best ones can have surprising finesse.

Morey-St-Denis

THE SWATHE OF *GRAND CRU* vineyards heading south from Gevrey-Chambertin continues into Morey-St-Denis, and some of those vineyards, notably Clos de la Roche and Clos St Denis, can be of truly outstanding quality. Unlike most Burgundian *crus,* which are divided into numerous parcels of vines with equally numerous owners, two of Morey-St-Denis' *grands crus* are monopolies with single owners. These monopolies are Clos des Lambrays and Clos de Tart, both now producing delicious wines after decades of mediocrity.

Chambolle-Musigny

MOREY-ST-DENIS segues so subtly into Chambolle-Musigny that the two villages share the *grand cru* Bonnes Mares. Chambolle-Musigny delivers the most elegant wines of the Côte de Nuits. They are perfumed and delicate, yet can age well. The other *grand cru* site, Le Musigny, is one of the most prized in all Burgundy, and its wines are admired for their extraordinary finesse and depth of flavour.

Vougeot

THIS HAMLET IS BEST known for its large (at 50ha, enormous by Burgundian standards) Clos de Vougeot *grand cru*, which sweeps up from

the main road to the celebrated château that stands within it. Because of its size and varied soils, this site produces wines of quality that range from the unexceptional to the magnificent. Here it is important to buy only from the best growers, such as Château de la Tour and domaines Anne Gros, Jacques Prieur, Grivot, and Méo-Camuzet.

Vosne-Romanée

THE WINES OF VOSNE-ROMANÉE are sturdy yet supple, perfumed yet rich, and full of body and vigour. Like Gevrey-Chambertin, this area is richly endowed with *grands crus* and superb *premiers crus.* Not surprisingly, the wines are highly sought after and expensive, but they are rarely disappointing.

Wine advertisement in Nuits-St-Georges

Nuits-St-Georges

IT IS SOMETHING OF AN ANOMALY that this famous village has no *grands crus*, possibly because its parsimonious growers back in the 1930s were reluctant to pay the higher taxes due from such sites. Spreading southwards through the hamlet of Prémeaux, Nuits-St-Georges is a large commune where quality can be variable. As is so often the case in Burgundy, the name of the producer tends to count for more than the name of the vineyard.

TOP PRODUCERS OF THE CÔTE DE NUITS

Domaine Armand Rousseau
Côte de Nuits

1 rue de l'Aumônerie, Gevrey-Chambertin 【 *03 80 34 30 55* W *www.domaine-rousseau.com* ◘ *by appt*

FEW GROWERS are as respected as the venerable Charles Rousseau. For decades he has produced some of the most profound wines of Gevrey-Chambertin, adapting his winemaking process to suit the structure of each one. His Clos St Jacques and Clos de Bèze are rich and oaky; but other wines have a lighter touch, with an intrinsic delicacy, aroma, and finesse. Sometimes simple in their

Charles Rousseau at Domaine Armand Rousseau

youth, these wines often require 10 years to show their irresistible elegance.
🔲 *red* 🔲 *2005, 2002, 2001, 2000, 1999, 1996, 1995* ★ *Gevrey-Chambertin Clos St Jacques, Ruchottes Chambertin, Chambertin*

Domaine Bernard Dugat-Py
Côte de Nuits

rue de Planteligone, Gevrey-Chambertin 【 *03 80 51 82 46* W *www.dugat-py.com* ◙

THE UNASSUMING Bernard Dugat-Py only began bottling his wines in 1989, but he is one of the best growers in Gevrey-Chambertin. Most of his vines are very old, he intervenes as little as possible during vinification and ageing, and he lets the grapes and soils speak for themselves. Bernard likes wines with flesh, which is an excellent description of his style.
🔲 *red* 🔲 *2005, 2002, 2001, 2000, 1999, 1996, 1995* ★ *Bourgogne Cuvée Halinard, Gevrey-Chambertin Coeur de Roy, Chambertin*

Domaine Bruno Clair
Côte de Nuits

5 rue du Vieux College, Marsannay 【 *03 80 52 28 95* W *www.bruno-clair.com* ◘

BRUNO CLAIR IS based in unfashionable Marsannay, but has vines in many of the best

sites in the Côte d'Or. His red Marsannays reveal just how good the area's wines can be, but his top bottlings are usually from Gevrey-Chambertin's Clos St Jacques and Clos de Bèze. The whites, from Morey-St-Denis and Marsannay, can be delicious too. With 21ha in as many appellations, Clair has a fine range to offer his enthusiastic aficionados.
🔲 *red, white, rosé* 🔲 *2005, 2002, 2001, 2000, 1999, 1996, 1995* ★ *Marsannay Longeroies, Gevrey-Chambertin Clos St Jacques*

Domaine Comte Georges de Vogüé
Côte de Nuits

Chambolle-Musigny 【 *03 80 62 86 25* ◘

NO DOMAINE CAN MATCH this one for the quality of its holdings in Chambolle-Musigny, which include the outstanding sites Les Amoureuses, Bonnes Mares, and Le Musigny. Some 70 per cent of Le Musigny is owned by this one estate. So exacting are its standards that the wines from vines under 20 years old are bottled under the lesser Chambolle *premier cru* appellation. De Vogüé aims for perfection and frequently attains it.
🔲 *red* 🔲 *2005, 2002, 2001, 2000, 1999, 1996, 1995* ★ *Chambolle-Musigny Amoureuses, Bonnes Mares, Le Musigny*

PERFECT CASE: CÔTE DE NUITS

🅡 Domaine Armand Rousseau Gevrey-Chambertin Clos St Jacques ££££

🅡 Domaine Bruno Clair Marsannay Longeroies ££

🅡 Domaine Comte Georges de Vogüé Le Musigny ££££

🅡 Domaine de la Romanée-Conti La Tâche ££££

🅡 Domaine de le Vougeraie Bonnes Mares £££

🅡 Domaine Denis Mortet Gevrey-Chambertin Vieilles Vignes £££

🅡 Domaine des Lambrays Clos des Lambrays £££

🅡 Domaine Dujac Clos de le Roche £££

🅡 Domaine Georges Roumier Chambolle-Musigny Les Cras ££

🅡 Domaine Henri Gouges Nuits-St-Georges Pruliers ££

🅡 Domaine Méo-Camuzet Vosne-Romanée Cros Parantoux ££££

🅡 Louis Jadot Chambertin Clos de Bèze ££££

Domaine de la Romanée-Conti

See p101.

Domaine de la Vougeraie
Côte de Nuits

rue de l'Eglise, Prémeaux 📞 *03 80 62 48 25* 🌐 *www.domainede lavougeraie.com* ⬜ *by appt*

NO MERCHANT has been more astute than Jean-Claude Boisset when it comes to acquiring properties in this region. By the late 1990s he had assembled some 37ha of vineyards. He then hired a brilliant winemaker, Pascal Marchand, and created this new domaine to produce and market the wines. From the outset, La Vougeraie has produced rich, modern-style burgundies, boldly flavoured and built to last. The current winemaker is Pierre Vincent.
🍷 *red, white* 📷 *2005, 2002, 2001, 2000, 1999* ★ *Pinot Noir Terres de Famille, Gevrey-Chambertin Les Évocelles, Bonnes Mares*

Domaine Denis Mortet
Côte de Nuits

22 rue de l'Eglise, Gevrey-Chambertin 📞 *03 80 34 10 05* 🌐 *www.denis-mortet.com* 🔲

BEFORE THE EARLY 1990s few had heard of Denis Mortet. On his father's retirement in 1991, the family estate was divided between him and his brother. Within a few years, Denis was a superstar, acclaimed for his rich, dense wines that often had more punch than elegance. Before long, the wines were showing finesse and vigour, as well as weight and power. Tragically, Mortet committed suicide in 2006, but his son Arnaud has been maintaining his

Domaine Denis Mortet

exacting standards. Most of his vineyards are village sites in Gevrey-Chambertin, but the vines are old and the quality sensational. There are also tiny quantities of *grands crus* Chambertin and Clos de Vougeot.
🍷 *red* 📷 *2005, 2002, 2001, 2000, 1999, 1995, 1995*
★ *Gevrey Vieilles Vignes, Clos de Vougeot*

Domaine des Lambrays
Côte de Nuits

31 rue Basse, Morey-St-Denis 📞 *03 80 51 84 33* ⬜

EXCEPT FOR one tiny parcel, this 9-ha *grand cru* domaine is owned by the German tycoon Günter Freund. Its exceptional site allows Thierry Brouin, who looks after the domaine and the winemaking, to produce equally exceptional wine. Anything he considers unworthy of the Lambrays label is bottled, modestly, as Morey-St-Denis Premier Cru.
🍷 *red* 📷 *2005, 2002, 2001, 2000, 1999, 1996, 1995* ★ *Morey-St-Denis Premier Cru, Clos des Lambrays*

Domaine Dujac
Côte de Nuits

7 rue de la Bussière, Morey-St-Denis 📞 *03 80 34 01 00* 🌐 *www.dujac.com* ⬜ *by appt*

THE 'JAC' IN DUJAC is Jacques Seysses, who abandoned banking for winemaking in 1969 and created this outstanding estate based in Morey-St-Denis. As an outsider who was anxious to learn, he sat at the feet of the region's best growers. Now he himself shares his experience and knowledge with

Cuverie at Domaine de la Vougeraie

winemakers the world over. As for his own wines, they demonstrate finesse rather than pure power, which does not prevent the best of them from ageing for 30 years.
🍷 *red, white* 📷 *2005, 2002, 2001, 2000, 1999, 1996, 1995* ★ *Gevrey-Chambertin Combottes, Bonnes Mares, Clos de la Roche*

Domaine Georges Roumier
Côte de Nuits

rue de Vergy, Chambolle-Musigny 📞 *03 80 62 86 37* 🌐 *www.roumier.com* ⬜ *by appt*

CHRISTOPHE ROUMIER is a super-star of Chambolle-Musigny. He knows that quality begins in the vineyard, to which he pays the closest attention. There is no hi-tech equipment in Roumier's winery; his winemaking is simple and traditional; and he takes care not to cosset his wines in too much new oak. The *premier cru* Chambolle-Musigny Les Amoureuses and the *grand cru* Bonnes Mares are usually his best wines, but even his simple *bourgogne rouge* has distinction.
🍷 *red* 📷 *2005, 2002 2001, 1999, 1996, 1995* ★ *Chambolle-Musigny, Les Amoureuses, Bonnes Mares*

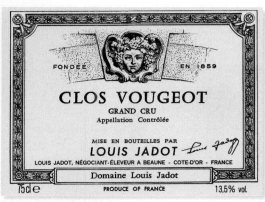

Louis Jadot *grand cru* label

Domaine Grivot
Côte de Nuits

6 rue de la Croix-Rameau,
Vosne-Romanée 🕾 03 80 61 05 95
🆆 www.domainegrivot.fr ☐ by appt

FOR A TIME Étienne Grivot
followed the advice of an
oenologist called Guy Accad,
whose techniques resulted in
very dark wines that lacked
true Burgundian character.
Some years ago Grivot
abandoned the system and
has been producing wonderful
wines, full of richness and
style, ever since. They are
perfect expressions of the
great *terroirs* of Nuits-St-
Georges and Vosne-Romanée.
🆁 red 📣 2005, 2002, 2001, 2000,
1999, 1996, 1995 ★ Vosne-Romanée
Beaux Monts, Échézeaux, Richebourg

Domaine Henri Gouges
Côte de Nuits

7 rue du Moulin, Nuits-St-
Georges 🕾 03 80 61 04 40
🆆 www.gouges.com ☐ by appt

FOR MANY YEARS Gouges
was acknowledged
as the top estate in
Nuits-St-Georges.
Then it lost its way,
and it was only in the
1990s, with a new
generation in charge,
that the domaine
has regained its

Domaine Grivot

supremacy. All the wines
are from Nuits-St-Georges,
offering a cross-section of the
best *premiers crus*. Gouges
also produces tiny quantities
of remarkably spicy white
wine from its vineyards.
🆁 red, white 📣 2005, 2002, 2001,
1999, 1996, 1995 ★ Nuits-St-
Georges: Pruliers, Les St Georges

Domaine Leroy
Côte de Nuits

rue du Pont Boillot, Auxey-Duresses
🕾 03 80 21 21 10
🆆 www.domaineleroy.com ◔

LALOU BIZE-LEROY, a determined
woman of a certain age
whose favourite recreation is
rock-climbing, has assembled
this magnificent estate,
which she runs alongside
her renowned *négociant*
business Maison Leroy.
She was one of the first
proprietors in Burgundy
to convert her vineyards
to biodynamism (*see
p105*), a somewhat
esoteric regime that
aims to restore health
and vigour to the over-
fertilized soils of
Burgundy – and other
regions. The wines,
from a wide range of
excellent vineyards,
are marvellous – and
very expensive.

🆁 red 📣 2005, 2002, 2001, 2000,
1999, 1996, 1995 ★ Vosne-Romanée
Brûlées, Pommard Vignots, Musigny

Domaine Méo-Camuzet
Côte de Nuits

11 rue des Grands Crus, Vosne-
Romanée 🕾 03 80 61 55 55
🆆 www.meo-camuzet.com ◔

NICOLAS MÉO could have
followed his father into the
advertising business, but
chose instead to devote
himself to the family domaine.
Working closely with legendary
Burgundian grower Henri
Jayer, he soon began producing wines every bit as good
as those from better known
estates in Vosne-Romanée.
These are not wines for the
faint-hearted: they are rich
and dense, and often remain
closed for five years or more.
Patience is, however, rewarded
with some of the most complex red wines of Burgundy.
🆁 red 📣 2005, 2002, 2001, 2000,
1999, 1996, 1995 ★ Vosne-Romanée
Cros Parantoux, Richebourg

Louis Jadot
Côte de Nuits

21 rue Eugène Spuller, Beaune
🕾 03 80 22 10 57
🆆 www.louisjadot.com ☐ by appt

DIRECTED FOR MANY years
by the Gagey family, this
famous merchant house
consistently produces firm,
tannic, long-lived wines from
the Côte de Nuits (as well as
sumptuous whites from the
Côte de Beaune). Jacques
Lardière has been the winemaker for almost 40 years,
which accounts for the even
and consistent quality of the
wines. Even in the most
difficult vintages, Lardière's
touch resulted in an
impressive range of wines.
🆁 red, white 📣 2005, 2002, 2001,
2000, 1999, 1996, 1995 ★ Fixin,
Clos de Vougeot, Clos St Denis

DOMAINE DE LA ROMANÉE-CONTI

With a production of just 7,500 cases a year, Domaine de la Romanée-Conti's ultra-silky red wines are some of the most sought after in the world. Anyone who has tasted the wines from the 2005, 1996, or 1990 vintage would have to agree that the estate merits its reputation and exorbitant prices. With overall standards of winemaking improving, however, the gap between other Burgundian estates and this one is narrowing all the time.

Domaine de la Romanée-Conti's status as Burgundy's greatest wine estate may be open to challenge, but what is beyond doubt is that it boasts the finest collection of vineyards: nothing but *grands crus*, mostly in Vosne-Romanée, but also a precious parcel in Montrachet. The domaine is run with unobtrusive brilliance by co-owner Aubert de Villaine.

The wines here are not blockbusters. They impress with subtlety and elegance rather than with power and tannin. These wines are rich, even sumptuous, but they are also wonderfully perfumed: initially an amalgam of violets and raspberries, with wet leaves and truffles and many other aromas developing with age.

Contact Information

1 rue Derrière-la-Four,
Vosne-Romanée
📞 *03 80 62 48 80* 📠

Wine Information

🍷 *red* 🗓 *2005, 2001, 1999, 1997, 1996, 1995, 1993*
★ *La Tâche, Richebourg, Romanée-Conti*

The Wines

The domaine's red wines all come from adjoining vineyards, but each has its own distinctive taste. Four of the *grand cru* sites are shared with other growers, but two – La Tâche and Romanée-Conti – are monopolies. There are no direct sales to consumers from the estate, but Romanée-Conti, by far the estate's most expensive wine, retails in the UK at more than £1,330 per bottle.

The Vineyards

There is nothing in the simplicity of this stone gatepost at the entrance to the fabled Romanée-Conti vineyard to suggest that you are about to step into one of the most famous, and valuable, vineyards in the world.

View over the village of Vosne-Romanée from above La Tâche vineyard

Parcels of vines owned by various growers in Savigny-lès-Beaune

WINEGROWING VILLAGES OF THE CÔTE DE BEAUNE

THE SWEEP OF THE Côte de Beaune vineyards curves gracefully around the small city of Beaune and continues south into Pommard, Volnay, and Meursault. These are Burgundy's only *grand cru* white vineyards outside Chablis, and the region is as famous for its white wines as for its elegant reds. Rising above the town of Aloxe-Corton is the great hill of Corton, with its celebrated Corton-Charlemagne vineyard. South of Beaune, set back from the villages of Puligny-Montrachet and Chassagne-Montrachet, are some other equally famous *grands crus*.

Côte de Beaune reds are quite varied: Pommard tends to be powerful and tannic; Volnay is more graceful; and the wines of

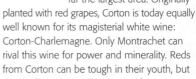

Traditional grape basket

Chorey-lès-Beaune and Savigny-lès-Beaune are usually medium-bodied and best drunk in the medium term. Wines hailing from villages up on the plateau sell as Hautes Côtes de Beaune, and wines from less prestigious villages such as Ladoix are sometimes labelled Côte de Beaune Villages. The soils are generally varied: limestone dominates, but is usually mixed with marl, clay, or pebbles. The following villages are some of the most important AOCs in the region.

limestone 🐦 *Pinot Noir* 🌿 *Chardonnay* 🍷 *red, white*

Chorey-lès-Beaune, Ladoix & Pernand-Vergelesses

THESE VILLAGES ARE grouped around the hill of Corton. Chorey-lès-Beaune is on fairly flat land and delivers reds that lack complexity but are very enjoyable when drunk young. Ladoix and Pernand-Vergelesses produce whites as well as reds. Very little wine is bottled as Ladoix as there are only about 120ha in production. Pernand-Vergelesses is also small, but it has some good hillside vineyards.

Aloxe-Corton

THIS PRETTY VILLAGE is also dominated by the mighty hill of Corton. A great sweep of *grands crus*, all known as Corton, are subdivided into sites such as Corton-Bressandes. Although the slopes are shared with Ladoix and Pernand-Vergelesses, Aloxe-Corton lays claim to by far the largest area. Originally planted with red grapes, Corton is today equally well known for its magisterial white wine: Corton-Charlemagne. Only Montrachet can rival this wine for power and minerality. Reds from Corton can be tough in their youth, but acquire haunting mellowness with age.

Beaune & Savigny-lès-Beaune

THE TOWN OF Beaune is flanked to the west by slopes studded with substantial vineyards, many of *premier cru* status. They are little known since there are few independent producers and most of the wine is sold by the town's merchant houses. Of greater fame is Beaune's annual charity wine auction, hosted by the Hospices de Beaune *(see p108)* as part of a 3-day festival. The village of Savigny lies in a valley north of Beaune, and produces sound, moderately-priced wine, most of it red. It is worth paying the slight premium for a *premier cru* from Beaune or Savigny. Clos des Mouches is Beaune's most remarkable white.

Pommard

IN GENERAL the Côte de Beaune gives lighter, more elegant wines than the Côte de Nuits, but Pommard is the great exception. Its richer soils deliver heady, dark, tannic reds, some of which never lose their initial toughness. The best wines, from growers such as Domaine du Comte Armand and Domaine de Courcel, are as structured and long-lived as those of the Côte de Nuit's Gevrey-Chambertin or Nuits-St-Georges. The best *premiers crus* are usually Rugiens and Épenots; these wines often need at least eight years to mature.

Volnay

UNLIKE BEAUNE, the hillside village of Volnay is crammed with excellent estates and here, the standard of winemaking is high. The wines tend to be perfumed and stylish: lighter and more elegant than Pommard. A century ago the wine of its neighbour Monthélie was sold as Volnay, which it resembles. At roughly half the price of Volnay, Monthélie (as it is now known) is among Burgundy's best-value wines, although it lacks the staying power of Volnay itself.

Tending grapes on the hill of Corton above the village of Pernand-Vergelesses

Auxey-Duresses, St-Romain & St-Aubin

THESE THREE VILLAGES lie in side valleys traversing the Hautes Côtes de Beaune. Auxey-Duresses and St-Romain lie behind Meursault. Auxey gives robust wines – both red and white – for medium-term drinking, while St-Romain, at a higher elevation, produces white wine that can be tart in tricky vintages. In general the whites of St-Aubin, which is tucked right behind the *grand cru* sites of Chassagne, are far better than its reds, and offer an attractive and inexpensive alternative to wines from the grander villages nearby.

Meursault

THIS LARGE VILLAGE is renowned for its sumptuous white wines; great Meursault is not just rich and hedonistic, it is also invigorating. There are no *grands crus* here but Meursault does have some exceptional *premiers crus* such as Les Perrières. Many growers single out village vineyards on their labels as they have an individual character, even though they are not *premiers crus*.

Puligny-Montrachet & Chassagne-Montrachet

THE WONDERFUL *premier* and *grand cru* vineyards belonging to these villages often adjoin one another, and it is not always easy to tell them apart. The wines are the quintessence of great white burgundy: noble, elegant, and profound. The greatest sites of all, the *grands crus* of Montrachet and Bâtard-Montrachet, are actually divided between Puligny and Chassagne. The high quality – and scarcity – of these wines mean they sell at a premium, so top *premiers crus* from both villages are better value. Whereas Puligny produces only white wines, almost half the production of Chassagne is of red wine.

Santenay & Maranges

SANTENAY COMPRISES A RANGE of vineyards just west of Chagny, and Maranges is its extension to the south, making it the most southerly vineyard of the Côte de Beaune. At their best, the wines from these sites are rich and fleshy, and, with quality steadily improving, they offer good value as both villages are little known.

TOP PRODUCERS OF THE CÔTE DE BEAUNE

Bouchard Père & Fils
Côte de Beaune

15 rue du Château, Beaune ☎ *03 80 24 80 24* ⊞ *www.bouchard-pereetfils.com* ◯ *by appt*

FOR DECADES this was one of Beaune's most celebrated merchant houses, blessed with a magnificent array of top vineyards. In the 1980s, however, quality slipped and scandals damaged the house's reputation. In 1995 it was bought by Champagne producer Joseph Henriot *(see p173)*, who improved quality across the board and restored the company to the ranks of Burgundy's top *négociants*.

PERFECT CASE: CÔTE DE BEAUNE

🔴 Bouchard Père & Fils Volnay Caillerets £££

⚪ Château de la Maltroye Chassagne-Montrachet Dent du Chien £££

⚪ Domaine Bonneau du Martray Corton-Charlemagne ££££

⚪ Domaine Chandon de Briailles Pernand-Vergelesses Île de Vergelesses ££

⚪ Domaine des Comtes Lafon Meursault Perrières £££

🔴 Domaine du Château de Chorey Beaune Les Cras ££

🔴 Domaine du Comte Armand Pommard Clos des Épeneaux £££

⚪ Domaine Leflaive Puligny-Montrachet £££

⚪ Domaine Marc Colin & Fils St-Aubin En Remilly ££

⚪ Domaine Michel Bouzereau & Fils Meursault Tessons ££

🔴 Domaine Michel Lafarge Volnay Vendanges Sélectionées ££

⚪ Olivier Leflaive Rully Rabourcé ££

🔲 red, white 🔁 2005, 2002, 1999, 1997 ★ Beaune Grèves Vigne de l'Enfant Jésus, Chevalier-Montrachet

Château de la Maltroye
Côte de Beaune

Chassagne-Montrachet
☎ *03 80 21 32 45* ◯ *by appt*

THE CHÂTEAU de la Maltroye stands out as one of the most handsome buildings in a rather plain village. Owned by Jean-Pierre Cornut since 1992, the 15-ha property is endowed with a fine selection of *premiers crus*. The wine is aged in one third new oak in unusually cold medieval cellars. The whites are rich and spicy, and the top *crus* have tremendous power. There is also some red Chassagne-Montrachet.
🔲 red, white 🔁 2005, 2002, 1999, 1996, 1995
★ *Chassagne-Montrachet: Clos de Château, La Romanée, Dent du Chien*

Domaine Albert Morot
Côte de Beaune

ave Charles Jaffelin, Beaune ☎ *03 80 22 35 39* ◯ *by appt*

THIS OLD-FASHIONED property was owned and run for years by Françoise Choppin who was succeeded in 2000 by her nephew Geoffroy. All the vineyards are *premier cru*, either in Beaune or Savigny. For a long time these wines were only known to insiders, but that has changed. Geoffroy has been modernizing the winemaking and introducing more new oak. Quality remains as high as ever, and the style is becoming increasingly sophisticated.

🔲 red 🔁 2005, 2002, 2001, 1999
★ Beaune: Marconnets, Teurons, Bressandes

Domaine Bonneau du Martray
Côte de Beaune

Pernand-Vergelesses
☎ *03 80 21 50 64*
⊞ *www.bonneaudemartray.com* ◯

JEAN-CHARLES Le Bault de la Morinière gave up his career as an architect in 1994 to manage his 200-year-old family estate, which produces red Corton and white Corton-Charlemagne. This makes it, together with Domaine de la Romanée-Conti, one of only two Burgundian estates to produce nothing but *grand cru* wines. With 9.5ha in Corton-Charlemagne, this estate is by far the largest producer of this *grand cru* and has for many years been the outstanding point of reference for the site. The white offers richness, mineral complexity, persistence, and a capacity to age for many years. The red is very refined, if less consistent.

Domaine Bonneau du Martray

🔲 red, white 🔁 2005, 2004, 2002, 2001, 1996, 1992
★ Corton-Charlemagne

Domaine Chandon de Briailles
Côte de Beaune

1 rue Soeur Goby, Savigny-lès-Beaune ☎ *03 80 21 52 31* ⊞ *www.chandon debriailles.com* ◯ *by appt*

RUN BY A mother-and-daughter team, Chandon de Briailles makes wines with a feminine touch. The whites from Pernand-Vergelesses and Savigny can be exquisite, and the red Savigny Lavières is minerally and elegant. The top wines come from the *grand cru* of Corton, with the emphasis on finesse and subtlety rather than power.

🟥 *red, white* 📆 *2005, 2000, 1999, 1996, 1995* ★ *Savigny Lavières, Pernand-Vergelesses Île de Vergelesses, Corton*

Domaine des Comtes Lafon
Côte de Beaune

Clos de la Barre, Meursault 📞 *03 80 21 22 17* 🔲 *www.comtes-lafon.fr* 🔲

SOME EXPERTS ON Burgundy consider Dominique Lafon the world's greatest producer of white wine, and it is hard to disagree. Meursault from elsewhere can often be soft and buttery; delicious, maybe, but not intrinsically Burgundian. With its vigour and raciness, and an abundance of rich, ripe fruit, Lafon's Meursault cannot be mistaken for anything but a burgundy. He is equally dextrous when it comes to red wine: his Volnay Santenots is one of the finest and best-balanced wines from that village.

🟥 *red, white* 📆 *2005, 2004, 2002, 2000, 1997, 1992* ★ *Meursault: Clos de la Barre, Perrières; Volnay Santenots*

Domaine du Château de Chorey
Côte de Beaune

Chorey-lès-Beaune 📞 *03 80 24 06 39* 🔲 *www.chateau-de-chorey.com* 🔲

CHOREY IS USUALLY overlooked because the village lies on the 'wrong' (eastern) side of the main road, the N74, away from the prestigious slopes of the Côte d'Or. The Germain family, whose wine formerly sold under the name Germain Père & Fils, is based at the village's château, and makes

BIODYNAMISM: MAGIC OR MADNESS?

In the 1920s the philosopher and educationalist Rudolf Steiner propounded the ideas that form the basis for biodynamic viticulture. The phases of the moon and stars are considered of primary importance – although this is nothing new, since traditional French winemakers have always timed their racking and bottling according to the lunar phases. More controversial is the use of homeopathic doses of unusual treatments such as animal compost, valerian, and boiled horsetail. Not surprisingly, many growers are deeply sceptical about the system, but essentially it all comes down to a method for restoring organic and microbial health to the soil and vines.

First adopted in 1980 by Nicolas Joly in the Loire Valley, biodynamism is now used by many leading estates in Burgundy and the Rhône Valley. Some of them, such as Domaine des Comtes Lafon, admit that they do not understand why the system works, but confirm that it does indeed improve the quality of both vines and wines.

delicious Chorey for early drinking, and a fine range of oaky Beaune *premiers crus*, which are among the best wines from these sites.

🟥 *red, white* 📆 *2005, 2002, 1999, 1997, 1996* ★ *Chorey-lès-Beaune, Beaune: Vignes Franches, Les Cras*

Domaine du Comte Armand
Côte de Beaune

place de l'Eglise, Pommard 📞 *03 80 24 70 50* 🔲 *www.domaine-comte-armand.com* 🔲 *by appt*

THE GLORY OF THIS Fommard property is its 5-ha Clos des Épeneaux, a top *premier cru*. It produces one of Burgundy's most powerful and tannic reds, and needs many years to reveal its multi-layered depths. Any wine not

considered worthy of the appellation is sold as simple Pommard and can be great value. Some less densely concentrated wine from Volnay and Auxey-Duresses is also produced here. In 2003 the estate converted all its vineyards to biodynamism.

🟥 *red* 📆 *2005, 2002, 2000, 1999, 1997, 1996, 1995* ★ *Pommard, Pommard Clos des Épeneaux*

Domaine Étienne Sauzet
Côte de Beaune

11 rue de Poiseul, Puligny-Montrachet 📞 *03 80 21 32 10* 🔲 *www.etienne-sauzet.com* 🔲 *by appt*

YEAR AFTER YEAR this estate has produced some of the most consistent wines of Puligny. Winemaker Gérard Boudot likes good acidity, and so the wines can take a few years to become harmonious. They are subtle rather than strident wines. Boudot has a wonderful range of *premiers crus*, as well as old vines in *grands crus* Bâtard-Montrachet and Chevalier-Montrachet.

🟥 *white* 📆 *2005, 2004, 2002, 1999, 1992* ★ *Puligny-Montrachet: Combettes, Champs Canet; Bâtard-Montrachet*

VIEILLES VIGNES

Beaune Les Cras
PREMIER CRU
APPELLATION BEAUNE 1ᵉʳ CRU CONTROLEE
1999
MIS EN BOUTEILLE AU
DOMAINE DU CHÂTEAU DE CHOREY
GERMAIN PROPRIÉTAIRE A CHOREY-LES-BEAUNE, CÔTE-D'OR, FRANCE

Domaine du Château de Chorey label

Domaine Françoise & Denis Clair
Côte de Beaune

14 rue de la Chapelle, Santenay
C 03 80 20 61 96 **⬜** by appt

THE CLAIRS' 11-HA property is divided between Santenay and St-Aubin, and excellent wines are made from both. Typical of his generation of Burgundian growers, Denis both cares for his vines and knows how to handle the grapes once they are brought into the cellars. Emerging from those cellars are succulent reds and spicy, lightly oaked, and good-value whites.

📷 *red, white* **📷** *2005, 2004, 2002, 2000* ★ *St-Aubin: En Remilly, Murgers des Dents de Chien*

Domaine Jacques Prieur
Côte de Beaune

6 rue des Santenots, Meursault
C 03 80 21 23 85
W www.prieur.com **⬜** by appt

THE 1970s AND 80s were a frustrating period for burgundy aficionados who knew about this domaine. It had sensationally good vineyards (including Montrachet, Musigny, and Chambertin), but made very dull wines. Then in 1990 the Prieur family went into partnership with the *négociant* house of Antonin Rodet *(see p112)* and quality soared. The wines are now dark, rich, and gutsy.

📷 *red, white* **📷** *2005, 2004, 2002, 2000, 1999, 1997* ★ *Corton Bressandes, Vosne Clos des Santenots, Le Montrachet*

Domaine Jean-François Coche-Dury
Côte de Beaune

9 rue Charles-Giraud, Meursault
C 03 80 21 24 12 **📷**

THIS HAS BEEN a legendary estate for some years, and

Domaine Jean-François Coche-Dury *grand cru* **label**

because owner Jean-François Coche-Dury has vines in many appellations, quantities of each wine are limited, so they can be costly and hard to find. They are snapped up by devotees from all over the world, who admire not only the Meursault but also the powerful Corton-Charlemagne, which benefits from prolonged ageing in oak barrels.

📷 *red, white* **📷** *2005, 2004, 2002, 2000, 1999, 1996, 1992* ★ *Meursault Perrières, Corton-Charlemagne, Volnay Clos des Chênes*

Domaine Leflaive
Côte de Beaune

place des Marronniers, Puligny-Montrachet **C** 03 80 21 30 13
W www.leflaive.fr **📷**

VINCENT LEFLAIVE was the first name to come to mind when speaking of white burgundy in the 1970s and 80s. But as he got older, the wines became less impressive. In the 1990s the domaine came into the hands of his daughter Anne-Claude, who converted the vineyards to biodynamism. The transformation has been astonishing, and bottles from the *premiers* and *grands crus* of Puligny-Montrachet are among the most profound and concentrated of all white burgundies.

📷 *white* **📷** *2005, 2004, 2002, 2000, 1999* ★ *Puligny-Montrachet Les Pucelles, Chevalier-Montrachet*

Domaine Marc Colin & Fils
Côte de Beaune

Gamay, St-Aubin **C** 03 80 21 30 43
⬜ by appt

THE GENIAL MARC COLIN and his three sons produce a range of wines from the underrated village of St-Aubin, as well as a tiny quantity of splendid Le Montrachet. All their St-Aubin vineyards are *premiers crus*, and the best are usually En Remilly and Chatenière. The wines are barrel-fermented and show exuberant fruit and a well-judged use of new oak.

📷 *white* **📷** *2005, 2004, 2002, 1999* ★ *St-Aubin: En Remilly, Chatenière; Le Montrachet*

Domaine Michel Bouzereau & Fils
Côte de Beaune

3 rue de la Planche-Meunière, Meursault **C** 03 80 21 20 74
⬜ by appt

ALTHOUGH NOT AS well known as some other Meursault producers, Michel Bouzereau and his son Jean-Baptiste produce impeccable wines both from their *premiers crus* and from their prized *village* sites such as Tessons and Limozin. The wines have richness and concentration, but also a sleek elegance complemented by skilful use of oak, and a spiciness that keeps them lively on the palate.

🍷 *white* 🔖 *2005, 2004, 2002, 2000, 1999* ★ *Meursault: Limozin, Charmes, Genevrières*

Domaine Michel Lafarge
Côte de Beaune

Volnay 📞 *03 80 21 61 61* 🌐 *www. domainelafarge.fr* ⏲ *by appt*

FOR MORE THAN 40 YEARS the modest Michel Lafarge made some of Volnay's most elegant wines, rich in fruit but never dense. His top bottlings are usually from *premiers crus* Clos des Chênes and Clos du Château des Ducs, the latter of which is under Lafarge's sole ownership.

Domaine Michel Lafarge

By 2001 Michel had handed the reins to his son Frédéric, and the estate had become fully biodynamic.

🍷 *red, white* 🔖 *2005, 2002, 2000, 1999, 1995* ★ *Volnay: Vendanges Sélectionées, Clos des Chênes, Clos du Château des Ducs*

Domaine Rémi Jobard
Côte de Beaune

12 rue Sudot, Meursault 📞 *03 80 21 20 23* ⏲ *by appt*

FRANÇOIS JOBARD, renowned for his rather austere wines, is better known than his nephew Rémi, but since 1997 Rémi has been making sensational white burgundies from his vineyards in Meursault. The wines that come out on top are usually Genevrières and Charmes: both *premiers crus*, they are vibrant, juicy and tightly structured.

🍷 *white* 🔖 *2004, 2002, 1999, 1996, 1995* ★ *Meursault: Genevrières, Charmes*

Domaine Vincent Girardin
Côte de Beaune

Les Champs Lins, BP 48, Meursault 📞 *03 80 20 81 00* 🌐 *www.vincentgirardin.com* 📧

FROM HIS BASE in the village of Meursault, Vincent Girardin has created a small but high-quality *négociant* business, supplementing the production of his own 14-ha estate with purchased wines from sites all over the Côte de Beaune. His Santenay reds are rich and supple, and there are also some increasingly impressive wines from Corton-Charlemagne and Pommard. Girardin likes a good deal of new oak, and so, it seems, do his numerous customers.

🍷 *red, white* 🔖 *2005, 2004, 2002, 1999* ★ *Santenay Gravières, Corton-Charlemagne, Pommard Rugiens*

Olivier Leflaive
Côte de Beaune

place du Monument, Puligny-Montrachet 📞 *03 80 21 37 65* 🌐 *www.olivier-leflaive.com* ⏲ *by appt*

WITH ANNE-CLAUDE Leflaive running the family domaine, which is also in Puligny-Montrachet, her cousin Olivier has set up this small *négociant* business specializing mostly in white wines, both from the great sites of Puligny-Montrachet and Meursault, and from lesser-known villages such as St-Aubin and Rully, which offer exceptional value.

These are modern-style burgundies, full in colour, creamy in texture, and accessible young.

🍷 *red, white* 🔖 *2005, 2004, 2002, 2000, 1999* ★ *Rully Rabourcé, Puligny-Montrachet Les Folatières, Bienvenues Bâtard-Montrachet*

LE MONTRACHET: AS GOOD AS IT GETS

The 8-ha site of Le Montrachet is the most famous white wine vineyard in the world. Even in modest vintages Montrachet is a wine of distinction, and in great years it has unparalleled richness. The wine's power is based on density of texture and concentration of flavour; its acidity is firm but not harsh, and allied to this is a capacity to age for many years, even decades. The quality level is kept extremely high by the producers who own vines here, most of whom are among the best in Burgundy: Domaine de la Romanée-Conti, Domaine des Comtes Lafon, Domaine Drouhin, Domaine Jacques Prieur and the two Leflaives. The wine is, however, overpriced; and a Bâtard-Montrachet or Chevalier-Montrachet from a renowned producer will be almost as fine and considerably cheaper.

WINE TOUR OF BURGUNDY

Burgundy is a region that effortlessly combines scenic beauty with a host of other attractions, from wine and gastronomy to magnificent medieval architecture. The prettiest part of the area lies in the south, among the rolling hills of Côte Chalonnaise and Mâconnais, but small villages such as St-Aubin and Chambolle-Musigny, which lie tucked among their vineyards on the Côte D'Or, also exude charm.

Puligny Montrachet

① Dijon
Dijon was the ancient capital of the powerful dukes of Burgundy, who took a keen interest in the region's wine. In 1385 they forbade the planting of the Gamay grape in Burgundy's vineyards, as they considered it inferior. Their former palace, which is now crammed with the fine collections of the Beaux-Arts Museum, is open to visitors.

② Route des Grands Crus ◁
This narrow road follows the mid-slope from Gevrey-Chambertin southwards to Morey-St-Denis *(left)* and beyond, passing through the most famous *grands crus* of northern Burgundy, including Le Chambertin.

③ Château du Clos de Vougeot ▽
Visit the medieval Château du Clos de Vougeot where Burgundian growers traditionally hold their ceremonies and banquets.
📞 03 80 62 86 09
🖥 www.closdevougeot.com

AUTU
LE CREUSOT
MONTCEAL-LES-MINE

④ Citeaux
The famous Abbaye de Citeaux is where the Cistercian order of monks was founded in 1098. In medieval times the monks controlled most of Burgundy's finest vineyards. Only vestiges of the abbey remain, but the interior can be visited. The monks' cheese is one of Burgundy's finest.
📞 03 80 61 32 58 🖥 www.citeaux-abbaye.com

THE HOSPICES DE BEAUNE

Founded in 1443, Beaune's magnificent Hôtel-Dieu is home to the Hospices de Beaune. The hospice's charitable activities are financed by the proceeds from the 58ha of vineyards with which it has been endowed over the centuries. Every year new wines are made by the hospice winemaker and auctioned off at a charity auction in November. The auction *(above)* is attended by wine lovers from around the world and many of the wines are bought by *négociants*. After the sale, the new oak barrels are transferred to cellars, where the wine is aged until it is ready for resale. The auction prices are closely monitored as a guide to market trends for the new vintage, but as a charitable event, high prices are encouraged and in truth, the auction is a combination of fundraising, promotion for merchants, and feasting.

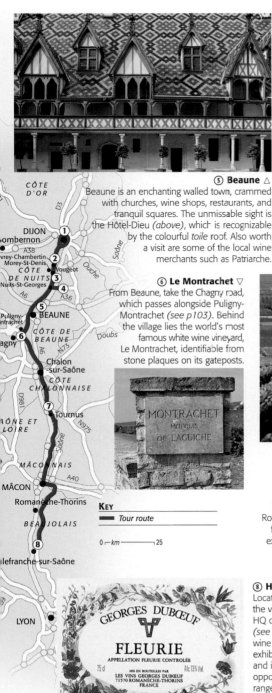

Visitors' Tips

Route: This 150km-tour begins in the north at Dijon and ends in Mâconnais. A motorway runs parallel to the Route Nationale, so it is easy to adjust the itinerary.

Duration: A full day is needed, or the tour can be taken at a more leisurely pace by including an overnight stay.

Wineries: In Beaune and Nuits-St-Georges, many *négociant* houses welcome visitors, but private wine estates are rarely open without an appointment.

Restaurant-Hotel Lameloise: 36 Place d'Armes, Chagny-en-Bourgogne ☎ 03 85 87 65 65 ⓦ www.lameloise.fr

⑤ **Beaune** △

Beaune is an enchanting walled town, crammed with churches, wine shops, restaurants, and tranquil squares. The unmissable sight is the Hôtel-Dieu *(above)*, which is recognizable by the colourful *toile* roof. Also worth a visit are some of the local wine merchants such as Patriarche.

⑥ **Le Montrachet** ▽

From Beaune, take the Chagny road, which passes alongside Puligny-Montrachet *(see p103)*. Behind the village lies the world's most famous white wine vineyard, Le Montrachet, identifiable from stone plaques on its gateposts.

Vineyards in the Côte de Beaune

⑦ **Tournus**

The main reason to visit this pretty little town is to tour the remarkable Romanesque abbey. Tournus is also a famous gastronomic centre, and an excellent base for visiting the villages and vineyards of Mâconnais.

KEY

▬▬ Tour route

0 ⌐ km ————— ⌐ 25

⑧ **Hameau en Beaujolais** ◁

Located on the edge of Beaujolais in the village of Romanèche-Thorins is the HQ of famous wine producer Duboeuf *(see p117)*. He has created a splendid wine museum here, with well-presented exhibits relating to the history of wine and its production process, plus the opportunity to purchase the entire range of Duboeuf wines.

☎ 03 85 35 22 22
ⓦ www.hameauenbeaujolais.com

Chardonnay grapes at Buxy co-operative in Montagny, Côte Chalonnaise

WINEGROWING VILLAGES OF THE CÔTE CHALONNAISE & MÂCONNAIS

Côte Chalonnaise

SET AMONG gently rolling hills between the Côte d'Or and the Mâconnais, the landscape of the Côte Chalonnaise is different from that of the Côte d'Or, and viticulture shares the land here with other forms of farming. Nor are the vineyards continuous; instead they are grouped around the five major villages. Both red and white wines are produced, and until recently the district had a reputation for rusticity. The efforts of quality-conscious *négociants* and a handful of excellent growers have raised standards considerably, and today the Côte Chalonnaise offers both good quality and good value. In addition to the basic Côte Chalonnaise appellation, there are the following five AOCs.

Domaine François Lumpp label

 limestone 🦋 Pinot Noir 🍂 Chardonnay
🍷 red, white

Bouzeron

A TINY COMMUNE OF only about 60ha, Bouzeron is best known for its acidic white grape variety, Aligoté *(see right)*. In 1997, the village received its own appellation, promoted from Aligoté de Bouzeron to simple Bouzeron.

Rully

THIS VILLAGE IS dominated by its splendid château, and its 340ha of vineyards are divided almost equally between Pinot Noir and Chardonnay.

Much of the wine is produced by *négociant* houses such as Antonin Rodet, Domaine Drouhin, and Olivier Leflaive, but private estates are beginning to produce wines of excellent quality. The *premiers crus*, both red and white, from growers such as Domaine Henri & Paul Jacqueson, are fruity, succulent, and excellent value.

Mercurey

THIS IMPORTANT AOC has 650ha in cultivation – almost 90 per cent of it red – and about one third of the vineyards enjoy *premier cru* status. The wines used to be rather coarse, but the ambition of local growers like Michel Juillot has led to a marked improvement. The *négociant* Domaine Faiveley is also a major proprietor here and it, too, sets high standards, increasingly followed by a new generation of growers in the village. White wines here are improving, but Mercurey's strength lies in robust, fruity reds.

Givry

THE QUIET VILLAGE of Givry has just over 200ha of vineyards. The efforts of a handful of ambitious and enthusiastic local growers are, however, showing that Givry is capable of producing supple Pinots and attractively aromatic Chardonnay (although only about 20 per cent of its production is white). The top growers include Domaine François

Lumpp, Domaine du Clos Salomon, Michel Sarrazin, Domaine Ragot, and Parizé & Fils.

Montagny

THE SOUTHERNMOST village in the Côte Chalonnaise, Montagny only produces white wine. Most of its vineyards are designated *premier cru*, but the wine is often dull. Much of it is produced by a sound co-op in Buxy, but there are better examples from Olivier Leflaive and Stéphane Aladame.

Mâconnais

THE STRENGTH OF THIS LARGE DISTRICT, northwest of Mâcon, lies in its fruity whites made from Chardonnay. The reds, usually from Gamay, are invariably inferior in quality and cannot compete with the best from Beaujolais. The most basic wines are sold as Mâcon or Mâcon Supérieur, but wines of much greater character are Mâcon-Villages, the *villages* often being replaced on the label by the name of one of the 27 villages entitled to the appellation.

Much of the wine is made by co-operatives, some of which are well equipped and produce wine to a good standard. Over the last decade, quality has improved dramatically, and the top wines of Pouilly-Fuissé and its nearby villages can rival some of the best from Chablis and the Côte de Beaune, although they are very different in style. The wines are broad, quite high in alcohol, and fleshy in texture. The following are the main AOCs within Mâconnais. *limestone* *Gamay* *Chardonnay* *red, white*

Vineyards and the Rock of Solutré, Pouilly-Fuissé

Viré-Clessé

THIS NEW AOC, created in 1999, replaced the two Mâcon-Villages appellations of Mâcon-Viré and Mâcon-Clessé. Around 400ha are in production and there are many good growers.

Pouilly-Fuissé

THIS IS BY FAR the best-known appellation within the Mâconnais, and with good reason, as its 760ha produce some of the area's most exciting wine. The vineyards lie beneath impressive cliffs, which help trap heat and project it onto the vines. The Chardonnay grown on these limestone soils tends to be richer and fatter than that from the Côte de Beaune, and vinification varies from unoaked (for clean fruity wines) to heavily new-oaked *cuvées*, which, in the hands of good wine-makers, can be sumptuous and opulent.

Pouilly-Vinzelles & Pouilly-Loché

THESE LESSER APPELLATIONS lie on the eastern fringes of Pouilly-Fuissé. Pouilly-Loché is often (legally) labelled as Pouilly-Vinzelles. Local co-operatives dominate production, which is limited since the two districts combined are only 81ha in area.

St-Véran

THIS 660-HA APPELLATION unites the wine of seven communes, and before 1971, when the AOC was created, it was usually sold as *Beaujolais blanc*. The production zones lie just north and south of Pouilly-Fuissé, and some of the better wines do resemble those from that well-known region. The wines are fresh and attractive, and can be good value.

THE CASE FOR ALIGOTÉ

Few wine lovers have a good word to say about Aligoté, other than as an essential ingredient in Kir, in which its asperity is softened by the addition of cassis liqueur. Many generations ago, however, Bouzeron was admired for its Aligoté, and when Aubert de Villaine, co-owner of Domaine de la Romanée-Conti *(see p101)*, bought a property here, he recognized the grape's potential. In 1979, de Villaine helped establish an AOC for Bouzeron and a good reputation for Aligoté. Fully ripe Aligoté can be delicious and refreshing, and a stimulating alternative to the ubiquitous Chardonnay in Burgundy.

TOP PRODUCERS OF THE CÔTE CHALONNAISE & MÂCONNAIS

Antonin Rodet
Côte Chalonnaise

Mercurey **☎** 03 85 98 12 12
Ⓦ www.rodet.com **❑**

RODET IS A WELL-RUN *négociant*, and the owner of 160ha in various parts of Burgundy. The company has always believed strongly in the Côte Chalonnaise and has close contact with two important properties (the Château de Rully in Rully and Château Chamirey in Mercurey), as well as owning Château de Mercey, which produces Mercurey and generic burgundy. Rodet is constantly fine-tuning the viticulture and winemaking in order to improve quality and give the wines more finesse. In good vintages they can be sensational, and excellent value; in difficult years a touch of coarseness can creep in.
▥ red, white **▨** 2005, 2002, 1999
★ *Rully Blanc (Château de Rully),*
Mercurey (Château Chamirey),
Mercurey (Château de Mercey)

Domaine du Clos Salomon
Côte Chalonnaise

Givry **☎** 03 85 44 32 24 **❑**

IN THE PAST, Clos Salomon was the most highly esteemed vineyard in Givry, but in recent decades the wine was unimpressive. However, for some years Ludovic du

Domaine Faiveley

Gardin and his brother have made enormous efforts to restore the 7-ha vineyard and improve the quality of the wine, and they have succeeded. The wine, which is more robust than many from this village, is aged in around 20 per cent new oak, allowing the richness of fruit to shine through.
▥ red **▨** 2005, 2002, 1999
★ *Givry Clos Salomon*

Domaine Faiveley
Côte Chalonnaise

8 rue de Tribourg, Nuits-St-Georges
☎ 03 85 61 04 55 **Ⓦ** www.
bourgognes-faiveley.com **◨**

FAIVELEY IS A MAJOR *négociant* house with well-located vineyards throughout Burgundy. Many of those vineyards are in Mercurey, and Faiveley has always regarded its holdings there with complete seriousness. It owns six sites, and most of the wines from each are vinified and bottled separately. La Framboisière and Les Mauvarennes are intended for early

drinking when their charm and fruit are most apparent; the most serious wine is from the *premier cru* site Clos du Roi, and is partly aged in new oak.
▥ red, white **▨** 2005, 2002, 1999
★ *Mercurey: La Framboisière, Clos du Roi*

Domaine François Lumpp
Côte Chalonnaise

36 ave de Mortières, Givry
☎ 03 85 44 45 57 **Ⓦ** www.
francoislumpp.com **❑** by appt

FRANÇOIS LUMPP owns vines in a variety of sites, including a number of *premiers crus*. His wines always respect the character of the Givry fruit, which is delicate rather than rich. This gives his whites an attractive herbal quality, and his reds a raspberry-scented fragrance. The best *cru* for red wine is usually Crausot, which has both freshness and concentration.
▥ red, white **▨** 2005, 2002, 1999
★ *Givry: Crausot, Petit Marole*

Domaine Henri & Paul Jacqueson
Côte Chalonnaise

5 rue de Chèvremont, Rully
☎ 03 85 91 25 91 **❑** by appt

HENRI JACQUESON AND his son Paul are justly regarded by many as the best producers in Rully. They have vines in some good *premiers crus*: Les Pucelles and Grésigny for whites, and Les Cloux and Chaponnière for reds. Although Jacqueson, like Rully itself, is probably better known for its rich spicy whites than for its reds, the red Les Cloux can be outstanding.
▥ red, white **▨** 2005, 2002, 1999
★ *Rully: Grésigny, Les Cloux*

PRODUIT DE FRANCE
GRAND VIN DE BOURGOGNE
Rully 1ᵉʳ Cru "Les Cloux"
APPELLATION CONTRÔLÉE
13% vol. Mis en bouteille à la Propriété par 750 mL
S.C.E.A. H.et P. Jacqueson, Viticulteur à Rully (S. & L.)
Domaine Henri & Paul Jacqueson label

Domaine Michel Juillot
Côte Chalonnaise

59 Grande rue, Mercurey
☎ 03 85 98 99 89
W www.domaine-michel-juillot.fr ☐

MICHEL JUILLOT was the first locally-based producer to put Mercurey on the map. Today the 27-ha domaine is run by his son Laurent. There are three sites of which they are particularly proud: Champs Martin, Clos de Tonnerre, and the exceptional Clos des Barraults. Although Juillot produces a good deal of white wine, it is the reds that are more arresting, with their red-fruit perfume and a sturdiness that is never rustic.
🔲 red, white 🔁 2005, 2002, 1999
★ Mercurey: Champs Martin, Clos des Barraults

Château de Fuissé
Mâconnais

Fuissé ☎ 03 85 27 05 90
W www.chateau-fuisse.fr ☐

FOR DECADES THIS property, owned by Jean-Jacques Vincent, set the pace for winemaking in Pouilly-Fuissé, although in recent years other estates have been hot on its heels in terms of quality. The vineyards are extensive, with

Château de Fuissé label

some 30ha. so different parcels are handled separately. The Cuvée Vieilles Vignes is the best-known bottling, but there are others from single parcels such as Le Clos and the very stony Les Combettes. The Vincents use new oak sparingly, and the result is a range of flavourful, well-structured wines, which age well.
🔲 white 🔁 2006, 2005, 2002, 2000
★ Pouilly-Fuissé: Cuvée Vieilles Vignes, Le Clos

Domaine de la Bongran
Mâconnais

Quintaine, rue Gillet, Clessé
☎ 03 85 36 94 03
W www.bongran.com ☐ by appt

THE MISCHIEVOUS Jean Thévenet is a man who defies tradition, or, as he sees it, returns to tradition – since he argues that he makes wine as his grandfather would have done. Yields are much lower than the official maximum, and he picks late. Consequently, the wines are enormously rich, often with a high percentage of alcohol. Thévenet's other estate, Domaine Emilian Gillet, produces similar results.
🔲 white 🔁 2006, 2005, 2004, 2002
★ Cuvée Tradition, Cuvée Botrytis

Domaine Guffens-Heynen
Mâconnais

Vergisson ☎ 03 85 51 66 00
☐ by appt

BELGIAN-BORN Jean-Marie Guffens-Heynen runs the highly regarded négociant house of Verget, which specializes in white burgundy. He also has this tiny domaine with vines in Mâcon Pierreclos and Pouilly-Fuissé. These are tended by his wife, while he takes care of the winemaking, which is both artisanal and exact. The wines are exceptionally rich and profound.
🔲 white 🔁 2006, 2005, 2004, 2002
★ Mâcon Pierreclos, Mâcon Pierreclos en Chavigne

Domaine J A Ferret
Mâconnais

Le Plan, Fuissé ☎ 03 85 35 61 56
☐ by appt

ONE OF THE STRENGTHS of this 15-ha property is that most of its vines are at least 30 years old, giving wines of considerable concentration. All the grapes are picked by hand and mostly fermented in barrique. Some parcels of vines are vinified and marketed separately, and the star turn is from Les Ménétrières, aged mostly in new oak and exceptionally rich.
🔲 white 🔁 2006, 2005, 2004, 2002 ★ Pouilly-Fuissé: Le Clos, Les Ménétrières

THÉVENET'S SWEET CHARDONNAY

Chardonnay is always dry, right? Not when Jean Thévenet of Domaine de la Bongran has a hand in it. Thévenet's vineyards sometimes attract botrytis (below), and in 1983, he decided to allow it to run riot. He vinified the grapes as if they were Sauternes (see p66), selecting only those grapes that had been affected by botrytis, and the result was a few thousand bottles of rich, honeyed wine, which attracted attention worldwide. Ever since, Thévenet has continued to make these wines whenever climatic conditions permit. There are two bottlings: Cuvée Levroutée, made from overripe grapes, and the rare Cuvée Botrytisée, which is made from nobly rotten grapes. So fine and distinctive are these wines that many of Thévenet's neighbours in Clessé are now following his example.

A windmill surrounded by Gamay vineyards at Moulin-à-Vent

WINEGROWING VILLAGES OF BEAUJOLAIS

THIS SOUTHERN district of Burgundy is a large and exceptionally pretty area with small villages and slopes planted almost exclusively with Gamay. It is often regarded as distinct from Burgundy in wine terms as its soil and grape variety, and therefore its wines, are different from those found elsewhere in the region.

Beaujolais made its reputation decades ago as a popular quaffing wine in the bistros of Paris and Lyon. Endlessly enjoyable and with no pretensions, it is all freshness and vivid, zesty fruit – a style that has been taken to a profitable extreme with Beaujolais Nouveau. Like some more 'serious' Beaujolais, this is made by a method known as carbonic maceration, which involves fermenting whole bunches of grapes under a protective layer of gas. The process emphasizes bright fruitiness at the expense of structure. At the same time, certain producers continue to vinify and age their wines in a traditional Burgundian fashion, aiming to create something more serious and age-worthy.

It seems that Beaujolais may have lost its way in recent years: in addition to the clusters of small family domaines, some excellent, others mediocre, it is dominated by co-operatives and merchants, some of whom have dragged down the quality of the wine. Markets have been shrinking and in 2002 the region saw part of its crop sent for distillation for lack of customers. Yet Beaujolais at its best is a unique

Domaine des Terres Dorées label, Beaujolais

wine that, if well made and well priced, will always find an enthusiastic following.

The basic appellation is AOC Beaujolais, of which on average some 80 million bottles are produced annually; a step up is AOC Beaujolais Villages, of which 45 million bottles are released. The rest of the production, around 48 million bottles, carries the AOCs of the 10 *crus* entitled to their own appellation, each with its own character. These *crus (below)* all lie in the northern half of the region on granitic soils.

🗺 *granite* 🍇 *Gamay* 🍷 *red*

Juliénas

THIS IS NOT usually one of the most immediately appealing of *crus*, as its 580ha give wines that are very high in tannins and acidity. On the other hand, it ages quite well, developing spiciness as it matures. In vintages where acidity levels are low, Juliénas shows a welcome vigour.

St-Amour

THE MOST NORTHERLY *cru*, St-Amour fetches a premium thanks to its romantic name. It can indeed be a charming wine, offering a mouthful of sweet, ripe fruit. However, it has less personality than some other Beaujolais *crus*.

Chénas

GRANITIC SUBSOILS beneath the 270ha of this village yield wines with more stuffing and ageing potential than many other Beaujolais *crus*. The wines are less overtly fruity and quaffable, but have weight and density, which give them added complexity.

Moulin-à-Vent

THIS 660-HA APPELLATION is the most serious of the Beaujolais *crus*. It produces wines that do not really conform to the stereotype of juicy purple wines to be knocked back with abandon. Its character derives from manganese in the soil. It also tends to be aged longer, and with a higher proportion of oak barrels than the other *crus*. It can keep well, and after 10 years or so comes to resemble Pinot Noir. Some wines from this *cru* can be slightly too serious and extracted, giving less pleasure than simpler, fruitier examples.

Fleurie

FLEURIE IS ONE OF THE MOST fragrant and elegant wines of Beaujolais. This, combined with its charming name, has made Fleurie one of the most expensive wines of the district, even though there is plenty of it to go round, with 870ha in production. Fortunately there are a good number of reliable producers.

Chiroubles

WITH ITS 360HA of vineyards located on some of the highest spots in the region, Chiroubles produces wine that is relatively light, though none the worse for that. It is best enjoyed young when its fruit is at its most vivid.

Harvesting Gamay grapes in Fleurie

THE NOUVEAU PHENOMENON

Beaujolais Nouveau is Beaujolais that has been vinified and bottled as fast as possible, to ensure the wine is bursting with youthful fruitiness. An excess of mediocre Nouveau has led to declining interest in the wine, but when all goes well, it can be delicious – and can also do wonders for the grower's cash flow.

As with some other types of Beaujolais, the wine is made by carbonic maceration. After a few days of maceration, the Gamay grapes are pressed and fermentation is finished in a vat, without grape skins to minimize astringency. When handled properly, the technique emphasizes colour and fruitiness, and keeps tannin to a minimum. The wine is ready to drink within a few weeks of harvest.

The vogue for Nouveau reached its peak in the 1960s when the annual Beaujolais Race developed, with producers competing to rush the newly released wines to restaurants and venues as quickly as possible each harvest.

Morgon

WITH 1,100HA under vine, this is an important *cru*, as well as one of the most distinctive, thanks to the schist and granite in the soil. Although it is not always the most appealing of wines when very young, Morgon can age well. Beaujolais fanciers look out for wines from the sub-district called the Côte du Py, where Morgon's best fruit is grown.

Régnié

THE MOST RECENT village to be promoted to *cru* status, Régnié became an AOC in 1988. With 640ha in the appellation, the wine should be more in evidence than it is. However, it has been slow to catch on, and a good deal of it is bottled as simple Beaujolais Villages.

Brouilly & Côte de Brouilly

THESE ARE BEAUJOLAIS' MOST southerly *crus*. Brouilly is quite a large village, with 1,300ha under vine; Côte de Brouilly, with just 300ha, is usually of slightly superior quality, since the vines are planted on slopes. Both wines often have an abundance of fruit and can be drunk with pleasure relatively young.

TOP PRODUCERS OF BEAUJOLAIS

Château des Jacques
Beaujolais

Romanèche-Thorins ☎ *03 85 35 51 64* W *www.louis-jadot.com* ☐ *by appt*

IN 1996 THE BEAUNE merchant house of Louis Jadot *(see p100)* acquired this important property in Moulin-à-Vent. From the start, Jadot has imposed a Burgundian style of vinification, with no carbonic maceration and discreet use of new-oak ageing. The 27-ha estate is divided into various sectors, which are vinified and sometimes bottled separately so as to demonstrate the varied styles and flavours of which Beaujolais is capable. But prices are Burgundian too – that is, considerably higher than the Beaujolais norm.
🍷 *red* 🔺 *2006, 2005, 2004, 2003*
★ *Moulin-à-Vent: Roche, Clos du Grand Carquelin*

Domaine Calot
Beaujolais

Villié-Morgon ☎ *04 74 04 20 55* W *www.domaine-calot.com* ☐

JEAN CALOT IS one of a growing number of Beaujolais wine-makers who no longer use carbonic maceration. He wants instead to highlight the depth

Domaine Calot label

of fruit from his 12ha. His vines' average age is 40 years, and there are even some centenarians. The latter are the source of his blackberry-scented Morgon Cuvée Vieilles Vignes. Another house special-ity is Morgon Cuvée Jeanne, made from overripe grapes, which is more full-bodied and plummy than most Beaujolais.
🍷 *red* 🔺 *2006, 2005, 2004, 2003*
★ *Morgon: Cuvée Vieilles Vignes, Cuvée Jeanne*

Domaine de la Madone
Beaujolais

La Madone, Fleurie ☎ *04 74 69 81 51* W *www.domaine-de-la-madone. com* ☐

LA MADONE IS ONE of a handful of good producers in Fleurie. Fleurie is, or should be, floral and charming, and Jean-Marc

Desprès makes wines that are very true to type. The regular bottling is simple and straightforward, and the Cuvée Vieilles Vignes is more vivid and concentrated. Both are best enjoyed young.
🍷 *red* 🔺 *2006, 2005, 2004, 2003*
★ *Fleurie, Fleurie Vieilles Vignes*

Domaine des Terres Dorées
Beaujolais

Crière, Charnay ☎ *04 78 47 93 45* ☐ *by appt*

JEAN-PAUL BRUN IS the region's most individual producer, a man who has challenged all the prevailing stereotypes about Beaujolais. He believes that the wine should be made in a Burgundian fashion, with natural yeasts and long fermentation. Appropriately, he calls this wine Cuvée à l'Ancienne. Brun does not confine himself to Gamay; he produces Chardonnay, both oaked and unoaked, as well as remarkably rich late-harvest wines. Brun is a one-off who has his own ideas and cour-ageously adheres to them.
🍷 *red, white* 🔺 *2006, 2005, 2004, 2003* ★ *Beaujolais Cuvée à l'Ancienne, Moulin-à-Vent*

Domaine Émile Cheysson
Beaujolais

Chiroubles ☎ *04 74 04 22 02* ☐

FOUNDED IN 1870, this estate is now owned by Jean-Pierre Large, and his 26ha of vineyards are dispersed among various sectors of Chiroubles. His wines can be muted when young, but reveal violet scents and silky textures if kept for a year or two.
🍷 *red* 🔺 *2006, 2005, 2004, 2003* ★ *Chiroubles: Traditionnelle, Cuvée Prestige*

A RETURN TO TRADITION

By the early 21st century, Beaujolais was in crisis. Although its top wines were highly prized, the bulk of run-of-the-mill Beaujolais was failing to attract buyers. The solution, many traditionalists argued, was to revert to more authentic forms of production with less reliance on high yields, chaptalization, and carbonic maceration. Previously, most commercial Beaujolais had been bottled as young as possible, but now traditionalists are returning to less hurried practices.

Today most conscientious Beaujolais producers are wisely steering a middle path, with lower yields, more selection in the vineyard, and ageing in old oak barrels to give more harmony and depth to their wines. Like other regions, Beaujolais is learning that hurriedly made, poor quality wines (however cheap) are no longer finding a market.

Domaine Louis-Claude Desvignes
Beaujolais

135 rue de la Voute, Villié-Morgon
☎ 04 74 01 23 35 W www.louis-
claude-desvignes.com ☐ by appt

THIS SEVENTH-GENERATION Morgon winemaker steers a clear path between the youthful hedonistic expression of Beaujolais and a more serious style. Louis-Claude Desvignes likes to harvest as late as possible for maximum ripeness, and then give the wine a long fermentation to extract colour and richness. Although these wines can be drunk young, they are among the few that benefit from two or three years in bottle.
🍷 red 📅 2006, 2005, 2004, 2003 ★ Morgon: Javernières, Côte du Py

Duboeuf
Beaujolais

BP12, Romanèche-Thorins
☎ 03 85 35 34 20
W www.duboeuf.com ☐

GEORGES DUBOEUF IS as well known as any wine producer in France, yet he has remained firmly planted on Beaujolais soil. Over 50 years ago he began his career by peddling his wines to local restaurants. Energy and luck brought him success, and he was soon established as a major *négociant*, working closely with 400 growers and 15 co-operatives, producing

Duboeuf

three million cases per year. Duboeuf still tastes for three hours daily with his son Franck to select the wines for his range. He has also done much for the region by creating his Hameau du Vin, a miniature wine village with an excellent museum and a large shop.
🍷 red, white 📅 2006, 2005, 2004, 2003 ★ Fleurie, Morgon, Moulin-à-Vent Prestige

Jean-Marc Burgaud
Beaujolais

Villié-Morgon ☎ 04 74 69 16 10
W www.jean-marc-burgaud.com
☐ by appt

JEAN-MARC BURGAUD, along with a few other growers, has moved away from the light but superficial style of Beaujolais in search of something more substantial and subtle, without losing that fruity Beaujolais character. The Morgon Les Charmes is light and fresh, and the more serious wine, aged for 12 months in oak casks, comes from the renowned Côte du Py, where Burgaud has old vines.
🍷 red 📅 2006, 2005, 2004, 2003 ★ Morgon: Côte du Py, Vieilles Vignes

Maison Mommessin
Beaujolais

Quincié-en-Beaujolais ☎ 04 74 69 09 30 W www.mommessin.com ●

FOUNDED IN 1865, this is a high-quality *négociant* house, blending and selling wines from all the Beaujolais *crus*. The basic bottlings are of sound quality, but there is a major step up to the single-vineyard *cuvées* such as the Moulin-à-Vent Réserve.
🍷 red 📅 2006, 2005, 2004, 2003 ★ Brouilly, Fleurie, Moulin-à-Vent Réserve

Maison Mommessin label

Paul & Eric Janin
Beaujolais

Romanèche-Thorins ☎ 03 85 35 52 80 ☐ by appt

THIS IS A very traditional 12-ha domaine that, unusually for Beaujolais, is partly cultivated biodynamically. Janin vinifies numerous parcels separately, ages them in large casks, and then blends them, arguing that the whole is more impressive than the individual wines that compose the blend. These are certainly complex wines, with aromas of cherry and liquorice, and the estate's top wine is usually the Clos du Tremblay, made from its oldest vines in Moulin-à-Vent.
🍷 red 📅 2006, 2005, 2004, 2003 ★ Beaujolais-Villages, Moulin-à-Vent Clos du Tremblay

THE RHÔNE VALLEY

THIS IS A REGION *of extreme contrasts. If the north is cool, discreet, noble, and expressed in different shades of just one red grape, the south is the antithesis: warm, exuberant, heartily earthy, with myriad grape varieties. The unifying factors are the Rhône River and the enduring appeal of all its wines.*

As the Rhône flows downriver from Lyon, it courses through a northern landscape of high, rocky hills which plunge to the water's edge: a mass of granite, schist, and gneiss, with vineyards clinging to the sides. The slope and erosion here necessitate dry-stone terraces and wooden stakes for trellising, and on this patchwork landscape just one red grape variety, Syrah, is allowed expression in five different vineyard areas or *crus*: Côte Rôtie, Hermitage, Cornas, St-Joseph, and Crozes-Hermitage.

Tying down vines, Côte Rôtie

In the 1960s Côte Rôtie, Hermitage, Cornas, and the Viognier-made white wine appellations Condrieu and Château Grillet were threatened with extinction through lack of interest and investment. They survived, regaining lustre and prestige as their true quality was identified, but production remains tiny. Producers farm only a few hectares and either bottle their own wines or sell the grapes to one of several important *négociants*.

The south, on the other hand, is a picture of largesse. Here, the Rhône Valley opens out into a broad panorama of river plain, rocky garrigue, oak and olive trees, and bush-grown vines offset by mountains. Over 90 per cent of the Rhône's 80,000ha is cultivated here. Estates are larger than in the north, and instead of just Syrah, the south grows a range of grapes, including Grenache and Mourvèdre.

Châteauneuf-du-Pape, with its warm, generous, mostly red wines, is the largest and most famous *cru*. Gigondas and Vacqueyras are its red wine cousins; rosé region Tavel and tri-coloured Lirac complete the list of *crus*. The volume, though, comes from wholesome Côtes du Rhône and Côtes du Rhône Villages, and 'younger' districts like Côtes du Ventoux.

View across the Rhône River to the vineyards on the hill of Hermitage

◁ **Individually staked Syrah vines on the steep terraces of the Côte Blonde, Côte Rôtie**

WINE MAP OF THE RHÔNE VALLEY

THE VINEYARDS OF the Northern Rhône trace the course of the river from the town of Vienne south to Valence. In descending order Côte Rôtie, Condrieu, Château Grillet, St-Joseph, Cornas, and St-Péray hug the left bank, while Hermitage and Crozes-Hermitage are located on the right. A distance of approximately 100km separates these Northern Rhône AOCs from the southern group of Châteauneuf-du-Pape, Gigondas, Vacqueyras, Lirac, and Tavel situated just to the north of Avignon. In between are the lesser-known districts of the Coteaux du Tricastin and Diois east of the river in the Drôme *département*, and Côtes du Vivarais to the west in the Ardèche. The Côtes du Ventoux and Côtes du Lubéron are ranged to the southeast of Avignon in the Vaucluse.

Domaine Bois de Boursan label, Châteauneuf-du-Pape

KEY

The Rhône Valley

CÔTE RÔTIE
CONDRIEU
CHÂTEAU GRILLET
ST-JOSEP
CROZES-HERMITAGE
HERMITAGE
Tain L'Hermitage ●
CÔTES DU RHÔNE
45°
CORNAS — Valence
ST-PÉRAY

Rhône

Dr

Rhône

● Montél

CÔTES DU VIVARAIS
COTEAUX TRICAST

VACQUEYR
Orange
CHÂTEAUNE
DU-PAPE
LIRAC
TAVEL
44°
AVIG

0 — km — 30

PERFECT CASE: THE RHÔNE VALLEY

Ⓡ Château de Beaucastel Châteauneuf-du-Pape £££

Ⓦ Château de Beaucastel Châteauneuf-du-Pape Roussanne Vieilles Vignes £££

Ⓡ Château Rayas Châteauneuf-du-Pape £££

Ⓡ Clos des Papes Châteauneuf-du-Pape £££

Ⓦ Domaine André Perret Condrieu Coteau de Chéry £££

Ⓡ Domaine Bois de Boursan Châteauneuf-du-Pape Cuvée des Félix £££

Ⓡ Domaine Clape Cornas ££

Ⓡ Domaine Jamet Côte Rôtie £££

Ⓡ Domaine Jean-Louis Chave Hermitage £££

Ⓦ Domaine Jean-Louis Chave Hermitage £££

Ⓡ Guigal Côte Rôtie La Mouline £££

Ⓡ Paul Jaboulet Aîné Hermitage La Chapelle £££

NORTHERN RHÔNE: AREAS & TOP PRODUCERS

CÔTE RÔTIE *p122*
Domaine Clusel Roch *p130*
Domaine Jamet *p130*
Guigal *p130*

CONDRIEU *p123*
Domaine André Perret *p130*
Domaine Georges Vernay *p130*
Domaine Yves Cuilleron *p131*

CHÂTEAU GRILLET *p123*

ST-JOSEPH *p124*

CROZES-HERMITAGE *p124*
Domaine Alain Graillot *p131*

HERMITAGE *p124*
Delas Frères *p131*
Domaine Jean-Louis Chave *p131*
M Chapoutier *p132*
Paul Jaboulet Aîné *p132*

CORNAS *p125*
Domaine Clape *p132*

ST-PÉRAY *p125*

Carrying Syrah grapes in the Northern Rhône

TERROIR AT A GLANCE

Latitude: 43.5–45.5°N.

Altitude: 0–450m.

Topography: The north is fairly rugged terrain with steep schistous slopes rising to a plateau 350m above the valley floor. The prime vineyard sites offer southerly or southeasterly exposure and shelter from the northerly winds. The south varies from sun-scorched alluvial river plain to the later-ripening limestone-and-clay slopes that rise to around 450m.

Soil: Granite, schist, sand, flint, chalk, mica, clay.

Climate: The north has a classic continental climate of hot summers and cold winters with clearly marked seasons: ideal for Syrah, which requires less intense heat. Cool, dry northerly winds and warmer, rain-bearing southerlies blow intermittently through the year. The climate of the south is pure Mediterranean with hot, dry summers and winter rain, good for varieties like Grenache and Mourvèdre that like the heat.

Temperature: July average is 22.5°C in the north and 23.5°C in the south.

Rainfall: Annual average is 600–650mm.

Wind: In the south, the mistral wind (see p129) aids ripening.

Viticultural hazards: Fungal disease; hail.

SOUTHERN RHÔNE: AREAS & TOP PRODUCERS

CÔTES DU VIVARAIS p126

COTEAUX DU TRICASTIN p126

CLAIRETTE DE DIE, CRÉMANT DE DIE & CHÂTILLON-EN-DIOIS p126

GIGONDAS p127
Domaine Raspail-Ay p133

VACQUEYRAS p127
Domaine de la Monardière p133

CHÂTEAUNEUF-DU-PAPE p128
Château de Beaucastel p133
Château la Nerthe p133
Château Rayas p134
Clos des Papes p134
Domaine Bois de Boursan p134
Domaine Bosquet des Papes p134
Domaine de la Janasse p134

LIRAC p128

TAVEL p128
Château d'Aquéria p135

CÔTES DU VENTOUX p129

CÔTES DU LUBÉRON p129

CÔTES DU RHÔNE & CÔTES DU RHÔNE VILLAGES p127
Domaine La Réméjeanne p135
Domaine Marcel Richaud p135

CLAIRETTE DE DIE, CRÉMANT DE DIE & CHÂTILLON-EN-DIOIS

CÔTES DU RHÔNE & CÔTES DU RHÔNE VILLAGES

GIGONDAS

△ Mont Ventoux

CÔTES DU VENTOUX

CÔTES DU LUBÉRON

View across the Rhône River to Tain L'Hermitage

Medieval chapel on the hill of Hermitage overlooking the Rhône River

WINEGROWING AREAS OF THE NORTHERN RHÔNE

THE NORTHERN RHÔNE is home to a single red grape variety, Syrah, seen in various guises according to the appellation. The tiny volume of white is produced from fragrant Viognier and subtle Marsanne and Roussanne.
Here you will find some of the finest wines produced in France – Hermitage, Côte Rôtie, and Condrieu. Unfortunately, quantities are limited by the restricted size of the vineyards, which are hemmed into a narrow valley with limited room for expansion.

Côte Rôtie

THE HILLSIDES OF AOC CÔTE RÔTIE, or the 'roasted slope', are an impressive sight: a stairway of narrow-terraced vineyards on vertiginous schistous slopes cascading down to the edge of the Rhône River. These are the most northerly vineyards in the Rhône, strung along 8km of the left bank of the river. Economic constraints and the physical difficulties of working the vineyards nearly led to their abandonment in the 1960s, but a revival of interest from a younger generation brought renewed planting. There are now 235ha under vine, producing just over a million bottles a year of this fabulous red wine. Deeply coloured, it has an exuberant aroma of dark fruits, violet, and spice; intensity of flavour; velvety texture; and lithe, rather than heavy, form. Although appealing when young, it also has the ability to age. All this is down to Syrah, grown on heat-retaining schistous soils at the limits of a continental climate. Up to 20 per cent of white Viognier

Rhône River and town of Condrieu

can officially be blended with Syrah in this appellation; the actual percentage used by producers is difficult to ascertain as the two varieties are often planted together, but it rarely, if ever, attains 20 per cent.

Côte Rôtie is divided into two segments. South of the town of Ampuis the silica-and-limestone soils of the Côte Blonde produce wines of great elegance, while in the Côte Brune to the north, located on darker, ferruginous, clay soils, the emphasis is on structure. Seventy-two specific vineyard sites have been officially designated within these zones, leading to a trend for single-vineyard bottlings that sell at a premium. The bulk of Côte Rôtie, however, is produced from vineyards in both the Côte Brune and Côte Blonde owned in small parcels by 100 or so growers who either bottle their own wine or sell to one of the major *négociants*.

▨ *schist, gneiss, limestone, clay* ▧ *Syrah*
▨ *Viognier* ▧ *red*

Condrieu

CONDRIEU HAS A SIMILAR ASPECT and history to that of neighbouring Côte Rôtie: steep slopes running to the river's edge, terraced vineyards, and a revival from virtual demise in the late 1970s. The big difference in this AOC is that it is white wine that is made here, from the Viognier grape. This variety has been grown in the region for centuries and seems to favour the continental climate and sandy, granite slopes which assist in producing one of the world's most original wines. Unctuous and heady, the aromatic spectrum hovers around a mix of apricot, peach, pear, and rose water for dry Condrieu, and candied citrus flavours for the rarer, sweeter wines. The volume and texture on the palate is provided by an imposing level of alcohol (13.5 per cent) and low acidity. These highly sought-after whites are best drunk young at two to three years. The problem is that Viognier is also a fickle variety in these climes, prone to difficult fruit set and with a history of low levels of production. This means that with only 130ha under vine, Condrieu is a rare wine and the price is consequently high. Of the 100 or so growers in the district, 30 make and bottle their own wines, the rest sell to the region's *négociants*. E Guigal is the most important of these, accounting for a third to a half of the district's output.

 granite, sand 　 Viognier 　 white

Château Grillet

WITH ONLY 4HA UNDER VINE, AOC Château Grillet is one of the smallest appellations in France. It is actually an enclave within Condrieu and forms a south-facing amphitheatre that offers shelter from the northerly winds. It has been owned by the same single family (Neyret-Gachet) since 1840. The wine is again made from Viognier but lacks the exuberance of Condrieu, being rather more reserved and austere, and in definite need of bottle age. This is due to the intensity of the wine and the lengthy time it spends in oak cask (20 to 22 months). Its high price is related to its rarity and reputation from the early 20th century of being one of France's greatest white wines.

granite, sand 　 Viognier 　 white

Jean-Luc Colombo label

1999
LES RUCHETS
CORNAS
APPELLATION CORNAS CONTRÔLÉE

RHÔNE REVOLUTIONARY: JEAN-LUC COLOMBO

Consultant oenologist Jean-Luc Colombo has played havoc in the small world of Rhône winemaking. When he arrived in the rather prosaic backwater of Cornas in 1984 to set up the Centre Oenologique, his outsider status alone was enough to set tongues wagging. Since then, his adherence to certain modern forms of winemaking has only caused further controversy. The use of cultured yeasts, destemming, rapid fermentation with a long period of maceration, and ageing in new oak barrels are all a far cry from what is deemed traditional here. The fact that Colombo also bottles wines from his Cornas domaine in Bordeaux bottles rather than the traditional Burgundy-shaped ones further upset the status quo. But that did not prevent a number of his clients from following his lead. Today, his lasting influence can be seen in the move towards cleaner, more controlled winemaking and an accessible style of wine. His detractors, however, regret the muting of regional style with modern techniques. In addition to his domaine in Cornas, Colombo also owns vines in St-Péray and the Côte Bleue in Coteaux d'Aix en Provence close to his native Marseille. He produces wines under the *négociant* label Jean-Luc Colombo and acts as a consultant all the way along the Rhône Valley from Switzerland to Châteauneuf-du-Pape.

W www.vinsjlcolombo.com

Steep terraces of Château Grillet

St-Joseph

St-Joseph is a difficult appellation to pinpoint, running from Condrieu to Cornas and extending for 60km along the left bank of the Rhône. The wines are over 90 per cent red, varying from light, fruity styles to a fuller, firmer, tannic form. Much depends on the aspect of the vineyard – as in Côte Rôtie the south-facing slopes are preferred – and on the winemaking techniques of the producer. Ideally, the wines

Harvesting Syrah grapes at Paul Jaboulet Aîné, Hermitage

should display the delicious dark fruit purity of the Syrah grape, making them good for drinking at two to five years. St-Joseph is one of the largest districts in the Rhône, with nearly 1,100ha, which means the wines are readily available. The small percentage of white is made mainly from Marsanne, with just a hint of Roussanne; the best of it is full-bodied with a lively acidity and faint floral bouquet.

granite, schist, sand, gravel **Syrah** *Marsanne, Roussanne* **red, white**

Crozes-Hermitage

The largest appellation in the Northern Rhône by some way, with just over 1,400ha under production, Crozes-Hermitage is centred on the flatlands surrounding the famous hill of Hermitage on the right bank of the Rhône. Essentially a red wine producing area, with only 10 per cent white, this is the value-for-

Crozes-Hermitage Syrah vineyards

money appellation of the Northern Rhône. Softer and fruitier than Hermitage, but with some of its august neighbour's robust intensity, Crozes-Hermitage is generally consumed young. Styles do vary with the soils, though: grapes grown on granite and the stony soils to the south produce longer-ageing wines than average. The efficient co-operative at Tain l'Hermitage accounts for 60 per cent of the production, and the rest comes from *négociants* such as Paul Jaboulet Aîné and a coterie of good individual producers. White Crozes-Hermitage is full bodied and floral, with the potential for a little more complexity at five to six years.

granite, gravel, sand, clay **Syrah** *Marsanne, Roussanne* **red, white**

Hermitage

Hermitage is the blue-blooded peer of the Northern Rhône, famous for its long-lived reds and complex whites. The vine was cultivated here in Gallo-Roman times, if not before, but the reputation of the wines dates from the 18th century, when they became as highly prized as Bordeaux's classed growths. Indeed, Hermitage was sometimes added to bordeaux to give extra strength, depth, and colour. The appellation Hermitage applies to a single granite hill that towers above the town of Tain l'Hermitage on the right bank of the Rhône. The name Hermitage stems, so the legend goes, from a wounded knight returning from the crusades who ended his days living as a hermit on the hill; a tiny medieval chapel on the summit, owned by *négociant* Paul Jaboulet Aîné, commemorates the myth.

As in Côte Rôtie, aspect and soil can vary over the 140ha – leading to a number of different *climats,* or designated vineyards, producing wines of varying nuance. Overall, though, rec Hermitage (75 per cent of the production) is a wine revered for its power and intensity. It needs at least a decade in bottle and it can age as long as, and in a similar style to, the great wines of Bordeaux. White Hermitage, made from Marsanne and Roussanne, is full-bodied with a honeyed bouquet in youth, maturing to a more mineral finish with bottle age. The co-operative in Tain l'Hermitage accounts for a third of Hermitage's output. The *négociant* houses of Chapoutier and Paul Jaboulet Aîné are the next in terms of production, and about 15 individual growers bottle their own wines.

Syrah grapes

granite, clay, loess *Syrah* *Marsanne, Roussanne* *red, white*

Cornas

CORNAS IS THE black sheep of the Northern Rhône. The Syrah-based wines from this AOC had a solid reputation in the 18th century but have recently been left out on a limb, stranded between acclaimed Côte Rôtie and Hermitage and 'good value' Crozes-Hermitage and St-Joseph. The size of the appellation (110ha) and lack of a superstar producer are perhaps part of the reason the wines have been a little underrated. The south-facing granitic vineyards an amphitheatre of vines sheltered from the wind, provide the potential for good ripeness, and the wines are generally concentrated and of a solid disposition. They have also been labelled as tannic in the past, but riper fruit

HERMITAGE CLIMATS

Hermitage gives the impression that it is a solid, uniform entity, but in reality this is far from the truth. The AOC refers to one single hill, but altitude (100–300m), varying exposures, and differing soil types add subtle nuances to the Syrah wines and have led to the recognition of designated vineyards or *climats*. There are about a dozen named sites. In the west, the granite of **Les Bessards** gives sturdy, upright wines with a tight, tannic structure. To the east, **Le Méal**'s stony limestone soils give flesh, volume, and a silky texture, while the clay at **Les Gréffieux** just below produces supple, fruity wines. **Péléat**, (owned almost entirely by producer Jean-Louis Chave) is known for its elegance, perfect for Syrah and whites Marsanne and Roussanne. Whites also do well on **Rocoule**'s limestone-and-clay slopes. The spicy side of Syrah can be found in the stony soils of **Beaume** and the higher site of **L'Hermite**, which also offers freshness. Most Hermitage is typically made from a blend of grapes from several *climats*, but occasionally there can be single-vineyard bottlings.

and less extraction have helped round out the tannins to a greater degree. A more modern style using new oak barrels and destemming also evolved in the late 1980s, following the arrival of consultant oenologist Jean-Luc Colombo *(see p123)*. In terms of ageability a decade is the ideal, providing a wine with satisfying expression and complexity.

granite, sand, limestone *Syrah* *red*

St-Péray

THIS IS THE LAST STOP on the voyage south down the Northern Rhône. The tiny volume of wine produced in this AOC is white, both still and sparkling, from Marsanne and Roussanne grapes. The sparkling wine is made by the traditional method and is mainly sold locally. It tends to lack the refreshing zip of good sparkling wines. The still white is soft and round with a floral fragrance, not dissimilar to white St-Joseph and appealing when drunk young.

granite, limestone *Marsanne, Roussanne* *white, sparkling*

Syrah vineyards in Cornas

Field of sunflowers and vines surrounding a ruined castle in the Southern Rhône

WINEGROWING AREAS OF THE SOUTHERN RHÔNE

THE WINES OF THE SOUTHERN RHÔNE are generally warm, hearty, and full-bodied – more akin to the style of Languedoc-Roussillon and Provence than that of the Northern Rhône. A range of grape varieties is permitted for these wines, which tend to be blends, but Grenache usually provides the foundation for the reds. There is also some fruity, full bodied rosé. The small percentage of white is soft and round with low acidity.

Côtes du Vivarais

THIS RATHER OBSCURE district in the Ardèche was given full appellation status in 1999. The climate is generally cooler and wetter than in the rest of the Southern Rhône, and the wines are therefore leaner in style. Reds are in the majority and are made principally from blends of Syrah and Grenache, which together must officially account for 90 per cent of the plantings. The co-operatives produce 85 per cent of the volume.

🔲 *limestone* 🔳 *Syrah, Grenache, Cinsaut, Carignan* 🔳 *Clairette, Grenache Blanc, Marsanne* 🔳 *red, white, rosé*

Coteaux du Tricastin

COTEAUX DU TRICASTIN is a fairly extensive AOC of 2,750ha located just south of Montélimar. The red wines, which represent 90 per cent of the production here, are like lighter styled Côtes du Rhône and should be drunk young. The high, open landscape is exposed to the full blast of the mistral and grapes like Grenache

do not ripen easily. Syrah fares better and, in accordance with AOC regulations, must represent 20 per cent of the plantings. A fruity quaffing rosé accounts for another eight per cent of production, while white is scarce but improving in quality.

🔲 *limestone-and-clay, sand* 🔳 *Grenache, Syrah, Cinsaut, Carignan, Mourvèdre* 🔳 *Grenache Blanc, Clairette, Marsanne, Roussanne, Viognier* 🔳 *red, white, rosé*

Grenache grapes

Clairette de Die, Crémant de Die & Châtillon-en-Diois

ABOUT 40KM EAST of the Rhône River, in the Drôme Valley, lies the region of Diois, where winemaking probably dates back to Roman times. Today, the best-known wine from the three AOCs here is the light, sweet, grapey sparkling Clairette de Die. This is made from Muscat Blanc à Petits Grains and Clairette grapes by the *méthode dioise*, a process in which a secondary fermentation in the bottle is initiated by residual grape sugars rather than by the addition of sugar as in the traditional method. The more regular dry white sparkling Crémant de Die is made exclusively from Clairette by the traditional method. A little still red and white is made in the zone of Châtillon-en-Diois. These wines are light in weight and frame; the red is mainly Gamay and the whites are from Aligoté and Chardonnay.

🔲 *stony* 🔳 *Gamay, Pinot Noir, Syrah* 🔳 *Muscat Blanc à Petits Grains, Clairette, Aligoté, Chardonnay* 🔳 *red, white, rosé*

Gigondas

GIGONDAS, LIKE VACQUEYRAS *(see below)*, lies in the shadow of the Dentelles de Montmirail hills. The two AOCs have similar soils, but Gigondas has most of its vineyards on limestone-and-clay slopes, which rise as high as 400m. These soils and the slightly cooler temperatures give additional intensity and volume, and a tighter structure, to the Grenache-based blends, making them firmer and longer ageing. A decade presents no problem to these powerful wines, and although the price has risen in recent years, Gigondas still offers excellent value.

limestone, clay, sand Grenache, Syrah, Mourvèdre, Cinsaut red, rosé

Vacqueyras

VACQUEYRAS IS THE MOST recent of the Rhône's *crus*, promoted from Côtes du Rhône Villages to full appellation status in 1990. Essentially a red wine district, it produces one of the great value wines of the region, with more weight and concentration than regular *villages* offerings. Grenache is the dominant grape variety, imparting a rich, warm, full-bodied generosity to the wine, which is best drunk between three and six years. A small percentage of white is also produced.

limestone, clay, sand Grenache, Syrah, Mourvèdre, Cinsaut Grenache Blanc, Clairette, Bourboulenc, Marsanne, Viognier red, white, rosé

Terraced vineyards in Gigondas

CÔTES DU RHÔNE

Vineyards in the AOC Côtes du Rhône

Côtes du Rhône, a name sometimes used to refer to the Rhône Valley, is also the label given to a broad base of generic wines. AOC Côtes du Rhône is a huge playing field of production accounting for over 40,000ha of vines and more than two million hectolitres of wine in an average year, most of it red. The district extends to areas in the Northern Rhône, but the south takes the lion's share. In such a large district there is naturally a great variety of style, from light and fruity to richer, fuller wines with lovely dark fruit character. Price is often the best indicator of quality. Grenache is the principal red variety and, in accordance with AOC rules, represents 40 per cent of the total plantings. Other red varieties include Syrah, Mourvèdre, Cinsaut, and Carignan, while the whites are produced from Grenache Blanc, Clairette, Bourboulenc, Marsanne, and Viognier. Co-operatives account for around 70 per cent of production.

CÔTES DU RHÔNE VILLAGES

Côtes du Rhône Villages is a distinct step up from generic Côtes du Rhône, implying limestone-and-clay or stony soils, stricter rules of production, and wines of greater depth. The percentage of Grenache, Syrah, and Mourvèdre in the blend is higher, and permitted yields are lower. The *villages* appellation covers 95 Southern Rhône communes, of which 19 are allowed to print their village names on the labels. The best wines are from Cairanne and Rasteau *(right)*: rich and full-bodied with a tannic structure. Côtes du Rhône Villages is almost always red, usually a blend of Grenache, Syrah, Mourvèdre, Cinsaut, and Carignan; the one per cent of white is soft, round, and floral for early drinking. Rasteau also makes a sweet, fortified *vin doux naturel* (VDN, *see p141*) from Grenache, as does Beaumes-de-Venise from Muscat.

Châteauneuf-du-Pape

THE RHÔNE'S MOST CELEBRATED wine takes its name from the location of a summer residence for the pope, built in the 14th century when the papal seat was temporarily moved to Avignon. By far the largest *cru* in the Rhône, Châteauneuf-du-Pape is a sizeable appellation of 3,200ha producing over 100,000hl of wine yearly. Many of the vineyards here are covered with *galets roulés* – large, smooth pebbles that retain heat, ensuring full ripeness and flavour. The wine itself, mostly red, is a powerful, heady libation, the best is sweet and smooth, packed with summer fruits and fine tannins, with a mineral freshness on the finish, and the ability to age. There is even a hint of top red burgundy about some examples. That said, the fact that 13 different grape varieties are allowed in the appellation *(see right)* and winemaking techniques vary, as do soils and exposures, means that style and quality vary considerably.

Château La Nerthe label, Châteauneuf-du-Pape

The present vogue for special *cuvées* – old vine fruit, less traditional blends (higher percentages of Syrah, for example), or wines aged in new oak – is even more irregular. The district is gathering pace, however, and with several great vintages (2007, 2005, 2001, and 2000) and a new generation of producers entering the fray, it is an ideal time to try these wines. White Châteauneuf, a varying blend of the four white varieties, is full and fruity with a delicate floral bouquet, and should be drunk young.

🕮 *sandy red clay, stones, limestone* 🌿 *Grenache, Syrah, Mourvèdre, Cinsaut, Counoise* 🍇 *Grenache Blanc, Clairette, Bourboulenc, Roussanne* 🍷 *red, white*

Vineyards in Tavel

THE 13 GRAPE VARIETIES OF CHÂTEAUNEUF-DU-PAPE

Châteauneuf-du-Pape unusually offers growers a choice of 13 different grape varieties: **Grenache, Syrah, Mourvèdre, Cinsaut, Counoise, Vaccarèse, Terret Noir, Muscardin, Bourboulenc, Clairette, Roussanne, Picardan,** and **Picpoul** – which probably all existed here pre-phylloxera. In theory, this allows for a huge range of styles, but in reality Grenache accounts for 75 per cent, imposing its big, warm-hearted flavours across the board. Plantings of Syrah and Mourvèdre have now increased to give added complexity and structure, but few producers other than Château de Beaucastel grow all 13 varieties.

The formula for the ideal blend, devised by the owner of Château la Nerthe in the early 1900s, involves 10 grapes: Cinsaut and Grenache for mellowness, warmth, and consistency, Mourvèdre, Vaccarèse, Muscardin, and Syrah for structure, freshness, ageing potential, and a thirst-quenching taste, Counoise and Picpoul for vinosity, pleasure, freshness, and bouquet, Bourboulenc and Clairette for vigour, finesse, and sparkle.

Lirac

ON THE OPPOSITE BANK of the Rhône River to Châteauneuf-du-Pape, the appellation of Lirac has grown to nearly 700ha. Its Grenache-based red is robust and meaty; some of it, with a higher percentage of Mourvèdre, is firmer in style and has the ability to age. The rosé is similar to that of neighbouring Tavel, full and heady and good with food. Like the fruity white, it should be consumed young.

🕮 *limestone, sand, stones* 🌿 *Grenache, Syrah, Mourvèdre, Cinsaut* 🍇 *Grenache Blanc, Clairette, Bourboulenc* 🍷 *red, white, rosé*

Tavel

THE REPUTATION OF THIS DISTRICT is based on a single style of wine – rosé – and with nearly 950ha under production, there is quite a lot of it. Grenache provides the base grape variety and is supplemented, according to

Galets roulés (large stones) in a Châteauneuf-du-Pape vineyard

producer, by a mix of other red and white grapes. This is a strong, full-bodied, fruity wine that finishes dry and is best drunk chilled with food. As an established name it usually demands a higher price than other rosés.

🗄 *limestone, sand, clay* 🎴 *Grenache, Syrah, Mourvèdre, Cinsaut, Carignan* 🎴 *Clairette, Bourboulenc* 🍷 *rosé*

Côtes du Ventoux

BY FAR THE LARGEST of the 'young' Rhône appellations, with over 6,600ha under production, Côtes du Ventoux is again dominated by red wine. The 1,900m-high Mont Ventoux is its focal point, with vineyards planted as high as 500m on its slopes. The altitude means a generally cooler than average climate with greater variation between day and night-time temperatures, resulting in wines that are fresh and fruity with a marked point of acidity. As a whole

THE MISTRAL

The cold, northerly mistral wind whistles down the Rhône Valley from the Alps and is a climatic feature of the region. In winter its influence can leave the Rhône Valley colder than central and northern Europe. In 1956, it blew for three weeks and temperatures dropped to -15°C, destroying the olive trees but not the vines. Its ferocity can cause havoc to vine trellising, particularly in spring, hence the tradition of bush-trained vines. On the positive side its dry, cool effect helps keep fungal diseases such as mildew and oidium at bay, and concentrates the grapes prior to harvesting.

they are made for drinking young, but a growing number of producers are now providing wines of greater structure which will age well for up to five or six years. The small percentage of white wine is usually light-bodied with a floral bouquet.

🗄 *limestone, clay, sandstone* 🎴 *Grenache, Carignan, Syrah, Cinsaut, Mourvèdre* 🎴 *Clairette, Ugni Blanc, Bourboulenc, Grenache Blanc, Roussanne* 🍷 *red, white, rosé*

Côtes du Lubéron

THE CÔTES DU LUBÉRON GAINED AOC status in 1988 and now has just over 3,000ha under vine. Its profile is similar to that of Côtes du Ventoux, with the added allure of a magical Provençal setting. Its vineyards are planted on the slopes of the Lubéron hills, surrounded by lavender, fruit orchards, and picture-postcard villages. The climate is slightly cooler here, and the red wines are generally light, fruity, and easy-drinking, although they occasionally display greater weight and frame. The cooler climate appears conducive to white varieties, and indeed Côtes du Lubéron produces more white wine than any other Rhône district. This tends to be round and fruity, although it is crisper than other whites from the Rhône region.

🗄 *limestone, sand* 🎴 *Grenache, Syrah, Carignan, Cinsaut, Mourvèdre* 🎴 *Grenache Blanc, Ugni Blanc, Vermentino, Clairette, Bourboulenc* 🍷 *red, white, rosé*

Costières de Nîmes

THIS AOC IS SOMETIMES considered to be part of the Rhône region. It is covered in this book within the Languedoc-Roussillon section (see p140).

TOP PRODUCERS OF THE NORTHERN RHÔNE

Domaine Clusel Roch
Côte Rôtie

15 rue Laclat, Verenay, Ampuis
☎ *04 74 56 15 95* ⬤ *by appt*

A HARDWORKING husband-and-wife team, Gilbert Clusel and Brigitte Roch produce one of the most finely textured and elegant wines in Côte Rôtie. Much of their success is due to the excellent quality of the fruit. There is a regular *cuvée* and a special selection, Les Grandes Places, a more structured wine made from 60-year-old vines. Quantities of both are limited to an average 12,000 and 2,500 bottles respectively. There is also a tiny volume of rich white Condrieu.
🔲 *red, white* 🔲 *red: 2006, 2003, 2001, 2000, 1999, 1998, 1995, 1991, 1990* ★ *Côte Rôtie, Côte Rôtie Les Grandes Places*

Domaine Jamet
Côte Rôtie

Le Vallin, Ampuis ☎ *04 74 56 12 57* ⬤ *by appt*

BROTHERS Jean-Luc and Jean-Paul Jamet make outstanding, long-lived Côte Rôtie from 25 parcels of vines scattered around the district. The lively fruit aspect of the wine is enjoyable up to five years' age, or it can be cellared for eight years for greater complexity. Production is limited to just 30,000 bottles a year.
🔲 *red* 🔲 *2006, 2003, 2001, 2000, 1999, 1998, 1997, 1995, 1991, 1990* ★ *Côte Rôtie*

Guigal
Côte Rôtie

Ampuis ☎ *04 74 56 10 22*
Ⓦ *www.guigal.com* ⬤ *by appt*

MARCEL GUIGAL is one of the key figures, if not *the* key figure, responsible for the revival of Northern Rhône wines. With quiet authority (and assisted by his son Philippe), he oversees a now burgeoning empire, which includes the *négociant* wines of E Guigal, Vidal Fleury, and de Vallouit, as well as the domaine wines from his own vineyards. Best known of these are the richly intense but expensive single-vineyard Côte Rôtie wines La Mouline, La Landonne, and La Turque, as well as Château d'Ampuis from six different sites, and the voluptuously fragrant Condrieu La Doriane. There is also a very fine St-Joseph from vineyards acquired from Jean-Louis Grippat.

🔲 *red, white* 🔲 *red: 2003, 2001, 2000, 1999, 1998, 1997, 1995, 1991, 1990* ★ *Côte Rôtie La Mouline, Côte Rôtie La Landonne, Condrieu La Doriane*

Domaine André Perret
Condrieu

Verlieu, Chavanay ☎ *04 74 87 24 74*
Ⓦ *www.andreperret.com* ⬤ *by appt*

THE AFFABLE André Perret is a master at producing great Condrieu. His recipe includes a small percentage of over-ripe Viognier grapes blended with the rest of the harvest, natural yeasts, and 12 months' ageing in barrels and tank. He has two *cuvées* of particular note, the aromatic Clos Chanson and the stunningly full-flavoured, elegant Coteau de Chéry. Perret also makes a juicy red St-Joseph, Les Grisières, which is the top wine.
🔲 *red, white* 🔲 *red: 2003, 2001, 2000, 1999, 1998* ★ *Condrieu Coteau de Chéry, St-Joseph Les Grisières*

Domaine Georges Vernay
Condrieu

1 rte nationale, Condrieu ☎ *04 74 56 81 81* Ⓦ *www.georges-vernay.fr* ⬤

GEORGES VERNAY is Mr Condrieu. Back in the 1950s and 60s, when the district was being abandoned, he was the one who stoically replanted the terraces here. Today, the domaine extends to 16ha and is run by George's daughter, Christine, producing some much-improved Côte Rôtie and St-Joseph as well as three *cuvées* of Condrieu. The Côte Rôtie Maison Rouge is an ample but elegant wine; Condrieu Chaillées de l'Enfer and Coteau de Vernon are rich, full, and exotic, the latter with greater depth; both

Château d'Ampuis, forming part of Guigal's estate

should preferably be drunk at three to six years.

🟥 *red, white* 🔴 *red: 2006, 2003, 2001, 2000, 1999, 1998*
★ *Condrieu Coteau de Vernon*

Domaine Yves Cuilleron
Condrieu

Verlieu, Chavanay
📞 04 74 87 02 37
🌐 www.cuilleron.com ⬜ by appt

THIS DOMAINE has increased considerably in size and notoriety since Yves Cuilleron took over in 1987 and it now totals 31ha. There is a complex catalogue of different *cuvées* from Condrieu, Côte Rôtie, and St-Joseph, all relating to specific parcels of vines. These are rich, dense, powerful wines, often marked by new oak in youth. The compellingly aromatic white Condrieu Les Chaillets is produced from the oldest parcels, and the sweet, citrus and marmalade Les Ayguets, also white, is made from late-harvested grapes. The top red *cuvées* include the St-Joseph Les Serines, and Côte Rôtie Terres Sombres and Bassenon. Yves Cuilleron is also involved in the Vins de Vienne-Seyssuel project *(see p132).*

🟥 *red, white* 🔴 *red: 2006, 2003, 2001, 2000, 1999, 1998, 1997, 1995, 1991, 1990* ★ *Condrieu Les Ayguets, Côte Rôtie Terres Sombres, St-Joseph Les Serines*

Domaine Alain Graillot
Crozes-Hermitage

Les Chênes Verts, Pont de l'Isère
📞 04 75 84 67 52 ⬜ by appt

A FORMER marketing manager for a large French industrial concern, Alain Graillot quickly settled into the life of a *vigneron* in the late 1980s and he now turns out consistently good Crozes-

Domaine Yves Cuilleron label

Hermitage. The red is ripe and fruity; the top wine, La Guiraude, richly concentrated and age-worthy; and the white is fresh and aromatic. There is also a little spicy red St-Joseph and a tiny volume of supple Hermitage made from a parcel of vines in the Les Gréffieux part of the appellation.

🟥 *red, white* 🔴 *red: 2006, 2003, 2001, 2000, 1999, 1998, 1997, 1995*
★ *Crozes-Hermitage, Crozes-Hermitage La Guiraude*

Delas Frères
Hermitage

Z A de l'Olivet, St-Jean-de-Muzols
📞 04 75 08 60 30
🌐 www.mmdusa.net ⬜ by appt

THIS NÉGOCIANT, owned by Champagne house Deutz *(see p172)* and therefore the Roederer group, has made huge strides in recent years under the direction of oenologist Jacques Grange, previously of M Chapoutier *(see p132).* The reds, in particular, are good across the range: they have taken on greater weight, purer fruit, and a finer structure. The top wines include the powerful Hermitage Les Bessards and dense Côte Rôtie La Landonne. The Hermitage Marquise

de la Tourette and Côte Rôtie Seigneur de Maugiron offer good value at a less excessive price.

🟥 *red, white* 🔴 *red: 2006, 2003, 2001, 2000, 1999, 1998, 1997, 1995, 1991, 1990* ★ *Hermitage Les Bessards, Hermitage Marquise de la Tourette, Côte Rôtie La Landonne*

Domaine Jean-Louis Chave
Hermitage

37 ave du St-Joseph, Mauves
📞 04 75 08 24 63 ⬛

THE NECK LABELS of bottles from Domaine Jean-Louis Chave display the phrase "Vignerons de Père en Fils depuis 1481" (winegrowers from father to son since 1481). Gérard Chave took up the torch from his father in the 1970s, turning the domaine's wines into a much sought-after commodity. Now with his son, Jean-Louis (the name appears every second generation), he continues to produce firm, fine, long-ageing Hermitage. The secret is the old vines located in seven different vineyard sites or *climats,* which are vinified separately and blended astutely. In what the Chaves consider exceptional years (most recently in 2000, 1998, 1995, 1991, and 1990), they make the more intense Cuvée Cathelin. The white Hermitage is also a long-ageing wine, and there is a little rich, fruity St-Joseph red for more immediate consumption.

Domaine Jean-Louis Chave

🟥 *red, white* 🔴 *red: 2006, 2003, 2001, 2000, 1999, 1998, 1997, 1995, 1991, 1990* ★ *Hermitage (red, white), Hermitage Cuvée Cathelin*

M Chapoutier
Hermitage

*18 ave Dr Paul Durand, Tain
l'Hermitage* **C** 04 75 08 28 65
W *www.chapoutier.com* **○**

THIS IS ANOTHER historic, family-owned *négociant* house run in a dynamic fashion by brothers Michel and Marc Chapoutier. The company owns an impressive number of vineyards up and down the Rhône Valley, including a large chunk in Hermitage, all of which have been converted to the bio-dynamic system of cultivation. The Hermitage sites produce the estate's best wines. From an extensive portfolio, the top *cuvées* include: the powerfully structured Ermitage Le Pavillon (from Hermitage) and Côte Rôtie La Mordorée, both made from very old vines; the richly opulent, oaky white Hermitage Cuvée de l'Orée; and a rather luxurious red Crozes-Hermitage called Les Varonniers. The company also produces wines in the Côtes du Roussillon, Banyuls, Coteaux d'Aix en Provence, and in South Australia.

🍷 *red, white* **🍾** *red: 2006, 2003, 2001, 2000, 1999, 1998, 1997, 1995, 1991, 1990* ★ *Ermitage Le Pavillon, Hermitage La Sizeranne, Côte Rôtie La Mordorée*

Paul Jaboulet Aîné
Hermitage

Les Jalets, RN 7, La Roche sur Glun, Tain l'Hermitage **C** 04 75 84 68 93
W *www.jaboulet.com* **○**

ANTOINE JABOULET established this legendary *négociant* house in the 19th century, and it remains very much a family affair. Although less consistent than it was in former years, it still has a number of eye-catching wines, particularly those sourced from the company's own vine-yards. The flagship wine is the powerful, long-ageing red Hermitage La Chapelle, produced from 25ha of vines dotted over the Hermitage hill. Crozes-Hermitage has always been a strong Jaboulet line and includes the well structured *cuvées* Domaine de Thalabert and Raymond

**Paul Jaboulet
Aîné**

Roure. The Domaine de St-Pierre, from Cornas, is a richly concentrated wine.

🍷 *red, white* **🍾** *red: 2006, 2003, 2001, 2000, 1999, 1998, 1997, 1995, 1991, 1990* ★ *Hermitage La Chapelle, Crozes-Hermitage Domaine de Thalabert, Cornas Domaine de St-Pierre*

Domaine Clape
Cornas

146 rte nationale, Cornas
C 04 75 40 33 64 **○** *by appt*

THE RESERVED and reticent Auguste Clape has been a pillar of Cornas for many years. Along with his son, Pierre-Marie, he produces an authentic, traditional Cornas brimming with ripe fruit but also firm and concentrated and without a trace of new oak. Since 1997 the young vines (12 to 16 years old) have been used for the *cuvée* Renaissance, while the older ones (25 to 60 years) make the top wine, simply called Cornas. Domaine Clape also produces a little generic Côtes du Rhône from Syrah, and an average 1,200 bottles a year of delicious St-Péray.

🍷 *red, white* **🍾** *red: 2006, 2003, 2001, 2000, 1999, 1998, 1995, 1991, 1990* ★ *Cornas*

THE NEW FACE OF SEYSSUEL

In 1996, three of the Northern Rhône's leading young producers, Yves Cuilleron, Pierre Gaillard, and François Villard, embarked on an ambitious project to resurrect the once famous vineyard of Seyssuel. Located just above the town of Vienne on the Rhône's right bank, the vineyard had been renowned as far back as Gallo-Roman times but disappeared with the arrival of phylloxera in the late 19th century. So far, 11ha have been successfully planted on the south-facing schistous slopes and two wines have been produced, the aromatic Taburnum made purely from Viognier and the 100 per cent Syrah Sotanum which is as rich and spicy as many a Côte Rôtie. These exceptional wines are labelled Vins de Pays des Collines Rhodaniennes, as Seyssuel is not an official appellation. To help finance the project the three friends also founded a small *négociant* house, called Les Vins de Vienne, to produce small quantities of top-quality Rhône wines from purchased grapes.
W *www.vinsdevienne.com*

Sotanum

M.M.

Cuilleron · Gaillard · Villard

TOP PRODUCERS OF THE SOUTHERN RHÔNE

Domaine Raspail-Ay
Gigondas

Gigondas 📞 *04 90 65 83 01*
☐ *by appt*

DOMINIQUE AY is a down-to-earth, no-nonsense *vigneron* who makes a traditional, ageworthy Gigondas at his 18ha domaine. There is no artifice here, just good fruit, careful vinification, and ageing in the classic large oak *foudres*. The wines have a firm tannic frame and need a minimum of four or five years' bottle age. There is also a small amount of excellent rosé.

🍷 *red, rosé* 📅 *red: 2007, 2005, 2001, 2000, 1998, 1995* ★ *Gigondas*

Domaine de la Monardière
Vacqueyras

Quartier les Grès, Vacqueyras
📞 *04 90 65 87 20* ☐ *by appt*

MARTINE AND CHRISTIAN Vache demonstrate the different expressions of Vacqueyras with a selection of *cuvées* from three soil types. All are Grenache-based, with a percentage of Syrah and Mouvèdre. Les Calades from clay soils is warm and generous and drinks well young. Réserve des 2 Monardes shows the freshness and finesse gained from sandier soils, while the Vieilles Vignes, produced from 60-year-old Grenache grown on the stony clay-and-limestone plateau, is richer, firmer, and suitable for longer ageing.

🍷 *red, white* 📅 *red: 2007, 2005, 2001, 2000, 1998* ★ *Vacqueyras Réserve des 2 Monardes, Vieilles Vignes*

Cellar at Château la Nerthe

Château de Beaucastel
Châteauneuf-du-Pape

Courthézon 📞 *04 90 70 41 00*
🌐 *www.beaucastel.com* ☐ *by appt*

THIS CHÂTEAU'S unique wine is simply one of the greatest in France. Rich, firm, concentrated, it has notes of dark fruits, spice, and game, and with age can reveal a tobacco-like complexity. The originality comes in the blend, where Grenache is reduced to 30 per cent and more prominence is given to Mourvèdre (30 per cent) and Counoise (10 per cent); the other 30 per cent is made up of a mix of varieties depending on the vintage. All 13 permitted grape varieties are cultivated at the 100-ha estate. In exceptional years, the tannic Cuvée Hommage à Jacques Perrin, (Jacques Perrin is the father of present owners François and Jean-Pierre), is produced from 60 to 70 per cent Mourvèdre. There are also two excellent white Châteauneufs, including the sumptuous Roussanne Vieilles Vignes, as well as red and white Côtes du Rhônes produced under the label Coudoulet de Beaucastel.

Château de Beaucastel

🍷 *red, white* 📅 *red: 2007, 2005, 2001, 2000, 1998, 1997, 1995, 1994, 1990* ★ *Châteauneuf-du-Pape (red), Châteauneuf-du-Pape Cuvée Hommage à Jacques Perrin, Châteauneuf-du-Pape Roussanne Vieilles Vignes*

Château la Nerthe
Châteauneuf-du-Pape

rte de Sorgues, Châteauneuf-du-Pape
📞 *04 90 83 70 11* 🌐 *www.chateau-la-nerthe.com* ☐ *by appt*

THIS MAGNIFICENT ESTATE is one of the oldest in Châteauneuf-du-Pape, and was bottling its own wines as far back as 1784. The modern era dates from 1985 when the property was bought by the Richard family, Parisian coffee and wine merchants, and Alain Dugas was installed as manager. The vineyard has been completely overhauled, yields reduced, and wines given a more contemporary approach. Both red and white wines are ripe, elegant, and polished. In exceptional vintages the longer ageing special selections, red Cuvée des Cadettes and white Clos de Beauvenir, are produced.

🍷 *red, white* 📅 *red: 2007, 2005, 2001, 2000, 1998, 1997, 1995, 1994, 1990* ★ *Châteauneuf-du-Pape (red, white), Châteauneuf-du-Pape Cuvée des Cadettes*

Château Rayas
Châteauneuf-du-Pape

Châteauneuf-du-Pape
☎ 04 90 83 73 09 ◉

AN IDIOSYNCRATIC domaine, Rayas is known for the eccentric manner of its former owner, Jacques Reynaud, and the quality and originality of its wines. Jacques's nephew, Emmanuel, has introduced a little more order and consistency, but the 100 per cent Grenache wine essentially remains the same: rich, sweet, and powerful, with the flavour of summer fruits. There is also an impressive second wine, Pignan, and a full, fresh white Rayas. Some delicious, concentrated red and white Côtes du Rhône is bottled under the label Château de Fonsalette.
🔲 red, white 🔼 red: 2007, 2005, 2001, 2000, 1998, 1995, 1994, 1991, 1990 ★ Châteauneuf-du-Pape (red), Châteauneuf-du-Pape Pignan, Côtes du Rhône Château de Fonsalette (red)

Clos des Papes
Châteauneuf-du-Pape

13 ave Pierre de Luxembourg, Châteauneuf-du-Pape
☎ 04 90 83 70 13 ❏ by appt

A DECEPTIVELY vigorous wine, Clos des Papes is one of the most consistent in the appellation. Owner Paul Avril started his search for the perfect blend back in 1976 and cultivates all 13 Châteauneuf varieties in parcels around the district. He and son Vincent have reduced the Grenache to 60 per cent in the blend

Château Rayas label

and added a generous amount of Mourvèdre and Syrah to produce a wine of elegant, cherry-raspberry ripeness with persistence and length. The white Châteauneuf is also very fine.
🔲 red, white 🔼 red: 2007, 2005, 2001, 2000, 1998, 1997, 1995, 1994, 1990 ★ Châteauneuf-du-Pape (red, white)

Domaine Bois de Boursan
Châteauneuf-du-Pape

Quartier St-Pierre, Châteauneuf-du-Pape ☎ 04 90 83 73 60
❏ by appt

THE FAMILY-OWNED business Bois de Boursan has burst onto the scene in recent years under the direction of Jean-Paul Versino. The domaine has 27 parcels of vines dotted all over the district, some 40 to 100 years old. The quality of the fruit can be seen in the wines, which explode with purity of flavour. The more intense Cuvée des Félix comes from the best low-yielding parcels of vines and is aged in small barrels, rather than the larger oak *foudres*.
🔲 red 🔼 2007, 2005, 2001, 2000, 1998, 1997, 1995, 1994, 1991, 1990 ★ Châteauneuf-du-Pape (red), Châteauneuf-du-Pape Cuvée des Félix

Clos des Papes

Domaine Bosquet des Papes
Châteauneuf-du-Pape

18 rte d'Orange, Châteauneuf-du-Pape ☎ 04 90 83 72 33
❏ by appt

THIS IS A GREAT location for Châteauneuf-du-Pape made in a classic mould. It comes mainly from Grenache, is vinified by the father and son team of Maurice and Nicolas Boiron, and is aged in large oak *foudres*. The regular *cuvée* has a cherry-raspberry fragrance, generous fruit, and a minerally freshness. There is greater intensity in the *cuvée* Chante le Merle, which exudes old vine depth and concentration, while La Gloire de Mon Grand-Père, introduced in 1998, has elegance and freshness of fruit. The small percentage of white wine is round, fruity, and for early drinking.
🔲 red, white 🔼 red: 2007, 2005, 2001, 2000, 1998, 1995, 1994, 1990 ★ Châteauneuf-du-Pape (red), Châteauneuf-du-Pape Chante le Merle

Domaine de la Janasse
Châteauneuf-du-Pape

27 Chemin du Moulin, Courthézon
☎ 04 90 70 86 29
🌐 www.lajanasse.com ❏

AIMÉ SABON created this domaine in 1973, but the wines really took off in 1991 when Sabon teamed up with his son Christophe (who had completed viticultural studies in Burgundy). A different approach to winemaking has given the essentially Grenache-based wines more finesse while retaining a soft, round, plummy fruit character. There are three *cuvées* of varying intensity: Tradition, Chaupin (100 per

THE RHÔNE RULE-MAKERS: FRANCE'S FIRST AOC SYSTEM

At the beginning of the 20th century, following the devastation of vineyards by phylloxera and mildew, the problem of fraudulent wine imitations was rife. As a means of protection against this commercial plague, Châteauneuf-du-Pape introduced a set of rules governing the production of wine. Devised by Baron Le Roy de Boiseaumarié, owner of Château Fortia *(right)* and a prominent lawyer, these were introduced in 1923. They later became the prototype for the French system of Appellation d'Origine Contrôlée (AOC), the first classification of its kind in the world, introduced in 1935. The essential elements included the geographical delimitation of the district, permitted grape varieties and methods of cultivation, and the minimum alcohol content. Châteauneuf-du-Pape also insists on a mandatory sorting of the grapes with a rejection of between 5 and 20 per cent of the crop according to the year.

cent Grenache, some planted in 1921), and Vieilles Vignes (60 to 100 years). Additionally, there is some good value Côtes du Rhône, particularly Les Garrigues. The white Châteauneufs are also of interest, especially the fleshy Roussanne-based Prestige.

🟥 *red, white* ➤ *red: 2007, 2005, 2001, 2000, 1998, 1995, 1994, 1990* ★ *Châteauneuf-du-Pape (red), Châteauneuf-du-Pape Chaupin, Côtes du Rhône Les Garrigues*

Château d'Aquéria
Tavel

Tavel 🄲 *04 66 50 04 56* 🆆 *www.aqueria.com* ⬜

THIS LARGE, RAMBLING estate of over 60ha has been a regular source of good fruity Tavel rosé for a number of years. There is a freshness in Château d'Aquéria's wines that is not always evident elsewhere. The estate also produces Lirac; the red is firmly structured and the white fresh and fragrant.

🟥 *red, white, rosé* ➤ *red: 2007, 2005, 2001, 2000* ★ *Tavel*

Domaine La Réméjeanne
Côtes du Rhône Villages

Cadignac, Sabran 🄲 *04 66 89 44 51* ⬜

AWAY FROM the Rhône Valley's viticultural hub in a remote village in the Gard *département*, Rémy Klein and his wife Ouahi provide a wonderful source of richly textured, vibrant, fruit-driven wines. Syrah provides the base for most of the reds and is the sole variety used in the intense, spicy top-of-the-range Côtes du Rhône Les Eglantiers. The Côtes du Rhône Villages Les Genevrières has weight and power, and like Les Eglantiers needs two or three years' bottle age. The fruity Les Chèvrefeuilles and Les Arbousiers are for earlier consumption. The white Arbousiers is clean and fruity and also for early drinking.

🟥 *red, white, rosé* ➤ *red: 2007, 2005, 2001, 2000, 1998* ★ *Côtes du Rhône: Les Eglantiers, Villages Les Genevrières*

Domaine Marcel Richaud
Côtes du Rhône Villages

rte de Rasteau, Cairanne 🄲 *04 90 30 85 25* ⬜

THE BUSTLING Marcel Richaud is a master at producing succulent, thirst-quenching wines that are bursting with ripe fruit flavours. The best are his good-value red Côtes du Rhône Garrigues, the firmer Cairanne, and the exemplary Cairanne l'Ebrescade made from a parcel of old-vine Grenache that has greater intensity and finer tannins, and can be aged for five or six years. The lightly oaked white Cairanne is full, fat, and creamy.

🟥 *red, white* ➤ *red: 2007, 2005, 2001, 2000, 1998, 1995* ★ *Côtes du Rhône Garrigues, Côtes du Rhône Villages Cairanne, Côtes du Rhône Villages Cairanne l'Ebrescade*

Domaine La Réméjeanne label

SOUTH OF FRANCE

BLUE SKIES, DAZZLING SUNLIGHT, *cypress, pine, and olive trees bowed by the force of the mistral wind, rocky terrain, and tiny villages with medieval towers – this is the South of France. Stretching along the Mediterranean coast between the Italian and the Spanish borders, this area is also an enormous viticultural zone, Languedoc-Roussillon alone representing a third of France's total vineyard area.*

The vinous history of the South dates back to 600BC, when first the Greeks, and then the Romans, cultivated vines here. Modern winemaking started up in the 1970s, when producers in Languedoc-Roussillon began to recognize that quality wine was needed to replace the cheap, mass-produced, rough red that had previously given the area its dubious reputation.

Sign for Rivesaltes wines

Red wines still account for nearly 90 per cent of production, but the style has changed beyond recognition. The hillside sites have been planted with Grenache, Syrah, and Mourvèdre, while mature vine Carignan has been nurtured to produce wine of greater character. These grape varieties, combined with increased investment and modern winemaking techniques, mean that Languedoc-Roussillon appellations now produce some of France's most exciting wines – rich, characterful blends with the distinctive imprint of this region. It has become France's answer to the New World. A new marketing initiative allowing Languedoc-Roussillon producers to add the term 'Sud de France' to their bottles is further proof of the progress that this giant wine region is making.

The French *vin de pays* classification has allowed stringent appellation rules to be stretched, enabling non-local varieties like Merlot, Cabernet Sauvignon, and Chardonnay to be planted.

The story in Provence is a little different. The buoyant tourism industry and warm climate here mean that heavy demands are made on rosé. Great reds can, however, be found in Mourvèdre-dominated Bandol, and increasingly from individual producers throughout the region who are making significant strides with a mix of Grenache, Syrah, and Cabernet Sauvignon grapes.

View of house surrounded by Provençal vineyards

◁ **Rows of vines in springtime in Provence**

FRANCE

WINE MAP OF THE SOUTH OF FRANCE

Bordered to the south by the Mediterranean and to the north by the foothills of the southern Alps and the Massif Central, the South of France is essentially one huge vineyard. To the east, Provence has some 27,000ha under vine, mostly in appellation Côtes de Provence. Moving west, the vineyards flow across the Rhône delta through Costières de Nîmes and on into the Languedoc and then Roussillon, which together are home to around 300,000ha of vines. Corbières is the appellation with the largest surface area, but Coteaux du Languedoc is the most important in terms of wine production.

Key
South of France

Cellar sign in Banyuls

PERFECT CASE: SOUTH OF FRANCE

Ⓡ Château de Pibarnon Bandol £££

Ⓡ Domaine Canet-Valette St-Chinian Maghani ££

Ⓡ Domaine d'Aupilhac Coteaux du Languedoc Montpeyroux £££

Ⓡ Domaine de la Rectorie Collioure Coume Pascole ££

Ⓡ Domaine de Trévallon VDP des Bouches-du-Rhône £££

Ⓡ Domaine du Clos des Fées Côtes du Roussillon Villages Vieilles Vignes £££

Ⓡ Domaine du Mas Blanc Banyuls Rimage La Coume ££

Ⓡ Domaine Gauby Côtes du Roussillon Villages Muntada £££

Ⓡ Domaine Peyre Rose Coteaux du Languedoc Syrah Léone £££

Ⓡ Domaine Tempier Bandol Cabassaou £££

Ⓡ Mas Bruguière Coteaux du Languedoc Pic St-Loup La Grenadière £££

Ⓡ Mas de Daumas Gassac VDP de l'Hérault £££

LANGUEDOC-ROUSSILLON: AREAS & TOP PRODUCERS

COSTIÈRES DE NÎMES *p140*

COTEAUX DU LANGUEDOC *p140*

Domaine d'Aupilhac *p144*
Domaine Canet-Valette *p144*
Domaine Peyre Rose *p144*
Mas Bruguière *p144*
Mas Jullien *p144*
Prieuré de St-Jean de Bébian *p144*

MINERVOIS *p141*

CORBIÈRES & FITOU *p142*

CABARDÈS & CÔTES DE MALEPÈRE *p142*

LIMOUX *p142*

CÔTES DU ROUSSILLON & CÔTES DU ROUSSILLON VILLAGES *p142*

Domaine du Clos des Fées *p145*
Domaine Gauby *p145*

Massif Central

Cévennes

Montpellier
COTEAUX DU LANGUEDOC

Montagne Noire

MINERVOIS
Canal du Midi
Sète

CABARDÈS & CÔTES DE MALEPÈRE Carcassonne

Boutenac · Narbonne

MEDITERRANEA

Lagrasse · **CORBIÈRES**

LIMOUX Durban

FITOU

Lesquerde Tautavel **CÔTES DU ROUSSILLON VILLAGES**
RIVESALTES & MAURY Agly · La Tour de la France
Caramany · Perpignan

CÔTES DU ROUSSILLON

BANYULS & COLLIOURE

SPAIN

0 — km — 50

Wall decoration, Provence

TERROIR AT A GLANCE

Latitude: 42.5°–44°N.

Altitude: 0–500m.

Topography: Varies from mountain ranges to flat, arid coastal plains. Languedoc hill sites are often sparse, rocky scrubland with some dense, bush-covered maquis.

Soil: Rich alluvial soils in the valleys; schist and limestone on the hillsides.

Climate: Mediterranean. Hot, dry summers and mainly winter rain.

Temperature: Although the July average is 22°C, daytime highs are often above 30°C in summer months. Temperatures on the coast are more extreme than those inland, and hill sites experience the greatest variation between daytime and night-time degrees.

Rainfall: Annual average is 500–700mm. In the west of the region, the Atlantic influence means rainfall is slightly higher.

Wind: Northerly winds known locally as the cers and tramontane, along with the mistral, accentuate the dry climate and help to prevent rot. Sea breezes can moderate temperatures near the coast.

Viticultural hazards: Storms; humidity; weather fluctuation.

RIVESALTES & MAURY *p143*

BANYULS & COLLIOURE *p143*
Domaine de la Rectorie *p145*
Domaine du Mas Blanc *p145*

VIN DE PAYS
Mas de Daumas Gassac *p145*

PROVENCE: AREAS & TOP PRODUCERS

BELLET *p146*

CÔTES DE PROVENCE *p146*
Château de Roquefort *p148*
Domaine Richeaume *p148*

COTEAUX VAROIS *p146*

BANDOL *p146*
Château de Pibarnon *p148*
Château Pradeaux *p148*
Domaine Tempier *p149*

CASSIS *p147*
Clos Ste Magdeleine *p149*

PALETTE *p147*
Château Simone *p149*

COTEAUX D'AIX EN PROVENCE *p147*

LES BAUX DE PROVENCE *p147*

VIN DE PAYS
Domaine de Trévallon *p149*

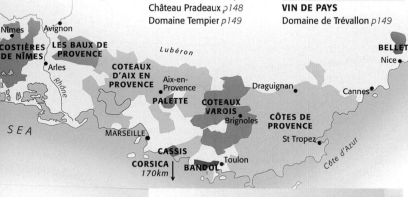

Nîmes · Avignon · COSTIÈRES DE NÎMES · LES BAUX DE PROVENCE · Arles · *Lubéron* · COTEAUX D'AIX EN PROVENCE · Aix-en-Provence · PALETTE · COTEAUX VAROIS · Brignoles · Draguignan · CÔTES DE PROVENCE · St Tropez · BELLET · Nice · Cannes · *Côte d'Azur* · *SEA* · MARSEILLE · CASSIS · CORSICA 170km · BANDOL · Toulon

---

Harvest time in Provence

VIN DE PAYS

Languedoc-Roussillon is the most important producer of *vin de pays* (VDP) in France, accounting for 80 per cent of the total. Much of it is labelled under the regional denomination Vin de Pays d'Oc, the rest under the names of local districts. VDP rules are less stringent than AOC, allowing producers to make varietal wines from non-traditional grapes, and to blend native and international varieties for fine wines. VDP status offers producers greater recognition than the basic *vin de table* status.

Market stall selling wine in the Coteaux du Languedoc

WINEGROWING AREAS OF LANGUEDOC-ROUSSILLON

RED WINES REIGN IN Languedoc-Roussillon. Almost all are made from the five classic southern varieties, and AOC regulations mostly demand a blend of all five grapes. Syrah, famous in the neighbouring Rhône Valley, is becoming increasingly popular; Catalan varieties Mourvèdre and Carignan give dark, tannic, spicy wines; and widely planted Grenache and Cinsaut are full of easy-going fruitiness.

Costières de Nîmes

SANDWICHED BETWEEN two regions, AOC Costières de Nîmes is often included in Languedoc appellations, but politically and administratively it is embraced by the Rhône. The name was changed from Costières du Gard in 1989 and there has been considerable progress since with new ownership of wineries, added investment, and improved winemaking. The climate is one of the hottest in France, the land low lying and covered with stones, or *galets roulés*, similar to those in Châteauneuf-du-Pape *(see p128)*, which radiate heat at night. Wines are similar in style to the powerful, fleshy reds of the Southern Rhône.

🌿 *sandy soils covered with large, smooth* galets roulés 🍇 *Grenache, Syrah, Carignan, Mourvèdre* 🍃 *Grenache Blanc, Marsanne, Roussanne* 🍷 *red, white, rosé*

Coteaux du Languedoc

NOW ONE OF FRANCE'S most exciting appellations, AOC Coteaux du Languedoc is a huge, diverse region with 15,000ha under vine. The land varies from the cooler, inland zones in the foothills of the Cévennes, where the wines – 90 per cent red and rosé – are fresher in style, to the warmer reaches near the Mediterranean seaboard, where the style is bigger and bolder. A constant feature of the landscape is the sparse, rocky, rosemary and thyme covered *garrigue*.

The Coteaux du Languedoc is such a large, multifarious region that guidance is needed in selecting the wines. Historically, 12 *terroirs* have been unofficially allowed to append their names to the label. Some, like St-Georges d'Orques, are noteworthy, others are rather more obscure. To help make sense of the region, a hierarchy is being established

ANIANE

Aniane is a highly sought-after area for producing quality grapes in the Coteaux du Languedoc. Mas de Daumas Gassac's high-profile *vin de pays* vineyards are located here. The local communist mayor refused to sell land to the late Robert Mondavi in California *(see p476)*, but French actor Gérard Depardieu *(right)* was allowed to purchase a plot. Depardieu's 2.5ha are planted with Syrah and Grenache, which are made into a garage wine. The 2003 harvest was literally made in a garage and grapes were hand-sorted by 15 obliging journalists.

for red wines. At base level there is 'generic' Coteaux du Languedoc with existing rules for production, such as yield and grape variety. At the next step up, seven climatic zones (Grès de Montpellier, Terrasses de Béziers, La Clape, Terres de Sommières, Pic St-Loup, Terrasses de Larzac, and Pézenas) have been defined as subregions and given stiffer controls. So far Pic St-Loup, La Clape, and Grès de Montpellier have been recognized and can officially use their names on the label. At the top level, climate and soil are taken into account, the rules again refined, and full AOC appellation status awarded.

A host of talented winemakers have instigated a sea of change in quality over the last 20 years. Styles vary but the overall theme is of ripe concentration, vigour, and a nuance of herbs. Within the region are fresh, minerally Faugères, slightly meatier St-Chinian, and dry and semi-sweet white Clairette du Languedoc, each with AOC status.

🗺 *limestone, schist, stony galets roulés* 🍇 *Syrah, Grenache, Mourvèdre, Carignan, Cinsaut* 🍇 *Grenache Blanc, Bourboulenc, Picpoul, Clairette, Roussanne* 🍷 *red, white, rosé*

Minervois

MINERVOIS AOC IS LIKE a huge, south-facing amphitheatre rising from the Canal du Midi in the south to the Montagne Noire in the north. Climatically there is an Atlantic influence in the west near Carcassonne, moving to Mediterranean in the east near Narbonne. Co-operatives are particularly influential here, although there are a number of good individual growers producing attractively fruity wines. Since 1997 Minervois La Livinière, in the centre of the district,

VIN DOUX NATUREL

Golden *vin doux naturel* (VDN) is the speciality of the Roussillon, which produces nearly 90 per cent of France's total output. It is not naturally sweet, as the name implies, but is a fortified wine made by the process of *mutage*, which involves adding neutral grape brandy (at 96 per cent alcohol) to partly fermented grapes. This stops fermentation, leaving a percentage of residual sugar and resulting in wines that are sweet and powerful in style. Some are bottled early to preserve the fruit character (Muscat de Rivesaltes, *below*; Vintage Maury; or Banyuls Rimage), others are aged in large oak barrels to acquire a more maderized flavour and aroma (Rivesaltes Hors d'Age or Banyuls Grand Cru). Red VDNs are made mainly from Grenache, while Muscat, Grenache Blanc, and Macabeo are used for the white.

has been awarded its own appellation. The rocky soils, hilly terrain, and warm, dry climate here produce wines (96 per cent red) that are fuller, firmer, and longer lived.

🗺 *stony limestone, sandstone, schist* 🍇 *Syrah, Carignan, Grenache, Cinsaut, Mourvèdre* 🍇 *Marsanne, Roussanne, Macabeo, Bourboulenc, Grenache Blanc* 🍷 *red, white, rosé*

Valley slopes and vineyards in Corbières

Corbières & Fitou

CORBIÈRES IS A WILD part of the world, a dramatic mix of mountain and valley with areas of sparse, rocky terrain. It is a vast area – over 15,000ha under vine, and 11 zones of production to denote the varying influence of mountain, soil, and sea. Boutenac, Lagrasse, and Durban are areas of particular note for the quality of their meaty and full-bodied reds. The best come from individual producers and a handful of the numerous co-operatives. The appellation Fitou, granted AOC status in 1948, is for red wines only, and these have much in common with Corbières. Fitou is produced in two zones within Corbières; those from vines grown in the rugged, hilly interior are more structured and capable of ageing than those from vineyards bordering the Mediterranean.

🏔 red sandstone, clay, limestone, schist, gravel 🍇 Grenache, Syrah, Mourvèdre, Carignan, Cinsaut 🍇 Grenache Blanc, Bourboulenc, Macabeo, Marsanne, Roussanne 🍷 red, white, rosé

Cabardès & Côtes de Malepère

THE CABARDÈS AND CÔTES DE MALEPÈRE AOCS are the two most westerly Languedoc-Roussillon appellations. Their location is reflected in the mix of southwest and Mediterranean varieties permitted. Wine styles vary considerably according to the blend: a greater percentage

Racks of Languedoc-Roussillon red wine

of Cabernet Franc or Cabernet Sauvignon gives wines a leaner, firmer, blackcurranty style more in tune with the wines of Southwest France, whereas Grenache offers more Mediterranean warmth.

🏔 limestone, schist, granite, clay 🍇 Merlot, Cabernet Franc, Grenache, Syrah, Cabernet Sauvignon 🍷 red, rosé

Limoux

THE COOLER, ATLANTIC influence in this hilly zone encourages good balance and acidity in white grapes and has played its part in establishing Limoux as the South's sparkling wine district. The wines are made by the traditional method (see pp166–7); Blanquette de Limoux has a minimum 90 per cent Mauzac, while Crémant de Limoux has a generous amount of Chardonnay. The AOC Limoux is for still white wines made mainly from Chardonnay. The best of these, from the important Sieur d'Arques co-operative, labelled Toques et Clochers, are sold in an annual charity auction in spring. Red AOC Limoux was officially recognized in 2003.

🏔 clay-and-limestone 🍇 Merlot, Malbec, Syrah, Grenache, Carignan 🍇 Mauzac, Chardonnay, Chenin Blanc 🍷 red, white, sparkling

Côtes du Roussillon & Côtes du Roussillon Villages

SOUTH TOWARDS THE Spanish frontier lies Côtes du Roussillon AOC. The fabric and culture of this border land is Catalan, which sets it apart from the Languedoc. The climate is hot and dry, the land swept almost continuously by

---

MUSCAT

The Muscat grape makes fortified vin doux naturel in a number of appellations. By far the largest area of production is Muscat de Rivesaltes in Roussillon, where Muscat d'Alexandrie and the nobler, smaller berried Muscat à Petits Grains produce a sweet but fresh, lively, aromatic wine for early consumption. The Languedoc Muscats are made exclusively from Muscat Blanc à Petits Grains. St-Jean-de-Minervois comes from the northeast corner of the Minervois, where the higher altitude and limestone soils give added finesse to the wine. The heavier wines of AOCs Muscat de Frontignan, Muscat de Mireval (right), and Muscat de Lunel are from the hotter coastal plain near Montpellier.

the northerly Tramontane wind, resulting in rich, warm, plummy wines. Mountains, particularly the snow-capped Canigou, dominate the skyline. Grapes for Côtes du Roussillon wines are grown in 118 communes throughout the district, whereas the superior Côtes du Roussillon Villages appellation is sourced specifically from hill sites in the valleys to the north. The wines here have more spice and concentration, and a softer texture. Four communes have the right to append their name to the *villages* label: Caramany, La Tour de France, Lesquerde, and Tautavel.

▨ *limestone-and-clay, granite, schist, gneiss*
▧ *Grenache, Carignan, Syrah, Mourvèdre, Cinsaut*
▨ *Grenache Blanc, Marsanne, Roussanne, Vermentino, Macabeo*
▨ *red, white, rosé*

Rivesaltes & Maury

WITH ITS HOT, dry climate, Roussillon has a historical reputation for strong, sweet, fortified *vin doux naturel*. Rivesaltes VDN comes in red, white, and occasionally rosé form, and is made by many of the same producers that make Côtes du Roussillon and Côtes du Roussillon Villages – including a number of large co-operatives. Rivesaltes Ambré comes from white grapes, Rivesaltes Tuilé from a minimum of 50 per cent red Grenache, and both are aged in barrel for

Domaine de la Rectorie label, Collioure

MAS DE SAPORTA

This useful address on the outskirts of Montpellier is the headquarters of the Coteaux du Languedoc winegrowers' association. It is a good source of information and has a wide range of wines available at domaine prices. Coteaux du Languedoc, St-Chinian, and Faugères are well represented with a smaller selection of Corbières, Fitou, and Minervois. There is also local food produce and a restaurant.
Lattes ☎ *04 67 06 04 44*
W *www.coteaux-languedoc.com*

two years. '*Hors d'Age*' means the wine has been aged for at least five years. Maury is a strong, tannic, Grenache-based *vin doux naturel* produced in the north of the district. It is either bottled when young and fruity (and usually labelled 'Vintage'), or aged for a few years before bottling.

▨ *limestone, schist* ▧ *Grenache, Syrah, Carignan* ▨ *Grenache Blanc, Grenache Gris, Macabeo, Bourboulenc* ▨ *fortified*

Banyuls & Collioure

AT THE EDGE of the Spanish border the foothills of the Pyrenees tumble to the Mediterranean Sea. On these steep, sun-baked hills terraced vineyards are held in place by 6,000km of dry stone walls. It is here that France's finest fortified wine, Banyuls, is produced. Vintage Banyuls, labelled Rimage, is bottled early to capture the power of the fruit. Banyuls aged for longer in large oak barrels or glass *bonbonnes* has a maderized flavour. Banyuls *grand cru* indicates 75 per cent Grenache and at least 30 months' ageing in barrel. There is also a small amount of white Banyuls. Collioure is produced in the same zone. Red and rosé are dry but full-bodied, and dry white Collioure has officially been recognized since the 2002 vintage.

▨ *schist* ▧ *Grenache, Mourvèdre, Syrah, Carignan* ▨ *Grenache Blanc, Grenache Gris, Malvoisie, Macabeo, Vermentino* ▨ *red, white, fortified*

Foothill vineyards and coast, Banyuls

TOP PRODUCERS OF LANGUEDOC-ROUSSILLON

Domaine d'Aupilhac
Coteaux du Languedoc

28 rue du Plô, Montpeyroux
📞 04 67 96 61 19
🖳 *www.aupilhac.com* ⬜ *by appt*

SYLVAIN FADAT began making wine with limited resources in 1989, initially vinifying in the reservoir of a wine tanker. He now has nearly 30ha of vines, including a vineyard he is developing at 350m. The range of wines includes the Coteaux du Languedoc Montpeyroux made from the five classic southern varieties (Syrah, Grenache, Mourvèdre, Carignan, Cinsaut). Two *vins de pays* also feature: Le Carignan, from vines that are over 50 years old, and Les Plos des Baumes, from Cabernet Sauvignon, Cabernet Franc, and Merlot planted in the highly prized region of Aniane.
🍷 *red, white, rosé* 🍾 *red: 2007, 2006, 2001, 2000, 1999, 1998, 1997, 1996, 1995* ★ *Coteaux du Languedoc Montpeyroux, VDP Le Carignan*

Domaine Canet-Valette
Coteaux du Languedoc

rte de Causses-et-Veyran, Cessenon-sur-Orb 📞 04 67 89 51 83 ⬜ *by appt*

MARC VALETTE IS an idealist whose dreams have come to fruition. He planted his vineyard in St-Chinian between 1988 and 1992 while still a member of the local co-operative, and added a new gravity-fed winery in 1999. He keeps his yields low, cultivates organically, and even physically treads most of the grapes. The wines are rich and concentrated, and have more finesse since he began destemming in 1997. Maghani, a blend of Syrah and Grenache, is the domaine's top wine.
🍷 *red* 🍾 *2007, 2006, 2001, 2000, 1999, 1998, 1997* ★ *Maghani*

Domaine d'Aupilhac label

Domaine Peyre Rose
Coteaux du Languedoc

St-Pargoire 📞 04 67 98 75 50
⬜ *by appt*

THE WINES MADE BY Marlène Soria from this isolated vineyard in the hinterland of La-Grande-Motte are truly special. Syrah-dominated and from extremely low yields, the two reds, Clos des Cistes and Syrah Léone, are aged for three years or more in vat, so they have already developed a certain maturity when sold. Dense, concentrated, and perfumed, they age admirably.
🍷 *red, white* 🍾 *red: 2007, 2006, 1998, 1997, 1996, 1995* ★ *Syrah Léone, Clos des Cistes*

Mas Bruguière
Coteaux du Languedoc

La Plaine, Valflaunes
📞 04 67 55 20 97 ⬜ *by appt*

ONE OF THE REGION'S early pioneers, Guilhem Bruguière replanted the family domaine with Syrah, Grenache, and Mourvèdre as far back as the 1970s. La Grenadière is his top red, matured in barrels and made to last. L'Arbouse is attractively spicy, and the white, Les Muriers, made from Roussanne, is one of

the most harmonious in the Coteaux du Languedoc.
🍷 *red, white, rosé* 🍾 *red: 2007, 2006, 2001, 2000, 1999, 1998, 1997, 1996, 1995* ★ *L'Arbouse, La Grenadière*

Mas Jullien
Coteaux du Languedoc

rte de St-André, Jonquières
📞 04 67 96 60 04 ⬜

OLIVIER JULLIEN is one of the Coteaux du Languedoc's early pioneers. In 1985, aged 20, he created this domaine from a small parcel of family-held vines; he is now a major reference point in the region. Smitten with the local soils and grape varieties, he makes a range of wines including Coteaux du Languedoc, a serious top red that ages well; Les États d'Âme, an easier drinking red; and the quirky, late-harvested Clairette de Beudelle.
🍷 *red, white, rosé* 🍾 *red: 2007, 2006, 2001, 2000, 1999, 1998, 1997, 1996, 1995* ★ *Coteaux du Languedoc, Les États d'Âme*

Mas Jullien

Prieuré de St-Jean de Bébian
Coteaux du Languedoc

rte de Nizas, Pézenas 📞 04 67 98 13 60 🖳 *www.bebian.com* ⬜ *by appt*

A 12TH-CENTURY CHAPEL highlights the antiquity of this site, although the domaine only made its mark in the 1980s. It was at this time that former owner Alain Roux replanted with vines acquired from top estates in Châteauneuf-du-Pape, Hermitage, and Bandol. The present owners, former wine writer Chantal Lecouty and her husband Jean-Claude Le Brun, arrived in 1994 and have continued Roux's legacy, producing rich, powerful, and relatively long-lasting wine.

🔴 red, white ⬛ red: 2007, 2006, 2001, 2000, 1999, 1998, 1997
★ Coteaux du Languedoc red

Domaine du Clos des Fées
Côtes du Roussillon Villages

69 rue du Maréchal-Joffre, Vingrau
☎ 04 68 29 40 00
🌐 www.closdesfees.com ☐ by appt

FORMER SOMMELIER, restaurateur, and wine writer Hervé Bizeul has proved that he can also turn his hand to winemaking. The progress of this domaine has been meteoric since the first vintage in 1998. Three blends are produced from Grenache, Syrah, Carignan, and Mourvèdre: Les Sorcières is rich and fruity, while Vieilles Vignes and Le Clos des Fées are more serious. La Petite Sibérie is an expensive limited edition of 2,000 bottles a year, made uniquely from Grenache grown on a single plot of land.

🔴 red ⬛ 2007, 2006, 2001, 2000
★ Vieilles Vignes, Le Clos des Fées

Domaine Gauby
Côtes du Roussillon Villages

Le Faradjal, Calce ☎ 04 68 64 35 19
☐ by appt

GÉRARD GAUBY is the down-to-earth star of Roussillon. He started bottling in the 1980s and his wines, once powerful and tannic, are now more refined in texture and quality of fruit. He has been cultivating the vines organically since 1996 and biodynamically since 2001. The red Vieilles Vignes and Syrah-dominated Muntada are superb, and there is also a very good range of whites.

🔴 red, white ⬛ red: 2007, 2006, 2001, 2000, 1999, 1998, 1997, 1996, 1995 ★ Vieilles Vignes, Muntada

Cabernet Sauvignon vines, Mas de Daumas Gassac

Domaine de la Rectorie
Banyuls & Collioure

54 ave du Puig-Delmas, Banyuls-sur-Mer ☎ 04 68 81 02 94
🌐 www.la-rectorie.com ☐ by appt

THE EXCELLENCE of this domaine is linked to the hard work in the vineyards. The Parcé brothers cultivate around 30 different terraced parcels at various altitudes from sea level to 400m. They then craft a range of wines: four Banyuls, three Collioures, two dry whites, and two rosés. The reds are made from a majority of Grenache, the long-lasting and elegant Collioure Coume Pascole with a little Syrah. The Banyuls cuvée Léon Parcé has a rich concentration of fruit and is aged in barrel for 12 months.

🔴 red, white, rosé, fortified
⬛ Collioure red: 2007, 2006, 2001, 2000, 1999, 1998, 1997, 1996 ★ Collioure Coume Pascole, Léon Parcé

Domaine du Mas Blanc
Banyuls & Collioure

9 ave du Général-de-Gaulle, Banyuls-sur-Mer ☎ 04 68 88 32 12 🌐 www.domaine-du-mas-blanc.com ☐ by appt

THE LARGER-THAN-LIFE personality of Dr André Parcé placed this family domaine firmly on the map in the 1970s. His son, Jean-Michel, has since maintained continuity. Collioure is produced, but the real interest is in the range of Banyuls:

the Rimage and Rimage La Coume are bottled early to preserve the fruit; Cuvée du Docteur Parcé is a blend of various years; and Hors d'Age de Sostréra is produced using a sherry-like solera system of fractional blending. The white Banyuls is made from Muscat, Grenache Blanc, and Malvoisie.

🔴 red, fortified ⬛ Banyuls Rimage: 2007, 2006, 2001, 2000, 1998
★ Banyuls Rimage La Coume

Mas de Daumas Gassac
Vin de Pays

Aniane ☎ 04 67 57 71 28
🌐 www.daumas-gassac.com ☐

THIS LEGENDARY domaine was created from nothing by former leather manufacturer Aimé Guibert in the 1970s. He discovered that his country retreat had amazing viticultural potential, hired top consultant Professor Émile Peynaud, and planted his vineyard. The first vintage, 1978, was acclaimed as the Château Lafite-Rothschild of the South, and the wine's reputation was made. Cabernet Sauvignon is the mainstay of the long-ageing red, and Viognier, Chardonnay, and Petit Manseng are used for the white, so the wines are labelled as vins de pays.

🔴 red, white ⬛ red: 2007, 2006, 2001, 2000, 1999, 1998, 1997, 1996, 1995 ★ VDP de L'Hérault

View of vineyard in the Côtes de Provence

WINEGROWING AREAS OF PROVENCE

THE LIFESTYLE, FOOD, AND CLIMATE of Provence have made rosé the principal wine to be made here. A growing number of individual producers are, however, making reds of note from blends of Syrah, Grenache, Mourvèdre, and Cabernet Sauvignon. Serious reds, made essentially from Mourvèdre, are found in Bandol.

Bellet

IN THE ALPINE foothills behind Nice, a handful of producers maintain the name of AOC Bellet. There were over 1,000ha of vineyards here in the early 19th century, but this has now dwindled to around 50. The cool hill sites are suited to the production of fresh, aromatic white wines made mainly from Vermentino (Rolle). Nice's Italian genealogy is seen in the use of the red grapes Folle Noire (Fuella) and Braquet (Brachetto). Most of the wine is consumed locally.

Wicker covered bottle

🏔 *gravel, sand, clay* 🍇 *Folle Noire, Braquet, Grenache, Cinsaut* 🍾 *Vermentino, Chardonnay* 🍷 *white, rosé*

Côtes de Provence

THE ONLY GENERALIZATION to be made about this appellation is that 80 per cent of the production is rosé. Otherwise, its sheer size – 20,000ha under vine – and diversity of topography and climate make it extremely disparate. Zones vary from the coastal area around St-Tropez to cooler hill sites north of Draguignan. The rosé is made mainly from Cinsaut and Grenache and is consumed by an insatiable local market. There are growing numbers of producers offering interesting reds from blends that can include Syrah, Cabernet Sauvignon, and Mourvèdre.

🏔 *sandstone, limestone, granite, schist* 🍇 *Cinsaut, Grenache, Syrah, Carignan, Cabernet Sauvignon* 🍾 *Clairette, Vermentino, Sémillon, Ugni Blanc* 🍷 *red, white, rosé*

Coteaux Varois

CENTRED AROUND THE TOWN of Brignoles, Coteaux Varois was upgraded to full AOC status in 1993. The grape varieties are much the same as in Côtes de Provence: what marks the difference is the location of the vineyards, which are inland away from the coast and all at a higher, cooler altitude, making the wines a little more intense. It is a district for which the potential has yet to be fully realized or a particular character of wine defined.

🏔 *limestone* 🍇 *Grenache, Cinsaut, Syrah, Carignan, Cabernet Sauvignon* 🍾 *Vermentino, Grenache Blanc, Clairette, Sémillon, Ugni Blanc* 🍷 *red, white, rosé*

Bandol

PROVENCE'S MOST SERIOUS appellation takes its name from the fishing port-cum-holiday resort of Bandol. Rosé provides the volume, but it is the red that holds the interest, a steely, tannic wine with a herbal nuance and good ageing potential. The vineyards form a terraced amphitheatre overlooking the

Mediterranean. The aspect and elevation, up to 400m, provide an annual average of 3,000 hours of sunshine, helping to ripen the grapes, while sea breezes temper the heat. The conditions are ideal for the awkward Mourvèdre, which represents at least 50 per cent of the blend for the red. The wine has to be aged in cask for a minimum of 18 months.
limestone-and-clay *Mourvèdre, Grenache, Cinsaut, Syrah, Carignan* *Clairette, Ugni Blanc, Bourboulenc, Sauvignon Blanc* *red, white, rosé*

Cassis

URBAN DEVELOPMENT poses the greatest threat to the pretty fishing port of Cassis and its wines. Located to the east of Marseille, AOC Cassis has just 175ha cultivated in a small arc, producing mainly white wines, which are fresh but low in acidity, and much in demand locally.
limestone *Grenache, Cinsaut, Mourvèdre, Carignan* *Ugni Blanc, Clairette, Marsanne, Sauvignon Blanc, Grenache Blanc* *red, white, rosé*

Palette

THE PARTICULARITY OF THIS tiny appellation of barely 35ha is a distinctive limestone soil called *calcaire de Langesse* and wines – red, white, and rosé – that benefit from bottle age. The principal reference here, Château Simone, produces firm, minerally whites and long-lived but rather idiosyncratic reds.
limestone *Grenache, Mourvèdre, Syrah, Cinsaut* *Clairette, Grenache Blanc, Ugni Blanc, Muscat* *red, white, rosé*

Coteaux d'Aix en Provence

THIS LARGE AOC stretches north to south from the Lubéron to the Mediterranean and east to

Vineyards and citadel in Les Baux de Provence

CORSICA

The mountainous island of Corsica lies 170km off the coast of France. Overall it has a dry, sunny climate, but there are local variations caused by altitude, the sea, and winds. Vermentino is the principal white grape, making soft, aromatic wines. Reds and rosés are made from traditional southern varieties Grenache, Carignan, and Cinsaut, as well as Nielluccio (Tuscany's Sangiovese), and the native Sciacarello. International grapes have gained steadily, producing varietal wines under the eyecatching Vins de l'Île de Beauté label.

Vin de Corse is the generic AOC for the island, to which five subregions can add their names. Ajaccio, noted for delicate reds made from Sciacarello, and Patrimonio, with rich, powerful reds from Nielluccio, are two specific AOCs.

west from the town of Aix-en-Provence to the Rhône Valley. In all, some 3,500ha of vines are planted at an altitude of anywhere between sea level and 400m. Rosé is the mainstay (55 per cent), with 40 per cent red and a complement of white. A diverse range of grapes is permitted, including Cabernet Sauvignon, Mourvèdre, and the more obscure Counoise, which make fresh, round rosés and reds with a certain depth and intensity.
limestone-and-clay, limestone-and-sand *Grenache, Cabernet Sauvignon, Carignan, Syrah, Cinsaut* *Bourboulenc, Vermentino, Clairette, Grenache Blanc, Ugni Blanc* *red, white, rosé*

Les Baux de Provence

LES BAUX DE PROVENCE used to be part of Coteaux d'Aix but was given independent AOC status for reds and rosés in 1995. Whites are still labelled Coteaux d'Aix en Provence. The vineyards are located in the foothills of the Alpilles Mountains with traditional southern grape varieties cultivated alongside Cabernet Sauvignon, which is permitted up to a maximum 20 per cent. There are only a dozen or so domaines in this tiny district, producing fruity reds with a little tannic grip. Many are run organically, the climatic conditions being conducive to this type of viticulture.
limestone *Grenache, Cinsaut, Syrah, Carignan, Mourvèdre* *red, rosé*

TOP PRODUCERS OF PROVENCE

Château de Roquefort
Côtes de Provence

Roquefort La Bedoule
☎ 04 42 73 20 84 ◗ by appt

THE EMERGENCE OF this estate near Bandol is relatively recent. Raimond de Villeneuve spent his childhood years here and returned in 1994 to take over the reins. He rapidly restructured the vineyard but continued the policy of organic cultivation. The wines are sumptuously fruity, with a fine-grained texture. The white Les Genêts is fresh and floral, and the rosés Corail and Sémiramis have red berry fruit. The red blends, Les Mûres and Rubrum Obscurum, are simply delicious, the latter with greater concentration and structure. In exceptional years La Pourpre is produced from Carignan and Syrah.
🔴 *red, white, rosé* 🔷 *red: 2007, 2006, 2001, 2000, 1999, 1998* ★ *Les Mûres, Rubrum Obscurum*

Domaine Richeaume
Côtes de Provence

Puyloubier ☎ 04 42 66 31 27 ◗ by appt

A JOB AS LECTURER at the University of Aix-en-Provence was the catalyst for Henning Hoesch establishing Domaine Richeaume in 1972. The estate has now grown to 20ha, and Henning has been joined by his son Sylvain, whose training has been more anglophone – Ridge Vineyards in California *(see p504)* and Penfolds in Australia *(see p571)* – than French. There is an aromatic white Blanc de Blancs made from Vermentino and Clairette, and a selection of very good reds. The Cuvée Tradition, a Cabernet

Château de Roquefort label

Sauvignon-Grenache blend, is dark, rich, and herbal, while the Cuvée Columelle (Cabernet Sauvignon-Syrah-Merlot) has greater depth and complexity.
🔴 *red, white, rosé* 🔷 *red: 2007, 2006, 2001, 2000, 1999, 1998, 1997, 1996, 1995* ★ *Cuvée Columelle*

Château de Pibarnon
Bandol

Chemin de la Croix-des-Signaux, La Cadière-d'Azur ☎ 04 94 90 12 73
🌐 *www.chateaupibarnon.com* ◗

IN 1977 Henri de St Victor exchanged a pharmaceuticals job in Paris for the life of a wine producer in Bandol. Château de Pibarnon was then only 3 or 4ha but now counts nearly 50. This magnificent estate overlooking the Mediterranean, currently run by Henri's son Eric, produces

one of the most elegant, complex, long-lived wines in the region. The red is made from Mourvèdre with just a splash of Grenache, the fruity rosé is a blend of Mourvèdre and Cinsaut, and the white is a mix of Clairette, Bourboulenc, Marsanne, Roussanne, and Viognier.
🔴 *red, white, rosé* 🔷 *red: 2007, 2006, 2001, 2000, 1999, 1998, 1997, 1996, 1995* ★ *Bandol red*

Château Pradeaux
Bandol

Chemin des Pradeaux, St-Cyr-sur-Mer
☎ 04 94 32 10 21 ◗ by appt

THE PORTALIS FAMILY has owned Château Pradeaux since 1752 and Cyrille Portalis is the present custodian. Old vines and low yields are part of the secret of his success. The Mourvèdre-dominated wine is totally uncompromising, firm, and structured, and needs several years in bottle to soften and unwind. It is a perfect example of the ageing potential of Bandol wines, displaying how they can develop great finesse and complexity over time.
🔴 *red, rosé* 🔷 *red: 2007, 2006, 2001, 2000, 1999, 1998, 1997, 1996, 1995* ★ *Bandol red*

Château Pradeaux label

Henri de St Victor, Château de Pibarnon

Domaine Tempier
Bandol

Le Plan du Castellet, Le Castellet 📞 04 94 98 70 21 ⓦ www.domainetempier.com ☐

DOMAINE TEMPIER HAS long been one of the guiding lights of Bandol. The estate was relaunched in the 1940s by Lucien Peyraud and is still owned by his family, although it is now managed by Daniel Ravier. A number of different red wines are made here: the Classique and Cuvée Spéciale are sourced from different sites around the estate, while La Migoua, La Tourtine, and Cabassaou are magnificent single-vineyard wines. All of them are produced from varying blends of Mourvèdre with a little Grenache, Cinsaut, and Syrah.
🔲 red, white, rosé 🔲 red: 2007, 2006, 2001, 2000, 1999, 1998, 1997, 1996 ★ Cuvée Spéciale, La Tourtine, Cabassaou

Clos Ste Magdeleine
Cassis

Cassis 📞 04 42 01 70 28 ☐ by appt

THE TERRACED VINEYARDS of the Clos Ste Magdeleine descend to the Mediterranean at this idyllic spot. This estate has consistently been one of the

top producers in the district for a number of years. Its wines, from grape varieties Marsanne, Clairette, and Ugni Blanc, have a floral, honeyed bouquet and ample soft, round fruit. They are best consumed young.
🔲 white, rosé 🔲 white: 2007, 2006, 2002, 2001, 2000 ★ Cassis white

Château Simone
Palette

Meyreuil 📞 04 42 66 92 58 ☐ by appt

OWNED FOR SEVEN generations by the Rougier family, this unique estate takes a very traditional approach to wine. The organically cultivated vineyard has never been replanted, and individual vines are replaced only when necessary. A collection of different grape varieties is

planted, but three principal ones are used: Grenache and Mourvèdre for the red, and Clairette for the white. The latter has a minerally freshness and improves with bottle age. The red, matured for upwards of three years in oak barrels, is light in colour, fine, and the antithesis of the modern, fruit-led wine.
🔲 red, white, rosé 🔲 white: 2007, 2006, 2001, 2000, 1999, 1998, 1997, 1996 ★ Palette white

Domaine de Trévallon
Vin de Pays

St-Etienne du Grès 📞 04 90 49 06 00 ⓦ www.trevallon.com ☐ by appt

ELOI DÜRRBACH makes a truly original red wine from an equal blend of Cabernet Sauvignon and Syrah. The texture is fine, the aromas are of laurel and *garrigue*, and the ageing potential is long. However, the percentage of Cabernet Sauvignon exceeds that authorized by AOC Les Baux-de-Provence, where the domaine is situated, and the wines are consequently labelled as *vins de pays*. There is also a good barrel-fermented white, produced from a blend of Marsanne, Roussanne, and Chardonnay.
🔲 red, white 🔲 red: 2007, 2006, 2001, 2000, 1999, 1998, 1997, 1996, 1995 ★ VDP red

ORGANIC ESTATES

Provence is the ideal location for organic cultivation. The generally sunny climate and dry, cleansing influence of the mistral wind means fewer problems with insects and fungal diseases in the vineyard, and hence suitability for an organic approach. Organically run domaines can be found throughout the region (although they do not always advertise the fact), in particular in the tiny appellation of Les Baux de Provence. Names to look out for here are Mas de la Dame, Mas de Gourgonnier, Domaine Hauvette, Château de Romanin, Domaine des Terres Blanches, and Domaine de la Vallongue.

THE LOIRE VALLEY

PARISIANS HAVE *long delighted in the wines of the Loire, but elsewhere in the world they tend to be undervalued. Yet, there is a fantastic diversity to be found in the region – from crisp, dry whites and good-value fizz to thirst-quenching rosé, light and food-friendly reds, and world-ranking sweet wines. The overall theme of wines from this region is one of harmony and easy drinkability.*

The proximity to France's capital city has provided a ready market for the Loire's wines since the Middle Ages, allowing the area's numerous small growers a direct source of trade. Links with Belgium and Holland were also established early on due to the excellent river connections, while ports on the western seaboard facilitated export to England, where the wines of Anjou were once preferred to bordeaux.

Sign depicting harvesting

The interconnecting thread through the whole region is the long, languorous Loire River, which covers a distance of some 1,000km from its source in the Massif Central. The upper reaches of the river are home to a handful of 'country' wines (St-Pourçain, Côte Roannaise, Côtes du Forez) rarely seen outside France. Serious winemaking begins further north at Pouilly-sur-Loire and continues west to Nantes. Along this stretch of the Loire some 13,000 family-run estates cultivate just over 50,000ha of Appellation d'Origine Contrôlée vines. The average holding is small – a little over 4ha-but with a total annual production of around three million hectolitres the Loire Valley is the third largest producer of AOC wines in France, behind Bordeaux and the Rhône Valley.

The majority of the Loire's wines are white, representing 52 per cent of the total volume, with just 26 per cent red, 16 per cent rosé, and 6 per cent sparkling. The northerly latitude for winemaking and generally temperate climate ensure good acidity and a refreshing nature in all the wines. The geographical extent of the Loire Valley, the many grape varieties cultivated, and the effect of vintage variation, however, mean that the wines are very varied in character.

Harvesting Sauvignon Blanc grapes outside the hill town of Sancerre

◁ **Château de Tracy and Sauvignon Blanc vineyard in Pouilly-Fumé**

WINE MAP OF THE LOIRE VALLEY

THE NORTHERN SECTION of the Loire River from the Atlantic Ocean east to Pouilly-sur-Loire in central France provides the focus for Loire wines. It can be broken down into four segments, each with its own distinct wines. The Pays Nantais on the Atlantic seaboard is home to Muscadet. Moving east, Anjou-Saumur produces luscious sweet wines (Coteaux du Layon) and long-ageing Chenin Blanc (Savennières). Touraine boasts the best Loire reds (Chinon, Bourgueil, and St-Nicolas-de-Bourgueil) and sweet forms of Chenin Blanc (Vouvray and Montlouis). The Central Loire is the hub for Sauvignon Blanc (Sancerre and Pouilly-Fumé).

KEY

▩ The Loire Valley

Vineyard in Pays Nantais

SAVENNIÈRES
QUARTS-DE-CHAUME
MUSCADET COTEAUX DE LA LOIRE
ANJOU
Angers
ST-NICOLAS-DE-BOURGUEIL
PAYS NANTAIS
Loire
COTEAUX DE L'AUBANCE
BOURGUEIL
Nantes
COTEAUX DU LAYON
MUSCADET SÈVRE ET MAINE
ANJOU-SAUMUR
Saumur
Vienne
CHINON
MUSCADET CÔTES DE GRANDLIEU
BONNEZEAUX
MUSCADET
ANJOU VILLAGES
SAUMUR
SAUMUR-CHAMPIGNY
47°
ATLANTIC OCEAN

0 ⊢ km ————————— 50

FOOD & WINE PAIRING IN THE LOIRE

Recognized as the 'garden of France', the Loire has a solid gastronomic tradition based on local produce. The wines provide an equally original and varied palette with just about every conceivable style available. There are many tantalizing food and wine combinations. Oysters, mussels, and other shellfish from the Atlantic are perfect with a crisp, dry, tangy Muscadet. Asparagus, fried whitebait, chicken liver mousse, or goat's cheese are the ideal partners to a clean, tangy Sancerre or Pouilly-Fumé. Poached

Local fish and seafood

river fish served in a creamy sauce – carp, pike, *sandre* (pike-perch) – pair well with a young, fruity red like Saumur-Champigny or the dry white Chenin Blanc-based wines of Vouvray and Savennières. Game dishes such as wild duck and pheasant are matched by the sufficient character of older vintages of red Chinon and Bourgueil. For dessert, what better than a home-made fruit tart with a sweet but tinglingly fresh Coteaux du Layon to round things off?

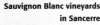

Sauvignon Blanc vineyards in Sancerre

TERROIR AT A GLANCE

Latitude: 47–48°N.

Altitude: 0–350m.

Topography The Loire River creates one long valley from west to east. The area is relatively flat with some hilly countryside in Anjou-Saumur and Touraine, where the Loire's tributaries create river valleys with gentle slopes. In the east, Sancerre is on a hill at 300m.

Soil: Schist, granite, gneiss, sand in the Pays Nantais; slate, schist, sandstone, tuffeau (limestone) in Anjou-Saumur; sand, clay, gravel, tuffeau in Touraine; kimmeridgian limestone soils similar to those of Chablis in the Central Loire.

Climate: Generally cool and temperate. A maritime influence prevails on the Atlantic seaboard and persists in varying degrees inland as far as Orléans. In the Central Loire the climate is more continental.

Temperature: July average is 19°C.

Rainfall: Annual average is 750mm.

Viticultural hazards: Spring frost.

Domaine Henry Marionnet label, Touraine

LOIRE VALLEY: AREAS & TOP PRODUCERS

PAYS NANTAIS p154

ANJOU-SAUMUR p154

TOURAINE p156

CENTRAL LOIRE p157

Domaine de la Taille label, Touraine

PERFECT CASE: THE LOIRE VALLEY

Ⓦ Château de Villeneuve Saumur Les Cormiers ££

Ⓦ Château Pierre Bise Coteaux du Layon Anclaie £££

Ⓦ Domaine de la Taille aux Loups Montlouis Cuvée des Loups *(moelleux)* £££

Ⓦ Domaine de l'Écu Muscadet Sèvre et Maine Expression de Granit ££

Ⓦ Domaine des Baumard Quarts-de-Chaume £££

Ⓦ Domaine Didier Dagueneau Pouilly-Fumé Silex ££££

Ⓦ Domaine du Clos Naudin Vouvray *(sec)* ££

Ⓦ Domaine Henri Bourgeois Sancerre La Côte des Monts Damnés ££

Ⓦ Domaine Huet Vouvray Le Clos du Bourg *(demi-sec)* ££

Ⓦ Domaine Huet Vouvray Le Mont *(moelleux)* £££

Ⓦ Domaine Patrick Baudouin Coteaux du Layon Maria Juby £££

Ⓦ Coulée de Serrant Savennières ££££

Picking Melon de Bourgogne grapes in Muscadet, Pays Nantais

WINEGROWING AREAS OF THE LOIRE VALLEY

THE LOIRE PRODUCES truly original wines in a gamut of styles: dry, medium-dry, and sweet white, red, rosé, and sparkling. White wines are in the majority, made principally from Chenin Blanc (known locally as Pineau de la Loire) in Anjou-Saumur and Touraine, Melon de Bourgogne in the Pays Nantais, and Sauvignon Blanc in the Central Loire and Touraine. Cabernet Franc is the red grape of the region, and is grown mainly in Touraine and Anjou-Saumur. Whatever the wine style, the northerly climes of the Loire place the emphasis on delicacy and flavour, rather than power and fruit-driven concentration.

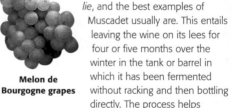

Melon de Bourgogne grapes

Pays Nantais

THE MOST WESTERLY of the Loire districts is the Pays Nantais, home of Muscadet, the crisp, cautiously neutral, dry white so often served as an accompaniment to seafood. The wine is made from the rather bland Melon de Bourgogne, a Burgundian grape variety introduced in the 17th century that had the fortitude to withstand the bitingly cold winter of 1709, which destroyed the previously dominant red varieties of the region.

The vineyards, some 13,000ha, are located around the city of Nantes and divide into four AOCs. **Muscadet Sèvre et Maine** is by far the largest, accounting for over 80 per cent of the production. The best of these wines have a fine, floral bouquet, a mineral edge, and occasionally the ability to age. **Muscadet**

Coteaux de la Loire is perhaps fuller bodied, while **Muscadet Côtes de Grandlieu**, the most recent designation – introduced in 1994 – is softer in style. There is also a small volume of generic AOC **Muscadet**. Throughout the region there is the potential to bottle the wine *sur lie*, and the best examples of Muscadet usually are. This entails leaving the wine on its lees for four or five months over the winter in the tank or barrel in which it has been fermented without racking and then bottling directly. The process helps to enhance flavour and, as the wine still contains a teasing sparkle of carbon dioxide, it emphasizes freshness and compensates for generally low acidity. Even drier than Muscadet is the VDQS Gros Plant du Pays Nantais made from Folle Blanche.

🏔 *schist, granite, gneiss, sand* 🍇 *Melon de Bourgogne, Folle Blanche* 🍷 *white*

Anjou-Saumur

THE GREATEST EXPRESSION of Chenin Blanc in the world, with the exception of Vouvray in Touraine, is found in Anjou. A combination of maritime climate, sheltered valleys, and schistous soils produce superlative dry and sweet styles, some with the potential to age for years, even decades.

Southwest of the town of Angers on the north side of the Loire River, the vineyards of AOC **Savennières** are planted on slate and schist soils that slope to the river's edge. A dry, minerally Chenin Blanc with great depth and persistence, Savennières needs at least four or five years to mellow. Medium-dry and sweet versions are occasionally produced in exceptional years. Within the district there are two sub-appellation AOCs, **Roche aux Moines** and the tiny **Coulée de Serrant**, a monopoly run in a resolutely biodynamic *(see p105)* fashion by owner Nicolas Joly.

The best of the sweet styles come from tributary valleys on the south side of the Loire in the AOCs **Coteaux de l'Aubance** and **Coteaux du Layon**. Chenin Blanc ripens to a fragrant sweetness on sites of varying aspect, assisted, when conditions are right, by the onset of botrytis *(see p66)*. Selective, late harvesting is therefore essential. The top wines have luscious fruit and floral aromas in youth, maturing to notes of honey and dried fruits, an unctuosity on the palate, backed by a mouth-tingling acidity. Two sites, **Bonnezeaux** and **Quarts de Chaume**, in the Coteaux du Layon, are considered superior for this style of wine and have been given individual AOC status.

Dry white and red is also produced throughout the AOC **Anjou**. The white invariably has an apple-quince flavour with a mineral note and is produced from Chenin Blanc, sometimes with a dash of Chardonnay and Sauvignon Blanc; the soft red is from Cabernet Franc. From a different red grape, light, quaffable **Anjou-Gamay** is mainly consumed within the region. **Anjou-Villages** and **Anjou-Villages Brissac** are uniquely red

Crémant de Loire

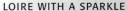

LOIRE WITH A SPARKLE

Sparkling wines are another facet of the Loire's varied showcase. The best are produced by the traditional method *(see pp166–7)* in the epicentres of Saumur and Vouvray. Sparkling Vouvray and Montlouis are produced solely from Chenin Blanc, and with its acidic bite are crisp and appley. A little bottle age adds a honeyed nuance. Saumur brut is based on Chenin Blanc but allows other varieties like Chardonnay, Sauvignon Blanc, and Cabernet Franc to round out the wine. Crémant de Loire is made from a similar range of grapes grown in Anjou, Saumur, and Touraine. Regulations for production are stricter than those for Saumur, and the wine is usually finer in style with a less aggressive fizz.

wine appellations from selected sites mostly south of the river. Produced from Cabernet Franc and Cabernet Sauvignon, they have a little more colour, intensity, and structure than regular Anjou and can represent excellent value. Rosé is another staple of Anjou and comes in various styles. **Cabernet d'Anjou** and **Rosé d'Anjou** are medium-dry while **Rosé de Loire** (also produced in Touraine) is dry.

The soft limestone or tuffeau soils of Saumur south of the river and further east have made the town and region of the same name a centre for sparkling wine *(see above)*. The town faintly resembles Épernay in Champagne with its large companies and galleries of cellars cut into the calcareous tuffeau rock. **Saumur** is the generic appellation for still red and white made, as in Anjou, from Cabernet Franc and Chenin Blanc respectively, although the chalky soils make the wines lighter. The best reds (also Cabernet Franc) come from **Saumur-Champigny**, a more limited AOC zone close to the town of Saumur. Raspberry- or violet-scented, they are usually fresh, fruity, and easy drinking.

🗺 *slate, schist, sandstone, tuffeau*
🍇 *Cabernet Sauvignon, Cabernet Franc, Grolleau, Gamay* 🍇 *Chenin Blanc, Chardonnay, Sauvignon Blanc*
🍷 *red, white, rosé, sparkling, dessert*

Chenin Blanc vineyards in the Coteaux du Layon, Anjou

Tubs of newly harvested Chenin Blanc grapes in Vouvray

Touraine

THE BEST LOIRE reds come from Touraine and specifically the appellations **Chinon, Bourgueil,** and **St-Nicolas-de-Bourgueil.** In general they are fresh, fruity, and invigorating, produced from Cabernet Franc, or Breton as it is known locally. What makes these wines so appealing is that they are digestible, convivial, not tiringly heavy, and above all they are food friendly. The lighter, youthful styles can, like Beaujolais *(see pp114–5),* be served slightly chilled (at 13 to 14°C) to emphasize the fruitiness. In great vintages (such as 1997 and 1996) and from certain soils, these wines can be firmer and longer lived and have the potential to age for at least 10 years.

Chinon is the largest of the three AOCs with 2,100ha located south of the Loire on either side of its tributary, the Vienne. The wines have a soft, rounded texture and weight, the lighter styles coming from the sandy, alluvial soils close to the river, those with greater vigour and structure being sourced from the clay-and-gravel plateaux or south-facing tuffeau (limestone) slopes. There is also a little rare, dry white Chinon made from Chenin Blanc. The tuffeau reappears north of the Loire at Bourgueil, giving firmness to the wines there, while the grapes grown on the predominantly alluvial soils at St-

Nicolas-de Bourgueil make lighter, fruitier wine. In all three districts, producers often present a number of different *cuvées,* each reflecting the soil type and age of the vines.

Touraine is the generic appellation for simple, lightweight white, red, and rosé wines produced in a zone that surrounds the town of Tours and that spreads east as far as Blois. A multitude of grape varieties are permissible, but the two most common, often used as varietal names on the label, are Gamay and Sauvignon Blanc. Three specific sectors are allowed to add their names to the label: **Touraine Mesland, Touraine Amboise,** and **Touraine Azay-le-Rideau,** while **Touraine Noble-Joué** (since 1999) accounts for a tiny production of pale pink, fruity *vin gris* made from Pinot Meunier, Pinot Noir, and Pinot Gris.

Just east of Tours are the two great white wine AOCs of Touraine, **Vouvray** and **Montlouis.** The mercurial Chenin Blanc again comes into its own producing dry *(sec),* medium-dry *(demi-sec),* sweet *(moelleux)* and sparkling wines *(see p155),* all with an appley, honeyed nuance and razor-edge streak of acidity. There is considerable vintage

Domaine Huet label, Vouvray

variation in this mid-continental, mid-maritime zone, and this affects the style of the wine. In ripe years, when botrytis takes hold, the pendulum swings towards the sweeter, quince and crystallized fruit-flavoured styles, whereas in leaner years sparkling and dry prevail. Whatever their character, these wines have incredible endurance and can age for decades. Vouvray is located on the north bank of the Loire and, with its tuffeau slopes, produces a wine of greater weight and intensity than Montlouis on the south bank, where the soils are generally sandier. Carved into the tuffeau at Vouvray are some impressive wine cellars and troglodyte homes. *tuffeau, sand, clay, gravel* *Cabernet Franc, Gamay, Côt, Cabernet Sauvignon* *Chenin Blanc, Sauvignon Blanc, Chardonnay* *red, white, rosé, sparkling, dessert*

SHOW-STOPPING SWEET LOIRE

The official guideline for sweetness in the Loire is outlined by European Union decree. Dry wines should have residual sugar of under five grams per litre, *demi-sec* or medium-dry between 5 and 14g/l and *moelleux* (sweet) between 14 and 45g/l. Anything higher should be referred to as *doux* (very sweet), a term most producers dislike, preferring the description *liquoreux*. However, this does not take into account the high levels of acidity found in wines like Vouvray and Montlouis, which counter sugar levels and make the wines seem drier. Producers often feel they can produce a more balanced wine by overstepping the statutory sugar levels and they are often reluctant, therefore, to precisely label the style of their wine. Hence it is not always easy to tell how sweet or dry the wine is from the bottle. Price can be an indicator, as sweeter wines are usually more expensive. Dry Vouvray with a high, but imperceptible, level of residual sugar is unofficially referred to as *sec tendre*. Whatever the residual sugar, though, the sweet wines of the Loire are unique world classics that age and retain their freshness for decades.

Domaine du Clos Naudin label

Central Loire

THE CENTRAL LOIRE is the Sauvignon Blanc capital of France, as demonstrated by the celebrated wines of **Sancerre** and **Pouilly-Fumé**. The vineyards are 360km upstream from the Atlantic coast, the climate decisively continental, and the wines crisp, dry, and tangy with a piercing redcurrant, gooseberry, and occasionally citrus aroma and flavour.

The hill town of Sancerre on the west bank of the Loire gives its name to the largest of the two appellations, some 2,600ha planted on hilly, limestone terrain. Pouilly-Fumé is produced on the opposite side of the river in the AOC **Pouilly-sur-Loire**. The land is flatter but the grape variety, Sauvignon Blanc, the same. Confusingly, there is also a white wine called Pouilly-sur-Loire, but it is made from Chasselas and is infinitely less memorable.

Tasting the difference between Sancerre and Pouilly-Fumé is not easy. The former can vary in quality but is perhaps fuller and a little fruitier, the latter with its greater percentage of flinty, limestone soils tends to be more minerally and intense. Both are particularly delicious when drunk young.

Whereas Pouilly-Fumé is a white wine-only district, Sancerre also produces a little red and rosé from Pinot Noir. The red is light-bodied with a cherry-like fragrance and is generally consumed locally or in Parisian bistros.

The other districts of the Central Loire, like Sancerre, fall within the left bank bend of the river. AOC **Menetou-Salon** immediately to the west of Sancerre is similar, producing pungent Sauvignon Blanc and light-bodied red and rosé from Pinot Noir. The wines are less well known but often represent excellent value. AOC **Reuilly**, too, produces reds and whites from the same grape varieties as well as a little rosé from Pinot Gris. The white is dry and a little more austere, the red lighter than Sancerre. Neighbouring AOC **Quincy** is a white wine-only district, the Sauvignon Blanc grown on sandy-gravel soils again producing fruity, aromatic wines that are soft in style.

🖾 *limestone, flint, sand, gravel* 🍇 *Pinot Noir* 🍇 *Sauvignon Blanc* 🍷 *red, white, rosé*

Sauvignon Blanc vineyards in Sancerre

THE WINE CASK

CASKS MADE OF OAK have been used for centuries to store wine, as wood was available in abundance and watertight barrels were easy to fashion. Fermenting or maturing wine in new oak barrels adds complex compounds that enhance a wine's aromas and flavours. As wood is porous, maturation in casks also permits subtle oxidation to soften the texture of the wine, while clarifying and stabilizing it before bottling.

Oak Forests of France
Oak from the USA, Russia, and the Balkans is used to create casks, but the forests of central France are widely accepted as yielding the finest wood for wine barrels. Wood from the Allier, Tronçais, and Nevers forests is particularly prized.

CRAFT OF THE COOPER

Casks are made according to the specific requirements of the client winery. Staves are positioned and then bent into shape with the aid of heat and metal retaining hoops. An open flame is used to 'toast' the inside of the new barrels. The degree of toasting – light, medium, or heavy – is directly linked to the level of smoky, spicy, vanilla aromas and flavours exhibited by the wine.

1. Assembling
Staves are tapered at each end and positioned in a circle with a hoop fitted to maintain their position.

2. Knocking down
The cooper then hammers down metal retaining hoops to begin shaping the cask.

3. Shaping
Fire and water are used to continue the shaping process, and more hoops are knocked tightly into position.

4. Toasting
The barrel is toasted inside to add character to the wine.

5. Finishing
Stave-ends are planed smooth before the barrel is released.

MODERN ALTERNATIVES TO OAK BARRELS

The relative expense of good quality casks has driven the wine industry to develop less costly means of achieving the influence of oak on wine. Alternatives include elaborate stave systems that are lowered into steel fermenting tanks. Even cheaper are nylon bags filled with oak chips that can be macerated like a teabag in the maturation vats.

With both of these methods, the wood's provenance and degree of toasting can be specified, just as with barrels.

Wood chips can be an inexpensive way to enhance wine aromas

Alternative Oxygenation
Mimicking the subtle oxygenation that softens and develops wine matured in oak requires no wood at all. Micro-oxygenation systems slowly inject measured streams of tiny air bubbles into stainless steel tanks of maturing wine, achieving much the same result as cask maturation.

BARREL SIZES

Cask size has a direct impact on the wine matured within it. The smaller the barrel, the faster the wine matures since there is a greater ratio of wood surface area to volume of wine, and therefore a greater ingress of air.

Fuder (1000L)

Pipe (550L)

Barrique (225L)

Gonci (136L)

TOP WINE PRODUCERS OF THE LOIRE VALLEY

Domaine de l'Écu
Pays Nantais/Muscadet Sèvre et Maine

La Bretonnière, Le Landreau
☎ 02 40 06 40 91 ☐ by appt

THERE COULD NOT be better publicity for biodynamic cultivation than Guy Bossard and the wines of the Domaine de l'Écu. He manages to put Muscadet on another plane with full, fragrant, complex wines that can even be aged. The regular Muscadet Sèvre et Maine *sur lie* is a classic, and then there are three exceptional *cuvées* nuanced by, and named after, the soils from which they come: Expression de Gneiss, de Granit, and d'Orthogneiss. Bossard also has a stunning traditional method sparkling wine labelled Ludwig Hahn made from Melon de Bourgogne, Folle Blanche, and Chardonnay.

🍷 white 🍾 2005, 2002, 2000, 1999, 1998, 1997 ★ *Muscadet Sèvre et Maine: Expression de Gneiss, Expression de Granit, Expression d'Orthogneiss*

Château de Villeneuve
Anjou-Saumur/Saumur-Champigny

3 rue Jean Brevet, Souzay-Champigny
☎ 02 41 51 14 04
ⓦ www.chateau-villeneuve.com ☐

THE IMPRESSIVE 18th-century château of Villeneuve was built from the local tuffeau stone. The wines are equally remarkable, made in an exacting manner by Jean-Pierre Chevallier. Rich, powerful, and deeply coloured, the red wines produced from Cabernet Franc are a wonderful example of the true potential of Saumur-Champigny. The regular *cuvée* is consistently good

SAUMUR CHAMPIGNY
APPELLATION SAUMUR CHAMPIGNY CONTROLÉE
LE GRAND CLOS
1 9 9 9
Château de Villeneuve
13% vol. 750 ML

Château de Villeneuve label

and in exceptional years (2001, 1999, 1997) the long-ageing Le Grand Clos and Vieilles Vignes are also produced. The Chenin Blanc Saumur Les Cormiers is rich and concentrated.

🍷 red, white 🍾 red: 2005, 2002, 2000, 1999, 1997, 1996 ★ *Saumur-Champigny, Saumur-Champigny Le Grand Clos, Saumur Les Cormiers*

Château Pierre Bise
Anjou-Saumur/Coteaux du Layon

Beaulieu-sur-Layon ☎ 02 41 78 31 44
☐ by appt

CLAUDE PAPIN KNOWS the *terroir* of his 54-ha estate like the back of his hand. This is the reason for the impressive array of wines, which are all linked to the site and soil of his various parcels located within Savennières and the Coteaux du Layon. Selective late harvesting gives the wines a generosity of fruit. Of particular note are the firm but succulent dry white Savennières Clos de Coulaine, the sumptuous sweet Coteaux du Layon Anclaie and Quarts de Chaume, and the concentrated red Anjou-Villages Sur Spilite, produced from Cabernet Sauvignon grapes grown on volcanic soils.

🍷 red, white, dessert 🍾 white: 2005, 2002, 2000,

1999, 1997, 1996 ★ *Coteaux du Layon Anclaie, Savennières Clos de Coulaine, Anjou-Villages Sur Spilite*

Clos Rougeard
Anjou-Saumur/Saumur-Champigny

15 rue de l'Église, Chacé
☎ 02 41 52 92 65 ☐ by appt

THE FOUCAULT BROTHERS, Charly and Nadi, may be a roisterous pair of lads, but they know how to make good wine. Incessant work in the vineyards, old Cabernet Franc vines, low yields, and ageing in oak *barriques* enables them to turn out rich, concentrated Saumur-Champigny that is a long way from the light, fruity red wines generally found in the district. The two top wines, Les Poyeux and Le Bourg, are as elegant, restrained, and structured as many a fine bordeaux. There is also a little full bodied, dry white Saumur.

🍷 red, white 🍾 red: 2005, 2002, 2000, 1999, 1997, 1996 ★ *Saumur-Champigny: Les Poyeux, Le Bourg*

Coulée de Serrant
Anjou-Saumur/Savennières

Château de la Roche-aux-Moines, Savennières ☎ 02 41 72 22 32
ⓦ www.coulee-de-serrant.com ☐

Coulée de Serrant

OWNER NICOLAS JOLY is the arch proponent of biodynamic viticulture *(see p105)* in France, and he advocates it in a proselytizing fashion. The 7-ha *grand cru* Coulée de Serrant is a monopoly, alongside which Joly also owns 3ha in *grand cru* Roche aux Moines and further parcels in regular Savennières. The wines are made in the simplest fashion relying on the quality of the Chenin Blanc grapes. Coulée de Serrant is always dry and full bodied with firm acidity and the aroma of honey and quince. It is best served decanted in advance.

🖼 white 🔲 2005, 2002, 2000, 1999, 1997, 1996, 1995 ★ Coulée de Serrant, Roche aux Moines Clos de la Bergerie

Domaine des Baumard
Anjou-Saumur/Coteaux du Layon

8 rue de l'Abbaye, Rochefort-sur-Loire
☎ 02 41 78 70 03
Ⓦ www.baumard.fr 🔲

THIS DOMAINE extends both sides of the Loire River in Savennières and the Coteaux du Layon giving Florent Baumard the opportunity to produce a wide range of delectable wines. The dry white Savennières Clos St-Yves is firm but rounded. In exceptional years (2000, 1997) there is also the Trie Spéciale, which is even more intense. From the Coteaux du Layon, the sweet Clos Ste-Catherine has marked elegance, while the Quarts-de-Chaume offers a huge concentration of rich, succulent fruit. In recent years the red Anjou has improved considerably.

🖼 red, white, rosé, dessert 🔲 white: 2005, 2002, 2000, 1999, 1997, 1996, 1995, 1993, 1990 ★ Coteaux du Layon Clos Ste-Catherine, Quarts-de-Chaume, Savennières Trie Spéciale

Domaine des Baumard label

Domaine Patrick Baudouin
Anjou-Saumur/Coteaux du Layon

Princé, Chaudefonds-sur-Layon
☎ 02 41 78 66 04 Ⓦ www.patrick-baudouin-layon.com 🔲 by appt

SELECTIVE HARVESTING has always been the dictum at this domaine, producing wines of natural richness and fruit concentration. According to the vintage, a number of Coteaux du Layon *cuvées* are produced from Chenin Blanc, with varying degrees of sugar. In order of richness, these are Après Minuit, Maria Juby, Grains Nobles, and Les Bruandières. This domaine also makes a wonderfully soft, fresh, minerally apple and quince dry Anjou Blanc and some fruity red Anjou-Villages.

🖼 red, white, dessert 🔲 white: 2005, 2002, 2000, 1999, 1997, 1996, 1995 ★ Anjou Blanc, Coteaux du Layon: Grains Nobles, Maria Juby

Domaine Bernard Baudry
Touraine/Chinon

13 Coteau de Sonnay, Cravant-les-Coteaux ☎ 02 47 93 15 79 🔲 by appt

BERNARD BAUDRY began in 1977 with just 2ha in Chinon and has since built this domaine – which he now runs with his son Matthieu – up to an impressive 30ha. The wines are aged in cellars excavated from the tuffeau rock. La Croix Boissée from Cabernet Franc grown on limestone soils and Grézeaux on gravel are structured and good for ageing, while Granges is a softer, fruitier Chinon. A new *cuvée*, Clos Guillot, made from ungrafted vines, was

Domaine Patrick Baudouin label

introduced in 2001, and a little fresh, white Chinon is also produced from Chenin Blanc.

🖼 red, white 🔲 red: 2005, 2002, 2000, 1999, 1997, 1996, 1995, 1993, 1990 ★ Chinon: Granges, Grézeaux, La Croix Boissée

Domaine de la Taille aux Loups
Touraine/Montlouis

8 rue des Aitres, Husseau, Montlouis-sur-Loire ☎ 02 47 45 11 11 🔲 by appt

FORMER WINE merchant Jacky Blot created this domaine in 1988 with the purchase of three tiny parcels of vines. He now has 16ha in Montlouis and Vouvray. The wines are elegant rather than powerful. Chenin Blanc grapes are carefully selected and vinified in oak barrels that are regularly renewed. There are two dry Montlouis: the pristine, linear Les Dix Arpents and the Cuvée Remus, which in youth has an atypical toasted oak flavour. Depending on the vintage there is also a *demi-sec* and the sweet Cuvée des Loups, as well as sparkling wines.

🖼 white, sparkling, dessert 🔲 2005, 2002, 2000, 1999, 1998, 1997, 1996 ★ Montlouis: Les Dix Arpents, Cuvée des Loups (demi-sec)

Domaine du Clos Naudin
Touraine/Vouvray

14 rue de la Croix Buisée, Vouvray **☎** *02 47 52 71 46*
○ *by appt*

PHILIPPE FOREAU describes the firm, minerally edge in older vintages of his Vouvray Chenin Blanc wines as almost "Chablisesque". Whether *sec*, *demi-sec*, *moelleux*, or – in exceptional years when botrytis appears – *moelleux réserve* (2005, 2003, 1997), all the wines are ripe, crystalline pure, and age for a considerable length of time. Some splendid traditional method vintage and non-vintage sparkling Vouvray is also produced.

▨ *white, sparkling* **▧** *2005, 2002, 2000, 1999, 1998, 1997, 1996, 1995, 1993, 1990* ★ *Vouvray (sec, réserve moelleux, sparkling)*

Domaine Henry Marionnet
Touraine/Vin de Pays

Domaine de la Charmoise, Soings **☎** *02 54 98 70 73* **ⓦ** *www.henry-marionnet.com* **○** *by appt*

HENRY MARIONNET has been something of a pioneer in his native Touraine, replanting his 60-ha vineyard, producing clean, modern style Sauvignon Blanc and fruity Gamay *nouveau*. Now he has taken to reviving forgotten grape varieties in the vineyard such as white Romorantin (first planted in 1850) in his Provignage and Gamay de Bouze in Les Cépages Cubliés (both *vins de pays*). There is also a wine called Vinifera from ungrafted Gamay. All three wines reveal a superb purity of fruit.

▨ *red, white* **▧** *white: 2005, 2002, 2000* ★ *Touraine Sauvignon Blanc, Provignage, Vinifera*

Domaine Henry Marionnet label

Domaine Huet
Touraine/Vouvray

11 rue de la Croix Buisée, Vouvray **☎** *02 47 52 78 87* **ⓦ** *www. huet-echansonne.com* **○**

GASTON HUET built the reputation of this Vouvray domaine after World War II. His son-in-law, Noël Pinguet, has carried on the tradition and turned the vineyard over to biodynamic cultivation along the way. The wines, made from Chenin Blanc, are produced from three superb sites: Le Mont, Le Haut-Lieu, and Le Clos du Bourg, and depending on the vintage can be either dry, medium-dry, or sweet. All three wines have tremendous ageing potential.

▨ *white* **▧** *2005, 2002, 2000, 1999, 1998, 1997, 1996, 1995, 1993, 1990* ★ *Vouvray: Le Mont, Le Haut-Lieu, Le Clos du Bourg*

Domaine Philippe Alliet
Touraine/Chinon

L'Ouche-Mondé, Cravant-les-Coteaux **☎** *02 47 93 17 62* **○** *by appt*

PHILIPPE ALLIET IS a reserved but determined man. After 20 years of extraordinary effort he and his wife Claude have made the Domaine Philippe Alliet the point of reference for red wine-making in Chinon. Much inspired by the techniques practised at the top estates in Bordeaux, Alliet has applied a number of these at his domaine, including ageing in Bordeaux *barriques*. Three wines are produced from Cabernet Franc – a light regular *cuvée* and the more structured and concentrated Vieilles Vignes and Coteau de Noiré.

▨ *red* **▧** *2005, 2002, 2000, 1999, 1998, 1997, 1996, 1995* ★ *Chinon: Vieilles Vignes, Coteau de Noiré*

Domaine Yannick Amirault
Touraine/Bourgueil

5 pavillon du Grand Clos, Bourgueil **☎** *02 47 97 78 07* **○** *by appt*

YANNICK AMIRAULT is such a dedicated *vigneron* that he still prunes the vines on his 18-ha estate himself. He produces a number of Cabernet Franc *cuvées* from different soils and ages of vine, all with a wonderful purity of fruit. From St-Nicolas-de-Bourgueil, there is Les Graviers and the firmer Les Malgagnes, while from Bourgueil he offers La Petite Cave, as well as the finely textured Les Quartiers and Le Grand Clos, all from vines of an honourable age.

Domaine Yannick Amirault

▨ *red* **▧** *2005, 2002, 2000, 1999, 1997, 1996* ★ *St-Nicolas-de-Bourgueil Les Malgagnes, Bourgueil: Les Quartiers, Le Grand Clos*

Château de Tracy
Central Loire/ Pouilly-Fumé

58150 Tracy-sur-Loire
📞 03 86 26 15 12 ☐ by appt

TRADITION IS WELL ingrained at Château de Tracy; the vine has been cultivated on the site since 1396, and the d'Estutt d'Assay family (of Scottish origin) have been resident since the 16th century. Over the past 10 years Henry d'Estutt d'Assay has replanted two-thirds of the 29-ha vineyard and steadily improved methods of cultivation. There is only one wine: produced from Sauvignon Blanc grapes grown on limestone and silex soils, and vinified and aged in stainless steel and concrete vats. It has a classic mineral and citrus intensity and is best with a year's bottle age.
🍷 white 🍇 2005, 2002, 2000, 1999, 1998 ★ Pouilly-Fumé Château de Tracy

Domaine Alphonse Mellot
Central Loire/Sancerre

Domaine de la Moussière, Sancerre
📞 02 48 54 07 41
🖥 www.mellot.com ☐ by appt

THERE HAVE BEEN 19 Alphonse Mellots, including the present winemaker and manager of the domaine. The *cuvée* Génération XIX, which comes as white (Sauvignon Blanc) and red (Pinot Noir) Sancerre, pays wry homage to this feat. The other Sauvignon Blancs from the 48-ha estate are all beautifully crafted and labelled. Domaine de la Moussière is the regular *cuvée*, all freshness and citrus fruit. The intense Cuvée Edmond comes from old vines and, like Génération XIX, is aged in oak cask. Its

Domaine Alphonse Mellot label

red double is as good as Pinot Noir gets in Sancerre.
🍷 red, white 🍇 white: 2005, 2002, 2000, 1999, 1998, 1997, 1996, 1995 ★ Sancerre: Domaine de la Moussière, Cuvée Edmond, Génération XIX (red)

Domaine Didier Dagueneau
Central Loire/ Pouilly-Fumé

1–7 rue Ernesto Ché Guevara, St-Andelain 📞 03 86 39 15 62 ☐ by appt

IT IS UNCLEAR EXACTLY what will happen to this domaine after Didier Dagueneau's untimely death in a microlite accident in September 2008. His wines are the finest expression of Sauvignon Blanc in Pouilly-Fumé. All are aged in oak barrels and are precise and finely honed.

En Chailloux is the softest and largest in volume, Buisson Renard citrous, Pur Sang generous, and Silex minerally and pure.
🍷 white 🍇 2005, 2002, 2000, 1999, 1998, 1997 ★ Pouilly-Fumé: Buisson Renard, Pur Sang, Silex

Domaine Henri Bourgeois
Central Loire/Sancerre

Chavignol, Sancerre
📞 02 48 78 53 20 🖥 www. bourgeois-sancerre.com ☐

THIS DYNAMIC COMPANY is located in the village of Chavignol, equally famous for its Sancerre as for its goats' cheese (Crottin de Chavignol). The primary production is Sancerre but the estate also has vineyards in Pouilly-Fumé, Quincy, and even Marlborough in New Zealand. A flattering range of Sancerres is produced from specific sites, soils, and Sauvignon Blanc vines of varying age. Among these, les Baronnes is a crisp, fresh standard *cuvée*, Le MD de Bourgeois more minerally and intense, while La Côte des Monts Damnés is long and complex.
🍷 red, white, rosé 🍇 white: 2005, 2002, 2000, 1999, 1998, 1997, 1996, 1995 ★ Le MD de Bourgeois, La Côte des Monts Damnés

Harvest time at Domaine Henri Bourgeois in Sancerre

CHAMPAGNE

*A*T ITS GLORIOUS BEST, CHAMPAGNE HAS NO PEERS. *It offers all the elements of a truly great sparkling wine: freshness and vivacity to lift the spirits, complexity of aroma, and richness on the palate balanced by fine acidity. While many winegrowing regions produce good sparkling wine, Champagne has a monopoly of the most celebrated brands and is the benchmark by which all other sparkling wines are judged.*

Champagne is France's most northerly established vineyard. Cool temperatures and long slow ripening of the fruit help to ensure high acidity levels, which are vital in champagne's long, slow ageing process. Its complexity, however, is not just a result of the marginal climate; a magical combination of climate, chalky soil, and three centuries of human endeavour have enabled a unique wine to emerge.

1930s champagne poster

Originally, Champagne was a red wine production area; wines were made in autumn and left to settle over winter, when the cold would halt fermentation. As spring arrived and the wines warmed up, they would begin to referment in the bottle – giving a slight spritz. These young, fizzy wines became fashionable in England in the mid-17th century. Later that century, Champagne's producers, led by Benedictine monk Dom Pérignon (who was in charge of the cellars at Hautvillier Abbey), found a way to refine and control this secondary fermentation. The modern era of champagne was born.

Today, champagne is usually a blend of two or three grape varieties (Pinot Noir, Pinot Meunier, and Chardonnay) but also a judicious mix from a number of vineyards *(crus)*. Additionally, unlike almost any other great wine, champagne is largely a blend of grapes from more than one harvest. Single vintage wine is made, but only in the best years.

With around 300 million bottles produced every year, sparkling wine is Champagne's *raison d'être*. Most of this valuable vineyard is in the hands of some 19,000 growers. Only about a tenth is owned by 264 *négociants*, who include among them the major international houses that have established Champagne's inimitable reputation worldwide.

Moët & Chandon's Château de Saran in the Côte des Blancs

◁ **Bottles of La Grande Dame in the cellars of Veuve Clicquot Ponsardin, Reims**

THE TRADITIONAL METHOD

T HE TRADITIONAL METHOD, *or* méthode traditionnelle *in France, is the most quality-focused way of producing sparkling wine. This costly and labour-intensive technique was pioneered in the region of Champagne and developed over many centuries. Now used all over the world, it is responsible for virtually all the finest bottles of fizz today. 'Champagne' applies exclusively to sparkling wine produced in the Champagne region, but the term 'traditional method' indicates that wines from outside the region have been manufactured with the same process and meticulous attention to quality.*

Louis Roederer and Pol Roger champagne

The Production Process

Grapes: Many grape varieties are used in sparkling wine, although the Champagne grapes Chardonnay, Pinot Noir, and Pinot Meunier are particularly popular around the world. Acidity is an important component, so grapes may be harvested earlier than usual. Hand-harvesting is a legal requirement in Champagne and helps growers avoid damaged black grapes staining the free-run juice.

Pressing: The gentler the pressing, the better, to avoid harsh flavours and tannins. In Champagne there are strict laws on how much juice can be extracted from each batch of grapes.

First Fermentation: The grape must, or juice, is fermented in stainless steel (or occasionally old oak casks) to produce an acidic white wine with moderate levels of alcohol. The still wines from different grape varieties and vineyards are normally fermented separately to allow a number of combinations at the blending stage. At this point most sparkling wine undergoes malolactic fermentation *(see p40)* – a natural process that converts hard malic acid into soft lactic acid and adds a creamy texture to the wine.

Blending: The vast majority of sparkling wines are made from a combination of grape varieties,

***Remueurs* at work in the cellars of Perrier-Jouët**

grown in different vineyards and – for non-vintage releases – from a number of years. In part, this practice originated in Champagne because the climate could not be relied upon to deliver healthy, ripe grapes every year. Blending different vintages helped a Champagne house to produce a consistent style of wine. There **Pinot Noir** is much more to blending **grapes** *(assemblage)* than attaining consistency, however. In the hands of a skilled winemaker, a range of wines with diverse flavours can be combined to produce an

overall blend that is far greater than the sum of its parts.

Second Fermentation: The blended wine is then bottled with a mixture known as *liqueur de tirage*, containing wine, sugar, and yeast. This initiates a secondary fermentation which happens inside the bottle, converting the sugar into alcohol and producing the gas carbon dioxide, which is responsible for the fizz. A crown cap is added to seal the bottle.

Maturation: This stage is absolutely crucial in the development of a quality sparkling wine. During maturation a process known as yeast autolysis occurs, where the

Sediments collected in cap

spent yeast cells or lees react with the wine, creating highly desirable bready, yeasty flavours.

Removal of Sediment: To allow the lees to be removed after maturation, the bottle is gradually rotated (over a period of six to eight weeks when done by hand) so that the sediment slides down to the neck, a procedure known as riddling or *remuage*. The neck containing the lees is then frozen, the bottle stood upright and the crown cap removed. The frozen sediment is then expelled under pressure – in a process known as disgorgement or *dégorgement*.

Dosage & Corking: *Dosage* is the name given to the replenishment of the small amount of wine which is lost during disgorgement. The liquid used to refill the bottle is known as *liqueur d'expédition* and contains a mixture of reserve wine and sugar. Nearly all sparkling wines will have some sugar added to balance their acidity, the amount varying according to the style. A large cork is forced into the bottle at considerable pressure to ensure a strong seal, and a wire basket is then normally fastened on top to reinforce it.

In the cellar at Alfred Gratien

CHAMPAGNE LABEL LAW

To distinguish between its numerous different styles, champagne has a range of terms all of its own.

Brut: The style of champagne depends on the amount of sugar added at *dosage* and ranges from extra brut (very dry) and brut (dry), to *demi-sec* (medium sweet) and *doux* (extremely sweet).

Non-vintage: Non-vintage (NV) is made from a blend of grapes from different years and matured for at least 15 months on its lees.

Vintage: Vintage champagne must come from a single harvest and requires at least three years of maturation. The best recent vintages across the whole of Champagne are 2002, 1999, 1998, 1997, 1996, 1995, 1990, 1989, 1988, 1985, 1983.

Krug's Grande Cuvée

Rosé: Champagne is one of the few appellations that allows rosé to be made from a blend of red and white wines.

Blanc de blancs: Made entirely from white grape varieties (almost always 100 per cent Chardonnay), this is the longest lived of all champagnes.

Blanc de noirs: Produced solely from black grape varieties (Pinot Noir and Pinot Meunier), *blanc de noirs* tends to have a fruitier flavour than conventional champagne.

Grande Marque: A term found on many champagne labels, meaning 'Great Brand'. Although a number of the leading houses use this phrase, it actually has little meaning as a guarantee of quality in isolation.

Bottle sizes: Champagne comes in a range of bottle sizes. Magnums (two x regular 75cl bottles) are considered the best for maturation. Larger sizes include Jeroboam (four x 75cl) and Methuselah (eight x 75cl), through to Melchior (24 x 75cl).

Cuvée de prestige: Many houses release top-of-the-range, no-expense-spared bottlings. Often released as single vintage wines, *cuvées* de prestige are made using the region's finest grapes and matured for lengthy periods before release. Examples include Dom Pérignon (Moët & Chandon) and La Grande Dame (Veuve Clicquot).

Veuve Clicquot Ponsardin Brut label

WINE MAP OF CHAMPAGNE

KEY

Champagne

THE CHAMPAGNE AOC extends 150km north to south and 115km east to west and is made up of five distinct vineyard areas. Épernay sits at the heart of the three largest and most prestigious production zones: Montagne de Reims, Vallée de la Marne, and Côte des

Picking grapes at Alfred Gratien

Blancs. Continuing south from the Côte des Blancs is the lesser-known Côte de Sézanne, while at the appellation's southerly extreme, some 100km from Épernay, is the Côte des Bar. The appellation includes 17 *grands crus*, 44 *premiers crus,* and a total vineyard area of 33,500ha.

Champagne flute

CHAMPAGNE'S NÉGOCIANT HOUSES

Champagne's many *négociant* houses buy in the majority of their grapes from growers spread all over the appellation, and their physical location usually reveals little about the style of wine they produce. Blending the wines to maintain a specific house style is a complex process, with major firms using as many as 100 different *crus* (as Moët does in its Brut Impérial *cuvée*), to create the desired taste. Very few houses grow all their own grapes; Bollinger and Louis Roederer are unusual in supplying around 75 per cent of their own needs. Some *négociants* buy in everything and have no vineyard holdings of their own.

Champagne's largest *négociants* tend to have their cellars based either in Reims or Épernay. Many line the Avenue de Champagne in Épernay, and in Reims a number (Ruinart, Veuve Clicquot Ponsardin, Taittinger, and Pommery) cluster around the Place du Général Gouraud. Most are open to visitors, offering tours that usually include a tasting. The next major centre, which boasts some of the best medium-sized producers, is Aÿ and adjoining Mareuil-sur-Aÿ where Bollinger, Billecart-Salmon, Deutz, Gosset, and Philipponnat are to be found.

The five best-selling champagne producers are: Moët & Chandon; Veuve Clicquot Ponsardin; Nicolas Feuillatte; Laurent-Perrier; and Piper-Heidsieck.

Viktor & Rolf's 'upside-down' bottle design for Piper-Heidsieck's Rosé Sauvage

CHAMPAGNE: TOP PRODUCERS

CHAMPAGNE *p170*
Billecart-Salmon *p172*
Champagne Alfred Gratien *p172*
Champagne Bollinger *p172*
Champagne Charles Heidsieck *p172*
Champagne Deutz *p172*
Champagne Drappier *p173*
Champagne Henriot *p173*
Champagne Jacquesson & Fils *p173*
Champagne Lanson *p173*
Champagne Perrier Jouët *p173*
Champagne Philipponnat *p174*
Champagne Salon *p174*
Champagne Taittinger *p174*
Champagne Veuve Clicquot Ponsardin *p174*
Krug *p174*
Laurent-Perrier *p175*
Louis Roederer *p175*
Moët & Chandon *p175*
Pol Roger *p175*
Ruinart *p175*

Vineyards and château in Champagne

TERROIR AT A GLANCE

Latitude: 48–49.5°N. The location at the northern edge of the winemaking belt means ripening can only be achieved by stretching the vine's growth cycle to the limit.

Altitude: 60–360m.

Topography: The landscape comprises a gently undulating, windswept plain intersected by rivers flowing east to west. Vineyards nestle on the hillsides and the gentler slopes of the river valleys, where there is protection from the westerly wind.

Soil: Porous chalky subsoil that drains well and holds water for the vine. Chalk breaks through the thin surface soil in places, reflecting sunshine onto the vines.

Climate: Champagne is a 'cool climate' appellation. It is exposed to storms and wind from the English Channel.

Temperature: July averages are 18.5°C in Reims and 19.5°C in Épernay.

Rainfall: Annual averages are 600mm in Reims and 670mm in Épernay.

Viticultural hazards: Spring frosts – in 2003, temperatures plunged below -6°C and more than half the harvest was lost.

PERFECT CASE: CHAMPAGNE

⑤ Billecart-Salmon Cuvée Nicolas-François Billecart Vintage ££££

⑤ Bollinger Grande Année Vintage Rosé ££££

⑤ Charles Heidsieck Brut Réserve NV (Mis en Cave) £££

⑤ Deutz Brut Classic NV £££

⑤ Duval-Leroy Les Clos des Bouveries Vintage Brut £££

⑤ Gosset Cuvée Célébris Extra Brut Blanc de Blancs ££££

⑤ Jacquesson & Fils NV Cuvée (individually numbered) £££

⑤ Krug Grande Cuvée NV ££££

⑤ Moët & Chandon Dom Pérignon Œnothèque ££££+

⑤ Philipponnat Clos des Goisses ££££

⑤ Pol Roger Blanc de Chardonnay Vintage ££££

⑤ Veuve Cliquot Vintage Brut Rare ££££

Moët & Chandon and Billecart-Salmon champagnes

0 ⊢ km ⟶ 100

Snow-covered Moët & Chandon vineyard on the Côte des Blancs

WINEGROWING AREAS OF CHAMPAGNE

THE CHAMPAGNE APPELLATION divides into five main production areas, each strongly associated with one of the three main grape varieties: Pinot Noir, Pinot Meunier, and Chardonnay. The majority of champagne is made from all three varieties from different *crus*, or villages, in differing proportions. There are nearly 12,900ha of Pinot Noir, just over 11,000ha of Pinot Meunier, and around 9,500ha of Chardonnay in the whole appellation.

In this marginal climate, slight *terroir* variations can significantly affect the quality of grapes. For this reason, the vineyards in Champagne are quality-rated under a system known as the Échelle des Crus ('ladder of growths'). All 319 villages in the appellation are classified, with the 17 *grands crus* all at 100 per cent, the 44 *premiers crus* between 90 and 99 per cent, and the rest in the lowest bracket, anywhere between 80 and 89 per cent.

Alfred Gratien label

🗌 *chalky* 🏵 *Pinot Noir, Pinot Meunier* 🏵 *Chardonnay* 🍾 *sparkling*

Montagne de Reims

MORE A WIDE PLATEAU than a mountain, the Montagne de Reims forms a U-shaped arc running south from Reims, with sheltered vineyards sloping down towards the Vesle and Marne rivers. This is not one homogeneous vineyard, but rather one where the differing microclimate, aspect, and exposure of individual sites result in a large range of

styles. Soil types may also vary, although all the *grands crus* are on the same chalky bed for which Champagne is rightly famous. Montagne de Reims is home to nine of the appellation's 17 *grands crus*.

This area is best known for Pinot Noir (41 per cent), and the reputation of the most famous *grand cru* villages of Mailly, Verzenay, Verzy, Ambonnay, and Bouzy is based on the quality of this variety. To the west of Ludes and in the Petite Montagne southwest of Reims, Pinot Meunier becomes more evident. There are also some important pockets of Chardonnay, most significantly in the *premier cru* villages of Villers-Marmery and Trépail.

Vallée de la Marne

THERE ARE VINEYARDS planted on the north side of the Vallée de la Marne from Tours-sur-Marne going west and on both sides to the west of Épernay all the way to Saacy-sur-Marne. The majority of plantings here are Pinot Meunier (63 per cent), which because of its late budbreak and early ripening is not as vulnerable in this low-lying, frost-prone valley. Less refined than Pinot Noir and Chardonnay, Meunier has a reputation for being Champagne's workhorse grape, and is widely used by the major houses because its fruitiness and early development help soften their non-vintage blends, making them more approachable when young.

Côte des Blancs

THE NAME OF THIS DISTRICT, which runs south from Épernay, comes from the fact that it is almost exclusively devoted to the cultivation of white grapes. The vineyards are predominantly east-facing and are mostly on the purest form of chalky belemnite subsoil, rich in minerals and trace elements. Ninety-seven per cent of the Côte des Blancs grapes are Chardonnay. Chardonnay grapes from the five *grands crus* – Cramant, Avize, Oger, Le Mesnil-sur-Oger, and Chouilly – are the most sought after in the appellation and command the highest prices. They give freshness and finesse to any blend, and when used unadulterated – as in the *blanc de blancs* of Salon – they can produce wines of great longevity and intensity.

Côte de Sézanne

THIS RAPIDLY DEVELOPING DISTRICT of just 1,360ha is virtually a continuation of the Côte des Blancs, separated from it only by the marshes of St Gond. The subsoil here is mostly clay and clayey silt with some pockets of chalk, and the vines are oriented towards the southeast. Like the Côte des Blancs, it is mainly planted with Chardonnay (62 per cent), with around 20 per cent given over to Pinot Noir. Thanks partly to the favourable aspect, the wines tend to be more forward and fruitier than those in the Côte des Blancs, some say slightly more rustic and less fine. Unusually, a general rating is given for this area on the Échelle des Crus: 87 per cent for white grapes and 85 per cent for red grapes.

Côte des Bar

THIS AREA IN THE AUBE *département* contains just over a fifth (7,105ha) of the total vineyard area in Champagne and is an important source for vigorous, full-flavoured, and ripe Pinot Noir. Nearly half Champagne's Pinot Noir comes from this area, and most of the major *négociants* source grapes from the region to blend in their non-vintage wines.

The three communes that make up Les Riceys (Ricey-Haut, Ricey-Haut-Rive, and Ricey-Bas) are the only places in France where wine may be produced under three different appellations, one sparkling (Champagne) and two still (red Coteaux-Champenois and Rosé des Riceys).

TOP CO-OPERATIVES

The co-operatives in Champagne have been radically overhauled in the past decade, and the best are now a valuable source of well-priced, quality champagne. A few of them are recommended below.

Champagne Beaumont des Crayères
Ⓦ www.champagne-beaumont.com

This medium-sized co-operative is located in Mardeuil, where most of the 200-odd growers work part-time tending their 80ha of vines at the weekends and on holidays. The well-made, characterful range hits a high point with its Nostalgie vintage, a classy act at the price (££–£££).

Champagne H Blin & Co
Ⓦ www.champagne-blin.com

The attractive, easy-drinking styles of champagne made by this co-op are based on Pinot Meunier and offer good value (££–£££).

Champagne Jacquart
Ⓦ www.champagne-jacquart.fr

Champagne Jacquart is now the preferred brand of three different co-operative groups that all operate under the Alliance umbrella, but also make their own wines under the Pannier and Veuve A Devaux, and Raoul Collet labels. Jacquart's rosé and vintage wines have been consistently good for a number of years and offer excellent value for money (££–££££).

Jacquart *cuvée* on ice

Champagne Nicolas Feuillatte CVC
Ⓦ www.feuillatte.com

This is the largest co-operative group in Champagne: its 4,900 members between them own nearly a fifth (over 6,000ha) of the appellation's vineyards. Most of its wines are Chardonnay-based blends, the youngest of which can be aggressive. Continued innovation has seen the introduction of zero-dosage Brut Extrem' and a vintaged, oak-aged Cuvée 225, while the six single *grands crus* wines will be blended together to produce one style in future (££–££££).

Union Champagne
Ⓦ www.de-saint-gall.com

The 1,800 members of this co-operative have the largest group holdings of *grands crus* (800ha) and *premiers crus* (400ha) in the Côte des Blancs. The de St Gall brand is a fine blend of wines from four Côte des Blancs *grand cru* villages: Avize, Cramant, Oger, and Le Mesnil-sur-Oger. The wines are well priced (££–£££).

TOP PRODUCERS OF CHAMPAGNE

Billecart-Salmon
Champagne

40 rue Carnot, Mareuil-sur-Aÿ
☎ 03 26 52 60 22
W www.champagne-billecart.fr

BILLECART-SALMON, established in 1818, is a small family-run house that makes a range of consistently fine wines. It is particularly admired for its delicate, beautifully balanced rosés, both the non-vintage style and the vintage Cuvée Elisabeth Salmon. Although not as well known as near neighbour Bollinger, Billecart-Salmon also makes excellent vintage champagne that ages very well, though in a very different style. In 2003 it launched a 100 per cent Pinot Noir from its walled vineyard (Clos St Hilaire) in Mareuil-sur-Aÿ; the first *cuvée* was made from the impressive 1995 vintage.
🍷 *sparkling* 🍇 *1999, 1998*
★ *NV Brut Rosé, Cuvée Elizabeth Salmon Rosé*

Champagne Alfred Gratien
Champagne

30 rue Maurice-Cerveaux, Épernay
☎ 03 26 54 38 20
W www.alfredgratien.com

ALFRED GRATIEN IS a traditional producer that still carries out the initial fermentation in oak barrels, giving a distinctive style. The Chardonnay-driven vintage wines are notably long-lived, partly because they do not undergo malolactic fermentation. They may be cellared for many years to good effect.
🍷 *sparkling* 🍇 *1998, 1997, 1996* ★ *Vintage*

Billecart-Salmon label

Champagne Bollinger
Champagne

18 blvd du Maréchal de Lattre de Tassigny, Aÿ ☎ 03 26 53 33 66
W www.champagne-bollinger.fr

THIS DEEPLY TRADITIONAL family-owned house is committed to the high production standards set out in its 1992 'charter of ethics and quality', which, with its stringent rules, has become a blueprint for quality in Champagne. Based in *grand cru* Aÿ, Bollinger has a 143-ha estate that supplies 70 per cent of its grapes. These underpin the high standard of its muscular, complex Pinot Noir-based wines, which age gracefully.

Bollinger RD (recently disgorged) is a vintage wine that is aged for longer on its lees, and only disgorged just prior to release to preserve freshness. Lovers of rich, mature vintage wines are advised to buy the considerably less expensive Grande Année and age it themselves. There is also a Vieilles Vignes Françaises – Blanc de Noirs from two tiny parcels of pre-phylloxera vines that has much in common with single-vineyard champagnes like Clos du Mesnil and Clos des Goisses.
🍷 *sparkling* 🍇 *2000, 1999, 1997, 1996, 1995*
★ *Grande Année (white, rosé)*

Champagne Bollinger

Champagne Charles Heidsieck
Champagne

4 blvd Henry Vasnier, Reims
☎ 03 26 84 43 50
W www.charlesheidsieck.com

MOST CHAMPAGNE houses like to be judged on the quality of their non-vintage Brut. On that basis alone, Heidsieck deserves its reputation for excellence; its Mis en Cave non-vintage regularly stands out in tastings. Other wines also delight including the vintage, the vintage rosé and the 100 per cent Chardonnay Blanc des Millénaires, the 1995 of which is still available. Winemaker since 2002, Régis Camus has maintained the high standards of his predecessor Daniel Thibault.
🍷 *sparkling* 🍇 *2000* ★ *NV Mis en Cave, Blanc des Millénaires*

Champagne Deutz
Champagne

16 rue Jeanson, Aÿ ☎ 03 26 56 93 96
W www.champagne-deutz.com

A DISTINGUISHED HOUSE in Aÿ that merits a much wider audience, Deutz has long enjoyed a good reputation among aficionados for its fine vintage Blanc de Blancs and delicate, beautifully balanced luxury *cuvée* William Deutz. The company was bought by Louis Roederer in 1993, and new owner Jean-Claude Rouzaud has invested wisely. He re-launched Deutz non-vintage Brut Classic in 1994, and has watched it become one of the best and most consistent performers in Champagne. The Brut Classic with extra cellar age has added complexity, and a new all-Chardonnay vintage luxury *cuvée*, L'Amour de Deutz,

should bring further acclaim.
■ *sparkling* ▲ *2002, 2000*
★ *NV Brut Classic, Blanc de Blancs*

Champagne Drappier
Champagne

Grand Rue, Urville ☎ *03 25 27 40
15* ⓦ *www.champagne-
drappier.com*

FAMILY-RUN *négociant*
Drappier is arguably the
best in the Côte des Bars –
an area that, according
to winemaker Michel
Drappier, is not the place
to make elegant and delicate
champagne. Instead he
produces wines with plenty of
character; and as this style has
gained popularity, the profile
of the company has been
raised dramatically. Drappier's
non-vintage *cuvée* Carte
D'Or is a gutsy, Pinot Noir-
dominated, structured wine.
The vintage wines, particularly
the single-parcel Grande
Sendrée, show the potential
of this underrated part of
the appellation. The range
also includes an excellent
Burgundian-style rosé, and
a no-dosage Brut Nature.
■ *sparkling* ▲ *2003, 2002, 2000*
★ *Grande Sendrée, NV Carte D'Or*

Champagne Henriot
Champagne

*3 place des Droits de l'Homme,
Reims* ☎ *03 26 89 53 00*
ⓦ *www.champagne-henriot.com*

JOSEPH HENRIOT is the man who
established Veuve Clicquot's
modern reputation. Since he
left Clicquot, he has restored
the standing of Bouchard
Père & Fils *(see p104)* and
William Fèvre *(see p95).* He
also runs this family company,
and although it is not well
known, its wines are worth
hunting out. There is an
attractive Blanc de Blancs
and a classy prestige line,
Cuvée des Enchanteleurs,

Various sized bottles of Drappier champagne

but the star of the range is
the Brut Vintage, capable
of long ageing and one of
Champagne's real bargains.
■ *sparkling* ▲ *2000, 1998* ★ *Brut
Vintage, Cuvée des Enchanteleurs,
NV Blanc de Blancs*

Champagne Jacquesson & Fils
Champagne

68 rue du Colonel Fabien, Dizy
☎ *03 26 55 69 11*

THIS SMALL, independently
minded producer is distancing
itself from the crowd by
making its non-vintage *cuvée*
a one-off, different each year,
but always the best possible
blend. Cuvée No 728, based
around the 2000 harvest,
launched the series in 2003,
and the wines that follow will
be numbered sequentially,
with Cuvée 732, based on
the 2004 harvest, launched in
2008. While a single blended
vintage is still produced, the
rest of the range has evolved
into four vintaged, single-
vineyard, varietal cuvées: Dizy
Corne Bautray (Chardonnay),
Aÿ Vauzelle Terme (Pinot
Noir), Avize Champ Caïn
(Chardonnay), and finally a
saignée pink fizz, Dizy Terres
Rouges Rosé.
■ *sparkling* ▲ *2002, 2000, 1997*
★ *NV Cuvée (individually
numbered), Signature*

Champagne Lanson
Champagne

12 blvd Lundy, Reims ☎ *03 26 78
50 50* ⓦ *www.lanson.fr*

LANSON'S BLACK LABEL *cuvée* is
one of the few non-vintage
champagnes not to under-
go malolactic fermen-
tation (which makes the
wines more approachable
in their youth), and it can
seem austere as a result.
However, a couple of
years' bottle age show
how well it is made.
Vintage Lanson can be very
good (as in 1995, 1989,
1988, and 1976), and the
brand's three prestige Noble
Cuvée styles, particularly the
vintage Blanc de Blancs,
show real elegance.
■ *sparkling* ▲ *1999, 1998, 1997*
★ *Blanc de Blancs, Noble Cuvée*

Champagne Perrier Jouët
Champagne

26 ave de Champagne, Épernay
☎ *03 26 53 38 00*
ⓦ *www.perrier-jouet.com*

AFTER SEVERAL CHANGES of
ownership, the future looks
more settled for Perrier Jouët
and its sister brand GH
Mumm. They are now both
run by French drinks giant
Pernod-Ricard, which has
already shown a keenness
to develop the premium
styles of each marque.
Improvements across the
range under winemaker
Hervé Deschamps, who took
over in 1993, have been
consolidated. *Prestige cuvée*
Belle Époque, packaged in
the famous flower-motif
bottle and now made in a
blanc de blancs style as well
as a white and rosé, has
become a more consistent
performer again.
■ *sparkling* ▲ *2002, 1999*
★ *Belle Époque (white, rosé)*

Champagne Philipponnat
Champagne

13 rue du Pont, Mareuil-sur-Aÿ
03 26 56 93 00
www.champagnephilipponnat.com

OWNER Bruno Paillard's first priority on acquiring this house was to restore its magnificent, steep south-facing vineyard, Clos des Goisses. Now Charles Philipponnat (who was working for Moët & Chandon in South America until Paillard bought him back to run the house his family used to own) is quietly adjusting and improving the other wines in the range. Philipponnat is a house whose reputation is likely to climb in the near future.
sparkling 2002, 2000, 1999
★ Clos des Goisses

Champagne Salon
Champagne

Le Mesnil-sur-Oger 03 26 57 51 65

SALON IS AN exceptional wine. It comes from *grand cru* Le Mesnil-sur-Oger in the Côte des Blancs, it is made solely from Chardonnay, and it is purely the product of one vintage. No more than 10,000 cases are made in any vintage and the wine is typically aged for at least a decade before release (the 1983, for example, was put

Taittinger label

on sale in 1996). Even at release, the wine still tends to be piercingly fresh, and it does not develop its full, often stunning complexity for a couple of decades or more.
sparkling 1997, 1996, 1995
★ Salon

Champagne Taittinger
Champagne

9 place St-Nicaise, Reims 03 26 85 45 35 www.taittinger.fr

TAITTINGER IS one of the bigger champagne houses still in family ownership. Its good vineyard holdings in the Côte des Blancs are put to excellent use in its Blanc de Blancs *cuvée de prestige*, Comtes de Champagne, which can develop richness and com-plexity with age. Sensibly, Taittinger is focusing on this wine, which also comes in a rosé style, and is no longer pushing its overpriced, flashily packaged Vintage Collection, which is now only available from the company's website.
sparkling 2002 ★ Comtes de Champagne Blanc de Blancs

Champagne Veuve Clicquot Ponsardin
Champagne

1 place des Droits de l'Homme, Reims 03 26 89 54 41
www.veuve-clicquot.fr

THE NEXT LARGEST producer of non-vintage Brut after Moët has suffered from its success. The increase in volume has meant sacrifices in quality and style, and wines have become younger and lighter over the past few years. However, the high quality of the muscular, Pinot Noir-based vintage wine, made in white and rosé versions that age particularly well, has continued. The *cuvée de prestige* La Grande Dame is consistently good too, although expensive.
sparkling 2002, 2000
★ Brut, Rosé, La Grande Dame

Krug
Champagne

5 rue Coquebert, Reims 03 26 84 44 20 www.krug.com

ESTABLISHED IN 1843 and formerly owned by Rémy-Cointreau, Krug is now in the hands of LVMH, which also owns the region's most celebrated brand, Dom Pérignon. Fears that LVMH would want to boost production, compromising on quality, appear to be unfounded. At Krug, even the non-vintage Grande Cuvée is matured for at least six years before release. Top wines are kept back much longer, but to fully appreciate what is special about a Krug vintage wine, it should be cellared for several years, perhaps even a decade, after its release. At a tasting in 2002 to celebrate Henri Krug's retirement, almost every released vintage that he was involved with (1962 to 1988) was opened, and the 1981

GROWER-PRODUCERS
There are around 5,000 grower-producers who make and market their own wines. The physical location of the grower-producers is more significant than that of the *négociants* as they often have holdings in just the village or *cru* where they are based. They are prohibited from buying in grapes, but they may swap five per cent of their harvest with another grower in order to make a blend. Recommended grower-producers are: *Chartogne-Taillet (03 26 03 10 17); Vilmart & Co (www.champagnevilmart.fr); René Geoffroy (03 26 55 32 31); Larmandier-Bernier (03 26 52 13 24); Serge Mathieu (03 25 29 32 58).*

vintage was the youngest wine to be nearing its peak.

🍷 sparkling 📈 *1998, 1996, 1995, 1990, 1989* ★ *NV Grande Cuvée, Krug*

Laurent-Perrier
Champagne

ave de Champagne, Tours-sur-Marne
☎ *03 26 58 91 22*
🌐 *www.laurent-perrier.fr*

LAURENT-PERRIER is probably best known for its non-vintage rosé, which was originally launched back in 1968, when very little pink champagne was made. However, its light, delicate, and refreshing Chardonnay-based non-vintage *cuvée* is also worthy of attention. It produces one of the few 'multi-vintage' *cuvées de prestige* (Krug is the other obvious example) in Grande Siècle, a blend of three harvests. Grand Siècle Cuvée Alexandra Rosé is much sought after.

🍷 sparkling 📈 *1998, 1997, 1996* ★ *Grande Siècle: La Cuvée, Alexandra Rosé; NV Brut*

Louis Roederer
Champagne

21 blvd Lundy, Reims
☎ *03 26 40 42 11*
🌐 *www.champagne-roederer.com*

ALONG WITH Bollinger's Ghislain Montgolfier, Jean-Claude Rouzaud is arguably the man who has done the most to encourage high standards in Champagne. The Roederer wines are exemplary; elegant, subtle, complex, and long-lived. A large holding of top quality *grand cru* vineyards forms the basis of the dazzling range. The delicious non-vintage Brut Premier puts most non-vintage champagne to

shame, while Louis Roederer's top wine, Cristal, is one of Champagne's three icons of excellence. (The others are Dom Pérignon and Krug's Grande Cuvée.) The vintage Blanc de Blancs is a beautifully refined, less celebrated star, for those who do not have the cash for Cristal.

🍷 sparkling 📈 *2003, 2002, 2000* ★ *NV Brut Premier, Blanc des Blancs*

Moët & Chandon
Champagne

18 ave de Champagne, Épernay ☎ *03 26 51 20 20* 🌐 *www.moet.com*

THE BEST KNOWN and biggest selling non-vintage brand by a mile is Moët & Chandon's Brut Impérial. Given the volume produced (over 16 million bottles a year), the consistent quality of this wine is laudable. Moët's recently introduced non-vintage rosé is good enough to rival Laurent-Perrier's, and its vintage wines can be classy and develop well with age. Moët's Dom Pérignon continues to excel under the talented hands of winemaker Richard Geoffroy, although unfortunately most is drunk long before its peak, rarely reached before 15 years of maturing.

Laurent-Perrier

🍷 sparkling 📈 *2003, 2002, 2000* ★ *Dom Pérignon, NV Rosé*

Pol Roger
Champagne

1 rue Henri Lelarge, Épernay ☎ *03 26 59 58 00* 🌐 *www.polroger.co.uk*

AFTER A PERIOD OF sensible re-investment in its winery, Pol Roger is back on top form. Its fine, long-lived vintage wines are much sought after and attractively

priced. They need time to reach their full potential, so anyone who has already drunk their 1998 vintage is missing a treat for the future. Prestige style, the vintage Sir Winston Churchill Cuvée, has few peers. The installation of Krug's former winemaker, Dominique Petit, is unlikely to set things back.

🍷 sparkling 📈 *2002, 2000, 1999, 1998* ★ *Sir Winston Churchill Cuvée*

Ruinart
Champagne

4 rue des Crayères, Reims ☎ *03 26 85 40 29* 🌐 *www.ruinart.com*

RUINART, THE OLDEST house in Champagne, was founded in 1729, and is the only producer in the LVMH camp to specialize in Chardonnay and Blanc de Blancs styles. With the launch of a non-vintage Blanc de Blancs and a seriously expensive top-of-the-range, multi-vintage blend named L'Exclusive in the past 10 years, it now has three such wines. However, it is the vintage Dom Ruinart Blanc de Blancs, unusually comprising a blend of Côte des Blancs *grands crus* with Chardonnay from the best villages in the Montagne de Reims, that has established the good reputation of this house.

🍷 sparkling 📈 *2000, 1998, 1996* ★ *Dom Ruinart Blanc de Blancs*

Statue of Dom Thierry Ruinart

ALSACE

POISED BETWEEN *French and German cultures, Alsace is quite unlike any other wine region. Its seductive ribbon of vineyards running through the foothills of the rugged Vosges Mountains produces versatile, fruity, and full-bodied wines, which, unusually for France, take their names from local grape varieties.*

The turbulent history of winemaking in Alsace can be traced back to Roman times. In the ensuing years, harvests were sometimes so successful that excess wine was allegedly used to wet building mortar, while other years' harvests were entirely destroyed, with caterpillars, phylloxera, frost, the bubonic plague, and, later, Napoleon, all playing their part.

Four centuries of territorial disputes between France and Germany – including German annexation after the Franco-Prussian War (1871), French retrieval of power after World War I (1918), and German occupation during World War II – have also made their mark on the identity of Alsace's wines. The vineyards face towards Germany, only 30km away, and, although Alsace has been firmly under French rule since 1945, Germanic influences are in evidence throughout the region, from village

Alsatian wine master

names to grape varieties. However, while the grapes, soil, and altitude are often similar to those of the Rheingau *(see pp354–6)* in Germany, the concentrated, powerful wines of Alsace are in a league of their own. With an effortless balance between fruit and acidity, Alsace wines are produced in both dry and sweet styles. Wood is rarely used in the vinification so the grape flavours are pure, and the varied microclimates, created by foothill topography, accentuate the wines' all-important acidity.

The majority of Alsace wine is white: Gewürztraminer, Riesling, Muscat Blanc à Petits Grains, and Pinot Gris are the signature grapes. Muscat and Pinot Gris are native to France, while the other two are rejected by AOC rules elsewhere in the country. Pinot Noir, the only red grown here, accounts for just nine per cent of total production.

Vintners' carts used as decoration in Dambach-la-Ville, Bas-Rhin

◁ **Ribeauvillé viewed from the Kirchberg de Ribeauvillé vineyard, Haut-Rhin**

WINE MAP OF ALSACE

Alsace's famed and beautiful route du vin runs through the heart of its two *départements* – Bas-Rhin and Haut-Rhin – which together have some 15,000ha of vineyards. The finest Alsace wines come from Haut-Rhin's central section, where the height of the Vosges Mountains protects the vines from Atlantic storms. There is also an isolated 2-ha pocket of Pinot Blanc and Pinot Noir at Wissembourg on the German frontier.

Gewürztraminer grapes

ALSACE WINE LAW

Alsace labels its wines *by grape variety, just as producers do in the New World. The four main grapes are Gewürztraminer (spelled Gewurztraminer in France), Muscat Blanc à Petits Grains (usually Muscat d'Alsace here), Riesling, and Pinot Gris (formerly called Tokay Pinot Gris). Another distinctive feature of wine from Alsace is the traditional, slender bottle required by law. Alsace's AOCs are outlined below:*

Alsace or Vin d'Alsace

This AOC was established in 1962. Grapes allowed for varietals are Gewürztraminer, Klevener de Heiligenstein, Muscat Blanc à Petits Grains, Pinot Blanc, Riesling, Silvaner (known as Sylvaner in Alsace), and Pinot Gris.

Edelzwicker

This is an inexpensive blend of Alsatian grapes. Since most wines from Alsace are varietals, this category allows winemakers to blend two or more varieties. The permitted grapes are Pinot Blanc, Auxerrois, Pinot Gris, Pinot Noir, Riesling, Gewürztraminer, Muscat Blanc à Petits Grains, Sylvaner, and Chasselas.

Alsace Grand Cru

This wine can be made using grapes from 50 designated vineyards, whose grapes must meet fixed criteria for ripeness and taste. The principal grapes allowed are Gewürztraminer, Muscat, Riesling, and Pinot Gris.

Vendange Tardive & Sélection de Grains Nobles

Vendange tardive, made from very ripe grapes picked late in the season, has a good balance of sweetness and acidity. *Sélection de grains nobles*, made from individually-picked berries, is intensely rich and sweet, and is only made in years when botrytis appears. Both can be labelled Alsace or Alsace *grand cru*. Grapes allowed are Gewürztraminer, Muscat, Riesling, and Pinot Gris.

Crémant d'Alsace

This is sparkling wine made using the traditional method (*see pp166–7*). Pinot Blanc is the main grape used, but Pinot Gris, Pinot Noir, Riesling, and Chardonnay are also permitted. Pinot Noir is also used to make a rare pink *crémant rosé*.

Domaine Marcel Deiss Alsace Grand Cru label

ALSACE
GRAND
CRU

SCHŒNENBOVRG
2000

MARCEL   DEISS

KEY
■ Alsace

Zinsel d

Saver

Mossig

Ploine   Bruch

Mittelbergh
And

Giessen

Fave   Séle

Bergheim
Ribeauvillé
Kaysersberg   Rique
Ammerschwihr
Turckheim   Co
Wintzenheim   Eguis
Munster   Husseren-   HAU
les-Châteaux   RH
Soultzmatt   Pfaffen
Orschwihr
Guebwiller
Thur   Wuenheim

Cernay
Thann
Mulhouse
Doller

Altkirch

Largue

0 km   20

SWITZERLA

BELGIUM GERMANY
Strasbourg
PARIS
Atlantic Ocean   49°
ITALY
SPAIN

Vosges

48°

TERROIR AT A GLANCE

Latitude: 47.5–49°N.

Altitude: 180–420m.

Topography: The wide valley follows the Rhin (Rhine) River and is protected from rain and wind by the Vosges Mountains to the west, the Jura Mountains to the south, and the Black Forest across the German border to the east.

Soil: Immensely varied range of soils. Mineral-rich granite, limestone, marly clay, schist, volcanic, and sandstone topsoils.

Climate: Moderate and sunny, with a long, cool growing season.

Temperature: July average is 24°C.

Rainfall: Relatively low, with an annual average of 400–500mm in the central town of Colmar.

Viticultural hazards: Hail; frost; drought; over-production.

ALSACE: AREAS & TOP PRODUCERS

BAS-RHIN *p180*

HAUT-RHIN *p180*
Clos St Landelin *p182*
Domaine Marcel Deiss *p182*
Domaines Schlumberger *p182*
Domaine Weinbach *p182*
Domaine Zind-
  Humbrecht *p182*
Hugel & Fils *p183*
Léon Beyer *p183*
Maison Trimbach *p183*

Maison Trimbach and Geisberg
grand cru vineyard, Ribeauvillé

Niedermorschwihr vineyard, Haut-Rhin

THE ROUTE DU VIN

Alsace's famous wine route meanders through this picturesque region from Marlenheim, just northwest of Strasbourg, to the tiny village of Thann, near Mulhouse, 100km further south. Along the way it takes in Alsace's many *grand cru* vineyards and passes through medieval towns and fairy-tale villages of cobbled lanes and timbered houses,

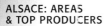

Traditional wine shop sign

where local wines and traditional Alsatian food are on offer. It can take a few days to explore the entire route, but those with less time to spare can make short trips out from the central town of Colmar. The vineyard paths are closed to visitors just before and during the harvest.

W *www.alsace-route-des-vins.com*

Harvesting white grapes in Haut-Rhin

WINEGROWING VILLAGES OF ALSACE

Bas-Rhin

THE VINEYARDS of this northern Alsace *département* surround fairy-tale villages of timbered houses and narrow lanes. The Vosges Mountains are relatively low in this area, giving limited protection against the westerly rains. This means that although wines here are reliable, they often lack the intensity and ripeness found further south. Bas-Rhin is split into two subregions below.

🏔 *granite, limestone, and clay mixtures* 🍇 *Pinot Noir* 🍇 *Gewürztraminer, Riesling* 🍷 *white*

Around Marlenheim

KNOWN FOR ITS LIGHT, fresh rosé, Marlenheim is where Alsace's historic Route du Vin *(see p179)* begins. Wolxheim's *grand cru* Altenberg, to the southeast, is reputed to have supplied Napoleon with his favourite wine, a *vin de paille* made from Chasselas grapes dried on straw mats. More popular these days are the dry wines made from Riesling, Gewürztraminer, and Pinot Blanc; the spicy Gewürztraminers from the rolling hills of Bergbieten are the most noteworthy.

Around Andlau

RIESLING IS THE GRAPE to look for in Andlau, which has more *grands crus* (Moenchberg, Wiebelsberg, and Kastelberg) than any other village in Bas-Rhin. This is because the soil is hard and rocky, and the climate hot and dry. To the north, Heiligenstein produces unique, racy Klevener de Heiligenstein. Just to the south,

Barr is known for its succulent Gewürztraminer, while Mittelbergheim, whose viticultural records date back to the 4th century, has a reputation for Sylvaner. Enjoyed young elsewhere, this variety creates a fuller and more age-worthy wine here as a result of the purity of the limestone soil in the area and the fact that the finest *grand cru* Zotzenberg wines are grown in a basin-like sun-trap. Rich Rieslings, on the other hand, characterize Eichhoffen; the best usually come from the Kritt vineyard.

Haut-Rhin

THIS AREA BOASTS a climate among the driest in France (second only to Perpignan in the far south), and has some 50 vineyards with *grand cru* status. As the Vosges rise ever higher, the foothills become steeper, the vines better, and the wines more powerful. The villages of the Haut-Rhin are listed in more detail below.

🏔 *limestone, sandstone, granite* 🍇 *Pinot Noir* 🍇 *Riesling, Gewürztraminer, Pinot Blanc, Pinot Gris* 🍷 *white*

Domaine Zind-Humbrecht, Haut-Rhin

Around Ribeauvillé

THIS BEAUTIFULLY PRESERVED village is famed for its classic, intense Rieslings, which thrive on the sandstone and marl soils here. There are three *grand cru* sites in the area: Geisberg, Kirchberg, and Osterberg. Age-worthy Gewürztraminer is the speciality of the fortified village of Bergheim to the northeast, while super-rich Muscat and concentrated Auxerrois come from Rorschwihr, to the north. Haut-Rhin's northernmost wine village, St-Hippolyte, is best known for its soft, cherry-flavoured Pinot Noir. In fact, this village, along with the nearby Rodern, prides itself on some of the most esteemed red wines in the region.

Around Riquewihr

WITH ITS STONE WALLS, cobbled streets, and ancient wine cellars, Riquewihr is situated among some of the area's best vineyards, including Schoenenbourg and Sporen *grands crus*. The speciality here is long-lived Riesling. The *grand cru* of warm Beblenheim to the east – aptly named Sonnenglanz, meaning sunshine – delivers ripe and fully aromatic wines that were among the first in Alsace to be singled out for special status. Gewürztraminer is the highlight here. Moving south to Mittelwihr, the star is once again Riesling: a steely version that oozes racy yet refined flavours – often put down to the mildness of the climate, as well as the perfectly suited gravel and limestone soil. Further south still, Kaysersberg produces fat, spicy Gewürztraminer from its steeply-sloping Schlossberg and Bixkoepflé vineyards.

Around Turckheim

TO THE WEST OF COLMAR lies the oldest and most famous of Alsace's *grand cru* vineyards: Kaefferkopf in the village of Ammerschwihr, which is renowned for its Rieslings and well-structured Gewürztraminers. Katzenthal, to the south, also produces some fine Rieslings. Meanwhile, the fortified village of Turckheim – where Brand is the *grand cru* – favours Pinot Gris and Pinot Noir. The high levels of sunshine allow the thicker skins of red grapes to ripen sufficiently here. Both rosé and red Pinot Noirs from this village are concentrated, rich, and delicious; the rosé is a local speciality. The powerful, intense Pinot Gris of Wintzenheim is well worth seeking out, especially the rare late harvest *sélection de grains nobles*.

Around Eguisheim

WITH THE THREE CASTLES of Husseren-les-Châteaux dominating the skyline, Eguisheim is the highest point on the Route du Vin. Around the walled village are some of Alsace's top vineyards for Riesling, Gewürztraminer, and Muscat. Superbly aromatic Muscat and intense Gewürztraminer are the highlights of the Goldert *grand cru* in Gueberschwihr; Pfaffenheim produces Alsace's richest Pinot Blanc; and Soultzmatt, tucked up into the mountains, is home to fresh, flavourful Pinot Blanc and the Gewürztraminer *grand cru* Zinnkoepflé. *Grand cru* Pfingstberg of Orschwihr also produces hugely powerful, and sublimely classy, Pinot Blanc and Pinot Gris.

Guebwiller & Thann

MANY OF ALSACE'S most concentrated wines come from this southerly part of the region, which boasts the Kessler, Kitterlé, Saering, and Spiegel *grands crus*. Some 75 per cent of Guebwiller's vineyards are owned by Domaines Schlumberger, whose specialities are Pinot Gris and Gewürztraminer; although they also deliver some elegant Riesling from Kitterlé. Wuenheim, to the south, produces crisp, fresh Riesling from *grand cru* Ollwiller. This village was the effective end of the Route du Vin for many years. However, since the vineyards of Thann, long abandoned because of their gradient, were replanted in the 1970s by Léonard Humbrecht of Domaine Zind-Humbrecht, great wines have been appearing further south. The best known site is the terraced *grand cru* Rangen, an immensely steep vineyard punctuated only by the tiny chapel of St-Urbain. Pinot Gris, which loves the sun, is the star variety here.

Picturesque village of Riquewihr

TOP PRODUCERS OF ALSACE

Clos St Landelin
Haut-Rhin

rte du vin, Rouffach
☎ 03 89 78 58 00
W *www.mure.com* ○

THIS ALSATIAN operation was established in 1630 by Michel Muré. Part of the *grand cru* Vorbourg in Rouffach, the wines here are truly special: well-balanced and concentrated whites include a powerful Riesling and a refreshing Muscat. There is also a surprisingly complex wood-aged Pinot Noir. The same family also owns René Muré, the brand for the *négociant* side of the business, which buys in grapes to make wines that can be drunk younger.
🍷 *red, white* 🍇 *2007, 2005, 2004, 2002, 2001, 2000, 1999* ★ *Riesling Vorbourg, Pinot Noir, Muscat Vendanges Tardives Vorbourg*

Domaine Marcel Deiss
Haut-Rhin

15 rte du vin, Bergheim ☎ 03 89 73 63 37 W *www.marceldeiss.com* ○

TERROIR IS everything to Jean-Michel Deiss. So strong is his belief in the vineyard that he goes against all the traditions of Alsace and labels his wine with the vineyard name rather than the grape variety. His wines not only have great balance and finesse, but also great concentration. Rieslings from *grands crus* Altenberg de Bergheim and Schoenenbourg are stunners; while the wines from *grand cru* Mambourg are hugely rich, and also hugely expensive.
🍷 *white* 🍇 *2007, 2005, 2004, 2001* ★ *Grand Cru Altenberg de Bergheim, Grand Cru Schoenenbourg, Grand Cru Mambourg*

Domaine Marcel Deiss label

Domaines Schlumberger
Haut-Rhin

100 rue Théodore-Deck, Guebwiller
☎ 03 89 74 27 00 W *www. domaines-schlumberger.com* ○

WITH 140HA of vines, Schlumberger is by far the largest producer in Alsace: its vineyards dominate the industrial town of Guebwiller. Nicolas Schlumberger assembled the estate's land in the 19th century, from what are now the *grands crus* Saering, Kessler, Kitterlé, and Spiegel, as well as sites such as Heissenstein and Schimberg. The domaine's most famous wine is Cuvée Christine – a Gewürztraminer *vendange tardive* that combines richness and power without ever becoming over-luscious, and can be kept for 10 years or more. Les Princes Abbés is a range of 10 wines: nine varietals and one blend, for early drinking.
🍷 *white* 🍇 *2007, 2005, 2004* ★ *Riesling Grand Cru Saering, Riesling Grand Cru Kitterlé, Gewürztraminer Grand Cru Kitterlé*

Domaine Weinbach
Haut-Rhin

Clos des Capucins, 25 rte du vin, Kientzheim ☎ 03 89 47 13 21 W *www.domaine weinbach.com* ○

MARKED OUT since 890 AD by the monks of Etival Abbey, the vineyard of Clos des Capucins is now the preserve of Colette Faller and her daughters, Laurence and Catherine. Their wines are among Alsace's best: pure and balanced, with a light touch of sweetness. Some say Laurence is one of the finest white winemakers in the world. Her crowning glory is the complex, concentrated, and racy Riesling *grand cru* Schlossberg, made from grapes grown on the dramatic slopes around the town of Kaysersberg.
🍷 *white* 🍇 *2007, 2005, 2004, 2001* ★ *Riesling Grand Cru Schlossberg, Riesling Réserve, Pinot Gris Cuvée Laurence*

Domaine Zind-Humbrecht
Haut-Rhin

4 rte de Colmar, Turckheim
☎ 03 89 27 02 05 ○ *by appt*

FORMERLY A SCIENTIST and engineer, Olivier Humbrecht was the first in France to gain the coveted Master of Wine title. He is now leading the charge into biodynamic techniques in Alsatian vineyards, mirroring those used in Burgundy *(see p105)*. He works some of the finest vineyards in the region, a collection that his father, Léonard, built up over many years. The wines are outstanding. The most basic are full and dry, and his finest is the very rich and sumptuous *vendange tardive* from Pinot Gris and Gewürztraminer.

🏳 white 📅 2007, 2005, 2004, 2002, 2001, 1998 ★ *Gewürztraminer Grand Cru Hengst, Vendange Tardive Pinot Gris Clos Windsbuhl, Muscat Herrenweg de Turckheim*

Hugel & Fils
Haut-Rhin

3 rue de la première armée, Riquewihr 📞 *03 89 47 92 15* 🖥 *www.hugel.com* 🔲

JEAN 'JOHNNY' HUGEL was, for many years, the public face of Alsace around the world. Now his sons Marc and Étienne, the 13th generation, have taken over the family firm, which dates back to 1639. Their classy and elegant wines remain benchmarks for Alsace wine lovers. Hugel excels at the late harvest wines, *vendange tardive* and *sélection de grains nobles*. One of the first to deliver these rich harvest styles, it remains one of the best. Gentil, which combines Gewürztraminer, Riesling, Pinot Gris, Muscat, and Sylvaner, is a great aromatic blend.

🏳 white 📅 2007, 2005, 2004, 2002 ★ *Riesling Cuvée Jubilee, Gewürztraminer Sélection de Grains Nobles, Tokay Pinot Gris Vendange Tardive*

Léon Beyer
Haut-Rhin

2 rue de la première armée, Eguisheim 📞 *03 89 21 62 30* 🖥 *www.leonbeyer.fr* 🔲

BEYER VINEYARDS first appeared in 1580, the firm in 1867, and the family tradition of making dry, 'food-friendly' wines for top-range restaurants

continues today. Marc Beyer and his son Yann-Léon now run this operation. The hallmark brand is Comtes d'Eguisheim, made only in the very best years. The Beyers' 20ha include *grand cru* vineyards in Eichberg and Pfersigberg, but they see no need to advertise the *grand cru* status, believing their own name is what counts. They also buy in grapes for their less expensive wines.

🏳 white 📅 2007, 2005, 2004, 2002 ★ *Riesling Les Écaillers, Riesling Comtes d'Eguisheim, Gewürztraminer Comtes d'Eguisheim*

Maison Trimbach
Haut-Rhin

15 rte de Bergheim, Ribeauvillé 📞 *03 89 73 60 30* 🖥 *www.maison-trimbach.fr* 🔲

Maison Trimbach

FOR FRESH, RACY, vibrant, and graceful Riesling, Trimbach is the name to look for. Riesling Clos Ste-Hune, from a tiny 1.3-ha vineyard, is arguably the finest Riesling in the world. Just 9,000 bottles are produced each year. It has perfume, steeliness, purity of fruit, and true elegance, and should be aged for at least five years. The Riesling Cuvée Frédéric-Émile is almost as high in quality. The standard continues right through the million-bottle range of Trimbach wines, many of which can be found in restaurants all over the world.

🏳 white 📅 2007, 2005, 2004, 2002, 2001 ★ *Riesling Clos Ste-Hune, Gewürztraminer Seigneurs de Ribecupierre, Pinot Gris Réserve*

PERFECT CASE: ALSACE

Ⓦ Cave de Turckheim Gewürztraminer Brand ££ (www.cave-turckheim.com)

Ⓦ Clos St Landelin Riesling Grand Cru Vorbourg £££

Ⓦ Domaine Marcel Deiss Grand Cru Mambourg ££££

Ⓦ Domaine Marc Kreydenweiss Riesling Clos Rebberg ££ (03 88 08 95 33)

Ⓦ Domaine Ostertag Riesling Grand Cru Muenchberg £££ (domaine-ostertag@wanadoo.fr)

Ⓦ Domaine Paul Blanck Riesling Grand Cru Furstentum Vieilles Vignes £££ (www.blanck.com)

Ⓦ Domaines Schlumberger Gewürztraminer Grand Cru Kitterlé £££

Ⓦ Domaine Weinbach Riesling Grand Cru Schlossberg Cuvée Ste-Catherine £££

Ⓦ Domaine Zind-Humbrecht Pinot Gris Clos Jebsal Sélection de Grains Nobles ££££

Ⓦ Hugel & Fils Tokay Pinot Gris Vendange Tardive £££

Ⓦ Léon Beyer Riesling Comtes d'Eguisheim ££

Ⓦ Maison Trimbach Riesling Clos Ste-Hune ££££

Hugel & Fils Gewürztraminer Sélection de Grains Nobles label

ITALY

ITALY

With a 3,000-year viticultural history, *Italy remains firmly at the forefront of world wine production. It produces and consumes more wine than any other nation, with the exception of France.*

THE EARLY YEARS

Originally introduced by the Greeks and the Etruscans to Sicily, Puglia, and Tuscany in the 4th century BC, the vine quickly carpeted Italy in its entirety. It was, however, the Romans who were responsible for its dissemination throughout Europe: a map of modern European viticulture is almost identical with another of the Roman Empire at its height *(see p14)*. Wine became an integral part of Roman life, fuelling infamous debauchery and inspiring both authors and poets. Many centuries ago, Roman citizens like Pliny documented key concepts in the production of quality grapes including site selection, training, pruning, yields, and ageing. While the claim that the Romans did more for wine production in

Roman relief depicting the storing of wine

200 years than the Italians have done in 2,000 is uncharitable, the reality is that the Romans raised both grape growing and winemaking to a level that remained unchallenged until the advent of such advances as pasteurization and temperature control.

MODERN HISTORY

The fall of Rome may have spelled the end of wine's golden age but the peninsula's inhabitants did not abandon viticulture. On the contrary, it flourished under the profusion of flags that ruled various parts of Italy until unification in 1861. One thousand years of bitter rivalry between these city-states led to extraordinary diversity in the vineyard as each federation fiercely protected local varieties and traditions. During this time viticulture in Italy gradually assumed the bewildering shape we know today, with a profusion of regional grape varieties, wine styles, and local winemaking techniques coming to the fore. Some wine zones, such as Chianti, have survived virtually intact since the 14th century, while others, such as Brunello di Montalcino, did not appear until 500 years later.

Although Italy's potential has always been formidable, there was little incentive to improve the quality of wine in a country so perfectly adapted to the vine and with such a high level of domestic consumption. The emergence of a true middle class after World War II meant that, for the first time, Italians

Caravaggio's portrayal of Bacchus, the Roman god of wine

◁ **Castello di Volpaia, with Radda in Chianti in the distance, Tuscany**

WINEGROWING REGIONS

Italy is blanketed in vines from head to toe. The country divides into four key winegrowing zones: the Northwest, Northeast, Central Italy, and the South & Islands, which neatly break down into 20 winegrowing regions. Within each of these regions a complicated series of DOC(G)s can often be found, including the famous names of Barolo and Barbaresco, and Soave and Valpolicella.

became interested in quality rather than just quantity. The 1950s saw both an unprecedented demand for better wines and the economic stability required for their production. Gradually, Italy's creaking, leviathan wine industry began to change course. Reliance on co-operatives declined, yields were reduced, and new technology was embraced.

The 1960s saw the emergence of the Super-Tuscans like Sassicaia *(see p261)*, a wine that changed the world's perception of Italian wines. Made from international varieties and produced outside the hallowed DOC system, the Super-Tuscans were so good that collectors from around the world rushed to buy them at prices that set new records. These wines showed other producers that Italian bottles could compete on the world stage. What began as a trickle of producers who decided to lower yields and improve technology is now a torrent from Valle d'Aosta to Sicily.

FOOD & WINE

L'abbinamento, or 'the match', is the Italian word reserved almost exclusively for the happy marriage of food and wine. The two have evolved together over the centuries. *Bistecca alla fiorentina* (steak) and Chianti Classico; risotto and Soave; *ossobuco* and Barolo are all perfect matches where the flavour of one adroitly complements that of the other. The combination of naturally crisp acidity and firm tannins make Italian wines perfect for rare beef, cream sauces, and salami. That is why Italian wines taste so good in Italy – they are drunk with the food they are intended to partner.

THE WINE INDUSTRY TODAY

Italy is the second largest producer and the largest exporter of wine in the world. With more than one million grape growers, each with an average holding of less than 1ha, the Italian wine industry is highly fragmented. It is therefore difficult to build the big international brands found in other winegrowing countries, offering consistency and volume. Italy's forgiving climate encourages generous yields, and the abundant grapes produced are often processed in the antiquated facilities of co-operatives. There is, however, another side to Italy's wine industry: modern, privately owned estates that control all aspects of production and bristle with armies of agronomists and oenologists, many of whom have been trained abroad. Not surprisingly, these producers are dismissive of bulk production, and some have gone so far as to label their wines outside the official DOC(G) system in order to escape its strict restrictions. Cult wines such as Tenuta San Guido's Sassicaia, although in the minority, have re-established the country's reputation. Italy's star is certainly in the ascendant.

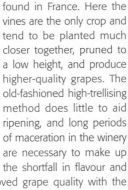

Grape picker, Tuscany

VITICULTURE & VINIFICATION

There are two main methods of training vines in Italy: high-trellising and the more quality-focused cane-pruning system. High-trained vines allow space for other crops underneath – an important advantage for Italian smallholdings – and are easier to manage on steep hillsides, which are often the norm. Yields from this method, however, tend to be high. Newer vineyards, on the other hand, often use the cane-pruning system, similar to that found in France. Here the vines are the only crop and tend to be planted much closer together, pruned to a low height, and produce higher-quality grapes. The old-fashioned high-trellising method does little to aid ripening, and long periods of maceration in the winery are necessary to make up the shortfall in flavour and colour. Improved grape quality with the cane-pruning system has, however, meant shorter maceration times. Temperature-controlled fermentation is now the rule rather than the exception, and the gleam of stainless steel can be seen even in some co-operatives. The use of new oak for maturation

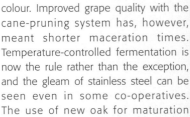

View of vineyards in Tuscany, one of Italy's key wine producing regions

remains controversial, with some producers swearing allegiance to large Slavonian oak *botti* while others have switched to smaller French oak *barriques*. Whatever the choice, long maturation times are on the wane in Italy.

RED GRAPE VARIETIES & WINE STYLES

Italy is a nation of red wine producers, and its reputation for vinous excellence rests firmly on

Mountainous vineyards in Alto Adige, Northeast Italy

the distinguished shoulders of Barolo (Piemonte), Brunello di Montalcino (Tuscany), Taurasi (Campania), and Chianti Classico (Tuscany). Italy's warm climate, moderated by the sea and mountains, and poor soils give its reds a rare combination of weight and elegance. Varieties like Nebbiolo, Sangiovese, and the Sicilian Nerello Mascalese each have the potential to produce wines rich in both extract and alcohol that are nevertheless stylish and age-worthy. Aglianico, Nero d'Avola, and Montepulciano, on the other hand, trade a little sophistication for muscle yet develop just as gracefully.

There is a huge flavour spectrum of Italian reds, but black fruit and a hint of earthiness approach ubiquity. There are many exceptions, however, particularly in the north where local varieties such as Teroldego, Refosco, and Freisa offer red fruit and even floral notes. Firm tannins and crisp acidity – the structural components that confer both longevity and an affinity for food – are more common in Italian reds than any individual flavour. Italy's great reds are a compelling expression of their *terroir* – they just *feel* Italian. The wines exude charm and authenticity while reflecting an agricultural heritage that reaches back two millennia.

WHITE GRAPE VARIETIES & WINE STYLES

Although the Roman taste was for white and sweet wine, modern Italy has swung in the opposite direction. Nevertheless, native white varieties (vast swathes of Trebbiano and pockets of Vernaccia, Garganega, and Greco) can be found from north to south, and each has adapted to the local climate. In the heat of the far south, where Chardonnay and Sauvignon Blanc are harvested by the end of July, local varieties Greco, Fiano, and Inzolia ripen to perfection two months later. More importantly, they ripen with moderate levels of potential alcohol, balanced acidity, and a wealth of aromatic intensity.

When yields are kept in check, Italian whites are characterized by a unique herbal note allied to a mineral edge that underpins the varietal character. Verdicchio's subtle nuttiness, Garganega's more pronounced floral intensity, and Greco's overt fruitiness are very individual, but all these wines are distinctly Italian. Aromatic intensity is frequently matched by similar weight on the palate and balanced by remarkably fresh acidity – an ideal foil for pasta, risotto, and fish. Wines with such natural balance and versatility at the table, long taken for granted, are now receiving the attention they deserve.

ITALY'S INDIGENOUS GRAPE VARIETIES

A T A TIME WHEN *the world of wine is increasingly dominated by a few, so-called international grapes, Italy remains a haven for obscure indigenous varieties. Its rich heritage of over 2,000 native grapes is a result of a long viticultural history with growers developing different varieties to take advantage of local conditions. Here are some of Italy's most important native grapes.*

Aglianico ◁
An ancient red variety mainly found in the south, this grape can make excellent, full-bodied wines with characteristic flavours of roasted cherries, chocolate, and tar.
🍇 *13,000ha* ★ *Taurasi DOCG, Aglianico del Vulture DOC*

Arneis
Full-bodied and dry in style, Arneis is recognized as one of Italy's finest white grapes. It is renowned for its attractively perfumed flavours of melon, pears, almonds, and dried herbs. Mainly grown in Piemonte.
🍇 *400ha* ★ *Roero Arneis DOCG, Langhe DOC*

Barbera ▽
Best in Piemonte, Barbera can produce wines that are full-bodied and packed with soft, sweet fruits and flavours of red berries, spices, and wood smoke. It is the second most planted red grape in Italy, but is mostly grown in the north.
🍇 *50,000ha* ★ *Barbera d'Alba DOC, Barbera d'Asti DOC*

Cortese ▽
A quality grape variety, Cortese produces full-bodied, refreshing white wines with appealing flavours of lime, greengages, and minerals. It is found in Piemonte, Lombardia, and the Veneto but the best examples are from Gavi DOCG.
🍇 *3,000ha* ★ *Gavi DOCG*

Corvina ▽
The most distinguished grape of Valpolicella DOC, Corvina provides the backbone for the region's cherry and herb scented wines and can, in the right hands, produce concentrated flavours and silky tannins. It really comes into its own in *amarone* and *recioto* styles.
🍇 *4,500ha* ★ *Valpolicella DOC*

Dolcetto △
Meaning 'little sweet one', Dolcetto makes deliciously drinkable wines with deep colour and vibrant cherry flavours. Most producers of Barolo and Barbaresco make Dolcetto to be drunk young and fruity, while others can be aged.
🍇 *4,500ha* ★ *Dogliani DOCG, Dolcetto d'Alba DOC*

Garganega
This grape variety is capable of exceptional quality, but its brilliance is quickly dulled by high yields. Late ripening and with an affinity for botrytis, it can produce medium- to full-bodied whites with notes of camomile and sweet almond.
🍇 *13,000ha* ★ *Soave Classico DOC, Soave Classico Superiore DOCG*

📷 Nebbiolo △

Nebbiolo makes the legendary wines of Barolo and Barbaresco, which have a gloriously perfumed nose of violets, roses, tar, and spices, with high acidity, sweet fruits, and powerful tannins.
📷 2,700ha ★ Barolo DOCG, Barbaresco DOCG, Roero Arneis DOCG

📷 Sangiovese ▷

The most widely planted red grape variety in Italy, Sangiovese can produce world class wines, which are medium to full-bodied, with soft, grainy tannins and earthy flavours of herbs, vanilla, and bitter cherry.
📷 100,000ha plus ★ Chianti Classico DOCG, Brunello di Montalcino DOCG

📷 Trebbiano △

Trebbiano (or Ugni Blanc) is a fairly ordinary grape producing large volumes of dry, crisp but ultimately undistinguished wine. It is the most planted white variety in Italy and is usually blended.
📷 100,000ha ★ Trebbiano di Romagna DOC, Trebbiano d'Abruzzo DOC, Lugana DOC

📷 Greco Bianco ▽

An ancient Greek variety, Greco is planted mainly in Campania. In its most famous incarnation, Greco di Tufo DOC, it makes a full-bodied dry white wine with a deep colour and flavours of pear, peach, and dried herbs.
📷 1,000ha ★ Greco di Tufo DOCG

📷 Primitivo ◁

Used in blends and as a single grape variety. Primitivo typically has high alcohol and a fruity, bitter cherry flavour. It is genetically identical to California's Zinfandel although it makes quite different wines.
📷 17,000ha ★ Primitivo di Manduria DOC

📷 Verdicchio

There are two DOCs in Le Marche in Central Italy that produce a dry, crisp white wine with flavours of lemons, grass, and almonds from this characterful white grape.
📷 2,400ha ★ Verdicchio dei Castelli di Jesi DOC, Verdicchio di Matelica DOC

📷 Montepulciano

Production is centred on Abruzzo, though it drifts into Le Marche and Puglia. In the right hands, Montepulciano makes wines with dizzying levels of acidity, alcohol, and tannins.
📷 31,000ha ★ Cónero DOCG, Montepulciano d'Abruzzo Colline Teramane DOCG

📷 Negroamaro ▽

Literally meaning 'black bitter', Negroamaro typically produces wines with a deep colour, concentrated tannins, and full-bodied flavours of bitter cherry, liquorice, and blackcurrant. Widely planted in the south, it is often used in blends.
📷 31,000ha ★ Salice Salentino DOC

📷 Vernaccia

Grown in various styles throughout Italy, this grape is most famous as Vernaccia di San Cimignano DOCG in Tuscany. Here it produces a crisp, dry white wine with distinctive flavours of nuts and spices.
📷 1,500ha ★ Vernaccia di San Gimignano DOCG

ITALIAN WINE LAW

A T FIRST GLANCE, *Italian wine law appears straightforward with just four categories of classification. At the top of the tree there* is *Denominazione di Origine Controllata e Garantita (DOCG) followed by Denominazione di Origine Controllata (DOC). These 'controlled wines with an additional guarantee' (DOCG) and 'controlled wines' (DOC) are produced from a specified region according to local regulations. At the next level is Indicazione Geografica Tipica (IGT) and* finally *vino da tavola (VdT) or table wine.*

In theory, *DOCG wines should be the best, followed by DOC, IGT, and finally* vino da tavola. *However, there are numerous complications.*

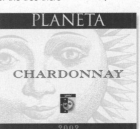

IGT label from Planeta, Sicilia

Firstly, *a DOC or DOCG classification is, despite the name, no guarantee of exceptional quality, as in many cases regulations are insufficiently stringent. Secondly, a DOCG wine is not necessarily superior to a DOC, as a number of regions have been promoted to the higher classification purely on political grounds. And thirdly, some Italian producers choose to avoid the DOC and DOCG framework altogether, either because they believe the system has little value, or* because they prefer to use grape varieties or techniques not permitted under existing regulations. Therefore a number of Italy's finest wines are released as IGT or even VdT.

Italian Wine Classification

All Italian wines are classified under four designations:

Denominazione di Origine Controllata e Garantita (DOCG): This is the highest classification for quality Italian wine. Some regions only possess DOCG status for certain wines: for example, Acqui can only label wines made from the Brachetto grape variety DOCG.

Denominazione di Origine Controllata (DOC): DOC is the quality classification equivalent to the Appellation d'Origine Contrôlée (AOC) in France.

Indicazione Geografica Tipica (IGT): This category is the same level as *vin de pays* in France. Many of the finest wines in Italy may be labelled IGT to avoid strict DOC or DOCG regulations, particularly when non-traditional grape varieties like Chardonnay, Cabernet Sauvignon and Merlot are used.

Vino da Tavola (VdT): Table wine accounts for the vast majority of Italian wine production. It is usually of low quality, but exceptions still exist.

ITALIAN DOCGS

Red
Barbaresco (Piemonte)
Bardolino Superiore (Veneto)
Barolo (Piemonte)
Brachetto d'Acqui (sparkling)
 (Piemonte)
Brunello di Montalcino
 (Tuscany)
Carmignano (Tuscany)
Cerasuolo di Vittoria (Sicilia)
Chianti Classico (Tuscany)
Chianti & subregions
 (Tuscany)
Cònero (Le Marche)
Dogliani (Piemonte)
Gattinara (Piemonte)
Ghemme (Piemonte)
Vino Nobile di
 Montepulciano (Tuscany)
Montepulciano d'Abruzzo
 Colline Teramane (Abruzzo)

CHIANTI CLASSICO DOCG

Chianti Classico DOCG label from Brancaia, Tuscany

Morellino di Scansano
 (Tuscany)
Roero (Piemonte)
Sagrantino di Montefalco
 (Umbria)
Taurasi (Campania)
Torgiano Riserva (Umbria)
Valtellina Superiore (and
 Sforzato) (Lombardia)

White
Albana di Romagna
 (Emilia-Romagna)
Asti (sparkling) (Piemonte)
COF Picolit (sweet)
 (Friuli-Venezia Giulia)
Gavi & subregions
 (Piemonte)
Greco di Tufo (Campania)
Fiano d'Avellino (Campania)
Franciacorta (sparkling)
 (Lombardia)
Moscato d'Asti (Piemonte)
Ramandolo (sweet)
 (Friuli-Venezia Giulia)
Roero Arneis (Piemonte)
Soave Superiore
 (and Recioto) (Veneto)
Vermentino di Gallura
 (Sardegna)
Vernaccia di San Gimignano
 (Tuscany)
Vernaccia di Serrapetrona
 (Le Marche)

READING AN ITALIAN WINE LABEL

If a bottle is labelled DOCG or DOC, the name of the region or district can generally provide a good indication of the style of wine. Both designations should in theory indicate a quality wine, but they are unfortunately no guarantee. Only the name of the producer can provide a more definitive insight.

If the wine is labelled IGT or *vino da tavola*, the name of the producer becomes much more important. Price can also be a guide, as a top quality IGT wine may cost two or three times that of a DOCG bottle produced in the same region. It may not offer better value, however.

The name of a grape variety can sometimes be found on Italian wine labels with the exception of VdT, and can provide a clue to the style. The word 'di' (or d') means 'of' in Italian, hence Barbera d'Alba translates as the Barbera grape variety from the region of Alba. The quality of vintages in Italian wine do vary, generally the further north the wine region, the greater the variation year upon year.

Badia a Passignano is the name of the estate, but this could equally be a brand name.

2000 indicates the vintage, the year the grapes were harvested.

Chianti Classico is the designated region, the 'heartland' or 'classic' zone of Chianti.

Denominazione di Origine Controllata e Garantita, also known as DOCG, is the official quality classification.

Riserva denotes the wine has been aged in barrel and bottle for at least three years before release.

Antinori is the name of the producer and, in this instance, owner of many of the finest estates in Italy.

Glossary of Label Terms

abboccato: lightly sweet.

anno/annata: vintage.

amabile: medium sweet.

amaro: bitter or dry.

amarone: a DOC red wine made in Valpolicella from dried (passito) grapes (see p229).

azienda/tenuta: estate.

azienda agricola: an estate that uses its own grapes to produce its wine.

bianco: white.

cascina: estate.

cantina: winery.

cantina sociale: co-operative.

chiaretto: pale red or dark rosé.

classico: the original zone of production within a DOC(G) region (generally better vineyards).

dolce: sweet.

fattoria: estate.

fermentazione naturale: sparkling wine where the 'fizz' has been produced by fermentation in tank or bottle.

frizzante: slightly sparkling.

imbottigliato all'origine: estate bottled.

metodo classico: a sparkling wine made using the same techniques as champagne.

passito: a strong, powerful wine made from dried grapes;

it can be sweet as in recioto, or dry as in amarone.

produttore: producer.

recioto: red or white sweet wine made from dried grapes; usually quite strong and a speciality of the Veneto.

ripasso: literally 'repassed', referring to the process of using amarone grape skins to initiate a secondary fermentation in an ordinary Valpolicella. The finished wine will have more body, alcohol and amarone flavours.

rosso: red.

rosato: rosé.

secco: dry.

spumante: sparkling.

Prosecco di Valdobbiadene DOC

Superiore: usually applied to DOC(G) wines with a higher alcoholic strength – not an indicator of quality.

vendemmia: vintage.

vino: wine.

vin santo: white dessert wine, a speciality of Tuscany. Made from dried grapes and aged in small casks for at least three years.

vino novello: literally 'new wine', a similar idea to Beaujolais Nouveau.

vigneto/vigna: vineyard.

NORTHWEST ITALY

F LANKED BY MOUNTAINS *on three sides, Northwest Italy retains a strong sense of its own identity. It is justly proud of producing a clutch of Italy's most prestigious wines, securing it a place in the hearts of wine lovers worldwide.*

The northwest offers a continuum of viticultural excellence, and has done more to keep Italy's flag flying than any other region. While quality is exceptionally high, this region is of relative insignif - cance in terms of volume.

The Romans introduced the vine to the northwest but the first references to viticulture as we know it today date from the 13th century. The grape's affinity for the region's cool climate, long autumns, and poor soils was soon recognized and it thereafter developed a loyal following. Centuries of economic prosperity ensured that here, as in Tuscany, wine production is dominated by independent estates rather than co-operatives. Generations of estate production have created a healthy and competitive industry, well equipped to exploit the region's huge natural potential. The Alps temper the hot summer sun, and the resulting cooler temperatures preserve acidity and encourage complexity in the

Barbaresco

grapes. Unfortunately for the grower, the steep slopes also ensure that viticulture here remains gruelling work.

Winemaking in the northwest, as elsewhere in Italy, suffered from the instability that dogged the country after World War II. Emerging in the 1980s from decades of viticultural indifference, Piemonte now vies with Tuscany to produce the nation's greatest red wines. Nebbiolo delivers a virtuoso, solo performance on the limestone slopes of the Langhe hills. No longer cast in supporting roles, Barbera and Dolcetto complete a Piemontese trio that can rival Bordeaux's three key varieties.

Today, the northwest offers more than just the famous names and lofty prices of the Langhe's Barolo and Barbaresco wines. The aromatic whites of Liguria and Valle d'Aosta, the celebrated sparklers of Lombardia, and Piemonte's forgotten outposts of Nebbiolo make for a distinguished patchwork.

Vineyard topped by a cedar of Lebanon tree in Barolo, Piemonte

◁ **Terraced vineyards surrounding the village of Manarola in the Cinque Terre, Liguria**

WINE MAP OF NORTHWEST ITALY

THE TERRACED PATCHWORKS of Valle d'Aosta's and Lombardia's DOC(G)s are some of Italy's most northerly vineyards. Further south, across the broad valley of the Po River, is the famous winegrowing region of the Langhe, including the powerhouses of Barolo and Barbaresco. Their end marks the start of the Alpi Liguri and the northern boundary of the maritime influence responsible for the breezy flavours of Liguria's whites. To the east, the fertile plains of Emilia are dominated by Lambrusco vines.

KEY

▨ Northwest Italy

Vineyards and medieval castle
in Barolo, Piemonte

PERFECT CASE: NORTHWEST ITALY

R Angelo Gaja Langhe Sorì Tildin ££

S Cà del Bosco Franciacorta Brut Rosé ££

R Domenico Clerico Barolo Percristina £££

D Ferrando Erbaluce di Caluso Cariola ££ (37.5cl)

R Giuseppe Mascarello Barolo Bricco £££

W Institut Agricole Régional Valle d'Aosta Pinot Gris ££

S La Spinetta Moscato d'Asti Bricco Quaglia ££

W La Zerba Gavi di Tassarolo Terrarossa ££

R Pecchenino Dolcetto di Dogliani Sirì d'Jermu ££

R Roberto Voerzio Barbera d'Alba Vigneto Pozzo £££ (0173 509196)

S Uberti Franciacorta Satèn Magnificentia ££

W Walter de Batté Cinque Terre ££

0 ⌐ km

Hillside vineyards in
Valtellina, Lombardia

TERROIR AT A GLANCE

Latitude: 44–46.5°N.

Altitude: Varies considerably from the Colli Piacentini to Valle d'Aosta (100–900m).

Topography: Vineyards in the northwest use the hills and mountains to best effect. Valle d'Aosta has the steepest slopes of all; Piemonte and Lombardia's northern vineyards are sited in the foothills of the Alps and face south, overlooking the broad valley of the Po River. Lower altitude and the southern exposure here ensure an ideal mesoclimate for grape growing.

Soil: Calcareous marl, clay, sand, gravel, limestone and glacial moraine.

Climate: Climate plays a decisive role in shaping the quality of each vintage in the northwest of Italy, where annual variation can be significant. In Valle d'Aosta and Lombardia the climate ranges from marginal to cool continental. Further south, the Mediterranean influence is felt with earlier budbreak and cooler evenings. The Langhe often enjoys a true Indian summer.

Temperature: July average is 22°C.

Rainfall: Annual average is 850mm.

Viticultural hazards: Mildew; hail; underripeness caused by fog; cool, cloudy weather; rain during September and October.

NORTHWEST ITALY: AREAS & TOP PRODUCERS

Cà del Bosco label, Lombardia

Wines from Giuseppe Mascarello
and Bruno Giacosa, Piemonte

Terraced Nebbiolo vineyard in Donnaz, Valle d'Aosta

WINEGROWING AREAS OF NORTHWEST ITALY

Valle d'Aosta

SMALL IN BOTH AREA and production, Valle d'Aosta is inevitably overlooked in the dash south to the famous wines of the Langhe *(see p206)*. This is a great shame as Aosta's viticultural history is as rich as any in Italy and the labour involved in coaxing grapes from the collage of steep, terraced vineyards is enough to threaten their very existence.

The long, narrow Aosta valley follows the Dora Baltea River. Agriculture here is backbreaking work as flat land is in short supply and there is little topsoil. The vine, however, boldly goes where other crops fear to tread and Valle d'Aosta has developed its own style of viticulture, albeit on a tiny scale. The fresh, elegant wines of Valle d'Aosta remain undiscovered and undervalued.

Bruna label, Liguria

Tucked up against the Piemontese border is the DOC of **Donnaz**, a natural extension of Piemonte's Carema. The grape common to both is Nebbiolo, and its perfumed scent is a defining feature throughout. Although the wines of Donnaz lack the power of Barolo or Barbaresco, they offer Nebbiolo of peerless elegance and purity.

As the valley turns east, the neat terraces of **Chambave** DOC come into view. Of late this area has developed an enviable reputation for dessert wines made from Moscato (Muscat) in the *passito* style *(see p280)*. Lighter and racier than those from the south, they are as fine as any in Italy. Chambave also produces

a modest red from Petit Rouge, a grape that increases in prominence further west up the valley. Well suited to the vagaries of the Aostan climate, Petit Rouge is the region's most common variety and the mainstay of the DOCs of **Enfer d'Arvier** and **Torrette**, near the city of Aosta. Firm acidity, moderate colour, and a bouquet reminiscent of redcurrant jelly go well with the local hearty mountain fare.

The vineyards of **Blanc de Morgex et de la Salle** DOC sit under the shadow of Mont Blanc. At 1,200m they are among the highest in Europe, and the wines, from the local Prié Blanc grape, combine high acidity with a firm mineral intensity.

To avoid relegation to IGT, the DOC of **Valle d'Aosta** permits varietal labelling for a number of grapes grown in the valley. There is a band of local stars in addition to the ubiquitous Chardonnay. Of these, the white Petite Arvine takes top place. Its mineral and gooseberry character can compete with flavours in the best wines of Sancerre or Pouilly-Fumé. The red Prëmetta appears to be staging a comeback here through the efforts of a handful of dedicated growers and offers an affable, fruity nose reminiscent of Beaujolais. There are also some compelling examples of Pinot Grigio (Pinot Gris), often, and confusingly, labelled as Malvoisie.

🗺 *gravelly, sand, clay* 🍇 *Nebbiolo, Petit Rouge, Prëmetta* 🍇 *Moscato, Prié Blanc, Chardonnay, Petite Arvine, Pinot Grigio* 🍷 *red, white, sparkling, dessert*

Piemonte

See p206.

Liguria

THE SWEEPING ARC OF Liguria stretches from the French Riviera to northern Tuscany and includes some of Europe's most valuable land. Tourism and all things maritime have kept the light of Ligurian winemaking under a bushel, but this is a region of enormous potential.

Liguria's rare combination of altitude and maritime influences create a mesoclimate ideally suited to the production of aromatic whites. Wine made from the Vermentino grapes of Liguria can rival the best from Sardegna (Sardinia) and many would argue that its freshness and concentration elevate it to a class of its own. Pear and apple flavoured Vermentino joins the local and equally distinguished almond and apricot flavoured Pigato. Rarely oaked, both are ideal with Ligurian seafood or as an accompaniment to *pesto*, another Ligurian creation.

Although justifiably famous for its whites, Liguria is also Italy's last outpost of Rossese, a red grape still prized for its light body and delicious aromas of redcurrant and strawberry. The versatility of this grape in terms of its ability to age and its uncanny affinity for seafood has earned it DOC protection in **Rossese di Dolceacqua**. Producers in this small enclave, huddled next to the French border, share a dedication to returning this variety to its rightful place in the wine world's canon of elegant reds. Rossese di Dolceacqua is the only denomination devoted entirely to this grape and is also Liguria's only red wine DOC.

Next door, the sprawling **Riviera Ligure di Ponente** DOC (which translates as 'Liguria's sunset coast') sweeps around to the city of Genova. It is Liguria's largest DOC in terms of both area and volume, and 80 per cent of production is white. Helpfully, the wines are varietally labelled, and Rossese appears again under the Riviera Ligure di Ponente banner, although the aristocratic Pigato and Vermentino are the main varieties.

Across the Golfo di Genoa is the Riviera di Levante, a beautiful and popular rocky coastline. The rugged peninsula of Cinque Terre and its five villages juts into the Mediterranean to the west of La Spezia. Clinging to these forbidding slopes is one of Italy's most improbable DOCs. **Cinque Terre** comprises a series of ancient terraces that have more in common with Valle d'Aosta than they do with the Mediterranean. The sacrifices necessary to work the slopes in this region act as a barrier to all but the most dedicated grower and production today for the entire DOC is less than that of some individual Bordeaux châteaux. These wines, however, make wine lovers wish for more hardy producers.

In Cinque Terre, Vermentino is blended with Bosco and Albarola. Their heady mix of herbal notes, ripe fruit character, and mineral hues together make for some of Liguria's finest white wines. The unpronounceable Sciacchetrà is a dessert wine made in the *passito* style *(see p280)* from Bosco, a grape that shares with Malvasia a herbal twist ideally suited to the production of sweet wine.

To the north of Cinque Terre lies the DOC of **Colline di Levanto**, a perennial under-achiever, and to the south, straddling the border with Tuscany, is the more noteworthy **Colli di Luni**. Reliable, rather than exciting, dry whites for enjoyable holiday drinking come from both DOCs.

🍇 *iron-rich clay, limestone* 🍇 *Rossese, Dolcetto, Sangiovese* 🍇 *Vermentino, Pigato, Bosco, Albarola* 🍷 *red, white, sparkling, dessert*

Harvest worker in the hills around Manarola, one of the five Cinque Terre villages, Liguria

Lombardia

THIS IS ITALY'S INDUSTRIAL HEARTLAND and home to the nation's fashion and financial capital, Milano. In geographical terms it comprises a sizeable chunk of Northwest Italy, including a vast swathe of the Po Valley and the lion's share of the Italian lakes. Overshadowed by the giants of Italian production – Piemonte, Emilia-Romagna, and the Veneto – Lombardia's fledgling wine industry has never quite developed a reputation to rival its illustrious neighbours. However, its profile has, in recent years, been boosted through the flurry of activity in the zone of **Franciacorta,** following its elevation to DOCG status in 1995. It remains the country's only denomination dedicated to sparkling wine production using the traditional method *(see p166).* Sparkling wine's aura of sophistication has acted as a magnet for both winemakers and investors keen to show the world that Italy can produce sparkling wines to compete with the best from Champagne. Rivalry aside, there is no doubt that Franciacorta is now the reference point for all Italian sparkling wines, and serious examples abound.

The quality of Franciacorta's wines is due to a number of factors, not least of which is the considerable investment made by many producers. Low yields, the latest technology, and the no-expense-spared dedication to quality also make considerable impact. The unrewarding, stony soil of these alpine foothills south of Lago d'Iseo is well-suited to the production of high-quality grapes. The soil's low fertility, combined with the area's continental climate and frequent fogs, goes some way to creating a sparkling wine *terroir.*

Finally, the DOCG regulations themselves impose stringent criteria: only three grape varieties (Chardonnay, Pinot Noir, and, to a lesser extent, Pinot Bianco) are permitted, and the minimum time spent on lees *(see p166)* must be 18 months for non-vintage wines and 30 months for vintage. Still wines made in this area are entitled to the **Terre di**

Vineyards in Valtellina, Lombardia

Franciacorta DOC, where the sparkling wine trio of grapes are joined by a host of international players, including Bordeaux varieties (mainly the two Cabernets and Merlot).

East of Lago d'Iseo and immediately south of Lago di Garda, straddling the Lombardia-Veneto border, the DOC of **Lugana** enjoys much the same climate and soil as its more illustrious neighbour. The DOC permits the production of sparkling wines, but Lugana's reputation is for its Trebbiano, a notoriously unimaginative white grape infamous for its prodigious yields. On the rolling hills of Lugana, however, Trebbiano undergoes a Cinderella-like transformation into a perfumed celebrity achieving unheard-of freshness and longevity.

Tenuta Roveglia label, Lugana

Between Lago d'Iseo and Lago di Como lies the DOC of **Valcalepio.** Next door to Franciacorta and sharing its natural advantages, there is little excuse for Valcalepio's lacklustre performance since its demarcation in 1976. The host of inter-national varieties planted here are capable of much more, but the apathy that gripped Italian winemaking during the 1970s and 80s continues to dominate production.

Some 100km north of Valcalepio and Franciacorta is the alpine valley of **Valtellina Superiore** DOCG. The Adda River runs through this area in much the same way as the Dora Baltea does in Valle d'Aosta and has carved a similarly steep valley. There are many other similarities between these two zones,

THE TRUTH ABOUT LAMBRUSCO

The dry, red, and slightly sparkling reality of a quality Lambrusco may come as a surprise to many who expect a sweet, frothy white. Prized as the ideal counterpoint to rich Parma ham and Parmesan, Lambrusco's overnight success in the 1980s encouraged gross overproduction until the final product bore no resemblance to the original. Producers removed the grape's natural colour (red), added unnecessary sugar, and bottled the sparkling wine under screwcap. A decline in sales and fall from grace were almost inevitable. Today, however, resurrection is afoot. Traditional DOCs such as **Sorbara** and **Grasparossa di Castelvetro** (Emilia) have recently been given a new lease of life. The best

examples of Lambrusco are sourced from vineyards in the foothills of the Apennines to the south of Modena. The north-facing slopes delay ripening and the grapes arrive at the winery with only moderate amounts of sugar and a bracing natural acidity. These features make good Lambrusco a perfect foil for the rich cooking of the region. A short maceration extracts colour rather than tannins, and the final part of the fermentation is completed in sealed tanks to preserve some carbon dioxide. Proper Lambrusco must be DOC, made from Lambrusco grapes, and bottled under a mushroom cork. It will almost always be dry with a light, refreshing sparkle, moderate alcohol, and immediate grapiness.

including a fascination with Nebbiolo (known here as Chiavennasca), which is far from its natural home in the Langhe. In contrast with the 2,000m peaks on all sides, the vineyards are planted at a more modest 300–400m and Nebbiolo, against the odds, reaches maturity during the brief, hot summer. Valtellina is divided into five subzones: Maroggia, Sassella, Grumello, Inferno, and Valgella; each may appear on the label. The designation *sforzato* indicates that the wine is made from dried grapes in the style of Valpolicella's *amarone* (see p229). **Sforzati di Valtellina** DOCG wines are inevitably high in alcohol and extract, and represent the pinnacle of Valtellinese winemaking.

In contrast to the immaculate vineyards of Valtellina, the sprawling DOC of **Oltrepò Pavese** is enormous (nearly as big as Soave). Confusingly, this DOC has 10 permitted

varieties and produces wines of variable quality, and there is little to encourage the unravelling of the arcane DOC legislation. To their credit, a few producers are attempting to turn the tide. Consumption of these wines is a local affair, and particular affection is shown for the lively wines made from the local Bonarda (Croatina) grape. These include Sangue di Giuda – a sparkling, sweet red wine which is not dissimilar to Piemonte's Brachetto d'Acqui.

limestone with clay, chalk, or gravel overlay; heavy clay ▨ *Nebbiolo, Barbera, Bonarda, Lambrusco, Cabernet Sauvignon, Cabernet Franc, Merlot, Pinot Nero* ▨ *Trebbiano, Cortese, Chardonnay, Pinot Bianco, Moscato, Pinot Grigio, Malvasia, Riesling, Riesling Italico* ▨ *red, white, rosé, sparkling, dessert*

Emilia

BARRING FRASCATI, the Malvasia grape's importance in **Colli Piacentini** – Emilia's key DOC – is unrivalled anywhere in Italy; and Gutturnio, produced from a blend of Barbera and Bonarda (Croatina), also enjoys huge local popularity. Emilia's other key DOCs include **Sorbara** and **Grasparossa di Castelvetro**, known for their production of traditional Lambrusco *(see above)*.

limestone, clay, chalk (hills); fertile clay, alluvial sand (plains) ▨ *Barbera, Bonarda, Cabernet Sauvignon, Pinot Nero, Lambrusco* ▨ *Trebbiano, Chardonnay, Pinot Grigio, Malvasia, Sauvignon Blanc* ▨ *red, white, rosé, sparkling, dessert*

La Stoppa vineyard in Colli Piacentini, Emilia

TOP PRODUCERS OF NORTHWEST ITALY

Institut Agricole Régional
Valle d'Aosta

regione La Rochère, 1A, Aosta **C** *0165 215811* W *www.iaraosta.it* ○ *by appt*

THE REGIONAL WINEMAKING college in Aosta has already made a name for itself by turning out some of the country's leading winemakers, but it has now gone a step further and begun to sell the products of its stunning new experimental winery. Unfettered by commercial considerations, the focus here is on quality alone and the results are extremely encouraging. Take the Pinot Gris (Pinot Grigio), for example. Weighing in at a hefty 14.5 per cent alcohol, it could easily appear top-heavy; but the broad streak of Aostan acidity keeps it on its toes. Most impressive, however, is the Nebbiolo sourced from steep-sloped vineyards at 900m. This explosive mix of ripe black fruit and smoky oak would shame many a Barolo.

red, white ★ most recent

★ *Valle d'Aosta: Pinot Gris, Petite Arvine; Trésor du Caveau VdT*

Bruna
Liguria/Riviera Ligure di Ponente

via Umberto I 81, Ranzo **C** *0183 318082* ○ *by appt*

THE WORLD NEEDS MORE Ligurian Pigato specialists and more first-class winemakers like Riccardo Bruna, who, after 30 years in the cellar, is as excited today about the prospect of making great Pigato and Rossese as he has ever been. His wines are intense, artisan interpretations of these grapes from vineyards high in the Ligurian

Selection of Bellavista wines

Alps. His top wine, Pigato U Baccan, is a lush expression of honeysuckle and almond supported by wonderful acidity that will keep it at its peak for a number of years. The Pigato Villa Torrachetta is slightly less complex but offers an abundance of moreish tropical fruit. Bruna also makes Rossese Le Russeghine: one of the best examples around of this light, elegant grape.

red, white ★ most recent

★ *Riviera Ligure di Ponente: Pigato U Baccan, Pigato Villa Torrachetta, Rossese Le Russeghine*

Walter de Batté
Liguria/Cinque Terre

via Trarcantu 25, Riomaggiore **C** *0187 920127* ○ *by appt*

THE FIRST PERSON to attempt any form of agriculture on the slopes of the Cinque Terre must have acted in desperation; to continue this folly in the 21st century takes an individual of uncompromising character.

'Uncompromising' only partly describes the tenacious character of Walter de Batté, who continues to tend his precious plots of local grapes Bosco and Albarola entirely by hand. His winery could double as an agricultural museum. The wines, however, silence all critics. The Cinque Terre develops slowly in the glass, eventually revealing freshness and layers of stone fruit that dance on the tongue. His Sciacchetrà is utterly captivating, with honeyed sweetness and crisp acidity playing one against the other.

white, dessert ★ most recent

★ *Cinque Terre, Cinque Terre Sciacchetrà*

Bellavista
Lombardia/Franciacorta

via Bellavista 5, Erbusco **C** *0307 762000* W *www.bellavistasrl.it* ○ *by appt*

THE JEWEL IN the Moretti family's crown, Bellavista is more like a way of life than a mere estate. Attached to its winery is one of Italy's most celebrated restaurants as well as one of its most sumptuous hotels. The Moretti family made their fortune in construction but their passion, clearly, lies in wine. Given

Modern label of Bruna's top wine

the amount of money invested here, it is not surprising that the quality is uniformly high. Although still wines are also made, the sparkling wines command all the attention. The vintage Gran Cuvée Brut offers levels of biscuity complexity that ought to send the people of Champagne running for cover.

🖼 red, white, sparkling

📷 2006, 2004, 2001, 1999

★ Franciacorta: Gran Cuvée Brut, Gran Cuvée Pas Operé

Cà dei Frati
Lombardia/Lugana

via Frati 22, Sirmione 📞 030 919468 🖳 www.cadeifrati.it 🔲

OTHER ESTATES IN Lugana may be nipping at its heels but Cà dei Frati remains the one to watch in the much-maligned DOC of Lugana. The Dal Cero brothers have invested heavily in the estate and produce a broad range of styles including still, sparkling, and dessert wines. Their trump card remains the Lugana Brolettino Grand' Annata, a wine with the potential to resuscitate the entire DOC. A strict selection of only the best grapes is fermented in *barriques* and then aged in both wood and bottle. This is Trebbiano at its finest, with a golden colour, a nose redolent of dried fruits and herbal notes, and an aromatic finish. The straight Lugana offers text-book aromas of melon and apple, with plenty of stuffing on the palate. A sparkling Lugana and the luscious IGT dessert wine Tre Filer, a *recioto* style made from Trebbiano, Sauvignon Blanc, and Chardonnay, round off an exemplary portfolio.

Cà dei Frati label

🖼 white, rosé, sparkling, dessert

📷 most recent ★ Lugana: Brolettino Grand'Annata, I Frati; Tre Filer IGT

Cà del Bosco
Lombardia/Franciacorta

via Case Sparse 20, Erbusco 📞 0307 766111 🔲 by appt

CÀ DEL BOSCO remains one of Italy's winemaking elite. The one million bottle annual production of both still and sparkling wines is of an extraordinarily high quality. It is the sparkling wines that receive most of the attention. These include the ethereal Annamaria Clementi, which is made only in the best vintages. The freshly baked bread character derived from more than three years on its lees mingles with elegant citrus fruit in a fitting tribute to the sophistication of Annamaria Clementi Zanella, the estate's founder. Cà del Bosco's Brut Rosé is easily the best in its class, with a fat, ripe, straw-berry fruit character and opulent finish balanced with a touch of residual sugar. Unusual for a sparkling wine producer, the still wines are every bit as thoroughbred as their more famous stablemates. The Cabernet Sauvignon Maurizio Zanella, sourced from a small block of high-density vines, can rival the best examples from Tuscany or Piemonte, while the modern and overtly oaky Chardonnay is a regular visitor to the awards podium.

🖼 red, white, sparkling 📷 2004, 2001, 2000 ★ Franciacorta Brut: Annamaria Clementi, Brut Rosé; Maurizio Zanella IGT

CÀ DEL BOSCO: LEADING THE WAY

In 1968, when Annamaria Clementi Zanella planted her first vines in the forested hills south of Lago d'Iseo, the property was nothing more than, literally, a house in the woods. The Franciacorta zone was one of the few parts of Italy where the vine had failed to gain a foothold, and the gently rolling hills were dotted with the summer homes of Milanese industrialists. Despite the absence of any established viticulture, Annamaria was certain that this area had huge potential for winemaking; unlocking its secret became her abiding passion. It took 10 years of resolve, hard work, and endless experimentation for Cà del Bosco, the 'House in the Woods', to establish – a most single-handedly – Franciacorta as the centre of excellence for Italy's fledgling sparkling wine industry. Today there are dozens of estates mounting credible challenges to Champagne's supremacy, but Cà del Bosco continues to lead the field.

Cavalleri
Lombardia/Franciacorta

via Provinciale 96, Erbusco 📞 *0307 760217* 🌐 *www.cavalleri.it* 🕐 *by appt*

A VISIT TO THE Cavalleri estate, with its turreted gates and stately drive, is like stepping back in time. Cavalleri's tradition of making excellent Franciacorta is both an object of great pride and a role that the family takes very seriously. The style is one of pleasing rusticity; the characters of both grape and winemaking are given equal billing. Long ageing on lees (four years for the vintage wines) confers additional complexity, but the primary fruit character is always in evidence. Cavalleri's vintage Satèn is the pick of the crop – the luxurious mousse and toasted brioche character make an idyllic summer sparkler.

🔲 *red, white, sparkling* 📷 *2001, 2000, 1998* ★ *Franciacorta Brut Satèn*

Mazzolino
Lombardia/ Oltrepò Pavese

via Mazzolino 26, Corvino San Quirico 📞 *0383 876122* 🌐 *www.tenuta-mazzolino.com* 🕐 *by appt*

THE OLTREPÒ PAVESE DOC produces oceans of wine, and most of it is best forgotten. Tenuta Mazzolino is the lone

Nino Negri label

beacon in this sea of mediocrity. International varieties are skilfully vinified by a team of French oenologists who have more than a passing familiarity with the likes of Pinot Nero (Pinot Noir) and Cabernet Sauvignon, and these sit alongside an impressive range of local specialities such as Bonarda. The Pinot Nero deserves separate mention – it is one of Italy's best, with Pinot's telltale red berry fruit and elegant mid-palate much in evidence.

🔲 *red, white, dessert*
📷 *white: most recent; red: 2004*
★ *Oltrepò Pavese: Chardonnay, Cabernet Sauvignon, Pinot Nero*

Nino Negri
Lombardia/Valtellina

via Ghibellini 3, Chiuro 📞 *0342 482521* 🌐 *www.giv.it* 🕐

THE NEGRI ESTATE is the undisputed king of Valtellina. Not only does it produce a complete range from each of the subdistricts, it also makes a range of *sforzati* – the *amarone*-style wines for which Valtellina is famous. Annual volumes are approaching one million bottles a year, which makes the extremely high quality across the board even more impressive. Top of the ladder is the Sfursat Cinque Stelle, an immortal Nebbiolo combining palate-numbing tannin with an immense concentration of tobacco, chocolate, and dried fruit. These are traditional renderings of Nebbiolo – lengthy maceration times and a couple of years' cask maturation result in the orangey rim and oxidized character associated with the Nebbiolo of yesteryear. This old-fashioned approach may have its critics, but older vintages show great balance and freshness.

🔲 *red, white* 📷 *2001, 1999, 1998* ★ *Valtellina Superiore Vigna Fracia, Valtellina Sfursat Cinque Stelle*

Tenuta Roveglia
Lombardia/Lugana

loc Roveglia, 1, Pozzolengo 📞 *030 918663* 🌐 *www.tenutaroveglia.it* 🕐

THE MANICURED exterior of Tenuta Roveglia hides one of Lombardia's most dynamic producers and one with a true passion for Trebbiano. The least expensive Lugana is a splendid

Racks of Franciacorta wine at Cavalleri

introduction to this DOC's affordable, nutty, and faintly aromatic pleasures. Up another notch from this in terms of quality is the Vigne di Catullo, from a plot of old-vine Trebbiano. Bitter almonds mingle with melon and a bracing citrus acidity provides focus; the length is extraordinary given the wine's humble origins and modest price.

🍷 white, sparkling 📆 most recent
★ Lugana Superiore Vigne di Catullo

Triacca
Lombardia/Valtellina

via Nazionale 121, Villa di Tirano
📞 0342 701352
🌐 www.triacca.com ◻ by appt

NEBBIOLO IS A DIFFICULT GRAPE to nurture successfully at the best of times, but coaxing it to ripeness in the Alpine conditions of the Valtellina is a labour of love. It must be frustrating to toil on steep, terraced vineyards, patiently wait for grapes to dry, and age wines in wood for long periods, only for the wine drinking fraternity to take precious little notice of your labour. Domenico Triacca, however, relishes a challenge and seems undaunted by the Valtellina's limited following among wine lovers. That these wines deserve wider appreciation is beyond doubt. Triacca's Valtellina *sforzato*, made from partially dried grapes, uses Nebbiolo's structure as a foil for truly decadent amounts of black fruit and mineral intensity. The Valtellina Prestigio replicates much of the *sforzato's* charms in a more accessible model best consumed with lashings of hearty mountain stew.

🍷 red, white 📆 2001, 2000, 1999
★ Valtellina Sforzato, Valtellina Superiore Prestigio

Uberti
Lombardia/Franciacorta

via Enrico Fermi 2, Erbusco 📞 0307 267476 🌐 www.ubertivini.it ◻ by appt

A FAR CRY FROM the glittering hobby estates typical of Franciacorta, Uberti remains a resolutely family concern, run with fastidious care by Agostino and Eleonora Uberti. Annual production is just 120,000 bottles a year, and these are sourced entirely from their own vineyards. The craftsmanship evident across the range catapults Uberti straight into the front ranks of Franciacorta's winemaking fraternity. Top marks go to the Extra Brut Comarì del Salem, a wine whose residual sugar is more than balanced by a wealth of apple and toasty complexity. The Satèn Magnificentia is a fusion of stone fruit and biscuity elegance with layers of flavour on the finish.

🍷 red, white, sparkling 📆 2004, 2000, 1997 ★ Franciacorta: Extra Brut Comarì del Salem, Satèn Magnificentia

La Stoppa label

La Stoppa
Emilia/Colli Piacentini

fraz Ancarano, Rivergaro 📞 0523 958159 🌐 www.lastoppa.it ◻ by appt

BY EMILIAN STANDARDS, the La Stoppa winery is quite small – making just 200,000 bottles from the company's own vineyards – but this gives owner Elena Pantaleoni control over every aspect of production. The bordeaux-style blend 'Stoppa' offers a well-judged mouthful of fruit and wood, but the Malvasia Passito Vigna del Volta is the real showstopper. Ten months in oak have added a lick of spicy vanilla to the herbal, honeyed, concentrated Malvasia. The Colli Piacentini could do with more wineries like this one.

🍷 red, white, dessert 📆 2004, 2001, 2000 ★ Colli Piacentini: Cabernet Sauvignon Stoppa, Malvasia Passito Vigna del Volta

La Tosa
Emilia/Colli Piacentini

loc La Tosa, Vigolzone
📞 0523 870727 ◻ by appt

THE COLLI PIACENTINI DOC is not an area renowned for quality wines. First-rate producers are few and far between, and this DOC is seldom included in the pantheon of great Italian wines. It is therefore all the more pleasing to taste the range of excellent, modestly priced wines from La Tosa, owned by Stefano and Ferruccio Pizzamiglio. The aim of purity of fruit together with varietal character is largely achieved, and the Malvasia, Sauvignon Blanc, and Cabernet Sauvignon are all hugely drinkable examples of this region's potential.

🍷 red, white, sparkling 📆 red: 2004, 2000, 1999; white: most recent ★ Colli Piacentini: Malvasia Sorriso di Cielo, Cabernet Sauvignon Luna Selectiva, Sauvignon Blanc

Hilltop village of Castiglione Falletto in Barolo, the Langhe

WINEGROWING AREAS OF PIEMONTE

PIEMONTE IS HOME to the pre-eminent DOCGs of Barolo and Barbaresco. Together they represent some of Italy's – and the world's – finest wines. The region's reputation is ineradicably linked to the grape Nebbiolo, but it also offers the wine lover much more than just the produce of its two most famous sons. Vineyards cover every inch of Piemonte, which is made up of a complicated series of interlocking DOCs. They break down into five key areas: Asti, Alba, the northern and eastern DOCs, and the Langhe – the heart of winegrowing in Piemonte.

Harvesting Nebbiolo grapes

▨ *morainic with gravel or stone outcrops (north); limestone (Langhe); limestone, loam, clay (Asti); limestone with alluvial gravel or iron-rich marl (east)* 🔲 *Nebbiolo, Dolcetto, Barbera, Freisa, Grignolino, Brachetto, Croatina (Bonarda)* 🔲 *Erbaluce, Moscato, Cortese, Arneis, Timorasso* 🔲 *red, white, sparkling, dessert*

The Langhe

THE LANGHE *terroir* is at the heart of northern Italy's finest red wines. The combination of climate, grape, and soil is every bit as potent as in Bordeaux or Burgundy, and the wines' balance and longevity are also a match. The Langhe, from the Latin for 'tongue', comprises the system of steep, narrow hills extending north from the Alpi Liguri, bounded to the west and north by the Tanaro River, and to the east by the Bormida River. Crucially, it drains to the north, preserving steep, south-facing slopes, and boasts a mix of soils not found elsewhere.

The summits of the Langhe hills have a lime-stone content unrivalled in northern Italy; marl dominates the middle slopes, while higher proportions of clay are found in the valley bottoms. These three soil types broadly correspond to the three key grape varieties planted in the Langhe: Nebbiolo, Barbera, and Dolcetto. Nebbiolo is the slowest to ripen and the finest quality. This grape takes pride of place on the top of steep south- or east-facing slopes and produces the area's star DOCG wines **Barolo** and **Barbaresco**. Barbera claims the middle ground, while Dolcetto is on the north- or west-facing slopes or the heavier, alluvial soils on the valley floor.

These two grapes make the wines of Asti and Alba important subregions in their own right (see pp208–9), as well as the wines of **Dogliani** DOCG. The **Langhe** DOC itself is a catch-all for the many good wines produced outside the famous DOCG areas.

Harvest dates are proof of the influence of the sea on the Langhe climate; Barbaresco is typically a week earlier than Barolo, despite being further north. Cooler sea air, particularly at night, stabilizes acidity levels, which would otherwise drop during the sweltering summer. Rainfall is a major concern. The wettest months are May and September, critical times for flowering and harvesting; and hail, encouraged by hot, dry weather, can wreak havoc. Despite Nebbiolo's robust constitution, vintage variation can be significant.

THE CLASSIC WINES OF THE LANGHE

ALTHOUGH THERE IS MUCH MORE TO THE LANGHE *than Barolo and Barbaresco, it is these two wines that have drawn the world's attention to the misty hillsides of this corner of Piemonte. The cantankerous Nebbiolo grape ripens to perfection here, making wines that are must-haves in every serious cellar. Barbera and Dolcetto, too, must be counted as modern classics (see also pp208–9).*

Barolo

BAROLO IS A GRACEFUL, sumptuous expression of the winemaker's art, and the Nebbiolo grape is key. When young, the daunting mass of tannins and acidity renders the wine impenetrable and aloof, although its perfume is already sublime. Violet, redcurrant, and liquorice aromas are prominent; it is intense and yet imprecise, hinting at impending greatness rather than characterized by a single element. With age (at least a decade for even the more modest wines) the bouquet develops an eloquence that is lacking in its youth – floral notes are joined by peppery tones, the fruit moves from red to black, and a liquorice tinge joins the tobacco, leather, and tar flavours. Nebbiolo's firm acidity comes into its own with extended ageing; it provides focus while the tannin's

Barolo from Domenico Clerico

rough edges gently soften. The best wines will easily last 20 years, perhaps more, but older examples in peak condition are thin on the ground. Relatively recent changes in vinification have established a new quality benchmark, and current examples are unquestionably the finest the region has ever made. The Barolo DOCG, in the west of the Langhe, comprises the five communes of La Morra, Barolo, Monforte d'Alba, Serralunga d'Alba, and Castiglione Falletto, and includes the vineyards of Cannubi, Brunate, La Serra, Monprivato, and Bussia.

Barbaresco

ALSO MADE FROM NEBBIOLO, Barbaresco, in the centre of the Langhe region, has a reputation as Barolo's 'sister'. However, although the wines from top producers are every bit as concentrated, structured, and impressive as Barolo, subtle differences do exist. The tannins are softer, the fruit is more red than black, and these wines evolve more quickly than Barolo. Admittedly, these factors are influenced as much by the winemaker as they are by the *terroir*. There are three communes within Barbaresco DOCG – Neive, Treiso, and Barbaresco itself – and production, at an average of three million bottles per year, is one third that of Barolo.

Dogliani

DOGLIANI DOCG is immediately south of Barolo. Dolcetto is planted on limestone summits here, and the wines produced are powerful and aromatic. Exceptional examples of Dolcetto, they are testimony to the strength of the Langhe *terroir*.

Barbaresco vineyards above the Tanaro Valley

Vineyards around Casorzo in the Monferrato hills, Asti

Asti

SURROUNDED BY HILLS covered with vines, the medieval city of Asti has been at the centre of Piemontese viticulture for centuries, and winemakers have exploited its natural potential to the full. It has, however, acquired a bewildering array of DOCs. Much of the confusion arises from the multiplicity of varieties grown in this small area: Asti is home to five permitted grapes, with Barbera and Moscato taking the lead roles.

The geography of the hills surrounding Asti plays a critical role in defining the DOC structure. To the north of the city, running in a broad band between the rivers Po and Tanaro, lie the Monferrato hills. This is Barbera country, and there is a separate DOC, **Barbera del Monferrato**, to recognize the grape's particular affinity for the clay and loam soils. Other grapes grown in this region, including Freisa, Dolcetto, and Cortese, must settle for the catch-all **Monferrato** DOC, to which the name of the grape may be appended. South of Monferrato and the Tanaro River and southeast of Asti lies **Barbera d'Asti** DOC. This district is essentially an extension of Barbaresco, although the soil here contains more clay and less limestone and is therefore unsuitable for Nebbiolo. Fortunately, Barbera excels in these heavier soils. Barbera d'Asti DOC, with the subzones of Nizza and Tinella, reveals the grape's finest moment, and Barbera grown here has an unrivalled richness and texture. Alcohol levels of up to 15 per cent are balanced by masses of black fruit and Barbera's telltale gaminess.

Older vintages suggest flawless balance and reflect the grape's oft-overlooked capacity for ageing.

Bordering Barbera d'Asti are the twin DOCGs of **Asti** and **Moscato d'Asti**, both reserved for sweet, sparkling wines made by the Asti method. These overlapping DOCGs account for an astonishing 65 million bottles of sparkling white wine per year. Asti is a wine of noble pedigree sullied by generations of shoddy vinification and overproduction. At its best it is unashamedly grapey and light in alcohol. As a rule, Moscato d'Asti tends to be lighter, finer, and more artisan than Asti. The neighbouring **Brachetto d'Acqui** DOCG produces a gloriously sweet, frothy red dessert wine which is redolent of strawberries.

Between Asti and Gavi are two DOCs dedicated exclusively to Dolcetto: **Dolcetto d'Acqui** and **Dolcetto di Ovada**, which produce fresh and uncomplicated versions that champion Dolcetto's sweet black fruit and youthful charms.

To the southwest of Asti, the DOCG of **Roero** is restricted to two main varieties, Nebbiolo and Arneis, although there are also significant plantings of Barbera in these sandy soils. Nebbiolo here is a great-value alternative to its neighbours Barolo and Barbaresco. Arneis, on the other hand, is pleasantly oily with aromas of quince. Finally, there are a number of DOCs that do not have a strong regional connection and are simply labelled after the

THE ASTI METHOD

Asti was the world's first sweet sparkling wine, and represented the height of technical sophistication when it was first made more than a century ago. It is produced by the Asti method, whereby grape-must ferments in sealed tanks until it reaches between five and seven per cent alcohol. By this stage the wine is fully sparkling, yet still contains significant amounts of unfermented sugar. It is then filtered under pressure to prevent further fermentation. Both Moscato d'Asti and Asti are designed for immediate consumption; the aim is to preserve as much freshness as possible.

variety from which they are made. These are scattered across numerous communes around Asti and include a trio of light reds designed for early consumption: **Freisa d'Asti**, **Dolcetto d'Asti**, and **Grignolino d'Asti**. At their best they show a marked red fruit intensity allied to a refreshing fizz.

Alba

ALBA'S DOCS MIRROR THE pattern found in Asti and extend over many communes around the town. Alba's varietal DOCs such as **Dolcetto d'Alba** and **Barbera d'Alba** produce superb wines which, when made by the top growers, represent exceptional value. There is also **Nebbiolo d'Alba**, a DOC of declining importance, even though its wines are good quality and modestly priced.

The North

PIEMONTE'S NORTHERN WINEGROWING DISTRICTS are little appreciated. North of Turin, **Carema** DOC is on the border with Valle d'Aosta, and the area's steep terraces produce Nebbiolo with a rare purity of flavour. Just to the south, where the gradients are more amenable, the DOC of **Erbaluce di Caluso** yields both dry and sweet wines from the grape of the same name. The dry version, faintly aromatic and with a fresh bite of acidity, is pleasant enough. The sweet Caluso Passito, however, ranks as one of Italy's foremost dessert wines. Made from grapes dried in the *passito* style *(see p280)*, it combines the natural acidity of Erbaluce with a gloriously oxidized nose of marmalade and honey. It is rarely encountered outside the DOC.

East of Caluso unfolds a succession of near-derelict DOCs planted on the south-facing slopes of the Po Valley. These are ideally suited to viticulture, and Nebbiolo, known locally as Spanna, has no trouble reaching maturity here. In the late 1960s, as Barolo and Barbaresco began their meteoric rise, Ghemme and Gattinara were similarly upgraded to DOCG status, but today they, and other local DOCs, are virtually unknown. **Ghemme**, **Gattinara**, **Boca**, **Bramaterra**, and **Lessona** all look to Nebbiolo for inspiration, and sell their wines at prices that seem increasingly modest.

Sparkling wine from Asti

TRADITIONAL VERSUS MODERN?

Piemonte's distinguished history of quality wine production includes a number of traditions. The debate focuses on two issues: maceration and maturation. In years gone by the grapes, riddled by viruses, had difficulty ripening. The unripe grapes were subjected to a long maceration in an attempt to extract some colour from the pale skins, but this had the unwanted side effect of extracting tannins, too. Faced with a surfeit of tannins the producers matured the wine for several years in oak. In great vintages the result was a wine of ample structure balanced by sufficient fruit, but in the majority of cases the wines were unbalanced. Recent viticultural advances now ensure that the grapes ripen fully, and maceration and maturation times are being reduced. This has resulted in fruitier, less tannic wines that are more approachable in their youth; but traditionalists argue that the pendulum has swung too far and that great wines may now lose the uncompromising character that initially won them hard-fought recognition.

The East

THE EASTERN PART OF PIEMONTE is home to one of Italy's handful of still, white DOCGs, **Gavi**. Rarely seen outside this DOCG, the local grape Cortese has an obvious affinity for the alluvial soil with its occasional outcroppings of iron-rich veins. The Gavi vineyards are sited north of Genoa, and the maritime influence preserves vital acidity. Gavi's lofty reputation perhaps surpasses the uncomplicated charms of its wines: inevitably light and fresh, Gavi allies a firm mineral backbone to a citrus character.

Sandwiched between Gavi and the Oltrepò Pavese, and sadly overlooked as a result, are the unassuming hills of the **Colli Tortonesi** DOC. Thanks to the unstinting efforts of a new generation of producers, this is one of the north's up-and-coming areas. Barbera lies at the heart of the DOC's reds, while the whites rely on both Cortese and local hero Timorasso. There is a cool elegance to all the wines; the reds are polished while the whites have all the class of Gavi at a fraction of the cost.

TOP PRODUCERS OF PIEMONTE

Angelo Gaja
Piemonte/Langhe

via Torino 36, Barbaresco
📞 0173 635158 🔲

THE GREAT Angelo Gaja, Piemonte's indefatigable ambassador, shrewd businessman, and winemaker extraordinaire is a legend in his own lifetime. His fame rests entirely on the reputation of his wines, which were unrivalled for decades. Since the late 1980s, however, there have been serious challenges to his position, and today he is first among equals. Gaja made his name with Barbaresco, and this still leads the field despite the fact that the single-vineyard wines Sorì Tildin, Sorì San Lorenzo, and Costa Russi are now bottled as generic Langhe DOC Nebbiolo, due to his disillusionment with the DOC system. The Sperss and Conteisa, Barolo to anyone else, are also known by this DOC. The quality of this estate's wines lies in the impeccable balance: acidity and tannins, while sufficient to provide focus and structure, never overshadow the wonderful complexities of the fruit. Gaja also owns vineyards in Bolgheri, Tuscany.
🔲 red, white 📅 2004, 2001, 2000, 1999 ★ Langhe: Sorì Tildin, Sperss, Conteisa

Braida
Piemonte/Barbera d'Asti & Brachetto d'Acqui

via Roma 94, Rocchetta Tanaro
📞 0141 644113 🔲 www.braida.it
🔲 by appt

BRAIDA AND BARBERA are inextricably linked in the minds of wine aficionados. The late

Giacomo Bologna devoted his life to raising the profile of the Barbera grape. It was he who first exploited the potential of the clay-rich soil in the hills east of Asti, and who lobbied for improved standards in the Barbera d'Asti DOC. His legacy includes one of the most respected estates in Piemonte and a range of wines that has established Barbera's reputation. Ai Suma is the top wine and can be a trifle oaky in some vintages, but the Bricco dell'Uccellone gets it right with lashings of black fruit and creamy oak. His Brachetto d'Acqui, Piemonte's neglected, frothy red, is the best around.
🔲 red, white, sparkling, dessert 📅 2004, 2001, 2000, 1998 ★ Barbera d'Asti: Ai Suma, Bricco dell'Uccellone; Brachetto d'Acqui

Angelo Gaja reds

Bricco Rocche
Piemonte/Barolo & Barbaresco

via Monforte 63, Castiglione Falletto
📞 0173 62867 🔲 www.ceretto.com
🔲 by appt

THE ESTATE NAME Bricco Rocche, taken from the most prestigious vineyard under its control, is the Barolo branch of the Ceretto family's empire. Bricco Asili, for similar reasons, is the aegis for its Barbaresco operation. The quality of Ceretto's production from both is consistently high. The Barolo and Barbaresco from the eponymous vineyards are the estate's pride and joy, but there is much to savour across an impeccable range.
🔲 red, white, sparkling 📅 2004, 2001,

2000, 1999, 1995, 1990 ★ Barolo Bricco Rocche, Barbaresco Bricco Asili

Bruno Giacosa
Piemonte/Barolo & Barbaresco

via XX Settembre 52, Neive 📞 0173 67027 🔲 www.brunogiacosa.it
🔲 by appt

PERFECTLY COMBINING traditional with modern, Bruno Giacosa displays an equal aptitude for both Barolo and Barbaresco, although his cellars are in the Barbaresco DOCG. The wines are magnificent. The Barolo Falletto, from the commune of Castiglione, is complex and classically proportioned. His Barbaresco Asili offers more delicacy but the telltale grip of Nebbiolo is never far away.
🔲 red, white 📅 2004, 2001, 2000, 1996, 1995 ★ Barolo Falletto, Barbaresco Asili

Cascina La Barbatella
Piemonte/Barbera del Monferrato

strada Annunziata 55, Nizza Monferrato 📞 0141 701434 🔲 by appt

ANGELO SONVICO'S small estate south of the Tanaro has made a name for itself with exemplary Barbera. The Sonvico sees a little Barbera blended with Cabernet Sauvignon to great effect. In the glass, the toasty oak steps aside long

Bricco Rocche label

enough to unveil pure red fruit mingled with nuances of Cabernet's vegetal edge. The structured Barbera Vigna dell'Angelo is also excellent.
🖾 red, white 🔼 2003, 2001, 2000, 1998 ★ Barbera del Monferrato Rosso Sonvico, Barbera d'Asti Superiore Vigna dell'Angelo

Cà Viola
Piemonte/Langhe

borgata San Luigi 11, Dogliani
📞 0173 70547 🔳 www.caviola.com
🔲 by appt

BEPPE CAVIOLA SPENDS so much time working as a consultant winemaker that it is difficult to see how he finds the time to turn out some of Piemonte's most consistent wines here at his own estate. Nevertheless 40,000 bottles a year of superb Barbera, Dolcetto, and Pinot Nero emerge from these atmospheric cellars. Of these, the Dolcetto Barturot is the favourite, an accomplished blend of sweet fruit, soft tannins, and aromatic notes.
🖾 red 🔼 2004, 2001, 2000, 1999, 1995 ★ Langhe Dolcetto Barturot, Langhe Rosso Bric du Luv

Domenico Clerico
Piemonte/Barolo & Langhe

loc Manzoni 67, Monforte D'Alba
📞 0173 78171 🔲 by appt

DOMENICO CLERICO has devoted a lifetime to raising the profile of Barolo. Although the rotary fermenters and new *barriques* in the cellar reflect modernity, the sinewy texture of his wines belie a love of the Langhe's traditional virtues. Deeply coloured and ferociously tannic when young, but endowed with divine complexity, Domenico's wines assert Barolo's outstanding quality among Italian reds. Two thirds of the estate's production comprises Dolcetto, Barbera, and

Ferrando label

Arte – a blend of 85 per cent Nebbiolo with Barbera and Cabernet – but, such is the quality of the Barolos, these are often overlooked. Three Barolos steal the show. The finest of these is Percristina, made from vines in the Mosconi vineyard and labelled in honour of Domenico's daughter. Pajana and Ciabot, the other two Barolo wines, are more muscular expressions, needing at least a decade to reach their peak.
🖾 red 🔼 2004, 2001, 2000, 1997, 1995 ★ Barolo: Percristina, Ciabot Mentin Ginestra; Langhe Rosso Arte

Elio Altare
Piemonte/Barolo & Langhe

fraz Annunziata 51, La Morra
📞 0173 50835 🔲 by appt

A STAUNCH MODERNIST, Elio Altare has shown beyond all doubt that the advent of stainless steel and *barriques* need not necessarily spell the end of Barolo as we know it. His vineyards are clustered in the commune of La Morra, home to Barolo's most elegant and perfumed wines. The flagship wine, Barolo Arborina, redefines avant-garde Barolo with a refined palate, ripe tannins, layers of fruit, and

not inconsiderable power.
🖾 red 🔼 2004, 2001, 2000, 1999, 1995 ★ Earolo Vigneto Arborina, Langhe Rosso Larigi

Enzo Boglietti
Piemonte/Barolo

via Roma 37, La Morra
📞 0173 50330 🔲

MODERN, ELEGANT, and eminently drinkable, the Langhe classics from this young estate have funky labels that reflect innovative intentions. Barolo is the centre of attention, with three versions in production. Brunate, from one of La Morra's top vineyards, is traditional with a tobacco and floral character; Case Nere is more overtly oaky, but with plenty of ripe fruit; and the Fossati combines the best of both worlds.
🖾 red 🔼 2004, 2001, 2000, 1999 ★ Barolo: Brunate, Case Nere, Fossati

Ferrando
Piemonte/Carema & Erbaluce di Caluso

via Torino 599/A, Ivrea 📞 0125 641176 🔳 www.ferrandovini.it 🔲

THE WINES FROM Roberto and Luigi Ferrando's estate represent a broad range of Piemontese winemaking. The highlights include a mesmerizing Carema Etichetta Nera that shows soft, ripe fruit and sensitive use of oak. The balance is exemplary and prices are modest. The sweet Caluso Passito Vigneto Cariola is utter magic. After four years in old oak, this unctuous nectar offers staggering complexity with rose, dried fruit, honey, spice, and vanilla coalescing into one hedonistic glass of dessert wine heaven.
🖾 red, white, sparkling, dessert 🔼 2003, 2001, 2000, 1997 ★ Carema Etichetta Nera, Erbaluce di Caluso Cariola, Caluso Passito Cariola

Giuseppe Mascarello

Giacomo Conterno
Piemonte/Barolo

loc Ornati 2, Monforte d'Alba 📞 0173 78221 🔲 www.cconterno.it ⬜

BORN IN ARGENTINA in 1895, Giacomo Conterno came to Italy in the early 20th century to establish a small restaurant and winery in the town of Monforte d'Alba. The wine was named Monforte or Monfortino, and Conterno's Barolo Monfortino Riserva is still made today. The Conterno cellars are now run by Giacomo's grandson Roberto, but the philosophy has not changed. Extended ageing can stay the release for up to a decade. The results, however, are worth the wait. Made only in good vintages, it can take up to 20 years to hit its stride and then stay on top form for as long again.
🟥 red 🔺 2004, 2001, 1996,1995, 1990, 1988, 1985 ★ Barolo Riserva Monfortino

Giuseppe Mascarello
Piemonte/Barolo, Dolcetto d'Alba & Barbera d'Alba

via Borgonuovo 108, Monchiero 📞 0173 792126 🔲 www.mas carello1881.com ⬜ by appt

MAURO MASCARELLO and his son Giuseppe are the self-appointed guardians of Piemonte's winemaking patrimony. Founded in 1881, the winery has admitted few concessions to the relentless march of technological advancement. Technology, however, can add little to vineyards like these. The Monprivato *cru* is the pride and joy of the Mascarello family – an outstanding *terroir* with a southern exposure and white marl soil. Barolo from Monprivato combines the elegance of La Morra with the power of Serralunga: a blissful marriage. Mascarello's Barolo Monprivato boasts remarkable longevity and grace. A Dolcetto with a generous helping of damson fruit and an alluring Barbera round off the list.
🟥 red 🔺 2004, 2001, 2000, 1999, 1997 ★ Barolo Monprivato, Dolcetto d'Alba Bricco, Barbera d'Alba Scudetto

La Spinetta
Piemonte/Barbaresco & Barbera d'Asti

via Annunziata 17, Castagnole delle Lanze 📞 0141 877396 ⬜ by appt

THOSE WHO CONTINUE to describe Barbaresco as Barolo's 'sister' have yet to meet the inky-black giants that lurk in Giorgio Rivetti's cellars here at La Spinetta. The result of tiny yields (in some vintages less than 20hl/ha) and ageing in 100 per cent new French oak, these are not wines for the faint-hearted. The impenetrable purple hue, explosive nose of cassis and vanilla, and 15 per cent alcohol allied to intense black fruit make for a taste sensation not easily forgotten. The bad news is that the 3.5ha of Barbaresco vineyards limit production. The good news is that Giorgio produces a Barbera d'Asti Superiore that is every bit as compelling as his Barbaresco. Few Piemontese producers can offer a credible challenge to the cult of La Spinetta.
🟥 red, white, sparkling, dessert
🔺 2004, 2001, 2000, 1999
★ Barbaresco Vigna Gallina, Barbera d'Asti Superiore, Monferrato Rosso Pin

La Zerba
Piemonte/Gavi

strada per Francavilla 1, Tassarolo 📞 0143 342259 ⬜ by appt

THE LORENZI family quickly established a reputation for excellence with their Gavi. Far too much Gavi is dilute and overpriced, but this, from a patch of 50-year-old Cortese vines planted on an outcrop of iron-rich *terra rossa* soil, bucks the trend. Ripe greengages and yellow plums herald the arrival of a Gavi that finally justifies the denomination's DOCG status.
🟥 white 🔺 most recent
★ Gavi di Tassarolo Terrarossa

Luciano Sandrone
Piemonte/Barolo & Langhe

via Pugnane 4 📞 0173 560023 🔲 www.sandroneluciano.com ⬜ by appt

IT HAS BEEN 25 years since Luciano Sandrone first released a bottle of Barolo. Not long in Langhe terms, but long enough to have established this estate firmly in Barolo's front ranks. His Barolo Cannubi Boschis hails from what many consider to be the finest slopes in the entire DOCG. Taut and finely crafted, it needs time to develop, but its pedigree

Luciano Sandrone label

is immediately obvious. Sandrone's blend of Barbera and Nebbiolo, Pe Mol, is a gloriously fat and oaky red with just enough tannins to corral the exuberant fruit.

🍷 red 📅 2004, 2001, 2000, 1999, 1995, 1990 ★ Barolo Cannubi Boschis, Nebbiolo d'Alba Valmaggiore

Matteo Correggia
Piemonte/Roero & Barbera d'Alba

case Sparse Garbinetto, via Santo Stefano Roero 124, Canale 📞 0173 978 009 🖥 www.matteo correggia.com 🕐 by appt

THE MAN who gave his name to this estate died a few years ago, but his spirit of uncompromising quality and endless innovation lives on. Much of the current vogue for all things Roeran can be attributed to Matteo Correggia's perseverance with the Nebbiolo and Arneis varieties. Today, his Roche d'Ampsej is a testimony to his sound judgement. This is Nebbiolo caught in a rare moment of uncharacteristic generosity, gushing Bacchanalian decadence and unbridled hedonism. His Barbera d'Alba Marun is almost as good. Arneis, the unsung hero of the Roero, is treated here to a Cinderella makeover and emerges resplendent in lively fruit and finesse.

🍷 red, white 📅 2004, 2001, 2000, 1999, 1997 ★ Roero Roche d'Ampsej, Barbera d'Alba Marun, Roero Arneis

Orsolani
Piemonte/Erbaluce di Caluso

via Michele Chiesa 12, San Giorgio Canavese 📞 0124 32386 🕐 by appt

THE ORSOLANI FAMILY began making wine in this area in the 19th century. Today, they produce more than 100,000 bottles annually, including the world's most captivating

dry Erbaluce. Redolent of green apple, quince, and with a herbal twist, this is not only alarmingly drinkable but also very well priced.

🍷 red, white, dessert 📅 most recent ★ Erbaluce di Caluso La Rustià

Paolo Scavino
Piemonte/Barolo

via Alba Barolo 33, fraz Garbelletto, Castiglione Falletto 📞 0173 62850 🕐 by appt

AT THIS LEGENDARY BAROLO ESTATE with vineyard holdings in the most enviable positions, Enrico Scavino seems incapable of putting a foot wrong. There is Bric del Fiasc from Castiglione, showcasing the muscularity and longevity for which this village is famous. Rocche dell'Annunziata reflects La Morra's elegance and perfume. Cannubi, perhaps the most sought-after vineyard in the entire DOCG, reflects Barolo's irresistible charms – the perfect balance of ripe tannins, sweet fruit, and unforgettable bouquet of spice, flowers, black fruit, and damp earth. Wine does not come any more seductive than this.

🍷 red, white 📅 2004, 2001, 2000, 1996, 1995 ★ Barolo: Bric del Fiasc, Rocche dell'Annunziata, Cannubi

Pecchenino
Piemonte/Dogliani

borgata Valdiberti 59, Dogliani 📞 0173 70686 🕐

NESTLED IN THE HILLS between Monforte d'Alba and Dogliani, the Pecchenino vineyards fall just outside the Barolo border. Not that this is a cause for concern for the brothers Orlando and Attilio – their ambition has always been to produce high quality Dolcetto, and the best vineyards are planted with this

Matteo Correggia label

amiable grape. Their Dolcettos are muscular wines – alcohol levels are often 14 per cent or more and the generous use of new oak may offend purists – but the masses of rich, brambly fruit will melt the heart of all but the sternest critics.

🍷 red, white 📅 2007, 2006 ★ Dogliani Sirì d'Jermu, Dogliani Bricco Botti

Vigneti Massa
Piemonte/Colli Tortonesi

piazza Capsoni 10, Monleale 📞 0131 80302 🕐 by appt

AS QUIET AND UNASSUMING as the gentle hills of the Colli Tortonesi, Walter Massa is nevertheless a truly passionate believer in this remote DOC, home to the local Timorasso variety. Massa's pet grape, this is an elegant white with a fragrant, floral character that belies its capacity for ageing. Barbera is another of Walter's strengths, and he makes two cracking examples. Bigolla, named after a vineyard, is a big, rather caky wine, but the lighter Monleale is a judicious blend of sweet black fruit and vanilla. Last but by no means least is the Croatina Pertichetta, the nation's finest example of wine from the often overlooked Croatina (Bonarda) red grape.

🍷 red, white, dessert 📅 2006, 2004, 2001, 2000, 1999 ★ Colli Tortonesi: Barbera Bigolla, Barbera Monleale; Timorasso Costa del Vento

NORTHEAST ITALY

S TRETCHING FROM the Alps to the Adriatic, with the quintessentially Italian Venezia (Venice) at its heart and bilingual regions on its borders, Northeast Italy is an area of enormous scenic and cultural diversity. Topographical extremes mean that there are growing conditions here for everything from rich, sun-loving red grapes to cool-climate, aromatic white ones.

Of the three geographical regions that make up the modern northeast, the Veneto boasts the oldest winemaking tradition. By the 2nd century BC, viticulture was flourishing here under the Romans. The dried grape red wines of Valpolicella are descendants of an age-old speciality from the hills above Verona. Winegrowing in the border regions has had a more chequered history. It flourished under the Austro-Hungarian empire, which ruled most of the Adige Valley and the far northeast until 1919. However, phylloxera and World War I devastated the vineyards, with long-lasting repercussions. In Friuli-Venezia Giulia (F-VG), the northeast's youngest wine region, recovery only began in the mid-1960s.

The key northeastern regions – Trentino-Alto Adige, the Veneto, and Friuli-Venezia Giulia – collectively grow around 50 officially approved grape varieties. There is a rich portfolio of local grapes, such as Lagrein and Refosco, but international grape varieties like Sauvignon Blanc, Chardonnay, and Pinot Grigio (Pinot Gris), introduced in the late 19th century, also have a consolidated presence.

The northeast produces everything from sparkling wines and dry whites to rosés, reds, and dessert wines, with the Veneto boasting by far the biggest production. *Amarone* (made in the Veneto; *see p229*) is one of Italy's richest and most successful reds; while the well-known Soave, Valpolicella, and Prosecco wines represent the classic Veneto easy-drinking style. Friuli-Venezia Giulia and Trentino-Alto Adige have younger wine-making industries and much smaller production quantities, but their top estate wines rank among the national elite. Unfortunately, local demand for them is huge and often only tiny quantities are left for export.

Grape picker in Trentino

Autumnal vineyards in the hills of the Valpolicella Classico area, the Veneto

◁ **The grand castle of Soave in the Veneto**

WINE MAP OF NORTHEAST ITALY

Maculan, Veneto

THE MAJORITY OF Northeast Italy's best vineyards lie in an area that begins in the northerly Valle dell'Isarco, stretches south through Trentino-Alto Adige to Verona, and then shadows the arc of the Alps across the Veneto and Friuli-Venezia Giulia to the Golfo di Trieste (Gulf of Trieste). Ironically, the area with the most varied soils and climates groups most of its wines under only two main DOCs – Alto Adige and Trentino – although there are some lesser-known DOCs within these. The Veneto and Friuli-Venezia Giulia, on the other hand, have a complex system of overlapping subzones.

KEY

▢ Northeast Italy

NORTHEAST ITALY: AREAS & TOP PRODUCERS

Foradori label, Trentino

TERROIR AT A GLANCE

Latitude: 45.3–47°N.

Altitude: 0–900m.

Topography: Vineyards benefit from the shelter of the Alps and the moderating influence of Lago di Garda (Lake Garda) and the Adriatic. The best sites are on south-facing slopes, mid-altitude hills, and valley sides.

Soil: Extremely varied, from glacial-alluvial to volcanic bedrock, limestone, and sandy gravel beds.

Climate: Generally hot summers and mild winters. Frost is rare thanks to mainly south-facing aspects, the shelter of the high mountains and the moderating influence of Lago di Garda and the Adriatic.

Temperature: July average is 23°C.

Rainfall: Average annual ranges from 500 to 1,450mm.

Viticultural hazards: Hail; unpredictable rainfall; drought.

Produttori San Michele Appiano's winery and vineyard, Alto Adige

Le Vigne di Zamò label, Friuli-Venezia Giulia

Tenuta San Leonardo vineyards, Trentino

PERFECT CASE: NORTHEAST ITALY

R Allegrini La Poja Corvina Veronese IGT £££

W Borgo del Tiglio Collio Bianco Ronco della Chiesa £££

R Cantina Produttori Bolzano Alto Adige Lagrein Riserva Taber £££

S Ferrari Giulio Ferrari Riserva del Fondatore Trento Brut £££

R Foradori Granato Vigneti delle Dolomiti Rosso IGT £££

W Gini Soave Classico Contrada Salvarenza Vecchie Vigne ££

R Le Due Terre Sacrisassi Colli Orientali del Friuli Rosso £££

D Maculan Acininobili Veneto Bianco IGT ££££

W Produttori Termeno Alto Adige Gewürztraminer Nussbaumerhof ££

R Romano Dal Forno Amarone della Valpolicella Vigneto di Monte Lodoletta ££££

W Schiopetto Mario Schiopetto Bianco IGT £££

W Vie di Romans Sauvignon Vieris Friuli Isonzo ££

Lush vineyards of Tenuta San Leonardo in Trentino

WINEGROWING AREAS OF TRENTINO-ALTO ADIGE

THE DISTRICTS OF TRENTINO AND ALTO ADIGE are jointly known as Trentino-Alto Adige for administrative purposes. They are, however, two distinct wine regions, with not only separate histories and characters, but also extreme soil and climate differences. Germanic influences are strong in bilingual Alto Adige, as is evident in many of the dual place and wine names here; while Trentino is much more traditionally Italian.

Alto Adige

ITALY'S NORTHERNMOST wine region, the Alto Adige (Südtirol) is a small and dynamic winemaking district, with only 5,030ha under vine. It has earned a cult following in Italy for its range of exclusive, limited production wines, but it also offers excellent value for money with its more widely available brands.

Part of the Austro-Hungarian empire until 1919, the Valle dell'Adige (Adige Valley) was extensively planted with the rather unexciting Schiava (Vernatsch) grape to ensure the empire had a supply of home-grown red wines.

The modern wine industry in Alto Adige dates from the start of the conversion to more interesting varietals in the late 1970s. Of the new arrivals, Sauvignon Blanc and Chardonnay express the tangy fruit quality of the Alto Adige well, but even better at communicating the region's character are the very dry Pinot Bianco (Pinot Blanc) and the aromatic Silvaner and Riesling. The other

Label from Cesconi, Trentino

authentic *terroir*-driven wine here is Gewürztraminer. Alto Adige's interpretation of this classic aromatic variety is full-bodied, bursting with fruit, flower, and spice aromas, and just off-dry to middling-sweet.

When it comes to reds, growers agree that Schiava, which still covers roughly half the region's total vineyard area, has to be cut back. However, a well-made example is light, soft, dry, and perfect for summer drinking. Lagrein, another local variety, is the grape of the moment. Aged in new oak to break down its chunky tannins, this very characterful variety makes dark, smoky reds with a lot of depth. The six per cent of vineyard area that it occupies is nowhere near enough to meet demand, but expansion is hampered by the fact that Lagrein is very particular about its habitat. The fussiest grape of them all, Pinot Nero (or Pinot Noir), has also found a home from home in the subregion. The cool slopes above the village of Egna offer one of the very few microzones in Italy capable of capturing the elusive varietal flavours of this superb grape.

Quality-oriented co-operative wineries dominate Alto Adige's production, but there are also increasing numbers of small grower-producers who make hand-crafted wines with lots of character. The majority of the wines are bottled under the generic **Alto Adige** (Südtirol) DOC. However, this denomination reserves some special subzone labels for: Lagrein from **Gries** on the edge of the provincial capital of Bolzano; Schiava wines from the picturesque village of **Santa Maddalena**; aromatic whites from the sub-alpine **Valle Isarco** and **Val Venosta**; and the intensely mineral-flavoured Pinot Bianco and Sauvignon Blanc of **Terlano**. All are worth seeking out.

from glacial-alluvial to volcanic Schiava, Lagrein, *Pinot Nero, Merlot, Cabernet Sauvignon* Pinot *Bianco, Gewürztraminer, Silvaner, Sauvignon Blanc, Chardonnay* red, white, rosé, sparkling, dessert

Trentino

TRENTINO IS THE entirely Italian-speaking part of the double-barrelled Trentino-Alto Adige region. It occupies the lower part of the Adige, as well as the side valleys that stretch toward Lago di Garda and the Alpi Dolomitiche (Dolomites). Clever planning and faultless winemaking (the region is home to Italy's top school of oenology) have created a very market-friendly wine industry here. **Trentino** DOC brings together 19 varietals and a couple of blends from different parts of the subregion. Eighty per cent of this production is handled by co-operatives, another 18 per cent by private bottling firms, and the rest by independent growers. Although the latter make up a mere two per cent of the wine bottled in the region, their mini-productions are among the most exciting wines to come out of Trentino today. Many of these private growers opt out of the DOC in favour of the less restrictive IGT Vigneti delle Dolomiti label.

The most planted grape in this region is Chardonnay, the vast bulk of which goes into **Trento** DOC Metodo Classico, a wine that

makes champagne-style wines affordable. Trentino is Italy's only serious producer of Müller-Thurgau, a grape that is associated with high vineyards, and that produces crisp white wines with a hint of grapefruit. Nosiola is another altitude-loving grape variety. It is not the world's most thrilling white in dry versions, but in the Mediterranean mesoclimate of the Valle dei Laghi it makes an explosively sweet, dried grape dessert wine called *vin santo*. On the red front, besides Cabernet Sauvignon and Merlot (Trentino was the first region in Italy to make Bordeaux-style Cabernet-Merlot blends), the region has its own share of local varieties. Potentially the most interesting is the dark, dry, and full-bodied Teroldego. This grows only in a small gravelly area on the floor of the Valle dell'Adige called the Campo Rotaliano, and makes **Teroldego Rotaliano** DOC. Then there is Marzemino, an easy-to-like red from the south of the region. Mozart's librettist Del Ponte rated it so highly that he wrote it into the final act of *Don Giovanni*.

deep gravel beds, grey marl, basalt Merlot, Cabernet *Sauvignon, Teroldego, Marzemino* Chardonnay, Müller-Thurgau, *Nosiola, Pinot Bianco* red, *white, sparkling, dessert*

Steep vineyards in Santa Maddalena, Alto Adige

TOP PRODUCERS OF TRENTINO-ALTO ADIGE

Abbazia di Novacella
Alto Adige/Valle Isarco

via Abbazia 1, Varna **C** 0472
836189 **W** www.abbazia
novacella.it **O** by appt

MONKS HAVE been making
wine in this subalpine
abbey since the 12th
century. The Abbazia's
reputation has faltered from
time to time, but the arrival
of a new winemaking team
in the late 1990s brought
more consistency. Alongside
the classic dry and citrus-
flavoured Valle Isarco
Silvaner, Novacella has
recently impressed with
the prize-winning, austere
single vineyard Lagrein
Riserva Praepositus.
📷 *red, white, dessert* **📷** *2007, 2006,
2005, 2004 (w); 2005, 2003 (r)*
★ *Alto Adige: Valle Isarco Silvaner
Brixner Praepositus, Lagrein
Riserva Praepositus*

Alois Lageder
Alto Adige

Tenuta Löwengang, vicolo dei Conti 9,
Magrè **C** 0471 809500
W www.aloislageder.eu **O** by appt

BOTH ALOIS LAGEDER and his
superb wines exude a sense
of real spontaneity. However,
behind that lies a deep

Label from Alois Lageder

philosophy which is evident
right through from the
environmentally friendly
management of his vineyards
to his use of solar power in the
winery. Lageder sources his
long list of single vineyard
selections from sites that are
legendary in the region for
their respective varieties.
Taste the concentrated cassis
flavours of the Cor Römigberg
Cabernet Sauvignon from
the hot, south-facing slopes
of Lago di Caldaro, and the
flinty, dry Lehenhof Sauvignon
Blanc from the high, volcanic-
soil terraces of Terlano for a
text-book introduction to *terroir*
differences in Alto Adige.
📷 *red, white* **📷** *2005, 2004, 2003
(w); 2004, 2001 (r)* **★** *Alto Adige:
Löwengang Chardonnay, Cor
Römigberg Cabernet Sauvignon,
Lehenhof Terlaner Sauvignon*

Arunda Vivaldi
Alto Adige

via Civica 53, Meltina **C** 0471
668033 **W** www.arundavivaldi.it
O by appt

SEPP REITERER makes
traditional bottle-
refermented bubbly in the
tiny Tyrolean village of
Meltina, 1,200m above
sea level. He ages the
wines for up to five years and
believes in minimum *dosage*
(added sugar at bottling) to
preserve the authentic dry,
tangy quality of the Alto
Adige. The result is a range
of *spumante* wines that are
among the most interesting
and long-lived in Italy.
📷 *sparkling* **📷** *2004, 2003, 1999,
1998* **★** *Alto Adige: Spumante
Arunda Brut Rosé, Spumante Arunda
Extra Brut Riserva, Spumante Arunda
Extra Brut Cuvée Marianna*

Cantina Produttori
Bolzano
Alto Adige

piazza Gries 2, Bolzano **C** 0471
270909 **W** www.cantinabolzano.com
O by appt

THE AMALGAMATION of Bolzano's
two leading co-operatives,
Cantina Gries and Produttori
Santa Maddalena, means

CO-OPERATIVE WINEMAKING IN ALTO ADIGE

Co-operatives are generally associated with
everyday drinking wine rather than exciting
quality. However, in Alto Adige, where
cantine produttori (the title most co-ops
have adopted) handle 70 per cent of the
output, they make many of the best wines.

In the mid-1980s, charismatic winery
directors Luis Raifer and Hans Terzer
updated the unwieldy co-op system from
the 19th century, making it the driving
force behind modernizing the regional wine
industry. Their drastic reduction of yields,
rigid selection of grapes, and exclusive
single vineyard bottlings took Alto Adige into

the top league of Italian winemaking.
A string of progressive *produttori* wineries
have since emerged to make the co-op
sector the most reliable and exciting in
the region. In addition to the co-ops
featured, look out for those listed below.

*Produttori Cornaiano (www.girlan.it);
Viticoltori Caldaro (www.kellereikaltern.
com); Produttori Cortaccia (www.kellerei-
kurtatsch.it); Erste e Neue (www.erste-
neue.it); Produttori Merano (www.meraner
kellerei.com); Cantina Valle Isarco
(www.cantinavalleisarco.it; left).*

that the cream of Lagrein production from the classic Gries subzone is now under one roof. Their joint list represents the best of both the old and the new in reds. The berry-flavoured Barone Carl Eyre selection is aged in big traditional barrels, while the dense, chocolaty Taber Riserva belongs to the modern, new *barrique* school of wine-making. Both are impeccable.

🔲 red, white, rosé, dessert 🔳 red: 2006, 2005, 2004, 2001, 1999

★ Alto Adige: Lagrein Scuro Taber Riserva, Lagrein Dunkel Riserva Collection Barone Carl Eyre, Lagrein Dunkel Riserva Prestige

Hofstätter
Alto Adige

piazza Municipio 7, Termeno
📞 0471 860161 🇼 www.hofstatter.com 🕒 by appt

NOT ONLY DOES Hofstätter own Italy's greatest Pinot Nero (Pinot Noir) vineyard – the Vigna Sant'Urbano – but it is also the owner of one of Alto Adige's best Gewürz-traminer estates. The sublimely long-lived Pinot Nero has had a faultless track record over the past 15 years, while the rich and peppery Gewürztraminer has moved up a gear in the last two or three. Both belong to the must-try category.

🔲 red, white, dessert 🔳 2007, 2004, 2003 (w); 2005, 2004 (r) ★ Alto Adige: Pinot Nero Riserva Barthenau Vigna Sant'Urbano, Gewürztraminer Kolbenhof Soll

Kuenhof
Alto Adige/Valle Isarco

loc Mahr 110, Bressanone 📞 0472 850546 🕒 by appt

SILVANER GRAPES usually make light, dry, and floral wines, perfect for summer drinking. Kuen Hof owner-winemaker Peter Pliger, however, looks

The fairy-tale setting of Produttori Colterenzio, Alto Adige

for another dimension in the variety. A grower of almost fanatical dedication, he works with minuscule yields, harvests late, and ages his wine in large acacia wood barrels to make full-bodied wines with layers of fruit and aromas which are made to stand the test of time. Equally impressive are his dry, peach-flavoured Gewürztraminer and his full-bodied Grüner Veltliner, made from an Austrian grape variety grown nowhere in Italy outside the Valle dell' Isarco.

🔲 white 🔳 2007, 2006, 2005, 2004 ★ Alto Adige Valle Isarco: Silvaner, Grüner Veltliner, Gewürztraminer

Josephus Mayr-Unterganzner
Alto Adige

Erbhof Unterganzner, via Campiglio 15, Cardano 📞 0471 365582 🕒 by appt

THE MAJORITY OF Alto Adige's farmers make a good living by selling their grapes to the region's 16 excellent co-operatives. So any small grower who takes on the risks involved in making and bottling his own wine needs to have guaranteed premium quality as well as something spectacular to say. Specialist Lagrein producer Josephus Mayr has both of these. In recent years he has won a keen following for his refined,

berry-flavoured *riserva* and his unique blockbuster Lamarein Vino da Tavola, which he makes in the *amarone* style *(see p229)*.

🔲 red 🔳 2005, 2004, 2001, 2000 ★ Alto Adige: Lagrein Dunkel Riserva, Vino da Tavola Lamarein (Lagrein)

Produttori Colterenzio
Alto Adige

strada del Vino 8, Cornaiano
📞 0471 664246
🇼 www.colterenzio.it 🕒 by appt

COLTERENZIO DIRECTOR Luis Raifer was one of the first to break down the scepticism of the outside world towards co-op wines by bringing quality here up to international standards. A key factor in this was his Cornell Chardonnay, which, beneath its lick of buttery oak, epitomizes the Alto Adige varietal style. In contrast, the Lafoa Sauvignon (from the Raifer family's own vineyard) takes a more subtle and personal approach to a stand-ard international variety, with its delicate quince flavours and dry, minerally finish. Schwarzhaus Pinot Nero is the winery's up-and-coming red, and there is also quality among the local varietals.

🔲 red, white, dessert 🔳 2007, 2006 (w); 2004, 2003, 2001 (r) ★ Alto Adige: Lafoa Sauvignon, Cornell Chardonnay, Cornell Pinot Nero Schwarzhaus Riserva

Produttori di Terlano
Alto Adige/Terlano

via Silberleiten 7, Terlano ☎ *0471 257135* W *www.cantina-terlano.com* ○ *by appt*

AMALGAMATION with the historic Produttori di Andriano cooperative has increased the potential of this high-quality winery specializing in exceptionally dry whites. It sources its grapes from high vineyards with sandy, quartz-rich soils that give amazingly intense and long-lived Pinot Bianco and Sauvignon Blanc. The cellar door list includes 10- and 12-year-old whites that still taste incredibly fresh. The very individual Lagrein combines the structure of wines from the Gries sub-zone with the intense aromas typical of Terlano.

🍷 *red, white* 📅 *2005, 2004, 1996, 1995 (w); 2003, 2001 (r)* ★ *Alto Adige: Terlaner Sauvignon Quarz, Terlaner Pinot Bianco Vorberg, Lagrein Riserva Porphyr*

Produttori San Michele Appiano
Alto Adige

via Circonvallazione 17/19, Appiano ☎ *0471 664466* W *www.stmichael.it* ○ *by appt*

THIS DYNAMIC CO-OP, which has the biggest turnover and the fastest growth of any winery in Alto Adige, was named Italian producer of the year in 2000 by wine guide *Gambero Rosso*. Winemaker Hans Terzer's style is up-front. He is best known for his dry whites, and in particular the sumptuous Sanct Valentin Sauvignon Blanc, but in the last few vintages he has also brought out spectacular Cabernet Sauvignon, and a Pinot Nero in the Sanct Valentin range.

🍷 *red, white, rosé, dessert* 📅 *2007, 2006, 2005 (w); 2004, 2000 (r)* ★ *Alto Adige: Sanct Valentin Sauvignon Blanc, Sanct Valentin Cabernet Sauvignon, Sanct Valentin Gewürztraminer*

Produttori Termeno
Alto Adige

strada del Vino 144, Termeno ☎ *0471 860126* W *www.tramin-wine.it* ○ *by appt*

WILLI STURZ IS currently the hottest winemaker in the Alto Adige. His magic touch has taken Produttori Termeno's single vineyard selections to the top of their category in the past two or three vintages. He has also worked magic on the mid-range and basic labels, so that this medium-sized co-op now delivers one of the most convincing all-round performances in the

La Vis label

region. The smooth, mellow fruit style of the whites is exemplified by the multiple award-winning Nussbaumerhof Gewürztraminer, while the stylish fruit and low-key oak of Sturz's reds shine in his Urbanhof Lagrein.

🍷 *red, white, dessert* 📅 *2007, 2006, 2005, 2004, 2000 (w); 2006, 2003 (r)* ★ *Alto Adige: Gewürztraminer Nussbaumerhof, Lagrein Urbanhof Terminum, Pinot Bianco Tauris*

Cesconi
Trentino/IGT

via Marconi 39, loc Pressano, Lavis ☎ *0461 240355* W *www.cesconi.it* ○ *by appt*

THIS YOUNG, family-owned estate debuted in 1998 with a range of whites that put it among the region's top independent growers. An equally impressive set of reds from the Mediterranean climate zone of Lago di Garda (Lake Garda) followed two years later. In the DOC range the winemaking style lets the ripe fruit speak for itself, while the IGTs – Olivar and Pivier – are serious oak-aged wines that hold promise for the future. Both excellent, Olivar is a fleshy blend of Chardonnay, Pinot Bianco, and Pinot Grigio, and Pivier is a rich and spicy Merlot.

🍷 *red, white* 📅 *2006, 2005, 2004 (w); 2003, 2000 (r)* ★ *Olivar Vigneti delle Dolomiti Bianco IGT, Pivier Vigneti delle Dolomiti Rosso IGT, Trentino Pinot Grigio*

Ferrari
Trentino

via del Ponte di Ravina 15, Trento ☎ *0461 972311* W *www.ferrari spumante.it* ○ *by appt*

GEWÜRZTRAMINER SYMPOSIUM

DNA studies finally seem to have established what the locals have always claimed on the basis of the grape name: that Gewürztraminer does actually originate from the Alto Adige commune of Tramin, now called Termeno. For a week in July every year, this picturesque Tyrolean village becomes the world centre for the spicy white varietal as it hosts a hedonistic International Symposium which bristles with food and wine events.

Over 200 Gewürztraminer wines from all over the world grace the main showroom. The meals are prepared by Michelin star chefs and the tastings are led by the current world champion sommelier. W *www.tramin.it*

THIS HISTORIC FIRM was founded in 1902 by a nursery owner with a head for business and a passion for viticulture. Ferrari's Chardonnay-based style is classic Trentino. Quality is impeccable right through from the ridiculously good value Brut to the breathtaking crystal elegance and complexity of the Riserva Giulio Ferrari, which is disgorged after eight years, released after 10, and still guaranteed to drink sublimely for another decade.

🍷 *sparkling* 📆 *1999, 1997, 1995, 1993, 1991* ★ *Trento: Giulio Ferrari Riserva del Fondatore, Perlé, Brut*

Foradori
Trentino/IGT

via Damiano Chiesa 1, Mezzolombardo 📞 *0461 601046* 🌐 *www.elisabetta foradori.com* 🚪 *by appt*

CERTIFIED BIODYNAMIC GROWER Elisabetta Foradori's IGT wine Granato takes the rustic Teroldego grape to a level no other producer can reach. Like its creator, it can be tough and uncompromising, but it more than makes up for it with its depth and complexity. Exasperated by the inertia of the DOC, Elisabetta decided to cross over to the IGT Vigneti delle Dolomiti with the 2000 vintage. Her dry, minerally second label remains Teroldego Rotaliano DOC.

🍷 *red, white* 📆 *2006, 2004, 2003, 2002, 2001, 1999* ★ *Granato Vigneti delle Dolomiti Rosso IGT, Myrto Vigneti delle Dolomiti Bianco IGT, Foradori Teroldego Rotaliano*

La Vis e Valle di Cembra
Trentino/IGT

via Carmine 7, Lavis 📞 *0461 440111* 🌐 *www.la-vis.com* 🚪 *by appt*

THIS PROGRESSIVE co-operative offers outstanding value across the whole of its extensive

**Owner and winemaker
Elisabetta Foradori**

range. La Vis was a pioneer in the cutting-edge research area of 'zoning', or matching sites to grape varieties in Trentino. Operating mainly on the cooler left (east) bank of the Adige, its traditional specialities are fruity white varietals such as the Chardonnay Ritratti and the deliciously scented Müller-Thurgau Maso Roncador; but it also turns out an IGT red Lagrein-Teroldego blend called Ritratti Rosso with inky depth of colour and lots of smoky fruit.

🍷 *red, white, dessert* 📆 *2007, 2006, 2004 (w); 2004, 2003 (r)* ★ *Trentino Müller-Thurgau Maso Roncador, Ritratti Rosso Vigneti delle Dolomiti IGT*

Pojer & Sandri
Trentino/IGT

loc Molin 4, Faedo 📞 *0461 650342* 🌐 *www.pojeresandri.it* 🚪 *by appt*

MARIO POJER AND Fiorentino Sandri run Trentino's most innovative winery. Since they launched in the early 1980s with a blush version of the local Schiava, this dynamic pair have never been without a new project and have generally kept one step ahead of the next trend. Their latest venture involves the production of *terroir*-focused wines, one red and one white, from the restored Maso Besler estate

in the Val di Cembra, where the combination of high altitude and complicated blends of rare local varieties produces wines with intense and highly original aromas of berry fruit and wild herbs.

🍷 *red, white, rosé, sparkling, dessert, grappa* 📆 *2004, 2001 (w); 2005, 2004, 2000 (r)* ★ *Spumante Extra Brut, Besler Bianck Vigneti delle Dolomiti Bianco IGT, Rosso Faye Vigneti delle Dolomiti Rosso IGT*

Tenuta San Leonardo
Trentino/IGT

fraz Borghetto all'Adige, loc San Leonardo 3, Avio 📞 *0464 689004* 🌐 *www.sanleonardo.it* 🚪 *by appt*

SAN LEONARDO has been described as Italy's equivalent of a Bordeaux *premier cru*. However, it is much more than a mere Médoc lookalike. The *barriques* and the grape varieties – mainly Cabernet Sauvignon, Cabernet Franc, and Merlot – are indeed French, but the soils and climate are quintessentially Trentino. These elements combine to produce a herb and liquorice nuance beneath the fruit – the hallmark of reds from the lower Valle dell'Adige. The classy second-label IGT wine is the plummy, Merlot-based Villa Gresti.

🍷 *red* 📆 *2004, 2003, 2001, 2000, 1999, 1997* ★ *San Leonardo Rosso delle Dolomiti IGT, Villa Gresti Vigneti Rosso delle Dolomiti IGT*

Tenuta San Leonardo label

Hillside vineyards in Prosecco di Valdobbiadene & Conegliano

WINEGROWING AREAS OF THE VENETO

THE WINES OF THE HILLS above Verona monopolize the scene in the Veneto. Soave and Valpolicella – the areas with the highest concentration of big-name producers – together make up 40 per cent of the region's DOC production. The performance outside these districts is varied, but not without its high points. Virtually every one of the region's other 20 DOC zones has at least one good (and sometimes great) producer. International-style reds from the quality pioneers in Colli Berici and Colli Euganei suggest that there could be a lot of interesting wines still waiting to happen here. Fans of dessert wines should keep an eye on the Gambellara DOC. However, it is the quality and style of producers that stand out in these fringe DOCs more than any *terroir* character. The Veneto's key DOCs are covered below.

Pieropan label, Soave

🗻 sand, limestone, marl, basalt 🍇 Corvina, Rondinella, Cabernet Sauvignon, Merlot 🍇 Garganega, Vespaiolo 🍷 red, white, rosé, sparkling, dessert

Bardolino

THE PALE RED WINE from **Bardolino** DOC, on the southeast shores of Lago di Garda (Lake Garda), is made from roughly the same Corvina-Rondinella-Molinara grape mix as Valpolicella and offers the same cherry fruit and almondy finish in a lighter and softer vein. A lot of the large annual production is channelled into the bouncy Beaujolais Nouveau-style *(see p115)*

Bardolino Novello. Chiaretto is the rosé version of standard DOC; **Bardolino Superiore** DOCG is a new and as yet under-utilized denomination.

Bianco di Custoza

THIS POPULAR TOURIST WINE comes from a small area south of Lago di Garda. It used to be made exclusively with the rather lack-lustre Trebbiano (Ugni Blanc), but recent amendments to the Bianco di Custoza DOC now allow more enterprising producers to brighten up their wines with the punchier Pinot Bianco, Chardonnay, and Riesling Italico, giving it a lightweight, early-drinking feel.

Prosecco di Valdobbiadene & Conegliano

THE BEST PROSECCO comes from the hills between the two towns that give their name to this DOC: Valdobbiadene and Conegliano. Prosecco grapes produce a vat-fermented *spumante* that is light, bubbly, fresh, and gently fragrant. Brut is the driest version, 'dry' is confusingly the sweetest, and 'extra dry' is somewhere in between. Prosecco DOC is an ideal summer tipple, so do not expect the body or complexity of a Chardonnay-based *spumante*.

Valpolicella

REGULATIONS IN THE Valpolicella DOC allow producers here to make four different red wine styles from the same vineyards and from the same basic blend of Corvina, Molinara, and Rondinella grapes. From the lightest to the most full-bodied, these are: Valpolicella, Valpolicella Superiore, *amarone (see p229)*, and *recioto*. Recioto and its dry counterpart *amarone* are powerfully alcoholic wines made from partially dried grapes. Straight Valpolicella is a dry, savoury, everyday wine made from fresh grapes. And Valpolicella Superiore is theoretically a fresh grape wine, although it often gets beefed up by a period of refermentation with the skins left over from *amarone*, or with a drop of *amarone* itself. Common to all Valpolicella wines is the cherry flavour with the bitter twist of the Corvina grape. In the best wines, there is also a dry tanginess traditionally attributed to the soils of the 'Classico' area – the original Valpolicella zone in the heart of the current DOC, which was established in 1968 and now accounts for less than half the area's production. The variations on the Valpolicella theme depend not only on whether fresh or dried grapes are used, but also on the secondary grape varieties chosen for the blend, and on the choice of barrels. French *barriques*, with their distinctive toast and vanilla aromas, are becoming an established feature.

Soave

THE BASIC GRAPE in **Soave** DOC is a local variety called Garganega, which has delicate lemon and almond flavours. With an annual production of over 60 million bottles, Soave is by far Italy's biggest white wine DOC. The credibility of the denomination was severely dented by an emphasis on quantity over quality through the 1980s. In the past five to ten years, however, the efforts of small grower-producers have brought Soave back into the realm of serious white wines, although the diversity of winemaking styles and the official sanctioning of Chardonnay as a blending variety have blurred its identity somewhat. Straight Soave DOC can be bland, but the new DOCG category of **Soave Superiore**, which came into effect with the 2002 vintage, should sort out the best from the rest. If in doubt, go for bottles labelled 'Classico', which come from the top hill sites in the communes of Soave and Monteforte d'Alpone, and which should have more body and flavour. Another Soave capable of greatness in the right hands is **Recioto di Soave** DOCG, a sweet white wine with honey and apricot flavours that is made from dried Garganega grapes.

Gambellara

THIS DOC IS A SMALL HILL ZONE in the province of Vicenza that uses the Garganega variety to make both a sweet white *recioto* and dry and flowery whites similar to Soave. Mineral-rich soils and a mild, sunny climate offer potential for quality whites, which, to date, has only been partially realized.

Colli Berici

THE LOW, WOODED HILLS of this DOC are more famous for their Palladian villas than their wines, although Cabernet Sauvignon and Merlot both ripen well here, and in recent years, quality producers have started to make convincing versions of Bordeaux-style wines. The local speciality is an original, light but tannic varietal with raspberry flavours called Tocai Rosso.

Colli Euganei

CABERNET AND MERLOT from this DOC have a distinctive ripe and mellow character. The area also has a long-standing relationship with Moscato (Muscat), which is made both in a dry version and in a dessert wine called Fior d'Arancio Passito.

Vineyards around Bardolino on Lago di Garda (Lake Garda)

TOP PRODUCERS OF THE VENETO

Adami
Veneto/Prosecco

via Rovede 27, Vidor 📞 *0423 982110,*
🌐 *www.adamispumanti.it* ⬜ *by appt*

THE DIFFERENCE BETWEEN good
Prosecco and the best is a
question of balance between
the fizz, the sweetness, and
the acidity. Franco Adami is
a master at the delicate
juggling of these three
elements in his sparkling
wines. His focus at the
moment is on the dry and
biscuity Brut, but the classic
from this family-run winery
remains the soft and floral
style of the Vigneto Giardino.
🍷 *sparkling* 🍇 *most recent*
★ *Prosecco di Valdobbiadene*
Spumante Brut Bosco di Gica,
Prosecco di Valdobbiadene
Spumante Dry Vigneto Giardino

Allegrini
Veneto/Valpolicella

via Giare 5, Fumane 📞 *045 6832011*
🌐 *www.allegrini.it* ⬜ *by appt*

FRANCO ALLEGRINI has
never ceased to challenge
the preconceptions of
Valpolicella, from the creation
of the varietal Corvina La
Poja in the early 1980s to
the modernization of the
grape drying process for
amarone, and the planting
of Cabernet and Merlot for

their Villa Giona IGT. Recent
vintages of the Allegrini
classics have seen more
and more body and fruit
flavours packed into
these superb wines.
🍷 *red, recioto*
🍇 *2004, 2001, 2000, 1999, 1998*
★ *La Poja Corvina Veronese IGT,*
Amarone della Valpolicella
Classico, La Grola Rosso
Veronese IGT

Anselmi
Veneto/IGT

via San Carlo 46, Monteforte
d'Alpone 📞 *045 7611488*
🌐 *www.anselmi.eu*
⬜ *by appt*

AFTER DECADES OF
questioning the official
denomination, Roberto
Anselmi dropped
out of the DOC in
2001. The standard
of his wines, from the heart
of the Soave Classico zone
is impeccable, from the
elegant, candied fruit
flavours of the Garganega
varietal I Capitelli Passito to
his Capitel Croce – Veneto's
first oak-aged Garganega –
with its tropical fruit nose
and long minerally finish.
🍷 *white, dessert* 🍇 *2007, 2006,*
2005, 2004, 2001 ★ *Veneto Bianco*
IGT: I Capitelli Passito, Capitel Croce,
Capitel Foscarino

Bisol Desiderio & Figli
Veneto/Prosecco

via Fol 33, fraz S Stefano,
Valdobbiadene 📞 *0432 900138*
🌐 *www.bisol.it* ⬜ *by appt*

THE MAJORITY of the wineries
in the Prosecco DOC zone
source their fruit from contract
growers. Bisol is the only
producer in the area with
sizeable vineyard holdings
of its own, and this
advantage of direct control
over grape supply shows
in the extra personality
that comes from lower
yields, particularly for
the special wines: dry
and biscuity Crede,
soft and creamy
Garnei, and floral
Vigneti del Fol.

Bisol Desiderio
& Figli

🍷 *sparkling* 🍇 *most recent*
★ *Prosecco di Valdobbia-*
dene Spumante Brut Crede,
Prosecco di Valdobbiadene Spumante
Dry Garnei, Prosecco di Valdobbiadene
Spumante Extra Dry Vigneti del Fol

Gini
Veneto/Soave

via G Matteotti 42, Monteforte d'Alpone
📞 *045 7611908* 🌐 *www.ginivini.com*
⬜ *by appt*

BENEATH SANDRO GINI'S modest
exterior and great enthusiasm
lie the skill and intelligence of
one of Soave's most talented
winemakers. He has great
raw material to work with, but
it still takes a special touch to
produce wines with the personality and sheer class of the
rich and complex Contrada
Salvarenza and the luscious
dessert wine Renobilis. This
family-run estate ranks among
Soave's best.
🍷 *white, recioto* 🍇 *2007, 2006, 2005,*
2001, 2000, 1999 ★ *Soave Classico*
Superiore Contrada Salvarenza Vecchie
Vigne, Recioto di Soave Renobilis,
Soave Classico Superiore La Froscà

VINITALY

This is *the* Italian wine fair. Every April trade buyers, producers, journalists, and vast numbers of dedicated wine
fans from around the world descend on Verona for a five-
day immersion in Italian wine. For anyone interested in an
intensive course in the wines of Italy, there is no better
opportunity. Four thousand producers, from the biggest
and most exclusive to the smallest, family-run ventures
present their wines for visitors to try. The programme of
around 75 guided tastings ranges from highly technical to
purely fun wine-food matching sessions, and includes
everything from regional overviews to sampling of rare
vintages from single producers. 🌐 *www.vinitaly.com*

Meticulous grape sorting at Maculan

Inama
Veneto/Soave & IGT

loc Biacche 50, San Bonifacio
☎ 045 6104343
🖳 www.inamaaziendaagricola.it
🕐 by appt

STEFANO INAMA produces wines that make an impact. In the context of Soave, the deep straw colours and ripe aromas sometimes look outspoken, but you have to admire their authenticity. And Inama's Vulcaia Fumé Sauvignon Blanc boasts outstanding fleshy texture and delicious fruit-and-mineral flavours. Look out too for the Carmenère-based Oratorio di San Lorenzo and the Cabernet Sauvignon Bradissimo, both from the Colli Berici.
🍷 red, white
🔟 2006, 2005, 2001 (w); 2004, 2001 (r)
★ Soave Classico Vigneto du Lot, Vulcaia Fumé Sauvignon Blanc Veneto IGT, Soave Classico Superiore Vigneti di Foscarino

Maculan
Veneto/Breganze & IGT

via Castelletto 3, Breganze ☎ 0445 873733 🖳 www.maculan.net
🕐 by appt

FOR THE PAST 20 YEARS Fausto Maculan has made one of Italy's greatest dessert wines, Acininobili, and by far the

Veneto's most convincing Cabernets, Fratta and Palazzotto. Yet this has not stopped him expanding his eclectic and increasingly international range with the rich and concentrated Crosara Merlot and the excellent-value Speaia and Brentino.
🍷 red, white, dessert 🔟 2005, 2004, 2001 (r); 2005, 2003 (w) ★ Veneto IGT: Acininobili Bianco, Fratta Rosso; Breganze Crosara Merlot

Masi
Veneto/Valpolicella & IGT

via Monteleone 26, fraz Gargagnago, Sant'Ambrogio di Valpolicella
☎ 045 6832511
🖳 www.masi.it 🕐 by appt

MASI BROKE NEW GROUND with its Toar, the first modern IGT alternative to Valpolicella, and the austerely structured Osar IGT from the Oseleta grape it rescued from virtual extinction. The focus in recent vintages has returned to the classic amarone range, with a subtle re-styling of the Costasera Riserva and the great single-vineyard wines Campolongo di Torbe and Mazzano.
🍷 red, white, recioto
🔟 red: 2004, 2003, 2001, 1999, 1997 ★ Amarone della Valpolicella Classico: Mazzano, Campolongo di Torbe; Oscr Rosso del Veronese IGT

Pieropan
Veneto/Soave

via Camuzzoni 3, Soave ☎ 045 6190171 🖳 www.pieropan.it
🕐 by appt

INDEPENDENT GROWER Leonildo Pieropan makes two single vineyard selections of uncompromisingly good quality. La Rocca is a late-harvested, oak-conditioned Soave. Calvarino, on the other hand, is a true representative of the fresh and dry style of vat-fermented Soave, with its spring flowers aroma and delicate fruit and almond flavours. Both wines are at the top of their categories. They are also great value for money.
🍷 white, dessert 🔟 2006, 2005, 2004, 2003, 2000 ★ La Rocca Soave Classico Superiore Calvarino, Soave Classico Superiore, Passito della Rocca Bianco del Veneto IGT

Quintarelli
Veneto/Valpolicella

via Cere 1, Negrar ☎ 045 7500016
🕐 by appt

GIUSEPPE QUINTARELLI is one of the patriarchs of Valpolicella. His amarone was a benchmark for the denomination for decades, but nowadays the mature raisiny flavours and very long barrel-ageing of his riservas (not to mention prices at the level of grand cru burgundy) divide opinion slightly. The Valpolicella Classico Superiore offers a more accessible introduction to the style, which might come across as a little rustic, but has a unique fascination.

Masi

🍷 red, recioto 🔟 2000, 1999, 1998, 1997, 1995 ★ Amarone della Valpolicella Monte Cà Paletta, Valpolicella Classico Superiore Monte Cà Paletta, Alzero VdT

Grape picking at Romano Dal Forno in Valpolicella

Romano Dal Forno
Veneto/Valpolicella

loc Lodoletta 1, Cellore d'Illasi
045 7834923 ☐ *by appt*

VALPOLICELLA THESE DAYS is by no means short of progressive producers, but Romano dal Forno is a revolutionary. Nobody else would dream of planting the heavy-bearing local varieties at a density of 13,000 plants per hectare and harvesting less than a kilo of fruit per vine. But then nobody else in the Veneto makes wines that combine monumental concentration with such class and elegance.
 red, recioto 2004, 2001, 1999, 1998, 1997, 1996 ★ *Amarone della Valpolicella Vigneto di Monte Lodoletta, Recioto della Valpolicella Vigneto di Monte Lodoletta, Valpolicella Superiore Monte Lodoletta*

Ruggeri
Veneto/Prosecco

via Prà Fontana, Valdobbiadene
0423 9092
 www.ruggeri.it ☐ *by appt*

RUGGERI IS ONE OF the biggest and also one of the best producers in the Valdobbiadene-Conegliano area. The round and fruity Giustino B represents the traditonal style of Prosecco, while the innovative Vecchie Viti and Extra Brut signal the trend towards drier, vintage-labelled wines.
 sparkling most recent
★ *Prosecco di Valdobbiadene Spumante Extra Dry Selezione Giustino B, Prosecco di Valdobbiadene Spumante, Prosecco di Valdobbiadene Brut Vecchie Viti*

Speri
Veneto/Valpolicella

via Fontana 14, fraz Pedemonte, San Pietro in Cariano 045 7701154
 www.speri.com ☐ *by appt*

SPERI IS A long-established Valpolicella producer with extensive vineyards that include the outstanding Vigneto Sant'Urbano. Like many family-owned wineries at the point of the hand-over between generations, its winemaking treads a careful path between tradition and innovation. Speri's complex and velvety *amarone* regularly competes with the best.
 red, recioto 2004, 2001, 1999, 1997 ★ *Amarone della Valpolicella Classico Vigneto Sant'Urbano, Recioto della Valpolicella Classico La Roggia*

Tedeschi

Tedeschi
Veneto/Valpolicella & IGT

via Verdi 4/A, fraz Pedemonte, San Pietro in Cariano 045 7701487
 www.tedeschiwines.com ☐ *by appt*

MANY PRODUCERS would agree that the most important challenge for Valpolicella today is to create a top-class international red from local varieties, without the help of dried grapes. Riccardo Tedeschi has succeeded at this. His Valpolicella Superiore La Fabriseria has all the cherry and plum fruit of the local Corvina-Rondinella blend, plus the structure that these varieties so often lack. He also makes two outstanding *amarones*: the velvety Capitel Monte Olmi and the highly concentrated La Fabriseria.
 red, recioto 2004, 2003, 2001, 2000, 1999, 1995 ★ *Valpolicella Superiore La Fabriseria, Amarone della Valpolicella Classico Capitel Monte Olmi, Amarone della Valpolicella La Fabriseria*

Tommaso Bussola
Veneto/Valpolicella

via Molino Turri 30, fraz San Peretto, Negrar 045 7501740
www.bussolavini.com ☐ *by appt*

TOMMASO BUSSOLA uses an incredible 6kg of fruit to make just a half bottle of his TB selection *recioto*. Most producers crush the fruit for this sweet, dried grape red wine in January or February, but Bussola leaves it to shrivel until the end of March, when the amount of juice left in the berries is reduced to a minimum, making the concentration of sugar and flavours truly breathtaking. His dry *amarones* are similarly statuesque.
 red, recioto 2004, 2003, 1999, 1998, 1997 ★ *Recioto della Valpolicella TB, Amarone della Valpolicella Classico TB Vigneto Alto, Amarone della Valpolicella Classico TB*

BLOCKBUSTER AMARONE

AMARONE IS ONE OF the world's biggest, fleshiest red wines, and boasts a unique gamut of flavours that recall cherry jam, plum pudding, raisins, rose petals, and spice. It is made from semi-dried grapes in a Verona hills tradition that dates back to the Byzantine period. Updated in 2007, the production norms stipulate a blend of Corvina and Rondinella with the addition of a maximum of other local or international varieties authorized for Valpolicella, the only DOC in which it is made. Alcohol levels range from 14 per cent to the more traditional 16 per cent. However, the trend since the early 1990s has been towards a shorter grape drying period than before to create fruitier wines with relatively lower alcohol, and to reduce the effect of botrytis *(see p66)*. *Amarone* is released a minimum of two years after the harvest, at which point it should be almost ready to drink, although it will continue to age well in bottle. Top vintages are 1990, 1995, and 1997.

Key Producers
The bulk of *amarone* production comes from Valpolicella Classico *(see p225)*, where the long list of quality estates includes established names like Allegrini, Masi, Quintarelli, Speri, and Tedeschi, as well as an up-and-coming generation represented by producers such as Tommaso Bussola. There are also a few excellent *amarone* makers outside of the Valpolicella Classico zone in the valleys of Illasi and Mezzane, including Romano Dal Forno, whose produce is generally recognized to be about as good it gets.

The Production Process
Traditionally, only grapes from the tops of bunches were selected. Today all the fruit is harvested, and unripe or broken berries are discarded. The grapes are laid out in shallow trays and left to dry at natural temperatures for at least three months – usually in an air-conditioned shed to prevent mould. By the end, the grapes have shrunk to half their original size and are ready for vinification.

Vineyards belonging to Masi, one of Italy's prime *amarone* producers

Harvest time in Friuli-Venezia Giulia

WINEGROWING AREAS OF FRIULI-VENEZIA GIULIA

TINY PRODUCTION, countless grape varieties, hair-splitting DOC zones, and many small producers make Friuli-Venezia Giulia (F-V G) the most complex district of Northeast Italy to grasp. The quality, however, is exceptional. Only Tuscany and Piemonte, which make two to three times more wine, pick up more prizes. Friuli-Venezia Giulia led the Italian white wine revolution at the start of the 1980s with its innovative fresh varietal styles. Since the mid-1990s it has also added super-selected, oak-aged whites and an increasingly convincing series of reds. Friuli-Venezia Giulia has nine DOC zones, all growing similar

Livio Felluga label

varieties. Understanding the region involves knowing the basic character of the grapes and seeing how they perform in various sub-regions. The classiest wines come from three DOCs in the east, while the south and west are known for more commercial styles.

🏔 *sandy loam, alluvial gravel, stony marl* 🍇 *Merlot, Refosco, Schioppettino, Pignolo* 🍇 *Tocai Friulano, Ribolla Gialla, Pinot Grigio, Pinot Bianco, Sauvignon Blanc, Chardonnay, Picolit* 🍷 *red, white, sparkling, dessert*

The Premium Zones

THE PRESTIGIOUS WINES all come from an area that takes in the hills of the Collio Goriziano ('Collio'), the Colli Orientali del Friuli, and the northern part of the Friuli Isonzo DOC. The historic zones of the **Collio** DOC and **Colli Orientali del Friuli** DOC have hot summers and mineral-rich soils. This makes for full-bodied whites packed with fruit and aroma, with more alcohol and lower acidity than wines from other parts of the northeast. The Collio specializes in dry whites, including original blends bottled under the Collio Bianco DOC label. Colli Orientali is more focused on varietals, producing everything from dessert wines to local reds, like Refosco and Schioppettino. The northern part of the **Friuli Isonzo** DOC competes at the same level as the hills, but has fewer top producers. Vines here grow in a climate that particularly favours dry whites.

TOKAY OR TOCAI?

After decades of wrangling, Hungary's claim to the exclusive right to the name Tokay was finally recognized by the EU in a ruling of 2004. This imposed a change of denomination on any other wine with the same or similar name, including Friuli's favourite white, Tocai. Despite the obvious differences between the Hungarian dessert wine and Italy's dry white, Friuli producers have had to bow to the principle established by the EU that place names (such as Tokay) must take precedence over grape varieties in the naming of wines. From the 2007 vintage, Tocai, which ironically probably takes its own name from a small river that flows through the traditional production area in the Collio, will be labelled Friulano.

Wine casks in a Friuli cellar

The Plains

THE REST OF THE REGION'S DOC zones, which make wines more for everyday drinking, are on flat lands along the Adriatic coast and on the central plain of Friuli, which stretches west towards the Veneto. With its 6,000ha of vineyards, **Grave del Fruili** DOC grows more wine than the rest of F-V G's DOCs put together. It is a source of good-value international varietals with zippy aromas, such as Sauvignon Blanc and Chardonnay.

The coastal plain is divided into three DOC zones: **Aquileia**, **Annia**, and **Latisana**. The light sandy and limestone soils here produce mainly light- to medium-bodied wines. Friuli-Aquileia is the biggest of the three DOCs and its tangy whites are also the most appetizing of the wines from the coast.

Often left out of the reckoning on account of its minuscule dimensions (it has less than 50ha of vineyards), **Carso** is a DOC zone situated on a windswept limestone plateau overlooking the bay of Trieste. The specialities here are startlingly dry wines from the local Vitovska and Refosco (Terrano) varieties.

Terraced vineyard in Colli Orientali del Friuli

Grape Varieties of Friuli-Venezia Giulia

It is not unusual for estates in Friuli-Venezia Giulia to grow 12 or more grape varieties, and bottle each separately. Some of the marginal ones are now being phased out, but the regional output remains varied.

Local Varieties

Malvasia: This is a Collio speciality, where it ripens to a spicy opulence and is called Malvasia Istriana. In Aquileia it makes a simpler but tangy white.

Picolit: A sweet white grape from the Colli Orientali, this enjoys local cult status despite (or maybe because of) a genetic disorder called floral abortion, which is capable of devastating entire crops, and makes the wine rare and expensive.

Pignolo: A seriously tannic, long-ageing, and expensive rarity, this red is creeping back into production in the Colli Orientali.

Refosco: Packed with berry fruit and soft tannins, the classiest examples of this red wine come from the Colli Orientali. Its full name is Refosco dal Peduncolo Rosso, and a sub-variety of it makes Terrano wine in Carso.

Ribolla Gialla: Planted in the Collio since the 12th century, this white grape has lost vineyard space over the years, but there is currently a revival of demand for its dry, citrus flavours.

Schioppettino: This red grape is dark and juicy with a touch of exotic aromas, and is made to be drunk young.

Tocai Friulano: This white grape is the area's most planted. It needs hill sites and careful handling but is one in which producers of the Collio and Colli Orientali have invested a lot over the past 10 years. Unoaked styles highlight its hedgerow aromas and dry, almondy finish.

Verduzzo: This apple-flavoured white grape from the DOC of the same name makes a reliable and affordable dessert wine. It is also the grape used for the micro-production Ramandolo DOCG.

International Varieties

Sauvignon Blanc is the most successful grape, doing best in the Collio-Colli Orientali-Isonzo triangle, where aromatic, vat-fermented versions are most typical. Pinot Grigio is the flagship variety of Isonzo. Producers from this DOC were the first in Italy to put Pinot Grigio into oak. The wines are big, tasty, and built to last. Pinot Bianco makes refined wines with orange blossom aromas and dry fruit in the Collio. Chardonnay styles range from elegant Burgundian to sunny Californian. The variety is strongest in Isonzo and Colli Orientali. Merlot ripens better than Cabernet Sauvignon and can make wines to match the best in the country.

TOP PRODUCERS OF FRIULI-VENEZIA GIULIA

Borgo San Daniele
F-V G/Friuli Isonzo & IGT

via San Daniele 16, Cormons
C 0481 60552 **W** *www.borgo sandaniele.it* **○** *by appt*

MAURO MAURI belongs to the young, trend-setting generation of Friuli growers who have abandoned crisp, dry whites in favour of wines that are richer and mellower. Mauro takes the rustic edge out of Tocai Friulano, and his Pinot Bianco-Sauvignon Blanc-Chardonnay-Tocai Friulano blend, called Arbis Blanc, is a luscious, not-quite-dry white with an Alsace-style character.
▨ *red, white* **▨** *2007, 2006, 2005, (w); 2003, 2001 (r)* ★ *Friuli Isonzo Tocai Friulano, Friuli Isonzo Bianco Arbis Blanc, Arbis Rosso Venezia Giulia IGT*

Borgo del Tiglio
F-V G/Collio

via San Giorgio 71, fraz Brazzano, Cormons **C** 0481 62166 **○** *by appt*

NICOLA MANFERRARI painstakingly selects wines from different microzones around his estate to create a range of highly personal and long-lived whites. Newcomers to his wines are bowled over by the power and originality of the classic Ronco della Chiesa

(made from Tocai Friulano), the rich and spicy oak-aged Malvasia, and the unique Studio di Bianco, which dares to blend Tocai Friulano, Sauvignon, and Riesling.
▨ *red, white* **▨** *2006, 2004, 2001 (w); 2004, 2001 (r)* ★ *Collio Bianco Ronco della Chiesa, Collio Bianco Studio di Bianco, Collio Malvasia Selezione*

Edi Keber
F-V G/Collio

loc Zegla 17, Cormons
C 0481 61184 **○** *by appt*

KEBER IS THE epitome of Collio grower-producers: jovial, hospitable, and very capable. He is the biggest producer of the Collio Bianco DOC, in force since the end of the 1990s. In 2008 Keber took the radical decision to concentrate all his white-grape production into a single-estate wine under the Collio Bianco DOC label. The result is a rich, multi-faceted white with great body, subtle oak influence, and huge personality. He no longer makes any red wine.
▨ *white* **▨** *white: 2007, 2006, 2005, 2004, 2001* ★ *Collio Tocai Friulano, Collio Bianco*

Girolamo Dorigo
F-V G/Colli Orientali del Friuli

via del Pozzo 5, Buttrio **C** 0432 674268 **W** *www.montsclapade.com* **○** *by appt*

DORIGO'S RANGE has a distinctly francophile note with its Cabernet Sauvignon-Merlot Montsclapade, Burgundy-style Ronc di Juri Chardonnay, and traditional-method bubbly. However, Girolamo Dorigo also makes the rare local dessert wine Picolit, as well as Friuli's tannic and long-lived red Pignolo, both of which are capable of greatness in the best vintages.
▨ *red, white, sparkling, dessert* **▨** *2005, 2004, 2001(r); 2006, 2004 (w)*
★ *Colli Orientali del Friuli: Rosso Montsclapade, Chardonnay Vigneto Ronc di Juri; Dorigo Brut VdT*

Girolamo Dorigo label

Jermann
F-V G/IGT

via Monte Fortino 21, fraz Villanova, Farra d'Isonzo **C** 0481 888080 **W** *www.jermann vinnaioli.it* **○** *by appt*

SILVIO JERMANN'S curriculum vitae – which stretches back to the mid-1970s – bulges

---

JOSKO GRAVNER: BACK TO THE FUTURE

Grower-producer Josko Gravner owns and runs a small estate in the village of Oslavia in the Collio. His Burgundy-style Chardonnays of the 1980s earned him a reputation as Italy's finest white wine producer, but in 1997 he began to experiment with alternative winemaking. His search for the ultimate natural wine led him to 5,000-year-old methods: making wine in round, 2m-high earthenware vessels called *kvevri*. After crushing the grapes, he puts the juice and the skins into these jars, which are

buried for seven months to ferment and mature. The wine then goes into large oak barrels to age for three and a half years before bottling without filtering. The wines are dry, concentrated, full-bodied, and unique. Gravner's production of around 40,000 bottles a year consists of a Merlot-based red called Rujno, a white varietal from Ribolla Gialla, and a Pinot Grigio-Chardonnay-Sauvignon blend called Breg. Only small quantities are exported.
W *www.gravner.it*

with great white wines, ranging from the genial Vintage Tunina blend and the oak-conditioned Capo Martino blend to a stylish Chardonnay with the enigmatic name Were Dreams. The Pignolo-based Pignacoluse shows his confident touch with reds. In 2008 the winemaking moved to spectacular, ultra-modern cellars at Ruttars.

🟥 red, white 🔺 2006, 2005, 2001, 2000, 1999 ★ Vintage Tunina VdT, Capo Martino in Ruttaris VdT, Pignacoluse Venezia Giulia IGT

Kante
F-V G/Carso

loc Prepotto 1A, Duino-Aurisina
📞 040 200255 🔲 by appt

EDI KANTE is the great producer of F-V G's smallest DOC zone, Carso. His output is tiny, but the dry, flinty intensity and aroma of his wines is unforgettable. If the Vitovska seems too subtle, or the Terlano made from Refosco too sharp, try the vibrant Sauvignon Blanc or the spicy Malvasia instead.

🟥 red, white 🔺 white: 2005, 2002, 2000, 1998 ★ Carso: Malvasia, Vitovska, Sauvignon Blanc

La Castellada
F-V G/Collio

fraz Oslavia 1, Gorizia 📞 0481 33670 🔲 by appt

THE VILLAGE OF OSLAVIA is home to some of F-V G's most serious whites, and is one of the few places in the region where the rare Ribolla Gialla grape ripens to its full potential, giving wines with hedgerow aromas and intense, citrus flavours. La Castellada's Bensa brothers make a Ribolla varietal and put the other six or seven varieties they grow into the chunky Bianco

Stylish label from Kante

della Castellada estate blend.

🟥 red, white 🔺 2004, 2003, 2000, 1999, 1998 ★ Collio Bianco della Castellada, Collio Ribolla Gialla

Le Due Terre
F-V G/Colli Orientali del Friuli

via Roma 68/B, Prepotto 📞 0432 713189 🔲 by appt

LE DUE TERRE produces a tiny amount of handcrafted wines with enormous personality. It is one of the few estates in F-V G – an area that built its reputation on whites – to concentrate on red wines. Sacrisassi Rosso is a blend of local varieties that combines the spicy character of Schioppettino with the berry fruit of Refosco, while the Colli Orientali Merlot is a rich, plummy monovarietal. The Sacrisassi Bianco – a white with the body of a serious red – is made from Tocai Friulano, Ribolla Gialla, and Sauvignon Blanc.

🟥 red, white 🔺 2005, 2004, 2000 (w); 2004, 2000 (r)

Le Due Terre

★ Colli Orientali del Friuli: Merlot, Sacrisassi Bianco, Sacrisassi Rosso

Le Vigne di Zamò
F-V G/Colli Orientali del Friuli

via Abate Corrado 4, loc Rosazzo, Manzano 📞 0432 759693 🌐 *www.levignedizamo.com* 🔲 by appt

PREVIOUSLY SITED on the historic Abbazia di Rosazzo estate, Zamò has been at the state-of-the-art winery across the road from the abbey since the mid-1990s. With vineyards now starting to mature, Zamò's basic Tocai Friulano and Malvasia varietals look very impressive. The superb, full-bodied Cinquant'anni selections come from tiny plots of 50-year-old Tocai Friulano and Merlot vines at the original family holdings.

🟥 red, white, dessert 🔺 2006, 2000 (w); 2003, 2001, 2000 (r) ★ Colli Orientali del Friuli: Tocai Friulano Vigne Cinquant'Anni, Pinot Bianco Tullio Zamò, Merlot Vigne Cinquant'Anni

Lis Neris
F-V G/Friuli Isonzo & IGT

via Gavinana 5, San Lorenzo Isontino 📞 0481 80105 🌐 *www.lisneris.it* 🔲 by appt

THE LIS NERIS estate has grown steadily in recent years, but owner-winemaker Alvaro Pecorari has gradually whittled down the range to focus on the varieties closest to his heart: Chardonnay, Sauvignon Blanc, and Pinot Grigio. The latter also features heavily in the two new, top quality IGT blends: Lis and Confini. Then there is Tal Lùc, which is one of Italy's greatest dessert wines, and the house red is pretty good too.

🟥 red, white, dessert 🔺 white: 2007, 2006, 2004, 2002, 2001 ★ Friuli Isonzo Gris Pinot Grigio, Lis Venezia Giulia Bianco IGT, Tal Lùc Verduzzo Passito VdT

Livio Felluga
F-V G/Colli Orientali del Friuli

via Risorgimento 1, fraz Brazzano, Cormons **C** *0481 60203*
W *www.liviofelluga.it* ☐ *by appt*

THIS FAMILY-RUN WINERY, which owns extensive vineyards in some of the best sites in the Colli Orientali, is one of the key players in the region. Look out for the Terre Alte Sauvignon/Pinot Bianco with oak-fermented Tocai, the red Sossó Riserva, and the oak-aged Pinot Bianco Illivio.
⬛ *red, white, dessert* **⬛** *2006, 2004, 2002, 2001, 1999 (w); 2004, 2001 (r)* ★ *Colli Orientali del Friuli: Rosazzo Rosso Sossó, Rosazzo Rosso Riserva Sossó, Rosazzo Bianco Terre Alte, Bianco Illivio*

Livon
F-V G/Collio

via Montarezza 33, fraz Dolegnano, San Giovanni al Natisone
C *0432 757173* **W** *www.livon.it* ☐ *by appt*

GOING AGAINST THE current trend in Italy for Mediterranean-type whites, the Livon family remains faithful to its elegant, lightly oaked house style, as displayed in its prize-winning Braide Mate Chardonnay and its dry, delicately aromatic Braide Alte (Moscato-Sauvignon Blanc-Chardonnay-Picolit). The same family owns the specialist Collio estate Tenuta Roncalto, and makes the great-value Villa Chiopris range of red and white wines for everyday drinking.
⬛ *red, white, dessert* **⬛** *2006, 2004, 2001 (w); 2004, 2000 (r)* ★ *Collio Braide Mate Chardonnay, Braide Alte VdT, Collio Merlot Tiare Mate*

Livon

Miani
F-V G/Colli Orientali del Friuli

via Peruzzi 10, fraz Vicinale, Buttrio **C** *0432 674327*
☐ *by appt*

ENZO PONTONI runs the ultimate one-man winery. The paucity of his yields is legendary: He makes 8,000 bottles from 16ha of vineyard. There is weight and concentration to his gutsy barrel-aged Tocai Friulano, Refosco Calvani and cassis-scented old-vines Merlot Filip. These are cult offerings that are hard to find but worth it.
⬛ *red, white* **⬛** *2004, 2002, 2000 (r); 2006, 2000 (w)* ★ *Colli Orientali del Friuli: Tocai Friulano, Ribolla Gialla, Merlot*

Ronco del Gelso
F-V G/Friuli Isonzo

via Isonzo 117, Cormons
C *0481 61310* **W** *www.roncodel gelso.com* ☐ *by appt*

GIORGIO BADIN's wines require patience. When they are young they offer lots of glossy texture with just an inkling of fruit; it is only after a couple of years in the cellar that their true fruit and aromas emerge. Alternatively, try unleashing the character of his young wines by decanting them. With a little air the Tocai Friulano will deliver ripe peach with wild herbs, fennel, and almond.
⬛ *red, white* **⬛** *2007, 2006, 2005, 2004, 2001 (w)* ★ *Friuli Isonzo: Pinot Grigio Sot Lis Rivis, Sauvignon, Tocai Friulano*

Russiz Superiore
F-V G/Collio

via Russiz 7, Capriva del Friuli
C *0481 99164* **W** *www.marco felluga.it* ☐ *by appt*

ALTHOUGH THE FELLUGA brothers went separate ways over 30 years ago, each has continued to have an influence at the quality end of Friuli-Venezia Giulia's wine industry. Livio Felluga (see p233), now run by Livio's children, sources most grapes from the Colli Orientali. Marco Felluga, on the other hand, is based in Collio, where son Roberto now manages the historic Russiz Superiore property. All the grapes from this no-expense-spared winery go into the top of the range single-estate selections, like the juicy varietal Collio Sauvignon Blanc. The same winemaking team turns out the Marco Felluga range from mainly bought-in grapes, which is only slightly below the single-estate wines in terms of quality.

Collio
Denominazione di Origine Controllata
Tocai Friulano
SCHIOPETTO
2002

Schiopetto Tocai Friulano label

red, white 📇 *2007, 2006, 2004 (w); 2004, 2001 (r)* ★ *Collio Bianco Disôre, Collio Sauvignon, Collio Rosso Riserva degli Orzoni*

Schiopetto
F-V G/Collio & IGT

via Palazzo Archivescovile 1, Capriva del Friuli 📞 *0481 80332*
Ⓦ *www.schiopetto.it* ⬚ *by appt*

THE SCHIOPETTO RANGE focuses on the classic Collio varietals – almondy Tocai Friulano, succulent Sauvignon Blanc, and orange-blossom Pinot Bianco – as well as two cuvèes. The lightly oaked Blanc des Rosis is made from Tocai Friulano, Pinot Grigio, Sauvignon Blanc, Malvasia Istriana, and Ribolla Gialla; and the Mario Schiopetto Bianco is a unique blend of Chardonnay and Tocai Friulano. This wine was created in honour of the late Mario Schiopetto, the man rightly considered the founder of modern winemaking in Friuli-Venezia Giulia. The two estate reds – Rivarosa and Poderi dei Blumei – are gaining an increasingly high profile.

red, white
📇 *white: 2007, 2006, 2003, 2002, 2000*
★ *Mario Schiopetto Bianco Venezia Giulia IGT, Collio Tocai Friulano, Collio Pinot Bianco*

Vie di Romans
F-V G/Friuli Isonzo

loc Vie di Romans 1, Mariano del Friuli 📞 *0481 69600*
Ⓦ *www.viediromans.it*
⬚ *by appt*

GIANFRANCO GALLO built his repuation on outstanding personal interpretations of the popular international whites of the Isonzo: Pinot Grigio,

Label from Volpe Pasini's Zuc di Volpe range

Sauvignon Blanc, and Chardonnay. Recent years have seen him return to his Friuli roots with new wines from Malvasia Istriana (Dis Cumieris) and Tocai Friulano (Dolèe), as well as exploring new ground with a Chardonnay/Sauvignon blend called Dut'Un. All three wines have made an instant impact, further enhancing the standing of one of the region's top grower-producers.

red, white 📇 *white 2006, 2004, 2002, 2001, 2000* ★ *Friuli Isonzo: Sauvignon Vieris, Chardonnay Vie di Romans, Sauvignon Pière*

Villa Russiz
F-V G/Collio

via Russiz 6, Capriva del Friuli 📞 *0481 80047*
Ⓦ *www.villarussiz.it*
⬚ *by appt*

WINEMAKER Gianni Menotti's wine style is full-bodied and crammed with varietal character. He held back from using oak for many years and still only makes one barrel-fermented white, but the de la Tour Chardonnay shows that he has thoroughly mastered the technique. The

Villa Russiz Merlot label

top selections at this benchmark Collio estate are named after the 19th-century owner Comte de la Tour, who was the first to introduce French grape varieties to this region.

red, white 📇 *2007, 2005, 2004, (w); 2005, 2003 (r)* ★ *Collio: Sauvignon de la Tour, Merlot de la Tour, Chardonnay Gräfin de la Tour*

Volpe Pasini
F-V G/Colli Orientali del Friuli

via Cividale 16, fraz Togliano, Torreano di Cividale 📞 *0432 715151*
Ⓦ *www.volpepasini.it* ⬚ *by appt*

EMILIO ROTOLO took over this dwindling winery in the mid-1990s, and in the space of just three vintages turned it into one of the region's real high flyers. The distinctly international-style Zuc di Volpe range is the work of Merlot specialist Riccardo Cotarella, one of Italy's most sought after consultant winemakers. The reds are crammed with velvet tannins and berry flavours, while the whites have fruit salad aromas and, in the case of Pinot Bianco, a very classy touch of oak.

red, white 📇 *2007, 2006, 2004, 2001 (w); 2001 (r)* ★ *Colli Orientali del Friuli: Merlot Focus Zuc di Volpe, Pinot Bianco Zuc di Volpe, Pinot Grigio Zuc di Volpe*

CENTRAL ITALY

THE VARIED REGIONS OF HILLY CENTRAL ITALY *turn out about a quarter of the national wine production. The combination of distinctive terroir, sunny Mediterranean climate, and expert producers results in some of the country's greatest wines.*

Differences in the history and styles of winemaking in the various regions of Central Italy are significant. Tuscany is the acknowledged leader here, boasting the greatest number of DOCs, and the largest and most varied output of wine. It vies with Piemonte for the title of the country's top quality region. Tuscany's Central Hills have been a fulcrum of winegrowing since the time of the Etruscans, but huge investments today are turning Tuscany's coastal zone, the Maremma, into the fastest growing prestige wine area.

Medieval fresco of a wine tavern, Umbria

Other regions in the centre of Italy have been traditionally associated with bulk production and everyday drinking, although this is beginning to change: the regions of Romagna, Le Marche, Lazio, Umbria, and Abruzzo are improving quality, and wines from small producers here are starting to make an impact.

The vineyards of Central Italy now cover over 200,000ha of land, growing a diverse range of fascinating local grapes. Red wines revolve around Sangiovese and Montepulciano, while Verdicchio, Trebbiano (mainly Trebbiano Toscano in this region), and Malvasia account for most whites. Cabernet Sauvignon and Merlot are firmly established in Tuscany and now appear in the top estate wines of other central regions, too.

Central Italy's traditional denominations such as the ever-consistent Chianti Classico, Sangiovese di Romagna and Le Marche's Rosso Piceno offer some of the best buys. Abruzzo's home-grown red Montepulciano and Umbria's rustic Sagrantino are starting to realize their potential now, too. As for whites, Verdicchio wins for personality and quality; but not everything worthwhile is inside the DOC. More and more producers are successfully experimenting with alternative French grape varieties permitted under the regional IGT labels.

Vineyards at Marchesi de' Frescobaldi in Tuscany

◁ **Hillside house and vineyards, Tuscany**

WINE MAP OF CENTRAL ITALY

THE LONG CENTRAL SECTION of the Italian peninsula extends from Tuscany's northwestern border with Liguria over seven regions to Molise in the deep southeast. The unifying feature is the dorsal chain of the Apennines, which runs the length of the central regions, dividing them down the middle. On the Adriatic flank an almost uninterrupted wine-growing belt stretches parallel to the coast through Romagna, Le Marche, Abruzzo, and Molise, occupying the plains and the hills which rise towards the mountains. On the western side of the Apennines, the key wine areas are dotted around hilly inland areas in Tuscany (see pp252–67), Umbria, and Lazio.

KEY

☐ Central Italy

PERFECT CASE: CENTRAL ITALY

Ⓡ Arnaldo Caprai – Val di Maggio Sagrantino di Montefalco 25 Anni ££££

Ⓦ Bucci Verdicchio dei Castelli di Jesi Classico Villa Bucci Riserva ££

Ⓦ Castello della Sala Cervaro della Sala Bianco dell'Umbria IGT ££

Ⓡ Falesco Montiano Lazio IGT £££

Ⓡ Fattoria Le Terrazze Chaos Marche Rosso IGT £££

Ⓓ Fattoria Zerbina Albana di Romagna Passito Scacco Matto £££

Ⓡ Lanari Rosso Conero Fibbio ££ (0712 861343)

Ⓡ Masciarelli Montepulciano d'Abruzzo Villa Gemma ££

Ⓦ Sartarelli Verdicchio dei Castelli di Jesi Classico Superiore Balciana £££

Ⓡ Stefano Berti Sangiovese di Romagna Superiore Calisto £££

Ⓦ Valentini Trebbiano d'Abruzzo ££££

Ⓦ Villa Simone Frascati Vigneto Filonardi £

Parma
Reno
Modena
Ferrara

ROMAGNA
BOLOGNA

SANGIOVESE Ra
DI ROMAGNA
COLLI DI   COLLI
FAENZA   IMOL
Faen

La Spezia

TREBBIANO DI
ROMAGNA

Ceser

ALBANA DI
ROMAGNA

Lucca

FIRENZE
(FLORENCE)

PISA

Livorno

**TUSCANY
(TOSCANA)**

Arezzo

Cecina

Siena

Lago
Trasimeno

Montepulciano

COLLI
TRASIME

Grosseto

ORVI

Orv

SEE TUSCANY MAP
pp252–3

Lago di
Bolsena

EST! ESTI
EST!!!
Le
di

Lago
Bracc

Civitavecchia

TYRRHENIAN SEA

Cornia

Maremma

Ombrone

Orbetello

Vineyards around Montefalco, Umbria

Grape pickers at Masciarelli, Abruzzo

TERROIR AT A GLANCE

Latitude: 41.5–45°N.

Altitude: 0–700m.

Topography: Central Italy stretches from the hills of northeast Tuscany to the coastal plain of Molise. Terrain and altitude vary greatly but vineyards tend to be found on the flat plains and foothill sites.

Soil: Calcareous clay in the Adriatic hill zones; very mixed stony marls in central Tuscany and sandy clays in the Maremma. Red grapes perform best here, but the chalky clay of Orvieto and the volcanic soils of Frascati allow some whites to thrive, too.

Climate: Varies but summers are generally hot and dry, followed by cool winters. Mediterranean climate in the south, and relatively cooler in the north of the region.

Temperature: July average is 24°C.

Rainfall: Annual average ranges from 600 to 900mm.

Wind: Cool maritime breezes from the Adriatic moderate the high summer temperatures on the east coast.

Viticultural hazards: Spring frost; hail; harvest rain.

Boccadigabbia label, Le Marche

CENTRAL ITALY: AREAS & TOP PRODUCERS

ROMAGNA *p240*

Fattoria Zerbina *p246*
La Berta *p246*
San Patrignano *p246*
Stefano Berti *p246*
Tre Monti *p246*

LE MARCHE *p240*

Boccadigabbia *p246*
Bucci *p247*
Fattoria Le Terrazze *p247*
Garofoli Gioacchino *p247*
La Monacesca *p247*
Monte Schiavo *p248*
Saladini Pilastri *p248*
Sartarelli *p248*
Umani Ronchi *p248*

UMBRIA *p242*

Arnaldo Caprai *p248*
Castello della Sala *p249*
Lungarotti *p249*
Palazzone *p249*

LAZIO *p244*

Castel de Paolis *p250*
Di Mauro Paola –
   Colle Picchioni *p250*
Falesco *p250*
Fontana Candida *p250*
Villa Simone *p250*

ABRUZZO *p244*

Fattoria La Valentina *p250*
Illuminati Dino *p251*
Masciarelli *p251*
Valentini *p251*

MOLISE *p245*

Di Majo Norante *p251*

The town of Loreto viewed from a Rosso Piceno vineyard, Le Marche

WINEGROWING AREAS OF CENTRAL ITALY

Romagna

THE BEST WINES IN ROMAGNA, both red and white, come from inland hills that rise to around 350m above sea level. Romagna wins the prize for the Italian region with the most easily comprehensible DOC system. The official labels communicate the essentials – the grape variety plus the region. To further simplify matters, there are only three important varieties: Trebbiano (Ugni Blanc), Albana, and Sangiovese.

The first of these shows up in the **Trebbiano di Romagna** DOC, which is responsible for dry, rather neutral wines produced mainly on the coastal plains. The second, **Albana di Romagna**, was Italy's first white DOCG. Its promotion to the country's highest official wine category in 1987 was greeted with scepticism. The *secco* version has a certain amount of body, but it does not exactly burst with flavour. What has given this wine prestige, however, is the *passito* style made from raisined grapes. This is a refined, concentrated, honey-sweet wine with peach and almond aromas. The most renowned production area is around the village of Bertinoro, where limestone soils give the wines an extra boost of aroma. The other local hero is **Sangiovese di Romagna** DOC. Both the Adriatic region and neighbouring Tuscany claim paternity of this, central Italy's most important red grape. Research shows

Sangiovese grapes

that each region probably developed its own clones. On sandy marl soils in the hills above the towns of Forlì, Faenza, and Cesena the Romagna version gives bright ruby-coloured wines with an aroma of violets and vigorous dry flavours. **Colli d'Imola**, **Colli di Faenza**, and **Colli di Rimini** are small, hillside DOCs launched at the end of the 1990s with the aim of giving specific identities to wines from these towns. All three allow the use of new arrivals Chardonnay and Cabernet alongside the traditional Sangiovese. The basic **Romagna** DOC is for everyday wines. The *superiore* version is a step up in concentration and fruit, and *riserva* wines age for two years and have a lot more soft tannin and berry flavours than they used to. Many other wines worth knowing about come from outside the DOC system. For reasons of prestige, some producers prefer to bottle the DOC-permitted variety Sangiovese under the recently-created IGT labels Forlì, Rubicone, and Ravenna, which are also increasingly used for alternative varietals or Chardonnay-Sauvignon blends.

🏝 *sandy marl, fossil-rich limestone* 🍇 *Sangiovese, Cabernet Sauvignon* 🍇 *Albana, Trebbiano, Chardonnay* 🍷 *red, white, dessert*

Le Marche

ALTHOUGH LE MARCHE has been flirting with international grapes in recent years, the region remains fundamentally faithful to local varieties. Verdicchio dominates the white wine scene. This unique Le Marche variety grows in two distinct DOC zones. The grapes for **Verdicchio dei Castelli di Jesi** DOC wine come from the hills northeast of Ancona, up to 500m above sea level. *Classico* on the label indicates that a wine originates in the historic production zone around the town of Jesi. *Superiore* wines have half a per cent more alcohol than *classico*, and *riservas* have half a per cent more than *superiore*. With an annual production of around 24 million bottles, Castelli di Jesi is Le Marche's biggest DOC by far, and the second biggest in Italy after Soave. **Verdicchio di Matelica** grows in a much smaller DOC zone, closer to the mountains in the neighbouring province of Macerata. Soils here are particularly rich in minerals and this, combined with the cooler mesoclimate, may account for the extra tangy intensity of Matelica wines. The *terroir* factor, however, has less of an influence than wine-making styles, which are many and various.

Verdicchio is a full-bodied white with a dry, nutty flavour. Basic label wines are unoaked and made for early drinking. The majority of producers, however, also turn out special selections, which could be barrel conditioned or late harvested, and in some cases can age comfortably for a decade or more. In this league there are flavours of ripe apple and apricot, and a whole range of wild herb aromas from thyme to fennel and aniseed.

On the red wine front the main grape is Montepulciano. The purest version of this hearty, berry-scented variety is **Rosso Conero**. Producers in this small-scale DOC on the edge of Ancona's residential suburbs tend not to blend their Montepulciano, which flourishes on the dry chalky soils of Monte Conero. The result is a serious but highly drinkable wine with a hallmark note of black-berry jam and hints of violets and rose petal. **Rosso Piceno** DOC, on the other hand, is generally made from a Montepulciano-Sangiovese blend that gives drier flavours, often with a touch of cherry or plum. In this DOC the term *superiore* denotes a wine from the top production area around Ascoli Piceno, which has the kind of hot, dry soils that Montepulciano thrives on. Rosso Piceno is the biggest red DOC in terms of quantity.

The smallest DOC is **Lacrima di Morro d'Alba**. This varietal wine, made from the grape of the same name, has an explosive up-front mix of fruit, spice, and perfumed floral aromas. To get the full effect, try the *novello* style – the light fruity wine released in the November after the vintage and made for immediate drinking. Production totals a mere 5,000 or 6,000 bottles, but is increasing as producers begin to replant the grape that only 10 years ago was on the brink of extinction. The other small but expanding sector is that of wines made from imported varieties bottled under the IGT Marche label. Neither the quality nor the quantity of the Chardonnay, Sauvignon Blanc, and Pinot Grigio currently made here is going to threaten Verdicchio producers, but Cabernet Sauvignon, Merlot, and Syrah might seriously test the region's loyalty to its own varieties in the future.

🏔 *sandy clay, chalky marl*
🍇 *Montepulciano, Sangiovese, Lacrima di Morro, Cabernet Sauvignon, Merlot* 🍇 *Verdicchio*
🍷 *red, white*

Verdicchio dei Castelli di Jesi Classico vineyard, Le Marche

Toscana (Tuscany)

See pp252–67.

Umbria

UMBRIA'S WINEMAKING REPUTATION used to rest solidly on the popular white Orvieto wine and, to a lesser extent, red Torgiano, but both have been overshadowed since the mid-1990s by a new generation of premium reds from the village of Montefalco. The region's DOC system remains substantially traditionalist, which means that producers who want to experiment with alternative grape varieties are obliged to use the IGT Umbria label which, in this region (as in other parts of Central Italy) collects more adherents and accolades every year. Umbria breaks down into the three key winegrowing areas that follow, as well as some smaller, lesser-known ones.

🗍 *fossil-rich calcareous clay, sandy calcareous clay*
▨ *Sangiovese, Canaiolo, Sagrantino, Gamay, Merlot*
▨ *Trebbiano (Procanico), Malvasia, Grechetto, Sauvignon Blanc* 🍷 *red, white, dessert*

Orvieto

A LOCAL SUB-VARIETY of Trebbiano called Procanico is used in combination with varying percentages of Grechetto, Verdello, Drupeggio (Canaiolo Bianco), and Malvasia in Orvieto DOC. The basic style is light and very

Picturesque monastery and vineyards, Orvieto

dry with a delicate almondy flavour. The production area, which spills over into neighbouring Lazio, is big and it is worth opting for the *classico* wines from the top sites on the hillsides up to 500m, just south of the spectacular cathedral town. Here, calcareous clays rich in fossils give extra body and a tangy intensity. The other advantage of the *classico* zone is the humidity that rises from the lakes and river below the town in autumn. This creates ideal conditions for late-harvest dessert wines, which are made from the same grapes as the dry versions. More and more producers are returning to their roots – historically Orvieto was sweet and not dry – by making wine in this style. Quantities are minimal, but the dessert wines, identified by the term *dolce,* are well worth looking for.

Torgiano

TORGIANO IS A WINE VILLAGE south of Perugia where they make a white DOC wine from Trebbiano and Grechetto, a red DOC wine from Sangiovese-Canaiolo and, from the same grapes, a red *riserva* with DOCG status. The vines are planted in sandy calcareous soils at an elevation of 200–300m. Both the white and the reds are dry, medium-bodied wines. **Torgiano Bianco** DOC wine has white melon and apricot flavours. The red **Torgiano Rosso** DOC is a cherry and violet-scented wine designed for early drinking. **Torgiano (Rosso) Riserva** DOCG, on the other hand, ages for three years in wood. It has the typical garnet shade of Sangiovese-based *riservas*, lots

---

TORGIANO WINE MUSEUM

The Museo del Vino at Torgiano, open since 1974, is one of the largest and most complete collections of wine artefacts in Europe. Established by passionate winemaker Giorgio Lungarotti *(see p249)* and his wife, the museum recounts the history of wine through objects that have been used over the past 2,000 years to produce, store, and serve it. Exhibits on display range from the drinking vessels of the second millennium BC used by the Hittite people of Anatolia and the Baccanalian chalices of ancient Rome to ingenious agricultural implements, bizarre domestic gadgetry, and artistic curiosities. Educational sections unravel the complexities of growing grapes and making wine, and there is a vast area dedicated to wine illustrations through the ages. There is also a museum store, well-stocked wine shop, and a restaurant which serves traditional local dishes.

🖳 *www.made-in-italy.com/winefood/wine/museum.htm*

of tannin, and complex spicy-floral aromas. For decades the only producer to bottle the wines of Torgiano was Lungarotti. There is now a wider choice of labels, but Lungarotti remains the standard bearer of the denomination.

Montefalco

THE TOWN OF MONTEFALCO gives its name to a red DOC blend (60–70 per cent Sangiovese, 10–15 per cent Sagrantino, plus a few other grapes) and a DOCG varietal wine made from Sagrantino. The vineyards are situated on hot, dry slopes with predominantly clay soils at the same altitude as Torgiano further north. The beefy entry level **Montefalco Rosso** DOC is an earthy-tasting wine which these days is often softened by a drop of Merlot. One step up, there is also a full-bodied Rosso Riserva which delivers the authentic Central Italy wood-aged style at a fraction of the cost of its Tuscan counterparts.

Castello della Sala label, Umbria

The superstar, however, is the immensely powerful **Sagrantino di Montefalco** DOCG. Sagrantino is a grape variety which grows only in this corner of Umbria. According to local legend it was cultivated by the Franciscan brothers of Assisi (the alternative spelling Sacrantino suggests an altar wine), but written records of the variety only go back to the late 19th century. Traditionally, the grape was dried to make a sweet *passito* wine (which still exists)

with a vague resemblance to Recioto di Valpolicella DOC in Northeast Italy *(see p224)*. Specialized production of dry Sagrantino only really took off in the 1990s, thanks mainly to the trail-blazing Arnaldo Caprai estate. It is a wine with a heady aroma of blackberries and toffee apple, and with massive tannins that need at least three or four years to mellow, especially since the top producers give their wines the full new oak treatment. Annual output of Sagrantino *secco* currently amounts to less than 500,000 bottles, but this is destined to multiply rapidly in the next few years as the significant players who have bought into the area – including Cecchi, Antinori, Frescobaldi, Lungarotti, and Livon from Friuli – come on line with their first vintages.

Umbria's Other DOCs

AMONG THE HALF A DOZEN lesser-known DOCs of the region, the **Colli del Trasimeno** is one worth looking out for as a source of modern, fruity Sangiovese-based reds. A curiosity of the hills around Lago Trasimeno is the long-established presence of the red grape Gamay (usually associated with Beaujolais), which occasionally turns up as a varietal wine, as well as contributing to the DOC blend.

Other French varieties planted in the region are destined for the increasingly significant IGT Umbria denomination. As with all IGTs, the front label may or may not specify the grape. Chardonnay has a certain following in the region, and Sauvignon Blanc is sometimes used in the Orvieto area to make Sauternes-inspired sweet wines *(see p66)*. It is the predictable Cabernet Sauvignon and Merlot, however, which tend to steal the scene, whether in varietals, Bordeaux-style blends, or in combination with the local Sangiovese.

Lungarotti vineyard, Torgiano

Lazio

ALMOST HALF THE WINE made in Lazio comes from a country district south of Rome called the Castelli Romani. The idyllic climate of the hills here has, for centuries, made them home to the summer residences of the Roman aristocracy (not to mention the Pope), as well as to numerous vines. Although the latitude ought to favour reds, the Castelli Romani is white wine country. The mix of fine-grained volcanic soils and elevations of up to 400m provide a habitat in which the traditional white varieties have always flourished. Chief among these are the prolific Trebbiano and Malvasia grapes, key components in Frascati, alongside a small optional percentage of Greco. The **Frascati** DOC has supplied the taverns and inns of the Eternal City with its everyday drinking wine for the last 2,000 years. The style is light, soft, and for drinking young. *Superiore* wines are fuller-bodied but, more importantly, have the slightly salty almond finish that gives good Frascati its undeniable touch of personality. Lazio's other historic white wine zone is on the northern border with Umbria. On volcanic slopes around the Lake of Bolsena, the same basic grape mix of Trebbiano and Malvasia is responsible for the DOC **Est! Est!! Est!!!** *(see right)*. The exclamation marks may seem something of an anomaly today, but modern winemaking technology produces a gentle, peachy-flavoured white wine that makes a lovely summer drink. If you are searching for more weight and up-front character in the region, then you have to look outside the traditional DOCs and explore the IGT Lazio wines. There are a growing number of boutique wineries here with ambitions that go

DRINK AS THE ROMANS DO

The Italian capital has boasted a buzzing wine trade ever since Roman times. Not only did the Romans export wine in bulk, but they also consumed vast amounts. Taverns provided the hub of the business, selling wine from the hills immediately south of Rome. The term *frascati* comes from the practice of hanging a leafy branch called a *frasca* at the inn door when a new vintage was ready.

The tradition of the wine tavern lived on through the Middle Ages – a census in 1425 recorded 1,022 of them in the capital – and is still strong today. Known variously as *osteria, vineria,* or *enoteca,* the modern wine bar serves wine by the glass and by the bottle, offers light meals, and is typically annexed to a wine shop. Nowhere else in the country offers such a vast selection of wines. Top addresses in Rome include:
Cavour 313, via Cavour 313 (06 7685496);
Cul de Sac 1, Piazza Pasquino 73
(06 68801094); Semidivino, via Alessandri
230 (06 44250795); Trimani Wine Bar,
via Cernaia 37b (06 4469630);
Gusto, Piazza Augusto Imperatore 9
(06 3226273); Simposio, Piazza Cavour 16
(06 3211502); Enoteca al Parlamento,
via dei Prefetti 15 (06 6873446).

beyond the local grapes into the realms of Chardonnay, Viognier, Cabernet Sauvignon, Merlot, Syrah, and Petit Verdot. In the field of red wine in particular, where the local tradition has never been strong, Lazio's future definitely lies with the international varieties.

🏞 *fine grained volcanic, tuffaceous clay, limestone*
🍇 *Cabernet Sauvignon, Merlot* 🍇 *Trebbiano,*
Malvasia (Toscana, del Lazio and di Candia)
🍷 *red, white*

Abruzzo

ABRUZZO USES A REGIONAL SYSTEM of wine classification that distinguishes between varieties, but not (with one recent exception) between subzones. Since the whole production revolves around just two grape types, this makes for very uncomplicated wine lists. The basic choice is between the red **Montepulciano d'Abruzzo** DOC and the white **Trebbiano d'Abruzzo** DOC. The only current exception to the catch-all system of wine denomination is the recent **Controguerra** DOC, created to accommodate

Vines among an olive grove, Frascati, Lazio

Masciarelli vineyards in the Abruzzo region

a range of local and international varieties grown in a specific and very interesting subzone around the town of the same name on the border with Le Marche. Production will need to increase considerably, however, before this denomination makes an impact. Montepulciano d'Abruzzo wines from the hills around Teramo have the right to specify the zone Colline Teramane on the label. Plans to promote the denomination to full DOCG status in its own right are in the pipeline. Montepulciano, a grape that is native to Abruzzo and has no link with the town of the same name in Tuscany, certainly deserves attention. Its dark, spicy fruit character and soft acidity make it inviting to drink young, but it can also make chunky and powerfully tannic wines with great ageing potential. It also makes a delicious, strawberry-flavoured rosé called Cerasuolo, ideal for summer quaffing.

The grape known locally as Trebbiano d'Abruzzo (Bombino Bianco) is a different variety from the Trebbiano (Trebbiano Toscano) found elsewhere in the central regions. It generally makes fresh, dry white wines with a

slightly grassy flavour. It is also capable of complex, full-bodied wines that see some oak and last for decades, but this style is pursued by only a couple of producers, principally the legendary Valentini. Alternative grape varieties do not attract anything like the following they have in the other regions of Central Italy, which means few producers have adopted the IGT Abruzzo label. Chardonnay does extremely well in Abruzzo, but producers may think twice before turning to an already over-exploited variety as an alternative to Trebbiano.

🗺 sandy clay, stony clay, limestone
🍇 Montepulciano 🍇 Trebbiano d'Abruzzo
🍷 red, white, rosé

Molise

MOLISE IS ITALY'S SECOND SMALLEST region after the Valle d'Aosta. Its winemaking identity is inextricably linked to that of its star producer, Di Majo Norante, the estate that single-handedly put the region on the map. Winegrowing is concentrated on the coastal plain, where hot, dry summers make irrigation essential. The region has two DOCs. The region-wide **Molise** permits around a dozen varieties, the most used of which are Falanghina and Aglianico from neighbouring Campania and the Calabrian Greco Bianco. Aglianico makes a dark, full-bodied red with black cherry and violet aromas. The other two varieties are mixed together by Di Majo Norante to make a peachy-flavoured white. The second DOC, **Biferno**, is a more restricted area in Campobasso province, where the focus varieties are the white Trebbiano and red Montepulciano d'Abruzzo.

🗺 sandy clay, clay, limestone 🍇 Montepulciano, Aglianico 🍇 Trebbiano d'Abruzzo, Greco Bianco, Falanghina 🍷 red, white

EST! EST!! EST!!!

The exclamation marks are an integral part of the Est! Est!! Est!!! label and refer to the story of a 12th-century imperial emissary who was charged with checking out the quality of the wine at the inns along the route of the emperor. He wrote 'Est', meaning 'here it is', on the doors of the places that served the best wine. In his enthusiasm for the wine of Montefiascone (or perhaps seeing triple) he chalked up the message Est! Est!! Est!!!, which gave its name to the local wine.

TOP PRODUCERS OF CENTRAL ITALY

Fattoria Zerbina
Romagna/Sangiovese di Romagna, Albana di Romagna & IGT

via Vicchi 11, Marzeno di Faenza
C *0546 40022* **W** *www.zerbina.com*
O *by appt*

CRISTINA GEMINIANI started a degree in economics, but switched to agriculture, studied oenology, and was managing her grandfather's wine estate by the age of 30. This estate makes Sangiovese in styles from the fruity, unoaked Ceregio to the majestic, old-vine Riserva Pietramora. The honey and apricot flavoured Scacco Matto is one of Italy's greatest dessert wines. Marzieno is a classy blend of Sangiovese, Cabernet Sauvignon, Merlot, and Syrah.
red, dessert *2006, 2004, 2001, 2000, 1999* ★ *Sangiovese di Romagna Superiore Riserva Pietramora, Albana di Romagna Passito Scacco Matto, Marzieno Rosso IGT*

La Berta
Romagna/Sangiovese di Romagna

via La Berta 13, Brisighella
C *0546 84998* **O** *by appt*

THIS LONG-ESTABLISHED, family estate started a replanting programme in the mid-1990s, which is now supplying consultant winemaker Stefano Chioccioli with first class raw materials. The Bordeaux influence here is clear from the dark colour, soft tannins, and ripe fruit of the Ca' di Berta Cabernet Sauvignon-Sangiovese blend. The Sangiovese Riserva Olmatello is just as smooth, but has more local character in its aromas.
red *2006, 2005, 2004, 2001, 2000* ★ *Colli di Faenza Rosso Ca' di Berta, Sangiovese di Romagna Superiore Riserva Olmatello*

San Patrignano
Romagna/Sangiovese di Romagna

via San Patrignano 53, Ospedaletto di Coriano **C** *0541 362362*
W *www.sanpatrignano.org* **O** *by appt*

SAN PATRIGNANO is a large, self-financing rehabilitation community. The professional wine-making operation here, led by top-flight consultant Riccardo Cotarella, sources grapes exclusively from its own vineyards, which now extend over 110ha. Key emphasis is on red wines, which bear the Cotarella hallmark of impenetrable colour, explosive fruit, and rich, deep textures. The Sangiovese di Romagna Riserva Avi has become a classic of the region, while the Colli di Rimini Cabernet Montepirolo is a great red from a little-known DOC.
red, white *2006, 2004, 2003, 2001, 2000* ★ *Sangiovese di Romagna Riserva Avi*

Stefano Berti
Romagna/Sangiovese di Romagna

loc Ravaldino in Monte, via la Scagna 18, Forlì **C** *0543 488074*
W *www.stefanoberti.com* **O** *by appt*

UNTIL 1999 Stefano Berti sold his grapes to a local co-op. Then in 2000 he decided to start making his own wine in the cellar of the family farm.

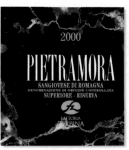

Fattoria Zerbina label

His first release of Sangiovese di Romagna, from a question-able vintage, was promising, but the 2001 was a knockout. The top selection, Calisto, has huge fruit and substance, but also a smoothness and balance that make it immediately drinkable. Ravaldo has less wood and concentration, but the same cherry and dried flower aromas as the senior wine.
red *2006, 2004, 2001, 2000* ★ *Sangiovese di Romagna: Superiore Calisto, Superiore Ravaldo*

Tre Monti
Romagna/Sangiovese di Romagna & Colli d'Imola

via Lola 3, Imola **C** *0542 657116*
W *www.tremonti.it* **O** *by appt*

TRE MONTI IS ONE OF a growing number of producers that now espouse the cause of the new Colli d'Imola DOC, designed to give an identity to wines from the hills around Imola, which would otherwise fall into the generic IGT category. The estate makes a range of very respectable whites from Chardonnay and Sauvignon Blanc, but the most interesting release to date is a full-bodied and spicy Cabernet Sauvignon-Sangiovese blend called Boldo. Among the more traditional wines, the Sangiovese Riserva Thea has plenty of class and nuance.
red, white *2006, 2004, 2001, 2000* ★ *Colli d'Imola Rosso Boldo, Sangiovese di Romagna Superiore Thea*

Boccadigabbia
Le Marche/Rosso Piceno & IGT

contrada Castelletta 56, Civitanova Marche **C** *0733 70728*
W *www.boccadigabbia.com* **O** *by appt*

ONCE THE PROPERTY OF Emperor Napoleon III, this estate has

revived a 19th-century tradition by specializing in French varietals. Akronte is a concentrated Cabernet Sauvignon that accumulates great depth through two years' ageing in new oak. The rich and spicy Pix is Le Marche's first high-profile Merlot. Owner Elvido Alessandri also makes good use of local grapes. Salta-picchio is a classy Sangio-vese with soft fruit aromas and the kind of depth and texture not always found in the variety's native Tuscany. The core business Rosso Piceno has delicious dry cherry fruit and lots of body.

🍷 red 🍷 2006, 2004, 2001, 2000 ★ Rosso Piceno; Marche IGT: Akronte, Saltapicchio, Pix

Bucci
Le Marche/Verdicchio dei Castelli di Jesi

fraz Pongelli, via Cona 30, Ostra Vetere 🍷 071 964179 🌐 www.villabucci.com 🔲 by appt

AMPELIO BUCCI and his veteran consultant winemaker Giorgio Grai use traditional methods for the Villa Bucci Riserva, which include fermenting at natural temperatures and long ageing in oak casks. The fruit for this legendary white comes from five different vineyards. Each parcel is vinified and aged separately before being assembled by master taster Grai to obtain the desired poise and complexity. The wine, which comes out after three years, is all about balance and aroma. A typical vintage has soft apricot fruit, a huge gamut of floral nuances, and a freshness which holds up for years in the bottle.

🍷 white 🍷 2006, 2004, 2001, 2000, 1999, 1998 ★ Verdicchio dei Castelli di Jesi Classico Villa Bucci Riserva

Boccadigabbia label

Fattoria Le Terrazze
Le Marche/Rosso Conero & IGT

via Musone 4, Numana 🍷 071 7390352 🌐 www.fattorieleterrazze.it 🔲 by appt

THE TERNI FAMILY have been making quality wines in the Rosso Conero DOC since 1862. The top selection is the Sassi Neri, with the blackberry aromas of Rosso Conero and a hint of leather in the back-ground. Chaos is the new IGT creation of owner Antonio Terni and his consultant Attilio Pagli. Made from Monte-pulciano, Merlot, and Syrah, it has an inky depth of colour and almost caricatured soft-ness and fruit concentration.

🍷 red 🍷 2006, 2004, 2001, 2000, 1998 ★ Rosso Conero Sassi Neri, Chaos Marche Rosso IGT

Garofoli Gioacchino
Le Marche/Verdicchio dei Castelli di Jesi & Rosso Conero

p.le G.Garofoli, Castelfidardo 🍷 071 7820162 🌐 www.garofolivini.it 🔲 by appt

THE GAROFOLI ESTATE is best known for Verdicchio, which winemaker Carlo Garofoli turns out in five distinctive versions. The Classico Superiore Podium delivers nectarine and acacia aromas and a soft round palate. The Riserva Serra Fiorese is released after a year's wood ageing, when it has begun to

develop honey on the nose and a long minerally palate. Look out too for the muscular Rosso Conero Agontano.

🍷 red, white, sparkling, dessert 🍷 2006, 2004 (w); 2001, 2000, 1999 (r) ★ Rosso Conero Riserva Grosso Agontano; Verdicchio dei Castelli di Jesi: Classico Superiore Podium, Riserva Serra Fiorese

La Monacesca
Le Marche/Verdicchio di Matelica

contrada Monacesca, Matelica 🍷 0733 812602 🌐 www.monacesca.it 🔲 by appt

THIS FAMILY-RUN ESTATE makes terroir-focused wines that bring out the tangy quality of the Matelica DOC zone, yet preserve the varietal character of the Verdicchio grape by ageing exclusively in stainless steel vats. The standard DOC wine boasts floral aromas and a long, dry finish. The top of the range Mirum Riserva is sourced from 30-year-old vines and released two years after the vintage. Expect a deep, glossy palate, and aromas of sweet aniseed, apricot, and hazelnut.

🍷 white 🍷 2006, 2004, 2001, 2000 ★ Verdicchio di Matelica: La Monacesca, Mirum Riserva

Garofoli Gioacchino vineyards

Monte Schiavo
Marche/Verdicchio dei Castelli di Jesi & Rosso Conero

Fraz Monteschiavo, via Vivaio, Maiolati Spontini **☎** *0731 700385* **W** *www.monteschiavo.it* **❑** *by appt*

MONTE SCHIAVO is a former co-op that was bought in 1994 by Pieralisi, one of Italy's largest agricultural machinery firms. Its range covers all the main DOCs of the region, but Verdicchio leads the way. The tasty basic label Coste del Molino is great value, while the barrel-aged Riserva Giuncare, the superb late-harvested Pallio di San Fioriano, and the new Nativo all compete for the top places in the Castelli di Jesi DOC. Also worth trying are the oaky Rosso Conero Adeodato selection and the fragrant and highly original Lacrima di Morro d'Alba.

■ *red, white* **➋** *2006, 2004 (w); 2004, 2001, 2000 (r)* ★ *Verdicchio dei Castelli di Jesi: Coste del Molino, Classico Superiore Pallio di San Floriano; Rosso Conero Adeodato*

Saladini Pilastri
Marche/Rosso Piceno

via Saladini 5, Spinetoli **☎** *0736 899534* **❑** *by appt*

SALADINI PILASTRI's mission is to elevate Rosso Piceno from rustic, cheap, and cheerful right up to super-premium status. The resources are not lacking, as the 120-ha estate occupies prime sites on the hills south of Ascoli Piceno. The top selection Vigna Monteprandone made its debut at the end of the 1990s. It took a couple of vintages to come into its own, but it has been highly consistent since the breakthrough 2000 vintage. The stablemate Montetinello

Arnaldo Caprai label

comes a close second in terms of quality. In the young red wine class, the astoundingly good basic label Rosso Piceno offers some of the best value drinking in Italy today.

■ *red* **➋** *2006, 2004, 2001, 2000* ★ *Rosso Piceno, Rosso Piceno Superiore Montetinello, Rosso Piceno Superiore Vigna Monteprandone*

Sartarelli
Marche/Verdicchio dei Castelli di Jesi

via Coste del Molino 24, Poggio San Marcello **☎** *0731 89732* **W** *www. sartarelli.it* **❑** *by appt*

SARTARELLI's SPECIALITY is the late-harvested Verdicchio Contrada Balciana. The idea behind this unique wine is to pick the grapes in November – when they are in the state of advanced over-ripeness usually reserved for dessert wines – and then vinify them completely dry, in a style that captures their huge aromatic concentration, without the distractions of oak ageing. The result is a spectacular white which takes Verdicchio into another realm. The succession of aromas wafts from peaches and mangos, to wild herbs and Thai spices, through to hints of mushroom and undergrowth. The palate is bursting with flavour, and the finish is almost infinite.

■ *white* **➋** *2004, 2001, 2000, 1999, 1998* ★ *Verdicchio dei Castelli di Jesi Classico Superiore: Tralivio, Balciana*

Umani Ronchi
Marche/Verdicchio dei Castelli di Jesi, Rosso Conero & IGT

via Adriatica 12, Osimo **☎** *071 7108019* **W** *www.umanironchi.com* **❑**

UMANI RONCHI is the biggest single producer of Rosso Conero, with a selection of wines that ranges from the unoaked Serrano through the great value San Lorenzo to the top selection Cùmaro. Each maintains the value-for-money and drinkability that are Umani Ronchi trademarks. The company's production Verdicchio is organized in this same three-tier range, led by the outstanding Riserva Plenio. The Cabernet Sauvignon-Montepulciano-Merlot blend called Pelago, a former winner of London's International Wine Challenge, is the top IGT.

■ *red, white* **➋** *2006, 2004, 2003 (w); 2004, 2001 (r)* ★ *Rosso Conero Cùmaro, Verdicchio dei Castelli di Jesi Classico Superiore Casal di Serra, Pelago Marche Rosso IGT*

Arnaldo Caprai
Umbria/Montefalco Rosso, Sagrantino di Montefalco & IGT

loc Torre Montefalco **☎** *0742 378802* **W** *www.arnaldocaprai.it* **❑** *by appt*

CAPRAI WAS THE FIRST to believe in the Sagrantino grape and to back it with a programme of vineyard research, clonal selection, and new planting (with 136ha, it is by far the biggest grower of the variety in the DOCG). The investment is now paying massive dividends. In the cellar, credit goes to consultant winemaker Attilio Pagli for harnessing Sagrantino's

intransigent tannins and developing the complex fruit style that sets this producer apart. The top label Sagrantino 25 Anni is immense, but the sibling Collepiano and the hugely improved Montefalco Rosso Riserva are not far behind. The latest release is an immensely structured Merlot-Cabernet Sauvignon blend called Outsider.
🔲 *red* 🔳 *2006, 2004, 2001, 2000, 1999* ★ *Montefalco Rosso Riserva; Outsider Umbria Rosso IGT; Sagrantino di Montefalco: Collepiano, 25 Anni*

Castello della Sala
Umbria/Orvieto & IGT

Castello della Sala, Ficulle 📞 *0763 86051* 🌐 *www.antinori.it* ●

QUALITY IS IMPECCABLE across the whole range of this Antinori-owned 160-ha estate, but the star is IGT Cervaro della Sala. This genial blend of oak-conditioned Chardonnay and Grechetto ranks among the country's top 10 whites. It has been around since the mid-1980s, but no other Italian producer has managed to match its unique style. Cervaro bursts with fruit and energy, which make it enjoyable two years after vintage, but it also has dauntless ageing potential.

MUFFA NOBILE
1999
ITALIA
12,5% vol.

Palazzone label

The sweet Muffato della Sala (a Sauvignon Blanc-Grechetto-Gewürztraminer-Riesling blend) is less consistent, but it, too, is capable of greatness.
🔲 *red, white, dessert* 🔳 *white: 2006, 2004, 2001, 2000, 1999* ★ *Cervaro della Sala Bianco dell'Umbria IGT, Muffato della Sala Umbria Bianco Passito IGT*

Lungarotti
Umbria/Torgiano & IGT

via Mario Angeloni 16, Torgiano 📞 *075 988661* 🌐 *www.lungarotti.it* ⬚ *by appt*

A PIONEER IN THE 1960s and 70s, Giorgio Lungarotti was the first Umbrian producer to plant Cabernet Sauvignon and to use *barriques* for white wine. For decades he was the sole bottler of the Chianti-inspired Torgiano DOC, and his Rubesco was largely responsible for putting Umbrian red wine on the map. The Riserva Vigna

Monticchio is part of the Lungarotti heritage. The new generation is represented by the oak-conditioned Aurente Chardonnay, as well as by an IGT red from a multi-grape blend called Giubilante (Cabernet-Sangiovese-Canaiolo-Montepulciano) and the monumental new Sagrantino di Montefalco.
🔲 *red, white* 🔳 *red: 2004, 2001, 2000, 1999, 1997* ★ *Aurente Chardonnay dell'Umbria IGT, Giubilante Rosso dell'Umbria IGT, Torgiano Rosso Riserva Rubesco Vigna Monticchio*

Palazzone
Umbria/Orvieto & IGT

loc Rocca Ripesena 68, Orvieto 📞 *0763 344921* 🌐 *www.palazzone.com* ⬚ *by appt*

PALAZZONE IS divided between innovation and representation of traditional local varieties. On one hand, there are mini-productions of the prize-winning Cabernet Sauvignon-Cabernet Franc blend called Armaleo, a young, fruity Viognier, and a late-harvested Sauvignon Blanc. On the other, there is the Orvieto Classico Campo del Guardiano, which is often top in its category and exploits the local white wine's largely unrecognized capacity for bottle ageing. Cellared for 16 months before release, it boasts aromas of wild flowers and herbs, and a poised palate. Muffa Nobile is a juicy, honey and sultana flavoured dessert wine made from Sauvignon Blanc.
🔲 *red, white, dessert* 🔳 *2006, 2004, 2001, 2000* ★ *Orvieto Classico Campo del Guardiano, Muffa Nobile Umbria IGT, Armaleo Umbria IGT*

UP–AND-COMING UMBRIANS

Behind the fairly short list of internationally-known Umbrian wineries there is a much longer one of excellent producers about to break onto the scene. The majority of these work with varieties not permitted within the DOC system, which means they have to use the IGT Umbria label. The most interesting wines here are red, many made with Merlot: *Cantina Monrubio, Palaia* (www.monrubio.com); *Castello delle Regine, Merlot* (www.castellodelleregine.com; right); *Sportoletti, Villa Fedelia* (www.sportoletti.com); *La Fiorita Lamborghini, Campoleone* (075 8350029); *Poggio Bertaio, Crovello* (075 956921)

I Quattro Mori

Castel de Paolis label

Castel de Paolis
Lazio/Frascati & IGT

via Val de Paolis 41, Grottaferrata
☎ 06 9413648 🌐 *www.castelde paolis.it* ⬚ *by appt*

CASTEL DE PAOLIS boasts innovative blends, low yields, and high prices. The basic Frascati is the fullest-bodied version of the DOC wine in circulation. The super-ripe Vigna Adriana, which is made from an exotic blend of Malvasia del Lazio, Viognier, and Sauvignon Blanc, also has a hefty 14 per cent alcohol. I Quattro Mori is a mature and peppery blend of Syrah, Merlot, Cabernet Sauvignon, and Petit Verdot.
🟥 *red, white* 📗 *2007, 2006, 2004* ★ *Frascati Superiore, Vigna Adriana Lazio Bianco IGT, I Quattro Mori Lazio Rosso IGT*

Di Mauro Paola – Colle Picchioni
Lazio/IGT

loc Frattocchie, via di Colle Picchione 46, Marino ☎ 06 93546329
🌐 *www.collepicchioni.it* ⬚ *by appt*

THE DI MAURO FAMILY inherited Bordeaux varieties when they bought this estate in the 1970s. At that time, making red wine in the Castelli Romani was considered eccentric, but Di Mauro's Vigna del Vassallo blend of Merlot, Cabernet Sauvignon, and Cabernet Franc has changed that view. This top-class IGT red has broken into the alternative national elite

since the arrival of consultant winemaker Riccardo Cotarella in 1996. Expect complex berry fruit, spice aromas, and rich, deep textures. Le Vignole is also good: a Malvasia-Trebbiano-Sauvignon Blanc blend with tropical fruit aromas.
🟥 *red, white* 📗 *2006, 2004, 2001, 2000, 1999* ★ *Le Vignole Lazio Bianco IGT, Colle Picchioni Il Vassallo Lazio Rosso IGT*

Falesco
Lazio/Est! Est!! Est!!! & IGT

zona Artigianale Le Guardie, Monte-fiascone ☎ 0761 834011 ⬚ *by appt*

CONSULTANT WINEMAKER Riccardo Cotarella runs this winery with his brother Renzo, Antinori's general director. Riccardo is Italy's number one specialist with Merlot, which he uses for his top wine, Montiano. The concentrated style explodes with fruit and spice aroma, backed by new oak nuances of cocoa and roasted coffee. The texture is dense, creamy, and multi-layered, and the fruit finish long and sweet. Est! Est!! Est!!! Poggio dei Gelsi is a bouncy white with candied peel and citrus aromas.
🟥 *red, white* 📗 *red: 2001, 2000 1999, 1998, 1997, 1996; white: most recent* ★ *Est! Est!! Est!!! di Montefiascone Poggio dei Gelsi, Montiano Lazio IGT, Vitiano Umbria Rosso IGT*

Fontana Candida
Lazio/Frascati & IGT

via Fontana Candida 11, Monte Porzio Catone ☎ 06 9401881
🌐 *www.fontanacandida.it* ⬚ *by appt*

LIKE ALL WINERIES owned by Gruppo Italiano Vini (GIV), Fontana Candida is run by oenologists. Director-cum-winemaker Francesco Bardi has a very hands-on approach. He is a great fan of the Malvasia del Lazio grape,

which is generally much less used than other, more pro-ductive Malvasia sub-varieties in the Castelli Romani, but which gives his Frascati a distinctive roundness and slightly aromatic fruit aroma. Try the varietal Terre de' Grifi Malvasia to get the full unblended flavour.
🟥 *white* 📗 *most recent* ★ *Frascati Superiore Terre de' Grifi, Terre de' Grifi Malvasia del Lazio IGT*

Villa Simone
Lazio/Frascati

via Frascati Colonna 29, Monte Porzio Catone ☎ 06 9449717
🌐 *www.periocostantini.it* ⬚ *by appt*

THE WINE STYLE at Villa Simone involves fresh, intense flavours that come from early picking and carefully controlled vinification. Besides a tasty basic Frascati, Villa Simone makes two single-vineyard selections: Filonardi has a lot of structure; while Villa dei Preti is a deliciously intense, dry white best enjoyed with fish. The whites are flanked by two serious-weight red wines made from the local Sangiovese and Cesanese varieties and released under the Lazio Rosso IGT label: La Torraccia and Ferro e Seta Villa Simone.
🟥 *white, red* 📗 *most recent (w); 2006, 2004 (r)* ★ *Frascati Vigneto Filonardi, Frascati Superiore Villa dei Preti*

Fattoria La Valentina
Abruzzo/Montepulciano d'Abruzzo & Trebbiano d'Abruzzo

via Torretta 52, Spoltore ☎ 085 4478158 🌐 *www.lavalentina.it*
⬚ *by appt*

THIS DYNAMIC WINERY produces only local varieties, including both a great-value Trebbiano and Montepulciano for every-day drinking. Since the late 1990s, when Tuscan consultant Luca D'Attoma began to oversee the winemaking, a series of heavyweight special selections has arrived, starting with the single-vineyard Spelt and followed by Binomio and the latest release Bellovedere. All three have impressive power and meaty flavours that will refine with bottle age.

🔴 red, white 📗 2006, 2004, 2001, 2000, 1999 ★ Montepulciano d'Abruzzo: Binomio, Spelt, Bellovedere; Trebbiano d'Abruzzo

Illuminati Dino
Abruzzo/Montepulciano d'Abruzzo & Controguerra

contrada San Biagio 18, Controguerra 📞 0861 808008 🌐 www.illuminati vini.it 🔾 by appt

THE ILLUMINATI WINERY was the first to sign up for the new Controguerra DOC when it was launched in 1996, and remains its principal champion. The Controguerra red is an impressive Montepulciano-Cabernet blend Riserva called Lumen which stands out for its plummy flavours and excellent ageing prospects. Ciafrè, the corresponding juicy white, is made from a complex mix of local varieties.

🔴 red, white 📗 2006, 2004, 2001, 2000, 1999 ★ Montepulciano d'Abruzzo Colline Teramane Zanna, Controguerra: Rosso Riserva Lumen, Bianco Ciafrè

Masciarelli
Abruzzo/Montepulciano d'Abruzzo, Trebbiano d'Abruzzo & IGT

via Gamberale 1, San Martino sulla Marrucina 📞 0871 85241 🌐 www.masciarelli.it 🔾 by appt

GIANNI MASCIARELLI, who died in 2008, demonstrated to the world that the sleepy backwater of the Abruzzo was capable of turning out great modern wines. The estate, now ably managed by his

Illuminati Dino

wife Marina Cvetic, continues to produce the range created by Gianni. The barrel-fermented Chardonnay gets its fruity intensity from the calcareous soils. The estate's other top white has a full-bodied ripeness of fruit that is rare in Trebbiano. And the multiple prize-winning Montepulciano Villa Gemma delivers wild fruit, spice, liquorice, and sophisticated toasty oak.

🔴 red, white 📗 2006, 2004, 2001, 2000, 1999 ★ Chardonnay Marina Cvetic VdT, Trebbiano d'Abruzzo Marina Cvetic, Montepulciano d'Abruzzo Villa Gemma

Valentini
Abruzzo/Montepulciano d'Abruzzo & Trebbiano d'Abruzzo

via del Baio 2, Loreto Aprutino 📞 085 8291138 🔾

THE LEGENDARY STATUS of wines here derives in part from their sheer splendour and in part from the mystery surrounding them. The late Edoardo Valentini used to make the odd cryptic statement about his winemaking philosophy (which was apparently inspired by ancient Roman authors), but his methods remained largely

obscure. His son Francesco now continues in his father's footsteps, vinifying in traditional-sized barrels without any temperature control, and he does not fine or filter his produce. The resulting wines have a unique and unforgettable length, complexity, and intensity.

🔴 red, white 📗 2004, 2001, 2000, 1999, 1997 ★ Montepulciano d'Abruzzo, Trebbiano d'Abruzzo

Di Majo Norante
Molise/Biferno, Molise & IGT

contrada Ramitelli 4, Campomarino 📞 0875 57208 🌐 www.dimajo norante.com 🔾 by appt

FOR DECADES, Di Majo Norante was the only Molise producer featured in Italian wine guides, and he is indisputably the best. The big (900,000 bottles per year) and great-value range is firmly anchored to local varieties: Falanghina and Greco for the whites, and Montepulciano and Aglianico for the reds. The wines have gained in fruit and body since the arrival of flying winemaker Riccardo Cotarella in 2000. Top of the range are the beefy Montepulciano Don Luigi, the Aglianico Contado, and the oak-aged white Biblos. The classic dry, berry-scented Ramitello is also worth trying.

🔴 red, white, dessert 📗 2001, 2000, 1999 ★ Biblos Terra degli Osci Bianco IGT Molise, Biferno Rosso Ramitello, Molise Montepulciano Don Luigi

One of Masciarelli's vineyards

WINE MAP OF TUSCANY

TUSCANY SPLITS FAIRLY neatly into two broad geographical areas: the Tyrrhenian coast zone – which stretches from the province of Livorno, past Grosseto, to the regional border with Lazio – and the Central Hills in the provinces of Florence and Siena. Most of the winegrowing areas of the provinces of Pisa and Lucca lie inland, but the warm, maritime climate produces wines similar to those of the coast. The broad geographical areas are divided into DOC zones, each with their own production norms and specified grape varieties. Producers who opt out of the DOC system use an alternative IGT label.

KEY

■ Tuscany

Hillside vineyards in Chianti Classico

THE COAST: AREAS & TOP PRODUCERS

LUCCA *p254*

PISA *p254*
Castello del Terriccio *p260*
Tenuta di Ghizzano *p260*

BOLGHERI *p254*
Le Macchiole *p260*
Michele Satta *p260*
Tenuta dell'Ornellaia *p261*
Tenuta Guado al Tasso
   p261

MAREMMA *p255*
Gualdo del Re *p261*
Le Pupille *p261*
Montepeloso *p262*
Moris Farms *p262*
Poggio Argentiera
   p262
Russo *p262*
Tua Rita *p262*

THE CENTRAL HILLS: AREAS & TOP PRODUCERS

CARMIGNANO *p256*
Tenuta di Capezzana *p263*

CHIANTI CLASSICO *p256*
Barone Ricasoli *p263*
Castello di Fonterutoli
   p263
Fattoria di Felsina *p263*
Fattoria Isole & Olena *p263*
Fontodi *p264*
La Massa *p264*
Marchesi Antinori *p265*
Riecine *p264*
Rocca di Montegrossi *p264*

CHIANTI *p256*
Marchesi de' Frescobaldi *p266*

VERNACCIA DI SAN GIMIGNANO *p257*
Montenidoli *p266*

BRUNELLO DI MONTALCINO *p257*
Biondi Santi (Il Greppo) *p266*
La Cerbaiola-Salvioni *p266*
Pieve di Santa Restituta *p267*
Siro Pacenti *p267*
Tenute Silvio Nardi *p267*

VINO NOBILE DI MONTEPULCIANO *p257*
Poliziano *p267*
Tenuta Valdipiatta *p267*

Grapes drying, Rocca di Montegrossi, Chianti Classico

TERROIR AT A GLANCE

Latitude: 42.5–44°N.

Altitude: 100–500m.

Topography: This area is one fifth mountain and two thirds hills. High vineyards share land with woods and olive groves. The coast and its immediate hinterland offer big open spaces on flat land, and gently rolling hills that are suitable for more intensive viticulture.

Soil: The basic soil type is sandy-calcareous marl. Variations in the mix of clay, stones, and minerals have a big influence on viticulture. The most prized soils contain a flaky compressed clay called

galestro and/or an ochre-coloured calcareous rock called albese.

Climate: The hills have hot, dry summers but unpredictable autumns with the risk of harvest rain. The coastal climate is warm and dry, which guarantees un-problematic harvests most years.

Temperature: July average is 24°C.

Rainfall: Annual averages are 690mm (coast) and 850mm (hills).

Viticultural hazards: Occasional spring frost; harvest rain in the Central Hills.

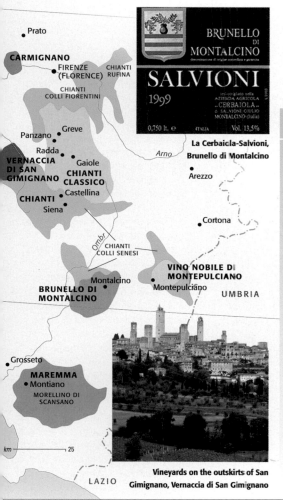

La Cerbaiola-Salvioni, Brunello di Montalcino

Vineyards on the outskirts of San Gimignano, Vernaccia di San Gimignano

PERFECT CASE: TUSCANY

🅓 Avignonesi Vin Santo ££££ (www.avignonesi.it)

🅡 Castello di Fonterutoli Siepi Toscana IGT ££££

🅡 Fattoria di Felsina Chianti Classico Riserva Rancia ££

🅡 Fattoria Isole & Olena Cepparello IGT Rosso Toscano ££

🅡 La Cerbaiola-Salvioni Brunello di Montalcino ££££

🅡 Le Pupille Saffredi Maremma Toscana IGT £££

🅡 Marchesi Antinori Solaia Rosso Toscana IGT ££££

🅡 Poliziano Vino Nobile di Montepulciano Riserva Asinone £££

🅡 Riecine Chianti Classico Riserva £££

🅡 Siro Pacenti Brunello di Montalcino ££££

🅡 Tenuta dell'Ornellaia Masseto Toscana IGT ££££

🅡 Tenuta San Guido Bolgheri Sassicaia ££££ (www.sassicaia.com)

Tenuta dell'Ornellaia vineyard in Bolgheri

WINEGROWING AREAS OF TUSCANY

THE COAST

THE TUSCAN COAST IS the fastest-growing wine area in Italy. Led by the elite aristocratic estates of Bolgheri and the boutique wineries in the Maremma, investment has poured into the coastal regions of Livorno and Grosseto over the past 10 years, which is also advantageous for the formerly little-known winegrowing areas around Pisa and Lucca. This is red wine country. Sangiovese is present in the longer-established DOCs, such as Morellino di Scansano, but the main focus is on international varieties such as Cabernet Sauvignon, Merlot, and Syrah. It is estate names here, rather than new and little-known DOCs, that give the best indication of quality and style.

Vine leaf

Lucca

HILLS TO THE NORTH and northeast of the quintessentially Tuscan town of Lucca make small quantities of deliciously drinkable and often original wines. Sandy soils make for whites and reds with a light to medium body, soft acidity, and appetizing fruit. **Colline Lucchesi** is the basic DOC for red wines based on Sangiovese. The most exciting wines of the denomination come from ambitious Tenuta di Valgiana. **Montecarlo** DOC is a white wine with good body and a soft nutty character. It is made from a complicated blend of the local Trebbiano with trans-Alpine varieties introduced into the area by a family of French aristocratic immigrants in the 1820s. This DOC is now re-emerging thanks to the gradual modernization of winemaking here.

🌾 sandy, sandy-calcareous 🍇 Sangiovese, Ciliegiolo 🍇 Trebbiano, Roussanne, Malvasia, Vermentino 🍷 red, white

Pisa

THE PROVINCE OF PISA has a variety of growing areas that stretch from an area southeast of the town of the famous leaning tower over various ranges of hills towards the coast. **Colline Pisane** is a traditional DOC based on Sangiovese grapes topped up with the local, cherry-scented Ciliegiolo. Merlot and Cabernet Sauvignon have also adapted well to the clay soils of the area, and IGT wines from up-and-coming estates like I Giusti e Zanza are starting to win a reputation for this previously little-known part of Tuscany. **Montescudaio** is a large and rather sleepy DOC located north of the elite Bolgheri zone. The maritime climate and mineral-rich soils give the wines an intensity of flavour. Cabernet and Merlot have been incorporated into the DOC here, and perform a lot better than the traditional Sangiovese. 🌾 sand, sandy clay 🍇 Sangiovese, Merlot, Cabernet Sauvignon, Ciliegiolo 🍷 red

Bolgheri

THIS WINEGROWING DISTRICT has grown up around the legendary Tenuta San Guido of Sassicaia fame *(see p261)*. The Bolgheri DOC, which is used by the majority of producers here, includes an exclusive, single-estate sub-denomination to accommodate Sassicaia. Huge investments over the past five years

mean that a production boom is in the pipeline as new owners (including Angelo Gaja,
see p210) bring out their first vintages.
Vineyards cover the mainly stony sand soils
in the communes of Bolgheri and Castagneto
Carducci, close to the coast. Conditions are
probably not ideal for Sangiovese, but Cabernet
Sauvignon, Merlot, and, more recently, Syrah
make wines with huge class and balance.

🔲 stony, calcareous sand, clay 🟦 Sangiovese,
Cabernet Sauvignon, Merlot, Syrah 🟦 Vermentino,
Chardonnay, Sauvignon Blanc 🔲 red, white, rosé

Hilltop town of Montiano, southern Maremma

Maremma

STRICTLY SPEAKING, THE MAREMMA is the name of
the coastal flats of the province of Grosseto,
but the term has been extended to refer to
the winegrowing districts along the whole of
the southwest coast and the hills just inland.
The area has been dubbed Italy's California.
Attracted by conditions for making premium
wines in commercially viable quantities, many
of the big names in Tuscan winemaking (and
others from further afield) have bought a
stake in the area over the past five years.

Morellino di Scansano is the traditional
Sangiovese-based DOC of the area. Look for
robust, plum-flavoured reds with Mediterranean
notes of spice and tobacco that do not call
for particularly long ageing. **Val di Cornia** is a
more recent DOC with its epicentre at Suvereto.
Soils similar to those of Chianti or the northern
parts of Montalcino give the reds here a lot

more power and ageing potential than the
generally low acidity wines of other parts of
the Maremma. Val di Cornia's reputation was
made by boutique estates with small produc-
tions, but the future is likely to see large-scale,
modern wineries such as the Moretti family's
Petra playing a major role. Cabernet Sauvignon
and Merlot are big in the area, but this is also
one of the few terroirs outside the Central Hills
that can put real excitement into Sangiovese.

Monteregio di Massa Marittima is a
relatively new DOC which covers a large
growing area north of Grosseto. The official
grape variety is Sangiovese, but on the whole
the most eye-catching bottles to come out of
these hills are IGTs that use Cabernet and/or
Merlot, either as varietals or in blends.

🔲 stony, calcareous clay 🟦 Sangiovese,
Cabernet Sauvignon, Merlot, Alicante
🟦 Trebbiano 🔲 red, white

THE SUPER-TUSCANS

The Super-Tuscan phenomenon
originated in the early 1980s
when producers, frustrated by
the outdated norms of the
DOC(G) system, turned to
alternative grape varieties to
create a new breed of top-of-the-
range wines outside the DOC.
These wines came to be labelled
as IGT or VdT, denominations
originally intended for everyday
plonk. The paradox is that they came to
represent the highly priced cream
of the region's production. Since the mid-
1990s, many of the traditional DOC(G)s have
been modified and others created to give
producers more freedom in their choice of
grape varieties. This means that many Super-

Tuscan wines would now be
eligible for DOC(G) status, but
many continue to prefer the IGT
label because of its trendy, elite
image and associated high prices.
Super Tuscans to look out for,
besides those with separate
entries, include: *Castello di Ama*:
L'Apparita (Merlot) 0577 746031;
Castello di Bossi: Girolamo (left;
Merlot) 0577 359330; *Brancaia*:
Brancaia Il Blu (Sangiovese-Cabernet Sauvignon-
Merlot) 0577 738353; *Castello di Rampolla*:
La Vigna di Alceo (Cabernet Sauvignon)
055 852001; *San Fabiano Calcinaia*: Cerviolo
Rosso (Sangiovese-Cabernet Sauvignon-Merlot)
0577 979232; *San Giusto a Rentennano*:
Percarlo (Sangiovese) 0577 747121.

THE CENTRAL HILLS

THE CENTRAL HILLS were the fulcrum of the wine renaissance of the 1980s, when progressive new estates set the standards for the rest of Italy. Today it remains the prestige growing district of Tuscany, with its classic Sangiovese-based DOCGs: Brunello di Montalcino, Carmignano, Chianti, and Vino Nobile di Montepulciano, as well as a plethora of Super-Tuscan estate wines.

Carmignano

GRAND DUKE COSIMO III included this tiny, hilly DOCG northwest of Florence in the official decree of 1716 that marked out Europe's first quality winegrowing zones. The wines are made from Sangiovese and Cabernet Sauvignon: a blend traditional to the area long before it became the mark of the Super Tuscans. The warm, mainly south-facing slopes here make sturdy wines with good ageing potential.

🗻 stony, calcareous clay
🍇 Sangiovese, Cabernet Sauvignon
🏛 Trebbiano, Malvasia 🍷 red, white, dessert

Chianti Classico

CHIANTI IS THE NAME of the hills that stretch south from Florence to Siena. Chianti Classico DOCG is the traditional heart of this area's wine production. Originally located around the villages of Gaiole, Radda, and Castellina, the *classico* area now includes the neighbouring communes of Greve, San Casciano, Barberino Val d'Elsa, and Castelnuovo Berardenga. Soils and mesoclimates vary considerably here. The best wines come from stony-calcareous terrain at an elevation of 350 to 450m, a combination which produces wines with body along with intense fruit and flower aromas. Sangiovese is the key variety, complemented traditionally by small percentages of the red-skinned Canaiolo, Colorino, and Mammolo as well as, in the case of everyday drinking wines, the white Trebbiano and Malvasia. This mix was devised by Baron Bettino Ricasoli in the 1860s, and his formula remained virtually unchanged until the revisions to the DOCG in the mid-1990s. These allowed producers to make Chianti from 100 per cent Sangiovese,

Fontodi vineyard in Chianti Classico

Fattoria di Felsina, Chianti Classico

but they also opened the door to the use of innovative blending varieties like Cabernet Sauvignon and Merlot. Purists grumble about the loss of Tuscan nuance in modern Chianti Classico – only a minority of producers now work exclusively with local varieties – but the quality is undeniable. From a non-*riserva*, expect plenty of berry fruit, a whiff of new oak, and a tangy, medium-bodied style; while the *riserva* is extremely full-bodied.

🗻 stony, calcareous marl, sandy clay
🍇 Sangiovese, Canaiolo, Cabernet Sauvignon, Merlot, Colorino, Mammolo
🏛 Trebbiano, Malvasia 🍷 red, dessert

Chianti

AROUND TWO THIRDS of the annual production of Chianti DOCG is made outside the classico zone. This production includes generic wines and others from specific subzones. Made from basically the same grape mix as *classico*, standard label Chianti is often not all that exciting, but there are gems to seek out in some sub-zones. Chianti Colli Fiorentini has a reputation for a lighter, iris-scented style of wine to drink young. Further south, Chianti Colli Senesi produces a beefier red wine. Chianti Rufina is the highest and coolest of the Chianti zones. Wines from these hills east of Florence have heavy acidity and powerful tannins, but also the true earthy, black cherry aromas of Sangiovese and great staying power.

🗻 calcareous clay, sandy clay 🍇 Sangiovese, Canaiolo, Cabernet Sauvignon, Merlot
🏛 Trebbiano, Malvasia 🍷 red, dessert

Vernaccia di San Gimignano

FIRST CITED IN 1276, **Vernaccia di San Gimignano** DOCG has the longest pedigree of any white varietal wine in Italy. The grapes are grown on the slopes around this medieval hill town, and everyday wines tend to be light and dry. For smoother textures and the variety's true violet and almond aromas, seek out the top-of-the range selections which include oak-aged *riservas* (Vernaccia is one of the very few white Italian DOCGs with a *riserva* category). A number of producers in the area also make serious red wines under the San Gimignano or Chianti Colli Senesi labels, or as IGTs.

chalky clay, sandy clay *Sangiovese* *Vernaccia* *red, white*

Brunello di Montalcino

BRUNELLO DI MONTALCINO – a DOCG since 1982 – originated with what nowadays would be called a clonal selection of Sangiovese Grosso. It was the work of a 19th-century farmer named Ferruccio Biondi Santi, who, by selecting cuttings of the best vines on his estate and propagating them, created a clone of the Brunello grape (alias Sangiovese) capable of making full-bodied wines for long ageing. From the date of his first bottling in 1888 to the 1950s, his family were virtually the only producers of Brunello di Montalcino. Production began to expand with the arrival of the DOC in 1966, but Biondi Santi remained the figurehead of the denomination. It was only with the up-grading of winemaking standards and a massive extension of vineyard area in the past 20 years that a new generation of producers has come to the fore. Brunello is Tuscany's only 100 per cent Sangiovese DOCG wine. It is also the one that has to be aged the longest: an obligatory four years, of which at least two must be in oak. The taste has changed from the pale, dry, minerally wines of the past to today's much fruitier, rounder, and deeper-coloured styles.

Brunello is by far Tuscany's most expensive DOCG wine. A good vintage delivers the full, ripe character of southern Tuscany and the complexity that extended ageing carries with it. These wines have depth of flavour, and aroma with black cherry and plum at the front and an array of spices and herbs in the background.

sandy clay, clay, galestro *Sangiovese (Brunello)* *red*

Vino Nobile di Montepulciano

MONTEPULCIANO IS A hill town southeast of Siena which makes DOCG wines from a grape mix based on Sangiovese, known locally as Prugnolo. These warm hillsides with lots of clay produce red wines with chunky tannins and earthy aromas. There are a couple of modernist estates, but the denomination generally has a more traditional image than Chianti and less kudos than Montalcino, which makes it a good source of hearty, value-for-money reds with real Tuscan character.

calcareous clay *Sangiovese, Canaiolo, Cabernet Sauvignon* *Trebbiano, Malvasia* *red, dessert*

VIN SANTO

Vin santo is the time-honoured dessert wine of the Tuscan countryside, made from raisined grapes crushed in the spring after the vintage. Traditionally, the juice is then fermented and aged in small wooden barrels with the precious yeasts (or *madre*) left over from the previous batch of wine. However, many winemakers now use *barriques,* and few trust the hygiene of the traditional yeasts. It still remains a strictly artisanal product, made in small quantities from the original Trebbiano-Malvasia grape mix. In Florentine *trattorie,* biscuits are dunked in *vin santo* for dessert. It is, nevertheless, capable of a more elevated status, too. The 10-year-old *vin santo* created in minuscule quantities by the Montepulciano producer Avignonesi has an explosive concentration that makes it one of the world's most sought-after sweet wines. *www.avignonesi.it*

Grapes drying for *vin santo*

WINE TOUR OF CHIANTI

THIS TOUR CROSSES THE heart of Chianti Classico DOCG, between the two great art cities of Florence and Siena. It combines top level wine tasting with spectacular countryside and glimpses of Tuscan rural life, still unspoilt by mass tourism. The cellar visits show the two faces of Chianti: international high-flyers Fonterutoli and the family-run Podere Capaccia. It also takes in elegant Renaissance villas such as Vignamaggio and fortified medieval hamlets like Volpaia with breathtaking views.

Family crest of Badia a Coltibuono

① Enoteca Pinchiorri
Try Annie Feolde's Tuscan- and French-inspired cooking at this two Michelin-starred restaurant in Florence. The mainly Italian and French wine cellar is mind-boggling for size and quality, and boasts Italy's biggest selection of magnums and historic vintages.
📞 055 242777

② Greve Market & Wine Estates ▽
Chianti's largest wine town has undergone some gentrification in the past few years, but the Saturday morning market still gives a feel of the real Tuscan country lifestyle. The Enoteca Gallo Nero (below) has the most complete selection of Chianti Classicos in the region. Castle wine estates to visit nearby include: Castello di Vicchiomaggio (055 854079); Castello di Verrazzano (055 854243); and Villa Vignamaggio (055 854661).
📞 055 853297 (Enoteca Gallo Nero)

Conca d'Oro below Panzano

③ Panzano ▷
Panzano's south-facing slopes, known as the Conca d'Oro, have the highest concentration of top-class, small-scale wineries in Chianti Classico. It has a roll call which includes Castello dei Rampolla (right), producers of one Tuscany's best single-vineyard Cabernets, the pioneering Fontodi (see p264), and the superstar estate La Massa (see p264).
📞 055 852725 (Producers' Association)

④ Castello di Fonterutoli
The Mazzei family have owned the castle in the heart of the medieval hamlet of Fonterutoli since 1435. This is a place to experience great wines in a quintessential Chianti setting. The castle is today the centre of a modern winery and estate, which offers sales and tastings plus cellar visits by appointment, and an osteria. See p263.
📞 0577 73571
🌐 www.fonterutoli.it

WINE-RELATED EVENTS IN TUSCANY
Tuscany's hottest wine show is the Corte del Vino held at San Casciano every year on the third weekend in May. A hundred of the region's very best producers pour their own wines, and there are master class tastings led by star winemakers. An enoteca (wine shop) sells all the wines on show (www.principecorsini.com). All the Chianti villages also have their own annual shows. The biggest and the best happens in Greve in the second week of September (www.chianticlassico.com). For estate visits, the big date is Cantine Aperte day in May when wineries across the country open their cellar doors for guided tours, hospitality, and tastings (www.movimentoturismovino.it).

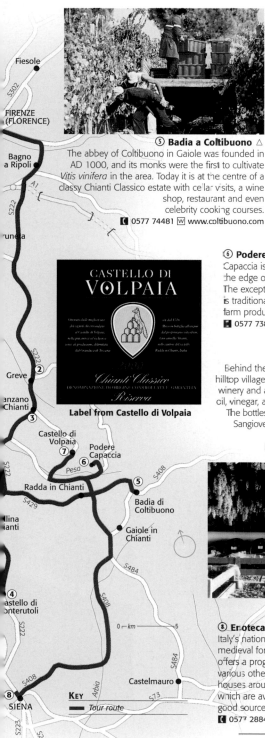

⑤ Badia a Coltibuono △

The abbey of Coltibuono in Gaiole was founded in AD 1000, and its monks were the first to cultivate *Vitis vinifera* in the area. Today it is at the centre of a classy Chianti Classico estate with cellar visits, a wine shop, restaurant and even celebrity cooking courses.

📞 0577 74481 W www.coltibuono.com

Label from Castello di Volpaia

Visitors' Tips

Route: This 117-km tour begins in Florence and ends in Siena.

Duration: The tour can be done in a day, but beware: Tuscan country roads are slow.

Wineries: Most wineries welcome visitors, but always telephone to check hours.

Restaurant recommendations: Lo Sfizio di Bianchi 📞 0577 749501 in Gaiole, and Mangiando Mangiando 📞 055 546372 in Greve.

Useful contacts: Wine Producers' Consortium W www.chianticlassico.com

⑥ Podere Capaccia

Capaccia is a small-scale family-run estate on the edge of a nature reserve outside Radda. The exceptionally good wine produced here is traditional-style Chianti. Olive oil and other farm products are also sold.

📠 0577 738385 W www.poderecapaccia.com

⑦ Castello di Volpaia ▽

Behind the perfectly restored walls of the tiny hilltop village of Volpaia is a surprisingly modern winery and a state-of-the-art olive oil mill (olive oil, vinegar, and wines are all sold here; *below*). The bottles to take home are the Super-Tuscan Sangiovese-Cabernet Balifico and the Chianti Riserva Coltassala.

📞 0577 738066 W www.volpaia.com

⑧ Enoteca Italiana

Italy's national wine museum is housed in a medieval fortress on the edge of Siena and offers a programme of exhibitions, tastings, and various other wine-related events. The collection houses around 1,100 wines, the majority of which are available for sale. The *enoteca* is a good source of local information.

📞 0577 288497 W www.enoteca-italiana.it

KEY

— Tour route

TOP PRODUCERS OF THE COAST

Castello del Terriccio
Pisa/IGT

via Bagnoli 16, Castellina Marittima
☎ 050 699709 ⓦ www.terriccio.it
🕐 by appt

BESIDES HAVING THE longest name in Tuscan winemaking, Gian Annibale Rossi di Medelana Serafini Ferri has one of the longest extended runs of five-star vintages in the region. His track record is testimony to the benign climate of these low hills facing the Tuscan coast and to the standards established by consultant winemaker Carlo Ferrini back in the early 1990s, when he came to Terriccio in his first job. Ferrini, now Tuscany's most sought-after consultant, continues to supervise the red wines made here from Sangiovese, Cabernet, and Merlot. Lupicaia, the Cabernet Sauvignon-Merlot senior label, is renowned for an almost antipodean note of eucalyptus. The second label, Tassinaia, is a softer, earlier drinking wine. The most recent addition to the range is the prize-winning, Rhône-style Castello del Terriccio based on Syrah, Mourvèdre, and Petit Verdot.
🖼 red 🍷 2005, 2004, 2001, 1999, 1998 ★ Toscana IGT: Tassinaia, Lupicaia

Tenuta di Ghizzano
Pisa/IGT

via della Chiesa 4, Ghizzano di Peccioli
☎ 0587 €30096 ⓦ www.tenuta
dighizzano.com 🕐 by appt

THIS ARISTOCRATIC ESTATE made a splash in the mid-1980s with a Sangiovese-Cabernet Sauvignon blend called Veneroso in the rich and velvety style of Antinori's Tignanello. It subsequently went through an uneventful patch until

Tenuta di Ghizzano label

Luca D'Attoma and then current consultant Carlo Ferrini injected life back into the winemaking through much stricter grape selection and fine-tuning of the oak ageing. Merlot has now become a key Ghizzano variety, lending plummy ripeness to the Veneroso and forming the basis of the prize-winning Bordeaux-style blend Nambrot.
🖼 red 🍷 2005, 2004, 2003, 2001, 2000 ★ Rosso Toscana IGT: Veneroso, Nambrot

Le Macchiole
Bolgheri/IGT

*loc Contessine, via Bolgherese 189/A,
Bolgheri* ☎ 0565 766092
ⓦ www.lemacchiole.it 🕐 by appt

EUGENIO CAMPOLMI used to run a general store until his passion for wine led him to found this model estate in 1981. After his death in 2002, his wife Cinzia took over. The winemaking mastermind at work here is consultant Luca D'Attoma. The flagship label, Paleo, originally a Bordeaux-style blend and now monovarietal Cabernet Franc, is one of a trio of wines (the others are the Merlot-based Messorio and the Syrah Scrio) that comprise an innovative range with a cult following. The style revolves around big,

concentrated fruit flavours superbly blended with oak.
🖼 red 🍷 2006, 2005, 2004, 2001, 1999 ★ Bolgheri Rosso Superiore Paleo; Rosso Toscana IGT: Messorio, Scrio

Michele Satta
Bolgheri/IGT

*loc Casone Ugolino 23, Castagneto
Carducci* ☎ 0565 773041
ⓦ www.michelesatta.com 🕐 by appt

MICHELE SATTA IS an independent producer whose winery has grown up in the shadow of the big league estates Ornellaia and San Guido. Originally based on the local Vermentino and Sangiovese, his production has grown to include a wide range of international varietals. Piastraia comes from an original Cabernet-Merlot-Syrah blend. The micro-production Bolgheri Superiore I Castagni is a more classic Bordeaux-style wine, while the highly acclaimed white Giovin Re is a full-on oak-conditioned Viognier (note the anagram).
🖼 red, white 🍷 2004, 2003, 2001, 2000, 1999 ★ Costa di Giulia Bianco Toscana IGT, Bolgheri Rosso Piastraia

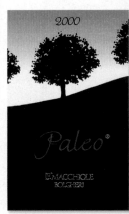

**Le Macchiole's flagship
wine, Paleo**

SASSICAIA: IN A LEAGUE OF ITS OWN

In the 1950s, the Tuscan aristocrat landowner Mario Incisa della Rocchetta took Cabernet Sauvignon cuttings from Château Lafite in Bordeaux. He planted them in a vineyard called Sassicaia on his Tenuta San Guido estate at Bolgheri to make wine for the family. When, in the 1960s, Rocchetta's nephew Piero Antinori – head of wine firm Antinori – tasted the wine he was bowled over, and persuaded his uncle to start selling it. He also sent him the Antinori oenologist Giacomo Tachis to help with the winemaking. In 1978 Rocchetta's wine came out top in a historic tasting of the world's leading Cabernets in London, and has never looked back. Sassicaia is arguably Italy's greatest wine. Its class and longevity – vintages like 1985 are still perfect today – give it investment ratings comparable with the best bordeaux. The other best vintages are 1988, 1995, 1997, 1999, 2001, and 2004. The blend is around 85 per cent Cabernet Sauvignon and 15 per cent Cabernet Franc. The style is silky and discreet, intensely flavoured, dry, and long. It is a wine that needs five or six years before it starts to deliver. Sassicaia has had its own DOC (Bolgheri Sassicaia) since 1994. W *www.sassicaia.com*

Tenuta dell'Ornellaia
Bolgheri/IGT

via Bolgherese 191, Bolgheri C *0565 71811* W *www.ornellaia.it* ☐ *by appt*

LUDOVICO ANTINORI founded this 70-ha estate on land that, together with the Tenuta San Guido of Sassicaia fame and Piero Antinori's Guado al Tasso, originally stretched over much of Bolgheri. Through the 1980s and most of the 90s, Ornellaia was the only producer on the Tuscan coast to make wines comparable with Sassicaia. The futuristic architecture at Ornellaia has a distinct Californian look, but the wines are Bordeaux-inspired. The estate-name label is a deep, soft Bolgheri DOC made from Cabernet-Merlot. The limited production IGT wine Masseto – coveted by collectors worldwide – is just Merlot. Compared with its eternal rival Sassicaia, the style is more upfront, with more immediate fruit and earlier-drinking tannins. Its form since 1995 has been faultless. After a period of joint ownership by Robert Mondavi and Marchesi Frescobaldi, the estate now belongs wholly to the latter.
■ *red* ▶ *2004, 2001, 1999, 1998, 1997* ★ *Bolgheri Rosso Superiore Ornellaia, Masseto Toscana IGT*

Tenuta Guado al Tasso
Bolgheri

loc Belvedere 140, Bolgheri C *0565 749735* W *www.antinori.it* ●

THIS 200-HA ANTINORI property south of Bolgheri fulfils a double role for the giant Florentine producer. It is the source of significant quantities of a fruity rosé called Bolgheri Rosato, which is made from Sangiovese, and a lightly perfumed white Vermentino. It also supplies Antinori with their version of the more serious new generation reds, based on Bordeaux varieties. Guado al Tasso is a classy, medium-bodied wine with Cabernet Sauvignon fruit and a touch of toasty oak.
■ *red, rosé* ▶ *2005, 2001, 1999, 1998, 1997* ★ *Bolgheri Rosso Superiore Guado al Tasso*

Gualdo del Re
Maremma/Val di Cornia

loc Notri 77, Suvereto C *0565 829 888* W *www.gualdodelre.it* ☐ *by appt*

OWNER NICO ROSSI has switched from blends to varietals for his top red and he has also dropped IGT labels in favour of the up-and-coming Val di Cornia DOC. Federico Primo is now made exclusively with Cabernet Sauvignon and l'Rennero with Merlot. These powerful, spicy wines have a lot of depth, and although they are hard to find, they are worth seeking out. Gualdo del Re also produce a respectable Val di Cornia DOC wine.
■ *red* ▶ *2005, 2004, 2001, 1999* ★ *Val di Cornia: l'Rennero Suvereto, Federico Primo*

Le Pupille
Maremma/Morellino & IGT

piagge del Maiano 92/A, Istia d'Ombrone C *0564 409517* W *www. elisabettageppetti.com* ☐ *by appt*

LE PUPILLE HAS ONE of the classiest ranges in the Maremma, from the basic label Morellino di Scansano DOC to the two top end selections: Morellino di Scansano Poggio Valente and Saffredi IGT. The single vineyard Poggio Valente, made from the Sangiovese-based DOC blend, has the combination of weight and plummy fruit that is the classic feature of southern Tuscany. Saffredi, on the other hand, takes a Bordeaux theme, with the local accent provided by the rich, broad tannins of the Alicante variety.
■ *red* ▶ *2006, 2005, 2004, 2001, 1999* ★ *Morellino di Scansano, Morellino di Scansano Poggio Valente, Saffredi Maremma Toscana IGT*

Montepeloso
Maremma/IGT

loc Montepeloso 82, Suvereto
☎ *0555 828180* ◉

LIKE SEVERAL OF ITS illustrious neighbours, Montepeloso started out as a hobby estate. With the arrival of the ambitious current owner Fabio Chiarelotto, however, things started to get much more scientific, both in the vineyard and the cellar. He delivers the power typical of wines from this corner of the Maremma and also adds a touch of elegance and definition, which can be missing in southern Tuscany. Nardo is 90 per cent Sangiovese with a top up of Cabernet Sauvignon and Montepulciano, while Gabbro is a Cabernet Franc-Sauvignon blend. Both are superb IGT wines, although with production of less than 3,000 bottles they are pricey and hard to find.
▥ *red* ⯈ *2005, 2004, 2002, 2001, 1999* ★ *Toscana IGT: Gabbro, Nardo*

Moris Farms
Maremma/Morellino di Scansano

loc Curanuova, Fattoria Poggetti, Massa Marittima ☎ *0566 918010* �𝗪 *www.morisfarms.it* ◌ *by appt*

MORIS FARMS, an Italian-owned winery despite the English name, set up in the Maremma before the area became fashionable, which means that it is a few steps ahead of the new generation of estates. The Morellino DOC wine is plummy, dry, and excellent value. Avvoltore was

the prototype Maremma Super-Tuscan IGT wine and remains one of the best in this category. With a drop of Syrah added to the original Sangiovese-Cabernet mix for extra spice, this is a wine that offers plenty of colour and big, ripe fruit aromas.
▥ *red* ⯈ *2006, 2004, 2003, 2002, 2001* ★ *Morellino di Scansano, Avvoltore Maremma Toscana IGT*

Poggio Argentiera
Maremma/Morellino di Scansano

loc Banditella di Alberese 2, Grosseto ☎ *0564 405099* ⟨𝗪⟩ *www.poggio argentiera.com* ◌ *by appt*

Moris Farms

POGGIO ARGENTIERA IS one of the first of the Maremma estates founded in the 1990s to really get into its stride. While other new producers focus on international grape varieties, owner-winemaker Gianpaolo Paglia has remained faithful to the local Morellino di Scansano DOC blend of Sangiovese and Alicante. His Morellino Capatosta is a rich Mediterranean-style red with barrow loads of fruit and spice, and plenty of mouth feel. The slightly less concentrated second label Bellamarsilia is only half a rung below it on the quality ladder.
▥ *red* ⯈ *2006, 2004, 2003, 2002, 2001* ★ *Morellino di Scansano Capatosta, Morellino di Scansano Bellamarsilia*

Russo
Maremma/Val di Cornia

via Forni 71, Suvereto
☎ *0565 845105* ◌ *by appt*

MICHELE AND ANTONIO RUSSO, with the help of consultant oenologist and Sangiovese expert Alberto Antonini, are among the few producers at Suvereto to keep faith with the local varieties Sangiovese and Colorino, which they use for the IGT Barbicone. This combines the punchy quality of the local soils with authentic Tuscan fruit and flower aromas, and guaranteed ageing potential. The excellent Sassobucato is a blend of Merlot and Cabernet Sauvignon.
▥ *red* ⯈ *2006, 2004, 2003, 2002, 2000* ★ *Barbicone Rosso Toscano, Sassobucato Rosso Toscano*

Tua Rita
Maremma/IGT

loc Notri 81, Suvereto ⟨𝗪⟩ *www.tuarita.it* ☎ *0565 829237* ◌ *by appt*

THIS BOUTIQUE WINERY started out as a retirement retreat and went on to spearhead the development of one of Tuscany's fastest growing and most exciting wine zones around the village of Suvereto. Stefano Chioccioli has now taken over from Luca D'Attoma, the winemaker who launched the estate in the early 1990s, but the Tua Rita style remains as powerful and concentrated as ever. Giusto di Notri IGT is a Cabernet-Merlot blend with inky tannins and enormous depth. Redigaffi IGT is a rich Merlot of top international quality but minute production.
▥ *red* ⯈ *2006, 2004, 2002, 2001, 2000* ★ *Toscana IGT: Giusto di Notri, Redigaffi, Syrah Rosso Toscano*

Poggio Argentiera label

TOP PRODUCERS OF THE CENTRAL HILLS

Tenuta di Capezzana
Carmignano/IGT

*loc Seano, via di Capezzana 100,
Carmignano* 📞 *055 8706005*
🅦 *www.capezzana.it* ⬚ *by appt*

CAPEZZANA is the longest-established estate in this tiny hill area north of Florence, which was the first DOC in Tuscany to make officially recognized Sangiovese-Cabernet blends. Since the arrival of consultant Stefano Chioccioli in 1998, it has taken on a new lease of life. Carmignano Villa di Capezzana has all the Chioccioli trademarks: depth of colour, abundance of fruit flavours, and soft tannins. Ghiaie della Furba is a no-holds-barred blend of Cabernet, Merlot, and Syrah, and the Capezzana *vin santo* has unforgettable smoothness and concentration.
🍷 *red, white, dessert* 🗓 *2005, 2004, 2001, 1999, 1997* ★ *Carmignano Villa di Capezzana, Ghiaie della Furba Toscana Rosso IGT, Carmignano Vin Santo Riserva*

Barone Ricasoli
Chianti Classico/IGT

loc Brolio, Gaiole 📞 *0577 7301*
🅦 *www.ricasoli.it* ⬚ *by appt*

THE CASTELLO DI BROLIO was where Baron Bettino Ricasoli first codified the grape blend for Chianti in the 1860s. The large 220-ha estate has seen periods of alternating fortunes, but since Francesco Ricasoli stepped in to run the winery in the early 1990s, it has become one of the modern leaders in Chianti Classico. Ricasoli replanted the best part of the estate, renewed the barrel cellar, and, together with agronomist-cum-winemaker Carlo Ferrini, revamped the production from top to bottom. The

Tenuta di Capezzana

Chianti Classico range now kicks off with the great value Brolio. The 100 per cent Sangiovese Castello di Brolio, with its smooth tannins and background of oak, is the top wine. The Super-Tuscan Casalferro is a very smart berry-flavoured blend of Sangiovese-Merlot-Cabernet.
🍷 *red, white* 🗓 *2005, 2004, 2001, 1999, 1997* ★ *Chianti Classico Brolio, Chianti Classico Castello di Brolio, Casalferro Toscana IGT*

Castello di Fonterutoli
Chianti Classico/IGT

loc Fonterutoli, via Ottone di Sassonia, Castellina 📞 *0577 73571*
🅦 *www.fonterutoli.it* ⬚ *by appt*

PRODUCTION AT FONTERUTOLI underwent a shake-up in the mid-1990s in a move to lift the profile of Chianti Classico in response to the rise of the attention-grabbing Super Tuscans. Top of the range since its debut in 1996, the Castello di Fonterutoli Chianti Classico is a modern, sophisticated version of this DOCG with loads of colour and soft tannins, and more than a whiff of Cabernet Sauvignon. The impeccable second label wine is called Fonterutoli. They also turn out around 25,000 bottles of a silky textured Sangiovese-Merlot blend called Siepi.
🍷 *red* 🗓 *2005, 2004, 1999, 1997, 1995* ★ *Chianti Classico Fonterutoli, Chianti Classico Castello di Fonte-rutoli, Siepi Toscana IGT*

Fattoria di Felsina
Chianti Classico/IGT

via del Chianti 101, Castelnuovo Berardenga 📞 *0577 355117*
🅦 *www.felsina.it* ⬚ *by appt*

FELSINA IS A CLASSIC. The rather austere house style reflects in part the convictions of owner Giuseppe Mazzocolin and his winemaker Franco Bernabei, and in part the local stony, calcareous soils. The Fontalloro was one of the prototype all-Sangiovese Super-Tuscan wines. Along with the Riserva Rancia it heads up a range of authentic *terroir*-driven Chianti Classico wines with enormous class. Felsina also makes an oaky-flavoured, barrel-fermented Chardonnay, called I Sistri.
🍷 *red, white* 🗓 *2005, 2004, 2001, 1999, 1997* ★ *Chianti Classico Riserva Rancia, Fontalloro Sangiovese di Toscana IGT, I Sistri Chardonnay di Toscana IGT*

Fattoria Isole & Olena
Chianti Classico/IGT

loc Isole, Barberino Val d'Elsa
📞 *055 8072763* 🅦 *www.isoleolena.it*
⬚ *by appt*

PAOLO DE MARCHI is one of Chianti's most respected winemakers. Cepparello is one of the trail-blazing 1980s generation of all-Sangiovese IGT wines that demonstrate that berry fruit and soft tannins are not exclusive to the French varieties. Under the Collezione de Marchi label, Paolo bottles limited quantities of Chardonnay and Syrah, as well as a Cabernet that has become a Tuscan classic. His *vin santo* is one of the region's best.
🍷 *red, white, dessert* 🗓 *2005, 2004, 2003, 2001, 1999* ★ *Cepparello Toscana IGT, Cabernet Sauvignon Collezione de Marchi Toscana IGT, Vin Santo del Chianti Classico*

Fontodi
Chianti Classico/IGT

via San Leolino 89, Panzano **C** *055 852005* **W** *www.fontodi.com* ○

SITUATED ON THE renowned slopes of Panzano, the Manetti family's estate was one of the first to demonstrate in the 1980s that there could be more to Chianti than raffia-covered bottles. Consultant winemaker Franco Bernabei delivers the trademark tight-packed tannins as well as subtle and intriguing aromas, which, thanks to sensitive barrel ageing, are not blurred by the flavours of oak. Flaccianello is the all-Sangiovese *terroir* wine which needs at least five years to open up. A drop of Cabernet Sauvignon adds depth and a more inter-national flavour to the long-lived Vigna del Sorbo Riserva. **☒** *red* **☒** *2005, 2003, 2000, 1999, 1997* ★ *Chianti Classico Riserva Vigna del Sorbo, Flaccianello della Pieve Colli della Toscana Centrale IGT*

Fontodi

La Massa
Chianti Classico/IGT

via Case Sparse 9, Panzano **C** *055 852722* ○ *by appt*

NEAPOLITAN GIAMPAOLO MOTTA came to Chianti to learn the winemaking trade in the late 1980s. He started at the bottom of the ladder as a grape picker and cellar hand at various wineries before buying a property of his own. In 1992 he jumped at the chance to acquire a struggling estate in a dream location at Panzano, and in the same year he produced his first wine. Despite this being one of the worst vintages in living memory in Tuscany, he pulled out an

amazingly ripe and concen-trated wine that launched him into the new-wave elite in the region, and he has never looked back. In 2003 the entry-level Chianto Classico La Massa moved over to IGT, and in 2008 the top-of-the-range Giorgio Primo also abandoned the DOCG. Both wines are made from the same basic mix of Sangiovese and Merlot, fine-tuned from vintage to vintage with Cabernet Sauvignon and Petit Verdot. **☒** *red* **☒** *2004, 2003, 2001, 2000, 1999* ★ *La Massa Toscana IGT, Giorgio Primo Toscano IGT*

Marchesi Antinori
Chianti Classico/IGT

See opposite.

Riecine
Chianti Classico/IGT

loc Riecine, Gaiole **C** *0577 749098* **W** *www.riecine.com* ○ *by appt*

ENGLISH BUSINESSMAN John Dunkley bought Riecine in the early 1970s before Chianti became so fashionable. With his wife, he turned the 8-ha property into a veritable gem of a winery. When he died in 1999, American Gary Baumann joined in partnership with the long-time winemaker Sean O'Callaghan to continue the tradition. They have maintained the style and the hands-on approach of the original owner and have kept standards as high, if not higher than ever. Now a certified organic grower, Riecine makes Chiantis with pure berry fruit, a medium body, and

a long, dry finish. La Gioia is a Sangiovese Super-Tuscan with a bit more upfront oak. **☒** *red* **☒** *2004, 2001, 2000, 1999, 1997* ★ *Chianti Classico, Chianti Classico Riserva, La Gioia di Riecine Rosso Toscana IGT*

Rocca di Montegrossi
Chianti Classico/IGT

fraz Monti, loc San Marcellino, Gaiole **C** *0577 747977* **W** *www.marcde grazia.com* ○ *by appt*

WHEN THE HISTORIC Cacchiano estate was divided between the Ricasoli-Firidolfi brothers in the mid-1990s, elder brother Giovanni got the castle and surrounding vineyards, while Marco took over an 18-ha estate in great need of attention lower down the hillside. With the advantage of rebuilding from scratch, Marco has created a gem of a winery and a very personal range of Chiantis with strong *terroir* character. This southwest corner of the commune of Gaiole makes a perfumed style of wine with medium-bodied elegance. The top selection is the Riserva San Marcellino. The IGT Geremia is a stylish Cabernet-Merlot blend. **☒** *red* **☒** *2005, 2004, 2001, 2000, 1999* ★ *Chianti Classico, Chianti Classico Vigneto San Marcellino Riserva*

Rocca di Montegrossi label

THE ANTINORI EMPIRE

PIERO ANTINORI WAS the first to recognize the need to internationalize Tuscan wine by raising technical standards and making its traditional hard, dry flavours softer and more appealing. In the early 1970s, his winemakers began to experiment with *barrique* ageing and alternative blends in search of a style closer to international tastes, but still authentically Tuscan. The result was Tignanello, a revolutionary blend of 80 per cent Sangiovese and 20 per cent Cabernet Sauvignon and Cabernet Franc, which appeared for the first time in its current form in 1975. The equally ground-breaking Solaia, which inverted the proportions of Sangiovese and Cabernet used in Tignanello, was released in 1978. Together, these two labels brought Tuscan wines into line with those from Bordeaux and California, the ultimate models of the 1970s, and, in so doing, they launched the Tuscan wine renaissance.

The Winemakers

Behind Antinori's success lie the talents of some of Italy's greatest winemakers. The epoch-making Tignanello and Solaia were the work of Giacomo Tachis, doyen of Italian oenologists. It was Tachis who invented the Sangiovese-Cabernet blend and taught Italy how to use *barriques*. His successor Renzo Cotarella *(right)* master-minded the Chardonnay-Grechetto Cervaro della Sala, and helped Antinori break into Montalcino with the Pian delle Vigne Brunello.

Contact Information

piazza degli Antinori 3, Firenze 📞
055 23595 🌐 *www.antinori.it* ●

Wine Information

🍷 *red, white, dessert, sparkling*
📅 *2006, 2005, 2004, 2001, 1999*
★ *Chianti Classico Badia di Passignano Riserva, Solaia Rosso Toscana IGT, Tignanello Rosso Toscana IGT*

Antinori Properties

Antinori realized that to be a contender on the world stage, he needed to put together a portfolio of premium wines that went beyond native Chianti. Empire building began with the acquisition of Umbrian Castello della Sala in 1940, and has remained a feature of the company strategy ever since. The Tuscan holdings include the Chianti estate of Badia di Passignano, the huge Guado al Tasso property at Bolgheri, the Brunello winery of Pian delle Vigne, and La Braccesca at Montepulciano. Outside the region, the Umbrian winery Castello della Sala makes one of Italy's best white wines, Cervaro della Sala. In Piemonte, Antinori owns the Barolo producer Prunotto, and in 1998 they snapped up the Tormaresca property in Puglia. He also owns vineyards abroad.

Antinori vineyard with rolling hills in the background

Marchesi de' Frescobaldi
Chianti/Chianti Rufina & IGT

via San Spirito 11, Firenze
☎ 055 27141 🖵 www.frescobaldi.it
🚪 by appt

MARCHESI DE' FRESCOBALDI is the biggest vineyard owner in Tuscany. Unlike rival Antinori, the company initially showed little inclination to expand outside the region. However, when it went global in the mid-1990s, it aimed straight for the top. A joint venture with Californian Mondavi produced a pricey, international-style Merlot-Sangiovese blend called Luce. Next came the headline-making takeover of the Ornellaia estate in Bolgheri, in partnership again with Mondavi. Meanwhile, big improvements in the wines from the historic family estate Castello di Nipozzano have raised the profile of the great value Chianti Rufina Riserva Nipozzano and the complex and austere single-vineyard Riserva Montesodi.

🟥 *red, white* 📅 *2005, 2004, 2001, 1999, 1997* ★ *Chianti Rufina Riserva Nipozzano, Chianti Rufina Montesodi, Lamaione Toscana VdT*

Montenidoli
Vernaccia di San Gimignano

loc Montenidoli, San Gimignano
☎ 0577 941565 🖵 www.montenidoli.com 🚪 by appt

ELISABETTA FAGIUOLI makes three versions of Vernaccia di San Gimignano. The Tradizionale is macerated with the skins, giving a deep straw-coloured wine with leafy aromas. Fiore is made in the modern soft press and cold fermentation style, which brings out the delicate fruit vein. Carato is a big, buttery, oak-conditioned wine. The common denominator for them all is the body and sweet almond flavour of authentic Vernaccia wine. Look out too for the beefy, long-lived red, Chianti Colli Senesi Montenidoli.

🟥 *red, white* 📅 *2007, 2006, 2005, 2004 (w); 2001 (r)* ★ *Vernaccia di San Gimignano: Tradizionale, Fiore, Carato*

Biondi Santi (Il Greppo)
Brunello di Montalcino/IGT

loc Greppo 183, Montalcino ☎ 0577 848087 🖵 www.biondisanti.it
🚪 by appt

FRANCO BIONDI SANTI continues – at his Greppo estate in Montalcino – to make the austere and phenomenally long-lived *riservas* that established Brunello's international reputation. His son Jacopo owns and runs the newly renovated Castello di Montepò winery in the Maremma, where he makes a range of more immediately accessible reds, led by a Sangiovese-Cabernet-Merlot Super Tuscan of silky elegance called Schidione. The top wine – Riserva Il Greppo – is very expensive, but has a proven track record. Biondi Santi Sr describes the 1997 Riserva as the wine of his lifetime, but the 2001 is not bad either.

🟥 *red* 📅 *2003, 2001, 1999, 1997, 1995* ★ *Brunello di Montalcino Riserva Il Greppo, Schidione Toscana Rosso IGT*

La Cerbaiola-Salvioni
Brunello di Montalcino

piazza Cavour 20, Montalcino
☎ 0577 848499 🚪 by appt

GIULIO SALVIONI OWNS 2ha of superb vineyard and a minuscule, low-ceilinged cellar in the town square of Montalcino. In a good year Giulio's production of Brunello might reach 4,500 bottles. The style is traditional in the best sense, with an accent on balance and the authentic flowers and spice aromas of Sangiovese aged in Slavonian oak barrels. Infallibly consistent and very long-lived, La Cerbaiola is a top buy.

🟥 *red* 📅 *2003, 2001, 1999, 1997, 1995* ★ *La Cerbaiola Brunello di Montalcino*

TUSCANY'S FLYING WINEMAKERS

The new generation of estate owners who flocked into Tuscany in the 1970s and 80s brought fresh capital, entrepreneurial spirit, and the cult of the expert. These new owners put winemaking into the hands of a new class of wine professionals: the travelling free-lance consultants. Franco Bernabei, Maurizio Castelli, and Vittorio Fiore were the key figures behind the resurgence of Tuscan wines in the 1980s. They were followed by a talented new generation including the likes of Luca D'Attoma, Alberto Antonini, and Attilio Pagli. The hottest name of the moment is Carlo Ferrini *(above)*, the man behind Fonterutoli, Brolio, Terriccio, and a score of other wineries. These experts, known as flying wine-makers, have become indispensable, not only to the production but also to the image of estates. There is, however, debate over whether the rise of the super-expert has concentrated influence in the hands of too few, stifling individuality and creating a culture of winemaking by numbers.

Pieve di Santa Restituta
Brunello di Montalcino

loc Chiesa di Santa Restituta, Montalcino 📞 *0577 848610* ⬤

PIEMONTESE CULT PRODUCER Angelo Gaja bought this estate outright from the original owner Roberto Bellini in 1996. He makes just two wines, both selections of Brunello di Montalcino, both in the sophisticated style of the Gaja empire. Of the two, Sugarille is richer, softer, and more complex. Rennina is drier and a little tougher, but is full of authentic Sangiovese character.

🔴 red 📆 2001, 2000, 1999, 1998, 1997 ★ *Brunello di Montalcino: Sugarille, Rennina*

Siro Pacenti
Brunello di Montalcino

loc Pelagrilli 1, Montalcino 📞 *0577 848662* ⬤ *by appt*

YOUNG GIANCARLO PACENTI created a stir in the late 1980s by launching this estate with a Rosso di Montalcino – in theory the second label wine of the DOCG zone – that scored higher than many Brunello DOCGs in blind tastings. His Brunello production got under way in 1993, and immediately placed him in the top three in the denomination. The style is big and fleshy, with wild berry and cherry aromas, and less oak than one would expect from a wine that ages in 90 per cent new *barriques*. The intense, fruit-driven Rosso continues to be Montalcino's best by a long way.

🔴 red 📆 2001, 2000, 1998, 1997, 1995 ★ *Rosso di Montalcino, Brunello di Montalcino*

TOSCANA
INDICAZIONE GEOGRAFICA TIPICA
Azienda Agricola
POLIZIANO

750ml ℮   13,5%vol-Italia

Poliziano label

Tenute Silvio Nardi
Brunello di Montalcino

loc Casale del Bosco, Montalcino 📞 *0577 808269* 🖥 *www.tenute nardi.com* ⬤ *by appt*

SINCE THE MID-1990s, the dynamic Emilia Nardi has totally restructured this 72-ha Brunello di Montalcino estate. A firm believer in research, she has replanted much of the estate with clones of old-vine Sangiovese selected from her own vineyards. The vinification and ageing show the Bordeaux-inspired influence of consultant winemaker Paolo Vagaggini, who delivers inky dark colours, soft tannins, and far more fruit than is traditional for Brunello, along with creamy new oak flavours. The prestige Manachiara has recently been joined at the top of the range by another single-vineyard selection Brunello, Poggio Doria.

🔴 red 📆 2001, 2000, 1997, 1995 ★ *Brunello di Montalcino, Brunello di Montalcino Manachiara*

Tenute Silvio Nardi

Poliziano
Vino Nobile di Montepulciano/IGT

via Fontago 1, Montepulciano Stazione 📞 *0578 738171* 🖥 *www. carlettipoliziano.com* ⬤ *by appt*

MONTEPULCIANO PRODUCES full-bodied but not always refined Sangiovese. At Poliziano the team of owner-cum-agronomist Federico Carletti and consultant winemaker Carlo Ferrini turns the local raw material into some of the smoothest modern wines in the region. The top selection Vino Nobile Riserva Asinone has ripe blackberry fruit and round, soft tannins that invite drinking as soon as the wine comes out, at three years from the vintage. Resist the temptation for another two or three years, and the pay off on the aromas is enormous. The Super-Tuscan Le Stanze (Cabernet-Sangiovese-Merlot) rivals top Bordeaux wines.

🔴 red 📆 2005, 2004, 2003, 2001, 2000 ★ *Vino Nobile di Montepulciano, Riserva Asinone, Le Stanze del Poliziano Toscana IGT*

Tenuta Valdipiatta
Vino Nobile di Montepulciano/IGT

via della Ciarliana 25, Montepulciano 📞 *0578 757930* 🖥 *www.valdipiatta.it* ⬤ *by appt*

THIS 25-HA ESTATE was upgraded through the 1990s with new, high-density planting and radical restyling of vinification methods. It now turns out some of central Tuscany's beefiest new-wave reds. Consultant oenologist Paolo Vagaggini crams more concentrated colour, fruit, and body into a bottle than any other winemaker in Montepulciano. Vigna d'Alfiero, first released in 1999, is the top vineyard selection DOCG. Trincerone is an interesting, berry-scented blend of Merlot, Cabernet Sauvignon, and Petit Verdot.

🔴 red 📆 2006, 2005, 2004, 2001, 1999 ★ *Vino Nobile di Montepulciano Riserva, Vino Nobile di Montepulciano Vigna d'Alfiero, Trincerone Rosso Toscana IGT*

SOUTH ITALY & THE ISLANDS

THE VINE HAS BEEN *a source of both solace and revenue in this region since the Greeks first landed in Sicily in the 8th century BC. Today, cheap land, an ideal climate, and, by European standards, permissive DOC(G) legislation have brought renewed interest in southern Italian wines.*

Having looked down their noses at the south for more than a century, giant concerns worldwide are now eager to exploit the region's huge viticultural potential. This investment brings with it much needed improvements in vine husbandry and the long-overdue introduction of stainless steel. However, modern techniques are, sadly, still the exception to the rule. The south's natural suitability for vines has led to proliferation rather than to improvement, and less than three per cent of production south of Naples is of DOC or DOCG standard.

Nevertheless, viticulture remains the economic bedrock for tens of thousands of subsistence farmers who have average holdings of less than a hectare each. In stark contrast to the prosperous estates of the affluent north, the south boasts few privately owned wineries

Roman wall painting of Bacchus, god of wine

that both grow their own grapes and bottle their own wine. Eighty per cent of the harvest continues to be vinified by immense local co-ops that sell the wine in bulk for blending. Volumes are huge: Puglia produces more grapes than the whole of Northwest Italy, and Sicily produces more grapes than all of Bordeaux.

The secret of the south's prodigious output lies in its near-perfect climate for viticulture and a plethora of supremely capable local grapes. This combination endows the south with a remarkable potential that is only now being unlocked. Armed with more technology than ever before and blissfully free from many of the legal restrictions concerning permitted varieties that weigh down Italy's more famous regions, the south is set to reinvent itself as Italy's hottest viticultural zone.

Sicilian farmers harvesting grapes

◁ **Hillside vines at Vettica Minora near Amalfi, Campania**

WINE MAP OF SOUTH ITALY & THE ISLANDS

No VINEYARD IN ITALY is far from the sea. Coastal sites at lower altitudes in the south experience the greatest maritime influence, while those planted further inland balance altitude with the impact of the sea. The fertile plains of Puglia form one of the country's largest wine producing areas. In contrast, winegrowing in hillier Basilicata, Campania, and Calabria is more difficult and there are only a handful of DOC(G)s. The islands of Sicilia (Sicily) and Sardegna (Sardinia) share both geographical isolation and viticultural diversity.

KEY

South Italy

VIGNA FLAMINIO
Brindisi
Denominazione di Origine Controllata

Rosso 2000

AGRICOLE VALLONE

75 cl℮   13% vol
Estate Bottled

Label from Vallone, Puglia

**PERFECT CASE:
SOUTH ITALY &
THE ISLANDS**

Ⓦ Cusumano Nadaría Inzolia IGT £

Ⓓ Donnafugata Passito di Pantelleria Ben Ryè ££ (37.5cl)

Ⓡ Felline Primitivo di Manduria ££

Ⓡ Feudi di San Gregorio Patrimo IGT £££

Ⓦ Firriato Chiaramonte IGT Sicilia £

Ⓕ Marco de Bartoli Vecchio Samperi ££ (50cl)

Ⓡ Molettieri Taurasi Vigna Cinque Querce £££

Ⓡ Montevetrano IGT ££££ (www.montevetrano.it)

Ⓡ Morgante Nero d'Avola Don Antonio IGT Sicilia ££

Ⓦ Odoardi Scavigna Bianca Pian della Corte ££

Ⓦ Planeta Cometa IGT Sicilia ££

Ⓦ Terredora Greco di Tufo Loggia della Serra ££

Tending Aglianico vines, Basilicata

Grape picker at D'Ambra, Campania

TERROIR AT A GLANCE

Latitude: 41.5–37°N.

Altitude: 10–600m.

Topography: The Apennine mountain range dominates the mainland, with the best vineyards situated in north-facing foothills. Many Sicilian vineyards are planted on the slopes of Monte Etna.

Soil: Predominantly volcanic and granite, with some clay and chalk.

Climate: The southern location and the Scirocco (a hot wind from Africa) ensure high ripening

temperatures, while the influence of the Mediterranean reduces nocturnal temperatures in coastal areas by anything up to 20°C.

Temperature: July average is 24.5°C.

Rainfall: Annual average is 600mm. The South's hardy grape varieties can ripen to perfection despite the absence of water during the growing season.

Viticultural hazards: Scirocco wind which can desiccate grapes; drought; rapid ripening.

SOUTH ITALY & THE ISLANDS: AREAS & TOP PRODUCERS

SARDEGNA

Vineyards near Menfi, Sicilia

Vineyard in Martina Franca, southern Puglia

WINEGROWING AREAS OF SOUTH ITALY

Puglia

FLAT AS A BILLIARD TABLE and sun-scorched throughout the long summer months, Puglia is Italy's answer to California's Central Valley or to Australia's Riverina. For grape growers, the living is easy: rain falls obediently during the winter months long after the grapes have been harvested; there is an abundance of ancient, non-irrigated vineyards planted with local varieties; grapes generally ripen beautifully with little annual variation; and land values are a tenth of what they are in the north. With such obvious advantages it is not surprising that some of Italy's biggest producers, including Antinori, GIV, and Casa Girelli, have decided to set up camp here.

**Leone de Castris label,
Salice Salentino**

Despite Puglia's natural advantages, the average quality of its wines has, until recently, remained resolutely low. Generations of winemakers have squandered the potential of this viticultural paradise through absurdly high yields and poor techniques. Puglia produces more wine than any other region in Italy – 14 per cent of the nation's total – yet just 2.5 per cent is DOC status. For decades northern Europe quietly absorbed the region's tanker loads of wines destined either for vermouth production or for blending into less robust offerings. Puglia's culture of over-production, however, has recently crashed headlong into Europe's general declining consumption and the current affection for New World wines. Together, these have spelled an end to the halcyon days of bulk sales and the Pugliesi have had to up their game.

The last 10 years have witnessed a veritable renaissance in Puglia's fortunes and, to their credit, the region's growers have been far from complacent. Two factors have played a crucial role in this regeneration. External investment, through both EU subsidies and private companies, brought much-needed capital to an area desperate for the advantages of refrigeration and stainless steel. The second factor was the arrival of flying winemakers, often from the New World, who brought both innovative ideas and a firm understanding of modern wine styles.

The concept of *terroir* is very much alive and well in Puglia. The patchwork of grape varieties, topographies, and philosophies have created a myriad of local wine styles reflected in the often arcane legislation of more than 25 DOCs. Consequently this region can offer something for every palate.

Northern Puglia marks the limit of cultivation of central Italian grapes – Trebbiano for the whites, and Montepulciano and Sangiovese for the reds – and the beginning of South Italy's viticultural empire. The local Bombino Bianco grape is capable of producing affable white wines with a citrus hint, while in careful hands the Verdeca variety can fashion serious dry whites with concentrated tropical fruit flavours. The white-only DOC of **Locorotondo** is the principal exponent of Verdeca, along with the lesser-known **Gravina** and **Martina Franca** DOCs.

It is the reds, however, that are grabbing the headlines, and Puglia has no shortage of superb raw material. In the north the elegant tannins and restrained fruit of Uva di Troia craft refreshingly patrician wines in the DOC of **Castel del Monte**. Further south into Italy's heel the broad plain of the Salento Peninsula opens and the ubiquitous Negroamaro begins to hold sway. True to its name (it translates as 'bitter black') Negroamaro offers a wine with a lush palate of black fruit and a bittersweet sting in its tail that goes admirably with the local cuisine. Negroamaro reaches its apogee in **Salice Salentino**, Puglia's most productive DOC. It also provides the backbone for **Brindisi**, **Copertino**, and **Squinzano**, where it is often softened with a little Malvasia Nera (Red Malvasia), and Primitivo.

Although quite insignificant in terms of volume, Primitivo, a clone of California's Zinfandel, seems to have hijacked Negroamaro's lead-role status. The overt jamminess of Primitivo allied to its optional labelling as Zinfandel has led to a meteoric rise in its fortunes. The best wines are **Primitivo di Manduria** DOC and originate from mature, non-irrigated vines trained low to the ground. Primitivo is occasionally used to make dessert wine, although the rare **Aleatico di Puglia** DOC remains in pole position in this field.

THE RISE OF THE MEZZOGIORNO

The change in the fortunes of the Mezzogiorno (South Italy) during the past 10 years is largely due to overproduction within the EU. Faced with an ever-deepening wine lake, Brussels first banned all new plantings and then instigated numerous vine-pull schemes. For the first time, producers in the south were

forced to face the reality of either ripping up their vineyards or producing commercially viable wines. The region's quality pioneers – Planeta *(above) et al* – demonstrated not only that it was possible to produce less and still make a profit, but more importantly, that producing less was the only way to make a profit. Now there is an ever-increasing number of producers who are adapting to the new economic conditions. Making great wine is never easy, but making good wine could never be easier than it is in the viticultural paradise of the Mezzogiorno.

This DOC zone covers the whole of Puglia and is its greatest secret. Made in the *passito* style *(see p280)* from red grapes of the same name, Aleatico vies with *recioto* for the title of Italy's greatest sweet red wine.

Since 1990 Puglia has divorced itself from a tradition of bulk production and actively sought to make the most of its huge potential. Along with Sicilia, it is unquestionably home to the most exciting recent vinous discoveries in all of Italy and now offers the consumer an unbeatable combination of quality and value.

🗒 sand and clay over limestone, outcrops of iron-rich, red loam

🗒 *Primitivo, Aleatico, Negroamaro, Malvasia Nera, Montepulciano, Sangiovese, Uva di Troia*

🗒 *Bombino Bianco, Verdeca, Trebbiano, Chardonnay* 🗒 *red, white, rosé, dessert, fortified*

Harvested grapes near Brindisi, Puglia

Farmhouse and vineyard in Aglianico del Vulture, Basilicata

Campania

MONTE VESUVIO TO THE SOUTH of the regional capital, Napoli (Naples), produces a soil that is ideally suited to viticulture. Rich in both trace elements and minerals yet poor in organic matter, the area around the volcano has been credited with producing some of Italy's finest wines since Roman times. It is still home to the ubiquitous Lacryma Christi, a wine available in red, white, sparkling, dessert, and fortified versions under the **Vesuvio** DCC, and which continues to trade on its reputation in the *trattorie* of Naples.

Just inland lies the dilapidated hamlet of **Taurasi**, home to both the south's first red DOCG and one of its most aristocratic red grapes, Aglianico. Well suited to prolonged ageing and combining fine tannins with fresh acidity, Aglianico has all the hallmarks of a classic variety. The best examples need a decade to reach their peak, when they develop an intense, violet perfume reminiscent of Mourvèdre. Aglianico is in its element when consumed with the south's delicious sausages and salami.

The volcanic soil surrounding Vesuvio is equally suited to the cultivation of white grapes, and the principal varieties include Falanghina, Greco, and Fiano, in order of increasing quality. With 2,000 years to adapt to both soil and climate these grapes eschew ponderous levels of alcohol and flabby acidity in favour of an elegant reflection of their *terroir*. They seldom achieve more than 12.5 per cent alcohol and are often harvested well into October – extraordinarily late given the hot climate. Fortunately, producers recognize that the delicate flavours of pear, quince, and dried apple are shown to best effect when untouched by oak. Principal DOCGs include **Fiano d'Avellino** and **Greco di Tufo**, both nestled in gently rolling hills.

The unassuming Falanghina, a grape that barely merits a mention in the environs of Taurasi, has been elevated to cult status; largely through the efforts of two producers in the obscure DOC of **Falerno del Massico**.

Vineyards in Savuto on Calabria's northern coast

Praise from all corners continues to be heaped upon the honeyed richness of Falanghina emanating from this forgotten corner of Campania. Red Falerno, blended from Aglianico and the local Piedirosso, has also been commended for its sappy red fruit.

Piedirosso is also planted on Ischia, an island in the bay of Naples. In its day Ischia rivalled Capri as a holiday destination, and it retains an air of verdant serenity. No doubt due in part to happy holiday memories, **Ischia** DOC wines have developed a certain following perhaps disproportionate to their quality. Nevertheless, against a backdrop of a Mediterranean sunset few could deny the simple pleasure of a glass of either the local cherry-scented Piedirosso or the equally unfamiliar white Biancolella, with its light, citrus charms. The d'Ambra estate dominates production here.

Lesser known Campanian DOCs include **Sannio** and **Taburno**, both sandwiched between Falerno and Avellino. Production here is dominated by the co-operatives, but improvements are now beginning to make a noticeable impact. Just to the north of Naples, in a curious mix of vineyards and industrial estates, is the **Campi Flegrei** DOC. That wines from here remain deeply unfashionable is a great shame as they offer an affordable introduction to the pleasures of Campania's native grapes.

volcanic tuffeau and limestone overlaid with clay, alluvial soils in valleys Piedirosso, Aglianico Falanghina, Greco, Fiano, Biancolella red, white, rosé, sparkling, dessert

Basilicata

NESTLED IN THE INSTEP of Italy's boot shape, between Puglia, Campania, and Calabria, the area of Basilicata is home to just one DOC of significance, **Aglianico del Vulture**. In contrast with Puglia, the vineyards here extend to more than 600m above sea level and produce correspondingly fresh, structured reds made from the Aglianico grape. While never hitting the heights of Taurasi (also made from the intense Aglianico variety), good Aglianico del Vulture offers excellent value for money.

clay, volcanic on Monte Vulture Aglianico red

ORIGINS OF WINE

Italy must thank both the Etruscans and the Greeks for its more than 2,500 years of uninterrupted wine production. The Etruscans struck land north of Rome and went on to settle most of modern-day Tuscany, while the Greeks colonized Puglia first, before capturing Sicilia from the Phoenicians. So impressed were they with how the vines they established took to their new home that they christened Italy *Enotria* or 'Land of the Vine'. Greco, a grape still widely planted in both Campania and Sicilia, is of Greek origin and would have been vinified at that time in earthenware pots

to make a cloudy wine for early drinking. Extended storage was a Roman invention, and adding seawater as a preservative was a Greek one. The Greeks trained their vines close to the ground to retain moisture, and most vineyards in the south are still trained in this way. The legacy of the Greek presence in Italy is far reaching, and it is easy to underestimate the impact that the vine has had on the country's agriculture, economy, and people. Today more than a million Italians are directly involved in wine production.

Calabria

CALABRIA APPEARS TO HAVE derived little benefit from the flood of financial assistance pouring into South Italy. The region's best-known DOCs cling to both coasts – **Melissa** and **Cirò** to the south, and **Savuto** (for reds only) and **Scavigna** to the north. The rustic and somewhat uncouth Gaglioppo is the driving force behind the dusty, tannic reds, although the Sicilian Nerello (mainly Nerello Mascalese but also Nerello Cappuccio) makes an occasional guest appearance. The whites rely on Greco but those accustomed to Campania's world-class examples will be disappointed by Calabria's efforts. Greco from Calabria remains a distant cousin and is best enjoyed by the pitcherful with the local seafood.

clay, sand, and marl Gaglioppo, Nerello Mascalese Greco red, white, rosé

TOP PRODUCERS OF SOUTH ITALY

Candido
Puglia/Salice Salentino & IGT

via Armando Diaz 46, San Donaci
☎ 0831 635674
W www.candidowines.it ▢

ANYWHERE BUT IN THE SOUTH of Italy Alessandro and Giacomo Candido's 140 ha of vineyards and two million bottle production would seem prodigious. Their reputation, however, has been built on quality rather than quantity, and their solid, sweet-and-sour Salice Salentino has served as the DOC's standard-bearer for decades. Negroamaro gets top billing here, although it is artfully blended with Cabernet Sauvignon in the modern Immensum and with Montepulciano in the oaky flagship wine, Duca d'Aragona. Small quantities of Chardonnay and Sauvignon Blanc are also produced, together with an exquisite example of the rare Aleatico, Puglia's answer to the Veneto's *recioto*.
▧ red, white, rosé, dessert
▨ red: 2005, 2003, 2001, 2000; white: most recent ★ Salice Salentino, Immensum IGT, Aleatico di Puglia, Duca d'Aragona IGT

Cantina del Locorotondo
Puglia/Locorotondo & IGT

via Madonna della Catena 99,
Locorotondo ☎ 080 4311644
W www.locorotondodoc.com ▢

QUANTITY AND PRICE are the watchwords of most co-ops, so the exceptionally good-value, well-made reds and whites from this forward-thinking cellar come as a welcome surprise. Founded in 1929 by a group of farmers who were tired of getting little recognition

Stylish label from Cantina del Locorotondo

for their hard work, it now controls more than 1,000ha of vineyards and produces 3.5 million bottles a year. From the crisp and correct entry-level Locorotondo to the Negroamaro-based Roccia Rosso and the oaky Cummerse, wines from this producer are as cheerful as they are cheap. With its enticing floral and citrus aromas, the single vineyard Verdeca Vigneti in Talinajo is a reminder that Italy can trade blows with the New World at every price point.
▧ red, white, rosé ▨ most recent
★ Roccia Rosso IGT, Cummerse IGT, Vigneti in Talinajo, Locorotondo

Felline
Puglia/Primitivo di Manduria & IGT

via Santo Stasi Primo, Manduria
☎ 0999 711 660 ▨

FELLINE IS THE FLAGSHIP label of the vast Pervini empire, a Puglian dynasty run by

Gregory Perucci. Low yields and a refusal to irrigate are just part of the great care lavished on the more than 80ha of vineyards under their control. In most years, just two wines are produced, the exceptionally good value Alberello, a moreish blend of Negroamaro and Primitivo, and the judiciously oaked DOC wine, Primitivo di Manduria. In great vintages, Roberto Cipreso, the consultant oenologist, will release limited quantities of a chunky Primitivo-Montepulciano blend, an IGT wine called Vigna del Feudo.
▧ red ▨ most recent
★ Primitivo di Manduria, Vigna del Feudo IGT, Alberello IGT

Leone de Castris
Puglia/Salice Salentino & IGT

via Senatore De Castris 26, Salice
Salentino ☎ 0832 731112
W www.leonedecastris.com ▢

FOUNDED IN 1665, Leone de Castris boasts an uninterrupted and unmatched viticultural history in Puglia. The current annual production of 3.5 million bottles is significant by anyone's standards, and all credit must be given to the family for their tireless efforts and successes. The fleshy and exuberant Five Roses Anniversario (IGT) merits special mention as Puglia's finest rosé, and the tightly wound DOC wine, Salice Salentino Riserva Donna Lisa, remains a winemaking *tour de force*.
▧ red, white, rosé, dessert
▨ red: 2007, 2005, 2003, 2001, 2000; white: most recent
★ Rosato Five Roses Anniversario IGT, Salice Salentino Rosso Riserva Donna Lisa

Rivera
Puglia/Castel del Monte

SS 98 km 19,800, Contrada Rivera,
Andria ☎ *0883 569501*
ⓦ *www.rivera.it* ◯ *by appt*

GIVEN THIS ESTATE'S investment in raising the profile of the local grape, Uva di Troia, given its determination to remain loyal to the Castel del Monte DOC, and given its tireless professionalism in the face of the south's lethargy, there is little doubt that it remains in the vanguard of Puglian wine-making. The winery, like the wines, is clean and modern, and no expense has been spared in Carlo de Corato's search for quality. The Il Falcone, a blend of 65 per cent Uva di Troia and 35 per cent Montepulciano, is aged in *barrique* for 12 months and offers a heady aroma supported by a silky, integrated palate of cherry and plum. It is one of Puglia's finest reds.

🍷 red, white, rosé, dessert ⮞ red: 2005, 2003, 2001, 2000; white: most recent ★ Castel del Monte Il Falcone Riserva

Vineyard near Locorotondo, Puglia

Taurino
Puglia/IGT

SS 605, Guagnano ☎ *0832 706490*
ⓦ *www.taurinovini.it* ◯

THE PASSAGE OF TIME and the whims of fashion appear to have neatly passed by Cosimo Taurino and his winery, both of indeterminate age. This is an estate for which Puglia's 2,000-year-old viticultural history is key. Traditional grapes such as Negroamaro and Malvasia Nera are treated to extended maturation in old oak for anything up to five

Rivera

years as part of Cosimo's admirable determination to preserve his heritage. The slightly oxidized but intensely flavoured Notarpanaro VdT wine provides a trip down Puglia's gloriously sun-drenched memory lane.

🍷 red, white, rosé ⮞ red: 2004, 2001, 1999, 1997; white: most recent ★ Salice Salentino Rosso Riserva, Notarpanaro VdT

Vallone
Puglia/Brindisi & IGT

via XXV luglio 7, Lecce
☎ *0832 308041*
ⓦ *www.agricolevallone.it* ◯ *by appt*

IN AN AREA where winemaking disappointments still vastly outnumber triumphs, the Vallone estate remains a welcome beacon of consistency. Since the estate was founded in 1934, its Brindisi Rosso Vigna Flaminio has more than satisfied consumers looking for a no-nonsense, hearty red. Vallone's premium wine, Graticciaia, is a late-harvest Negroamaro that just manages to marry palate-numbing levels of alcohol with fresh acidity and suitably robust tannins. Beware, however: this is not a wine for the faint-hearted.

🍷 red, white, rosé, dessert ⮞ red & dessert: 2004, 2000, 1997; white: most recent ★ Brindisi Rosso Vigna Flaminio, Graticciaia IGT

THE ROLE OF CO-OPS IN THE SOUTH

Before Italy joined the EEC, South Italy was starved of capital investment and had only a few privately owned wineries. Subsistence farming was the only option for millions, who managed to eke out a living on smallholdings. In an effort to improve the agricultural economy, successive governments threw farmers the lifeline of agricultural co-operatives. The co-ops represented a guaranteed market for their winegrowing members, who were paid according to how much they produced. Over time, production levels soared and domestic wine consumption fell, resulting in a glut known as the 'wine lake'. Co-ops are still important in the south, where they represent 80 per cent of production by volume, although much less by value. The majority continue to champion quantity over quality but a few have initiated schemes that reward growers for producing higher quality grapes. Among the most respected are:
Cantina del Locorotondo (Puglia), Cantina del Taburno (Campania; www.cantinadeltaburno.it), Settesoli (Sicilia); 0925 77111), Cantina Gallura (Sardegna), and Cantina di Santadi (Sardegna).

Caggiano
Campania/Taurasi

contrada Sala, Taurasi 📞 *0827
74723* 🌐 *www.cantinecaggiano.it* 💻

ANTONIO CAGGIANO makes
utterly compelling Taurasi
DOCG wine. For now it
remains the pick of the crop,
but with his passion for all
things Campanian, it is only
a matter of time before his
other wines show the same
integration and concen-
tration. Taurasi's 18 months
in oak soften the Aglianico
grape's ferocious tannins
and harmonize both its
structure and fruit.
🍷 *red, white, dessert* 📅 *red: 2001,
2000, 1999; white: most recent;
dessert: 2000* ★ *Taurasi Vigna
Macchia dei Goti*

D'Ambra
Campania/Ischia

*loc Panza, SS 270 Via Mario d'Ambra,
Forio* 📞 *0819 07210*
🌐 *www.dambravini.com* 💻

THE ISLAND OF ISCHIA is home
to D'Ambra, one of the

D'Ambra label

south's leading estates; one
glass of the overtly fruity
Biancolella Frassitelli, sourced
from terraced vineyards at
500m, confirms this. Where
the estate scores most highly,
however, is in its devotion to
native varieties, of which many,
like Biancolella, are seen only
on Ischia. Forastera, San
Lunardo, and Guarnaccia
grapes are also lovingly
selected, grown, and vinified
by the D'Ambra family.
🍷 *red, white* 📅 *white: most recent;
red: 2006, 2004, 2001* ★ *Ischia
Biancolella Tenuta Frassitelli*

Fattoria Villa Matilde
*Campania/Falerno del
Massico*

*Strada Statale Domitiana 18,
frazione località Parco Nuovo-Cellole*
📞 *0823 932088* 🌐 *www.fattoria
villamatilde.com* 💻

THE WINES OF FALERNO have
been celebrated since Pliny
first drew attention to them
in the first century AD. Two
thousand years later, the Ava-
llone family decided to focus
all their efforts on rekindling
Falerno del Massico DOC's
former glory. Falanghina, a
poor cousin to Fiano and
Greco elsewhere, is here
elevated to heroic status in the
Falerno Bianco Vigna Caracci,
a hedonistic blend of peach
and apricot allied with exotic
spiciness. The red Vigna
Camarato, from 80 per cent
Aglianico and Piedirosso, is
equally impressive, with its
essence of blackberry and
juicy redcurrant.
🍷 *red, white, rosé, dessert* 📅 *red:
2004, 2001, 2000; white: most recent*
★ *Falerno del Massico Bianco: Vigna
Caracci, Vigna Camarato*

Feudi di San Gregorio
Campania/IGT

contrada Cerza Grossa, Sorbo Serpico
📞 *0825 986611*
🌐 *www.feudi.it* 💻

AT THE FOREFRONT of Campanian
winemaking for more than 20
years, there is little doubt that
Feudi di San Gregorio
continues to set the standard.
The winemaker is the
redoubtable Riccardo Cotarella,
who has worked his usual
magic over a full range of
Campanian classics. The
popular Falanghina, Fiano,
Greco, and Taurasi are all
here, and all exemplary, but
it is the estate's own inven-
tions that attract the most
interest. The white Campanaro, a blend of Greco and

MONTEVETRANO: TOP OF THE CHARTS

Silvia Imparato, one of Italy's leading photographers,
inherited her family's small wine estate in the hills behind
the fashionable resort of Sorrento in 1985. The vineyards on
the estate soon became a passion. Although not a winemaker by trade, Silvia applied considerable diligence and
resource to the complete renovation of both vineyards and
winery. A portion of her considerable investment went to
employing the services of Riccardo Cotarella, one of
Italy's most celebrated winemakers. The combination of
his expertise, Silvia's uncompromising search for perfection,
and the superb *terroir* of the estate culminated in the
1993 Montevetrano IGT Colli di Salerno, a wine that
leapt straight to the top of the charts in both Italy and
America. Today it enjoys cult status as one of Italy's most
sought-after reds. A seductive Bordeaux-meets-Napoli
blend of Cabernet Sauvignon,
Merlot, and Aglianico, Montevetrano
offers flavours of new oak and
cassis, and has an impressive track
record of older vintages. Its success
has propelled both the modest
Silvia and the estate to stardom.
🌐 *www.montevetrano.it*

Fiano from selected parcels, offers a panoply of lush, tropical fruit supported by discreet barrel maturation. Serpico, from century-old Aglianico, remains a paragon of restraint and fills the mouth with elegant tannins and concentrated fruit, but it is pipped to the post by the monumental Patrimo wine, fashioned from a small parcel of ancient Merlot.

Molettieri vineyards, Campania

🍷 red, white, dessert 🍇 red: 2004, 2001, 2000; white: most recent ★ Fiano Campanaro IGT, Serpico IGT, Patrimo IGT

Molettieri
Campania/Taurasi

via Musanni 19, Montemarano
📞 0827 637224
🆆 www.salvatoremolettieri.it ◻

ACCORDING TO Salvatore Molettieri, he has always made great Aglianico but it is only in the past few years that the rest of the world has begun to take any notice. It is impossible to disagree when confronted with the concentrated black cherry and damson character of his powerful Taurasi DOCG. The Riserva just manages to cloak Aglianico's Herculean form with ripe black fruit and creamy new oak, and needs a decade to show at its best.
🍷 red 🍇 2004, 2001, 2000, 1999, 1997, 1996 ★ Taurasi Vigna Cinque Querce, Vigna Cinque Querce Riserva

Terredora
Campania/Greco di Tufo

via Serra, Montefusco 📞 0825 968 215 🆆 www.terredora.com ◻ by appt

TERREDORA OWES its existence to an acrimonious split within one of Campania's leading wine families, Mastroberardino. In 1996 the two brothers parted company; one (Paolo) retained the winery and the name, and the other kept

the vineyards – some of Campania's finest. In short order, Lucio Mastroberardino built a new winery (Terredora) and released his first vintage entirely from his own vineyards. The wines reflect Lucio's insight gathered during a lifetime devoted to expressing his beloved *terroir*. Terredora's range is of uniformly high quality. The elegant Fiano d'Avellino and opulent Greco di Tufo both eschew oak in favour of concentrated fruit, while the refined Taurasi skilfully blends the two.
🍷 red, white, rosé, dessert 🍇 red: 2001, 2000, 1998; white: most recent ★ Greco di Tufo Loggia della Serra, Fiano d'Avellino Terre di Dora, Taurasi Fatica Contadina

Librandi
Calabria/Cirò & IGT

SS 106 C da San Gennaro, Cirò Marina 📞 0962 31518 🆆 www.librandi.it ◻

SOLID, RELIABLE, and for decades the only Calabrian estate that had the faintest pretence to quality, a quaint sense of the old-fashioned still pervades the winery, but there is also a new and purposeful air. In addition to the substantial holdings within the Cirò DOC, Librandi have recently bought new vineyards within the forgotten region of Melissa DOC. This spells good news for devotees of indigenous varieties, as Librandi have always championed local grapes despite its recent

success with the Chardonnay varietal, Critone. The real star, however, continues to be the Gravello, a blend of Gaglioppo's structure with Cabernet Sauvignon's fruitiness.
🍷 red, white, rosé, dessert 🍇 red: 2004, 2000, 1997, 1990; white: most recent ★ Critone IGT, Gravello IGT, Cirò Duca Sanfelice

Odoardi
Calabria/Scavigna & Savuto

viale della Repubblica 143, Cosenza 📞 0984 29961 ◻

THE RADIOLOGIST Dr Gregorio Odoardi was the first Calabrian to experiment with high-density planting and new oak barrels. This, together with the help of consultant winemaker Stefano Chioccioli, has raised the standard of Calabrian wines. In addition to low yields, vineyards here benefit from a strong maritime influence that preserves the black fruit and floral subtleties of the Scavigna DOC Vigna Garrone, a clean interpretation of Aglianico, Merlot, Cabernet Sauvignon, and Cabernet Franc aged in new oak for 12 months. Other highlights include the charms of the white Scavigna, and red Savuto DOC Vigna Mortilla. Odoardi is the most exciting estate to have emerged from sleepy Calabria in many a moon.
🍷 red, white, dessert 🍇 red & white: most recent ★ Scavigna Vigna Garrone, Savuto Vigna Mortilla

Vineyards in Marsala, Sicilia

WINEGROWING AREAS OF SARDEGNA & SICILIA

Sardegna (Sardinia)

THREE QUARTERS OF SARDEGNA'S (Sardinia's) vines have been uprooted in the past 15 years as a result of EU-funded schemes to reduce the size of Europe's wine lake. Despite this, an ever-widening circle of decent wines is produced here. Carignano (Carignan) from **Carignano del Sulcis** DOC can be tamed to make an obediently juicy red, and Cannonau (Grenache), the island's best-known wine, can be similarly jammy and moreish. Curiously, South Italy's first white DOCG is also found here. Inevitably overlooked, **Vermentino di Gallura** DOCG has had a lonely existence despite its considerable talents. The best examples are concentrated and ripe with a flinty, floral dimension. The local white grape Nuragus finds expression in the **Nuragus di Cagliari** DOC. Sardegna also retains a few producers who stubbornly refuse to cease production of the old-fashioned oddity that is **Vernaccia di Oristano** DOC – a dry, sherry-like apéritif from the eastern coast, which is now in danger of extinction.

🗺 granite subsoil with clay and sand 🍇 Carignano, Cannonau 🍇 Vermentino, Vernaccia 🍷 red, white, rosé, dessert, fortified, sparkling

Sicilia (Sicily)

SICILIA'S ABUNDANCE of native grape varieties, allied to enormous climatic variation, has given rise to a plethora of wine styles, with no shortage of more raw material. Despite the EU's incessant clamouring for vine grubbing, Sicilia (Sicily), with its 158,000ha of vines, still boasts a greater vineyard area than any other region in Italy.

Stunning examples of both IGT and DOC wines can be found in Sicily. There is one IGT for the entire island (IGT Sicilia), and this grants the freedom to both blend grapes from anywhere on the island and label products varietally – great for experimental vineyards and for producers wanting to make large volumes of inexpensive wines from international varieties.

PASSITO WINES

The blistering climate of the south lends itself perfectly to the production of one of Italy's national treasures: luscious dessert wine made from carefully dried grapes *(passito)*. Producers in the Mezzogiorno joke that the strong winds and low humidity allow them to achieve in two weeks what it would take two months to accomplish in the north. Most *passito* wines are made from either Moscato or Malvasia and hail from **Passito di Pantelleria** and **Malvasia delle Lipari** DOCs, both from islands off Sicilia. The grapes are harvested when fully mature and laid on straw mats to desiccate under the sun. Sixty per cent of the juice may be lost through this process. As the water evaporates, the sugar levels soar. The syrupy liquid can take months to ferment but the resulting wine is rich in both sugar and alcohol. The Italians refer to these as *vini da meditazione*, indicative of the contemplative mood that ought to accompany their consumption.

In the extreme northeast, crumbling basalt terraces march up the foothills of the Peloritani Mountains. This is the home of the near-derelict red DOC of **Faro**, as well as one of the unsung heroic Italian grapes, Nerello Mascalese. Something of a cult in Italy, Faro manages to retain Burgundian elegance in the face of Sicilia's wilting heat. The delicate red fruit aromas and refined palate are rather unexpected from a Sicilian wine.

Just south of Faro the modest peaks of the Peloritani give way to Monte Etna, Europe's largest active volcano, which soars to more than 3,300m, and dominates the horizon. Vineyards race up Etna's slopes from sea level to almost 1,000m; these are some of the highest in Europe and the altitude delays ripening which tends to concentrate aromas. The Carricante grape, which creates ageworthy whites with a focused mineral quality and dried fruit character, joins Nerello in the eponymous **Etna** DOC.

Sicilia's southeast corner is Italy's driest and hottest zone. Rain falls intermittently and often not for months at a time, while the Scirocco wind regularly sends temperatures soaring up to 40°C plus. Only the very hardiest vines can survive this punishing climate, such as the red variety Nero d'Avola, which is the mainstay of the DOC of **Eloro**.

Nero d'Avola now ranks as Sicilia's most widely planted red variety and demands to be included in the canon of Italy's finest indigenous grapes. The flavour profile is characterized by a certain aristocratic nervosity comprising sappy acidity, fine and occasionally aggressive tannins, and a dryish mulberry note. Low yields confer powerful alcohol and a prune and cinnamon character. It has some affinity for oak and blends well with Frappato in the DOCG of **Cerasuolo di Vittoria**. Cultivated for generations in isolated pockets around Vittoria in the south of the island, the red Frappato must compose at least 40 per cent of DOCG Cerasuolo di Vittoria. Frappato, with its pale colour, soft tannins, and a generous mouthful of redcurrant and strawberry fruit, is the Mediterranean's answer to Beaujolais's Gamay. It has fresh acidity, is rarely oaked, and is designed for

MARSALA

Delicate yet assertive, fortified Marsala is the serendipitous product of a chance encounter. The 1770 arrival in Marsala of John Woodhouse – a British wine importer who happened to be born in Sicily – coincided with a boom in popularity of fortified wines in Georgian England. Woodhouse's flourishing business already imported sherry and port, and he wasted no time in establishing an Italian equivalent, which came to count Lord Nelson among its devotees. Always fortified, Marsala was originally dry and matured using the solera system, already well established for sherry. Grillo is still considered the Marsala grape *par excellence* but Inzolia, Catarratto, and Damaschino are also permitted. After its 19th-century heyday, faltering sales in the 20th century led to attempts at varying the styles, which now include dry, medium, and sweet *(secco, semisecco*, and *dolce)*, as well as gold, amber, and red *(oro, ambra*, and *rubino)*. Such confusing nomenclature sounded the death knell for Marsala. Quality production has dropped by 97 per cent since the late 1970s. The Vergine and Vergine Stravecchio are the oldest and most interesting versions, but even these now struggle.

Marsala wine

early consumption. Although red varieties remain Sicilia's stock-in-trade, a couple of white grapes are worthy of separate mention. The earthy aromas and prodigious alcohol of Catarratto usually consign it to **Marsala** production *(see above)*, but it occasionally treats the faithful to flashes of zesty brilliance when yields are restricted. DOC **Alcamo** is its spiritual home. The ubiquitous Moscato (known here as Zibibbo) reaches its zenith in glorious dessert wines such as **Passito di Pantelleria** DOC *(see left)*. The deep amber colour and dried fruit nose are harbingers of an intensely sweet palate resolutely balanced by natural freshness. **Malvasia delle Lipari** DOC offers a refreshingly herbal variation on the *passito* theme *(see left)*.

chalk and clay, volcanic basalt, sand

Frappato, Nerello Mascalese, Nerello Cappuccio, Nero d'Avola *Moscato, Malvasia, Grillo, Inzolia, Catarratto, Damaschino, Carricante*

red, white, rosé, sparkling, dessert, fortified

TOP PRODUCERS OF SARDEGNA & SICILIA

Argiolas
Sardegna/IGT & Nuragus di Cagliari

via Roma 56/58, Serdiana █ 0707
40606 ⓦ www.vinidocsardegna.it ⬚

TO GIVE CREDIT where credit is due, Argiolas had already discovered the potential of Sardegna's *terroir* when the current crop of headline-grabbers were still in short trousers. Fine producers are still in short supply, and the Argiolas pedigree deserves as much recognition as the wines. The flagship Turriga, an IGT wine, comprises a majority of Cannonau stiffened with a little Malvasia Nera. Its ripe, jammy character framed by toasted oak would embarrass many a Châteauneuf-du-Pape. Equally impressive are the sweet Angialis, the dry Costamolino from Vermentino, and a rare white Nuragus di Cagliari DOC. If Argiolas were in Tuscany the wines would be three times the price.
🍷 *red, white, dessert* 📆 *red: 2004, 2002, 2000, 1998, 1997, 1995; white: most recent* ★ *Turriga IGT, Angialis IGT, Nuragus di Cagliari*

Cantina Gallura
Sardegna/Vermentino di Gallura

via Val di Cossu 9, Tempio Pausania
█ 0796 31241
ⓦ www.cantinagallura.it ⬚

A LONELY OUTPOST of Sardinian viticulture, the co-op in Gallura continues to exhort its members to show due care and attention in the vineyards. Over the years these fine words have seeped into the members' consciousness and, phoenix-like, decent Vermentino has emerged from this region. The three versions on offer (Canayli, Piras, and Mavriana),

Argiolas label

are all richly aromatic and expressive. Vermentino di Gallura DOCG remains one of Italy's best value whites, and this modest co-op one of its principal exponents.
🍷 *red, white, rosé, dessert* 📆 *most recent* ★ *Vermentino di Gallura: Canayli, Mavriana, Piras*

Cantina di Santadi
Sardegna/Carignano del Sulcis

via Su Pranu 12, Santadi █ 0781
950127 ⓦ www.cantinadisantadi.it ⬚

FAR FROM AN AVERAGE co-op, Santadi consistently serves up not only some of the best wines on the island but some of the best wines in Italy. That they remain resolutely affordable is a source of continuing delight to those who have discovered the pleasures of the little-known DOC of Carignano del Sulcis. Santadi's Terre Brune is jam-packed with tarry, blackberry fruit allied to supple tannins and great length. Its younger brother Rocca Rubia is nearly as impressive, and both wines look increasingly good value.
🍷 *red, white, rosé, dessert*
📆 *red & white: most recent*
★ *Carignano del Sulcis Superiore Terre Brune, Carignano del Sulcis Riserva Rocca Rubia*

Capichera
Sardegna/IGT

SS Arzachena, S Antonio, 5km,
Arzachena █ 0789 80800
ⓦ www.capichera.it ⬚ by appt

IN AMONG the parched, rocky scrub of northern Sardinia lies the immaculate estate of Capichera. The Ragnedda family's relentless search for quality may not be unique in Sardegna but it is still in sharp contrast to the majority of producers. The family recently took the difficult decision to turn their back on Sardinia's only DOCG, Vermentino di Gallura, and label all their wines as IGT. This is a great pity as Capichera's unstinting efforts with Vermentino did much to elevate the reputation of the region as a whole. The Vendemmia Tardiva remains one of Vermentino's finest moments, showing nutty aromas overlaid with wild flowers and rare complexity. The Capichera offers a more affordable introduction to the pleasures of this grape. The estate has recently added a range of sound, if a little pricey, reds.
🍷 *red, white* 📆 *most recent* ★ *Capichera Vendemmia Tardiva IGT, Capichera IGT*

Contini
Sardegna/Vernaccia di Oristano

via Genova 48/50, Cabras █ 0783
290806 ⓦ www.vinicontini.it ⬚

ATTILIO CONTINI's determination to produce one of Italy's least fashionable wines, Vernaccia di Oristano DOC, is to be applauded by supporters of vinous diversity. Gently oxidized, indestructible, and peerless with soups and anti-pasto, Vernaccia di Oristano is

Italy's answer to fine *amontillado* sherry *(see p328)*, with a delicate nose of hazelnut and honey and a warming caramel note on the finish. Attilio's magnificent, multi-vintage Antico Gregori is still resolutely undiscovered.

🔲 red, white, dessert
🔲 red & white: most recent;
dessert: 2002, 2001 ★ *Vernaccia di Oristano Antico Gregori*

Benanti
Sicilia/Etna & IGT

via G Garibaldi 475, Viagrande
📞 0957 893 533 🔲 www.benanti.it
🔲 by appt

HIGH DENSITY PLANTINGS, low yields, and hand-plunging during fermentation are just a few of the steps the Benanti family have taken to establish their estate at the forefront of viticulture in Etna DOC. The high altitude and volcanic soil of the vineyards yield a small crop of aromatic local grapes. The white Pietramarina, made from 80-year-old Carricante vines planted at 850m, is a concentrated, blissfully oak-free mélange of almond, apple, and liquorice. The Rosso di Verzella is an equally impressive rendering of Nerello Mascalese.

🔲 red, white, dessert 🔲 2004, 2001, 2000, 1999 ★ *Etna Bianco Superiore Pietramarina, Minella IGT Sicilia*

Calatrasi
Sicilia/IGT

loc San Cipirello, contrada Piano Piraino, Palermo 🔲 www.calatrasi.it
📞 0918 576 767 🔲

A HEART-WARMING success story, Calatrasi was established in 1980 by Maurizio Miccichè, a Sicilian doctor who started the estate as the sales arm of the local co-op he had encouraged local farmers to create. Today, it controls

Contini label

three wineries and more than 500ha of vineyards near Palermo, with a further 240 in Puglia and 200 in Tunisia. Calatrasi exports both local and indigenous varieties to more than 25 countries under labels including Terre di Ginestra, Accademia del Sole, Allora, and D'Istinto. All wines are bottled as IGT Sicilia.

🔲 red, white 🔲 most recent
★ *D'Istinto IGT Sicilia range*

Colosi
Sicilia/Malvasia delle Lipari

via Militare Ritiro 23, Messina
📞 0905 3852 🔲 www.cantine colosi.com 🔲 by appt

PIERO COLOSI is a tireless champion of one of the south's near-extinct dessert wines, Malvasia delle Lipari DOC. He makes this in both a *naturale* and a *passito* style, but the sun-drenched island of Lipari specializes in the *passito* method *(see p280)*. This process exaggerates the herbal character of the grape, and creates a wine with a pleasing eucalyptus and apricot bitterness.

🔲 red, white, dessert 🔲 most recent ★ *Malvasia delle Lipari Passito di Salina*

Cusumano
Sicilia/IGT

con San Carlo, Partinico 📞 0918 903456 🔲 🔲 www.cusumano.it

BROTHERS Diego and Alberto Cusumano have

been experimenting with different grape varieties on their father's 140-ha farm since 1989. It took them until 2001 before they were happy enough with the results to release their first wine. This is an estate that does not put a foot wrong, and Diego's larger-than-life personality shines through all the wines from the jolly Inzolia Cubìa to the dramatic Noà, a blend of Nero d'Avola, Merlot, and Cabernet. They have recently purchased a 160-ha parcel of vines at 700m to experiment with cool-climate varieties. All wines are released under IGT Sicilia.

🔲 red, white 🔲 most recent
★ *IGT Sicilia: Inzolia Cubia, Noà*

Donnafugata
Sicilia/Passito di Pantelleria & Contessa Entellina

via S Lipari 18, Marsala 📞 0923 724 200 🔲 www.donnafuga.it 🔲

DONNAFUGATA has an exemplary range of Sicilian classics, many of which are Contessa Entellina DOC. Vigna di Gabri is a pure expression of the summer fruits and acacia for which the Inzolia grape is prized. The unctuous Ben Ryè has raised the bar for devotees of traditional, unfortified Passito di Pantelleria DOC.

🔲 red, white, dessert 🔲 white: 2004; red: 2004, 2002, 2001 ★ *Contessa Entellina Vigna di Gabri, Passito di Pantelleria Ben Ryè*

Donnafugata label

Firriato
Sicilia/IGT

via Trapani 4, Paceco 📞 *0923 882755* Ⓦ *www.firriato.it* ◻

THE DI GAETANC FAMILY have invested heavily in keeping both vineyards and winery fighting fit. Maintaining quality across 16 wines and four million bottles cannot be easy but all the wines that emerge from their unassuming premises are eminently presentable. The well-priced Chiaramonte, made from the Catarratto grape, offers a wealth of attractive lemon and stone fruit flavour. Moving up the scale, the dual-varietal Santagostino Bianco fattens 70 per cent Catarratto with a dollop of oak-aged Chardonnay. The Santagostino Rosso does much the same with 65 per cent Nero d'Avola balanced by Syrah's spiciness. Both offer a modern take on traditional Sicilian flavours. All wines are released as IGT Sicilia.

🟥 *red, white* 🔂 *most recent* ★ *IGT Sicilia: Chiaramonte, Santagostino Bianco, Santagostino Rosso*

Morgante label

Gulfi
Sicilia/IGT

loc Roccazzo, via Maria Santissima del Rosario, Chiaramonte Gulfi 📞 *0932 921 654* Ⓦ *www.gulfi.it* ◗

VITO CATANIA, a local boy made good through working with Formula One motor racing, has returned to his home town determined to produce Nero d'Avola that can take the world by storm. Since 1996 he has planted 90ha with dry-farmed, bush-vine Nero d'Avola at an incredible density of 8,500 vines per hectare. The estate's first inky-black release is a Nero d'Avola just as it ought to be – redolent of tangy black fruit

layered with balsamic new oak. There is no doubt that this estate will evolve into one of the most dynamic forces in Sicilia.

🟥 *red* 🔂 *2007, 2005* ★ *Nero d'Avola Rosso Ibleo IGT Sicilia*

Marco de Bartoli
Sicilia/Marsala

contrada Fornara Samperi, 292, Marsala 📞 *0923 962 093* Ⓦ *www. lilibeo.com/debartoli* ◻ *by appt*

LOST IN A SEA of mediocrity, Marco de Bartoli has been a lone voice championing the potential of Marsala *(see p281)*. And what a siren call. At the top of the tree is the sublime Marsala Vecchio Samperi 20-year-old Riserva, a gently sweet, extraordinarily complex fortified wine that immediately confers respectability upon the entire Marsala family. The vintage-dated Marsala Superiore and Vigna la Miccia are similarly refined. Not content with making benchmark Marsala, Marco also produces an exquisite Passito di Pantelleria, Bukkuram.

🟨 *white, dessert, fortified* 🔂 *dessert & fortified: 2004, 2001, 2000, 1998; white: most recent*

PLANETA'S METEORIC RISE

Just 20 years ago, the achievements of the Planeta family would have been unthinkable. Their metamorphosis from anonymous grape supplier to one of Italy's most respected wine producers is a tale of hard work and unwavering belief in the potential of Sicily's unique *terroir*. In 1985 Diego Planeta, president of Cantina Settesoli – the island's largest co-operative cellar – and one of its 6,000 members, decided to experiment with both local and international varieties to see if it was possible to coax anything but inevitably cheap and not so cheerful wine from Sicily's unrewarding soils. He planted more than 50 different combinations of variety, clone, and rootstock in a tireless campaign to raise the quality of the island's wines through their raw material. His project marked a turning point in Sicilian viticulture. Planeta's first release, a Chardonnay grown from this experimental vineyard, was greeted with unanimous praise from both sides of the Atlantic and offered proof of the south's potential. Today, Planeta produces more than a dozen wines with an increasing emphasis on local varieties.

★ *Marsala Vecchio Samperi 20-year-old Riserva, Marsala Superiore, Passito di Pantelleria Bukkuram*

Morgante
Sicilia/IGT

contrada da Racalmare, Grotte
☎ *0922 945579*
W *www.morgante-vini.it* ▢

IT IS DIFFICULT to imagine a more unassuming winery than this utilitarian building behind Agrigento. The wines, however, are testimony to Carmelo and Giovanni Morgante's quiet determination to bring Nero d'Avola to the world's attention. Just two, modestly-priced wines are produced from Nero d'Avola: a gluggable version with just four months in oak, and the more contemplative Don Antonio, aged for a year in new oak. The Don Antonio offers an additional dimension of ripe fruit and spicy complexity that more than justifies the higher price.
■ *red* ■ *most recent*
★ *Nero d'Avola Don Antonio IGT Sicilia*

Murana
Sicilia/Passito di Pantelleria

contrada Khamma 276, Pantelleria
☎ *0923 915231*▢

SALVATORE MURANA, the unofficial prince of Pantelleria DOC, is the island's foremost exponent of its luscious sweet wines, made from sun-dried Moscato grapes. The Martingana reveals divine concentration of Moscato's signature orange blossom and sultana aromas, complemented by peach and honey. The Khamma is similar, but a very brief period in oak adds a spicy note.
■ *red, white, dessert* ■ *most recent*
★ *Passito di Pantelleria Martingana, Passito di Pantelleria Khamma*

Palari
Sicilia/Faro

loc Santo Stefano Briga, contrada Barna, Messina ☎ *0906 94281*
W *www.vinipalari.it* ▢ *by appt*

IN 1990, the noted Italian wine journalist Luigi Veronelli approached Salvatore Geraci, an architect from Messina, with an ambitious undertaking: he asked Salvatore to save the DOC of Faro from extinction. At that time there were only two producers of Faro; under Italian law there must be a minimum of three if a DOC is to remain in existence. Geraci's family owned 4ha of terraced vineyards but had always sold the wine locally in demijohn. Fortunately, Salvatore took up the challenge, experimenting from 1990 to 1994, then releasing his first wine, which went on to scoop one of Italy's top awards. Crafted from low-yielding Nerello Mascalese and Nerello Cappuccio, Palari's Faro is an elegant composition of new oak and sweet berry fruit.
■ *red* ■ *2004, 2001*
★ *Palari Faro*

Planeta
Sicilia/IGT

via Michele Amari, Palermo ☎ *0913 27965* W *www.planeta.it* ▢ *by appt*

YEAR AFTER YEAR, the supremely confident Planeta clan deliver the goods. Although the obvious, international charms of the Chardonnay and Cabernet Sauvignon win the awards, the family are most proud of their achievements with Italian varieties. The white Cometa, a 100 per cent Fiano, aged partly in *barrique*, delivers an unforgettable performance with an intense palate of dried fruit and spice. Santa Cecilia is their version of Nero d'Avola, and it is suitably impressive with refined tannins and good persistence. Given the quality of the wines and the hype surrounding the Planeta estate, the wines continue to offer exceptional value and are released as IGT Sicilia.
■ *red, white* ■ *red: 2006, 2004, 2001; white: most recent*
★ *IGT Sicilia: Cometa, Santa Cecilia*

Valle dell'Acate
Sicilia/Cerasuolo di Vittoria

contrada Bidini, Acate
☎ *0932 874166*
W *www.valledellacate.com* ▢ *by appt*

THE ACATE RIVER has carved a series of broad, alluvial terraces through the arid plains of Sicily's southeastern tip. Valle dell'Acate is a mini-co-operative comprising just seven members, each with vineyards planted on these terraces. The unrewarding, stony soil and proximity to the sea create an ideal meso-climate for Inzolia, Nero d'Avola, and Frappato, all skilfully vinified by Gaetana Jacono. The delicate red fruit and fresh acidity of her Cerasuolo di Vittoria make it an ideal summer red.
■ *red, white* ■ *most recent*
★ *Inzolia IGT Sicilia, Cerasuolo di Vittoria DOC*

Valle dell'Acate label

SPAIN

SPAIN

SPAIN IS WESTERN EUROPE'S *second-oldest wine-producing country, but 3,000 years on, it is producing wines that are among the most modern in Europe. From cheerful, fruity everyday wines to impressive, world-class classics of enormous complexity and ageing potential, Spain has reinvented itself in the vineyard and in the winery, and it now boasts a wine industry more dynamic and diverse than ever.*

BACKGROUND

WINE WAS FIRST MADE in Andalucía between 1100 and 500 BC. Initially produced by traders from Phoenicia, it was later made by Greeks fleeing the power struggles in the eastern Mediterranean, which had sparked war on the Aegean coast. With them, the Greeks brought their families, livestock, and vines. The Romans arrived in 200 BC and set about turning vinegrowing from a largely domestic industry into something that could supply their legions and Rome itself. Thus, Spain's first real export market evolved.

1920s Cava poster

The Moors invaded Spain in AD 711 and the wine business went into abeyance for several centuries under Muslim rule. By the 14th century, sherry, in particular, had become an important export item, and was sold in capitals all over Europe. The burgeoning Spanish empire in the Americas brought more export opportunities after 1492, and especially later in the 17th and 18th centuries.

The next major change came in Rioja in the 1850s *(see p302)*, when Bordeaux methods were first used for making Spanish red wine. The export market was boosted by the phylloxera disaster in the late 19th century, when many of the French vineyards were wiped out and France looked to Spain for wine supplies.

It was in the late 20th century that Spain's wine industry made the biggest leap forward. The country prospered after the return to democracy in 1978, particularly after joining the European Union in 1986, and investment consequently flooded in. Dramatic changes took place in the vineyard and winery with improved methods of vine planting, training, and pruning, new stainless steel equipment, and better education – all of which resulted in a commensurate advance in the quality of Spanish wine. A major drought in 1992–3 encouraged many growers to experiment with irrigation (at that time forbidden by DO regulations), and this was allowed within the new DO law in 2003.

THE WINE INDUSTRY TODAY

FOR MANY YEARS SPAIN has had the largest area under vine (1.2 million

Harvesting a Torres-owned vineyard in Catalunya

◁ **Vineyards and farmhouse near Valdepeñas, Ciudad Real, Castilla-La Mancha**

WINEGROWING REGIONS

Spain has 17 autonomous regions and 70 quality wine (VCIG/DO/DOCa) zones, plus six DO Pagos. The country divides into three parts: the Northwest, which includes the cool coastal areas of Galicia and the warm inland highlands of Castilla y León; the Northeast, which encompasses La Rioja, Aragón, Navarra, and Catalunya; and Central and Southern Spain, which includes Castilla-La Mancha, Valencia, Andalucía, and the Canarias.

Bay of Biscay

NORTHERN SPAIN
pp292–3

France

Galicia

País Vasco

Navarra

La Rioja

Castilla y León

Duero

Ebro

Aragón

Catalunya

Barcelona

Baleares (Balearic Islands)

MADRID
Madrid

Atlantic Ocean

42°

40°

38°

28°

Portugal

Extremadura

Castilla-La Mancha

Valencia

Murcia

Murcia

Mediterranean Sea

Sevilla (Seville)

Andalucía

Málaga

Gibraltar

CENTRAL & SOUTHERN SPAIN
pp314–15

Canarias (Canary Islands)

Atlantic Ocean

ha) of any country in the world. With so many of the vineyards in dry, low-producing areas, however, it remains only the world's third-largest wine producer with an annual output of 34.8 million hl. There are more than 10,000 wineries in the country, 76 DO zones, and 17 autonomous regions producing regional or district wines. In the old days many bodegas (wineries) were co-

Harvest girl at Festival of the Grape, Andalucía

ops owned and run by their members, but there has been a trend since the mid-1990s to turn them into limited companies, with the former members as shareholders. This has led to a significant leap in quality and efficiency.

GRAPE VARIETIES & WINE STYLES

THE CLASSIC SPANISH wine is typically red and made from the Tempranillo grape, with a strawberry-raspberry fruit flavour and a little toasty oak. It has achieved international fame largely because of the outstanding work that has been done in Rioja. Today, however, Spain has a great deal more to offer. Among the star regions are Navarra, with its bright, cherry-fresh Cabernet Sauvignon and

Merlot; the internationally famous Ribera del Duero with its highly-extracted, complex, and rich reds from Tempranillo; and Catalunya, with world-class red wines such as Penedès and Priorat, which are made using Garnacha (Grenache) and Cariñena (Carignan) grapes from ancient, low-yielding vineyards.

Of the white wine regions, Rueda (Castilla y León) makes some of Spain's best white wines from Verdejo and Sauvignon Blanc. Rías Baixas (Galicia) competes for the title of Spain's classic white with cool, crisp, clear wines made from the Albariño grape. Aragón has old plantations of Garnacha and produces wines offering astonishing value. La Mancha is another good source for bargain red wines (mostly Tempranillo) and some quality surprises (such as the lovely, oaky reds of Valdepeñas). Adding more diversity to Spain's impressive portfolio are Cava and sherry, the world's oldest fine wine. Made from the Palomino grape in Andalucía, sherry ranges from the palest, driest most delicate fino to the richest, most pungent oloroso.

SPANISH WINE LAW

THE SPANISH SYSTEM of wine law was overhauled in June 2003, tightening up existing regulations and introducing two new categories: DO Pago and VCIG. As in every country of the European Union, Spanish wines are divided into 'quality' wine, which comes from named areas under fairly strict regulations, and 'table' wine (vino de la tierra and vino de mesa), which is less regulated or virtually unregulated. The four categories of quality are Pago DO, DOCa, DO, and VCIG. These are normally monitored by a consejo

Terra Alta DO label

regulador, which enforces specific viticultural and winemaking standards, including regulations on grape varieties, maximum yields, specifications on ageing, and on the information that must be given on the label. The stamps of the various consejo reguladors (see below), guaranteeing the wine's origin, may be found on the label or the capsule. Standards within each DO are now overseen by an independent committee, which has the power to regulate the production and quality of wine within each region.

Spanish Wine Classification

Denominación de Origen de Pago (DO Pago): This small category is reserved for the finest wines from single estates with a track record for quality.

Denominación de Origen Calificada (DOCa): These should be wines of consistently high quality, which have proved for at least 10 years that they can maintain that standard.

Denominación de Origen (DO): This category is roughly equivalent to the French Appellation d'Origine Contrôlée (AOC) and represents wine produced from a designated region according to local regulations. DO wines can vary in quality, but should offer a style commensurate with their

Consejo regulador Rioja stamp

region. This and the categories above are regulated by a *consejo regulador* and independent standards committee.

Vino de Calidad con Indicación Geográfica (VCIG): This new category, introduced in 2003, is for high-performing wines seeking promotion from VdlT (see below), and is roughly equivalent to the French Vin Délimité de Qualité Supérieure (VDQS). VCIG wines may apply for promotion to DO after a minimum of five years, and are regulated by an *órgano de gestión* (management committee).

Vino de la tierra (VdlT): These country wines, roughly equivalent to *vins de pays* in France, are less regulated than those from DOs and VCIGs and can cover quite large areas. Plans for a *Viñedos de España* category are currently on hold.

Vino de mesa (VdM): Under European law, basic table wine is prohibited from giving any indication of regional origins, grape variety, or vintage on the label.

Rioja DOCa *gran reserva* label

Empordà-Costa Brava DO *reserva* label

Rueda DO label

Navarra DO label

READING A SPANISH WINE LABEL

The first thing to establish on a Spanish wine label is the name of the region, which should give a fairly clear indication as to the style and quality of the wine. In this example the wine is from Penedès, which is of DO status and has an excellent reputation. Terms such as *crianza*, *reserva*, and *gran reserva* indicate how long the wine has been aged and are a further pointer towards quality, as is the name of the producer. The grape variety is not always labelled, but is often implied in the DO name.

1870 is the year the winery was founded.

Torres is the name of the producer.

Gran Coronas is the name of the wine.

Cabernet Sauvignon is the grape variety.

Volume

Penedès Denominación de Origen confirms the wine is of DO quality level from the area of Penedès.

Alcoholic strength

Reserva means the wine has spent a minimum of three years in barrel and bottle before release.

Embotellador Miguel Torres confirms that this wine was bottled on the estate.

1999 indicates the vintage, the year the grapes were harvested.

Glossary of Label Terms

añejo: *a wine that has been aged for at least 12 months.*

año: *year.*

blanco: *white.*

bodega: *winery.*

brut: *dry (used for sparkling wines).*

Cava: *a DO or appellation for sparkling wine produced in designated regions in Spain according to the traditional method.*

cosecha: *harvest or vintage.*

coto: *estate.*

crianza: *a wine that has spent at least 6 months in oak and at least 18 months in bottle before release (used for reds).*

dulce: *sweet.*

elaborado: *produced.*

embotellado: *bottled.*

espumoso: *sparkling wine – any method can be used to produce the fizz.*

finca: *estate.*

generoso: *fortified wine.*

granja: *estate.*

gran reserva: *a wine that has spent at least 18 months in oak and the balance of five years before release (used for reds). In theory this should only be made in the finest vintages.*

noble: *a wine which has been aged for at least 24 months.*

pálido: *pale (used for fortified wines).*

reserva: *wine that has spent at least one year in oak and the balance of three years in bottle before release (used for reds).*

rosado: *rosé.*

seco: *dry.*

semi-seco: *medium dry*

tinto: *red.*

vendímia: *vintage.*

viejo: *wine that has been aged*

Rueda DO label

for at least 36 months, with marked oxidative effect.

viña/viñedo: *vineyard.*

viñas viejas: *old vines.*

vino: *wine.*

vino joven: *'young wine', designed for early consumption with little or no oak maturation.*

WINE MAP OF NORTHERN SPAIN

THE MAJORITY OF SPAIN'S finest wines come from the
northern half of the country where the mountainous
landscape provides cool vineyard sites even in the
hottest of summers. The most significant wine areas are
along the banks of Spain's two most important
wine rivers: the Duero and the Ebro. The Duero
flows west through the winelands of Castilla y
León – most famously Ribera del Duero;
while the Ebro flows southeast through the
well-known regions of La Rioja and Navarra
and on to Aragón and Catalunya.

KEY

Northern Spain

**Torres,
Catalunya**

BAY OF BISCAY

A Coruña

Oviedo

Santander

Santiago

Cordillera Cantábric

43°

Miño

RIBEIRA
SACRA

BIERZO

León

RIBEIRO

Sil

Montes
de León

Burgo

Vigo

RÍAS
BAIXAS

Ourense

VALDEORRAS

GALICIA

42

MONTERREI

CASTILLA Y LEÓN

CIGALES

Valladolid

RIBER
DU

ATLANTIC OCEAN

PORTUGAL

Duero

TORO

RUEDA

41

Salamanca

MADR

NORTHWEST SPAIN:
AREAS & TOP PRODUCERS

GALICIA *p294*
Fillaboa *p296*
Martín Códax *p296*

CASTILLA Y LEÓN *p294*
Aalto *p296*
Abadía Retuerta *p296*
Alejandro Fernández *p296*
Álvarez y Díez *p297*
Castilla la Vieja *p297*
Descendientes de
  J Palacios *p297*
Emilio Moro *p297*
Fariña *p298*
Hacienda Durius *p298*
Hacienda Monasterio *p298*
Marqués de Riscal *p298*
Mauro *p298*
Maurodos *p299*
Valdelosfrailes *p299*
Vega Sicilia *p299*
Viña Bajoz *p299*

Hacienda Durius vineyards in Castilla y León, Northwest Spain

Vineyards and church in La Rioja

TERROIR AT A GLANCE

Latitude: 41–43.5°N.

Altitude: Varies from 0 to 2,600m; vineyards are at sea level along the Catalan coast, in the lowlands in Aragón and Navarra, and in the highlands in other areas of Navarra, La Rioja, Penedès, and Ribera del Duero.

Topography: The Cordillera Cantábrica mountain range dominates the north.

Soil: Mainly limestone, mixed with sandstone or calcareous clay.

Climate: Varies from temperate Atlantic influences north of the Cordillera Cantábrica to more continental south of these mountains. Lowlands are hot and dry, with semi-arid spots, while the highlands of Ribera del Duero, La Rioja, and Navarra are cooler. Heading east, the climate becomes more Mediterranean, with complex mesoclimates in the highlands of Catalunya and humid and temperate areas towards the coast.

Temperature: July average is 22°C.

Rainfall: Annual average is 1,200mm.

Viticultural hazards: Frost in highlands of La Rioja, Navarra, and Aragón; rain and wind at harvest time in Galicia and País Vasco; fungal infections in Catalunya.

NORTHEAST SPAIN: AREAS & TOP PRODUCERS

Vineyards above the Miño River in Ribeiro, Galicia

WINEGROWING AREAS OF NORTHWEST SPAIN

NORTHWEST SPAIN HAS just two wine regions, both of which are rapidly growing in importance. In the cool northwest corner, the region of Galicia produces some of the country's freshest and most delightful white wines. The dry interior of the vast area of Castilla y León, meanwhile, is home to the internationally known Ribera del Duero DO, which is currently witnessing the seemingly unstoppable rise of its blockbuster reds.

Galicia

WITH ITS DEEP RIVER VALLEYS, soaring granite peaks, and secluded coastal coves, this region lying to the north of Portugal is among the most beautiful in Spain. Conditions are ideal for the production of fresh, dry, fruity, white wines due to the cool, wet climate and versatile granite soils. The most important whites are made from the Albariño grape.

Of the region's five DO zones, **Rías Baixas** produces the Galician wine most likely to feature in export markets, though small-scale production tends to make it rather expensive. Rías Baixas' best wines are 100 per cent Albariño. The vineyards tend to be small parcels of land dotted around the steep slopes of the river valleys, with the vines usually trained on pergolas so that the grapes hang below a blanket of leaves, protecting them from the sun and preventing over-ripeness. This also has the benefit of keeping them clear of the soil: with 1,600mm of rain each year, damp can be a problem.

Albariño grapes

While Rías Baixas is the most prominent DO, the others have their own strengths and are starting to make inroads into international markets. **Ribeiro** is centred on the lovely town of Ribadavia on the Miño River, and is the next most important. It too makes very good white wines, the best principally from the Godello grape, which is not quite as peachy as Albariño, but has a delicate, herby scent nonetheless. Excellent Godello also originates from **Valdeorras**, which together with Ribeiro is the oldest established Galician DO. The area lies alongside the Sil River in the east of the region, and it is also responsible for some worthwhile light reds made from Mencía.

Ribeira Sacra is a tiny region around the town of Monforte de Lemos where grape varieties Albariño, Loureira, and Godello are grown for aromatic whites, and Mencía for delicate reds. Around the town of Verín, **Monterrei** is the smallest Galician DO, making wines similar to those of Ribeira Sacra.
🏞 *alluvial, granite, and slate* 🍇 *Mencía*
🍇 *Albariño, Godello* 🍷 *red, white*

Castilla y León

THE ANCIENT HEARTLAND OF Castilian Spain is a land of cathedrals, monuments, and castles – the legacy of the nobles and government officials who lived here, and for whom Castilla y León's big red wines were originally produced. It is a very large area (covering almost one fifth of the country), sheltered from the excesses of the Atlantic climate by the mountains of León. The area has some impressive peaks, and some of the best vineyard sites benefit from altitudes exceeding 800m, resulting in long hot days in the ripening season combined with cool nights to 'rest' the vines. Wine production here was generally fairly basic (with a few notable exceptions) until the 1980s, when Ribera del Duero won its DO status and started to make its presence felt.

Ribera del Duero is unquestionably the most important of Castilla y León's five DO zones, and its most famous wine, Vega Sicilia (*see p299*), has proved since the mid-19th century that it is possible to make world-class red wines in this area. However, despite being granted DO status in 1982, it was only in 1989 that its wines began to be noticed internationally. Suddenly, everybody wanted a piece of the action and land prices shot up – and are continuing to do so. Its principal advantages are the altitude (up to 900m) and chalk-rich soils over a schistous bedrock, which is perfect for vines. Vineyards tend to be 100 per cent Tempranillo (here called Tinto Fino or Tinto del País), though a little Cabernet Sauvignon is also grown. The wines are bold, powerful, full of fruit, and have impressive ageing qualities. At their best, they are among Spain's very finest – with prices to match.

Rueda is Castilla y León's most important

ALBARIÑO: A RISING STAR

The lipsmackingly crisp fruit, peachy aromas, and wonderful zest of Albariño make it the perfect accompaniment to Galician seafood. This distinctive grape is claimed by both Galicia and Portugal (where it is known as Alvarinho) but there are those – Miguel Torres among them – who believe that Albariño is actually the Riesling grape, brought by German monks along the Camino de Santiago in the 11th century. Whatever its provenance, Albariño is responsible for one of Spain's – and the world's – truly great white wines.

DO for white wines: in fact, these wines challenge the Albariños of Rías Baixas for the title of Spain's finest whites. Since the late 1970s, there has been an upsurge in fresh, delicate, fruity, crisp, dry whites made from the local Verdejo grape and, since the 1980s, Sauvignon Blanc. Rueda's reds (mainly Tempranillo) can also be strikingly good, although they are not in the block-busting style of Ribera del Duero.

The three remaining DO zones are less well-known outside Spain, but this is set to change. Slightly lower in altitude than Ribera del Duero (at 650–830m), **Toro** has a hotter climate and ripens Tempranillo (here known as Tinta de Toro) to considerable strengths – up to 15 per cent potential alcohol in some cases. It is famed for its big red wines, which have tremendous heat, power, and richness. Many of the major producers from more expensive Ribera del Duero are buying land here, and Toro has become a major player in the DO. **Cigales** will probably follow: the grape is the same, the style is similar, the altitude on a par, and it has a very stony soil, which some growers think can be perfect for ripening Tempranillo. **Bierzo**, in the far north, mainly specializes in light reds made from Mencía and is now making some of the region's most interesting wines.

🏷 alluvial, limestone, chalk

🍇 Tempranillo 🍇 Verdejo, Sauvignon Blanc 🍷 red, white

Vineyard in Ribera del Duero, Castilla y León

TOP PRODUCERS OF NORTHWEST SPAIN

Fillaboa
Galicia/Rías Baixas

Lugar de Fillaboa, Salvaterra do Miño, Pontevedra 986 658 132 W *www.fillaboa.es*
🚪 *by appt*

THIS SMALL (32-ha), corporately owned but family-run estate produces exemplary, fragrant Albariño wines. It is one of the few bodegas in Rías Baixas that makes some wines for keeping, as well as those for instant drinking: either way, they are among the finest to emerge from the DO, conjuring a great deal of subtlety from the grape and regularly winning prizes.
🍷 *white* 📆 *most recent*
★ *Fillaboa, Selección de la Familia*

Martín Códax
Galicia/Rías Baixas

Burgáns 91, Vilariño, Cambados, Pontevedra 986 526 040
W *www.martincodax.com* 🚪

FOUNDED IN 1986, Martín Códax is now housed in a smart, new, state-of-the-art winery. All 190ha are planted with Albariño, but, as is common in Galicia, these are spread out over 1,200 separate plots. Two basic wines are made (the Burgáns is from premium selected grapes) plus the barrel-fermented Organistrum and a fabulous late-harvest *semi seco* (medium dry) Gallaecia.
🍷 *white* 📆 *most recent*
★ *Burgáns, Organistrum, Gallaecia*

Martín Códax

Aalto
Castilla y León/ Ribera del Duero

ctra de Peñafiel, Roa de Duero, Burgos 947 540 781 W *www.aalto.es* ⬤

AALTO IS AN AMBITIOUS project run by two of Ribera del Duero's best-known names. Mariano García was head winemaker at Vega Sicilia for 30 years, and Javier Zaccagnini was director of the *consejo regulador* (from 1992–8), so their combined expertise is impressive. The first wines from this producer founded in 1999 show astonishing maturity, richness and finesse, but they claim that it will be 15 to 20 years before production reaches its full potential. Aalto is a member of Grandes Pagos de España, Spain's most elite wine producers' organization.
🍷 *red* 📆 *2004, 2001, 1999*
★ *Aalto, Pagos Seleccionados*

Abadía Retuerta
Castilla y León

ctra de Soria, Sardón de Duero, Valladolid 983 680 314
W *www.abadia-retuerta.com* 🚪

THE STUNNINGLY restored former abbey of Santa María de la Retuerta has a 1996-built winery with technology that goes beyond up-to-date and into space-age. Mainly Tempranillo is grown, as well as some Cabernet Sauvignon, with wines made from hand-selected grapes. This independent winery operates outside the DO system, but even the basic *cuvée* Primicia outperforms many wines from Ribera del Duero DO.
🍷 *red* 📆 *2005, 2004, 2001*
★ *El Campanario, Pago Negralada, Pago Valdebellón*

Alejandro Fernández
Castilla y León/ Ribera del Duero

Real 2, Pesquera de Duero, Valladolid 983 870 037
W *www.pesqueraafernandez.com* 🚪

FERNÁNDEZ IS THE man whose blockbusting 1986 vintage made the world take note of Ribera del Duero. He has 150ha of vines in Pesquera and a further 200ha at the Condado de Haza, a purpose-built estate in Roa de Duero, about 20km to the east. The

Fillaboa label from Rías Baixas

wines (all Tempranillo) are truly magnificent; positively glowing with fruit and ripeness. Unsurprisingly they are also suitably expensive.

🟥 *red* 🔺 *2004, 2002, 2001, 1999*
★ *Pesquera, Condado de Haza, Alenza*

Álvarez y Díez
Castilla y León/Rueda

Juan Antonio Carmona 16, Nava del Rey, Valladolid 📞 *983 850 136*
🆆 *www.alvarezydiez.com* ⬜

THIS LONG-ESTABLISHED *bodega* reinvented itself in 1994 to make cool-fermented white wines in the modern style from Verdejo, Sauvignon Blanc, and a little Viura. There is also a heady, yet delicate barrel-fermented Verdejo, but the bestseller is the Mantel Blanco, a slightly drier style than some wines made by other companies in Rueda DO, but with the classic Verdejo fruit and herbs.

🟥 *white* 🔺 *most recent*
★ *Mantel Blanco*

Castilla la Vieja
Castilla y León/Rueda

ctra La Coruña, km 170.6, Rueda, Valladolid 📞 *983 868 116*
🆆 *www.bodegasdecastilla.com* ⬜

A MEMBER OF Rueda's first family of wine, Antonio Sanz farms 200ha and has been in the business since 1976. Palacio de Bornos is his flagship wine: pure Verdejo and very fragrant. Bornos is 100 per cent Sauvignon

Castilla la Vieja label

Blanc, with that typical grassy, gooseberry fruit, given a warm Spanish twist. Sanz also makes a beguiling late-harvest semi-sweet Verdejo called Exxencia de Bornos. Other branches of the Sanz family make wine at Sitio de Bodega and Félix Sanz in Rueda.

🟥 *white* 🔺 *most recent*
★ *Palacio de Bornos, Bornos*

Descendientes de J Palacios
Castilla y León/Bierzo

Calvo Sotelo 6, Villafranca del Bierzo, León 📞 *987 540 821* ⬛

THIS IS ANOTHER collaboration between pioneering wine-maker Álvaro Palacios, creator of Finca Dofi in Priorat *(see p311)* and his nephew Ricardo Pérez, a former student at Château Margaux in Bordeaux. Both are, as the name indicates, descendants of José Palacios, a venerable local legend in Rioja. They came to Bierzo in 1999 to tame the difficult Mencía grape, and bought 11ha of old vines in 45 separate parcels. The duo make a first (Corullón) and a second wine (Bierzo), and their early vintages are showing exceptionally well. Old vine (low-yield) Mencía has an elegant structure with crisp, brambly fruit.

🟥 *red* 🔺 *2005, 2004, 2002, 2001*
★ *Petalos del Bierzo, Viña de Corullón*

Emilio Moro
Castilla y León/ Ribera del Duero

ctra Peñafiel-Valoria, Pesquera de Duero, Valladolid
📞 *983 878 400*
🆆 *www.emiliomoro.com* ⬜

EMILIO MORO HAS 7Cha of Tempranillo vines, including the single-vineyard Finca

Resalso, which was planted in 1933, the year Moro was born. His Malleolus is made from old-vine grapes, while the Malleolus de Valderramiro is the product of an 80-year-old vineyard of the same name and is one of Ribero del Duero's finest wines, with superb fruit and complexity.

🟥 *red* 🔺 *2005, 2004, 2003, 2002, 2001* ★ *Finca Resalso, Malleolus, Malleolus de Valderramiro*

Tempranillo vineyard, Emilio Moro

PERFECT CASE: NORTHWEST SPAIN

🅡 Aalto £££

🅡 Abadía Retuerta Pago Negralada ££££

🅡 Alejandro Fernández Alenza ££££

🅦 Castilla la Vieja Palacio de Bornos £

🅡 Descendientes de J Palacios Bierzo ££

🅡 Durius Alto Duero Hacienda Zorita 2000 £

🅡 Emilio Moro Malleolus de Valderramiro ££££

🅦 Fillaboa Selección de la Familia ££

🅦 Marqués de Riscal Reserva Limousin ££

🅦 Martín Códax Gallaecia £££

🅡 Valdelosfrailes £

🅡 Viña Bajoz Gran Bajoz £££

Fariña
Castilla y León/Toro

Camino del Pal, Toro, Zamora
☏ *980 577 673*
🌐 *www.bodegasfarina.com* ☐

MANUEL FARIÑA IS arguably the man who put the Toro DO on the map. His father founded this business in 1942, but it was Manuel who brought new technology and new thinking to the winemaking. His 250ha are mainly planted with Tempranillo, and his wines are legendary: big, powerful, and plummy, they are the perfect match for the area's robust, meaty cuisine.
🍷 *red* 📅 *2005, 2004, 2003, 2002, 2001, 1999* ★ *Colegiata, Gran Colegiata, Primero*

Hacienda Durius
Castilla y León/Arribes

ctra Zamora-Fermoselle, km 56, Fermoselle, Zamora ☏ *980 613 163*
🌐 *www.arcobu.com* ●

THIS MODERN *bodega* was purpose-built by the ARCO Group, which has projects all along the river Duero and into Portugal's Douro region. The first vintage on this site was in 2003, under the Durius brand name, which had previously been produced elsewhere. The Tempranillo fruit style is rather cooler here than further south, and judicious cask ageing gives the wines a softer edge.
🍷 *red* 📅 *2005, 2004, 2003*
★ *Durius, Hacienda Zorita*

Hacienda Monasterio
Castilla y León/ Ribera del Duero

ctra Pesquera-Valbuena, Pesquera de Duero, Valladolid ☏ *983 484 002*
🌐 *www.haciendamonasterio.com* ☐

THIS MODERN winery has achieved singular fame in a very short time thanks to the vision of its dynamic owner,

Danish winemaker Peter Sisseck. Tempranillo is the dominant grape, with some Cabernet Sauvignon and Merlot. Sisseck has developed the Dominio de Pingus at Quintanilla de Onésimo, some 20km to the west, where he claims to make wine with the "maximum expression of the Tempranillo". The wine (Pingus) from this site is, at €800 a bottle, Spain's most expensive, but even the cheaper wines are supremely concentrated and beautifully structured.
🍷 *red* 📅 *2005, 2004, 2001, 1999*
★ *Hacienda Monasterio, Pingus, Flor de Pingus*

Marqués de Riscal
Castilla y León/Rueda

ctra N-IV, km 172.600, Rueda, Valladolid ☏ *983 868 029*
🌐 *www.marquesderiscal.com* ☐

THIS WAS the *bodega* that re-invented Rueda DO in 1972. Francisco Hurtado of Marqués de Riscal *(see p309)* wanted to make a white wine, but was unimpressed by white Riojas, so he began looking for an alternative location. After many pilot plantings he settled on Rueda as having the best native white grape (Verdejo). He built a new winery, and also persuaded the *consejo regulador* to permit plantings of Sauvignon Blanc. His Verdejo has a crisp, herby freshness that is very appealing. A 100 per cent Verdejo Reserva Limousin with six months in cask and a non-DO Tempranillo red, simply called Riscal, are also made.
🍷 *red, white* 📅 *red: 2006, 2005, 2004, 2003; white: most recent* ★ *Marqués de Riscal, Reserva Limousin*

Mauro
Castilla y León/VdlT

Cervantes 12, Tudela de Duero, Valladolid ☏ *983 521 439* 🌐 *www.bodegasmauro.com* ☐ *by appt*

THIS IS MARIANO GARCÍA'S family *bodega (see also* Aalto *p296),* established in 1980. Lying some 20km from the western boundary of the

Picker at Marqués de Riscal

Ribera del Duero DO, this vineyard's wines are classified as VdlT Castilla y León: nevertheless they are exemplary. Tempranillo predominates, but there is a sprinkling of both Garnacha and Syrah (banned within the DO). All the wines have the García touch: ripe, complex, and judiciously oaked.

🟥 red 🔺 2005, 2004, 2003, 2001 ★ Mauro

Maurodos
Castilla y León/Toro

ctra N-122, km 412, Villaester, Valladolid 📞 983 521 972
🆆 www.bodegasmauro.com 🔳

THIS IS ANOTHER venture by Mariano García's family, with the singular aim of creating the Toro DO's finest wine. The first vintage – Viña San Román 1999 – was 100 per cent Tempranillo with 22 months in cask and is already showing superb quality. In line with all Garcia's wines, San Román is a modern classic: rich, structured, and powerful, yet with a subtle delicacy. Like his Aalto estate (see p296), Maurodos is a member of Grandes Pagos de Castilla.

🟥 red 🔺 2006, 2005, 2004, 2003, 2001, 1999 ★ Viña San Román, Prima

Valdelosfrailes
Castilla y León/Cigales

ctra Cubillas, Cubillas de Santa Marta, Valladolid 📞 983 485 028
🆆 www.valdelosfrailes.es 🔳

VALDELOSFRAILES is part of the Matarromera group, which originated in neighbouring Ribera del Duero and controls six bodegas and a distillery. It makes a delicious Tempranillo joven as well as two even better cuvées with a year or more in oak. The basic

Valdelosfrailes is a fine example of a good, young wine with plenty of fruit, designed to be enjoyed the year after the vintage.

🟥 red 🔺 2006, 2005, 2004, 2003, 2002, 2001, 2000 ★ Valdelosfrailes, Prestigio, Vendímia Seleccionada

Vega Sicilia
Castilla y León/Ribero del Duero

ctra N-122, km 323, Valbuena de Duero, Valladolid 📞 983 680 147
🆆 www.vegasicilia.com 🔳

RIBERA DEL DUERO'S oldest, most prestigious fine wine bodega was founded in 1864, although the first commercial bottle appeared only in 1915. It still turns out immaculate wines of the quality for which it became famous – before anyone had even heard of Ribera del Duero. The 200ha of vines are mainly Tempranillo, with a substantial minority of Cabernet Sauvignon, Merlot, and Malbec. Typically wines are 80 per cent Tempranillo:

the five-year-old Valbuena is aged for 30 months in oak, while the legendary Único is matured for anything up to 15 years. Vega Sicilia also owns nearby Alión, which makes wines in a more modern style from 100 per cent Tempranillo with just 12 months in oak.

🟥 red 🔺 1998, 1996, 1994, 1991, 1989 ★ Valbuena, Alión, Único (1989)

Viña Bajoz
Castilla y León/Toro

av de los Comuneros 90, Morales de Toro, Zamora 📞 980 698 023
🆆 www.vinabajoz.com 🔳

FOUNDED IN 1962, this co-op in the Toro DO has reinvented itself in the past few years, improving all stages of production. Now, its 1,000ha of Tempranillo are producing wines approaching world-class status – though for the most part, still at co-op prices. Gran Bajoz is a stunning, elegant, powerful, structured example.

🟥 red 🔺 2006, 2005, 2004, 2003, 2001 ★ Bajoz, Gran Bajoz

THE EVOLUTION OF VEGA SICILIA WINES

In the early 20th century Vega Sicilia was in the hands of a Basque winemaker, Domingo Garramiola. He had carte blanche with investment, time, and winemaking style and soon established a reputation for quality. He used grapes from the oldest, lowest-producing vines to make a wine with deep, perfumed fruit and tremendous staying power. The wine traditionally spent 10 years in the cask before release. Mariano García became winemaker in 1966 and gradually the wine evolved away from the original heavily-oaked styles, maintaining its great concentration,

perfume, and depth in order to preserve the essential character. Then in 1982 David Álvarez bought Vega Sicilia and invested heavily to modernize the bodega and put the wines on a proper commercial basis. Now with winemaker Xavier Ausás at the helm, the work continues. Vega Sicilia Único, if not quite the heavy, oaky giant of the past, remains beautifully constructed, and harmonious, with dark, powerful fruit and a long bottle life.

Vineyards among barley fields in Navarra

WINEGROWING AREAS OF NORTHEAST SPAIN

NORTHEAST SPAIN includes four of the most dynamic wine-producing regions in the country – La Rioja, Navarra, Aragón, and Catalunya – with 19 DO zones, including two DO Pagos in Navarra. Proximity to France and the ports of Bilbao and Barcelona have helped to establish many DOs as household names, while others in the area have yet to reach such heights of public recognition.

País Vasco

PAÍS VASCO, or the Basque Country (Euskadi in Basque) consists of three provinces: Bizkaia (Vizcaya in Castilian Spanish) and Gipuzkoa (Guipúzcoa), west–east along the north coast, and Araba (Álava), located between them in the south. The southern part of this province is devoted to making Rioja (Alavesa). The traditional Basque wine is called 'Chacolí' in Castilian, followed by the name of its province – for example, 'Chacolí de Guetaria'. However, wines are much more likely to be labelled in Basque, as 'Getariako Txakolina', 'Bizkaiko Txakolina', and 'Arabako Txakolina'. In each case, the grapes are the same, unique to Basque viticulture: the Hondarribi Zuri (white) and Hondarribi Beltza (red). The wines are mainly white, very fresh and crisp, clean, and delicious on a hot day, especially with the local seafood.

Marqués de Riscal label, La Rioja

🗞 sandy soil over clay 🍇 Hondarrabi Beltza, Tempranillo 🍇 Hondarrabi Zuri 🍷 red, white

La Rioja

SPAIN'S FLAGSHIP WINE, Rioja, takes its name from this region. Even before the Romans were here in the second century BC, the grapes for this easy-drinking, fresh red were grown on freestanding bush vines and pressed by foot in stone troughs. The tradition remained for nearly 2,000 years. The 1850s saw the introduction of new technology by inspired Bordeaux pioneers *(see p302)*, including high-quality oak vats for fermenting and well-made casks for ageing. These slowly began to bring out a complexity and longevity in what had, until then, been a simple country wine. This was the start of **Rioja** as we know it today.

Since the mid-1980s, there has been enormous investment to maintain the integrity and quality of this wine. The time, energy, and money invested proved worthwhile when Rioja was promoted in 1991 to Denominación de Origen Calificada (DOCa) – a special higher grade of classification than DO, assigned only to wines that have shown consistent quality over many years. Not every Rioja vintage since then has been worthy of the accolade, but in great years the quality is truly exceptional.

Only four grape varieties are permitted in red Rioja wines, and they come from three subregions: Rioja Alta in the northwest, Rioja Alavesa (in the País Vasco), and Rioja Baja in the southeastern part of Rioja and those parts of Navarra that fall within Rioja DOCa. Rioja

Alta and Alavesa's vines are grown at altitudes of up to 600m, and share clay soils rich in chalk and iron, where the best Tempranillo and Graciano grapes are found. Rioja Baja is lower (down to 300m) and hotter, with alluvial soils: Cariñena (Carignan or Mazuelo) and Garnacha (Grenache) grapes are grown here.

Rioja reds are ripe with strawberry-raspberry Tempranillo fruit, underpinned with a warm, oaky note: the result of barrel-ageing in the winery. There are four main types: *jóven*, *crianza*, *reserva*, and *gran reserva (see p291)*. However, Rioja also produces some white and rosé *(rosado)*. The whites are usually young and fresh from Macabeo (known locally as Viura) grapes, but there is also a traditional oaked style of white Rioja, most often made from Macabeo and Malvasía. These wines can age for many years, and tend to be something of an acquired taste.

iron-rich clay, chalk-rich clay Tempranillo, Garnacha, Cariñena, Graciano Macabeo, Malvasía, Garnacha Blanca red

Navarra

NAVARRA LIVED IN THE shadow of its more famous Rioja neighbour for years, turning out good to excellent rosé that sold (and still sells) well locally, but hardly at all outside Spain. Things started to change in the 1980s however, when new regulations allowed the planting of more grape varieties. Today, Navarra DO is making its mark with an eclectic array of wines including Cabernet Sauvignon, Chardonnay, Garnacha Blanca (White Grenache), Malvasía, Moscatel (Muscat), and Merlot, as well as the seven Rioja varieties. The creation of a local government centre, EVENA (first established in 1981) to research the vine-soil relationship has also helped the area's progression. Navarra divides into five regions: Valdizarbe, Tierra Estella, Ribera Alta, Baja Montaña, and

Ribera Baja. Altitudes vary from around 600m in Valdizarbe to less than 350m in Ribera Baja. The climate gets warmer as the land gets lower, making the highlands good for international grape varieties and the lowlands better for Garnacha and Cariñena.

It is almost impossible to sum up the wines of Navarra, but some of the best are still classic oaky Tempranillos, which age with consummate grace. Also to be found are rich-textured, barrel-fermented Chardonnay; perfumed, elegant Cabernet Sauvignon; and, more recently, delicious sweet white wines made from late-harvested Moscatel (Muscat). And Navarra is still experimenting: look out for Pinot Noir, Syrah, and Gewürztraminer, especially those from the cooler northern vineyards. Navarra is only the second region in Spain to ratify DO Pago legislation, and it has two such estates.

mostly gravel over chalk, sandy in lowlands Tempranillo, Cabernet Sauvignon Macabeo, Chardonnay red, white, rosé

Flat-topped vineyards of Rioja Alta, La Rioja

Aragón

THE OLD KINGDOM of Aragón is a relatively recent performer on the international wine market, even though its oldest DO, Cariñena, was established in 1960. There are four DO regions within the area's two provinces: **Campo de Borja**, **Calatayud**, and **Cariñena** in the province of Zaragoza, and **Somontano** further north in the province of Huesca.

The *terroir* of Zaragoza's three DOs is very similar: hot and dry, with intense summers and cold winters, soft, sandy soils over limestone bedrock, and altitudes from 350m to over 800m. Campo de Borja grows Garnacha, Tempranillo, and Cariñena, as well as Cabernet Sauvignon, Merlot, and Syrah. The best wines tend to be Garnacha-Tempranillo blends with minimal oak-ageing: these can be delicious, fresh, fruity, and good value. Lying to the southwest, Calatayud is Aragón's smallest DO, and it has the potential to produce quality wines at budget prices. The best here are also usually young, fresh Garnacha-Tempranillo blends, but there is some impressive work being carried out with varietal Cabernet Sauvignon, too. Then to the east is Cariñena, which gave its name to the Cariñena grape (Carignan), despite the fact that very little is actually planted in this area. More common is a very pleasant dry white made from Macabeo (Viura). Reds from Tempranillo and Garnacha (and, perhaps, Monastrell and Cabernet Sauvignon) seem to be the way of the future.

Castillo de Milmanda, Conca de Barberá, set in the vineyards of Catalunya

Somontano is completely different from the DOs in Zaragoza. The vineyards are scattered up the southern face of the Pyrénées. New investment and rebuilding have made this one of Spain's most dynamic new winemaking areas. The local grapes are Moristel (red) and Alcañón (white), but Tempranillo, Macabeo, Cabernet Sauvignon, Pinot Noir, Chardonnay, and even Gewürztraminer are grown here. Somontano wines are usually varietals, and the modern-style whites tend to be clean, fresh, and fruity.

▨ *sandy over brown limestone, sandstone with carbonates* ▧ *Garnacha, Tempranillo, Moristel, Cabernet Sauvignon* ▨ *Viura, Macabeo, Alcañón, Chardonnay* ▧ *red, white*

RIOJA: THE FRENCH CONNECTION

Historically, France has played a fundamental role in Rioja's success story. In 1852 Spanish nobleman Luciano de Murrieta (later the Marqués de Murrieta) borrowed quality oak casks from Bordeaux to create what is viewed as the first 'modern' Rioja. Nobleman Camilo Hurtado de Amézaga (later the Marqués de Riscal) also looked to Bordeaux for inspiration. He went on to establish a vineyard in 1856, and Spain's first industrial-scale *bodega* in 1860 (see p309). His success was largely due to the use of giant oak fermenting vats and expensive casks of French origin: beautifully coopered, airtight, and robust so that wine could be shipped to the Americas without detriment.

Marqués de Riscal barrel

A second French connection came about in the late 19th century when phylloxera (see pp528–9) struck, destroying vast tracts of French vineyards. With dwindling supplies of their own wine, the French looked to neighbouring Spain and discovered something akin to Bordeaux (albeit made mainly from Tempranillo). Such was their enthusiasm for Rioja that several French investors set up their own *bodegas* there to ensure continued supplies. This established an export market which continues today; Rioja is still France's foreign wine of choice.

Catalunya

A REGION with a truly independent spirit, Catalunya (Catalonia) has produced successful wines for more than half a century, not least thanks to the considerable efforts of the Torres family *(see p313)*. White grape vines have always grown in the largely Mediterranean climate here, and the local white wine – made from the area's 'big three' white grapes Parellada, Macabeo, and Xarel-lo – is the ideal match for local seafood. Yet when the tourism boom began in the 1960s, winemakers started making red wine in order to reduce the need to buy reds from elsewhere in Spain. Catalunya was among the first areas in the country to plant international varieties such as Cabernet Sauvignon. More adventurous producers planted awkward corners of the cool-climate Alt-Penedès area and a distinctive Catalan style of wine was soon established to rival that of any wine-producing area in Europe. Some of the wines are now among the most highly prized –

Freixenet label, Penedès

and highly priced – in Europe, and although the region still makes more white than red, it is the reds that usually boast international fame.

Catalunya has 11 DO zones, more than any other Spanish region. The most significant (and the largest with 27,500ha) is **Penedès** in the province of Barcelona. The second most prominent is **Priorat**, which with 1,800ha is in fact one of the smallest wine areas. It lies in the province of **Tarragona**, which is also a DO in its own right. More recent DO zones **Montsant** and **Costers del Segre** are also noteworthy. The other Catalan DOs are of mainly local significance, although their wines can be found on world markets. They are **Empordà-Costa Brava**, **Pla de Bages**, **Alella**, **Conca de Barberá**, and **Terra Alta**. The region of Catalunya is unique in that it also has the **Catalunya** DO, launched in 1999, which allows the blending of DO wines from several Catalan regions without losing DO status.

▨ *alluvial, sandy, clay over limestone, some granite and schist* ▧ *Cabernet Sauvignon, Merlot, Tempranillo* ▧ *Parellada, Macabeo, Xarel-lo, Chardonnay* ▧ *red, white*

Priorat

PRIORAT (PRIORATO) IS THE second-smallest wine area in Catalunya, yet it boasts one of the best reputations. Until the mid-1980s, this area was known for only one wine – Cartoixa Scala Dei Negre, an enormous, opaque red made with grapes from ancient Garnacha vines. This blockbusting wine is rumoured to last for 50 years, and is still a Priorat classic. Between 1987 and 1989, however, half a dozen young winemakers established vineyards around the rocky mountain-top town of Gratallops. They planted international varieties such as Cabernet Sauvignon, Merlot, Syrah, and Pinot Noir, and also took over old plantations of the local Garnacha. Most of them terraced their vineyards into the steep slopes of the river valley (up to 700m) where outcrops of schist make up the bedrock, providing excellent drainage. The result was a host of impressive classics called 'Clos'. Their wines, however, were completely outside the DO system and had to be sold initially as simple *vino de mesa* (table wine). In the most high-profile example, Álvaro Palacios *(see p311)* established two properties: first Clos Dofi (now Finca Dofi) and then Clos L'Ermita (now L'Ermita), making astonishingly complex and powerful wines. It was not long before the DO authorities offered these successful newcomers unconditional membership. More of these 'new-wave' producers have established themselves here since then.

Ploughing at Álvaro Palacios in Priorat

Raïmat's *bodega* built in 1918, Costers del Segre

Montsant

MONTSANT LIES IN THE foothills beneath Priorat and was, until 2001, part of the immense Tarragona DC. Winemakers here felt that they could emulate their elevated neighbours by making wines from old, low-yield vines using modern fermentation technology. They lobbied hard for a classification of their own, distinct from the vast Tarragona, and their efforts were rewarded with the demarcation of the Montsant DO in 2002. Montsant set out from the start to make something palpably better than the low-cost, everyday wines for the supermarket trade, made throughout Tarragona. Early results suggest that they are succeeding, with potential to become an affordable alternative to the wines of Priorat. Montsant reds are excellent, with inventive blends of traditional

Vineyards and the Sierra de Montserrat, Penedès

and international varieties, such as the Mas Collet from Celler de Capçanes, which combines Garnacha, Cariñena, Tempranillo, and Cabernet Sauvignon in a rich and elegant style.

Costers del Segre

THIS DO CAME INTO BEING as recently as 1987, largely due to one successful producer: Raïmat. Owned by Codorníu (of Cava fame), this large estate has 1,000ha planted mainly with Chardonnay, Cabernet Sauvignon, Merlot, and Tempranillo. The California-style wines – with plenty of easy-drinking, rich, ripe fruit – set the tone for the whole area, which is made up of seven subzones around the city of Lledia. As other producers set up, it is becoming one of Catalunya's most exciting wine zones.

Penedès

PENEDÈS IS THE HEART OF Spain's booming Cava industry *(see right)*. Located on a vast central plateau some 600m high, it is surrounded by mountain ranges which rise to 900m. The landscape has three main graduated levels of land, each making very different types of wine.

Baix-Penedès (below 250m) is where the grapes for everyday wines are grown. The light, crisp whites are made from the three regional favourites (Parellada, Macabeo, and Xarel-lo), and the early-drinking, fruity reds, which are enjoyed locally, are usually from Tempranillo and Garnacha. Mitja-Penedès (250–500m) is quite noticeably cooler and tends to produce grapes of better quality with fresher acidity yet perfect ripeness. Many of the vineyards supplying the Cava industry are in this part of Penedès.

Tempranillo from this level is among the best in the region, making lovely fresh wines with ripe, strawberry-raspberry fruit and a hint of spice. Finally, Alt-Penedès (over 500m) is where individual vineyard microclimates come into their own, promoting the successful ripening of varieties such as Pinot Noir, Chardonnay, and even Riesling. The climate here is cooler still and the mountainous outcrops provide nooks and crannies up to 800m altitude, all with their own characteristics. Yields tend to be lower and frost is more of a danger, but some of Catalunya's finest wines are made from grapes grown in this area.

Baleares

UNTIL THE 1980s all wine made in the Balearic Islands was drunk only locally, but that did not stop wine producers in Mallorca campaigning for their own DO, led by the biggest player, Bodegas Franja Roja (José L Ferrer). Their efforts paid off when the area of **Binissalem** was awarded DO status in 1991.

Surrounding the town of the same name, Binissalem DO sits on a gently rolling plain in the centre of Mallorca. Grapes grown here are mostly local – Manto Negro and Callet for robust reds, and Moll for light, fresh whites – as well as a little Monastrell, Cabernet Sauvignon, and Merlot. The wines are noticeably different from those on the mainland, and have a more artisanal feel: the Manto Negro may not be as sophisticated as Tempranillo, but it has a ripe richness that goes well with the local cuisine. In 1999, Binissalem was joined by a new DO, **Pla i Llevant de Mallorca**, which includes most of the eastern half of the island, with Manacor and Felanitx the main towns. These vineyards are lowland – from sea level to about 100m – with wines similar to those of Binissalem. However, several *bodegas* are doing some fascinating work with Tempranillo, as well as Cabernet Sauvignon and Merlot, especially Miquel Oliver, who makes a stunning Cabernet-Merlot called Ses Ferritges, which is aged for at least 18 months in oak.

light topsoil over alluvial, clay over limestone
Manto Negro, Callet, Tempranillo, Monastrell
Moll, Macabeo, Parellada, Chardonnay
red, white

CAVA: A CAUSE FOR CELEBRATION

Freixenet's estate in Sant Sadurní d'Anoia

Cava has been made by the traditional method *(see pp166–7)* since the 1860s, and although most of it is sold at low prices, there is a growing interest in premium quality wines. Cava is now the world's second best-selling sparkling wine, after champagne. The town of Sant Sadurní d'Anoia in Penedès is the source of about 90 per cent of Spain's Cava production. However, unlike other Spanish wine DO classifications, Cava is not confined to one geographic area. Grapes are grown all over Catalunya and may be blended from different areas, as long they come from registered Cava vineyards.

Styles & Grape Varieties
The main grapes are Parellada, which provides a creamy, soft body; Macabeo for crispness and acidity; and Xarel-lo for ripeness, structure, and complexity. Other permitted grape varieties include Chardonnay (some Cavas may be 100 per cent Chardonnay), and the red grapes Garnacha, Monastrell, Trepat, and Pinot Noir. Classic Cava brut has soft, creamy acidity, and is bone dry but with a gentle, sparky fruit; older wines may have a hint of game on the nose. Cava's other main characteristic is its affordability.

Recommended Producers
The two dominant companies in the business are Codorníu and Freixenet. Some of the smaller, independent houses also turn out wine of great individuality and style in smaller quantities – look out for the following:
Agustí Torelló (*www.torello.es*)
Mont-Ferrant (*www.montferrant.com*)
Gramona (*www.gramona.com*)
Juvé y Camps (*www.juveycamps.com*)
Giró Ribot (*www.giroribot.es*)
Rovellats (*www.cavasrovellats.com*)

Gramona Cava label

WINE TOUR OF LA RIOJA

L A RIOJA IS SPAIN'S largest red-wine producing region, with more than 11,000 growers, nearly 600 wineries, and an annual production approaching three million hectolitres (400 million bottles). The region centres on the bustling city of Logroño, but the many *bodegas* are found in the small towns and on grand private country estates. The landscape is spectacular, with mountains sloping down to the valley of the Ebro River and a number of old fortified towns and ancient villages.

Marqués de Riscal
Gran Reserva

① **Rioja Wine Museum**
This museum tells the whole story of Rioja wine and gives a good introduction to what can be seen on *bodega* visits. There are exhibits relating to wine as part of the local culture as well as descriptions of the land, soil, and viticultural practices, plus the opportunity to taste some of the region's superlative wines.
C 941 310 547

② **La Rioja Alta** △
This 'classic' house in Haro offers a comprehensive visitors' centre (and shop), with regular guided tours. Many of the winemaking tasks are still carried out by hand here, and there is the opportunity to see ancient and modern methods working side by side. *See p309.*
C 941 310 346 **W** www.riojalta.com

③ **Bodegas Miguel Merino**
One of the rising stars of La Rioja, this *bodega* was founded in 1993 and the first vintage (1994) was sold in 2000. The family-run winery is one of La Rioja's smallest, producing limited volumes of high-quality *reservas*. The pretty town of Briones is also worth visiting.
C 941 322 263 **W** www.miguelmerino.com

WINE FESTIVALS

During the summer months, La Rioja hosts a number of wine-related festivals. Every year on 11 June, the **Fiesta de San Bernabé** in Logroño commemorates a siege of 1521. Deprived of supplies, the locals resorted to eating fish caught in the Ebro River, with bread and wine. Today, the siege is commemorated with the handing out of fish, bread, and flasks of wine. Soon after, on 29 June, **La Batalla del Vino** in Haro forms part of the celebration of the fiestas of San Juan, San Felices, and San Pedro. The 'battle' involves participants throwing wine at each other.

La Batalla del Clarete (25 July) is the equivalent 'battle' in San Asensio in celebration of the fiesta of Santiago (*clarete* is a young, light red wine made locally). On 21 September Logroño's week-long **Fiesta de la Vendímia** sees the first grapes trodden ceremonially *(left)* in the city centre square on the feast day of San Mateo. The first wine of the new season is traditionally offered to the Virgen de Valvanera before the revelry begins. Find out more about the wine fiestas and local events at the Logroño tourist office *(see Visitors' Tips)*.

④ Bodegas LAN

Established in 1974, this *bodega* has gained a reputation for exemplary, classic Rioja. The impressive 640-sq-m vaulted barrel cellar has no internal columns. The wines, especially the Culmen de Lan Reserva, are equally noteworthy.

☎ 941 450 950
W www.bodegaslan.com

⑤ Bodegas Ortañón

This modern *bodega* (opened in 1985), makes excellent, well-priced *reservas*, and has also pioneered the region's new, sweet Moscatel wines. A small museum displays wine-related mosaics, statues, paintings, and stained glass by local artist Miguel Angél Sáinz.

☎ 941 234 200
W www.ontanon.es

A glass of Rioja

⑥ Laguardia ▷

Laguardia is a beautiful, fortified hilltop town with stunning views over the surrounding countryside. Its narrow, cobbled streets have dozens of tiny bars offering *cosechero* Rioja, a young, fresh, fruity – and very cheap – wine, made by the growers themselves.

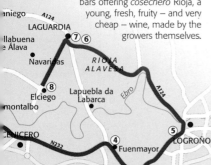

⑦ Bodegas Ysios ▽

This spectacular new winery, created in 1998 by the Valencia architect Santiago Calatrava, reflects the burgeoning confidence of La Rioja. The wood and steel construction was inspired by the Sierra de Cantabria mountains, which lie behind it. Deliciously tender wines reflect a return to the principles of *terroir*.

☎ 945 600 640 W www.comecqbodegas.com

KEY

━━ Tour route

0 ⌐ km ━━━━━━━━ 10

⑧ Marqués de Riscal ◁

One of the DO's oldest purpose-built *bodegas* is now also home to the newest architectural phenomenon. The stunning new company HQ, designed by Frank Gehry, incorporates a visitors' centre, museum, and restaurant. In the winery, ancient basket presses (still in use) exist alongside stainless steel fermenting vats. *See p309.*

☎ 941 606 000 W www.marquesderiscal.com

TOP PRODUCERS OF NORTHEAST SPAIN

Bodegas Marqués de Murrieta
La Rioja/Rioja

Castillo de Ygay, Ctra Logroño-Zaragoza, Rioja Alta **☎** *941 271 370*
W *www.marquesdemurrieta.com*
☐ *by appt*

THIS WONDERFUL old *bodega* was founded by Luciano de Murrieta, the first man to make modern-style Rioja in 1852 *(see p302)*. The Cebrán family have owned the estate since 1983, and have lovingly restored and extended it, introducing new wines and experimenting with single-vineyard plots. They have also brought the winemaking up to date, while preserving the traditions established by the original founder. Capellanía is a single-vineyard white wine made from old-vine Viura in the traditional oaky style. The flagship range is Ygay, boasting magnificent, deep, complex, perfumed *reservas* and *gran reservas*.
🍷 *red, white* 📅 *2006, 2005, 2004, 2001, 1998, 1996, 1995, 1994*
★ *Gran Reserva Castillo Ygay, Dalmau, Marqués de Murrieta, Capellanía*

Contino
La Rioja/Rioja

Finca de San Gregorio, Laserna, Álava **☎** *941 600 201*
W *www.cvne.com* **☐** *by appt*

THIS *BODEGA* not only makes one of the region's most respected wines – the eponymously named Contino – but also produces consistently high-quality single-vineyard wines. These include the rich, concentrated Viña del Olivo from a small vineyard around an olive tree, and the stunning, elegant yet powerful varietal Graciano,

La Rioja Alta label

made from one of Rioja's rarest grapes. Fifty per cent of Contino has been owned by CVNE since it was founded in 1974.
🍷 *red* 📅 *2005, 2004, 2001, 1998, 1996, 1995, 1994*
★ *Contino, Viña del Olivo*

CVNE
La Rioja/Rioja

Barrio del Estación, Haro, Rioja Alta **☎** *941 304 800*
W *www.cvne.com*
☐ *by appt*

ONE OF RIOJA'S OLDEST *bodegas*, established in 1879, CVNE (Compañía Vinícola del Norte de España) has recently invested heavily in new, state-of-the-art winery equipment. Its basic range comes from its own 560ha, but the best wines – Viña

Contino label

Real and Imperial Reserva – are made mainly from bought-in grapes. The first is from Rioja Alavesa and shows the freshness of ripe Tempranillo, while the second is mostly from Rioja Alta, with the classic mixture of Graciano and Garnacha.
🍷 *red* 📅 *2006, 2005, 2004, 2001*
★ *CVNE Imperial Reservas, Viña Real*

La Rioja Alta
La Rioja/Rioja

av Vizcaya, Haro, Rioja Alta
☎ *941 310 346*
W *www.riojalta.com* **☐** *by appt*

THIS 1890 VETERAN has always been owned and financed by the Aranzábal family. The best wines are still hand-made in the traditional manner, although some modern techniques have now been adopted, and stainless steel vats exist alongside old oak in the *bodega*. Viña Ardanza is widely regarded as the benchmark for *reserva* Riojas, with classic Tempranillo fruit, toasty American oak, and a long period in the cask.
🍷 *red* 📅 *2005, 2004, 2001, 1998, 1996, 1995, 1994*
★ *Viña Ardanza, Gran Reservas*

Marqués de Cáceres
La Rioja/Rioja

ctra Logroño, Cenicero, Rioja Alta
☎ 941 455 064 ⊞ *www.marques
decaceres.com* ◗

ENRIQUE FORNER, who founded
this house in 1970, learned
his trade in Bordeaux. The
company, officially known
as Unión Vitivinícola, was
the first to introduce
stainless-steel equipment
to Rioja, and has earned
itself a reputation for
consistency and quality.
The basic Marqués de
Cáceres is very reliable.
In 1996 a premium
wine called Gaudium
was introduced from
hand-selected grapes.
It combines the warmth
and power of traditional
Rioja with tremendous
ripeness and fragrance.
🔴 red, white 🍷 red: 2006,
2005, 2004, 2001, 1998;
white: most recent ★ Marqués
de Cáceres, Gaudium, Antea, MC

Marqués de Riscal
La Rioja/Rioja

c/Torrea 1, Elciego, Álava
☎ 945 606 000
⊞ *www.marquesderiscal.com* ◻

ESTABLISHED BY and named
after one of the original Rioja
pioneers *(see p302)*, this
company, now run by head of
the family Francisco Hurtado,
is still at the forefront of Rioja
production. One of the first
grape-sorting tables in Rioja
was installed here in 1995,
and a new HQ designed by
Frank Gehry (of Guggenheim
Bilbao fame) opened in 2006,
incorporating a visitor centre,
restaurant, and hotel behind
the *bodega (see p307)*. The
company also has one of the
oldest plantations of Cabernet
Sauvignon in Rioja. The Barón
de Chirél label, launched to
great acclaim in 1991,

combines Rioja spiciness
with Cabernet ripeness and
appealing aroma. Riscal's
reputation has been won by
assiduous attention to quality
and detail, and a willingness
to invest heavily when
investment is needed.
🔴 red 🍷 2005, 2004, 2001, 1998,
1996, 1995, 1994 ★ Marqués de
Riscal, Barón de Chirél

Guelbenzu
Navarra

San Juan 14, Cascante
☎ 948 850 055 ⊞ *www.
guelbenzu.es* ◻ *by appt*

**Julián
Chivite**

THIS COMPANY'S
vineyards were
replanted in the
1980s, but it was
virtually unheard-of
until wines began to
appear under the
Guelbenzu label in
the early 1990s. The
bodega withdrew
from the DO Navarra in
2002 in order to mix grapes
from other holdings in
difficult years and therefore
maintain its excellent
reputation. So the wines are
now labelled Vino de Mesa
del Ribera del Queiles. The
wines are made from
mature, low-yielding vines
and they are exemplary. Of
particular note is Lautus: a
Tempranillo-Merlot-Cabernet
Sauvignon-Garnacha blend
with 12 months in cask,
which is simply sublime.
🔴 red 🍷 2006, 2005, 2004, 2003,
2001, 1999 ★ Azul, Evo, Lautus

Irache
Navarra

Monasterio de Irache 1, Ayegui
☎ 948 551 932 ⊞ *www.irache.com*
◗ *by appt*

THIS IS AN OLD-ESTABLISHED
(1891) *bodega* right beside
the Camino de Santiago, and
it incorporates a courtyard

with a wine fountain for
passing pilgrims to help
themselves, as well as a
wine museum. The wines of
the basic range, Castillo de
Irache, represent excellent
value for money. The flagship
wine is Prado de Irache, a
Cabernet-Merlot-Tempranillo
mix with 12 months in French
oak. The grapes come from
a single 30-ha estate in the
northern part of Navarra. In
2008 the site was awarded
DO Pago status – the
second in Navarra and
only the sixth in Spain.
🔴 red, white, rosé 🍷 red: 2007, 2006,
2005, 2004, 2003, 2001, 1999, 1995;
white/rosé: most recent ★ Irache,
Castillo de Irache, Prado de Irache

Julián Chivite
Navarra

Ribera 34, Cintruénigo ☎ 948 811
000 ⊞ *www.bodegaschivite.com*
◻ *by appt*

FOUNDED IN 1647, Julián
Chivite is the oldest winery
in Navarra, and until the mid-
1980s it was responsible for
three quarters of all exports
from the DO. The basic range,
Gran Feudo, offers good
quality at modest prices. The
best wines, however, are a
buttery barrel-fermented
Chardonnay called Chivite
Colección and a Tempranillo-
Cabernet *reserva* titled
Colección 125, which boasts
impressive fruit and an oaky,
elegant, spicy aroma. In 1988
the family bought a single
estate, Señorío de Arínzano,
with 300ha of vines and an
ambition to make Navarra's
finest wine. The estate
became the first DO Pago
in the region in 2007. The
wines are spectacular – and
more than £100 per bottle.
🔴 red, white 🍷 red: 2007, 2006,
2005, 2004, 2003, 2001, 1999, 1995;
white: most recent ★ Gran Feudo,
Colección 125, Señorío de Arínzano

Grape picking, Ochoa

Ochoa
Navarra

Alcalde Maillata, 2, Olite ☎ 948 740
006 ⓦ www.bodegasochoa.com ⬚

THIS SMALL but dynamic
bodega founded in 1847 is
still run by the Ochoa family.
Javier, who makes the wine
with his daughter Adriana,
has contributed greatly to the
advancement of oenological
research in Navarra. The
company's 130ha of vines
deliver Tempranillo, Garnacha,
Cabernet Sauvignon, and
Merlot. One of the flagship
wines is Ochoa Tempranillo,
which is beautifully expressive
of the grape. Javier also
pioneered the lovely, flowery,
sweet Moscatel wines of
Navarra, which regularly win
awards. He has also produced
Navarra's first Moscato, a
low-strength Muscat wine
in the Italian style.
🟥 red, white, dessert 🔼 red: 2006,
2005, 2004, 2003, 2001; white: most
recent ★ Ochoa, Moscatel Dulce

Blecua
Aragón/Somontano

ctra Barbastro-Naval, Barbastro,
Somontano, Huesca ☎ 974 302 216
ⓦ www.bodegablecua.com
⬚ by appt

AN OFFSHOOT of Viñas del Vero,
this *bodega* makes a single
wine called Blecua from
Cabernet Sauvignon, Merlot,
and Garnacha, with up to 24

months in cask. Since the
2000 start-up, the aim has
been to make Somontano's
greatest wine, and the result
is an elegant nose hiding a
hefty, rich, smoky, powerful
palate that will probably take
several years to tame.
🟥 red 🔼 2003, 2002, 2001, 1998
★ Blecua

Bodega Pirineos
Aragón/Somontano

ctra Barbastro-Naval, Barbastro,
Somontano, Huesca ☎ 974 311 289
ⓦ www.bodegapirineos.com ⬚

SINCE THIS former co-operative
became a limited company in
1993, it has made enormous
strides with technology and
winemaking. The basic range
here is Bodega Pirineos; the
best wines are reds called
Señorío de Lazán, Montesierra,
and Marboré. The latter is
the finest: an eclectic mix
of Tempranillo, Cabernet
Sauvignon, Merlot, Moristel,
and Parraleta, with powerful
fruit and elegant, spicy tannins.
🟥 red 🔼 1998, 1997, 1996, 1995,
1993, 1990 ★ Señorío de Lazán,
Montesierra, Marboré

Bodegas San Alejandro
Aragón/Calatayud

ctra Calatayud-Cariñena 4, Miedes
de Aragón, Calatayud, Zaragoza
☎ 976 892 205
ⓦ www.san-alejandro.com ⬚ by appt

THIS CO-OPERATIVE *bodega* has
offered real quality and value
for money since the
mid-1990s. Its members
work some 1,300ha
of vineyards, mostly
growing the Aragón
staples Tempranillo and
Garnacha. The wines
are astonishingly good,
especially the Baltasar
Gracián Crianza, a
sublime Garnacha-
Tempranillo-Cariñena
mix with 12 months

in cask. In Spain it sells for
under €4 a bottle, though
some consider it to be worth
three times that amount.
🟥 red 🔼 2006, 2005, 2004, 2003,
2002, 2001 ★ Baltasar Gracián
Crianza

Covinca
Aragón/Cariñena

ctra Valencia, Longares, Cariñena,
Zaragoza ☎ 976 142 653 ⬚ by appt

COVINCA IS A LARGE, modern
co-operative with 3,000ha of
vineyards that has invested
heavily in modern winemaking
equipment. The best wines
are Garnacha-Tempranillo
blends. The estate's premium
Marqués de Ballestar range is
significantly better than the
basic Torrelongares range.
Made up to *gran reserva* level,
often with some Graciano
added to the very best wines,
it offers excellent value.
🟥 red 🔼 2006, 2005, 2004, 2003,
2002, 2001 ★ Marqués de Ballestar

Viñas del Vero
Aragón/Somontano

ctra Barbastro-Naval, Barbastro,
Somontano, Huesca ☎ 974 302 216
ⓦ www.vinasdelvero.es ⬚ by appt

FOUNDED IN 1986 as an
experimental facility for
Somontano, this company
expanded within just a few
years into one of the most
modern *bodegas* in Spain.
It now has 1,000ha and an
impressive reputation, making

Bodegas San Alejandro label

wines with international grapes as well as local varieties. The quality is uniformly high – especially the Gran Vos Reserva (Merlot-Cabernet-Pinot Noir), which is arguably one of Spain's finest reds.

🍷 *red, white* 🍷 *red: 2007, 2006, 2005, 2004, 2001, 2000, 1998, 1996; white: most recent*
★ *Viñas del Vero, Gran Vos Reserva*

Álvaro Palacios
Catalunya/Priorat

Aforès, Gratallops, Tarragona
📞 *977 839 195* ●

ÁLVARO PALACIOS, son of the Rioja family of the same name, was the most successful one of a group of pioneers who planted vines on the inhospitable slopes around Gratallops in the late 1980s. In doing so he helped to change the perception of Priorat's wines forever. All of the wines produced from his 25ha are impressive

examples of meticulous vine husbandry and skilful wine-making. Standing out from the crowd is the fabulously fragrant, complex, and rich L'Ermita. This is produced mainly from 100-year old Garnacha vines from steeply sloping vineyards, as well as a little Cabernet. It has now become one of the most sought-after, and most expensive, wines in Spain.

🍷 *red* 🍷 *2004, 2003, 2001, 1999, 1998, 1997, 1996, 1995* ★ *Les Terrasses, Finca Dofi, L'Ermita*

Álvaro Palacios

Agustí Torelló
Catalunya/Cava

La Serra, Sant Sadurní d'Anoia, Barcelona 📞 *938 911 173*
🌐 *www.torello.com* ○ *by appt*

ARGUABLY SPAIN'S FINEST Cava, Mata is classic *gran reserva* made from Parellada, Macabeo, and Xarel-lo. Mata Reserva Barrica is barrel-

fermented for a richer flavour, and crisp, fruity Kripta comes in a torpedo-shaped bottle (with a round base), priced at about €40.

🍷 *sparkling* 🍷 *2006, 2005, 2004, 2003, 2002, 2001, 2000*
★ *Mata, Kripta*

Celler de Capçanes
Catalunya/Montsant

Llaberia, Capçanes 📞 *977 178 319*
🌐 *www.cellercapcanes.com* ○ *by appt*

ANOTHER FORMER co-operative, now reconstituted as a limited company, Celler de Capçanes has helped lead the way for the Montsant DO. It has 300ha of vineyards and grows Garnacha, Mazuelo, Tempranillo, and Cabernet Sauvignon. Its best wine is Mas Tortó, a Garnacha-Merlot-Syrah-Cabernet Sauvignon blend matured for 14 months in cask, in which pure quality shines through.

🍷 *red* 🍷 *2006, 2005, 2004, 2003, 2002, 2001* ★ *Cabrida, Mas Collet, Mas Tortó*

---

12 NEW WAVE WINES FOR THE FUTURE

A selection of wines from a new generation of winemakers, who are making names for themselves in Northeast Spain:

🅱 Finca Allende Aurus
This Rioja is made from traditional grapes yet boasts concentration and complexity. ££££
📞 *941 322 301*

🅱 Castillo de Monjardín Merlot
A voluptuous Merlot made the toasty oak Navarra way. £
🌐 *www.monjardin.es*

🅱 Bàrbara Forés Coma d'en Pou
A rich, spicy Garnacha-Cabernet-Merlot-Syrah with 18 months in cask,

this wine is showing the way in Terra Alta. £££
📞 *977 420 160*

🅱 Viticultores Mas d'En Gil Coma Vella
An intense, powerful, fruity wine from Priorat (mainly Cariñena and Garnacha) with exotic, cigar-box aromatics. ££
🌐 *www.masdengil.com*

🅱 Bodegas Aragonesas Coto de Hayas Garnacha Centenaria
A new-wave red from an old Campo de Borja firm. Smoky-spicy old-vine Garnacha with a touch of oak. £
🌐 *www.bodegas aragonesas.com*

🅱 Vall-Llach Embruix
A Priorat wine that reveals the pure fruit

and ripeness of Cariñena and Garnacha. ££
🌐 *www.masmartinet.com*

🅱 Finca Valpiedra Classic
A ripe, Tempranillo-style Rioja with 16 months in oak. £££
🌐 *www.familiamartinez bujanda.com*

🅱 Castillo Perelada Gran Claustro
A Cabernet-Merlot from Empordà-Costa Brava with classic Catalan ripeness and fruit of tremendous power. £££
🌐 *www.perelada.com*

🅱 Castell del Remei Oda
A powerful Cabernet-Merlot-Tempranillo with toasty American oak – one of the rising stars of

Costers del Segre. ££
🌐 *www.castell delremei.com*

🅱 Roda Roda I
A tender, fruity, delicately structured Tempranillo which benefits from the Rioja Alta *terroir*. £££
🌐 *www.roda.es*

🅱 Miquel Oliver Ses Ferritges
A rich Cabernet-Merlot with 18 months oak, which leads the field for the Pla i Llevant de Mallorca DO. £
🌐 *www.miqueloliver.com*

🆆 Txomín Etxániz
A fabulously cool, crisp white from Getariako Txakolina, made from Hondarrabi Zuri. £
🌐 *www.txomin etxaniz.com*

Clos Mogador
Catalunya/Priorat

Camí Manyetes, Gratallops, Tarragona
☎ 977 839 171 ☐ *by appt*

RENÉ BARBIER was one of the Gratallops pioneers of 1987, and after building his winery there, he also decided to build himself a house on the side of a hill nearby. He only makes one wine here – Clos Mogador – although he also makes others through Europvin Falset *(see right)*. The Clos Mogador is a Garnacha-Cabernet Sauvignon-Syrah-Cariñena blend, aged for up to 16 months in cask, and, at its best, one of the greatest wines of Spain.
▧ *red* ▧ *2005, 2004, 2003, 2002, 2001, 2000* ★ *Clos Mogador*

Codorníu
Catalunya/Cava

av Jaime Codorníu, Sant Sadurní d'Anoia, Barcelona ☎ 938 183 232
ⓦ *www.codorniu.es* ☐

FOUNDED IN 1551, Codorníu is one of the two giants to have dominated the Spanish Cava scene. In 1872, it was the first company to create a cellar in which to make Cava in industrial quantities. Today the vast cellars house millions of bottles of bubbly, and the company controls 3,000ha of vineyards. Most production is of the traditional Parellada, Macabeo, and Xarel-lo, but Codorníu has always used a minimum of 40 per cent Chardonnay in all its wines. In the flagship wine, Jaume de Codorníu, the richness of the Chardonnay is counter-balanced by the sheer fresh-ness of the native varieties Macabeo and Parellada.
▧ *white, sparkling* ▧ *current vintage or non-vintage (NV)*
★ *Jaume de Codorníu, Cuvée Reina María Cristina, Non Plus Ultra*

Riddling racks of Cava in the cellar at Freixenet

Europvin Falset
Catalunya/Montsant

ctra Bellmunt, Falset, Tarragona
☎ 977 831 712 ◉

BORDEAUX-BASED Englishman Christopher Cannan and Priorat's René Barbier set up this *bodega* in 1999, and have demonstrated just how close Montsant can come to Priorat in terms of quality. The aromatic and complex Laurona is mainly a Garnacha-Cariñena mix with a little Syrah and Cabernet and has tremendous concentration. The other wine – 6 Vinyes de Laurona – is better still and could seriously challenge Montsant's famous mountainside neighbour.
▧ *red* ▧ *2005, 2004, 2003, 2002, 2001, 2000* ★ *Laurona, 6 Vinyes de Laurona*

Freixenet
Catalunya/Cava

Joan Sala 2, Sant Sadurní d'Anoia, Barcelona ☎ 93 891 7096
ⓦ *www.freixenet.es* ☐ *by appt*

SPAIN'S OTHER major Cava player, Freixenet, was founded in 1889. It is strictly tradition-alist, and vigorously opposes the use of any grapes other than the big three – Parellada, Macabeo, and Xarel-lo – for

white Cava. Their most famous wine is Cordón Negro, yet the best is Reserva Real, originally created for a royal visit to mark Freixenet's centenary. With a special reserve of old wine as part of its blend, this *reserva* reveals exceptional complexity.
▧ *white, sparkling* ▧ *current vintage or non-vintage (NV)*
★ *Cuvée DS, Reserva Real, Siglo XX*

Raïmat
Catalunya/Costers del Segre

Afueras, 25111 Raïmat, Lleida
☎ 973 724 000
ⓦ *www.raimat.com* ☐ *by appt*

THIS GIANT, 3,000-ha estate kick-started winemaking in the province of Lleida in 1918 and was the principal reason for the creation of the Costers del Segre DO in 1987. The owners of this positively space-age winery are the Raventós family of Codorníu. The style is Californian (the winemakers trained there), and the best wine is the stunning Raïmat 4 Varietales Gran Reserva: a blend of Cabernet, Merlot, Tempranillo, and Pinot Noir with 24 months in cask.
▧ *red, white* ▧ *red: 2007, 2006, 2005, 2004, 2003, 2001, 1998, 1997; white: most recent* ★ *Raïmat Abadía, Raïmat El Molí, Raïmat 4 Varietales*

THE TORRES EMPIRE

The most prominent producer in Catalunya, Torres has been in existence since 1800. It was, however, the late Miguel Torres Carbó, the third generation to run the business, who put the Torres name on the international map. During the 1940s and 50s, he travelled extensively to establish the Torres brand name worldwide. Torres was among the first to bring international grape varieties to Catalunya, and famously trumped the Gault-Millau Wine Olympics in Paris in 1970, when the Cabernet Sauvignon Gran Coronas Black Label (now known as Mas la Plana) beat all the top Bordeaux wines in a blind tasting. The company has never hesitated to innovate, promote, experiment, and develop its wines or its markets, and has interests in Chile and California. The fifth Torres generation is now at work: Miguel Carbó's grandson, another Miguel, looks after Jean León (now part of the Torres portfolio); while his granddaughter Mireia develops a new range of fresh, citrus whites and rich, spicy-peppery reds under the Nerola label.

Miguel Agustin Torres

The current head of the firm, Miguel Agustín Torres trained in Madrid, Montpellier, and Dijon, meticulously studying vine husbandry and winemaking. In 1962, he established Spain's first winery with stainless steel equipment to control fermentation, and has worked tirelessly in the vineyards ever since.

Practical Information

M Torres 6, Vilafranca del Penedès, Barcelona 🕾 938 177 400 🆆 www.torres.es ☐ by appt

Wine Information

🖼 red, white 📷 red: 2006, 2005, 2004, 2003, 2002, 2001, 2000, 1999, 1998; white: most recent ★ Gran Coronas, Mas Borras, Mas la Plana, Fransola, Gran Viña Sol, Milmanda

The Wines

Classic Torres wines tend to be varietals, including Sauvignon Blanc, Chardonnay, Moscatel (Muscat), Gewürztraminer, and Riesling, as well as Pinot Noir and Cabernet Sauvignon (the latter for the flagship wine Mas la Plana). Over the years, several almost-extinct Catalan species have also been carefully coaxed back into cultivation, and one of the wines – Crans Muralles – is made from a selection of ancient Catalan grape varieties, including Garró.

The Torres' Mas la Plana vineyard, Baix-Penedès

WINE MAP OF CENTRAL & SOUTHERN SPAIN

THIS IS A VAST AREA encompassing five autonomous regions, which break down into 35 DOs, including four of Spain's six Pagos (single estates). Some DOs are only of local interest; others, such as Jumilla and Yecla, boast a few star producers; and a couple, most notably La Mancha and Valencia, are making waves in the outside world, especially in terms of value-for-money wines. Of most significance is the Jerez DO, producing sherry, Spain's oldest and (now) second best-selling wine.

Piqueras rosé

KEY

Central & Southern Spain

CENTRAL SPAIN: AREAS & TOP PRODUCERS

MADRID & EXTREMADURA
p316

CASTILLA-LA MANCHA
p316

Dehesa del Carrizal *p319*
Dominio de Valdepusa *p319*
Félix Solís *p319*
Finca Élez *p319*
Pago Guijoso *p319*
Piqueras *p320*
Vinícola de Castilla *p320*

VALENCIA & MURCIA *p317*

Agapito Rico *p320*
Casa Castillo *p320*
Enrique Mendoza *p320*
Mustiguillo *p320*

SOUTHERN SPAIN: AREAS & TOP PRODUCERS

ANDALUCÍA *p318*

Alvear *p321*
Bentomiz *p321*
Emilio Lustau *p321*
González Byass *p321*
Hidalgo-La Gitana *p321*
Perez Barquero *p321*

CANARIAS (CANARY ISLANDS) see *p318*

Vineyards on La Mancha plain, Castilla-La Mancha

TERROIR AT A GLANCE

Latitude: 36–40.5°N (Mainland); 28°N (Canarias).

Altitude: 0–3,432m.

Topography: Central Spain is a vast *meseta* (plateau), dominated by Madrid at an altitude of 650m. The *meseta* climbs towards the mountainous area of Andalucía in the south. From there, land falls in a series of plateaux towards sea level. The Canarias (Canary Islands), volcanic in origin, have some of the highest vineyards in the world (over 1,500m).

Soil: Sandy clay throughout, with rich limestone in places.

Climate: Harsh, with huge temperature ranges. Andalucía is hot-Mediterranean, (although the highlands are much wetter than the lowlands) and the Canarias are subtropical.

Temperature: Annual July average is 33°C in Córdoba on the mainland and 28°C in the Canarias.

Rainfall: Annual average is 625mm in Córdoba on the mainland and 200mm in the Canarias.

Viticultural hazards: Summer drought.

Harvesting grapes, Andalucía

PERFECT CASE: CENTRAL & SOUTHERN SPAIN

Ⓡ Agapito Rico Carchelo £

Ⓓ Bentomiz Ariyanas Dulce £££

Ⓡ Casa Castillo Pie Franco £££

Ⓡ Dehesa del Carrizal Cabernet Sauvignon ££

Ⓡ Dominio de Valdepusa Eméritus ££££

Ⓓ Enrique Mendoza Dolç de Mendoza ££

Ⓡ Félix Solís Viña Albali Gran Reserva £

Ⓡ Finca Élez Manuel Manzaneque Nuestro Syrah ££

Ⓕ González Byass Tío Pepe £

Ⓡ Mustiguillo Quincha Corral £££

Ⓡ Piqueras Castillo de Almansa £

Ⓡ Vinícola de Castilla Guadianeja Reserva ££

Vines in albariza soil, Jerez, Andalucía

Vines in sandy clay, Valdepeñas, Castilla-La Mancha

WINEGROWING AREAS OF CENTRAL & SOUTHERN SPAIN

CENTRAL SPAIN

IN THE VAST AREA that lies between Madrid and the Andaluz border, there are 16 DO zones and four DO Pagos (single estates). Over the past two decades, the *bodegas* here – especially in La Mancha DO – have been working steadily to improve quality. The best have proved beyond doubt that Central Spain is an area capable of producing world-class wines.

Madrid & Extremadura

THE AREA SOUTH of Madrid and continuing south and west towards the Portuguese border falls in **Vinos de Madrid** DO, which tends to grow Malvar for white wines and Garnacha for reds. In the last five years, work with other varieties (especially Tempranillo) has produced some world-class wines here. To the west, Extremadura's **Ribera del Guadiana** DO is an area to watch. Created in 2001, a couple of producers have made investments here, and as a result have been able to make inroads into export markets.

Emilio Lustau label, Jerez, Andalucía

🍇 *sandy clay over limestone and chalk*
🍷 *Tempranillo, Monastrell, Bobal* 🍇 *Airén, Merseguera* 🍷 *red, white*

Castilla-La Mancha

THIS VAST REGION, sprawling to the south-southwest of Madrid, has enormous viticultural potential. Vast quantities of wine are produced here, but of its eight DOs, only **La Mancha** and **Valdepeñas** are producing large quantities of fine wine. La Mancha was long regarded as a source of cheap wine for the capital, but low land prices in the 1970s attracted massive investment. So, while the area is still producing simple, value-for-money wines, there are also a number of *bodegas* turning out some superlative examples. The main grape here is Tempranillo (known locally as Cencibel), which is spicy, rich, and redolent of summer fruit. Complex Tempranillo-based reds, some-times with a dash of Cabernet Sauvignon or even Syrah, are judiciously aged in cask. The main white grape in La Mancha is Spain's most planted white variety, Airén, which is light, fresh, and aromatic. To the south of La Mancha, in the dry, hot enclave of Valdepeñas at the edge of the *meseta* (plateau), the main grape is Tempranillo and the wine style is very much oaky and mature, with rich fruit. This is one of Spain's best-value DO zones, where prices are usually ridiculously low and the latest technology has often yielded fantastic results.

The other six DOs are: **Almansa**, which has the occasional star producer; **Méntrida**, struggling, with quite a way to go; **Manchuela**, created in 2000 and starting to show promise; **Mondéjar**, promoted to DO status in 1997 and on the up; **Ribera del**

Júcar, set up in 2003 as a result of some promising work and producing interesting results; and the small **Uclés**, around the town of the same name, which followed in 2005 for the same reasons. Four of Spain's six DO Pagos (single-estate wines) are also situated in Castilla-La Mancha *(see p319).*

red-brown sandy clay, some limestone/chalk *Tempranillo, Garnacha, Monastrell* *Airén, Macabeo* *red, white*

Valencia & Murcia

THIS REGION (ALSO KNOWN AS THE LEVANT) has six DO zones but fine wines are scarce. The emphasis has always been on export (with quantity winning over quality), and many supermarkets around the world will have something cheap and cheerful from this area simply labelled as 'Spanish white' or 'Spanish red'. One of the three DO zones in Valencia, **Alacant** (Alicante) grows Merseguera for white wines as well as Monastrell grapes for heavy reds. These are good, wholesome wines, if not very exciting. The vineyards of **Utiel-Requena** DO show slightly more promise due to the high altitude (up to 800m), which gives more flexibility to the wine-makers. There seems to be potential here for some excellent-quality wines made from the native red grape Bobal, formerly thought fit only for bulk wines. The **Valencia** DO, too, produces reds and whites (Monastrell and Merseguera) for the masses, immaculately made and at bargain prices. There is also an

Harvesting Airén grapes in La Mancha

ANDALUCÍA'S HEIGHTS

In the deep south, where wines have traditionally been fortified, altitude is the new attitude: the higher up you get from the scorched lowlands, the better it is for viticulture. Some shrewd investors have consequently started to buy land here for the production of non-fortified wines. Work in the Alpujarras vineyards – at over 1,500m, the highest in mainland Europe – is showing that Garnacha and Tempranillo can be grown in Andalucía without over-ripening. Elsewhere in the Sierra Nevada, Señorío de Nevada, an estate in Villamena, is successfully growing Syrah and Merlot. In Ronda to the west, even an altitude of 750m facilitates fascinating experiments with Tempranillo and Petit Verdot. Several *bodegas* have come in to exploit the opportunities here, including El Chantre, Descalzos Viejos, and Bentomiz, all in Málaga. Judging by positive results so far, other producers and investors will no doubt soon follow.

enthusiastic market for the local sweet wine – the often stellar Moscatel de Valencia.

Murcia's three DO zones all make wines in a similar style to those of neighbouring Valencia, primarily growing Monastrell for reds and Merseguera or Macabeo for whites. **Jumilla** is the region that successfully rehabilitated the Monastrell grape and has a few star producers such as Agapito Rico, while **Yecla** is a one-town DO with the occasional stand-out *bodega*. To the southwest, **Bullas** is the most recent DO and is starting to show good work with Monastrell.

red-brown soil over limestone, some clay *Tempranillo, Garnacha* *Merseguera, Malvasía* *red, white*

SOUTHERN SPAIN

ANDALUCÍA IS WHERE winemaking in Spain, and indeed in western Europe, began around 500 BC. The wines were robust, strong, and sweet, and they evolved into what is now known as sherry. Today, sherry and its sister wines from Montilla and Málaga are still being made, but the region is also beginning to produce impressive red and white wines, especially in cooler mountain highlands *(see above).*

Andalucía

ANDALUCÍA IS THE HOME of sherry, a wine unique in the world both for the way it is made and its numerous styles (see pp322–3). Since the mid-1990s the term sherry, formerly a generic term for a range of fortified wines, can – within the EU – only be applied to wines produced in the **Jerez** DO. These range from the palest, most delicate manzanilla, drunk as a dry white wine and best accompanied by the local seafood, to the opaque, midnight-black, and richly sweet Pedro Ximénez. Most sherry is made with the Palomino grape, which thrives in the very chalky *albariza* soils of the vineyards around the three sherry towns: Jerez de la Frontera in the centre, and Puerta de Santa María and Sanlúcar de Barrameda on the coast.

Montilla-Moriles' best wines are made just like sherry: in fact, Montilla lends its name to *amontillado* sherry for the resemblance between the two wines. However, here the base grape is Pedro Ximénez rather than Palomino, and Montilla wines are naturally strong and may be unfortified, whereas sherry is always fortified. Montilla wines come in 'dry', 'medium', and 'cream' styles as well, and they are bidding strongly to win back their market, especially with the sweet Pedro Ximénez wines. The **Condado de Huelva** DO, between Jerez and the Portuguese border, makes fortified wines from the local Zalema grape, while further east, **Málaga** DO is known for its lovely, dark, toffee-caramel flavoured fortified wine from Pedro Ximénez. Sadly, land in Málaga is more valuable for holiday homes than for vines, and the area given over to vineyards is shrinking.
🗺 sand or clay over limestone, very chalky in the west 🍇 Palomino, Pedro Ximénez 🍷 fortified

Barrels of Montilla

Harvesting Palomino grapes in Andalucía

Canarias (Canary Islands)

THERE ARE NO FEWER than 11 DO zones in the Canarias, scattered across all the islands with the exception of Fuerteventura. However, only two produce enough wine to tap into the export market. **Tacoronte-Acentejo** (Tenerife) is the oldest and most important DO zone on the islands, making warm, robust reds and fresh, clean whites with the local Listán Negro and Gual grapes, as well as classic sweet whites from Malvasía. The reds have most potential – at their best they have a rich, perfumed style and can age well in oak.

Lanzarote DO, where the vines are planted in pits carved out of the lava bedrock, is the home of the ancient, sweet white wines known in Shakespeare's time as 'Canary Sack' and made from Malvasía and Moscatel. Though producers now make more mainstream reds and whites, the sweet wines are still produced, and can be superb – delicately perfumed and gently sweet with a freshness which prevents cloying. The other DOs are of little significance, although their wines are widely enjoyed locally. Most of them make reds and whites from the local Listán Negro and Malvasía, and some grow grapes such as Bujariego (Vijariego) and Gual – long near-extinct on the mainland.
🗺 volcanic 🍇 Listán Negro, Negramoll
🍇 Pedro Ximénez, Malvasía, Moscatel, Verdello, Vijariego 🍷 red, white, dessert

TOP PRODUCERS OF CENTRAL & SOUTHERN SPAIN

Dehesa del Carrizal
Castilla-La Mancha/ Pago DO

Retuerta del Bullaque, Ciudad Real
☎ *925 421 773*
Ⓦ *www.dehesadelcarrizal.com* ☐

LOCATED IN the Montes de Toledo region, this *bodega* was promoted to DO Pago status in 2006, a move justified by its outstanding record. It was established in 1987, with 22ha growing Chardonnay, Cabernet, Merlot, and Syrah, which is showing extremely well.
🍷 *red* 🍇 *2003, 2002, 2001, 2000, 1999* ★ *Chardonnay, Cabernet Sauvignon*

Dominio de Valdepusa
Castilla-La Mancha/ Pago DO

ctra San Martín de Pusa, km 6.5, Malpica de Tajo, Toledo ☎ *914 114 202* Ⓦ *www.pagosdefamilia.com* ◕

THE VISIONARY CARLOS FALCÓ put Toledo on the wine map in the 1970s with this estate, He produces stunning Cabernet Sauvignon, Syrah, and Petit Verdot – a variety he introduced to Spain. In 1998 Falcó produced Eméritus, a Syrah-Cabernet Sauvignon-Petit Verdot blend, aged for 13 months in barrel, which possesses tremendous warmth and complexity.
🍷 *red* 🍇 *2003, 2002, 2000, 1999, 1997* ★ *Dominio de Valdepusa Eméritus*

Félix Solís
Castilla-La Mancha/ Valdepeñas

Autovía Andalucía, km 199, Valdepeñas, Ciudad Real ☎ *926 322 400* Ⓦ *www.felixsolis.com* ☐

SPAIN'S BIGGEST single wine producer is an ultra-modern outfit with a vast ware-

Selection of Félix Solís wines

house worked by robots. Red wines are made entirely from Tempranillo: the more basic ones are Soldepeñas, Los Molinos, and Viña Albali – arguably Spain's best-value red, full of fruit and warmth.
🍷 *red* 🍇 *2007, 2006, 2005, 2004, 2003, 2002, 2001, 2000* ★ *Viña Albali*

Finca Élez
Castilla-La Mancha/ Pago DO

ctra Ossa de Montiel-Bonillo, El Bonillo, Albacete ☎ *967 585 003* Ⓦ *www.manuelmanzaneque.com* ☐

IN 1992, FILM AND THEATRE director Manuel Manzaneque established himself in the Sierra de Alcaraz, overseeing a different kind of production. His vineyards, now DO Pago status, are located at around 1,000m, where the cooler microclimates allow

the Syrah, Chardonnay, Merlot, Cabernet Sauvignon, and Tempranillo vines to flourish. The best and most widely available wines are the big, barrel-fermented Chardonnay and the warm, spicy Syrah.
🍷 *red, white* 🍇 *red: 2005, 2004, 2003, 2002, 2001, 2000, 1999; white: most recent* ★ *Manzaneque Finca Élez, Manuel Manzaneque Nuestro Syrah*

Pago Guijoso
Castilla-La Mancha/ Pago DO

Ctra Ossa de Montiel-El Bonillo, km 11, Albacete ☎ *967 370 750* Ⓦ *www.sanchez-muliterno.com* ☐

EDUARDO SANCHEZ MULITERNO is the chairman of this family-owned company with 99ha of vines at a dizzying 1,000m altitude. It grows Cabernet, Merlot, Tempranillo, Syrah, Chardonnay, and Sauvignon and produces a range of four wines under the DO Pago. The flagship wine is Magnificus, a 100 per cent Syrah with 12 months in French (Alliers) oak. There is also a 'second wine' under the VdlT Castilla.
🍷 *red, white* 🍇 *2005, 2004* ★ *Divinus, Vega Guijoso, Viña Consolación, Magnificus*

SPAIN'S DO PAGOS

In 2001, Dominio de Valdepusa became the first DO Pago, recognized only by the regional government of Castilla-La Mancha. In 2003, DO Pago was endorsed as Spanish wine's highest category, reserved for single-estate wines bottled on the estate and with a strong international reputation. Regional governments must ratify the legislation individually, and so far only Navarra has followed Castilla-La Mancha. As of 2008, there were six DO Pagos in those regions: Dominio de Valdepusa (since 2003, Toledo), Finca Élez (2003, Albacete), Pago Guijoso (2004, Albacete), Dehesa del Carrizal (2006, Ciudad Real), Señorío de Arínzano (2007, Navarra), and Prado de Irache (2008, Navarra).

Piqueras
Castilla-La Mancha/ Almansa

Zapateros, Pol Ind El Mugrón, Almansa, Albaccete
☎ 967 341 482
Ⓦ www.bodegaspiqueras.com ▢

FOR MANY YEARS this was the only noteworthy *bodega* in the DO zone of Almansa, and certainly the only one with even a toehold in the export market. The winery has 220ha under cultivation, and makes Monastrell and Tempranillo reds to *reserva* standard. Piqueras has shown the way for numerous up-and-coming new producers in Almansa. All the Piqueras wines are good, but the *reserva* – well-structured, big, and rich – positively shines.
▨ red ⤷ 2005, 2004, 2003, 2002, 2001 ★ Castillo de Almansa

Vinícola de Castilla
Castilla-La Mancha/ La Mancha

Pcl Ind Calle 1, Manzanares, Ciudad Real ☎ 926 647 800
Ⓦ www.vinicoladecastilla.com ▢

ONE OF THE FIRST newcomers to build a state-of-the-art *bodega* (in 1976), this estate has 150ha of vines producing mostly red wines, principally from Tempranillo, with some Cabernet Sauvignon and Merlot. The wine-making is impecca-ble. If money is no object, the best of their range is the big, spicy Señorío de Guadianeja Reserva.
▨ red ⤷ 2005, 2004, 2003, 2002, 2001, 2000, 1999 ★ Castillo de Alhambra, Señorío de Guadianeja Reserva

Emilio Lustau label

Agapito Rico
Valencia & Murcia/Jumilla

Casa de la Hoya, Paraje El Carche, Jumilla, Murcia ☎ 968 435 137
Ⓦ www.carchelo.com ▢

ONLY IN THE mid-90s was it shown that Monastrell could make a world-class wine – a discovery that made Agapito Rico wonder what else the high-altitude land around Jumilla could be persuaded to do. The fine result is Carchelo, a delicious and judicious mix of Monastrell and Tempranillo. He also planted Cabernet Sauvignon, Merlot, and, most notably, a huge, spicy Syrah, which makes his flagship wine with just a 'bite' of three months in cask.
▨ red ⤷ 2005, 2004, 2003, 2002, 2001, 2000, 1999 ★ Carchelo

Casa Castillo
Valencia & Murcia/ Jumilla

ctra Jumilla-Hellin, km 15.7, Jumilla, Murcia
☎ 968 781 691
Ⓦ www.casacastillo.es ▢

THIS COMPANY started producing wine from its own four vineyards in the high plateau of Jumilla in 1993, with an ambition to let each vineyard's terroir 'speak for itself'. They grow Monastrell, Garnacha,

Piqueras

Syrah, and Cabernet Sauvignon, and produce four wines, one from each vineyard. The flagship wine is Pie Franco, from ungrafted vines. Casa Castillo is a member of the prestigious Grandes Pagos de España.
▨ red ⤷ 2006, 2005, 2004, 2003, 2002, 2001, 2000 ★ Monastrell, Valtosca, Las Gravas, Pie Franco

Enrique Mendoza
Valencia & Murcia/ Alacant

Partida El Romeral, L'Alfás del Pi, Alicante ☎ 965 888 639
Ⓦ www.bodegasmendoza.com ▢

ESTABLISHED IN 1989, Enrique Mendoza is another producer that aimed high, planting 85ha of vines including Chardonnay, Pinot Noir, and Moscatel at an altitude of 600m. Mendoza's Santa Rosa is a prizewinning Cabernet Sauvignon-Merlot-Syrah blend, and his 100 per cent Syrah has also garnered accolades. The sweet blended red Dolç de Mendoza is a modern take on the traditional Garnatxa wines that were once the staple of production along the east coast.
▨ red ⤷ 2007, 2006, 2005, 2004, 2003, 2002, 2001, 2000 ★ Enrique Mendoza, Dolç de Mendoza

Mustiguillo
Valencia & Murcia/VdlT

ctra N-330, km 191, Las Cuevas de Utiel, Valencia ☎ 620 216 227
Ⓦ www.bodegamustiguillo.com ◓

THOUGH IT LIES within the DO Utiel-Requena, this award-winning *bodega* (founded in 1999) prefers to remain independent. The local Bobal grape dominates, and the winemakers are working veritable miracles with it. Staying outside the system, however, has allowed them to take a more experimental approach and use 'forbidden' grape varieties. The basic Terrazo wines are excellent; one of the best is Quincha Corral, a superb Bobal-Tempranillo blend.

🍷 red 🗒 2006, 2005, 2004, 2003, 2002, 2001 ★ *Finca Terrerazo, Quincha Corral*

Alvear
Andalucía/Montilla-Moriles

av María Auxiliadora 1, Montilla, Córdoba ☎ *957 650 100* 🌐 *www.alvear.es* ◯ *by appt*

THIS FAMILY-OWNED *bodega* within DO Montilla-Moriles was founded in 1729 and continues to invest heavily in quality wines. The unfortified wines are best known on the export market, but at home it is the classic fortified wines that are most popular. Well worth seeking out are: the delicate Capataz Fino; rich Oloroso Asunción; best-selling, crisp, dry Fino CB; and the most delicate Fino en Rama (only available locally).

🍷 red, white, fortified ★ *Fino Capataz, Fino CB, Solera 1910*

Bentomiz
Andalucía/Málaga

Pago Cuesta Róbano, Sayalonga, Málaga ☎ *952 115 939* 🌐 *www.bodegasbentomiz.com* ◖

HUSBAND-AND-WIFE team André Both and Clara Verheij bought a small vineyard in the mountains of Málaga, with ancient Moscatel vines growing in rocky outcrops. They started with a sweet wine that, unlike the traditional Málaga, isn't fortified, so it's called *naturalmente dulce* (naturally sweet). The *bodega* also produces a dry white and red under the DO Sierras de Málaga.

🍷 red, white, sweet 🗒 red: 2006, 2005; white: most recent ★ *Ariyanas*

Emilio Lustau
Andalucía/Jerez

Calle Arcos, 53, Jerez de la Frontera, Cádiz ☎ *956 341 597* 🌐 *www.lustau.es* ◯

ESTABLISHED IN 1896, Lustau now belongs to industry giant Luís Caballero, but still functions as an independent producer. The standard range – though of far from 'standard' quality – is Solera Reserva, which features sherries such as the very pale, dry Puerto Fino and the rich, old East India. The Almacenista range is stunning, featuring handcrafted, single solera wines of which the Manzanilla Amontillada is a shining example.

🍷 fortified ★ *Puerto Fino, Cuevas Jurado, Old East India*

González Byass
Andalucía/Jerez

Manuel María González 12, Jerez de la Frontera, Cádiz ☎ *956 357 000* 🌐 *www.gonzalezbyass.es* ◯ *by appt*

A FAMILY FIRM operating since 1835, González Byass boasts perhaps the region's most impressive *bodega* – a whole slice of the old town of Jerez de la Frontera. It also lays claim to possibly the most impressive range of fortified wines in Jerez. They are of impeccable quality, and include the world bestseller – Tío Pepe. The old wines include the magnificently nutty Amontillado del Duque, the rare Apóstoles Palo Cortado, and the venerable, rich Matúsalem.

🍷 fortified ★ *Tío Pepe, Apóstoles Palo Cortado, Matúsalem*

Hidalgo-La Gitana
Andalucía/Manzanilla

Banda de Playa 42, 11540 Sanlúcar de Barrameda, Cádiz ☎ *956 385 304* 🌐 *www.lagitana.es* ◯

ONE OF THE PREMIER producers of manzanilla sherry (called *La Gitana*), this family firm, established over 200 years ago, also has an impressive array of older fortified wines. Pastrana Manzanilla Pasada is a single-vineyard wine and arguably the best example of its kind in Sanlúcar. The Jerez Cortado Hidalgo is a sublime libation dispensed from ancient casks discovered in another Hidalgo family *bodega* a few years ago.

🍷 fortified ★ *La Gitana, Pastrana, Manzanilla Pasada, Napoléon*

Hidalgo-La Gitana

Perez Barquero
Andalucía/Montilla-Moriles

av Andalucía 27, Montilla, Córdoba ☎ *957 650 500* 🌐 *www.perez barquero.com* ◯

THIS BODEGA produces excellent value-for-money wines. The Gran Barquero range offers a cross section that reveals what Montilla wines are all about: from the excellent *fino* to a dark, spicy, dried-fruit Pedro Ximénez.

🍷 fortified ★ *Gran Barquero*

González Byass label

SHERRY & THE SOLERA SYSTEM

SHERRY HAS BEEN PRODUCED, *in one form or another, for more than 2,000 years. It is Spain's most labour-intensive and complex wine, made by a unique process of fractional blending of old and new wines in a network of barrels known as a solera system. Sherry is astonishingly versatile, with a spectrum of styles ranging from pale, delicate, bone-dry wines to ancient, powerful sweet elixirs with exotic perfumes. It is a wine style that has been imitated by many regions but never really succeeded outside Jerez. Within the EU, the name may only be legally applied to wines from Jerez.*

Selection of sherry

Vineyards & Grapes: The vineyards of Jerez (Sherry) form a triangle between the three towns of Jerez de la Frontera, Puerto de Santa María, and Sanlúcar de Barrameda in Andalucía. The special characteristic of this area is the high chalk content in the soil (*albariza*), which soaks up water in the rainy season and conserves it for the vine roots throughout the scorching hot summer months. The most important sherry grape is the relatively bland Palomino, which makes all the main styles of wine. Pedro Ximénez (PX) has a richer juice and is used in sweeter wines, and Moscatel is made purely as a sweet wine.

Rolling the sherry barrels through the *bodega*

Winemaking & Fortification: Grapes are harvested and the wine is made in exactly the same way as any other dry white wine. Then, in the year following the harvest, the wine is lightly fortified with a mixture of pure alcohol and wine to raise the strength to 14.5 per cent (for the best wines). This stabilizes the wine and also provides nutrients for the growth of flor.

Flor: Flor is a naturally-occurring yeast that is a problem in many wine areas, but in the region of Jerez, it is beneficial to wines that will become *finos*. It grows as a film across the surface of the wine and feeds on residual sugars, fusel oils, and other trace elements in the wine. It also forms a physical barrier between the wine and the air in the head space of the cask, protecting from oxidization and giving it a nutty, yeasty tang. Those barrels that develop a lot of flor will go into a *fino* solera *(see below)*. Those that do not will go into an *oloroso* solera. Later the same year, the final selection will be made, with wines destined for *fino* refortified to 15.5 per cent, and those for *oloroso* to 17.5 per cent, which will kill off any residual flor.

The Solera System: The intricate solera system is the key to quality control – mixing young

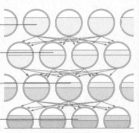

THE SOLERA SYSTEM

Final *criadera* is replenished with new wine each year

Second *criadera* is replaced with wine from the final criadera

First *criadera* is replaced with wine from the second criadera

Solera scale: the final blend is drawn from here and the scale is replaced with wine from the first *criadera*

Crushing Palomino grapes

wines with older wines of a similar style to maintain consistency. Typically there will be four or five rows of oak barrels (known as scales or *criaderas: see left*), and each year two thirds of the wine in each row will be blended with one third from the row from the following year. Wine leaves from the oldest row to be sold; this is then topped up from the next row and so on. Eventually, the final *criadera* is replenished with the new wine of the year.

Fino soleras are emptied periodically to maintain the freshness of the wine, and a decent *fino* will have spent around five years in the system before release. *Oloroso* soleras, on the other hand, may never be completely emptied, and it is very difficult to know how old a sherry is when it finally emerges. Every barrel will contain traces of wine that dates from when the solera was established. For this reason, producers often indicate the year the solera was formed. Each style of sherry has its own solera: in a *fino* solera the new wine will refresh the flor growth each time, in an *oloroso* solera the new wine will rapidly take on the richness and maturity of the older wine.

Amontillado sherry label

SHERRY STYLES

Sherry comes in a number of styles – the very best of which fall into the following categories.

Fino: These are the palest and driest wines of Jerez. *Manzanilla* is *fino* matured in the cool seafront town of Sanlúcar de Barrameda, which has its own unique oceanic mesoclimate. It is the most delicate and freshest sherry of all, sometimes with a hint of citrus zest on the nose, but always with that almond-nutty savouriness. *Finos* from Puerto de Santa María also have a lightness and delicacy that makes them perfect with the local seafood. Jerez *finos* tend to be a little heavier and more perfumed, but they are still fresh, crisp, bone-dry, and nutty.

Amontillado: As a *fino* ages beyond about five years in the solera, it becomes a *fino-amontillado*, in which the flor has died and the wine has begun to oxidize and turn a delicate shade of almond. The palate is richer and more pungent, but still completely dry. In Sanlúcar these wines are called *manzanilla-pasada*. After 10 years the wine has darkened considerably to a walnut hue, and is called *amontillado*. True *amontillado* is still bone dry but with a mellow richness on the mid-palate and a pungent, spicy nose.

Oloroso: These are rich and pungent in style when mature – after about 10 years in the solera – but still completely dry. They are less pungent than *amontillado* and are suited to sweetening with some Pedro Ximénez to make 'cream' styles. Most 'cream' sherries are, unfortunately, a commercial blend.

Palo cortado: This rare and expensive style is made when the flor yeast dies unexpectedly.

Manzanilla sherry label

These wines are aged separately and take on the nuttiness of the *fino* smoothed over by the richness of the *oloroso*.

Varietals: These tend to be the sweetest sherries. Moscatel wines are fortified during fermentation to retain as much of the grapes' natural sugar as possible, and are rich and voluptuous. Old PX wine is made from Pedro Ximénez laid out in the sun to shrivel before pressing, and can be nearly black, opaque, and one of the world's richest, sweetest wines.

Age-dated sherries: Old wines may be classified by their age. There are 12-, 15-. 20-, and 30-year-old styles. A complex mathematical formula is used to work out the 'average' age of the wines while they are in the solera; they must also pass a tasting and approval test before they can claim these age categories.

Vintage & Single Cask Sherries: A few producers also make individual vintages and keep them separate from the solera wines, and one or two also produce 'single cask' wines, bottling one individual barrel that is showing particularly well.

Palomino grapes

PORTUGAL

PORTUGAL

FEW COUNTRIES THE SIZE OF PORTUGAL can boast such a fascinating and varied array of wines from a wealth of native grape varieties. This small country is covered with enough vines to put it among the world's 10 largest wine producers.

BACKGROUND

THE IBERIAN PENINSULA has a long and distinguished history of producing wine, which pre-dates the foundation of Portugal. Although vines may have been planted in western Iberia by the Tartesians as early as 2000 BC, it was the Phoenicians who are thought to have introduced winemaking. The Romans continued the tradition, but wine suffered a huge setback under Muslim occupation from the 8th to the 12th centuries. The Portuguese nation emerged between the 10th and 13th centuries when the Christians in the north forced their way south along the narrow strip of land that forms Portugal today.

The country's success as a wine-producing nation was founded on overseas trade. The alliance between Britain and Portugal, sealed by the Treaty of Windsor in 1386, made Portugal a natural home for British traders, some of whom settled here as early as the 15th century. By the 16th century, merchant firms – many of them

Madeira barrel

British – were already prospering in the north and, slightly later, on the island of Madeira. A number of the port houses are still British-owned to this day.

By the 18th century, port and madeira had emerged as two of Portugal's leading exports. These wines found favour with the British, particularly when periodic skirmishes with France made the wines of Bordeaux and Burgundy unavailable.

Then, in the late 19th century, Portugal suffered, along with numerous European countries, from phylloxera. Many indigenous grape varieties were lost, and some wine regions have never fully recovered. The situation was hindered further in the mid-20th century by Portugal's dictator, António d'Oliveira Salazar, who encouraged farmers to grow wheat rather than vines in a drive to make the country self-sufficient. After 48 years in power, his regime was finally overthrown in 1974 and, after a brief period of damaging

Stained-glass window depicting men loading boats with port barrels

◁ **The village and vineyards of Vale de Mendiz in the Douro Valley** political instability, Portugal became a member of the European Union (EU) in 1986. Entry into the EU resulted in a newly demarcated DOC system, modelled on the French AOC structure. Money has since poured into rural areas and the wine industry has been one of the chief beneficiaries.

Portugal's wineries are now some of the most up-to-date in Europe and, although vineyards have been slower to adapt, many of the country's unique native grape varieties *(see p335)* are well on the way to being rediscovered.

Terraced vineyards in the Douro Valley

THE WINE INDUSTRY TODAY

FOR YEARS, PORTUGAL was known only for its great fortified wines, but recently unfortified wine production has been catching up with modern winemaking elsewhere in the world. Portugal now lays claim to around 240,000ha of vines split between approximately 300,000 growers. Vineyards, particularly in the more densely populated north of the country, are extremely fragmented due to Napoleonic inheritance laws, and because of this many growers supply their grapes to local co-operatives – of which there are around 100 in total. There are a handful of large, privately-owned firms, notably Sogrape, José Maria da Fonseca, J P Vinhos, Caves Aliança, and Quinta da Aveleda, many of which have substantial vineyard holdings. Since funds became available from the EU, a number of small private estates, or *quintas*, have left the co-operatives and now make their own, much more individual, wines *(see p340)*.

Portugal's total annual production averages around seven million hectolitres, but this figure hides the huge fluctuations resulting from the vagaries of the Atlantic climate. Of Portugal's total wine production around 60 per cent is red,

rosé, and fortified and 40 per cent is white. Exports account for nearly half of annual production, with Angola (an ex-Portuguese colony), France, Spain, Italy, and the United Kingdom the principal markets.

GRAPE VARIETIES & WINE STYLES

THROUGHOUT THE TRANSFORMATION of the wine industry that has taken place over the past decade, the Portuguese have been careful to safeguard their heritage, and most wines still reflect their *terroir*. The granite soils of the cool northwest produce crisp, minerally Vinho Verde, while the warmer schists inland give rise to the berry-fruit flavours associated with port and unfortified Douro reds. Wines from the coastal littoral tend to be light, and become steadily riper inland and towards the south. The plains of the deep south represent Portugal's New World, producing wines with lashings of full-favoured fruit. Offshore, the volcanic island of Madeira has its own distinctive *terroir*, making some of the world's most enduring wines. While much wine today is dominated by a handful of international grapes, Portugal's isolation from world trends has helped to preserve its heritage of distinctive indigenous grape varieties.

PORTUGAL'S FORTIFIED WINES

L IKE SO MANY *life-enhancing creations, port and madeira were invented by accident. In the 17th and 18th centuries, when wines were shipped over vast distances, it became common practice to add brandy as a preservative. Eventually grape spirit was added during the winemaking process, arresting the fermentation to leave the natural grape sugars. Over the years, port and madeira have developed their own styles, reflecting the different growing conditions of northern Portugal's Douro Valley and the island of Madeira in the Atlantic.*

Tawny port & Verdelho madeira

Port

Port emerged as a sweet, rich fortified wine at the start of the 19th century. Since then there has been no looking back.

Grapes

Port may be made from a choice of over 80 different grapes. Since the 1970s, there has been a focus on Touriga Franca, Tinta Roriz, Tinta Barroca, Touriga Nacional, and Tinto Cão. Currently, however, there is renewed interest in other red varieties including Sousão, Tinta Amarela, Tinta Francisca, and Tinta da Barca. Each of these has different attributes, but colour and sweetness are prized above all.

Winemaking Process

The fermentation period for port takes as little as 48 hours, during which the winemaker has to extract as much flavour, colour, and tannin from the grape skins as possible. Since the grape juice spends very little time in contact with the skins, a vigorous maceration process is essential.

Treading grapes for port in a traditional *lagar*

View across the Douro to Porto from Vila Nova de Gaia

Traditionally this was achieved by treading the grapes by foot in large stone tanks (*lagares*). Today only the very finest wines are made this way, and other methods are used to simulate the traditional process. When about half the natural grape sugar has fermented into alcohol, fermentation is arrested by the addition of a colourless grape spirit (with a strength of 77 per cent).

Classification

In the spring following the harvest the young wine was traditionally shipped downstream to the cooler, more humid climes of Vila Nova de Gaia, but a growing amount of port is now aged in air-conditioned lodges in the Douro. Gaia is still the centre of the port business,

and it is here that the wines are tasted and classified. There are many different styles of port *(see right)*, but there are two basic categories. 'Wood ports', including ruby, most LBV, tawny, and *colheita* ports, are those aged for varying periods in wood (from 2 up to 40 or more years) and bottled when ready to drink. 'Bottle-matured' ports are those aged for a shorter period in wood before continuing to develop in bottle. All vintage, crusted, and some (unfiltered) LBVs are in this category. With the notable exception of single-*quinta* ports (from a single property), all ports are complex blends, and exporters (shippers) use tasters charged with maintaining and developing the house style.

Madeira

The Portuguese island of Madeira produces a unique fortified wine made in a number of styles with varying levels of sweetness.

Grapes & Styles

The most highly prized classic madeiras are varietal wines, made from the so-called *nobre* (noble) white grape varieties. The driest are made from Sercial, medium-dry from Verdelho, medium-rich from Bual, and the sweetest wines, called Malmsey, come from the Malvasia grape. The majority of madeiras (nearly all 3- and 5-year-old dry to sweet style wines), however, are made from pale red Tinta Negra Mole, which is the most widely planted variety on the island, accounting for around 80 per cent of production.

Winemaking Process

Wines are partially or wholly fermented (according to sweetness) prior to fortification with grape spirit of 95 per cent. Then the wines are slowly heated. The best wines age in cask at Madeira's warm ambient temperatures for 20 years or more, until they take on ethereal 'maderized' aromas and flavours. Initially they are aged on the warm upper floors of the wine lodges, and as the wines age they are brought down to the cooler lower floors. For inexpensive wines, the effects of this long ageing are replicated by heating artificially in huge vats *(estufas)* at up to 55°C for a minimum of 90 days. The wines often taste soft, rich, and caramelized by comparison. The extreme maturation process, together with the high natural acidity from the grapes, makes madeira virtually indestructible.

Casks of Verdelho madeira

PORT STYLES

There are many different styles of port, distinguished from each other by the source and quality of the wine and the manner in which they are aged. Wines which are ready to drink have a stoppered cork, those for ageing have a driven cork.

Ruby: The youngest and fruitiest style of port, ruby is rich and peppery in style but sometimes raw and spirity. A multi-year blend, it is aged for two or three years before bottling. Rubies made with premium quality grapes are bottled with the designation reserve (*reserva*) and are aged for an average of three to five years. They are smoother and have more concentration of flavour than basic ruby.

Tawny: In theory, this is a wine which has been aged for longer than ruby, although much inexpensive tawny is the same age as basic ruby and is little more than attenuated ruby. Aged tawnies (usually labelled with an indication of age: 10, 20, 30, or 40 years old) are the real thing, having gained silky complexity from long ageing in cask, with flavours akin to liquid fruit cake.

Vintage: This is the very best wine from a single fine harvest, aged in wood for around two years before bottling. Bottled without filtration, the wines continue to age in bottle for 20 or more years, throwing a 'crust' or deposit. Vintage ports should be decanted before serving. Young vintage port tends to be opaque in colour with lashings of ripe berry fruit and cast-iron tannins. With age these wines soften and open up to reveal a floral character that combines both power and elegance. Vintage wines are only 'declared' in the finest years.

Graham's vintage port 1977

Late Bottled Vintage (LBV): Wine from a single year or harvest, produced in much larger quantities than vintage port and aged for four to six years in wood before bottling. With more depth and concentration of flavour than reserve ruby port, LBV is very popular. Unlike vintage port, most LBVs are filtered and bottled ready to drink.

Colheita: A wine from a single harvest, aged in wood for a minimum of seven years – by which time it takes on a smooth, silky tawny character. Some *colheitas* spend 30 years or more in wood, and take on a rich, maderized quality.

Vintage and tawny port

Crusted: This blend of wines from more than one harvest is bottled unfiltered like a vintage port. They share some of the power and concentration of vintage port and are often great value for money.

White Port: a port made from a host of white grapes (mostly Codega, Malvasia Fina, Malvasia Rei, Rabigato, Gouveio, Moscatel, and Viosinho), usually off-dry and drunk as an aperitif.

WINE MAP OF PORTUGAL

With the exception of the very highest mountain peaks, wine regions virtually cover Portugal in its entirety. The country extends just 200km from east to west at its widest point, and some 600km from north to south. It also includes the winegrowing island of Madeira, 1,000km southwest of the mainland. There are 24 DOCs, 5 IPRs, and 8 *vinhos regionais*. Porto, where port has been made for over two centuries, is Portugal's most famous DOC.

Vineyards and the village of Lapela in Vinho Verde

Casks of wine being loaded onto a ship at Funchal port in Madeira

PORTUGAL: AREAS & TOP PRODUCERS

VINHO VERDE *p332*
Quinta da Aveleda *p338*

VINHO DO PORTO *p332*
A A Ferreira *p338*
Churchill *p338*
Cockburn *p338*
Croft *p339*
Dow *p339*
Fonseca Guimaraens *p339*
Gran Cruz Porto *p339*
Niepoort *p340*
Quinta do Noval *p340*
Ramos Pinto *p340*
Sandeman *p340*
Taylor, Fladgate & Yeatman *p341*
W & J Graham *p341*
Warre *p341*

PERFECT CASE: PORTUGAL

🅡 A A Ferreira Barca Velha ££££

🅕 Churchill's Dry White Port ££

🅕 Henriques & Henriques 15-Year-Old Verdelho ££

🅦 Herdade do Esporão Branco ££

🅡 Luís Pato Vinha Pan £££

🅕 Madeira Wine Company Blandy's 1954 Bual £££

🅦 Niepoort Redoma Branco ££

🅡 Quinta do Crasto Maria Teresa £££

🅡 Quinta do Mouro ££

🅕 Quinta da Pellada £££

🅡 Quinta do Vale Meão £££

🅕 W & J Graham's 1970 Vintage Port ££££

Minho

42°

Lima

Cávado

Costa Verde

VINHO VERDE

Porto (Oporto)

Serra do Marão

PO DO

41°

Vila Nova de Gaia

Douro

Dão

ATLANTIC OCEAN

BAIRRADA

DÃO

Serra Estre

Mondego

Coímbra

40°

Serra de Aire

Serra da Montejunto

LISBOA (ESTREMADURA)

Serra de Tejo (Tagus)

RIBATEJO

BUCELAS

PORTAL

39°
ALENQUER

ARRUDA

ALENTE

COLARES

LISBOA (LISBON)

BORBA

PALMELA

SETÚBAL

REDONDO

SETÚBAL PENINSULA

ÉVORA

Sado

REGUE

GR

AM

VIDIGUEIRA

38°

MOU

Guadiana

MADEIRA

ATLANTIC OCEAN

Porto Moniz

Pico Ruivo

MADEIRA

Machico

Câmara de Lobos

FUNCHAL

0 ⌐km ———— 30

ALGARVE

Faro

37°

Painted tiles depicting workers gathering grapes in the vineyard

-km ⌐⎯⎯⎯⎯⎯⎯⎯⎯⎯ 100

TERROIR AT A GLANCE

Latitude: 37–42°N.

Altitude: 0–1,990m.

Topography: The Tejo (Tagus) River divides Portugal into asymmetric halves. The land north of the Tejo is mountainous, rising to nearly 2,000m in the Sera da Estrela, with a narrow coastal littoral. South of the Tejo the countryside is much flatter, seldom reaching over 500m.

Soil: Granite and schist in the interior; limestone, clay, and sand along the coastal littoral.

Climate: Coastal regions are strongly influenced by the Atlantic, with high rainfall. Inland and to the south, the climate becomes more continental, and near the Spanish border drought is a continual problem. The marked variation in climate is a major factor in creating many different styles of wine.

Temperature: July average is 22.5°C in Lisboa; 21.3°C in the Douro.

Rainfall: Annual average is 670mm in Lisboa, 1,130mm in Oporto, and as little as 400mm at the border with Spain.

Wind: Coastal winds can cause damage. Easterly winds have a drying effect in the summer months.

Viticultural hazards: Frost; harvest rain; fungal diseases.

PORTUGUESE WINE LAW

*S*INCE JOINING *the EU in 1986, a large number of new wine regions have been recognized, and Portuguese wine law has gradually been brought into line with other European countries. There are four levels of quality, and grape varieties, maximum yields, and (in some instances) minimum ageing requirements are controlled at both DOC and IPR levels.*

Denominação de Origem Controlada (DOC)
Equivalent to AOC in France, DOC is the highest category of wine in Portugal. Wines must originate from a designated area and be produced according to local regulations.

Indicação de Proveniencia Regulamentada (IPR)
A category for wines with the potential to achieve DOC status.

Vinho regional
Regional wines, produced from a broad but legally defined area. Equivalent to *vin de pays* in France, this category permits the blending of wines across a wide area and is much more flexible in the range of grape varieties allowed. In the south many producers prefer to use this category.

Vinho de mesa
Table wine.

Quinta da Aveleda label

Glossary of Label Terms

adega*: winery.*
branco*: white.*
colheita*: vintage.*
doce*: sweet.*
engarrafado*: bottled.*
garrafa*: bottle.*
garrafeira*: a term that may indicate extra quality; wines will be matured in both cask and bottle for minimum periods before release. The regulations are more stringent than for reserva.*
maduro*: old or mature.*

quinta*: vineyard or wine estate.*
reserva*: wines which have achieved at least an extra 0.5 per cent alcohol. Unlike in Spain, there are no requirements for barrel and bottle maturation.*
rosado*: rosé.*
séco*: dry.*
tinto*: red.*
verde*: literally 'green' but normally used to mean young.*
vinho*: wine.*

Village of Sabrosa set among vineyards of the Douro Valley

WINEGROWING AREAS OF PORTUGAL

THE NORTH

THE NORTH OF PORTUGAL is home to the country's best-known wines. Some, like port and Vinho Verde, are already household names. There are four well established DOCs here, and three large but much less significant *vinhos regionais*: Minho, Trás-os-Montes, and Beiras.

Vinho Verde

THE COASTLINE NORTH OF THE CITY of Porto is aptly titled the Costa Verde (Green Coast). Inland from the white sandy beaches is a patchwork of vineyard known as Vinho Verde, still the nation's largest DOC, covering the entire northwestern corner of Portugal. Vinho Verde is best drunk young, in its first flush of youth; most is bottled without a vintage date on the label and it is assumed that the wine being drunk is from the previous year's harvest.

Tile depicting boat ferrying port

Vinho Verde is predominantly dry and slightly fizzy, low in alcohol (8.5 to 11.5 per cent) but with searingly high levels of acidity. Wines destined for export are often sweetened a little to mask this. Red Vinho Verde, which is still popular locally, has plenty of tannin, but these rasping reds pair well with local cuisine. Most Vinho Verde is made from a field blend – vineyards interplanted with many different grape varieties – but an increasing number of wines are made solely from Loureiro and/or Trajadura, two of the leading white varieties in the region. In the far north along the Minho

River, the Alvarinho grape produces a fuller flavoured, aromatic dry white, which goes wonderfully with Atlantic shellfish.

🌾 mostly granite-based 🍇 Vinhão, Azal Tinto 🍇 Loureiro, Trajadura, Padernã, Avesso, Azal, Alvarinho 🍷 red, white

Vinho do Porto (Port Wine)

PORTUGAL'S SECOND LARGEST CITY, Porto (Oporto), lends its name to one of the world's most famous fortified wines: *vinho do porto*, or port wine. The vineyards of Porto DOC are found 100km or so inland in a tightly delimited area that corresponds to an outcrop of schist. Like the granite-based soils in most of northern Portugal, the schistous soils of the Douro are infertile and gruelling to work. However, unlike granite the schist fractures vertically allowing the vines to root deeply in search of water and nutrients. In recognition of its unique *terroir*, the Douro Valley was among the first wine regions in the world to be officially demarcated, when the Portuguese government, led by the Marquês de Pombal, imposed strict boundaries on port vineyards in 1756.

Over the years, the steep slopes of the Douro and its tributaries (the Corgo, Tedo, Távora, Torto, and Pinhão rivers) have been worked into tiny terraces, each supporting just a few rows of vines. This breathtakingly beautiful terraced landscape could be added to the list of wonders of the world, such is the feat of three centuries of engineering, and it is in fact now recognized as a World Heritage Site. In recent years, however, the drive towards increased mechanization has meant that many vineyards have had to be replanted, and some of the high retaining walls have been destroyed and replaced. Modern vineyards are either planted on *patamares* (terraces gouged from the slope with earth banks rather than retaining walls) or increasingly as *vinha ao alto*, rows of vines planted up and down the slope.

The upper Douro Valley is protected from rain-bearing Atlantic westerlies by a range of mountains rising to 1,400m called the Serra do Marão. Within the region there are three distinct and officially recognized subregions. The most westerly of these, the Baixo Corgo, is the smallest, wettest, and most densely planted. It produces the bulk of inexpensive ruby and tawny port *(see p329)*. The second of the three subregions, the Cima Corgo, is significantly drier. Centred on the small town of Pinhão, it is the source of the greatest of ports (vintage, LBV, and aged tawny) as well as an increasingly significant quantity of unfortified Douro wine *(see below)*. The third and most easterly subregion is the Douro Superior.

The hub of the port business is the city of Vila Nova de Gaia, on the estuary of the Douro River facing Porto. In the spring following the harvest, the young wine was traditionally shipped to the cooler, more humid Vila Nova de Gaia, but today an increasing proportion of port is aged in air-conditioned *armazens* (lodges) in the Douro. However, wines are still tasted and classified in Gaia.

schist *Touriga Nacional, Touriga Franca, Tinta Roriz, Tinta Barroca, Tinto Cão, Tinta Amarela* *fortified*

Douro

THE PORT TRADE STILL DOMINATES in the Douro region, but winemakers are increasingly diverting more of their attention to unfortified quality wines, which have had their own demarcation (Douro DOC) since 1979. Wines from Douro DOC share the ripeness and concentration of a fine port, and this region is now producing some of Portugal's most impressive reds, made primarily from port grapes. The finest wines are made in small, sometimes minute, quantities and frequently command a high price on the domestic market. But the sheer richness and intensity of a red wine sourced from low yielding, 70-year-old vines is worth paying for.

schist *Touriga Nacional, Touriga Franca, Tinta Roriz, Tinta Barroca, Tinto Cão, Tinta Amarela* *Gouveio, Viosinho, Rabigato, Malvasia Fina, Donzelinho* *red, white*

Dão

LONG MARKETED AS Portugal's best red wine, Dão DOC has often failed to live up to expectations. But now that the co-operatives have lost their stranglehold on the region, there are a number of enterprising producers intent on proving that Dão can make wines of note. Sheltered on nearly all sides by high granite mountains, Dão (like much of the Douro) is in the transition zone between maritime and continental climate, and it has the capacity to produce great wine. It shares many of the same grape varieties as the Douro, the best wines revealing the floral character of Touriga Nacional.

Most vineyards are small and scattered amid the pine and eucalyptus forests. At the moment there are only two producers of any size here, Sogrape and Dão Sul, both of which make good, spicy, well-balanced reds. A number of *quintas* (Quintas dos Roques, da Maias, de Saes, and das Carvalhas) are already producing red wines with structure, power, and intensity.

granite *Touriga Nacional, Tinta Roriz, Alfrocheiro Preto, Jaen, Tinta Pinheira* *Encruzado, Bical, Malvasia Fina, Rabo de Ovelha* *red, white*

Picking grapes from vines on pergolas in Vinho Verde

Bairrada

THE COASTAL REGION OF BAIRRADA DOC makes the best and worst of Portugal's wines. It is all down to the capricious red grape Baga, which dominates here. When fully ripe, Baga makes dense reds with a wonderful bramble character and the capacity to age in bottle for years, sometimes decades. Luís Pato, Casa da Saima, Quinta do Baixo, and Caves São João are Baga's most convincing producers. All too often, however, the grapes are picked under-ripe when rain threatens at harvest time, and the wines taste astringent and weedy. More attention to viticulture is needed in this region to help the grapes ripen earlier. Like so much of northern Portugal, however, Bairrada is divided up into tiny holdings tended by weekend farmers who sell their grapes to the co-operatives to make the wine. Much of the region's crop ends up in Mateus rosé *(see p339)*, which is made at Anadia in the heart of this area. White wines are also produced, largely for the benefit of the local sparkling wine industry.

🏔 *limestone-based clay, some sand* 🍇 *Baga, Castelão* 🍇 *Maria Gomes, Bical, Rabo de Ovelha* 🍷 *red, white, rosé, sparkling*

CENTRAL PORTUGAL

WITH THE EXCEPTION of a few historic enclaves, central Portugal has long been a source of wine quantity rather than quality. Two regions, Lisboa (known as Estremadura until 2008) and the Ribatejo, produce nearly a third of the nation's output of wine. Things are changing, however, and a number of promising *terroirs* within these regions now have their own DOCs.

Vineyards near Arruda in Lisboa (Estremadura)

Lisboa (Estremadura)

THIS STRIP OF MARITIME COUNTRYSIDE is colloquially known as the Oeste (West). The entire region includes around 50,000ha of vineyard, but less than a third of this qualifies as DOC or IPR (of which there are seven, Alenquer and Arruda being the best known) or *vinho regional*. Although the proportion of wine entitled to these geographic designations is on the increase, most wine from Lisboa is still sold as *vinho de mesa*, with 19 large co-operatives producing the bulk. Helped by funds from the EU, these establishments have undergone a transformation in recent years. With a certain amount of guidance from consultant wine-makers, they are now capable of producing some inexpensive, characterful reds. The best wines come from the leeward side of the Serras Aire, Candeiros, and Montejunto. Here, particularly around the town of Alenquer, there are a number of *quintas* already producing world-class wine. Best of all is Quinta do Monte d'Oiro, with a Syrah that competes with the greatest of the northern Rhône.

🏔 *mostly limestone-based* 🍇 *Castelão, Tinta Miuda, Cabernet Sauvignon, Syrah, Merlot* 🍇 *Antão Vaz, Arinto, Bical, Chardonnay, Fernão Pires* 🍷 *red, white, rosé*

Colares

THIS TINY DOC on the Atlantic coast west of Lisbon is the haven for one of Portugal's most historic wines. Planted in sandy cliff-top soil, the Ramisco vines here survived the phylloxera epidemic that swept through Europe in the 19th century. Phylloxera cannot complete its life cycle in sand and therefore does not attack the roots of the vines. Production has declined in recent years, but the few gnarled vines that remain continue to grow on their own roots without the need to be grafted onto phylloxera-resistant rootstock. Good Colares, mostly red, is now hard to find; older vintages hint at greatness with wonderful fragrance and finesse.

🏔 *sand* 🍇 *Ramisco* 🍇 *Arinto, Jampal, Malvasia* 🍷 *red, white*

Bucelas

DESPITE BEING LESS THAN 25km from the hub of Lisbon, Bucelas DOC has still managed to hang onto and even reclaim some of its rural heritage. The region was well known in the

Harvesting Merlot grapes in Ribatejo

of the largest and most prosperous wine estates in Portugal. Fertile soils, frequently inundated by the river itself, support all manner of produce, including a huge crop of grapes.

This is an area for large quantities of wine at low prices. There is, however, now a welcome transfer of vineyards to the higher land on either side of the Tejo, where yields are naturally lower and quality improved. Much of the region's wine is white, made from the versatile Fernão Pires grape and a legacy from the time when Ribatejo produced the spirit for fortifying port.

It is the reds, however, that are now

19th century for the production of Portuguese hock, a white wine which was often fortified with brandy. Bucelas is still white, but is now bottled unfortified. The main grape here is the lemony-lime Arinto, one of Portugal's leading white grapes. Often in partnership with the ferocious Esgana Cão, it produces dry, fruity white wine balanced by crisp natural acidity.
🌾 limestone-based 🍇 Arinto, Esgana Cão, Rabo de Ovelha 🍷 white

Ribatejo

THE RIBATEJO STRADDLES the Tejo (Tagus) River upstream from Lisbon and is Portugal's agricultural heartland. The smallholdings that dominate the north overflow from Lisboa (Estremadura) into the western margins of the province. To the south and east are some

attracting the most attention with substantial plantings of international grapes (Cabernet Sauvignon, Merlot, and Syrah) alongside the best indigenous varieties like Trincadeira and Touriga Nacional. In the warmer southeast of the region, many of the wines share an affinity with those from the neighbouring and hugely successful Alentejo. The entire Ribatejo is now covered both by DOC and *vinho regional*, the latter known somewhat confusingly as Ribatejano. Six subregions, **Tomar**, **Chamusca**, **Santarém**, **Almeirim**, **Cartaxo**, and **Coruche**, can add their names to the Ribatejo DOC.
🌾 varied: limestone-based clays, alluvium, sand 🍇 Castelão, Camarate, Preto Martinho, Tinta Miuda, Trincadeira, Touriga Nacional, Cabernet Sauvignon, Merlot, Syrah 🍇 Fernão Pires, Talia, Boal de Alicante, Arinto, Chardonnay, Sauvignon Blanc 🍷 red, white

PORTUGAL'S UNIQUE GRAPE VARIETIES

What do a red dog, a cat's tail, a ewe's tail, fly droppings, and a dog strangler have in common? They are all names of Portuguese grape varieties. Portugal has evolved like a viticultural island and boasts a fascinating array of native grapes. Many are of little note, but in the viticultural work that has been gathering pace over the past decade, a number of excellent indigenous varieties have emerged. Due to the interplanting of different grape varieties in the same plots, most Portuguese wines are traditionally blends, but since varietal planting has became more commonplace since the 1980s, varietal wines

Touriga Nacional

are now making their mark. Although there are a handful of promising white grapes (Loureiro, Arinto, Encruzado, Antão Vaz), most are red and can now be found as varietal wines. Some of the best are the traditional port grapes: Touriga Nacional, Touriga Franca, and Tinto Cão. Also capable of good, or even great, results are the spicy, peppery Trincadeira, raspberry-flavoured Castelão, and Baga with its wonderful wild berry, bramble character, as well as Alfrocheiro and Tinta Miuda. Other than Spain's Tempranillo (known here as Tinta Roriz and Aragonez), foreign grape varieties have made comparatively few incursions into Portugal.

THE SOUTH

MUCH OF SOUTHERN PORTUGAL used to be a no-man's land for wine. A quarter of a century ago, there was virtually nothing fit to drink. The hot climate made much of the wine taste stewed, fruitless, and unpalatable. With financial help from the EU, the introduction of stainless steel, accompanied by temperature-controlled fermentation, has transformed the fortunes of this area and the province of Alentejo in particular is now a wine region to be taken seriously.

Vineyard around Vidigueira in Alentejo

Setúbal Peninsula

THE LAND BETWEEN the Tejo and Sado rivers juts out into the Atlantic. Known unofficially as the Setúbal Peninsula, it is home to two of Portugal's leading winemakers, José Maria da Fonseca and J P Vinhos (alias João Pires). The region produces numerous different wines, each with their own overlapping demarcations.

Setúbal DOC applies to a sweet, fortified wine made from the local Muscat grape (Moscatel de Setúbal). Aged in cask, sometimes for decades, before bottling, the wine turns from amber-orange after about five years to mahogany brown after 20, then ebony with 50 or more years in wood. Candied fruit notes take on a hint of butterscotch and eventually develop a richness resembling molasses. At its best at around 20 years old, Setúbal is the wine to drink with Christmas pudding.

The **Palmela** DOC covers much the same ground as Setúbal, but extends eastwards to cover more of the plain. The area has two very distinctive *terroirs*: the north-facing limestone hills seem more suited to white grapes (as well as Cabernet Sauvignon and Merlot); whereas on the sandy soils inland and to the east, the red Castelão grape dominates. Here the climate seems to have just the right maritime and continental mix for this grape to produce wines with some depth and ageing capacity. Raspberryish and often astringent when young, the wines gain a note of tar-like complexity with age.

Terras do Sado is the name of the *vinho regional* that covers the Setúbal Peninsula in its entirety as well as the coastline southwards

towards the Algarve. It embraces around 60 grape varieties, and there are a growing number of innovative wines combining both indigenous and international grapes. Most of the wine production is concentrated in the north, but there is a prison near Grandola, 70km south of Setúbal, that keeps its inmates occupied with tending vines and making wine.

limestone in hills, sandy on plains Castelão, *Trincadeira Preta, Aragonez, Touriga Nacional, Touriga Franca, Cabernet Sauvignon, Merlot, Syrah* *Moscatel de Setúbal, Fernão Pires, Arinto, Chardonnay, Sauvignon Blanc* *red, white, rosé, fortified*

Alentejo

THE LARGEST PROVINCE IN PORTUGAL, the Alentejo stretches from the Tejo in the north to the Algarve in the south, taking up almost a third of the country. It has a mere sixth of Portugal's population, and agriculture is extensive, with estates *(latifúndios)* extending to hundreds, sometimes thousands, of hectares. Cork has long been one of the region's most important products, but the barren plains are now interrupted by huge swathes of green vines.

The moderating effect of the Atlantic diminishes sharply inland, and low summer rainfall is a continual problem. Irrigation (once forbidden by the EU) is now considered essential. With super-ripe, sun-drenched flavours coming from charismatic grapes like Aragonez and Trincadeira, red wines from the Alentejo have become hugely marketable for their easygoing, ripe flavours. Large producers such as Esporão and Cartuxa, and well-run co-ops at Redondo and Reguengos are able to produce huge volumes of consistent wine that would be difficult to replicate further north. There are also one or two good whites made from Antão Vaz and Roupeiro. The entire Alentejo province is now covered by a *vinho regional* called Alentejano, and there are eight distinct enclaves with DOC status: **Portalegre**, **Borba**, **Redondo**, **Évora**, **Reguengos**, **Granja-Amareleja**, **Moura**, and **Vidigueira**. Each of these regions has the right to bottle wines under their name preceded by 'Alentejo'.

varied with schist, granite-and-limestone-based soils Trincadeira, Aragonez, Castelão, Moreto, Cabernet Sauvignon, Syrah, Alicante Bouschet Antão Vaz, Roupeiro, Diagalves, Manteudo, Perrum, Chardonnay *red, white*

Algarve

PORTUGAL'S SOUTHERNMOST COAST is a world-renowned tourist destination, but it has never been recognized for its wine. Singer Sir Cliff Richard established a winery here and now seems set to change the Algarve's image with a red wine made from Aragonez, Trincadeira, and Syrah. First released in 2001, it is not a great wine for the price, but it is significantly better than anything else the Algarve has ever produced. This has led to renewed interest in the Algarve as a wine region, and more producers are now following Sir Cliff's lead.

limestone-based clay Negra Mole, Bastardo, Castelão, Aragonez, Trincadeira, Syrah Arinto, Diagalves, Perrum, Rabo de Ovelha *red, white*

Madeira

TWO SWORN ENEMIES of most winemakers – heat and air – conspire to turn madeira into one of the world's most enthralling wines, as well as the most resilient. Due to the island's strategic position in the Atlantic (1,200km southwest of Lisbon), Madeira became an important sea port soon after it was colonized by the Portuguese in the early 15th century. Vines were planted on the island, and wine was taken on board ships possibly as an antidote to scurvy. It was soon found that these wines, fortified to prevent spoilage, took on a different character when they were shipped across the tropics, and in the late 18th century, a fashion for madeira developed in the US and UK.

Nowadays wines are no longer shipped in cask across the tropics, but the wines are still heated, either artificially in giant vats *(estufas)*, or in cask, for many years at the warm ambient temperatures that prevail on the island. The soil here is entirely volcanic, and vines fight for space with other crops on tiny, step-like terraces known as *poios*. There are four main grape varieties officially classified as 'noble': Sercial, Verdelho, Bual, and Malvasia. Individually these white grapes are used to make varietal wines ranging in style from bone-dry to rich and sweet. However, the most planted variety on the island is the versatile Tinta Negra Mole, which is used to make wines in a range of styles imitating the so-called 'noble' grapes.

Due partly to the soil, partly to the grapes themselves, but also high yields, all madeiras have distinctively crisp acidity. The driest wines, made from Sercial, can be quite austere in style, but in the medium-dry Verdelho and the richer Bual and Malvasia (Malmsey) the acidity helps to counter-balance the sweetness.

Wicker-covered madeira bottle

Due to the heating process, which the wines undergo before bottling, madeira is the world's most long-lived wine, and it is possible to find wines from the late 18th century which are still incredibly alive and enjoyable today. Once opened the wines do not deteriorate for months, even years.

volcanic Tinta Negra Mole Sercial, Verdelho, Bual, Malvasia *fortified*

Terraced vineyards and farmland around the village of Curral das Freiras, Madeira

TOP PRODUCERS OF PORTUGAL

Quinta da Aveleda
Vinho Verde

Apartada 77P, Penafiel 📞 *255 718
200* 🅦 *www.aveleda.pt* 🔲

THIS BUCOLIC estate just 30km from Porto makes Portugal's bestselling Vinhos Verdes. With 200ha of vines, Aveleda's vineyards are by far the largest and most technically advanced in northwest Portugal. Casal Garcia, the main brand, is exported worldwide. Light, spritzy, and off-dry, it is made from fruit grown by hundreds of nearby farmers. At the other end of the spectrum, Grinalda is made only from grapes grown on the estate and is properly dry with a wonderful fresh, floral character. The dark, astringent red Vinho Verde is strictly for aficionados.
🍷 *red, white, brandy* 🔲 *most recent*
★ *Quinta da Aveleda, Grinalda, Alvarinho, Aveleda Follies*

Sogrape
Douro and other regions

Apartado 3032, Aldeia Nova, Avintes
📞 *227 850 300* 🅦 *www.sogrape.pt*
🔲 *some establishments*

BY FAR the largest producer in Portugal, Sogrape was built up on the back of Mateus rosé *(see right)*. The HQ is in the Douro but the company has diversified and now has interests in most of the country's main wine regions (Vinho Verde, Dão, Bairrada, and Alentejo) as well as in Argentina. It is still controlled by the founding family, the Guedes, who own Quinta do Azevedo near Barcelos. This is the source of crisp, spritzy Gazela Vinho Verde, and there is some consistently good red and white Dão under the Duque de Viseu label. Most recently, Sogrape has moved into Alentejo, where it makes

Quinta da Aveleda label

a deliciously juicy red, Vinho da Monte, and a range of very good varietal reds from the Herdade do Peso estate.
🍷 *red, white, rosé* 🔲 *2008, 2007, 2004* ★ *Quinta das Carvalhas, Duque de Viseu, Callabriga*

A A Ferreira
Vinho do Porto (Port Wine)

rua da Carvalhosa 19/105, Vila Nova de Gaia 📞 *223 745 292* 🔲

THE DOUGHTY Dona Antónia Ferreira (1811–1896) built up an empire in the Douro that can still be seen today. The firm remained in family hands until 1987, when it was sold to Sogrape. The brand leader in Portugal, Ferreira has earned a fine reputation for tawny ports and Barca Velha, an unfortified Douro red which commands the same price as a top vintage port. Barca Velha is made from port grapes (mostly Tinta Roriz, with some Touriga Franca, Tinta Barroca, and Tinta Amarela). It is only made in the best years and there have only been 15 vintages since it was first made in 1952.
🍷 *red, fortified* 🔲 *2000, 1997, 1995, 1994* ★ *Barca Velha (2000, 1999, 1995, 1991, 1985), Dona Antónia Reserva Pessoal, Duque de Bragança 20-Year-Old Tawny, Esteva*

Churchill
Vinho do Porto (Port Wine)

rua da Fonte Nova 5, Vila Nova de Gaia 📞 *223 703 641*
🅦 *www.churchills-port.com* 🔲

FOUNDED IN 1981 by the Graham brothers, Churchill has quickly established a reputation for good, dense LBV and vintage ports. The nutty Dry White Port, which spends 10 years ageing in wood and takes on the character of a tawny, is one of very few white ports worth drinking.
🍷 *fortified* 🔲 *2000, 1997, 1994*
★ *Dry White Port, LBV, Quinta da Gricha 2001 Vintage Port, Quinta da Gricha Douro Red*

Cockburn
Vinho do Porto (Port Wine)

rua das Coradas, Vila Nova de Gaia
📞 *223 776 500*
🅦 *www.cockburns-usa.com* 🔲

Churchill

COCKBURN (pronounced 'Co-burn') was established in 1815 and has become one of the best-known names in port. It was taken over by Harvey's of Bristol in 1962 and later by Jim Beam Global, who sold everything except the brand to the Symington family (see Dow, *opposite*). As a result of the purchase, the Symingtons now have huge holdings in the Douro Superior, including in the relatively flat Vilariça estate, which was planted in the 1970s to supply Special Reserve, a rich, full-bodied *reserva* ruby, softened by five years' ageing in wood. This is the bestselling port in the UK.
🍷 *fortified* 🔲 *2000, 1983, 1963*
★ *Special Reserve, LBV, Cockburn's 20-Year-Old Tawny*

Croft
Vinho do Porto (Port Wine)

Largo Joaquim Magalhães 23, Vila Nova de Gaia 223 305 514
W *www.croftport.com*

ESTABLISHED IN 1678, Croft is one of the oldest and most distinguished names in the business. It suffered a rough ride under the ownership of Diageo but has now found a loving new home in the Fladgate Partnership alongside Taylor's and Fonseca. Croft's estate, Quinta da Roeda, is currently being restored. The wines improved in the 1990s, and the vintage ports have regained the richness and concentration of flavour for which they were famed until the 1960s. Pink, the first pink port, was launched in 2008.
fortified 2000, 1994, 1991, 1963 ★ *Croft Distinction, Croft 20-Year-Old Tawny, Croft 2003 Vintage Port*

Dow
Vinho do Porto (Port Wine)

Silva & Cosens Lda, Trav Barão de Forrester, Vila Nova de Gaia 223 396 063 W *www.dows-port.com*

ONE OF THE SIX port producers owned by the Symington family, Silva & Cosens dates back to 1798 when it was founded in London by Bruno da Silva. The Dow's brand name was introduced nearly a century later and has been associated ever since with some outstanding vintage ports. These are dense and concentrated, but drier in style than those from most other producers. Dow's crusted ports are nearly as rich and impressive, but cost a fraction of the price.
fortified 2003, 2000, 1997, 1994, 1980, 1970 ★ *Dow's Midnight, LBV, Quinta do Bomfim 1987 Vintage Port*

Fonseca Guimaraens
Vinho do Porto (Port Wine)

rua Barão de Forrester 404, Vila Nova de Gaia 223 742 800
W *www.fonseca.pt*

FONSECA GUIMARAENS (not to be confused with José Maria da Fonseca) was founded by Manuel Pedro Guimaraens in 1822. Although Fonseca now forms part of the Fladgate Partnership, the Guimaraens family is still actively involved. The late Bruce Guimaraens and his son David have been responsible for some of the finest ports on the market. With the exception of 1983 and 1980, Fonseca arguably

Selection of ports from Fonseca Porto

makes better vintage port than its sibling Taylor. Deliciously dense in youth, it opens up to reveal great finesse.
fortified 2003, 2000, 1994, 1992, 1985, 1970, 1966, 1963 ★ *Fonseca Bin 27, 20-Year-Old Tawny, Quinta do Panascal 2005 Vintage Port*

Gran Cruz Porto
Vinho do Porto (Port Wine)

Sociedade Comercial de Vinhos, Rua José Mariani 390, Vila Nova de Gaia 223 746 490

WITH HUGE SALES in France (the world's largest market for port), Cruz is Portugal's biggest single port brand. The company is best known for its simple, inexpensive tawnies. Quantity has the tendency to override quality.
fortified 2000
★ *Tribute Reserve LBV*

PORTUGAL'S ROSÉ PHENOMENON

In 1942, in the darkest days of World War II, fortified wine exports were at an all-time low. A group of businessmen decided to use the surplus port grapes to make a new style of rosé wine. They rented a winery and asked a nearby landowner if they could label the flagon-shaped bottle with a picture of his baroque palace. The wine was a fresh, slightly fizzy, off-dry rosé called Mateus. It was initially exported to Brazil, but when that market collapsed in the late 1940s, the producer, Sogrape, turned to the UK, which became much more receptive to wine after World War II. Sales peaked in the early 1980s, but Mateus still exports 16 million litres a year to 130 countries on four continents. Its smaller rival, Lancers, produces a similar fizzy rosé, made by José Maria da Fonseca. The Mateus range now includes a Tempranillo rosé from Spain and a Syrah rosé from France. The Sparkling Mateus emanates from Portugal. Unlike the Spanish, the Portuguese have never developed a taste for rosé.

Mateus rosé

Niepoort
Vinho do Porto (Port Wine)

rua Infante D Henrique 16 2° Frt, Porto ☎ *222 001 028* ○ *by appt*

FIVE GENERATIONS of the Niepoort family have been hoarding wines in a cramped lodge in the heart of Vila Nova de Gaia since this company was first established in 1842. Although Niepoort's reputation is for fine old tawnies and *colheitas*, the wines are excellent across the range – from simple ruby to great vintage port. Unfortunately, they are only shipped in small quantities. Dirk Niepoort has now turned his hand to producing some impressively full, concentrated, unfortified wines under the Redoma, Charme, and Batuta labels.
🍷 *fortified* 🍇 *2005, 2003, 2000, 1994, 1970* ★ *LBV, 20-Year-Old Tawny, 1994 Colheita*

Quinta do Noval
Vinho do Porto (Port Wine)

av Diogo Leite 256, Vila Nova de Gaia ☎ *223 770 270*
🅦 *www.quintadonoval.com* ○

QUINTA DO NOVAL is one of the most spectacular properties in the Douro Valley, and it lends its name to a shipper with a very good range of ports. Wines labelled Quinta do Noval are produced from grapes grown on the estate, and those labelled Noval are sourced from other growers. After a dip in quality during the 1980s, Noval's vintage ports are truly back on form. Noval Naçional, made in tiny amounts from a plot of ungrafted vines, holds the record for the most expensive bottle of vintage port ever sold: the 1931 vintage went for US$5,900 a bottle in 1983.
🍷 *fortified* 🍇 *2004, 2003, 2000, 1997, 1994* ★ *LBV, Quinta do Noval 1994 Vintage Port, Quinta do Noval Naçional*

Quinta do Noval label

Ramos Pinto
Vinho do Porto (Port Wine)

av Ramos Pinto 380, Vila Nova de Gaia ☎ *223 707 000* ○

ADRIANO RAMOS PINTO made his name in the late 19th century selling port to Brazil, helped by a series of posters of scantily clad women. The firm remained in family hands until 1990, when it was sold to Champagne house Louis Roederer *(see p175)*, but the winemaker is still a direct descendant of the founder. Ramos Pinto is best known for its fine single *quinta* tawnies. Quinta da Ervamoira 10-Year-Old has a tawny colour with a rich raisin and sultana character and a hint of toasted almonds. Quinta do Bom Retiro 20-Year-Old is a pale amber tawny with soft,

seductive flavours and great poise. Toasted almond and brazil nut complexity are a result of ageing in wood.
🍷 *fortified* 🍇 *1983* ★ *Quinta da Ervamoira 10-Year-Old Tawny, Quinta do Bom Retiro 20-Year-Old Tawny*

Sandeman
Vinho do Porto (Port Wine)

Largo de Miguel Bombarda 3, Vila Nova de Gaia ☎ *223 740 500*
🅦 *www.sandeman.com* ○

FOUNDED BY Scotsman George Sandeman in 1790, this producer is forever identified by the silhouette of the don, one of the most instantly recognizable logos in the wine world. The company is still managed by a Sandeman – also named George – but now belongs to Sogrape. Sandeman releases small amounts of beautifully balanced tawnies and makes a vintage port named Vau Vintage, which is packed with mulberry fruit. Consumers are encouraged to drink Vau Vintage young, although it is capable of 10 years' age.
🍷 *fortified* 🍇 *2003, 2000, 1994* ★ *Imperial Tawny, 20-Year-Old Tawny, Vau Vintage 2000*

THE RISE OF THE QUINTA

Small is becoming increasingly beautiful in Portugal as an increasing number of private estates, or *quintas*, gain the wherewithal to make and market their own wines. Although a number of *quintas* may share the same consultant winemaker, this independence has brought about much greater diversity and individuality. Quinta do Ameal in Vinho Verde, and Quinta de Covela in Minho, are among the estates already known for their distinctive wines; in the Douro, it is Quintas do Crasto, do Cotto, de la Rosa, do Vale Meão, and do Vallado. Further south in Dão, Quinta dos Roques has made a name for itself, while in Estremadura, Quintas do Monte d'Oiro and de Pancas are well worth seeking out. Ribatejo's top *quintas* are Quinta de Alorna, Quinta do Casal Branco, and Casa Cadaval; and in Alentejo, the shining lights are Quinta do Mouro, Cortes de Cima, and Herdade de Mouchão.

Taylor, Fladgate & Yeatman
Vinho do Porto (Port Wine)

rua do Choupelo 250, Vila Nova de Gaia ☎ *223 742 800* ⓦ *www.taylor.pt* ◯

TAYLOR'S HAS BUILT a reputation as one of the most prestigious port producers of all. The company can trace its roots back to 1692 and remains the only British producer to have never been sold or taken over. Now the senior member of the Fladgate Partnership (alongside Fonseca and Croft), Taylor's makes vintage ports that consistently fetch some of the highest prices at auction. This was also the first company to popularize LBV, one of the bestselling styles of port. The range is huge; vintage ports are tight-knit and concentrated in youth, and develop an opulent floral character (akin to violets) with about 20 years' bottle age.

🍷 *fortified* 🔺 *2000, 1983, 1980, 1977, 1966, 1963* ★ *Taylor's First Estate, LBV, Vintage Ports: Quinta de Vargellas 2005, Quinta da Terra Feita 2005*

W & J Graham
Vinho do Porto (Port Wine)

rua Rei Ramiro 514, Vila Nova de Gaia ☎ *223 776 300* ⓦ *www.grahams-port.com* ◯

THE GRAHAMS were textile manufacturers who came into port as a result of a bad debt. Their shipping firm was then bought by the Symingtons (also owners of Dow and Warre), who have continued to make wines in the characteristically rich Graham's style. The phenomenally good range includes a delicious fruit-driven LBV that is popular in both the UK and the US.

🍷 *fortified* 🔺 *2003, 2000, 1997, 1994, 1991, 1983, 1977, 1970, 1966, 1963* ★ *Six Grapes, Malvedos 1998 Vintage Port, 1985 Vintage Port, 30-Year-Old Tawny*

Warre
Vinho do Porto (Port Wine)

Trav Barão de Forrester 85, Vila Nova de Gaia ☎ *223 776 300* ⓦ *www.warre.com* ◯

ESTABLISHED IN 1670, Warre (pronounced 'war') is the oldest of the British-owned houses. The firm joined the Symington group in the 1960s, but the Warre family continued to be associated with the business until 1991. Although it has a well-established reputation for vintage port, Warre recently raised its profile with Otima, a very soft, seductive 10-year-old tawny with a pronounced flavour of dried fruit and a nutty finish.

🍷 *fortified* 🔺 *2003, 2000, 1991, 1983, 1970* ★ *Warre's Warrior, Otima 10-Year-Old Tawny, Quinta da Cavadinha 1995 Vintage Port*

Caves Aliança
Bairrada

rua do Comércio, Sangalhos ☎ *234 732 000* ⓦ *www.caves-alianca.com* ◯

ESTABLISHED IN 1927, this large Bairrada-based company has reinvented itself in recent years. After investing heavily in a new winery in the 1980s, Aliança has now turned its attention to the vineyards. With holdings in Trás-os-Montes, the Douro, Dão, and Alentejo as well as

Caves Aliança label

Bairrada, these amount to 350ha in total. Aliança was the first Bairrada producer to move towards a modern style of winemaking. Bordelais consultant Michel Rolland has been recruited to accelerate the process, and Aliança is now making ever more accessible, easy drinking reds. T da Quinta da Terrugem, from the Alentejo, has quickly become one of Portugal's most sought-after reds, with a price tag to match.

🍷 *red, white, rosé, sparkling* 🔺 *2008, 2007, 2006* ★ *Galeria (red & white), Alabastro, T da Quinta da Terrugem*

W & J Graham

Luís Pato
Bairrada

Ois de Bairro, Anadia ☎ *231 528 156* ◯ *by appt*

LUÍS PATO HAS DONE MORE to put Bairrada (and perhaps Portugal) on the map than any other winemaker. He only began bottling wine under his own label in 1980, after inheriting 70ha of vines from his father, and he has worked tirelessly to promote his own good name ever since. After a decade or more of trial and error, Pato has established a successful formula based on the variations in the local *terroir*. With over 20 plots scattered on sandy-clay and chalky-clay soils around the region, he now reserves the sandier soils for white wines and lighter reds, and makes a range of intense, full-bodied reds on the heavier clays, mainly from the capricious Baga grape.

🍷 *red, white, sparkling* 🔺 *2008, 2007, 2005, 2004, 2003* ★ *Vinha Barrosa, Vinha Pan, Pé Franco*

D F J Vinhos
Ribatejo

Quinta Fonte Bela, Vila Cha de Ourique, Cartaxo
☎ 243 704 701 ◑

THE LATE DINO VENTURA and Fausto Ferraz were working as wine importers in London when they met winemaker José Neiva. In a short space of time, the three men built up one of the most successful wine ventures in Portugal. With grapes from Lisboa (formerly Estremadura) and Ribatejo, they make a huge range of wines, largely for the UK market but increasingly popular in Portugal. Although Neiva's wines tend to owe more to the winemaker than to *terroir*, they are accessible and easy to drink. The dynamic range includes bargain wines made by local co-ops under Neiva's guidance – these sell under a variety of labels, of which Portada and Segada are the best known. Varietal wines (both red and white, made from indigenous and foreign grapes) are mostly bottled under the Grand'Arte label.
🔲 *red, white*
🔺 *most recent*
★ *Segada, Grand'Arte*

José Maria da Fonseca
Setúbal Peninsula

Vila Nogueira de Azeitão, Azeitão
☎ 212 197 500
🔲 www.jmf.pt ◻

DESCENDANTS OF José Maria da Fonseca, who settled on the Setúbal Peninsula in 1834, still own and manage this historic firm. Brothers António and Domingos Soares Franco are president and winemaker respectively, looking after the 650ha of vineyard. The company's reputation was built on the back of Periquita, a brand that was established in 1850 and is still one of Portugal's bestselling reds. After World War II, Fonseca followed Sogrape into the rosé business, creating its own answer to Mateus *(see p339)*, Lancers. This grew so fast that the company briefly split in two, but came back together again in 1996. This company has one of the most advanced wineries in Portugal, and makes an ever-changing range of wines, including innovative reds that combine local and foreign grapes. It is also the biggest producer of fortified Setúbal and has stocks of this magnificently concentrated wine dating back to 1884.
🔲 *red, white, rosé, sparkling, fortified* 🔺 *2008, 2007, 2004, 2003*
★ *Periquita Classico, José de Sousa, Hexagon, Trilogia*

J P Vinhos
Setúbal Peninsula

Vila Nogueira de Azeitão, Azeitão
☎ 212 198 060
🔲 www.jpvinhos.com ◻

JOÃO PIRES WAS an Algarvean who cleverly established a winery by the main north-south railway line on the Setúbal Peninsula to quench the thirst of the Algarve fishermen. The company has since undergone a number of reincarnations and was put on the international map in the early 1980s by Australian winemaker Peter Bright. Although Bright has now moved on to establish his own business, many of the wines he created remain successful. For years, the company's signature wine was João Pires, a deliciously aromatic dry Muscat. This brand has now been sold, and J P Vinhos has turned to making solid, southern reds like Tinta da Anfora and Só Syrah, most recently under the guiding hand of Madeiran businessman Jo Berardo. There are also sweet, fortified Setúbal wines and Loridos sparkling wines.
🔲 *red, white, sparkling, fortified*
🔺 *2008, 2007, 2004, 2003*
★ *Serras de Azeitão, Tinta da Anfora, Só Syrah*

Herdade do Esporão
Alentejo

Finagra, Reguengos de Monsaraz
☎ 266 509 270
🔲 www.esporao.com ◻

WITH 550HA OF VINES, Esporão has the largest single vineyard in Portugal. It is the result of a decade of investment by banker and all-round businessman José Roquette. The winemaking here is the responsibility of David Baverstock, an Australian with 30 years' experience in Portugal. Although made mainly from super-ripe local grape varieties, the wines have a

Periquita grapes being unloaded at J P Vinhos

ripe, sometimes minty flavour that hints at the New World reds. Monte Velho, the principal brand, has consistently sound red and white wines that seem to be on every restaurant wine list in Portugal.

🍷 red, white, rosé, sparkling 📅 2008, 2007, 2004, 2003 ★ Esporão (red & white), Vinha da Defesa, Trincadeira

Quinta do Carmo
Alentejo

Herdade das Carvalhas, Gloria, Estremoz 📞 *268 33 73 20* 🖥 *www.lafite.com* 🔲 *by appt*

ONCE PART OF a large family estate, the winemaking interests at Quinta do Carmo are now run as a joint venture between Les Domaines Baron de Rothschild – owner of Château Lafite-Rothschild in Bordeaux *(see p68)* – and Jo Berardo of J P Vinhos. A large swathe of vineyard has been replanted, and although quality dipped in the 1990s, it seems to be on the up again as the vines reach maturity. Cabernet and Syrah are planted alongside local grape varieties to make a wine that combines the power and ripeness of the Alentejo with French finesse.

🍷 red, white 📅 2008, 2007, 2004, 2003 ★ Quinta do Carmo, D Martinho

Henriques & Henriques
Madeira

Sítio de Bélem, Camara de Lobos 📞 *291 941 551* 🔲

WITH THE LARGEST vineyard holding on the island, Henriques & Henriques has all the raw material needed to make an excellent range of wines. The 10- and 15-year-old blends made from each of the four 'noble' grape varieties are bench-mark madeiras. Henriques &

Private Selection

ESPORÃO

Garrafeira 2000 - Alentejo - D.O.C.
Denominação de Origem Controlada-Reguengos
Vinho Tinto / Red Wine / Vin Rouge

Alc.14% by vol. Produced and bottled par FINAGRA S.A. - Lisboa - Produce of Portugal 75cl

Herdade do Esporão label

Henriques also has some absolutely remarkable vintage wines that even pre-date the company's original foundation in 1850.

🍷 fortified 📅 1954, 1944, 1934, 1927 ★ 10-Year-Old Bual, 15-Year-Old Verdelho, Monte Seco

Justino Henriques
Madeira

Parque Industrial de Cancela, Caniço 📞 *291 934257* 🔴

NOW THE LARGEST Madeira shipper, Justino Henriques mostly bottles large quantities of inexpensive wine under the Cruz label for export to France. The company used to own traditional lodges in the centre of Funchal, but it has moved to more practical, purpose-built premises on an industrial estate outside town. It produces a full range of styles including a number of vintage wines dating back to the early years of the 20th century. These have a rich, baked, toasted quality that is characteristic of traditional madeira.

🍷 fortified 📅 1964, 1954 ★ 10-Year-Old Malmsey

Madeira Wine Company
Madeira

rua dos Ferreiros 191, Apartado 295, Funchal 📞 *291 470 100* 🖥 *www.madeirawinecompany.com* 🔲

FORMED FROM the amalgamation of a number of small firms in 1913, the 'Madeira Wine Association', as it used to be called, grew in stature when Blandy's, Leacock, Miles, and Cossart Gordon joined its ranks. These remain the four main brands. The company is now run by the Symington family from Porto in partnership with Blandy's, who retain a strong presence on the island. The company boasts wonderful stocks of vintage madeira both in cask and in bottle, the latter dating back well into the 19th century. Blandy's Alvada is an unusual five-year-old blend of Bual and Malvasia. Medium-rich, smooth, and raisiny in style, it is made to go with sticky puddings and blue cheese.

🍷 fortified 📅 1972, 1958, 1954 ★ Blandy's Alvada, Cossart Gordon Colheitas, Blandy's 1954 Bual

Vinhos Barbeito
Madeira

Estrada de Ribeira Garcia, 9300–324, Câmara de Lobos 📞 *291 761829* 🔲

THIS FAMILY-RUN FIRM was given a new lease of life when a younger member of the Barbeito family, Ricardo Diogo, joined in 1990 and entered into a joint venture with Kinoshita, a large Japanese client. Barbeito is now bottling small amounts of innovative cask-aged madeiras.

🍷 fortified 📅 1957, 1901 ★ Single-cask colheitas, 20-Year-Old Malvasia

Vinhos Barbeito

GERMANY, AUSTRIA & SWITZERLAND

GERMANY

THIS IS THE HOMELAND OF RIESLING, *regarded by many wine experts as the noblest white grape variety. Germany earns its place as one of the world's great wine regions by producing wines in a range of styles from sensational, sweet, and rare* Trockenbeerenauslese *(TBA) to racy* Kabinett. *The major development of recent years, however, has been the resurgence of red wines from Germany.*

BACKGROUND

THE ROMANS BROUGHT organized viticulture to this northerly European region, and in the early Middle Ages the Church owned and developed huge vineyards here. According to legend, the Emperor Charlemagne stood on the river bank opposite the Rheingau in the 8th century, noting where the winter snows melted first. He then commanded that vines be planted on those warmer sites.

Crest of Weingut Geheimer Rat Dr von Bassermann-Jordan

By the late Middle Ages, many aristocratic estates had been established both in the Rheingau and to the south. Some still remain in the hands of the same families. It is estimated that at the end of the 16th century, the area under vine was three times larger than it is today. Conflicts, such as the Thirty Years' War (1618–48), devastated vast regions of vineyards, and in times of hardship peasants often replaced vines with other edible crops. However, the wine industry recovered, and by the late 19th century the Rheingau's best wines fetched prices as high as those of Bordeaux *premiers crus*. Unfortunately, standards plummeted during the 1960s and 70s as many producers opted for maximum yields, and only in the past decade has there been a sustained effort by top estates to recover the once enviable reputation of German wine.

THE WINE INDUSTRY TODAY

GERMANY IS NOT A major player in international terms, with just 102,000ha in production – nine times less than France or Italy. The image of German wine has suffered badly due to the large amount of mediocre sweetish white wine that has

View of the Mosel-Saar-Ruwer winegrowing area

◁ **Terraced vineyards line the steep banks of the Rhein (Rhine) River at Kaub, Mittelrhein**

WINEGROWING REGIONS
Most of Germany's key winegrowing areas are clustered along the Rhein (Rhine), Mosel, and Main rivers to the southwest of the country. There are two additional pockets on the Elbe and Saale rivers in the former East Germany.

GRAPE VARIETIES & WINE STYLES

RIESLING REMAINS THE major grape variety of southern Germany – specifically of the Mosel and Rhein regions. A long growing season and a high incidence of botrytis *(see p66)* allow the Riesling vineyards here to produce some of the world's most sensational sweet wines. Germany's finest wines are its estate-bottled Rieslings, which range from steely and bone-dry to sweet and racy, and are usually underpriced for their quality.

In the south, especially in Baden, Pinot varieties reign supreme. Weissburgunder (Pinot Blanc) is found across Germany's viticultural areas, while Spätburgunder (Pinot Noir) is grown in northerly regions such as the Ahr, with steadily improving results. Silvaner is not held in high esteem, but in Franken it can achieve great heights.

Bone-dry wines are easily produced in southern regions such as the Pfalz and Baden. In cooler climes further north, however, dry styles can be too austere for most palates because of the grapes' naturally high acidity. Instead, the wines here are often balanced with residual sugar, resulting in a refreshing fruitiness.

Oak barrels play a part in red wine production, but on the whole the whites are unoaked. This means that they often reflect their soil origins and microclimatic conditions far better than wines that have been cosseted in costly French oak, and allow a purity of flavour – and often their mineral vigour – to shine through.

been unleashed onto export markets over recent decades. Consequently, many consumers associate German wine with the worst quality that the country has to offer. This problem has been exacerbated by the structure of the industry, which is based on very small estates and large co-operatives. The small estates, many of them of world-class stature, have limited quantities of wine to sell; the larger producers are rarely focused on high quality, so their wines do little to improve the image of German wines abroad.

Local wine laws and archaic labelling regulations have also made life difficult for the consumer *(see pp348–9)*. Thousands of vineyards have the right to be identified on a label, and in addition to the well known grape varieties there are numerous crosses. But if the range of varieties and wine styles can be a marketing handicap, it can also be a positive consideration, since few countries are able to offer such diversity of styles.

Wine shop in Meersburg, Baden

GERMAN WINE LAW

TO AN UNTRAINED EYE, *few things in life can appear quite as baffling as a German wine label. Even the most accomplished expert occasionally struggles with the finer nuances. This is information overload at its most extreme – grape variety, ripeness level, vineyard, village, region, producer name and address, not to mention the Gothic lettering or Amtliche Prüfungsnummer (AP number), which shows that the wine has been officially tested.*

Weingut Freiherr Heyl Zu Herrnsheim label, Rheinhessen

All of Germany's grape growing areas are legally defined and designated, whether a single vineyard (Einzellage) or a collection of vineyards (Grosslage). Unlike in France and much of Europe, however, the vineyards are not classified according to quality.

Instead, individual wines are rated according to the ripeness of the grapes at harvest. Thus any Einzellage can achieve the highest ranking in German wine, Qualitätswein mit Prädikat (QmP), in a particular vintage.

In theory this is fine – riper grapes generally produce the best wine. Yet flaws in the system (chiefly the planting of inferior grapes to achieve high levels of ripeness) mean that roughly 90 per cent of production is classified as QmP or the next best quality level, Qualitätswein bestimmter Anbaugebiet (QbA). So the hierarchy is both ambiguous and seriously top-heavy – with world-class bottles sharing the same classification as bog-standard, barely drinkable plonk.

German Wine Classification

German wines are classified according to the ripeness of the grapes at harvest.

Qualitätswein mit Prädikat **(QmP)**: This literally means 'quality wine with special characteristics' and is German wine's highest classification. To qualify for QmP status, grapes must meet minimum ripeness levels – from *Kabinett* (the lowest natural sugar readings) to *Trockenbeerenauslese* (TBA; the highest). The levels of ripeness stipulated vary according to region and grape variety. Chaptalization (the addition of sugar during fermentation to increase alcohol levels) is not permitted for QmP wines.

Kabinett: Unless labelled *trocken* or *halbtrocken*, this wine will normally be medium dry.

Spätlese: A 'late harvest' wine, normally medium to medium sweet in style.

Auslese: A medium to sweet wine where some of the grapes may have been affected by botrytis.

Beerenauslese **(BA)**: A sweet wine, where many of the grapes will have been affected by botrytis.

Eiswein: An intensely sweet wine made from grapes that have naturally frozen on the vine. Ice wines tend to have very pure, rich flavours.

A *Spätlese* from Domänenweingut Schloss Schönborn, Rheingau

Trockenbeerenauslese **(TBA)**: An intensely sweet wine made only from grapes affected by botrytis. Do not be confused by the word 'trocken', meaning dry.

Qualitätswein bestimmter Anbaugebiet **(QbA)**: This is the second-ranked German classification, for quality wine made within a designated region. Chaptalization is permitted for this category.

Landwein: Germany's equivalent of the French *vin de pays*, a 'country wine' can come from any one of 17 designated areas.

Deutsche Tafelwein: This category is for table wine, which can only come from Germany itself.

Note: In Austria, even higher ripeness levels are required to produce *Beerenauslese* (BA) and *Trockenbeerenauslese* (TBA) wines.

GROSSES GEWÄCHS

The *Grosses Gewächs*, or great growth, system was designed to solve some of the problems created by the existing German wine regulations. First introduced in the mid-1990s by the VDP, the association of Germany's leading growers, the system classifies all the outstanding vineyards and covers all German wine regions with the exception of the Rheingau, which has its own classification system, with the best sites labelled as *Erstes Gewächs*. To use the designation on their label, producers must use only permitted grape varieties and keep yields low to bring out the true quality of the vineyard. If the wine is an *Auslese* level or below, it must be dry in style. Although far from perfect, the classification has been widely adopted.

Grosses Gewächs symbol

READING A GERMAN WINE LABEL

If faced with German wine from an unfamiliar producer, the following techniques can help unravel the style and potential quality: look for a grape variety – in Germany the best wines are usually Riesling QmP wines and will generally be medium dry *(Kabinett)* through to extremely sweet *(Trockenbeerenauslese)*, unless the words *trocken* or *halbtrocken* appear. Avoid QbA wines unless you are confident of the producer.

Alcoholic strength may help to confirm the style: less than 12 per cent (and especially less than 10.5 per cent), expect a medium or sweet style of wine. It also helps to be familiar with the styles of the major German regions: wines tend to become fuller and drier as you move from north to south. Lastly, price is a reasonable guide to quality. There are bargains to be had in German wine, but expect to pay a bit more for the top producers.

Glossary

Bereich: *a district within one of the wine regions covered in this chapter. Approach with caution: if you see this on a label, as quality can be poor.*

Classic: *a wine that is reasonably dry in style and made from a traditional grape variety such as Riesling, Silvaner, or Rivaner. This term was introduced in an attempt to make the labelling of German wines easier.*

Einzellage: *single vineyard.*

Grosslage: *a group of vineyards.*

halbtrocken: *literally 'half dry' or off dry.*

Rotwein: *red wine*

Sekt: *sparkling wine.*

trocken: *dry.*

Weingut: *wine estate.*

Weisswein: *white wine.*

Rotling: *rosé.*

Selection: *related to Classic, this is meant to denote a premium wine that is produced in limited quantities. The term is rarely seen on exported wines.*

Ursprungslage: *another new term, meant to replace Grosslage. The wine must not just originate from a designated area, it must also be produced in a specific style using registered grape varieties.*

Detail from Weingut Reichsrat von Buhl label

Weingut Juliusspital label

Gutsabfüllung denotes the wine is bottled by the producer.

Müller-Catoir is the name of the producer.

Weingut

2216

feit 1744

Müller-Catoir

Gutsabfüllung · D-67433 Neustadt/Weinstrasse-Haardt

2002er Riesling

Haardter Bürgergarten Spätlese
alc. 9,0%vol. · **Pfalz** · **750 mle**
Qualitätswein mit Prädikat · Amtl.Prüf.Nr. 5174079 603

Address of producer

Riesling is the name of the principal grape variety.

2002 – the vintage.

Vineyard

Alcoholic strength

Spätlese means 'late harvest', this indicates the ripeness of the grapes and therefore the sweetness of the wine.

Volume

Qualitätswein mit Prädikat (QmP) is the quality classification.

Pfalz is one of the 13 specified quality regions in Germany.

Amtliche Prüfungsnummer (AP number) confirms the wine has passed official testing procedures. The standards in Germany are very low, however.

WINE MAP OF GERMANY

1998
Riesling Kabinett trocken

**Weingut Geheimer Rat
Dr. v. Bassermann-Jordan**

**Riesling label from Weingut
Geheimer Rat Dr von Bassermann-
Jordan, Pfalz**

ALTHOUGH GERMANY'S *TAFEL-* AND *LANDWEIN (see p348)* regions stretch as far north as Mecklenburg, near the Baltic coast, the majority of the country's quality wine is made in the southwest. From just south of Bonn to the Swiss border, the Rhein River meanders through a long series of wine regions, many of whose names reflect the importance of this great river and its tributaries – which include the Ahr, Mosel, Saar, Ruwer, and Nahe. Rheinhessen is the largest wine region, but the most favoured sites are located on the steep, south-facing slopes of the Rheingau. Franken, just to the east, spreads out along the Main River, and much further east are the two small outposts of Saale-Unstrut and Sachsen. Across the whole country, most of the wines produced are white, and the grape of choice is Riesling.

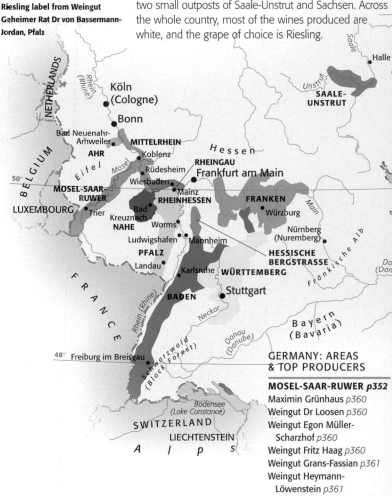

GERMANY: AREAS & TOP PRODUCERS

MOSEL-SAAR-RUWER *p352*
Maximin Grünhaus *p360*
Weingut Dr Loosen *p360*
Weingut Egon Müller-
  Scharzhof *p360*
Weingut Fritz Haag *p360*
Weingut Grans-Fassian *p361*
Weingut Heymann-
  Löwenstein *p361*
Weingut J J Prüm *p361*

Harvesting Riesling grapes in the Mosel-Saar-Ruwer

TERROIR AT A GLANCE

Latitude: 47–5 °N.

Altitude: 65–380m.

Topography: Most vineyards are planted along river valleys. South-facing slopes are favoured, and some are remarkably steep.

Soil: Varies widely including loess, loam, limestone, sandstone, marl, clay, slate, volcanic and granite.

Climate: Generally damp and cool. More northerly regions such as Mosel-Saar-Ruwer, and especially

Saale-Unstrut and Sachsen, have very marginal and variable conditions. Southern regions such as the Pfalz have consistently sunnier and warmer climates.

Temperature: July average is 18.5°C.

Rainfall: Annual averages range from 490–880mm.

Viticultural hazards: Spring frost; autumnal rain; fungal diseases; underripeness.

Dresden

gebirge
Mountains)

POLAND

CZECH REPUBLIC

HSEN

⊢— km ——————¬ 100

Weingut Georg Breuer's Rheingau plot

Bereich Bernkastel vineyards and a ruined castle, Burg Landshut, overlooking the Mosel River

WINEGROWING AREAS OF GERMANY

Mosel-Saar-Ruwer

THE MOSEL-SAAR-RUWER IS a large region, broken down into five districts (*Bereiche*). Remains of Roman press-houses in this region's vineyards are evidence of cultivation stretching back 2,000 years. The wine produced here was almost all consumed locally until the early 20th century, when the area became better known abroad for its fresh, charming wines. It is an exceptionally beautiful region, with vineyards planted on steep slopes rising from the river bank. The gradient allows the vines to enjoy maximum exposure to the sun, while the slate soils retain warmth and help the grapes to ripen. There are many vineyards on flatter land away from the river, but these are mostly planted with Müller-Thurgau and produce simple wines without the elegance or longevity of Riesling. The winegrowing areas along the Mosel, and its tributaries the Ruwer and Saar, produce a unique style of Riesling: low in alcohol, usually balanced with natural grape sweetness, and refreshed by racy acidity.

Despite its renown, the region is under increasing threat. Tending and harvesting its vineyards is back-breaking work, and labour shortages mean that the least accessible sites are gradually being abandoned. The prices of these wines need to rise to make the sites economically viable in the long term.

Among the most delicate of all white wines, Mosel Riesling can nonetheless age superbly;

HEYMANN-LÖWENSTEIN

Logo, Weingut Heymann Löwenstein

40-year-old examples can still be mouth-wateringly fresh. In general, the Mosel itself gives relatively rich, fruity, and succulent wines, whereas those of the cooler Saar and Ruwer are more steely and intense. There is a growing vogue for dry Rieslings from these regions, but in difficult vintages such wines can be tart. However, growing expertise and global warming are resulting in much more successful dry styles. In exceptional years, magnificent botrytis wines (*see p66*) are produced throughout the Mosel-Saar-Ruwer. TBA (*see p348*) is the rarest, as it is made from individually picked berries, and few estates can produce more than a few hundred bottles. Not surprisingly, these wines fetch high prices at regional auctions. Capable of remaining fresh and vigorous for a century, they are miracles of intensity and flavour.

🗔 *blue slate, Devonian slate* 🮐 *Spätburgunder (Pinot Noir)* 🯁 *Riesling, Elbling* 🮕 *red, white, sparkling, dessert*

Bereich Burg Cochem

THIS NORTHERN STRETCH OF THE MOSEL is also known as the Untermosel or, increasingly, as the Terrassenmosel, a reference to the fact that many of its steep vineyards are terraced. There are few producers of note here, but the area's reputation has been growing in recent years thanks to the hard work of a few individuals. Drier styles of Riesling from more innovative growers such as Weingut Heymann-Löwenstein can be very successful. Wine lovers with an eye for a bargain can find some excellent bottles in this district, which is considered less fashionable than the neighbouring Mittelmosel.

Bereich Bernkastel

STRETCHING FROM PÜNDERICH TO SCHWEICH, this is the largest of the Mosel *Bereiche*, and well known for its vineyards. Its central portion – roughly from Urzig to Trittenheim, and usually known as the Mittelmosel, although the term has no strict geographical or legal definition – is the source of the finest wines. The most famous vineyards, including Wehlener Sonnenuhr, Bernkasteler Doktor, and Brauneberger Juffer-Sonnenuhr, all lie along this stretch, though there is a growing band of producers making excellent wines from less well-known sites in Pünderich and Enkirch. The Prüm family has long been the most famous set of growers, but today there is no shortage of outstanding producers.

Bereich Ruwer

JUST EAST OF TRIER IS THE small Ruwer River, whose vineyards were created over 1,000 years ago, mostly by monastic estates. Exceptionally steep and hard to work, the vineyards are, regrettably, declining in area. Their wines, from wineries such as Maximin Grünhaus and Weingut Karlsmühle are among the most exquisite in the entire region. Dry as well as sweet Rieslings are produced, but almost all are consumed by the domestic market.

Weingut Reinhold Haart on the bank of the Mosel River

BERNKASTELER DOKTOR: THE MIRACLE CURE

This south-facing vineyard perched above Bernkastel is said to be the most valuable agricultural land in Germany. It is a small patch of land with only four producers: Wegeler-Deinhard, Reichsgraf von Kesselstatt, and the two Thanisch estates. The wines from its few hectares are among the most expensive in Germany. Legend has it that the vineyard got its name in the 14th century from Archbishop Boemund of Trier who owned a castle above the town, and one day fell ill there. Medicines proved of no avail, but a glass of wine from a nearby vineyard cured him. Out of gratitude the archbishop gave the name 'Doctor' to the site. It later acquired additional renown as the vineyard from which the Mosel's first TBA was produced in 1921.

Bereich Saar

AT KONZ, THE SAAR RIVER joins the Mosel: the Saar region stretches from here south to Serrig, an area larger than the Ruwer but far smaller than Bereich Bernkastel. The Saar has the most extreme climate, with bitterly cold winters, and there are years when the grapes do not ripen fully and the wines are over-acidic. When they do ripen, however, these can be the finest wines of the region, better even than those of the Mosel. The celebrated Egon Müller estate at Scharzhof sets the standards to which most other estates here aspire. Powerful dry wines can also be produced in the Saar, but only by limiting yields to scarcely economic levels.

Bereiche Obermosel & Moseltor

THE OBERMOSEL LIES west of Trier and fringes the border with Luxembourg. Elbling rather than Riesling is the most commonly planted variety. While it has a very long history, Elbling is today usually grown to provide a base wine for sparkling *Sekt*. The dry wines can be thin and tart as yields are often excessively high. Spring frosts are a common climatic hazard. Bereich Moseltor, the small southerly extension of the Obermosel, is of little significance.

Ahr

LOCATED JUST SOUTH OF BONN, this is one of Germany's – and Europe's – most northerly winegrowing regions, and the speciality here is Spätburgunder (Pinot Noir), which can ripen fully on the dark cliffs that hem in the river valley. The wines used to be made in a sweetish style, but now all the best producers aim for rich, dry wines with density and elegance. Production is limited, and prices tend to be high, but that does not seem to deter the day-trippers from Bonn and Koblenz, who come here in droves on summer weekends to taste and buy. Other grape varieties are also grown in the Ahr region but result in wines of considerably less interest.

Bingen, at the confluence of the Nahe and Rhein rivers

slate, loam Spätburgunder (Pinot Noir), Portugieser Riesling red, white

Mittelrhein

AFTER RÜDESHEIM the Rhein (Rhine) River flows north once again, through the narrow, castle-studded valley of the Mittelrhein wine region. The slopes here are very steep, and many former vineyard sites have been abandoned over recent decades because they are inaccessible and therefore extremely costly to cultivate. Overshadowed by its neighbours the Rheingau to the south and the Mosel to the southwest, this is an underestimated and undervalued region, but one fully capable of producing exciting Rieslings. The region is popular with tourists, however, and too many growers content themselves with producing overcropped wines for sale in the local wine taverns and restaurants. This undermines the efforts of the few more serious producers to achieve the quality that the Mittelrhein can produce.

slate Spätburgunder (Pinot Noir) Riesling, Müller-Thurgau red, white, sparkling, dessert

Nahe

THE NORTHERNMOST FRINGES of the Nahe region lie opposite the Rheingau on the south bank of the Rhein, and its vineyards stretch in a southwesterly direction in side valleys off the Nahe River. It is a very mixed region in terms of soils and grape varieties, so it is hardly surprising that it lacks identity. There are a handful of excellent local producers, but there are also many estates that produce run-of-the-mill wines. The Nahe is less well known than it ought to be, so prices, even for the finest wines, are usually reasonable given their quality.

The best vineyards lie on steep, stony slopes around the villages of Niederhausen and Schlossböckelheim: the Rieslings from here are midway in style between examples from the Mosel and those of the Rheingau, and can be exceptionally good. The vineyards closer to the Rhein River have fairly rich, fertile soils, and their wines can be rather soft and lacking in zest.

porphyry, slate, clay, loam, sandstone Spätburgunder (Pinot Noir) Riesling, Müller-Thurgau, Silvaner red, white, sparkling, dessert

Rheingau

AT MAINZ THE MIGHTY Rhein turns a corner and heads due west for some 32km. Lining the north bank are south-facing vineyards that stretch for a few kilometres inland until forests on the higher slopes mark the end of the land suitable for viticulture. Riesling has been grown on these slopes for centuries, and on the region's western fringes, around Assmannshausen, Spätburgunder (Pinot Noir) can claim an equally long tradition. More than any other region, the Rheingau is dominated by large aristocratic and ecclesiastical estates that have survived from medieval times.

In the 19th century, wines from the Rheingau were as sought after, and as expensive, as the finest growths of Bordeaux, but more recently the region's reputation has slipped, as yields have risen and winemaking standards declined. The top producers have now reversed the trend, but still argue among themselves over stylistic issues. In the 1980s some forward-looking local growers, notably the late Bernhard Breuer of Weingut Georg Breuer and the late Graf Matuschka-Greiffenclau of Schloss Vollrads, founded the Charta Association, which sought to promote dry Rieslings with a good acidic structure as ideal wines to accompany food. They were, they asserted, the German equivalents of fine Chablis. Charta only had limited success, but it launched a series of vital debates, first about wine styles, and then about vineyard classification. Breuer and others believed that the Rheingau's only chance of recovering its reputation was by focusing on its outstanding sites – those with *Erstes Gewächs* (first growth) status. But who was to determine which were the top sites? Inevitably, discussions on the subject became both political and personal, but eventually a

GEORG BREUER
1999
BERG SCHLOSSBERG
RÜDESHEIM

**Weingut Georg Breuer
wine label**

list of first growth vineyards was published in 2000. Unfortunately, compromise ruled the day, so that one third of all the viticultural land in the Rheingau emerged as worthy of *Erstes Gewächs* classification, which some growers thought was a ridiculously high proportion. In practice, however, estates have been cautious about mentioning the designation on their labels, sensibly reserving its use for one or two outstanding wines in each vintage. The prevailing style is essentially dry with a good backbone of acidity, and, in exceptional vintages, there are also some breathtaking dessert wines made from grapes affected by botrytis.

Although the top wines of the Rheingau are superb, they tend to lack consistency. The naturally high acidity can be difficult to balance, and there is less stylistic uniformity here than in the Pfalz, for example. Moreover, many estates remain in the hands of absentee aristocratic landlords, who employ managers to run the properties. And since managers are less likely to take the risks necessary for outstanding quality than owner-winemakers, the overall standard suffers. But it is not for nothing that the Rheingau vineyards were revered. Riesling, whether dry or sweet, can attain true magnificence here, and will continue to do so.

Burg Stahleck with the village of Lorch and its vineyards, Rheingau

The Rheingau Villages

AT THE EASTERN LIMIT of the Rheingau, just across the river from Mainz, Hochheim's vineyards rise gently up from the river bank to the charming main street of the old town. The mesoclimate here, warmer than the rest of the Rheingau, usually results in wines of considerable body and power. Further west, behind the extensive but unremarkable vineyards of Eltville on slopes set back from the river, is Rauenthal, boasting a number of outstanding sites including Baiken, Gehrn, and Nonnenberg. Kiedrich, one of the Rheingau's loveliest villages and home of the Gräfenbach vineyard, is also tucked back into the foothills of the Taunus Mountains, while Erbach, best known for its distinguished Marcobrun vineyard, is unusual in that it lies very close to the river bank. Even more unusual is the Schloss Schönborn Estate in Hattenheim, which has vineyards on an island in the middle of the Rhein. Oestrich is joined to Winkel and Mittelheim to the west. The best known sites here are Schloss Vollrads, on the slopes well away from sprawling Winkel, and Lenchen and Doosberg, closer to Oestrich itself. Hallgarten's vineyards, to the northwest, are the Rheingau's highest – but the only well-known vineyard here is Schönhell, and the wines are perhaps not as well known as they should be.

More a hamlet than a village, Johannisberg is famous worldwide for its *Schloss* (castle) and abbey, both reconstructed after bombardment during World War II. The best-known vineyard stretches below the *Schloss* and its terrace, where the soils have a high quartzite content. In summer, the narrow lanes of Rüdesheim are thronged with tourists, few of whom cast more than a glance at the vast sweep of vineyards that lie above and to the west of the town. The vines here suffer easily from drought stress, so, unusually, they fare better in wet years than in very dry ones. Located between Johannisberg and Rüdesheim, the town of Geisenheim has some good vineyards, such as Kläuserweg, but is best known for its wine college and research institute, which studies everything from new crossings to viticultural practices, and attracts students from the world over.

Furthest west and hidden around the bend of the river, Assmannshausen and Lorch are detached from the other Rheingau villages – as much in their wines as in their location. In Assmannshausen the slate soils are almost entirely planted with Spätburgunder (Pinot Noir), while Lorch, right on the border with the Mittelrhein region, produces clean, racy Rieslings that in fact have more in common with those of the Mittelrhein than the Rheingau. These wines are underestimated and comparatively underpriced.

loam, clay, quartzite

Spätburgunder (Pinot Noir) *Riesling*

red, white, sparkling, dessert

Drosselhof wine bar, Rüdesheim, Rheingau

KLOSTER EBERBACH

In 1155 the Archbishop of Mainz gave a Hattenheim vineyard known today as the Steinberg to the Cistercian order. The monks built a monastery, Kloster Eberbach, nearby, and its vineyards proliferated. After being seized by Napoleon, it became a ducal property, and was then taken over by the Prussian state. Today the monastery is the headquarters of Hessen's State Domaine *(see p363)* and a popular location for wine auctions, which attract bidders from all over the world. The monastic ruins, the attractive wooded grounds, and the restaurant and wine shop all add up to an appealing tourist attraction.

Rheinhessen

THIS IS THE MOST MALIGNED of the country's wine regions, since its interior, west of the Rhein, is devoted to industrial vineyards that churn out tanker-loads of the cheap, undistinguished white wines that have marred Germany's reputation worldwide. Many crossings are planted here, especially new varieties that have been bred to ripen early and give high yields. This may satisfy the many growers who are oriented towards quantity rather than quality, but the wine itself is usually bland and dilute. The chief example is known as Liebfraumilch – which is legally defined as a *Qualitätswein* from the Rheinhessen, Pfalz, Nahe, or Rheingau. Liebfraumilch must contain at least 70 per cent Riesling, Kerner, Silvaner, or Müller-Thürgau, and have between 18 and 40g of residual sugar. Depressingly, this nondescript concoction still mops up much of all Rheinhessen's production.

Weingut Wittmann's crest, Rheinhessen

Thankfully, this is not all that the region produces. Closer to the river, along the so-called Rheinfront between the villages of Nierstein and Nackenheim, are remarkable red-soiled slopes that produce rich, mineral, and mostly dry Rieslings. Very impressive wines are also made further south around Flörsheim-Dalsheim, Westhofen and Bechtheim. Silvaner is another Rheinhessen speciality: a dry, tangy wine that is consumed in vast quantities during the asparagus season. And almost 30 per cent of the vineyards in the Rheinhessen grow red varieties, with an expansion of Dornfelder plantings making it the second most popular grape across the region.

clay, loam, slate, iron, sand *Portugieser, Dornfelder* *Müller-Thurgau, Silvaner, Riesling* *red, white, sparkling, dessert*

Pfalz

THE PFALZ, OR PALATINATE, is the southerly extension of Rheinhessen. A relatively warm region, protected by the Haardt Mountains to the west, it produces many of Germany's finest dry Rieslings, with impressive weight and power. Riesling dominates the area between Bad Dürkheim and Neustadt, particularly around the villages of Wachenheim, Forst, Deidesheim, and Ruppertsberg. Elsewhere other varieties thrive: Scheurebe, Gewürztraminer, Rieslaner, and, further south, the Pinot family.

Until 15 years ago, the southern Pfalz had a poor reputation, but standards have risen swiftly. Much of Germany's finest Spätburgunder (Pinot Noir), Chardonnay, and Weissburgunder now comes from here, as do some vigorous Rieslings. The balmy climate encourages the production of rich, rounded wines, with little of the sometimes strident acidity that is found in the more northerly regions. These are wines well in tune with modern tastes, and the Pfalz is enjoying great success. In no other region has overall quality improved as dramatically as in the Pfalz over recent years.

loam, sand, basalt, loess, limestone *Portugieser, Spätburgunder (Pinot Noir), Dornfelder* *Riesling, Scheurebe, Weissburgunder (Pinot Blanc)* *red, white, sparkling, dessert*

Vineyards around the village of Wachenheim in the Pfalz region

Franken

A LARGE AREA IN northern Bavaria, Franken (sometimes known as Franconia) consists of 6,000ha of vineyards that cling to the banks of the Main River as it twists around the city of Würzburg. Although a third of the viticultural land here is planted to Müller-Thurgau, the region is best known for some excellent Silvaner and Riesling. Only a small fraction of production is devoted to red wine, but very convincing examples of Spätburgunder (Pinot Noir) come from the western part of the region, near Bürgstadt. Franken's continental climate brings with it the challenge of hard frosts, and historically this has meant widely varied harvests. However, conditions over the past decade have permitted consistently good vintages. Much of the region's wine is easily recognizable, as it comes in traditional squat, flagon-shaped bottles known as *Bocksbeutel*. There is a strong local market for wines from Franken, so they tend to be expensive. In style they are mostly dry and full-bodied, with vigorous acidity. Sweet wines such as *Eiswein* and TBA are rare, but can be of superb quality.

🏔 *limestone, sandstone, clay, loess*
🍇 *Spätburgunder, Frühburgunder (both Pinot Noir)*
🍷 *Müller-Thurgau, Silvaner, Riesling* 🍾 *red, white, sparkling, dessert*

Hessische Bergstrasse

THE VINEYARDS OF THE Hessische Bergstrasse begin just north of the city of Heidelberg and extend in a narrow band some 30km further north, following the route of an old Roman mountain road. Around half of the region's 450ha are planted to Riesling; the rest are scattered with small amounts of Müller-Thurgau and other traditional varieties. This is a pretty, old-fashioned stretch where small vineyards are interspersed with orchards and tended by individual grape growers. Since few of the local growers have the means to vinify their own fruit, most of the wine made here comes from local co-operatives, and almost all of it is sold to the weekend tourists and hikers who flock to the Bergstrasse all year round.

🏔 *loess, clay, granite, sandstone* 🍇 *Spätburgunder (Pinot Noir), St-Laurent* 🍷 *Riesling, Müller-Thurgau, Grauburgunder (Pinot Gris)* 🍾 *red, white, dessert*

Württemberg

ALTHOUGH THE WINE region of Württemberg broadly follows the course of the Neckar River, most of its vineyards are concentrated in the area just north of Stuttgart. With 11,500ha, this southerly region is the fourth-largest in Germany. Nearly 70 per cent of the wine produced here is red, with the largest share coming from Trollinger. This grape (known as Schiava in Italy, Vernatsch in Tyrol), is used in light, almost rosé-like, wines that are consumed in large quantities by the local population but rarely found elsewhere. More conventional and impressive reds are made from Schwarzriesling (Pinot Meunier), Lemberger, and Spätburgunder (Pinot Noir). One group of winemakers uses the label 'Hades' to identify some of the region's most ambitious reds, made from

Vineyard above the village of Unterhambach in the Hessische Bergstrasse

low-yielding vines and aged in barriques. A significant amount of Riesling is also made, but only a handful of producers offer noteworthy examples.

🏛 marl, limestone, sandstone
🍇 Trollinger, Schwarzriesling (Pinot Meunier), Lemberger, Spätburgunder (Pinot Noir)
🍷 Riesling 🏺 red, white, sparkling, dessert

Baden

THIS IS GERMANY'S most southerly wine region, but that statement is deceptive since Baden is vast – stretching 400km from the edge of the Franken region, near Würzburg, down along the Rhein Valley to the border with Switzerland, and covering almost 16,000ha along the way. Baden's size brings with it a lack of coherence in terms of soils, climate, and grape varieties, which can make the wines difficult to market. Müller-Thurgau dominates the northern Tauberfranken district, while Riesling thrives in the more central Ortenau area, just south of Baden-Baden. Further south, Kaiserstuhl and Tuniberg are the showpiece districts of the region. It is here, with lots of sunshine and volcanic soils, that the three Pinot varieties excel. There is great potential for deep and fruity examples of Spätburgunder (Pinot Noir), the most planted grape in Baden. Markgräflerland and Bodensee are the final, most southerly sections of the Baden region, and they are best known for light whites made from Gutedel (known as Chasselas in Switzerland) and Müller-Thurgau.

🏛 loess, limestone, volcanic, granite
🍇 Spätburgunder (Pinot Noir) 🍷 Müller-Thurgau, Grauburgunder (Pinot Gris), Weissburgunder (Pinot Blanc), Riesling, Gutedel (Chasselas) 🏺 red, white, sparkling, dessert

Saale-Unstrut

SOUTHWEST OF LEIPZIG, the confluence of the Saale and Unstrut rivers marks the centre of the most northerly winegrowing region in Europe. The northerly latitude and harsh continental climate both contribute to regular frosts, so viticulture is limited to pockets of land on south-facing slopes that total just

Gutedel (Chasselas) grapes

650ha. Nevertheless, this is double the amount that was under vine 15 years ago, as new vineyards have been cultivated and many old ones re-established since German reunification in 1990. Plantings are mainly white grape varieties, and Müller-Thurgau is the most important of them. For visitors to the region, there is a tasting room in the historic town of Naumburg.

🏛 limestone, loess, clay
🍇 Spätburgunder, Portugieser
🍷 Müller-Thurgau, Weissburgunder (Pinot Blanc), Silvaner 🏺 red, white, rosé, sparkling, dessert

Sachsen

THE VINEYARDS OF SACHSEN (Saxony) cover more than 400ha along the banks of the Elbe river northwest of Dresden. This is the most easterly wine region in Germany and, like nearby Saale-Unstrut, it is plagued by severe frosts. Plantings are led by Müller-Thurgau, and the wine is made in an easy-drinking style – making it popular both with locals and with visitors to the area's riverside villas and the rugged rock formations known as the Saxonian Switzerland.

🏛 granite, loess, sand, clay 🍇 Spätburgunder (Pinot Noir), Dornfelder 🍷 Müller-Thurgau, Riesling, Weissburgunder (Pinot Blanc), Traminer 🏺 red, white, dessert

Monument depicting St Urban, the patron saint of winegrowners, in one of Baden's vineyards

TOP PRODUCERS OF GERMANY

Maximin Grünhaus
Mosel-Saar-Ruwer

Mertesdorf ☎ *0651 5111*
🖳 *www.vonschubert.com* ⬜ *by appt*

THIS ESTATE, NOW owned by the von Schubert family, is a monastic foundation from the 10th century, and its vineyards are still divided into three sections: the Abtsberg (the abbot's section), the Herrenberg (the lord's section), and the Bruderberg (the brothers' section). About half the production is of dry wines, for which the estate has an excellent reputation, but outside Germany it is known for its exquisite and immensely long-lived sweet wines.
🍷 *white, dessert* 🍇 *2007, 2005, 2004, 2002, 1999, 1997* ★ *Maximin Grünhäuser: Herrenberg Riesling Kabinett, Abtsberg Riesling Auslese, Abtsberg Riesling Eiswein*

Weingut Dr Loosen
Mosel-Saar-Ruwer

St Johannishof, Bernkastel
☎ *06531 3426*
🖳 *www.drloosen.de* ⬜ *by appt*

THE LOOSEN ESTATE is blessed with exceptional vineyards in some of Mittelmosel's best villages: Graach, Wehlen, Bernkastel, Erden, and Urzig. Ernst Loosen has always understood that high prices, essential for economic survival, are dependent on producing wines of a very high quality. By reducing

Weingut Dr Loosen, Label

ERNST LOOSEN

From the moment he took over the family estate in 1987, Ernst Loosen has worked tirelessly to improve its wines. The trick, he realized from the start, was to improve the quality of the grapes and pick at the right moment. Unlike most Mosel growers, he has been an active promoter of his wines, and thus of Mosel wines as a whole, but in the late 1990s he leased the J L Wolf estate in the Pfalz in order to try his hand at dry Rieslings, to which he believes the Mosel is not well suited. While Loosen's exasperation with the cumbersome German wine laws has made him few friends within the country's wine establishment, his enthusiasm – and the quality of his wines – have made him one of the most internationally respected German producers.

Ernst Loosen

yields and introducing a stringent selection process, he has allowed the personality of each site to emerge, and the happy result, year in and year out, is a brilliant range of Rieslings, from *Kabinett* through to TBA.
🍷 *white, dessert* 🍇 *2007, 2005, 2004, 2001, 1999, 1997* ★ *Wehlener Sonnenuhr Riesling Kabinett, Erdener Prälat Riesling Auslese, Urziger Würzgarten Riesling TBA*

Weingut Egon Müller-Scharzhof
Mosel-Saar-Ruwer

Wiltingen ☎ *06501 17232*
🖳 *www.scharzhof.de* ◐

BETWEEN OBEREMMEL and Wiltingen rises the great hump of the Scharzhofberg vineyard. At its foot stands the elegant Scharzhof manor house, home since 1797 to the Müller family, which still owns the finest sections of this world-famous Saar vineyard. Since 1961 the estate has deservedly been best known for its glorious sweet wines, such as *Eiswein* and TBA, both of

which fetch phenomenally high prices at auction.
🍷 *white, dessert* 🍇 *2007, 2005, 2004, 2002, 1999, 1997*
★ *Scharzhofberger: Riesling Kabinett, Riesling BA*

Weingut Fritz Haag
Mosel-Saar-Ruwer

Dusemonder Str 44, Brauneberg
☎ *0653 4410* 🖳 *www.weingut-fritz-haag.de* ⬜ *by appt*

WILHELM HAAG IS the leading producer from one of the Mittelmosel's top vineyards, Brauneberger Juffer-Sonnenuhr. If Mosel wines can be considered muscular, these have muscle and vigour, carrying immense minerally flavour on a relatively light frame. Haag likes to bottle casks with different characters separately, so in any vintage there could potentially be four or five different *Auslesen*. As a general rule, the higher the price the more painstaking the selection.
🍷 *white* 🍇 *2007, 2005, 2004, 2001, 1999, 1997* ★ *Brauneberger Juffer-Sonnenuhr Riesling Kabinett, Brauneberger Juffer-Sonnenuhr Riesling BA*

Weingut Grans-Fassian
Mosel-Saar-Ruwer

Römerstr 28, Leiwen 📞 *06507 3170*
🌐 *www.grans-fassian.de* 🕐 *by appt*

GERHARD GRANS IS the latest of his family to run this estate founded in 1624. More than other local producers, he has proven that the lesser known vineyards of Leiwen and Trittenheim can produce world-class Rieslings. Over one third of his wines are dry, but the sweet wines are the most delectable offerings, especially the *Eiswein*. They combine full-throttled fruitiness with a zesty acidity.
🍷 *white, dessert* 📅 *2007, 2005, 2004, 2001, 1999, 1997* ⭐ *Trittenheimer Apotheke Riesling Spätlese, Leiwener Klostergarten Riesling Eiswein*

Weingut Heymann-Löwenstein
Mosel-Saar-Ruwer

Bahnhofstr 10, Winningen
📞 *02606 61919* 🌐 *www.heymann-loewenstein.com* 🕐 *by appt*

REINHARD LÖWENSTEIN has put Winningen on the map since he took over the property in 1980. He has demonstrated how well this stretch of the river is suited to dry wines as well as to sweet wines of at least *Auslese* quality. Some *terroir*-based blends of dry wine are produced: Schieferterrassen ('slate terraces') and Von Blauem Schiefer ('from blue slate'). Of the single-vineyard wines, Winninger Uhlen is invariably the finest, though all of the wines here are beautifully rich and superbly concentrated.
🍷 *white* 📅 *2007, 2005, 2004, 2003, 2002, 2001*
⭐ *Riesling Schieferterrassen, Winninger Röttgen Riesling, Winninger Uhlen BA*

Weingut J J Prüm
Mosel-Saar-Ruwer

Uferallee 19, Wehlen 📞 *06531 3091*
🌐 *www.jjpruem.com* 📧

THE MANY-BRANCHED Prüm family has dominated quality wine production in the Mittelmosel for a century or more, and this is their finest estate. Now owned by Dr Manfred Prüm, it includes exceptional vineyards in Wehlen and Graach. The wines do not always show well when young, but after four years they emerge from their shell and can keep for 20 years or more. Light in body but intense in flavour, they are effortlessly elegant. For many Riesling lovers, the Prüm wines epitomize all that is best about the Mosel style.
🍷 *white* 📅 *2007, 2005, 2004, 2001, 1999, 1997, 1995* ⭐ *Graacher Himmelreich Riesling Spätlese, Wehlener Sonnenuhr Riesling Auslese*

Weingut Reichsgraf von Kesselstatt
Mosel-Saar-Ruwer

Schlossgut Marienlay, Morscheid
📞 *06500 91690* 🌐 *www.kesselstatt.com* 🕐 *by appt*

LARGE ARISTOCRATIC estates are rare in the Mosel. This one was sold in 1978 to wine wholesaler Günther Reh, and it is run by his daughter Annegret Reh-Gartner. She leased out the second-rank sites and focused on the top vineyards in Scharzhofberg, Josephshof, Piesporter Goldtröpfchen, and Kaseler Nieschen in the Ruwer. Though a most half the wines are dry, the best tend to be those with some residual sugar. Given the estate's size, there are occasional

Weingut Reichsgraf von Kesselstatt

disappointments, but few other properties offer such a wide range of Mosel wines at such a high quality level.
🍷 *white* 📅 *2007, 2005, 2004, 2001, 1999, 1998, 1997* ⭐ *Piesporter Goldtröpfchen Riesling Kabinett, Scharzhofberger BA, Palais Kesselstatt Riesling Trocken*

Weingut Reinhold Haart
Mosel-Saar-Ruwer

Ausoniusufer 18, Piesport 📞 *06507 2015* 🌐 *www.haart.de* 🕐 *by appt*

THEO HAART'S CELLARS look across the river to the mighty slopes of Piesport, where he has important holdings within the renowned Goldtröpfchen. Thanks to low yields and a scrupulous insistence on harvesting only completely healthy grapes, Haart has long been the best producer in this village. His style is pure, mineral, and vigorous.
🍷 *white* 📅 *2007, 2005, 2004, 2001, 1999, 1998, 1997* ⭐ *Piesporter Goldtröpfchen Riesling Kabinett, Riesling Auslese*

Weingut St Urbans-Hof
Mosel-Saar-Ruwer

Urbanusstr 16, Leiwen
📞 *06507 93770*
🌐 *www.weingut-st-urbans-hof.de* 🕐

FOUNDED SOME 50 years ago, this estate has shot into the top tier of producers under the management of Nik Weis. Although based in Leiwen, it also has important Saar vineyards, and a parcel in Piesporter Goldtröpfchen. The dry wines from Wiltinger Schlangengraben are sleek and mineral, but the sweeter styles are exceptional, of a mouth-watering raciness and purity, the quintessence of fine Riesling.
🍷 *white* 📅 *2007, 2005, 2004, 2001, 1999, 1997* ⭐ *Piesporter Goldtröpfchen Riesling Kabinett, Ockfener Bockstein Riesling Auslese*

One of Weingut Meyer-Näkel's vineyards in Ahr

Weingut Deutzerhof
Ahr

Mayschoss ☎ *02643 7264*
Ⓦ *www.weingut-deutzerhof.de*
◻ *by appt*

THE DEUTZERHOF vineyards are dominated by Spätburgunder (Pinot Noir) but also contain some Dornfelder, Portugieser, Chardonnay, and Riesling. Co-owner Wolfgang Hehle makes characterful wines from all of them. The top two, Altenahrer Eck and Grand Duc, derive their quality from low yields and old vines rather than from tricks in the winery, and no more than one third new oak is used. Most of Hehle's wines are dry, but he sometimes makes high-quality Riesling *Auslese* and *Eiswein*.

🖼 *red, white, dessert* 📥 *2007, 2006, 2005, 2003, 2001, 1999* ★ *Grand Duc Spätburgunder, Altenahrer Eck Spätburgunder Grosses Gewächs Trocken*

Weingut Meyer-Näkel
Ahr

Hardtbergstr 20, Dernau ☎ *02643 1628* Ⓦ *www.meyer-naekel.de*
◻ *by appt*

WERNER NÄKEL HAS set the pace in the Ahr, proving that good quality Früh- and Spät-burgunder (Pinot Noir) can be produced in this region. His simplest *cuvées* are the Trocken and Trocken G, followed by the Blauschiefer,

named after the blue slate soils on which it is grown. The best blended selection of Spätburgunder is labelled 'S'. Finally there are three single-vineyard Pinots. The wines are tightly structured and quite oaky, and, unlike most Ahr wines, they are built to last.

🖼 *red, white* 📥 *2007, 2006, 2005, 2003, 2001, 1999* ★ *Frühburgunder Trocken, Spätburgunder S*

Weingut Ratzenberger
Mittelrhein

Blücherstr 167, Bacharach
☎ *06743 1337*
Ⓦ *www weingut-ratzenberger.de* ◻

JOCHEN RATZENBERGER has demonstrated that the Mittel-rhein is fully capable of producing lean, elegant,

yet long-lived Rieslings, with fragrant aromas of pears and minerals. His basic bottling is called Caspar R, a wine with high acidity balanced by residual sugar. This estate has also been making good traditional-method Riesling *Sekt* since 1997.

🖼 *white, sparkling, dessert* 📥 *2007, 2005, 2004, 2002* ★ *Bacharacher Wolfshöhle Riesling, Bacharacher Kloster Fürstental Riesling Eiswein*

Schlossgut Diel
Nahe

Burg Layen ☎ *06721 96950*
Ⓦ *www.schlossgut-diel.com* ◻

ARMIN DIEL IS well known in Germany as a leading wine and restaurant critic as well as a wine producer. His vineyards are in the northern Nahe, and are planted not only with Riesling but with Burgundian varieties too. The wines are made to a high standard across the board. The Dorsheimer Goldloch is often the best Riesling, and the *barrique*-aged Weisser Burgunder can be excellent.

🖼 *white, sparkling* 📥 *2007, 2005, 2004, 2002, 2001, 1999* ★ *Weisser Burgunder Barrique, Dorsheimer Goldloch Riesling Spätlese*

A SWEET HISTORY

For every region where sweet wines are made from botrytized fruit *(see p66)* there is a legend to explain how this style of wine came into being. The Rheingau is no exception. In the 18th century Schloss Johannisberg was the property of the absent Prince Bishop of Fulda, who decided when the harvest should begin. In 1775, his messenger, it is said, arrived very late, by which time the vineyards had succumbed to botrytis, an unsightly fungal infection that concentrates sugar, acidity, and glycerol. The grapes were picked and pressed, and the result was nectar: sublimely sweet, succulent wines. Such wines continued to be produced when climatic conditions permitted, and ancient vintages of BA and TBA survive in the Schloss cellars: the 1862 TBA was still alive and well in 2001.

Weingut Hermann Dönnhoff
Nahe

Bahnhofstr 11, Oberhausen
☎ *06755 263*
Ⓦ *www.doennhoff.com* ☐ *by appt*

EVER SINCE Helmut Dönnhoff took over the family property in 1971, he has steadily aimed for greatness. His excellent vineyards in Niederhausen, Oberhausen, Norheim, and Schlossböckelheim are mostly on volcanic soils. Yields are low, the harvest late, and the winemaking traditional. What marks out all his wines is their purity and limpidity. The Rieslings are rich but balanced and never heavy. Dönnhoff is rightly celebrated for brilliant *Eisweine* that have few peers anywhere in Germany.
🍷 *white, dessert* ▶ *2007, 2005, 2004, 2002, 2001, 1999*
★ *Niederhäuser Hermannshöhle Riesling Spätlese, Oberhäuser Brücke Riesling Eiswein*

Domänenweingut Schloss Schönborn
Rheingau

Hauptstr 53, Hattenheim ☎ *06723 91810* Ⓦ *www.schoenborn.de* ☐

THE NOBLE SCHÖNBORN family has owned this large, 50-ha estate, together with another estate in Franken, for centuries. Its cellars are in Hattenheim, but its vineyards are dispersed throughout the region. Quality has been uneven, but vintages such as 2005 showed that Schloss Schönborn could produce magnificent sweet wines. In recent years the estate has wisely focused on its best sites – such as Hattenheimer Pfaffenberg and Erbacher Marcobrunn.
🍷 *white, dessert* ▶ *2007, 2005, 2004, 2002, 2001, 1999* ★ *Hattenheimer Pfaffenberg Riesling Erstes Gewächs, Erbacher Marcobrunn: Riesling Kabinett, Riesling BA*

Hessische Staatsweingüter Kloster Eberbach
Rheingau

Schwalbacher Str 52–62, Eltville
☎ *06123 92300* Ⓦ *www.weingut-kloster-eberbach.de* ☐

THIS GREAT monastic estate is now owned by the state of Hessen. This means it is often affected by local politics, which can be tiresome for the winemaker and director. But it also means that the Kloster Eberbach estate enjoys considerable resources and nationwide renown. There are six domaines, in both the Rheingau and the Hessische Bergstrasse *(see p368)*. The excellent vineyards include Steinberg, a monopoly site that predates the 12th-century monastery. Quality has been patchy in the past, which is not surprising given the scale of the operation. But director Dieter Greiner is determined to ensure that a domaine with so many top sites produces consistently, rather than occasionally, outstanding wines.
🍷 *white* ▶ *2007, 2005, 2004, 2002, 2001, 1999* ★ *Erbacher Marcobrunn Riesling Kabinett, Steinberger Riesling Erstes Gewächs, Rüdesheimer Berg Schlossberg Riesling Erstes Gewächs*

Domänenweingut Schloss Schönborn

Schloss Johannisberg
Rheingau

Geisenheim-Johannisberg
☎ *06722 70090*
Ⓦ *www.schloss-johannisberg.de* ☐

THIS ANCIENT PROPERTY sprawls across a plateau overlooking vineyards where, since 1720, Riesling alone has been cultivated; legendary sweet wines have been produced here from 1775 onwards. At the highest level – BA and TBA – Schloss Johannisberg can still turn out stunning wines, but the lower qualities are less exciting. Fortunately, vintages since 1999 have shown some welcome signs of improvement.
🍷 *white, dessert* ▶ *2007, 2005, 2004, 2002, 2001, 1999*
★ *Schloss Johannisberger Riesling Spätlese Trocken, Schloss Johannisberger Riesling BA*

Schloss Vollrads
Rheingau

Oestrich-Winkel ☎ *06723 660*
Ⓦ *www.schlossvollrads.com* ☐

DURING THE 1980s and through much of the 1990s, Graf Matuschka-Greiffenclau was one of the most forceful personalities on the German wine scene. He owned the sprawling estate of Schloss Vollrads, but sadly he neglected the quality of its wines. When financial difficulties led to the Graf's suicide in 1997, the property was acquired by a local bank, which appointed an excellent new team to restore it to greatness. They are on their way: late selective harvesting has improved quality, and the wines – some of which are outstanding – are balanced and concentrated.
🍷 *white, dessert*
▶ *2007, 2005, 2004, 2001*
★ *Schloss Vollrads Riesling, Schloss Vollrads Riesling Eiswein*

Weingut Franz Künstler
Rheingau

*Freiherr-von-Stein Ring 3,
Hochheim* ☎ 06146 82570
🖳 *www.weingut-kuenstler.de* 🖸

HOCHHEIM'S WARM mesoclimate
results in wines of unusual
richness and power, and no
local producer can better the
efforts of Gunter Künstler. His
sweet wines are exceptional,
but Hochheim is perfectly
suited to dry Rieslings, and
Künstler produces a range of
them from the village's top
sites. His Spätburgunders
(or Pinot Noirs) sell for high
prices, but they lack the
harmony of his Rieslings.
🖷 *red, white, sparkling* 🗲 *2007,
2005, 2004, 2002, 2001, 1999*
★ *Hochheimer Stielweg Riesling
Spätlese Trocken, Hochheimer Hölle
Riesling Auslese Trocken*

Weingut Georg Breuer
Rheingau

Grabenstr 8, Rüdesheim ☎ 06722
1027 🖳 *www.georg-breuer.com* 🖸

BERNHARD BREUER was always
a passionate advocate of
drier styles of Rheingau
Riesling; until his
untimely death in
2004, he put his
ideas into practice
at the family estate,
though he also made
BAs and TBAs in
suitable vintages.
The estate's top
vineyards are   **Riesling grapes**
Rüdesheimer Berg
Schlossberg and Rauenthaler
Nonnenberg, and these
single-vineyard wines are
rich, serious, and expensive –
although the village Rieslings
are excellent value for money.
🖷 *red, white, sparkling*
🗲 *2007, 2005, 2004, 2002, 2001,
1999* ★ *Rüdesheim Estate Riesling
Trocken, Rauenthaler Nonnenberg
Riesling Trocken, Rüdesheimer Berg
Rottland Riesling Auslese*

Weingut Johannishof
Rheingau

Grund 63, Johannisberg
☎ 06722 8216
🖳 *www.weingut-johannishof.de* 🖸

THERE HAVE BEEN Esers in
Johannisberg since 1685, and
today this property is run by
Hans Hermann Eser and his
son Johannes. They also
have vineyards in Winkel and
Geisenheim, as well as substantial sites in Rüdesheim.
The Johannishof style is
balanced and fresh, rather
than powerful or muscular.
🖷 *white* 🗲 *2007, 2005, 2004, 2002,
2001, 1999* ★ *Johannisberger Klaus
Riesling Spätlese, Rüdesheimer Berg
Rottland Riesling Erstes Gewächs*

Weingut Peter Jakob Kühn
Rheingau

Mühlstr 70, Oestrich ☎ 06723 2299
🖳 *www.weingutpjkuehn.de* 🖸

PETER JAKOB KÜHN'S relentless
quest for improvement has
transformed his family estate
into one of the Rheingau's top
names. His main recreation
is visiting other wine regions
to see whether he can use
or adapt their practices. He
makes dry Rieslings from
Oestricher Doosberg
and sweeter ones
from Oestricher
Lenchen: his BAs
and *Eisweine* are among
the region's finest.
🖷 *red, white, dessert*
🗲 *2007, 2005, 2004,
2001, 1999* ★ *Oestricher Doosberg
Riesling Erstes Gewächs, Oestricher
Lenchen Riesling BA*

Weingut Robert Weil
Rheingau

Mühlberg 5, Kiedrich ☎ 06123 2308
🖳 *www.weingut-robert-weil.com* 🖸

ALTHOUGH SUNTORY HAS owned
this estate since 1988, the
Japanese company shrewdly

Weingut Peter Jakob Kühn

hired young Wilhelm Weil
to manage the property.
This he has done brilliantly.
The speciality here is a
range of ripe Rieslings from
the Gräfenberg vineyard.
No expense is spared during
harvest, with a team of 70
pickers going through the
vineyards repeatedly, seeking
only the ripest berries. The
majority of the wines made
here are dry, but Weil also
produces large quantities
of very sweet wine each
year. No other Rheingau
estate has succeeded in
producing TBAs in so many
consecutive vintages.
🖷 *red, white, dessert* 🗲 *2007, 2005,
2004, 2003, 2001, 1999* ★ *Riesling
Spätlese Trocken, Kiedricher
Gräfenberg Riesling Auslese*

Weingut Freiherr Heyl zu Herrnsheim
Rheinhessen

Langgasse 3, Nierstein
☎ 06133 57080
🖳 *www.heyl-zu-herrnsheim.de* 🖸

UNDER ITS FORMER owner,
this estate pioneered the
production of dry wines
and organic viticulture in
the Rhein regions. In 2006
the property was leased to
Detlev Meyer, who has
maintained the estate

philosophy and further improved quality. Most of the Heyl zu Herrensheim vineyards are on remarkable red soils near the river, and a range of bottlings called Rotschiefer ('red slate') are the product of these slopes. The top Rieslings, which come from Niersteiner Brudersberg and Pettental, have the bracing earthiness characteristic of wines from the very best Rheinhessen sites.

🍷 white, dessert ⭐ 2007, 2004, 2002, 2001, 1998 ★ Rotschiefer Silvaner Trocken, Niersteiner Brudersberg Riesling Grosses Gewächs, Niersteiner Brudersberg Riesling TBA

Weingut Gunderloch
Rheinhessen

Carl-Gunderloch Platz 1, Nackenheim ☎ 06135 2341 🌐 www.gunderloch.de ⬜

HALF THE GUNDERLOCH vines lie within the superb red-soiled Nackenheimer Rothenberg vineyard, which is equal in quality to the better known Nierstein sites. The wine-making at this estate is utterly traditional – with very low yields, no cultivated yeasts, and an unusually long ageing period in cask before bottling. The result is a collection of some of Rheinhessen's most complex Rieslings, in both

Weingut Wittmann label

dry and ultra-sweet styles. This estate has also created an off-dry wine called Jean-Baptiste for restaurants and export markets.

🍷 white, dessert ⭐ 2007, 2005, 2004, 2003, 2002, 2001 ★ Jean-Baptiste Piesling Kabinett, Nackenheimer Rothenberg Auslese

Weingut Keller
Rheinhessen

Bahnhofstr 1, Flörsheim-Dalsheim ☎ 06243 456 🌐 www.keller-wein.de ⬜

THIS RISING STAR has emerged, rather surprisingly, in one of the least-esteemed stretches of southern Rheinhessen. The Kellers painstakingly identified their best sites (Dalsheimer Hubacker for Riesling, Dalsheimer Bürgel for Spätburgunder), and then made the most of them by severely reducing yields. The dry Rieslings are exceptional, as are the rich, multi-layered BAs and TBAs from Riesling and Rieslaner.

🍷 red, white, dessert ⭐ 2007, 2005, 2004, 2002, 2001 ★ Dalsheimer Hubacker Riesling Trocken Max, Dalsheimer Bürgel Spätburgunder Felix, Riesling TBA

Weingut Wittmann
Rheinhessen

Mainzer Str 19, Westhofen ☎ 06244 905036 🌐 www.wittmannweingut.com ⬜ by appt

THE CELLARS AT Weingut Wittmann are filled with the family's modern art collection, some of which is reproduced on the wine labels. This is a forward-looking, organic estate, and all the dry wines are crisp and sharply defined. Low yields are the secret of the quality here, in addition to the constantly evolving winemaking techniques and skilful handling. As well as spicy Grosses Gewächs

Rieslings, there are imposing dry wines made from Weissburgunder (Pinot Blanc) and Chardonnay. The outstanding bottlings in any vintage are designated 'S', which stands for Selection. The Westhofener Morstein site is the source of some superlative sweet wines.

🍷 white, dessert ⭐ 2007, 2005, 2004, 2003, 2001 ★ Weisser Burgunder S, Westhofener Morstein Riesling Grosses Gewächs, Westhofener Morstein Riesling BA

PERFECT CASE: GERMANY

Ⓦ Weingut Dr Bürklin-Wolf Forster Ungeheuer Riesling Erstes Gewächs ££

Ⓦ Weingut Dr Loosen Wehlener Sonnenuhr Riesling Kabinett £

Ⓓ Weingut Emrich-Schönleber Monzinger Frühlingsplätzchen Riesling Eiswein ££££ (www.schoenleber.de)

Ⓦ Weingut Franz Künstler Hochheimer Kirchenstück Riesling Spätlese Trocken ££

Ⓦ Weingut Freiherr Heyl zu Herrnsheim Niersteiner Brudersberg Riesling Trocken ££

Ⓦ Weingut Georg Breuer Rüdesheim Estate Riesling Trocken £

Ⓦ Weingut Hermann Dönnhoff Oberhäuser Brücke Riesling Spätlese ££

Ⓦ Weingut Keller Dalsheimer Hubacker Riesling Auslese £££

Ⓦ Weingut Müller-Catoir Mussbacher Eselshaut Rieslaner Auslese £££

Ⓦ Weingut Ökonomierat Rebholz Chardonnay Spätlese Trocken R ££

Ⓦ Weingut Robert Weil Kiedricher Gräfenberg Riesling Auslese £££

Ⓦ Weingut St Urbans-Hof Ockfener Bockstein Riesling Auslese ££

Weingut Christmann
Pfalz

Peter-Koch Str 43, Gimmeldingen
☎ 06326 6039
🌐 *www.weingut-christmann.de* ▢

AFTER STEFFEN CHRISTMANN took over the family estate in 1994, quality soared. An enthusiastic supporter of the new classification, he has won the right to *Grosses Gewächs* (great growth, *see p348*) status for sites in Ruppertsberg, Deidesheim, Königsbach, and his native Gimmeldingen. The quality of his dry Rieslings is matched by that of his opulent sweet wines from botrytized fruit. Christmann is also getting to grips with Spätburgunder (Pinot Noir), but his yields need to be tiny to achieve the concentration required for his heavily oaked wines.

🍷 *red, white, dessert, sparkling*
📋 *2007, 2005, 2004, 2002, 2001, 1999* ★ *Gimmeldinger Mandelgarten Riesling Grosses Gewächs, Ruppertsberger Reiterpfad Riesling TBA, Königsbacher Idig Spätburgunder Grosses Gewächs*

Weingut Dr Bürklin-Wolf
Pfalz

Weinstr 65, Wachenheim ☎ *06322 95330* 🌐 *www.buerklin-wolf.de* ▢

IN 1875 LUISE WOLF married Dr Albert Bürklin, thereby creating what was to become Germany's largest private estate. As with the Pfalz's other great producers, quality slipped in the 1980s when things were left in the hands of a general manager – who valued productivity and high yields above quality, and allowed the estate to coast on its reputation. But the current owner, Bettina Bürklin, has been determined to restore its reputation. Dr Bürklin-Wolf's portfolio of vineyards includes just about

Weingut Christmann

every good site in the Mittelhaardt, and since 2005 the viticulture has been biodynamic. Although some Spätburgunder and Dornfelder are produced, the estate's reputation rests on its dry Rieslings: Bürklin-Wolf has rather lost interest in the sumptuous sweet wines for which it used to be well known.

🍷 *red, white* 📋 *2007, 2005, 2004, 2003, 2002, 2001, 1999, 1998* ★ *Forster Ungeheuer Riesling Grosses Gewächs, Forster Kirchenstück Riesling Grosses Gewächs*

Weingut Geheimer Rat Dr von Bassermann-Jordan
Pfalz

Kirchgasse 10, Deidesheim
☎ 06326 6006
🌐 *www. bassermann-jordan.de* ▢

THIS MAJOR ESTATE oozes history: within its maze of cellars are niches filled with Roman amphorae and other antiquities discovered within the region. By the 1980s, wine standards had declined, but in the late 1990s a new winemaker, Ulrich Mell, turned things around and today Bassermann-Jordan is back in the top rank. Mostly dry Rieslings are made from outstanding

sites in Ruppertsberg, Deidesheim, and Forst. In exceptional vintages fabulous TBAs are also produced, with rich flavours of stewed peaches and figs.

🍷 *red, white, dessert* 📋 *2007, 2005, 2004, 2002, 2001, 1999* ★ *Pechstein Forst Riesling Spätlese Trocken, Reiterpfad Ruppertsberg Riesling TBA*

Weingut Josef Biffar
Pfalz

Niederkirchener Str 13, Deidesheim
☎ 06369 67629
🌐 *www.biffar.com* ▢

ALTHOUGH THE BIFFARS came to Deidesheim from Lyon in 1723, their estate only achieved celebrity status in the 1990s, thanks to a new winemaker. Their vineyards lie among the top villages of the Mittelhaardt, with Deidesheimer Grainhübel and Wachenheimer Gerümpel as their leading sites. Over two thirds of the wines are dry, but the *Auslesen* can be delicious too. The dry Weissburgunder (Pinot Blanc) is also worth looking out for.

🍷 *white* 📋 *2007, 2004, 2002, 2001, 1999* ★ *Deidesheimer Herrgottsacker Riesling Spätlese Trocken, Wachenheimer Gerümpel Grosses Gewächs*

Label from Weingut Geheimer Rat Dr von Bassermann-Jordan

Weingut Knipser
Pfalz

Hauptstr 47, Laumersheim
☎ 06328 742
W www.weingut-knipser.de ○

WERNER KNIPSER LIKES to dabble: he has produced unusual wines from the obscure Gelber Orleans variety, which he has revived at his northern Pfalz estate, as well as Chardonnay and Sauvignon Blanc. However, the local dry mesoclimate also allows the production of red wines with plenty of stuffing: Spätburgunders have vigour and spice, but wines produced from Bordeaux varieties and from Syrah are inconsistent. In a region dominated by Riesling, however, this estate, with its emphasis on innovation, has found many avid supporters.

red, white 2007, 2005, 2004, 2003, 2002, 2001

★ Weissburgunder Spätlese Trocken, Laumersheimer Kirschgarten Spätburgunder Spätlese Trocken

Weingut Koehler-Ruprecht
Pfalz

Weinstr 84, Kallstadt
☎ 06322 829 ○

BERND PHILIPPI IS an international wine consultant but in his native Kallstadt he produces powerful and long-lived Rieslings under the Koehler-Ruprecht label. He also produces an entirely different range under the Philippi label: barrel-fermented wines from Riesling, Chardonnay, and the Pinot family. These are wines with a personal stamp, not bound by rules and regulations, but they lack the consistency of his Rieslings.

red, white 2005, 2004, 2002, 2001, 1998 ★ Kallstadter Saumagen Riesling Spätlese Trocken, Philippi Spätburgunder R

Weingut Müller-Catoir
Pfalz

Mandelring 25, Neustadt ☎ 06321 2815 W www.mueller-catoir.de ○

THIS ESTATE OF Huguenot origin was brought to the highest level by its brilliant former winemaker, Hans-Günther Schwarz. The achievement was all the more astonishing because the estate does not own exceptional vineyards. Riesling is dominant, but there are significant parcels of Grauburgunder (Pinot Gris), Scheurebe, Muskateller, Gewürztraminer, and Rieslaner too. At a time when much German oenology was aimed at minimizing risk by cleaning up musts and wines, Schwarz argued in favour of using natural yeasts and for minimal intervention. He also insisted on late and selective harvesting. The resulting wines combine intensity of flavour with exoticism. The brilliant Rieslings are sometimes surpassed by the house speciality of Rieslaner, a crossing with higher acidity than Riesling, yielding superb sweet too. Martin Franzen is the new winemaker.

red, white, dessert
2007, 2005, 2004, 2002, 2001, 1999, 1998 ★ Riesling Spätlese Trocken, Haardter Bürgergarten Muskateller Trocken

Weingut Ökonomierat Rebholz
Pfalz

Weinstr 54, Siebeldingen
☎ 06345 3439
W www.oekonomierat-rebholz.de ○

HANSJÖRG REBHOLZ RUNS the finest estate of the southern Pfalz. All the wines here are dry, and the Chardonnay and Spätburgunder are aged in barrique. The Rieslings can be austere when young, but have formidable intensity and longevity. The top Riesling sites are Birkweiler Kastanienbusch (more classic) and Siebeldinger Im Sonnenschein (more exotic). The Weissburgunder, fermented in older barriques, can be delicious, and so is the flowery Muskateller.

red, white 2007, 2005, 2004, 2003, 2002, 2001, 1999

★ Siebeldinger Im Sonnenschein: Riesling Grosses Gewächs, Weisser Burgunder Grosses Gewächs; Spätburgunder R

Weingut Reichsrat von Buhl
Pfalz

Weinstr 16, Deidesheim
☎ 06326 965010
W www.reichsrat-von-buhl.de ○

THIS LARGE ESTATE, with sites in most of the Pfalz's top vineyards, was bought in 2005 by Achim Niederberger. It had previously been leased to a Japanese company that had invested steadily and ensured the winemaking was in competent hands. Quality soared from the mid-1990s and has been maintained ever since. The dry Rieslings from the Forst vineyards are magnificent, and so are the sweet wines in suitable vintages. Red wine production is also taken seriously, and in top vintages the Spätburgunder is aged in a good deal of new oak.

Weingut Reichsrat von Buhl

red, white, dessert 2007, 2005, 2004, 2002, 2001, 1999

★ Forster Pechstein Riesling Grosses Gewächs, Forster Kirchenstück Riesling Grosses Gewächs, Forster Ungeheuer Riesling TBA

Weingut Rudolf Fürst label

FÜRST

Parzival
2002

Weingut Horst Sauer
Franken

Bocksbeutelstr 14, Escherndorf
☎ 09381 4364 Ⓦ www.weingut-horst-sauer.de ◻ by appt

HORST SAUER has been called
the wizard of Silvaner – with
good reason. A third of his
14ha are planted to this grape,
from which he crafts thrilling
wines. Silvaners and Rieslings
from the south-facing Lump
vineyard – one of Franken's
best sites – are consistently
impressive, but Sauer's
meticulous and delicate
approach makes even his
basic wines a treat to drink.
🔳 white, dessert 🔁 2006, 2005,
2004, 2003 ★ Escherndorfer Lump
Silvaner Spätlese trocken

Weingut Rudolf Fürst
Franken

Hohenlindenweg 19, Bürgstadt
☎ 09371 8642 Ⓦ www.weingut-rudolf-fuerst.de ◻ by appt

SOME OF GERMANY'S best wines
come from this 17-ha estate
in western Franken. Paul and
Monika Fürst make expressive
Weissburgunder (Pinot Blanc)
and Riesling, but are admired
most for their well-balanced,
oak-aged reds. The reserve
Spätburgunder (Pinot Noir)
from the Centgrafenburg
vineyard is simply excellent.
🔳 red, white, sparking, dessert
🔁 2006, 2005, 2004, 2003 ★ Bürg-
stadter Centgrafenburg Spätburgunder
trocken R, Parzival trocken R

Hessische Staatsweingüter Domaine Bergstrasse
Hessische Bergstrasse

Grieselstr 34–36, Bensheim
☎ 06251 3107 Ⓦ www.weingut-kloster-eberbach.de ◻

THIS LARGE, STATE-OWNED winery
is run as a subsidiary of Kloster
Eberbach (see p363). Most
of its wines are Rieslings, and
the sweet examples are the
most impressive. The efforts
of Volker Hörr, the estate
director, seem set to
maintain this estate's
position as the best in the
Hessische Bergstrasse.
🔳 red, white, dessert 🔁 2007, 2005,
2004, 2001 ★ Heppenheimer
Centgericht Riesling TBA

Weingut Graf Adelmann
Württemberg

Burg Schaubeck, Kleinbottwar
☎ 07148 921220
Ⓦ www.graf-adelmann.com ◻

A FAMILY WINERY based just north
of Stuttgart, Graf Adelmann
has given more than a quarter
of its land to Riesling, but the
best-known wines are the reds
based on Lemberger. The top
cuvée is Vignette, a stunning
blend of Lemberger, Samrot,
Dornfelder, and Cabernet aged
in oak for up to two years.
🔳 red, white, dessert
🔁 2007, 2006, 2005, 2003, 2001
★ Vignette trocken (Hades)

Weingut Bernhard Huber
Baden

Heimbacher Weg 19, Malterdingen
☎ 07644 1200 Ⓦ www.weingut-huber.com ◻ by appt

SPÄTBURGUNDER (Pinot Noir)
is Bernhard Huber's calling
card: 70 per cent of his 26ha
are devoted to this variety,
from which he creates four
different wines. Most of them
are made in a bold style, and
some need a little time to
open up. Huber is also
known for his characterful
oaked Chardonnays, while
limited amounts of good *Sekt*
come from Weissburgunder

RED WINE: ON THE UP?

Germany has a long tradition of red wine production, but
the national taste in reds has traditionally been for light and
even sweet wines – to the dismay of international wine
lovers. In the 1990s, the best growers realized that the
secret of good, rich, complex red wine lay in the vineyards
– the right clones in the right places, low yields, selective
harvesting – and in the winery, where wines were given
longer maceration. Although the grape known as Früh- or
Spätburgunder (France's Pinot Noir, first brought by monks
from Burgundy) is still Germany's key red variety, some
interesting wines are also made from native grapes such as
Schwarzriesling (Pinot Meunier) and
Lemberger, as well as international
varieties like Merlot and Cabernet
Sauvignon. In southern Germany and
the Ahr there are serious reds that are
now beginning to attract attention.
Red wine specialists include Weingute
Meyer-Näkel (see p362), Rudolf
Fürst (above) and August Kesseler.
Ⓦ www.august-kesseler.de

(Pinot Blanc) blended with Spätburgunder.

red, white, rosé, sparkling, dessert ★ *2007, 2005, 2004, 2003, 2002* ★ *Spätburgunder trocken R*

Weingut Dr Heger
Baden

Bachenstr 19–21, Ihringen *07 66 82 05* *www.heger-weine.de* *by appt*

HALF OF THE HEGER vineyards, on the volcanic slopes of the Kaiserstuhl district, are planted with Spätburgunder (Pinot Noir) and Riesling, although the significant plots of Grauburgunder (Pinot Gris) and Weissburgunder (Pinot Blanc) have done more for Heger's fabulous reputation. The top plots are in the Winklerberg and Schlossberg vineyards; almost every wine that Heger makes from these parcels shows remarkable richness and elegance. Second-tier wines, labelled Weinhaus Joachim Heger, also offer great quality.

red, white, dessert ★ *2007, 2005, 2004, 2002* ★ *Achkarrer Schlossberg Grauburgunder Auslese trocken*

Weingut Lützkendorf
Saale-Unstrut

Saalberge 31, Bad Kösen *03446 361000* *www.weingut-luetzkendorf.de* *by appt*

UWE LÜTZKENDORF has 10ha of vines at the southwest corner of Saale-Unstrut. The largest portion of the estate is planted with Silvaner, but he also makes good Weissburgunder (Pinot Blanc) and Riesling, and excellent Traminer.

white, dessert ★ *2007, 2005, 2003, 2002* ★ *Karsdorfer Hohe Gräte Traminer Spätlese trocken*

Weingut Pawis
Saale-Unstrut

Lauchaer Str 31c, Freyburg/Unstrut *03446 428315* *www. weingut-pawis.de*

SINCE TAKING OVER his family farm in 1998, Bernard Pawis has put in a lot of careful work in the vineyard – and it shows in the wines. Riesling is the main draw here, but the Grau- and Weissburgunder (Pinots Gris and Blanc) show class, too. Pawis wine bar is very popular with the locals.

red, white, dessert ★ *2007, 2005, 2003, 2002* ★ *Freyburger Edelacker Riesling Spätlese trocken*

Weingut Klaus Zimmerling
Sachsen

Bergweg 27, Dresden-Pillnitz *03512 618752* *by appt*

KLAUS ZIMMERLING farms his 5ha organically and manages his vineyards for remarkably tiny yields (20hl/ha) – resulting in wines that are true reflections of the local terroir. They are also extremely well made, especially the Grauburgunders (Pinot Gris) and Rieslings. Zimmerling's wife is a sculptor, and images of her work adorn the estate's wine labels.

white, dessert ★ *2007, 2005, 2004, 2003* ★ *Riesling trocken R*

Weingut Martin Schwarz
Sachsen

Weinbergstr 34, Radebeul *03518 956072*

NOT CONTENT with his day job as winemaker at Schloss

Logo of Weingut Schloss Proschwitz, on a gate leading to one of the estate's vineyards

Proschwitz, in 2003 Martin Schwarz began to make wines under his own name from a steep, single-hectare plot in Radebeul. His work with Traminer, Spätburgunder (Pinot Noir), Weissburgunder (Pinot Blanc), and Grauburgunder (Pinot Gris) is truly inspiring, though sadly the wines are of very limited availability – for now. This is a star on the rise.

red, white ★ *2007, 2005, 2004, 2003* ★ *Weissburgunder-Grauburgunder trocken*

Weingut Schloss Proschwitz
Sachsen

Dorfanger 19, Zadel *0352 1767 60* *www.schloss-proschwitz.de*

A BEAUTIFUL BAROQUE castle and the oldest wine estate in Sachsen, Schloss Proschwitz owns 70ha of vineyards. They are planted with Grauburgunder (Pinot Gris), Weissburgunder (Pinot Blanc), Spätburgunder (Pinot Noir), and Riesling, among other varieties. Many of the wines are quite racy, and best drunk after a year or two in bottle.

red, white, dessert ★ *2007, 2005, 2004, 2003* ★ *Traminer Eiswein*

AUSTRIA & SWITZERLAND

S NOW-CAPPED MOUNTAINS *are widely associated with both Austria and Switzerland, but the vineyards that cover their foothills, and the wines they make, are much less well known. This obscurity is especially true of Switzerland, as barely a drop of its production leaves the country. Austria, however, is capturing international attention with its range of expressive styles. The wines of both nations offer great discoveries for the inquisitive enthusiast.*

AUSTRIA

VITICULTURE IN THIS part of the world pre-dates both Christianity and the Romans, and Austria's first grapes were planted by the Celts. After the Dark Ages, however, it was Christian monks who first planted vines in quantity. From the Middle Ages, Austria's political might meant that its viticultural influence spread across central Europe. The Austro-Hungarian Empire left a rich heritage, not least from the research and experimentation carried out by the country's first wine school, established at Klosterneuburg in 1860. After World War I, the empire was reduced to its core, and Austria was sustained by tourism. Wine production was firmly bound up with the country's touristy image: German visitors wanted little more than *Gemütlichkeit* – ladies in folk costumes serving mugs of semi-sweet wine to the accompaniment of cold pork and *Schrammelmusik*.

St Urban, Austrian patron saint of winemakers

It was not until the 1950s that a small group of growers based in Wachau began to reform Austria's image by making some serious wines. The process was accelerated by the repercussions of the wine scandal of 1985, when the country's sweet and semi-sweet wines were discredited by the crooked practices of a handful of merchants who had added chemicals to their musts. The

Austrian wine industry was shaken from top to bottom – a process that fortunately proved beneficial in the long term.

The past two decades have been a major success story for Austria. The country's Rieslings are now acknowledged to be some of the best in the world, Grüner Veltliner has gained recognition, and local unoaked Chardonnays and the sappy Steiermark Sauvignon Blancs have taken on a character all of their own.

There are now around 46,000ha of vines in Austria, making its production about a quarter that of Germany, with 75 per cent of wines being white. The home market is the main consumer of Austrian wines, but Germany is ready to buy up any leftovers. There are also buoyant export markets to the USA, Sweden and Japan.

Wine village of Weissenkirchen in Wachau, Austria

WINEGROWING COUNTRIES

These two small, land-locked countries share a position at the centre of Europe. The Alps dominate much of the landscape in both nations, so wine production is limited to the relative geographic margins.

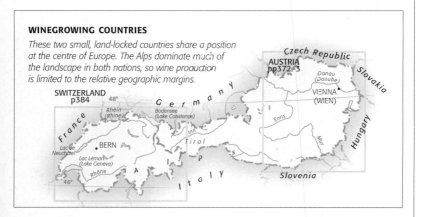

SWITZERLAND

THE SWISS WINE TRADITION probably also pre-dates the Romans, although, just as in Austria, winemaking was very much a small-time activity until the Middle Ages, when viticulture expanded under the influence of Cistercian monks. Winemaking then thrived until phylloxera and other vine-growing blights all but destroyed it in the late 1800s. Its recovery was stymied by the advent of industrialization and a new market for cheap, imported wine. Even by the middle of the 20th century, the Swiss wine industry was still a shadow of its historic self.

Recent decades have revived its fortunes. Switzerland's seven million residents are enthusiastic wine consumers, drinking 380 million bottles each year. Such demand far exceeds domestic capacity, but it has spurred dynamic change. The Swiss now produce about 149 million bottles annually, split almost equally between reds and whites. The country's 15,000ha of vineyards are distributed among almost all of the 26 cantons, though they are concentrated in three regions: the French-speaking west, the German-speaking east, and the Italian-speaking south.

Valais, in the Francophone region, is the undisputed star of Swiss wine, and it is widely planted with the country's most popular variety, Chasselas (also called Fendant here). This white grape gives a light, dry wine that can range in style from fairly neutral to pleasantly aromatic. Potentially more interesting indigenous whites include Petite Arvine and Amigne. Reds in Valais include Pinot Noir and Gamay; wine blended from the two is called Dôle. Indigenous red varieties include the spicy, tannic Cornalin and the excellent Humagne Rouge.

In the German-speaking east, production is overwhelmingly red. Most wines are light and made from the area's leading red variety, Blauburgunder (Pinot Noir). For whites, the light and floral Müller-Thurgau is most common. The Italian-speaking south, or Ticino (Tessin), is dominated by Merlot. Styles vary, but many of the (often oak-matured) wines from here are world class.

Because Swiss wines are highly prized in the domestic market, less than one per cent is exported – which is a great shame as, despite relatively high prices, this country offers variety and character that are more than welcome in today's increasingly homogenous wine world.

Vineyards in Valais, Western Switzerland

WINE MAP OF AUSTRIA

A USTRIA'S VINEYARDS are located in the east of the
country along the Czech, Slovakian, Hungarian,
and Slovenian borders. The key winegrowing region
is Niederösterreich (Lower Austria), on the fertile
Donau (Danube) plain in the northeast. The small
but significant districts of Wachau and Kremstal, in
the west of Niederösterreich, are associated with
some of Austria's most experimental producers.

AUSTRIA: AREAS & TOP PRODUCERS

NIEDERÖSTERREICH *p374*

Bernhard Ott *p378*
Franz Proidl *p378*
F X Pichler *p378*
Nikolaihof *p378*
Rudi Pichler *p378*
Stift Göttweig *p379*
Weingut Bründlmayer *p379*
Weingut Familie Nigl *p379*
Weingut Familie Pitnauer *p379*
Weingut Franz Hirtzberger *p379*
Weingut Hiedler *p379*
Weingut Högl *p380*
Weingut K Alphart *p380*
Weingut Knoll *p380*
Weingut Ludwig Neumayer *p380*
Weingut Malat *p380*
Weingut Prager *p380*
Weingut Undhof Salomon *p380*

VIENNA (WIEN) *p375*

Weingut Wieninger *p381*

BURGENLAND *p376*

Ernst Triebaumer *p381*
Josef Pöckl *p381*
Umathum *p381*
Uwe Schiefer *p382*
Weingut Familie Gesellmann *p382*
Weingut Gernot & Heike Heinrich *p382*
Weingut Juris *p382*
Weingut Prieler *p382*
Weingut Velich *p383*
Weinlaubenhof Kracher *p383*

STEIERMARK (STYRIA) *p377*

Tement *p383*
Weingut Erich & Walter Polz *p383*
Weingut Gross *p383*

KEY

Austria's eastern wine areas

Weingut Prieler, Burgenland

CZE

Retz
Pulkau

Zöbing
Langenlois   KAMPTAL
           ● Strassertal
    Krems   ● Brunn im Felde
         KREMSTAL
Durnstein   ● NIEDERÖSTERREI
       ● Krems

WACHAU   DONAULAND
         TRAISENTAL

Danau (Danube)

48°   Bad Vös

THERMENREGION

A l p e n
(A l p s)

Mur

STEIERMARK
(STYRIA)

SUDÖST STEIERMARK
● Graz

WESTSTEIERMARK   Riegersburg

47°   Kapfenstein

                   St Annaam Aigen
Mur   Straden ●
SÜDSTEIERMARK   Tieschen ●
   Gamlitz ●
Spielfeld ● Bad Radkersb
           SLOVENI A

GERMANY
Salzburg ●
               VIENNA ■
               (WIEN)
ITALY   SLOVENIA
CZECH
REPUBLIC
         CROATIA

Farmhouse overlooking sloping vineyards near Graz, Steiermark

TERROIR AT A GLANCE

Latitude: 46.5–49°N.

Altitude: 115–550m.

Topography: Varied, from flat lakeside areas around the large shallow Neusiedler See in the east of Burgenland to rolling hills in Steiermark.

Soil: Generally stony schist, limestone, and gravel.

Climate: Continental, with relatively mild autumns that often allow late ripening into October or November.

Temperature: July average is 19.5°C.

Rainfall: Annual average is 603mm. Rainfall is lowest in the western Weinviertel and highest in the eastern Weinviertel.

Wind: Warm Pannonian winds blow along the Danau (Danube) off the Hungarian Plains, resulting in higher temperatures for riverside vineyards.

Viticultural hazards: Spring frosts, rain.

Top Austrian Grape Varieties

There are a number of grape varieties that are native to Austria and reflect the country's special character.

White Grape Varieties

Grüner Veltliner: This key variety has a vegetal aroma, and white pepper and grapefruit flavours emerge when it is very ripe. A few of the best come from the Wachau; some people say it can rival Chardonnay and Riesling.

Welschriesling: Unrelated to the well-known Riesling variety, this grape produces light, aromatic wines. Its seam of lemony acidity makes it the Austrians' favourite for sparkling wine, or *Sekt*.

Zierfandler: Spicy Zierfandler was traditionally mixed with Rotgipfler to produce *Gumpoldskirchner*, a white from the Thermenregion. Today, it can be found on its own.

Rotgipfler: This was the other half of the pairing used for *Gumpoldskirchner*, but can now be found as a varietal. It sometimes smells of brown bread.

Neuburger: Most often found in the Wachau region, this is a

Blaufränkisch grapes

cross between Weissburgunder (Pinot Blanc) and Silvaner. It tends to be full-bodied, and at its best has a nutty flavour.

Red Grape Varieties

Blaufränkisch: Widely planted and very popular in Austria, this grape produces robust, good-coloured reds with a flavour of raspberries and a touch of white pepper. It is sometimes said to be Austria's answer to Cabernet Sauvignon – especially in its weightier Burgenland versions – but there is a zip of acidity that always distinguishes it.

Zweigelt: Also grown all over Austria, this grape is the creation of Dr Zweigelt, who crossed St-Laurent and Blaufränkisch. It can be a heavy cropper, but kept under control it makes attractive, juicy, cherry-flavoured wines.

Blauer Wildbacher: This dark-red grape, native to Steiermark, is used almost exclusively for the region's crisp rosé, *Schilcher*.

Grüner Veltliner grapes

Vineyards along the Donau (Danube) Valley, Wachau

WINEGROWING AREAS OF AUSTRIA

Niederösterreich

WITH 33,650HA UNDER VINE, Niederösterreich (Lower Austria) accounts for 58 per cent of Austrian wine production. Most of the wines produced here are dry whites and Grüner Veltliner is the most popular variety, occupying nearly half the vineyards. Niederösterreich breaks down into eight key winegrowing districts.

Wine cellar sign, Vienna

🏔 *various* 🍇 *Portugieser, Zweigelt, St-Laurent* 🍇 *Grüner Veltliner, Müller-Thurgau, Welschriesling* 🍷 *red, white, dessert*

Weinviertel

THE LARGEST WINE DISTRICT in Austria with 18,000ha under vine, the Weinviertel ('wine quarter') was formed after 1985 and was Austria's first EU-approved appellation or DAC *(Districtus Austria Controllatus)*. The climate here varies greatly, from the aridity of Retz to the more humid areas along the March River, where much of Austria's classic Grüner Veltliner is produced. Base wines for Austria's flourishing *Sekt* industry (usually from Grüner Veltliner, Weissburgunder (Pinot Blanc), or Riesling) come mainly from Poysdorf to the northeast, and exemplary still wines are produced here too – notably peppery Grüner Veltliners and deliciously sappy Weissburgunders. The Pulkautal, in the north along the Pulkau River, is home to the Hardegg estate, which is known for having produced Austria's first port-style wine and the first commercial Viognier.

Kamptal

CLIMATE AND SOIL COMBINE to make this one of the country's best winegrowing areas, above all for dry white wines made from Grüner Veltliner, Riesling, and Weissburgunder (Pinot Blanc). The Kamptal centres on the small town of Langenlois, home of first-rate winemakers such as Willi Bründlmayer. There are also groups of important growers in the Strassertal and Zöbing, who exploit the area's greatest geological feature, the Heiligenstein. This south-facing Permian rock is made up of a mixture of shaley sandstone and volcanic soils that produce top-class Grüner Veltliner, impressive Weissburgunder, and racy Riesling. Kamptal growers have even elaborated their own classification based on soil: *Grosse Erste Lage (grand cru)*, *Erste Lage (premier cru)*, and *Klassifizierte Lage (cru classé)*.

Kremstal

THE 1,000-YEAR-OLD TOWN OF KREMS is home to some of the best growers in Niederösterreich. The sandy soils to the east are ideal for lively Grüner Veltliners, but more serious wine – above all lime-scented Riesling – is made on the primary rock soils of Stein and Senftenberg. There are two more pockets of quality vineyards: around Rohrendorf and Brunn im Felde; and across the Donau (Danube) in Furth and Palt. Wines here are chiefly Grüner Veltliner, but Riesling also makes an appearance. The Kremstal now has its own DAC.

Wachau

WACHAU HAS BECOME Austria's most famous wine district for its powerful, lime-scented Rieslings. Even so, Riesling only accounts for around 10 per cent of production here. Grüner Veltliner is still the main grape, and the area's granite soils mean these wines can be every bit as good as Riesling.

With vineyards either side of the Donau (Danube) and a dramatic patchwork of terraces hewn out of the granite, gneiss, and mica, there are few wine regions in the world that can rival Wachau's beauty. Wines from the south-facing slopes below Dürnstein tend to be more powerful than those from further west. There is also a small cluster of good growers in Mautern, south of the river. The Vinea Wachau organization has developed its own system of classification: *Steinfeder* is a light, unchaptalized wine; *Feder-spiel* a medium *Kabinett*; and *Smaragd* is a powerful dry *Kabinett* or *Spätlese (see p348)*.

Traisental

AUSTRIA'S NEWEST AND SMALLEST wine district was born in 1995, with 700ha between the Donau (Danube) and St Pölten, but has been slow to present any particular identity. The flagship was, and is, Ludwig Neumayer's 7-ha estate in Inzersdorf ob der Traisen, which is known for its impressive Weissburgunders.

Wagram

THIS REGION CENTRES ON KLOSTERNEUBURG – best known for its monastery – and the Wagram itself, west of Vienna. The monastery is the biggest vineyard owner in Austria and owns some stunningly steep slopes on the western fringes of the capital, with considerable potential for Grüner Veltliner and Riesling. The best wines, however, still come from the Wagram, a long loess ridge where growers make some of the country's most delightfully peppery, lentil-scented Grüner Veltliners.

Carnuntum

THIS PROMISING AREA – above all for red wines – runs along the north bank of the Donau (Danube) and benefits from the warm Pannonian winds. Most of the good growers are around Göttlesbrunn. Zweigelt is the best

A typical *Heurige* or inn, Vienna

grape in the west of the region, producing rich, cherry-scented wines. But Cabernet Sauvignon and even Syrah are made here too. Blaufränkisch dominates in the east, but it lacks the weight of its Burgenland cousin.

Thermenregion

IN THE OLD DAYS, the demand in Vienna's pubs or *Beisls* was for sweet, white *Gumpoldskirchner* or red *Vöslauer* – both produced in the Thermenregion. *Vöslauer*, from the deep gravel soils around Bad Vöslau, used to be a thin wine made largely from Portugieser, but these days it is as likely to be Cabernet Sauvignon, St-Laurent, or Blauburgunder (Pinot Noir). *Gumpoldskirchner* comes from the rolling hills that are the last outriders to the Alps. Classically it was made from Zierfandler and Rotgipfler, which give broad-shouldered whites; around Baden in the north there was more Neuburger, which is allegedly part of the Burgundian vine family and makes plump wines that become nutty with age. When the region was badly hit by the 1985 wine scandal *(see p370)*, growers responded by trying Chardonnay instead – although successful, producers are now returning to tradition.

Vienna (Wien)

VIENNA HAS many vineyards on its rustic fringes to supply the city's *Heurigen* (inns) with fresh young white wine, also called *Heurige* ('this year's'). When it passes its first birthday, this wine is designated *Altwein* ('old wine') and replaced by the newly harvested *Heurige*. As the locals and tourists are relatively undemanding, winemaking can be sloppy, but a few serious growers are now producing Rieslings and Weissburgunders that show potential.

 limestone, loess, brown soils, loam, gravel

Zweigelt Grüner Veltliner, Riesling red, white

Decorated barrel, Burgenland

Burgenland

BURGENLAND IS AUSTRIA'S second-biggest wine region, and virtually every type of wine is made here. Part of Hungary until 1921, it is not surprising that it has little in common with Niederösterreich, or that Welschriesling, as opposed to Grüner Veltliner, is the most planted grape. As in Hungary, Blaufränkisch is the main red variety, particularly in Mittelburgenland. The Hungarian influence is also found in Ruster Ausbruch, Austria's answer to Tokay. Burgenland divides into four winegrowing districts.

🏞 *gravel, sand, loam, chalk, limestone*
🍇 *Blaufränkisch, Zweigelt, Cabernet Sauvignon, Syrah, Nebbiolo, Tempranillo* 🍇 *Welschriesling, Weissburgunder, Chardonnay* 🍷 *red, white, dessert*

Neusiedlersee (Seewinkel)

NEUSIEDLERSEE IS OFTEN ASSOCIATED with luscious sweet wines made from Welschriesling, Scheurebe (Sämling 88), Traminer, Grauburgunder (Pinot Gris), Weissburgunder (Pinot Blanc), and Bouvier. These grapes are grown closest to the shallow lake, the Neusiedler See, around the villages of Illmitz and Apetlon. The autumn mists here are important for production of these wines as they encourage botrytis *(see p65)*, which is also helped by a belt of largely stagnant ponds with appropriate names – like the upper and lower Stinkersee. But even in misty Apetlon it is possible to make some rich, dry whites, as the Velich family proves.

Further back from the lake shores, sweet wines give way to other styles. Gols, halfway up the eastern shore, has become famous for its great reds. This is the home of the Pannobile organization, whose members specialize in blending native grapes such as Blaufränkisch, St-Laurent, and Zweigelt with imported cultivars. To the north is Jois, where Austria's most convincingly Burgundy-style Blauburgunders (Pinot Noirs) are made.

Neusiedlersee-Hügelland

THIS AREA CENTRES on the small town of Rust, on the west bank of the Neusiedler See, and Eisenstadt, Burgenland's capital in the Leitha Hills. Since the early 17th century, Rust has been associated with sweet *Ausbruch* wine. At that time, when Burgenland was under the Hungarian crown, it was the Western counterpart of Tokay's famous Aszú *(see p397)*. Unlike the sweet wines from the eastern side of the lake, *Ausbruch* is made by just adding botrytized grapes to the wine or must. The result is more vinous – closer to the French Sauternes *(see p66)*. Today this Hungarian tradition is most readily apparent in the wines of Robert Wenzel. Up in the hills above the lake, producers have pioneered the development of western-style Bordeaux-blends and dry whites from Chardonnay and Sauvignon Blanc.

Mittelburgenland

SOMETIMES CALLED BLAUFRÄNKISCHLAND after its dominant grape variety, this is essentially a red wine area that now benefits from a new DAC. Red wine grapes traditionally make up two thirds of the total planted around the small towns of Horitschon, Neckenmarkt, and Deutschkreuz. The 1980s and 90s were a time of experimentation here: the French oenologist Philippe Ricôt converted many local growers to Merlot, and the late Hans Igler brought in Cabernet Sauvignon. In the early 1990s new oak *barriques* were also introduced and wildly over-used. Their use has now been moderated, and the wines have benefited from the mellowed oak flavours. In fact, a collection of exemplary Blaufränkisch wines has recently been released from Neckenmarkt co-operative. Near the Hungarian border in Lutzmannsburg, meanwhile, Roland Velich of Apetlon has created another new (and fashionable) wine, Moric, using century-old Blaufränkisch vines.

Südburgenland

THIS WILD AND REMOTE DISTRICT in the south of Austria only produces a small amount of wine, most of it red. The best comes from Deutsch Schützen, where Weingut Krutzler makes one of the country's best reds, Perwolf, by blending Blaufränkisch with a small amount of Cabernet Sauvignon. Other villages of note are Eisenberg and Rechnitz. In Heiligenbrunn and Moschendorf, there are still several growers who make *Uhudler* – a wine from ungrafted American hybrids – which, like the Italian Fragola, has a strawberry bubblegum flavour.

Steiermark (Styria)

AFTER VIENNA, Steiermark is the smallest region in terms of wine production. The fact that one in 10 growers has a *Buschenschank* (country inn) gives an indication of the sort of wine that is made here – simple stuff for local consumption. The climate is warm and most of the wine produced in Steiermark's three districts is dry and white, although some sweet wines are made in good years. Recently the region's wines have won a reputation in Austria for their sappy fruitiness, and their fame is now spreading.

volcanic Zweigelt Welschriesling, Sauvignon Blanc, Chardonnay, Grauburgunder (Pinot Gris), Weissburgunder (Pinot Blanc), Gelber Muskateller red, white, rosé, sparkling

Südost Steiermark

PRINCIPALLY, WHITE GRAPES, such as Welschriesling, are grown on the volcanic knolls and outcrops of this district, especially along a strip of land that protrudes into Slovenia around Bad Radkersburg. The villages to look out for are Kapfenstein (a fief of the Winkler-Hermadens who make Austria's most monumental Zweigelt, Olivin), St Anna am Aigen, Straden, Tieschen, Riegersburg, and Klöch – which specializes in off-dry Gewürztraminer.

Südsteiermark

THIS IS ONE of the country's most beautiful wine districts, and the wines here are a match for the scenery. The pioneer was the elder Willi Sattler, who began making dry white wine in Gamlitz in the 1970s. In those days, this area made semi-sweet wines to sate the German tourists, but after 1985 everyone followed Sattler's lead. Wines to look out for are Sauvignon Blanc, Chardonnay (Morillon), and Grauburgunder (Pinot Gris), preferably vinified in a dry, not-too-oaky style that brings out the fruitiness. Welschriesling is the mainstay of most vineyards – its delicate acidity and refreshing clarity of fruit can be a revelation here.

Weststeiermark

WITH ONE OR TWO EXCEPTIONS, Weststeiermark means *Schilcher*: a darkish rosé with a searing acidity made as a red wine from the Blauer Wildbacher grape. The *Sekt* is best. Every now and then a hot year allows growers to vinify Blauer Wildbacher as a Merlot-like red wine, which can be worth trying.

HEINRICH

Pannobile 2001

BURGENLAND

Weingut Gernot & Heike Heinrich label, Burgenland

Vineyards surrounding the village of Kapfenstein, Südost Steiermark

TOP PRODUCERS OF AUSTRIA

Bernhard Ott
Niederösterreich

Neufang 36, Feuersbrunn 📞 *02738 22 57* 🖰 *www.ott.at* 🔾 *by appt*

FROM HIS BASE in Donauland, Bernhard Ott cultivates Grüner Veltliner and almost nothing else. The success of this focus has quickly made him a star in Austrian and German wine circles. His top bottling is the dense and textured Rosenberg Reserve, but Ott is best known for his 'Fass 4', a balanced wine blended from just a handful of great sites that is an unalloyed pleasure to drink.

🖼 *white* ➋ *2007, 2005, 2003, 2002, 2001, 2000, 1999*
★ *Grüner Veltliner Fass 4, Grüner Veltliner Rosenberg Reserve*

Franz Proidl
Niederösterreich

Oberer Markt 5, Senftenberg 📞 *02719 24 58* 🔾 *by appt*

FOR DECADES, THE terraced site of Ehrenfels lay abandoned below the ruined Senftenberg castle in northwest Kremstal. Then, in the late 1980s, Franz Proidl rescued the vineyard and began growing powerful Riesling and Grüner Veltliner grapes on its mineral soils. When conditions permit, he also produces some stunning botrytized dessert wines.

🖼 *white, red, dessert* ➋ *2007, 2005, 2003, 2002, 2001, 2000, 1999* ★ *Riesling Senftenberger Ehrenfels*

Painted sign on the wall at Franz Proidl's winery

Hillside vineyard in Krems, Niederösterreich

F X Pichler
Niederösterreich

Oberloiben 27, Loiben 📞 *02732 85 3 75* 🔾

LIKE FRANZ HIRTZBERGER, F X has celebrity status in Austria. He only has a 7.5-ha vineyard, but supplements his production with bought-in Riesling and Grüner Veltliner grapes. His top *Smaragde* are modern legends – particularly those marked 'M' for monumental. Look out for the powerful Grüner Veltliners from the Kellerberg and the Loibner Berg. Like all his wines, the Rieslings can be austere when young, but they develop magnificently: Loibner Berg and Kellerberg are leaders here too. There is also a rare sweet wine, made only in exceptional years.

🖼 *white, dessert* ➋ *2007, 2005, 2003, 2002, 2001, 2000, 1999, 1998, 1997* ★ *Kellerberg Riesling, Loibner Berg Grüner Veltliner*

Nikolaihof
Niederösterreich

Mautern 📞 *02732 82 901* 🖰 *www.nikolaihof.at* 🔾 *by appt*

IT MAY BE TUCKED AWAY on the south side of the Danube, but Nikolaihof is not to be ignored. The wines are

organic, grown in 16ha of the Wachau and Stein. Owners Nikolaus and Christine Saahs make austere, angular Rieslings from Vom Stein, Im Weingebirge, and the Steiner Hund, and there are some interesting blends, such as the Chardonnay-and-Neuburger Cuvée Elisabeth (named after one of the Saahs' daughters). In season, the family runs a serious restaurant in the beatiful, old house.

🖼 *white* ➋ *2007, 2005, 2003, 2002, 2001, 2000, 1999, 1998, 1997*
★ *Steiner Hund Riesling, Cuvée Elisabeth*

Rudi Pichler
Niederösterreich

Marienfeldweg 122, Wösendorf 📞 *02715 2267* 🖰 *www.rudipichler.at* 🔾 *by appt*

RUDI PICHLER has now made it to the top flight of Wachau growers with a superb series of wines in 2007. The top Veltliners are from Hochrain, while a magnificent Weissburgunder is made from the Kollmütz site. Rudi Pichler's Smaragds from Kirchweg and Achleiten are as good as any Rieslings in Austria.

🖼 *white* ➋ *2007, 2006, 2005*
★ *Crus Kirchweg, Kollmütz, Achleiten*

Stift Göttweig
Niederösterreich

Göttweig 1, Furth ☎ *02732 801 440*
Ⓦ *www.weingutstiftgoettweig.at*
○ *by appt*

THERE HAS BEEN A CHANGE of management at this great Benedictine monastery that dominates the Danube Valley south of Krems: Fritz Miesbauer has taken over from the Ungers, and the wines have leapt up in quality. In the difficult 2007 vintage, Miesbauer made a brilliant series including the delicious Messwein, Veltliners from the Berg and Gottschelle sites, and Rieslings Berg and Silberbichl.
🍷 *white* 🍾 *2007* ★ *Göttweiger Berg, Gottschelle, Silberbichl*

Weingut Bründlmayer
Niederösterreich

Zwettler Str 23, Langenlois
☎ *02734 21 720*
Ⓦ *www.bruendlmayer.at* ○

AUSTRIA'S BEST ALL rounder, Willi Bründlmayer makes over a dozen wines on this 50-ha estate. His top bottlings are the powerful Alte Reben (old-vine) Grüner Veltliners and Rieslings, but it would be hard to fault his creamy Chardonnay or oak-aged Grauburgunder. Delicious dessert wines occasionally feature, and there are also some good reds, particularly Blauburgunder. The *Sekt* is one of the most measured in Austria – the best home-grown alternative to champagne.
🍷 *red, white, sparkling, dessert* 🍾 *2007, 2006, 2005, 2003, 2002, 2001, 2000, 1998, 1997, 1995, 1994, 1993, 1992, 1990*
★ *Alte Reben: Riesling, Grüner Veltliner; Sekt*

Weingut Familie Nigl
Niederösterreich

Priel 7, Senftenberg ☎ *02719 26 09*
Ⓦ *www.weingutnigl.at* ○ *by appt*

THE FAMILIE NIGL is a top producer of Grüner Veltliner and Riesling from primary rock soils above Senftenberg. Look out for the Kremsleiten, Senftenberger Piri, and Hochäcker sites – their wines compare with Wachau's best. There is also some occasional dessert wines made from Chardonnay.
🍷 *white, dessert* 🍾 *2007, 2006, 2005, 2003, 2002, 2001, 2000, 1999*
★ *Senftenberger Piri Riesling, Senftenberger Hochäcker Riesling*

Weingut Familie Pitnauer
Niederösterreich

Weinbergstr 6, Göttlesbrunn
☎ *02162 82 49* Ⓦ *www.pitnauer.com*
○ *by appt*

THE SENIOR MEMBER of the local Göttlesbrunn pack, Hans Pitnauer excels at full-bodied red wines like Bienenfresser, a pure Zweigelt, and Franz Josef (named after Pitnauer's father and grandfather), a blend of Zweigelt, Cabernet Sauvignon, and St-Laurent or Syrah. He also produces experimental wines such as Grüner Veltliner vermouth.
🍷 *red, white* 🍾 *2007, 2005, 2003, 2002, 2001, 2000, 1999, 1998*
★ *Bienenfresser, Franz Josef*

Weingut Bründlmayer label

Weingut Familie Nigl wines

Weingut Franz Hirtzberger
Niederösterreich

Kremserstr 8, Spitz an der Donau
☎ *02713 22 09* ○ *by appt*

HIRTZBERGER IS a key figure in the Wachau and the second generation of dry winemakers on the family estate. His powerful, sometimes very alcoholic, Honivogl Grüner Veltliner is a model for all other *Smaragde*. Superbly long, complex Rieslings come from Hochrain and the Singerriedl.
🍷 *white* 🍾 *2007, 2006, 2005, 2003, 2002, 2001, 2000, 1999, 1998, 1997*
★ *Honivogl Grüner Veltliner Smaragd*

Weingut Hiedler
Niederösterreich

Am Rosenhugel 13, Langenlois ☎ *02734 24 68* Ⓦ *www.hiedler.at* ○ *by appt*

LUDWIG HIEDLER AND his Spanish wife Maria Angeles are gaining global recognition for their work in Kamptal. A single hectare in the Heiligenstein vineyard near the village of Zöbing is the source of some brilliantly focused Rieslings, but the Hiedlers also produce six different expressions of Grüner Veltliner – from the light and crisp Löss to the amazingly complex Maximum. Each wine reflects its *terroir*.
🍷 *white, red* 🍾 *2007, 2006, 2005, 2003, 2002, 2001, 2000, 1999*
★ *Riesling Maximum, Grüner Veltliner Maximum*

Weingut Högl
Niederösterreich

Viessling 31, Spitz an der Donau
📞 *02713 84 58* 🆆 *www.weingut-hoegl.ct* 🄲 *by appt*

TEN YEARS AGO it was inconceivable that any other Wachau grower should break in on the big four (Pichler-Hirtzberger-Prager-Knoll), but Högl has succeeded with the magnificent wines he makes in Spitz and Loiben. Look out for Rieds Schön Grüner Veltliner and Bruck Riesling.
🍷 *white* 🔜 *2007, 2006, 2005, 2003, 2002, 2001, 2000, 1999* ★ *Rieds Schön Grüner Veltliner, Bruck Riesling*

Weingut K Alphart
Niederösterreich

Wiener Str 46, Traiskirchen 📞 *02252 25 3 28* 🆆 *www.alphart.com* 🄲

THE BEST GROWER in the Thermenregion, Karl Alphart has found a middle way between tradition and modernity. Most of his wines, made from Zierfandler, Rotgipfler, or Neuburger, are bone-dry, but in a good year he makes the best spicy BAs and TBAs around *(see p348)*.
🍷 *white, dessert* 🔜 *2007, 2006, 2005, 2002, 2001, 2000, 1999, 1998* ★ *Zierfandler, Rotgipfler, Neuburger*

Weingut Knoll
Niederösterreich

Unterloiben 10, Loiben 📞 *02732 79 3 55* 🆆 *www.knoll.at* 🄲 *by appt*

THE QUIET VOICE of distinction in the Wachau, Knoll makes some of the best Grüner Veltliners and Rieslings in this area. Look out for the Schütt Veltliner in particular, which in a good year has a wonderful scent of pineapples. The Loibenberg wine is also magnificently structured. Knoll's best results with Riesling come from the Loibenberg and the Kellerberg

sites. Occasional dessert wines are also produced.
🍷 *white, dessert* 🔜 *2007, 2006, 2005, 2003, 2002, 2001, 2000, 1999, 1998* ★ *Schütt Grüner Veltliner*

Weingut Ludwig Neumeyer
Niederösterreich

Dorfstrasse 37, Inzersdorf on der Traisen 📞 *02782 82985* 🆆 *www.weinvomstein.at* 🄲 *by appt*

LUDWIG NEUMEYER is the man who put the Traisental on the map. A dignified winemaker, he gives the impression of having thought long and hard before making each wine. Everything seems to turn to gold in his hands, but particularly recommended are his Veltliner, Riesling, and Weissburgunder wines. The latter is one of Austria's best.
🍷 *white* 🔜 *2007, 2006, 2005, 2003* ★ *Rafasetze, Wein vom Stein*

Weingut Malat
Niederösterreich

Lindengasse 27, Furth bei Göttweig 📞 *02732 82 9 34* 🆆 *www.malat.at* 🄲 *by appt*

FORMER SKIER AND racing car driver Gerald Malat produces a dazzling array of wines from his 30-ha vineyard. His reds – a Blauburgunder (Pinot Noir) and an internationally inclined Bordeaux blend – are very exciting; his whites are not far behind. There is a

new-wave, oaky Chardonnay, and a Weissburgunder inspired by Italy, as well as Riesling and Grüner Veltliner wrought in a more local idiom.
🍷 *red, white, sparkling, dessert* 🔜 *2007, 2006, 2005, 2003, 2002, 2001, 2000, 1999, 1998* ★ *Blauburgunder*

Weingut Prager
Niederösterreich

Weissenkirchen 48 📞 *02715 22 48* 🆆 *www.weingutprager.at* 🄲 *by appt*

FRANZ PRAGER WAS one of the pioneers of dry wines in the Wachau. Now made by his son-in-law, Toni Bodenstein, complex, opulent Riesling dominates here, with the best wines coming from Achleiten, Klaus, and Steinriegl. Prager likes to claim its land in Ried Ritzling as the origin of the grape variety.
🍷 *white* 🔜 *2007, 2006, 2005, 2003, 2002, 2001, 2000, 1999, 1998, 1997* ★ *Riesling Achleiten, Riesling Klaus, Riesling Steinriegl*

Weingut Undhof Salomon
Niederösterreich

Undstr 10, Krems-Stein 📞 *02732 832 26* 🆆 *www.undhof.at* 🄲 *by appt*

AFTER THE DEATH of his brother Erich, Bert Salomon continues to work the family's 20ha at the western edge of Kremstal. Half of the estate is devoted to Riesling, and the wines crafted with this variety

pinot noir   2001

MALAT

RESERVE

Weingut Malat Pinot Noir (Blauburgunder) label

Cellar at Weingut Wieninger on the outskirts of Vienna

show real elegance. Most of the remaining land is given over to Grüner Veltliner, which produces wines with pronounced minerality. Bert also makes red wines in South Australia under the Salomon Estate label.

🗺 white 📷 2007, 2006, 2005, 2003, 2002, 2001, 2000, 1999 ★ Riesling Kremser Koegl Reserve, Grüner Veltliner Von Stein

Weingut Wieninger
Vienna (Wien)

Stammersdorfer Str 80, Stammersdorf 📞 01290 1012
🌐 www.wieninger.at ⬜

FRITZ WIENINGER makes modern, sophisticated wines that sell in top wine shops and distinguished restaurants in Vienna. His business now spans both sides of the Donau (Danube). He makes an old-fashioned Gemischter Satz in Nussdorf — a blend of all the grapes in the vineyard, some of which are unidentified. His most famous wines, however, are the creamy, international-style Chardonnays (Select and Grand Select). It is hard to imagine that wines like his Pinot Noir and Cabernet-Merlot blend come from a Viennese Heurige, or inn.

🗺 red, white 📷 2007, 2006, 2005, 2002, 2001, 2000, 1999 ★ Nussdorf Gemischter Satz, Select Chardonnay

Ernst Triebaumer
Burgenland

Raiffeisenstr 9, Rust 📞 02685 528
🌐 www.triebaumer.com ⬜ by appt

THE WINE BOTTLES FROM this estate display the letters 'ET'. The Spielberg connection is unintentional, but the quality of Ernst Triebaumer's wine might well be considered out of this world. Triebaumer is fastidious and consistent — as are those who work with him: some members of his crew have completed 25 harvests at the estate. Triebaumer is also a founding father of the small red-wine revolution taking place in Austria. His intense Blaufränkisch Mariental is a standard against which domestic reds are judged, as it has been since 1986.

🗺 red, white, dessert 📷 2007, 2006, 2005, 2003, 2002, 2001, 2000, 1999 ★ Blaufränkisch Mariental, Ruster Ausbruch

Josef Pöckl label

Josef Pöckl
Burgenland

Baumschulgasse 12, Mönchhof
📞 02173 80 2 58
🌐 www.poeckl.com ⬜ by appt

PÖCKL IS acknowledged to be one of the best, if not the best, red winemaker in the whole of Austria. His repertoire includes Zweigelt. Syrah, Nebbiolo, and Zinfandel, but the estate's top wines are the multi-faceted Admiral (Zweigelt blended with Cabernet Sauvignon and Merlot) and Rosso e Nero (Zweigelt, Cabernet Sauvignon, Blaufränkisch, Syrah, Merlot, and St-Laurent). Rosso e Nero is justifiably one of the most sought-after wines in the country today.

🗺 red, dessert 📷 2007, 2006, 2005, 2002, 2001, 2000, 1999, 1998 ★ Admiral, Rosso e Nero

Umathum
Burgenland

St Andräer Str 7, Frauenkirchen
📞 02172 24 4 00 🌐 www.umathum.at ⬜ by appt

PEPPI UMATHUM WAS one of the movers and shakers in the 1980s, when he created some of the first red blends in Burgenland, and they are still some of his best wines: Haideboden (from Zweigelt and Merlot) and Hallebühl (Zweigelt-Blaufränkisch-Cabernet Sauvignon). His raspberry-scented St-Laurent and his latest release, a chunky Pinot Noir from the Jois site, are also superb.

🗺 red, white, dessert 📷 2007, 2006, 2005, 2002, 2001, 2000, 1999, 1998, 1997 ★ Haideboden, Hallebühl, Jois Pinot Noir

Uwe Schiefer
Burgenland

Welgersdorf 3 📞 *03362 2464* 💻
www.weinbau-schiefer.at 🕐 *by appt*

THE RISING STAR in South Burgenland, Uwe Schiefer has a little over 5.2ha of the schistous Eisenberg on the Hungarian border and is in the process of converting his production to biodynamism. His wines are issued under the Eisenberg, Königsberg, Szapary, and Reihburg labels. The Reihburg is the top cru; with its ancient vines, it makes one of the most individual Blaufränkisch wines of all: grapefruit and minerals with a long, persistent taste of raspberries.

🟥 *red* 📅 *2007, 2006, 2005, 2002, 2001, 2000, 1999, 1998, 1997*
★ *Eisenberg, Königsberg, Szapary, Reihburg*

Weingut Familie Gesellmann
Burgenland

Langegasse 65, Deutschkreutz
📞 *02613 80 360*
💻 *www.gesellmann.at* 🕐

THE WINES HERE ARE now made by Albert Gesellman, who cut his teeth in South Africa and California and so brings an international perspective to this family estate. There are whites, but the delights

here are the reds, particularly the rich Blaufränkisch Creitzer, the deep-coloured Pinot Noir from Ried Siglos, and the Bordeaux blend, Bela Rex – possibly the most admired of its type in Austria.

🟥 *red, white* 📅 *2007, 2006, 2005, 2003, 2002, 2001, 2000, 1999, 1998*
★ *Bela Rex, Blaufränkisch Creitzer, Ried Sigloss Pinot Noir*

Weingut Gernot & Heike Heinrich
Burgenland

Baugarten 60, Gols 📞 *02173 31 7 60*
💻 *www.heinrich.at* 🕐 *by appt*

GERNOT HEINRICH IS young and impatient and has already made wine in a variety of styles. Every year a wine is lost, but it is always replaced by something new. The consolation is that whatever he hatches turns out to be good, from his well-balanced Chardonnay to his more complex Pannobile Weiss blend; from his Zweigelt to his Salzberg Cuvée (Zweigelt-Blaufränkisch-Merlot-Syrah), currently one of the most trendy wines in Austria. This is made in garage wine *(see p83)* quantities and sells at an outrageous price.

🟥 *red, white* 📅 *2007, 2006, 2005, 2003, 2002, 2001, 2000, 1999, 1998*
★ *Pannobile Weiss, Salzberg Cuvée*

Weingut Juris
Burgenland

Marktgasse 12-18, Gols 📞
02173 22 03 💻 *www.juris.at*
🕐 *by appt*

AXEL STIEGELMAR HAS taken over from his father Georg at Juris, which was one of the first estates in Austria to gain a reputation for red wines. Those wines are still there: exemplary rich St-Laurent and weighty Pinot Noir,

PERFECT CASE: AUSTRIA

Ⓦ Bründlmayer Alte Reben Riesling ££

Ⓦ Franz Hirtzberger Singerriedl Riesling Smaragd £££

Ⓦ F X Pichler Loibner Berg Riesling Smaragd £££

Ⓡ Gesellmann Creitzer £££

Ⓡ Gernot & Heike Heinrich Salzberg Cuvée ££££

Ⓡ Josef Pöckl Rosso e Nero £££

Ⓡ Juris St-Laurent £££

Ⓦ Knoll Loibenberg Grüner Veltliner Smaragd £££

Ⓦ Polz Hochgrassnitzberg Sauvignon Blanc £££

Ⓦ Prager Riesling Steinriegl £££

Ⓦ Tement Zieregg Sauvignon Blanc £££

Ⓓ Weinlaubenhof Kracher Zwischen den Seen £££

Inamera (Cabernet-Merlot) and St Georg (Pinot Noir, St-Laurent, and Zweigelt). As for the whites, he makes classy Chardonnay and Sauvignon Blanc, and some very good, luscious *Strohwein* and other sweet wines.

🟥 *red, white, dessert* 📅 *2002, 2001, 2000, 1999, 1998, 1997* ★ *Strohwein*

Weingut Prieler
Burgenland

Hauptstr 181, Schützen im Gebirge
📞 *02684 22 29*
💻 *www.prieler.at* 🕐 *by appt*

OFTEN OVERLOOKED at home, Engelbert Prieler and daughter Sylvia are consistently good winemakers and dab hands with the difficult Blaufränkisch grape, managing to preserve its delicate flavour despite their use of new oak. The whites are Weissburgunder (Pinot Blanc) and Chardonnay, which are vinified in an international way while retaining a fine acidity. Prieler also excels at Cabernet

Weingut Juris label

Sauvignon, which is sometimes mixed with Zweigelt.

Vineyard of Weinlaubenhof Kracher

🟥 red, white 🔁 2007, 2006, 2005, 2003, 2002, 2001, 2000, 1999, 1998, 1997 ★ Prieler Blaufränkisch Goldberg, Weissburgunder

Weingut Velich
Burgenland

Seeufergasse 12, Apetlon 📞 02175 3187 Ⓦ www.velich.at 🔲 by appt

HEINZ AND ROLAND VELICH farm nine hectares of land within the beautiful Neusiedlersee-Seewinkel national park. Their exclusively white production is dominated by Chardonnay. The estate's flagship bottling is the single-vineyard Tiglat, a rich expression of Chardonnay that is fermented and matured in French oak barrels. And when the conditions are right, Weingut Velich also produces an outstanding dessert wine from Welschriesling.

🟥 white, dessert 🔁 2007, 2006, 2005, 2003, 2002, 2001, 2000, 1999 ★ Chardonnay Tiglat, Welschriesling TBA

Weinlaubenhof Kracher
Burgenland

Apetloner Str 37, Illmitz 📞 02175 33 77 Ⓦ www.kracher.at 🔲 by appt

ALOIS 'LUIS' KRACHER was the best-known face of Austrian wine. He died in his prime in 2007, and the wines are now made by his son Gerhard. At home in Illmitz the Krachers preside over a tiny patch of land, but buy in botrytis-affected grapes from all over Austria to make their sumptuous sweet wines: Zwischen den Seen – the traditional range vinified in acacia casks – and Nouvelle Vague, made in new French barriques. Varietal Welschriesling, Scheurebe, and Traminer all give him

wonderful results too, but these days a Kracher BA or TBA is often a blend.

🟥 red, white, dessert 🔁 2007, 2005, 2003, 2002, 2001, 2000, 1999, 1998, 1997 ★ Zwischen den Seen, Nouvelle Vague

Tement
Steiermark

Berghausen, Zieregg 13, Ehrenhausen 📞 03453 410 10 Ⓦ www.tement.at 🔲 by appt

MANFRED TEMENT is one of the most popular producers in Austria. He manages to make wonderful wines while also keeping abreast of the trends. The Tement series starts with the L u T (light and dry) Welschriesling, and works its way up in price and quality to the Zieregg Morillon (Chardonnay), made using malolactic fermentation and lashings of oak. In the middle of the range is an aromatic Zieregg Sauvignon Blanc, which is vinified in steel to preserve its freshness.

🟥 white 🔁 2007, 2002, 2001, 2000, 1999, 1998 ★ Zieregg Morillon, Zieregg Sauvignon Blanc, L u T Welschriesling

Weingut Erich & Walter Polz
Steiermark

Grassnitzberg 54a, Spielfeld 📞 03453 23 010 Ⓦ www.polz.co.at 🔲

BROTHERS ERICH and Walter Polz produce good quantities of superlative Steiermark wines at this family winery. Among them are a steely Welschriesling, finely structured

Weingut Erich & Walter Polz wine

Grauburgunder (Pinot Gris), Weissburgunder (Pinot Blanc) from the Grassnitzberg, and their workhorse – a multi-layered Chardonnay (Morillon) from the Hochgrassnitzberg. The same vineyard also yields a wonderfully perfumed Sauvignon Blanc, and an oaky Chardonnay is produced from Ried Obegg. They are all superb.

🟥 white 🔁 2007, 2002, 2001, 2000, 1999, 1998 ★ Grassnitzberg Weissburgunder, Hochgrassnitzberg: Morillon, Sauvignon Blanc

Weingut Gross
Steiermark

Ratsch a d Weinstrasse 26, Ehrenhausen 📞 03453 2527 Ⓦ www.gross.at 🔲 by appt

THE QUIET MAN of the South Styrian Wine Road, Alois Gross hasn't put a foot wrong these last 20 years. He is now in a position to challenge all the other top growers in the region with his crus: the lyrical Muskateller from Perz, his Weissburgunder from Kittenberg, and three wines from the Nussberg: Morillon (Chardonnay), Sauvignon Blanc and Gewürztraminer.

🟥 white 🔁 2007, 2006, 2005 ★ Nussberg

WINE MAP OF SWITZERLAND

Switzerland is a land divided by languages and unified by mountains – and Swiss wine can be viewed in much the same way. Yet while the Alps are a factor for all of the country's wine regions, their influence is not uniform. In fact, they create a wide variety of sub-climates and soil profiles, which in turn yield the great stylistic diversity of Swiss wines.

SWITZERLAND: AREAS & TOP PRODUCERS

WESTERN REGION
Jean-René Germanier
Louis Bovard
Marie-Therese Chappaz

EASTERN REGION
Daniel & Martha Gantenbein

SOUTHERN REGION
Luigi Zanini (Castello Luigi)

WINEGROWING AREAS OF SWITZERLAND

Western Region

THE FRENCH-SPEAKING CANTONS in the western part of Switzerland are the hub of the country's wine industry. More than 11,000ha of vines are planted in the cantons of Valais, Vaud, Genève (Geneva) and Neuchâtel. Valais, with almost half of this total, is by far the most important. The vineyards here follow the banks of the Rhône River, and are concentrated along south-facing slopes. This is a mountainous region, so typical vineyard altitudes vary from 400–700m. Viticultural challenges include frost and soil erosion – the latter is a reflection of the steep, terraced plots that typify the area. (Some vineyards have slopes of up to 85 per cent.) As with all of Switzerland, this long stretch of land is farmed by hundreds of smallholders. The majority of the plantings are Chasselas and Pinot Noir, although Syrah is also on the rise here. Even so, there are dozens of fascinating local varieties that are found nowhere else in the world. White grapes include Amigne and Petite Arvine, while Cornalin and Humagne Rouge can make remarkable red wines.

🏞 alluvial, gravel, glacial moraine, limestone, clay 🍇 Pinot Noir, Gamay, Syrah, Cornalin, Humagne Rouge 🍇 Chasselas, Sylvaner, Pinot Gris, Amigne, Petite Arvine 🍷 red, white, rosé, sparkling, dessert

Snow-covered vineyards in the canton of Valais, Western Region

Wine château in Vaud, Western Region

Eastern Region

THERE ARE MORE THAN 2,500ha of vineyards spread across the 17 German-speaking cantons known collectively as Eastern Switzerland. Winter and spring frosts are a challenge on this side of the Alps, although an extensive network of lakes and rivers greatly moderates the climate for viticulture. In spite of the cold climate, the region is largely devoted to red wine production – in particular, Pinot Noir. Although conditions are difficult, some of the Pinot Noirs from this region (generally labelled as Blauburgunder) are considered the best wines in the entire country. Of the white grapes, Müller-Thurgau is most common. In fact, Dr Hermann Müller, who was responsible for developing this (in)famous Germanic crossing in 1882, came from the canton of Thurgau, in this very region.

limestone, sandstone, slate, glacial moraine

Pinot Noir (Blauburgunder) *Müller-Thurgau, Pinot Gris, Pinot Blanc, Gewürztraminer, Chardonnay*

red, white, rosé, sparkling, dessert

Southern Region

TICINO IS AN ITALIAN-SPEAKING canton on the southern slopes of the Alps. It is the sunniest region in Switzerland and, thanks to a local wind known as the Föhn, it is also the warmest. The almost-Mediterranean conditions make this clear red-wine country. More than 1,000ha of vines grow in the area, and nearly 90 per cent of them are Merlot. Ticino's northern wine zone, Sopraceneri, is home to the indigenous Bondola variety, which is used in a rustic red called Nostrano. The southern zone, Sottoceneri, produces a range of excellent Merlots. Most of the best wines from anywhere in Ticino are marked with the local quality seal 'VITI'.

granite (north); limestone, clay (south)

Merlot, Bondola, Pinot Noir, Cabernet Sauvignon *Chardonnay, Chasselas, Semillon, Sauvignon Blanc* *red, white, rosé, sparkling*

TOP LOCAL PRODUCERS

Jean-René Germanier, *Western Region*
W www.jrgermanier.ch

This family estate is perhaps the most dynamic in the Valais. The production includes award-winning Chasselas (Fendant), Pinot Noir, Humagne Rouge, a very impressive Syrah called Cayas, and Mitis – an outstanding sweet wine from the indigenous Amigne grape. Jean-René Germanier also distills the popular Bon Père William pear brandy.

Louis Bovard, *Western Region*
W www.domainebovard.com

This winery in Cully, on Lake Geneva, has 17ha spread out over the winemaking appellations of the Canton of Vaud. There are 17 wines as well, ranging from the zinging Chasselas Grand Cru Dézaley La Médinette to more experimental wines made from Sauvignon Blanc and the simply named Rouge (a Merlot-Syrah blend).

Marie-Thérèse Chappaz, *Western Region*
W www.chappaz.ch

Marie-Thérèse Chappaz began renovating her great uncle's 7-ha estate in the Valais about 15 years ago, after formal training in oenology and several years of related research in the Vaud. She is truly devoted to her work, and crafts wines of tremendous character from Chasselas (Fendant), Pinot Noir, and Humagne Rouge, plus fabulous examples of Marsanne (Ermitage) and Petite Arvine.

Daniel & Martha Gantenbein, *Eastern Region*
C 081 302 47 88

The Gantenbeins farm 6ha of vines in Bündner Herrschaft, between the Rhine and the border with Liechtenstein. This district, known as the Burgundy of Switzerland, produces some excellent Pinot Noir, and it is no exaggeration to say that Daniel and Martha Gantenbein make the best. They also produce a rich and compelling Chardonnay. From a humble start in 1982, the couple say they have learned that nothing can improve the fruit that comes from the vineyard; what happens in the cellar can only preserve (or lose) that potential.

Luigi Zanini (Castello Luigi), *Southern Region*
W www.zanini.ch

Luigi Zanini set up the Castello Luigi estate almost 20 years ago, and his commitment to excellence has made him the leading producer in Ticino. His Merlot vines are carefully managed to produce fruit with maximum colour and flavour – yielding just a third of the harvest of other vineyards in the region. Zanini then vinifies his world-class wines in an immaculate, spiral cellar that curls 18m below a rather elaborate château.

CENTRAL & EASTERN EUROPE

CENTRAL & EASTERN EUROPE

*O*nce important in terms of wine culture, today this region is struggling to regain its former glory. In the Communist era the focus was on quantity rather than quality, and wine suffered from a chronic lack of investment. Many of the countries have recently joined the European Union, which may offer their producers a brighter future.

HUNGARY

HUNGARY USED TO be one of the principal wine sources for quality wine within the Austro-Hungarian Empire. The famous sweet wine Tokaji, as well as other wines such as the tangy Somló, graced the tables of the rich and noble at home and abroad. After 1945 wine production went into decline; a malaise brought about by the imposition of co-operatives and state farms under communism, and only since 1990 have the tables begun to turn. Hungary's vineyards are more akin to the Western model than other countries in the old Eastern bloc, as the *kolkhoz* (co-operative) system had already begun to fall apart before the Iron Curtain came down, and some growers already owned medium-sized plots of vines.

Clock decorated with grapes at Tokaj station, Hungary

Today Hungary is a mixture of former state co-operatives and individual producers owning, or farming, plots of under 10ha. There are currently 85,220ha under vine, producing around 4.8 million hectolitres. Over a quarter of Hungarian wine is exported, and Germany is the biggest market. As elsewhere in the old Eastern bloc, foreign investment has dropped in recent years. The only areas that might be pronounced a success story are Tokaj and Hilltop's Riverview brand.

Hungary has many indigenous grape varieties with evocative names. The most popular is Kékfrankos (Blaufränkisch or Lemberger) with just under 10 per cent of plantings, followed by Olasz Rizling (or Welschriesling). International varieties are proving a boon for the branded market, and Chardonnay comes in third. There are substantial plantings of Cabernet Sauvignon, Sauvignon Blanc, Pinot Noir – which is considered to have potential in Eger – and Merlot. After Kékfrankos and Olasz Rizling, the most widely grown indigenous grape is the Tokaji grape Furmint, followed by the Muscat-like Irsai Oliver. There are also significant plantings of the Austrian Zweigelt cultivar. Although branded wines are naturally made in a style to suit Western palates, Hungarian tastes are echoed in the

White wine is important around Lake Balaton, west Hungary

◁ **Vineyard at Klanjec, Kontinentalna (inland) Croatia**

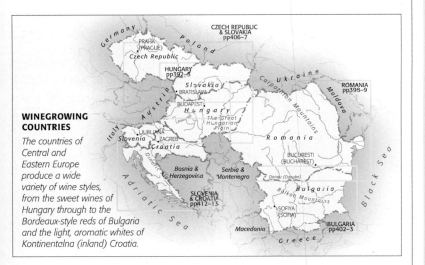

WINEGROWING COUNTRIES

The countries of Central and Eastern Europe produce a wide variety of wine styles, from the sweet wines of Hungary through to the Bordeaux-style reds of Bulgaria and the light, aromatic whites of Kontinentalna (inland) Croatia.

sharp wines of Somló, the luscious sweet wines of Tokaji, and Bikavér, the chunky blend known as Bull's Blood.

ROMANIA

ROMANIA IS A LATIN NATION among Slavic neighbours, and wine has been a part of its culture for 4,000 years. More than 95 per cent of the country's production is drunk at home, and Romania became a net importer in 2006, bringing in largely inexpensive wines from Italy and Spain. Leading export destinations were Germany, Russia, and Estonia.

Romania joined the EU in 2007, and its wine industry has benefited from pre-accession investment in new equipment, vineyard consolidation, and replanting. In 2008, the vineyard area was estimated at around 190,000ha (seventh largest in Europe) and wine production was 6.3 million hectolitres. Wine from noble varieties (rather than hybrids) accounts for less than 50 per cent of production, and the local market drinks around two-thirds white wine, usually semi-sweet in style. Consumption is changing towards reds and drier whites along with increasing wealth and the development of an aspirational middle class that is increasingly exposed to imported wines.

By 2001, privatization of the state-owned vineyards and wineries was mostly completed. This included 180,000ha being returned to private individuals in holdings of less than 1ha each. The issues of this fragmentation of vineyards have largely been overcome, at least by the larger commercial wineries, which have bought significant consolidated plots, and control picking time and quality of purchased fruit through contracts. The domestic market is dominated by five large producers, but quality improvements have been led by mid-sized and small boutique wineries that often have foreign investment or ownership. The image of Romania's wines in export markets remains low due to lack of promotion, but it is buoyant in the local market thanks to improved quality and customers prepared to pay higher prices.

The country's vineyards fall either side of the Carpathian Mountains. To the west, grape varieties such as Fetească Albă and Olasz Rizling are often the same as those found in Austria or Hungary. East of the Carpathians, Dealul Mare has built a reputation for smooth, ripe red wines. International varieties have been present in Romania since phylloxera caused devastation in the late 1800s, but plant

Bulgaria's warmest wine region lies in the southwest around Melnik

material is rarely high quality except in new vineyards. Romania does, however, boast some interesting indigenous grapes, most notably the black 'maiden grape' Fetească Neagră, which has the potential to make rich, well-structured reds. The white cross Fetească Regală makes good sparklings, while Tămaioasă Românească (or frankincense grape) and Grasă are both used for the sweet white wines of Cotnari.

Romania's wine industry still has a fair way to go, but this is definitely a country to watch.

BULGARIA

FEW COUNTRIES CAN claim an older tradition of winemaking than Bulgaria, with some vineyards believed to date back to the time of the Ancient Greeks. The state of Bulgaria was established in AD681 and viticulture became widespread, though the arrival of the Turks in the 14th century shifted winemaking to the monasteries. After 500 years of Ottoman rule, Bulgaria became independent in 1878, though, as in most of Europe, phylloxera devastated the country's vineyards soon after.

Since World War II, politics has been the major force in shaping Bulgaria's wine industry. It became part of the Soviet bloc after 1945, and the new communist government collectivized land and wineries to supply wine to Comecon countries. Around this time, vineyards were moved away from the hills and on to flat land so that the industry could be mechanized, and international grape varieties were planted in preference to native cultivars. These changes made Bulgaria the sixth-biggest wine producer in the world at its peak. Prior to land reforms in the 1990s, 80 per cent of the country's wine was made by Vinprom, the state wine trust. The Russians deserted Bulgaria in 1985, when Gorbachev unleashed his anti-alcohol campaign, but the state-run export organization Vinimpex turned to the Western European market, where soft, ripe, and cheap Bulgarian Cabernet Sauvignons made an impact.

Bulgaria has just over 70,000ha in production for wine grapes, two-thirds of which are planted with red varieties. It was Cabernet and Merlot that made Bulgaria's name in the 1980s and 90s; these remain important, but recent plantings have included a greater range of varieties, such as Shiraz, Petit Verdot, and Cabernet Franc. Most exciting of all is the revival of indigenous red grapes like Mavrud, Melnik, and Rubin, which are showing real promise, both in blends and on their own.

Ahead of joining the EU in 2007, Bulgaria's industry attracted more than €100 million in subsidies. This has drawn both foreign and local investments into the vineyards and wineries, and the results are showing in improved quality. Most leading wineries have their own

Vineyard worker, Tokajská (Slovak Tokaj) region

vineyards, allowing them better control over fruit sourcing. This had become essential, since poorly handled privatization had left viticulture in a very bad state by the end of the 1990s. A new wave of boutique and quality-focused wineries has set new standards for the industry, and the arrival of high-profile names like Michel Rolland has added credence to the country's claim to great conditions for producing wine. Bulgaria continues to export the majority of its production, though exports to the west have fallen considerably. Its major customers are Russia and Poland, while at the same time there is increasing demand in the domestic market for Bulgaria's best wines.

CZECH REPUBLIC & SLOVAKIA

SLOVAKIA HAS A long tradition of wine production stretching back around 3,000 years in Malokarpatská (Little Carpathians) region; the Czech Republic is a more recent producer – vines were first planted in Bohemia in the 9th century. In the Communist era private vineyard holdings were turned into large collective farms that concentrated on low quality, bulk production. After the fall of Communism, attempts were made to return vineyards to their original owners but this proved problematic. Entry into the European Union in 2004 for both countries is beginning to bring much-needed investment into the wine industry, allowing private companies to focus more on quality and also to demonstrate their potential. The climate of both the Czech Republic and Slovakia is more suited to the production of white wine rather than red; the long, dry autumns also allow some excellent sweet wines to be made.

SLOVENIA & CROATIA

THE VINOUS HERITAGE of these countries dates back over 2,000 years. Both nations were part of the former Communist state of Yugoslavia, but in the aftermath of its dissolution, Slovenia escaped relatively unscathed, whereas Croatia endured a brutal civil war. Today, Slovenia has a more successful wine industry, although world-class producers can be found in both. In the warmer coastal Adriatic wine regions, red wines tend to dominate, such as the Merlot-based reds from Goriška Brda, Slovenia, and the powerful reds from the Plavac Mali grape from Dingac, Croatia. Inland, dry white wines become more important, such as Pinot Gris, Šipon, and Laski Rizling from Ljutomer-Ormož, Slovenia, and Graševina (Welschriesling) from Slavonija in Croatia.

Vineyard in Haloze, Podravje region, Slovenia

WINE MAP OF HUNGARY

THERE ARE SEVEN WINE REGIONS in Hungary, replacing the 22 that formerly existed: Balaton, Duna, Eger, Észak-Dunántúl, Pannon, Sopron and Tokaj-Hegyalja. Not all produce quality wines. The country's most famous wine, Tokaji, comes from the northeast, as does Bikavér (Bull's Blood) of Eger. In the south, Villány and Szekszárd are highly regarded for reds, together with Sopron in the west. Important white winegrowing areas include Somló and Ászár-Neszmély in the northwest. Central Hungary's Great Plain once produced bulk wines for export to Soviet Russia and has struggled since this market disappeared with reforms in 1985.

KEY

Hungary

Tokaji Aszú label

1997
TOKAJI ASZÚ
5 PUTTONYOS
Tokaji édes, fehér borkülönlegesség • High quality sweet white wine
Termelte és palackozta • Produced and bottled by
Degenfeld Bt. Tarcal
10% alc/vol.   PRODUCT OF HUNGARY   0,5l

PERFECT CASE: HUNGARIAN WINE

R Attila Gere Cabernet Sauvignon Barrique ££ (072 492 195)

R Béla Vincze Cabernet Franc ££ (036 427 515)

D Disznókő Esszencia Aszú 6 Puttonyos ££££

D Graf Degenfeld 6 Puttonyos ££££ (047 380 173)

R Huba Szeremley, Kéknyelü £££

D István Szepsy Aszú 6 Puttonyos ££££

R Jozséf Bock Cabernets Sauvignon-Franc ££

D Oremus 6 Puttonyos ££££

D Royal Tokaji Mezes Maly 6 Puttonyos ££££

R St Andrea Marengo Egri Bikavér Superior £££

R Vesztergombi Szekszárdi Bikavér ££

S Vinarium Château Vincent Extra Brut Vintage £ (012 265 133)

Vineyards on the slopes of an extinct volcano in the Badacsony region on the north shore of Lake Balaton

Harvest time in Badacsony

TERROIR AT A GLANCE

Latitude: 45.5–48.5°N.

Altitude: 80–500m.

Topography: Mainly flat and arid, although the hills of Tokaj rise to 300m. Hungary contains Europe's largest lake, Balaton. Volcanic hills constitute the Northern Massif. The suffix '-alja' indicates a hilly region.

Soil: Sand on Great Plain; basalt around Lake Balaton; clay, loess, and volcanic subsoils in Tokaj and the Northern Massif.

Climate: Continental with predictably cold winters and hot summers. Prolonged, sunny autumns favour botrytis.

Temperature: July average is 21.5°C.

Rainfall: Ranges from 410–1,210mm per annum.

Viticultural hazards: Spring frost; September rain; inadequate fog, cool autumns, and excess rain can prevent the formation of botrytis required for Tokaji.

HUNGARY: AREAS & TOP PRODUCERS

THE NORTHEAST *p394*
Disznókő *p396*
István Szepsy *p396*
Oremus *p396*
Royal Tokaji *p396*
St Andrea *p396*

THE WEST *p394*
Huba Szeremley *p397*

THE SOUTH *p395*
József Bock *p397*
Vesztergombi *p397*

BIKAVÉR: THE BLOOD OF BULLS

The name Bikavér (Bull's Blood) allegedly dates back to the siege of the fortress of Eger (1552), when the attacking Turks took fright at the dark red wine stains on the Magyar soldiers' uniforms, believing that they drank bull's blood to give them strength.

Bull's Blood is a blended red wine, made from at least three grape varieties. Traditionally it included a high proportion of Kadarka, but this is a tricky grape to grow and is often replaced by Kékfrankos, plus Kékoportó and Cabernet Sauvignon or Zweigelt. Bikavér's reputation plummeted after 1945, and in the 1960s and 70s it was one of the most widely distributed cheap red wines in Western Europe. Today, there is a move to establish a new Bikavér tradition with origin, yield, and minimum time in oak all specified by law. Certain growers are keen to promote it as a wine of real quality, most notably St Andrea in Eger and Vesztergombi in Szekszárd.

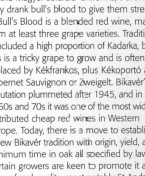

Egri Bikavér, Bull's Blood

Bottle cellar of Disznókő winery, Northeast Hungary

Vineyards on the hill behind the town of Tokaj

WINEGROWING AREAS OF HUNGARY

The Northeast: Eger

THE MOST FAMOUS REGION for the production of Bikavér is **Eger**, where the loess, tuffeau, and clay soils at the foot of the Matra Hills help to make these robust reds. As in Szekszárd, before World War II the wine's key ingredient was Kadarka: now the mainstay is Kékfrankos (Blaufränkisch) with Kékoportó (Portugieser) and Zweigelt. However, the loss of the Kadarka has meant a less complex wine, lacking in a vital element of spice. Thummerer and St Andrea are producers to look out for.

Matráalja, just to the south, is Hungary's second largest wine region, and yet only a couple of producers have a good reputation. The Gyöngyös Estate's Chardonnay and Sauvignon Blanc caused a stir when first produced in an international style by flying winemakers. Today the Chardonnay is still reliable, and moderately priced. Nagyrede is the other well-known name, with a good range of attractive, if simple, varietal wines. However, Tokaj-Hegyalja is the area's most important wine region.

🎞 clay, loess, tuffeau 🖼 Cabernet Sauvignon, Merlot, Kékfrankos, Kékoportó, Zweigelt 🖼 Furmint, Chardonnay, Hárslevelű, Muscat, Olasz Rizling, Szürkebarát (Pinot Gris), Pinot Blanc, Zenit 🍷 red, white, dessert

**Sign of a *Borház*
(wine house), Villány**

Tokaj-Hegyalja

THIS IS HUNGARY'S MOST FAMOUS vineyard region, known for Tokaji – a luscious, sweet, white wine. The area's rolling volcanic hills centre on the little town of Tokaj, where the rivers Bodrog and Tisza meet. It is this confluence that can create the autumnal mists which encourage the growth of botrytis. This fungus, which causes noble rot (see p66), needs just the right combination of cool, humid mornings and warm afternoons to work its magic, and is crucial for making Tokaji. However, dry wines are a commercial necessity, as the mists cannot be guaranteed every year, and so neither can the wine. For most of the 15,000-odd growers, 70 to 100 per cent of their crop will not make Aszú (the most famous Tokaji style) quality in any year. Making good dry wine needs a change in attitude from managing vines for rot development, to understanding how to grow healthy fruit for dry wines. The former state winery Kereskedoház (Crown Estates) has brought in international consultants to work on the dry whites with promising results.

The West: Balaton, Észak-Dunántúl, and Sopron

THE CLIMATE OF THIS PART OF HUNGARY is moderated by both Lake Balaton and the Duna (Danube) River. Most appellations here specialize in white wines: **Ászár-Neszmély** is an increasingly important area thanks to the success of the revamped Hilltop winery (which makes the Riverview range), whose wines are clean and fresh. Szürkebarát (Pinot Gris), Gewürztraminer (Tramini), Chardonnay, and

Sauvignon Blanc are planted, along with local specialities like Csersegi Főszeres, an aromatic spicy white with soft acidity. Volcanic **Somló** almost rivals Tokaj for historical clout. They are supposed to 'guarantee' a male heir when drunk at weddings. Today this is Hungary's smallest wine region with full-bodied, high-extract dry whites from grapes like Furmint, Hárslevelű, and Juhfark — the latter produces firm mineral whites with green apple notes and marked acidity. Due east, the district of **Etyek Buda** is traditionally the source for base wines for the production of sparkling wine and is also increasingly recognized for its lean, elegant, and aromatic whites, especially Szűrkebarát, Chardonnay, and Sauvignon Blanc. On the sunnier, northern side of Lake Balaton, **Badacsony** is home to the unique and deliciously floral Kéknyelő, and also produces rich and spicy Szűrkebarát as well as Olasz Rizling. To the south of the lake is **Balatonboglár**, where international varieties such as Szűrkebarát, Chardonnay, and Muscat are grown with great commercial success. The Balatonboglár winery, with its Chapel Hill range, was one of the pioneers in importing Australian winemaking know-how represented by Kym Milne in the early 1990s.

Lying close to the Austrian border on the eastern side of Lake Fertű (Neusiedler See to the Austrians), **Sopron** is predominantly a red wine-producing area: the climate here is more temperate than the rest of Hungary, with cooler summers and wetter winters. Kékfrankos dominates, and the wines tend to be tannic, with firm acidity. Cabernet Sauvignon and Merlot are also grown, along with the white Zőldvetelini (Grüner Veltliner).

🏔 *basalt, red sandstone, chalk, loess, clay, brown forest soil, crystalline shale, limestone, gravel* 🍇 *Kékfrankos, Merlot, Cabernet Sauvignon, Zweigelt, Kadarka* 🍇 *Olasz Rizling, Chardonnay, Szűrkebarát, Sauvignon Blanc, Ezerjó, Furmint, Juhfark, Müller-Thurgau* 🍷 *red, white, sparkling*

The South: Duna and Pannon

REAL POTENTIAL FOR quality emerges in **Szekszárd** on the west of the Great Plain, now Hungary's largest red grape-growing region. Traditionally, this area produced Bikavér (Bull's Blood), but it was banned during the communist era and Szekszárd has only recently re-established its right to make this famous blend. The mineral-rich loess and *terra rossa* soils here are believed to be responsible for the wines' paprika-like spicy quality. There has been some replanting of Kadarka, a red grape formerly believed indispensable for making Bikavér, though today a blend including Kékfrankos and Zweigelt is more popular. The region likes to claim it makes Hungary's best Merlots, and Cabernet Franc is also showing a lot of potential. Nearby, the new region of **Tolna** is exhibiting enough promise for Italian producer Antinori *(see p265)* to invest in the Bátaapáti estate, making Chardonnay, Gewürztraminer, and a Bordeaux-style red named Talentum.

To the south, **Siklos** concentrates on whites, notably from Leányka, while better-known **Vlány** is the viticultural success story of post-communist Hungary, with a concentration of hardworking growers achieving excellent red wines at impressive prices. Its most famous vineyards are on the slopes of a rocky mound called Számsomlyó, the site of the hottest vineyard in Hungary, with summer temperatures comparable with those of France's Rhône Valley. The principal grapes used here are Kékfrankos (which makes purplish, juicy, cherry-fruited reds inclined to high acidity) and Kékoportó (lively, easy drinking reds with berry notes and velvety tannins), but there are a lot of foreign cultivars making Bordeaux-style wines of good weight, and even some promising Pinot Noirs.

🏔 *loess, terra rossa* 🍇 *Merlot, Cabernet Sauvignon, Cabernet Franc, Kékfrankos, Kékoportó, Kadarka* 🍇 *Chardonnay, Olasz Rizling, Pinot Blanc, Leányka, Gewürztraminer* 🍷 *red, white*

Vineyards on the slopes of Mount Badacsony

TOP PRODUCERS OF HUNGARY

Disznókő
The Northeast/Tokaj

Disznókő Szőlőbirtok Pincészet, Tokaj
📞 047 361 371 ⏰ by appt

OWNED BY French insurance company AXA, Disznókő is a trend-setting example in Tokaj, but it has been criticized for making wines too similar to Sauternes *(see p66)*. However, there is no denying the quality of the individual *crus*. A fully mature 5 or 6 *puttonyos (see right)* wine will give similar flavours to Western European dessert wines: apricots, peaches, and dried herbs. The vineyard is a single plot around the winery on a site of great first growth *(see right)* quality. Sweet wines are bottled as *Szamorodni* or 4, 5, or 6 *Puttonyos*. There is also a dry *Szamorodni*, oxidized the traditional way and barrel aged under a thin sheen of yeast.
🍷 white, dessert 📅 *2003, 2000, 1999, 1997, 1995* ★ *5 Puttonyos, 6 Puttonyos, Dry Furmint*

István Szepsy
The Northeast/Tokaj

Táncsics u 37, Mád
📞 047 348 349 ⏰ by appt

ISTVÁN SZEPSY'S FAMILY has been making wine in Tokaj since the 1300s. He started

Glass of Tokaji in the barrel cellar of István Szepsy

with the co-operative in the 1970s, and even before the old regime died, Szepsy was quietly piecing together his estate. He now has over 20ha, with a high proportion in the classified growths. Szepsy's wines are a marriage of tradition and modernity: he believes in long cask ageing for the best, but he does not look for oxidation, and he also makes a luscious Szepsy Cuvée.
🍷 dessert 📅 *2003, 2002, 2000, 1999, 1996, 1993* ★ *Aszú 6 Puttonyos, Szepsy Cuvée*

Oremus
The Northeast/Tokaj

Tokaj-Oremus Szőlőbirtok Es Pincészet Kft, Bajcsy Zs út 45, Tolcsva
📞 047 384 504 ⏰ by appt

OREMUS IS OWNED by Pablo Álvarez, the proprietor of Vega Sicilia *(see p299)*, which produces one of Spain's most prestigious (and expensive) wines. On his 45ha, he claims to own the plot where the first Aszú wine was made, and has just installed a state-of-the-art winery. Oremus makes good, dry Furmint and elegant Noble Late Harvest Furmint, as well as a dry *Szamorodni* with its nutty *fino* tang, and a full range of Aszú wines. They also have stocks of Tokaji from the communist era, including a wonderful 1972 6 *puttonyos*, reminiscent of toffee and oranges, and a sublime 1975 Esszencia.
🍷 white, dessert 📅 *2003, 2000, 1999, 1995, 1993, 1989, 1975* ★ *5 Puttonyos, 6 Puttonyos, Aszú Esszencia*

Royal Tokaji
The Northeast/Tokaj

Royal Tokaji Borászati Kft, Rákóczi út 35, Mád 📞 047 348 011 ⏰ by appt

Royal Tokaji

SOME 100 shareholders, under the chairmanship of British wine writer Hugh Johnson, own this company, which is at the top of the market in born-again Tokaji. Royal Tokaji makes only Aszú wines from its holdings in the first growth vineyards of Betsek, Birsalmas, Nyulászo, and Szent Tamás, while its pride and joy is a stake in the great first growth of Mézes Mály. Royal Tokaji is rare in labelling the best wines with the names of the growth: lesser wines are simply bottled with blue labels.
🍷 dessert 📅 *2003, 2000, 1999, 1995, 1993, 1991, 1990* ★ *Mézes Mály, Szent Tamás, Betsek, Birsalmas, Nyulászo*

St Andrea
The Northeast

3394 Egerszalok, Jokai u 28, Eger
📞 036 47 40 18 🌐

GYORGY LORINCZ started his estate in partnership with Tibor Gál, Hungary's most famous winemaker, who died in a car accident in 2006. Like Gál, Lorincz is determined to revive the fortunes of Bikavér. He has around 20ha now and is keen to make the best from his vines, particularly his Pinot Noir. He has also planted Csokaszolo and Kadarka for Bikavér. Once this is added to the Merengo blend, the wine will get better and better.
🍷 white, red 📅 *2006, 2005, 2003, 2002* ★ *Egri: Napbor, Orokke (white blends), Pinot Noir, Kékfrankos, Bikavér, Bikavér Superior*

Huba Szeremley
The West

8262 Badacsonylábdihegy, Romai u 93 **☎** *036 87 432 352* ◉

TWENTY YEARS AFTER the collapse of communism, Szeremley is the grand old man of Hungarian wine, with three large estates, including 115ha on the volcanic soils of Badacsony. He inspires a new generation with his mission to revive the lost glories of Hungarian wine and food.

◪ *white, red* ▨ *2007, 2006, 2005, 2003* ★ *Badacsony Bakalor, Budai Zöld, Kéknyelű; many Sopron reds*

József Bock
The South

Bock Pince, Batthyány u 15, Villány **☎** *072 492 919* ○ *by appt*

ONE OF VILLÁNY'S leading lights, József Bock makes very good, peach-like Hárslevelű from his land in Siklós. However, his best wines are the local reds, especially Kékoportó and the Cabernets Sauvignon-Franc blend. In their smoothness, these are model wines for the new Eastern Europe.

◪ *red, white* ▨ *2006, 2005, 2003* ★ *Kékoportó, Bock Grand Selection*

Vesztergombi
The South

V & V Borázati Bt (Vesztergombi Pince), Muncácsy u 41, Szekszárd **☎** *074 316 059* ○ *by appt*

FERENC VESZTERGOMBI and his son Csaba have been leading the revival of Kadarka in Szekszárd with a view to making proper Bikavér. They blend it with Kékfrankos, Merlot, and Cabernet Sauvignon to make a charming, cinnamon-scented wine. The Merlot and Cabernet Sauvignon varietals are also worthwhile.

◪ *red* ▨ *2006, 2005, 2003, 2000* ★ *Szekszárdi: Bikavér, Merlot, Cabernet Sauvignon*

TOKAJI: A NATIONAL TREASURE

First recorded in the mid-1600s, Tokaji, declared the "wine of kings and king of wines" by Louis XIV, is today so important for Hungary that it even figures in the national anthem.

Making Tokaji

The jewels in Tokaji's crown are the sweet Aszú wines, made from botrytis-affected grapes that have shrivelled on the vine – mostly Furmint for structure and acidity, with some sweet Hárslevelű and Muscat Blanc a Petits Grains (Muskotály). The grapes are picked individually and traditionally put into a *puttony* (wooden tub), though today stainless steel vats are also used, and stored until the base wine or must is ready for the next stage. While the Aszú berries are being stored, a small quantity of intensely sweet liquid seeps out – the 'essence' or *Esszencia*. Very rarely it will be fermented apart to make the legendary wine of that name; more usually it will be added back to the Aszú wine to adjust sweetness. The Aszú grapes are then pressed into a paste before being added to a *gönc* (a 136-l barrel) of white wine or fermenting must. The measure of sweetness on the label is shown as 3, 4, 5, or 6 *puttonyos*. The mixture is left to macerate for 1–5 days, and then the liquid is drawn off to ferment in barrels in underground cellars. The walls are covered in a thick black growth of the fungus *Racodium cellare*, which helps maintain the humidity vital in allowing Tokaji to mature.

Botrytized Furmint grapes

Other Styles of Tokaji Wines

Szamorodni is made from whole bunches rather than individual berries, and may contain variable proportions of Aszú grapes depending on the year. It comes in both a dry *száraz* style, made a little like *fino* sherry *(see p328)*, and a sweet *(édes)* style, made from partially botrytis-affected bunches and fermented in wood.

A modern style of sweet late-harvest wine is now made by many producers, where late-picked, botrytis-affected bunches are fermented in stainless steel and bottled early – typically deliciously fresh and floral, such as the stunning Szepsy Cuvée.

Fordítás is a sweet but more tannic wine made by soaking the leftover Aszú paste with fresh must and fermenting again.

Máslás is a dry wine made by adding must to Aszú lees and fermenting.

The Growth System

Tokaj was the first place in the world to draw up a system of vineyard classification in 1730, predating those of Bordeaux and Burgundy. The Tokaji Renaissance movement is keen to revive this system, which identified two great first growths: Mézes Mály and Szarvas. Disznókő, Hetszolo, Nyulászo, Nagyszolo, Szent Tamás, Kiraly, Betsek, Messzelato, and Pajzos are some of the better known first growths.

***Racodium cellare* mould-covered bottles of Tokaji wine**

WINE MAP OF ROMANIA

ROMANIA IS DOMINATED by the Carpathian Mountains, which sweep across the country from the Ukrainian border towards Serbia, enclosing the Transylvanian Plateau in the centre of the range. The country has seven main wine regions: the northeastern province of Moldova includes the famous region of Cotnari, whose sweet wines once rivalled Hungary's Tokaji in reputation, while in the southeast, the district of Murfatlar in Dobrogea, on the

Black Sea coastal plain, is best known for white wines. On the south-facing slopes of the Carpathians, Oltenia-Muntenia includes Dealul Mare – Romania's most famous red wine-producing district.

Picking grapes near Murfatlar, Dobrogea

PERFECT CASE: ROMANIA

🅡 Carl Reh La Cetate Shiraz £££

🅦 Davino Domaine Ceptura Blanc ££

🅡 Davino Flamboyant £££

🅦 Halewood Hyperion Fetească Neagră ££ (www.halewood.com.ro)

🅓 Halewood Tămaioasă Românească ££

🅦 Murfatlar Tre Hectari Chardonnay ££ (www.murfatlar.com)

🅦 Prince Stirbey Cramposie Selectionata £

🅡 Prince Stirbey Negru de Dragasani ££

🅦 Recaş La Putere Fetească Regală Barrique ££

🅦 SERVE Cuvée Amaury ££

🅡 SERVE Cuvée Charlotte £££

🅡 Vinarte Prince Matei Merlot £££

ROMANIA: AREAS & TOP PRODUCERS

MOLDOVA p400

BANAT & TRANSYLVANIA p400
Recaş Winery p401

OLTENIA-MUNTENIA p400
Carl Reh Winery p401
Davino p401
Prince Stirbey p401
SERVE p401
Vinarte p401

DOBROGEA p400

ROMANIA'S SWEET HEART

Produced for 500 years, the once famous Cotnari wine may be made from any of the four white grape varieties grown in the region, or produced as a blend. Grasă gives body and sweetness with notes of honey and sultana; Tămaioasă Românească (frankincense grape) gives perfume and spice; Fetească Albă gives fresh floral notes; and Frâncuşă has crisp appley acidity. Grasă can ripen to incredible levels of sweetness, and every three to four years botrytis develops, making the intensely sweet Cotnari. In other years late-harvest, sweet wines (also called Cotnari) are still made. Both styles are aged in barrel for one year and, unlike the more traditional styles of Tokaji, are protected from oxygen and retain a greenish tinge.

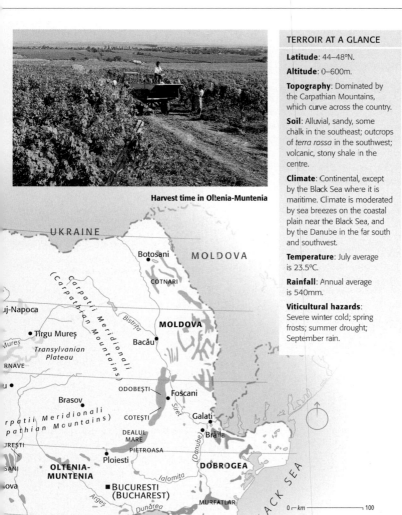

Harvest time in Oltenia-Muntenia

TERROIR AT A GLANCE

Latitude: 44–48°N.

Altitude: 0–600m.

Topography: Dominated by the Carpathian Mountains, which curve across the country.

Soil: Alluvial, sandy, some chalk in the southeast; outcrops of *terra rossa* in the southwest; volcanic, stony shale in the centre.

Climate: Continental, except by the Black Sea where it is maritime. Climate is moderated by sea breezes on the coastal plain near the Black Sea, and by the Danube in the far south and southwest.

Temperature: July average is 23.5°C.

Rainfall: Annual average is 540mm.

Viticultural hazards: Severe winter cold; spring frosts; summer drought; September rain.

FETEASCĂ NEAGRĂ : THE NEW GREAT RED HOPE

A few years ago, Pinot Noir seemed to have the potential to create Romania's best reds, but it has rather fallen off the radar, let down by poor plant material. Today the best examples are from new French clones planted in cooler zones like Transylvania and Banat.
The grape set to give Romania a new sense of pride is the local Fetească Neagră. With its wild berry fruit and structured tannins, it can make some serious reds. Most

Fetească Neagră grapes

leading wineries (Davino, Recaş, SERVE, Murfatlar, Prince Stirbey, and Halewood's Hyperion) produce a varietal Fetească Neagră, and they are learning to bring its sometimes fierce tannins under control. Some of Romania's best reds are blends of international grapes such as Cabernet and Merlot with Fetească Neagră to give a true Romanian identity. Look out for SERVE's Cuvée Charlotte and Davino's Flamboyant and Domaine Ceptura Red.

WINEGROWING AREAS OF ROMANIA

Moldova

MOLDOVA, EAST OF THE CARPATHIANS, is Romania's biggest wine region with a third of the country's vineyard area (85,000ha). Two thirds is devoted to white wine production, with vineyards typically planted on south-facing slopes protected from harsh north winds, especially in its most famous district, **Cotnari** *(see p398)*. **Odobeşti** is Romania's oldest viticultural area, but it tends only to produce high-volume whites for local consumption. The southernmost district, **Coteşti**, is better known for its deep-coloured reds, but its white wines also show promise.

Vineyard at Dealul Vei in the foothills of the Carpathian Mountains, Dealul Mare

🗻 *marl and clay on limestone, black forest* 🍇 *Cabernet Sauvignon, Băbească Neagră, Merlot, Fetească Neagră* 🍾 *Fetească Regală, Muscat Ottonel, Aligoté, Tămaioasă Românească, Grasă* 🍷 *red, white, dessert*

Banat & Transylvania

BANAT, ON THE SERBIAN BORDER, is Romania's smallest wine region, with just one winery in operation. To the east, the high (with altitudes up to 300m) central Transylvanian plateau is the country's coolest region, and one where vines are often planted on steep slopes. The area was once part of the Austro-Hungarian Empire, and the influence shows in the wines, which tend to be Germanic in style with crisp acidity. **Tarnave** is the most important sub-district.

🗻 *sandy, stony, black earth, alluvial, acid brown* 🍇 *Pinot Noir, Cadarcă, Merlot, Burgund Mare* 🍾 *Fetească Albă, Traminer Rose, Olasz Riszling, Sauvignon Blanc, Muscat Ottonel, Fetească Regală* 🍷 *red, white*

Recaş Winery, La Putere Fetească Neagră

Oltenia-Muntenia

AT JUST OVER 110,000HA, these two areas combined are similar in size to Bordeaux. On the eastern slopes of the Carpathians, Muntenia includes **Dealul Mare,** the best known red wine area in the country, with vineyards planted with Cabernet Sauvignon, Merlot, some Pinot Noir, and Fetească Neagră at 130–600m. **Pietroasa** is a small subdistrict, producing lusciously sweet, perfumed, golden white wines. Oltenia continues into the southern mountains covering the extensive vineyards (for red

and white wine production) of **Drăgăşăni**, said to date back to Roman times. **Sâmburesti** is a smaller wine region specializing in the production of full-bodied, structured reds. **Plaiurile Drancei**, to the southwest, includes the subregions of **Vanju Mare-Orevita** and **Oprisor**, both very promising areas for high quality reds, including Romania's first plantings of Shiraz.

🗻 *forest brown, clay, iron hard pan, podsols, stony, chalky, terra rossa* 🍇 *Cabernet Sauvignon, Pinot Noir, Merlot, Burgund Mare, Fetească Neagră* 🍾 *Fetească Albă, Olasz Rizling, Pinot Gris, Muscat Ottonel, Sauvignon Blanc, Tămaioasă Românească* 🍷 *red, white, rosé*

Dobrogea

THIS REGION ON the Black Sea coast has up to 300 days of sunshine a year. Its most important district is **Murfatlar,** best known for its white wines (some 75 per cent of production). Many local producers cannot afford modern vinification equipment, but where this exists, some expressive, fruity, dry Pinot Gris and Chardonnays (a variety introduced as early as 1907) are produced. Due to the low summer rainfall, botrytis is rare, but Murfatlar is also noted for its late-harvest sweet wines.

🗻 *black earth on limestone subsoil* 🍇 *Cabernet Sauvignon, Pinot Noir, Merlot* 🍾 *Pinot Gris, Chardonnay, Muscat Ottonel, Olasz Rizling, Sauvignon Blanc* 🍷 *red, white, dessert*

TOP PRODUCERS OF ROMANIA

Recaş Winery
Banat & Transylvania

Str Lugojului 322, Recas 📞 *0256 330 296* 🆆 *www.recaswine.ro* 🅾 *by appt*

PHILIP COX AND his Romanian wife Elvira bought 660ha of vineyards in 1999, adding this modern winery in 2002. The couple have replanted the vineyards with new, high-quality clones of Pinot Noir and released their first Fetească Neagră and Shiraz, made under the supervision of Australian consultant Hartley Smithers of Yellow Tail.
🅆 *red, white* 🅿 *red: 2007, 2006, 2005; white: most recent* ★ *Shiraz Limited Release, Fetească Regală Barrique, Sole Chardonnay*

Carl Reh Winery
Oltenia-Muntenia

Oprisor, Meheolinti 📞 *0252 391 310* 🆆 *www.reh-kendermann.de* 🅾 *by appt*

IN 2001 GERMAN COMPANY Reh Kendermann bought 292ha of abandoned vineyard near Oprisor, attracted by the iron-rich *terra rossa* soil. The organically managed estate is being planted with high-quality clones, including Pinot Noir and Shiraz. The La Cetate estate Merlot hints at the potential for rich, velvety reds.
🅆 *red, white, rosé* 🅿 *red: 2007, 2006, 2004; white: most recent* ★ *La Cetate Shiraz, La Cetate Pinot Noir, Val Duna Pinot Grigio*

Davino
Oltenia-Muntenia

Str Arh Stefan Burcus nr 6, Parter, Sector 1, Bucharest 📞 *031 805 3745* 🆆 *www.davino.ro* 🅾

DAVINO WAS FOUNDED in 1992 by Dan Balaban. Grapes are hand-picked from just 68ha in the Ceptura zone of Dealul Mare. The winery believes in the potential of local grapes such as Fetească Albă and Fetească Neagră. Flamboyant is the top red blend (Fetească Neagră, Merlot, Cabernet), while Purpura Valahica is a great example of pure Fetească Neagră.
🅆 *red, white* 🅿 *red: 2007, 2006, 2003; white: 2007, 2006* ★ *Flamboyant, Domaine Ceptura, Purpura Valahica*

Prince Stirbey
Oltenia-Muntenia

36 Alexandru Donici St, Ap 8, Bucharest 📞 *031 103 5610* 🆆 *www.stirbey.com* 🅾 *by appt*

THIS FAMILY have owned vineyards in the Drăgasăni region since the 1700s; Prince Stirbey's descendant Baroness Kripp-Costinescu was able to recover her family holdings in 2001. Today, 20ha are planted to vines. The winery specializes in reviving historic varieties, such as whites Cramposie Selectionata, Fetească Regală, and Tămaioasă Românească, and red grapes Novac and Negru de Drăgasăni.
🅆 *red, white* 🅿 *red: 2007, 2006, 2005; white: most recent* ★ *Cramposie Selectionata, Tămaioasă Românească, Negru de Dragasani*

The Carpathian Winery's logo

SERVE
Oltenia-Muntenia

Comuna Ceptura 125C, Judet Prahova 📞 *021 224 2131* 🆆 *www.serve.ro* 🅾

FOUNDED IN 1994 by French Corsican Count Guy de Poix, SERVE set new standards in quality with a philosophy of low yields, careful selection of the best vineyards, and gentle handling in the ultra-modern winery. The top red wine Cuvée Charlotte remains the model others aim for. The winery also makes a fine white blend (Cuvée Amaury) and good varietal wines under the Terra Romana label.
🅆 *red, white, rosé* 🅿 *red: 2006, 2004, 2003; white & rosé: most recent* ★ *Cuvée Charlotte, Cuvée Amaury, Terra Romana Sauvignon*

Vinarte
Oltenia-Muntenia

Terase Danubiane, Comuna Rogova, Judetul Mehedinti 📞 *052 352 206* 🆆 *www.vinarte.com* 🅾

AN ITALIAN-BACKED investment now producing 2.6 million bottles including some of Romania's most expensive (and impressive) red wines. These include the rich, velvety, cedar-scented Prince Matei Merlot and intense, brambly Swallowtail Fetească Neagră.
🅆 *red, white* 🅿 *2000, 1999* ★ *Merlot Prince Matei, Swallowtail Fetească Neagră, Cabernet Sauvignon Soare*

Sampling wine from the barrel at a winery

WINE MAP OF BULGARIA

BULGARIA is split into two regions covering wine with regional geographic indication: the Danube Plain, to the north of the Balkans, and the Thracian Valley, to the south. In addition, there are 47 specified regions for quality wine production. The southwest is warmer and drier than the rest of the country, while the Black Sea moderates the climate in the eastern region where whites are more common.

Damianitza The northwest also has its own distinctive *terroir* with rolling hills and the influence of the Danube giving long autumns and cool nights, for good sparkling wines and elegant reds.

KEY

Bulgaria

BULGARIA: AREAS & TOP PRODUCERS

DANUBE PLAIN *p404*

Chateau de Val *p405*
Valley Vintners *p405*

THRACIAN LOWLANDS *p404*

Bessa Valley *p405*
Damianitza *p405*
Katarzyna Estate *p405*
Santa Sarah *p405*
Telish (Castra Rubra) *p405*
Terra Tangra *p405*

MAKING WAVES AMONG THE VINES

Bulgaria's potential has attracted much foreign interest. Bessa Valley, for example, is owned by Stephan Von Niepperg of Château Canon-la-Gaffelière and his German partner; the general manager is French winemaker Marc Dworkin, who also consults for Katarzyna Estate, Belvedere's investment near the Greek border. Michel Rolland is acting as consultant to Telish, which has planted a new vineyard and built

Merlot grapes

its brand-new Castra Rubra winery in the south. Italian textile magnate Edoardo Miroglio has built a state-of-the-art winery near Sliven and is making Bulgaria's best bottle-fermented sparkling wine. On a smaller scale, boutique producers like Maxxima (the first to make a super-premium wine in Bulgaria), Santa Sarah, Chateau de Val, and Valley Vintners show what passionately committed people can achieve in Bulgaria.

Harvest time, Northern Region

TERROIR AT A GLANCE

Latitude: 41–44°N.

Altitude: 100–1,000m.

Topography The Stara Planina (Balkan Mountains) range stretches across the centre of the country and protects the south of Bulgaria from cold winds blowing off the Russian Steppes. The highest altitudes are in the Rhodope Mountains in the southwest.

Soil: Loess over limestone on the Dunav Plain, alluvial soils on the Thracian Plain; forest soils near the mountains.

Climate: Continental climate in the north, Mediterranean in the south and maritime on the Black Sea coast.

Temperature: July average is 23°C.

Rainfall: Annual average is 630mm.

Viticultural hazards: Hail; fungal diseases; September rain.

A tasting room in a Bulgarian winery

PERFECT CASE: BULGARIA

- **Ⓡ** Bessa Valley BV by Enira £££
- **Ⓡ** Chateau de Val Grand Claret £££
- **Ⓦ** Chateau de Val Sauvignon ££
- **Ⓡ** Damianitza No Man's Land Melnik Rosé ££
- **Ⓡ** Domaine Boyar Solitaire Merlot £££ (www.domaine boyar.com)
- **Ⓢ** Edoardo Miroglio Brut Metodo Classico ££ (www.emiroglio-wine.com)
- **Ⓡ** Katarzyna Estate Question Mark by ££
- **Ⓡ** Maxxima Private Reserve ££ (032 649 493)
- **Ⓡ** Santa Sarah Privat Mavrud & Cabernet Sauvignon £££
- **Ⓡ** Telish Castra Rubra ££
- **Ⓡ** Terra Tangra Grand Reserva £££
- **Ⓡ** Valley Vintners Dux £££

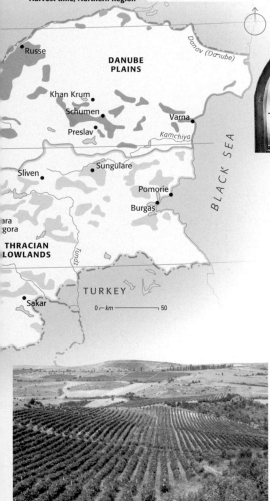

View of vineyards near Melnik, Southwestern Region

Map labels:
- Russe
- DANUBE PLAINS
- Danav (Danube)
- Khan Krum
- Schumen
- Preslav
- Varna
- Kamchiya
- BLACK SEA
- Sliven
- Sungulare
- Pomorie
- Burgas
- ...ara ...gora
- THRACIAN LOWLANDS
- Tundzha
- TURKEY
- Sakar
- 0 — km — 50

Grape pickers at Suhindol, Danube Plain

WINEGROWING AREAS OF BULGARIA

Danube Plain

THE NORTHERN PART OF BULGARIA is cooler than the south, its temperatures moderated by the River Danube to the north and the Black Sea to the east. The Danube Plain includes two distinct zones that, in the past, were identified as separate viticultural regions: the Eastern Region and the Northern Region. The former is the only one where white varieties dominate, benefiting from the freshness that the maritime influence brings. Local Misket and Dimiat wines can be grapey and appealing, and there are some bright, fresh, well-handled Chardonnays and Traminers from areas like Preslav, Khan Krum, Russe, and Schumen.

In what used to be the Northern Region, reds predominate, with Gamza, Cabernet Sauvignon, Merlot, and Pamid all important. The northwest, especially around Vidin, is developing a reputation for elegant reds and crisp, fresh whites, which benefit from hilly sites, long sunshine hours, and cool nights.

loess over limestone, sandy to loamy soils
Cabernet Sauvignon, Merlot, Gamza, Pamid
Dimiat, Misket, Chardonnay, Muscat *red, white*

Thracian Valley

THE SOUTHERN PART OF BULGARIA is warmer, with plenty of sunshine during the growing season. Red varieties predominate here, though there are successful whites, too. The southwestern area, or Struma Valley, is the hottest part of the country, a mountainous zone near the Greek border with its own microclimate. Here the vineyards lie around the town of Melnik and are dominated by the local broad-leaved Melnik vine, which produces full-bodied, tannic, and potentially long-lived reds. There's also an early-ripening Melnik that is juicier and more approachable when young (try Damianitza's Uniqato or Logodaj) and a unique Bulgarian crossing of Nebbiolo and Syrah called Rubin. The south of Bulgaria includes such famous areas as the mountainous Sakar district, with its long reputation for rich, fruity Merlots, and nearby Lyubimetz and Haskovo. There has been considerable investment in new vineyards in this part of Bulgaria, with extensive plantings of Cabernet and Merlot, but also Shiraz/Syrah, Mavrud, Rubin, and even Viognier. In the foothills of the Balkans, the district of Sliven is notable and has seen several high-profile investments, especially at Elenovo, with Pinot Noir looking promising and fine Merlots. The area to the south of Plovdiv has a very long growing season, which is essential for Bulgaria's best native grape, the deep-coloured Mavrud. Traditionally, it is made in a very tannic style for long ageing, but with modern vinification it can produce some impressively concentrated, black-cherry-ish wines. It is also appearing in top blends, where it can add a real sense of Bulgarian identity.

sand, loam, limestone bedrock in southwest and south *Cabernet Sauvignon, Merlot, Mavrud, Melnik, Syrah, Pinot Noir* *Misket, Chardonnay, Traminer* *red, white*

TOP PRODUCERS OF BULGARIA

Chateau de Val
Danube Plain

Gradetz, Vidin **☎** *094 607 960*
W *www.chateaudeval.com*
☐ *by appt*

AT THIS SMALL but quality-focused winery, Val Markov aims to revive local wine traditions. One of the first to develop true *terroir* wines in Bulgaria, he works as naturally as possible in the winery, and with great care in the vineyard. His top red Claret is a blend of up to 12 grapes, including Saperavi, Pamid, Merlot, and Cabernet.
▨ *red, white* **▧** *red: 2006, 2004, 2003; white: 2007, 2006, 2005* ★ *Grand Claret, Cuvée, Sauvignon Blanc*

Valley Vintners
Danube Plain

21 Lyule Burgas St, Plovdiv
☎ *0887 806 222* **◉**

THIS WINERY IS OWNED by Ognyan Tzvetanov, who launched Sensum, the country's first *terroir* wine, and Dux, its most expensive red. Tzvetanov has planted Marsanne, Rousanne, Viognier, Marsellan, and Teroldego, so expect to see more exciting stuff over the next few years.
▨ *red, white* **▧** *red: 2006, 2004, 2003; white: 2007, 2006* ★ *Dux, Sensum, Le Cubiste*

Bessa Valley
Thracian Lowlands

Ognianovo Village, Pazardjik
☎ *0889 499 992*
W *www.bessavalley.com* **☐** *by appt*

STEPHAN VON NIEPPERG and Karl Hauptmann were drawn to the foothills of the Rhodope Mountains by the great *terroir* and potential for fine red wine. They now have 140ha

planted with Merlot, Syrah, Petit Verdot, and Cabernet Sauvignon. The small but impressive range of red wines is sold under the Enira name.
▨ *red* **▧** *2007, 2006, 2005*
★ *BV by Enira, Enira Reserva, Enira,*

Damianitza
Thracian Lowlands

2813 Damianitza, Sandanski District **☎** *074 630 090*
W *www.melnikwine.bg*
☐ *by appt*

PHILIP HARMANDJIEV arrived at Damianitza in 1998. He was meant to help out for three months but stayed on, eventually buying (and overhauling) the winery. He switched from cheap bulk exports to high quality and was among the first to make a premium wine in Bulgaria, Redark. Today the winery has over 200ha under vine and focuses on local grapes such as Early Melnik, Rubin, and Ruen.
▨ *red, rosé* **▧** *2007, 2006, 2005* ★ *No Man's Land Rosé, Uniqato Melnik, Redark*

Katarzyna Estate
Thracian Lowlands

PO Box 5833, 23 September St, Svilengrad **☎** *024 911 732*
W *www.katarzyna.bg*
☐ *by appt*

Damianitza

A MAJOR NEW INVESTMENT by the French-owned Belvedere group, Katarzyna has 365ha planted in the "no man's land" border zone between Bulgaria and Greece. Its single-estate wines reflect the excellent *terroir*. The first vintage in 2006 made a big impression. One to watch.
▨ *red, white* **▧** *2007, 2006*
★ *Question Mark, Reserve, Les Fleurs Chardonnay*

Santa Sarah
Thracian Lowlands

1 Hadji Dimitar Asenov St, Stara Zagora Goritsa **☎** *042 649 669*
W *www.santa-sarah.com* **◉**

IVO GENOWSKI'S quality handcrafted wines have made Santa Sarah one of Bulgaria's top producers. He is currently building a biodynamic winery on the Black Sea coast. The top wine is Privat (Cabernet Sauvignon-Mavrud); he also makes a "snow wine" from frozen red grapes.
▨ *red, white, dessert* **▧** *red: 2007, 2006, 2004; white: 2007, 2006*
★ *Privat, Snow Wine, Bin 41 Merlot*

Telish
Thracian Lowlands

Castra Rubra Winery, 6460 Kolarovo
☎ *038 510 170* **☐** *by appt*

THIS IS ONE OF BULGARIA'S leading producers, with wineries and vineyards in the north and south. Michel Rolland has been consulting here since 2006, and they aim to show that Bulgaria can make great wine through hard work in the vineyards and minimal intervention in the winery.
▨ *red, rosé* **▧** *2007, 2006*
★ *Castra Ruba, Via Diagonalis, Pendar Rubin, Merlot*

Terra Tangra
Thracian Lowlands

35 Nikola Petkov, 6450 Harmanli
☎ *0888 309 303* **W** *www.terra tangra.com* **◉**

TERRA TANGRA'S 300HA are cultivated organically, and owner Emil Zaychev plans to go biodynamic in the next few years. The wines show lovely balance and purity of fruit.
▨ *red, white* **▧** *2007, 2006, 2005*
★ *Grand Reserva, Roto, Traminer*

WINE MAP OF THE CZECH REPUBLIC & SLOVAKIA

THE VINEYARDS OF THE Czech Republic are situated in two locations: a small but historic region around the city of Praha (Prague) in Bohemia and a much larger area in Moravia on the border with Austria and Slovakia. The vineyards of Slovakia begin at the Czech Republic border in the far west and run almost continuously eastwards along the southernmost part of the country adjoining Hungary. In the west there is the dynamic Malokarpatská (Little Carpathians) region; in the far east, Tokajská (Slovak Tokaj), is an extension of the world-famous Hungarian Tokay region.

KEY

Czech Republic & Slovakia

Harvesting grapes, Moravia, Czech Republic

PERFECT CASE: CZECH REPUBLIC & SLOVAKIA

S Bohemia Prestige Brut ££

W Château Belá Riesling ££

D Mikros-vin Mikulov Ryzlink Vlassky Icewine £££

W Nové Vinařství Cuvée Lange´Warte ££

D Ostrozovic Tokaj 6 putňový £££

W Pomfy Martin-Mavino Grüner Veltliner Late Harvest ££

D Sonberk Palava £££

D Tokaj & Co Tokajská Esencia ££££

W Vinařství Baloun Grüner Veltliner ££

W Víno Borik Pinot Blanc ££

R Víno Masaryk ENEM Cuvee ££

D Znovin Znojmo Riesling Straw Wine £££

51°

GERMANY

Liberec

ZERNOSECKA / ROUNDNICKÁ

MOSTECKA

Ohre

MĚLNICKÁ

BOHEMIA

PRAŽSKÁ

Elbe

Su d e t e

CASLAVSKÁ

PRAHA (PRAGUE)

Plzen

Vltava

C Z E C H

R E P U B L I C

Jihlava

M

BRNEN

49°

Dyje

ZNOJEMSKÁ

VELKOPAVLOVICKÁ

MIKULOVSKÁ

PO

AUSTRIA

Vineyards in Hradcany, Praha (Prague), Bohemia, Czech Republic

TERROIR AT A GLANCE

Latitude: 48–5⊃°N.

Altitude: 115–2,655m.

Topography: In the west of the Czech Republic, in Bohemia, there are plains and plateaux surrounded by low mountains. In the east around Moravia the terrain is more hilly. In Slovakia there are rugged mountains in the centre and north, with lowlands in the south.

Soil: Diverse.

Climate: Temperate with maritime and continental influences. Cool summers with cold winters.

Temperature: July average in Praha (Prague) is 18°C. In Slovakia the average is nearer 20°C.

Rainfall: Annual average is around 690mm in the Czech Republic and between 530–650mm in Slovakia.

Viticultural hazards: Low temperatures

St-Laurent is widely planted

Vineyards around Kosice, Eastern Slovakia

CZECH REPUBLIC: AREAS & TOP PRODUCERS

BOHEMIA p408
Bohemia Sekt p409

MORAVIA p408
Mikros-Vin p409
Nové Vinařství p409
Sonberk p409
Vinařství Baloun p409
Znovin Znojmo p409

Ostrava

POLAND

Carpathian Mountains

OVSKÁ
IUTENICKÁ

UHERSKOHRADISTSKA
BZENECKÁ
STRÁZNICKÁ

Váh

Torysa

Ondava

49°

SLOVAKIA

Kosice
VÝCHODOSLOVENSKÁ

UKRAINE

KARPATSKÁ

Nitra

TOKAJSKÁ

Nitra
NITRANSKÁ
STREDOSLOVENSKÁ

ATISLAVA

ZNOSLOVENSKÁ

HUNGARY

Dunaj (Danube)

SLOVAKIA: AREAS & TOP PRODUCERS

MALOKARPATSKÁ (LITTLE CARPATHIANS) p410
Borik Vino p411
Mavín p411
Vino Masaryk p411

JUZNOSLOVENSKÁ (SOUTHERN SLOVAKIA) p410
Château Belá p411

NITRANSKÁ (NITRA) p410

STREDOSLOVENSKÁ (CENTRAL SLOVAKIA) p410

VYCHODOSLOVENSKÁ (EASTERN SLOVAKIA) p410

TOKAJSKÁ (SLOVAK TOKAJ) p410
J & J Ostrozovic p411

J & J Ostrozovich, Slovakia

Moravian vineyards produce most of the Czech Republic's wine

WINEGROWING AREAS OF THE CZECH REPUBLIC

THE CZECH REPUBLIC joined the European Union on 1st May 2004, bringing much-needed investment into its vineyards and wineries. In the lead up to EU membership, plantings of vineyards increased significantly.

Bohemia

THIS SMALL WINE REGION of just 550ha is set on the banks of the Labe (Elbe), Vltava, and Berounka rivers around Praha (Prague) and to the north of the city. The key wine areas are **Mostecka**, **Zernosecká**, **Roundnická**, **Melnická**, **Prazká**, and **Caslavská**. Vines were first planted in Bohemia in the 9th century. Today the tourist trade is an important market for local producers. Riesling is considered the best grape, and wines tend to show some Germanic style, being relatively light, crisp, and aromatic. Bohemia Sekt is the country's largest wine producer.

Vineyard, Havraniky, Moravia

🏔 *limestone, sandstone, volcanic* 🍇 *Riesling, Müller-Thurgau, Rizling Vlassky (Welschriesling), Chardonnay, Gewürztraminer, Pinot Gris* 🍇 *Frankovka (Blaufränkisch), Pinot Noir, Portugieser* 🍷 *red, white*

Moravia

NINETY-FIVE PER CENT of Czech wine comes from Moravia in the south. The key areas are **Brneská**, **Kyjovska**, **Mutenická**, **Uherskohradistka**, **Bzenecká**, **Stráznická**, **Podluzí**, **Mikulovská** – the largest wine region in the Czech Republic – **Velkopavlovicka**, and **Znojemská**. While average temperatures here are warmer than in Bohemia, Moravia's continental climate favours white wines which account for around 75 per cent of production. The dry whites tend to be relatively aromatic, with a lean, mineral structure and noticeably high acidity. The Austrian grape, Grüner Veltliner, is the most widely-planted variety, followed by the undistinguished German variety, Müller-Thurgau. However, perhaps the most successful wines come from Riesling, as well as Pinot Gris, Moravian Muscat, and Pinot Blanc. The relatively dry Czech autumns and cold winters also encourage the production of sweeter styles: rich, decadent ice wines and luscious, complex straw wines made from partially-dried berries. Red wine production is dominated by St-Laurent (locally known as Svatovavrinecke) which accounts for more than half of all plantings. The most interesting red wines come from Frankovka (Blaufränkisch) which produces relatively light and fruity wines but with plenty of character. The dark-coloured German grape, Dornfelder, is also successful here, as well as Portugieser.

🏔 *clay, sand, limestone* 🍇 *Grüner Veltliner, Müller-Thurgau, Rizling Vlassky (Welschriesling), Riesling, Pinot Blanc, Moravian Muscat* 🍇 *St-Laurent, Frankovka (Blaufränkisch), Zweigeltrebe, Portugieser* 🍷 *red, white, sparkling, dessert*

TOP PRODUCERS OF THE CZECH REPUBLIC

Bohemia Sekt
Bohemia

Smetanova 220, Stary Plzenec
📞 377 197 111
🌐 www.bohemia sekt.cz ⏲ by appt

THIS IS BOTH the largest wine producer in the Czech Republic, as well as one of its most important companies. Around 30 million bottles are produced annually, the majority of which are sparkling, under a number of different brand names. An extensive investment programme has been undertaken in the past three years to improve quality and volume. Although their most important sparkling wine is called Bohemia Sekt, grapes are sourced from south Moravia.
🍷 sparkling, white, red 🍇 2006, 2005, 2004 ★ Bohemia Prestige, Louis Gerardot

Mikros-Vin
Moravia

Nadrazni 29, Mikulov 📞 515 238 342 🌐 www.mikrosvin.cz ⏲ by appt

MORAVIA'S LARGEST VINEYARD owner, Mikros-Vin has adopted largely organic principles. Numerous grape varieties and wine styles are produced, and the winemaking involves minimal intervention

Wine cellar, southern Moravia

to create a pure, fruit-driven style across the range.
🍷 dessert, white 🍇 2007, 2006, 2005 ★ Ryzlink Vlassky Icewine, Legio X Gemina Ryzlink Vlassky, Chardonnay Barrique

Nové Vinařství
Moravia

Výsluní 613, 69183 Drnholec 📞 519 519 082 🌐 www.novevinarstvi.cz ⏲ by appt

LOCATED SOUTH OF BRNO, Nové Vinařství (meaning 'new winery') has 102ha in sites at Langewarte in Nový Přerov and Slunecný Vrch near Drnholec. The winery is committed to high quality through diligent vineyard work and low yields. The focus is on white wines and blends with fantasy names, and the first vintage was 2005.
🍷 white, dessert 🍇 2007, 2006, 2005 ★ Cuvée Lange'Warte, Cuvée To'No, Cuvée Gabriel

Sonberk
Moravia

Sonberk 1, 69127 Popice 📞 777 630 434 🌐 www.sonberk.cz ⏲ by appt

THIS NEW, MODERN WINERY in the Mikulov region of south Moravia was set up by award-winning young winemaker Oldřich Drápal, who claims to be the first to produce and market straw wines in the Czech Republic. These are made by drying grapes on straw mats over the winter until they shrivel into raisins, giving a fabulously sweet rich wine.

🍷 white, red, dessert 🍇 2007, 2006, 2005 ★ Traminer Straw Wine, Rulandské Šedé (Pinot Gris), Palava

Vinařství Baloun
Moravia

Nádražní 2/4, 68186 Velké Pavlovice 📞 519 428 236 🌐 www.baloun.cz

RADOMIL BALOUN learned to make wine from his grandfather, and founded this, his own winery, in 1991. The cellars had originally been built in 1750 by Empress Marie Theresa and required massive investment to modernize. Today he has 60ha of vineyards and has collected quite an array of international medals – a reflection of his philosophy of producing exceptional wines with soul.
🍷 white, red, dessert 🍇 2007, 2006, 2005 ★ Grüner Veltliner, Riesling, Merlot, Chardonnay Selection

Znovin Znojmo
Moravia

Šatov 404, 67122 Znojmo 📞 515 266 610 🌐 www.znovin.cz ⏲ by appt

THIS IS ONE of the bigger wineries in the Czech Republic, with about 3.5 per cent market share. It has worked hard on researching terroirs in the stunning Znojmo region, and has developed its own selections of yeast for its top wines. A wide range of wine styles runs from dry to sweet, but the crown jewels are the lusciously sweet straw wines and the ice-wines made from frozen grapes.
🍷 dessert, white, red 🍇 2007, 2006, 2005 ★ Riesling Icewine, Riesling Straw Wine, Pinot Gris

Vineyard near Pezinok, Slovakia

WINEGROWING AREAS OF SLOVAKIA

THE EASTERN PART OF former Czechoslovakia is only slowly coming to terms with the privatization of its state wineries and vineyards. Slovakia joined the European Community in 2004 and faces numerous challenges and opportunities. At its best, its wine has world-class potential, but the poor quality, bulk-production side of the market may struggle to compete in the longer term.

Malokarpatská (Little Carpathians)

ALSO KNOWN AS the Little Carpathians, this dynamic wine region accounts for about one-third of all Slovakia's vineyards. The quality can be variable, but there are hundreds of family wineries in Pezinok and villages such as Devin and Vajnory. Visitors can take the Little Carpathian Wine Road, sampling red Frankovka and St-Laurent, and local whites.
clay, sand *Pinot Blanc, Müller-Thurgau, Grüner Veltliner, Welschriesling, Devin* *Frankovka (Blaufränkisch), St-Laurent* *red, white, sparkling, dessert*

Juznoslovenská (Southern Slovakia)

SOUTHERN SLOVAKIA IS best known for the superb Château Belá, a joint venture involving Egon Müller from the Mosel Valley in Germany, which has rapidly established a reputation for world-class Riesling. The warm temperatures and long autumns help to produce a rich and full-bodied Riesling which bears comparison with the best in Alsace and Austria. If other producers follow Château Belá's lead, this will be a region to watch.

volcanic *Riesling, Tramin (Gewürztraminer)* *Cabernet Sauvignon, Frankovka, St-Laurent* *red, white*

Nitranská & neighbours

NITRANSKÁ (NITRA), STREDOSLOVENSKÁ (**Central Slovakia**) and Vychodoslovenská (**Eastern Slovakia**) together account for around 20 per cent of the wine production. One of the country's most diverse wine regions, Nitranská produces several different styles and quality levels from full-bodied reds, to crisp, aromatic whites, and sparkling wines. Stredoslovenská produces crisp, fresh whites.
diverse, the best are volcanic in origin. *Grüner Veltliner, Müller-Thurgau, Welschriesling, Pinot Blanc, Tramin* *Frankovka, St-Laurent, Cabernet Sauvignon* *red, white, sparkling, dessert*

Tokajská (Slovak Tokaj)

THE HISTORIC SWEET WINE of Tokajská is better associated with Hungary, but there are around 900ha of Tokaji vineyards that belong to Slovakia. Under an agreement in 2004, a proportion of these vineyards now have the right to use the name 'Tokaji'. There are currently seven Slovakian Tokaji wineries but the quality of their wines is largely a pale imitation of Hungarian versions. However, with new regulations, and if the region manages to attract much-needed investment, it possesses the potential to become one of the most exciting wine regions in the country.
volcanic *Furmint, Lipovina, Yellow Muscat* *white, dessert*

TOP PRODUCERS OF SLOVAKIA

Borik Vino
Malokarpatská

Jilemnického 2a, Pezinok
☎ *0905 525 759*
Ⓦ *www.borikvino.com* 🔲 *by appt*

THIS IS ONE many small-scale, good-quality producers in and around the city of Pezinok in the Malokarpatská region (Little Carpathians). Although Borik Vino made wine for private consumption only during the Communist regime, Peter and Magdalena Borik only established their wine company in 1998. They produce just over 15,000 bottles a year of soft, oak-aged reds from varieties such as Cabernet Sauvignon as well as light, crisp whites from Riesling, Chardonnay, and Tramin.

🔳 *red, white* 📥 *2007, 2006, 2005*
★ *Riesling, Pinot Blanc*

Vino Masaryk
Malokarpatská

Pod Kalvariou 45, Skalica
☎ *0346 646 960*
Ⓦ *www.vino-masaryk.sk* 🔲 *by appt*

THIS TINY PRODUCER is situated near the Czech border in Skalica. Although the winery was only founded in 1996, Alojz Masaryk spent 30 years in the communist wine industry. With the help of new equipment, Masaryk produces a range of ripe, fruity whites and deep, concentrated reds.

🔳 *white, red, dessert* 📥 *2007, 2006, 2005* ★ *ENEM Cuvée, Traminer, Pinot Blanc*

Château Belá
Juznoslovenská

Kastiel Belá, 94353 Belá, Muzla
☎ *0367 586 112*

THIS WORLD CLASS Riesling is produced by a joint venture between the Baron Ullman family and the renowned German producer Egon Müller. Situated in Juznoslovenská (Southern Slovakia) along the Hungarian border, one of the warmest parts of the country, Château Belá is a historic estate that fell into ruin in the aftermath of World War I. The company is still in the process of buying its vineyard but the winery is now fully-functioning in the capable hands of cellarmaster Miroslav 'Miro' Petrech. With several vintages under its belt, Château Belá is delivering on its early promise and has settled into a consistent style of intense, dry Riesling with wonderful mineral undertones. The château itself has been developed into a hotel, spa and restaurant complex, too.

🔳 *white* 📥 *2006, 2004, 2003*
★ *Riesling*

Mavín (Martin Pomfy)
Malokarpatská

Pezinská 7, 90201 Vinosady
☎ *0908 777 066* ◉

MAVÍN WAS ESTABLISHED in 2001 in a typical winegrowing village. It's very much a family business, following Martin Pomfy's childhood traditions, but with a focus on quality, through using modern equipment and oak casks. Pomfy sees himself as still at the start of his journey and admits to having great plans for the future. He certainly appears to have set out in the right direction and has been creating quite a splash, winning top awards for wines from the 2006 and 2007 vintages.

🔳 *white, dessert* 📥 *2007, 2006*
★ *Grüner Veltliner Late Harvest Dry, Devín, Late Harvest Riesling*

J & J Ostrozovic
Tokajská

Velká Trna 233 ☎ *0566 793 322*
Ⓦ *www.cstrozovic.sk* 🔲

ALTHOUGH THE wines that are produced in the Slovakian part of Tokaj are generally inferior to their Hungarian counterparts, J & J Ostrozovic is one of the better producers. The company was founded by husband-and-wife team Jaroslav and Jaromira in 1990 with, in their words, "nothing more than five wooden barrels and an unquenchable drive for hard work". Today they produce a range of classic Tokajska wines, as well as late-harvest and straw wines.

🔳 *white, dessert* 📥 *2006, 2005, 2002* ★ *Tokaj Cuvée, Tokaj 6 Putňový, Lipovina Straw Wine*

Ostrozovic wine cellar

WINE MAP OF SLOVENIA & CROATIA

BECAUSE THEIR GEOGRAPHY is so diverse, the wine regions of Slovenia and Croatia vary dramatically within each country. The regions adjoining the Adriatic in Primorje in Slovenia and Kontinentalna (coastal) Croatia both have warm, Mediterranean climates and favour the production of red wines. In the Alpine foothills of Podravje in Slovenia – where temperatures are much cooler – crisp, aromatic whites are the speciality. In the rolling hills of Kontinentalna (inland) Croatia, white wines are also produced in a relatively light, refreshing style, although reds, normally from the grape variety, Frankovka, can also be found.

KEY

Slovenia & Croatia

Vineyards in Posavje, Slovenia

SLOVENIA: AREAS & TOP PRODUCERS

PODRAVJE *p414*
PraVino *p415*

POSAVJE *p414*

PRIMORJE *p414*
Edi Simčič *p415*
Jakončič *p415*
Marjan Simčič *p415*
Movia *p415*
Sutor *p415*
Tilia *p415*

CROATIA: AREAS & TOP PRODUCERS

PRIMORSKA/COASTAL *p416*
Grgich Vina *p417*
Tomic *p417*
Zlatan Otok *p417*

KONTINENTALNA/INLAND *p416*
Ivan Enjingi *p417*
Krauthaker *p417*

Edi Simčič, Primorje, Slovenia

Vineyards beneath a medieval hilltop town, Istria, Croatia

TERROIR AT A GLANCE

Latitude: 42–47°N.

Altitude: 0–2,364m.

Topography: Slovenia is a mountainous terrain dominated by the Alps and the Dinaric Alps with a coastal strip to the west joining the Adriatic. Croatia has rolling hills in its northeast and a rocky coastline where it meets the Adriatic in the west. Between them are the Dinaric Alps and a few smaller mountain ranges.

Soil: Diverse.

Climate: Mediterranean along the Adriatic coast with mild winters and hot summers. Cooler in the mountainous areas. Continental further inland.

Temperature: In July from 21°C in northeast Slovenia to 25°C in south Primorska (coastal) Croatia.

Rainfall: Annual average is 800–1,350mm.

Viticultural hazards: Frost and low temperatures in cooler regions; harvest rains; fungal diseases.

Spraying vines at Klanjec, Kontinentalna (inland) Croatia

Ljutomer-Ormož, Podravje, Slovenia

HUNGARY

46°

Osijek

ONTINENTALNA   *Vuka*   SERBIA & MONTENEGRO

SLAVONIJA

PODUNAVLJE

Vrbas   *Bosna*

BOSNIA & ERZEGOVINA

0 — km ——————— 30

44°

TIAN LAND

I P S

Dubrovnic •

PERFECT CASE: SLOVENIA & CROATIA

D Dveri Pax Šipon/ Chardonnay TBA ££££ (www.dveri-pax.com)

R Edi Simčič Kolos ££££

W Ivan Enjingi Venje £££

W Jakončič Carolina Bela ££

W Krauthaker Graševina ££

W Marjan Simčič Teodor Rdece £££

R Movia Pinot Noir ££££

D PraVino Šipon Ledeno Vino (Ice Wine) ££££

W Sutor Chardonnay ££

R Tilia Pinot Noir ££

D Tomic Prosek Hektorvich £££

R Zlatan Otok Zlatan Plavac Grand Cru ££££

Autumn vineyard in Kras where the renowned Teran is produced

WINEGROWING AREAS OF SLOVENIA

SLOVENIA GAINED ITS independence from former Yugoslavia in 1991, and was relatively unscathed by the civil wars that scarred her neighbours. Its wine tradition dates back some 2,400 years. There are around 17,000ha of registered vineyards, and a growing number of high-quality wine estates.

Podravje

PODRAVJE IS IN THE ALPINE foothills of the northeast, bordering Austria. It is the largest wine region, making mainly aromatic whites with lively acidity. **Maribor** is the best district for aromatic whites, especially Renski Riesling. Maribor is also famous for Europe's oldest productive vine, a 400-year-old Žametovka. The number of districts has recently gone from seven to two: Prekmurje and Stajerska Slovenija. The hills of Jeruzalem produce particularly good dry whites from Beli and Sivi Pinots and are also known for Šipon and Laški Rizling; late harvest, ice wine, and noble sweet wines. **Haloze** produces fresh Pinots, Renski Riesling, and Traminec (Gewürztraminer).

sedimentary, marl, clay, volcanic around Maribor *Žametovka, Modra Frankinja (Blaufränkisch), Modri Pinot (Pinot Noir)* *Laški Rizling, Renski Riesling (Rhein Riesling), Sivi Pinot (Pinot Gris), Beli Pinot (Pinot Blanc), Šipon (Furmint)* *red, white, dessert*

Posavje

POSAVJE TOWARDS THE southeast is least well-known internationally. Blended wines are the staple, though ice wines made from Laški Rizling are well regarded. The three wine-growing regions are **Bizeljsko**, **Dolenjska**, and **Bela Krajina**. Cvicek is a staple of Dolenjska, traditionally a light, fresh, tart blend of four grapes (two red and two white). Bela Krajina is best known for Metliška mina, a blend including Frankinja and Žametovka. Chardonnay, Beli Pinot, and Sauvignon are grown in Bizeljsko, as well as Laški Rizling, and bottle-fermented sparkling wines are a local speciality.

marl, clay, sandstone, loess *Modra Frankinja (Blaufränkisch), Žametovka, Modri Pinot (Pinot Noir)* *Laški Rizling, Šipon (Furmint), Chardonnay, Rumeni Muskat (Yellow Muscat)* *red, white, sparkling, dessert*

Primorje

PRIMORJE (OR PRIMORSKA) means 'by the sea'. This region of Slovenia has the largest number of leading producers and reds are as important as whites. It is divided into four districts: **Brda**, **Vipava**, **Kras**, and **Koper**. Brda, also known as Goriška Brda, is a continuation of Italy's renowned Collio (*see p230*), with vineyards straddling the border. Vipava Valley is best for whites and looks promising for elegant Pinot Noir. The local Refošk is important around Koper, producing a lively raspberry-style wine. A unique strain of Refošk is grown around Kras on rich *terra rosa* soil, where it makes the renowned Teran.

marl, shale, sandstone, terra rossa at Kras *Merlot, Refošk, Cabernet* *Rebula, Malvazija, Sivi Pinot (Pinot Gris), Chardonnay, Sauvignon* *red, white*

TOP PRODUCERS OF SLOVENIA

PraVino
Podravje

Čurin-Prapotnik Winery, Kog 15, 2275 Kog **C** *027 196 277* **W** *www.curin.net* **□** *by appt*

STANKO ČURIN is a legend in Slovenia: he was the first to make high-quality sweet wines, and the first to bottle under a private label in 1971. Today his son-in-law and grandson continue his legacy. World-class sweet wines are this family's passion, and it shows in their gorgeous Šipon (Furmint) and amazingly luscious Laški Rizling ice wines.

■ *white, dessert* **■** *2005, 2004, 2003* ★ *Šipon Ledeno Vino, Laški Rizling Ledeno Vino, Rumeni Muscat*

Edi Simčič
Primorje

Vipol e 39A, Dobrovo **C** *053 039 591* **□** *by appt*

FATHER-AND-SON team Edi and Aleks Simčič have taken quality to a new level at their 5.5ha vineyard, resulting in some of central Europe's finest wines. Aleks recently released two excellent single-vineyard wines, Kozana Chardonnay and Kolos Red.

■ *red, white, dessert* **■** *red: 2004, 2003, 2002; white: 2007, 2006* ★ *Kolos, Kozana Chardonnay, Sivi Pinot Riserva*

Jakončič
Primorje

Kozana 5, 5212 Dobrovo **C** *053 041 215* **□** *by appt*

THE JAKONČIČ ESTATE has 160 years of winemaking history behind it but is still a family business. The vineyards pro-duce both red and white wines. The white Carolina Bela is a wonderful blend of local Rebula (Ribolla) with Chardonnay, while its red partner is based on Cabernet and shows lovely balance and complexity.

■ *white, red* **■** *red: 2006, 2004, 2003; white: 2006, 2005, 2004* ★ *Carolina Bela, Carolina Rdece*

Marjan Simčič
Primorje

Ceglo 3B, Medana, Dobrovo **C** *053 959 200* **W** *www.simcic.si* **□** *by appt*

WITH HIS ROCK-STAR looks, Marjan seems unlikely to be one of Slovenia's top wine-makers. He won't trust any-one else with his barrels, taking just one snowboarding trip in February when all is quiet. His whites are big, rich, and intense, including an intriguing Rebula fermented on skins like a red wine. In contrast, Simčič's reds are

Cellar, Marjan Simčič

remarkably elegant and finely handled and age superbly.

■ *red, white, dessert* **■** *red: 2003, 2002, 2000; white: 2006, 2005, 2004* ★ *Teodor Rdece, Rebula, Leonardo Passito*

Movia
Primorje

Ceglo 18, Dobrovo **C** *053 959 510* **W** *www.movia.si* **□** *by appt*

SET IN THE Slovenian part of Collio, Movia was established in 1820. Winemaker Ales Kristančič uses a combina-tion of traditional and mod-ern – biodynamic viticulture with computers programmed to follow phases of the moon. Wines mature in oak for long periods but have the fruit quality to stand up to it.

■ *red, white* **■** *2000, 1998* ★ *Modri Pinot, Veliko Rdece, Veliko Belo*

Sutor
Primorje

Podraga 30-31, Podnanos **C** *053 669 367* **W** *www.sutorvino.com* **□** *by appt*

BROTHERS PRIMO AND MITJA Lavrenčič are rising stars in Slovenian wine. Their estate is in the coolest area of the Vipava Valley and the main focus here is whites. They have identified that their location is best for Pinot Noir as a red variety, and the first release in 2006 seemed to live up to this billing, silky and Burgundian in style.

■ *red, white* **■** *2006, 2005, 2004* ★ *Chardonnay, Pinot Noir, Burja*

Tilia
Primorje

Kotoce 41, 5263 Dobravlje **C** *053 646 684* **W** *www.tilia premiumwines.com* **□** *by appt*

HUSBAND AND WIFE Matjaz and Melita Lemut have just 7ha of vines in the heart of the Vipava Valley, an area known for balanced whites with good acidity, but Pinot Noir is also looking promising.

■ *white, red* **■** *red: 2007, 2006, 2004; white: most recent* ★ *Pinot Noir, Pinot Gris, Zelen*

Hvar Island, Primorska, is an historic winegrowing area

WINEGROWING AREAS OF CROATIA

ALTHOUGH CROATIA HAS a lengthy winegrowing tradition stretching back to the 4th century BC, today its wine industry is still coming to terms with the aftermath of civil war. The country has two distinct wine regions split by a mountain range – Kontinentalna (inland) and Primorska (coastal) – each with their own unique climate, soils, and wine styles. Active vineyard holdings are once again increasing thanks to initiatives such as the Roots of Peace organization, which has been working hard to clear mines and replant vineyards.

Primorska (coastal) Croatia

THE PRIMORKSA (COASTAL) region of Croatia runs from Istria in the northwest down along the Adriatic to Dalmatia in the southeast, and includes the Dalmatian Islands. The climate here is Mediterranean with a maritime influence and the hilly terrain produces a number of different microclimates. The four main subregions are: **Istria and the Croatian Sea**, **North Dalmatia**, **Central and Southern Dalmatia plus Islands**, and the **Dalmatian Hinterland**. Red wines account for around 70 per cent of production in the region; in Istria, in the north, it is the Bordeaux grape varieties of Cabernet Sauvignon and Merlot that are important, as well as Malvasia Nera and Teran, better known under its Italian guise of Refosco. Further south there are numerous indigenous red grape varieties that have adapted to the local conditions. The best known is Plavac Mali, which makes full-bodied, robust wines. Recent DNA research

by Dr Carole Meredith at the University of California revealed that Plavac Mali is a cousin of Zinfandel as both grapes share a parent in the rare Croatian Crljenak. The best-known established appellations for Plavac Mali are Dingac and Postup on the Peljesac peninsular, but some of Croatia's best examples of the grape now come from the island of Hvar. A number of different white varieties are grown in the Primorska region, most notably around 6,000ha of Malvasia Istriana and indigenous varieties such as Marastina further south. Marastina is one of the more interesting, producing wines which are fresh, light, and slightly herbal in character.

🗻 *rocky* 🍇 *Malvasia Nera, Teran (Refosco), Cabernet Sauvignon, Merlot, Plavac Mali* 🍇 *Malvasia Istriana, Marastina, Pošip, Grk* 🍷 *red, white*

Kontinentalna (inland) Croatia

EXTENDING FROM THE northwest to the south-east along the Drava River towards the Dunaj (Danube), Kontinentalna (inland) Croatia specializes in the production of white wines. This region has hot, arid summers and cold winters. Graševina (Welschriesling) is the dominant grape variety. The main subregions are **Zagorje-Medimurje**, **Prigorje-Bilogora**, **Plesivica**, **Moslavina**, **Pokuplje**, **Slavonija**, and **Podunavlje**, and the district of Kutjevo has become particularly noted for its top quality wines.

🗻 *various* 🍇 *Frankovka* 🍇 *Graševina (Welschriesling), Riesling, Gewürztraminer, Pinot Blanc, Chardonnay* 🍷 *red, white*

TOP PRODUCERS OF CROATIA

Grgich Vina
Primorska

Trstenik 78, Trstenik
📞 *20 748 090* ⬜ *by appt*

MILJENKO 'MIKE' GRGICH of Grgich Hills in the Napa Valley is one of Croatia's most famous expat winemakers. In 1996 he returned to his homeland to establish a tiny winery in the seaside village of Trstenik. Mike Grgich is an enthusiastic fan of Zinfandel in California *(pp487)* and specializes in its close relation, Plavac Mali, in Croatia. The wine is matured in French oak barrels to help produce tiny quantities of a deep-coloured, surprisingly elegant style. He also makes a light, lively white from the Pošip grape variety. As well as sharing his extensive technical expertise with local wine producers, Mike Grgich is also actively involved in the replanting of vineyards through the Roots of Peace organization.

🍷 *red, white* 🍇 *2004, 2003, 2002* ★ *Plavac Mali, Pošip*

Tomic
Primorska

Bastijana, Jelsa, Hvar Island 📞 *21 768 160* Ⓦ *www.bastijana.hr* ⬜ *by appt*

FROM THE DALMATIAN island of Hvar, this forward-thinking estate produces some superb wines ranging from a rich and complex Plavac Mali through to a unique sweet wine made from dried grapes – Prošek Hektorovich. Winemaker Andro Tomic was born on this historic grape-growing island before continuing his career on the mainland. Determined to help revive Hvar's great winemaking heritage, Andro sources his grapes from his own vineyards, as well as those of various carefully selected local growers.

🍷 *red, white, dessert* 🍇 *2005, 2004, 2003* ★ *Plavac Barrique, Plavac Mali, Prošek Hektorovich*

Zlatan Otok
Primorska

Sveta Nedilja 21455 Jelsa 📞 *20 745 709* Ⓦ *www.zlatanotok.hr* ⬜ *by appt*

ZLATAN PLENKOVIĆ is widely regarded as the King of Plavac Mali and was named Croatia's Winemaker of the Year 2005. The winery has 75ha of vineyards and is in the process of gaining organic certification. Most of the vineyards are planted to local red grape Plavac Mali, producing hugely concentrated, powerful wines, most notably the Zlatan Plavac Grand Cru. There's also a richly sweet Prošek, unusually made from dried Plavac Mali grapes.

🍷 *red, white, dessert* 🍇 *2004, 2003, 1999* ★ *Zlatan Plavac Grand Cru, Zlatan Plavac Barrique, Prošek*

Ivan Enjingi
Kontinentalna

Hrnjevac, Vetovo 📞 *34 267 200* ⬜ *by appt*

THIS SMALL BUT ESTABLISHED estate in the region of Slavonija was recently catapulted into the international limelight with its spectacular success in the Decanter World Wine Awards 2004. Ivan was awarded two trophies for his *barrique*-matured, blended wine, Venje, and single varietal, Graševina, in the face of extremely challenging competition from across the globe. The estate owns around 50ha of vineyards planted with a range of grape varieties such as Gewürztraminer, Riesling, and Zweigelt, but there are also plans in the pipeline to expand their plantings.

🍷 *red, white* 🍇 *2004, 2003, 2002* ★ *Graševina, Rajnai Rizling, Venje*

Krauthaker
Kontinentalna

John Jambrovica 6, 34340 Kutjevo
📞 *34 315 000* Ⓦ *www.krauthaker.hr* ⬜ *by appt*

VLADO KRAUTHAKER has worked hard to improve the quality at his winery and was one of the first to use green harvesting to reduce yields. He has 22ha of his own and manages another 35ha, most planted to whites, especially Graševina, which is a benchmark in Croatia. He also makes stylish Chardonnay and Sauvignon, as well as reds from Syrah and Pinot Noir.

🍷 *white, red* 🍇 *2007, 2006, 2005* ★ *Chardonnay Rosenberg, Graševina Mitrovac, Sauvignon Blanc*

Ivan Enjingi wine

Grgich label

SOUTHEASTERN EUROPE

SOUTHEASTERN EUROPE

S OUTHEASTERN EUROPE IS THE CRADLE OF VITICULTURE. *Historians believe the birth of winemaking and wine culture took place here, in what was Asia Minor, between 6,000 and 8,000 years ago. Immersed in ancient history, modern winemaking in this corner of Europe combines the finest of the old with the best of the new to create some of the most beautiful and fascinating wines in the world.*

GREECE: BACKGROUND

THE HISTORY OF WINEMAKING in Greece can be traced back as far as 4,000 years, and the wine export industry to as long ago as 1,000 BC, when the ancients were shipping their highly popular product to most of Europe. Wine was transported in two-handled airtight vessels called amphorae. There is evidence on these artefacts of the first ever appellation system, ensuring authenticity rather than governing methods of production. The shape of the container indicated the city or region that produced and traded the wine, and the year of production was inscribed on it. On either handle of the amphora was the **Greek amphora** stamp of the winemaker and the local ruler.

Around 730 BC, the ancient Greeks began to colonize many parts of the Mediterranean. They took their vines with them, thus laying the foundations for much of the wine industry in Europe today. Their legacy can still be seen, especially in parts of southern Italy, where the names of ancient grape varieties indicate their Greek origins.

GREECE: THE WINE INDUSTRY TODAY

GREECE PRODUCES only a tiny proportion of the world's wine – around 3.9 million hectolitres per year – of which about 350,000hl is exported. The area under vine stands at around 66,000ha, with white grapes accounting for 68 per cent and red grapes 32 per cent. There are around 500 commercial producers, including 54 co-operatives. Production as a whole has fallen since the early 1980s, but the commercial output has remained constant. A new generation of growers

RETSINA: AN ANCIENT TRADITION PRESERVED

Greece has been exporting what is now known as retsina for more than 2,000 years. In order to prevent oxidation, pine resin was originally used to seal the tops of the amphorae in which wine was transported. Later, this resin was added to the wine to prevent and then conceal oxidation, and resin-flavoured retsina wine emerged. This curious wine was, in the main, made in Attica from over-cropped, flavourless white Savatiano grapes, and was heavily treated with resin to impart a strong flavour.

Gaia Wines retsina label

The home market began to turn its back on this ancient tradition in favour of conventional wine, and a new wave of lightly resinated, fresh-tasting, easy-drinking retsina has emerged to replace it. This is made with high quality, low yield, native grapes from all over Greece. Quality examples of this much-maligned style of wine can be exceptional, especially with spicy foods. **Gaia Wines**, **Tsantali**, **Kechri** *(23107 51283)*, **Boutari**, **Sitia Co-operative** *(www.sitiacoop.gr)*, and **Papagianakos** *(21066 26146)* produce some of the finest examples.

◁ **Vineyard on the Ionian Island of Cephalonia, Greece**

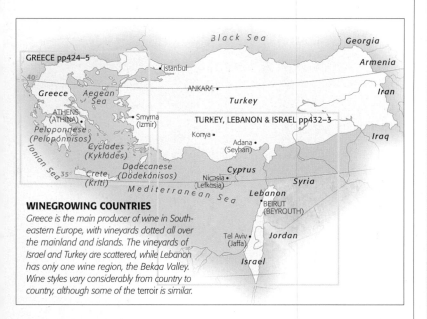

WINEGROWING COUNTRIES

*Greece is the main producer of wine in South-
eastern Europe, with vineyards dotted all over
the mainland and islands. The vineyards of
Israel and Turkey are scattered, while Lebanon
has only one wine region, the Bekaa Valley.
Wine styles vary considerably from country to
country, although some of the terroir is similar.*

has also now come to the fore, many of
whom have been trained abroad.

GREECE: GRAPE VARIETIES & WINE STYLES

GREECE HAS INHERITED more than 300
indigenous grape varieties, although in
reality only around 20 per cent of these
are being utilized in today's wine industry.
Those that are provide refreshing diversity
in a world market awash with uniformity.
Vintage by vintage, more and more of
these ancient cultivars are being
called to the world stage to sate the
need for variety, and each year
Greece's quality revolution continues
to gather pace.

Today's producers choose from a
wide range of native and international
grape varieties in order to express the
individual *terroir* of each locale, to make
every style of wine imaginable. Some
of the best and most prolific of the
indigenous varieties are the red
Xinomavro, Aghiorghitiko, Kotsifali, and
Krasato, and white Assyrtiko, Roditis,
Savatiano (the traditional retsina
grape), and Vilana. The most successful

international varieties are Syrah, Cabernet
Sauvignon, Merlot, Chardonnay, Sauvignon
Blanc, Viognier, and Sémillon. Pioneering
work is being done here in re-establishing
ancient grape varieties such as the white
Malagousia (initially from Gerovassiliou)
and red Mavrotragano (in Santorini).
Ancient vineyards such as the historical
Marónia site in Thrace (mentioned in the
writings of Homer) are also being
resurrected by ground-breaking
companies like Tsantali.

Estate Biblia Chora vineyard in Macedonia

LEBANON

THE CULTURE OF WINEMAKING in Lebanon is one of the oldest and most continuous in the world, dating back at least six millennia. Even the recent 15-year-long civil war was not able to halt a steady output from the most established producers of the area. It is thanks to this continuity that the world-class winemakers of this tiny country have managed to hang on to the very best of the old, while cherry-picking the finest of the new, to keep this rich viticultural country firmly on the international stage. Approximately 90 per cent of Lebanon's wine is now exported.

Harvesting at Château Ksara, Lebanon

The indigenous grape varieties of the area have remained unchanged since the time of the Phoenicians. Some even predate this era – the white grapes Obaideh and Merwah, for example, have existed in Lebanon for around 4,000 years. It is the country's strong links with France, however, that have really shaped Lebanon's modern wine industry and winemaking style. Today, the best producers are firmly entrenched in the Old World ways, using the finest noble varieties from France as well as their own indigenous grapes. Fruit-driven boldness is emphatically rejected in favour of balance, restraint, and understatement. With relative peace and stability having returned to the country since 1990, new innovative producers are now beginning to add diversity to a region that is already the envy of many a winemaker around the world.

ISRAEL

ALTHOUGH ISRAEL IS historically home to one of the world's oldest viticultural areas, it was not until the 1880s that Baron Edmond de Rothschild set up the first wine company, thereby establishing a modern wine industry in the country. Even then, Israel languished far behind the rest of the world. Blighted by war and instability for decades, the neglected industry made

Vineyard of Golan Heights Winery, Katzrin, Israel

very ordinary wine, mainly from just one red variety – Carignan – to provide kosher wine for its people and for orthodox Jews around the world. In the mid-1980s, however, a serious quality revolution began to shift into top gear. Large-scale plantings of many high quality international varieties and massive investment in state-of-the-art technology have enabled this tiny country to begin extracting the very best its *terroir* has to offer. As the region's indigenous grape varieties have long since died out, imported Cabernet Sauvignon, Chardonnay, Merlot, Sauvignon Blanc, Cabernet Franc, and Muscat are now the most cultivated grapes here. Expertise brought in, mainly, from California has also left its indelible mark, giving many of the region's wines a definite New World signature. Israel's is still very much a fledgling industry, but it is beginning to produce winemaking talent and turn out some promising wines that will soon make other winemaking countries take note.

TURKEY

TURKEY IS CONSISTENTLY one of the top five grape producing nations in the world, with nearly 600,000ha under vine. However, only around two per cent of its crop is made into wine.

Although it is believed that Turkey is one of the areas in which *Vitis vinifera* was originally cultivated, the wine industry flagged lethargically until Kemal Atatürk, the founder of the Turkish republic and its first president, gave it a boost in the 1920s. Large amounts of wine are still being made purely for local consumption (and therefore cater to local tastes), but today Turkish wine is experiencing a real revival, benefiting from great investment over the past 20 years. The best wines today are ripe and modern, produced from Turkey's fascinating and unique local grapes, as well as international varieties and blends of both.

Native Grape Varieties of Southeastern Europe

Red Grape Varieties

Aghiorghitiko (Greece): This native grape of the Peloponnese makes wines that are soft, roundly structured, and supple.

Boğazkere (Turkey): A producer of big, muscular, tannic wines that age well, this variety is often blended with Öküzgözü.

Mandelaria (Greece): The red variety of the islands (known as Amorghiano on Rhodes) makes fruity, medium-bodied wines with plenty of backbone that pair well with Greek food.

Xinomavro

Öküzgözü (Turkey): Öküzgözü produces intense, fleshy wines. It is often blended with Boğazkere to give a softer edge.

Xinomavro (Greece): Grown in northern and central parts of Greece, this grape gives big, muscular, tannic wines that age superbly.

White Grape Varieties

Assyrtiko (Greece): Santorini's native grape is used to create both minerally dry and seductively sweet whites.

Athiri (Greece): Grown mainly on the Dodecanese, Cyclades, and Aegean islands, Athiri is used in deliciously textured, fruit-scented wines.

Assyrtiko

Merwah (Lebanon): Very similar in both appearance and flavour to Sémillon, this grape is used for blending in Château Musar's white wine.

Moschofilero (Greece): Mainly found in the Peloponnese, Moschofilero gives wonderfully dry, elegant, rose-scented wine.

Narince (Turkey): This makes fresh-tasting, bone-dry, lemony wines.

Obaideh (Lebanon): Blended in the white wine of Château Musar, Obaideh has a palate very similar to that of Chardonnay.

Robola (Greece): The grape of Cephalonia gives concentrated, focused, elegant wines.

Roditis (Greece): Roditis is planted all over mainland Greece to create firm, dry, punchy, fruit-filled wine.

Savatiano (Greece): Savatiano makes soft, round, fat, and supple wines. It is also used for retsina.

Vilana (Greece): This Cretan variety's best wines are fresh-tasting, supple, and lemony.

WINE MAP OF GREECE

Gaia Wines label, Peloponnese

THE VINEYARDS OF GREECE stretch the length and breadth of the country, from the cooler, greener northern areas of Thrace and Macedonia to the hot, dry island of Crete in the south, and from Cephalonia and the Ionian Islands in the west to Rhodes in the east. The whole country is officially divided into 11 regions *(see below)*, each with its own special attributes. Within these, there are 33 quality growing areas, called Appellations of Origin or AOs. Of these, 25 are Appellations of High-Quality Origin, or OPAPs, the other eight are Appellations of Controlled Origin (OPEs), producing sweet wine. In addition, there are more than 80 *topikos oenos*, or regional wine designations.

GREECE: AREAS & TOP PRODUCERS

THRACE *p426*

MACEDONIA *p426*
Boutari *p429*
Domaine Constantine
 Lazaridi *p429*
Domaine Gerovassiliou *p429*
Estate Biblia Chora *p429*
Estate Kyr-Yanni *p429*
Tsantali *p429*

EPIRUS *p426*

THESSALY *p427*

CENTRAL GREECE & ATTICA *p427*
Domaine Evharis *p430*
Domaine Vassiliou *p430*
Harlaftis *p430*

PELOPONNESE *p427*
Achaia Clauss *p430*
Gaia Wines *p430*
Papantonis Winery *p430*
Tselepos *p431*

THE CYCLADES ISLANDS *p427*
Hatzidakis *p431*
Santo Wines *p431*

RHODES *p428*
CAIR *p431*

CEPHALONIA & THE IONIAN ISLANDS *p428*
Gentilini *p431*

LÍMNOS, SÁMOS & THE AEGEAN ISLANDS *p428*
Sámos Co-operative *p431*

CRETE *p428*

KEY

Greece

MACEDONIA

GOÚMENISSA

AMINDEO   NÁOUSSA   Thessalo

ALBANIA

MACEDONIA (MAKEDONÍA)
Mount Olympus

RAPSÁNI

MESSENIKOLA

Corfú (Kérkyra)

ZITSA

EPIRUS (ÍPEIROS)

THESSALY (THESSALÍA)
Lárisa

Vólos

ANHIALOS

Levkás

CEPHALONIA (KEFALLINÍA) & THE IONIAN ISLANDS (IÓNIOI NÍSOI)

Pátra

CENT GREE & ATT (ATTI

CEPHALONIA (KEFALLINÍA)

PATRAS

Zákinthos

NEMEA

MANTINIA

PELOPONNESE (PELOPÓNNISOS)

0 — km ————— 100

Harvesting grapes in Macedonia

TERROIR AT A GLANCE

Latitude: 35–41.5°N.

Altitude: 0–800m.

Topography: The northern mainland is dissected by high mountains (such as the Pindos range) that extend southwards towards a landscape of pine-forested uplands, craggy, scrub-covered foothills, and fertile plains. The islands account for one fifth of the land area of the country.

Soil: Limestone subsoils on the mainland and volcanic soils on the islands. In general, fertility is low.

Climate: Mediterranean, but with cooler continental influences in the mountains. The variation from north to south can be extreme. Cold, snowy, wet winters and warm, slightly rainy summers in the north. Extremely mild winters and arid summers on Rhodes and Crete in the south.

Temperature: July average is 26.5°C.

Rainfall: Annual average is 720mm.

Wind: Maritime breezes.

Viticultural hazards: Drought; sudden storms.

Vineyard owned by Tsantali in Rapsáni, Thessaly

PERFECT CASE: GREECE

D Achaia Clauss Mavrodaphne Grand Reserve 1979 £££

R Boutari Naoussa Grand Reserve ££

S CAIR Rosé Réserve 10 Ans Brut £

W Domaine Costa Lazaridi Amethystos Sauvignon Blanc ££

R Domaine Gerovassiliou Syrah ££

W Estate Biblia Chora ££

R Estate Kyr-Yanni Yianakohori ££

R Gaia Estate ££

W Hatzidakis Santorini ££

D Sámos Co-operative Sámos Nectar ££

R Tsantali Rapsáni Reserve £

W Tselepos Moschofilero ££

Vineyards overlooking the Aegean Sea at Sithonia, Macedonia

WINEGROWING AREAS OF GREECE

Thrace

IN THIS AREA (known locally as Thráki) bordering Bulgaria and Turkey, extensive efforts have been made in recent years to reconstruct the ancient vineyard of Marónia. Another promising new winegrowing area has also been established, in the frontier area along the Turkish border. Mild Aegean breezes during the winter and cool northerly winds in summer make extreme temperature fluctuations rare. The best whites, mostly from foreign grape varieties, are soft, fruity, and freshly perfumed. Elegance and finesse dominate the bouquet and palate of the first-rate Syrah-based reds now made in this improving region.

calcareous 🍇 *Limnio, Mourvèdre, Grenache, Syrah, Merlot* 🍇 *Malvasia, Sauvignon Blanc, Chardonnay, Muscat, Viognier* 🍷 *red, white, rosé*

Macedonia

GREECE'S MOST IMPORTANT wine region has within its boundaries four OPAPs: **Amindeo**, **Côtes de Meliton**, **Goumenissa**, and **Naoussa**, and 21 *topikos oenos* (country wine) areas, each with its own unique mesoclimate. Generally Greece's most temperate region, with cold, rainy, sometimes snowy winters and pleasantly warm summers, Macedonia (Makedonía) has a reputation for producing the largest amount of – and some of the best – high-quality wine in Greece. It is in the mountainous areas of the region, towering

high above the peach-tree covered flatlands, that the native Nebbiolo-like red grape Xinomavro thrives at all altitudes to give dense, tannic, magnificently long-lived reds. White wines, especially from Sauvignon Blanc, draw supreme freshness of acidity and fruit from the varied Aegean and cooler climate influences, while the international varieties Cabernet Sauvignon, Syrah, and Merlot are also thriving at altitude in this part of Greece, giving stylish, fleshy, fruit-packed varietals and blends.

sandy clay 🍇 *Xinomavro, Negoska, Limnio, Cabernet Sauvignon, Syrah, Grenache, Merlot* 🍇 *Roditis, Assyrtiko, Athiri, Malagousia, Sauvignon Blanc* 🍷 *red, white, rosé, dessert*

Papantonis Winery, Peloponnese

Epirus

EPIRUS (ÍPEIROS), on the west coast opposite Corfu, is the smallest, least inhabited, and most rugged region of mainland Greece. Four fifths of its terrain is mountainous, with mostly calcareous soils, which yield concentrated, powerfully structured red wines and crisp, fruity whites. The climate changes as you move from east to west, though in general it is continental with cold winters and warm summers. The unusual green apple-scented Debina grape is cultivated around the region's single OPAP, **Zitsa**, for high-quality still and sparkling wine.

calcareous 🍇 *Cabernet Sauvignon, Merlot, Vlachikó, Bekiari* 🍇 *Debina, Chardonnay, Traminer* 🍷 *red, white, rosé, sparkling*

Thessaly

HERE, ON THE EASTERN SHORES of the mainland, vines are cultivated anywhere between sea level and 600m, from low-lying Anhialos to the slopes of Mount Olympus. Right across Thessaly (Thessalía), winters are cold with heavy rainfall and summers are extremely hot. The whites produced here can be pleasantly fresh and fruity, but it is the exquisite, full-bodied red wines, with their tobacco scent and velvet tannins, that are the region's real joy. Usually a blend of Xinomavro, Krassato, and Stavroto grapes, these benefit from both the influences of the Aegean and the cool water of the melted mountain ice-caps.

🗺 iron-rich schist underlaid with sandy clay 🍇 Xinomavro, Krassato, Stavroto, Cabernet Sauvignon, Merlot 🍇 Roditis, Savatiano, Batiki 🍷 red, white, rosé

Central Greece & Attica

ALTHOUGH, LIKE THRACE, THEY HAVE NO AO status vineyards, Central Greece and Attica (Attíkí) are hugely important. A significant proportion of Greek production originates here and has recently included a considerable quantity of world-class wine from Attica, Euboea, Boeotia, and Atalanti. Although Savatiano and Roditis are the only real indigenous grape survivors of a severe bout of phylloxera in the mid-20th century, key work is now being done with international grapes and native varieties transplanted from other areas. Warm, wet winters and oven-hot, dry summers give the wines plenty of concentration and flavour, and the varietal wines tend to display textbook characteristics.

🗺 calcareous, clay 🍇 Cabernet Sauvignon, Syrah, Merlot, Grenache 🍇 Savatiano, Roditis, Assyrtiko, Athiri, Chardonnay, Sauvignon Blanc 🍷 red, white, rosé

Pruning in a vineyard at Emborio, Santorini

Peloponnese

A HUGE AMOUNT OF Greek wine – much of it mass-produced – comes from this most southerly part of the mainland. Most of the high-quality grapes are from six appellations: OPAPs **Mantinia**, **Nemea**, and **Patras**, and OPEs **Muscat of Patras**, **Muscat of Rio of Patras**, and **Mavrodaphne of Patras**. The Peloponnese (Pelopónnisos) in general enjoys mild, rainy winters and hot, dry summers, but each area has a unique mesoclimate, and Mantinian winters can be exceptionally cold. Among the region's best wines are: crisp, lemony Roditis; firm, soft, succulent Savatianos; rose-scented, fruity Moschofileros; expansive, velvet-structured, full-bodied Aghiorghitikos; sturdy, penetrating, sweet Muscats; and magnificent, opulent, deep, sweet Mavrodaphnes.

🗺 deep clay, calcareous 🍇 Aghiorghitiko, Mavrodaphne, Cabernet Sauvignon, Merlot 🍇 Roditis, Moschofilero, Savatiano, White Muscat, Chardonnay 🍷 red, white, rosé, sparkling, dessert

The Cyclades Islands

THIS ISLAND GROUP (known as Kykládes in Greek) includes two main winegrowing islands, **Santorini** and **Páros**, both with AO status. Volcanic Santorini's half-moon shaped bay delivers a panorama of high, rolling terraces of coloured rock, and white cliffs plunging to the sea. Mild winters and warm, dry summers combine perfectly with the volcanic soil to give steely, fresh, mineral whites and intense, sternly backboned sweet *vin santos* (made from the Assyrtiko grape), the dessert wines that take their name from this vinously rich island. Growers protect against dry conditions by weaving their vines into basket shapes to trap moisture from the night air and shield grapes from the hot, gusting island winds.

Páros is another wind-blown island where vines find it difficult to survive. Growers here train their vines low along the ground to escape the damaging effects of the strong Aegean breezes. The ancient white grapes Monemvasia and Aidani are grown here, as well as the more widely known varieties Assyrtiko and Mandelaria – all at low altitude – making very pleasant, uncomplicated wine.

🗺 volcanic 🍇 Mandelaria, Mavrotragano 🍇 Assyrtiko, Monemvasia, Athiri, Aidani 🍷 red, white, rosé, dessert, fortified

Rhodes

The island of **Rhodes** (Ródos) benefits from the finest viticultural conditions in the Aegean, with mild winters and cool summers that bring out the best in the local grapes. Its 1,200ha of vines, on the eastern slopes of Mount Attavyros, are ideally positioned to obtain excellent yields and sturdy acidity from Athiri, the island's main variety. This results in fresh, fruit-crammed sparkling wines and crisp, refreshing, dry and off-dry whites. The finest reds are softly tannined, medium-bodied, creamily textured, and fruit-driven. Rhodes also makes good dessert wines – the honey and citrus White Muscats never

Vineyard near Argostólion, Cephalonia

fail on fine acidity and depth, and the firm-backboned reds from Mandelaria (known here as Amorghiano) have delicious raisin and citrus peel flavours.

🗻 calcareous 🍇 Mandelaria, Grenache, Syrah, Cabernet Sauvignon 🍇 Athiri, Muscat 🍷 red, white, rosé, sparkling, dessert

Cephalonia & the Ionian Islands

THE IONIAN ISLANDS (Iónioi Nísoi) of Cephalonia, Zákinthos, Corfu (Kérkyra), and Levkás all make wine, but **Cephalonia** (Kefallinía) – home of the firm, mellow, seductive Robola grape – is the main player. The native varieties Tsaoussi, Goustoulidi, Zakynthino, and Mavrodaphne are all important here too. Muscat (White Muscat) and Mavrodaphne have their own dessert wine appellations. Most grapes are grown at altitude – between 200 and 800m – in stony limestone soil, which gives the wines a clean-tasting acidity and steely backbone.

🗻 limestone 🍇 Mavrodaphne, Aghiorghitiko 🍇 Robola, Tsaoussi, Goustoulidi, Zakynthino, Muscat 🍷 red, white, rosé, dessert

Límnos, Sámos & the Aegean Islands

THE ONLY NORTHERN Aegean Island to produce wine of any consequence, **Límnos** has two AO designations, one for dry and one for dessert wines. Muscat d'Alexandrie is the grape most planted here, for enjoyable, floral-scented, mineral dry whites and excellent flowery, honey-flavoured dessert wines backed up with tasty acidity. Most of Límnos' 900ha of vines are at sea level, but some are as high

as 430m. The island's slightly acidic, volcanic soil yields gentle-tannined, round, approachable reds from the indigenous Limnio grape.

Winemaking on **Sámos**, further south, goes back about three millennia. Since the 17th century, Muscat Blanc à Petits Grains (now called Muscat of Sámos by many ampelographers) has been grown on steep terraces at up to 800m, making some of the world's most profound dessert wines. The climate allows this variety to produce magnificent, long-lived, heady, full-bodied dessert wines that metamorphose from honey-sweet youth into deep, complex, fresh fig and date-flavoured giants that can live for up to a century.

🗻 volcanic, calcareous 🍇 Limnio 🍇 Muscat d'Alexandrie, Muscat Blanc à Petits Grains 🍷 red, white, rosé, dessert

Crete

CRETE (Kríti) IS GREECE'S MOST SOUTHERLY point. Its mild, slightly rainy winters and baking hot summers are important to viticulture, but it is the mountain range stretching from east to west that plays the biggest part, providing altitude, protection from the warm Mediterranean currents, exposure to the cooling Aegean winds, and water from the melting ice caps in summer. The results are light, fruity, Vilana-based whites, and reds that range from soft, forward, and fruit-driven to the big, muscular, ripely concentrated Kotsifali-Mandelaria blends.

🗻 limestone 🍇 Kotsifali, Mandelaria, Liatiko 🍇 Vilana, Daphni, Plyto, Thrapsathiri, Athiri 🍷 red, white, rosé, dessert

TOP PRODUCERS OF GREECE

Boutari
Macedonia

Stenimachos, Naoussa ☏ *23320 41666* W *www.boutari.gr* ⬚

BOUTARI, ONE OF GREECE'S oldest producers, has seen massive expansion from its small roots in Naoussa. Now one of the largest players in Greece with an output of over 11 million litres annually, Boutari acquired the Attican producer Cambas in 1992. Although now publicly owned, it remains firmly under family control, and the quality of the *terroir*-driven wines is as consistently high as ever. Boutari boasts one of the largest arrays of indigenous and international grape varieties in Greece.

🍷 *red, white, rosé, dessert, retsina* 🍇 *2006, 2005, 2004, 2003, 2001, 2000, 1999, 1997, 1993, 1990* ★ *Domaine Seliadia, Naoussa Grande Reserve (red)*

Domaine Costa Lazaridi
Macedonia

Adriani, Drama ☏ *25210 82231* ⬚

AT THIS WINERY in Macedonia, both native and international varieties are used to make a dynamic range of varietals and blends, from fresh, pinpoint accurate whites to dense, long-lived, barrel-aged *cavas* (aged wines). For many years, Costa Lazaridi has been one of the region's most internationally respected names.

🍷 *red, white, rosé* 🍇 *2006, 2005, 2004, 2003, 2001, 2000, 1999* ★ *Château Julia Assyrtiko, Amethystos: White, Cava*

Tsantali's wine cellar

Domaine Gerovassiliou
Macedonia

Epanomi, Thessaloniki ☏ *22860 32466* W *www.gerovassiliou.gr* ⬚

EVANGELOS GEROVASSILIOU is one of the great pioneers of the Greek wine industry, and arguably the finest winemaker in Greece. Very skilled with both native and international varieties, he resurrected the long-forgotten white Mala-gousia grape together with the late Professor Logothetis. His wines are consistently excellent: elegant, stylish, and fresh. The beautifully concentrated, harmonious Syrah is superlative.

🍷 *red, white* 🍇 *2006, 2005, 2004, 2003, 2001, 2000* ★ *Syrah, Domaine Gerovassiliou*

Estate Biblia Chora
Macedonia

Kook Kinohori, Kavala ☏ *25920 44974* ⬚

FORMED BY MAESTRO winemaker Vassilis Tsaktsarlis and the legendary Gerovassiliou in 2001, this estate is the result of one of the most important partnerships in the modern Greek wine industry. Decades of expertise have had an immediate impact. Old World-style mineral whites and rosés with enchanting fresh acidity, and medium-

Estate Biblia Chora

bodied, gloriously scented, elegant reds add a flourish to this talent-filled estate.

🍷 *red, white, rosé* 🍇 *2006, 2005, 2004, 2003, 2001* ★ *Biblia Chora (red, white)*

Estate Kyr-Yanni
Macedonia

Yanakohori, Naoussa ☏ *23320 51100* ⬚

HIGH IN THE MOUNTAINS of Naoussa, Yiannis Boutari (of the Boutari clan) has won worldwide acclaim as the finest producer of the lean, tannic, acidic Xinomavro grape. He has managed to soften the wine from his old vines, giving it an unusually seductive body, without losing any of the leathery, tobacco, minty, medium-weight fruit characteristics of the grape. Diaporos, a Xinomavro-Syrah blend, has staggering depth and excellent ability to age.

🍷 *red, white, rosé* 🍇 *2006, 2005, 2004, 2003, 2001, 2000, 1999, 1997* ★ *Yianakohori, Ramnista, Diaporos*

Tsantali
Macedonia

Aghios Pavlos, Halkidiki ☏ *23990 76100* W *www.tsantali.gr* ⬚

THIS MASSIVE producer focuses mainly on northern and central Greece, but has interests scattered all over the country. It has an annual output of 23 million litres and an impressive range of wines, from the bottom-level easy-drinking Makedonikos and Thessalikos labels to some of the most hedonistic, powerful yet supple, long-lived Xinomavro-Krassato reds.

🍷 *red, white, rosé, dessert, retsina* 🍇 *2006, 2005, 2004, 2003, 2001, 2000, 1999, 1997, 1994, 1990* ★ *Rapsáni Reserve, Metoxi*

Domaine Evharis
Central Greece & Attica

Mourtiza, Megara 📞 22960 90346
Ⓦ *www.evharis.gr* ▢

THIS GRAND, VERY influential Attican estate is owned by entrepreneur Haris Antoniou and his partner Eva Boehme. This quality-driven pair cut no corners: a state-of-the-art winery and masterful use of oak mean world-class wines every vintage. The replanting of indigenous grapes has been successful, and the estate's delicate Merlot and Syrah are wrought in a fine Old World style.

🍷 *red, white, rosé, sparkling*
📅 *2006, 2005, 2004, 2003, 2001*
★ *Merlot, Syrah. Assyrtiko*

Domaine Vassiliou
Central Greece & Attica

26 Klm Av Lavriou, Koropi
📞 *21066 26870*
Ⓦ *vww.vassilioudomaine.gr* ▢

ONE OF ATTICA'S fastest-rising stars, George Vassiliou wins more competitions with every vintage. He makes fresh, complex Savatiano, Roditis, and Moschofilero whites and intense, brooding, solidly structured Aghiorghitiko wines from his new venture, Nemeion Estate, in Nemea, especially Igemon.

🍷 *red, white, rosé, retsina*
📅 *2006, 2005, 2004, 2003* ★ *Fumé, Mantinia, Nemea Reserve, Igemon*

Harlaftis
Central Greece & Attica

Leoforos Stamatas 11, Stamata Atticis, Attica 📞 *21062 19374*
Ⓦ *www.harlaftis.gr* ▢

PILOT DIOGENIS HARLAFTIS and his wife Adda restarted this family winery in Attica in 1979 and it is now run by their son Nikos. Harlaftis has expanded

Domaine Evharis at the foot of the Gerania Mountains

into the Peloponnese, and makes an excellent red from Aghiorghitiko – Argilos Ghi – a soft, heady wine that captures the region's unique *terroir* perfectly. From Attica, Château Harlaftis Cabernet Sauvignon, with its multitude of complex flavours elegantly wrapped in new oak, and some mouthwateringly oaked whites are very appealing.

🍷 *red, white, rosé*
📅 *2006, 2005, 2004, 2003, 2001*
★ *Château Harlaftis Cabernet Sauvignon, Argilos Ghi, Domaine Harlaftis Chardonnay*

Harlaftis

Achaia Clauss
Peloponnese

Petroto, Patras 📞 *26103 25051* ▢

BAVARIAN NOBLEMAN Gustav Clauss founded this beautiful estate in 1859. The story goes that he fell in love with one of his workers – Daphne – and, when she died having never learned of his feelings, he created the red Mavrodaphne grape in her memory. Though it is now widely grown, Achaia Clauss still makes some of the finest wine from this grape. The fragrant, complex, opulent, sweet Mavrodaphne Grand Reserve was casked in 1979 and only a small amount is bottled every year.

This huge producer also makes a vast range of other styles, sourcing native and international grapes from growers all over Greece.

🍷 *red, white, rosé, dessert, retsina*
📅 *2006, 2005, 2004, 2003, 1985, 1979* ★ *Château Clauss, Mavrodaphne Grand Reserve 1979*

Gaia Wines
Peloponnese

Themistokleous 22, Maroussi 📞 *21080 55642* ▢ *by appt*

SINCE ERUPTING onto the scene in 1994, winemakers Yiannis Paraskevopoulos and Leon Karatsalos have been two of the leading lights of the Greek wine export market. Zesty whites from Santorini and a popular range of Nemea reds (fruity Notios and intense Gaia Estate among them) are consistently excellent, bringing out the best in Greece's indigenous grape varieties. The Ritinitis Nobilis Retsina gives a modern, surprisingly likeable twist to this unusual style.

🍷 *red, white* 📅 *2006, 2005, 2004, 2003, 2001, 2000, 1999, 1998, 1997* ★ *Gaia Estate, Gaia S*

Papantonis Winery
Peloponnese

Kanari 48, Argos 📞 *27510 23620* Ⓦ *www.papantonis.gr* ▢ *by appt*

ANTHONY PAPANTONIS built this winery in 1993 for his 11-ha (now 30-year-old) vineyard, which became one of Greece's leading exponents of the Aghiorghitiko grape. Older vintages of his first wine, Meden Agan, are profoundly complex, yet rich and soft in style. The dessert wine Lysimelis, first created in 2002, also looks promising.

🖾 *white, red, dessert* 🔖 *2006, 2005, 2004, 2003, 2001, 2000, 1999, 1998, 1997* ★ *Meden Agan*

Tselepos
Peloponnese

14th Klm Tripolis-Kastri NR Rizes, Arcadias 🔲 *27105 44440* 🔲

DIJON-TRAINED winemaker Yiannis Tselepos is probably best known for his dense, concentrated, blockbuster Cabernet Sauvignon and Merlot. His wonderful dry, elegant, round, lemon-and-rose-scented Moschofilero whites also help to mark out this producer.

🖾 *white, rosé, red* 🔖 *2006, 2005, 2004, 2003, 2001, 2000* ★ *Mantinia, Moschofilero, Nemea Driopi Reserve, Cabernet-Merlot*

Hatzidakis
The Cyclades Islands

Pyrgos Kallistis, Santorini 🔲 *22860 32466* 🔲 *by appt*

IT MAY BE EARLY DAYS, but this young winemaker is one of Greece's brightest prospects. Assyrtiko, Aidini, and Athiri are Haridimos Hatzidaki's tools, and steely, minerally, finely-balanced dry whites and fruity, fresh-tasting *vin santos* are his speciality. He is also pioneering the recovery of long-forgotten red grape Mavrotragano, from which he makes firm, fruit-packed, beautifully scented wines.

🖾 *red, white, dessert* 🔖 *2007, 2006, 2005, 2004, 2003, 2001, 2000, 1999, 1997* ★ *Santorini, Santorini Barrel, Vin Santo*

Santo Wines
The Cyclades Islands

Pirgos, Santorini 🔲 *22860 22596* 🔲 *www.santowines.gr* 🔲

SINCE 1947 – long before today's clutch of exciting new winemakers came to Santorini – this large co-operative has been making delicately balanced, steely, mineral-lemon flavoured, but little known, Assyrtiko wines. It is still a quality producer, crafting sweet, firm, super-rich, spicy, dried-fruit-flavoured *vin santos* that can age for several years.

🖾 *red, white, rosé, dessert, retsina* 🔖 *2007, 2006, 2005, 2004, 2003, 2001, 2000, 1999* ★ *Santorini Nykteri, Vin Santo*

CAIR
Rhodes

2nd Klm Rhodes-Linaos 🔲 *22410 68770* 🔲 *www.cair.gr* 🔲

BY FAR THE LARGEST producer on Rhodes, this company refuses to let quantity interfere with quality. Every year, CAIR sets the standard for Rhodes' aromatic, fruit-driven, succulent Athiri white and sparkling wines. The tobacco-scented, opulently textured Cabernet-Grenache reds are firmly

CAIR label

backboned honey-sweet Muscats are excellent.

🖾 *red, white, rosé, sparkling, dessert, retsina* 🔖 *2006, 2005, 2004, 2003* ★ *Ródos 2400, Pathos White and Red, Rosé Réserve 10 Ans Brut*

Gentilini
Cephalonia & the Ionian Islands

PO Box 137, Minies, Cephalonia 🔲 *26710 41618* 🔲 *www.gentilini.gr* 🔲 *by appt*

SPIROS COSMETATOS founded Gentilini in 1984, and it was quickly acknowledged as one of Greece's most innovative wineries at that time. Spiros' daughter Marianna and son-in-law Petros Markantonatos took over in 2002, and Gentilini goes from strength to strength, making far and away the best Robola, mineral whites, and complex, *terroir*-focused reds.

🖾 *red, white, rosé* 🔖 *2007, 2006, 2005, 2004, 2003* ★ *Robola of Cephalonia, Syrah*

Sámos Co-operative
Limnos, Sámos & the Aegean Islands

Union of Vinicultural Co-operatives of Sámos, Malagari, Sámos 🔲 *22730 27381* 🔲 *www.samoswine.gr* 🔲

WINE HAS BEEN MADE on Sámos for thousands of years but, although there are many growers supplying grapes, this is now the only licensed commercial producer on the island. Muscat Blanc à Petits Grains is the only variety used here, and although dry wines are produced, the aromatic, heroically structured, complex, date-fig-raisin flavoured dessert wines are the real glory. These can age for a staggering 80 or 90 years.

🖾 *white, dessert* 🔖 *2005, 2004, 2003, 2001, 2000, 1999, 1997, 1995, 1990, 1975* ★ *Sámos: Nectar, Anthemis, Vin Doux Naturel Grand Cru*

WINE MAP OF LEBANON, ISRAEL & TURKEY

CLUSTERED AROUND THE EASTERN SHORES of the Mediterranean are three nations that, despite their cultural and religious differences, all share a historical attachment to wine. Vines have been cultivated in Lebanon, Israel, and Turkey for centuries, and as modern practices penetrate these areas, the wines are becoming increasingly accessible to the world market. The growing conditions in these countries could not be more diverse; from the cooler northern areas of Turkey to the near desert-like Negev in Israel, high quality wines are now showing what the unique *terroirs* of Southeastern Europe have to offer.

KEY

Lebanon, Israel & Turkey

Harvesting grapes at Château Ksara in Lebanon

PERFECT CASE: LEBANON, ISRAEL & TURKEY

- **R** Château Clos St Thomas Château St Thomas ££
- **R** Château Kefraya ££
- **R** Château Kefraya Comte de M £££
- **W** Château Ksara Chardonnay ££
- **R** Château Musar ££
- **R** Château Musar Hochar Père et Fils ££
- **W** Dalton Winery Reserve Sauvignon Blanc ££
- **R** Doluca Karma Merlot/ Bogazkere ££
- **R** Domaine du Castel Grand Vin £££
- **O** Golan Heights Winery Yarden Heights Wine ££
- **R** Golan Heights Winery Yarden Syrah £££
- **R** Kavaklidere Egeo Syrah £££

LEBANON, ISRAEL & TURKEY: AREAS & TOP PRODUCERS

LEBANON *p434*
Château Clos St Thomas *p436*
Château Kefraya *p436*
Château Ksara *p436*
Château Musar *p436*
Domaine Wardy *p436*
Massaya *p436*

ISRAEL *p434*
Amphorae Vineyard *p437*
Barkan Wine Cellars *p437*
Carmel *p437*
Dalton Winery *p437*
Domaine du Castel *p437*
Galil Mountain Winery *p437*
Golan Heights Winery *p438*
Recanati Winery *p438*

TURKEY *p435*
Doluca *p438*
Kavaklidere *p438*

Château Musar label, Lebanon

Sorting grapes at Kavaklidere's winery in Turkey

TERROIR AT A GLANCE

Latitude: 31.5–42°N.

Altitude: 0–1,250m.

Topography: Lebanon is dominated by the Bekaa Valley at a height of around 900m. In Israel there are coastal plains, central hills, the Great Rift Valley, and the Negev Desert, and in Turkey, a high central plateau, narrow coastal plain, and several mountain ranges.

Soil: No dominant soil type.

Climate: Mediterranean with hot dry summers and cooler rainy winters, except at higher altitudes where it can be much colder.

Vineyards situated inland are subjected to much harsher winters.

Temperature: July average in the wine regions of Lebanon and Israel is 26°C. Summer averages range from 25 to 40°C in Turkey.

Rainfall: Annual average is 600–650mm in Lebanon and Israel, higher in Turkey.

Wind: Coastal regions are heavily influenced by warm and cool sea breezes.

Viticultural hazards: Violent storms; flooding; drought.

Domaine Wardy's red wines from Lebanon

Domaine du Castel vineyard in the Judean Hills, Israel

Women harvesting grapes at Château Ksara in Lebanon

WINEGROWING AREAS OF LEBANON, ISRAEL & TURKEY

Lebanon

ONE OF THE OLDEST winemaking countries in the world, Lebanon is strongly influenced by the Old World – which is hardly surprising given its historical links with France. The seven million bottles of wine that come from Lebanon's tiny viticultural area each year are made by just 16 producers. French varieties reign supreme, and the outstanding quality of the wines has been recognized for decades.

The **Bekaa Valley** is Lebanon's only winegrowing region, and it could well be the place where wine was first made. The Phoenicians made and exported their wine from this historical land over 3,000 years ago. There is even evidence of winemaking at Bekaa's ancient archaeological site Baalbek, where the impressive 2,000-year-old Roman ruins include a temple to Bacchus, the Roman god of wine. The Bekaa Valley stretches from the Lebanon Mountains around 30km east of Beirut (Beyrouth) to the Anti-Lebanon Mountains some 120km further east. The combination of soil, altitude (900 to 1,100m), and plenty of sunshine gives the wines freshness without loss of concentration, so that balance and elegance can be achieved. These are perfect conditions for producing fresh-tasting, fruity white wines with excellent acidity – and opulent, dense, elegant, roundly structured, concentrated reds, some of which are admired worldwide.

Massaya label, Lebanon

🏞 gravel, clay, chalk, limestone 🍇 Cinsaut, Carignan, Cabernet Sauvignon, Merlot, Syrah 🍇 Chardonnay, Sauvignon Blanc, Clairette, Merwah, Obaideh 🍷 red, white, rosé, dessert, fortified

Israel

AS ISRAEL'S NATIVE GRAPE VARIETIES are sadly long gone, this country now relies solely on international varieties. Californian influences have given Israel's wines a distinct and appealing New World feel, which contrasts wonderfully with the Old World winemaking styles of Lebanon.

Extending south from the border with Lebanon, **Galilee** (Tiberias) is the most important Israeli wine region in terms of quality. It contains the viticultural districts of Lower Galilee, Upper Galilee, Golan Heights (Israel's coldest region), and Tabor. The northernmost vineyards of the Golan Heights are up to 1,200m above sea level, while in Upper Galilee they reach around 700m.

Snow is common on the upper reaches of Galilee during winter, and summer heat is tempered by cool breezes from Mount Herman. This, combined with long periods of sunshine, gives the wines a sheer concentration of fruit which is difficult to find anywhere else in the country. Cabernet Sauvignon, Merlot, Syrah, Chardonnay, Sauvignon Blanc, and Muscat are the varieties that benefit most from the exquisite growing conditions of Galilee.

To the south, on the Mediterranean coastal

plain, **Samaria** (Shomron) is Israel's largest wine region. The typically Mediterranean climate gives the best wines suppleness and an intense aromatic quality. Chardonnay and Sauvignon Blanc are the main white grapes here; Cabernet Sauvignon and Merlot are the dominant reds. These varieties reappear further south in the area of **Samson** (Shimshon), where the white wines tend to be full-bodied and intensely fruity, and the reds are big, dense, and robust.

Moving inland, the **Judean Hills** (Harey Yehuda) are still relatively undeveloped and consist of small clusters of vineyards that lie just north of Jerusalem. Vines are grown mainly on terraces or in narrow valleys on thin, limey, stony ground, which results in some exceptionally fine examples of Old World-style winemaking. Burgundy-like whites and Bordeaux-style reds characterize the best of this region's wines.

🖊 *clay, limestone, calcite alluvium, sandstone*
🍇 *Cabernet Sauvignon, Merlot, Pinot Noir, Cabernet Franc, Sangiovese, Syrah* 🍇 *Chardonnay, Sauvignon Blanc, Gewürztraminer, Muscat, Riesling*
🍷 *red, white, rosé, sparkling, dessert, fortified*

Turkey

ALTHOUGH THIS REGION HAS A LONG history of winemaking, very few of the grapes grown here today are used for wine. Around 60 of the official 1,250 grapes are used commercially, with native varieties concentrated in the east and international varieties in the west. Wines are becoming more modern, though still retaining local character.

Bordering Greece and Bulgaria is the region of **Thrace and Marmara**, which forms the heart of Turkey's wine industry with some 40 per cent of production. The region's hot, humid, sunny summers and freezing cold winters lead to lightish wines from a wide range of grapes. The best are fresh-tasting, with good balance and acidity.

Further east is Turkey's 1,700km stretch of lush **Black Sea** coast. The native red grapes Boğazkere and Öküzgözü dominate, giving sturdy, attractive, fruity reds, while Narince and Kabarcik make surprisingly well-structured whites. **Central Anatolia**'s plateau of vineyards suffers severe temper-

ANCIENT ORIGINS OF WINE

According to the Bible, winemaking began in the foothills of the Caucasus Mountains, between the Black and Caspian seas. It is here that Noah's Ark is said to have settled when the floods subsided, and where Noah supposedly became the first man to plant vines.

Evidence of ancient viticulture in the region suggests that there may be some truth in this story. Until 5600 BC, the Black Sea was a small lake surrounded by lush, rich land which, according to ancient texts, sustained many different peoples. Then the sea level rose considerably and the Mediterranean broke over the strip of land bounding the lake, flooding it with salt water to form the Black Sea. It is thought that the survivors of this flood fled into Europe, the Ukraine, and Anatolia, taking their viticultural knowledge with them. The reason many cultures use a similar word for wine may be that it originated from this one lakeside, thousands of years ago.

ature extremes, yet manages to produce 28 per cent of the country's wine, especially from native varieties including Narince and Kalecik Karasi.

On an arid plain at 600m, **Southeastern Anatolia** sees temperatures soar to 46°C in summer and fall to a numbing -11°C in winter. Reds from the Boğazkere grape respond best to these conditions. Darkly tannic, robust, and full-bodied, these are often given a little more elegance with the addition of the fruitier, more delicate Öküzgözü.

🖊 *loam, clay, sand* 🍇 *Boğazkere, Öküzgözü, Papazkarasi, Kalecik Karasi* 🍇 *Narince, Sémillon*
🍷 *red, white, rosé, fortified*

Vineyard overlooking the Sea of Galilee in Israel

TOP PRODUCERS OF LEBANON, ISRAEL & TURKEY

Château Clos St Thomas
Lebanon/Bekaa Valley

Kab-Elics, Main St, Bekaa Valley 📞 *08 500 814* 🌐 *www.closstthomas.com* ⬜

ONE OF THE Bekaa Valley's new estates, this exciting family-run venture planted its first vines (all French varieties) in 1993 and sold its first vintage in 1998. The wines are the most New World in style of all Bekaa wines, although this does not detract from their reflection of the all-important *terroir*. The white wines are terrifically clean and balanced, with tasty acidity. The harmonious, hedonistically scented, soft, velvety reds – the best example of which is called Château St Thomas – are world-class.
🟥 *red, white, rosé* 📅 *2006, 2003, 2002, 2001, 2000* ★ *Les Gourmets Blanc, Les Emirs, Château St Thomas*

Château Kefraya
Lebanon/Bekaa Valley

Zahlé 📞 *08 645 333* 🌐 *www.chateaukefraya.com* ⬜

FRENCH STYLE merges with rich Bekaa *terroir* at this world-class estate. A survivor of the vicious civil war, Kefraya originally sold grapes from its now 50-year-old vines to Château Musar. Since 1979, it has been making its own magnificent wines under the direction of Michel de Bustros. White dessert wines are crisp, fruit-led, and pleasantly honeyed; red masterpieces such as Comte de M are complex, beautifully weighted, monumentally concentrated, and simply blossom with elegance and finesse as they age.
🟥 *red, white, rosé, dessert* 📅 *2006, 2003, 2002, 2001, 2000, 1999, 1998, 1997, 1996, 1995, 1994, 1993* ★ *Le Château Kefraya Blanc de Blancs, Château Kefraya, Comte de M*

Château Ksara
Lebanon/Bekaa Valley

Charles Malek Av, Nakhle Hanna Bldg 📞 *01 200 715* 🌐 *www.ksara.com.lb* ⬜

THIS OLD ESTATE, built on the site of a crusade fortress (ksar), is steeped in history. It was acquired by the Jesuit Fathers in 1857, who continued the winemaking tradition of the property until they had to sell up on the orders of the Vatican. They also maintained the Roman tunnels that are still used as natural cellars. Today, the winemaking is distinctly Old World – the zesty, adroitly oaked Chardonnay epitomizes the skilful winemaking, and the best reds rival the finest bordeaux.
🟥 *red, white, rosé, dessert* 📅 *2006, 2003, 2002, 2001, 2000, 1999, 1998, 1997, 1996, 1995, 1994, 1993* ★ *Chardonnay, Château Ksara, Cabernet Sauvignon*

Château Musar
Lebanon/Bekaa Valley

Baroudy St, Sopenco Bldg, Beirut 📞 *01 328 111* 🌐 *www.chateaumusar.com.lb* ⬜

IT IS THE ETHOS and sheer imagination of Serge Hochar that single out his wines for so much world acclaim. Rarely will the first wine, Château Musar – a blend of Cabernet Sauvignon, Cinsaut, and Carignan – be the same from one vintage to the next. Some years Cabernet will dominate, giving the wine a deep, Médoc-like quality, while in others Cinsaut may prevail to give it an air of the Rhône. It is one of the most interesting and individual wines of all time.
🟥 *red, white, rosé* 📅 *2006, 2003, 2002, 2001, 2000, 1999, 1998, 1997, 1996, 1995, 1994, 1993*

★ *Château Musar (red, white), Hochar Père et Fils*

Domaine Wardy
Lebanon/Bekaa Valley

Cité Industrielle, Zahlé, Bekaa Valley 📞 *08 930 141* 🌐 *www.domaine-wardy.com* ⬜

THIS ESTATE launched its first commercial vintage in 1997, although the parent company (Solifed) has a history, under various names, of producing arak spirit from its own vines since 1893. Owner Salim Wardy continues to plant vines – mostly noble varieties – but the estate crops from vines planted as far back as 1989. The white wines are crisp, fruity, and easy-drinking; the reds are well made and medium-weight, and the finest examples, like the Château Les Cèdres, have plenty of complexity, perfect balance, good fruit, and a pleasingly firm, round structure.
🟥 *red, white, rosé* 📅 *2006, 2003, 2002, 2001, 2000, 1999* ★ *Wardy Clos Blanc, Château Les Cèdres, Cabernet Sauvignon*

Massaya
Lebanon/Bekaa Valley

Tanail Property, Bekaa Valley 📞 *08 510 135* 🌐 *www.massaya.com* ⬜

MASSAYA IS A promising four-way Franco-Lebanese venture that began in 1998, and involves a number of prestigious French châteaux. The Bekaa's unique *terroir* has been impeccably imprinted on the noble variety wines; the whites have an attractive, easy-drinking feminine side, and the chunky, masculine, long-lived reds are jam-packed with fruit.
🟥 *red, white, rosé* 📅 *2006, 2003, 2002, 2001, 2000* ★ *Silver Selection (red, white), Gold Reserve*

Amphorae Vineyard
Israel/Galilee

3 Hasadnaot St, Herzlia 📞 *04 984 0702* 🌐 *www.amphorae-v.com* 🔲

TUCKED AWAY in the heart of the Carmel Mountains, but not far from Haifa and the Mediterranean, this new winery produces dense, heavyweight, firmly tannined reds that seem to draw the best characteristics of Galilee and neighbouring Samaria. Already world-class, these wines have the potential to age extremely well.

🍷 *red, white* 📅 *2005, 2003, 2002, 2001* ★ *Chardonnay, Merlot, Cabernet Sauvignon*

Barkan Wine Cellars
Israel/Samson

Kibbutz Hulda, DN Sorek 📞 *03 936 4520* 🌐 *www.barkan-winery.co.il* 🔲

ONE OF ISRAEL'S largest estates, Barkan was established as a private company in 1990, but in 1994 issued 25 per cent of its corporate shares to the public. A brand new winery was built in Kibbutz Hulda in the Samson region in 1999 where Barkan now makes excellent modern-style wines that tend to be big, intense, and robust. There are also some excellent wines bottled under the Segal label.

🍷 *red, white, rosé, dessert* 📅 *2005, 2003, 2002, 2001, 2000, 1999, 1998, 1997, 1996, 1995, 1994, 1993* ★ *Segal Dry White Wine, Barkan Reserve Merlot*

Carmel
Israel/Samson

25 Hacarmel St, Rishon Le Zion 📞 *03 948 8851* 🌐 *www.carmel-winery.co.uk* 🔲

CARMEL IS ONE of the largest producers and exporters of wine in Israel. Also one of the oldest, it was founded in 1882 by Baron Edmond de Rothschild, and has been part of the turbulent history of the modern Israeli wine industry. The wines are well made and New World in style, with grapes sourced from Israel's best areas, including Galilee. The Private Collection Chardonnay and Cabernet Sauvignon are particularly good. Both are full-bodied and masculine, firmly structured with plenty of concentration and tonnes of fruit.

Carmel

🍷 *red, white, sparkling, dessert, fortified* 📅 *2005, 2003, 2002, 2001, 2000, 1999, 1998, 1997, 1996, 1995, 1994, 1993* ★ *Private Collection: Chardonnay, Cabernet Sauvignon*

Dalton Winery
Israel/Galilee

52 Bezalel St, Ramat Gan 📞 *03 751 8922* 🌐 *www.dalton-winery.com* 🔲

THIS SMALL, family-owned concern is being hailed as one of Israel's rising stars – and rightly so. Located in Upper Galilee at an altitude of 850m, Dalton grows Sauvignon Blanc, Cabernet Sauvignon, Merlot, Shiraz, and Chardonnay. The emphasis is on complexity and elegance in the wines, but careful winemaking also retains the wonderful power and concentration of fruit found in this region. The medium-bodied, intensely fruity, beautifully balanced Sauvignon Blanc and the rich, full-bodied, densely packed Reserve Cabernet Sauvignon are this producer's best wines.

🍷 *red, white* 📅 *2005, 2003, 2002, 2001, 2000, 1999, 1998, 1997, 1996, 1995* ★ *Reserve: Sauvignon Blanc, Cabernet Sauvignon, Merlot*

Domaine du Castel
Israel/Judean Hills

Ramat Raziel 📞 *02 534 2249* 🌐 *www.castel.co.il* 🔲

WHEN ELI BEN ZAKEN founded this family-owned winery in the Judean Hills, he brought with him a philosophy of winemaking that stands out as unique in Israel. His aged *(sur lie)* Chardonnay could easily be mistaken for a fine burgundy, and his elegant, subtle, stylish reds, for some of the best that Bordeaux has to offer. In a country where wines are mostly New World-style, Ben Zaken's love of the Old World makes Castel's wines truly unique, while his skill in both the vineyard and the winery sets him apart as one of Israel's finest individual winemakers.

🍷 *red, white* 📅 *2005, 2003, 2002, 2001, 2000, 1999, 1998, 1997, 1996, 1995, 1994, 1993* ★ *Castel C Blanc du Castel Chardonnay, Petit Castel Red, Castel Grand Vin*

Galil Mountain Winery
Israel/Galilee

Kibbutz Yiron, MP Merom Galil 📞 *04 686 8740* 🌐 *www.galilmountain.co.il* 🔲

THIS IS AN EXCITING new joint venture in the Upper Galilee between the large Golan

Domaine du Castel vineyard

Heights Winery and the co-operative Kibbutz Yiron. New plantings of Cabernet Sauvignon, Merlot, Pinot Noir, and Chardonnay in the Kadesh Valley area, near the Lebanese border, supplement the older vine-yards that have been making complex, intensely fruity wines since the 1980s. The Yiron red, hedonistically tobacco-scented, elegantly full-bodied, and intensely concentrated, has all the hallmarks of the region.

🎞 *red, white* 📷 *2005, 2003, 2002*
★ *Yiron*

Golan Heights Winery
Israel/Galilee

Katzrin 📞 *04 696 8400*
🔲 *www.golanwines.co.il* 🔲

THIS MODERN WINERY, founded in 1983, is situated in the town of Katzrin, high in the Golan Heights. Vines have been planted here since 1976, but the grapes were originally sold on to large coastal co-ops. In 1982, local experimental wine-making by four kibbutzim (collective farms) and four *moshavs* (co-operative farms) produced excellent results, prompting all eight to team up and build what is now the region's most important, and largest, winemaking facility. Expertise, chiefly from California, gives their intense, weighty, fruit-packed wines – all from international grapes – a definite Californian slant. This world-class producer is now winning many awards at prestigious competitions and shows around the world. Yarden is the flagship brand.

🎞 *white, sparkling, dessert*
📷 *2005, 2003, 2002, 2001, 2000, 1999, 1998, 1997, 1996, 1995, 1994, 1993* ★ *Yarden Syrah, Yarden Cabernet Sauvignon, Yarden Heights Wine*

Galil Mountain Winery label

Recanati Winery
Israel/Samaria

Industrial Zone Emek Hefer
📞 *04 622 2288*
🔲 *www.recanati-winery.com* 🔲

RECANATI WINERY is in the Samaria region, but sources most of its Merlot, Cabernet Sauvignon, and Chardonnay grapes from high-altitude vineyards in the Upper Galilee and the mountains around Jerusalem. Recanati is the only producer left in Israel that hand-harvests all its grapes. Most of the emphasis is on red wines, which tend to be modern and New World-style – elegant, supple, and round – and develop great complexity over time. The one to try is the superbly balanced, elegant, gloriously complex Reserve Merlot.

🎞 *red, white* 📷 *2005, 2003, 2002*
★ *Cabernet Sauvignon, Reserve Merlot*

Doluca
Turkey/Thrace & Marmara

Halkali Caddesi 218 Sefakoy, Istanbul 📞 *0212 698 9830*
🔲 *www.doluca.com* 🔲

THIS IS ONE of the truly 'old-school' private producers in Turkey, which dates back to the 1920s. Though based in the northeast near Istanbul, Doluca creates interesting blends from indigenous grapes sourced from across Turkey. Doluca also produces wine from international varieties,

blended with local grapes under the Karma label. For international varietal wines they have created a completely separate label called Sarafin. Reliable, interesting, and enjoyable are the lasting impressions of Doluca's wines.

🎞 *red, white, rosé, sparkling*
📷 *2007, 2006, 2005* ★ *Karma Merlot/Boğazkere, Sigium, Kav Narince*

Kavaklidere
Turkey/Central Anatolia

Akyurt, Ankara 📞 *0312 847 5073*
🔲 *www.kavaklidere.com* 🔲

ESTABLISHED IN 1929 by the Austrian-trained winemaker Cenap And, this is one of the oldest privately owned producers in Turkey, and the largest. Kavaklidere focuses strongly on indigenous varieties based on its philosophy of "Anatolian grapes from Anatolia". It has had a partnership with a French company since 2005 to improve vineyard management and winemaking, and has launched a range called Egeo based on French grapes. The quality is consistently high across the company's wide range of labels.

🎞 *red, white, rosé, sparkling, fortified* 📷 *2007, 2006, 2005*
★ *Egeo Syrah, Vin-Art Narince/ Chardonnay, Vin-Art Syrah/Kalecik Karasi, Ancyra Öküzgözü*

CYPRUS: AN ISLAND TRANSFORMED

Cyprus may be better known for its tourist beaches than for its wines, but grape growing here is pretty much unique in Europe. Its island status, strict quarantine, and sunny dry climate mean the island is phylloxera-free, with lots of venerable and naturally low-yielding vines growing on their own roots. The location of vineyards at altitude on the slopes of the Troodos Mountains mitigates the summer heat, bringing cooler nights and protecting fruit flavours and acid levels. Indeed, one of the island's best producers, Kyperounda, has measured its vineyards to over 1,480m, possibly the highest in Europe.

The island has a long history in wine, with archaeological finds dating back to around 3500 BC, and it also claims the oldest named wine still in production – the sweet, golden-brown Commandaria, made from sun-dried grapes. The industry has changed dramatically in the last few years, not least due to the effect of joining the EU in 2004. This brought a sudden end to the heavily subsidised, low-quality bulk exports that the four biggest producers had relied on.

Today, vineyards cover around 15,000ha, with more than 50 registered wineries. There is a new emphasis on quality and pride in local production, and several wineries are now producing genuinely exciting wines. The big four of SODAP, Loel, Etko, and Keo have also all changed direction, investing in wineries in the mountains close to the vineyards and bringing in consultants to help them produce a new generation of wines.

Wines to Try

Ayia Mavri Muscat, Rosé
 W www.ayiamavri.com
Domaine Hadjiantonas
 Chardonnay
 W www.hadjiantonas.com.cy
Kyperounda Petritis, Chardonnay
 W www.pp-group.com.cy
Olympus Winery Shiraz
 W www.etkowines.com
SODAP St Barnabas
 Commandaria, Island Vines
 W www.sodap.com.cy
Tsiakkas Cabernet Sauvignon,
 Xynisteri
Vasa Maratheftiko, St Timon
 W www.vasawinery.com
Vlassides Shiraz, Xynisteri,
 Maratheftiko
 W www.cyprusvines.com
Zambartas Lefkada/Cabernet
 Franc Rosé, Xynisteri

More information about the island's wines can be found at:
 W www.cypruswineries.org

Early spring flowers in a Cypriot vineyard

Grapes on Cyprus

Production is still dominated by two local varieties: the nondescript black Mavro and the white Xynisteri. The latter has real potential for attractive whites, if grown at altitude to protect its subtle flavours and acidity, or blended with small amounts of Sémillon or even Sauvignon (try Vlassides, Tsiakkas, Zambartas or Aes Ambelis). There are also successful examples with partial barrel fermentation, such as Kyperounda's impressive Petritis. International varieties have been on the island for several decades, and Mediterranean grapes such as Syrah/Shiraz are particularly well suited to the island's climate. Of the other local varieties, Maratheftiko has the greatest potential to be the island's 'signature'. Wines made from this distinctive, deep-coloured grape are definitely improving, though there is still a steep learning curve to be tackled in how best to grow and vinify it.

SOUTH AFRICA

SOUTH AFRICA

THE BREATHTAKINGLY BEAUTIFUL *Cape winelands are spread over a relatively small area, but the diversity of the winegrowing sites ensures that the country can produce an extensive range of wines to excite the tastebuds of wine lovers the world over.*

BACKGROUND

IT IS SOMEWHAT IRONIC that South Africa is known as one of the New World wine countries, as winegrowing here is anything but 'new'. The first vines were planted in the Cape of Good Hope by Commander Jan van Riebeeck of the Dutch East India Company as long ago as 1655. Although van Riebeeck was the first to make wine in South Africa, Simon van der Stel was the founder of winegrowing in both Stellenbosch (in 1679) and Constantia (in 1685). He is viewed as establishing South Africa as a successful wine-growing country, and is also responsible for creating Constantia's world-famous dessert wine (*see* Vin de Constance, *p456*), which became renowned as far away as Holland by 1698.

Chenin Blanc grapes

However, the country's wine business subsequently suffered many setbacks. The industry floundered when the UK – South Africa's main importer – dropped protective tariffs on French wines in the 1860s, making them cheaper than the South African wines. The spread of phylloxera in 1885 then destroyed many vines. This was followed by the problem of over-production in the early 20th century, when a wine farmer's success was associated with high yields. By 1918, almost 87 million vines had been planted by independent farmers, creating some 56 million litres of wine – most of which was un-saleable. A giant ruling co-op, the Koöperatiewe Wijnbouwers Vereniging (KWV), was consequently formed, with government backing, to control sales and stabilize prices. A quota system was introduced in 1957, which limited attempts to plant vines in new places, and the KWV quarantine system strictly dictated which new vine material could be imported. This limited producers' growing options, and failed to take into account the quality of the wine being made. The final blow to the Cape wine industry was the introduction of international trade sanctions in the 1980s as a protest against the apartheid regime.

Vergelegen's winery in the prime winegrowing area of Stellenbosch

◁ **Dramatic aerial view of Constantia Ward**

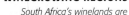

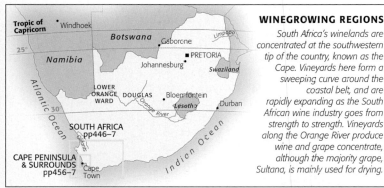

WINEGROWING REGIONS

South Africa's winelands are concentrated at the southwestern tip of the country, known as the Cape. Vineyards here form a sweeping curve around the coastal belt, and are rapidly expanding as the South African wine industry goes from strength to strength. Vineyards along the Orange River produce wine and grape concentrate, although the majority grape, Sultana, is mainly used for drying.

THE WINE INDUSTRY TODAY

THE SITUATION HAS CHANGED dramatically since the end of apartheid, with South Africa's re-entry into world markets *(see pp444–5)* in the 1990s and with the KWV relinquishing its regulatory role in 1997. South Africa is now the world's ninth largest wine producer. The co-operative movement still produces the bulk of the annual crop (just under 80 per cent). However, more and more independent, quality-driven producers are now setting up here, and the country competes and wins at the highest level, whether at international wine shows or in the crucial race for winelovers' wallets.

Rupert & Rothschild Vignerons, Paarl District

GRAPE VARIETIES & WINE STYLES

CHENIN BLANC IS South Africa's most widely grown grape variety. Though mainly important in the past for the production of brandy, it still retains dominance in the vineyards. However, many better, often international, varieties have been replacing less suitable ones since the end of the quota system in 1992. The top seven varieties after Chenin Blanc are now Cabernet Sauvignon, Colombard (another key brandy variety), Shiraz, Chardonnay, Sauvignon Blanc, Merlot, and Pinotage (South Africa's own grape; *see p451*). The emerging importance of reds is another significant change: up from 15.5 per cent of total vineyard area in 1990 to 44.2 per cent in 2007. Smaller, often experimental, areas of French, Spanish, Portuguese, and Italian varieties are also broadening the scope of South African wines. Styles now cover the spectrum from sparkling to fortified, and from big and showy to more refined and elegant. A definitive South African style has yet to emerge, though. Like the country itself, the wines are often described as being halfway between the Old World and the New: with the structure and restraint of the former and the fruit intensity of the latter. As the many new, *terroir*-focused vineyards mature, and winemakers gain more understanding of the harvest, the sense of place in their wines will surely increase.

SOUTH AFRICA'S TURNING POINT

Hardly any aspect *of South Africa's wine industry has remained untouched by the events that have unfolded in the country since the end of apartheid in 1990. On 2nd February of that year, a speech given by the then President F W de Klerk began the dismantling of this repressive regime, and simultaneously laid the foundations for the re-opening and success of the Cape's wine industry.*

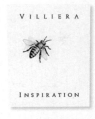

Modern Villiera label

Thriving Glen Carlou vineyards, Paarl District

Nelson Mandela's Role

Nelson Mandela's release from prison followed nine days after F W de Klerk's historic speech; and South Africa's first democratic elections were then held in 1994. Mandela's support for South African wines formed the necessary political stepping stone for the true re-emergence of Cape wine onto the international scene. Mandela also toasted his 1993 Nobel Peace Prize with Cape wine.

The Wind of Change

A tremendous increase in the number of South African private cellars as well as the KWV's *(see p442)* transformation from co-op to private company means that both competition and quality in wine have increased dramatically. Export figures alone tell the transition story. In 1991, South Africa's wine exports totalled 23 million litres; by mid-2008 that figure had escalated to over 363 million litres, ahead of projected figures. The weaker rand currency

Mzokhona Mvemve, Stellenbosch graduate

and a far wider geographic export base both played roles in this impressive growth, as well as the marketing skills of organizations such as Wines of South Africa (WOSA).

Empowerment Initiatives

Real success within the South African wine industry will only come about when open minds and racial equality reign on every level. While the Black Association of the Wine and Spirits Industry (BAWSI) work firmly towards this objective, individuals are also making a difference. Among other schemes, wine farmers, such as Charles Back of Fairview *(see p464)*, are assisting their workers to buy their own houses and to set up their own wine operations. Some companies are also offering scholarships to enable young black South Africans to study viticulture and oenology at Stellenbosch University, such as Mzokhona Mvemve – the first black Stellenbosch graduate in this field, in 2001.

New Developments

Since the quota system *(see p442)* was scrapped in 1992, the search for cooler, quality vineyard sites has taken entre-preneurs right to the tip of Africa and even to elevations on the snowline. Between 1992 and 2007, the five classic varieties (Shiraz, Cabernet Sauvignon, Merlot, Chardonnay, and Sauvignon Blanc) have increased their share of the total vineyard area from 10.5 to 45.9 per cent. Quality varieties from other areas, especially the Rhône Valley, are also putting down roots in Cape soil. Vineyards and viticulturists, including foreign consultants, have taken on new importance since apartheid ended. There is now a better understanding of *terroir*, and of managing vines and irrigation to produce better fruit.

Exchange visits between local and foreign winemakers have also led to many new ideas being trialled in Cape cellars – among them techniques such as micro-oxygenation and finishing fermentation of red wines in small oak barrels. In recent years, cellars such as Tokara, Morgenster Estate, and Quoin Rock have become increasingly high-tech.

With the knowledge gained in the past decade, some winemakers now have the confidence to return to more traditional methods. For instance, techniques like fermenting in large open wooden vats, creating wines naturally without adding yeast, and leaving them as untouched as possible, with no fining or filtration, are once again becoming more commonplace.

Oak barrels at Vergelegen in Stellenbosch

Château Pichon-Lalande, which has acquired Stellenbosch vineyard Glenelly; and Chablis's Michel Laroche, who now owns the Stellenbosch property L'Avenir. Foreign investors bring new ideas and increase exports through native country contacts.

Foreign Investment

OF THE DRINK INDUSTRY'S worldwide giants, only Constellation and Pernod-Ricard have been attracted to invest in South Africa, but many individuals from around the globe have become involved in the country's progressive wine industry since 1990. Some have set up joint ventures, such as husband-and-wife team Phil Freese (viticulturist) and Zelma Long (highly-regarded US winemaker). Others have bought wineries outright, like Anne Cointreau, a member of the famous Cointreau family, who owns Morgenhof winery in Stellenbosch; the French company

The Wines

THE BENEFITS of vastly improved vineyard sites, better management techniques, and South African winemakers' broader experience are evident in the wines currently on the market. Winemakers are learning to take a more hands off approach, letting the wines express their specific vineyard origins. Varietal wines remain consumer favourites, although blends are now becoming more popular, with quality white blends receiving much positive attention. Stylish packaging, contemporary label design, and new non-cork closures all reflect South Africa's coming of age in the current international marketplace.

Harvesting at Charles Back's successful Fairview estate, Paarl District

WINE MAP OF SOUTH AFRICA

Grape picker at Paul Cluver Estate

SOUTH AFRICA'S KEY winegrowing regions are located in the southwestern corner of the country, known as the Cape. The West Coast areas have recently found their feet with commercial wines from Olifants River, bold, age-worthy reds from inland Swartland, quality whites from coastal Darling, and modern reds from Tulbagh. Southern interior regions like Klein Karoo have raised standards with specialization in port-style wines as well as good everyday reds and whites, and new, cooler South Coast winegrowing areas, such as Elim, have recently been taking off in a big way. The Cape Peninsula region, however, still remains the country's key winemaking zone, Stellenbosch in particular *(see p460)*.

KEY

South Africa

SOUTH AFRICAN WINE LAW

SOUTH AFRICA'S WINE OF ORIGIN *(WO)* labelling system guarantees variety, vintage (both to be 85 per cent of that stated on the label), and origin (all grapes must be from the named place of origin, but with conditions, more than one origin may be noted). The areas of origin that can appear on a label divide broadly into three (below). There are two further, smaller WOs. An estate wine is grown, vinified, and bottled on a single piece of land registered under a particular name. A single-vineyard wine is made using only grapes from a block no larger than 6ha, planted to a single variety.

Regions

The largest units of viticultural land, these are defined by all-embracing area names: principally Olifants River, Klein Karoo, Breede River Valley, and the Coastal Region (encompassing Swartland, Darling, Tulbagh, Paarl, Tygerberg, Stellenbosch, and Cape Point). All regions contain districts and/or wards, but not all districts and wards necessarily fall within a region.

Districts

Smaller than regions, these are mainly delimited along geopolitical lines. Among the most well-known are Stellenbosch, Paarl, and Swartland.

Wards

These even smaller areas of land are determined according to *terroir*. Wards that fall within districts include Elgin and Klein River in Overberg. New wards outside established areas now exist too, such as Cederberg.

Only after official analysis and tasting is a final WO certification granted, at which point seals are placed on the bottles. Some 52 per cent of South Africa's wine was certified in 2007.

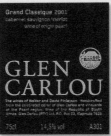

Wine of Origin Paarl District

Paul Cluver Estate guesthouse, Overberg District

TERROIR AT A GLANCE

Latitude: 3˚–34.5°S.

Altitude: 0–1,100m.

Topography: Vines are grown on low hills in Swartland; valley floors or east-facing slopes in Tulbagh; on fertile riverbanks; and in Breede River Valley's foothills. The Olifants River irrigates around 10,000ha of vineyards.

Soil: Vineyards are limited to the deepest moisture-retaining soils, and sites are chosen according to irrigation availability.

Climate: Mediterranean climate. Inland vineyards tend to be hotter and drier, with more drastic differences between summer and winter temperatures.

Temperature: January average is 22.5°C.

Rainfall: Annual average varies from 140mm in the Olifants River Region to 1,042mm in the Overberg District.

Wind: The West Coast is cooled by the north-flowing Benguela Current in the Atlantic; while southeasterly winds on the South Coast bring cloud cover and summer rain.

Viticultural hazards: Wind; drought.

WEST COAST: AREAS & TOP PRODUCERS

OLIFANTS RIVER REGION *p448*

CEDERBERG WARD *p448*
Cederberg Cellars *p450*

SWARTLAND DISTRICT *p448*
Lammershoek Winery *p450*
Sadie Family Wines *p450*

DARLING DISTRICT *p449*
Darling Cellars *p451*
Groote Post *p451*

TULBAGH DISTRICT *p449*
Rijk's Private Cellar *p451*

SOUTH COAST & INTERIOR: AREAS & TOP PRODUCERS

KLEIN KAROO REGION *p452*
Axe Hill *p454*
De Krans Wine Cellar *p454*

Groote Post wines, Darling District

BREEDE RIVER VALLEY REGION *p452*
Graham Beck Wines *p454*
Springfield Estate *p454*

OVERBERG DISTRICT *p453*
Paul Cluver Estate *p455*

CAPE AGULHAS DISTRICT *p453*

WALKER BAY DISTRICT *p453*
Bouchard Finlayson *p455*
Hamilton Russell Vineyards *p455*
Newton Johnson *p455*

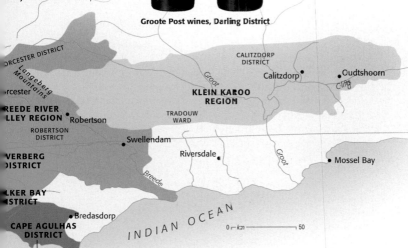

Groote Post in the newly designated Darling District

WINEGROWING AREAS OF THE WEST COAST

CO-OPERATIVES, AND THE PRODUCTION of bulk volumes of wine, used to completely dominate South Africa's West Coast winegrowing areas. However, quality wines are now being made here as more private producers open up cellars and invest in vineyards.

Olifants River Region

AS ITS NAME SUGGESTS, Olifants River Region takes the name of the major waterway running through it. Vineyards on the flattish land either side of the river have plentiful irrigation, so high yields are easily attainable. This explains why the area was previously associated with poor quality bulk wines. However, better viticultural practices have been established and farmers are increasingly being paid on graded fruit quality rather than sugar levels, which means yields are now much lower. Consequently wines with added character are made here, despite still being of commercial, early-drinking style. This positive turn is also reflected in the grape varieties planted. In 1990, the top five were all white, headed by Chenin Blanc *(see p450)* and Colombard; but by 2007, Shiraz, Cabernet Sauvignon, and Pinotage *(see p451)* had edged their way onto the list, with Shiraz showing great promise.

Recently, more sites with higher quality potential have been identified. These include: **Lutzville Valley District** in the most northerly part of the region; **Koekenaap Ward,** a coastal area near Vredendal; the wards of **Bamboes**

Label from Rijk's, Tulbagh District

Bay and **Lamberts Bay**, where the vineyards are close to the beach; **Piekenierskloof Ward,** in the new **Citrusdal Mountain District;** and its neighbour, **Citrusdal Valley District**.

Despite all this progress, co-operative cellars still dominate the area; Vredendal, the dedicated white wine cellar for Namaqua Wines, is the country's biggest under one roof, its annual white wine harvest alone topping a phenomenal 85,000 tonnes.

alluvial, red soils and lime, red sands 🍇 *Shiraz, Cabernet Sauvignon, Pinotage, Merlot, Ruby Cabernet* 🍷 *Chenin Blanc, Colombard, Sauvignon Blanc, Chardonnay, Hanepoot (Muscat d'Alexandrie)* 🍾 *red, white, sparkling, dessert, fortified*

Cederberg Ward

CEDERBERG IS A SMALL WARD that lies just to the east of the Olifants River Region's southern end. The winery of the same name, with its 51ha of vineyard, lies 1,100m up in the Cederberg Mountains. It is a stark, beautiful conservation area blessed with clean air and often covered in snow during winter, all of which adds to the character of its sleek wines.
sandstone 🍇 *Shiraz, Merlot, Pinotage, Cabernet Sauvignon* 🍷 *Sauvignon Blanc, Chardonnay, Chenin Blanc, Bukettraube* 🍾 *red, white*

Swartland District

SWARTLAND – THE 'BLACKLAND' – gets its name from the black bushes that dot the area's gentle hilltops. Traditionally known as wheat country,

Swartland has seen the development of many new vineyards during its emergence as premium wine country in the last decade. Sites here have to be carefully selected due to the long, hot summers and the minimal irrigation available. Untrellised bush vines are common; their naturally smaller crop produces the big, powerful wines for which the interior of the district is known. Wines for which it is now becoming known are Rhône-style red blends and flavoursome, rich, dry white blends; grape varieties are changing to complement this trend. In 1990, the frontrunners were Chenin Blanc, White French (Palomino), Cinsaut, Colombard, and Pinotage. Today the list of top five grapes reads Chenin Blanc, Cabernet Sauvignon, Shiraz, Pinotage, and Chardonnay – sure signs of a recognized quality area.

red-brown with granite *Cabernet Sauvignon, Shiraz, Pinotage, Merlot, Cinsaut* *Chenin Blanc, Chardonnay, Sauvignon Blanc, Colombard* *red, white, sparkling, dessert, fortified*

Darling District

The principal ward within the newly designated Darling District, **Groenekloof** really reaps the benefit of the Benguela Current, which carries in cool air from the Southern Oceans. This, in conjunction with its complementary slopes and aspects, helps to retain the all-important fruity acids in the wines here. White varieties, particularly Sauvignon Blanc, shine in Darling. While none of the wines lack alcohol, their natural acids give a fresher, more elegant

View of Swartland District, the 'Blackland'

impression than is usual in wines with high alcohol levels.

red-brown with granite *Cabernet Sauvignon, Cinsaut, Shiraz, Pinotage, Merlot* *Chenin Blanc, Sauvignon Blanc, Chardonnay* *red, white, dessert*

Tulbagh District

Famous for the 1969 earthquake that destroyed many of the town's old houses, Tulbagh was rather a neglected wine area for quite some time. Until recently, it was best known for Cap Classique sparkling wine *(see p459)* from just one producer, Twee Jonge Gezellen. Otherwise, it was associated with everyday-drinking white wines. With the opening up of the industry in the 1990s, however, newcomers, all private wineries dedicated to quality, saw the potential for red varieties here. Now, Shiraz, Merlot, Cabernet Sauvignon, and Pinotage are all starting to shake up the 'white varieties only' philosophy, with just over half of all viticultural land here being occupied by red grapes. Many of the newcomers are proving themselves on the show circuit and attracting enthusiastic consumers. While much of this focus is on red wines, Sauvignon Blanc is also performing well, showing that there are spots here where even such cool-climate grapes can succeed.

boulder beds of large stones *Cabernet Sauvignon, Shiraz, Pinotage, Merlot, Pinot Noir* *Chenin Blanc, Colombard, Chardonnay, Sauvignon Blanc, Muscat Blanc à Petits Grains* *red, white, sparkling, dessert*

TOP PRODUCERS OF THE WEST COAST

Stacked barrels in a Swartland cellar

Cederberg Cellars
Cederberg Ward

PO Box 84, Clanwilliam **C** *027 482 2827* **W** *www.cederbergwine.com* **O**

IT IS A LONELY business for wine-maker David Nieuwoudt – the sole producer in this lofty region, 1,100m up in the Cederberg Mountains. Five generations of Nieuwoudts have farmed this land, and their wines are among the best in the country. The whites vibrate with natural acid and pure fruit; while the reds combine the pared sleekness of traditional Europe with the bright flavours so redolent of the New World. Cabernet Sauvignon was a regular award winner for David's grandfather; and David's V Generations Cabernet continues the award-winning tradition. David also makes striking Sauvignon Blanc and Sémillon in the Elim ward.
🍷 *red, white* 🍾 *2008, 2007, 2006* ★ *V Generations Cabernet Sauvignon, V Generations Chenin Blanc, Ghost Corner Sémillon (WO Elim), Shiraz*

Lammershoek Winery
Swartland District

PO Box 597, Malmesbury **C** *022 482 2835* **W** *www.lammershoek.co.za* **O**

Lammershoek farm dates back to the early 1700s, vines appearing by 1750, but its modern era began in the early 21st century, when present owners the Kreztel family decided to make wine from some of their 130ha. Both whites and reds are made traditionally; no cultured yeasts are used, and neither style is fined or filtered. The Rhône influences the reds: the Syrah is full-bodied yet delicate, and the red Roulette is in a rich, savoury Côtes du Rhône style. The white Roulette is a blend of Chenin Blanc with Chardonnay, Viognier, Clairette Blanche, and Hárslevelú, oaked with a touch of sugar. The varietal Chenin Blanc is full-bodied but with varietal charm.
🍷 *red, white, dessert, fortified* 🍾 *2008, 2007, 2006* ★ *Roulette (red), Roulette Blanc, Syrah, Chenin Blanc Barrique*

Sadie Family Wines
Swartland District

PO Box 1019, Malmesbury **C** *021 482 3138* **O** *by appt*

EBEN SADIE EPITOMIZES the new South African winemaking generation: brimming with passion, whether he is paying minute attention to his vines, wine, or surfing style. After a winemaking stint at nearby producer Spice Route, Sadie went solo in 2001. Columella, his Swartland Shiraz merged with Mourvèdre, is a wine of great delicacy, despite being from this very warm region. And the secret to its success is ruthless selection from vine to bottle; only the most natural of treatments; fermentation on native yeasts; judicious oaking; and finally, bottling with no filtration. Palladius, his white blend featuring Viognier and Chenin Blanc with Chardonnay and Grenache Blanc,

---

CHENIN BLANC: ON THE COMEBACK

Chenin Blanc's dominance in the Cape was originally a result of its suitability for brandy, but plantings of the variety (once commonly known as Steen) have decreased from 32 per cent of South Africa's total vineyard area in 1990 to just under 19 per cent in 2007. Local aficionados founded the Chenin Blanc Association (*www.chenin.co.za*) in 1999 to rescue it. This, as well as increased consumer interest, shows that Chenin is on the comeback. Key producers, including Kanu (*www.kanu.co.za*), Rudera (*www.rudera. co.za*), Ken Forrester Wines (*www.kenforresterwines.com*), De Trafford Wines, and Villiera Wines, are developing a new style that is unlike the previously mass-produced wines in that it shows true varietal character: delicacy with concentration. Chenin Blanc is also being used increasingly in serious white blends, particularly in the richer, riper styles of the Swartland. Whether as a varietal wine or as part of a blend, Chenin Blanc is capable of developing with age.

HOME HERO: PINOTAGE

When Professor Abraham Perold crossed Pinot Noir with Cinsaut in 1924, he created South Africa's national grape, Pinotage. Some 35 years passed before it was hailed as a champion at the Cape Wine Show, though it was not until 1961 that it appeared commercially. International interest in Pinotage was only stirred when South Africa re-emerged on the global wine scene in the early 1990s: wine drinkers wanted to try something typically South African. This led to the formation of the Pinotage Association (www.pinotage.co.za), whose main aims are to research and promote this grape. They even hold an annual Top Ten Pinotage competition to find the best of the Cape breed. Modern Pinotage has its inherent astringency well-managed; it offers ripe red plum, raspberry fruits and a rich texture, and produces wines from light, dry, and fruity, through to oaked, full-bodied, and long-lived. A blended red including Pinotage is often called a Cape Blend, but this is not an official category.

Eben Sadie topping up barrels

was a pioneer in this now popular Mediterranean/Rhône style. Variations on these themes are explored under the Sequillo label. Sadie weaves similar magic on a small vineyard in Priorat, Spain.

🖼 red, white ▶ 2007, 2006, 2005
★ Columella, Palladius, Sequillo Red, Sequillo White

Darling Cellars
Darling District

PO Box 114, Darling 📞 022 492 2276 ⌨ www.darlingcellars.co.za ⬚

DARLING CELLARS REPRESENTS one of South Africa's great transformation stories. The name change in 1997 from Mamreweg Co-op to Darling Cellars brought with it a total revamp of the business, and a shift in emphasis from quantity to quality. The focus is now on winning international markets. New vine plantings have introduced international favourites like Merlot and Chardonnay; and viticulture has been improved to ensure limited yields. Big-hearted reds, Shiraz in particular, come from Darling Cellars' warmer, inland vineyards; while ever-better Sauvignon Blanc stems from their cooler spots.

🖼 red, white, rosé ▶ 2007, 2006, 2005 ★ Onyx Cabernet Sauvignon, Pinotage, Darling Cellars Shiraz

Groote Post
Darling District

PO Box 13, Darling 📞 C22 492 2825 ⌨ www.grootepost.com ⬚

GROOTE POST'S HILLSIDE vineyards, a mere 6km from the Atlantic, enjoy the bracing sea air. The vines here used to compete with a Holstein dairy herd for the attention of owners Peter and Nick Pentz, but this is no longer the case. The herd's milk was great, but nowhere near as talked-about as the wines the Pentz family now produce. Groote Post Sauvignon Blanc is delicate yet intensely fruited, and the barrel-fermented Chardonnay they make is full of fresh, citrous vibrancy. Equally fresh, yet generously proportioned, Shiraz leads Groote Post's reds but no-one is giving up on the temperamental Pinot Noir either.

🖼 red, white ▶ 2008, 2007, 2006
★ Sauvignon Blanc, Chardonnay

Rijk's Private Cellar
Tulbagh District

PO Box 400, Tulbagh 📞 023 230 1622 ⌨ www.rijks.co.za ⬚

CONVENTIONAL WISDOM used to have it that Tulbagh was white wine-only territory: strange given this mountain-enclosed valley's reputation for such hot summers. But businessman Neville Dorrington turned this belief on its head when he bought Rijk's farm in 1997. Early success came with the rich, fine-tannined Pinotage and opulent, French oak-fermented Sémillon; both set the standard for the range. Now Pierre Wahl's attention is turning to a Bordeaux-style white blend and Rhône-style red including Pinotage.

🖼 red, white
▶ 2008, 2007, 2006
★ Pinotage, Sémillon

Groote Post

Vineyards on the Paul Cluver Estate in Elgin

WINEGROWING AREAS OF THE SOUTH COAST & INTERIOR

THE SOUTH COAST AND INTERIOR present two quite different sides of South African wine. The interior areas of Klein Karoo and the Breede River Valley are traditional, hot winegrowing areas; while Overberg and the areas south to Cape Agulhas typify modern viticulture in South Africa, where the search is for cooler growing conditions and quality is the only goal.

Klein Karoo Region

ALSO KNOWN AS LITTLE KAROO, this region has long been associated with fortified wines. The area's reputation is today centred on port-style fortifieds, with **Calitzdorp District** as the country's unofficial HQ in this field. Production tends to be traditional here, the grapes trodden by barefoot workers in shallow, open cement tanks. The area's climatic similarity to the Douro region in Portugal *(see p333)* was the inspiration for local producers, and it is this hot, dry climate that makes irrigation a must. Water is the major limitation on vineyard planting, hence the relatively small area under vine in this large region (almost 3,000ha). Nevertheless, there is plenty of varietal diversity, and most grapes are grown on an experimental basis by a mix of independent and co-operative wineries.

Tradouw Ward is a smaller, more recently discovered area, which enjoys an unhindered view of the sea, some 45km to the south. Its cooling influence assists in the making of

Graham Beck Wines label, Breede River Valley region

elegant Bordeaux-style reds and refined Chardonnays from the ward's limited 115ha. 🗺 *silty alluvial, shale, sandstone* 🌿 *Ruby Cabernet, Shiraz, Merlot, Red Muscadel (red Muscat Blanc à Petits Grains), Pinotage* 🌿 *Colombard, Chenin Blanc, Chardonnay, Hanepoot (Muscat d'Alexandrie)* 🍷 *red, white, sparkling, dessert, fortified*

Breede River Valley Region

THE BREEDE RIVER VALLEY is tracked along its northern bank by the Langeberg Mountains. The area's two principal winegrowing districts – Worcester and Robertson – straddle the banks of this river; but just as important is Brandvlei Dam, the all-important irrigation source.

With approximately 20,588ha, the district of **Worcester** boasts the largest area of vineyards in the country. Most vines here were initially planted along the fertile riverbanks, with brandy production their chief purpose. However, the varietal mix, vineyard sites, wine styles, and, most importantly, producer attitudes are now changing. While Chenin Blanc and Colombard remain the major varieties, Chardonnay, Sauvignon Blanc, Cabernet, and Shiraz are not far behind. Hillside vineyards are now producing lower yields of better fruit, from which the main co-ops make pleasant wines. Oak staves and chips are sometimes used to add extra flavour to those destined for early drinking. And many wines are custom-designed for UK supermarkets or local *négociants* for sale under their own labels. There is also a slice of history to be found in the area's traditional dessert and fortified wines, made from Muscat grapes, that made the old Constantia wine famous.

The region's other main district, **Robertson**, has a lot of limestone, which is ideal for Chardonnay, both as a still wine and in Cap Classique sparkling styles *(see p459)*. White varieties have dominated, but Shiraz and Cabernet Sauvignon also do well now, with bright, fresh fruit and firm but friendly tannins. *alluvial, shale, limestone* *Cabernet Sauvignon, Shiraz, Merlot, Ruby Cabernet, Pinotage, Cinsaut* *Chenin Blanc, Colombard, Chardonnay, Sauvignon Blanc, Hanepoot (Muscat d'Alexandrie), Muscat Blanc à Petits Grains* *red, white, sparkling, dessert, fortified*

Overberg District

THE WARDS OF ELGIN AND KLEIN RIVER provide the main quality wine interests in Overberg. Their importance, however, hugely exceeds the tiny percentage of the Cape's wine crop that they produce. Small, independent companies make up the winery count here, though bigger players, such as Neil Ellis Wines, also buy in grapes from this area.

Apple orchards dominate highland **Elgin Ward**, lying at 305m above sea level. The area under vine has increased more than fourfold, from 150ha in 2002 to 711.23ha in 2007, helped by its cooler climate and longer ripening period. Pioneers such as Paul Cluver and Iona proved the area's suitability for white wines – Sauvignon Blanc in particular – though other aromatic whites are showing promise, as are Pinot Noir and Shiraz among red varieties. Oak Valley, Elgin Vintners, and South Hill have added to Elgin's vinous prestige, as have high-profile producers from other areas, such as Thelema and Tokara from Stellenbosch. The **Klein River Ward**, at sea level and closer to Walker Bay, currently has only two wineries and just 85.57ha of vines, dominated by Cabernet Sauvignon, Shiraz, Merlot, and Sauvignon Blanc. One winery, Raka, has already shown much promise with its red wines. *gravelly, sandstone with shale and granite* *Cabernet Sauvignon, Shiraz, Merlot, Pinot Noir, Pinotage* *Sauvignon Blanc, Chardonnay, Chenin Blanc, Viognier, Sémillon* *red, white, dessert*

PINOT NOIR ON THE RISE

Early results with Pinot Noir encouraged more South African growers to give it a try; even a Burgundian (Paul Bouchard) has joined forces with a local winemaker (Peter Finlayson) to focus on the variety. The opening of new areas, improved vine material from France, extensive exposure and tasting abroad, and sheer determination have all helped Pinot Noir's huge transformation in South Africa. Not only the Hemel-en-Aarde Valley in Walker Bay, but highland Elgin, Constantia, parts of Stellenbosch, and even Paarl now make individual still wines. The variety also continues to play an important role in the Méthode Cap Classique sparkling wines *(see p459)*. Hamilton Russell Vineyards and its neighbour Bouchard Finlayson are considered leaders in the Pinot pack.

Cape Agulhas District

THIS IS HOME to Africa's most southerly vineyards, with just over half the 254ha lying within the ward of **Elim**. The benefits of the cooler climate are challenged by birds, wind, and summer rain, which causes rot. Nevertheless, hard graft is seeing Sauvignon Blanc and Sémillon hauling in awards. Shiraz is the dominant red, but early examples of Pinot Noir suggest this is the one to really keep an eye on. *shale* *Shiraz, Merlot, Cabernet Sauvignon, Pinot Noir* *Sauvignon Blanc, Sémillon, Chardonnay* *red, white*

Walker Bay District

THIS DISTRICT fronts Walker Bay and is dominated by the wards of **Hemel-en-Aarde Valley** and **Upper Hemel-en-Aarde; Sunday's Glen Ward** is a new addition. This valley was the original area to be opened up in the 1970s (then illegally, before dropping of the quota system in 1992), when Tim Hamilton Russell was searching for cooler conditions, for Pinot Noir and Chardonnay. Since then many other wineries have arrived, mostly concentrating on the Burgundian duo but also finding success with Sauvignon Blanc, Pinotage, and Shiraz. *shale, granite, sandstone* *Shiraz, Cabernet Sauvignon, Pinot Noir, Merlot, Pinotage* *Sauvignon Blanc, Chardonnay, Chenin Blanc, Sémillon* *red, white*

TOP PRODUCERS OF THE SOUTH COAST & INTERIOR

Axe Hill
Klein Karoo Region

Wesoewer Road, Calitzdorp
C 044 213 3585
W www.axehill.co.za **O** by appt

THIS 'PORT' SPECIALIST winery passed into new hands after the death of founder Tony Mossop in 2005. The new owners aim to maintain its quality and reputation. The slightly cooler hillside site in the otherwise hot Calitzdorp District encourages later-ripening grapes. Mossop's 'ports' reflect Old World originals, and some of the earliest have shown they can age. The keen interest of the Portuguese indicates they are on the right track.
fortified 2006, 2005, 2004 ★ *Cape Vintage*

De Krans Wine Cellar
Klein Karoo Region

PO Box 28, Calitzdorp **C** 044 213 3314 **W** www.dekrans.co.za **O**

BOETS AND STROEBEL NEL'S flagship Vintage Reserve, made since 1990, blends four Portuguese varieties, echoing Euro-

pean originals with high alcohol and low sugar levels. They make White, Ruby, Tawny, and Vintage variations. Aside from the range of port-style wines, the Nels are also emulating the growing reputation for Portuguese red table wines; their 'work-in-progress' Red Stone Reserve blends Touriga Nacional with Cabernet Sauvignon. De Krans White Muscadel Jerepigo upholds the Klein Karoo's high reputation for this traditional style, yet has slightly lower alcohol and sugar levels.
red, white, rosé, sparkling, fortified 2006, 2005, 2004 ★ *Vintage Reserve Port*

Graham Beck Wines
Breede River Valley Region

PO Box 724, Robertson **C** 023 626 1214 **W** www.grahambeckwines.co.za

A DEVASTATING 1981 flood denuded this riverside farm of topsoil; but this did not deter entrepreneur Graham Beck from purchasing the land and setting up a winery. Now, 28 years on, chief winemaker Peter Ferreira and

Abrie Bruwer, winemaker at Springfield Estate

his team are leaders in Cap Classique sparkling wine. They have also proven that Robertson, an area long considered suitable only for white wines, can produce equally smart reds, especially Shiraz, which thrives here. Among the other beauties are Pinotage and Cabernet Sauvignon, made by Erika Obermeyer at the company's Franschhoek cellar.
red, white, fortified, sparkling 2008, 2007, 2006, 2005, 2004 ★ *The Ridge Syrah, Pinotage, Blancs de Blancs Cap Classique, Pheasant's Run Sauvignon Blanc*

Springfield Estate
Breede River Valley Region

PO Box 770, Robertson **C** 023 626 3661 **W** www.springfieldestate.com **O**

DETERMINED TO let his vineyards express themselves in his wines, winemaker Abrie Bruwer takes such a hands-off approach that some of his wines do not make it to the bottle. Méthode Ancienne Chardonnay, for instance, can ferment for 55 days on native yeast, spend a year in oak without sulphur, and be bottled with no further treatment. To date only six out of 13 attempts with this have been successful; but when it works, the results are truly

---

THE SUCCESS OF CAPE 'PORT'

'Port' styles in the Cape used to be sweet and made from Tinta Barroca, Cinsaut, and even Cabernet Sauvignon and Shiraz. But with the creation of the South African 'Port' Producers Association in 1993 came drier styles, higher alcohol levels, and a mix of the best grapes, including the king of 'port' varieties, Touriga Nacional. European legislation since 2002 means the actual word 'port' is being phased out on all South African versions, thus the creation of names with a Cape identity like Cape Vintage, Cape Late Bottled Vintage, Cape Ruby, Cape Tawny, and Cape Vintage Reserve. The unofficial South African 'port' capital is Calitzdorp in the Klein Karoo Region but great examples are also made in Paarl and Stellenbosch. Even leading Portuguese port houses now respect South African versions. Among the best producers are **Axe Hill**, **Boplaas** *(044 213 3326)*, **De Krans**, and **J P Bredell** *(021 842 2478)*. Although Cape 'port' has similar sugar and alcohol levels to its Portuguese cousin, the former tend to be fruitier.

worth it. The first Cabernet made in this risky way has recently joined his range too. And for those who think all Sauvignon Blanc is the same, compare Bruwer's riverside vineyard, Special Cuvée, with his Life From Stone – which hails from a flinty escarpment site. Two very different wines.

red, white 2008, 2007, 2006, 2005, 2004, 2003
★ Méthode Ancienne: Chardonnay, Cabernet Sauvignon

Paul Cluver Estate
Overberg District

PO Box 48, Grabouw 021 844 0605 www.cluver.com

HIGHLAND ELGIN IS prime apple-producing country, but early success with wines has seen increased plantings over the past few years. The Cluvers were among the pioneers, and having proved the suitability of this cooler climate, they are now testing other sites on their farm with vine plantings. Summer cloud results in a longer ripening period, so grapes here have more intense flavours. Chardonnay, Riesling, and Sauvignon Blanc are Cluver's main white strengths. Of the reds, Pinot Noir also shows great promise.

red, white, dessert 2008, 2007, 2006, 2005 ★ Seven Flags Pinot Noir, Chardonnay, Gewurztraminer, Riesling Noble Late Harvest

Bouchard Finlayson
Walker Bay District

PO Box 303, Hermanus
028 312 3515
www.bouchardfinlayson.co.za

PETER FINLAYSON CAN aptly be described as the Pinot Noir pioneer of the Hemel-en-Aarde Valley. He worked with the variety for a dozen

Bouchard Finlayson vineyards in Walker Bay District

years at Hamilton Russell, before joining Burgundian Paul Bouchard to set up this winery next door. His focus remains on Pinot Noir on the home farm. Some Chardonnay is also drawn from here, as well as being bought in from nearby Villiersdorp. Do not imagine, however, that Finlayson's classic leanings stifle his experimental nature. His Hannibal wine, an unusual but great-tasting Sangiovese-Nebbiolo-Pinot Noir blend, panders to his love of Italian varieties.

red, white 2008, 2007, 2006
★ Tête de Cuvée Pinot Noir, Galpin Peak Pinot Noir, Missionvale Chardonnay

Hamilton Russell Vineyards
Walker Bay District

PO Box 158, Hermanus
028 312 3595 www. hamiltonrussellwines.com

FOUNDER TIM HAMILTON RUSSELL used to long for a cool-climate farm where his favourite Pinot Noir and Chardonnay grapes could shine. He found the best South Africa could offer here, where he produced exceptional wines from those same varieties. Son and present owner Anthony – with winemaker Hannes Storm – have since built on

Paul Cluver

that success. They tend good vine material in an environmentally friendly way to great effect, and keep firmly abreast of the current trends in wine styles. A stronger sense of place and quality are the highly pleasing results.

red, white 2007, 2006, 2005
★ Pinot Noir, Chardonnay

Newton Johnson
Walker Bay District

PO Box 225, Hermanus
028 312 3862
www.newtonjohnson.com

BACKED BY WINE-SAVVY parents, the young Johnson brothers, Gordon (winemaker) and Bevan (marketing manager), are full of adventurous spirit. Based in the Hemel-en-Aarde Valley, they are part of the Pinot Noir brigade, but they also get individual results from Sauvignon Blanc. Attention to detail is evident in their elegant, harmonious Chardonnay, matured in custom-designed Burgundian small oak barrels, while the Syrah-Mourvèdre blend has a pleasing delicacy. The entire range is food-friendly, the primary objective of this family winery.

red, white, rosé 2008, 2007, 2006 ★ Syrah-Mourvèdre, Pinot Noir, Chardonnay

WINE MAP OF THE CAPE PENINSULA & SURROUNDS

THESE SOUTHERLY AREAS are the heart of the South African wine industry, producing wine that is quality-driven throughout. With its varied *terroirs*, Stellenbosch is pre-eminent, although Paarl is now also breaking onto the scene; both specialize mainly in red wines. Since the 1980s, Constantia has been regaining status, not only with its much publicized Vin de Constance but with its fine Sauvignon Blanc and Merlot, too: varieties which are also gaining recognition in Tygerberg. Cape Point, planted only in the mid-1990s, has meanwhile got off to a very successful start. These areas are likely to remain the leaders in quality South African wine for the foreseeable future.

KEY

Cape Peninsula & Surrounds

Cape Point Vineyards, Cape Point District

VIN DE CONSTANCE

Governor of the Cape from 1679 to 1699, Simon van der Stel was granted a farm in 1685 by the Dutch East India Company, which he named Constantia. Among other grapes, he planted Muscat de Frontignan, and soon made a sweet wine. But it was not until the Cloete family bought the farm at the end of the 18th century that this delicious dessert wine gained international fame. The honeyed liquid, known simply as Constantia, was relished by European royalty and even Napoleon.

The wine then disappeared when the Cape government purchased the estate in 1885 as an experimental farm. Fast forward to 1980, when the Jooste family bought Klein Constantia, part of van der Stel's original farm, and set about re-creating the fabled wine. Low crops of very ripe Muscat de Frontignan grapes, slowly fermented, aged in oak barrels, and sold in 19th-century replica bottles, have been made into what is now known as Vin de Constance *(right)*. This modern Cape classic enjoys international recognition, matching that attained by Cloete's initial masterpiece.

Grape picker, Fairview, Paarl District

TERROIR AT A GLANCE

Latitude: 33–34.5°S.

Altitude: 0–550m.

Topography: Mountains dominate – vineyards are planted on slopes and lush valley floors.

Soil: Varies dramatically, with over 50 types of soil in the Stellenbosch region alone but predominantly highly acidic and clay based.

Climate: Mediterranean. Long hot summers and cold, wet winters. Snowfall on the higher mountains.

Temperature: January average is 23°C.

Rainfall: Annual average ranges from 735mm in Stellenbosch to 1,070mm in Constantia. Irrigation is often necessary.

Wind: Summer wind from the southeast, also known as the Cape Doctor, cools down vineyards and helps prevent disease.

Viticultural hazards: Humidity; heat stress; strong winds.

CAPE PENINSULA & SURROUNDS: AREAS & TOP PRODUCERS

PAARL DISTRICT *p458*

Boekenhoutskloof *p464*
Fairview *p464*
Glen Carlou *p464*
Rupert & Rothschild Vignerons *p464*
Veenwouden Private Cellar *p465*
Vilafonté *p465*

TYGERBERG DISTRICT *p459*

STELLENBOSCH DISTRICT *p460*

De Trafford Wines *p465*
Jordan Wines *p465*
Kanonkop *p466*
Le Riche Wines *p466*
Meerlust Estate *p466*
Morgenster Estate *p466*
Mulderbosch Vineyards *p466*
Neil Ellis Wines *p467*
Rustenberg Wines *p467*
Rust en Vrede Estate *p467*
Saxenburg *p467*
Thelema Mountain Vineyards *p467*
Vergelegen *p469*
Villiera Wines *p468*

CONSTANTIA WARD *p461*

Klein Constantia Estate *p468*
Steenberg Vineyards *p468*

CAPE POINT DISTRICT *p461*

Cape Point Vineyards *p468*

Rupert & Rothschild Vignerons label, Paarl District

PERFECT CASE: CAPE PENINSULA

Ⓡ Boekenhoutskloof Syrah £££

Ⓦ Cape Point Vineyards Isliedh ££

Ⓦ De Trafford Wines Chenin Blanc ££

Ⓡ Fairview Primo Pinotage ££

Ⓦ Jordan Wines Chardonnay ££

Ⓕ J P Bredell Wines Cape Vintage Reserve Port £££ (021 842 2478)

Ⓦ Ken Forrester The FMC Chenin Blanc ££

Ⓓ Klein Constantia Estate Vin de Constance £££

Ⓡ Neil Ellis Wines Cabernet Sauvignon ££

Ⓦ Steenberg Vineyards Sauvignon Blanc Reserve ££

Ⓡ Thelema Mountain Vineyards Cabernet Sauvignon ££

Ⓡ Vergelegen Flagship Red Blend £££

Jordan Wines vineyards, Stellenbosch District

WELLINGTON WARD
Wellington

R PAARDEBERG WARD

Paarl

PAARL DISTRICT

Simonsberg Mountain
SIMONSBERG-PAARL WARD
FRANSCHHOEK WARD

MONSBERG-ELLENBOSCH WARD

Stellenbosch
BANGHOEK WARD

JONKERSHOEK VALLEY WARD

ELLENBOSCH DISTRICT

AAIBERG ARD
Helderberg Mountains

Somerset West

Strand

Berg

A vineyard in the landlocked Paarl District

WINEGROWING AREAS OF THE CAPE PENINSULA & SURROUNDS

THE CAPE PENINSULA and surrounding areas are home to some of the Cape's oldest wine farms. The highest concentration of wineries in the country, mainly small and privately-owned, is also found here. Among them are some of the most famous names and the best wines. The proximity of Cape Town and the beneficial effects of the maritime climate in the coastal areas are two of the main reasons these well-known areas have led the advance in quality.

Paarl District

PAARL (MEANING PEARL) is landlocked and therefore generally quite warm. Important in terms of both quantity and quality, it has just under 17,500ha of vines, second in size only to Worcester. Every type of winery from the huge KWV company right down to small, private and merchant cellars are found in Paarl, and many are at the cutting edge of winemaking.

In keeping with its varied topography, soils, and meso-climates, Paarl is able to produce excellent wines right across the range, from Méthode Cap Classique sparkling to 'port' styles. Varieties proving particularly successful include Viognier, Sémillon, and Chardonnay among whites; and Shiraz, Mourvèdre, Cabernet Sauvignon, and Merlot among reds. The district is currently home to four official wards.

Old-style wine press, Franschhoek

Downstream, beyond Paarl town, lies the ward of **Wellington**, which extends from the folds of the Hawekwaberg and Groenberg mountains to the other side of the Berg River. Traditionally seen as a centre for good sherry-style wines made from Chenin Blanc – the majority grape here – Wellington has recently revealed a talent for full-bodied reds, both varietals and blends incorporating Shiraz, Cabernet Sauvignon, Merlot, and Pinotage.

The vineyards in **Simonsberg-Paarl** stretch along the Paarl side of Simonsberg Mountain. Well-exposed, gentle slopes – generally north-facing – and deep soils prove ideal for both white and red grapes, with the whites usually planted above the reds to make the best of any cool airflow. Classic varieties and local Pinotage dominate, but there are also experimental blocks, including Sangiovese, Verdelho, Tannat, Tempranillo, and Nebbiolo.

The cigar-shaped ward of **Franschhoek**, meaning French corner in Afrikaans, is one of the most picturesque parts of Paarl. It lies at the southeastern end of the district in a narrow valley encircled by high mountains. The Berg River rises here and runs through both Paarl and Swartland districts to its mouth at the Atlantic. Vineyards are planted along its alluvial riverbanks and on the generally better mountain slope sites. Sémillon has strong historical links to Franschhoek, with several century-old bush vines still bearing fruit. Red varieties are more recent introductions, but Cabernet Sauvignon, Merlot, and Shiraz are already doing well.

Paarl is fairly flat in the north, except for Paarl Mountain and the Perdeberg. **Voor Paardeberg** in the northwestern part of the district, on the border with Swartland, is the latest ward. With a much drier climate than the rest of the district, it produces predominantly red wines, strongly featuring big and booming Pinotage and Shiraz, though some interesting rich white blends, combining Chenin Blanc, Chardonnay, and Viognier, are adding to the ward's quality image.

Glen Carlou vineyards in Paarl District

reddish-yellow in foothills, coarse soil over granitic clay in exposed sites, dark alluvial by river, bleached sand on mountainside ✦ *Cabernet Sauvignon, Shiraz, Merlot, Pinotage, Cinsaut* ✦ *Chenin Blanc, Chardonnay, Sauvignon Blanc, Colombard, Crouchen Blanc* ✦ *red, white, sparkling, dessert, fortified*

Tygerberg District

TYGERBERG DISTRICT is at the northern tip of Greater Cape Town. Rural **Durbanville Ward**, like Constantia, would be under great threat from urban growth if it were not for the area's quality wine potential, which has so far kept further encroachment into vineyard land at bay. Its position in an open-ended tunnel created by the Tygerberg Hills means that breezes from the Atlantic, and to a lesser extent False Bay, act as an air-conditioner during the hot summer months in this ward. These conditions are perfect for the main white variety, Sauvignon Blanc. Leader of the reds, Cabernet Sauvignon receives the full benefit of long sunlight hours on well-exposed sites, though Merlot, too, does better here than in many other places in South Africa. The newish ward of **Philadelphia**, at the northern end of Tygerberg District, also benefits from the Atlantic's cooling influence. Some of the vineyards are planted up to 260m above sea level, resulting in a significant difference in diurnal temperatures and thus slower ripening. Cabernet-led blends and Sauvignon Blanc show promise at the ward's only two wineries.

shale, red granite, schist ✦ *Cabernet Sauvignon, Merlot, Shiraz, Pinotage* ✦ *Sauvignon Blanc, Chenin Blanc, Chardonnay* ✦ *red, white, sparkling*

MÉTHODE CAP CLASSIQUE

Champagne's ruling body (CIVC) ruled out the name champagne for Cape sparkling wine long before the European Union trade agreement in 2002. South African sparkling wine producers therefore came up with the term Méthode Cap Classique (MCC) to describe their style of making bubbly. 'Méthode' and 'Classique' still suggest the classic Champagne method *(see pp166–7)*, while 'Cap' points to the geographical South African origin.

Quality MCCs are produced in all of the country's major wine regions. Many are made from Chardonnay and Pinot Noir, the classic champagne grapes; a little Pinot Meunier is often used; and some even incorporate a touch of Chenin Blanc or Pinotage. All follow the original method used in Champagne as closely as possible, though the results generally show riper New World fruit flavours. All the familiar champagne styles are made, as well as MCC Red from both Shiraz and Pinotage.

Simonsig *(www.simonsig.co.za; left)*, **Villiera Wines**, and **Graham Beck Wines** are three of the leading South African cellars producing top-quality MCC wines.

Stellenbosch District

THE HUB of South Africa's wine industry, Stellenbosch has more private cellars than any other Cape area. The district is also the centre for viticultural research and training, as well as being home to Distell, the country's largest wine and spirits producer. And quality has always been key here.

Stellenbosch District follows closely behind Worcester and Paarl in terms of area under vine. Like Paarl, it benefits from varied mesoclimates, aspects, elevations, and soil types. But Stellenbosch also has the advantage of its frontage onto False Bay. The summer Cape Doctor wind works its magic here, keeping the vineyards cool and helping to control disease. All of this allows for the production of quality wines across the whole stylistic spectrum, making up 8.4 per cent of South Africa's total wine production in 2007.

Although many vines in this area stretch up mountain slopes, the lower, undulating land provides the thickest carpet of vine. The fact that land here is among the most expensive in the Cape winelands does not deter winemakers from innovation and cutting-edge experimentation. The holy grail chased by all is a sense of *terroir* in their wines, already discernible in places.

Stellenbosch contains seven official wards: **Simonsberg-Stellenbosch Ward**, northwest of the town of Stellenbosch, incorporates the whole of the south-facing side of Simonsberg Mountain, and some of the lower-lying land beneath its towering 1,000m peaks. On the highest, most exposed slopes (up to 450m), white varieties perform best, but are vulnerable to the strong southeasterly wind. The foothills, on the other hand, are much more sheltered, allowing red varieties to produce full and generous wines.

ORGANIC WINES

Political isolation during apartheid left South African winegrowers unaware of organics, but they are now waking up to this trend, with a few even turning to bio-dynamics *(see p105)*. Most Cape wine-lands enjoy hot, dry summers, which are beneficial for the no-pesticides approach that organic farming demands. In good years, well-exposed spots in Paarl and Stellenbosch make quality organic wines. Every year, more producers convert at least part of their vineyards to organic farming, though few have turned to it completely. Organic producers include: *African Terroir (www.africanterroir.co.za), Bon Cap (www.boncaporganic.co.za), Fairview, Laibach (www.laibach.co.za), Reyneke Wines (www.reynekewines.co.za), Rozendal (www.rozendal.co.za), Stellar Organics (www.stellarorganics.com)*

The warm northerly and westerly slopes of the hills in **Bottelary Ward** favour Shiraz. The contiguous **Devon Valley Ward** – accessible only by a single, narrow winding lane – includes a horseshoe of slopes: the southerly side favours Chardonnay, while the remaining vineyards are stronger on reds, Cabernet Sauvignon in particular. Adjoining Devon Valley is the ward of **Papegaaiberg** – Afrikaans for Parrot Mountain. This area is home to a mix of both reds and whites, but fewer producers here means there are no real stand-out varieties. **Jonkershoek Valley Ward** is towered over by both the Jonkershoek and Stellenbosch mountains. This inhospitable terrain, and the early loss of sunlight, means it is possible to plant vineyards only on south- or west-facing slopes at the valley mouth. There is a mix of white and red varieties under vine here; but it is the Cabernets in this area that display the most refined nature. **Banghoek** and **Polkadraai Hills** are two new wards in the Stellenbosch District. Banghoek straddles the *nek* across Helshoogte, running up the Simonsberg on the north side and the Jonkershoek mountain on the south. The variety of aspects and elevations allow for a wide spread of varieties – everything from

View from the Jordan Wines estate in Stellenbosch District

Riesling to Cabernet does well here, with the latter the dominant red. Shiraz, Merlot, Sauvignon Blanc, and Chardonnay also produce wines of a quality that upholds their vineyard dominance. There is only a handful of wineries in this ward, but quality is common to all. The Polkadraai Hills run to the south and east of the Bottelary Hills. With their good exposure to the cooling effects of False Bay, this latest Stellenbosch ward produces some pure, crisp Sauvignon Blancs, though Cabernet Sauvignon is again the most planted variety.

Helderberg is not yet a designated Wine of Origin area in its own right, but the reds grown here tend to be fine and elegant thanks, again, to the cooling False Bay breezes. Cabernet Franc in particular does well.

🗺 *reddish-yellow, granite, coarse soil over granitic clay, shale* 🍇 *Cabernet Sauvignon, Shiraz, Merlot, Pinotage, Cabernet Franc* 🍇 *Sauvignon Blanc, Chenin Blanc, Chardonnay, Sémillon, Viognier, Crouchen Blanc* 🍷 *red, white, sparkling, dessert, fortified*

Constantia Ward

A WARD FAMED FOR its historic sweet wine (*see p456*) rather than its size, Constantia is an upmarket residential suburb, limited in its winegrowing by the pressures of urban development as well as by the dominating physical presence of two peaks in the Cape Peninsula mountain chain: Constantiaberg and Vlakkenberg, along the slopes of which vineyards meander. The limited number of independent producers is growing, though quality remains the common goal.

Generally facing in a southeast direction, Constantia vineyards catch the full benefit of cooling breezes blowing off False Bay. Despite these breezes, cloud cover and overnight condensation often lead to the development of botrytis. A strict viticultural regime is therefore necessary to avoid fungus. The ward has made

Steenberg Vineyards in Constantia Ward

its name with Sauvignon Blanc, by far the principal variety, but reds on the warmer, lower slopes and recent plantings on northwest-facing slopes at the northern end of the ward receive longer sunlight hours and may soon need to be taken as seriously as the whites.

🗺 *red-brown sandstone on granite* 🍇 *Cabernet Sauvignon, Merlot, Cabernet Franc, Shiraz* 🍇 *Sauvignon Blanc, Chardonnay, Sémillon, Hanepoot (Muscat d'Alexandrie), Muscat Blanc à Petit Grains* 🍷 *red, white, sparkling, dessert*

Hout Bay Ward

THIS IS THE NEWEST and one of the smallest wards, named after the fishing village tucked around the slopes at the back of Table Mountain. Between the current five producers and grape growers, they have a mere 4.62ha planted across various aspects and on varying soils, with no one vineyard covering more than 1ha. Many vines have yet to start bearing; in the meantime, grapes are bought in from other areas. This boutique scenario is unlikely to change given both the pressure from urbanization and the inhospitable, steep mountain slopes.

🗺 *alluvial sand, sandstone, weathered granite* 🍇 *Pinot Noir, Shiraz, Merlot, Cabernet Sauvignon* 🍇 *Chardonnay, Muscat d'Alexandrie, Sauvignon Blanc, Viognier* 🍷 *red, white, sparkling*

Cape Point District

IN ALL RESPECTS, Cape Point represents the new face of South African wine. For a start, the vines, all under the ownership of Cape Point Vineyards, have been planted on new winegrowing territory on the Atlantic side of the Cape Peninsula mountain chain, where *terroir* is key. The Noordhoek vineyards feature Sauvignon Blanc, Sémillon, and Chardonnay, while further south, Redhill's old gravel quarry location is planted with Cabernet, Shiraz, and a few rows each of Cabernet Franc and Merlot. It is early days yet for the sole red, a well-structured Cabernet-Shiraz blend with bright fruit, but the validity of this new and emerging area has been proven, with the early vintages of Sauvignon Blanc and Sauvignon Blanc-Sémillon blend regularly winning awards.

🗺 *sandstone on bleached granite* 🍇 *Cabernet Sauvignon, Shiraz, Pinot Noir* 🍇 *Sauvignon Blanc, Chardonnay, Sémillon* 🍷 *red, white*

WINE TOUR OF STELLENBOSCH

Vergelegen

STELLENBOSCH, founded in 1679, is a bustling university town. It is probably also the most widely recognized of South Africa's wine-growing areas, outside as well as inside the country. There are at present close to 100 wineries open to the public, all within easy reach of the town centre. A drive around this area affords some of the best views of South Africa's stunning winelands.

① **Vergelegen** △
This property has a beautifully restored 18th-century manor house, spacious gardens, and a centre depicting the farm's history. It produces some of South Africa's best wines. *See p469*.
☎ 021 847 1334 🅦 www.vergelegen.co.za

③ **Spier**
One of the first wine farms to be founded in Stellenbosch (in 1767), Spier features old Cape Dutch buildings, gardens running down to the river's edge, an excellent wine shop, restaurants, and a winery producing modern-style varietal wines.
☎ 021 881 3690 🅦 www.spierwines.co.za

④ **Stellenbosch** ▽
Dorp Street is known for its Dutch settler buildings as well as its wine shops and bars, including Stellenbosch Wine Export Centre and an old general dealer-style store, 'Uncle Samie's (*below*). For a wealth of winemaking history under one roof, the Stellenryck Wine Museum is also on R44/Plankenberg Road.
☎ 021 883 3584 (Tourist Information)

② **Morgenster Estate** △
Owned by Italian Giulio Bertrand, this winery is as well known for its olive products as it is for its classic, Bordeaux-style red wines. The modern one-storey cellar offers spectacular views over the Helderberg Mountain. *See p466*.
☎ 021 852 1738 🅦 www.morgenster.co.za

LOCAL WINE FESTIVALS

The first Stellenbosch wine and food festival was held in the town in 1976. Today, a bigger version takes place every August, featuring local restaurants, delicatessens, and wine and food personalities, as well as Stellenbosch wines, in an extravagant three-day feast. Smaller areas within the region also promote their own wine and food. Contact the local tourist office for further information.
🅦 *www.istellenbosch.org.za*

⑤ **Neil Ellis Wines**
A winding country lane leads to this Tuscan-style winery, complete with a stream running through it. A dam, colourful gardens, and a fabulous mountain backdrop provide a bucolic setting in which to enjoy the polished wines. *See p467*.
☎ 021 887 0649 🅦 www.neilellis.com

⑥ **Thelema Mountain Vineyards** ▷
Taste some of South Africa's most sought-after wines here, while soaking up the view of the dramatic Groot Drakenstein Mountains. *See p467.*
📞 021 885 1924
🆆 www.thelema.co.za

PAARL
10km

Simonsberg Mountain

KEY
━━━ Tour route

⑦ **Tokara**
Enjoy a combination of impressive views and modern architecture at this recently built winery. Art exhibits, home-grown olive oil, and a well-rated restaurant all make it worth the trip. So too will the classy Tokara wines.
📞 021 808 5900 🆆 www.tokararestaurant.co.za

Dorp Street
STELLENBOSCH

Eerste

Helderberg Mountain

0 ─km─ 5

Somerset West

⑧ **Rustenberg Wines** △
This historic property, dating from 1692 and surrounded by many old Cape Dutch buildings, oozes charm, and the cellar is brimming with stellar modern wines. *See p467.*
📞 021 809 1200 🆆 www.rustenberg.co.za

⑨ **Kanonkop** ◁
The Krige brothers (Johan, *left*), grandsons of one-time member of the South African Cabinet Paul Sauer, own this farm, and the tasting room is packed with family memorabilia. The red wine range here is headed by the internationally renowned Paul Sauer Bordeaux-style blend. *See p466.*
📞 021 884 4656 🆆 www.kanonkop.co.za

TOP PRODUCERS IN THE CAPE PENINSULA & SURROUNDS

Boekenhoutskloof
Paarl District

PO Box 433, Franschhoek Valley
☎ *021 876 3320*
W *www.boekenhoutskloof.co.za* ☐

THE FIRST LOVE OF winemaker Marc Kent is Shiraz. Until the young vines behind his Franschhoek cellar are more mature, his Shiraz comes from warmer Wellington (also in Paarl), its rich spiciness unhindered by any new oak. New oak is, however, used for his taffeta-textured Sémillon, which includes fruit from some 100-year-old Franschhoek vines, and the polished Cabernet Sauvignon; the scent of spicy French oak complements the wine's vibrant, sweet fruit flavours. The hedonistic, Shiraz-led Chocolate Block is a local take on Côtes du Rhône.
🍷 *red, white, dessert* 🗓 *2007, 2006, 2005* ★ *Shiraz, Cabernet Sauvignon, Sémillon*

Fairview
Paarl District

PO Box 583, Suider-Paarl ☎ *021 863 2450* W *www.fairview.co.za* ☐

ALL THINGS RHÔNE-influenced pour forth here. The easy-flow Goats do Roam range targets the fun-drinking market; while a sophisticated, spicy Shiraz is their flagship. Led by Charles Back, Fairview was the first in South Africa to crack Viognier, a richly-textured grape here. The Back team also produces sumptuous Sémillon, satin-tannined Pinotage, and a very smart Chardonnay. Sauvignon Blanc and Cabernet Sauvignon from the new, cooler vineyards in Darling and Stellenbosch are already augmenting the quality of this range.

CHARLES BACK

Charles Back is a man of admirable business ethics who loves life and revels in hard work. After training at Elsenburg Agricultural College, he joined his father, Cyril, on the Fairview family farm in 1978, and has been there ever since. Ideas are his lifeblood and he runs with them at his own pace. In the 1990s, Back uprooted every grape variety – even fashionable ones – that did not perform well on Fairview and replaced them with those that he believed would – mainly Rhône varieties. This brave move paid dividends, as his silky-textured Viognier and easy-drinking Goats do Roam (a play on words with Côtes du Rhône) range show. Having conquered the lower-priced end of the market, Back has now turned to what he hopes will prove an icon wine at his Swartland-based Spice Route winery: Malabar, a rich yet refined blend of Shiraz, Merlot, and Grenache.

🍷 *red, white, rosé* 🗓 *2007, 2006, 2005, 2004* ★ *Fairview: Viognier, Sémillon, Shiraz*

Glen Carlou
Paarl District

PO Box 23, Klapmuts ☎ *021 875 5528* W *www.glencarlou.co.za* ☐

THE HESS GROUP now owns this Paarl farm, which was started by Walter Finlayson in 1988. His son David remains as cellarmaster. The fresh, age-worthy Chardonnay is now complemented by the complex, single-vineyard Quartz Stone Chardonnay. Cabernet Sauvignon also comes in standard and single-vineyard versions, with the structured Gravel Quarry French-oaked. David loves experimenting: Pinot Noir, Zinfandel, and Shiraz are part of the range, and more are on the way.
🍷 *red, white* 🗓 *2007, 2006, 2005* ★ *Quartz Stone Chardonnay, Gravel Quarry Cabernet Sauvignon, Grand Classique*

Rupert & Rothschild Vignerons
Paarl District

PO Box 412, Franschhoek Valley ☎ *021 874 1648* W *www.rupert-rothschildvignerons.com* ☐ *by appt*

FOUNDED IN 1690, this farm now joins two illustrious winemaking families – one South African and one French. In deference to these families, the environmentally friendly wines ooze a certain grandeur.

The Baroness Nadine Chardonnay wine is opulent, yet elegant and dry. And the farm also produces two Cabernet Sauvignon-led blends: Baron Edmund and Classique. The former can take over two years' ageing in new French oak barrels, while the latter is lighter-textured, more accessible, and sees less oak.
🍷 *red, white* 🗓 *2006, 2005, 2004* ★ *Baron Edmund, Classique, Baroness Nadine Chardonnay*

Rupert & Rothschild Vignerons

Veenwouden
Private Cellar
Paarl District

PO Box 7086, Noorder-Paarl
📞 *021 872 6806* ⬜ *by appt*

AFTER ITS FIRST VINTAGE in 1993, Veenwouden quickly reached cult status. Sadly, a family tragedy curtailed some of the success, though the expanded range is improving each year. Ex-golf pro, now winemaker, Marcel van der Walt gleaned most of his wine knowledge from a 1994 harvest with Michel Rolland (famed wine consultant).

The focus here is on Bordeaux varieties expressed in three wines: the Classic, a Cabernet Sauvignon-led blend; an opulent Merlot; and, under the Thornhill label, Vivat Bacchus, a Merlot-Shiraz-Cabernet blend. A vigorous Syrah has recently joined the range, while the Chardonnay Special Reserve remains a creamy, well-oaked favourite.
🍷 *red, white* 📅 *2007, 2006, 2005*
★ *Classic, Merlot*

Vilafonté
Paarl District

7c Lower Dorp Street, Bosman's Crossing, Stellenbosch 📞 *021 886 0483* 🌐 *www.vilafonte.com* ⬜ *by appt*

CALIFORNIAN HUSBAND AND WIFE Phil Freese (viticulturist) and Zelma Long (winemaker) first visited the Cape in 1990. They immediately recognized the potential and bought 42ha in the Simonsberg Paarl ward; 15ha are currently planted solely to Bordeaux red varieties. Two blends are made: Series C, Cabernet-based with Merlot and Cabernet Franc; and Series M, usually Merlot-dominated with Malbec and Cabernets Sauvignon and Franc.
🍷 *red* 📅 *2006, 2005, 2004*
★ *Series C, Series M*

500ml PRODUCT OF SOUTH AFRICA Alc 13.5% Vol.

de Trafford
VIN DE PAILLE
Wine from naturally dried grapes
WINE OF ORIGIN STELLENBOSCH
1999
MONT FLEUR · PO BOX 495 · STELLENBOSCH · FAX 021 8801611

**Hand-painted label,
De Trafford Wines**

De Trafford Wines
Stellenbosch District

PO Box 495, Stellenbosch 📞 *021 880 1611* 🌐 *www.detrafford.co.za* ⬜

VINEYARDS HIGH in the Helderberg provide most of the fruit for De Trafford's range of 10 wines, all of which are big in flavour yet exude elegance. Owner and winemaker David Trafford specializes in two styles from local white star Chenin Blanc. One is dry and fermented with native yeasts; the other, a lusciously sweet *vin de paille*. De Trafford's reds, including a big, supple Shiraz and a majestic Cabernet, are equally individual, as are Rita Trafford's beautiful, hand-painted labels.
🍷 *red, white, dessert* 📅 *2007, 2006, 2005* ★ *Chenin Blanc, Shiraz, Cabernet Sauvignon, Vin de Paille*

Jordan Wines
Stellenbosch District

PO Box 12592, Die Boord
📞 *021 881 3441*
🌐 *www.jordanwines.com* ⬜

TED JORDAN purchased this farm in 1982, selecting sites to suit grape varieties, with a future international market in mind. Then California-seasoned winemakers Jordan Junior (Gary) and his wife Kathy arrived in the early 1990s. Production has soared since the first harvest under their own label in 1993, yet they have managed to maintain high quality. Stars of their strong range include a welcomingly consistent Chardonnay, an expressively ripe, barrel-fermented Sauvignon Blanc, a modern-classic Cabernet Sauvignon, and the flagship, Cobblers Hill Bordeaux-style blend. All mature admirably.
🍷 *red, white* 📅 *2007, 2006, 2005*
★ *Nine Yards Chardonnay, Chardonnay, Cabernet Sauvignon, Cobblers Hill*

Winery worker packing wine bottles into cases

Kanonkop
Stellenbosch District

PO Box 19, Elsenburg 📞 *021 884 4656* 🌐 *www.kanonkop.co.za* ⬤

THIS VENERABLE ESTATE, founded in 1910 by Senator Sauer, is now owned by his descendants, the Krige brothers. The national grape, Pinotage, has been given modern appeal here by former winemaker Beyers Truter. Winemaking methods, though, remain traditional. The juice is fermented in open tanks and the heavy cap of skins has to be pushed through the juice regularly by hand. But it is Paul Sauer, Kanonkop's Cabernet-based Bordeaux-style blend, that has made critics worldwide take notice. Made from the grapes of 30-year-old vines, it is named after the Krige brothers' grandfather.

🔴 *red* 📆 *2006, 2005, 2004* ★ *Paul Sauer, Cabernet Sauvignon, Pinotage*

Le Riche Wines
Stellenbosch District

PO Box 6295, Stellenbosch 📞 *021 887 0789* 🌐 *www.leriche.co.za* ⬤

AUTHORITATIVE YET ELEGANT is a summary of the approach that Etienne le Riche has brought with him from his years of experience at Rustenberg. His range is sourced from several parts of Stellenbosch – some designed for early drinking and others for a few years of ageing. The Cabernet Reserve is full, supple, and enriched with top quality French oak; while the regular Cabernet, with a splash of Merlot, is softer and with less new oak. Etienne's first white, a Chardonnay, reflects the understated elegance of its red counterparts.

🔴 *red, white* 📆 *2006, 2005, 2004* ★ *Cabernet Reserve, Cabernet Sauvignon, Cabernet Sauvignon-Merlot*

Punching down grape skins at Kanonkop

Meerlust Estate
Stellenbosch District

PO Box 7121, Stellenbosch 📞 *021 843 3587* 🌐 *www.meerlust.co.za* ⬤

EIGHT GENERATIONS of the Myburgh family have lived here since 1693. Chris Williams took over as winemaker from Giorgio Dalla Cia in 2004. (Dalla Cia has since set up his own winery and grappa distillery.) Williams has freshened up the range without losing its traditional style. Based on Bordeaux and Burgundy varieties, the wines receive an unhurried upbringing in good French oak and are released older than many. The first release of the Bordeaux-style, Cabernet-led blend Rubicon was from the 1980 vintage.

🔴 *red, white* 📆 *2007, 2006, 2005, 2004*
★ *Rubicon, Merlot, Chardonnay*

Morgenster Estate
Stellenbosch District

PO Box 1616, Somerset West 📞 *021 852 1738* 🌐 *www.morgenster.co.za* ⬤

PERFECTION DOES NOT come easily: it took the Italian owner, ex-textile magnate Giulio Bertrand, 10 hard years to transform this neglected farm, originally part of Vergelegen estate, and to release his first flagship Bordeaux-style wine. The vineyards on the wind-blown, rock-strewn Schaapen-berg slopes had to be carved from virgin soil. The wine-making team here is one of South Africa's most experienced, including Pierre Lurton, manager of Château Cheval Blanc *(see p80)* in St-Émilion. Morgenster's flagship wine, a Cabernet Franc-Cabernet Sauvignon blend, is sleek, fresh, and elegant. There are also a supple, Merlot-led red, Lourens River Valley, and two 'Italian Collection' wines, one based on Nebbiolo, the other on Sangiovese.

🔴 *red* 📆 *2006, 2005, 2004*
★ *Morgenster, Lourens River Valley*

Mulderbosch Vineyards
Stellenbosch District

PO Box 548, Stellenbosch 📞 *021 865 2488* 🌐 *www.mulderbosch.co.za* ⬤ *by appt*

Meerlust Estate

THIS IS A GREAT property to visit, as much for the entertaining winemaker (Mike Dobrovic) and the beautiful landscape as for the masterful wines it makes. The farm and Dobrovic's name were made on pure Sauvignon Blanc. Tentative steps with the use of oak were then taken with Chenin Blanc, Chardonnay, and a riper Sauvignon Blanc, but as an extra rather than a key flavour. Fully barrel-fermented Chardonnay is also made, but only in years when it achieves adequate concentration. An understated Cabernet Sauvignon-Cabernet Franc-Merlot leads the trio of reds.

🔴 *red, white, dessert* 📆 *2001, 2000, 1999, 1998* ★ *Sauvignon Blanc, Barrel-fermented Chardonnay*

Neil Ellis Wines
Stellenbosch District

PO Box 917, Stellenbosch 📞 *021 887 0649* 🌐 *www.neilellis.com* ⬜

ONE OF THE COUNTRY'S most respected winemakers, Neil Ellis set the trend for *négociant* (see p97) trading nearly 20 years ago. As well as growing grapes around his own cellar, he has contracts with others who grow the varieties most suited to their sites: he buys Sauvignon Blanc grapes from Groenekloof, overlooking the Atlantic; Chardonnay from highland Elgin; and more Chardonnay, Shiraz, Merlot, and Cabernet Sauvignon from warmer Stellenbosch, close to HQ. With his careful handling, each wine bears the stamp of its origin and exemplifies modern refinement with great ageing potential.
🟦 *red, white* 🔼 *2007, 2006, 2005*
★ *Cabernet Sauvignon Reserve, Elgin Chardonnay, Groenekloof Sauvignon Blanc*

Rustenberg Wines
Stellenbosch District

PO Box 33, Stellenbosch 📞 *021 809 1200* 🌐 *www.rustenberg.co.za* ⬜

OWNED BY THE BARLOWS since 1941, Rustenberg underwent a complete re-vamp in the mid-1990s: a new cellar was formed out of the old dairy, and new vine material was imported to improve quality. The wines are already showing the benefit of this input and of Randolph Christians, previously Adi Badenhorst's assistant, who took over in the cellar when Badenhorst resigned. The majestic single-vineyard Peter Barlow Cabernet Sauvignon leads the range. And the Bordeaux-style John X Merriman blend is worth a try.
🟦 *red, white* 🔼 *2008, 2007, 2006, 2005* ★ *Peter Barlow, Rustenberg John X Merriman*

Winery at Neil Ellis Wines

Rust en Vrede Estate
Stellenbosch District

PO Box 473, Stellenbosch 📞 *021 881 3881* 🌐 *www.rustenvrede.com* ⬜

THE GOAL here is to produce just one red wine – the flagship Estate Blend – as the best expression of each Rust en Vrede vintage. Old, virused vineyards have been replaced and a new barrel maturation cellar has been built in the continuing pursuit of this dream, and the young team at the helm are sure they can make it happen. Until then, this prize-winning Estate Blend takes its place alongside the other wines in the estate's range: a savoury Cabernet Sauvignon, a rich Shiraz, and a fleshy Merlot.
🟦 *red* 🔼 *2007, 2006* ★ *Estate Blend*

Saxenburg
Stellenbosch District

PO Box 171, Kuils River 📞 *021 903 6113* 🌐 *www.saxenburg.com* ⬜

SHIRAZ MIGHT BE the variety favoured by an increasing number of Cape producers, as it is here by Nico van der Merwe, but not many have the depth of experience that Nico has with this grape. His first Saxenburg vintage was in 1991. And since 1996, he has enjoyed the luxury of creating two versions a year at Saxenburg: the refined, dark-berried Private Collection and the con-centrated Saxenburg Shiraz Select. The popularity of this duo reflects his great success.
🟦 *red, white, dessert, sparkling*
🔼 *2008, 2007, 2006, 2005*
★ *Saxenburg Shiraz Select, Private Collection Shiraz, Private Collection Cabernet Sauvignon*

Thelema Mountain Vineyards
Stellenbosch District

PO Box 2234, Dennesig 📞 *021 885 1924* 🌐 *www.thelema.co.za* ⬜

VIRTUALLY EVERY RANGE here since 1988 has sold out less than two months after its release. Winemaker Gyles Webb's philosophy is simply to grow good fruit and get it into the bottle with as little fuss as possible. His tasting skills keep this mountainside farm at the cutting edge, producing some of the Cape's best Cabernet Sauvignon, Chardonnay, and Sauvignon Blanc. The list also includes a Riesling that matures magnificently. The range has recently been expanded by fruit from Thelema's Elgin vineyards; the Sutherland Sauvignon Blanc and Chardonnay both show a fine thread of freshening minerality.
🟦 *red, white, fortified*
🔼 *2008, 2007, 2006*
★ *The Mint Cabernet Sauvignon, Cabernet Sauvignon, Chardonnay, Sauvignon Blanc, Riesling*

Vergelegen
Stellenbosch District

See right.

Villiera Wines
Stellenbosch District

PO Box 66, Koelenhof 📞 *021 865 2002* 🌐 *www.villiera.com* ⬜

THE GRIER FAMILY manage to achieve consistent quality in a range that, at last count, numbered 21 wines. No pesticides or insecticides are used on the vineyards here; ducks and guinea fowl clean up any destructive life, and good vine husbandry helps restrict mildew. The wines respond with great personality, whether it is the speciality bubblies or the silky-fruited dessert wine, Inspiration.

🟥 *red, white, sparkling, dessert*
📅 *2008, 2007, 2006, 2005, 2004, 2003* ★ *Bush Vine Sauvignon Blanc, Monro Brut Première Cuvée, Brut Natural MCC*

Klein Constantia Estate
Constantia Ward

PO Box 375, Constantia 📞 *021 794 5188* 🌐 *www.kleinconstantia.com* ⬜

IN 1986 KLEIN CONSTANTIA'S slopes opened up a whole new perspective on Cape Sauvignon Blanc. The matching of variety to site and careful

Carrying wine, Villiera Wines

vine canopy management were major contributors to its success. Winemaker Adam Mason has built on the wine's reputation since his arrival in 2003, introducing the single-vineyard Perdeblokke. Mason and the Jooste family (who own the farm) are also world renowned for their apricot-scented Vin de Constance. This unfortified dessert wine from Muscat de Frontignan grapes is a re-creation of the Constantia wine that originally earned the Cape its international acclaim. Riesling has also proved a consistent though unsung performer. Reds struggle in these cool climes, but better vine stock is beginning to improve this.

🟥 *red, white, dessert, sparkling* 📅 *2008, 2007, 2006, 2005, 2004* ★ *Vin de Constance, Sauvignon Blanc, Perdeblokke Sauvignon Blanc, Riesling*

Steenberg Vineyards
Constantia Ward

PO Box 224, Steenberg 📞 *021 713 2211* 🌐 *www.steenberg-vineyards.co.za* ⬜

STEENBERG'S SAUVIGNON BLANC has a little more richness surrounding its minerally core than most in Constantia, and the best vintages of this unoaked wine age well for several years. The barrel-fermented Sémillon is delicious too. These two varieties are combined in the flagship white Magna Carta; the maiden 2007 promises elegant maturity several years hence. And Steenberg's warmer slopes benefit red grapes: Merlot in particular, but also some experimental Nebbiolo. All the Chardonnay and Pinot Noir here are now channelled into the Steenberg 1682 Brut, a non-vintage dry bubbly commemorating the year the farm was set up.

🟥 *red, white, sparkling* 📅 *2008, 2007, 2006* ★ *Magna Carta, Sauvignon Blanc Reserve, Sémillon, Merlot*

Cape Point Vineyards
Cape Point District

PO Box 100, Noordhoek 📞 *021 785 7660* 🌐 *www.capepointvineyards. co.za* ⬜ *by appt*

THE ORIGINALITY of Cape Point wines lies in the lone position of its two vineyards, west of the Peninsula mountain chain. A four-year-old Sauvignon Blanc vineyard produced the wine of the year at the 2000 South Africa National Wine Show, and other awards have followed. The grassy, oaked Sémillon is also much-awarded, but the Sauvignon-Sémillon blend Isliedh eclipses both in intensity and complexity. The Scarborough Red is well structured.

🟥 *red, white* 📅 *2007, 2006, 2005* ★ *Isliedh, Sauvignon Blanc, Sémillon*

Harvesting grapes, Steenberg Vineyards

VERGELEGEN'S SUCCESS STORY

FOUNDED IN 1700 by Willem van der Stel, Vergelegen is one of the Cape's most magnificent farms. When the company Anglo-American purchased the property in 1987, no vines remained. Extensive studies to determine the best vineyard sites resulted in plantings of Cabernets Sauvignon and Franc, Merlot, Sauvignon Blanc, Sémillon, plus a little Shiraz and Chardonnay, around the hilltop winery. These vines have rapidly produced wines of international repute. A gravity flow system from grape delivery to the barrel cellar ensures gentle handling throughout the winemaking process.

It was Vergelegen's pure, powerful Sauvignon Blanc that started the run of awards here. This was then followed by the beautifully-polished flagship Bordeaux-style red blend, and more recently a new, barrel-fermented Bordeaux-style white blend (Sémillon-Sauvignon Blanc), which promises to develop great complexity with time. Two winemakers with profound ability have headed the cellar since 1987; André van Rensburg took over from Martin Meinert in 1998. His dream is to eventually make just one superb white and one top-notch red.

Contact Information

PO Box 17, Somerset West
☎ 021 847 1334
🖥 www.vergelegen.co.za ⬜

Wine Information

🍷 red, white, dessert
📅 2008, 2007, 2006, 2005, 2004
★ Vergelegen V, Vergelegen Red (Bordeaux-style blend), Vergelegen White (Bordeaux-style blend), Sauvignon Blanc Reserve

The Camphor Trees

Van der Stel transformed the uncultivated property he named Vergelegen into an international garden of Eden. Trees were a special love of his, and several of the Chinese camphors he planted still thrive. As the oldest living, officially documented trees on the subcontinent, they have now been declared a national monument.

The Homestead

Careful restoration by successive owners has ensured that the original 18th-century van der Stel homestead has remained in harmony with the rest of the impressive Vergelegen property. A landmark in its own right, it is complemented by the beautiful landscape that surrounds it.

View from Vergelegen's hilltop winery

USA

USA

THE USA IS *blessed with a wide variety of vineyards, from the sun-drenched slopes of California to the more Burgundian climes of Oregon and the frosty Finger Lakes region of New York State. Each has its own captivating set of wine styles.*

BACKGROUND

GRAPE CUTTINGS were first brought to the USA in the 18th century by Spanish missionaries, who planted them in order to produce communion wines. It was only in the mid-19th century that serious attempts were made to improve quality by importing top-quality cuttings from Europe. These thrived throughout California and in various eastern states as well. By the end of the 19th century, the red wines from the Napa Valley were already recognized as being of outstanding quality.

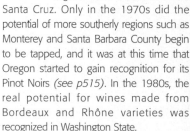

Grape picker at Robert Mondavi's vineyards

Two disasters then struck. The first was phylloxera *(see pp528–9)* in the late 19th century; the second, equally damaging, was Prohibition *(see pp474–5)*. The ban on alcohol was widely evaded, but even so, the vineyards of California were neglected and wineries were closed. By the time the ban was repealed in 1933, the industry had virtually collapsed: cheap fortified wines were being produced in California,

and only a handful of fine red wines existed. Eastern states such as New York found a market for poor sparkling wines and sweet reds from inferior grape varieties.

It was not until the 1960s that new influences came to the fore, with mentors such as Russian winemaker André Tchelitscheff and Robert Mondavi *(see p476)*. In 1966, Mondavi built the first new winery in the Napa Valley since Prohibition. Others followed, and quality-conscious wineries were established in other California regions such as Sonoma and Santa Cruz. Only in the 1970s did the potential of more southerly regions such as Monterey and Santa Barbara County begin to be tapped, and it was at this time that Oregon started to gain recognition for its Pinot Noirs *(see p515)*. In the 1980s, the real potential for wines made from Bordeaux and Rhône varieties was recognized in Washington State.

Despite occasional problems, such as an oversupply of grapes and a new outbreak of phylloxera in the 1980s, the USA has never looked back. Quality, and prices, reach exceptional heights in California. Some states, namely Ohio, Michigan, New York, and Virginia, have shown that they too are capable of producing serious wines.

THE WINE INDUSTRY

THE USA is the fourth-largest wine-producing country in the world, and California alone is responsible for 94 per cent of its output. After Italy and France, it is the world's largest wine-

Vineyard and school house in St Helena, Napa Valley

◁ **Autumnal vineyards and Mayacamas Mountains in Napa Valley, California**

Washington PACIFIC NORTHWEST pp510–11

NEW YORK pp522–3

NORTH COAST CALIFORNIA pp480–81

CENTRAL & SOUTHERN CALIFORNIA pp496–7

WINEGROWING REGIONS

California dominates the USA's wine industry, but there are significant wine-producing areas in almost all states. Of most viticultural significance are Washington and Oregon in the northwest and New York State in the east. Many other states have been dogged by a poor reputation, but Michigan, Ohio, and Virginia are steadily improving the quality of their wines.

consuming nation. However, only eight per cent of the population is responsible for consuming 80 per cent of all American wine. Although there are about 1,500 wineries, the market is dominated by a few major producers: Ernest & Julio Gallo alone accounts for 30 per cent, with Beringer Blass, Constellation Brands, and Mondavi also producing a significant percentage.

The wine regions are divided into zones known as American Viticultural Areas (AVAs), of which there are over a hundred. Some embrace an entire county; others may encompass fewer than 100ha. AVAs are distinct from the European AOC or DOC systems in that they are simply geographical descriptors with no qualitative criteria. The absence of European-style regulation and the industry's dependence on market forces means that occasionally the USA over- or under-produces, as occurred in 2003 when there was a major glut, resulting in tens of thousands of hectares being pulled up in California. Such periods of instability, however, tend to be short-lived.

Cabernet Sauvignon grapes

GRAPE VARIETIES & WINE STYLES

CABERNET SAUVIGNON is by far the most important red variety in California,

accounting for almost one quarter of all red grapes in the state. For some years Zinfandel and Merlot have been neck and neck in second place. The former was close to extinction 20 years ago, but was saved by the invention of blush wine *(see p487)*. Merlot's popularity peaked in the late 1990s, but many weak, overcropped wines have marred its reputation. Pinot Noir meanwhile, has made great strides in the past decade in cool regions such as Oregon, and Syrah seems to be thriving everywhere.

California's red wines tend to be made in a rich, almost burly, fruit-driven style with relatively high alcohol, which is an unavoidable consequence of the balmy Californian climate. Reds from the Pacific Northwest and Long Island in New York State often show balance rather than power.

Chardonnay remains overwhelmingly the first choice among white grapes. Rich and opulent, its popularity has never diminished. Other white grapes such as Viognier, Roussanne, Pinot Gris, and Riesling produce some excellent wines, but quantities are minute compared with the all-conquering Chardonnay. Only Sauvignon Blanc offers itself as a viable alternative in terms of quantity.

PROHIBITION

Americ an prohibition outlawed the manufacture and sale of intoxicating liquors in the USA from January 1920 to December 1933. This 'noble experiment' reflected a variety of historical and cultural forces, but it was a clear disaster for the domestic wine industry. Even beyond these 14 'dry' years, Prohibition dramatically influenced America's relationship with alcohol. Its legacy continues through a complex legal framework for alcohol sales.

Prohibition-era drinks tray

Concealed corkscrew

Collapse

The 18th Amendment to the US Constitution ushered in national Prohibition, and the American wine industry immediately collapsed. But there were legal loopholes that permitted a few wineries to continue limited operation. Some survived by providing consumers with dried 'grape bricks' for home wine production, which was permitted. A few producers were designated to make wine for sacramental and medicinal purposes.

GRASS-ROOTS PROTEST

Prohibition advocates march in Washington, DC in 1913

THEIR SECURITY DEMANDS
YOU VOTE **REPEAL**

BALLOT BOX

WOMEN'S ORGANIZATION NATIONAL PROHIBITION REFORM

Prohibition reform poster

America's 'Wild West' expansion and industrial development made the late 1800s and early 1900s a chaotic time. World War I intensified the sense of social strife. Popular reactions to these events included the Progressive political movement and a Protestant religious revival. Some grass-roots protest groups also began targeting alcohol abuse. However, many leaders of this temperance movement called for reform after it became clear that Prohibition did more harm than good.

Supplies of alcoholic beverages were seized and destroyed

Illegal drinking

Despite the efforts of police, Prohibition was widely flouted. The production and sale of wine, beer, and spirits were widespread. Speakeasies, underground drinking establishments, soon sprang up. The supply of bootleg liquor was largely in the hands of criminals.

Aftermath

The 21st Amendment to the Constitution ended Prohibition. Each state is now responsible for its own system of alcohol distribution and sales. All states operate a tiered system, whereby producers must sell to wholesalers, who sell to retailers, who then sell to consumers. In some areas, known as control states, it is the state itself that is the wholesaler and retailer. In others, license states, the state designates who may fulfill these roles. Recent court challenges now question the system's legality.

Early confiscation efforts drew vast community support

INFLUENTIAL 20TH-CENTURY WINEMAKERS

Y THE END OF PROHIBITION, *there was little left of the once-renowned US wine industry. Many wineries had closed, and there was a shortage of modern equipment and trained winemakers. A gallant handful of enthusiasts – led by Beaulieu Vineyards and winemaker André Tchelitscheff – were responsible for initiating the industry's revival. Tchelitscheff's ideas and practices influenced generations of California winemakers, who in the 1950s and 1960s put California firmly back on the international stage.*

Beaulieu Vineyards

André Tchelitscheff in Beaulieu Vineyards

André Tchelitscheff (1901–94)

Russian-born but French-trained oenologist Tchelitscheff was hired in 1938 to revamp Beaulieu Vineyards' *(see p490)* corroded Napa Valley winery. Beaulieu had survived Prohibition by supplying wine for liturgical purposes. Moreover, it was one of the few California estates with substantial plantings of mature Cabernet Sauvignon vines. Tchelitscheff overhauled the winery and produced a series of famous Cabernets, known as the Georges de Latour Private Reserve. His main achievement was to recognize the importance of viticultural practices such as frost protection, temperature controlled fermentation, and malolactic fermentation. He imparted his knowledge to countless US winemakers, who collectively improved the overall quality of California wine dramatically.

Martin Ray (1905–76)

Martin Ray bought the Paul Masson winery in 1936, sold it to Seagram in 1943, and then established his own vineyards and winery at Mount Eden, over 600m up in the Santa Cruz Mountains. Even though US wine law allows a varietal wine to include up to 25 per cent of a different grape, Ray insisted that his wines should be 100 per cent varietal. He also campaigned against the use of chemical additives and concentrates, which were widely employed by other wineries at that time. He vehemently believed that California should adopt European viticultural and winemaking practices, a view widely accepted today, but regarded as eccentric in the 1950s.

Robert Mondavi (1913–2008)

Mondavi came from a traditional wine-producing family, but his visits to Europe persuaded him that quality throughout California needed to be improved so that the wines could rival European models. His family did not agree, so after a bitter dispute

Robert Mondavi in the cellar of his Napa Valley winery

he set up his own winery in Napa Valley in 1966 *(see p491)*. Within a few years he was producing some of California's most sophisticated wines. His passion for excellence was inspirational to other winemakers, and he was unstintingly generous in sharing the results of his research into techniques such as oak-ageing. He also strongly believed in educating consumers on the virtues of responsible wine consumption as a life-enhancing experience. Even into his 90s, Mondavi was an energetic international crusader for the value of wine, food, and the arts.

Warren Winiarski (1928–)

In 1970, Winiarski, a thoughtful political scientist from Chicago, left for California, took a lowly job as a cellarhand at Mondavi, and eventually acquired vineyards and a winery in Napa's Stags Leap district *(see p492)*. His Cabernet Sauvignon soundly beat the grandest French opposition at the famous 'Judgment of Paris' tasting *(see p492)* in 1976. Winiarski never looked back. He produced impeccable Cabernets, which demonstrated that although Napa wines have their own character, they have won the right to be regarded alongside the greatest wines of France.

Paul Draper (1936–)

Paul Draper has been the winemaker at Ridge Vineyards *(see p504)* in Santa Cruz since 1969. His achievement has been twofold; he created an American wine classic in his long-lived Monte Bello Cabernet Sauvignon; and he has demonstrated that Zinfandel can be more than a brawny, rustic red wine, and that it can take its place among the world's most desirable reds. For 30 years he has shown that old-vine Zinfandel can produce simply delicious wines that are stylistically unique to California.

David Lett (1940–2008)

The great American winemakers are not confined to California. If it wasn't for David

Lett's conviction that Pinot Noir was better suited to Oregon than California, Oregon might have remained a viticultural backwater. The Pinots he made in the 1970s triumphed when blind-tasted alongside burgundies *(see p515)*, and Oregon has gone from strength to strength.

Randall Grahm (1953–)

Randall Grahm of Bonny Doon Vineyard *(see p505)* in Santa Cruz has the most original and inventive mind of any American winemaker. In the early 1980s, he attempted a revolution by turning his back on the ubiquitous Cabernet and Chardonnay to focus instead on Mediterranean varieties, primarily from the Rhône, and unfashionable grapes such as Riesling. He is an amazingly gifted publicist for the like-minded group known as the Rhône Rangers *(see p501)*, and has persuaded drinkers worldwide to re-evaluate the potential of California wine.

David Lett first planting vines in 1966

Helen Turley (1946–)

Helen Turley is a consultant winemaker who has established the dominant style for top-flight California wine since the early 1990s: made from ultra-ripe grapes, with richness of oaky flavour compensating for low acidity and high alcohol, and bottled without filtration. Turley is the best known of the growing band of consultants who have become important in the USA as more and more wealthy people establish vineyards and wineries having had no hands-on experience.

Warren Winiarski

CALIFORNIA

THIS VITICULTURAL PARADISE *has been a source of rich, hedonistic wines for well over a hundred years. Not only is it a mecca for producers of top-class Chardonnay and Cabernet Sauvignon, but its rich terroir is capable of producing a wine collection as diverse as you might find anywhere in Europe.*

The first to plant vines in California were the Spanish missionaries, who arrived around 1770. By the mid-19th century, settlers from Italy and Germany were planting high on sun-drenched slopes in an attempt to reproduce their European landscape. Many areas soon began producing commercially successful wines. Then the double blows of phylloxera *(see pp528–9)* in the late 19th century and Prohibition *(see pp474–5)* in the early 20th century devastated the industry. Americans do not give up easily, however, and once Prohibition had ended and the prosperous postwar era began, the California wine industry gradually recovered.

The industry remained small until the 1960s, when the real renaissance in California wines began. World-famous wine producer Robert Mondavi established his own winery in 1966, and then in the early 1970s two California wines scored a stunning victory over top French *cuvées* in the so-called 'Judgment of Paris' *(see p492).* The stage was set and California winemakers never looked back.

Quady Winery, Central Valley

Today, there are at least 1,300 wineries stretching from Mendocino in the north to Malibu in the south and beyond. Producers range from boutique wineries making a few hundred cases of wine a year to vast industrial operations such as Ernest & Julio Gallo and Kendall-Jackson. With over 200,000ha planted, California produces 90 per cent of the USA's wine.

Although by no means California's largest wine region, the richly-endowed Napa Valley is deservedly its most celebrated, offering full-bodied Cabernet Sauvignons that bear comparison with top bordeaux. Of the other key regions: neighbouring Sonoma has a more diverse climate and range of grapes; Monterey is ideal for Chardonnay and Riesling; Santa Barbara County is showing potential for dazzling Chardonnay, Pinot Noir, and Syrah; and more rural inland California is home to brawny Zinfandels and fortified wines from the Sierra Foothills, as well as vast quantities of basic but drinkable wines from the blisteringly hot Central Valley.

View over Byron vineyard and winery to the Sierra Madre Mountains in Santa Barbara

◁ **Vineyard in the foothills of the Mayacamas Mountains, Knights Valley, Sonoma**

WINE MAP OF NORTH COAST CALIFORNIA

THE NORTH COAST STRETCHES northwards from San Francisco encompassing four counties: Napa Valley, Sonoma, Mendocino, and Lake. The North Coast AVAs are mostly coherent and distinctive topographical entities. In Sonoma, however, the boundaries are more complicated; some (Green Valley, Chalk Hill) are in fact subregions within the much larger Russian River AVA, whereas the Sonoma Coast AVA, by contrast, is a vast coastal swathe extending from the far south to the far north of the county.

KEY

North Coast California

Navarro vineyards in Mendocino

Coastal Range

Fort Bragg

REDWOOD VALLEY
POTTER VALLEY
Lake Mendocino

MENDOCINO

UKIAH VALLEY

Philo

ANDERSON VALLEY

Hoplar

MENDOCINO RIDGES

YORKVILLE HIGHLANDS

PACIFIC OCEAN

Coastal Range

SONOMA COAST

39°

Navarro

Anderson

NORTH COAST CALIFORNIA: AREAS & TOP PRODUCERS

NAPA VALLEY *p482*
Araujo *p490*
Beaulieu Vineyards *p490*
Beringer *p490*
Château Montelena *p490*
Dominus *p490*
Duckhorn *p490*
Frog's Leap *p491*
Joseph Phelps *p491*
Merryvale *p491*
Robert Mondavi *p491*
Spottswoode *p491*
Stag's Leap Wine Cellars *p492*

SONOMA *p484*
Château St Jean *p492*
Cline *p492*
Ferrari-Carano *p492*
Gallo of Sonoma *p492*
Gary Farrell *p493*
Gloria Ferrer *p493*
Kendall-Jackson *p493*
Kenwood *p493*
Kistler *p494*
Marimar Torres *p494*
Peter Michael *p494*
Ravenswood *p495*

MENDOCINO *p486*
Fetzer *p494*
Greenwood Ridge *p494*
McDowell Valley
   Vineyards *p495*
Monte Volpe *p495*
Navarro *p495*
Roederer Estate *p495*

LAKE COUNTY *p487*

Beaulieu Vineyards label, Napa Valley

Gloria Ferrer wines, Sonoma

Pruning vines in Beringer's vineyards, Napa Valley

TERROIR AT A GLANCE

Latitude: 38–40° N.

Altitude: 20–700m. Valley floor districts in all counties are close to sea level, while Pacific ridgelands in Sonoma and Mendocino can be as high as 600m. Vineyards on Spring Mountain above Napa are higher still.

Topography: Vines are planted on the floors and lower slopes of valleys that run mostly from north to south. Napa is the major river of Napa Valley, and the Russian River flows through parts of Sonoma and Mendocino; land close to the rivers tends to be too fertile for good grape production, but bench-lands set back from the river-banks often offer ideal conditions.

Soil: Loam and clay dominate, but soils are extremely varied.

Climate: Winters can be quite rainy, summers tend to be very hot, and autumns are usually balmy and dry.

Temperature: July average is 22°C.

Rainfall: Annual average is 950mm.

Viticultural hazards: Spring frosts; drought; Pierce's Disease.

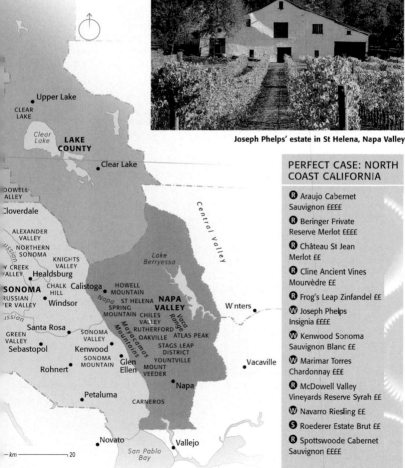

Joseph Phelps' estate in St Helena, Napa Valley

PERFECT CASE: NORTH COAST CALIFORNIA

Ⓡ Araujo Cabernet Sauvignon ££££

Ⓡ Beringer Private Reserve Merlot ££££

Ⓡ Château St Jean Merlot ££

Ⓡ Cline Ancient Vines Mourvèdre ££

Ⓡ Frog's Leap Zinfandel ££

Ⓦ Joseph Phelps Insignia ££££

Ⓦ Kenwood Sonoma Sauvignon Blanc ££

Ⓦ Marimar Torres Chardonnay £££

Ⓡ McDowell Valley Vineyards Reserve Syrah ££

Ⓦ Navarro Riesling ££

Ⓢ Roederer Estate Brut ££

Ⓡ Spottswoode Cabernet Sauvignon ££££

Map labels: Upper Lake, CLEAR LAKE, Clear Lake, LAKE COUNTY, Clear Lake, MCDOWELL VALLEY, Cloverdale, ALEXANDER VALLEY, NORTHERN SONOMA, KNIGHTS VALLEY, DRY CREEK VALLEY, Healdsburg, Central Valley, Lake Berryessa, SONOMA, RUSSIAN RIVER VALLEY, CHALK HILL, Calistoga, HOWELL MOUNTAIN, ST HELENA, SPRING MOUNTAIN, NAPA VALLEY, CHILES VALLEY, Windsor, Winters, Santa Rosa, SONOMA VALLEY, RUTHERFORD, OAKVILLE, ATLAS PEAK, GREEN VALLEY, Sebastopol, SONOMA MOUNTAIN, Kenwood, STAGS LEAP DISTRICT, YOUNTVILLE, Vacaville, Rohnert, Glen Ellen, MOUNT VEEDER, Napa, Petaluma, CARNEROS, Novato, San Pablo Bay, Vallejo, Mayacamas Mountains, Vaca Range, km 20

Rows of autumnal vines in Carneros, Napa Valley

WINEGROWING AREAS OF NORTH COAST CALIFORNIA

Napa Valley

NAPA HAS BEEN PRODUCING America's finest red wines for over a century, and its best examples are so prized that they fetch thousands of dollars at charity auctions. Napa has also become a playground for the rich, who enjoy the glamour of being associated with a wine estate. Almost every pocket of potential land is now in production, so there is little room for expansion. Competitiveness between owners, and the need to recoup the extremely high costs of land and planting, have led many to conclude that most Napa wines are very overpriced.

Frog's Leap label, Rutherford

Cabernet Sauvignon reigns supreme, combining opulent fruit with firm tannic structure and more power and flesh than the wines of Bordeaux, but there are also excellent wines from Merlot, Syrah, and Zinfandel. Although there are around 18,000ha planted, this accounts for only 11 per cent of California's vineyards, and, due to low yields – only four per cent of its wine production. Napa is climatically varied, and the northern part, around Calistoga, is significantly hotter than southern districts such as Yountville and Carneros. There are also marked differences between the low benchlands flanking the valley floor and the mountainside vineyards high above. The following are Napa's most important AVAs.

gravel, loam, sand, silt, clay, volcanic, shale, tuffeau
Cabernet Sauvignon, Syrah, Merlot, Pinot Noir, Sangiovese, Zinfandel Sauvignon Blanc, Chardonnay red, white, sparkling

Rutherford

THIS IS THE HISTORICAL core of Napa Valley, where the celebrated Beaulieu and Inglenook vineyards were planted in the 19th century. This AVA retains some of the most prized viticultural land in America and is home to some of California's top wineries. The wines are highly sought after and very expensive. Cabernet Sauvignon performs marvellously here, giving sumptuous wines of great profundity and longevity: some Rutherford Cabernets from the 1940s and 50s are still very enjoyable. It is thought that the secret to Rutherford's success lies in the gravelly loam soil and the well-drained benchlands at the foot of the Mayacamas Mountains, just west of the town of Rutherford. The vineyards that lie closer to the Napa River in the centre of the valley have richer soil and can be overproductive.

St Helena

IMMEDIATELY NORTH of Rutherford, the St Helena AVA stretches some way north of the little town of the same name. Like Rutherford, this is red-wine territory, though some white grapes are also planted. St Helena is slightly warmer than Rutherford, but is still capable of delivering Cabernet Sauvignon with striking elegance as well as richness. Many of Napa Valley's historic wineries are based here: among them, Beringer, Charles Krug, and Freemark Abbey. The northern continuation of St Helena is the hot area around Calistoga, which, although not an AVA, is nonetheless renowned for its powerful red wines from estates such as Château Montelena and Araujo.

Oakville

IT WAS ROBERT MONDAVI who put the Oakville AVA on the map when he built his Spanish-style winery here in the 1960s. The district is home to some of the valley's best-known vineyards: To-Kalon, largely owned by Mondavi, and Martha's Vineyard, which supplies grapes to Heitz Winery in the Napa Valley. These benchland sites are similar to the more celebrated examples within Rutherford. It is also where the vineyards of the Mondavi/Rothschild joint venture, Opus One, are planted. Oakville Cabernet Sauvignon often shows more spice, if less power, than that from Rutherford. The climate is slightly fresher here than further north, so white grapes, especially Sauvignon Blanc and Chardonnay, can give excellent results.

Yountville

YOUNTVILLE AVA is the most southerly of the red-wine regions of Napa Valley and it is distinctly

Robert Mondavi's Oakville winery

cooler than Oakville and regions further north. Dominus is its best known winery, showing that muscular Bordeaux-style reds can be produced on its well-drained loamy soils.

Stags Leap District

LYING TO THE EAST of Yountville and tucked against the Vaca Range, this AVA has become renowned for the elegance of its Cabernets. The soils are distinctive and reddish in colour, with volcanic subsoil on the slopes. Wineries here, such as Shafer and Stag's Leap Wine Cellars, often attribute the stylishness of their wines to the wind that funnels in cool air from San Pablo Bay during the afternoon and prevents the vines from becoming too hot and baked. The wines are consequently supple, yet have the structure to age well.

Howell Mountain & Atlas Peak

THESE TWO DISTRICTS lie up in the Vaca Range. Howell Mountain AVA overlooks St Helena; Atlas Peak is high above Stag's Leap. Their meso-climate differs from the valley floor regions not only because of their elevation (between 300 and 600m), but because they are above the fog line. They therefore lack the 'air-conditioning' that the fog provides lower down, but altitude gives cooler night-time temperatures. Howell Mountain is renowned for its Cabernets and Zinfandels, which emerge in a big, brawny style. They may lack elegance but make up for it with power and intensity. The major Atlas Peak estate bears the same name as the district. It was founded by the Tuscan producer Antinori (*see p265*) but has since changed hands more than once. The Chiles Valley AVA is another winegrowing region in these mountains, but it has very few vineyards of note.

CULT WINES

Every year the press reports another astronomical price paid for a bottle of cult Napa Cabernet. In 2000, a magnum of 1996 Screaming Eagle fetched over US$10,000 at a Napa charity auction. Most of the cult wines are produced in minute quantities by consultant wine-makers hired at enormous salaries. These rich oaky wines are awarded near perfect scores by American wine critics, making them highly desirable – and scarcely obtainable. Most are of exceptionally high quality, even if they tend to come from the same mould: highly concentrated and steeped in new French oak. Much of the hype is due to the extravagance (and wealth) of American wine collectors, who assemble every year at the Napa Valley Wine Auction to outbid each other.

PINOT NOIR: THE HEARTBREAK GRAPE

Pinot Noir label

Admirers of this impossibly difficult grape love to debate over which California wine region produces the best Pinot Noir. There is no definitive answer, but the main contenders are generally thought to be Sonoma Coast, Carneros, and Russian River Valley. Sonoma Coast is too recently planted for anyone to be certain about its potential, but its Pinot Noirs can have exquisite perfume and considerable finesse and purity; Carneros, while fresh and fruity, is rarely complex or long-lived; and Russian River Valley delivers more layered wines, with Burgundian nuances and an ability to age for the medium term. There are other areas of note, especially Santa Barbara, but it is the North Coast that has the longest track record. Californian Pinot Noir rarely emulates Burgundy, but the combination of selected sites, good clones, and sensitive winemaking is beginning to produce some world-class wines.

Mount Veeder & Spring Mountain

THESE TWO AVAS are located up in the Mayacamas Mountains, hugging the border with Sonoma County. They face onto Howell Valley and Atlas Peak on the other side of Napa Valley, with similar elevation and fog-free conditions. Mount Veeder is planted with Cabernet, Merlot, and some Chardonnay. Its reds can be burly and tannic. The exceptionally beautiful Spring Mountain, with its eroded volcanic soils, produces wines that are slightly more supple than those from Mount Veeder. Its best known wineries include Newton, Kennan, Cain, Togni, and Stony Hill.

Carneros

THE GRASSY HILLS of the Carneros AVA, close to San Pablo Bay, comprise Napa's most southerly winegrowing area, a district shared with Sonoma County. Far cooler than the valley floor because of proximity to Pacific breezes and fog, Carneros is not suited to Cabernet Sauvignon, although in some sheltered pockets Merlot and Syrah can give good results. It is mostly planted with Chardonnay and Pinot Noir, which are vinified as both still and sparkling wine. French and Spanish sparkling wine houses have set up American outposts here: Taittinger *(see p174)* and Codorníu *(see p312)* have estates in the Napa part of Carneros.

Sonoma

UNTIL A DECADE AGO Sonoma was clearly overshadowed by its more sophisticated cousin, Napa Valley, but today it is producing wines to rival those of its world-famous neighbour. Sonoma is the most diverse of the North Coast counties, with an enormous range of soil types, mesoclimates, and elevations. Broadly speaking, the subregions closer to the Pacific are cooler and better suited to Burgundian varieties (Chardonnay and Pinot Noir), whereas the valley floor and eastern slopes are hotter and ideal for Bordeaux red grapes and Zinfandel. The subregional structure is extremely complicated, since AVAs overlap.

While just about all suitable land in Napa Valley is already planted, new areas in Sonoma are still being developed, and none is more exciting than the cool,

Gloria Ferrer's winery in the Sonoma section of Carneros

lofty ridgetops of the Sonoma Coast. In total, there are around 26,000ha in production, and over 250 wineries, ranging in size from tiny boutique operations to the vast ranches set up by the Gallo family. Alongside the numerous established Italian families of the region – Seghesio, Foppiano, Martinelli – are relative newcomers equally dedicated to making the most of Sonoma's varied and generous climate. Chardonnay from this region can be exceptional, and Pinot Noir from Russian River Valley is probably the best expression of this tricky variety in the whole of California. The following are Sonoma's most important AVAs.

🏞 *gravel, sandy loam, shallow sedimentary, clay, sandstone, gravel, shale* 🍇 *Cabernet Sauvignon, Zinfandel, Merlot, Pinot Noir, Syrah* 🍃 *Chardonnay, Sauvignon Blanc, Gewürztraminer* 🍷 *red, white*

Harvesting Chardonnay grapes in Sonoma

Alexander Valley & Knights Valley

ALEXANDER VALLEY AVA can be extremely hot, so many of the 6,000ha of vineyards lie at higher elevations in the foothills of the Mayacamas Mountains. On the valley floor, Zinfandel thrives. The valley is also an increasing source of succulent, rich Cabernet Sauvignon and Merlot.

The adjoining Knights Valley AVA twists through the mountains to Calistoga in northern Napa Valley. There is only one important winery based here, Peter Michael, although Beringer has substantial plantings too. Red vines flourish down on the valley floor, while Chardonnay gives impressive results at much higher elevations.

Kendall-Jackson label, Sonoma

Dry Creek Valley

THIS CELEBRATED REGION (4,000ha of vineyards) runs northwest from Healdsburg, and most of its estates and wineries are strung out along Dry Creek Road. There is a good deal of splendid old-vine (often century-old) Zinfandel planted here; but like other Sonoma regions, Dry Creek Valley is versatile, and some excellent Cabernet Sauvignon and even some white wines can be found. Most of the estates are quite small, but over the past decade the Gallo family *(see p506)* has developed vast holdings throughout Sonoma and has its main base in Dry Creek Valley.

Russian River Valley, Green Valley & Chalk Hill

THE RUSSIAN RIVER VALLEY AVA has around 4,000ha under vine and is renowned as a cool region, prone to maritime fog incursions. One sector, where producers Williams-Selyem, Rochioli, and Davis Bynum are based, is certainly the source of some of California's best Pinot Noir. The texture of the wine can be silky and sensuous, and nowhere else in California does Pinot develop that seductive damp undergrowth character typical of burgundy. The region is, however, far from uniform, and there are areas where Zinfandel has been established for decades.

Green Valley, although an independent AVA, is in fact an enclave within southern Russian River Valley. Here it can be cool, and in some vintages the grapes struggle to ripen. Marimar Torres, sister of the renowned Catalan wine producer Miguel Torres *(see p313)*, grows Burgundian varieties here, while Iron Horse is the best known of the sparkling wine producers. Chalk Hill AVA is another pocket within Russian River Valley, mostly given to the winery and estate of the same name. This is warmer territory just north of Santa Rosa, but it is nonetheless well known for its Chardonnay and Sauvignon Blanc.

Aerial view of Navarro's vineyards in Anderson Valley, Mendocino

Sonoma Valley & Sonoma Mountain

EXTENDING FROM Santa Rosa to Carneros *(see p484),* Sonoma Valley AVA is home to some of the county's best-known producers (Kenwood, Landmark, St Francis, and Château St Jean). Their wineries are located on the valley floor, though their vineyards are sometimes planted on side valleys. It is a versatile region, producing good Chardonnay, Zinfandel, and red Bordeaux varieties. The loftier Sonoma Mountain AVA lies just to the west. Few wineries are based here; the best known is Laurel Glen, which produces tannic and long-lived Cabernets from vineyards at 250m.

Sonoma Coast & Northern Sonoma

THE VAST AND ALMOST meaningless Sonoma Coast AVA stretches some distance inland from the long Sonoma County coastline. However, over recent years, vineyards have been planted on high ridges just inland from, and sometimes overlooking, the Pacific, all with the intention of finding the perfect cool-climate location for Chardonnay and Pinot Noir. Flowers is the only important winery located here, but many top producers buy fruit from the area. Sonoma Coast wines often have an intensity and purity that is reminiscent of fine burgundy. Another vast appellation within Sonoma Coast is Northern Sonoma, which exists at the behest of Gallo of Sonoma, as a catch-all AVA to include wines they blend from various districts within Sonoma.

Mendocino

FOR DECADES THE MAIN ROLE of Mendocino, California's most northerly growing area, was to supply grapes to larger producers based further south, who appreciated the county as a source of first-rate grapes that could be purchased at attractive prices. Today large wineries – Robert Mondavi, Beringer, Duckhorn – have all developed their own vineyards here. Much of the land had originally been settled by Italian families, who had planted dry-farmed Zinfandel, Petite Sirah, and other varieties. Today Mendocino is gaining renown as many growers establish their own wineries. Mendocino shares Sonoma's versatility, producing good Chardonnay and Viognier, robust reds, and fine sparkling wines. Although a relatively small region, with 7,000ha planted and around 60 wineries, it is one of considerable diversity, with chilly Anderson Valley close to the Pacific, and warmer valleys, such as Redwood and McDowell, further inland. Hidden away in all these regions are very old vineyards that are still in production and are increasingly valued by winemakers throughout California. Organic viticulture, pioneered by the Fetzer family, has been pursued avidly throughout the county, and about 25 per cent of all vineyards are certified as organic. Mendocino's most important AVAs are listed below.

▨ *clay, gravel, volcanic, red clay, loam, alluvial* ▣ *Cabernet Sauvignon, Zinfandel, Petite Sirah, Pinot Noir, Syrah, Barbera* ▣ *Gewürztraminer, Riesling, Chardonnay, Pinot Gris, Sauvignon Blanc* ▨ *red, white, sparkling*

Anderson Valley, Mendocino Ridges & Yorkville Highlands

THE ANDERSON VALLEY AVA follows the Navarro River, and is the closest region to the Pacific coastline, with some sectors that are distinctly cool and foggy thanks to the maritime influence. In some years the region is so cool that the grapes do not ripen, or they succumb to rot due to damp weather conditions.

Although a host of varieties are grown here, grapes such as Riesling, Gewürztraminer, and Chardonnay can do particularly well, as does Pinot Noir. Exceptionally good sparkling wine is also made, notably by the American branch of champagne house Louis Roederer (*see p175*), which set up here in 1982.

A few excellent old vineyards between Anderson Valley and the Pacific have their own AVA called Mendocino Ridges. These are planted mostly with Zinfandel at over 350m. Yorkville Highlands AVA is the southern extension of Anderson Valley and is considerably warmer. It only represents about 10 per cent of Anderson Valley's 800ha.

Redwood Valley & Potter Valley

SOME OF MENDOCINO'S oldest vineyards are in the Redwood Valley AVA, which is showing immense versatility. Cooler than neighbouring Ukiah, it is nonetheless warm enough to ripen Zinfandel and Italian varieties, as well as a wide range of white grapes. The Potter Valley AVA, to the east, is at around 300m, so white grapes (Chardonnay, Sauvignon Blanc) and some Pinot Noir are most commonly planted. Much of the fruit is destined for sparkling wine houses.

Ukiah Valley

NOT AN AVA, Ukiah Valley is a large region stretching northwards from Hopland to Ukiah, producing a substantial proportion of Mendocino's grapes. The best vineyards, red and white, are planted on benchlands flanking the Russian River. Higher up are older vineyards planted with Italian and Rhône varieties.

In the Fetzer winery, Mendocino

ZINFANDEL: CALIFORNIA'S INDIGENOUS GRAPE

California is fortunate in that its vinous calling card, Zinfandel, is a fascinating grape variety. It is of Croatian origin and identical to the southern Italian Primitivo, but in California it has taken on its own personality. It was very widely planted by immigrants, mostly Italian, who settled in the North Coast in the 19th century, delivering robust, full-bodied wines that resembled those from southern Europe. Many of the old vineyards survive; being dry-farmed, they give relatively small crops of intensely flavoured grapes. Zinfandel can suffer from uneven ripening: pick too early and it tastes green; pick too late, and it can taste like jam. The trick is to pick it fully ripe. There is an unfortunate vogue for Zinfandels with very high alcohol levels and for sweet pink 'blush' Zinfandel.

Zinfandel label

McDowell Valley

THIS SMALL AVA in South Mendocino is more or less the fiefdom of McDowell Valley Vineyards, which specializes almost entirely in Rhône varieties. Its vineyards are planted with some of the oldest Syrah in California, which still produces first-rate wine. The McDowell Reserve Syrah is smoky and spicy, and sometimes displays a gamey or even slightly jammy character.

Lake County

THIS COUNTY HAS ONLY ONE IMPORTANT subregion, the **Clear Lake** AVA, situated east of Ukiah Valley and named after the large lake fringed by vineyards. Although a warm region, it has long been known for its Sauvignon Blanc and Cabernet Sauvignon, which are widely planted. Hot days are tempered by nights cooled by cold air descending from the mountains. In 2004 the Red Hills AVA was created for vineyards at a high elevation. It is likely to gain in importance, thanks to plantings by major growers.

volcanic, alluvial *Cabernet Sauvignon, Zinfandel, Merlot* *Sauvignon Blanc, Chardonnay* *red, white*

WINE TOUR OF THE NAPA VALLEY

THIRTY YEARS AGO, Napa Valley was a rural backwater. The celebrity of its vineyards and its proximity to San Francisco, however, have since combined to make it one of the greatest tourist attractions in the USA. Visitors flock to the many hospitable tasting rooms, as well as to the fine delis and restaurants, country clubs, and luxurious inns. The most direct route follows the main highway, Highway 29. However, if this is overcrowded, take the alternative Silverado Trail, which has retained its charming rural character.

Sterling Vineyards

① Copia
Napa's lavish centre for wine, food, and the arts is located along the banks of the Napa River. The admission charge includes wine tuition, and the centre hosts special exhibitions, dinners, blind tastings, and other events.
707 259 1600
W www.copia.org

③ Hess Collection
The early 20th-century Christian Brothers stone winery was leased by Swiss tycoon Donald Hess in 1986. There are wine tastings and tours of the winery as well as of Hess's remarkable contemporary art collection.
707 255 1144
W www.hesscollection.com

② Napa Wine Train △
The luxurious Napa Wine Train offers the most effortless way to view the valley – at a price. The train takes a non-stop tour from Napa station to St Helena and back again. There are wine tastings and meals to divert passengers during the three-hour ride.
707 253 2111 W www.winetrain.com

④ Robert Mondavi ▽
The Mondavi winery is not only a local landmark, it also offers the best and most detailed winery tours in the valley. Some focus on technical aspects, others on the mysteries of wine tasting or matching food and wine. Advance booking is essential. *See p491.*
1 888 766 6328 W www.robertmondavi.com

⑤ Rubicon △
Film-maker Francis Ford Coppola has bought some of Rutherford's most historic vineyards, and the former Inglenook winery, which he has converted into a museum devoted to the history of the estate. The museum also includes a collection of Coppola's movie memorabilia, including his five Oscars.
1 800 782 4266 W www.rubiconestate.com

KEY
▬▬ *Tour route*

⑦ Clos Pegase △

When the architect Michael Graves won the competition to build this winery, some neighbours tried to block its construction. The Minoan-style structure, surrounded by owner Jan Shrem's modern sculpture collection, was built in 1987. It is Napa's most controversial winery, both loved and loathed. Take one of the daily tours and decide for yourself. ☎ 707 942 4981 ⓦ www.clospegase.com

⑥ Tra Vigne Restaurant

This lofty, spacious, long-established restaurant in St Helena is an excellent, reasonably-priced choice for lunch and dinner. Mediterranean-style cooking is accompanied by a good list of wines sold by the bottle and the glass. Reservations are essential.
☎ 703 963 4444
ⓦ www.travignerestaurant.com

⑧ Sterling Vineyards △

Sterling Vineyards' spectacular winery is based on the whitewashed buildings typical of the Greek islands. Access to the hilltop site is by a cable car, and tours and tastings of an excellent range of varietal wines are available daily. ☎ 1 800 726 6136 ⓦ www.sterlingvineyards.com

⑨ Calistoga

Calistoga's numerous attractions include hot springs with therapeutic mud baths and the opportunity to enjoy a tranquil two-hour balloon ride over the vineyards while enjoying a champagne breakfast.
ⓦ www.caohwy.com

Visitors' Tips

Route: This 65km tour begins in Napa and follows Highway 29 to Calistoga. For a circular route, return to Napa on the quieter Silverado Trail.

Duration: It will take a full day, or for a more leisurely visit stop off overnight.

Wineries: Most Napa wineries have a tasting room, and some have picnic tables where you can enjoy an alfresco lunch. Many producers make a small charge for tasting, refundable if you make a purchase.

Hotel recommendations:
Hotel Meadowood Resort in St Helena offers the ultimate in luxury and spaciousness ⓦ www.meadowood.com; Rancho Caymus in Rutherford has a cosy ambience and central location ⓦ www.ranchocaymus.com; Inn at Southbridge in St Helena is cheap, modern, comfortable, and functional
☎ 707 967 9400

TOP PRODUCERS OF NORTH COAST CALIFORNIA

Araujo
Napa Valley

2155 Pickett Rd, Calistoga
C 707 942 6061
W www.araujoestatewines.com ●

KNOWN AS THE Eisele Vineyard in the 1970s and 80s, this estate was the source of outstanding Cabernet Sauvignon for Ridge and Phelps. In the early 1990s it was bought by Bart and Daphne Araujo, who added Sauvignon Blanc and Syrah to the range. Although the Araujos are typical of the new generation of rich entrepreneurs buying vineyards in Napa, they have firmly set their sights on making superb wines from this exceptional site. The wines are consistently outstanding, especially the reds, with typically Calistogan flavours of blackcurrant, chocolate, and black olives.
▦ *red, white* **▨** *2003, 2004, 2000, 1999, 1997* ★ *Cabernet Sauvignon, Syrah*

Beaulieu Vineyards
Napa Valley

1960 St Helena Hwy, Rutherford
C 707 967 5230
W www.beaulieuvineyards.com ▢

THIS LEGENDARY PROPERTY was founded by Frenchman Georges de Latour in 1899. Its equally legendary winemaker André Tchelitscheff *(see p476)* crafted some magnificent Cabernets in the 1950s and 60s. Quality plummeted in the 1970s, but today, under corporate giant Diageo, things have improved substantially. The basic varietal ranges are correct if unexciting, but the Signet Collection series offers Rhône-style blends and Sangiovese of real character.
▦ *red, white, sparkling* **▨** *2006, 2005, 2004, 2001, 1999, 1997* ★ *Private Reserve Cabernet Sauvignon*

Beringer's Nightingale wine

Beringer
Napa Valley

2000 Main St, St Helena **C** 707 963 4812 **W** www.beringer.com ▢

THIS HISTORIC WINERY dates from the 1880s and has been owned by a succession of corporations, most recently the Australian Foster's group. Until 2007 Ed Sbragia was chief winemaker, fashioning a rich, generous, oaky style for all the wines. Although Beringer buys fruit from all over California, it owns substantial holdings in Napa. The finest wines are the Bordeaux-style blends known as Alluvium, and the Private Reserves, which have excellent ageing capability. A curiosity here is Nightingale, a sweet wine made from Sauvignon Blanc and Sémillon grapes artificially induced with botrytis.
▦ *red, white* **▨** *2006, 2005, 2004, 2001, 1999, 1997* ★ *North Coast Zinfandel, Private Reserve Merlot*

Château Montelena
Napa Valley

1429 Tubbs Lane, Calistoga **C** 707 942 5105 **W** www.montelena.com ▢

THIS 19TH CENTURY winery was restored by James Barrett, whose son Bo has been winemaker since 1981. The top wine is the intense, magisterial Estate Cabernet Sauvignon, while the cheaper Napa Cuvée is made from bought-in grapes. The atypical Chardonnay sees hardly any new oak, and though austere when young, it can age well.
▦ *red, white* **▨** *2005, 2004, 1999, 1997, 1994* ★ *Estate, Cabernet Sauvignon, Zinfandel*

Dominus
Napa Valley

2570 Napanook Rd, Yountville
C 707 944 8954
W www.dominus estate.com ●

DOMINUS STANDS IN the middle of a historic vineyard that was once a source of legendary Inglenook Cabernet. In 1982 it was acquired by the Moueix family, owners of Château Pétrus *(see p83)*. At first the top wine, made in Bordelais fashion, was tough, but the team soon adapted to Napa conditions and today the wine is better balanced, showing great power and depth. The second wine, Napanook, is intended for earlier drinking.
▦ *red* **▨** *2005, 2004, 2002, 1996, 1994* ★ *Dominus, Napanook*

Duckhorn
Napa Valley

1000 Lodi Lane, St Helena
C 707 963 7108
W www.duckhorn.com ▢

LONG BEFORE MERLOT became fashionable in California, Dan Duckhorn was producing rich, powerful examples with imposing tannic structure. He also invented a style he calls Paraduxx, an appealing blend of Zinfandel, Cabernet, and Merlot. He also expanded operations by buying land in Mendocino, from which a fine Pinot Noir, called Goldeneye, is produced.
▦ *red, white* **▨** *2005, 2004, 2001, 1999, 1997* ★ *Paraduxx, Three Palms Vineyard Napa Merlot, Napa Cabernet Sauvignon*

Duckhorn's estate in St Helena

Frog's Leap
Napa Valley

8815 Conn Creek Rd, Rutherford
707 963 4704
www.frogsleap.com

JOHN WILLIAMS TURNS out elegant Sauvignon Blanc, Cabernet Sauvignon, and Zinfandel, as well as a Cabernet Sauvignon-Cabernet Franc blend called Rutherford. The wines are often undervalued because Williams aims for style and balance rather than power and overt oakiness. The result is a range of eminently drinkable, as well as serious, wines that are made from organic grapes.
red, white 2005, 2004, 2001, 1999, 1997 ★ *Cabernet Sauvignon, Zinfandel, Rutherford*

Joseph Phelps
Napa Valley

200 Taplin Rd, St Helena 707 963 2745 www.jpvwines.com by appt

PHELPS MADE ITS NAME with sweet Rieslings and was one of California's earliest producers of Syrah. Although it has a fine reputation for Cabernet and its prestigious Insignia, former winemaker Craig Williams developed Rhône-style wines of great appeal. But today the emphasis is on Cabernet and Pinot Noir from cool Sonoma vineyards.
red, white, rosé 2005, 2004, 2001, 1999, 1997, 1994 ★ *Insignia, Napa Valley Cabernet*

Merryvale
Napa Valley

1000 Main St, St Helena 707 963 2225 www.merryvale.com

NOW OWNED BY Swiss and Californian partners, Merryvale has benefited from excellent winemakers and the advice of consultant winemaker Michel Rolland. Substantial volumes of wine are made here, all to an impressively high standard. The top ranges – Reserve and Prestige – are outstanding, but Profile, an elegant Bordeaux-style blend aged in new oak, is usually the best wine.
red, white, fortified 2006, 2005, 2004, 2001, 1999, 1997 ★ *Silhouette Chardonnay, Carneros Merlot, Profile*

Robert Mondavi
Napa Valley

7801 St Helena Hwy, Oakville 707 226 1395 www.robertmondavi.com

ROBERT MONDAVI *(see p476)* was such a Californian insti-

Spottswoode label

tution that it is hard to believe he only founded his winery in 1966, and went through many tough years. His secret was simple: indefatigable curiosity and steely determination to excel. He created the Fumé Blanc style of oaked Sauvignon Blanc and pioneered research into oak ageing and vineyard density, sharing the results with other wineries. Fanatical about education, he was also the major financial backer of Napa's Copia Center *(see p488)*. Mondavi's extensive vineyards in the Central Coast and Santa Barbara mostly provide fruit for the less expensive blends. The wines from the Napa vineyards are of high quality, in particular those with subregional designations from Oakville, Stags Leap, and Carneros. The Reserve wines are significantly superior to the regular bottlings.
red, white 2006, 2005, 2004, 2001, 1999, 1997 ★ *Pinot Noir Reserve, Oakville Cabernet Sauvignon*

Spottswoode
Napa Valley

1902 Madrona Ave, St Helena 707 963 0134 www.spottswoode.com by appt

SINCE THE DEATH of founder Dr Jack Novak many years ago, his widow Mary and daughter Beth have run this outstanding organic estate. Despite the renown and consistency of its wines, Spottswoode still has a family atmosphere, with no pretensions to grandeur. Consultant winemaker Tony Soter established a reputation for immensely stylish Cabernet and lively Sauvignon Blanc. Current winemaker Rosemary Cakebread has maintained this approach since 1997.
red, white 2005, 2004, 2002, 2001, 1999, 1995 ★ *Sauvignon Blanc, Cabernet Sauvignon*

THE JUDGMENT OF PARIS

In 1976, British wine merchant Steven Spurrier organized a blind tasting at which the best wines of California were pitted against the top growths of Bordeaux and Burgundy. The mostly French team of tasters discovered that they gave pride of place to a Stag's Leap Wine Cellars Cabernet and a Château Montelena Chardonnay. The French were mortified when the story hit the international press. The comparison was unequal, as only recent vintages were tasted and French wines are generally less open and expressive in youth than their California rivals. However, a repeat of the tasting in 2006 yielded results close to those of 30 years earlier.

with traditional grapes, notably Mourvèdre, Zinfandel, and Carignane (Carignan). In 1991 they moved to southern Sonoma and planted Rhône varieties. Anyone weary of Chardonnay and Cabernet should try their sensibly priced Zinfandel, Mourvèdre, Syrah, and Viognier, as well as Carignane and Marsanne.
🟥 red, white, sparkling 🔲 2006, 2005, 2004, 2001 ★ Sonoma Viognier, Ancient Vines Mourvèdre

Ferrari-Carano
Sonoma

8761 Dry Creek Rd, Healdsburg
📞 707 433 6700
🌐 www.ferrari-carano.com ⬛

THE CARANOS ARE hoteliers from Nevada, and their showman-ship is fully in evidence at this lavish Dry Creek estate, which is enjoyed by visitors as much for its gardens and hospitality centre as for its wines. Nonetheless, the wines are among Sonoma's best, thanks to the skill of long-term winemaker George Bursick. At first, the winery was known for its elegant, oaky Chardonnay and Sauvignon Blanc, but now the reds win equal acclaim. In addition to standard varietals, there is a fine Cabernet-Sangiovese blend called Sienna and a rich Bordeaux blend called Tresor.
🟥 red, white 🔲 2005, 2004, 2001, 1999, 1995 ★ Fumé Blanc Reserve, Siena

Gallo of Sonoma
Sonoma

3387 Dry Creek Rd, Healdsburg
📞 707 431 5500
🌐 www.gallosonoma.com ⬛

TO THE ASTONISHMENT, and even irritation, of small-scale Sonoma growers, the power-ful Gallo family came out of its Central Valley lair in the mid-1980s and bought

Stag's Leap Wine Cellars
Napa Valley

5766 Silverado Trail, Napa 📞 707 944 2020 🌐 www.cask23.com ⬛

WARREN WINIARSKI'S *(see p477)* famous winery produces a wide range of wines, but made its name with its sumptuous Cabernets including a Napa appellation wine from bought-in grapes; the SLV from the estate vineyard; and the often sublime reserve called Cask 23. They are quintessential Stag's Leap reds – rich but elegant, supple, balanced, and age-worthy. In 2007 the property was sold to a group that included Tuscany's Antinori.
🟥 red, white 🔲 2005, 2004, 2001, 1999, 1997, 1994 ★ Sauvignon Blanc, SLV Cabernet Sauvignon, Cabernet Sauvignon Cask 23

Château St Jean
Sonoma

8555 Hwy 12, Kenwood
📞 707 833 4134
🌐 www.chateaustjean.com ⬛

IN THE 1970s, this property's first winemaker, Richard Arrowood (who now has his own winery), produced dazzling dry and sweet white wines from individual vine-yards. Today Château St Jean is part of the Foster's empire,

and the range is no longer so extensive, though the Chardonnay and Sauvignon Blanc are still impressive. The winemakers also introduced some excellent reds: Merlot and the Cabernet-dominated Cinq Cépages. The style is richly fruity and the emphasis is on wines that are best drunk young.
🟥 red, white 🔲 2006, 2005, 2004, 2001, 1999 ★ Robert Young Vineyard Chardonnay, Cinq Cépages

Cline
Sonoma

24737 Hwy 121, Sonoma 📞 707 963 4310 🌐 www.clinecellars.com ⬛

THE CLINE BROTHERS come from Oakley, in Contra Costa County, where they still own a splendid old vineyard planted

Cline label

1,200ha of land in Sonoma. Since the first releases in 1991, wine critics have been surprised by the high quality of the wines. In addition to the single-vineyard labels, the Gallos released very limited quantities of varietal wines known, confusingly, as the Estate Range; although expensive, they are not significantly better than the well-priced regular bottlings.

🔴 red, white 📆 2006, 2005, 2004, 2001, 1999 ★ *Laguna Chardonnay, Frei Ranch Zinfandel, Stefani Vineyard Cabernet Sauvignon*

Gary Farrell
Sonoma

10701 Westside Rd, Healdsburg
📞 707 433 6616
🌐 *www.gary farrell.com* ⭕ *by appt*

Since 1982, the self-effacing Gary Farrell has been the winemaker fashioning some of the finest Pinot Noirs for Russian River wineries such as Davis Bynum. He has also produced a range of wines under his own label, and in 2000 set up his own winery. However, the property soon changed hands – repeatedly – and in 2007 Farrell himself left.

🔴 red, white 📆 2005, 2004, 2001 ★ *Russian River Valley Pinot Noir, Dry Creek Zinfandel*

Gloria Ferrer
Sonoma

23555 Hwy 121, Sonoma 📞 707 996 7256 🌐 *www.gloriaferrer.com* ⭕

A few european sparkling wine houses set up wineries in Carneros in the 1980s, and this one was established by the Ferrer family, which owns the Freixenet *(see p312)* cava business. Some of the simpler wines are a touch broad and too overtly fruity to attain real elegance, but the top *cuvées* are impres-

sive. The crisp Royal Cuvée spends six years on the yeast before disgorgement, and the more toasty Carneros Cuvée is aged for even longer. Sparkling wines remain hard to sell, so like other producers here, Gloria Ferrer has been increasing its output of still wines. As well as Pinot Noir and Chardonnay, Ferrer also offers Merlot and Syrah.

Gloria Ferrer's Royal Cuveé

🔴 red, white, sparkling 📆 2003, 2000, 1997, 1991 ★ *Royal Cuvée, Carneros Cuvée*

Kendall-Jackson
Sonoma

5007 Fulton Rd, Santa Rosa 📞 707 544 4000 🌐 *www.kj.com* ⭕

Jess jackson only started producing wines from his small Lake County vineyards in 1982. The company grew swiftly, acquiring enormous vineyards and making Jackson a billionaire, partly thanks to the success of his off-dry Vintner's Reserve Chardonnay. Today his wines come from all over California, and his empire includes many other wineries that operate independently. The Sonoma properties include Hartford Court, La Crema, Stonestreet, and Matanzas

Creek. From the beginning, Jackson used only coastal fruit, scorning grapes from the Central Valley. The winemakers blend in the Australian mode, taking components from various regions to make stylistically consistent wines.

🔴 red, white 📆 2006, 2005, 2004, 2001

★ *Vintner's Reserve Cabernet Sauvignon, Grand Reserve Pinot Noir, Verité Sonoma Merlot*

Kenwood
Sonoma

9592 Hwy 12, Kenwood 📞 707 833 5891 🌐 *www.kenwoodvineyards.com* ⭕

For almost 40 years, Kenwood has maintained its reputation for good-quality wines at all price ranges, from the basic Sonoma Series to the more prestigious Jack London and Reserve ranges. Sauvignon Blanc is not an easy grape to grow and vinify in California, but Kenwood has rightly enjoyed a high reputation for this wine. The top Cabernet Sauvignon is the outstanding new-oaked Artist Series, and other very good red wines are made from the Jack London Ranch, leased by Kenwood.

🔴 red, white 📆 2006, 2005, 2004, 2001, 1999 ★ *Jack London Zinfandel, Sonoma Sauvignon Blanc*

Kenwood's tasting room in Sonoma

Kistler
Sonoma

4707 Vine Hill Rd, Sebastopol
☎ 707 823 5603
ⓦ www.kistlervineyards.com 🔵

COLLABORATORS Mark Bixler and reclusive winemaker Steve Kistler specialize in Pinot Noir and Chardonnay. They own some vineyards but mostly source fruit from top vineyards in Sonoma, all bottled separately. From the outset, Kistler wines have enjoyed a cult following, and they can be in a league of their own, showing a concentration and mineral complexity rarely encountered in California. Best known for its fruity Chardonnays, Kistler also produces Pinot Noir of remarkable purity and intensity.

🟥 *red, white* 📖 *2006, 2005, 2004, 2003, 2001* ★ *Vine Hill Chardonnay, Chardonnay Cuvée Cathleen, Cuvée Elizabeth Pinot Noir*

Marimar Torres
Sonoma

11400 Graton Rd, Sebastopol ☎ *707 823 4365* ⓦ *www.marimar estate.com* 🔵 *by appt*

MARIMAR TORRES is a member of the renowned Catalan Torres clan *(see p313)* and she bought this property in 1986. The cool climate of its Green Valley vineyards makes it ideal for Chardonnay and Pinot Noir. Production has expanded since the acquisition of additional land along the Sonoma Coast. Torres aims for finesse and balance, and though she does not overtly aim to produce burgundy-look-alikes, her wines do have the elegance and length of flavour often found in fine burgundy. Since 2003 the estate has been organic.

🟥 *red, white* 📖 *2005, 2004, 2002, 2001, 1999, 1995* ★ *Chardonnay, Pinot Noir*

Greenwood Ridge label

Peter Michael
Sonoma

12400 Ida Clayton Rd, Calistoga ☎ *707 942 4459* ⓦ *www.peter michaelwinery.com* 🔵

ENGLISH ELECTRONICS TYCOON Sir Peter Michael bought land in Knights Valley in 1981, and harvested his first vintage in 1987. The estate is noted for its range of single-vineyard Chardonnays, which can be remarkably intense and complex; the Sauvignon Blanc (L'Après-Midi) and Cabernet Sauvignon (Les Pavots) can also be first-rate. All are expensive.

🟥 *red, white* 📖 *2006, 2005, 2004, 2003, 2002*
★ *Clos du Ciel Chardonnay, Les Pavots*

Ravenswood
Sonoma

See right.

Fetzer
Mendocino

13601 Eastside Rd, Hopland ☎ *707 744 7600* ⓦ *www.fetzer.com* 🔵

THE FETZER FAMILY no longer owns this winery, but even under the control of the Brown Forman corporation, it has remained true to its principles. Fetzer was a pioneer of organic viticulture in California, and the winery still produces

organic wines under its Bonterra label. Although many of the grapes come from Mendocino, some ranges are sourced elsewhere. Fetzer sells four million cases of wine each year, and the secret of this success is the outstanding value the wines offer. The basic range is called Bel Arbor; the Barrel Select and Reserve ranges are higher in quality. The white wines are lean and fresh; the reds packed with fruit flavour.

🟥 *red, white* 📖 *2006, 2005, 2004, 2003, 2002* ★ *Bonterra Viognier, Barrel Select Zinfandel*

Greenwood Ridge
Mendocino

5501 Hwy 128, Philo ☎ *707 895 2002* ⓦ *www.greenwood ridge.com* 🔵

MANY OF Allan Green's vineyards are high in the hills surrounding Anderson Valley. He inadvertently became a pioneer of the Mendocino Ridges AVA, created to recognize sites at high elevations. Green's Riesling, Pinot Noir, Cabernet, and Merlot come from the ridges, and he buys in fruit from other vineyards for Zinfandel and Sauvignon Blanc.

🟥 *red, white* 📖 *2006, 2005, 2004, 2002* ★ *Estate Merlot, Estate Chardonnay*

Fetzer

McDowell Valley Vineyards
Mendocino

3811 Hwy 175, Hopland 📞 *707 744 1053* 🌐 *www.mcdowellsyrah.com* ⬤

THE SYRAH VINES planted here date from 1948 and 1959, making them among the oldest Syrah in California. These old vines are used for the superb Reserve, but the regular bottling of Syrah is also juicy and beguiling. All the other wines are from Rhône varieties; including an excellent example of the notoriously tricky Viognier, as well as an enjoyable dry Grenache rosé.

🍷 *red, white* 📗 *2006, 2005, 2004, 2002, 2001* ★ *Viognier, Reserve Syrah*

Monte Volpe
Mendocino

1170 Bel Arbres Rd, Redwood Valley 📞 *707 485 9463* 🌐 *www.grazianofamilywines.com* ⬤

GREG GRAZIANO'S ancestors were typical Mendocino immigrant farmers, and he honours their traditions by specializing in Italian varietal wines. It is impossible to replicate the hills of Piemonte or Friuli in the Mendocino highlands, so not every wine is successful. Overall, however, Graziano (who shows the passion of

McDowell Valley Vineyards label

a missionary) does an excellent job, and has the courage to produce fine versions of wines that cannot always be easy to sell. He has two other labels: Domaine St Gregory releases wines from the Pinot family, while Enotria focuses on Piemontese varieties such as Nebbiolo and Barbera.

🍷 *red, white* 📗 *2006, 2005, 2004, 2002, 2001* ★ *Monte Volpe Pinot Bianco, Enotria Barbera*

Navarro
Mendocino

5601 Hwy 128, Philo 📞 *707 895 3686* 🌐 *www.navarrowine.com* ⬤

IN 1973, TED BENNETT and Deborah Cahn bought a sprawling sheep ranch in

Anderson Valley, and planted 34ha with cool-climate varieties. Their Rieslings are among California's finest, always backed with vivid acidity. The Pinot Noir is aged in small French barrels, and can be impressive.

🍷 *red, white* 📗 *2006, 2005, 2004, 2003, 2002* ★ *Riesling, Pinot Noir Méthode à l'Ancienne*

Roederer Estate
Mendocino

4501 Hwy 128, Philo 📞 *707 895 2288* 🌐 *www.roedererestate.net* ⬤

MOST FRENCH champagne houses looking for Californian vineyards choose Carneros or southern Napa, but Jean-Claude Rouzaud, when head of Louis Roederer *(see p175)*, chose Anderson Valley instead. The cool, even uncertain, climate gives the wines the acidic backbone needed for great sparkling wine, so his decision has been vindicated. The Estate Brut is the basic bottling, and it sometimes seems just as good as the more expensive *prestige cuvée*, the vintage L'Ermitage. Many Californian sparkling wines have fruit but lack finesse; the Roederer Estate wines have both.

🍷 *sparkling* 📗 *2002, 2000, 1999, 1998* ★ *Estate Brut, Rosé, L'Ermitage*

THE RAVENSWOOD STORY

Joel Peterson, an immunologist by profession, caught the wine bug in the 1970s. He produced 327 cases in 1976, and by 1991 his outfit, Ravenswood, had become recognized for its superb red wines. Production expanded and Peterson bought a defunct winery in Sonoma. The tasting room was soon packed with visitors, sampling wines and buying T-shirts with the Ravenswood motto: "No Wimpy Wines". In the 1990s, Ravenswood continued producing single-vineyard wines, but prospered with a cheap, cheerful range

called Vintners Blend, known by Peterson as Château Cash Flow. In 2001, the vast Constellation Brands bought Ravenswood. Peterson remained in place, and the folksy tasting room continues to be thronged. Few visitors realize that the annual production has soared to over 700,000 cases. It is a great California success, but no one knows what the future holds, now that a boutique winery has become a stitch in a corporate tapestry.

18701 Gehricke Road, Sonoma 📞 *707 933 2332* 🌐 *www.ravenswood-wine.com* ⬤

WINE MAP OF CENTRAL & SOUTHERN CALIFORNIA

ALTHOUGH THE NORTH COAST boasts California's most famous wine regions, there are extensive vineyards extending south of San Francisco. In the Central Coast region, Monterey County is home to California's largest commercial vineyards, and AVAs such as Carmel Valley and Chalone are gaining renown for quality. San Luis Obispo County, especially Paso Robles, produces supple red wines, and further south, Santa Barbara County is making huge strides with Chardonnay, Pinot Noir, and Rhône varieties. Inland lie the Sierra Foothills and the immense Central Valley, home to America's bulk wine industry.

Quady Winery, Central Valley

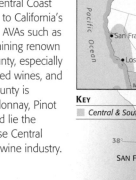

KEY

Central & Southern California

CENTRAL & SOUTHERN CALIFORNIA: AREAS & TOP PRODUCERS

SAN FRANCISCO BAY p498
Ridge Vineyards p504
Testarossa p504
Wente Vineyards p504

MONTEREY p498
Calera Wine Company p504
Chalone Vineyard p504
Paraiso Vineyards p505

SAN LUIS OBISPO p500
Alban Vineyards p505
Justin Vineyards & Winery p505
Meridian Vineyards p505
Tablas Creek Vineyard p505
Wild Horse Winery & Vineyards p506

SANTA BARBARA COUNTY p501
Alma Rosa p506
Andrew Murray Vineyards p506
Arcadian Winery p506
Au Bon Climat Winery p506
Byron p507
Firestone Vineyard p507

SIERRA FOOTHILLS p502
Domaine de la Terre Rouge p507

CENTRAL VALLEY p502
Quady Winery p507

SOUTHERN CALIFORNIA p503
Moraga Vineyards p507

PERFECT CASE: CENTRAL & SOUTHERN CALIFORNIA

Ⓡ Alban Vineyards Reva Syrah ££££

Ⓡ Andrew Murray Vineyards Tous Les Jours Syrah ££

Ⓡ Arcadian Winery Bien Nacido Pinot Noir ££££

Ⓦ Au Bon Climat Winery Talley Vineyard Chardonnay £££

Ⓡ Byron Pinot Noir ££

Ⓦ Chalone Vineyard Viognier ££

Ⓡ Domaine de la Terre Rouge Pyramid Block Syrah £££

Ⓡ Justin Vineyards & Winery Isosceles £££

Ⓕ Quady Winery Essensia ££

Ⓡ Ridge Vineyards Monte Bello Cabernet Sauvignon ££££

Ⓡ Tablas Creek Vineyard Esprit Red £££

Ⓦ Testarossa Michaud Vineyard Chardonnay £££

Autumnal vineyards and the Santa Lucia Mountains, San Luis Obispo

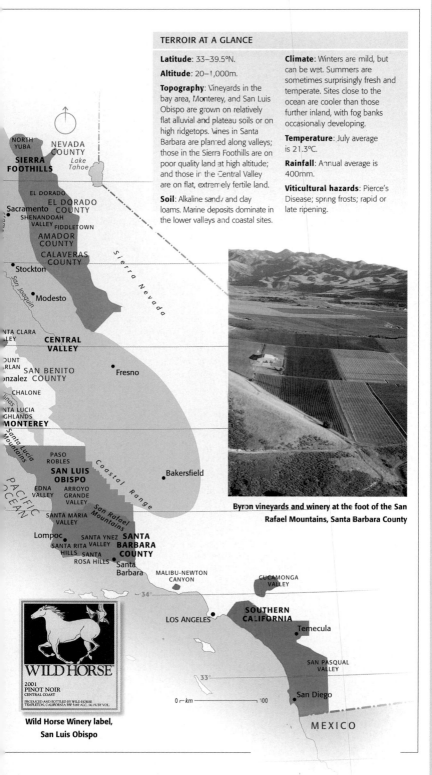

TERROIR AT A GLANCE

Latitude: 33–39.5°N.

Altitude: 20–1,000m.

Topography: Vineyards in the bay area, Monterey, and San Luis Obispo are grown on relatively flat alluvial and plateau soils or on high ridgetops. Vines in Santa Barbara are planted along valleys; those in the Sierra Foothills are on poor quality land at high altitude; and those in the Central Valley are on flat, extremely fertile land.

Soil: Alkaline sandy and clay loams. Marine deposits dominate in the lower valleys and coastal sites.

Climate: Winters are mild, but can be wet. Summers are sometimes surprisingly fresh and temperate. Sites close to the ocean are cooler than those further inland, with fog banks occasionally developing.

Temperature: July average is 21.3°C.

Rainfall: Annual average is 400mm.

Viticultural hazards: Pierce's Disease; spring frosts; rapid or late ripening.

Byron vineyards and winery at the foot of the San Rafael Mountains, Santa Barbara County

Wild Horse Winery label, San Luis Obispo

Chalone Vineyard below the Pinnacles National Monument, Gavilan Mountains

WINEGROWING AREAS OF CENTRAL & SOUTHERN CALIFORNIA

San Francisco Bay

THIS WAS ONCE a very important wine region, well developed by the time phylloxera hit in the late 19th century. Many vineyards were not replanted, and proximity to San Francisco meant that only the most remote were spared from the encroachment of suburbia. Today the region is dotted with AVAs so small and marginal that their names are rarely encountered on labels.

The most important district to the east of San Francisco Bay is the **Livermore Valley** AVA, largely planted with white grapes – including Sauvignon Blanc, which originally derives from Château d'Yquem cuttings *(see p75)* imported in the 1880s – and dominated by the Wente group of wineries.

Wente Vineyards in Livermore Valley

To the south of the bay the key district is the **Santa Cruz Mountains** AVA, which produces excellent Cabernet Sauvignon and other grapes at high elevations. Most of the vineyards in this area are remote and dispersed. Between San Jose and Gilroy lies the **Santa Clara Valley** AVA, whose wine industry is now close to extinction due to urban sprawl. Many of the wineries based south of the bay, including Bonny Doon Vineyard and Ridge Vineyards, bring in grapes from other regions to supplement local production.

gravel, loam, shale *Cabernet Sauvignon, Pinot Noir, Zinfandel* *Chardonnay, Sauvignon Blanc, Sémillon* *red, white, sparkling*

Monterey

THE MONTEREY REGION BEGINS at Watsonville and continues in a southeasterly direction down Salinas Valley. In the 1960s, viticultural experts recommended the valley as a good site for Cabernet Sauvignon. They calculated that there were sufficient hours of sunshine to ripen Cabernet, but they had overlooked the strong cool winds that roar down the valley and inhibit ripening. Many of the wines turned out to have an unpleasant vegetal character. The errors of the past have been corrected, and Monterey is now best known for its white varietal wines: Chardonnay, Riesling, and others. There are a few subregions where Bordeaux red grape varieties can ripen, but in terms of red wine Monterey as a whole is better suited to Pinot Noir and Syrah.

The county-wide Monterey AVA applies mostly to Salinas Valley, which is well known for its extensive vegetable farms. The northern end is very cool, but the valley becomes progressively warmer towards the southeast, as the maritime influence diminishes. Large-scale investment has been important here, with hundreds and even thousands of hectares being planted by individual companies. Kendall-Jackson alone owns 1,000ha here and the San Bernabe Vineyard in the south is the largest in California, with 3,500ha under vine.

Relatively few producers are based in Monterey, and much of the fruit is sold to very large wineries elsewhere. Chardonnay is the most important variety, and the wines often display a tropical fruit character. The following AVAs are the most significant.

 silt, loam, well-drained sandy loam, clay, alluvial loam, decomposed granite, clay, limestone
 Pinot Noir, Syrah, Merlot, Cabernet Sauvignon
 Chardonnay, Riesling, Pinot Blanc, Sauvignon Blanc, Viognier red, white

Carmel Valley

THE VINEYARDS OF THIS AVA lie in a verdant valley between the Salinas Valley and the ocean to the west. The mesoclimate here is warmer than in the Salinas, and is largely free from fog. Even though the vineyards are planted at elevations of up to 600m, red Bordeaux varieties do well here and account for 70 per cent of plantings. The wines are rich and fleshy, and modestly structured. Some Chardonnay is also grown. Large-scale wineries of note in this district include Joullian, Heller, and Georis.

Santa Lucia Highlands

NEAR GONZALEZ ON the western side of Salinas Valley is a series of terraces, slightly elevated over the side of the valley, known as the Santa Lucia Highlands AVA. Somewhat sheltered from the cold Pacific blasts that roar down Salinas Valley, and hovering just above the fog line, these highlands are where some of Monterey's top vineyards are located. Few wineries are based here, but the extensive and highly regarded vineyards sell their fruit to many producers. Some North Coast wineries have even bought land here. Pinot Noir and Syrah can be excellent, as can Riesling, but low market prices for the latter mean that many vineyards are being grafted over to more fashionable and lucrative grape varieties.

Chalone

CHALONE IS A ONE-WINERY AVA high in the Gavilan Mountains, at an altitude of 550–600m, on the eastern side of Salinas Valley. It took courage to plant vines here back in 1919, when there was no electricity or adequate water supply. The surviving vines

from 1919 are the oldest Chardonnay and Chenin Blanc in Monterey. The vineyards were obscure until wine entrepreneur Dick Graff purchased them in 1965. With the help of drip irrigation and barrel-fermentation (rare in those days), Graff produced some exceptional and long-lived wines. Today, some 200ha are in production, and after a mediocre patch and a change of winemakers, the Chalone Vineyard estate is once again on top form.

Mount Harlan

ON THE EASTERN SIDE of the Gavilan Mountains, within San Benito County, are four tiny AVAs; Mount Harlan is the only one of any significance. Although not officially in Monterey County, it is only just across the county border and deserves consideration because of its very unusual *terroir*. The site was selected in the mid-1970s by Burgundy enthusiast Josh Jensen for its limestone soil, which he believes to be one of the secrets of great burgundy. The only winery here is Jensen's Calera Wine Company, renowned for its Chardonnay and Pinot Noir, both planted at 700m, high above the fog line. The Chardonnays are reliable, and the Pinots have on occasion been exceptional; on the other hand, certain vintages have been angular or marred by off-flavours.

Calera Wine Company vineyard in the Gavilan Mountains, Mount Harlan

San Luis Obispo

THIS COUNTY ENCOMPASSES 11,000ha of vineyards and three excellent AVAs, of which the best known is Paso Robles. The mesoclimatic conditions vary greatly; many vineyards are planted on fairly flat land, while others are high in the Santa Lucia Mountains. Generalizations are difficult, but the red wines (notably Cabernet Sauvignon, Syrah, and Zinfandel) from Paso Robles tend to be supple and seductive, while Arroyo Grande and Edna Valley, being cooler, favour the Burgundian grape varieties. Unlike Monterey, which ships most of its grapes to wineries beyond its borders, San Luis Obispo

Tablas Creek Vineyard label, Paso Robles

has a host of small, thriving wineries, which attract many visitors. There is a growing interest in Rhône varieties in the area. The most significant AVAs are elaborated on below.

🗺 sandy loam, silty clay, marine deposits, marine sediment, degraded granite and tuffeau, clay, light clay 🍇 Cabernet Sauvignon, Zinfandel, Merlot, Syrah, Pinot Noir 🍇 Chardonnay, Sauvignon Blanc, Viognier 🍷 red, white

Paso Robles

VINEYARDS LIE BOTH east and west of this laid-back little town, and there are around 170 wineries within the AVA. To the east there stretches a large plateau, where the majority of vineyards are planted. To the west the terrain is quite different: more mountainous, with vineyards on isolated slopes among the forests of the coastal mountains. The mesoclimates are also different, since the so-called Westside vineyards receive much more rainfall than those on the plateau. The plateau can be very hot during the day, but its elevation of 400m means that nights are relatively cool, so the grapes never become baked. Broadly speaking, plateau wines have supple tannins, are medium-bodied, and

show a great deal of youthful charm. Zinfandel, Cabernet Sauvignon, and Syrah are best drunk within five years, but they can often be kept longer. Westside wines reflect the more rugged terrain, have fiercer tannins, and often need up to five years in bottle to reveal their complexity and profundity. There is a plethora of small wineries here, ranging from decidedly rustic in quality to sophisticated boutique operations. Some of them benefit from ownership of very old Zinfandel vineyards, and newer plantings of Bordeaux and Rhône varieties show great promise. Adjoining the Westside is the very small York Mountain AVA, which has a cooler mesoclimate and is best known for red varieties, although ripening can be problematic here.

Edna Valley

JUST SOUTH OF THE TOWN of San Luis Obispo is the Edna Valley AVA, which has little in common with Paso Robles. Open to the Pacific to the south and west, it has a strongly maritime climate and a very long growing season. Fog can provoke botrytis and other maladies. Chardonnay dominates, and the wines tend to be rich and plump. There are about 550ha in production, with little room for further expansion. The region is dominated by a single winery, the eponymous Edna Valley.

Vineyards in the dramatic Arroyo Grande Valley, San Luis Obispo

CALIFORNIA'S RHÔNE RANGERS

Since the 1970s, a few wine producers have argued, persuasively, that California's hot climes are far better suited to Mediterranean grapes than to the usual Burgundy and Bordeaux varieties. These 'Rhône Rangers' have cropped up across California. Founder member Randall Grahm *(see p477)* of Bonny Doon winery pays homage in his wines and labels to celebrated Mediterranean wines, while the Perrin family, owner of Châteauneuf's best known estate, Château de Beaucastel *(see p133)*, has planted the best clones of Rhône varieties in the hills of San Luis Obispo's Westside *(right)*. Syrah, the archetypal Rhône grape, is enjoying a boom here and in Santa Barbara, where the climate is warm but not excessively hot. There are also some stunning Syrahs emerging from the rustic Sierra Foothills. Grenache is often used to make richly fruity rosés, while Viognier has proved more difficult – perhaps because of the Californian propensity to throw everything into new oak and overcharge for the result. Even so, exciting Viogniers are emerging from places as diverse as Mendocino, Napa, and Santa Barbara. Less familiar whites like Marsanne and Roussanne are also being cultivated, and some North Coast growers are showing interest in old-vine Carignane just when many southern French growers are grubbing the variety up from their vineyards. Producers include **Fetzer, McDowell Valley Vineyards, Joseph Phelps, Tablas Creek Vineyard, Alban Vineyards**, and **Sierra Vista**.

Arroyo Grande Valley

THIS IS, IN EFFECT, the southeastern extension of Edna Valley. Much of this AVA has a mesoclimate similar to that of its neighbouring AVA, though slightly warmer and less breezy, and both Chardonnay and Pinot Noir are grown here with great success. Further inland, where the temperatures are higher, there are small pockets of Zinfandel. Alban Vineyards on the western edge of the sub-region is an outpost of Rhône varieties of exceptional quality.

Santa Barbara County

IN 1969, THE TOTAL VINEYARD surface in this county was less than 5ha; today there are over 8,500ha under vine. This used to be ranching country, with undulating grassy hills, so it was not difficult to convert some of those gentle slopes and valley floors to vineyards. East-west valleys let in maritime breezes that made this territory promising for Burgundian varieties, although the more inland sites are warm enough for Merlot. Syrah, Sauvignon Blanc, Riesling, Cabernet Franc, and even Cabernet Sauvignon can also ripen here, but only in specific sites. Given the cool climate, sun exposure is of primary importance and vineyards planted in poorly exposed spots risk grapes not ripening. Growers like to point out that Santa Barbara was producing exciting wines from the outset, even when vines were planted more or less at random, without any great knowledge of clonal selection and other viticultural practices. Now that these issues are far better understood, quality is likely to improve even further.

🏞 marine sediment, sandy loam, clay loam, silty loam, shale, calcium 🍇 Pinot Noir, Merlot, Syrah 🍇 Chardonnay, Riesling, Pinot Blanc, Sauvignon Blanc, Viognier 🍷 red, white, sparkling

Santa Maria Valley

MARITIME INFLUENCES ENSURE that the vineyards planted in this AVA are among the coolest in California. Most of them lie on terraces or shelves above the valley floor, but not on the exposed ridgetops of the San Rafael Mountains just to the north. Many of these vineyards are very large, and are owned by producers based on the North Coast such as Robert Mondavi, Kendall-Jackson, and Beringer. There are also large commercial vineyards, such as Bien Nacido, that sell fruit to a wide range of wineries throughout the state. Chardonnay is by far the dominant variety; the fruit can have a firm acidic structure, which is unusual in California, and this acidity consolidates the grapes' intensity of flavour. The wine often has an exotic or fruit-salady flavour, which can be an acquired taste. Pinot Noir is also successfully grown here.

Santa Ynez Valley

THIS VALLEY IS LOCATED south of Santa Maria Valley, and curves inland from the town of Lompoc. With every 3km from the ocean, average temperatures increase by about 0.5°C, so there is a marked difference between westerly sites such as the Sanford and Benedict vineyards and easterly locations like those of the Firestone and Zaca Mesa vineyards. This means that a wide range of grape varieties can be grown, with Burgundian varieties and Riesling doing well towards the cooler west, and Bordeaux and Rhône grapes flourishing in the warmer east. Merlot and Cabernet Franc are more reliable than Cabernet Sauvignon, which can display vegetal tones here. Rainfall is low – in fact non-existent – in summer, and spring frosts are very rare.

Sanford, Santa Rita Hills

Santa Rita Hills

THIS AVA WAS CREATED in 2001, at the urging of leading growers such as Richard Sanford and Bryan Babcock. It lies between the Purisima Hills to the north and the Santa Rosa Hills to the south. Almost the entire region is an enclave within the larger Santa Ynez Valley AVA. With about 1,000ha under cultivation, it is cooler than the larger region, experiencing maritime fogs. Consequently, the grape variety with the greatest potential here is Pinot Noir, which is dark-coloured and potent, yet fragrant.

Sierra Foothills

THE PLANTING OF THE Sierra Foothills area was a by-product of the Gold Rush of the 1850s, when farmers and entrepreneurs planted vines to service the thirsty prospectors. By the late 1860s, there were 4,000ha under vine. Although only half that area is in production today, some of the vineyards date back to the late 19th century, and the area is arguably the most fascinating of California's wine regions. What makes the Foothills area so intriguing is its combination of lofty terrain, long winemaking history (still in evidence within truly ancient vineyards), and remaining links with the Gold Rush days, especially at wineries such as Kautz Ironstone, where an enormous gold nugget is on proud display.

The vineyards are high, between 400 and 900m, and elevation moderates the heat of this inland region, east of Sacramento. There are four AVAs. **El Dorado** is the largest, with no vineyards below 400m. It produces a range of grapes, including Zinfandel, Barbera, Cabernet Sauvignon, Merlot, Chardonnay, and Viognier. Just south of El Dorado, within Amador County, are **Shenandoah Valley** and **Fiddletown**, both renowned for their old-vine Zinfandel. The southernmost area is Calaveras County, which has no AVA, but is home to some important wineries nonetheless. The growers of the Foothills are generally open-minded, and there are substantial plantings of Rhône and Italian varieties. Fortified wines can be outstanding, with port-style wines from Zinfandel and Barbera, and rich Muscats. Winemaking standards vary, with state-of-the-art facilities alongside decidedly rustic and mediocre wineries.

A few vineyards lie on the fringes of the Foothills, such as the handful of wineries within Nevada County. The impressive terraced vineyards of the Renaissance Winery, which enjoy their own AVA, **North Yuba**, successfully produce a very wide range of varieties, from Riesling to Cabernet Sauvignon. *granite, volcanic deposits* *Syrah, Zinfandel, Cabernet Sauvignon, Barbera* *Chardonnay, Sauvignon Blanc* *red, white, rosé, fortified*

Central Valley

THIS IS CALIFORNIA'S wine factory. With 80,000ha under vine, the Central Valley is by far the largest of California's wine regions, producing around 60 per cent of all the state's grapes. The region encompasses the vast San Joaquin Valley and areas to the south and north. The soils are rich and the climate is blisteringly hot and dry; this is one of the world's sunniest regions, so irrigation is essential. The heat means that high-quality grapes are virtually impossible to cultivate; instead, the valley is a source of fruity, easy-drinking wines that give plenty of pleasure at an affordable price. A handful of producers make excellent port-style and Muscat wines, but they are a drop in the ocean of Chardonnay, Chenin Blanc, French Colombard, Merlot, and Zinfandel. A few northerly regions around Sacramento can make some claim to quality: Zinfandel from Lodi and Chenin Blanc from Clarksburg are certainly worth a try.

Autumnal vineyard in Santa Ynez Valley, Santa Barbara County

▨ alluvial loam ▩ Merlot, Cabernet Sauvignon, Zinfandel ▩ Chardonnay, Chenin Blanc, Colombard, Sauvignon Blanc ▨ red, white, rosé, sparkling, dessert, fortified

Southern California

IN THE 19TH CENTURY, vineyards were flourishing in Los Angeles itself, but they were wiped out by Pierce's Disease, a bacterial malady spread by insects, for which there is no cure. In recent years, this disease has destroyed a substantial proportion of vineyards elsewhere in southern California, notably in Temecula, a former Chardonnay stronghold midway between Los Angeles and San Diego. Vines have not entirely vanished from metropolitan Los Angeles, and there is even a tiny AVA called **Malibu-Newton Canyon**. Around San Bernardino is the **Cucamonga Valley** AVA, dominated by Zinfandel; and there is another AVA in the far south, consisting of 30ha around San Diego, called **San Pasqual Valley**. With a few exceptions, none of these regions are strongly focused on quality, and the wineries survive by catering to the thirst and recreational needs of the enormous local population. Zinfandel, Chardonnay, Syrah, and Sauvignon Blanc are the dominant grape varieties in this area.

▨ varied ▩ Zinfandel, Syran ▩ Chardonnay, Sauvignon Blanc ▨ red, white

THE FORTIFIED WINE TRADITION

A few decades ago, California's wine industry was dominated by fortified wines, which gave drinkers more alcohol for their money. Quality was usually dismal, as producers took short cuts to simulate sherry and port styles. Today such wines may be out of fashion, but there are some superlative examples.

Port-style wines are sometimes made from Zinfandel, Petite Sirah, or even Cabernet Sauvignon, and a handful of wineries, including the vast Mondavi Woodbridge operation in Lodi AVA, produce good fortifieds from Portuguese grapes such as Touriga Nacional.

Quady Winery Muscat label

The Sierra Foothills region, which has never abandoned the tradition of fortified wine production, is also a good source of these wines, and of rich Muscats. In the Central Valley, where quality rarely rises above mediocre, Ficklin has always specialized n port-style wines that are regularly among California's best. The standard bearer for elegant Muscats is Quady Winery in the Central Valley, which has mastered the difficult craft of producing highly perfumed Muscats and – thanks in large part to brilliant packaging (left) – has made them an international success.

TOP PRODUCERS OF CENTRAL & SOUTHERN CALIFORNIA

Ridge Vineyards
San Francisco Bay

17100 Monte Bello Rd, Cupertino
【 408 867 3233
ⓦ www.ridgewine.com ⚪

THIS FAMOUS WINERY was founded on the site of an 1880s vineyard by Stanford University professors in 1959. In 1969, Paul Draper became winemaker, and he is still at the helm. His finest wine is the estate Cabernet Sauvignon from grapes grown in the 600m high Monte Bello vineyard. One of California's undisputed first growths, it is aged, unusually, in American oak. Ridge also produces some stunning Zinfandels from old vineyards in Sonoma and Paso Robles.

Ridge Vineyards

🍷 red, white 🔀 2006, 2005, 2004, 2003, 2001, 2000
★ Santa Cruz Mountains Chardonnay, Monte Bello Cabernet Sauvignon, Geyserville Zinfandel

Testarossa
San Francisco Bay

300-A College Ave, Los Gatos 【 408 354 6150 ⓦ www.testarossa.com ⚫

THIS NÉGOCIANT winery was founded by Rob and Diana Jensen in 1993. Based near San Jose, they own no vineyards and so they buy in grapes from nine top sites in Monterey and Santa Barbara County. The Chardonnays tend to be rich and toasty, with good acidic bite. The Pinot Noirs are spicy and well structured, with a distinctively California style. The Syrah is excellent, too.
🍷 red, white 🔀 2006, 2005, 2004,
2002 ★ Rosella's Vineyard Chardonnay, Sleepy Hollow Vineyard Pinot Noir, Subasio Syrah

Wente Vineyards
San Francisco Bay

5565 Tesla Rd, Livermore 【 408 456 2300 ⓦ www.wentevineyards.com ⚪

THIS FAMILY-OWNED estate, founded in 1883 by Carl Wente, dominates Livermore Valley and has substantial holdings in Monterey, planted with Pinot Noir and other varieties. The wines are commercial in the best sense – made in large quantities to a consistent level of quality. The standard varietals are labelled Family Selections and estate-grown wines are bottled as Vineyard Selections. Wente also makes a fine sparkling wine aged for five years before disgorgement.
🍷 red, white, sparkling 🔀 2006, 2005, 2004, 2003, 2002 ★ Estate Chardonnay, Late Harvest Riesling, Brut Reserve

Calera Wine Company
Monterey

11300 Cienega Rd, Hollister 【 831 637 9170 ⓦ www.calerawine.com ⚫

AN ADMIRED ESTATE with a style of its own, Calera is one of the few wine estates planted to test a theory. Josh Jensen often visited Burgundy in the early 1970s and was convinced that the secret of great Pinot Noir was the limestone soil. Back in California, he found limestone 670m up in the Gavilan Mountains, and planted four different sites there with the grape. Results were mixed: some vintages were magnificent; some earthy and stewed. The limestone soils do offer excellent drainage, but bacterial problems undermine fruit quality in certain vintages. However, the Viognier, made since 1987, is splendid.
🍷 red, white 🔀 2006, 2005, 2003, 2002, 2000 ★ Viognier, Mount Harlan Chardonnay, Selleck Mount Harlan Pinot Noir

Chalone Vineyard
Monterey

Stonewall Canyon Rd & Hwy 146 W, Soledad 【 831 678 1717 ⓦ www.chalonevineyard.com ⚪ by appt

THIS REMOTE mountainside property dates from 1919, but the wines were first bottled in 1960. Chardonnay and Pinot Noir dominate; Syrah and Viognier were planted in the late 1990s. Bacterial problems in the winery damaged Chalone's reputation in the 1990s, but today the winery is back on form. The old-vine Chenin Blanc here shows just how stunning it can be.
🍷 red, white 🔀 2005, 2004, 2003, 2002 ★ Chenin Blanc, Viognier, Pinot Noir

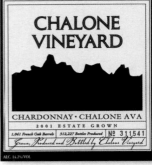

Chalone Vineyard label

Paraiso Vineyards
Monterey

38060 Paraiso Springs Rd, Soledad
C *831 678 0300*
W *www.paraisovineyards.com* ●

RICH SMITH IS PRIMARILY a grape farmer, but he sets aside certain blocks of land from his 1,200ha to make his own wine. He creates uncomplicated wines of great purity and direct fruit flavours. Pinot Blanc has sadly been phased out for commercial reasons, but the Chardonnay, Pinot Noir, and Syrah show the intense fruitiness of which Monterey is capable.

⬛ *red, white* **⬛** *2006, 2005, 2004, 2003* ★ *Pinot Noir, Syrah*

Alban Vineyards
San Luis Obispo

8575 Orcutt Rd, Arroyo Grande
C *805 546 0305*
W *www.albanvineyards.com* ●

JOHN ALBAN WAS converted to Rhône varieties when he visited Condrieu, and from 1990 onwards he dedicated his vineyard to the varieties of the Rhône. Low yields give his wines immense concentration, and whether he is turning his hand to Roussanne or Viognier, Syrah or Grenache, Alban is incapable of making a bad wine. It is no wonder that other producers queue up to buy his grapes.

⬛ *red, white* **⬛** *2006, 2005, 2004, 2003, 2002* ★ *Viognier, Reva Syrah, Grenache*

Justin Vineyards & Winery
San Luis Obispo

11680 Chimney Rock Rd, Paso Robles
C *805 238 6932*
W *www.justinwine.com* ●

FORMER BANKER Justin Baldwin bought this Westside Paso

RANDALL GRAHM & BONNY DOON

The witty and intellectual Randall Grahm wandered into the California wine industry and became its most admirable gadfly. His Bonny Doon Vineyard in Santa Cruz is his way of demonstrating that California's climate is far better suited to Rhône and Mediterranean varieties than to holy cows Cabernet Sauvignon and Chardonnay. His wines are acts of homage to Châteauneuf-du-Pape and Bandol, and idiosyncratic acts of courage, such as the attempt to produce a 'Pacific Rim' Riesling from West Coast regions. These are not California's best wines, but Grahm's rejection of conventional wisdom about varieties, wines, and markets has stimulated others to redefine the future of the industry.

Tasting rooms: 328 Ingalls St, Santa Cruz
C *831 425 4518 or 2485 W Hwy 46, Paso Robles*
C *805 239 5614* **W** *www.bonnydoonvineyard.com*

Bonny Doon Syrah

Robles property in 1982 and now has 33ha in production. Over the years he has experimented to see which varieties work best in these virgin sites. His Cabernet Sauvignon and Syrah varietals have proved successful, as have his Bordeaux blends called Isosceles and Justification. High quality and skilful marketing have brought Justin swift recognition.

⬛ *red, white, fortified* **⬛** *2006, 2005, 2004, 2003* ★ *Sauvignon Blanc, Syrah, Isosceles*

Meridian Vineyards
San Luis Obispo

7000 Hwy 46 E, Paso Robles
C *805 237 6000*
W *www.meridianvineyards.com* ●

FOUNDED BY veteran wine-maker Chuck Ortman, Meridian has been through many changes in ownership, and at present the winery is part of the Foster's group. Production at this already large winery is set to expand further. With thousands of hectares at his disposal, Meridian makes a wide range of wines that offer exceptional value for money.

⬛ *red, white* **⬛** *2006, 2005, 2004, 2003* ★ *Limited Release Pinot Noir, Limited Release Syrah, Dusi Vineyard Zinfandel*

Tablas Creek Vineyard
San Luis Obispo

9339 Adelaida Rd, Paso Robles
C *805 237 1231* **W** *www.tablascreek.com* ● *by appt*

FOR MANY YEARS the Perrin family and American wine importer Robert Haas searched for the perfect place to grow Rhône varieties in California. Eventually they chose the Westside of Paso Robles, as its soils and rugged terrain resembled those of the family's estate in Châteauneuf-du-Pape, Château de Beaucastel (see p133); they imported vines from France, and grew them organically. Since 1997, they have produced varietal wines and complex blends called Esprit de Beaucastel. The red is based on Mourvèdre and Grenache; the white on Roussanne and Grenache Blanc.

⬛ *red, white* **⬛** *2006, 2005, 2004, 2003* ★ *Esprit de Beaucastel, Esprit de Beaucastel Blanc*

Wild Horse Winery & Vineyards
San Luis Obispo

1437 Wild Horse Winery Ct, Templeton ☎ *805 434 2541*
W *www.wildhorsewinery.com* ○

For 20 years, the irrepressible Ken Volk produced an astonishing range of wines from his own land and from various Central Coast vineyards. He became renowned for his Pinot Noir and wines from Rhône varietals, but also delighted in producing highly individual wines from rare varieties such as Blaufränkisch, Négrette, and Verdelho. In 2003 Volk sold the winery, which is now owned by Constellation. But Wild Horse remains a fine source of some of California's most quirky wines.

red, white* 2006, 2005, 2004, 2003 ★ *Malvasia Bianca, Viognier, Cheval Sauvage Pinot Noir

Alma Rosa
Santa Barbara County

7250 Santa Rosa Rd, Buellton
☎ *805 688 9090*
W *www.almarosawinery.com* ○

Richard Sanford was one of the first Pinot Noir growers in the county, establishing his vineyard in 1971 and his winery 10 years later. But in 2006 he was forced out by shareholders who did not have his organic vision, so, retaining 42ha of his original vineyards, he set up this new winery, making charming Chardonnay and Pinot Noir.

red, white* 2006, 2005 ★ *El Jabali Chardonnay, La Encantada Pinot Noir

Andrew Murray Vineyards
Santa Barbara County

5095 Zaca Station Rd, Los Olivos
☎ *805 686 9604* W *www.andrewmurrayvineyards.com* ●

Wild Horse Winery & Vineyards label

Andrew Murray became acquainted with Rhône wines on family trips to France. The family planted Rhône varieties on hilly land in the Santa Ynez Valley from 1990, and also bought fruit from selected vineyards. Murray developed a fine range of Syrahs. In 2005 a family dispute led to Andrew losing his vineyards, but the brand continues using purchased fruit of high quality.

red, white* 2006, 2005, 2004, 2003 ★ *Viognier, Tous Les Jours Syrah

Arcadian Winery
Santa Barbara County

Santa Ynez ☎ *805 688 1876*
W *www.arcadianwinery.com* ●

Joseph Davis does not own any vineyards. Instead, he leases plots of land from grape growers in Santa Barbara County and Monterey, and farms them himself. This is the only way to ensure the grapes are of the quality he desires. Having worked in Burgundy, France remains his model for Chardonnay and Pinot Noir. Davis uses a great deal of new oak, but the wines have sufficient concentration for the wood not to be dominant. These are Burgundy-style wines of purity and intensity.

red, white* 2005, 2004, 2002, 2001 ★ *Sleepy Hollow Chardonnay, Pisoni Vineyard Pinot Noir, Stolpman Syrah

Au Bon Climat Winery
Santa Barbara County

Rte 1, Santa Maria Mesa Rd, Santa Maria ☎ *805 937 9801*
W *www.aubonclimat.com* ●

Jim Clendenen is one of the great pioneers of Santa Maria Valley. For over 25 years, he

THE GALLO PHENOMENON

Gallo's lavish advertising features a family company that is content to tend its vineyards and invite the public to enjoy the results. In reality, this is a wine industry phenomenon, the world's largest wine producer, a reclusive and protective company that makes about as much wine as the whole of Australia, although much of it is sold under other labels.

Founded by brothers Ernest and Julio Gallo, the business took off just as Prohibition ended in the mid-1930s. Thanks to a well developed distribution network, market awareness, and ruthless promotion, Gallo grew fast and by 1967 had a third of the US market. It is still based deep in the Central Valley, where it produces tens of millions of cases each year; but it was the domaine in Sonoma *(see p492)*, set up by the founders' grandchildren, that saved Gallo from a reputation for mediocrity in the 1980s, and keeps up the image today, offering sound quality at a fair price.

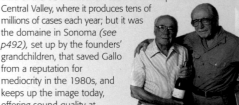

Ernest & Julio Gallo

has produced some very fine Chardonnay and Pinot Noir, both from his own vineyards and from those of the region's leading growers. He favours restraint over power, yet the wines remain Californian in their generosity and richness. Clendenen also produces a range of Italian varietals under the Clendenen Family Vineyards label.

🟥 red, white ▶ 2006, 2005, 2004, 2003, 2001 ★ Bien Nacido Vineyard Chardonnay, Isabelle Pinot Noir

Byron
Santa Barbara County

5230 Tepusquet Rd, Santa Maria
📞 805 937 7288
🖳 www.byronwines.com ⬜

KEN BROWN FOUNDED this winery in the 1980s, and although it was sold to Robert Mondavi in 1990, Brown remained in charge until 2005, when the property was sold. Today it belongs to Jackson Family Estates, but still focuses on Chardonnay and Pinot Noir. Byron has over 250ha of vineyards, but also buys fruit from other top sites in Santa Barbara. The wines are perfect examples of the elegantly poised Santa Maria style.

🟥 red, white ▶ 2006, 2005, 2004, 2003, 2002 ★ Nielson Vineyard Chardonnay, Bien Nacido Pinot Noir

Firestone Vineyard
Santa Barbara County

5000 Zaca Station Rd, Los Olivos
📞 805 688 3940
🖳 www.firestonewine.com ⬜

SET UP BY Brooks Firestone in the 1970s, this Santa Ynez Valley estate is now owned by local insurance man William Foley, who also has an estate under his own

name. The winery soon won a reputation for outstanding value. Production has expanded considerably, and many grapes are now bought in, so quality can be variable. Sauvignon Blanc has always been reliable, as are the Merlot and much improved Cabernet Sauvignon. Wines can lack concentration and length, but are well crafted and remain good value.

🟥 red, white ▶ 2006, 2005, 2004, 2003, 2002 ★ Gewürztraminer, Late Harvest Riesling, Merlot Reserve

Domaine de la Terre Rouge
Sierra Foothills

10801 Dickson Rd, Fiddletown
📞 209 245 3117
🖳 www.terrerougewines.com ⬜

FOUNDED IN 1987 by William Easton, Terre Rouge produces the Sierra Foothills' best wines from Rhône varieties. The finest Syrah comes from a parcel of land called Pyramid Block, and the best grapes are usually reserved for the very oaky Ascent bottling. Whites include a Rhône-style blend called Enigma and a rich Viognier. Under the Easton label, there are some powerful yet elegant Zinfandels and juicy Barberas.

🟥 red, white, fortified ▶ 2006, 2005, 2004, 2003 ★ Enigma, Sentinel Oak Syrah, Estate Zinfandel

Quady Winery
Central Valley

13181 Rd 24, Madera 📞 559 673 8068 🖳 www.quadywinery.com ⬜

ANDREW QUADY dabbled with port-style wines in the late 1970s while working for other wineries. He also experimented with fortified Muscats, and

Assistant winemaker Herb Quady in the lab at Quady

in 1981, released Essensia, an enchanting, beautifully packaged, orange-scented Orange Muscat, which was a smash hit. He then created other wines: Elysium, a rose-scented Black Muscat; sweet and dry vermouths; and fortified wines from Zinfandel and Portuguese varieties. This area is too hot for fine table wines, but Quady has proved Madera is an ideal location for world-class sweet wines.

🟥 fortified ★ Essensia, Elysium

Moraga Vineyards
Southern California

650 Sepulveda Blvd, Los Angeles
📞 310 471 8560
🖳 www.moragavineyards.com ⬛

TOM JONES'S small Moraga Canyon plot in Los Angeles' exclusive Bel Air suburb must be the most unlikely spot in the USA for a quality-oriented vineyard. The canyon's meso-climate has the advantage of higher rainfall and cooler nights than downtown LA. There is only one red and one white wine: the Cabernet Sauvignon-dominated Bordeaux-style blend made in an opulent and oaky style is as expensive, and as impressive, as a fine Napa Cabernet.

🟥 red ▶ 2004, 2003, 2002, 2001 ★ Moraga Cabernet

Byron

PACIFIC NORTHWEST

Although Oregon *and Washington are as diametrically opposed to one another as Bordeaux is to Burgundy, they are both more closely allied to France than to other US winegrowing states. Lying, like their French counterparts, between 43 and 47° latitude, they are separated from each other by the great Columbia River and divided in two by the Cascade Mountains. The interplay between sun, weather, and these geological features defines regional wine styles.*

Unique in the history of wine, Oregon's wine industry was established in the 1960s purely to produce Pinot Noir. Its founders were convinced that in order to re-create the delicately spiced perfume, velvety texture, and fine structure of burgundy, Pinot Noir had to have a long ripening period. After undertaking an almost kamikaze-like pursuit to that end, Oregon's winemakers eventually gave birth to cool-climate viticulture in the New World (see p515).

Ranked fourth in the USA in terms of production, Oregon's 393 Burgundy-sized wineries and 7,042ha of vineyards produce around two million cases per year. Most wineries cluster west of the Cascades within the coastally influenced, cool, wet Willamette Valley. The focus here is primarily on cool-climate grapes: Pinot Noir, Pinot Gris, Sauvignon Blanc, Gewürztraminer, Riesling, and Pinot Blanc.

In sharp contrast, Washington State's industry is much grander in scale. In the past 20 years it has grown from 19 wineries to more than 600, and from 2,025ha to over 12,545. Now ranked second in the USA, output tops 757,000hl annually and is exported to over 40 countries. Situated in a semi-desert, high-plains environment, Washington's wine regions mainly follow river valleys in the east of the state, and they could not survive without irrigation. Endless sun allows a wide range of grape varieties to ripen consistently, and production is centred on Chardonnay, Riesling, Cabernet Sauvignon, Merlot, and Syrah.

Pinot Gris grapes

Cabernet Franc vineyard at Woodward Canyon Winery in Walla Walla, Washington

◁ **Willamette Valley vineyard with Mount Hood in the background, Oregon**

WINE MAP OF THE PACIFIC NORTHWEST

Tucked in the northwest corner of the USA are the wine-growing states of Washington and Oregon. To the east of the Cascade Mountains lie Washington's nine AVAs: the all-encompassing Columbia Valley AVA, with six smaller AVAs within its borders; Columbia Gorge AVA, standing alone; and Puget Sound AVA, which produces relatively small quantities. Oregon's 16 AVAs lie to the west, set between the Coastal Range and the Cascades. They run 320km from north to south. Willamette Valley AVA has six subregional AVAs; Southern Oregon AVA has four. Three further AVAs are shared with Washington, and a fourth with Idaho.

Woodward Canyon Winery label, Washington

PERFECT CASE: PACIFIC NORTHWEST

WASHINGTON

🔴 Cayuse En Cerise Vineyard Syrah

🔴 Woodward Canyon Old-Vine Cabernet

🔴 DeLille Cellars Chaleur Estate D2

⚪ L'Ecole No 41 Barrel-Fermented Sémillon

⚪ McCrea Non Sequitur/ Roussanne

⚪ Chateau Ste Michelle Canoe Ridge Chardonnay

OREGON

🔴 Cristom Jesse Vineyard Pinot Noir

🔴 Domaine Drouhin Cuvée Laurène Pinot Noir

⚪ Domaine Drouhin Chardonnay

🔴 Elk Cove La Bohème Vineyard Pinot Noir

🔴 Ken Wright Single Vineyard Pinot Noirs

🔴 Ponzi Reserve Pinot Noir

WASHINGTON: AREAS & TOP PRODUCERS

COLUMBIA VALLEY AVA p512
Columbia Winery p516
McCrea Cellars p516
Ste Michelle Wine Estates p516

YAKIMA VALLEY & RED MOUNTAIN AVAs p513
DeLille Cellars p516
Hogue Cellars p516
Hedges Family Estates p517

WALLA WALLA AVA p513
Canoe Ridge Vineyard p517
Cayuse Vineyards p517
L'Ecole No 41 p517
Woodward Canyon Winery p517

Domaine Drouhin's gravity-fed winery, Willamette Valley, Oregon

TERROIR AT A GLANCE

Latitude: 45–43.5°N. (Washington); 42–45.5°N (Oregon).

Altitude: 0–270m in Washington; 90–800m in Oregon.

Topography: In Washington, the Cascade Mountains act as a barrier to the moist, moderate marine weather patterns of the Pacific Ocean. Oregon's wine regions are further west, sandwiched between the Coastal Range and the Cascades.

Soil: Basaltic sand, loess, and river gravel in Washington; volcanic, granite, and clay in Oregon.

Climate: Only 200mm of rain makes it past the mountains to fall on Washington's bone-dry wine regions. Summers are hot here, but dramatic diurnal temperature shifts preserve acidity and ensure slow ripening. In Oregon, the Pacific influence means cool summers and damp autumns.

Temperature: July average is 21°C in Washington; 19°C in Oregon.

Rainfall: Annual average is 200mm in Washington; 1,100mm in Oregon.

Viticultural hazards: Occasional vine-damaging hard freezes in Washington; fungal diseases, underripeness in Oregon.

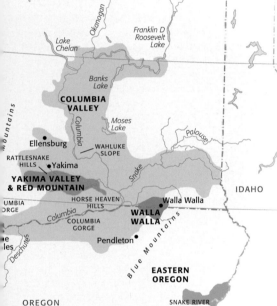

OREGON: AREAS & TOP PRODUCERS

GEOLOGICAL MAKE-UP

The geology of the Pacific Northwest has been shaped by monumental flood erosion as well as ongoing volcanic activity (Mount St Helen last erupted in 1982). As glaciers retreated 16,000 years ago, one of antiquity's greatest inland lakes, Lake Missoula, burst its ice dam, releasing a tsunami-sized wave 60m high and 20km wide. It flowed at 320km per hour, scouring out the massive Columbia Gorge, blasting westward through the Cascades' ancient basalt, and eventually depositing truck-sized boulders and silt onto the Willamette Valley floor. In its wake it left a 75m deep gravel bed covering Columbia Valley, and shallow, stone-studded, free-draining, highly infertile, phylloxera-free, sandy topsoil, which is perfect for grape growing.

Vineyard planted on infertile riverbed in Walla Walla, Washington

WINEGROWING AREAS OF THE PACIFIC NORTHWEST

WASHINGTON

BOLSTERED BY FRENCH, German, and Italian immigrants in the 19th century, vines, grapes, and wine have long played a part in Washington's history. Today the state's wine industry is dominated by two Seattle-based giants, Stimson Lane and Corus Brands, which together account for over 70 per cent of production. Historically, Washington's wine industry resembles the massive, agri-business approach common to Australasia. Large wineries grew up in populated areas around Seattle and were supplied by grapes shipped over the mountains from sun-blessed and dry eastern Washington. This allowed efficient production and cross-regional blending between a range of subclimates. Starting with large volumes of consistently good-quality, well-priced, everyday wine, wineries then added reasonably priced mid-range, reserve, and super premium labels.

Originally, white varieties dominated; but now reds account for 56 per cent of output. Over the past 30 years, Washington's wine industry has earned a strong reputation for its varietals, consistently delivering character-filled flavours, smooth textures, and finely honed structure – usually at relatively steep prices.

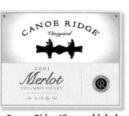

Canoe Ridge Vineyard label

Columbia Valley AVA

CONTAINING 98 PER CENT of Washington's total production and roughly a third of its landmass (some 4.4 million ha), Columbia Valley AVA was established in 1984 as a catch-all to facilitate cross-regional blending. Its own designated vineyards cover 2,709ha and encompass the state's widest range of sub-climates – from the hottest vineyards along the Wahluke Slope AVA (Mattawa, Saddle Mountains, Frenchman Hills, and Indian Wells), to the cooler south, where relatively temperate, frost-free vineyards dot the upper slopes of the Columbia Gorge AVA (1,794ha) and Horse Heaven Hills AVA (2,444ha), with its important vineyards Alder Ridge, Zepher Ridge, and Canoe Ridge.

Generally, soils range from highly infertile ancient gravels to sand, clay, and basalt. Out of necessity, vineyards are planted on slopes between 20 and 310m above sea level, close to the Columbia River to keep frost at bay in winter and vines cool in summer.

This all-encompassing AVA was first recognized for its high-quality, delicately perfumed, racy Rieslings in the early 1970s. Although eclipsed by Chardonnay and Merlot in the 1980s, the dry, medium- and late-harvested Rieslings remain among the best in the USA. Matured-on-the-vine ice wines are made when conditions are suitable. Sadly, Washington's early success with vibrantly fruited, razor-sharp, highly unfashionable Sémillon and Chenin Blanc is under-appreciated. The refreshingly crisp Sauvignon

Blancs are among the country's better versions, and are often ridiculously cheap.

Merlot has been Washington's star red since 1976. It is generally richer, riper, and more alcoholic than in bordeaux, and more finely structured and juicier than in Californian wines. Now the state's most planted grape, Cabernet Sauvignon ripens equally consistently, producing concentrated, powerful wine. The two grapes marry well, often forming a blend with Cabernet Franc or Malbec – or both, in full Meritage glory. All can appear remarkably bordeaux-like in style and structure.

The 1990s saw phenomenal growth in plantings of Syrah. Now the fifth most-planted grape, its style is very much that of France's northern Rhône Valley. In this spirit, Washington's own Rhône Ranger movement, mirroring that of California (see p501), has been known to add a seven per cent dash of Viognier for aromatic lift and structure.

Less well known but trendy varieties such as Marsanne, Roussanne, Malbec, Mourvèdre, Nebbiolo, Sangiovese, Barbera, Zinfandel, Grenache, and Cinsaut are starting to produce exciting wine. Unique in the USA, Lemberger is making a strong comeback. Big, brash, and fruity, it may turn out to be Washington's answer to California's Zinfandel. 🏔 *gravels, sand, clay, basalt* 🍇 *Merlot, Cabernet Sauvignon* 🍇 *Chardonnay* 🍷 *red, white*

Yakima Valley & Red Mountain AVAs

HEMMED IN BY Rattlesnake Hills AVA (607ha) and Horse Heaven Hills AVA (2,444ha), the relatively cool Yakima Valley AVA, established in 1983, now has around 4,450ha under vine. Silt loam soils dominate in the famous

Sémillon vineyard in Yakima Valley

> ### A COOL ADVANTAGE
>
> Washington's growing conditions are occasionally marred by vine-killing freezes, but the cold has its up side. The phylloxera louse cannot cope with the extreme cold or sandy soils common to the Columbia basin, so Washington remains phylloxera-free, allowing vinifera vines to be grown ungrafted on their own roots. Many believe that this may mean healthier vines and grapes, producing purer varietal characteristics akin to those found in 19th century French wines before phylloxera devastated the vines (see pp528–9).

Otis, Red Willow, Sagemoor, Wycoff, Boushey, and Elerding vineyards. These focus on Chardonnay, Riesling, Merlot, Cabernet Sauvignon, and Cabernet Franc, but newcomers Pinot Gris, Sangiovese, Barbera, Syrah, Malbec, and Viognier are on the increase. Red Mountain's relatively hot 1,619ha straddle a sharp bend in the Yakima River, made famous for producing ultra-ripe Bordeaux and Rhône varieties on its 'roasted slopes.' The free-draining vineyards are well suited to Cabernet Sauvignon, Cabernet Franc, Merlot, Malbec, Syrah, and Viognier; Ciel du Cheval is its most famous vineyard. 🏔 *gravels, sand, clay, basalt* 🍇 *Merlot, Cabernet Sauvignon* 🍇 *Chardonnay* 🍷 *red, white*

Walla Walla AVA

ESTABLISHED IN 1984, Walla Walla AVA has the highest concentration of boutique wineries. Ripe with potential, around 486ha are planted on ancient, infertile river beds peppered with cobbles. With Walla Walla's wide range of hot and cool mesoclimates, the harvest of a single variety can take up to three weeks from one side of the valley to the other. Pepper Bridge and Seven Hills Vineyards, among others, produce bold Cabernet Sauvignon and Merlot alongside frilly, racy Viognier and rich, smooth Syrah. The small wine industry of neighbouring Idaho State functions as a cooler extension of the Walla Walla AVA. 🏔 *gravels, loess-based soils* 🍇 *Cabernet Sauvignon* 🍇 *Chardonnay* 🍷 *red, white*

OREGON

FROM THE OUTSET, Oregon wineries have been mainly tiny, family-run operations that hand-pick their own fruit, often grown in small plots. Winemaking and grape growing have closely followed traditional Burgundian practices, and as in Burgundy, producers have adapted to extreme vintage variations. Over time, steadily improved viticulture, better clonal selection of grape varieties, lower yields, and the influence of 20- to 35-year-old vines have evened out annual variations and delivered increasingly high levels of concentration and complexity. In a world favouring reliably ripe, predictably homogeneous, highly manufactured New World wine styles, Oregon refuses to sell out.

Willamette Valley AVA

THE COOL, WET, PINOT-FOCUSED Willamette Valley AVA holds nearly three quarters of Oregon's wineries within its six subregional AVAs. Forty years into the adventure, distinct *terroir* can now be readily observed through single-vineyard bottlings from grapes grown around the Dundee Hills, McMinnville, Ribbon Ridge, Eola-Amity Hills, Chehalem Mountains, and Yamhill-Carlton District, which has led to their AVA status. Mature, multi-clone vineyards are planted in relatively infertile soil, mostly sited on gentle slopes, 90–215m above sea level.

With focused fruit, delineated structure, and intense aromatics, Oregon's better Pinot Noirs lean toward the wines of Burgundy more than to the New World. Often needing four to seven years to open up, many can evolve over two decades. Other reds also look promising.

Pinot Noir vines

Dry, freshly fruited, and richly textured, Pinot Gris is the state's signature white and second most planted grape, although Pinot Blanc could eventually trump it. Aromatic Rieslings and Gewürztraminers can show intensely focused, Alsace-like characters. Oregonians adopted Dijon clones of Chardonnay after plantings of Californian clones delivered tart, fruitless wine. Current models wear Côte de Beaune-like fruits undercut by earthy aromatics and steely acidity.
volcanic, granite, clay, marine sediment
Pinot Noir *Pinot Gris* *red, white*

Southern Oregon AVA

THE SOUTHERN OREGON AVA encapsulates four sub-regional AVAs: Umpqua Valley, Red Hill Douglas County, Rogue Valley, and Applegate Valley.

Sandwiched between the north's warmer, wetter Pinot country and the higher, drier, Syrah vineyards to the south, Umpqua Valley's complicated mixture of transitional climates has shown potential for Tempranillo, Syrah, Grenache, Merlot, Dolcetto, Malbec, Cabernet Franc, Viognier, and Albariño, whereas the slightly wetter and cooler subregional AVA Red Hill Douglas County focuses on Pinot Noir, Riesling, and Chardonnay.

Dwarfed by the Pinot Noir-dominated north, Rogue Valley AVA and its subregion Applegate Valley AVA have come of age. They are far drier than the Willamette Valley, and their huge range of highly elevated (310–780m) vineyards and soil types presents limitless possibilities. Early focus on Pinot Gris, Chardonnay, Sauvignon Blanc, and Pinot Noir has shifted positively into Sangiovese, Viognier, Syrah, Tempranillo, and Bordeaux varieties. Especially noteworthy are the ripe, finely structured, claret-like blends of Cabernet Sauvignon, Cabernet Franc, Merlot, and Malbec. The climate encourages these varieties to ripen slowly, the way Pinot Noir does further north. The varietal characters and finer structures are more typical of Washington than of Oregon. The aromatic, fine-bodied, tangy Viognier and richly ripe, tightly structured Syrah could make the Rogue Valley Oregon's response to California's Rhône Rangers (*see p501*).
metamorphic, sedimentary, volcanic, alluvial, granite, loams, clay *Merlot, Cabernet Sauvignon, Pinot Noir* *Pinot Gris, Chardonnay* *red, white*

Eastern Oregon

THE COLUMBIA GORGE, Columbia Valley, and Walla Walla AVAs straddle Washington and Oregon's borderline and are shared by both states. Similarly, Oregon's easternmost AVA, Snake River Valley shares its AVA with Idaho. It is elevated, dry, and relatively cool.
silts, loams, loess, sand, volcanic, sedimentary *Cabernet Sauvignon, Merlot* *Riesling, Chardonnay, Gewürztraminer* *red, white*

THE BIRTH OF COOL-CLIMATE VITICULTURE

THE THOROUGHLY MODERN *New World concept of cool-climate viticulture found its first footing in Oregon. Vitis vinifera was introduced here by Henderson Luiellen in 1847 and Peter Britt in 1852, but few of the earliest wineries survived beyond Prohibition (see pp474–5). It was not until the 1960s that serious winegrowing in Oregon really took off.*

Believing California's hotter climates were unsuited to varieties from Burgundy, Alsace, and Germany, two visionary winemakers, Richard Sommer and David Lett, bucked conventional beliefs that Oregon was far too cool and damp to grow grapes, and headed north in search of slower, gentler ripening conditions, more akin to those of Northern Europe.

Richard Sommer explored the Umpqua Valley first, successfully establishing the Hillcrest vineyard and the Riesling variety there in 1961. Taking a giant leap of faith into the considerably cooler, wetter Northern Willamette Valley, David Lett planted Pinot Noir, Pinot Meunier, Pinot Gris, Riesling, and Muscat there in 1965. Others soon followed.

David Lett's hunch ultimately paid off. In 1979, his 1975 Eyrie Vineyards Pinot Noir won second place at the Gault-Millau Wine Olympics in Paris, competing against a top flight of *cru* class burgundies. Surprising experts, Oregon was cast into the limelight as the first region outside Burgundy to produce Burgundy-style Pinot Noir.

Having bought heavily into a 'Burgundian' climate, the Oregonians soon felt its down-

Pinot Noir label, Eyrie Vineyards

side: frost, rot, harvest rains, under-ripe and high-acid grapes, and extreme vintage variations. Turning to Burgundy, Switzerland, and Alsace for practical help, instead of to the hot regions of Australia and California, the Oregonians effectively opened up the first beachhead for traditional, low-tech, Old World winemaking practices outside Europe. During the 1970s the Swiss taught them to micro-manage vines, exposing the fruit to light and wind through leaf plucking; and from the French they learned the importance of site selection and microclimates, planting on slopes, drainage, close planting, gentle handling, 'cold soak' pre-fermentation maceration, and non-filtered, gravity-fed production. Eventually jettisoning their original 'hot climate' Pinot Noir vines, Oregonian growers imported better suited 'cool-climate' Dijon clones from Burgundy.

With hindsight, it was Pinot Noir first forcing the issues in Oregon that brought about the codification of cool-climate practices now commonly used throughout the New World. *Eyrie Vineyards* 503 472 6318

Young Pinot Noir vines in the cool Willamette Valley

TOP PRODUCERS OF THE PACIFIC NORTHWEST

Columbia Winery
Columbia Valley

14030 NE 145th St, Woodinville, WA
☎ *425 488 2776*
🅦 *www.columbiawinery.com* ☐

COLUMBIA WINERY WAS created by visionary amateur winemakers in 1962 and is now owned by Ascentia Wine Group. Taking over from founding winemaker David Lake MW, Kerry Norton continues Columbia's reputation for making characterful, varietally correct, flavour-filled wines. Columbia always pushes the boundaries: after introducing Cabernet Franc, Syrah, and Pinot Gris to Washington, it helped establish exotic varieties such as Sangiovese and Barbera, and led the way with *terroir*-distinct, single-vineyard, long-lived wines.
🍷 *red, white* 🍇 *2007, 2005, 2003, 2002, 1999, 1998, 1995, 1994, 1992* ★ *Cabernet Franc, Syrah, Viognier*

Hogue Cellars
Columbia Valley

Wine Country Rd, Prosser, WA
☎ *509 786 4557*
🅦 *www.hoguecellars.com* ☐

HOGUE IS A LARGISH WINERY with a smallish feel to it. Its sharply priced, three-tier range (named Hogue, Genesis, and Reserve) all show crystal-clear varietal characters, vibrantly stated fruit, and a degree of linearity and elegance. The winery's varietal strengths include Chenin Blanc, Chardonnay, Fumé Blanc, Syrah, and Merlot.
🍷 *red, white* 🍇 *2007, 2005, 2004, 2002, 2001, 2000, 1999* ★ *Chenin Blanc, Syrah, Riesling*

DeLille Cellars vineyard in Yakima Valley

McCrea Cellars
Columbia Valley

13443 SE 118th Ave, Rainier, WA
☎ *800 378 6212* 🅦 *www.mccrea cellars.com* ☐ *by appt*

SAXOPHONIST turned Northern Rhône Ranger Doug McCrea now riffs through Grenache, Syrah, Viognier, Mourvèdre, Roussanne, Grenache Blanc, Bourblanc, and Counoise, sometimes blending, sometimes not. With fruit grown primarily on Red Mountain, his range includes several elegant, single-vineyard Syrahs; Shiraz-like Amerique; Châteauneuf-du-Pape-influenced Sirocco and Non Sequitur; and low-cropped, spicy Roussanne.
🍷 *red, white* 🍇 *2007, 2005, 2002, 2001, 2000, 1999* ★ *Syrah, Grenache-Syrah-Mourvèdre, Roussanne*

Columbia Crest, Ste Michelle Wine Estates

Ste Michelle Wine Estates
Columbia Valley

Château Ste Michelle, 14111 NE 145th St, Woodinville, WA ☎ *425 488 1133*
🅦 *www.ste-michelle.com* ☐

THIS SMARTLY BRANDED COMPANY includes Château Ste Michelle, Columbia Crest, and inexpensive Snoqualmie, Spring Valley, and Northstar (all in Columbia Valley), together producing over half of Washington's wine. Château Ste Michelle won a reputation in the early 1970s for consistent budget varietals. Now its comprehensive portfolio of single-vineyard Chardonnays, Merlots, and Cabernets ranks among the USA's finest. Columbia Crest, set up as a volume label in 1984, is now a high-quality producer in its own right. Still growing, Ste Michelle Wine Estates has collected quality Californian and Oregon wineries and collaborated with Antinori (Italy, *see p265*) and Dr Loosen (Germany, *see p360*).
🍷 *red, white* 🍇 *2007, 2005, 2002, 2001, 2000, 1999, 1997, 1995, 1994, 1990* ★ *Merlot, Riesling, Chardonnay*

DeLille Cellars
Yakima Valley

14208 NE Redmond Rd, Woodinville, WA ☎ *425 489 0544*
🅦 *www.delillecellars.com* ☐ *by appt*

DELILLE PRODUCED Washington's first Meritage, and continues to make densely packed, unfiltered, long-lived Bordeaux-style blends from impeccably grown, site-specific fruit. Low yields, ruthless grape sorting, and rigorous declassification ensure consistency and excellence. Chaleur and Harrison Hill, both intense, savoury Cabernet blends, complement D2, a smooth, gamey Merlot-led wine. The vibrant Viognier, peachy Roussanne, Graves-like Sauvignon-Sémillon and the peppery, dusty tannined Doyenne (97.5 per cent Syrah) are equally compelling.
🍷 red 🔖 2008, 2007, 2006, 2005, 2002, 2001, 2000, 1999 ★ Chaleur, D2, Doyenne, Chaleur Estate Blanc

Hedges Family Estates
Red Mountain

195 NE Gilman Blvd, Issaquah, WA
📞 425 391 6056
🌐 www.hedgescellars.com ◻

HEDGES' WINES are built to last: densely packed with savoury aromas, condensed flavours, juicy textures, and firm tannins. Top wines include a sweetly ripe, early-drinking CMS (Cabernet Sauvignon-Merlot-Syrah); a meaty, tightly wound Three Vineyards (Cabernet Sauvignon-Merlot); and a complex, floral Red Mountain Reserve (Cabernet-Syrah-Merlot blend). The two Single Vineyard varietals (Malbec and Syrah) are also noteworthy. Red Mountain Fortified is a port-style wine made with genuine Portuguese grapes.
🍷 red, fortified 🔖 2007, 2005, 2003, 2002, 2001, 2000, 1999 ★ Cabernet Sauvignon, Merlot, Blends

Canoe Ridge Vineyard
Walla Walla

1102 W Cherry, WA
📞 509 527 0885
🌐 www.canoeridgevineyard.com ◻

ArtistSeries #8   Larry Pirnie

woodward canyon
1999
Washington Cabernet Sauvignon

Alcohol by Volume 13.9%   Contains Sulfites

Woodward Canyon Winery artist series label

THIS IMPORTANT vineyard in the upper Columbia Gorge was named by 19th-century explorers Lewis and Clark for its resemblance to an overturned canoe. California's Chalone Group, which runs it today, makes deeply perfumed, velvety, Pinot Noir-like Merlots and crisp, delicate Chablis-style Chardonnays.
🍷 red, white 🔖 2002, 2001, 2000, 1999, 1997, 1935, 1994, 1990 ★ Merlot, Chardonnay, Cabernet Sauvignon

Cayuse Vineyards
Walla Walla

17 E Main, WA 📞 509 526 0686
🌐 www.cayusewineyards.com
◻ by appt

ONCE DUBBED the 'Bionic Frog' in the Barossa Valley, and now proudly sporting WWSYRAH licence plates on his Ford pick-up, *terroir*-ist vigneron Christophe Baron infuses Walla Walla with Gallic flair and charm. Farmed biodynamically and fermented with indigenous yeasts, his unfiltered, unfined, single-vineyard wines reek of originality, personality, and authenticity. Abhorring "Mike Tyson-style wines that knock you out". Baron creates food-friendly styles that "excite the taste buds and stimulate the intellect" in abundance.
🍷 red, white 🔖 2002, 2001, 2000, 1999 ★ Syrah, Syrah-Viognier

L'Ecole No 41
Walla Walla

41 Lowden School Rd, WA 📞 509 525 0940 🌐 www.lecole.com ◻

INHABITING Lowden's original schoolhouse, long-established L'Ecole makes some of the best age-worthy barrel-fermented Sémillons this side of Hunter Valley. The top reds include an expansive, creamy, elegant Seven Hills Perigee (Cabernet Sauvignon-Merlot-Franc blend), which counterpoints a bolder, brasher Pepper Bridge Apogee (similar mix, with a dash of Malbec). Other reds include several finely structured Merlots, a meaty, slick Walla Walla Cabernet Sauvignon, and an inky Syrah packed with dried black fruits and well-managed tannins.
🍷 red, white 🔖 2008, 2007, 2005, 2004, 2003, 2002, 2001, 2000, 1999 ★ Sémillon, Syrah, Apogee, Perigee

Woodward Canyon Winery
Walla Walla

11920 W Hwy 12, Lowden, WA
📞 509 525 4129
🌐 www.woodwardcanyon.com ◻

THE HIGH-DENSITY, low-yield vineyard of this pioneering boutique winery produces complex, silky, seamless, long-lived wines. The winemaking here is non-interventionist: wines are unfiltered, unfined, never acidified, and never over-done. Famous for elegantly styled, earthy Celilo Chardonnay; floral, velvety Merlot; seriously complex, bordeaux-like Estate Red; and powerful, tannic, Old Vines Cabernet Sauvignon, Woodward now also does some dandy Barbera and Dolcetta.
🍷 red, white 🔖 2008, 2007, 2006, 2005, 2004, 2003 ★ Chardonnay, Cabernet Sauvignon, Merlot, Syrah

Amity Vineyards
Willamette Valley

18150 Amity Vineycrds Rd, Amity, OR **C** *888 264 8956*
W *www.amityvineyards.com* ☐

THIS QUIRKY, VETERAN, 1970s-era producer consistently makes complex, age-worthy, old-vine Pinot Noir, richly fruited Gamay, and exemplary, varietally correct aromatics: dry Riesling, Gewürztraminer, and Pinot Blanc. It is also noteworthy for one of the world's first sulphite-free wines, the organic Eco-Wine Pinot Noir, as well as for the winery's early period Oregon-funk architecture.
red, white *2005, 2003, 2002, 2001, 2000, 1999, 1998* ★ *Pinot Noir, Gewürztraminer, Riesling, Gamay*

Argyle Winery
Willamette Valley

691 S Pacific Hwy, Dundee, OR **C** *888 417 4953*
W *www.argylewinery.com* ☐

AUSTRALIA'S FIRST adventure into the USA focused the attention of winemaker Brian Croser (of Petaluma; *see p570*) on making top-quality Oregon sparkling wine using the traditional method (*see pp166–7*). Current winemaker Rollin Soles now gathers accolades for richly fruited Chardonnays and Pinot Noirs. The portfolio includes well-balanced Blanc de Blancs, rosés, and vintaged sparkling wines, all with clear cool-climate character and rich autolytic notes.
red, white, sparkling *2005, 2003, 2002, 2001, 2000, 1999, 1998, 1994* ★ *Méthode Champenoises, Nuthouse Chardonnay, Reserve Pinot Noir*

Cristom Vineyards
Willamette Valley

6905 Spring Valley Rd NW, Salem, OR **C** *503 375 3068*
W *www.cristomwines.com* ☐

Elk Cove Vineyards label

LONGTIME WINEMAKER for California's Calera, Steve Doerner is one of Oregon's under-recognized artists. His entry-level Mt Jefferson Cuvée Pinot Noir is an overture of pure fruit, back-palate concentration, and thoughtful structure, whereas Cristom's eight individual Pinots are symphonic masterpieces. The same vineyard produces an equally good Côtes-Rôtie-like Syrah-Viognier blend, a mineral-infused Chardonnay, and a visceral Pinot Gris.
red, white *2008, 2005, 2002, 1999, 1998, 1996* ★ *Pinot Noir*

Domaine Drouhin
Willamette Valley

6750 Breyman Orchards Rd, Dundee, OR **C** *503 864 2700* **W** *www.domainedrouhin.com* ☐ *by appt*

DOMAINE DROUHIN marks the first Burgundian foray into the New World. In 1987, *négociant* Joseph Drouhin planted a plot of Chardonnay and Pinot Noir with double the usual US vine density and filled his gravity-fed winery with state-of-the-art French technology. Marrying French soul to Oregon soil, Drouhin produces elegant, under-played benchmark Pinot Noirs, and highly under-rated, understated, earthy Dijon-clone Chardonnays. Expensive but worth it, the

reserve Pinot, Laurène, is only made in the best years.
red, white *2006, 2005, 2002, 2001, 2000, 1999, 1998, 1994, 1993* ★ *Pinot Noir, Chardonnay*

Elk Cove Vineyards
Willamette Valley

27751 NW Olson Rd, Gaston, OR **C** *877 355 2683*
W *www.elkcove.com* ☐

TYPICAL OF OREGON'S early quality producers, Elk Cove's output evolved from estate-bottled Pinot Noir into five sub-regionally distinct single-vineyard wines, including the famed La Bohème, Roosevelt, and Windhill. The Pinot styles err on the side of subtlety, balance, and elegance, often with an impressive silkiness. The best will age for 20 years. Finely focused, dry Riesling, Pinot Gris, and Pinot Blanc, and late-harvested Riesling, can be great value. The Southern Oregon Syrah and Viognier also show promise.
red, white *2006, 2003, 2002, 2001, 2000, 1999, 1998, 1994, 1990* ★ *Pinot Noir, Pinot Gris, Riesling*

Ken Wright Cellars
Willamette Valley

236 N Kutch St, Carlton, OR **C** *503 852 7070* **W** *www.kenwrightcellars.com* ☐ *by appt*

OREGON'S LEADING *terroir*-ist, Ken Wright produces 8–12 very low-yield single-vineyard Pinot Noirs, each delineating a wide range of soil types and microclimates. His Tyrus Evan Rogue Valley label offers a massively fruited, structured Cabernet Franc, a fine-grained Malbec, a savoury, claret-like Bordeaux blend, and a creamy, super-ripe Syrah. All suggest that Rogue Valley could rival Willamette's reputation for Pinot Noir.
red, white *2005, 2003, 2002, 1999, 1998* ★ *Pinot Noir, Pinot Blanc*

Ponzi Vineyards
Willamette Valley

14665 SW Winery Lane, Beaverton OR 📞 503 628 1227 🌐 www.ponzi wines.com 🔲

ONE OF THE EARLY 1970s pioneers, Ponzi continues to improve the quality and breadth of its wine range. Its Pinot Noir consistently ranks as one of Oregon's most reliable and complex: silky smooth and dressed in smoky bacon and mushroom savouriness. Chardonnay, Pinot Gris, Arneis, and late-harvest Riesling all show rich texture and clean, well-outlined ripe fruit.

🍷 red, white 🗓 2005, 2003, 2002, 2001, 2000, 1999, 1998 ★ Pinot Noir, Pinot Gris, Arneis

Rex Hill Vineyards
Willamette Valley

30835 N Hwy 99W, Newberg, OR 📞 800 739 4455 🌐 www.rexhill.com 🔲

REX HILL IS RENOWNED for multi-layered, complex Pinot Noirs with nicely focused fruit, but the whites include a crisp, unoaked Sauvignon, varietal Pinot Gris and Riesling, and a silky Chardonnay. Established in 1982, Rex Hill was taken over in 2007 by A to Z Wineworks, which functioned along the lines of a traditional Burgundian *négociant*, blending wine from a variety of sources. With a former Chehalem Winery winemaker, and newly committed to bio-dynamic production, Rex Hill promises great things in the future. A to Z's 'aristocratic wines at democratic prices' are well made, easy drinking, and sharply priced.

The barrel store at a Willamette Valley winery

🍷 red, white 🗓 2006, 2003, 1999 ★ Pinot Noir, Pinot Gris, Chardonnay, Riesling

WillaKenzie Estate
Willamette Valley

19143 NE Laughlin Rd, Yamhill, OR 📞 503 662 3280 🌐 www.willa kenzie.com 🔲

BURGUNDIAN Bernie Lacroute traded his career developing computer companies for one growing vines organically. His handsome gravity-fed winery makes richly fruited Pinots Gris, Blanc, and Meunier, and eight densely fruited Pinot Noirs. The wines over-deliver at good prices.

🍷 red, white 🗓 2005, 2002, 2001, 2000, 1999, 1998, 1996 ★ Pinot Noir, Gamay, Pinot Meunier

2001
Viognier
GRIFFIN CREEK

Rogue Valley
Southern Oregon

Willamette Valley Vineyards label

Willamette Valley Vineyards
Willamette Valley

8800 Enchanted Way SE, Turner, OR 📞 503 588 9463 🌐 www.willamette valleyvineyards.com 🔲

NASDAQ-LISTED, with 2,782 shareholders, this winery is committed to carbon-neutral, salmon-safe, sustainable

production. Organically managed mature vines are used for distinguished Pinot Noirs. The spicy, pear-infused Pinot Gris is a consistent star. Second label Griffin Creek makes a ripely fruited, plump Syrah and a delicately styled Viognier. Visionary manage-ment and smart winemaking deliver reasonably priced, well-made wine.

🍷 red, white 🗓 2008, 2006, 2005, 2003, 2002, 1999, 1998, 1994 ★ Pinot Noir, Pinot Gris, Syrah, Viognier

Abacela Vineyards & Winery
Southern Oregon (Rogue River)

12500 Lookingglass Rd, Roseburg, OR 📞 541 679 6642 🌐 www.abacela.com 🔲

AFTER A LONG SEARCH through-out America for a suitable climate for Tempranillo, Abacela settled on the Rogue Valley's sunny, south-facing, rocky hillsides. It produces sexy whites like Albariño and Viognier, and it is hard to find anything crab in the rest of the portfolio: Syrah, Merlot, Dolcetto, Cabernet Franc, Sangiovese, Grenache, and Malbec. Watch this space.

🍷 red, white 🗓 2008, 2007, 2005, 2002, 2000, 1998 ★ Syrah, Tempranillo, Malbec

NEW YORK STATE

A RENAISSANCE IS UNDER WAY *in New York State, a developing wine region that is rapidly gaining recognition and respect. The state's reputation for sweet, cheap, and kosher wines for immigrant Jews is history. Instead, handcrafted European-style Riesling, Chardonnay, Merlot, and Cabernet Franc now rule the day.*

Grapes were first planted on Long Island in the 17th century. By the 1800s hybrids flourished across the state, thanks to horticulturalists who crossed thousands of European *(Vitis vinifera)* varieties with sturdier native vines *(Vitis labrusca)*. Then the temperance movement emerged, blaming alcohol for the nation's social ills. In 1919, Prohibition *(see pp474–5)* effectively crushed the wine industry; until the law changed in 1933, gangsters, bootleggers, and speakeasies flourished, while winegrowers survived by making juice and sacramental wines and selling grapes to underground winemakers.

The 1950s saw the revival of serious winemaking in New York State. Ukrainian professor of plant science Konstantin Frank began expounding his beliefs that Old World vinifera like Riesling, Pinot Noir, and Chardonnay could thrive in the inhospitably cold Finger Lakes area. Charles Fournier, the president of Gold

Dr Konstantin Frank label, Finger Lakes

Seal, New York's top winery at the time, took a gamble and hired the visionary émigré as director of research. Frank successfully grafted vinifera vines onto hardy American rootstock, dubbing his victory "the second discovery of America".

In 1976, new legislation permitted small wineries to sell direct to customers, making them more economically viable. The industry exploded and by 2003 there were 177 wineries statewide, compared with 19 in 1976; most are small and family-run.

New York's output is now third in the US after California and Washington. Although many local wines can compete in terms of quality, New York will never match the West Coast's vast production. The boutique winemakers here work for passion and prestige, not profit. Made by careful, clean methods with few chemicals, most wines are designed for early drinking and cater mainly to a local market.

Vineyard above Canandaigua Lake in the Finger Lakes

◁ **Vineyards and winery, Keuka Lake in the Finger Lakes**

WINE MAP OF NEW YORK STATE

Between the shores of Lake Erie and the eastern tip of Long Island are four major American Viticultural Areas (AVAs). Lake Erie is the biggest, but 90 per cent of its output is grape juice. Some 500km west of New York City, near Ithaca, is the scenic, noteworthy Finger Lakes area, north of Manhattan is the Hudson River Valley, and to the east is 'New York's Bordeaux' – Long Island's North Fork – and the South Fork, known as The Hamptons. Central New York State is developing as a wine region, but has not yet been designated an AVA.

KEY

New York State

Merlot and Chardonnay vines on Long Island's North Fork

Lake Ontario

- Niagara Falls
- Buffalo
- Rochester

FINGER LAKES

CANADA

Canandaigua Lake
Keuka Lake
Seneca Lake
Ithaca

Lake Erie

- Erie

LAKE ERIE

Allegheny Plateau

PENNSYLVANIA

Appalachi

Port Clinton
Cleveland
OHIO

0 ⊢ km ⎯⎯⎯⎯⎯ 100

EXPLORING NEW YORK STATE'S WINERIES

New York State's picturesque wine districts are well worth exploring by car. Wineries that are open to the public are clearly signposted by road signs bearing clusters of grapes.

Scores of wineries hug the shores of the Finger Lakes, particularly Lake Seneca. Among them are celebrated Riesling master **Hermann J Wiemer Vineyard** offering self-guided vineyard walks, and **Wagner Vineyards** with a restaurant and tasting room (try the smoky, plummy Meritage, a Bordeaux blend, and tangy, spicy Riesling ice wine). Also in the Finger Lakes is **Glenora Wine Cellars**, which features a fine restaurant and inn with breathtaking views. It

Millbrook Vineyards & Winery

is a leader in the region for its impressive sparkling wines, especially Riesling, and Gewürztraminer.

Millbrook Vineyards & Winery, in the Hudson River Valley, hosts concerts, outdoor films, and giant harvest parties. On the Long Island tasting circuit, **Pindar** and **Pellegrini Vineyards** are key players, with live music, food festivals, and deluxe wine-and-food pairing dinners.

Hermann J Wiemer Vineyard: www.wiemer.com; Wagner Vineyards: www.wagnervineyards.com; Glenora Wine Cellars: www.glenora.com; Millbrook Vineyards & Winery: www.millbrook wine.com; Pindar: www.pindar.net; Pellegrini Vineyards: www.pellegrinivineyards.com

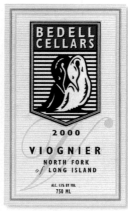

Bedell Cellars label from Long Island's North Fork

TERROIR AT A GLANCE

Latitude: 40.5–43°N.

Altitude: 0–245m.

Topography: Diverse terrain. Ice-age glaciers left behind a landscape of sloping hillsides, deep valleys, and bodies of water ranging from the carved-out Finger Lakes to the wide, majestic Hudson River.

Soil: Deep, well-drained, glacial soils, silt and loam composition.

Climate: Cool nights and warm, but not hot, days characterize these

wine districts, all of which benefit from a lake, river, or ocean effect.

Temperature: July average is 24°C.

Rainfall: Annual average is 915–1,120mm.

Wind: Lake and ocean breezes keep wine regions cooler in summer. In winter, warm southwesterly winds from the Atlantic moderate temperatures.

Viticultural hazards: Black rot; insects; bird damage; hurricanes.

Vineyards above Canandaigua Lake in the Finger Lakes

PERFECT CASE: NEW YORK

Ⓦ Bedell Cellars Corey Creek Chardonnay ££

Ⓡ Bedell Cellars Merlot ££

Ⓡ Château LaFayette Reneau Cabernet Sauvignon ££££

Ⓦ Château LaFayette Reneau Johannisberg Riesling ££

Ⓢ Dr Konstantin Frank Château Frank Brut ££

Ⓦ Dr Konstantin Frank Rkatsiteli ££

Ⓦ Johnson Estate Vidal Blanc ££

Ⓦ Paumanok Vineyards Chenin Blanc ££

Ⓦ Standing Stone Vineyards Gewürztraminer ££

Ⓡ The Lenz Winery Old Vines Merlot ££££

Ⓦ The Lenz Winery White Label Chardonnay ££

Ⓕ Wölffer Estate Rosé ££

NEW YORK STATE: AREAS & TOP PRODUCERS

LONG ISLAND p524

HUDSON RIVER VALLEY p525

FINGER LAKES p525

LAKE ERIE p525

Vineyard on the west side of Lake Keuka

WINEGROWING AREAS OF NEW YORK STATE

Long Island

TODAY, BURGEONING LONG ISLAND lays claim to 52 vineyards on two peninsulas, exclusively growing classic European grapes. The North Fork, a slim strip bounded by Long Island Sound, Peconic Bay, and the Atlantic, holds the majority. So far, no problem with phylloxera has emerged and as troubled California replants its old louse-weakened vines, the relatively young Long Island vines will ironically surpass them in maturity.

🌿 fertile sand, loam, silt 🍇 Merlot, Cabernet Sauvignon, Cabernet Franc 🍇 Chardonnay, Gewürztraminer, Riesling 🍷 red, white, rosé, sparkling, dessert

North Fork

RAVE REVIEWS are pouring in for North Fork wines, which are now offered in many of Manhattan's best restaurants. Vineyards were attempted here in the 17th century, but it was not until 1973 that Alex and Louisa Hargrave successfully planted the first vinifera vines on their potato farm in Cutchogue. Over the years they battled droughts, diseases, and hurricanes but in 2003, Long Island grandly celebrated the 30th anniversary of their victory (though they sold the winery in 1999). Their pioneering spirit inspired other winemakers who now produce world-class Cabernet Sauvignon, Merlot, Bordeaux-style blends, and Chardonnay. The top producers –

Bedell Cellars label, North Fork

Bedell Cellars and The Lenz Winery among them – exhibit elegant European-style leanings over bold California-style wines. With a long growing season of 215–235 days, the North Fork has an extended period of freeze-free temperatures. Salt-spraying hurricanes and sporadic droughts continue to pose a threat to the harvest, but flocks of ravenous starlings and robins are actually more destructive. Netting the vines seems to be the best solution, albeit an expensive one.

The Hamptons

FAMOUS FOR swanky mansions and glamorous summer parties, The Hamptons is also a productive agricultural area settled by European immigrant farmers in the 17th century. The deep, well-drained soil is loam-rich, needing less irrigation than the North Fork. Of the three wineries on the South Fork – Wölffer Estate, Channing Daughters, and Duck Walk – Wölffer is the most ambitious and accomplished; its Chardonnay and Merlot show satisfying depth and balance. Perhaps the reason The Hamptons lacks more wineries is the prohibitive cost of property here. What was once a charming collection of sleepy maritime villages is now swimming with boutiques, restaurants, and nightclubs. It is a particularly heady place on summer weekends, even without wine.

Hudson River Valley

GRAPES HAVE BEEN GROWN in the lush, bountiful Hudson River Valley for 300 years. The region is home to Brotherhood, America's oldest continuously operating winery; it is one of the few that lasted through Prohibition by making sacramental and 'medicinal' wines. Native American Concord, Catawba, Delaware, and Niagara grapes dominate here, as well as the French-American hybrid Seyval Blanc. The vast valley is scattered with lovely river cities, its latitude parallel to northern Spain but with a shorter growing season. Nearly 30 wineries are in operation, focusing on light-bodied, fruity wines. Millbrook Vineyards and Winery is the region's flagship producer, making a sprightly Tocai Friulano and textbook Cabernet Franc, among other varietals.

🗺 glacial deposits of shale, slate, limestone 🍇 Pinot Noir, Cabernet Franc 🍇 Chardonnay, Tocai Friulano, Seyval Blanc 🍷 red, white

Finger Lakes

ICE-AGE GLACIERS GOUGED OUT the 11 narrow, deep Finger Lakes in west central New York. The four largest resemble the long, tapered fingers of the hand of the Great Spirit described by Iroquois tribal legend – hence the lakes' native names. Over 80 wineries have tamed this former wilderness, taking advantage of the ideal growing conditions for a staggering variety of grapes. Lakes with sloping hillsides buffer extremes in temperature during winter and summer, and the 190-day-plus growing season contributes to outstanding ripening conditions for Riesling, Gewürztraminer, and Pinot Noir. Sparkling wines are another forte; Glenora Wine Cellars is one of the largest producers in the east USA. Along the southeastern shore of Seneca Lake is the so-called 'banana belt', a viticultural phenomenon boasting the highest degree days and longest growing season of all the Finger Lakes. The heaviest concentration of wineries is in this pocket, including Château LaFayette Reneau, Wagner Vineyards, Standing Stone Vineyards, Silver Thread Vineyard, and Red Newt Cellars. The mesoclimate seems to coax Riesling and Gewürztraminer to more vibrant, honeyed heights, and adds intensity to Merlot and Cabernet Sauvignon.

Central New York, a region of pastoral farmland just to the east of the Finger Lakes region, is now also undergoing strong development as a viticultural area, but it has yet to win AVA status. With well over a dozen wineries currently in operation – some of which buy in grapes from other regions – the area is starting to show promise.

🗺 shallow topsoil on sloping shale beds 🍇 Cabernet Franc, Pinot Noir, Merlot, Cabernet Sauvignon 🍇 Chardonnay, Riesling, Gewürztraminer 🍷 red, white, sparkling, dessert

Lake Erie

LAKE ERIE IS A MULTI-STATE AVA, covering 16,188ha in New York, Pennsylvania, and Ohio. Since the 19th century, native labrusca grape producers have cornered the market, making this the grape juice capital of the US. The juicy, sweet local wines reflect that tradition. These days French-American varieties, such as Seyval Blanc and Vidal Blanc, and noble grapes like Riesling and Chardonnay, are being more widely planted. Of the dozen or so wineries here, Johnson Estate and Merritt Estate are the biggest, oldest, and most respected. The lake provides a unique macroclimate – extended summer sunlight, few thunderstorms, constantly flowing air that minimizes botrytis and other fungal problems – but severe winter weather menaces vines about every three years.

🗺 gravel-and-shale soils of glacial origin 🍇 Chancellor, Merlot, Cabernet Sauvignon 🍇 Chardonnay, Riesling, Vidal Blanc 🍷 red, white, sparkling, dessert

Trellising system at Millbrook Vineyards, Hudson River Valley

TOP PRODUCERS OF NEW YORK STATE

Bedell Cellars
Long Island/North Fork

36225 Main Rd, Cutchogue
📞 *631 734 7537*
🌐 *www.bedellcellars.com* ⬜

FROM SMALL BEGINNINGS making wine in his basement, Kip Bedell founded this acclaimed winery in 1980. He realized that the North Fork's cool climate and well-drained soils were ideal for Merlot. His wines are consistently delicious: mouth-filling and silky with hints of raspberry and black cherry. He has now ventured into plummy Bordeaux-style wine, complex Cabernet Sauvignon, and lightly oaked Chardonnay. When Michael Lynne, co-CEO of New Line Cinema, acquired Bedell Cellars in 2000, Kip agreed to stay on as part of a winemaking team now led by Pascal Marty, formerly of Château Mouton Rothschild. Lynne has also bought the Corey Creek and Wells Road vineyards, signalling a new era of big business.

🍷 *red, white, rosé, dessert* 🍾 *red: 2007, 2005, 2004, 2001; white: 2007, 2005, 2004* ★ *Merlot, Corey Creek Chardonnay, C-Block South Merlot*

Palmer Vineyards
Long Island/North Fork

108 Sound Ave, Aquebogue
📞 *631 722 9463*
🌐 *www.palmervineyards.com* ⬜

PALMER MAKES SOME of Long Island's best-known wines. Owner Robert Palmer's experience as an ad man helps, but the round-but-not-opulent Chardonnay and silky, smoky, black cherry Cabernet Franc live up to the hype. The tasting house, an 18th-century farmhouse in period style, is worth a visit.

Bedell Cellars Corey Creek label

🍷 *red, white, rosé, sparkling* 🍾 *red: 2007, 2005, 2004, 2001; white: 2007, 2005, 2004* ★ *Cabernet Franc Reserve, Chardonnay Reserve*

Paumanok Vineyards
Long Island/North Fork

1074 Main Rd, Rte 25, Aquebogue
📞 *631 722 8800*
🌐 *www.paumanok.com* ⬜

TAKING ITS NAME FROM the Native American word for Long Island, Paumanok, founded by Ursula and Charles Massoud in 1983, is a real family affair. Ursula was born into a line of German winemakers, and the couple's three sons are also passionately involved in the winery. Charles' smooth Merlot and rich Cabernet Sauvignon are consistently good, as is his juicy, melony Chardonnay; the Cabernet Franc is supple with savoury hints of tobacco. Charles is also one of the few in New York State to make Chenin Blanc, with crisp citrus and peach flavours.

🍷 *red, white* 🍾 *2001, 2000, 1998 (w), 1995 (r)* ★ *Merlot, Chenin Blanc*

The Lenz Winery
Long Island/North Fork

Main Rd, Rte 25, Peconic 📞 *631 734 6010* 🌐 *www.lenzwine.com* ⬜

FOUNDED IN 1978, Lenz has some of the most mature vineyards on Long Island. The amazing Old Vines Merlot, from some of the oldest Merlot vines in North America, is spicy and voluptuous with hints of charcoal. In 1996, owners Peter and Deborah Carroll were so confident that Lenz wines could compete with the world's best, they instigated public blind tastings to prove it. Indeed, the Merlots and Chardonnays made news by standing up to higher-priced French and Californian rivals. Long Island wines had landed, and the Carrolls have never looked back.

🍷 *red, white, sparkling* 🍾 *red: 2007, 2005, 2004, 2001; white: 2007, 2005, 2004* ★ *Old Vines Merlot, Gewürztraminer, White Label Chardonnay*

Wölffer Estate
Long Island/The Hamptons

139 Sagg Rd, Sagaponack 📞 *631 537 5106* 🌐 *www.wolffer.com* ⬜

INTERNATIONAL BUSINESS magnate Christian Wölffer spent millions on this Tuscan-style winery and equestrian centre in the heart of The Hamptons before his death in a swimming accident on New Year's Eve 2008. German-born winemaker Roman Roth's European-style, food-friendly wines are classically elegant. They range from well structured US$100 Premier Cru Merlot, with lush berry flavours that promise to age well, to a more modest rosé evoking roses and citrus, perfect for a picnic.

🍷 *red, white, rosé, sparkling* 🍾 *red: 2007, 2005, 2004, 2001; white: 2007, 2005, 2004* ★ *Estate Selection Merlot, Reserve Chardonnay, Cabernet Franc*

Château LaFayette Reneau
Finger Lakes

Rte 414, Hector ☎ 607 546 2062
Ⓦ www.clrwine.com ▢

THE *TERROIR* of south Seneca Lake enriches LaFayette Reneau's structured, German-style Riesling, and full-bodied Merlot with mocha and black cherry undertones. The Pinot Noir has lively hints of raspberry and cherry, and the Cabernet Sauvignon is layered with plum, leather, and chocolate. Winemaker Tim Miller often wins medals, and owners Dick and Betty Reno run a small inn with panoramic lake views.

Château LaFayette Reneau logo

🍷 red, white, rosé, sparkling, dessert 🍷 red: 2007, 2005, 2002; white: 2007, 2005, 2003 ★ Cabernet Sauvignon, Merlot, Johannisberg Riesling

Dr Konstantin Frank
Finger Lakes

9749 Middle Rd, Hammondsport
☎ 607 868 4888
Ⓦ www.drfrankwines.com ▢

A PROFESSOR of plant science, Dr Frank, who founded this seminal winery in 1962, knew how to farm with minimal use of chemicals. So does his grandson Fred: he spreads hay across fields to restore soil nutrients and builds birdhouses to encourage birds which control insects. The wines include full, earthy reds, crisp, ripe Rieslings, Rkatsiteli, a vibrant, appley grape of Georgian origin, and toasty sparkling wines that often outscore pricier French examples.

🍷 red, white, sparkling 🍷 red: 2007, 2005, 2002; white: 2007, 2005, 2003 ★ Château Frank Brut, Rkatsiteli, Cabernet Sauvignon

Standing Stone Vineyards
Finger Lakes

9934 Rte 414, Hector
☎ 800 803 7135
Ⓦ www.standingstonewines.com ▢

STANDING STONE'S SPICY, golden, pungent Gewürztraminer is arguably the best in the USA. Tom and Marti Macinski's wines are beautifully complex. The garnet-hued, redcurrant-flavoured Pinnacle (a Bordeaux-style blend), and cherry-chocolatey Cabernet Franc are of particular note.

The couple wisely bought the pioneering Gold Seal winery land in 1991, inheriting New York State's first vinifera plantings. Though the site is small – only 16ha – it is bursting with potential.

🍷 red, white, dessert 🍷 red: 2007, 2005, 2002; white: 2007, 2005, 2003 ★ Gewürztraminer, Pinnacle, Cabernet Franc

Johnson Estate
Lake Erie

8419 West Main Rd, Westfield
☎ 716 326 2191
Ⓦ www.johnsonwinery.com ▢

AURORE, CHAMBOURCIN, Ives Noir – the tradition of weird-sounding but well-made Native American and French-American hybrids is proudly upheld at Johnson, the oldest family-owned estate winery in the state (1961). Semi-sweet, fruity wines such as the fun and lively Seyval Blanc are the speciality. The Freelings Creek Merlot evokes cherry pie, and the French-American hybrid Chancellor is an austere red with good acidity. The Vidal Blanc ice wine is luscious.

🍷 red, white, rosé, sparkling, dessert 🍷 red: 2007, 2005, 2002; white: 2007, 2005, 2003 ★ Vidal Blanc, Chancellor, Seyval Blanc

UP-AND-COMING PRODUCERS

Some of New York State's finest producers remain obscure due to limited supplies or the newness of the establishment. **Schneider Vineyards** is a North Fork Cabernet Franc specialist of note with under 3ha. In the Finger Lakes, **Shalestone Vineyards** and **Silver Thread Vineyard** have 4ha or less each, and sell 90 per cent of the wine they make on site. Shalestone produces five stirring, well-structured vinifera reds, and Silver Thread is the only winery to take a wholly organic approach, making delicious Riesling and Pinot Noir. Finger Lakes winemaker David Whiting is another one to watch: having done stints at Château LaFayette Reneau and Standing Stone Vineyards, he opened **Red Newt Cellars** in 1999 and makes compelling, diverse varietals. **Fox Run Vineyards** *(left)*, also in the Finger Lakes, excels at floral, fruity Riesling, and is expanding its output with recently planted Gamay, Gewürztraminer, Merlot, and Cabernet Franc.

Schneider Vineyards: www.schneider-vineyards.com; Shalestone Vineyards: www.shalestonevineyards.com; Silver Thread Vineyard: www.silverthread wine.com; Red Newt Cellars: www.rednewt.com; Fox Run Vineyards: www.foxrunvineyards.com

PHYLLOXERA

P*HYLLOXERA VASTATRIX* IS A TINY APHID that nearly destroyed the European wine industry. Native to eastern North America, the vine-killing louse was accidently introduced into southern France on imported American vines in the 1860s. The blight spread rapidly throughout Europe and infected vines were uprooted and burnt. The endemic, and its resolution, have changed how vines are cultivated forever.

Phylloxera aphid

Great wine blight
When French vines began to wither and die in the 1860s, it gave rise to wild theories – from climate change, or 'tired soil' to the wrath of God.

Identifying phylloxera
The French botanist Jules-Emile Planchon first identified that yellow insects found on the roots of withered French vines were the source of the devastation. He also deduced that American vines seemed to have a natural resistance to this parasite. By the time Planchon's theories were finally accepted the blight had already begun to spread throughout other vine-growing regions of Europe.

A collaborative solution
In the 1870s Planchon collaborated with English-born scientist Charles Riley, the state entomologist of Missouri, on the solution to the blight: grafting together phylloxera-resistant roots of American vines and the fruit-bearing shoots of European vines.

GRAFTING ROOTSTOCK

Grafting is a simple procedure. The rootstock of a North American vine species, such as *Vitis riparia*, is joined to the shoot of the desired vine variety of the European species, *Vitis vinifera*. When planted, the phylloxera-resistant root both protects and sustains the grape-producing shoot. Most of the world's vines are now grafted in this way, and intense effort is made to ensure its success. Shoot varieties and rootstocks are also carefully matched for a variety of characteristics.

A COMPLEX LIFE CYCLE

The life cycle of the phylloxera aphid is extremely complex. As this 19th-century illustration below shows, it includes eggs, nymphs, male and female adult forms that reproduce above ground, asexual adults that live and reproduce underground, and even a winged form. Reproduction is prolific in even a single season. It has been calculated that as many as 25 billion aphids may follow from one female in seven months.

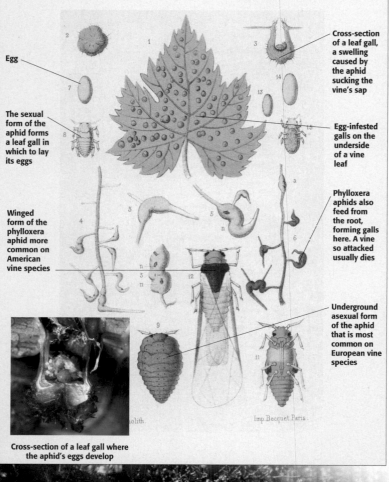

Egg

The sexual form of the aphid forms a leaf gall in which to lay its eggs

Winged form of the phylloxera aphid more common on American vine species

Cross-section of a leaf gall, a swelling caused by the aphid sucking the vine's sap

Egg-infested galls on the underside of a vine leaf

Phylloxera aphids also feed from the root, forming galls here. A vine so attacked usually dies

Underground asexual form of the aphid that is most common on European vine species

Imp.Becquet.Paris.

Cross-section of a leaf gall where the aphid's eggs develop

CHILE & ARGENTINA

CHILE & ARGENTINA

*A*FTER HUNDREDS *of years of winemaking experience, Chile and Argentina are poised on the edge of a winemaking revolution. Both countries have massive natural advantages in terms of climate and controllable irrigation, and now, with a new wave of technical expertise combined with a real understanding of terroir, the wines of Chile and Argentina are set to become serious players on the world market.*

CHILE

AS IN MANY LATIN AMERICAN countries, vines arrived in Chile with the Spanish invaders in the 16th century, but it was an invasion of another kind – that of French culture and ideas – which created the real foundation for a quality wine industry in the 19th century. Enthusiasm for all things French led to the appointment of many French winemakers and the planting of vineyards stocked with European cuttings. These had been taken just decades before phylloxera swept though Europe. In its isolation, cut off behind the Andes and sandwiched between the Atacama desert in the north and the ice of the Antarctic in the south, Chile is still unaffected by phylloxera and its bank of European vines remains the backbone of the country's wine industry today.

Cabernet Sauvignon grapes

Political changes in Chile since 1989 have opened the doors to foreign investment, while the export market for Chilean wine has grown rapidly. The country now ranks 11th in the world for wine production and while much of it is everyday wine, quality is steadily improving. All the major wine companies and most of the smaller family-run estates have made dramatic improvements in the wineries and now the focus is on the vineyards and searching out the best sites for each grape variety. Casablanca Valley led the way with Sauvignon Blanc, while Leyda in San Antonio Valley is producing excellent Pinot Noirs, and the calcium soil of Limarí gives Chardonnay wines a crisp, minerally edge. The area of vines grown organically is also expanding.

One of the most important steps for Chile in recent years has been the identification of the Carmenère grape *(see p538)*. Previously confused with Merlot, this full-flavoured, soft, plummy old Bordeaux variety is now carving its own niche within Chile's range of wines. Equally important for the region has been the differentiation between low-quality Sauvignonasse, which was widely planted, and pure Sauvignon Blanc. New plantings are now 100 per cent Sauvignon Blanc, and the quality of this variety has improved enormously, particularly in Casablanca Valley.

Cabernet Sauvignon is by far the most widely planted variety in Chile, having

Aconcagua Valley vineyards and the Andean foothills, Chile

◁ **Catena Zapata's winery in Upper Mendoza River, Argentina**

doubled its hectarage in the past 10 years. Merlot plantings have also increased dramatically, while the area of Chardonnay, Sauvignon Blanc, and Pinot Noir vines is growing steadily. New plantings of Syrah are proving very successful, particularly in Colchagua and Aconcagua valleys, while Viognier, Gewürztraminer, and Sangiovese are beginning to add diversity to Chile's range. Grape ripeness is never a problem in Chile, and the reds exhibit generous ripe fruit.

Vineyards in Argentina's Upper Mendoza River

Increasing reliance on cool-climate sites, such as Casablanca Valley and Leyda, has dramatically raised the quality of Chilean white wine, and Pinot Noir is also beginning to show great promise in these cooler areas.

ARGENTINA

IT WAS PROBABLY JESUIT missionaries who planted the first vines in the Mendoza region of Argentina in the mid-16th century, making use of irrigation channels carved out centuries earlier by the local population. Successive waves of immigrants from wine-producing countries during the 19th and early 20th centuries brought new vine varieties and better winemaking skills. These became the foundations of the new Argentine wine industry, which is now the fifth largest in the world. The real change came with the building of the railway from Buenos Aires to Mendoza, which was then extended to San Juan. This opened the market for wine and led to a massive expansion in vineyard area.

The Argentine wine industry survived the dramatic economic and political changes of the 20th century, but towards the end of the 1990s, as the local consumption fell, new markets had to be found. A massive vine-pull scheme reduced the vineyard area by a third

while the focus shifted to exports. Wine quality needed to rise, and investment was required. Some of this came from local business, but more significantly, investment flowed in from around the world, much of it from established wine producers who delighted in the natural climatic advantages that Argentina offers. They brought expertise, enthusiasm, and routes to market, kick-starting Argentina's new wine revolution.

Local grape varieties such as País and Moscatel still dominate plantings, but these are not generally used for export-quality wine. Malbec is the variety which is carving out a reputation in Argentina. Brought from France in the early 20th century, it ripens fully in the southern hemisphere sunshine, giving deep, damsony flavours which it never achieves in Europe. Torrontés is also widely planted and modern winemaking techniques have improved this variety to show its light, aromatic style. Argentina's strength, however, lies in the diversity of its vineyards. Sangiovese, Tempranillo, Bonarda, Nebbiolo, and Viognier all show good results; the reds achieving robust, ripe flavours, while the whites are crisper with more fruit. New cooler areas such as the Uco Valley have been planted as the drive upmarket continues.

WINE MAP OF CHILE & ARGENTINA

Haras de Pirque

WITH THE ANDES TO the east and the Pacific to the west, Chile forms a long thin sliver of land. Most vineyards are concentrated in the Central Valley between the Coastal Range and the Andes, and in smaller river valleys which run to the sea. From Atacama in the north to Malleco Valley in the south, grapes are grown in valleys over a distance of 1,300km. Over the Andes, hugging their leeward side, are the vineyards of Argentina. From Salta in the north, through La Rioja, San Juan, and Mendoza to Río Negro in the south, they cover a distance of 1,600km.

KEY

Central Chile & Argentina

CHILE: AREAS & TOP PRODUCERS

LIMARÍ VALLEY *p536*

ACONCAGUA VALLEY *p536*
Errázuriz *p540*

CASABLANCA & SAN ANTONIO VALLEYS *p536*
Viña Indomita *p540*
Viña Veramonte *p540*

MAIPO VALLEY *p537*
Antiyal *p540*
Concha y Toro *p543*
Cousiño-Macul *p540*
Haras de Pirque *p541*
Santa Carolina *p541*
Santa Rita *p541*
Viña Ventisquero *p542*

RAPEL VALLEY *p537*
Casa Lapostolle *p542*
Viña La Rosa *p542*
Viña Montes *p542*

CURICÓ VALLEY *p538*

MAULE VALLEY *p538*

ITATA VALLEY *p538*

BÍO-BÍO VALLEY *p538*

MALLECO VALLEY *p538*

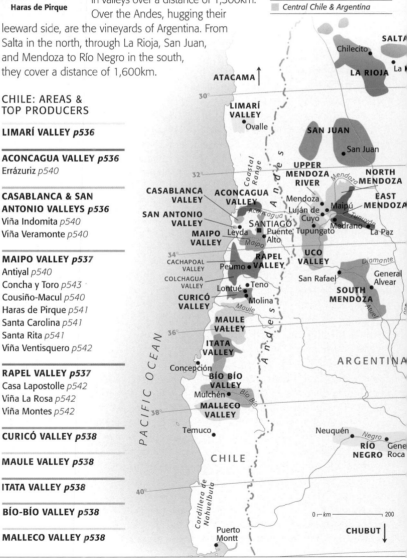

Sorting grapes at Fabre Montmayou, Mendoza, Argentina

TERROIR AT A GLANCE

CHILE

Latitude: 30–38°S.

Altitude: 400–1,000m.

Topography: Vineyard areas are situated between the Coastal Range and the Andes.

Soil: Limestone-and-clay with alluvial silt near rivers.

Climate: Maritime and extremely varied with intense heat in the north and high rainfall in the south. Close to the mountains, night-time temperatures fall significantly.

Temperature: January average is 30°C.

Rainfall: Annual average is 380mm.

Viticultural hazards: Frost; excessive rain.

ARGENTINA

Latitude: 26–42°S.

Altitude: 300–2,200m.

Topography: Vineyards are located in the west of Argentina, in the rain shadow of the Andes.

Soil: Sand, clay, and deep loose alluvial soil.

Climate: Continental and semi-desert. High daytime temperatures fall dramatically at night, especially in the mountain foothills.

Temperature: January average is 28°C.

Rainfall: Annual average is 100–300mm.

Viticultural hazards: hail.

ARGENTINA: AREAS & TOP PRODUCERS

NORTH MENDOZA p544

Familia Zuccardi p548

UPPER MENDOZA RIVER p544

Bodega Benegas p548
Bodega Norton p548
Catena Zapata p548
Dominio del Plata p548
Fabre Montmayou p549
Finca Flichman p549
Terrazas de los Andes p549
Weinert p549

PERFECT CASE: CHILE & ARGENTINA

Ⓡ Antiyal £££

Ⓡ Casa Lapostolle Clos Apalta £££

Ⓡ Catena Zapata Angélica Zapata Malbec Alta ££££

Ⓡ Catena Zapata Caro ££££

Ⓡ Clos de Los Siete ££££

Ⓦ Concha y Toro Terrunyo Sauvignon Blanc ££

Ⓡ Concha y Toro Almaviva ££££

Ⓡ O Fournier Bodegas y Viñedos A Crux ££££

Ⓡ San Pedro de Yacochuya Yacochuya ££££

Ⓡ Seña ££££

Ⓡ Terrazas de los Andes Cheval des Andes ££££

Ⓡ Viña Montes Alpha M £££

Catena Zapata vineyard in Mendoza, Argentina

Immaculate Don Maximiano vineyards of Errázuriz in Aconcagua Valley

WINEGROWING AREAS OF CHILE

COQUIMBO

GEOGRAPHICALLY, the northern region of Coquimbo should be far too hot and dry for the successful cultivation of grapes, but its proximity to the Pacific and the influence of the Antarctic Humboldt Current provides cooling sea breezes to create the right climate. Of Coquimbo's three valleys, Elqui, Limarí, and Choapa, the latter is of most interest for wine grapes.

Limarí Valley

UNTIL 1993 the semi-arid region of Limarí Valley was used only for growing grapes for the local spirit *pisco*, but recent plantings of wine grapes, mainly Cabernet Sauvignon, Merlot, Carmenère, Chardonnay, and Viognier, have been successful. Around 1,700ha of vines are now grown on valley floors and slopes around the towns of Ovalle and Punitaqui. Here, daytime sea breezes and night-time fogs moderate temperatures, while water for irrigation comes from La Paloma reservoir. Companies such as Casa Tamaya, Tabalí, and Maycas del Limarí have established reputations for clean, fruity, supple wines from this region.

Seña, Aconcagua Valley

🌾 stony clay 🍇 Cabernet Sauvignon, Merlot 🍃 Chardonnay, Viognier 🍷 red, white

ACONCAGUA

THE GREATER AREA of Aconcagua encompasses the warm valley of the same name, as well as Casablanca Valley and San Antonio Valley.

Aconcagua Valley

LINKED TO THE ANDES and the Pacific by the Aconcagua River, this area has a warm, dry climate favouring red wine production. The valley channels cool air from the sea, so warm days and cool nights allow slow ripening, giving generous fruity wines with intense colour and concentrated flavours. Aconcagua Valley is relatively small, with around 1,000ha of vines, 90 per cent of which are red. Most of the vineyards are around **Panquehue**, where Errázuriz is the key producer. Shallow, rocky, well-drained soils provide good growing conditions for Cabernet Sauvignon, Merlot, and Carmenère, while Syrah thrives on warm, north-facing slopes, and Sangiovese does well on the cooler sites. Nearer the coast at Ocoa, the northeast-facing Seña vineyard *(see p541)* has been planted to provide grapes for one of Chile's premium red wines.

🌾 well-drained, rocky, shallow soils 🍇 Cabernet Sauvignon, Merlot, Syrah, Carmenère 🍷 red

Casablanca & San Antonio Valleys

DISCOVERED AS A POTENTIAL viticultural region in the 1980s, Casablanca Valley has quickly run out of suitable viticultural land. It lies west of the Coastal Range, within reach of the cooling Pacific, and has some of Chile's best cool-climate growing conditions. Spring frosts, however, can be a hindrance. Irrigation is also a problem since the area is too far from the Andes to obtain meltwater, so the supply comes from more limiting bore-holes. The wines from Casablanca were soon recognized for their vibrant, fresh flavours, and now Chardonnay, Sauvignon Blanc, and Pinot Noir have come to dominate the 4,000ha of vines here. At the eastern end of the valley, temperatures are about 4°C higher than in the west, and some success is seen with Merlot and Carmenère.

San Antonio Valley is an even more recent discovery. It is strongly influenced by the Antarctic Humboldt Current, and long, cool summers allow grapes to ripen slowly and develop concentrated, lively fruit flavours. In particular, the rolling hills of **Leyda** offer good conditions for Chardonnay and Pinot Noir, although Merlot, Gewürztraminer, and Riesling are also planted. Expansion has only been possible since the installation of a pipeline bringing water from the Maipo River.

shallow sandy soils *Pinot Noir, Merlot, Syrah* *Chardonnay, Sauvignon Blanc* *red, white*

CENTRAL VALLEY

THE CENTRE OF CHILE'S wine production runs 320km south from Santiago and occupies the land between the Andean foothills and the Coastal Range. In some places, there are wide open valleys; in others the mountains almost meet. Crossing the valley are a number of rivers that create four subregions: Maipo, Rapel, Curicó, and Maule valleys.

Maipo Valley

THIS IS THE TRADITIONAL heart of Chilean wine-making, home to its first generation of serious wines. Planted by wealthy families in the mid-19th century with vines from Bordeaux, Maipo Valley still has many grand estates as a reminder of its prosperous past. However, the sprawl of Santiago is encroaching on older vineyards and many companies are moving further out.

There are 8,500ha of vines in Maipo, with vineyards stretching from the foothills of the Andes, east of Santiago, in a sweep through **Puente Alto**, **Pirque**, **Buin**, and **Isla de Maipo**, falling from 1,000m to around 400m. A higher, cooler location can need days or weeks more than lower sites to ripen grapes, allowing for the development of complex aromas and finer tannins. With a variety of mesoclimates and soil types, each area produces slightly different nuances of flavour in the wines.

Maipo Valley established Chile's reputation for fine, supple Cabernet Sauvignon, particularly around Puente Alto, where companies such as Concha y Toro and Errázuriz source grapes for some of their best Cabernet-based wines. Chilean Cabernet Sauvignon achieves its richest, lushest flavours here: the wines are known for their intense blackcurrant fruit, hints of eucalyptus, and soft, silky tannins.

Further south at Pirque, temperatures are kept low by a wind that flows along the river, while towards Buin, grapes ripen more rapidly, giving rich, soft, minty flavours to the Cabernet vines that dominate the area.

infertile alluvial clays on rock *Cabernet Sauvignon, Merlot* *red*

Rapel Valley

RAPEL VALLEY'S 30,000ha under vine represent over a quarter of Chile's vineyards. Essentially a red wine area, Rapel divides into two districts, **Cachapoal Valley** and **Colchagua Valley** (*see p539*), each centred on a river that flows into Lake Rapel. Cachapoal is the smaller of the two, extending from the cool foothills of the Andes across the narrow Central Valley to Peumo. Cabernet Sauvignon and Merlot dominate the hotter inland areas around Rancagua and Rengo, while in Requinoa, where temperatures are cooler, Cabernet grapes produce fresher, fruitier styles. Whites such as Chardonnay and Sauvignon Blanc are also showing good potential. Beyond the Coastal Range, around Peumo, temperatures are cooler and this area is developing a reputation for fine quality Merlot.

from fertile alluvial soil to shallow rocky slopes *Cabernet Sauvignon, Merlot, Carmenère* *red*

Harvesting Cabernet Sauvignon, Maipo Valley

GRAPE SURVIVOR

Carmenère is Chile's signature grape variety. Rediscovered in 1994, it was thought to be a variant of Merlot from the last century, despite having a slightly different leaf shape and ripening two weeks later. Recent DNA tests have, however, shown that Carmenère is derived from cuttings of Grand Vidure vines taken in Bordeaux in the late 19th century. Bordeaux Grand Vidure was virtually wiped out by phylloxera, but in Chile its progeny thrive, producing deep-flavoured, bramble-and-chocolate-tasting wines often with high levels of alcohol. Carmenère makes up around 6 per cent of Chile's planted area to Merlot's 11 per cent.

Curicó Valley

THIS AREA IS THE POWERHOUSE of Chilean wine production, with over 19,000ha of vineyards and the presence of almost every large Chilean wine company. Many good-value wines come from this region. Vines are mainly grown on the rich fertile plains around **Lontué** and on the slopes of the Coastal Range, where a long growing season produces good fruit concentration from a range of grape varieties. Cooler areas around Molina in the east and Teno in the north are particularly suited to white grapes.

fertile alluvial plains Cabernet Sauvignon, Merlot, Carmenère Sauvignon Blanc, Chardonnay *red, white*

Maule Valley

THE MOST SOUTHERLY part of the Central Valley, this area of wide, flat plains and low hills has been important for viticulture for 200 years. There are around 31,000ha of vineyards, a quarter of which still grow the native, rustic red grape País, which is made into wine for local consumption. The rest is planted with Cabernet Sauvignon, Merlot, and Sauvignon Blanc. This is also the land of Carmenère, which develops its rich, spicy flavours particularly well around San Clemente. Rainfall is higher here, and in some places, around Cauquenes in particular, there is no need for irrigation.

fertile alluvial plains Cabernet Sauvignon, Merlot, Carmenère Sauvignon Blanc, Chardonnay *red, white*

SOUTHERN REGION

WITH AROUND ONE FIFTH of Chile's vineyards, the south is an important region for volume. Local grapes such as País and Moscatel de Alejandría dominate here, but it is the small areas of Pinot Noir and Chardonnay that are of most interest.

Itata Valley

ONE OF THE ORIGINAL winegrowing areas, this southern region was left behind a century ago with the introduction of noble grapes further north. Local varieties País and Moscatel de Alejandría still dominate the vineyards, although there are some newer plantations of Cabernet Sauvignon and Chardonnay. Hot, dry summers and great temperature variations between day and night mean that this could be a region to watch in the future.

fertile loam País, Cabernet Sauvignon Moscatel de Alejandría, Chardonnay, Torontel *red, white*

Bío-Bío Valley

BÍO-BÍO VALLEY RECEIVES HIGHER RAINFALL than the more northerly areas, which have greater protection from the Coastal Range. Cooler summer temperatures and slower ripening conditions favour the production of aromatic whites. The harvest here can lag three weeks behind the Central Valley. Although extensively planted with the native País grape, Bío-Bío has great potential for fresh, lively wines from Pinot Noir, Gewürztraminer, Chardonnay, and Riesling, in particular from the area around Mulchén.

fertile alluvial loam País, Pinot Noir Moscatel de Alejandría, Chardonnay *red, white*

Malleco Valley

DISCOVERED ONLY RECENTLY as a suitable place for grape growing, this area is located between the Andes and Cordillera de Nahuelbuta, around 480km south of Santiago. Rainfall is high and temperatures are cool, with good sunshine and strong winds from the south assisting ripening. So far, Chardonnay is showing most promise in producing wines with crisp, aromatic flavours.

shallow rocky soil Chardonnay *white*

CREATING AN IMAGE IN COLCHAGUA VALLEY

Colchagua Valley has become Chile's most fashionable wine region, with wine producers and tourist agencies working together to develop an international image that sets it apart from other areas. Many important producers have vineyards located here, and some have now made it their flagship area.

The valley follows the Tinguiririca River from the Andes to the Pacific. Flanked north and south by extensions of the Andes, it forms a 30km-wide corridor. The terrain is varied with deep, loamy, fertile soils close to the river, and shallow soil, rocks, and gravel on the hillsides. Overall this is a warm area, but with the Andes exerting a cooling effect from the east and the sea moderating temperatures in the west, there are a number of mesoclimates. The variation in daytime and night-time temperatures gives Colchagua wines firm tannins and intense aromas. This is a red wine area dominated by Cabernet Sauvignon, with appearances from Merlot, Carmenère, and Syrah.

Colchagua Valley Districts
Near the coast, Lolol and Marchihue are becoming increasingly important as a source of good-quality Colchagua Valley whites. One of the key areas, however, is Apalta (above), with its steep rocky slopes, where producers Casa Lapostolle and Viña Montes have their most important vineyards. In places, it is so steep that terraces for vines have been cut into the hillside. Apalta is the source of Cabernet Sauvignon grapes for Montes' top wine, Alpha M, and Casa Lapostolle's Cabernet-based Clos Apalta. These structured, complex, and concentrated reds are two of Chile's most exciting wines, revealing the region's potential to compete on the world stage.

Top Producers
A number of excellent producers are helping to make a name for this up-and-coming region. Among those of particular note are Casa Lapostolle, Cono Sur, Montes, Viñedos Emiliana (www.emiliana.cl), Los Vascos (www.lafite.com), and Viu Manent (www.viumanent.cl).

Hillside vineyard in Colchagua Valley, Rapel Valley

TOP PRODUCERS OF CHILE

Errázuriz
Aconcagua Valley

Panquehue, Aconcagua
034 590 139
www.errazuriz.com

With an old-style winery building and wicker armchairs on the veranda, this estate seems to have barely changed since it was established in 1870 by Don Maximiano Errázuriz. Inside, however, the winery is completely up to date. The perfectly groomed Don Maximiano vineyard adjoining the winery was one of the first in Chile to take to the slopes. Some of it is now organically worked, and the best varieties are Merlot, Cabernet Sauvignon, and Syrah. Other Aconcagua Valley vineyards have been selected for different properties. Warmer El Ceibo provides fruity Cabernets and Merlots, while cooler Las Vertientes yields more structured Cabernets and Syrahs. Today Errazuriz is still owned by descendents of Don Maximiano who also own Caliterra and Seña *(see right)*.

red, white* *2006, 2005, 2003
★ Viñedo Chadwick, Don Maximiano, Errázuriz Single Vineyard Carmenère

Errázuriz's 19th-century winery

Viña Indomita
Casablanca Valley

Ruta 68, km 64, Casilla 162, Casablanca *032 275 4400*
www.indomita.cl

Viña Indomita sits high on a hillside at the inland end of Casablanca Valley. Established in 2000, it is an ambitious project aiming to create a top-class winery with a restaurant and visitor centre. The 220ha of vines are split between Casablanca, Maipo, Rapel, and Maule valleys, and the 1.5-million-litre capacity gravity-fed winery has space to double its output. The wines show promise, particularly the Pinot Noir and Chardonnay.

red, white* *2006, 2005
★ Indomita Reserva Cabernet Sauvignon, Indomita Chardonnay

Viña Veramonte
Casablanca Valley

Ruta 68, km 66, Casablanca *032 232 9924* *www.veramonte.cl*

With its striking architecture, Veramonte offers a Napa-style welcome, reflecting the Californian roots of its parent company. The wines, however are distinctly Chilean. Syrah, Merlot, Carmenère, and Pinot Noir are planted on 450ha of valley floor and slopes in the hottest part of the Casablanca Valley, with another 100ha in Colchagua. The estate is moving towards organic status, and the ever-increasing care in the vineyard, in terms of less irrigation and better pruning, is showing in the complexity of its wines and greater definition of fruit.

red, white* *2006, 2005, 2004
★ Primus, Merlot Reserva

Antiyal
Maipo Valley

Padre Hurtado 68, Paine, Santiago
02 821 4224
www.antiyal.com

This is a tiny operation owned by Alvaro Espinoza, who is widely recognized as one of Chile's most respected winemakers and as a leading exponent of organic grape growing. In between various consultancies and projects, including VOE *(see p543)*, with major companies, he works his own vineyards according to biodynamic principles, using specialist composts. Antiyal is Cabernet Sauvignon-based with a dash of Syrah and Carmenère, and it demonstrates great depth of flavour and style.

Antiyal

red* *2005, 2003* ★ *Antiyal

Concha y Toro
Maipo Valley

See p525.

Cousiño-Macul
Maipo Valley

Macul, Maipo *02 351 4100*
www.cousinomacul.cl

When Cousiño-Macul first planted vines in 1856, Macul was on the outskirts of Santiago, but city sprawl has overtaken the prized vineyards. Now a new vineyard has been planted at Buin in the Maipo Valley, with closer planting densities and drip irrigation. Cuttings were selected from the best of the original vines to maintain continuity of style. A high-tech winery at the new site completes the move for this traditional estate, whose

Cabernet-based wines maintain their firm texture and long-lived style. The original Cousiño-Macul estate, with its manicured gardens, old winery, and a few surviving vineyards, remains in Macul.

🖼 red, white 📆 2005, 2004, 2003
★ Lotae, Finis Terrae, Antiguas Reservas

Haras de Pirque
Maipo Valley

Camino San Vicente, Casilla 247, Correo Pirque 📞 02 854 7910
🌐 www.harasdepirque.com 🗓 by appt

BUILT ON THE SIDE of a horseshoe shaped hill, this is one of the most visually dramatic of the new-era Chilean wineries. Vines climb the slopes making the most of different aspects and ripening conditions. The aim of the owning Matte family to establish a quality company is reflected in the state-of-the-art gravity-fed winery, with its grape selection tables and new wooden vats. Top consultants have ensured the best winemaking from the start. The reds reveal careful treatment and have rich, deep, radiant fruit with silky tannins and developing complexity. Haras de Pirque also has a joint venture with Italian producer Antinori to make an icon wine, Albis.

🖼 red, white 📆 2006, 2005, 2003
★ Haras Elegance Cabernet Sauvignon, Haras Character Chardonnay

Haras de Pirque's impressive winery in Maipo Valley

Santa Carolina
Maipo Valley

Tiltil 2228, Macul, Santiago
📞 02 450 3000
🌐 www.santacarolina.com
🗓 by appt

SANTA CAROLINA may be based at one of Chile's national monuments – a 19th-century winery in Macul – but it is one of the nation's most forward-looking companies. With 2,000ha of vines in Casablanca, Maipo, and Colchagua valleys, plus a network of contracted growers, this large producer has strict control over quality. Wines are consistently good, but the Chardonnays and Merlots show particular depth and ripe fruit. The Sauvignon Blanc is one of Chile's best, with bright, lively herbaceous flavours.

🖼 red, white 📆 2007, 2006, 2003
★ Barrica Selection Carmenère, VSC, Santa Carolina Sauvignon Blanc

Santa Rita
Maipo Valley

Buin, Maipo 📞 02 362 2000
🌐 www.scntarita.com
🗓 by appt

WITH 2,000HA OF vineyards spread across Maipo, Casablanca, Rapel, and San Antonio valleys, as well as recently acquired land in Limarí and the Rapel Valley, Santa Rita is the second largest land-owning winery in Chile. Sustainable agriculture, better clone material, and improved trellising and irrigation techniques have helped Santa Rita control and improve quality across the wide range of wines – from the commercial but good 120 level (named for the 120 soldiers who hid in the cellars during Chile's war of independence), through Reserva, Medalla Real, and Floresta, to Casa Real, a single-vineyard wine planted 50 years ago. At the heart of this estate is a 30-ha haven of trees, lawns, and lakes, complete with a luxury hotel and newly restored chapel. Santa Rita owns the neighbouring winery Carmen, which pioneered organic viticulture in Chile.

🖼 red, white 📆 2008, 2006, 2005
★ Casa Real Cabernet Sauvignon, Floresta Apalta Cabernet Sauvignon, Floresta Syrah

---

SEÑA: THE SEAL OF QUALITY

The Chadwick and Mondavi families co-own the Seña ('Seal') project, which was created to show that Chile could produce a wine capable of competing with the best on the world market. No effort has been spared in the densely planted, rocky Seña vineyard in Aconcagua Valley, which is angled away from the hot afternoon sun to prolong ripening. The graceful wine is a blend of six classic red varietals – Cabernet Sauvignon, Merlot, Carmenère, Cabernet Franc, Petit Verdot, and Malbec – and shows complexity, finesse, and great ageing potential.

Viña Ventisquero
Maipo Valley

Rancagua 📞 *072 201 240*
🌐 *www.ventisquero.cl* ⬜ *by appt*

THE ENVIRONMENTAL CREDENTIALS of this company are excellent, with low-energy buildings, water recycling, lightweight glass bottles, and carbon-offsetting used to reduce its carbon footprint. With more than 1,500ha of vineyards planted in the key areas of Maipo, Colchagua, and Casablanca, this is a large operation, yet manages to deliver quality wines at all price points. The value varietals offer clean, fresh, well-made fruit, but at the top end, Vertice, made with the combined talents of Ventisquero's Felipe Tosso and Australian winemaker John Duval, shows that this company can also deliver deep, complex wines.
🍷 *red, white* 📅 *2008, 2007, 2006*
★ *Grey Carmenère, Vertice*

Casa Lapostolle
Rapel Valley/
Colchagua Valley

Santa Cruz, Colchagua
📞 *02 426 9960*
🌐 *www.casalapostolle.com*
⬜ *by appt*

THE LATEST TREND at this premium winery is to de-stem the grapes by hand. It is time consuming, but the quality shows in the silky texture of the wines. Casa Lapostolle has become a focused operation based on a plantation of 80-year-old Cabernet Sauvignon in Colchagua Valley. Vines have been extended up the slope of Clos Apalta, and a breathtaking new winery has been built solely for this top cuvée wine. There are also vineyards in the Casablanca and Rapel valleys. Low yields,

A vineyard in Chile's Colchagua Valley

ripe fruit, and the expertise of consultant Michel Rolland ensure that these wines maintain high standards.
🍷 *red, white* 📅 *2006, 2005, 2004* ★ *Clos Apalta, Cuvée Alexandre Merlot*

Viña La Rosa
Rapel Valley/
Cachapoal Valley

Camino de la Fruta,
Ruta 66, km 28, Comuna de Peumo
📞 *02 670 0600*
🌐 *www.larosa.cl* ⬜ *by appt*

TUCKED AWAY IN a hidden valley and surrounded by palm trees, Viña la Rosa's vineyard at La Palmeria de Cocolán is not only stunningly beautiful but it also has a mesoclimate ideal for viticulture. Carmenère, Merlot, and Cabernet Sauvignon have been planted here. This is just one of la Rosa's vineyards, which are spread over 700ha in three Rapel Valley sites. The company is part of the larger La Rosa Sofruco fruit-growing operation and has recently invested in a new winery, visitors' centre, and vineyards. Quality has moved up, especially at the top end of the range, where single vineyard wines show a deep, velvety fruit quality.
🍷 *red, white, rosé* 📅 *2007, 2006, 2005* ★ *Don Reca Cabernet Sauvignon, La Capitana Carmenère*

Viña Montes
Rapel Valley/
Colchagua Valley

Colchagua Estate, La Finca de Apalta,
Apalta, Santa Cruz, Colchagua
📞 *02 248 4805* 🌐 *www.montes wines.com* ⬜ *by appt*

"IT WAS LOVE AT FIRST SIGHT," says owner Aurelio Montes about the steep rocky slope of Finca de Apalta in Colchagua Valley. That was in 1972, but it was 16 years before Viña Montes – the company he formed with three partners – bought the land and uprooted the pear and plum trees that grew here. Now with 140ha at Apalta and another 350ha at Marchigue (both in Colchagua Valley) as well as vineyards in Curicó, this company has established a reputation for quality at all levels – particularly for its Alpha range. Syrah is the latest challenge; by planting higher up the slope, the vines are stressed at the right time to achieve great concentration and complexity of flavour. Montes is a highly respected winemaker who also acts as consultant to other companies. His top wines, the rich, peppery, spicy Folly (Syrah) and rounded, elegant Alpha M (Cabernet blend) are two of the finest in Chile.
🍷 *red, white* 📅 *2007, 2006, 2005* ★ *Alpha M, Folly, Alpha Syrah*

THE CONCHA Y TORO EMPIRE

As Chile's largest wine company, and one of the oldest (founded 1883), Concha y Toro has the resources to show the strengths of Chilean wine across a wide range. With over 3,500ha of vineyards in the main growing regions, it controls the supply of grapes for all the premium quality wines. Two of Chile's best winemakers, Marcelo Papa and Ignacio Recabarren, are in charge of the eight winemaking teams at locations close to the vineyards.

Concha y Toro has a number of associated wine companies in Chile and Argentina. The Cono Sur winery was established in 1993 in Chimbarongo (Rapel) to make fresh and fruity New-World style wines. With a slogan of "no family trees, no dusty bottles, just quality wine", it has carved a name

for an affordable, high-quality product, and the company now has a strong environmental agenda.

Other companies include Viña Maycas del Limarí, which is based in the Limarí Valley and makes elegant, minerally wines, particularly Chardonnay.

Marcelo Papa

Almaviva

This joint project between Concha y Toro and French producer Baron Philippe de Rothschild was established to create one of Chile's finest wines. Almaviva comes from a 50-ha vineyard at Puente Alto in Pirque, planted with Carmenère, Cabernet Sauvignon, Cabernet Franc, Merlot, and Petit Verdot. Low yields and classic winemaking result in a firm-structured, elegant wine, which reflects its half-French parentage.

Practical Information

Pirque, Maipo ☎ 02 476 5269
🖳 www.conchaytoro.com
🖸 by appt

Wine Information

🍷 red, white
📷 2006, 2005, 2004
★ Don Melchor, Terrunyo

The Concha y Toro Range

Concha y Toro's wines continue to improve in quality. From the lively, fruit-driven Casilliero del Diablo range, which covers all key Chilean grape varieties, moving up through the ranges of Trio, Marqués de Casa Concha, Terrunyo, Amelia, and Don Melchor (above), there is an increasing link to terroir. Terrunyo Sauvignon Blanc, sourced from cool Casablanca Valley and Leyda (San Antonio Valley), shows how far Chile can progress in terms of defining fruit characteristics in relation to vineyard location. Oak is judiciously used across the range, with the emphasis on fine-grained quality.

Almaviva's winery in Pirque, Maipo Valley

Merlot vineyards and the Andes in Upper Mendoza River

WINEGROWING AREAS OF ARGENTINA

MENDOZA

FROM THE AIR, Mendoza appears as a stretch of green in a vast area of brown scrubland, in the arid rain shadow to the east of the Andes. Most of Mendoza remains a desert, but parts of it were turned into an oasis 700 years ago by the diversion of mountain-fed rivers through irrigation canals. Designed by the Incas, these canals were extended over the centuries by the indigenous Huarpe Indians. Now Mendoza is Argentina's most important viticultural region, producing 70 per cent of the country's wine grapes from 140,000ha. Most of the large companies are based in Mendoza although some also have vineyards and facilities elsewhere. There are five distinct areas within Mendoza.

Bodegas Salentein label, Uco Valley

North Mendoza

LYING TO THE NORTH and east of the city of Mendoza, this plain is around 600 to 700m above sea level and includes the districts of Lavalle, Guaymallén, Las Heras, San Martín, and part of Maipú. The poor, sandy loam soil is irrigated by the Mendoza River. High salinity in the soil leads to low acidity in the wine, and this area favours light reds such as Bonarda and Sangiovese for early drinking, and whites such as Chenin Blanc and Pedro Giménez. There are around 14,000ha of vines here, including a small area of 100-year-old Malbec vines.

alluvial sandy loam *Bonarda, Sangiovese* *Chenin Blanc, Pedro Giménez* *red, white*

Upper Mendoza River

THIS CENTRAL AREA CLOSE TO THE CITY of Mendoza is regarded as one of the best places to grow grapes in Argentina. To the south of the city, stretching along the Andean foothills, the area of **Luján de Cuyo**, which includes Vistalba, Perdriel, and Agrelo, is one of Argentina's three recognized Denominatión de Origen (DO). It is a visual delight, with a backdrop of snow-topped mountains and a gentle slope of vines. Malbec was planted here 100 years ago, and this area remains the best place in Argentina to achieve low yields and concentrated flavours. Key wineries such as Fabre Montmayou, Bodega Norton, and Catena Zapata are based here, and many others source grapes from the area. At an altitude of 1,000m, big differences between daytime and night-time temperatures lead to fine aromas and good acidity. Soils are varied according to their position on the complex layers of alluvial loam, rock, and gravel that form this northeast-facing slope.

Maipú, to the east and southeast of Mendoza city, includes the subdistricts of Cruz de Piedra, Lunlunta, and Las Barrancas. This area, located at around 800m, has rocky soil, particularly around Las Barrancas, where large stones cover the surface of the vineyards. Malbec is the main grape here, although Cabernet Sauvignon can shine, giving high quality wines with structure, elegance, and deep flavours.

🍇 complex alluvial, stony 🔴 Malbec, Syrah, Cabernet Sauvignon 🟡 Sémillon, Chardonnay 🍷 red, white

Uco Valley

LOCATED 80KM SOUTH OF THE CITY of Mendoza and stretching for another 80km, Uco Valley is Argentina's most exciting new development. An area between **Tupungato** and **Pareditas** is gradually being planted on the lower slopes of the Andes at altitudes of 900 to 1,500m, and state-of-the-art wineries are beginning to dot the landscape. This is where Clos de los Siete, Bodegas Salentein, and O Fournier Bodegas y Viñedos have chosen to invest, taking advantage of naturally low temperatures, long ripening periods, and scant, stony soil. Red grapes such as Malbec, Syrah, Cabernet Sauvignon, Merlot, and Pinot Noir show strong varietal character backed up by crisp acidity. Among the whites, Sémillon, Riesling, Pinot Gris, and Chardonnay provide clear fruit flavours, with a backbone of acidity that is sometimes lacking in wines from other regions. Uco Valley has space to expand even further, and is likely to become one of Argentina's premier wine districts.

🍇 poor, stony 🔴 Malbec, Cabernet Sauvignon, Merlot 🟡 Sémillon, Chardonnay, Riesling 🍷 red, white

East Mendoza

EAST MENDOZA IS THE BIGGEST wine producing area in the province. Spreading along the banks of the Tunuyán River as far as La Paz, this essentially flat, warm area is extensively planted with vines. Altitudes range from 750m in the west around **Medrano** to 560m near **La Paz**, and soil types vary,

MIGHTY MALBEC

Malbec is faring better in Argentina than it ever did in its French homeland. The vines were probably brought to Argentina in the late 19th century by immigrant workers from Southwest France, where it is known as Côt. Versatile, able to blend with other varieties and distinctive in style, this grape ripens well in the South American sunshine, producing rich, lush, damsony wines. Malbec is Argentina's second most widely planted variety, with about 17 per cent of the total vineyard area.

with a greater concentration of sand in the west and deep, rich soils to the east.

Some of the 60,000ha of vines are still trained in the traditional way, on overhead trellises called *parrals*. In parts of Mendoza, the *parral* system is indicative of large crops and low quality, but here, where daytime temperatures are high, controlled pruning and training can be used to shade the developing grapes and slow down ripening, leading to high quality, rich-tasting wines. This vast area is home to a wide range of red grape varieties, as well as new plantings of Viognier.

🍇 rich, deep, alluvial 🔴 Bonarda, Syrah, Sangiovese 🟡 Torrontés, Chardonnay, Viognier 🍷 red, white

South Mendoza

SOME 130KM TO the southeast of Mendoza lies **San Rafael Valley**, the first Argentinian region to attain DO status. Here, irrigated by the Diamante and Atuel rivers, 20,000ha of vines are grown on a gentle slope that descends from Las Parades in the west at 800m to General Alvear in the east at 450m. Soils are alluvial over limestone rock, and while rainfall is low, hail is a major hazard. Warm daytime temperatures during summer favour the production of full-flavoured Malbec, Syrah, and Cabernet Sauvignon, while Chenin Blanc is the most widely planted white grape.

🍇 fertile, alluvial limestone 🔴 Malbec, Barbera, Cabernet Sauvignon 🟡 Chenin Blanc 🍷 red, white

Harvesting Malbec in Luján de Cuyo, Upper Mendoza River

Michel Torino Bodega La Rosa in Salta

BEYOND MENDOZA

WHILE THE MAJORITY of Argentina's vineyards are in Mendoza, there are substantial plantings in San Juan (22 per cent) and La Rioja (3.8 per cent), as well as small areas in Salta, Catamarca, and Río Negro. Each of these areas has its own specific mesoclimate, ideal for viticulture, and as Argentina's wine exports grow, the search for even more suitable areas is set to continue.

Salta

WITH COOL NIGHTS and hot days, tempered by a wind that switches on like air conditioning at the hottest part of the day, Salta province would be the perfect place to grow grapes if it were not so remote. Situated 1,000km north of Mendoza, in the foothills of the Andes, this high-altitude region is a long but beautiful drive from everywhere. Vineyards are planted in the Calchaquíes valleys of Salta Province, which continue into the northern part of neighbouring provinces Tucumán and Catamarca. The mountain resort of **Cafayate** in Salta is the main viticultural production area – where vineyards are planted at around 1,700m and new plantations climb even higher up the mountain slopes, challenging grapes to ripen at altitudes of up to 2,200m. At these altitudes, the diurnal temperature variation is significant. This develops complex aromas and flavours in the grapes, while the naturally

Michel Torino Bodega La Rosa label, Salta

high levels of UV here develop intense colour and fine tannins in red grapes.

Traditionally, 90 per cent of plantings have been the light, aromatic Torrontés variety, although small amounts of Cabernet Sauvignon and Malbec have also been grown here for many years. It is these red grapes, plus Syrah and Tannat, which are being revitalized and replanted at properties such as San Pedro de Yacochuya and Bodega Colomé.

🗺 *well-drained sandy gravel* 🍇 *Malbec, Cabernet Sauvignon, Bonarda* 🍃 *Torrontés, Chenin Blanc, Chardonnay* 🍷 *red, white*

La Rioja

LA RIOJA'S VINEYARDS are concentrated on the west side of the province between Sierra de Famatina and Sierra de Velasco. Chilecito, named after the Chileans who mined gold there a century ago, is the main production area, with Coronel Felipe Varela, Famatina, Castro Barros, and Arauco as other important centres. This hot, dry area is totally dependent on irrigation, and while wine grapes (mainly Torrontés) are important, it is also an area of table grape production. The Famatina Valley is one of Argentina's oldest wine-producing zones. It is a dry, windy region that lies between 800 and 1,400m.

High temperatures mean that white grapes are generally picked early to retain their fresh, aromatic qualities. Torrontés is the main white variety, while Bonarda, Cabernet Sauvignon, Barbera, and Syrah dominate red-grape planting. The quality of these wines is gradually improving as irrigation and pruning become more controlled.

🗺 *deep alluvial loam* 🍇 *Bonarda, Cabernet Sauvignon, Syrah* 🍃 *Torrontés, Moscatel de Alejandría* 🍷 *red, white*

San Juan

SAN JUAN IS the traditional heartland of Argentina's grape production and, historically, the place where the country's fortified wines have been made. Established by European immigrants in the late 19th century, it includes about a quarter of Argentina's vineyard area –

although much of this is given over to the production of table grapes and raisins. This is a hot, dry region, frequently scorched by a wind so fierce that it can dry the flowers on the vines, preventing fruit set. Grapes grow in a succession of six valleys from west to east at 900 to 600m, each irrigated by the San Juan River. Of these, the stony Ullum-Zonda Valley at 900m and the alluvial Tulum Valley at 600m are the most important. This is where workhorse varieties such as Pedro Giménez, Moscatel de Alejandría, Torrontés, and vast amounts of the local pink grape Cereza are grown, occupying over 80 per cent of the vineyard area. There are also small plantings of Cabernet Sauvignon, Malbec, and Syrah. Further south, the infertile El Pedernal Valley, at 1,340m, is a recent high-quality wine outpost within San Juan. Mild summers and cool nights provide grapes such as Chardonnay, Sauvignon Blanc, Merlot, and Malbec with ideal conditions to ripen slowly and develop fine aromas and flavours.

poor, stony, alluvial **Syrah, Bonarda, Cabernet Sauvignon, Barbera** *Pedro Giménez, Moscatel de Alejandría, Torrontés* *red, white, fortified*

Río Negro

SOME 640KM SOUTH OF MENDOZA on the northern edge of Patagonia, where the flat desert land stretches almost to infinity, lies the viticultural zone of Río Negro. In the early 20th century a team of British engineers diverted part of the Negro River to irrigate a valley and turned it into a prime production area for apples, pears, and quinces. Grapes are less important here

For some wine producers it is not enough to run a wine business. Situated out in the countryside, and often the largest – if not the only – employers in their districts, many companies not only provide jobs, but also houses, communities, and most importantly, schools. Producers such as José Alberto Zuccardi at La Agrícola are proud of the number of employees working on their land. Four hundred people tend the vines on this estate, providing much-needed employment in the countryside. This means that vines are tended and pruned, and grapes picked, by hand; and instead of the usual European vineyard sight of a solitary worker on a tractor, there are groups of 20 people employed tying up shoots or planting new vines. With many workers living on site, and buses servicing the local schools, companies such as this provide stability for whole rural communities.

than these other fruits – but even so, the particular climate proves perfect for some grape varieties. Late frost is a problem, but once that danger is over the region enjoys warm days and cool nights, giving a long ripening period which is particularly good for fresh-tasting whites and soft, ripe reds. Around 2,500ha of vines are planted in this area, mainly around Neuquén and General Roca, and many Mendoza producers have experimental vineyards here that may be expanded in the future. At just 300m above sea level, this area relies less on altitude and more on its southerly location to keep temperatures down. However, this is not Argentina's most southerly wine region; Bodegas Weinert is planting an area 320km further south in the province of Chubut at 42°S, and other companies are also exploring this area's potential.

alluvial sand, gravel **Merlot, Malbec, Syrah, Pinot Noir** *Pedro Giménez, Torrontés, Sémillon, Chardonnay, Sauvignon Blanc* *red, white*

Harvesting Sémillon grapes in Río Negro

TOP PRODUCERS OF ARGENTINA

Familia Zuccardi
North Mendoza

Ruta Provincial 33, km 7.5, Maipú
C *0261 441 0010*
W *www.familiazuccardi.com* ☐

INNOVATION IS THE KEY at this dynamic company, one of the largest family-owned wineries in Argentina. The usual grapes (Malbec, Cabernet Sauvignon, Merlot, and Chardonnay) are well represented, but it is the willingness to innovate with varieties such as Tempranillo, Viognier, Barbera, Grenache, Marsanne, and Zinfandel that sets Zuccardi apart. An increasing proportion of the 600ha of vineyards is cultivated organically, meanwhile the range of wines continues to expand at all price levels.
🍷 *red, white* 🔟 *2006, 2005, 2004* ★ *Q Malbec, Q Tempranillo, Santa Julia Viognier*

Bodega Benegas
Upper Mendoza River

Araoz 1600, Mayor Drummond Luján de Cuyo **C** *0261 496 0794* **W** *www.bodegabenegas.com* ☐ *by appt*

BENEGAS is one of the oldest names in Argentine wine. In 1883, Tiburcio Benegas, then governor of Mendoza, promoted agriculture in the region by extending the network of waterways. He also bought a vineyard here, El Trapiche, and founded the successful wine company named after it. This was sold in the 1970s and the family involvement in wine dwindled. Now, however, Federico Benegas Lynch has revived the family estate in Luján de Cuyo, where 40ha of stony soil are planted with Cabernet Franc, Sangiovese, Petit Verdot, and other grapes. The winery itself may be old, but the

Catena Zapata label

fermentation tanks are newly restored and produce wines of amazing depth and concentration. A range of varietals is made, plus a Bordeaux-style blend known as Meritage.
🍷 *red, white, rosé* 🔟 *2005, 2004, 2003* ★ *Meritage, Sangiovese, Malbec*

Bodega Norton
Upper Mendoza River

Ruta Provincial 15, km 23.5, Perdriel, Luján de Cuyo **C** *0261 488 0480* **W** *www.norton.com.ar* ☐

ESTABLISHED IN 1895 by an English engineer who helped to build Argentina's railways, this company took a century to gather steam. In 1989 it was bought by the Austrian Swarovski family, who built a new winery and revitalized the vineyards. With 680ha of vines, including some precious 90-year-old Malbec, which gives tiny amounts of top-quality wine, Norton is experimenting with trellising, irrigation, and pruning to become organic.
🍷 *red, white* 🔟 *2005, 2004, 2003* ★ *Reserva Malbec*

Catena Zapata
Upper Mendoza River

Calle J Cobos, Agrelo, Luján de Cuyo **C** *0261 413 1100* **W** *www.catenawines.com* ☐ *by appt*

THIS IS ARGENTINA'S most prominent wine empire, now

with a spectacular brand-new winery in Agrelo which resembles a Mayan pyramid. The company has changed direction in the last 20 years and is now clearly focused on creating quality, fruit-driven wines in the mid- to upper-price sector. The top of the range wine, named after owner Nicolás Catena Zapata, can challenge the best bordeaux in a blind tasting. With 425ha of vineyards and access to double that through contracts, Catena are researching the effects of planting density, clones, and yields on quality, but it is their work with altitude that is giving remarkable results. With vineyards planted at between 940m and 1,500m, they can produce complex, vibrant wines.
🍷 *red, white* 🔟 *2007, 2006, 2005* ★ *Catena Zapata Adrianna Vineyard, Alta Malbec, Alta Chardonnay*

Dominio del Plata
Upper Mendoza River

Cochabamba, Agrelo Luján de Cuyo **C** *0261 498 6572* **W** *www.dominio delplata.com.ar* ☐ *by appt*

OENOLOGIST Susana Balbo and her viticulturalist husband Pedro Marchevsky struck out on their own with this new venture in 2001. With 22ha of young vines in Agrelo planted to Malbec and Cabernet Sauvignon, a well-designed winery, and good grower contracts, they have access to some of the region's best grapes. The project is committed to quality, and the first wines show great potential with vibrant fruit, harmony, and elegance.
🍷 *red, white* 🔟 *2003, 2002* ★ *Susana Balbo Malbec, Ben Marco Expresivo, Crios Torrontés*

Fabre Montmayou
Upper Mendoza River

Roque Saenz Peña, Vistalba, Luján de Cuyo ☎ *0261 498 2330* ☒ *www.fabremontmayou.com* ⏰ *by appt*

WHEN DIANE AND Hervé Joyaux moved from Bordeaux in the early 1990s, they searched various locations in Chile and Argentina for the ideal *terroir*. They found what they were looking for in Luján de Cuyo, on gentle slopes planted with century-old Malbec vines. Densely planted and deeply rooted, these low-yielding vines form the core of their 80-ha Mendoza estate produce deep-flavoured, ripe, lush wines with an unmistakable French accent. A second estate in Río Negro, Patagonia, produces elegant, harmonious wines under the Infinitus label.

🍷 *red* 🍾 *2006, 2005, 2004*
★ *Grand Vin, Malbec, Infinitus Merlot*

Finca Flichman
Upper Mendoza River

Munives 800, Barrancas, Maipú ☎ *0261 497 2039* ☒ *www.flichman.com.ar* ⏰ *by appt*

BASED IN THE BARRANCAS REGION of Maipú, one of Mendoza's prime viticultural areas, Finca Flichman has extensive vineyards surrounding the winery, and further plantings in the high-altitude area of Tupungato. Since it was bought by Portuguese wine company Sogrape in 1998, this estate has seen substantial investment in both its vineyards and winery, in terms of cutting yields and increasing plant density. The result is a dramatic hike in wine quality across the range. In particular, the Gestos range blends wines sourced from vineyards at different altitudes to provide complexity while retaining

freshness of flavour. Two new Cabernet-blends, the dense, spicy Paisaje Barrancas (with Syrah) and the rich, chewy Faisale Tupungato (with Malbec), are the first attempts to relate wines to specific *terroirs*.

🍷 *red, white* 🍾 *2007, 2006, 2005* ★ *Dedicado, Paisaje Barrancas, Paisaje Tupungato*

Terrazas de los Andes
Upper Mendoza River

Cochabamba y Thames, Perdriel, Luján de Cuyo ☎ *0261 490 9921* ☒ *www.terrazasdelosandes.com* ⏰ *by appt*

THE BUILDING HERE IS an old-style Spanish *bodega*, but when the doors roll back, the glint of stainless steel is almost blinding. The first vintage from this revitalized winery was 1999, and since then quality has been steadily improving. Terrazas de los Andes was the first Argentinian winery to make the vital link between vineyard altitude and grape variety. With Syrah planted at 800m, Malbec at 1,080m and Chardonnay at 1,200m, each grape gets the perfect balance of

temperature and sunshine to achieve optimum ripeness. An 'icon' wine, made with Bordelais winemaker Pierre Lurton of Cheval Blanc *(see p80)*, bears the name Cheval de los Andes.

🍷 *red, white* 🍾 *2006, 2005, 2004* ★ *Malbec Reserva, Afincado*

Weinert
Upper Mendoza River

San Martin 5923, Luján de Cuyo ☎ *0261 496 0409* ☒ *www.bodegaweinert.com* ⏰ *by appt*

Weinert

THIS OLD ARGENTINIAN company, established by Bernardo Weinert in 1975, is still ageing its rich, concentrated wines in large oak vats, which gives them a delicious burnished complexity. Weinert is one of the first companies to investigate a new area for vines in Chubut in the dramatic wilderness of Patagonia, which has been planted with cool-climate varieties such as Pinot Noir, Sauvignon Blanc, Riesling, and Chardonnay.

🍷 *red, white* 🍾 *2006, 2005, 2004* ★ *Weinert Malbec, Cavas de Weinert Cabernet Sauvignon*

Hervé Joyaux at Fabre Montmayou

Bodegas Salentein
Uco Valley

Ruta 89, Los Arboles, Tunuyán
C *0262 242 9000*
W *www.bodegasalentein.com* ◻

IN 1998, THIS COMPANY led the way for international investment into the cool Uco Valley, and now it has a 2,000-ha estate with 700ha of vines. Malbec, Merlot, Cabernet Sauvignon, and Syrah are planted between 1,000 and 1,250m while cooler-climate grapes Pinot Noir and Sauvignon Blanc are higher up at around 1,700m. A new winery, impressive in size, appearance, and technology, has been built, while a cultural centre and restaurant are situated nearby. The wines are developing with each vintage, in particular the Reserve Pinot Noir with its balanced, harmonious fruit, and the dense, velvety Merlot.
🍷 *red, white* 📦 *2006, 2005, 2004* ★ *Salentein Malbec, Numina Gran Reserva*

Clos de Los Siete
Uco Valley

Vista Flores, Tunuyán
C *02614 234230* ◉

LIKE A WELL-ORGANIZED upmarket co-operative, this estate is made up of six investors, including top winemaker Michel Rolland, who have banded together to plant 800ha of land on the lower Andean hills in the Uco Valley. Originally there were seven investors, hence the name. This initiative was among the first to make a significant investment here, but more have followed, turning this former scrubland into some of Argentina's most desirable vineyards. Each of the six producers has their own wine, but a blend from

Vines at Bodegas Salentein

all the vineyards, representing the whole estate, is a concerted effort to produce one of Argentina's top wines through a combination of careful site, vine, and grape selection. With each vintage, the Malbec-led blend has become deeper and more complex and supple.
🍷 *red* 📦 *2007, 2006, 2005* ★ *Clos de Los Siete*

Finca La Celia
Uco Valley

Circunvalacion, Eugenio Bustos, San Carlos **C** *0261 413 4400*
W *www.fincalacelia.com.ar* ◉

BOUGHT BY CHILEAN wine company San Pedro in 2000, Finca La Celia is rapidly being overhauled with massive investment in its vineyards and winery. Based in the cool Uco Valley, at around 1,000m, the vineyards have been extended to 600ha. Grapes are additionally sourced from growers. The winery has seen the addition of barrel storage and a new cooling system, plus the replacement of old vats. The aim is to establish an export-focused company, and initial results are favourable. The range of wines is well made and structured, in particular the top blend, Supremo.
🍷 *red, white* 📦 *2007, 2006, 2005* ★ *La Celia Malbec Reserva, La Celia Supremo*

Jacques & François Lurton
Uco Valley

Ruta Provincial 94 km 21, 556 Tunuyán
C *02614 248400*
W *www.jflurton.com* ◉

ONE OF THE FIRST to establish a winery in the cool-climate Uco Valley, this French company chose a site close to the mountains at around 1,000m. There are 275ha of vines on the poor stony soil of Vista Flores, with another 100ha planted in the warmer area of Las Barrancas in the Upper Mendoza River area. Rather than the usual glittering array of stainless steel found in most new wineries, this company has chosen traditional concrete fermentation tanks in which the grapes can be hand-punched down to give good extraction of flavours. The wines, particularly the whites and the Bonarda, have clear, lively flavours, while the other reds are developing complexity with each vintage.
🍷 *red, white* 📦 *2006, 2005, 2004* ★ *Reserve Malbec, Chacayes*

O Fournier Bodegas y Viñedos
Uco Valley

Calle Los Indios, La Consulta
C *02622 451579*
W *www.bodegasofournier.com* ◉

THIS INVESTMENT PROJECT in the Uco Valley by the Spanish Ortega Fournier family has become one of the new stars of Argentina. With 94ha of vines already planted and long-term contracts on older vineyards, the focus is on Tempranillo, with Merlot and Malbec taking supporting roles in the blend. The wines, A Crux and B Crux, named after the Southern Cross stars, show deep

raspberry and chocolate flavours with great potential.
🖼 red 📆 2006, 2005, 2004
★ A Crux Malbec, B Crux Blend

Bodega Colomé
Salta

4419 Molinos, Salta ☎ *03868 494044* 🌐 *www.bodegacolome.com* ⬜ *by appt*

WITH VINEYARDS planted between 1,700 and 3,002m, Bodega Colomé in the northwest of Salta claims to be the highest in the world. This is a new venture, bought in 2001 by Swiss businessman and art collector Donald Hess as part of the international Hess Group, which owns wineries on three continents. The vast mountainous estate includes 110ha of old Malbec vines with Cabernet Sauvignon, Tannat, and Syrah. The location offers moderate daytime temperatures with cold nights, and high UV sunshine, which gives deep coloured grapes. Organic viticulture and traditional winemaking mark this property out as one to watch in the future.
🖼 red 📆 2005, 2004
★ Colomé Estate Malbec

Michel Torino Bodega La Rosa
Salta

Ruta 68 y 40, Cafayate, Salta ☎ *03868 421139* 🌐 *www.michel torino.com.ar* ⬜ *by appt*

THIS HISTORIC ESTATE was founded in 1892 by brothers David and Salvador Michel. The marriage of David to Gabriela Torino gave the company its name. Recently taken over by the Peñaflor group, an investment programme is transforming the beautiful old winery into a luxury hotel,

while the winery alongside is being revitalized. There are plans to extend the 360ha and develop better training methods including conversion to organic cultivation. Traditionally Torrontés has dominated production, but now Cabernet Sauvignon, Malbec, Merlot, Tempranillo, and Tannat feature significantly. The wines, which include a premium Don David selection and a top wine, Altimus, are steadily improving.
🖼 red, white 📆 2003, 2002, 2001 ★ Altimus, Don David Malbec, Michel Torino Colección Syrah

San Pedro de Yacochuya
Salta

Ruta Provincial 2, km 6, Yacochuya, Cafayate ☎ *03858 421233* 🌐 *www.yacochuya.com* ◉

THIS TINY PROPERTY halfway up a hillside in remote Salta makes a statement for the whole of Argentina. With just 40ha of vines, this venture between Argentinian Arnaldo Etchart and French consultant Michel Rolland shows the faith that these two giants of the wine industry have in Salta, where vast differences between daytime and night-time temperatures bring out complexity and perfume in the grapes. At 2,000m, this is one of Argentina's

highest vineyards, parts of it planted 80 years ago, and it is harvested several weeks after Mendoza. The Malbec-based wine, with a splash of Cabernet Sauvignon, is aged in small barrels for 12 months. The wines are intended to age for at least five years but show intense flavours, rich complexity, and harmony even when young. Just 2ha of Torrontés vines are also planted on the property.
🖼 red, white
📆 2005, 2004, 2003
★ Yacochuya, San Pedro de Yacochuya, San Pedro de Yacochuya Torrontés

Humberto Canale

Humberto Canale
Río Negro

Casilla de Correo 2, Chacra 186 – J J Gómez, General Roca, Pcia ☎ *02941 430415* 🌐 *www.bodega hcanale.com* ⬜ *by appt*

A FAMILY BUSINESS since 1913, this winery is based in the Upper Valley of Río Negro in Patagonia, where cold nights and warm days combine to give the vines individual ripening characteristics. The winery is a glorious mix of old wooden vats and new stainless steel, and the wines demonstrate sheer intensity of fruit and depth of flavour.
🖼 red, white 📆 2006, 2005, 2004
★ Humberto Gran Reserva Malbec, Humberto Canale Estate Merlot

Bodega Colomé's estate in Salta

AUSTRALIA

AUSTRALIA

USTRALIA HAS BECOME THE PIN-UP *of the New World of wine. This is a country that breaks free from the traditions and rules of the Old World. It is technologically innovative, consumer-oriented, internationally competitive, and above all, produces reliably sun-drenched, fruit-driven wines. In 2003, Australia was rated as the world's sixth biggest wine producer and the fourth biggest exporter of wine.*

THE EARLY YEARS

GOVERNOR ARTHUR PHILLIP stepped ashore at Sydney Cove in 1788 and is said to have planted Australia's first grapevine in his garden. Other 18th- and 19th-century pioneers also made their mark but it was an energetic Scot, James Busby, who collected some 543 different vines from Europe (of which 362 survived the voyage) and had them planted in Sydney's Botanic Gardens. Cuttings from these vines were distributed across Australia and provided the basis of the country's wine industry.

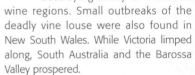

Governor Arthur Phillip

British-born landed gentry who settled in New South Wales, Victoria, and South Australia dominated the early 19th-century wine industry. Key figures with enduring wine names like Lindeman, Wyndham, Penfold, Reynell, and Hardy were soon joined by an influx of European immigrants. Swiss, Germans, and Silesians, including the de Castellas, de Purys, Henschkes, and Gramps, who were attracted to this new land of opportunity. The last half of the 19th century saw tremendous growth in vineyards and the establishment of a strong domestic market as well as a fledgling export trade to Britain. Then disaster arrived in Victoria when phylloxera struck in 1875, and quickly spread across the state. Hundreds of vineyards had to be uprooted and burned, all but destroying many of Victoria's wine regions. Small outbreaks of the deadly vine louse were also found in New South Wales. While Victoria limped along, South Australia and the Barossa Valley prospered.

The young Australian wine industry went through a series of booms and busts based on economic depressions, two world wars, and an on-going battle over protective tariffs between the individual states and bounties involving its biggest market, Britain. With rich soils and plenty of sunshine, red wines and fortifieds flourished, enabling Australia's strong market with Britain to build and grow. By the mid-1960s, although the wines barely resembled those seen today, the industry could be said to have begun its upswing.

Hardy Wine Company vineyard, Adelaide Hills, South Australia

◁ **Wolf Blass vineyard on the eastern slopes of South Australia's Barossa Valley**

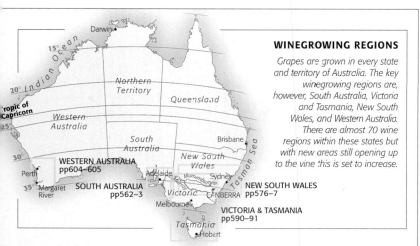

WINEGROWING REGIONS

Grapes are grown in every state and territory of Australia. The key winegrowing regions are, however, South Australia, Victoria and Tasmania, New South Wales, and Western Australia. There are almost 70 wine regions within these states but with new areas still opening up to the vine this is set to increase.

WESTERN AUSTRALIA
pp604–605

SOUTH AUSTRALIA
pp562–3

NEW SOUTH WALES
pp576–7

VICTORIA & TASMANIA
pp590–91

MODERN HISTORY

IN 1966, 78 PER CENT of Australian wine consumption centred on fortifieds. That was also the year Hunter Valley pioneer Max Lake wrote *Classic Wines of Australia*. He argued that the industry's future was not in producing "Olympic size pools of sweet fortifieds" but in greater quantities of quality wines made from proven grape varieties. Lake's analysis was perfect. European immigration following World War II influenced Australian tastes with new wines and foods foreign to their Anglo-Celtic roots. These immigrants were regularly buying wine and demanding just the qualities Lake had advocated. Some, like de Bortoli, Miranda, Sergi and Casella, were even getting into wine production themselves.

By the 1970s, the modern wine industry had been born. It was led by small pioneering producers like Cullen, Cape Mentelle, Pipers Brook, Stonier, and Mount Mary, which explored cooler areas like Margaret River, Tasmania, Mornington Peninsula, and the Yarra Valley. At the top end of the industry some serious rationalization was taking place. The building blocks of future wine empires like Southcorp Wines, Beringer Blass, and Orlando Wyndham were being pieced together through takeovers and mergers. The industry as we know it began to emerge: stainless steel was widely adopted, and new techniques for

controlling fermentation temperatures meant that red wine flavours became fruitier. White wine production became possible even in Australia's hottest regions. The advent of wine boxes and easy to recognize varietally labelled Chardonnay and Cabernet Sauvignon clinched the deal. During the 1980s and 90s, the country's wine industry blossomed until Britain was not the only market taking notice. In quality terms, both its ripe, fruity everyday wines and top-vineyard niche wines had made Australia a global phenomenon.

GEOGRAPHIC INDICATIONS

Introduced in 1994, the Geographic Indications, or GI, system of labelling Australian wines is based on state and regional boundaries. Wines carrying GI definitions must comply with the 85 per cent rule: if a label has a single vintage, region, or variety listed, it must contain 85 per cent of the wine stated. The GI system breaks down as follows: **South Eastern Australia** is the broadest definition and takes in all winegrowing states except Western Australia. **State** obviously refers to wines produced within a state. **Zone** comprises one or more regions. **Region** is an area within a zone that comprises a minimum of five vineyards of at least 5ha without common ownership and producing at least 500 tonnes of fruit. A subregion has the same requirements but falls within a region.

THE WINE INDUSTRY TODAY

THE AUSTRALIAN WINE industry has experienced incredible expansion over the past two decades: 20 years ago, there were only 534 wineries; today there are an incredible 2,299, and the number is rising. Vast areas of countryside have been turned over to the vine. The industry's blueprint for the future – known as Vision 2025 – aims to increase Australia's percentage of the global wine trade. That the Australian winemaker is focused on seducing the world with his wines is beyond question. Wine exports (695 million litres) now exceed domestic sales (449 million litres). The big Australian winemakers like Constellation Wines Australia and Foster's Group have strong US connections, while

View of the Hunter Valley, New South Wales

Orlando Wines is owned by French firm Pernod-Ricard. Medium-size winemakers are also consolidating their position with vineyard expansion and innovative production techniques and marketing. Even the smallest Australian winemaker, with barely

Hand-picking grapes

enough bottles to satisfy local demand, now exports wine.

This growth has led to the exploration of new wine regions like Mount Benson in South Australia (for Shiraz), Orange and Hilltops in New South Wales (for Chardonnay), the Canberra district (for Riesling and Shiraz), and even the cooler, higher altitudes of tropical Queensland (for Chardonnay). Areas that would once have been considered unsuitable for winegrowing are now under vine.

VITICULTURE & VINIFICATION

AUSTRALIAN WINEGROWERS and producers have always embraced change and employed the latest practices to improve wine quality. The emphasis today is on maximizing the use of water for irrigation and eradicating diseases in the most environmentally responsible way. There is also a growing debate about the reliance on machines for pruning and harvesting versus the benefits of performing these operations by hand.

In the winery, there is an increasing emphasis on making wines attractive and drinkable early. Wines are being released younger and younger, and practices like micro-oxygenation (the slow diffusion of tiny bubbles into wine during winemaking) can increase colour and texture, highlight fruitiness, and mimic the effect of barrel maturation. The traditional cross-regional blending practices, so commonplace in the past, are still popular for lower-priced wine. However, at the top end the emphasis is on making a strong regional or single vineyard statement.

Winemakers, too, are divided over old versus new: the adoption of computer-driven, technologically-smart devices in the winery as opposed to the old-fashioned, handmade approach. Concern, and often criticism, regarding high levels of alcohol and oak in Australian wines are also a source of constant debate. The challenge for producers is to prove that they are not only capable of making good, all-rounders but also fine wines.

RED GRAPE VARIETIES & WINE STYLES

AUSTRALIA HAS ONE of the world's largest plantings of Shiraz (or Syrah) with 43,417ha under vine. South Australia's Barossa Valley and McLaren Vale regions produce what is considered the archetypal Australian style, high in sun-ripened flavour and alcohol with generous oak support. In the Hunter Valley (NSW), the grape takes on a more idiosyncratic earthy, sun-baked character. Shiraz's nearest rival is **Chardonnay grapes** Cabernet Sauvignon with 27,909ha planted. It is capable of producing some world-class styles, particularly from Coonawarra and Margaret River, but further expansion of the variety seems to be overshadowed by its regular blending partner, Merlot (10,790ha). More producers are discovering that Merlot can stand by itself, although the style is far from defined as yet. Then there is the spotlight-hogging super-star, Pinot Noir. In a little more than 30 years, Pinot Noir has gone from zero to 4,393ha, securing a high public profile along the way thanks to passionate winemakers in southern Victoria and Tasmania.

WHITE GRAPE VARIETIES & WINE STYLES

WHEN IT COMES TO WHITE wine in Australia, no other grape variety comes close to Chardonnay, with more than 32,000ha under vine. Traditionally, Australian Chardonnay's great strength has been seen in sun-ripened, luscious wines to drink early. Today, the emphasis is also on producing top-class Chardonnays with complexity and ageing ability. Australian Sémillon (6,752ha) and Riesling (4,432ha) have proven their ability to make top-quality wines, too. Classic unwooded Hunter Valley Sémillon is arguably Australia's greatest white wine style; whereas the dynamic Clare and Eden valleys produce some of the country's best Rieslings.

With a Chardonnay- and Shiraz-saturated industry, Australians are looking at other grapes, too. Verdelho and Marsanne provide interesting white alternatives, while the reds Grenache, Mourvèdre (or Mataro), and Petit Verdot are equally at home. Mediter-ranean varieties Tempranillo, Graciano, Sangiovese, Barbera, Cortese, Primitivo (Zinfandel) and Pinot Gris are yet to be fully explored. Even after more than 200 years of winemaking, Australia is still a relative youngster.

View from modern winery restaurant, Yarra Valley, Victoria

AUSTRALIAN PRODUCERS: THE BIG & SMALL OF IT

THE AUSTRALIAN WINE INDUSTRY *is growing at an incredible rate – since 2000, a new wine producer has been set up every 61 hours. The majority are small and family-owned, reflecting a lifestyle move into wine. The growth in the number of small producers highlights another industry phenomenon in Australia: the growing gap between the big and the small.*

THE BIG FIVE

The industry is dominated by five produc-ers *(below)* who see themselves as global corporations with global ambitions. Over the past 20 years they have systematically taken over smaller wine producers, becoming stronger, more efficient wine-making machines. Their national and international success is based on producing well-made, fruit-driven wines of mass appeal at competitive prices, but they also produce quality wines. Between them, the Foster's Group and Constellation Wines Australia account for almost 50 per cent of branded wines sold in Australia.

Foster's Group △
In 2005, the Foster's Group (then owner of Beringer Blass) merged with Australia's biggest wine producer, Southcorp. The latter held some of the world's largest plantings of premium vineyards and super-premium brand Penfolds. Foster's had a good foothold in the US market and a strong range of wines.
Producers: *Seppelt Great Western, Wynn's Coonawarra Estate, Penfolds, Lindemans, Coldstream Hills, Wolf Blass, St Hubert's, Saltram, Mildara Coonawarra* **Brands:** *Koonunga Hill, St Henri, Grange, Leo Buring, Fifth Leg, Yellowglen, Eaglehawk, Annie's Lane, Pepperjack, Robertson's Well*

Casella Wines △
After a decade of spectacular growth fuelled by its Yellow Tail brand, Casella Wines is now one of Australia's largest wine companies both in sales of wine and in wine-grape intake. In 2008, it processed 124,306 tonnes of fruit. Owned by the Casella family, it has its headquarters in the small wine town of Yenda in the Riverina.
Producers: *Casella Wines* **Brands:** *Yellow Tail, Casella Estate, Yendah, Crate 31, Mallee Point*

McGuigan Simeon Wines △
CEO Brian McGuigan and his family are all involved in this publicly listed company. Fast-moving and ambitious, it has plans to be the most efficient wine producer in the world.
Producers: *McGuigan, Tempus Two, Miranda* **Brands:** *Genus 4, Black Label, River Run, Earth's Portrait, High Country, Vine Vale, Hermitage Road, Cowra Crossing, Howcroft Estate, Pewter Label*

Constellation Wines Australia ▽
Originally a joining of two major South Australian companies – Hardy Wines and Berri Renmano Ltd – BRL Hardy merged with US giant Constellation Brands in 2003 to form the world's biggest wine producer. In 2008, it officially became Constellation Wines Australia.
Producers: *Hardy's, Leasingham, Renmano, Houghton, Moondah Brook, Banrock Station, Reynell, Yarra Burn* **Brands:** *Omni, Sir James, Arras, Stonehaven, Tintara, Eileen Hardy*

Orlando Wines ◁
Orlando Wines, owned by French drinks giant Pernod-Ricard, is the face of Australian wine in major markets around the world through its mega-successful Jacob's Creek brand.
Producers: *Wyndham Estate, Richmond Grove, Poet's Corner, Morris* **Brands:** *Jacob's Creek, Triology, Gramps, Jacaranda Ridge, Centenary Hill, Lawson's, RF Range, St Hilary, St Helga, Russet Ridge, Carrington*

SMALL IS BEAUTIFUL

The top 22 big and medium-size Australian wine producers like McWilliam's, Brown Brothers, Tyrrell's, Riverina Estate and Peter Lehmann Wines now control 90 per cent of domestic wine sales. That leaves 2,279 producers fighting it out for the remaining 10 per cent of sales of bottled wine. However, what small Australian winemakers lack in size they more than make up for in other ways. They are the creative heart of the Australian wine industry. Almost every wine region in Australia owes its initial development to small makers willing to sink vines into virgin soil to see what succeeds.

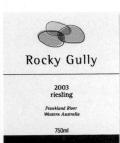

Rocky Gully

2003
riesling

*Frankland River
Western Australia*

750ml

Frankland Estate Riesling

Grosset Wines ▽
Jeffrey Grosset is one of the foremost Riesling makers in Australia. In 2000, he headed a group of his fellow Clare Valley (South Australia) winemakers in bottling Riesling under screwcap, and is now a spokesman for the growing movement away from cork. *See p568.*

Clonakilla ▽
Before it became trendy to blend Shiraz and Viognier in Australia, before Viognier was looked at seriously, and before Canberra was noted for its Riesling, Clonakilla was doing all these things, and doing it with style. Today, Tim Kirk and his father John are rightly viewed as leading exponents of these wines. *See p584.*

Clonakilla

2002
CANBERRA DISTRICT
VIOGNIER

750 ml

pizzini

Sangiovese
— 2002 —

KING VALLEY

This destiny's child has been quietly flourishing in the heart of thrilling Valley. Sanguis Jovis, the Latin root translates as "blood of Jove".

13.5 Alc   PRODUCT OF AUSTRALIA   750 ml

Pizzini △
If the secrets of Italian grape varieties are ever to be fully revealed in Australia, it will be by Fred Pizzini, an Australian-Italian winegrower and maker from the King Valley (Victoria). His quest for authenticity in Nebbiolo and Sangiovese makes for exciting drinking. *See p599.*

Frankland Estate
Western Australia's rating as a serious maker of Riesling has much to do with the success of Judi Cullam and Barrie Smith's Frankland Estate. They hit the jackpot with Riesling in this far-flung vineyard in the state's southwest. The company now sponsors an annual Riesling tasting and travel award. *See p611.*

Yalumba
Behind Yalumba's old establishment image lies a company on the move. There is little that does not attract the interest or study of this most enterprising company. Whether it be Viognier, Riesling, Shiraz, or potentially exciting varieties like Cienna (a cross between Cabernet Sauvignon and the Spanish grape Sumoll), Tempranillo, Petit Verdot, and Marsanne, they are all sold under the Vinno-vation label. *See p570.*

Giaconda Vineyard
Beechworth-based Rick Kinzbrunner is one of the most influential winemakers in Australia today. His Chardonnay is the standard by which other makers judge their own. He is noted for his commitment and passion, and there are few varieties he cannot convert into something special. *See p598.*

Yalumba's Pewsey Vale vineyard, Eden Valley, South Australia

SOUTH AUSTRALIA

WINE IS BIG BUSINESS *in South Australia. Many of the Australian industry's key players are headquartered in this hilly state, where flat valley floors rise to beautifully terraced vineyard vistas. A great number of these major wine brands have built their reputation on the high quality of South Australian grapes.*

South Australia's Barossa Valley was the beating heart of the early Australian wine industry. In the mid-1800s this area was settled by industrious immigrants who built impressive wine empires, many of which still stand today. By 1903, Barossa was home to the biggest producer in South Australia, Seppelt, and the valley was responsible for more than half of the state's total wine crush. However, McLaren Vale has always been a rival to Barossa. The area's early history was dominated by three men: John Reynell, Dr Alexander Kelly, and Thomas Hardy, whose company Thomas Hardy & Sons grew into the Australian giant Hardy Wine Company, largely through trade with Britain.

Finding your bearings in the world of wine

In fact, the British taste for strong, sweet fortified wines and equally strong, heavy reds kept the South Australian wine economy ticking along for almost 100 years. By the 1950s, clever winemaking and a series of smart investments were to cement the state's wine dominance. The introduction of German stainless steel fermentation tanks by Orlando Wines in 1953 brought a fresh aromatic quality to Barossa white wines, notably Riesling. In 1956, Orlando launched Barossa Pearl, Australia's first naturally fermented sparkling wine.

Today, big names dominate South Australia's winescape. These include the Foster's Group, which is a consolidation of old-time South Australian wine companies such as Penfolds and Leo Buring along with relative new chums like Wolf Blass, Annie's Lane, Jamiesons Run, and Maglieri. Orlando Wines and Constellation Wines Australia also still call South Australia home.

Over the years, these brands, and the many copies that followed, introduced millions of Australians and – from the 1970s onwards – international wine drinkers – to South Australian wine.

Yalumba's Heggies vineyard, Eden Valley

◁ **Cool-climate vineyards in the Adelaide Hills**

WINE MAP OF SOUTH AUSTRALIA

Sрефreshing maritime to warm Mediterranean and hot
OUTH AUSTRALIA has a range of climates, from
desert. South Australia's hotter regions are naturally
suited to ripening red grapes, notably Shiraz. So much
so that 53 per cent of Australia's reds are produced
here, and Shiraz is the speciality of the Barossa Valley,
McLaren Vale, and Clare Valley. Riesling, too, is top-class
from Clare, Eden, and Barossa. Coonawarra, on the other
hand, is the long-time home of some of Australia's finest
Cabernet Sauvignon. The Riverland area – Australia's
biggest single wine-producing region – can grow
anything the industry requires thanks to irrigation.
Meanwhile, the cool Adelaide Hills area is the state's
leading Sauvignon Blanc and Pinot Noir producer.

KEY

South Australia

SOUTH AUSTRALIA: AREAS & TOP PRODUCERS

CLARE VALLEY *p564*
Grosset Wines *p568*
Jim Barry Wines *p568*
Wendouree Cellars *p568*

RIVERLAND *p564*
Banrock Station *p568*

BAROSSA VALLEY *p565*
Orlando Wyndham *p568*
Penfolds *p571*
Peter Lehmann Wines *p569*
Seppelt Winery *p569*
Wolf Blass Winery *p569*
Yalumba *p570*

EDEN VALLEY *p565*
Henschke Wines *p570*
Mountadam Vineyards *p570*

ADELAIDE HILLS *p566*
Petaluma Limited *p570*
Shaw & Smith *p572*

MCLAREN VALE *p566*
Clarendon Hills *p572*
Constellation Wines Australia *p572*
Coriole *p573*
D'Arenberg *p573*

LANGHORNE CREEK *p566*
Casa Freschi *p573*

**Label from Peter Lehmann
Wines, Barossa Valley**

MOUNT BENSON *p567*

PADTHAWAY *p567*

WRATTONBULLY *p567*

COONAWARRA *p567*
Bowen Estate *p573*
Wynns Coonawarra Estate
  Winery *p573*

View of Barossa Valley vineyards

Kangaroos among the vines, Padthaway

TERROIR AT A GLANCE

Latitude: 33.5–37.5°S.

Altitude: 20–500m.

Topography: Expanses of flat terrain in Riverland. Mount Lofty Ranges and adjoining Adelaide Hills provide higher and cooler conditions for winegrowing.

Soil: Free-draining limestone and sandy soils, with a constant table of pure water 2m below.

Climate: Varies greatly, but generally intensely hot and dry. Cooler temperatures near the coast and in the hilly areas.

Temperature: January average 18°C.

Rainfall: Annual average 51.5mm. In the north the Murray River provides irrigation; in the south vines are irrigated by pipeline from Lake Alexandrina.

Wind: Cooling maritime breezes from Gulf St Vincent provide relief for McLaren Vale, and can travel as far inland as Clare Valley.

Viticultural hazards: High winds; spring frosts.

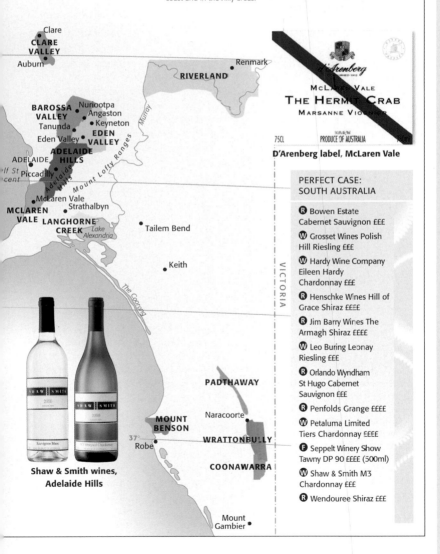

D'Arenberg label, McLaren Vale

Shaw & Smith wines, Adelaide Hills

PERFECT CASE: SOUTH AUSTRALIA

Ⓡ Bowen Estate Cabernet Sauvignon £££

Ⓦ Grosset Wines Polish Hill Riesling £££

Ⓦ Hardy Wine Company Eileen Hardy Chardonnay £££

Ⓡ Henschke Wines Hill of Grace Shiraz ££££

Ⓡ Jim Barry Wines The Armagh Shiraz ££££

Ⓦ Leo Buring Leonay Riesling £££

Ⓡ Orlando Wyndham St Hugo Cabernet Sauvignon £££

Ⓡ Penfolds Grange ££££

Ⓦ Petaluma Limited Tiers Chardonnay ££££

Ⓕ Seppelt Winery Show Tawny DP 90 ££££ (500ml)

Ⓦ Shaw & Smith M3 Chardonnay £££

Ⓡ Wendouree Shiraz £££

Vineyards in the scenic Clare Valley region

WINEGROWING AREAS OF SOUTH AUSTRALIA

Clare Valley

CLARE VALLEY IS MANY THINGS to many drinkers. It is the source of some of Australia's finest and zestiest Riesling. Its honeyed Sémillon has long been admired, while enthusiasts of hearty red wine have traditionally looked to the valley for succulent but firm Cabernet Sauvignon and gentle, spicy Shiraz. The contrast between the delicacy of its whites and the sheer opulence of its reds could not be any greater: a reflection of the variety of sub-climates. While the region is warm, there are cooling factors like southwesterly sea breezes (all the way from Gulf St Vincent) and the higher altitudes of individual vineyards, with some subregions climbing to 550m. Winegrowing in the Clare Valley started early: Mount Horrocks Wines

THE BEST RIESLING?

Clare and Eden valleys both have a strong history of making quality Riesling. Clare Valley Riesling is resoundingly mineral with citrus and lime aromas and bracing acidity. That acidity brings an austere, taut line and length, which is Clare Riesling's signature trait. In Eden Valley, the grape has generous floral, citrus, and (in some years) even ripe tropical fruit overtones. Elegance is Eden Valley Riesling's main attribute. Most makers keep wines from the two valleys separate, but others, like Wendy Stuckey, chief white winemaker at Wolf Blass *(see p569)*, has proven they go well together, getting the best of both worlds in her top-selling Gold Medal label.

commemorates the first settler, John Horrocks, who planted vines here in 1840. But the golden age of the Clare Valley was in the 1890s with the creation of companies like Wendouree and Stanley (now part of the Hardy Wine Company). *red to brown-grey soils with limestone* *Cabernet Sauvignon, Shiraz, Grenache* *Riesling, Chardonnay, Sémillon* *red, white, fortified*

Riverland

THE 'RIVER' IN RIVERLAND is the mighty Murray, which stretches right across South Australia and Victoria, bringing life to this hot, arid region. Irrigation from the river sustains 21,947ha of vineyards, producing an amazing 401,300 tonnes of wine grapes annually, and making Riverland Australia's biggest wine producing region. Every major Australian wine producer sources fruit from this area, and one, Constellation Wines Australia, even has its roots here. It is a major presence in the Riverland, with a 500-strong grower base. The combination of sun, available water, and large-scale winegrowing brings the kind of economies of scale that big companies appreciate, enabling them to deliver generous fruit-filled wines in the lower price range. In a strong line-up of wines led by ripe, sunny Chardonnay, a most promising newcomer is spicy Petit Verdot. This red grape, noted for its marked acidity, retains firmness and structure in the Riverland heat. *red-brown sandy loam over limestone* *Shiraz, Mourvèdre, Grenache, Petit Verdot* *Chardonnay, Colombard* *red, white, sparkling*

Barossa Valley

THE BAROSSA IS THE HEARTLAND of the Australian wine industry. Many companies that today stride the world wine stage originated here: Penfolds, Orlando, Wolf Blass, Henschke, Seppelt, Yalumba. A lot of these were started by a colourful mix of early settlers in the mid-1800s: some British landowning gentry and a number of German and Silesian Lutherans fleeing religious intolerance in Prussia. All were from wine drinking cultures, so wine-growing was naturally adopted as part of general farming here. By the 1870s many of these original vineyards were well established, and came to dominate not only the region, but Australian winemaking as a whole. Exports of solid, dry reds and heavy fortifieds to England helped build Barossa Valley into a major winemaking force. However, as tastes began to change from red to white wines after World War II, the Barossa changed too. Refrigeration, the first German pressure fermentation tank, imported by Orlando in 1953, and stainless steel tanks helped transform this warm region's white wines into crisp, fruity styles. Throughout its history, however, Barossa Valley has always excelled at one grape: Shiraz. It achieves levels of power and fruit intensity here that are unmatched elsewhere in Australia, and possibly the world. And it is the cornerstone of Australia's greatest red, Penfolds Grange, first made in 1951.

🏞 brown, loamy sand, grey-brown sand 🍇 Shiraz, Cabernet Sauvignon, Grenache 🍷 Riesling, Chardonnay, Sémillon 🍾 red, white, sparkling, fortified

Eden Valley

ALSO KNOWN (confusingly) as the Barossa Ranges, Eden Valley is the cooler, hillier extension of the Barossa Valley. Its history is closely aligned with that of the Barossa, with British and German settlers planting vineyards here between the 1840s and 1860s. From that time, two producers have come to dominate Eden Valley: Yalumba and Henschke wines. Yalumba was founded by Samuel Smith at Angaston in 1849, and Johann Henschke planted vines near Keyneton in 1862. Both companies, and others since, have found that the relatively warmer northern areas of Angaston, Moculta, and

HENSCHKE HILL OF GRACE

In a quiet area of the Eden Valley is an 8-ha vineyard of gnarled Shiraz vines planted in the 1860s. Around 1960 Cyril Henschke decided to make a special wine from these grapes for the emerging restaurant scene. He called it Hill of Grace, and half a century later it represents one of the great, enduring Australian reds. An important part of its success is the vineyard: the vines are dry-grown in sandy and clay loams, sinking their roots

deep into ironstone and quartz gravels, giving the wine an extraordinary depth of flavour. Yields are low, so a typical Hill of Grace is intensely concentrated, with black-berry and violet aromas. It also has silky tannins, and contains liquorice, choco-late, and savoury flavours highlighted by American oak. The wine ages very well: the 1962 vintage was still going strong at the 40th anniversary tasting in 1998.

Keyneton bring out the best in Shiraz. While as full-bodied as Barossa Shiraz, wines like the silky Henschke Hill of Grace show a finer structure. Meanwhile, in the cooler, higher southern areas (up to 550m) around the towns of Eden Valley and Springton grow some of the best Riesling in Australia. Highly floral and citrussy, Eden Valley Riesling ages beautifully over a decade into a toasty, golden wine.

🏞 sandy, clay loams with subsoils of ironstone and quartz gravels 🍇 Shiraz, Cabernet Sauvignon, Pinot Noir 🍷 Riesling, Chardonnay, Sémillon 🍾 red, white

Barrels at Yalumba winery, Barossa Valley

Adelaide Hills

TURN BACK the clock to the 1970s and Adelaide Hills was filled with fruit orchards. The region had experienced its great wine boom in the 1870s and had moved on due to the public's growing taste for fortified wines, which this cool area could not deliver. But when cool-climate viticulture was being explored in the 1970s, the Hills took off again. The biggest name to drive the change was Brian Croser, the former Thomas Hardy winemaker. He chose pretty Piccadilly to set up his Petaluma wine operation. The 100 per cent Adelaide Hills Chardonnays he has made from 1990 onwards have been among the best in Australia. During the 1990s, go-getter cousins Martin Shaw and Michael Hill-Smith (Shaw & Smith) also showed the area's potential for creating stunning Sauvignon Blanc. The high hills, up to 730m, also produce a soft, elegant, berry-rich Pinot Noir.

grey-brown loamy sands, clay loams **Pinot Noir, Cabernet Sauvignon, Shiraz** *Chardonnay, Sauvignon Blanc, Sémillon* **red, white, sparkling**

McLaren Vale

THE MCLAREN VALE made its name producing wine. Walk down the busy main street of McLaren Vale, the town that gives its name to the region, and next to the pub is one of the great wineries of Australia – Tintara – made famous by Thomas Hardy. Hardy, an Englishman, founded the firm that is now known as the Hardy Wine Company. The region is on the outer suburban fringes of Adelaide, rimmed by Gulf St Vincent to the west and the Mount Lofty Ranges to the east. The former cools this warm grape-growing region, while the latter offers higher altitudes (up to 350m), which are increasingly being explored. The main varieties here are sun-drenched Chardonnay and big, bold Shiraz. Well-rounded Cabernets and crisp, medium-bodied Riesling and Sauvignon Blanc can also be found.

red-brown loamy sands **Shiraz, Cabernet Sauvignon, Grenache** *Chardonnay, Sémillon, Riesling* **red, white, sparkling, dessert, fortified**

Langhorne Creek

LANGHORNE CREEK always seems to take a back seat in Australian winemaking. Major wine companies source its soft, well-rounded, earthy Cabernet Sauvignon and Shiraz, among other varieties, for top-selling wines like Penfolds Bin 389 Cabernet Shiraz and Wolf Blass Black Label Cabernet Sauvignon, but rarely as stand-alone styles. Its great asset – as a blending tool – is also its greatest drawback in terms of better recognition. Three of the country's major producers have vineyards here (the Foster's Group, Orlando Wines, and Constellation Wines Australia), but it is the small local wineries that have developed the real Langhorne Creek style. The Potts family of Bleasdale Vineyards are the keepers of the regional flame and have made wine – Shiraz and Verdelho – here since the 1850s. In fact, these two varieties, along with Cabernet, are the real strength of the region today.

deep, alluvial sand loams **Cabernet Sauvignon, Shiraz, Merlot** *Chardonnay, Verdelho, Riesling* **red, white**

D'Arenberg's winery in McLaren Vale

Coonawarra's famous *terra rossa* soils

Mount Benson

THIS FAST-DEVELOPING REGION came to prominence after Rhône winemaker M Chapoutier (*see p132*) planted a vineyard here in 1998, indicat-ing a potential future for Shiraz and Rhône styles. Most big Australian companies now buy in grapes from here.

🗓 sandy clay to clay loams over limestone and siliceous sands 🟪 Shiraz, Cabernet Sauvignon, Merlot 🟩 Chardonnay, Sauvignon Blanc, Sémillon 🟥 red, white

Padthaway

PADTHAWAY originally attracted the attention of wine firms in the 1960s as a cheaper source of grapes than Coonawarra. It has taken time for the area to achieve recognition in its own right. The establishment of Constellation Wines' Stonehaven Winery in the 1990s finally gave Padthaway the acknowledgement it deserves.

🗓 loamy sand soils with isolated limestone 🟪 Shiraz, Cabernet Sauvignon, Merlot, Pinot Noir 🟩 Chardonnay, Riesling, Sémillon 🟥 red, white

Wrattonbully

BORDERING COONAWARRA, this area has traditionally grown elegant Shiraz and Cabernet Sauvignon, which was sometimes bottled as Coonawarra. It is now a completely separate area under the Geographical Indications system (*see p555*).

🗓 sandy clay to clay loams over limestone 🟪 Cabernet Sauvignon, Shiraz, Merlot 🟩 Chardonnay, Sauvignon Blanc, Sémillon 🟥 red, white

Coonawarra

COONAWARRA IS RED: the wines are mainly red and the soil is a dazzling red-brick hue. Known simply as *terra rossa,* it is this soil that is behind Coonawarra's claim as Australia's greatest red wine region. The *terra rossa* strip – 15km long and varying in width from 200m to 1.5km – is likened to a cigar in shape. This 'cigar' is topped with a thin layer of well-draining, rich red soil, and beneath it lies soft limestone, allowing the vines to reach underground water reserves. The region is classified as cool (hard to believe during summer), with a long ripening period. This gives Cabernet Sauvignon a firm tannic quality, making it excellent for ageing. The style is concentrated, firm, and the most Bordeaux-like of all Australian Cabernet, although often with an distinct touch of mint. There is an impressive array of names, est-ablished from the 1950s onwards, who excel with the variety: Wynn's, Bowen, Hollick, Lindemans, Jamiesons Run, Majella, Brand's, and Katnook. It is hard for other varieties to make a showing here, but the region does make highly underrated earthy Shiraz and floral, easy-drinking Riesling.

🗓 red soil and black clays over limestone 🟪 Cabernet Sauvignon, Shiraz, Pinot Noir 🟩 Chardonnay, Riesling, Sauvignon Blanc 🟥 red, white

THE COONAWARRA BOUNDARY DISPUTE

The long-running dispute to define the official boundary of Coonawarra – a pre-eminent Cabernet Sauvignon region – began in 1984. It focused on a cigar-shaped area of rich, red soils known as *terra rossa*. As the famous 'cigar' became planted out, makers moved into adjoining soils where small pockets of *terra rossa* could be found. Over time, these producers considered the wines here to be comparable with those from the 'cigar'. This was the basis for the great boundary battle. A 1999 court decision saw 46 producers, including Petaluma and Beringer Blass (as was), fall outside the boundary. They appealed. In 2001, a tribunal allowed 24 of the makers back in, including Petaluma. After a further appeal in 2002, the Federal Court let five more growers in (including Beringer Blass, now part of the Foster's Group).

TOP PRODUCERS IN SOUTH AUSTRALIA

Grosset Wines
Clare Valley

Stanley St, Auburn 🔌 08 8849 2175
🌐 www.grosset.com.au ⭕

JEFFREY GROSSET'S approach to winemaking is all about attention to detail. And never more so than when artfully blending batches of Riesling. His Polish Hill (tight and minerally) and Watervale (citrus and aromatic) Rieslings are at the top of the Australian tree for this German grape. He has also ventured into new territory with a Piccadilly Chardonnay from the Adelaide Hills and a complex Clare Valley Cabernet Sauvignon blend called Gaia.
🍷 red, white 🍇 2006 (r), 2005, 2003 (w), 2002, 1998 (r) ★ Polish Hill Riesling, Watervale Riesling, Gaia

Jim Barry Wines
Clare Valley

Craigs Hill Rd, Clare
🔌 08 8842 2261 ⭕

THE BARRY BOYS – Jim and Brian, and their respective wine businesses – are institutions in Clare Valley. Jim Barry Wines is the better known, largely through the international success of its powerful The Armagh Shiraz, from the vineyard of the same name, which was planted by Jim himself in 1968. It is a shame that demand for this explosive wine has placed it out of reach for most. However, stepping in to fill the breach is the McRae Wood Shiraz, strong in blackberry fruits with a touch of mintiness, as well as the approachable McRae Wood Cabernet Sauvignon. But Jim

Jeffrey Grosset, winemaker at Grosset Wines

Barry does not excel only at reds: the fragrant Jim Barry Watervale Riesling is a fantastic bargain.
🍷 red, white 🍇 2006, 2005 (w), 2002, 2001 (w), 2000, 1999, 1998, 1996, 1995, 1994 (w), 1993, 1992, 1991, 1990 ★ Watervale Riesling, The Armagh Shiraz, McRae Wood Shiraz

Wendouree Cellars
Clare Valley

Wendouree Rd, Clare
🔌 08 88422896 ⭕

TONY BRADY TOOK over this 19th-century vineyard in the 1970s. A rarity in today's fast-moving Australian wine industry, Brady seeks no publicity, yet his wines sell out regardless; a fact that reflects their quality. He fashions extraordinarily powerful Shiraz and complex Cabernet Sauvignon (and assorted blends) around vice-like tannic structures that require time in the cellar.
🍷 red, fortified 🍇 2005, 2004, 2002, 1998 ★ Shiraz, Cabernet Sauvignon, Cabernet Sauvignon-Malbec

Jim Barry Wines

Banrock Station
Riverland

Holmes Rd, Kingston on Murray
🔌 08 8583 0299
🌐 www.banrockstation.com.au ⭕

OVERLOOKING THE Murray River, Banrock is a wine and wetland centre – an initiative of the Hardy Wine Company (now Constellation Wines Australia), which bought the 18,000-ha property in 1994. It produces a consumer-friendly range of boxed and bottled wine, and a higher-priced reserve range. The stars are the reds: Shiraz, Merlot, and Petit Verdot. But best of all is a lively sparkling Shiraz that belies its moderate price with great depth of flavour.
🍷 red, white, sparkling 🍇 2007, 2006, 2004, 2001, 2000, 1998 ★ Sparkling Shiraz, Cave Cliff Merlot, Ball Island Shiraz

Orlando Wyndham
Barossa Valley

Barossa Valley Way, Rowland Flat
🔌 08 8521 3000
🌐 www.orlandowines.com ⭕

THE CREEK that has flooded international wine markets – Orlando Jacob's Creek wines – began life here. In 1976, the first Jacob's Creek Shiraz-Cabernet Sauvignon was revolutionary: a fruit-driven, early drinking, good-value red. Today, there are nine standard and four reserve members of the Jacob's Creek family, representing some 5.3 million cases of wine annually. The brand and its maker outgrew the Barossa Valley a long time ago, but their roots still lie here.

The Orlando Wines range now spreads across a number of regions: the austere Steingarten Riesling and the more subtle and

Label from Peter Lehmann Wines, Barossa Valley

citrussy St Helga Riesling from Eden Valley; Padthaway's tropical St Hilary Chardonnay; plus the aristocratic, oaky Jacaranda Ridge Cabernet Sauvignon and the well-rounded St Hugo Cabernet Sauvignon from Coonawarra. These contrast well with the warm single-vineyard Centenary Hill Shiraz from the Barossa homeland.

🍷 *red, white, sparkling, dessert, fortified* 📋 *2006, 2005 (w), 2004 (w), 2002 (w), 2001 (w), 2000, 1998, 1997, 1996, 1995 (w), 1994, 1992, 1990* ★ *Centenary Hill Shiraz, St Hugo Cabernet Sauvignon, Steingarten Riesling*

Penfolds
Barossa Valley

See p571.

Peter Lehmann Wines
Barossa Valley

Off Para Rd, Tanunda 🕿 *08 8563 2500* 🖳 *www.peterlehmannwines. com.au* ⬜

BIG, WARM, HOSPITABLE Peter Lehmann is a Barossa wine legend, although sons Doug and Philip and winemakers Andrew Wigan, Ian Hongell, and Kerry Morrison now run the business. The company specializes in traditional Barossa styles, and they don't come any bigger than Peter Lehmann Shiraz, with its full fruit flavours and oak punch. Then there is the deep, seductive Black Queen sparkling Shiraz, and the

long-lived Stonewell Shiraz. The most heavenly exotic flavours, however, are found in the gorgeous Eight Songs Shiraz. In addition, there is a Vintage 'port', again predominantly Shiraz. Lehmann's subtle, aromatic Riesling and lemony Sémillon show, in contrast, great subtlety.

🍷 *red, white, sparkling, dessert, fortified* 📋 *2006, 2005 (w), 2004, 2002, 2001 (w), 1998, 1997 (w), 1996 (r), 1994, 1993 (w), 1991 (r), 1990 (r)* ★ *Black Queen Sparkling Shiraz, Blue Eden Riesling, Eight Songs Shiraz*

Seppelt Winery
Barossa Valley

PMB 1 Seppeltsfield via Nuriootpa 🕿 *08 8568 6217* 🖳 *www.seppelt.com.au* ⬜

SEPPELTSFIELD IS WHERE German businessman Joseph Seppelt laid the foundations for his mighty empire in 1867, building a grand wine estate which grew and grew. By the 1970s, Seppelt was making sparkling, still, and fortified wines across three states. The Seppelt family maintained control of the company until 1984, when it merged with South Australia Brewing, which in turn morphed into Southcorp and finally the Foster's Group. In 2006, Foster's put the Seppeltsfield showpiece Barossa winery on the market. A group, led by Kilikanoon Wines, bought the winery and stocks, leasing the vineyard back to Foster's.

Seppelt's fortifieds are legendary, led by the annual release of a 100-year-old liqueur tawny priced at around AUS$3,000 a bottle. Its first release was an 1878 wine in 1978. Top billing is shared by an extraordinary trio: a super-tangy Show Fino; an elegant, nutty Show Tawny; and a dry, complex Show Amontillado.

🍷 *red, white, sparkling, fortified* 📋 *2006, 2005, 2004, 2001, 1998 ('ports')* ★ *Show Fino DP 117, Show Amontillado DP 116, Show Tawny DP 90*

Wolf Blass Winery
Barossa Valley

97 Sturt Hwy, Nuriootpa 🕿 *08 8568 7300* 🖳 *www.wolfblass.com.au* ⬜

GERMAN-BORN winemaker Wolf Blass is a brash but endearing self-promoter. One of his renowned quotes is: "My wines make weak men strong and strong women weak". The winemaker, who migrated to Australia in 1961, brought a touch of chutzpah to winemaking, and it has rewarded him with a hugely successful wine business built around an old army shed-cum-winery at Nuriootpa in the Barossa. Today, that same shed site houses a AUS$30 million super-winery, which is an integral part of the Foster's Group empire. In 1991, Wolf Blass sold his company to Mildara Wines (now part of Foster's). The core of Wolf Blass wines today remains the same as ever: a highly approachable range of striking Rieslings and strong, oak-driven Shiraz and Cabernet Sauvignon.

🍷 *red, white, sparkling, dessert, fortified* 📋 *2006, 2005 (w), 2004 (r), 2002 (w), 2001 (w), 1999 (r), 1998 (r), 1997 (r), 1996, 1995 (r), 1993 (w), 1992 (w), 1991 (r), 1990* ★ *Platinum Label: Barossa Cabernet Sauvignon, Barossa Shiraz, Gold Label Riesling*

Yalumba
Barossa Valley

Eden Valley Rd, Angaston 📞 *08 8561 3200* 🌐 *www.yalumba.com* ⬜

SAMUEL SMITH, an Englishman, founded Yalumba (Aboriginal for 'all the country around') in 1849. Today, his great-great-grandson Robert heads the innovative company, which has sustained incredible growth through the family purse alone. With its warm and friendly style, Barossa Shiraz is the headliner red. The Eden Valley is home to Yalumba's Pewsey Vale and Heggies vineyards, which produce strong Riesling and Viognier respectively. The Pewsey Vale Riesling has delicate, citrussy notes, while the Viognier comes in many guises, from the drink-now Heggies Vineyard Viognier to the opulent, ginger-spiced The Virgilius.

🍷 *red, white, sparkling, dessert, fortified* 📅 *2006, 2005 (r), 2004, 2002 (w), 2001 (w), 2000 (w), 1999 (w), 1998, 1996, 1995, 1993, 1992, 1991* ★ *Barossa Shiraz-Viognier, The Virgilius Viognier, Pewsey Vale Riesling*

Henschke Wines
Eden Valley

Henschke Rd, Keyneton 📞 *08 8564 8223* 🌐 *www.henschke.com.au* ⬜

STEPHEN AND PRUE HENSCHKE make a formidable team: Stephen is a winemaker who treasures the 19th-century vineyard he has inherited from the Henschke generations before him; and Prue, his wife, is a viticulturist with an excellent understanding of the winemaking process. When they took over here in 1980, they set out to make their own mark by improving trellising in the vineyards, and opening up the vines to sunlight. The fruit intensity achieved since then, coupled

Label from Petaluma Limited

with the complexity that comes from low-yielding old vines, has resulted in red wines of great finesse. The richly concentrated Hill of Grace flagship *(see p565)*, developed by Stephen's father, Cyril, is followed by the fleshy Mount Edelstone Shiraz and the elegant Cyril Henschke Cabernet Sauvignon.

🍷 *red, white* 📅 *2006, 2005 (w), 2004, 2002 (w), 2001 (w), 1999 (r), 1998, 1997 (w), 1996 (r), 1995 (w), 1994, 1993, 1992, 1991 (r)* ★ *Hill of Grace Shiraz, Mount Edelstone Shiraz, Cyril Henschke Cabernet Sauvignon*

Mountadam Vineyards
Eden Valley

High Eden Rd, Eden Valley 📞 *08 85 64 1900* 🌐 *www.mountadam.com.au* ⬜

FOUNDED IN 1972 by the late David Wynn and his son, Adam, Mountadam was always going to be different. David was the man responsible for the development of the first commercial wine cask or bag-in-a-box in Australia, and was also behind Wynn's Coona-warra Estate. He and his son were among the first to promote unwooded Chardon-nay in Australia, as well as an unwooded Shiraz. In 2000, Adam accepted a takeover bid by LVMH, but by 2005 it was sold again, this time to Adelaide businessman David Brown, who brought in former Petaluma winemaker Con Moshos to revive its ailing

wine portfolio. Moshos has rejuvenated Riesling, created a fresher, leaner style of Chardonnay, and worked to reprise the flagship red, The Red (a blend of Merlot and Cabernet Sauvignon), Shiraz, and Cabernet Franc.

🍷 *red, white, sparkling, dessert* 📅 *2007 (w), 2006, 2005 (w), 2001, 1998, 1997, 1996 (r), 1994, 1993, 1992 (w), 1991, 1990* ★ *Eden Valley Riesling, Chardonnay, The Red*

Petaluma Limited
Adelaide Hills

Spring Gully Rd, Piccadilly 📞 *08 8339 9300* 🌐 *www.petaluma.com.au* ⬜

FOR NIGH ON THREE DECADES, Petaluma and Brian Croser were one and the same. In 1976 the charismatic Croser, a former Hardy winemaker, went it alone and set up Petaluma, aspiring to create the best wines from prime locations. He sourced pristine Riesling from the Clare Valley, and elegant Cabernet Sauvignon from Coonawarra, which is used in a red blend named after the area. He made his HQ at Bridgewater in the then little-known Adelaide Hills and planted Chardonnay in the nearby Piccadilly Valley. Within a decade, these three varieties were Australian benchmarks, reflecting what to many Australian drinkers was a new concept: *terroir* – or as Croser noted, "distinguished vineyard sites". In 2001 brewer Lion Nathan bought Petaluma and retained Croser as its chief winemaker until he retired to concentrate on his family vineyard Tappa-nappa in the Adelaide Hills.

🍷 *red, white, sparkling, dessert* 📅 *2006 (w), 2005 (w), 2004, 2003, 2002, 2001 (w), 2000, 1999, 1998, 1997, 1996* ★ *Hanlin Hill Riesling, Tiers Chardonnay, Coonawarra*

THE PENFOLDS SUCCESS STORY

No other wine company in the world can match Penfolds for the sheer quality and variety of wines across all price categories – from the AUS$10 Rawson's Retreat to the AUS$400 bottle of Grange. As part of Australia's biggest winemaker, Southcorp, Penfolds has an unequalled range of vineyard and winemaking resources at its disposal. Thousands of hectares of vines across all states are accessed; although South Australia remains its base.

Dr Christopher Rawson Penfold arrived at Magill near Adelaide in 1844 and planted vines, mostly Grenache. Palomino, Muscat, and Frontignac were also grown around the Penfold family's cottage, 'The Grange'. Dr Penfold believed in the medicinal value of wine and used it as a tonic for his patients. After his death, generations of the family continued his work in the vineyard, cementing a Penfolds winemaking tradition. In 1911, a winery was built in the Barossa Valley, which became Penfolds HQ in partnership with the original Magill winery.

Winemakers

Continuity of the Penfolds style has been maintained by the fact that since Max Schubert – the creator of the Grange wine range – was at the helm in the 1950s, there have been only been four chief winemakers. The latest, Peter Gago *(left)*, is keenly aware that the market expects Penfolds' traditions to be maintained.

Contact Information

Tanunda Rd, Nuriootpa
☎ 08 8568 9408
W *www.penfolds.com.au* ○

Wine Information

🍷 *red, white, fortified* ☒ *1998 1996, 1994, 1992, 1991, 1990*
★ *Penfolds Grange, Bin 707 Cabernet Sauvignon, Yattarna Chardonnay, Bin 389 Cabernet Sauvignon-Shiraz*

Penfolds Wine

While multi-regional blending has brought consistency to the wines, the heart and soul of almost all of them remains the Barossa Valley. As such, the Penfolds style could never be described as shy and retiring. It is ripe, rich, sweet fruit, often oak influenced, with rounded tannic structure. At the heart of the Penfolds brand is a strong range of individual styles. There is the peppery Bin 128 Shiraz and the ripe, full-flavoured Bin 389 Cabernet-Shiraz, but Bin 707 Cabernet Sauvignon is most elegant. St Henri Shiraz-Cabernet is the alter-ego to Penfolds' majestic Grange, a Shiraz of monumental power.

Dr Penfold's first vineyard at Magill, Adelaide in 1958

Shaw & Smith
Adelaide Hills

Lot 4, Jones Rd, Balhannah
📞 *08 8398 0500*
🌐 *www.shawandsmith.com* ⬜

MICHAEL HILL-SMITH was Australia's first Master of Wine, and his cousin Martin Shaw was one of Australia's first flying winemakers. They came together in 1989 to create Shaw & Smith, firing winelovers' imaginations with a bright and tropical Sauvignon Blanc. The crusading duo then went on to cement the Adelaide Hills' reputation as a serious Chardonnay region – first with an appley unwooded version and then with a wooded style generous in stone fruits. In 2001, they came out with a noticeably lean and citrous Chardonnay, M3 Vineyard.
🟥 *red, white* ▶ *2006 (w), 2005, 2004, 2003, 2002, 2001, 2000, 1999, 1997, 1995* ★ *Sauvignon Blanc, M3 Vineyard Chardonnay, Merlot*

Clarendon Hills
McLaren Vale

Brookmans Rd, Blewitt Springs
📞 *08 8364 1484* 🌐 *www.clarendon hills.com.au* ⬜ *by appt*

THE WINES of Clarendon Hills are among the biggest and most concentrated reds Australia can offer. These goliaths – mostly Shiraz, Cabernet Sauvignon, and Grenache – are the creation

Michael Hill-Smith and Martin Shaw of Shaw & Smith

of media-shy winemaker Roman Bratasiuk. He sources old vine, low-yielding grapes from the subregions of McLaren Vale. This has spawned a growing range headed by the super-rich Astralis Shiraz, which now enjoys cult status with collectors. As it heads out of most people's price range there are other reds filling the gap, notably the lovely Liandra Shiraz and the rustic Roma's Vineyard Old Vine Grenache.
🟥 *red, white* ▶ *2006, 2004, 2003 (r), 2002 (r), 2001 (r), 2000 (w)* ★ *Astralis Shiraz, Liandra Shiraz, Roma's Vineyard Old Vine Grenache*

Constellation Wines Australia
McLaren Vale

Reynell Rd, Reynella 📞 *08 8392 2222* 🌐 *www.cwines.com.au* ⬜

IN 2003, BRL Hardy signed a multi-billion-dollar merger with US wine company Constellation Brands to form the biggest wine business in the world – Hardy Wine Company. This was a far cry from 1992, when one of Australia's great family-run wine empires, Thomas Hardy & Sons, was in serious financial trouble and was taken over by Berri Renmano.

The road back to the top started with buying prestigious producers in desirable areas: Yarra Burn (Yarra Valley); Brookland Valley (Margaret River); Nobilo (New Zealand). The purchase of Banrock Station in the Riverland fuelled spectacular growth in the wine box and quaffing markets. Add in a sprucing up of old-time brands Houghton, Leasingham, and Château Reynella, and Constellation Wines Australia is the consummate Australian wine success story. Over the past decade, there has been a huge surge in sparkling wines under winemaker Ed Carr. The good-value Omni range segues into the mid-range Sir James with its top-notch appley-citrus vintage and a spicy sparkling Shiraz, finishing with the top-line Arras from Champagne grapes Pinot Noir and Chardonnay. The Eileen Hardy brand name represents the flagship white – a complex

---

SHIRAZ: MCLAREN VALE SPECIALITY

Some of the roundest and biggest Australian Shiraz wines can be found in McLaren Vale. Reaching high alcohol levels – 14 per cent is now almost the norm – is effortless in this warm climate. With such high alcohols, the riper tasting spectrum of Australian Shiraz is explored: blackberry, liquorice, chocolate, raisin, cinnamon, and nutmeg. The traditional American oak is often raised, sometimes too enthusiastically, to deal with such opulent fruit. In the early 1900s, McLaren Vale Shiraz was hailed for its iron qualities and even prescribed by doctors to restore the vitality of anaemic patients.

Chardonnay – and red, a hearty McLaren Vale Shiraz.

red, white, sparkling, dessert, fortified ▶ *2006, 2005, 2004, 2003, 2002, 2001, 2000, 1999, 1998 (r), 1997 (r), 1996* ★ *Arras Vintage Sparkling, Eileen Hardy: Chardonnay, Shiraz*

Coriole
McLaren Vale

Chaffeys Rd, McLaren Vale 📞 *08 8323 8305* 🌐 *www.coriole.com* 🔲

CORIOLE IS a little slice of Tuscany in Australia, with its terraced vineyards, olive trees, and fine Sangiovese wines. Coriole owners Mark and Paul Lloyd were among the first to plant Sangiovese in Australia (in the 1980s). They embrace the wine both as a stand-alone style, rich in savoury cherry fruit, and as an earthy blending tool. The red ironstone here weaves a subtle mineral quality into the red wines, which are beautifully balanced with gentle tannins. Top of the tree is the Lloyd Reserve Shiraz, a good example of what McLaren Vale does best. Coriole also does well with the easy-drinking white Lalla Rookh Sémillon.

red, white ▶ *2006, 2004 (r), 2003, 2002, 2001, 1998, 1997, 1996 (r)* ★ *Lalla Rookh Sémillon, Sangiovese-Shiraz, Lloyd Reserve Shiraz*

D'Arenberg
McLaren Vale

Osborn Rd, McLaren Vale 📞 *08 8329 4888* 🌐 *www.darenberg.com.au* 🔲

D'ARENBERG HAS BEEN coming up with lots of memorable reds – and names – since the brand was revamped in the 1990s. Among these are Dead Arm Shiraz, Iron Stone Pressings, The Laughing Magpie Shiraz-Viognier, and High Trellis Cabernet Sauvignon. They have now been joined by a bevy of white wines too, such as the mineral-rich Olive Grove Chardonnay and The Hermit Crab Marsanne-Viognier – with its honeysuckle undertones shining through.

red, white, sparkling, dessert, fortified ▶ *2006, 2005 (w), 2004 (r), 2002, 2001, 1996, 1995 (r), 1994 (w)* ★ *The Hermit Crab Marsanne-Viognier, Dead Arm Shiraz, Ironstone Pressings Grenache-Shiraz-Mourvèdre*

Casa Freschi
Langhorne Creek

Lot 2 Ridge Rd, Summertown 📞 *08 8390 3232* 🌐 *www.casafreschi.com.au* 📷

CASA FRESCHI sounds Italian, and the planting of Nebbiolo here confirms the Italian connection, but the exciting reds from this newcomer are more international in flavour. Perhaps that is because winemaker David Freschi has worked in Italy, California, and New Zealand. He returned to Langhorne Creek in 1998 to set up his own winemaking patch on his parents' 2.5-ha vineyard. Casa Freschi's first release wines were a huge success. La Signora ('the lady') is an unusual Cabernet Sauvignon-Shiraz-Nebbiolo-Malbec blend with chocolate and liquorice flavours. While Profondo Shiraz-Cabernet is one opulent, velvety wine that lives up to its name.

red ▶ *2006, 2005, 2004, 2002, 2001, 2000* ★ *La Signora, Profondo*

Bowen Estate
Coonawarra

Riddoch Highway, Coonawarra 📞 *08 8737 2229* 🔲

DOUG BOWEN ADMITS to not doing much with Cabernet Sauvignon, which he says pretty much makes itself – yet his cedary, blackberry Bowen Cabernet is a little more generous than many. Bowen has found Shiraz to be a winemaker-responsive variety, and he is regarded as its champion in Cabernet-crazy Coonawarra. There are some mighty tannins and alcohol at work in a young Bowen Shiraz that need at least five years mellowing. His 1998 Ampelon Shiraz is from a single low-yielding vineyard, with the resulting flavours deeply concentrated and rich.

red, white, sparkling ▶ *2006 (w), 2005 (r), 2004 (r), 2003 (r), 2002, 2001, 2000, 1998, 1996* ★ *Ampelon Shiraz, Shiraz, Cabernet Sauvignon*

Wynns Coonawarra Estate Winery
Coonawarra

Memorial Dr, Coonawarra 📞 *08 8736 3266* 🌐 *www.fosters.com.au* 🔲

WYNNS has steered away from the Bordeaux style aspired to by so many Coonawarra producers, and has instead created the quintessential laid-back Australian Cabernet. Known widely as Wynns Black Label, it is bold, fruity, and warm, with a hint of cedary oak. Move up a notch to the John Riddoch Cabernet and everything, especially the oak, is amplified. The standard, earthy Wynns Shiraz is welcoming everyday fare, but the Michael Shiraz demands at least 10 years to quieten down those oak tannins. Long-time winemaker Sue Hodder turns out a quality, lemony Riesling too.

Wynns Shiraz

red, white ▶ *2005, 2004 (r), 2003, 2002, 2001 (w), 1999, 1998, 1997 (r), 1996* ★ *Riesling, John Riddoch Cabernet Sauvignon, Michael Shiraz*

NEW SOUTH WALES

A STATE OF EXTREMES, *New South Wales is no Garden of Eden for vines. From the tropical north to the snow-capped Alps in the south, winegrowers here have succeeded against the odds, yet many of the great names of the Australian wine industry now call New South Wales home.*

The Australian wine industry actually began in New South Wales (NSW) in 1788, but it was determined 19th-century wine pioneers, like George Wyndham and Dr Henry Lindeman, who planted vineyards in outpost settlements like the Hunter Valley.

By 1850, the quality and suitability of grapes like Shiraz and Sémillon were already apparent in the Hunter Valley. Mudgee also had vines by 1858, but it was the expansion of well-known producer Orlando Wyndham's Hunter facilities (*see p558*) to Mudgee in 1997 that really helped promote the region. A sense of pride in Mudgee wines, led by Shiraz, Cabernet Sauvignon, and Chardonnay, has been growing ever since.

The 1912 Murrumbidgee Irrigation Scheme brought vineyards to hot, dry Riverina, which supplied huge volumes of cheap wine for the boxed wine market of the 1970s and 80s. Today,

Wine pioneer Vittorio De Bortoli

however, Riverina produces ripe, clean fruit for more palatable drinking.

Latter-day pioneers, such as Italian-born Vittorio De Bortoli (*see p585*), were still carving out vineyards in the most unlikely of areas right up to the 1950s. And since the 1970s, the rise of cool-climate viticulture in NSW has seen exploration of many other regions, such as Hilltops, Orange, and the enclave of Canberra (ACT). These areas now produce some of the region's most exciting wines with firmer tannin structures, more pronounced acidity, and less of the usual sun-baked fruity character.

Today New South Wales is the country's second largest wine state. It boasts 43,728ha of vines grown by well-known producers such as Lindemans (*see p587*), Wyndham, Tyrrell's, and McWilliam's: a feat that would not have been thought possible two decades, never mind two centuries, ago.

Grape picking at Tyrrell's in the Hunter Valley

◁ **View of the Hunter Valley, the key winegrowing region in New South Wales**

WINE MAP OF NEW SOUTH WALES

NEW SOUTH WALES boasts Australia's number one wine destination: the Hunter Valley. The Lower Hunter produces two world-class varietal wines – age-worthy Sémillon and earthy Shiraz. The Upper Hunter and Mudgee are associated with rich Chardonnay, while the newly emerging Orange and Hilltops areas, further south, are delivering more minerally examples of Chardonnay, as well as fleshy Shiraz. The larger Riverina area, known for its bulk production, also makes a generous Shiraz, and Sémillon excels here too. Towards the coast, the emerging Canberra district is delivering floral Rieslings, peppery Shiraz, and excellent Pinot Noir.

McWilliam's Mount Pleasant Wines

KEY

New South Wales

NEW SOUTH WALES: AREAS & TOP PRODUCERS

UPPER HUNTER VALLEY p578
Rosemount Estate *p582*

LOWER HUNTER VALLEY p578
Brokenwood Wines *p582*
Hope Estate *p582*
McGuigan Wines *p582*
McWilliam's Mount Pleasant Wines *p583*
Poole's Rock Wines *p583*
Tower Estate *p583*
Tyrrell's *p583*

MUDGEE p579
Botobolar Vineyard *p584*
Poet's Corner Wines *p584*

ORANGE & COWRA p579
Hamiltons Bluff Vineyard *p584*

HILLTOPS p580
Barwang Vineyard *p584*

CANBERRA DISTRICT p580
Clonakilla *p584*
Helm Wines *p585*
Lark Hill Winery *p585*

TUMBARUMBA p580

RIVERINA p581
Casella Wines *p585*
De Bortoli Wines *p585*
Nugan Estate *p585*

Water pump surrounded by vineyards, Mudgee

TERROIR AT A GLANCE

Latitude: 32–36.5°S.

Altitude: 10–900m.

Topography: The Hunter Valley, Canberra, and Mudgee are characterized by undulating hills and flood plains, while Orange, Cowra, Hilltops, and Tumbarumba are mountainous, and vineyards are therefore at higher altitudes. The Murrumbidgee River provides a lifeline in the hot winegrowing region of Riverina.

Soil: Mostly red clay or sand, with rich volcanic soil in the Orange region.

Climate: The Lower Hunter is warm and humid; the Upper Hunter is drier. Moderate climate (Mudgee); cool in the foothills of Mount Canobolas (Orange); warm and dry (Cowra). Riverina is hot and dry – irrigation here is vital whereas Canberra alternates between warm and cool.

Temperature: January average 27°C.

Rainfall: Annual average 630–75Cmm.

Viticultural hazards: Spring frosts; harvest rain; diseases resulting from excessive humidity.

Aerial view of vineyards, Lower Hunter Valley

Winemaker testing wine at De Bortoli Wines, Riverina

PERFECT CASE: NEW SOUTH WALES

Ⓡ Barweng Vineyard Shiraz ££

Ⓡ Brokenwood Wines Graveyard Shiraz ££££

Ⓡ Clonakilla Shiraz-Viognier ££££

Ⓓ De Bortoli Wines Noble One Botrytis Sémillon £££

Ⓦ Helm Wines Riesling ££

Ⓡ Lark Hill Winery Exaltation Pinot Noir £££

Ⓦ McWilliam's Mount Pleasant Wines Elizabeth Sémillon ££

Ⓦ Poole's Rock Wines Chardonnay £££

Ⓦ Rosemount Estate Hill of Gold Chardonnay ££

Ⓡ Tower Estate Hunter Shiraz £££

Ⓦ Tyrrell's Vat 1 Sémillon £££

Ⓦ Tyrrell's Vat 47 Chardonnay £££

The 150-ha Roxburgh Vineyard of Rosemount Estate in the Upper Hunter Valley

WINEGROWING AREAS OF NEW SOUTH WALES

Upper Hunter Valley

THE NORTHERNMOST OF the well-known Hunter Valley regions, the Upper Hunter is the baby in viticultural terms. It took until 1960 for a producer, namely Penfolds, to venture out of the successful Lower Hunter into this area around the farming town of Denman. However, the Upper Hunter is no longer a mere extension of its southern relative. This region has taken on a character very much its own, in particular since the arrival of Arrowfield in 1968 and Rosemount Estate in 1969. These producers showed that white wines are this region's main strength, namely butter-rich Chardonnay and soft Sémillon. Both varieties share a rounded character and are full of plump, ripe fruit. For reds, the flavoursome Cabernet Sauvignon has a natural juiciness, and Shiraz, while lacking the striking individuality of the Lower Hunter version, is warm and textured.

🌾 fertile black silty loams, red-brown duplex soils

🍇 Cabernet Sauvignon, Shiraz, Merlot

🍇 Chardonnay, Sémillon, Sauvignon Blanc

🍷 red, white, sparkling

Lower Hunter Valley

THE LOWER HUNTER VALLEY is a wine region recognized the world over for its distinctive, archetypal Australian styles. With more than 80 wineries, the region's winemaking epicentre is Pokolbin. To its west lies the sub-region of Broke Fordwich, where there are another 20-odd wineries. The area mostly follows the Hunter

River, with the rugged Brokenback Range forming the western boundary.

The Lower Hunter Valley finds its greatest expression in Sémillon, a white variety that is traditionally picked at low sugar levels (by Australian standards) of around 11 to 12 per cent and vinified to reveal crisp delicacy and extraordinary intensity when young, but developing into a rich, complex, honeyed wine with time. The Lower Hunter's great red, of almost rustic

HUNTER VALLEY SÉMILLON

Traditional Hunter Valley Sémillon does not appear to be much of a classic in its youth, but with age it is a masterpiece. In fact, a young Sémillon looks watery in the glass, there is a vague aromatic and lemony tang about it, and it has a striking acidity and dryness. It is unoaked and alcohols are generally on the low side. Some producers have tinkered with the style to make it more drinkable early on, but true Hunter Sémillon fans buy the wine to age. Left in the bottle, it develops a gorgeous golden toastiness and becomes rich and complex. The high acidity of its youth keeps the wine firm as it ages. It is not uncommon for Hunter Sémillon to age beautifully for a decade or more, but it is often enjoyable after five years. The Hunter's masters of the style – McWilliam's, Tyrrell's, Lindeman's – have examples still drinking superbly at 15 and 20 years of age.

Brokenwood Wines

appeal, is Shiraz. These two world-class wines are unlikely heroes in a climate that can be anything but conducive to winemaking. The Hunter is hot, often has rain during the harvest, and can be humid, making disease an ever-present problem. But these grapes obviously do not mind a little heat, and winemakers have discovered that the rich red soils – well-draining red clays –– are highly suited to Shiraz, while the creek bed sandy loams and yellow clays are best suited to white varieties like Sémillon.

The success of these grapes in the Lower Hunter Valley attests to the vision of two main pioneering Hunter winemakers: James Busby and George Wyndham, both of whom took the initiative and planted vineyards in the early 1800s. By 1843, an ex-Royal Navy doctor called Dr Henry Lindeman – who was soon destined to become a household name – had also planted vines in the Valley. Today the Lindeman name graces many wines under the Southcorp banner, and is a global brand.

Of the more recent pioneers, Dr Max Lake, founder of Lake's Folly, deserves a mention for planting Cabernet Sauvignon in 1963, when there was none in the Valley, and for seeing its potential as an equally earthy, savoury partner to Shiraz. The late Murray Tyrrell of Tyrrell's, similarly insightful, achieved even greater recognition for Hunter Chardonnay. Then there is Len Evans, founder of Rothbury Estate (1968), who was a passionate spokesman on all things Hunter until his death in 2006.
🗻 *well-drained red duplex and loam soils* 🍇 *Shiraz, Cabernet Sauvignon, Pinot Noir* 🍃 *Chardonnay, Sémillon, Verdelho* 🍷 *red, white, sparkling, dessert, fortified*

Mudgee

MUDGEE IS AN Aboriginal term meaning 'nest in the hills', an apt description for this hilly area on the western slopes of the Great Dividing Range, which is home to many small, family-owned vineyards. History has it that some of Australia's earliest Chardonnay cuttings (brought by James Busby in 1838) ended up here at Craigmoor vineyard, where they were

HUNTER VALLEY SHIRAZ

Hunter Shiraz smells and tastes like the sun-baked earth it comes from. Perhaps the most easily recognizable Shiraz in Australia, it is definitely a different beast from the rich, peppery Shiraz found in other states. Firstly, it does not share the same intensity or power. Hunter Shiraz is medium-bodied, and even when there is no rain at harvest and the grapes ripen longer on the vine, the style is never a blockbuster. That, in turn, means the wines do not cry out for high levels of new oak. In fact, traditional Hunter Shiraz rarely sees or needs new oak. Instead big, old oak casks provide the right environment to soften tannins and impart a little extra complexity, thus preserving all those distinctly Hunter smells and flavours.

called White Pineau. Pioneering Mudgee winemaker Alf Kurtz of Mudgee Wines took cuttings from Craigmoor and planted them in 1963. Only later, when a French vine expert visited his vineyard, were they identified as an exceptional, virus-free Chardonnay. This generous, peach-melon variety was then the source for many of the country's future plantings. Kurtz also pioneered a full-bodied chocolatey Cabernet Sauvignon in the region. Although these are Mudgee's two most suited varieties, the high demand for strong, leathery Shiraz has seen this grape thrive here, too.
🗻 *sandy loam topsoils over clay subsoils* 🍇 *Shiraz, Cabernet Sauvignon. Merlot* 🍃 *Chardonnay, Sémillon, Sauvignon Blanc* 🍷 *red, white*

View of vineyards in the Mudgee region

Orange & Cowra

ORANGE SITS WELL INLAND from Sydney in the foothills of the 1,426m-high Mount Canobolas. This area is high and cool, and – despite a late start to winegrowing in the 1980s – it has moved quickly to establish a reputation for finely structured Chardonnays and Cabernet Sauvignon. Its greatest promoter is Rosemount Estate, which was among the first to highlight the area's potential. To the south of Orange is Cowra, a warm and dry region with a special affinity for producing lively, peach-rich Chardonnay. Rothbury Estate and Petaluma were the first to really capitalize on Cowra Chardonnay in the 1970s. Styles are far from subtle, but they are very appealing.

🏞 *well-drained, red-brown clays with volcanic ash and clay loam over shale,* terra rossa *(Orange), loamy sand and clay with red clay subsoils (Cowra)* 🍇 *Shiraz, Cabernet Sauvignon, Cabernet Franc* 🍾 *Chardonnay, Sémillon, Verdelho* 🍷 *red, white*

Hilltops

FEW DRINKERS HAVE heard of Hilltops, but one range of wines from here has had huge success: McWilliam's Barwang, which took off in the 1990s. The Barwang wines are stylish and elegant, a surprise to many who assumed this was a hot inland spot. Just 80km south of Cowra, Hilltops actually enjoys a

AUSTRALIA'S SWEET HEART

It is a testament to the determination of local winemakers that flat, hot Riverina should produce something so decadently rich as botrytis dessert wine. After a long, hot summer Sémillon grapes are left out to ripen longer, and as humidity levels rise in autumn they become infected with botrytis, which shrivels the grapes reducing their water content and concentrating their sugars. Infection rates vary, but makers like to get 90 per cent coverage. Fresh berries are then added to the wine for a touch of zing and freshness. Riverina producer De Bortoli pioneered botrytis Sémillon in 1982. Its Noble One is the benchmark, delivering complex marmalade, citrous peel, and sweet apricot flavours.

continental climate with a long, even ripening period. These conditions seem particularly well-suited to making smooth, fleshy, and deep-hued Shiraz and Cabernet Sauvignon, but it is still early days. Hunter-based companies Allandale and Hungerford Hill (Southcorp) source grapes from here, too.

🏞 *dark red granitic clays with basalt* 🍇 *Shiraz, Cabernet Sauvignon* 🍾 *Sémillon, Chardonnay, Riesling* 🍷 *red, white*

Canberra District

THE CAPITAL OF AUSTRALIA, this is home to the Federal Parliament and a plethora of accompanying government industries. In fact, it was government research scientists who planted

Lark Hill Winery label, Canberra District

many of the first hobby vineyards here during the 1970s, around Murrumbateman to the north of the city and Lake George to the east. The early years for these small producers were hard: few had winemaking experience and there was no history of wine-growing in the area. Nevertheless, today, many of them are full-time winemakers, with companies like Clonakilla, Helm, Brindabella Hills, and Lark Hill making some of the region's best wines.

In 1997, the decision by Australia's second largest wine producer, the Hardy Wine Company, to build a large 2,000-tonne winery in the heart of Canberra brought a smile to the faces of the local winemakers. The winery, along with a 250-ha vineyard, was recognition, at last, from a major producer of the area's ability to make quality wines.

These are still early days for Canberra wines, but the whites are fine-textured with gentle aromatics, evident in the delicate, floral Rieslings. The reds tend to be elegant with fine tannin structures, such as the peppery Shiraz and opulent Pinot Noir.

🏞 *hard red duplex* 🍇 *Cabernet Sauvignon, Merlot, Pinot Noir* 🍾 *Chardonnay, Riesling, Gewürztraminer* 🍷 *red, white, dessert*

Tumbarumba

SINCE THE 1980s, when Tumbarumba was first planted, companies like Southcorp, the Hardy Wine Company, and Orlando Wyndham have sourced grapes from here for their premium bubblies. This cool-climate, high-altitude area is well-suited to producing Chardonnay, Pinot Noir, and Pinot Meunier for sparklings. Most wines are subsequently blended, but Hungerford Hill has supported the region since the 1990s, giving Tumbarumba recognition on its labels.

 granite, basalt  Pinot Noir, Cabernet Sauvignon, Merlot, Pinot Meunier  Chardonnay, Sauvignon Blanc  red, white, sparkling

Riverina

RIVERINA IS AUSTRALIA'S second biggest wine-producing area, with 23,000ha of vines producing 321,000 tonnes of fruit annually. Its forte is low-cost grapes. Growers, many with Italian heritage, settled here after World Wars I and II and now farm huge tracts of rich red earth, some over 400ha, irrigated with water from the Murrumbidgee River. Many, such as De Bortoli, Riverina Estate, and Casella Wines, have built sizeable empires by supplying the cheap and cheerful end of the market from their vast estates. In fact McWilliam's, the country's eighth biggest producer, whose Hanwood winery was started in 1877, calls Riverina home.

Makers here have worked hard to improve quality and concentrate fruit flavours, allowing them to move up into the premium price brackets. Generous Shiraz and full-bodied, sun-soaked Chardonnay are the all-round favourites, but since the 1990s some producers have explored Durif (De Bortoli), Sémillon (Riverina Wines), and Viognier and Tempranillo (Casella). However, the star of the region is not a dry table wine but a gorgeous, golden botrytized Sémillon of astonishing intensity.

 sandy loam over sandy clay loam  Shiraz, Cabernet Sauvignon, Mourvèdre  Sémillon, Trebbiano, Chardonnay  red, white, dessert

De Bortoli's fermentation tanks in Riverina

Winegrowing in Queensland

It may come as a surprise to many that tropical Queensland has made wine since 1863. Producers here avoid the heat and humidity by seeking out high altitudes or areas cooled by sea breezes. The Granite Belt around Stanthorpe and Ballandean in southern Queensland reaches altitudes of 810m and produces quality Sémillon and Cabernet Sauvignon, but its most consistent performer is Shiraz. The sprawling Burnett area, north of Brisbane, is still quite new to viticulture. Altitudes are not as high here, and the hot weather makes irrigation a must. Full-bodied, creamy Chardonnay is this area's most attractive style.

Albert River Wines, label

Albert River Wines
 www.albertriverwines.com.au

Founded in 1997, Albert River Wines has Peter Scudamore-Smith, Master of Wine, making a range of well-priced wines under the Private Reserve label, including a rich Chardonnay, a plummy Merlot, and an unusual red berry-charged Shiraz-Cabernet-Merlot blend matured in oak.

Ballandean Estate Wines
 www.ballandean-estate.com.au

This Granite Belt producer works hard to make some of the region's most consistent, full-bodied Chardonnays. Run by the energetic Angelo Puglisi, Ballandean also makes two separate releases under the Ballandean and Sundown Valley vineyards labels.

Rimfire Vineyards & Winery
 www.rimfirewinery.com.au

Grown on just 12ha of a 1,500-ha cattle stud, Rimfire Vineyards' quality Chardonnay, Verdelho, and Shiraz enjoyed great wine show success in the late 1990s.

Sirromet Wines
 www.sirromet.com

This large, no-expense-spared winery – with 142ha of vineyards under Adam Chapman – arrived with a bang in 1998. The market-driven brand delivers wines in all price ranges, with sunny Chardonnay, well-rounded Shiraz, and smooth Pinot Noir leading in terms of quality.

Stone Ridge Vineyards
 07 4683 4211

Jim Lawrie, the owner here since 1981, caused a stir in 2003 by releasing Queensland's most expensive Pinot Noir: AUS$100 for each fruit-packed bottle. He has also been highly regarded for his spicy Shiraz.

TOP PRODUCERS OF NEW SOUTH WALES

Rosemount Estate
Upper Hunter Valley

Rosemount Rd, Denman
☎ *02 6549 6400*
🌐 *www.rosemountestates.com* ☐

MURRAY TYRRELL may have pioneered Chardonnay in Australia, but it was this estate, founded in 1969 by Bob Oatley, that gave the grape mass appeal. Through shrewd marketing and good wine-making, he established a faultless range of wines. After noticing the superior quality from its Roxburgh vineyard, Rosemount released a premium Roxburgh Chardonnay in 1984: a rich, buttery wine that was lauded as the new pinnacle of Australian Chardonnay. Rosemount's premium wines are now sourced from several regions, among them Mudgee (Hill of Gold and Mountain Blue) and McLaren Vale (Traditional and Balmoral ranges).

🍷 *red, white, sparkling* 🍾 *2005 (w), 2004 (w), 2003, 2001, 2000 (r), 1999, 1998, 1997, 1996, 1995, 1993* ★ *Giants Creek Chardonnay, Roxburgh Chardonnay, Hill of Gold Chardonnay, Balmoral Syrah*

Brokenwood Wines
Lower Hunter Valley

McDonalds Rd, Pokolbin
☎ *02 4998 7559*
🌐 *www.brokenwood.com.au* ☐

BROKENWOOD, founded in 1970, was the dream of three Sydney professionals – including noted wine writer James Halliday – who managed to turn a weekend hobby into a respected Hunter concern. The original owners left and were replaced by a number of investors and, in 1982, CEO-winemaker Iain Riggs took the helm. He is

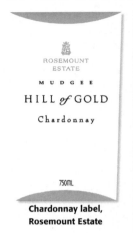

**Chardonnay label,
Rosemount Estate**

largely responsible for the emergence of Graveyard Vineyard Shiraz as one of Australia's great reds. This wine is sourced from a single vineyard (which was once chosen as a site for a grave-yard but never used), and shows a most un-Hunter-like restraint and elegance. His Sémillon is warm and lemony in its youth and ages beautifully. And a second label, Cricket Pitch, offers great value for money.

🍷 *red, white* 🍾 *2008 (w), 2005 (w), 2004 (w), 2002, 2001, 2000, 1999, 1998, 1997, 1996, 1995* ★ *Sémillon, Graveyard Vineyard: Shiraz, Chardonnay*

Hope Estate
Lower Hunter Valley

Broke Rd, Pokolbin ☎ *02 4993 3555* 🌐 *www.hope estate.com.au* ☐

IN 2006, PHARMACIST-CUM-WINEMAKER Michael Hope bought the famed Rothbury Estate from Foster's, vowing to return the grand old dame to its former glory. He was after a little magic – the kind that once inhabited one of the great Hunter vineyards of

modern times. In 1968, Len Evans and Murray Tyrrell formed Rothbury, planting a vineyard on Tyrrell's land specializing in Hunter favourites like Shiraz, Chardonnay, and Semillon. The wines were released under single-vineyard labels direct to members of its Rothbury Society. Membership brought invitations to Evans-inspired dinners and tastings that were gloriously decadent affairs. In 1996, the company was taken over by Mildara Blass. Without Evans, Rothbury lost much of its shine and, sadly, reputation. Under Michael Hope, there is a new beginning.

🍷 *red, white, rosé, dessert* 🍾 *2008 (w), 2006 (w), 2005, 2004* ★ *Shiraz, Chardonnay, Sémillon*

McGuigan Wines
Lower Hunter Valley

Corner Broke & McDonalds Rds, Pokolbin ☎ *02 4998 7400* 🌐 *www.mcguigan wines.com.au* ☐

BRIAN MCGUIGAN, a powerful mover and shaker in the Australian wine industry, started McGuigan Wines in 1992. Its policy is to produce easy drinking wines of mass appeal. In 2003 McGuigan Wines joined forces with major wine processor Simeon to form Australia's seventh largest wine company. It is now a formidable producer of wines for the domestic and international markets.

McGuigan Wines

🍷 *red, white* 🍾 *2008 (w), 2005 (w), 2004 (w), 2003, 2002, 2001, 2000* ★ *Genus 4 Old Vine Cabernet Sauvignon, Personal Reserve Hunter Valley Shiraz, Bin 9000 Sémillon*

THE TYRRELL WINEMAKING DYNASTY

The Tyrrell family has moulded not only the fortunes of the Hunter Valley but also those of the Australian wine industry as a whole. Third-generation winemaker Murray Tyrrell jumped his neighbour's fence one moonlit night in 1967 and 'borrowed' 1,000-odd Chardonnay cuttings – enough to plant half a hectare of his own. Vat 47 Chardonnay was born – a wine that brought Australian Chardonnay on to the world stage. In 1973, Tyrrell's became the first in Australia to mature Chardonnay in new, French oak hogsheads (300-l barrels). In 1979, another Tyrrell's pioneering effort, a 1976 Pinot Noir, made the cover of *Time* magazine after winning first place in the Paris Wine Olympics (*see p21*). Murray died in 2000, leaving his son, Bruce, a shrewd wine marketer, to carry on his legacy.

complex in 1999. The wines are very Evans, boasting strong personalities and luxurious, opulent, hedonistic styles. Evans passed away in 2006, but his dream goes on. The emphasis remains on strong regional styles, using grapes from interstate, as well as from the Hunter.

🍷 *red, white* 🕒 *2008 (w), 2006 (w), 2005, 2004* ★ *Hunter Valley Shiraz, Clare Riesling, Barossa Shiraz*

Tyrrell's
Lower Hunter Valley

Broke Rd, Pokolbin 📞 *02 4993 7000* 🌐 *www.tyrrells.com.au* ◯

TYRRELL'S HAS A deep connection with the Hunter Valley: no other wine company has the tradition, the feel for the land, or the passion and faith that Tyrrell's displays. Chardonnay, Sémillon, and Shiraz are still the company's cornerstone, and they come in a variety of styles. The Vat wines – the elegant Vat 47 Chardonnay, the nutty, honeyed Vat 1 Sémillon, and the earthy Vat 9 Shiraz – are examples of the Hunter at its best. Then there is a plethora of excellent, individual styles: from the Lost Block Sémillon to be enjoyed in its youth and the sherbety Moon Mountain Chardonnay, to the fruit-packed, old-vine Brokenback Reserve Shiraz.

🍷 *red, white, sparkling, dessert, fortified* 🕒 *2008 (w), 2006 (w), 2005, 2004* ★ *Vat 1 Sémillon, Vat 47 Chardonnay, Vat 9 Shiraz*

McWilliam's Mount Pleasant Wines
Lower Hunter Valley

Marrowbone Rd, Pokolbin 📞 *02 4998 7505* 🌐 *www. mcwilliams.com.au* ◯

MOUNT PLEASANT IS synonymous with Maurice O'Shea, one of Australia's top winemakers. He made wines of great elegance from Shiraz and Sémillon with no oak maturation, and gave them names like Anne, Florence, Philip, and Richard. O'Shea died in 1956, but the styles he inspired remain a feature of these wines to this day: Elizabeth Sémillon is the top-selling Sémillon in the country, released after four to five years in the bottle and showing a warm, buttered toastiness. The flagship Sémillon is Lovedale, an extraordinarily complex wine, also released with some age. The Maurice O'Shea Shiraz is a modern interpretation of an original O'Shea wine: with plenty of oak but also great finesse.

🍷 *red, white, sparkling, dessert, fortified* 🕒 *2008 (w), 2005 (w), 2004, 2000 (w), 1999, 1998, 1997 (w), 1996, 1995, 1994 (r), 1991 (r)* ★ *Elizabeth Sémillon, Maurice O'Shea Shiraz, Lovedale Sémillon*

Poole's Rock Wines
Lower Hunter Valley

DeBeyers Rd, Pokolbin 📞 *02 4998 7501* 🌐 *www.poolesrock.com.au* ◯

DAVID CLARKE started Poole's Rock as a personal venture, making wines that he liked to drink himself, but it has grown considerably. The focus here is Chardonnay: bright, clean, minerally and elegant. The Cockfighter's Ghost Vineyard and brand joined the stable in 1994 as a cheery second label, and Firestick, a well priced multi-regional brand, was added to the Poole's Rock portfolio in 2002.

🍷 *red, white* 🕒 *2008 (w), 2005, 2004, 2003 (r), 2002 (r), 2001* ★ *Poole's Rock Chardonnay, Cockfighter's Ghost: Unwooded Chardonnay, Verdelho*

Tower Estate
Lower Hunter Valley

Corner Broke & Halls Rds, Pokolbin 📞 *02 4998 7989* 🌐 *www.towerestate wines.com.au* ◯

AFTER LOSING Rothbury Estate in a hostile takeover, Len Evans started again with investor friends and built this magnificent winery-accommodation

TOWER
ESTATE
Hunter Valley
SHIRAZ
2002
WINE OF AUSTRALIA   750ml

Tower Estate label

Poet's Corner wine cellar

Botobolar Vineyard
Mudgee

89 Botobolar Lane, Mudgee **C** *02 6373 3840* W *www.botobolar.com* ○

THIS WAS ONE of Australia's first organic vineyards, established in 1971 by journalist Gil Wahlquist. Sheep graze on grass between the vines, copper sulphate and lime sulphur are used in sprays to keep disease at bay, and birds take care of the caterpillars and moths. Kevin and Trina Karstrom took over from Wahlquist in 1994 and, fortunately, have chosen to continue his work. They have now ventured into low-preservative wines, but the best results remain the reds where sulphur dioxide is used as a preserver of fruit aromas and flavours and an anti-oxidant.
🍷 *red, white* 🍇 *2006 (r), 2005 (w), 2004, 2002 (r), 2001* ★ *Shiraz, Cabernet Sauvignon, Marsanne*

Poet's Corner Wines
Mudgee

Craigmoor Rd, Mudgee **C** *02 6372 2208* W *www.poets cornerwines.com* ○

THE NAME OF THIS winery is a homage to Henry Lawson, Mudgee poet and writer. Established in 1989, Poet's Corner was then bought by Hunter Valley-based Wyndham Estate (which in turn was taken over by Orlando in

1990). Orlando-Wyndham saw in Poet's Corner a chance to infiltrate the mass market with a well-priced, consumer-friendly range. It offers good everyday-drinking wines in a range of three whites (notably a zesty Chardonnay) and three reds (the smooth Shiraz is great value). A Henry Lawson range was added a few years ago, while the Montrose label shows the best of Mudgee with some top quality wines led by a rich Black Shiraz.
🍷 *red, white* 🍇 *2006 (r), 2005 (w), 2004, 2002* ★ *Montrose: Black Shiraz, Sangiovese; Poet's Corner Unwooded Chardonnay*

Hamiltons Bluff Vineyard
Orange & Cowra

Longs Corner Rd, Canowindra **C** *02 6344 2079* W *www.hamiltonsbluff.com* ◉

ORANGE AND COWRA are fast developing a name for their cool-climate, sultry Cabernet Sauvignon-Merlot and Chardonnay. Some detect a European wine style emerging here: light, medium-bodied, and gently tannic; these are qualities that can be found in the produce of Hamiltons Bluff. This vineyard, started in 1995 by the Andrews family, is planted with the obligatory Chardonnay, Cabernet Sauvignon, and Shiraz, as

well as Viognier, Riesling, Sémillon, and Sangiovese. The Chardonnay comes in three styles: Reserve, Chairman's Reserve, and unwooded.
🍷 *red, white* 🍇 *2006 (r), 2004, 2003, 2002 (w)* ★ *Sangiovese, Canowindra Grossi Unwooded Chardonnay, Chairman's Reserve*

Barwang Vineyard
Hilltops

Barwang Rd, Young **C** *02 6382 3594* W *www.mcwilliams.com.au* **C** *02 6382 3594* ◉

MCWILLIAM'S BOUGHT Barwang in 1989 believing that this cool-climate region on the southwest slopes of the Great Dividing Range could have a successful future. They were right. Barwang wines are well received for their combination of generous flavour and reasonable prices. It is hard to choose between the company's two stalwarts: Shiraz (elegant and spicy with plums) and Cabernet Sauvignon (equally elegant but with blackcurrant and vanilla notes). Both show smooth tannic structures and the ability to age well. The Barwang Chardonnay is also beautifully restrained.
🍷 *red, white* 🍇 *2005 (w), 2003 (w), 2002 (r), 2001, 2000, 1998, 1997, 1996, 1994 (w), 1993* ★ *Shiraz, Cabernet Sauvignon, Chardonnay*

Clonakilla
Canberra District

Crisps Lane, Murrumbateman **C** *02 6227 5877* W *www.clonakilla. com.au* ○

SINCE TAKING OVER winemaking from his father in 1997, Tim Kirk has fashioned some of the most exciting Shiraz in Australia. He blends his intensely peppery Shiraz with a touch of the white grape Viognier to give a breathtaking fragrance and translucent appearance. In fact, everything Kirk turns his hand to is a gem, from his lively Riesling to the flowery delicacy of his varietal Viognier.

🟥 *red, white* 📆 *2007, 2006, 2005, 2004, 2003, 2002, 2001, 1998, 1997, 1995 (w), 1994* ★ *Shiraz-Viognier, Riesling, Viognier*

Helm Wines
Canberra District

Butts Rd, Murrumbateman
📞 *02 6227 5953* 🖵 *www.helm wines.com.au* 📞 *02 6227 5953* ⬜

A FORMER SCIENTIST and expert in phylloxera, Ken Helm has been making wine here since 1973, and is a keen supporter of the emerging Canberra wine region. His winemaking reflects a purist's scientific eye and emphasizes the region's clean fruit and firm acids. This is seen in a tightly structured Cabernet Sauvignon-Merlot, an unwooded Chardonnay bristling with citrus zest, and Helm's passion: a strong lime and mineral Riesling.

🟥 *red, white, dessert* 📆 *2007, 2006, 2005, 2004, 2003, 2002, 2001, 2000* ★ *Riesling, Cabernet Sauvignon-Merlot, Unwooded Chardonnay*

Lark Hill Winery
Canberra District

Bungendore Rd, Bungendore
📞 *02 6238 1393*
🖵 *www.larkhillwine.com.au* ⬜

DR DAVID AND SUE CARPENTER first made their name in the 1980s with fresh, aromatic cool-climate Rieslings from their 860m-high vineyard near Lake George. This was then followed by a subtle, firm-structured Chardonnay. The 1990s brought a flagship Lark Hill wine: a powerful, rich, and velvety Pinot Noir. In exceptional years a super-premium Pinot is made –

Detail of Clonakilla label

Exaltation (the term for a group of larks in flight).

🟥 *red, white* 📆 *2007, 2006, 2005, 2004, 2001, 2000, 1999 (r), 1997 (r), 1996 (r), 1995, 1994* ★ *Exaltation, Pinot Noir, Riesling, Shiraz*

Casella Wines
Riverina

Wakley Rd, Yenda 📞 *02 6961 3000*
🖵 *www.casellawine.com.au* ⬛

CASELLA WINES' 2001 launch of the Yellowtail range, with its easy-going (and slightly sweet) Chardonnay and peppery Shiraz saw its sales soar. Wines from this quiet company's Cottler's Bridge, Yendah Vale, and Carramar Estate ranges reflect what the Riverina is best at: clean, fruity, simple wine styles at reasonable prices. However, winemaker John Casella is now ready to explore the top end of the market, and has started sourcing wines from areas outside the Riverina region too.

🟥 *red, white* 📆 *2006, 2005, 2004 (r), 2002, 2000* ★ *Yendah Vale: Durif, Tempranillo; Caramar Estate Merlot*

De Bortoli Wines
Riverina

De Bortoli Rd, Bilbul 📞 *02 6966 0100* 🖵 *www.debortoli.com.au* ⬜

DE BORTOLI IS a very successful wine empire built on the passion and hard work of

Italian immigrant Vittorio De Bortoli, who arrived in Australia in 1924. Today, his grandson Darren oversees the company, now the sixth largest in Australia with an annual crush of 70,000 tonnes. Its wines run from the everyday Deen De Bortoli range to the truly extraordinary, luscious Noble One Botrytis Sémillon. Since the mid-1980s De Bortoli has established roots in the Yarra Valley, producing premium wines like velvety Pinot Noir and an elegant Chardonnay. In 2002, it also moved into the Lower Hunter Valley. De Bortoli wines always deliver over-and-above what their price tag suggests.

🟥 *red, white, sparkling, dessert, fortified* 📆 *2006, 2005, 2004 (r), 2002, 2001 (w), 2000, 1999 (w), 1998, 1997 (w), 1996 (w), 1995 (w), 1994, 1993 (r), 1992 (w)* ★ *Noble One Botrytis Sémillon, Yarra Valley: Chardonnay, Pinot Noir*

Casella Wines

Nugan Estate
Riverina

Darlington Point Rd, Willbriggie
📞 *02 6962 1822* ⬜

SINCE 1999 BUSINESSWOMAN Michelle Nugan has built a 600-ha wine empire that manages to show irrigated Riverina fruit as it is rarely seen: rich, supple, well-structured, and complex. Cookoothama Pigeage Merlot is luxurious in fruit flavour. Frasca's Lane Chardonnay avoids ripe Riverina style, instead displaying citrus and stone-fruit overtones. And Durif becomes a wine rich in savoury plumminess at Nugan.

🟥 *red, white, dessert* 📆 *2006, 2005, 2004 (r)* ★ *Cookoothama Pigeage Merlot, Manuka Grove Vineyard Durif, Frasca's Lane Vineyard Chardonnay*

WINE TOUR OF THE LOWER HUNTER VALLEY

JUST NORTH OF SYDNEY, the Lower Hunter Valley is dominated by the dramatic blue-green silhouette of the Brokenback Range. This region hosts millions of tourists annually, yet still manages to retain a relaxed country feel and charm. Grand multi-million dollar wineries rub shoulders with small, family-run enterprises, and architecture varies from Tuscan-inspired lodgings and Provençal villas to traditional Australian homesteads. The main wine hubs are Pokolbin, a town full of fine eateries and wineries, and the old mining town of Cessnock.

Lower Hunter Valley vineyards with a view of the Brokenback Range beyond

① Allandale Winery
Bring a picnic or throw a prawn on Bill Sneddon's barbeque, savour a glass of his deliciously steely Sémillon or scrumptious, food-friendly Matthew Shiraz, and enjoy the wide-screen valley vista.
📞 02 4990 4526
🌐 www.allandalewinery.com.au

② Tower Estate
The late Len Evans' love of international art and antiques meshes seamlessly into a modern context at Tower Estate. Marvel at the amazing architecture, enjoy dinner in the restaurant, sample the fine multi-regional wines and even stay at The Lodge. *See p583.*
📞 02 4998 7989 🌐 www.towerestatewines.com.au

③ Pepper Tree Wines ◁
Boasting the prettiest cellar door in the Hunter Valley, Pepper Tree Wines' complex includes a lawned picnic area, the Convent guesthouse, and Robert's Restaurant. For Merlot fanciers a visit here is a must.
📞 02 4998 7539
🌐 www.peppertreewines.com.au

KEY

━━━ Tour route

④ Tyrrell's ▷
The slab hut at the entrance is the 1850s 'homestead', erected by Edward Tyrrell, the current manager's great-grandfather. Wines in all price brackets are made here but pride of place goes to the Vat wines. Daily wine tours run from Monday to Saturday. *See p583.*
📞 02 4998 7989 🌐 www.tyrrells.com.au

⑤ McGuigan Wines ◁

This is the centre for the Hunter Valley Cheese Company and a great spot to stock up on picnic food, as well as McGuigan's ripe, sun-drenched styles like the Génus 4 Chardonnay and Personal Reserve Hunter Shiraz. *See p582.*

☎ 02 4998 7402 Ⓦ www.mcguiganwines.com.au

⑥ **Brokenwood Wines** ▷

CEO/winemaker Iain Riggs started this venture as a weekend hobby. The boutique winery produces quality Hunter Shiraz. The cellar door is totally unpretentious and boasts some exclusive releases. *See p582.*

☎ 02 4998 7559
Ⓦ www.brokenwood.com.au

Greta

Camp Road

Lovedale Road

Road

Majors Lane

Bishop's Hill

State Forest

km ⊢⊣ 5

①

Visitors' Tips

Route: This 34-km tour is centred around the Lower Hunter Valley.

Duration: This tour will take a day to complete.

Wineries: Almost all wineries here are open to the public daily and few charge for tastings.

Restaurant recommendation: Chez Pok ☎ 02 4998 7596 at Peppers Guest House, Pokolbin.

Useful contacts: Wine Country Visitor Information Center in Pokolbin Ⓦ www.winecountry.com.au

⑦ **Lindemans** ▽

Lindemans no longer has a working winery here but this handsome wine museum is housed in the historic Ben Ean building. Wine exhibits date back as far back as the 1800s and tastings can be enjoyed in a garden setting.

☎ 02 4998 7684
Ⓦ www.lindemans.com.au

⑧ **McWilliam's Mount Pleasant Wines** ▽

The vineyard is organized in easily navigable blocks inviting picnickers and walkers to roam round this estate. Or visitors can enjoy local exotica – like emu, crocodile, and kangaroo – at the café. The wines to try are the top-level Sémillons, the Merlot, and the earthy Maurice O'Shea Shiraz. *See p582.*

☎ 02 4998 7505 Ⓦ www.mcwilliams.com.au

⑨ **Bimbadgen Estate** △

Re-launched with an expanded winery-restaurant complex, this estate has a strong core range of Sémillon, Verdelho, and Shiraz. This is the bold new face of the Hunter Valley, also catering for tutored tastings at the cellar door, as well as providing accommodation.

☎ 02 4998 7585
Ⓦ www.bimbadgen.com.au

VICTORIA & TASMANIA

W HAT VICTORIA LACKS IN SIZE *it makes up for in diversity. There are more designated wine regions in Victoria – 21 in total – than in any other state, and more producers, 687 and rising. The landscape bristles with vineyards: small, family-run operations, which are the backbone of the industry here.*

Vineyards were first planted in Victoria in the wake of the great 1850s gold rush, but the arrival of the vine louse phylloxera via Geelong in 1875 wiped out many of these early establishments. It was not until the late 1960s that a great new confidence returned after more than half a century of decline.

As in most wine states in Australia, plantings of Shiraz and Chardonnay dominate Victoria's vineyards, which stretch from the Murray River to the Southern Ocean. However, some styles remain quintessentially Victoria: peppery Shiraz from the Pyrenees, the fruit-driven Pinot Noir of Mornington Peninsula, classy Yarra Valley Chardonnay, the Grampians' sparkling Shiraz, and the honeysuckle Marsanne of the Goulburn Valley. Then there are the fortified wines of the Northeast: these world-class Tokays (Muscadelles) and Muscats can reach the pinnacle of flavour intensity and concentration, and are rightly regarded as national treasures.

Barrel of Victoria's luscious Muscat

To the south of Victoria is Australia's smallest wine state – Tasmania. The island's wine industry only got started in the 1950s when Frenchman Jean Miguet planted vines in the north and Italian-Australian Claudio Alcorso started work in the south. For years, these two struggled alone in the cold winegrowing conditions until they were joined by more pioneers, such as Dr Pirie at Pipers Brook in 1974. Four varieties account for 87 per cent of the state's production: Chardonnay, Pinot Noir, Riesling, and Sauvignon Blanc. The region's suitability as Australia's premier sparkling wine source has only been discovered over the last 25 years.

Pipers Brook Vineyard, one of Tasmania's most prominent producers

◁ **View of vineyards in the cool winegrowing region of the Yarra Valley**

WINE MAP OF VICTORIA & TASMANIA

IN VICTORIA AND TASMANIA, every imaginable winegrowing variable is covered. Temperatures can soar up to 42°C on the mainland, but in total contrast there is breathtaking chill in Tasmania, where frost can be the vine's greatest enemy. Between these two extremes exists a multitude of viticultural areas: the warmer climes of Northeast Victoria are the source of world-class fortifieds, central Victoria is spicy Shiraz country, and southern Victoria is the realm of Pinot Noir and Chardonnay.

KEY

Victoria & Tasmania

Brown Brothers Milawa Vineyard label, Northeast Victoria

Yarra Yering vineyard and winery, **Yarra Valley**

Scotchmans Hill, **Geelong**

Handpicking Chardonnay grapes in the Yarra Valley

TERROIR AT A GLANCE

Latitude: 34–38.5°S.

Altitude: 15–800m (Victoria); 50–210m (Tasmania).

Topography: Extremely varied, from mountain ranges to valleys and coastal plains.

Soil: Red loam and volcanic soils in Victoria. Clay and peat in Tasmania.

Climate: Maritime. North of the Great Divide is warm and dry. South of the Great Divide is wet and cool. In Tasmania, temperatures are lower and humidity is higher than in other Australian regions.

Temperature: January average is 19°C (Victoria); 17°C (Tasmania).

Rainfall: The annual average is 638mm (Victoria); 1,032mm (Tasmania).

Wind: Southern Ocean provides breezes and high humidity. Windbreaks on seaward slopes protect vines from sea winds in Tasmania.

Viticultural hazards: Drought; sea wind and frost in Tasmania.

VICTORIA & TASMANIA: AREAS & TOP PRODUCERS

NORTHWEST VICTORIA p592

Zilzie Wines p596

GRAMPIANS p592

Mount Langi Ghiran Wines p596

Seppelt Great Western p596

PYRENEES p592

Dalwhinnie p596

Redbank Winery p596

BENDIGO & HEATHCOTE p593

Jasper Hill Vineyard p597

Wild Duck Creek Estate p597

GOULBURN VALLEY p593

Mitchelton Wines p597

Tahbilk Wines p597

NORTHEAST VICTORIA p593

Brown Brothers Milawa Vineyard p598

Giaconda Vineyard p598

Morris Wines p598

KING & ALPINE VALLEYS p594

Chrismont Wines p598

Pizzini Wines p599

GIPPSLAND p594

Bass Phillip Wines p599

Nicholson River Winery p599

YARRA VALLEY p594

Mount Mary Vineyard p599

Yarra Yering p600

MORNINGTON PENINSULA p594

Crittenden Wines p600

Stonier Wines p600

GEELONG p595

Bannockburn Vineyards p600

Scotchmans Hill p600

TASMANIA p595

Freycinet Vineyard p601

Jansz p601

Kreglinger Wine Estates p601

Stefano Lubiana Wines p601

TASMANIA

Bass Strait

Cradle Mountain

Tamar Valley

Launceston

Mount Ossa

Esk

Derwent

Gordon

Derwent Valley

Lake Gordon

Lake Pedder

HOBART

TASMAN SEA

42°

0 — km — 400

Murray

Great Divide

Australian Alps

Snowy

Stefano Lubiana Wines in the Derwent Valley, Tasmania

Yarra Valley, known for its wide range of wines

WINEGROWING AREAS OF VICTORIA & TASMANIA

Northwest Victoria

THE NORTHWEST IS one of the great engine rooms of the Australian wine industry. Wineries the size of small towns dominate the flat landscape, surrounded by thousands of hectares of vineyards that thrive in the region's hot conditions. Irrigation, essential in these parts, comes courtesy of the Murray River.

Big-name producers the Foster's Group and Constellation Wines Australia (*see p558*) have large winemaking operations here, which are involved in producing either boxed wine or cheap and cheerful bottled wines. In the 1970s, Sultana and Muscat of Alexandria made up the bulk of cheap blends. Today, it is usually Chardonnay, Sémillon, Shiraz, Colombard, and Cabernet Sauvignon. High yields, plenty of water, and lots of sun make big, flavoursome, and affordable wines, which have led the Australian wine invasion overseas.

 *brown loamy sand* *Shiraz, Cabernet Sauvignon* *Chardonnay, Colombard* *red, white*

Grampians

THE GRAMPIANS HAS few producers by Australian standards, but it yields an amazing 5,000 tonnes of fruit each vintage. In wine terms, the region's influence belies its size: Seppelt Great Western, part of the vast Southcorp group, has built up the country's biggest sparkling wine facility in the Grampians. All of Southcorp's sparkling wines are blended and matured here.

With the exception of Seppelt, the producers are small-scale makers. The area is also home to sparkling Shiraz, a bubbly with bite, made from super-ripe grapes. And then there is Shiraz as a still wine, a medium-bodied gentle giant that can be deceptively intense in the glass.

grey-brown loamy sands *Shiraz, Cabernet Sauvignon, Pinot Noir* *Chardonnay, Sauvignon Blanc, Riesling* *red, white, sparkling*

Pyrenees

THE PYRENEES AREA TAKES in the quiet hamlets of Moonambel and Avoca. But there is nothing quiet about the region's robust reds. Pyrenees Shiraz is strong and minty with a spice-filled perfume. Cabernet Sauvignon is the overlooked younger sibling but, like Shiraz, shows good ageing potential. It has taken 40 years for the region to find its real strength. In the 1960s, the first modern-day Australian winery, Château Rémy, was founded here for brandy production with input from drinks giant Rémy Martin. When brandy lost ground, there was a push towards sparkling as well as still wines. The cooler slopes of the Pyrenees were explored for these sparklings. With its rich textural appeal Chardonnay is more suited as a still wine here, and is now gradually taking over. A fuller style of Sauvignon Blanc is also made.

grey-brown sandy loam *Shiraz, Cabernet Sauvignon, Pinot Noir* *Chardonnay, Sauvignon Blanc* *red, white, sparkling*

> ℞
>
> **Sally's Paddock**
> **2000**
> Pyrenees
>
> Produced and bottled on the property
> Redbank Winery, Sally's Lane
> Redbank, Victoria
>
> 13.5% VOL.   PRODUCE OF AUSTRALIA   750ml

Sally's Paddock label from Redbank Winery, Pyrenees

Bendigo & Heathcote

IN 1864 THERE WERE more than 40 vineyards in Bendigo. That is what a gold rush can do for a region. But by 1893 the end was in sight with the arrival of the deadly phylloxera. From the early 1970s, however, Bendigo including neighbouring and ever-growing Heathcote found its feet again as winemakers rediscovered the region's ability to produce fine wine. Cabernet Sauvignon, Shiraz, and Chardonnay are the staples. The reds are strong and firm, with forceful tannins. Where there is quartz (the gold-bearing kind) there is a mineral quality to the wines. Chardonnay here is warm and round.

🔲 brown loamy sand, clay loam, patches of quartz gravel 🍇 Shiraz, Cabernet Sauvignon, Pinot Noir 🍃 Chardonnay, Riesling 🍷 red, white

Goulburn Valley

VIOGNIER, MARSANNE, ROUSSANNE, SHIRAZ, and Mourvèdre are the main grapes of France's Rhône Valley. They are also stalwarts of Australia's Goulburn Valley. Shiraz has been grown here since the 1860s, Marsanne from the 1930s, while other equally robust varieties suited to the warm climate arrived later. Vineyards follow the course of the Goulburn River through hard, dry grazing country, where irrigation is essential. Early wineries kept close to the river at Nagambie, which also boasts a large lake system. Two of the biggest wineries here, Tahbilk Wines and Mitchelton Wines, believe the nearby lake moderates temperatures, thereby favouring viticulture. The flavours of Shiraz and Cabernet are highly distinctive in this area: rustic, chocolate, dusty, red berries and the smell of baked earth.

Mount Langi Ghiran Wines' vineyard, Grampians

AUSTRALIA'S BUBBLY HEART

Seppelt Great Western is now the biggest sparkling wine operation in the southern hemisphere, producing 18 million litres annually. It stores another 19 million bottles under the various labels of Australia's biggest maker Southcorp. Minchinbury, Kaiser Stuhl, Killawarra, Seaview, Fleur de Lys, Salinger, and the truly indigenous, individual Seppelt Sparkling Shiraz are all made in this mini city of stainless steel. The first owner, Joseph Best, planted the vines and built the impressive winery, employing out-of-work gold miners to dig the cellars. In 1887, the second owner, Hans Irvine, imported winemakers and equipment from Champagne, and in 1918 the third owner, Benno Seppelt, helped expand the company into the giant we see today.

🔲 red and brown sandy clay loams, gravelly quartz sand 🍇 Shiraz, Cabernet Sauvignon, Merlot 🍃 Viognier, Marsanne, Roussane 🍷 red, white

Northeast Victoria

NORTHEAST WHITES ARE regarded as the entrée before a big main meal of powerful fruit, awesome tannins, and potent alcohols – otherwise known as Shiraz, Cabernet Sauvignon and Durif (California's Petite Sirah), a regional speciality. Originally from the Rhône Valley, Durif has been grown here for decades and produces a heady, spicy mix of deeply tannic wine. Centred around Rutherglen, the area is warm to hot, perfect for the production of hearty reds and exceptional fortifieds. Muscat Blanc à Petits Grains and Tokay (Muscadelle) are recognized as some of the most concentrated and luscious dessert wines in the world. The classification system divides these Rutherglen dessert wines into separate quality tiers: starting with Rutherglen, then Classic, Grand, and finally Rare.

🔲 friable red soil, free-draining gravelly quartz sands, red alluvial loam over river gravel 🍇 Shiraz, Cabernet Sauvignon, Durif 🍃 Chardonnay, Riesling, Tokay 🍷 red, white, fortified

King & Alpine Valleys

THE KING VALLEY vineyards, in the heart of Victoria's Alps, are planted to around 800m, making them some of the highest in the state. This is the home of finely-structured Chardonnay and Pinot Noir, as well as more aromatic whites. Further down the valley there is a little corner of Italy, with robust reds like Marzemino and Sangiovese made with firm astringency. Cabernet and Merlot are well-suited too, with a supple, fleshy quality and some of the deepest colours imaginable.

In the Alpine Valleys, towards Bright, the scenery is somewhat similar but the wines are not. This is warmer territory; perfect for Shiraz, which comes in either firm and spicy, or – from producers on the northern border at Beechworth – more savoury and minerally. Durif and Marzemino grapes also look promising in the Alpine Valleys, while Chardonnay from here tends to be very mellow.

fertile, deep red clay loams, sandy loams **Cabernet Sauvignon, Shiraz, Merlot** *Chardonnay, Riesling, Sauvignon Blanc* **red, white**

Gippsland

THE SPRAWLING GIPPSLAND ZONE is usually divided into west, south, and east. The west, around Moe, is possibly the driest and warmest of the three (relatively speaking, for Gippsland is very much cool-climate winemaking), with enough sunshine to ripen Shiraz and Cabernet Sauvignon. The south, around Leongatha, is the coolest, the wettest, and the windiest, with strong breezes whipped up from Bass Strait. Viticulture is demanding, but the results can be excellent Pinot Noir and Chardonnay. The east, around Bairnsdale, has a more moderate Mediterranean climate. Chardonnay is best-suited here, although pockets of Pinot Noir and even Cabernet Sauvignon can be found. Despite its size, Gippsland has fewer than 30 wineries and produced just 290 tonnes of fruit in 2001.

dark black loams to lighter sandy soils **Cabernet Sauvignon, Pinot Noir, Shiraz** *Chardonnay, Sauvignon Blanc* **red, white**

Pizzini Wines label, King & Alpine Valleys

Yarra Valley

MODERN YARRA VALLEY history begins in the 1960s with the revival of St Hubert's and Yeringberg wineries. Its success has been built on a phenomenal ability to make quality wines – from Pinot Noir, Chardonnay, Cabernet Sauvignon, and Shiraz, to great sparkling. It is only possible to produce such a range here as this is a cool winegrowing area – generally considered cooler than Bordeaux but warmer than Burgundy – with a variety of sub-regional climates. The further north you go, the (relatively) warmer and drier it becomes; the further south, the cooler and wetter it is. Yarra Valley Chardonnay is elegant, with flavours of stone fruits and figs. Pinot Noir, in the hands of the best producers, is complex, with cherry and forest fruit flavours. Both Chardonnay and Pinot Noir are the basis of tightly structured sparklings of real delicacy. The Yarra Valley produces great Cabernet Sauvignon, noted for its fine tannins and ageing ability. Shiraz, from the better sites, is taut and elegant.

hard, red duplex, deep, highly fertile red volcanic soils **Pinot Noir, Cabernet Sauvignon, Merlot** *Chardonnay, Sauvignon Blanc, Riesling* **red, white, sparkling**

Mornington Peninsula

ANY WINE LOVER'S wish-list of Australian Chardonnay or Pinot Noir would definitely include one or more Peninsula wines. This area,

Vineyards of Stonier Wines, Mornington Peninsula

only rediscovered for wine in the 1970s, has moved quickly to cement its place as a top Australian region. Through the efforts of producer Elgee Park, it also pioneered the charismatic white Rhône Valley variety, Viognier, in Australia, as well as the rich Alsatian-style Pinot Gris at T'Gallant. Surrounded by water on three sides, the Peninsula is highly maritime, with sea breezes providing a cooling effect on viticulture. This might help to explain why cool-climate Burgundy grape varieties, and not the normal Bordeaux ones, do best here. From its late start, there are now 920ha under vine and 50 cellar doors dotted around the Peninsula from Rosebud and Boneo in the south to Mornington in the north.

well-drained clay, fertile red volcanic, brown duplex, sandy *Pinot Noir, Shiraz* *Chardonnay, Pinot Gris, Sauvignon Blanc* *red, white*

Kreglinger's Pipers Brook Vineyard, Tasmania

Geelong

GEELONG WILL BE REMEMBERED in Australian wine history as the landing place for phylloxera. It was first recorded here in 1875 and brought Geelong winegrowing to an end by 1882. Fast forward to 1966, when there was a wine rebirth thanks to the arrival of Dr Daryl, a veterinary surgeon, and Dr Sefton, whose great grandparents had been members of the Swiss community that had turned Geelong into a major winegrowing district in the first place. To this day, the phylloxera threat is very real here, but most vineyards now use quarantine procedures and phylloxera-resistant rootstock to control it.

The modern emphasis here has been on red wines: Shiraz and Pinot Noir both vie for attention. The warm inland Anakie area is highly suited to generous Shiraz, while the cooler, maritime-influenced Bellarine Peninsula is making inroads with Pinot Noir and Chardonnay. Between these two areas is Bannockburn, home to the highly individual, gamey, and complex Bannockburn Pinot Noir.

red-brown clay loam over hard clay *Cabernet Sauvignon, Shiraz, Pinot Noir* *Chardonnay, Sauvignon Blanc, Riesling* *red, white*

Tasmania

GROWING AND MAKING wine in Tasmania is hard work. No other Australian wine state is cooler, more maritime, or has vineyards more prone to late spring frosts or gusty winds. Site selection becomes highly specialized, and trial and error a common occurrence. In 1972, Dr Andrew Pirie received Australia's First PhD in viticulture for his pioneering work in identifying the Pipers Brook region as a suitable area for fine, aromatic European-style wines. His feasibility study created a template for the future success of Pipers Brook Vineyard, now one of the island's largest and most influential producers. With mountainous terrain on the west and central parts of the island, vineyards (and people) tend to cling to the north, east, and south coastal fringes, which make up the three principal winegrowing districts. The north – Tamar Valley and Pipers Brook – specializes in crisp Chardonnay and highly aromatic whites like Riesling and Pinot Gris, as well as being the home to specialist sparkling winemakers. Selected individual sites on the east coast are proving excellent for ripening Chardonnay and Pinot Noir. Meanwhile, southern Tasmania, around Derwent Valley and Coal River, is extremely marginal – the next major land-mass is Antarctica – and yet can produce fine-textured Cabernet Sauvignon as well as generous Riesling, Chardonnay, and Pinot Noir.

deep red-brown soils, gravelly basalt on clay, ironstone, shallow, sandstone-based, peaty alluvial soils *Pinot Noir, Cabernet Sauvignon* *Chardonnay, Riesling* *red, white, sparkling*

TOP PRODUCERS OF VICTORIA & TASMANIA

Zilzie Wines
Northwest Victoria

Lot 66 Kulkyne Way, Karadoc
☎ 03 5025 8100
🖥 www.zilziewines.com.au ◑

THE FORBES FAMILY only started winemaking in 1999 and now, incredibly, owns one of the largest wine farms in the region. The Zilzie range includes Premium, Show Reserve, and the more commercially attractive Buloke Reserve. Zilzie scored a marketing coup in 2002 by signing up Australian cricketing hero Shane Warne, and putting his name to both a Chardonnay and an excellent Cabernet-Merlot-Petit Verdot. Both are easy-drinking, and well-priced too.
🖼 red, white 📷 2006, 2005, 2004 (r) ★ Show Reserve Chardonnay, Premium Merlot, Shane Warne Collection Cabernet-Merlot-Petit Verdot

Mount Langi Ghiran Wines
Grampians

80 Vine Rd, Bayindeen ☎ 03 5354 3207 🖥 www.langi.com.au ◑

WINEMAKER TREVOR MAST creates a leading example of a modern Australian Shiraz here: medium-bodied, clean, and fine. Mast is a pacesetter and has been an influential convert to minimal chemical intervention in the vineyard, as well as promoting Italian varieties like Pinot Grigio. His early training in Germany has also made him a deft hand with aromatic Riesling. He has even attracted the interest of like-minded top Rhône Valley maker Chapoutier (see p132), and now has a joint venture in place to develop Shiraz.
🖼 red, white 📷 2006, 2005, 2004 (r) ★ Shiraz, Pinot Grigio, Riesling

Seppelt Great Western
Grampians

Moyston Rd, Great Western ☎ 03 5361 2222 🖥 www.seppelt.com.au ◑

SEPPELT HAD TWO of the great Australian wine names guiding its early fortunes: Hans Irvine and Colin Preece. Irvine laid the roots for sparklings in the 1890s by importing winemakers and machinery from Champagne; while Preece made the company's reputation as a serious producer of reds in the 1940s, with brand names like Chalambar and Moyston. Now part of the giant Southcorp wine group, Seppelt Great Western's strengths remain sparkling wines, led by flagship

Seppelt Great Western

Salinger Sparkling and its red equivalent, Show Sparkling Shiraz. There is a range of Shiraz-based still wines too. Chalambar is an everyday red, while the St Peters Shiraz is the best red in the region.
🖼 red, white, sparkling, dessert, fortified 📷 2006, 2005, 2004 (r), 2003 ★ Show Sparkling Shiraz, Salinger Sparkling, St Peters Shiraz

Dalwhinnie
Pyrenees

Taltarni Rd, Moonambel ☎ 03 5467 2388 🖥 www.dalwhinnie.com.cu ◑

IT WAS CHARDONNAY that first attracted attention to Dalwhinnie, but it turns out that this producer's real strengths are Cabernet Sauvignon, Shiraz, and, to a lesser extent, Pinot Noir. An extraordinary vineyard location – up to 670m in the Pyrenees

– enables owners Jenny and David Jones to produce both warm and cool grape varieties. David looks after the Pinot Noir and Shiraz himself, preferring intensive French-inspired methods that deliver complex flavours. His highly concentrated premium Eagle Series Shiraz is one of the priciest reds in the state.
🖼 red, white 📷 2006, 2005, 2004, 2003, 2000, 1999 (w), 1998, 1997 ★ Chardonnay, Cabernet Sauvignon, Eagle Series Shiraz

Redbank Winery
Pyrenees

1 Sally's Lane, Redbank
☎ 03 5467 7255
🖥 www.redbank wines.com ◑

SALLY'S PADDOCK FROM Redbank Wines is the quintessential Victoria red. 'Sally' is the wife of owner Neill Robb, and the 'paddock' is their 4-ha vineyard, which is planted

---

PERFECT CASE: VICTORIA & TASMANIA

🅡 **Bass Phillip Wines Reserve Pinot Noir** ££££

🅡 **Dalwhinnie Eagle Series Shiraz** ££££

🆆 **Freycinet Vineyards Chardonnay** ££

🆆 **Giaconda Vineyard Chardonnay** ££££

🆂 **Jansz Vintage Sparkling** ££

🅡 **Jasper Hill Georgia's Paddock Shiraz** ££££

🅓 **Morris Wines Old Premium Liqueur Muscat** ££££

🅡 **Mount Langi Ghiran Wines Shiraz** ££££

🅡 **Mount Mary Vineyard Cabernet** £££££

🆆 **Pipers Brook Riesling** ££

🆂 **Seppelt Great Western Show Sparkling Shiraz** ££££

🆆 **Stefano Lubiana Wines Chardonnay** ££

with five red varieties – Cabernet Sauvignon, Merlot, Cabernet Franc, Malbec, and Shiraz – all, or some, of which are used to make this elegant blend, depending on the year. Robb revels in low-technology winemaking, retaining an earthiness that makes his wines both original and popular. In 2005, the Robbs sold the Redbank brand to Yalumba, which, under the name Redbank Victoria, now sources its grapes from the King Valley.

🖼 red, white, sparkling 📊 2006, 2005, 2004, 2001, 2000, 1998, 1997 ★ Sally's Paddock, Redbank Winery

Jasper Hill Vineyard
Bendigo & Heathcote

Drummonds Lane, Heathcote
📞 03 5433 2528 🗓 by appt

RON LAUGHTON staked a claim in this area in 1976, and with just two wine styles – Riesling and Shiraz – both the man and the region have become stars. The Georgia's Paddock Shiraz, bold and exotic, tends to steal the limelight, while the refined Emily's Paddock Shiraz-Cabernet Franc has a more elegant taste. Laughton's biodynamic approach to wine has brought him in contact with like-minded Rhône Valley maker Michel Chapoutier *(see p132)*, and the two now have a nearby vineyard planted with French and Australian Shiraz clones.

MITCHELTON

PRINT SHIRAZ
1998
750ml

Mitchelton Wines label

The distinctive Tahbilk Wines winery

🖼 red, white 📊 2006 (r), 2005, 2004, 2002, 2001, 2000 ★ Georgia's Paddock: Riesling and Shiraz

Wild Duck Creek Estate
Bendigo & Heathcote

Spring Flat Rd, Heathcote
📞 03 5433 3133 🗓 by appt

DUCK MUCK SHIRAZ has been one of the wines responsible for creating a new breed of cult Australian wines – so-called 'new classic' styles. Big and bold, this wine has true character – with a name like that, it really has to. Made by David 'Duck' Anderson, who has a delicious sense of the ridiculous, Duck Muck can have an alcohol content as high as 17.5 per cent, with lashings of succulent fruit and oak to match. His other reds, Shiraz and Cabernet Sauvignon, are just as well-made, strong, and highly individual.

🖼 red 📊 2006 (r), 2005, 2004, 2003 (r), 2002 ★ Duck Muck Shiraz, Alan's Cabernet Sauvignon, Springflat Shiraz

Mitchelton Wines
Goulburn Valley

Mitchellstown Rd, Nagambie
📞 03 5736 2222
🌐 www.mitchelton.com.au 🗓

SINCE ITS INCEPTION in 1969, Mitchelton has had just three winemakers; the latest is Ben Haines, the Wine Society's 2008 Young Winemaker of the Year. Owned by drinks giant Lion Nathan, Mitchelton has a strong portfolio of wines concentrating on Rhône grape varieties. The Crescent Shiraz-Grenache-Mourvèdre and Airstrip Marsanne-Viognier-Roussanne are contemporary takes on Rhône blends. For many years, Marsanne was a stalwart, but Mitchelton has recently turned its sights on Viognier. However, the earthy, spicy Shiraz continues to enjoy flagship status.

🖼 red, white, sparkling, dessert 📊 2007 (w), 2006 (r), 2005, 2004 (r), 2003 ★ Viognier, Crescent Rhône red blend, Airstrip Rhône white blend

Tahbilk Wines
Goulburn Valley

Nagambie 📞 03 5794 2555
🌐 www.tahbilk.com.au 🗓

TAHBILK BOASTS a French-inspired château and a classic mix of Rhône varieties. Yet the wines are unequivocally Australian: the reds are earthy and direct, the oak rarely new and intrusive; the whites are mostly unwooded, subtle, and inviting. It has been that way for three generations of Purbrick makers. Changes at Tahbilk are very low-key, like the move to a fruitier Marsanne, and the quiet launch in the late 1990s of its current superstar, Viognier.

🖼 red, white, sparkling, dessert, fortified 📊 2007 (w), 2006 (r), 2005, 2004 (r) ★ Marsanne, 1860 Vines Shiraz, Cabernet Sauvignon, Viognier

Taking barrel samples, Morris Wines

Brown Brothers Milawa Vineyard
Northeast Victoria

Meadow Creek Rd, Milawa 🕻 *03 5720 5500* Ⓦ *www.brownbrothers.com.au*

NAME JUST ABOUT any grape variety and the odds are that this company grows it. The Browns are a family of inveterate experimenters, who have been at the forefront of working with new wave European varieties, and who even created a 'kindergarten' at their Milawa winery in the 1980s to try out wines like the Italian Dolcetto and Sangiovese, Spanish Tempranillo, and the Rhône's Viognier. But Brown Brothers roots are firmly based in tannic, hearty reds, and excellent fortifieds from the Northeast. Its move into the King Valley successfully explored new sparkling and

white wine territory. And in 2003, the first super premium wines (red, white, and sparkling) from the Patricia Vineyard in Heathcote also came on stream.

🖪 *red, white, sparkling, dessert, fortified* 🗷 *2006 (r), 2005, 2004* ★ *King Valley Barbera, Patricia Pinot Noir-Chardonnay Vintage Sparkling, Shiraz-Malbec-Cabernet Sauvignon*

Giaconda Vineyard
Northeast Victoria

McClay Rd, Beechworth 🕻 *03 5727 0246* Ⓦ *www.giaconda.com.au* ☐ *by appt*

WINEMAKING GENIUS Rick Kinzbrunner founded Giaconda in 1985. His apprenticeship in California's Napa and Sonoma valleys was influential in developing methods like handling wild yeasts and fermenting all wine in new oak barrels: a cream-

textured Chardonnay is the result. An Australian classic, it contains flavours of grilled nuts, charred oak, and stone fruits. The Giaconda range also includes equally well-crafted Roussanne, Pinot Noir, Shiraz, and Cabernet Sauvignon.

🖪 *red, white* 🗷 *2006 (r), 2005, 2004* ★ *Chardonnay, Nantua Les Deux (Chardonnay-Roussanne), Shiraz*

Morris Wines
Northeast Victoria

Mia Mia Rd, Rutherglen 🕻 *03 6026 7303* Ⓦ *www.orlandowyndham group.com* ☐

FOUNDED by Englishman George Morris in 1859, this estate was one of the earliest in the area. Old Rhône variety Durif is a long-time Rutherglen and Morris speciality. The company's top Muscats and Tokays (Muscadelles) are also high quality thanks to generations of winemakers putting down blending material. The great Mick Morris's son David is now in charge. The laid-back country feel he gives the place makes it hard to believe that it is actually part of the very businesslike Orlando Wines, and indeed has been since 1970.

🖪 *red, white, sparkling, dessert, fortified* 🗷 *2006, 2005, 2004 (r), 2003 (r), 2002* ★ *Durif, Old Premium Liqueur Muscat, Liqueur Tokay*

Chrismont Wines
King & Alpine Valleys

Lake William Hovell Rd, Cheshunt 🕻 *03 5729 8220* Ⓦ *www.chris montwines.com.au* ☐

THE ENTERPRISING PIZZINI family, descended from early Italian settlers, owns two wineries: Arnie is behind Chrismont, while cousin Fred runs Pizzini. Both have extraordinarily green fingers in the vineyard, as well as intuitive powers in the winery. Arnie is responsible

THE BROWN FAMILY PROFILE

Brown Brothers is an age-old institution in Victoria. From small beginnings in a Milawa vineyard planted in 1889 by John Francis Brown, the company is now the nation's ninth largest seller of wine. John Brown Senior, son of the founder, originally kept everything in the family (hence the winery name). When John died in 2004, Ross Brown took the reins, and his brother Peter left to run his own business at All Saints, establishing a new branch of Brown wine men and women. The family was among the first to capitalize on export opportunities in the 1970s; to explore cool-climate viticulture in the now blossoming King Valley; to produce new wines like the light-bodied red varietal Tarrango; and to push the boundaries with Spanish and Italian grape varieties. In the 1990s, a new generation of Browns – men and women – started in the business, making the name somewhat dated.

FAMOUS LIQUEUR: MUSCAT & TOKAY

Word has finally got out about the great fortified wines from Northeast Victoria: Muscat (the luscious, raisined one) and Tokay (the butterscotch, nuttier one). No other Australian region achieves the same delicious intensity in the glass. The warm climate needed to ripen the grapes Muscat Blanc à Petits Grains and Tokay (Muscadelle) is one key factor. More important are the devoted generations of winemakers who have put down wines for ageing – some cellars hold stocks going back 80 years. Just a splash of an 80-year-old unctuous nectar in the blend and you are made! Then there is the role of the master blender using skills handed down from father to son. Astounding complexity is attained through blending parcels of separate wines: young and old, dry and sweet, solera-blended *(see pp322–3)* and barrel-aged into the final wine. That is why not just anyone can make them.

---

for what is quite possibly the best medium-priced Riesling in Victoria, and with his new Italian-style range (Pinot Grigio, Barbera, and Marzemino), La Zona, he is entering into exciting new territory making very drinkable wines for the table. No heavy alcohols here, just lots of smooth fruit with a touch of bitter astringency.

red, white 2006 (r), 2005 (w), 2004, 2002 ★ *Riesling, La Zona: Pinot Grigio, Barbera*

Pizzini Wines
King & Alpine Valleys

King Valley Rd, Whitfield 03 5729 8278 www.pizzini.com.au

IN THE 1990s, it was only the Pizzini white wines that were impressive. The truth is that owner Fred Pizzini just needed some time to get his wine-making mind around his homeland Italian varieties – reds like Nebbiolo and Sangiovese, as well as the odd white like Vernaccia. Pizzini goes for texture, depth, and complexity in his wines, which are medium-bodied and generously fruit-filled. His passion is Nebbiolo, and he is the first Australian maker to really uncover its hidden depths.

red, white 2006 (r), 2005 (w), 2004, 2003, 2002 ★ *Riesling, Vernaccia, Sangiovese, Nebbiolo*

Bass Phillip Wines
Gippsland

Hunts Rd, Leongatha South 03 5664 3341 *by appt*

REGARDED AS Australia's foremost maker of Pinot Noir, Phillip Jones has suffered for his passion. He lived in a caravan while developing his vineyard and it was 12 years before he sold his first bottle of wine. It was worth the wait though. The perfectionist in Jones looks for ridiculously low yields (a crazy average of one tonne of fruit to every 0.4ha) to concentrate flavour. In his hands, Pinot Noir can be strong but also surprisingly subtle in flavour.

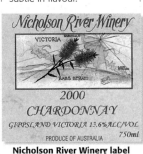

2000
CHARDONNAY
GIPPSLAND VICTORIA 13.6% ALC/VOL 750ml
PRODUCE OF AUSTRALIA

Nicholson River Winery label

red, white 2006, 2005, 2004, 2002, 2001, 1998 ★ *Standard, Premium and Reserve Pinot Noir*

Nicholson River Winery
Gippsland

Liddell's Rd, Nicholson 03 5156 8241 www.nicholsonriver winery.com.au

NICHOLSON RIVER WINERY is definitely out in left-field when it comes to wine. Winemaker Ken Eckersley rejoices in non-conformity. He does not make wines for the Australian wine show circuit (a popular winemaker pastime in this country) but for those after rich mouthfuls of flavour. The flagship Chardonnay, so powerfully rich, ripe, and toasty, and sometimes combined with a touch of botrytis, tends to polarize opinion in wine circles.

red, white 2006, 2005, 2004 ★ *Riesling, Chardonnay, Pinot Noir*

Mount Mary Vineyard
Yarra Valley

22–24 Coldstream West Rd, Lilydale 03 9739 1761

MOUNT MARY's wines offer a truly exceptional experience for those lucky enough to get hold of the tiny amounts produced. Founder and winemaker Dr John Middleton, who died in 2006, maintained the highest standards. His Quintet Cabernet (a blend of five Bordeaux red varieties) is the real jewel in his crown, a classically-structured wine built on glorious blackcurrant fruit, generous but never overstated oak, and fine-grained tannins. Mount Mary wines often take years to reveal their true personality – a style Dr Middleton's son David continues to pursue.

red, white 2006, 2005, 2004, 2003, 2002, 2001 ★ *Quintet Cabernet, Chardonnay, Pinot Noir*

Yarra Yering
Yarra Valley

Briarty Rd, Gruyere
☎ 03 5964 9267 ☐

WITH THE PASSING of founder and winemaker Dr Bailey Carrodus in 2008, one era for Yarra Yering comes to a close but another awaits. Carrodus came to the Valley in 1969 – not only to promote the elegance associated with cool-climate winegrowing, but also to highlight the complex flavours that develop with a wine's maturity. His Dry Red Number One (Cabernet-Malbec-Merlot) and Dry Red Number Two (Shiraz-Viognier) are excellent and should never be tackled young. Carrodus caused a stir by producing Australia's first AUS$100 Merlot.
🖼 *red, white* 🔎 *2006, 2005, 2004 (r), 2002, 2001* ★ *Dry Red Number One, Dry Red Number Two, Pinot Noir*

Yarra Yering

Crittenden Wines
Mornington Peninsula

25 Harrisons Rd, Dromana
☎ 03 5981 8322 🌐 *www.crittenden wines.com.au* ☐

OVER THE LAST 25 YEARS, Garry Crittenden has shown that the Peninsula is a truly exciting place for Chardonnay, Pinot Noir, and even Cabernet Sauvignon – impressive in such a cool climate. He began his winemaking career as founder of Dromana Estate, creating the Schinus range in the mid-1980s and the 'i' label for Italian wine styles in the 1990s. Today, with his winemaker son Rollo, Crittenden runs Crittenden Wines, concentrating on a strong range of Peninsula stalwarts and Italian grapes (under the Pinocchio label).

His latest passion is the Spanish white grape Albariño.
🖼 *red, white, rosé* 🔎 *2007, 2006, 2005 (r), 2004* ★ *Chardonnay, Pinot Noir, 'i' Sangiovese*

Stonier Wines
Mornington Peninsula

2 Thompsons Lane, Merricks
☎ 03 5989 8300
🌐 *www.stoniers. com.au* ☐

FEW PRODUCERS ON the Mornington Peninsula have been able to match Stonier Wines on quality or price. With an enviable record, its multi-layered Chardonnay and fleshy, dark-berried Pinot Noir, both standard and reserve, are consistently among Victoria's best. Little wonder then that the vineyard, established in 1978 by publishing executive Brian Stonier, caught the eye of Australian industry leader Brian Croser of Petaluma: a friendly takeover was completed in 1998. Stonier (like Petaluma Limited; *see p570*) is now part of Lion Nathan but continues to set a blistering pace. Long-time winemaker Geraldine McFaul left in 2008. Mike Symons continues in her footsteps.
🖼 *red, white* 🔎 *2007, 2006, 2005 (r), 2004* ★ *Pinot Noir, Chardonnay*

Bannockburn Vineyards
Geelong

Midland Highway, Bannockburn ☎ 03 5281 1363 🌐 *www.bannockburn vineyards.com* ●

FOR MORE THAN three decades, Bannockburn Vineyards has been at the forefront of super-premium Pinot Noir in the Geelong region. First under winemaker Gary Farr, and now under Michael Glover, Bannockburn enjoys a reputation as one of Australia's finest small makers. Its Pinot is highly perfumed with a noted spicy savouriness. The Chardonnay and Shiraz should not be under-rated either.
🖼 *red, white* 🔎 *2005 (r), 2004, 2003, 2002* ★ *Pinot Noir, Chardonnay, Shiraz*

Scotchmans Hill
Geelong

190 Scotchmans Rd, Drysdale
☎ 03 5251 3176
🌐 *www.scotchmans hill.com.au* ☐

IT TOOK TWO DECADES of making well-priced, easy-drinking Pinot Noir and Chardonnay before the Browne family released its first single vineyard wines from

STEVE WEBBER

In 1987, De Bortoli arrived in the Yarra Valley, and with it came a young winemaker who would leave an indelible mark on Valley winemaking and viticulture. Steve Webber has shown that big-company winemaking can adapt to produce ultra-premium wines. His constant questioning and willingness to experiment have produced some of the region's most stunning individual styles. While others concentrated on Cabernet Sauvignon, Webber championed Shiraz and, later, an elegant Shiraz-Viognier Rhône blend. He also saw the potential for quality Pinot Noir and employed a separate Pinot Noir winemaker. The results speak for themselves. Lately, he has turned his attention to a reserved, less herbaceous style of barrel-fermented Sauvignon Blanc, while his Chardonnay is evolving into something less overtly varietal, with lower alcohol and less new oak.

the same grapes in 2002. Ageing potential has never figured strongly, but wine-maker Robin Brockett has fashioned the reserve styles with tighter complexity which should see them age well.

red, white 2007, 2006, 2005 (r), 2004 (w), 2003 (r) ★ Pinot Noir, Reserve Chardonnay, Shiraz

Freycinet Vineyards
Tasmania

15919 Tasman Hwy, Bicheno
03 6257 8574
www.freycinetvineyard.com.au

GUT INSTINCT told Geoff Bull in 1980 that a 182-ha parcel of land he had bought was suited to vines. He planted a selection of grapes to see if he was right, and almost all (with the exception of Müller-Thurgau) were successful. His son-in-law, Claudio Radenti, transformed the grapes into some of the best, most consistent wines in Tasmania. The Freycinet style is clean and fresh with razor-sharp fruit.

red, white, sparkling 2007, 2006, 2005, 2004 ★ Radenti Sparkling, Chardonnay, Pinot Noir

Jansz
Tasmania

1216B Pipers Brook Rd, Pipers Brook
03 6382 7066
www.jansz.com.au

IT ALL STARTED in 1985 when a leading Tasmanian producer,

Kreglinger Wine Estates wines

Jansz, one of Tasmania's leading producers

Heemskerk, announced a joint venture with Champagne house Louis Roederer (see p175) to make sparkling wine in Tasmania, and a vineyard was planted specially at Pipers Brook. Today, winemaker Natalie Fryar concentrates on three styles: the creamy vintage sparkling, released after three years' ageing on lees; the sherbety non-vintage Chardonnay-Pinot Noir blend, and the late disgorged style for those who like their sparklings rich and honeyed.

sparkling 2005, 2004, 2002, 2000 ★ Jansz Vintage, Jansz Non-Vintage, Jansz LD (Late Disgorged)

Kreglinger Wine Estates
Tasmania

1216 Pipers Brook Rd, Pipers Brook
03 6382 7527
www.kreglingerwineestates.com

KREGLINGER ESTATES is one of Tasmania's biggest wine producers, with well-known brands such as Pipers Brook Vineyard (PBV) and Ninth Island. Kreglinger, an international trading company, bought PBV in 2003 and since then has maintained the PBV bent towards Burgundian and Alsatian styles while also increasing the portfolio of the top-selling Ninth Island. Aromatic varieties such as Riesling, Pinot Gris, and

Gewürztraminer are vibrant, while Chardonnay and Pinot Noir are supremely elegant. Kreglinger also releases an eponymous top-line sparkling wine.

red white, sparkling 2008 (w), 2007, 2006, 2005, 2004, 2003, 2002, 2001, 2000, 1999, 1998 ★ Pirie, Riesling, Chardonnay

Stefano Lubiana Wines
Tasmania

60 Rowbottoms Rd, Granton
03 6263 7457
www.stefanolubiana.com

STEFANO LUBIANA'S move to Hobart, Tasmania, brought him national recognition for his elegant sparkling, and Pinot Noir and Chardonnay varietals. In one of Australia's coldest wine regions, he manages to achieve incredibly ripe fruit with potential alcohol levels of up to 14.5 per cent, which is transformed into some of Tasmania's most complex wines and released under the flagship Signature label. Any wine made by Lubiana is highly individual in style, and none more so than his full-bodied Pinot Grigio, first made in 2000.

red, white, sparkling 2007, 2006, 2005, 2004 (w), 2003 ★ Sparkling Brut Non-Vintage, Signature: Chardonnay, Pinot Noir, Pinot Grigio

WESTERN AUSTRALIA

I N THIS STATE *of sun-seared plains and rugged mountain ranges, it is incredible that a wine industry has not only survived but flourished. This has been achieved by keeping plantings to the temperate south and focusing on the land around the coastal towns and cities, with only a few vineyards slightly inland.*

Western Australia (or WA) may be vast but only 13,091 ha of it are actually under vine, yielding 7.5 per cent of Australia's total wine output. However, it is the quality rather than the quantity that counts here.

In the 1920s the emergence of luscious fortified wines from the hot Swan District revealed that the region had real possibilities for wine, but it was Houghton Wine Company's 1930s 'White Burgundy' – a flavoursome golden white – which really put Western Australia on the wine map. The state's potential was fulfilled some 30 years later. It was kick-started by a 1965 research report *(see p607)* that highlighted Margaret River as an exciting new wine area – somewhat similar to Bordeaux. Ten years later, 11 vineyards had already been planted there, and the rest is history. Today, Margaret River stands as Western Australia's pre-eminent wine region, although promising new viticultural areas like Great Southern could be set to rival it in the future.

The subtle qualities of many Western Australian wines come as a surprise. Unlike the mainstream bold Australian style, they tend to be generous in fruit flavour, medium- rather than full-bodied, and supported by an ultra-fine structure. Chardonnay, Sauvignon Blanc, Sémillon, and, increasingly, Riesling are the most planted white varieties. The state has been highly successful with Bordeaux reds too – Cabernet Sauvignon, Merlot, and Cabernet Franc – producing some world-class examples. However, it is Shiraz that is gaining most recognition, with cool-climate examples showing a highly attractive spicy pepperiness and a new exciting weight that is rare in Australian reds.

Shiraz grapes

Vineyards near Mount Barker, Great Southern

◁ **View of riverside vineyards in the Margaret River region**

WINE MAP OF WESTERN AUSTRALIA

WESTERN AUSTRALIA MAY be the largest state in the country, but in wine terms it is a mere minnow. With the exception of those in the blazingly hot Swan District, wineries tend to be concentrated mostly south of the capital, Perth. They hug the coastal areas, where the sea breezes keep temperatures sufficiently cool to produce fine wines, especially in the prime winegrowing area of Margaret River. Regional differences have started to reveal themselves: the emerging Pinot Noirs of Pemberton and Manjimup, the Rieslings of Mount Barker, and the Shiraz and Cabernet Sauvignons of Great Southern are now among the most exciting wines produced in the state.

KEY

Western Australia

**Plantagenet Wines,
Great Southern**

PERFECT CASE:
WESTERN AUSTRALIA

W Cape Mentelle Sémillon-Sauvignon Blanc ££

R Cullen Wines Cabernet Sauvignon-Merlot ££££

W Frankland Estate Riesling ££

R Houghton Wine Company Pemberton Merlot ££

W Leeuwin Estate Art Series Chardonnay £££

R Moss Wood Winery Cabernet Sauvignon Blend ££££

R Plantagenet Wines Mount Barker Shiraz ££

G Sandalford Wines Sandalera ££

W Smithbrook Wines Sauvignon Blanc ££

S Stone Bridge Estate Sparkling ££

D Vasse Felix Botrytis Sémillon ££

W Voyager Estate Chardonnay ££

WESTERN AUSTRALIA: AREAS & TOP PRODUCERS

SWAN DISTRICT *p606*
Houghton Wine Company *p608*
Sandalford Wines *p608*

GEOGRAPHE *p606*

MARGARET RIVER *p606*
Cape Mentelle *p608*
Cullen Wines *p609*
Leeuwin Estate *p609*
Moss Wood Winery *p609*
Vasse Felix *p609*
Voyager Estate *p610*
Xanadu Wines *p610*

MANJIMUP *p607*
Chestnut Grove Wines *p610*
Stone Bridge Estate *p610*

PEMBERTON *p607*
Picardy *p610*
Smithbrook Wines *p611*

GREAT SOUTHERN *p607*
Alkoomi Wines *p611*
Frankland Estate *p611*
Plantagenet Wines *p611*
Wignalls Wines *p611*

Hand picking grapes in Margaret River

TERROIR AT A GLANCE

Latitude: 30–35°S.

Altitude. 40–400m.

Topography: Flat alluvial river plains, hills and ridges dominate.

Soil: Sandy and gravelly loams with overlying clay or granite of moderate fertility. Swan River irrigates the less fertile sandy soil in Swan District.

Climate: Maritime; the growing season is lengthened by reduced diurnal and seasonal temperature fluctuations. Swan District and Great Southern are the hottest, driest parts of the state, and irrigation remains a priority in these regions.

Temperature: January average is 20.5°C.

Rainfall: Annual average is 1,145mm.

Wind: Sea breezes moderate temperatures. Swan District: cooling afternoon wind known as the Fremantle Doctor. Great Southern: icy Antarctic current brings icy winds called The Roaring Forties.

Viticultural hazards: Wind damage; birds; drought.

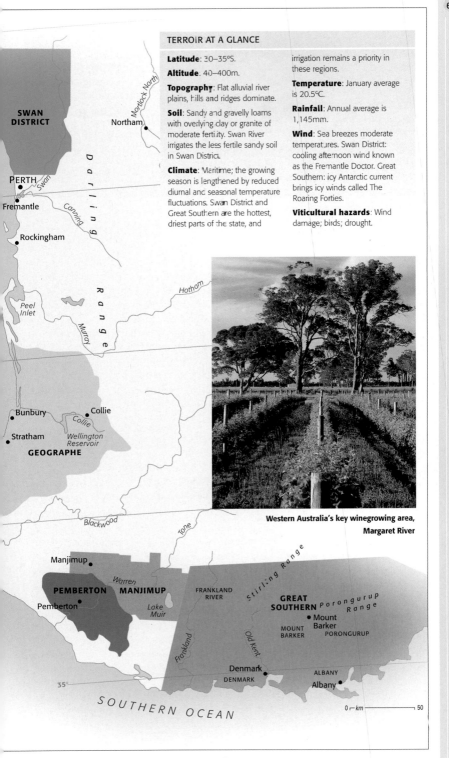

Western Australia's key winegrowing area, Margaret River

SWAN DISTRICT

Mortlock North

Northam

Darling

PERTH

Swan

Fremantle

Canning

Rockingham

Range

Hotham

Peel Inlet

Murray

Bunbury

Collie

Collie

Stratham

Wellington Reservoir

GEOGRAPHE

Blackwood

Tone

Manjimup

Warren

PEMBERTON

MANJIMUP

Pemberton

Lake Muir

FRANKLAND RIVER

Stirling Range

GREAT SOUTHERN

Porongurup Range

Mount Barker

MOUNT BARKER

PORONGURUP

Frankland

Old Kent

Denmark

DENMARK

ALBANY

Albany

35°

SOUTHERN OCEAN

0 — km — 50

Voyager Estate's winery in Margaret River

WINEGROWING AREAS OF WESTERN AUSTRALIA

Swan District

THE WESTERN AUSTRALIAN wine industry was born in the Swan District in 1829. Olive Farm at Guildford, north of Perth, has the distinction of having planted the first vineyard, but it is Houghton Wine Company, founded in 1859, which is recognized as truly marking the start of the commercial wine industry here.

The region boasts a hot climate, making it perfect for the production of the luscious fortified wines that gained prominence in the 1920s. Other wine styles then followed in the 1930s – tending to be full-bodied with a soft, mouth-filling generosity. Swan District has enjoyed greater success with white wines than reds, and the search for higher and cooler areas, such as Moondah Brook in the north, has definitely been rewarded with some high-quality wines, like Verdelho and Chenin Blanc.

Cape Mentelle label, Margaret River

🌄 yellow-brown loamy soil, sandy yellow duplex 🖳 Crenache, Shiraz, Cabernet Sauvignon 🍇 Chenin Blanc, Chardonnay, Verdelho 🍷 red, white, fortified

Geographe

THIS AREA TAKES ITS NAME from Geographe Bay, a popular seaside resort. While grapes have been cultivated here since the 1920s, the modern resurgence of the area on the wine scene dates back to 1973 when Dr Barry Killerby established Leschenault Wines (now Killerby Wines) at Stratham, close to the Indian Ocean. He was followed by Capel Vale in 1975, and it is still these two producers that dominate this coastal strip north of Margaret River. The climate is warm and dry, yet influenced by ocean breezes that have a cool and humidifying effect on winegrowing. Chardonnay is the most consistent performer and it runs the gamut of styles from fine to full-bodied. New red stars on the rise are robust Shiraz and full-bodied Merlot.

🌄 free-draining sands over limestone, sandy loams 🖳 Shiraz, Merlot, Cabernet Sauvignon 🍇 Chardonnay, Sémillon, Sauvignon Blanc 🍷 red, white

Margaret River

MARGARET RIVER HAS IT ALL: buckets of sunshine, surf, and world-class wines. The region comprises a coastal strip of low ridges from Cape Naturaliste in the north to Cape Leeuwin in the south. The star of Western Australia's winegrowing areas, it is one of the most maritime-influenced regions in the country, with ocean winds moderating the warm climate. Identified back in 1965 by agronomist Dr John Gladstones (*see p607*) as an exciting new wine region, Margaret River has developed fast. From one vineyard (Vasse Felix) in 1967, the region now has more than 114 producers. Gladstones compared the climate with Pomerol and St-Émilion in Bordeaux and it is certainly the red and white Bordeaux grape varieties that stand out here, as well as a lively Sauvignon Blanc and a creamy, complex Chardonnay.

 *gravelly sandy loams with underlying granite*
 *Cabernet Sauvignon, Shiraz, Merlot, Pinot Noir*
 *Sémillon, Sauvignon Blanc, Riesling, Chardonnay*  *red, white*

Manjimup

IT IS STILL EARLY DAYS in Manjimup, a wine region that only dates from the late 1980s. Vineyards are thin on the ground and most run as small family concerns. The only sizeable player is Cape Mentelle, a Margaret River producer that set up a joint venture in 1998 with Fonty's Pool Farm, a local grower. The venture is producing a range of well-priced wines (Chardonnay, Pinot Noir, and Shiraz). The region, warmer than Pemberton to the south, is showing potential as a source of quality Chardonnay and Pinot Noir for exciting sparklings. It is also creating some vibrantly fruity still wines led by exuberant Verdelho and easy-drinking Chardonnay in the whites, and smooth Pinot Noir and Merlot in the reds.
gravelly sands and loams *Cabernet Sauvignon, Pinot Noir, Merlot* *Chardonnay, Verdelho* *red, white, sparkling*

Pemberton

LIKE MARGARET RIVER, Pemberton has agronomist Dr John Gladstones to thank for highlighting its winegrowing potential. His report declared Pemberton to be one of the state's better sites for Pinot Noir and Chardonnay as a result of its relatively low temperatures, reduced sunshine hours, and high rainfall and humidity. His assessment has been proven correct. Site selection is vitally important in Pemberton because of its generally cool climate. The most consistent and successful wine is Chardonnay. Pinot Noir has put in the odd great performance but lacks general consistency. The low-lying mountains, northeast of Pemberton, where

Houghton's vineyards in the Swan District

AUSTRALIA'S BORDEAUX

In 1965, agronomist Dr John Gladstones put forward the tantalizing theory that Margaret River had the potential to become an Australian Bordeaux. He found close climatic analogies between the regions, although Margaret River had the advantage of less spring frost, more reliable summer sun, and less risk of excessive rain during ripening. Consequently, in the 1970s, 20 vineyards were established in Margaret River. Another 23 were planted in the 1980s and, true to Gladstones' report, a strong Bordeaux connection was made. Sauvignon Blanc and Sémillon, traditional Bordeaux white varieties, adapted well to produce Margaret River's signature white. But it is the principal red varieties of Bordeaux – Cabernet Sauvignon, Merlot, Cabernet Franc, and Petit Verdot – that excel here. The wines are generous in fruit and smooth in tannin but are also well-structured. The words used most often to describe Margaret River Cabernet? Stylish and elegant.

Salitage and Picardy have vineyards, is showing great potential for elegant, medium-bodied wines. Watch this space.
gravelly sands and loams, fertile loams *Cabernet Sauvignon, Pinot Noir, Merlot* *Verdelho, Chardonnay, Sauvignon Blanc* *red, white*

Great Southern

HERE, THE EMPHASIS is on 'Great', for this is the biggest wine region in Western Australia. Great Southern has five subregions now developing individual styles. **Frankland River**, in the west, is gaining a reputation for elegant Riesling and Cabernet Sauvignon. **Mount Barker**, to the southeast of Frankland, is making a delightful spicy Rhône-style Shiraz; while **Albany**, in the south, is characterized by fleshy Pinot Noir and Chardonnay. **Denmark**, to the west of Albany, is producing fragrant whites and juicy reds. **Porongurup**, dominated by the Porongurup Range, is the latest up-and-coming region and is showing promise with aromatic Riesling, generous Chardonnay, and opulent Pinot Noir.
hard, mottled yellow duplex *Cabernet Sauvignon, Shiraz, Pinot Noir* *Chardonnay, Riesling, Sauvignon Blanc* *red, white*

TOP PRODUCERS OF WESTERN AUSTRALIA

Houghton Wine Company
Swan District

Dale Rd, Middle Swan
☎ 08 9274 9450
🖰 www.houghton-wines.com.au ❑

LEGENDARY WINEMAKER Jack Mann established Houghton with his sherry styles and a big, ripe Chenin Blanc called White Burgundy. This became one of the most successful wines in Australia. Houghton's success saw a takeover by Thomas Hardy & Sons (now BRL Hardy) in 1976. The company's Jack Mann Cabernet oozes vibrant plum aromas, while the velvety Margaret River Cabernet, from Houghton's premium regional selection, delivers flavours of blackcurrant with underlying oak-defined spices.
🔳 red, white, sparkling, dessert, fortified 🔳 2006, 2005, 2004 (r), 2003 (r) ★ Pemberton Chardonnay, Jack Mann Cabernet Sauvignon, Margaret River Cabernet Sauvignon

Sandalford Wines
Swan District

3210 West Swan Rd, Caversham
☎ 08 9374 9374
🖰 www.sandalford.com ❑

THE LATE 1970s and early 80s were a golden age for Sandalford Wines. Winemaker Dorham Mann dominated

Vanya Cullen of Cullen Wines

the wine shows, as his father Jack had previously done for Swan Valley rival Houghton. His Riesling, Chenin Blanc, Verdelho, and Cabernet Sauvignon found huge consumer appeal. When Mann retired, competition saw the firm's market share dwindle and the company was sold, and sold again. The Sandalford name is no longer as big as it used to be but its Element range is a strong all-rounder (from creamy Chardonnay to soft, fruity Cabernet-Shiraz, while its fortifieds, led by Sandalera – made from old Verdelho vines and similar to sweet madeira – are sensational.
🔳 red, white, dessert, fortified 🔳 2006 (w), 2005 ★ Element Chardonnay, Element Cabernet-Shiraz, Sandalera

Cape Mentelle
Margaret River

Wallcliffe Rd, Margaret River
☎ 08 9757 0888
🖰 www.capementelle.com.au ❑

THE SISTER COMPANY of Cloudy Bay (see p625), Cape Mentelle was founded in 1971 in the belief that Margaret River and Cabernet Sauvignon were made for each other. Owner-winemaker David Hohnen was proved right in the 1980s with two successive wins of the coveted Jimmy Watson red wine trophy. Cabernet Sauvignon is the leader in a strong red range. Inspired by his time in California, Hohnen pioneered Zinfandel in Australia and makes an intense style. The Sémillon-Sauvignon Blanc blend is zesty, the Chardonnay is fruit-focused, and the well-structured Cabernet has hints of coffee and vanilla. Veuve Clicquot (see p174) invested in Cape Mentelle in 1988, but Hohnen continued to call the shots until his retirement in 2003. Today, talented young winemaker Robert Mann oversees wine production.
🔳 red, white 🔳 2006 (w), 2005, 2004 (r), 2003 (w), 2002 (w), 2001 ★ Cabernet Sauvignon, Chardonnay, Sémillon-Sauvignon Blanc

MARGARET RIVER SÉMILLON

Think of Australian Sémillon and the Hunter Valley springs to mind, but Margaret River is also producing a quality statement with this grape. Here, in a more temperate climate, Sémillon (right) is often tropical with a herbal edge, and rounder in flavour than in the Hunter Valley. In cooler years, it has more in common with Sauvignon Blanc, offering grassy herbal notes and an edgy acidity. Producers, notably Moss Wood Winery, who keep it as a varietal, make styles capable of ageing. Of more immediate appeal, however, is Margaret River's signature Sémillon-Sauvignon Blanc blend. No Australian region does it better: this Sémillon-Sauvignon is vibrantly fruity with a generous palate. Producers like Cape Mentelle and Cullen Wines have even barrel-fermented some Sauvignon Blanc for increased complexity.

Cullen Wines
Margaret River

Caves Rd, Cowaramup 📞 *08 9755 5277* 🌐 *www.cullenwines.com.au* ⬛

IF AUSTRALIA HAS a premier boutique winemaker it is Cullen Wines. The Cullen family touch is mesmerizing, whether it be in the subtlety of a Sémillon-Sauvignon Blanc or in the complex power of their Australian icon, Cullen Cabernet Sauvignon-Merlot. Dr Kevin Cullen established the vineyard in 1971, and when his medical practice proved too time-consuming he handed winemaking duties to his wife, Di. She wove her magic in what was then one of the most remote winemaking regions in Australia. When daughter Vanya took over in 1989, experimentation increased, and her refining of the Chardonnay in particular has led to its worldwide recognition. It is not only richly complex, but so finely structured and balanced that it is one of the few Australian Chardonnays worthy of cellaring for a decade.

🟥 *red, white* 📲 *2006 (w), 2005, 2004 (r), 2002, 2001* ★ *Cabernet Sauvignon-Merlot, Chardonnay, Sémillon-Sauvignon Blanc*

Leeuwin Estate
Margaret River

Stevens Rd, Margaret River 📞 *08 9759 0000* 🌐 *www.leeuwinestate.com.au* ⬛

THE BRAINCHILD OF Perth couple Denis and Tricia Horgan, Leeuwin Estate was originally bought in 1969 as a cattle farm. But a meeting with noted Californian wineman Robert Mondavi in 1973 changed all that and a grand plan was hatched.

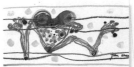

Leeuwin Estate Art Series: Riesling and Chardonnay labels

Leeuwin's Art Series Chardonnay is extraordinary in its fruit intensity, and one of the few Australian Chardonnays to age well; it is rightly regarded as one of the best in the land. Other wines are dwarfed in its shadow, but deserving of greater recognition are the fine-tannined Art Series Cabernet Sauvignon and the delicate Riesling.

🟥 *red, white* 📲 *2005 (w), 2004 (r), 2003, 2002* ★ *Art Series: Chardonnay, Cabernet Sauvignon, Riesling*

Moss Wood Winery
Margaret River

Metricup Rd, Wilyabrup 📞 *08 9755 6266* 🌐 *www.mosswood.com.au* ⬛ *by appt*

WINEMAKER Keith Mugford supposedly came to Margaret River for the surfing, yet ended up staying for the wine. He has never sought the limelight, but his wines have become classics nonetheless. Since buying Moss Wood in 1985, he has crafted Chardonnay, Sémillon, Pinot Noir, and Cabernet Sauvignon to an astonishingly consistent level of quality. Moss Wood's star is its ripe berry Cabernet Sauvignon, which has been modified over the years with Cabernet Franc, Merlot, and Petit

**Moss Wood Winery
Cabernet Sauvignon**

Verdot. Many new releases come from their Ribbon Vale vineyard, also in Margaret River.

🟥 *red, white* 📲 *2006 (w), 2005, 2004 (r), 2003, 2002 (w)* ★ *Cabernet Sauvignon, Chardonnay, Sémillon*

Vasse Felix
Margaret River

Harmans Rd South, Cowaramup 📞 *08 9756 5000* 🌐 *www.vassefelix. com.au* ⬛

TOM CULLITY, a Perth cardiologist with the viticultural passion of a true visionary, started Vasse Felix in 1967, making him Margaret River's first commercial winegrower. In 1987 it was bought by millionaire Robert Holmes à Court. The injection of family money into the winery and fine restaurant has contributed to its preeminent status. It is hard to say which is most impressive, the sweet-berried Shiraz or the Heytesbury Cabernet Sauvignon blend. In a great year, the Heytesbury shines with a good fruit generosity, softness and elegant Margaret River herbals. There is also the top-of-the-line creamy Heytesbury Chardonnay, and the impressive, honeyed Noble Riesling.

🟥 *red, white, sparkling, dessert* 📲 *2006, 2005, 2004 (r), 2002 (w), 1999 (r)* ★ *Heytesbury: Cabernet Sauvignon and Chardonnay, Shiraz*

Voyager Estate
Margaret River

Stevens Rd, Margaret River
☎ *08 9757 6354*
W *www.voyagerestate.com.au* ○

VOYAGER ESTATE IS owned by multi-millionaire mining magnate Michael Wright. Said to be virtually teetotal, he is very serious about wine and has spent large sums on making Voyager Estate a regional landmark, both in architecture (it is very Cape Dutch) and premium wine quality.

The groundwork was laid by Stuart Pym, a talented winemaker who was the architect of the Voyager Chardonnay style – elegant, rich, and textured. The company also makes a serious barrel-fermented Sémillon-Sauvignon Blanc called Tom Price. Today, current winemaker Cliff Royle shows a deft hand with oak, noticeable in both the peppery Shiraz and the tightly structured Cabernet Sauvignon.

🍷 *red, white* 📆 *2006 (w), 2005, 2004 (r)* ★ *Chardonnay, Tom Price Sémillon-Sauvignon Blanc, Cabernet Sauvignon*

Xanadu Wines
Margaret River

Boodjidup Rd, Margaret River
☎ *08 9757 2581* W *www.xanaduwines.com.au* ○

DURING THE 1990S Xanadu enjoyed a wine ride like few others, producing a strong range of well-made wines with potential for growth. In 1999, the Lagan family founders sold to a group of investors, and by 2001 the company was listed on the stock exchange. Ambitious expansion (including the purchase of Normans Wines) brought Xanadu to its knees and eventual sale in 2005

The family-run Picardy winery in Pemberton

to the Rathbone wine group. The once-proud label is back to better things these days. The Dragon range is great value.

🍷 *red, white* 📆 *2006 (w), 2005, 2004, 2003, 2002, 2001* ★ *Reserve Cabernet Sauvignon, Chardonnay, Secession Sauvignon Blanc-Sémillon*

Chestnut Grove Wines
Manjimup

Chestnut Grove Rd, Manjimup
☎ *08 9368 0099*
W *www.chestnutgrove.com.au* ○

CHESTNUT GROVE was established in 1991 with a gorgeous range that helped to put Manjimup on the map. A passion-fruit-infused Verdelho made the biggest noise, followed by a Merlot, weighty in alcohol, power, and body, which belies this region's reputation for being cool and marginal. But cool it definitely is, as shown in the Chestnut Grove Pinot Noir and Cabernet-Merlot, which vary with the vintage. In 2002, the Chestnut Grove brand was bought by Australian Wine Holdings. However, the Kordic family founders still own the vineyard and winery.

🍷 *red, white, sparkling* 📆 *2006 (w), 2005 (w), 2004 (r), 2002 (w)* ★ *Verdelho, Sémillon-Sauvignon Blanc, Merlot*

Voyager Estate Chardonnay

Stone Bridge Estate
Manjimup

189 Holly's Rd, Manjimup
☎ *08 9773 1371* ○ *by appt*

KATE HOOPER LEARNED much of her winemaking trade in Champagne, Bordeaux, and Burgundy before coming home to the family winery. Her experience is invaluable when dealing with the equally cool climate of Manjimup. Kate's sparkling wine is her strongest card, a full-flavoured style that usually sees at least 30 months on lees – a considerable investment for a small producer, but one that proves its serious intentions.

🍷 *red, white, sparkling* 📆 *2006 (w), 2005 (w), 2004 (r), 2002 (w)* ★ *Sparkling, Shiraz*

Picardy
Pemberton

Vasse Hwy & Eastbrook Rd, Pemberton
☎ *08 9776 0036* W *www.picardy.com.au* ○ *by appt*

AFTER HELPING pioneer Cabernet Sauvignon at Moss Wood in Margaret River, Bill and Sandra Pannell sold out and moved on to establish Picardy in 1993. Their dream was to see how Chardonnay and Pinot Noir, as well as Shiraz and Cabernet Sauvignon, fared in the cooler Pemberton region. With the couple's keen interest in Burgundy, it was not surprisingly a minerally Chardonnay and racy Pinot Noir that made an impressive start. A deep-coloured, spicy, rich Shiraz has also been made.

★ red, white 🗷 2006 (w), 2005, 2004, 2003 (w), 2002 (r), 2001 (w) ★ Chardonnay, Pinot Noir, Shiraz

Smithbrook Wines
Pemberton

Smithbrook Rd, Middlesex
☎ 08 9772 3557
🅦 www.smithbrook.com.au 🔾 by appt

THIS LITTLE-KNOWN COMPANY used to supply big name producers with grapes from its large holdings in the awakening Pemberton region. However, a small amount was kept aside to make wine under the Smithbrook label, including a fresh and lively Sauvignon Blanc and a peachy Chardonnay. Bought by Brian Croser of Petaluma in 1997, the label was revamped and, importantly, the company's Pinot Noir plantings were replaced by Merlot, which proved to be inspired. Soft, plummy, and – like all Smithbrook wines – great value, the Merlot is now the flagship.

★ red, white 🗷 2006 (w), 2005, 2004, 2003, 2001 (r), 2000 (w) ★ Merlot, Chardonnay, Sauvignon Blanc

Alkoomi Wines
Great Southern

Wingebellup Rd, RMB 234, Frankland
☎ 08 9855 2229 🅦 www.alkoomi
wines.com.au 🔾

RIESLING HELPED establish Alkoomi Wines and the Frankland area. The early Rieslings showed the kind of flavour intensity normally associated with the Clare and Eden valleys, and sparked immediate interest. Sea breezes help prolong the growing season here, giving the grapes time to accumulate incredible richness. But

the climate seems to suit every variety that winemaker Merv Lange grows: Cabernet Sauvignon is deep in colour and rich in fruit, and the black pepperiness of the Shiraz is also very appealing.

★ red, white 🗷 2006, 2005, 2004, 2003, 2002, 2001, 1999 ★ Shiraz, Cabernet Sauvignon, Riesling

Frankland Estate
Great Southern

Frankland Rd, Frankland 🅦 www.
franklandestate.com.au
☎ 08 9855 1544 🔾 by appt

JUDI CULLAM AND BARRIE SMITH call one of their wines Isolation Ridge. It is easy to see why: Frankland is one of the last great pioneer winegrowing regions in Australia. Cullam and Smith were farmers and wine enthusiasts who moved into winegrowing. Apprenticed in France, they even managed to lure Bordeaux producer Jenny Dobson here as an early winemaker. The restrained, elegant feel to their Cabernet Sauvignon makes it stand out in the Australian Cabernet crowd, and Olmo's Reward is a Bordeaux-style blend. The Shiraz can be vibrantly peppery, while the powerful Riesling has become an unofficial flagship.

★ red, white 🗷 2007 (w), 2005, 2004, 2003 (w), 2001 ★ Riesling, Isolation Ridge Shiraz, Olmo's Reward

Alkoomi Wines label

Plantagenet Wines
Great Southern

Albany Hwy, Mount Barker
☎ 08 9851 3111
🅦 www.plantagenetwines.com 🔾

PLANTAGENET STARTED LIFE in an apple-packing shed in Mount Barker township in 1974, and established the area's early wine history. The locals considered the building of a winery quite mad, but owner Tony Smith, a bespectacled Englishman, persisted, and Plantagenet survived. First came a fresh, aromatic Riesling, which looked and tasted unlike anything grown in Western Australia before. The Shiraz also wowed drinkers: all peppery and bouncy. As the fruit quality is so remarkably clean and fresh, Smith has pioneered an unoaked Chardonnay too.

★ red, white, dessert 🗷 2006, 2005, 2004, 2003 (w) ★ Omrah: Shiraz and, Unoaked Chardonnay; Mount Barker Cabernet Sauvignon

Wignalls Wines
Great Southern

Chester Pass Rd, Albany ☎ 08 9841 2848 🅦 www.wignallswines.com 🔾

BILL AND PAT WIGNALL were thinking about growing Pinot Noir before many Australian drinkers had even heard of the grape. They believed that King River near Albany shared many similarities with Burgundy's Côte de Nuits (see p95) and pressed on with Pinot Noir, Chardonnay, and a little Cabernet Sauvignon. In 1998 the Wignalls spent AUS$1 million on a vast new winery and they now employ Ben Kagi, formerly of Rippon Vineyard, New Zealand (see p627) to oversee their dream.

★ red, white 🗷 2005, 2004, 2002 (r), 2001, 1999, 1993 (r) ★ Shiraz, Pinot Noir, Chardonnay

NEW ZEALAND

NEW ZEALAND

N EW ZEALAND'S WINE JOURNEY *from obscurity to international renown has taken place only over the last 20 years. This is quite a formidable feat for a small country with a population of only four million.*

BACKGROUND

New Zealand's first vines were planted by English missionary Reverend Samuel Marsden in 1819 at Kerikeri on North Island. The first recorded wine was made some 20 years later in Waitangi by James Busby, the country's first resident British envoy. For the next century, winegrowers' efforts amounted to little. However, the 1960s saw a fresh start with government backing for the industry and an influx of international wine companies like Penfolds, McWilliam's, and Seagram. With increased investment and enthusiasm came better viticulture, better grape varieties, and better wines.

Sauvignon Blanc grapes

Like Australia, New Zealand built its wine industry in the warmer northern regions where ripening could be assured: Auckland on North Island's west coast and Hawke's Bay on the east laid the early foundations. During the 1970s, however,

the challenge was to see what South Island could do. Cooler sites were tried for the first time in Australia and New Zealand for varieties like Sauvignon Blanc, Chardonnay, Merlot, Cabernet Sauvignon, and Pinot Noir. New Zealand's biggest producer, Montana, is credited with planting the first vines in Marlborough in 1973. Its zesty 1980 Sauvignon Blanc was a revelation, and proved to be a catalyst for New Zealand's wine industry. It was responsible for stimulating the tastebuds of Australian winemaker, David Hohnen of Cape Mentelle *(see p608)*. After tasting a Marlborough Sauvignon, he travelled across the Tasman Sea to set up Cloudy Bay. The first release here, created by winemaker Kevin Judd in 1985, caused an international sensation. Other regions on the chilly South Island then opened up to winegrowing, including Nelson, Central Otago, and Canterbury. By 1990, there

The dramatic backdrop to Montana Wines' vineyards in Auckland and Northland

◁ **Mountain views from Cloudy Bay's vineyards, Marlborough**

Sign for Nigel Greening's successful Felton Road winery in Central Otago

were almost 5,000ha under vine. This was the start of an incredible boom, which today shows few signs of easing, with 24,660ha on the two islands combined.

THE WINE INDUSTRY TODAY

New Zealand has become a quality player on the international wine scene. It currently boasts over 500 wineries. The industry crushed a record 205,000 tonnes of fruit in 2007, although this was a mere splash in the ocean compared with its big brother winemaking neighbour, Australia, which crushed an incredible 1.3 million tonnes in the same year.

The export market is definitely driving the boom times, having risen to a record level of NZ$698 million in 2007. Large companies are leading the way: Pernod-Ricard (Montana) is the giant on the New Zealand wine scene; Constellation (Nobilo) is in the number two spot; with Delegats, one of the country's largest family-owned wineries, in third place. The heart and soul of New Zealand's wine industry remains in the many family-run wineries that dot the landscape. They may be small in size but they make up the bulk of wineries and have been responsible for opening up whole new winegrowing regions like Central Otago.

GRAPE VARIETIES & WINE STYLES

The country's most popular variety is Sauvignon Blanc. It has now surpassed Chardonnay as the most widely planted grape, accounting for 42 per cent of the total vineyard area. Chardonnay, with 16 per cent, is still holding its own and is capable of producing a wide range of styles. There is also a trend toward more red varieties. This has been led by the success of Pinot Noir, now the third most planted grape in the country with more than 4,000ha under vine. The chances of producing vibrant varietal Pinot flavours tend to increase on the cooler South Island, which is where the main growth has been. Merlot represents around six per cent of total plantings, and Pinot Gris and Riesling are, despite fierce competition, gaining a foothold.

Yet the success of New Zealand wines, with their clear, almost pristine fruit flavours and freshness, has far from dulled the New Zealand winegrowers' sense of exploration. The future of white varieties like Pinot Gris looks very promising, and some makers are willing to explore territory that was once unheard of – Syrah and Italian red varieties. There are still plenty more areas and grape varieties to be discovered.

Kumeu River Wines, Auckland and Northland

WINE MAP OF NEW ZEALAND

Tʜᴇ ᴛᴡᴏ ɪsʟᴀɴᴅs that make up New Zealand – North and South – are bristling with vineyards across the country's nine main winegrowing regions. North Island boasts five, including the second largest region, Hawke's Bay. South Island has four, but includes the biggest region, Marlborough. Winegrowing areas here span the latitudes of 35° to 46° south, covering more than 1,600km and taking in the most southerly vineyards in the world. The diversity of climate and terrain here is immense, and harvests in the warmer northern areas can finish up to seven weeks earlier than those in the cooler south.

Entrance to Dry River, Wairarapa

NORTH ISLAND: AREAS & TOP PRODUCERS

AUCKLAND & NORTHLAND p618

Babich Wines p622
Goldwater Estate p622
Kumeu River Wines p622
Montana Wines p622
Nobilo Wine Group p623
Stonyridge Vineyard p623
Villa Maria Estate p623

Sauvignon Blanc from well-known producer Cloudy Bay, Marlborough

WAIKATO & BAY OF PLENTY p618

GISBORNE p618

HAWKE'S BAY p618
C J Pask Winery p623
Corbans Winery p624
Craggy Range Winery p624
Te Mata Estate p624

WELLINGTON & WAIRARAPA p619
Ata Rangi p624
Dry River p624
Martinborough Vineyard p625
Palliser Estate p625

SOUTH ISLAND: AREAS & TOP PRODUCERS

NELSON p619
Neudorf Vineyards p625

MARLBOROUGH p619
Cloudy Bay p625
Huia Vineyards p626
Isabel Estate Vineyard p626
Wither Hills Vineyards p626

CANTERBURY & WAIPARA p619
Pegasus Bay p626

CENTRAL OTAGO p619
Chard Farm p627
Felton Road p627
Gibbston Valley Wines p627
Rippon Vineyard p627

SAUVIGNON BLANC: WORLD BEATER

Drinking Marlborough Sauvignon Blanc has been likened to jumping naked into a gooseberry bush. It is an exhilarating wine rush. The area's first Sauvignon Blanc, from Montana Wines, caused quite a stir in 1973 with its cut-grass pungency. It was seen as uniquely New Zealand, unable to be replicated elsewhere, not even in the grape's native French region, the Loire. Marlborough has a number of things that sit right with Sauvignon: plenty of sunshine and a long growing season that ensures grapes ripen fully. Soil is important too: the region's fertile silty soils produce a zingy style of Sauvignon, while the stony sites, where the heat is trapped during the day and released at night, result in a less aggressive wine. Virtually every one of Marlborough's 68 wineries now produces Sauvignon Blanc, but styles differ: some are fiercely herbal, others ripe and tropical.

PACIFIC OCEAN

TASMAN SEA

Ahipara Bay Kerikeri
  ●Waitangi
**AUCKLAND &
NORTHLAND**
  Portland

  ●Matakana
  Hauraki
AUCKLAND *Gulf*
  ●Waiheke
Kumeu■   Island
  Manurewa
  Lake Waikare
35°

37°

Kaimai Range

Waikato

  Hamilton●   *Bay of
Plenty*
WAIKATO   **BAY OF
PLENTY**   **GISBORNE**
*Lake
Taupo*
  ●Gisborne
38°
**NORTH
ISLAND**   *Poverty
Bay*
**HAWKE'S
BAY**
  Napier●   *Hawke's
Bay*
39°
Wanganui
  Hastings●
40°

  Otaki●
*Tasman
Bay*   **WELLINGTON
& WAIRARAPA**
*Lake
Wairarapa*
  Nelson●   ●Martinborough
NELSON   *Cloudy* **WELLINGTON**
  Blenheim●   *Bay*
MARLBOROUGH
41°

42°

Wairau

**SOUTH
ISLAND**

  Waikari●
Waimakariri   ●Waipara
*Pegasus
Bay*
43°

Rakaia
  ●Christchurch
*Lake
Ellesmere*
*Canterbury
Bight*
44°

OCEAN

45°

46°

0 ⊢ km ————— ┤ 150

Maté's Vineyard, Kumeu River Wines in
Auckland & Northland

TERROIR AT A GLANCE

Latitude: 35–46°S.

Altitude: 0–3,750m.

Topography: Dramatic variations, with high mountains and deep valleys running out to broad plains. Vines are mainly grown on flat or gently sloping land.

Soil: From fertile alluvial to infertile and sandy soil.

Climate: Cool maritime. North Island is warmer; South Island is cooler but drier. Marginal sites, frosts, and scarcity of water make winegrowing on South Island more problematic.

Temperature: January average is 23°C (North Island); 18°C (South Island).

Rainfall: Annual average is 1,240mm (North Island); 810mm (South Island). Heavy rains on North Island mean grapes are prone to damage and rot.

Wind: Mainly westerly. North Island has a moderating influence from sea breezes; South Island's prevailing winds come from the Southern Alps.

Viticultural hazards: Phylloxera; fanleaf degeneration; leafroll viruses.

Isabel Estate Vineyard, Marlborough

PERFECT CASE: NEW ZEALAND

Ⓦ Chard Farm Judge & Jury Chardonnay ££

Ⓦ Cloudy Bay Sauvignon Blanc ££

Ⓡ Felton Road Block 5 Pinot Noir £££

Ⓡ Goldwater Estate Esslin Merlot ££££

Ⓦ Huia Vineyards Riesling ££

Ⓦ Isabel Estate Vineyard Sauvignon Blanc ££

Ⓦ Kumeu River Wines Maté's Vineyard Chardonnay £££

Ⓡ Martinborough Vineyard Reserve Pinot Noir £££

Ⓢ Montana Wines Marlborough Deutz Cuvée £

Ⓡ Stonyridge Vineyard Larose ££££

Ⓡ Te Mata Estate Bullnose Syrah ££

Ⓦ Villa Maria Estate Reserve Noble Riesling ££

Sheep grazing in a vineyard near Kumeu, Auckland and Northland

WINEGROWING AREAS OF NEW ZEALAND

NORTH ISLAND

THE FIRST VINES WERE planted in the Bay of Islands in 1819 and, almost two centuries on, the wine industry is flourishing across five key zones.

Auckland & Northland

THIS REGION IS SMALL in terms of the area of vines actually grown but big in political power thanks to the huge number of wineries (125 in total). All the major producers are headquartered in Auckland and process grapes sourced from both inside and outside the area. There are seven districts with contrasting wines: the newest, Matakana, is promising for reds, Waiheke Island makes some of the best Cabernet-based wines, and exciting Chardonnay hails from Kumeu.

Huia Vineyards label, Marlborough

▨ *red-brown clays* 🋏 *Merlot, Cabernet Sauvignon* 🋏 *Chardonnay, Pinot Gris* 🯁 *red, white*

Waikato & Bay of Plenty

THE BEAUTIFUL ADJOINING WINE areas of Waikato and Bay of Plenty are backwaters on the New Zealand wine scene. However, this was not always the case: Waikato was the country's viticultural heart in the early 1900s thanks to the Te Kauwhata Viticultural Research Station. With just one per cent of the country's vineyards, the area's glory days may now have passed. However, producers like Mills Reef, Rongopai, and Morton Estate still do the region proud, especially with their Chardonnays.

▨ *free-draining brown-orange soils* 🋏 *Cabernet Sauvignon* 🋏 *Chardonnay, Sauvignon Blanc* 🯁 *red, white, dessert*

Gisborne

GISBORNE, ALSO KNOWN AS Poverty Bay, is warm and sunny: ideal for creating well-rounded, friendly wines. It has carved a strong national reputation for its whites, Chardonnay and Gewürztraminer in particular. It is also one of the last areas in New Zealand to have significant plantings of the old – now passé – white favourite, Müller-Thurgau. This grape is often used, along with Muscat varieties, in cheap commercial brands.

▨ *grey-brown river silts* 🋏 *Chardonnay, Müller-Thurgau, Muscat varieties, Gewürztraminer* 🯁 *white*

Hawke's Bay

BEFORE MARLBOROUGH ARRIVED on the scene in the mid-1970s, Hawke's Bay was New Zealand's key winegrowing region. The area has history (Te Mata is the site of the oldest New Zealand winery), suitable climate and soils, and pioneering spirit. Most wineries are located to the south around Hastings where the famous Gimblett Road gravels are found. This generally warmer site produces some of the richest and ripest fruit in the region and is outstanding for its Cabernet Sauvignon and Merlot. Hawke's Bay is New Zealand's second biggest winegrowing region with 100 wine producers. It is renowned for its rich Chardonnays and Cabernet Sauvignon blends, whose structure puts them in the Bordeaux league.

▨ *brown hill soils and river silts* 🋏 *Merlot, Cabernet Sauvignon* 🋏 *Chardonnay, Sauvignon Blanc* 🯁 *red, white*

Wellington & Wairarapa

THIS IS IDEAL PINOT NOIR TERRITORY: the Burgundy grape represents almost half of the plantings here, and is what originally put Wairarapa on the map. The region is now a strong all-rounder where Sauvignon Blanc and Chardonnay can also be world class. Major producers are heavily concentrated in the town of Martinborough, which explains why this winegrowing area is often referred to by that name.

light grey-brown loess Pinot Noir Sauvignon Blanc, Chardonnay red, white

SOUTH ISLAND

WINEGROWING ON SOUTH ISLAND started much later than in the north. Although cooler and more marginal for vines, the four southern regions are expanding fast.

Nelson

NELSON SHARES SOME SIMILARITIES with its near neighbour, Marlborough. It is warm and sunny, but hindered by autumn rains so that ripening can definitely be more of a challenge. Hermann Seifried planted his first vines here in 1974 and the Seifried Estate is still the region's biggest producer. Nelson falls into two distinct climate and soil areas: the river silt flats of the Waimea Plains and the higher reaches of the Upper Moutere Hills.

yellow-grey stony silts (river), clay loam (hills) Pinot Noir, Cabernet Sauvignon Chardonnay, Sauvignon Blanc, Riesling red, white

Marlborough

FROM A STANDING START in 1973, Marlborough has burst forth as a premier wine region and now boasts 53 per cent of all New Zealand's vineyards. Its attractions are: a long, slow ripening season; masses of sunshine; cool nights; and low rainfall. Little wonder it has far more vineyards (around 170) than any other South Island region. Early expansion was due to one grape variety – Sauvignon Blanc – which is best exemplified by the runaway success of Cloudy Bay. In the 1980s, the region delivered the nation's best sparkling wines and proved it was skilled at Pinot Noir

and Chardonnay too. However, this is not the perfect wine region. Frosts and lack of water for irrigation, especially in the arid hill regions, are a constant problem. Winegrowing centres on the Wairau Plains, but subregions in nearby valleys – Brancott, Hawkesbury, and Waihopai – are now opening up too.

stony, yellow-grey river silts Pinot Noir Sauvignon Blanc, Chardonnay, Riesling red, white, sparkling

Canterbury & Waipara

WITH ITS PROXIMITY TO the Southern Alps, little wonder this region used to be considered too cold for grapes. It is borderline for some varieties, but not for Pinot Noir and Chardonnay – especially in Waipara, which is set among the lush, protective hills around Pegasus Bay.

grey alluviums, stony yellow-grey sediments Pinot Noir Chardonnay, Riesling, Sauvignon Blanc red, white

Central Otago

THIS WINTER PLAYGROUND lies in the rain shadow of the Southern Alps, where vines often have to be planted on hillsides to maximize sunshine and escape frosts. It was one of the last regions to fall to the vine, but now it is catching up fast. Its reputation is based largely on Pinot Noir (see p624), although the area also produces exceptional Chardonnay, Pinot Gris, and Riesling. The continental climate produces wines of elegance and finesse, but the winemaking costs in Central Otago's difficult climate are the country's highest.

yellow-brown from alpine terrain Pinot Noir Chardonnay, Pinot Gris, Riesling red, white

View from Tim Finn's Neudorf Vineyards in Nelson

CORKSCREWS AND CLOSURES

THE USE OF CORK STOPPERS in wine bottles dates from the 1600s. However, the advent of standardized, cylindrical bottles in the 1700s changed the way these closures were used. As the new bottles had to be stored on their sides in 'bins', it became necessary to drive the corks fully into the necks of the bottles to prevent leakage. With this tight seal, a tool was needed to extract the cork. Corkscrews of myriad designs have been developed ever since.

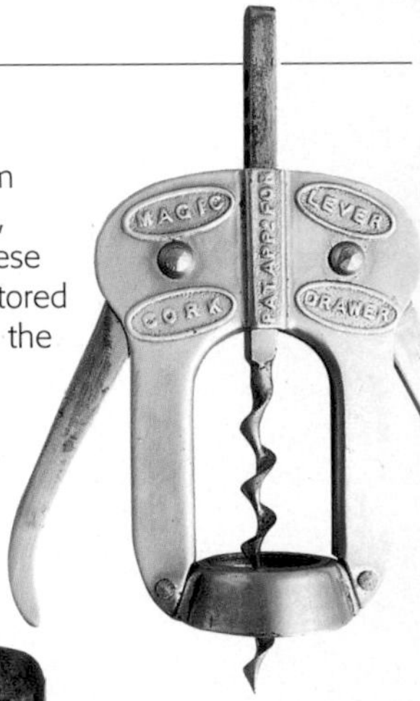

Magic Lever corkscrew c.1920

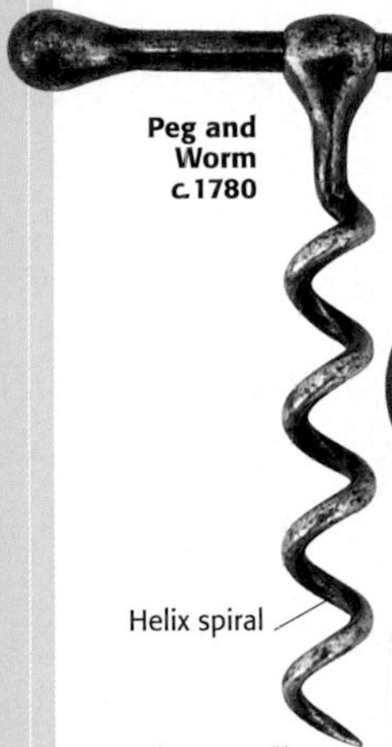

Mechanical
Mechanical corkscrews use levers, fulcrums, or ratchets to reduce the force needed to extract a cork.

Peg and Worm c.1780

Helix spiral

Direct-pull
Simple, or direct-pull, corkscrews are formed by a handle, shaft, and 'worm' (spiral).

American Clough corkscrew c.1920s

Folding Fancy c.1800s

1920s Bacchus corkscrew

1920s steel corkscrew

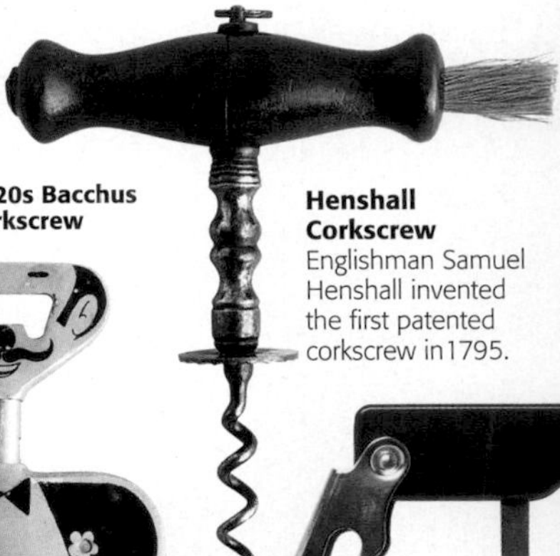

Henshall Corkscrew
Englishman Samuel Henshall invented the first patented corkscrew in 1795.

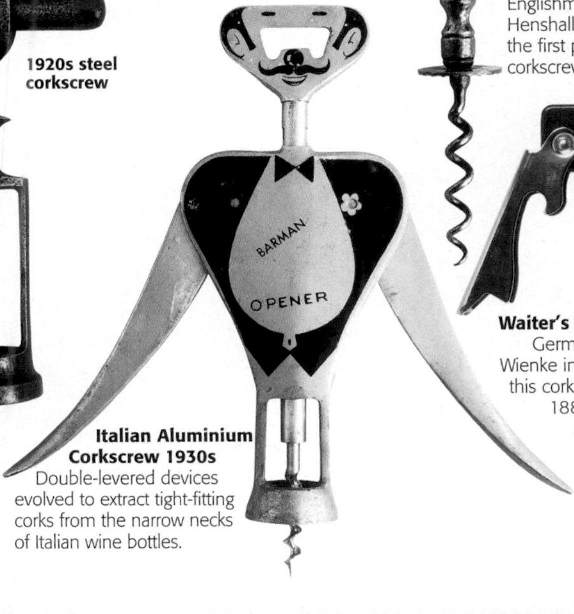

Italian Aluminium Corkscrew 1930s
Double-levered devices evolved to extract tight-fitting corks from the narrow necks of Italian wine bottles.

Archimedean spiral

Waiter's Friend
German Karl Wienke invented this corkscrew in 1882, and it is still used today.

BARMAN

OPENER

Pemberton Corkscrew
English craftsman Samuel Pemberton made this mother-of-pearl and silver device in 1810.

Silver corkscrew cap

Weir's Concertina Corkscrew
This mechanical unit was created in England by J. Heeley & Sons in the 1880s.

Zigzag Concertina Corkscrew c.1920

Thomason type with turned bone handle by Wilmot & Roberts c.1810

Eight tool folding bow corkscrew c.1820
This early device included a leather punch and a boot hook.

GES Geschultz Mermaid 1900

Screwpull
Sleek corkscrews were developed in the 1970s by American aerospace engineer Herbert Allen.

MODERN CLOSURES

Most wine bottles are sealed with traditional, natural cork. However, there is a range of alternatives. One popular choice is the synthetic plastic cork. Another option is the Stelvin screwcap. Once associated with low-quality wines, screwcaps are now the choice of many leading wine producers – especially in New Zealand. The crown cap often seen on soft drink and beer bottles is not yet common on wine bottles, but offers a reliable seal.

Screwcap (*left*), **artifical cork** (*middle*), **crown cap** (*right*)

TOP PRODUCERS OF NEW ZEALAND

Babich Wines
Auckland & Northland

Babich Rd, Henderson **C** *09 833 7859* W *www.babichwines.co.nz* ⬛

BABICH HAS BEEN A big name on the local wine scene since the family patriarch, Joe, founded the company in 1916. Long regarded as an industry stalwart – albeit a conservative one – Babich has been on a spending spree. In 1998, this medium-sized winery invested in a 40-ha vineyard in Awatere Valley, Marlborough, followed by 65ha in the nearby Waihopai Valley, as well as a quarter interest in Rapaura Vintners in Marlborough. The Patriarch and Mara (the family matriarch) brands do their namesakes proud, while the Irongate Chardonnay is one of the country's best.
⬛ *red, white* 📷 *2007 (w), 2006 (w), 2005, 2004, 2003 (w)*
★ *Irongate Chardonnay, Patriarch Cabernet Sauvignon, Marlborough Sauvignon Blanc*

Goldwater Estate
Auckland & Northland

18 Causeway Rd, Waiheke Island **C** *09 372 7493* W *www.gold waterwine.com* ⬛

AN HOUR'S FERRY RIDE from Auckland lies the temperate and strongly maritime-influenced island of Waiheke, where some of New Zealand's best Cabernet Sauvignon can be found. The similarities between Waiheke Island and Bordeaux were lost on many until founder Kim Goldwater planted the first vines there in 1978. Goldwater Estate made its name with a Cabernet-Merlot blend but more recently the silky Esslin Merlot has grabbed drinkers' attention worldwide.

View from Goldwater Estate on Waiheke Island

⬛ *red, white* 📷 *2007, 2006, 2005, 2004, 2003* ★ *Marlborough Chardonnay, Esslin Merlot, Cabernet Sauvignon-Merlot*

Kumeu River Wines
Auckland & Northland

550 State Highway 16, Kumeu **C** *09 412 8415* W *www.kumeuriver.co.nz* ⬛

NEW ZEALAND'S first Master of Wine, Michael Brajkovich, is one of the country's premier Chardonnay makers; he seeks out the rich complexities in the grape that few producers can match. In Maté's Vineyard Chardonnay, named after his late father, Brajkovich reaches the height of his craft. While Chardonnay is what the company is known for, its Pinot Gris, Pinot Noir, and Bordeaux red blends are also finely structured wines. After years of enduring cork taint as a necessary evil, Michael Brajkovich has taken the bold step of using screw caps across his entire range.
⬛ *red, white* 📷 *2007, 2006, 2005, 2004, 2003* ★ *Maté's Vineyard Chardonnay, Pinot Gris, Pinot Noir*

Kumeu River Wines

Montana Wines
Auckland & Northland

333 Apirana Ave, Glen Innes **C** *09 570 8400* W *www.montanawines.com* ⬛

THE MOST ARRESTING image of Montana Wines, seen around the world in glossy magazines, is of its Brancott Vineyard in Marlborough, nearly all its 295ha devoted to one grape – Sauvignon Blanc. It was Montana's Sauvignon Blanc that first alerted the world to the great potential of this region. That is not the first time this firm – New Zealand's biggest – has led the way. Its Marlborough Deutz Cuvée sparkling, made with input from Champagne house Deutz *(see p172)*, was the first serious sparkling wine made in the country. Montana's wine-making relationship with Bordeaux producer Cordier has helped contribute to considerable improvements in its reds.

The company, started in 1944 by Croatian immigrant Ivan Yukich (*montana* is Croatian for 'mountain'), has its star performers but stays essentially a loyal friend to consumers, as everyday drinking wines are its forte. In 2005, Pernod-Ricard acquired Montana through its takeover of Allied Domecq.

🔲 red, white, sparkling, dessert
📊 2007, 2006, 2005, 2004, 2003
★ Marlborough Deutz Cuvée, Reserve Marlborough Chardonnay, Hawke's Bay Cabernet Sauvignon-Merlot

Nobilo Wine Group
Auckland & Northland

45 Station Rd, Huapai ☎ 09 412 6666
🌐 www.nobilo.co.nz ☐

FOUNDED BY Dalmatian immigrant Nikola Nobilo in 1943, Nobilo's early national prominence was built on the success of the aromatic white variety Müller-Thurgau. However, times have changed and so has Nobilo. With an eye on popular tastes it created White Cloud in the 1980s, an easy drinking Müller-Thurgau-Chenin Blanc blend produced in a distinctive misty bottle. It sold like hot cakes and inspired many copies – notably Australian producer Seppelt Great Western's *(see p596)* Glass Mountain.

BRL Hardy *(see p572)* took 100 per cent ownership of Nobilo in 2000: an injection of capital has meant new planting programmes in Marlborough and Hawke's Bay, making Nobilo the second largest winery in New Zealand.

🔲 red, white, dessert
📊 2007, 2006, 2005, 2004, 2003 ★ Icon Series Chardonnay, Icon Series Riesling, House of Nobilo Marlborough Sauvignon Blanc

Stonyridge Vineyard
Auckland & Northland

80 Onetangi Rd, Waiheke Island
☎ 09 372 8822
🌐 www.stonyridge.co.nz ☐

THERE IS A distinctly Mediterranean feel at Stonyridge. Founder Stephen White says it is in keeping with Waiheke's climate, which is around 4°C warmer than any other New Zealand wine region. White, a sailor-cum-surfer-cum-winemaker, was inspired to plant Bordeaux red grape varieties after working for Mas de Daumas Gassac *(see p145)*. Wine writers put Larose – a blend of five red varieties and one of the country's most expensive and in-demand wines – in the Bordeaux league.

🔲 red, white 📊 2007, 2006, 2005, 2004, 2003 ★ Larose, Syrah

Villa Maria Estate
Auckland & Northland

118 Montgomerie Rd, Mangere
☎ 09 255 0660
🌐 www.villamaria.co.nz ☐

FOUNDED IN 1961, Villa Maria Estate is a wine giant, now third in New Zealand after Montana and Nobilo. The driving force is the hugely modest but determined owner, George Fistonich. His winemaking philosophy is focused on cheap and cheerful wines in keeping with the relative immaturity of the New Zealand wine industry. As the industry has grown, so too has Villa Maria Estate. The empire now embraces every price point and almost every

Villa Maria Estate label

Stylish C J Pask Winery label

major winegrowing region, with the Villa Maria Reserve label proudly leading the way.

🔲 red, white, sparkling, dessert
📊 2007, 2006, 2005, 2004, 2003
★ Wairau Reserve Sauvignon Blanc, Reserve Hawke's Bay Cabernet Sauvignon-Merlot, Reserve Noble Riesling

C J Pask Winery
Hawke's Bay

1133 Omahu Rd, Hastings
☎ 06 879 7906
🌐 www.cjpaskwinery.co.nz ☐

CHRIS PASK, a crop-spraying pilot, and Kate Radburnd, an award-winning winemaker, got together professionally in 1990 and have proven to be a great team ever since. Pask was one of the first people to recognize the potential of the now famous Gimblett Road gravel soils and planted a range of both red and white varieties here. While pretty good at white winemaking, Radburnd's forte is red – her Merlot is one of the best in the country. Her Cabernet Sauvignon blend is consistent but interest is high in what she will do with Syrah.

🔲 red, white 📊 2007, 2006 (w), 2004 ★ Reserve Merlot, Reserve Cabernet Sauvignon-Merlot, Reserve Chardonnay

Corbans Winery
Hawke's Bay

91 Thames St, Pandora, Napier
☎ 06 833 6830
⊞ *www.montanawines.co.nz* ⬜

WINE DRINKERS may well know Corbans through one or more of its many different guises: Longridge of Hawke's Bay, Stoneleigh Vineyard, Robard and Butler, Cook's Winemaker Reserve, International Cellars, and, of course, Corbans' own brand. Part of the huge Montana empire, Corbans has long been a major player in New Zealand's wine industry, even when it was still owned by the Corban family. Corbans delivers an extraordinary range of wines, from the economical white label to the exclusive, flagship Cottage Block brand, which includes a stone fruit-rich Chardonnay.

🍷 *red, white, sparkling, dessert* 📥 *2007, 2006, 2004* ★ *Cottage Block Chardonnay, Marlborough Sauvignon Blanc, Private Bin Noble Riesling*

Craggy Range Winery
Hawke's Bay

253 Waimarama Rd, RD12, Havelock North ☎ 06 873 7126
⊞ *www.craggyrange.com* ⬜

CRAGGY RANGE was set up in 1998 by successful businessman Terry Peabody, who had a growing desire to make premium wines. Early releases suggest he is well on track. The project's linchpin is the progressive viticulturist and winemaker Steve Smith. A Master of Wine, Smith has planted vineyards in Martinborough and Hawke's Bay, including Syrah at the Gimblett Road site – an exciting addition to the region's red wine arsenal. That Smith is a believer in the importance of site selection is obvious from the name of the Craggy Range restaurant: Terroir.

🍷 *red, white* 📥 *2007, 2006, 2004* ★ *Sauvignon Blanc, Chardonnay, Pinot Noir*

Te Mata Estate
Hawke's Bay

Te Mata Rd, Havelock North ☎ 06 877 4399
⊞ *www.temata.hb.co.nz* ⬜

THE FIRST VINES, Pinot Noir, were planted here as early as 1892. Today, red is still the colour that makes Te Mata one of the country's top producers. Cabernet Sauvignon, Merlot, and Cabernet Franc are the focus of owner John Buck's commitment to making wines of elegance and finesse. They also enjoy a reputation for longevity, an elusive dream for some New Zealand red wine producers. Te Mata's long-time winemaker, Peter Cowley, has now moved into new, exciting territory with Syrah: his Bullnose Syrah virtually explodes with spice.

Bullnose Syrah, Te Mata Estate

🍷 *red, white* 📥 *2007, 2006, 2004* ★ *Elston Chardonnay, Coleraine Cabernet Sauvignon-Merlot, Bullnose Syrah*

Ata Rangi
Wellington & Wairarapa

Puruatanga Rd, Martinborough ☎ 06 306 9570
⊞ *www.atarangi.co.nz* ⬜

IN MAORI, ATA RANGI translates as 'new beginning' – fitting for a vineyard that helped to pioneer a modern era of winemaking in Martinborough. Founder Clive Paton and his wife, Phyllis, a former Montana winemaker, planted Burgundy varieties following a report by soil scientist Dr Derek Milne that the region would be suited to them. By the 1990s, Ata Rangi was winning high esteem for its luxuriously big and silky Pinot Noir.

🍷 *red, white, dessert* 📥 *2006 (w)* ★ *Pinot Noir, Craighall Chardonnay, Lismore Pinot Gris*

Dry River
Wellington & Wairarapa

Puruatanga Rd, Martinborough ☎ 06 306 9388 ◉

In 2003, Dr Neil McCallum stunned Dry River fans by selling his 8-ha vineyard to

---

THE RISE & RISE OF PINOT NOIR

Twenty years ago most New Zealand Pinot Noir was thin and rosé-like. Early clones of the Burgundy grape were unsuitable, many early sites more so. As viticulture improved, so did the wines. Pinot is now the most planted red grape (almost 3,000ha) in New Zealand. Martinborough led the way, and continues to do so, with wines deep in colour and showing black cherry and savoury aromas, and a distinct gaminess in taste. More than 40 per cent of Pinot plantings are now found in Marlborough. Here, the grape splits into both sparkling and still wine production. Marlborough Pinot is the most approachable in style (and price). For a Pinot with real bite, there are only two words you need to remember: Central Otago.

American buyers. However, the good news is that McCallum, the founder, inspiration and winemaker, stayed on. He is considered a legend in Pinot Noir circles, and as a result, Dry River wines are some of the hardest to buy. His secret is obsessive attention to detail. Dry River shows the rich and complex side of the Pinot Noir grape. In fact, every grape McCallum touches should be tried.

🍷 red, white, dessert 📅 2006, 2003
★ Pinot Noir, Craighall Amaranth Riesling, Gewürztraminer

Martinborough Vineyard
Wellington & Wairarapa

Princess St, Martinborough
📞 06 306 9955
🌐 www.martinborough-vineyard.co.nz ☐

MARTINBOROUGH VINEYARD put Martinborough on the map. Or is it the other way round? Whichever way, it is responsible for some of the most opulent Pinot Noir made in Australasia. Fruit ripeness is the key, something the company has worked long and hard on: great care has been taken over trellising and pruning techniques, as well as sourcing the best clones of grapes. Top results can also be seen in the extremely powerful Chardonnay. During the 1990s, Martinborough was associated with winemaker Larry McKenna, a guru to Pinotphiles. Now that he is left, the aim will be to maintain the high standard. No problem so far.

🍷 red, white 📅 2006, 2003
★ Reserve Pinot Noir, Chardonnay, Riesling

Martinborough Vineyard label

Palliser Estate
Wellington & Wairarapa

Kitchener St, Martinborough
📞 06 306 9019
🌐 www.palliser.co.nz ☐

LIKE MOST MARTINBOROUGH producers, Palliser made its name in the 1990s with Pinot Noir. But today the company is an all-rounder with a cache of top-rung wines from Riesling to Chardonnay to Pinot Gris and Sauvignon Blanc. There is even a sparkling. Razor-sharp fruit intensity is the Palliser trademark. In fact, the unwooded Sauvignon Blanc is so good it gives Marlborough a run for its money. With 85ha under vine, Palliser Estate is now one of the region's largest wineries.

Sauvignon Blanc, Palliser Estate

🍷 red, white, sparkling
📅 2005, 2003
★ Sauvignon Blanc, Riesling, Pinot Noir

Neudorf Vineyards
Nelson

Neudorf Rd, Upper Moutere 📞 03 543 2643 🌐 www.neudorf.co.nz ☐

NELSON HAS something its superstar neighbour, Marlborough, does not: Neudorf Vineyards. In this tiny vineyard belonging to the Finns lies a fully fledged, red-hot Chardonnay of international repute: the Cloudy Bay of Chardonnays. Immensely approachable, combining flavour-rich power and elegance, Neudorf is consistently rated as one of New Zealand's greatest versions of this grape. Tim Finn approaches his task like an architect – structure is everything. His eye for detail applies equally to his highly regarded Pinot Noir.

🍷 red, white 📅 2007, 2006, 2004 (w), 2003 ★ Moutere Chardonnay, Sauvignon Blanc, Moutere Reserve Pinot Noir

Cloudy Bay
Marlborough

Jacksons Rd, Blenheim 📞 03 520 9140 🌐 www.cloudybay.co.nz ☐

IN 1985, CLOUDY BAY defined the archetypal New Zealand Sauvignon Blanc and became an international celebrity. Fruit sweetness countered with tangy gooseberries set the benchmark, and in warm years a splash of Sémillon did wonders. Winemaker Kevin Judd's style (the 2009 vintage was his 25th and his last for the company) has been widely copied but it still sets the pace. A world-class sparkling, Pelorus, was released in 1992. But that is not all. The Cloudy Bay portfolio is full of great wines: classy Chardonnay, Pinot Noir, an avant-garde wooded Sauvignon Blanc, a late-harvested Riesling, and a stunning Gewürztraminer. There is virtually nothing Cloudy Bay does not do well. Of course, it helps being part of the giant Louis Vuitton Moët Hennessy group.

🍷 red, white, sparkling, dessert 📅 2007 (w), 2004 (w), 2003 ★ Pelorus Vintage Sparkling, Sauvignon Blanc, Pinot Noir

Huia Vineyards
Marlborough

Boyces Rd, RD3, Blenheim ☎ *03 572 8326* 🖳 *www.huia.net.nz* ▢

A BOTTLE OF Cloudy Bay Sauvignon Blanc tasted in 1989 was career defining for Claire and Mike Allan. The wine's explosive flavours convinced the couple, studying winemaking in Australia, to head to Marlborough. It could be argued that in Huia (pronounced who-ya) they have created some of the most spine-tingling Sauvignon Blancs in the region, and they have now followed with a fabulous sparkling wine. Huia's hallmark is a firm structure with a bone-dry finish. The unusual name honours a now extinct kiwi songbird.

🖼 *red, white, sparkling* 📅 *2007, 2004, 2003* ★ *Huia Brut, Sauvignon Blanc, Riesling*

Isabel Estate Vineyard
Marlborough

72 Hawkesbury Rd, Renwick ☎ *03 572 8300* 🖳 *www.isabelestate.com* ▢

WE CAN THANK the late Isabel Tiller for the wines from this exciting Marlborough vineyard. She planted the first vines in 1982 and encouraged her son Michael to take up wine-growing. Everything has been planned, slow and steady, with the Tillers (Michael and wife Robyn) first growing grapes for other producers before establishing a winery of their own in 1997. The wines are noted for their great flavour concentration and persistence in the mouth. Quality is outstanding across the range.

🖼 *red, white, dessert* 📅 *2007 (w), 2004, 2003, 2002 (r)* ★ *Sauvignon Blanc, Riesling, Noble Sauvage (botrytis white: Sauvignon Blanc or Riesling depending on year)*

Wither Hills Vineyards
Marlborough

211 New Renwick Rd, Blenheim ☎ *03 520 8270* 🖳 *www.witherhills.co.nz* ▢

THIS USED TO BE a successful, smallish player on the New Zealand wine scene, run by founder and winemaker Brent Marris. Enter beer and drinks giant Lion Nathan in 2002 with some NZ$52 million, and Wither Hills became part of this growing Australasian empire. Current winemaker is Ben Glover. Wither Hills concentrates on just three wines – Sauvignon Blanc, Chardonnay, and Pinot Noir – and projects a rare consistency, offering outstanding value for money.

🖼 *red, white* 📅 *2007, 2004* ★ *Sauvignon Blanc, Chardonnay, Pinot Noir*

Pegasus Bay
Canterbury & Waipara

Stockgrove Rd, Amberley ☎ *03 314 6869* 🖳 *www.pegasusbay.com* ▢

IVAN DONALDSON, an associate professor of neurology as well as a winemaker, certainly has an enquiring mind, which in Pegasus Bay's

Pegasus Bay wine label

formative years was responsible for pursuing not just fruit flavour but complexity and texture. A family enterprise, Pegasus makes strong winemaking statements. Whether it is the Sauvignon Blanc-Sémillon, Riesling, Chardonnay, or Pinot Noir, flavours are rich and dramatic – in keeping with the Donaldsons' love of opera (and operatic wine names, such as their late-picked Riesling, Aria, and their unfiltered Pinot Noir, Prima Donna). No other Waipara maker comes close to exploring the inner mysteries of the region.

🖼 *red, white* 📅 *2007, 2005, 2004 (r), 2003 (r)* ★ *Sauvignon Blanc-Sémillon, Chardonnay, Prima Donna Pinot Noir*

STEVE SMITH: LIVING THE DREAM

Steve Smith has a dream, and so far it's all going to plan. He wants to see the full potential of New Zealand wines explored at home and applauded internationally. As a Master of Wine and chairman of the Air New Zealand Wine Awards, he is an influential ambassador for New Zealand's wines, believing its aromatic whites are among the world's best. He is the co-owner, managing director, winemaker, and viticulturist of Craggy Range Winery in Hawke's Bay, releasing small parcels of wine off individual vineyards. He sources the best grapes from Martinborough, Marlborough, Nelson, and Central and North Otago, as well as from his own bit of dirt, the amazing Gimblett Gravels region in Hawke's Bay. His wines speak with passion – none more so than his Le Sol Syrah, a wine that reveals just how serious (and seriously good) New Zealand Syrah can be.

Chard Farm
Central Otago

Chard Rd, Gibbston Valley, Queenstown
C *03 442 6110*
W *www.chardfarm.co.nz* ▢

BUNGEE JUMPING originated in the gorges near Chard Farm, which gives some idea of the dramatic local landscape. It was started in 1987 by brothers Rob and Greg Hay, and this cool site is perfect for aromatic Riesling, as well as for Burgundy soul mates Chardonnay and Pinot Noir. Ripening can be a problem though, and Rob (Greg left in 1998) can, and does, chaptalize to boost alcoholic strength. The Riesling is stunning, but the Chardonnay and Pinot Noir fight it out for flagship honours. Hay makes a number of styles of each variety: Judge and Jury Chardonnay and Finla Mor Pinot Noir reach heady climaxes.
▓ *red, white* ▨ *2007, 2006, 2005 (r), 2003* ★ *Riesling, Judge and Jury Chardonnay, Finla Mor Pinot Noir*

Felton Road
Central Otago

Bannockburn, RD2
C *03 445 0885*
W *www.feltonroad.com* ▢

FELTON ROAD IS to Central Otago what Cloudy Bay was to Marlborough. Planted in 1991, the first releases of Pinot Noir here startled tastebuds with an energized fruit intensity. Central Otago Pinot Noir, and Felton Road in particular, became hot property. The wine developed a legion of fans, especially in the UK from where owner Nigel Greening hails. He believes that Central Otago's fruit quality is due to a huge shift in temperatures between night and day: from 3° to 33°C.

Rippon Vineyard on Lake Wanaka, Central Otago

Winegrowing here is largely organic; and winemaking is definitely minimalist and Old World focused. The wines are strongly individual, showing exceptionally bright, pristine fruit.
▓ *red, white, dessert* ▨ *2005, 2003* ★ *Block 5 Pinot Noir, Dry Riesling, Barrel-Fermented Chardonnay*

Gibbston Valley Wines
Central Otago

Queenstown-Cromwell Hwy, Gibbston
C *03 442 6910*
W *www.gvwines.co.nz* ▢

AFTER THE TWIN attractions of skiing and bungee jumping there is yet another reason to visit Queenstown: the wine. From being unheard of 15 years ago, Gibbston Valley Wines has become a leading Pinot Noir maker in Central Otago. The climate here is very cool and marginal for grapes so the expertise of Otago-born, Napa Valley-trained winemaker Grant Taylor is vital. Expect wines of great vibrancy and purity of fruit. Gibbston Valley does well with the aromatic white variety Pinot Gris, which could ultimately prove the best white grape for the region. Pinot

Noir is supple and one of the more full-blooded wines made here: its reserve is the flagship.
▓ *red, white, dessert* ▨ *2007, 2006, 2005, 2003* ★ *Riesling, Chardonnay, Reserve Pinot Noir*

Rippon Vineyard
Central Otago

Mount Aspiring Rd, Lake Wanaka
C *03 443 8084*
W *www.rippon.co.nz* ▢

RIPPON VINEYARD IS breathtakingly beautiful with its shimmering blue Lake Wanaka, and the snow-capped Buchanan Range backdrop. With an undisputed pristine, alpine-fresh fruit quality, the wines are every bit as awe-inspiring as the view. Of course, when the first experimental plot of some 30 varieties was planted at Rippon in 1974, there was a great sense of the unknown. Ten years later, after making experimental batches, the final choices were made. Pinot Noir it was, as well as a clutch of aromatic whites.
▓ *red, white, sparkling* ▨ *2006, 2005 (r)* ★ *Pinot Noir, Riesling, Gewürztraminer*

OTHER WINE-PRODUCING COUNTRIES

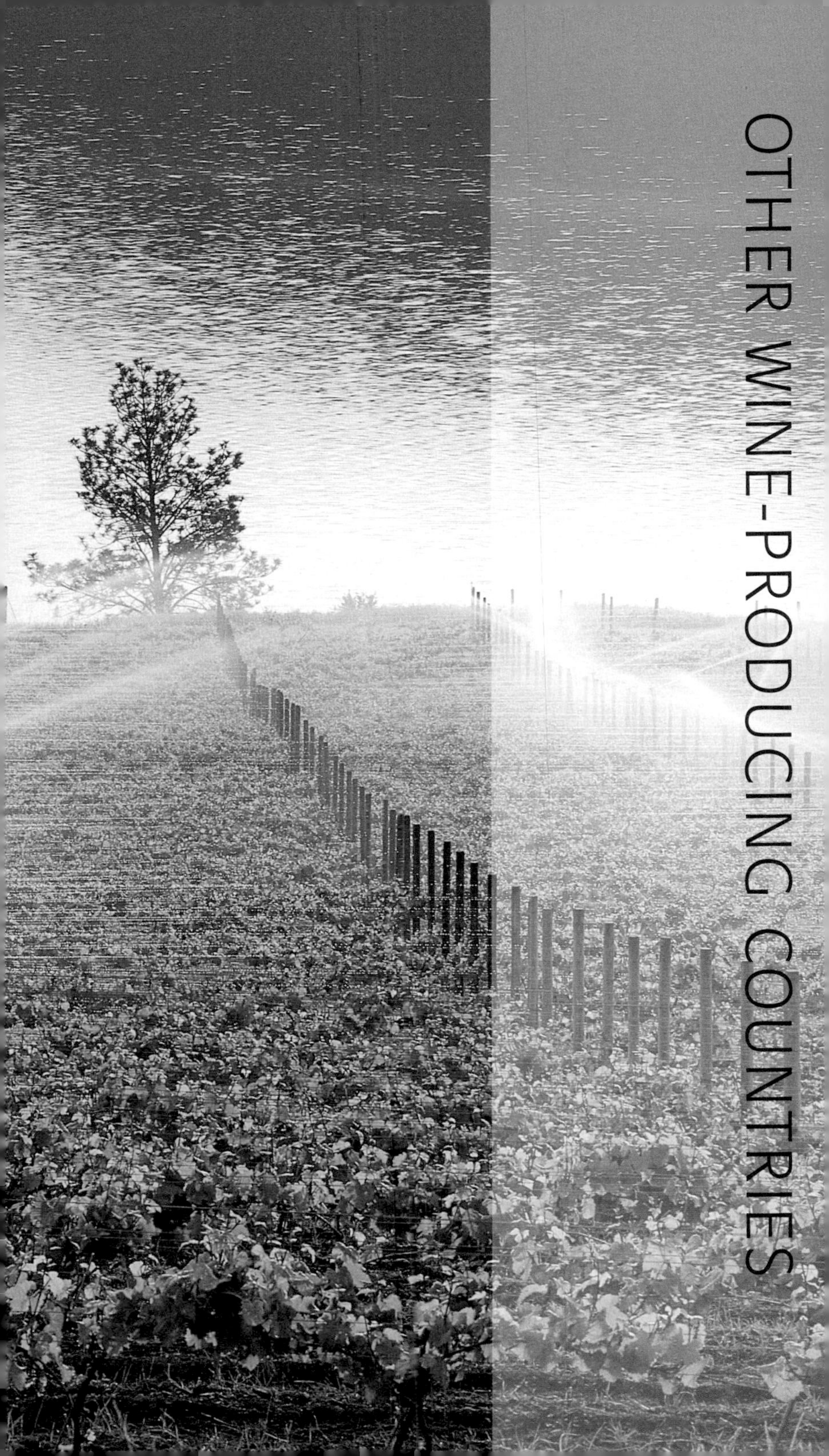

EUROPE

THE SMALLEST WINE-PRODUCING *countries in Europe live in the shadow of their more famous neighbours. The annual harvest of these countries combined would barely register next to the yields of giant producers such as France, Italy, and Spain. Yet these smaller European winegrowing nations all have important industries in their own right, some of which are going from strength to strength.*

Luxembourg

THE GRAND DUCHY OF LUXEMBOURG has produced small quantities of wine since the first century AD. For many years, much of Luxembourg's annual output was sent to Germany for its sparkling *Sekt*. Today the majority of its wines are consumed locally or exported to Belgium. Luxembourg has a challenging climate for successful grape growing. Production is limited to just 1,300ha of vines along the west bank of the Mosel River bordering Germany. Viticulture is difficult and labour intensive, with spring frosts and low temperatures common. Most of the wine produced in Luxembourg is dry, fruity, and white. The unremarkable Rivaner (the local name for Müller-Thurgau) is the most widely planted grape variety, although its popularity is waning. So, too, is the ancient Elbling, which, despite its uses in sparkling production, is generally too acidic and neutral as a still wine. Riesling makes perhaps Luxembourg's finest bottles, particularly from the limestone slopes of Ahn in the district of Grevenmacher. Other grape varieties that show promise include Pinot

Auxerrois label, Luxembourg

Blanc, Pinot Gris, and Gewürztraminer. Pinot Noir is used for an increasing amount of red and rosé production, although the cool climate can dilute its flavour. Two thirds of all wine in Luxembourg is produced by the co-operative Les Domaines de Vinsmoselle.

🎞 *Pinot Noir* 🍷 *Rivaner, Elbling, Riesling, Pinot Blanc, Pinot Gris* 🏔 *Remich, Grevenmacher* ☷ Les Domaines de Vinsmoselle (www.vinsmoselle.lu)

Pinot Noir vineyards, southern England

United Kingdom

ALTHOUGH THE VINE HAS BEEN grown in the UK for many thousands of years, wine production had all but died out by the beginning of the 20th century. The industry was then revived by Hambledon vineyard in the 1950s, and since then UK wine has made considerable progress. The country remains the smallest producer in Europe, but now has 98 wineries and nearly 400 vineyards. While the majority are concentrated in the south of England, there are also outposts in Wales, Yorkshire, and even as far north as Durham. Commercial viticulture is only possible at such northerly latitudes because of the moderating effects of the maritime climate and the Gulf Stream current. Fairly low temperatures throughout the season mean that growers often harvest their grapes as late as October or November. The quantity and quality of the crop can vary significantly between vintages due to the effects of spring frosts, rot, and problems achieving full ripeness.

The grape varieties planted in the UK are selected to cope with these difficult conditions. Varieties developed in Germany are especially popular, such as the early ripening Müller-Thurgau, plus Reichensteiner, Huxelrebe, and Schönburger. Madeleine Angevine is also commonly found, as is the hybrid Seyval Blanc. The typical style of wine in the UK is dry, medium-bodied, and aromatic.

◁ **Irrigation of Burrowing Owl vineyards, Okanagan Valley, Canada**

Some producers have demonstrated the potential of more conventional grapes such as Chardonnay, Riesling, and even the red variety Merlot. These perform particularly well in warmer vintages, such as 2003, and, if global warming gathers pace, they may become strong performers. Estates have also been experimenting with late harvest, dessert styles of wine and reds made from Pinot Noir or Teinturier. At the moment, the most promising avenue probably lies in sparkling wine. Neutral, acidic wines are relatively easy to achieve in this cool climate, and provide the perfect base for the production of high-quality fizz.

🎖 *Pinot Noir, Teinturier* 🎖 *Müller-Thurgau, Reichensteiner, Schönburger, Madeleine Angevine, Seyval Blanc* 🎋 *Kent, Sussex, southern Wales* 🎗 English Wines Group *(www.english winesgroup.com)*; Nyetimber Vineyard *(www.nyetimber-vineyard.com)*

Serbian producer Navip

Serbia, Montenegro & Kosovo

WAR, ITS AFTERMATH, and the sanctions that followed have brought about a decline in the wine industry of the former Republic of Yugoslavia – once one of the biggest exporters of bulk wine in the world. In the Union of Serbia and Montenegro 64,000ha under vine were recorded in 2001, plus some 5,000ha in the autonomous province of Kosovo, where the UN runs a support programme to enable the wine industry to restructure and attract investment. North of Belgrade, the province of Vojvodina is viticulturally an extension of inland Croatia *(see p416)* with – for the most part – similar grapes and wine styles, though the local white variety Smederevka produces large quantities of ordinary whites. The most promising vineyards are in the rolling hills of Fruska Gora, with plantings of Merlot and Cabernet Sauvignon, though large-scale old-fashioned wineries lack the equipment and/or expertise to realize their full potential.

Serbia used to produce around one third of Yugoslavia's wine and is generally recognized as making better reds: the local red variety Prokupac is grown in all Serbia's wine regions, but predominates in Zapadna Morava, while near the Bulgarian border Cabernet Sauvignon and Merlot are grown in Juzna Morava. Montenegro only ever produced around two per cent of Yugoslavia's wine and is best known for its robust, full-flavoured, red Vranac made from the grape of the same name.

🎖 *Prokupac, Vranac, Cabernet Sauvignon, Merlot* 🎖 *Smederevka* 🎋 *Fruska Gora, Zapadna Morava, Juzna Morava, Vranje*

A vineyard belonging to the English Wines Group, based in southern England

Republic of Macedonia

THERE HAVE BEEN vines in Macedonia since Roman times. Today around 80 per cent of the country's 22,400ha are planted with local red Vranec and white Smederevka, though the area of international grapes is increasing. Its warm summers are moderated by altitude, giving a very long growing season and potential for intense flavours. Macedonia's industry is fully privatized with 38 wineries and an increasing emphasis on improved quality in line with EU requirements as the country negotiates accession.

Vineyards near Negotino, Macedonia

🍷 *Vranac, Cabernet Sauvignon, Merlot* 🍷 *Smederevka* 🏔 *Povardarje, Pchinya-Osogovo, Pelagonija-Polog* 🔲 Fonko *(www.fonkowines. com.mk)* Cekorov *(www.cekorovi.com.mk)*

CIS States

A NUMBER OF THE former Soviet republics make substantial quantities of wine, although the vineyard area has been reduced since former president Gorbachev's 1980s anti-alcohol campaign. Like the rest of Eastern Europe, winemaking here is fraught with difficulties.

Moldova

GRAPES HAVE BEEN CULTIVATED in Moldova for at least 3,000 years. Viticulture is very important today, accounting for around 30 per cent of the country's export income in 2005. There is great potential for quality wine in Moldova, which has four demarcated regions, a gently undulating landscape, and a climate moderated by breezes from the Black Sea.

At one time Moldova was the eastern half of Romanian Moldavia, and the population here is still nearly two thirds Romanian-speaking. The country was first annexed by Russia in 1812, and the Tsars encouraged the planting of European grape varieties. The local wine industry used to rely heavily on the Russian market, a legacy of the Communist era, when 240,000ha of vines were planted to slake the thirst of the Soviet Union. That market was abruptly lost in 2006, when the Russians imposed a ban on all imports of Moldovan wine. As a result, the vineyard area is now greatly reduced, at just over 100,000ha, and the remaining producers are refocusing their attention on Western markets. Cricova-Acorex, which owns 3,000ha of vineyard, much of it organic, has led the way, employing an Italian winemaker to oversee the production of, among other things, an Amarone-style red and deliciously fresh Sauvignon Blanc and Pinot Gris. Dionysos-Mereni, owned by an American Moldovan, makes a ripe, if slightly earthy, Cabernet and an oak-aged Chardonnay. Political instability and the unreliable infrastructure mean foreign investment remains limited.

🍷 *Merlot, Cabernet Sauvignon, Pinot Noir* 🍷 *Aligoté, Rkatsiteli, Sauvignon Blanc, Feteasca Alba* 🏔 *Balti, Codru, Nistreana (or Purcari), Cahul* 🔲 Chateau Vartely *(www.vartely.md);* Acorex *(www.acorex.net);* Purcari *(www. purcari.md);* Dionysos-Mereni *(www.dionysos-mereni.com)*

Poster from Gorbachev's anti-alcohol campaign: 'where he drinks is where he fights'

Georgia

GEORGIA HAS STRONG CLAIMS to being the birthplace of wine, with archaeological remains dating back around 7,000 years. Its vineyards are mostly on the south-facing slopes of the Caucasus, which protects them from the harsh winters of the Russian Steppes. The key winegrowing areas include Kakheti in the east, the smaller Imereti in the centre-west, and central Kartli. Georgia has 35 different authorized grape varieties, most of them local, but the red Saperavi grape is the most popular. A deep-coloured grape, with brambly, black-fruit flavours, it has the potential to make very high quality wine, but needs careful vinification to suit Western palates Important white grapes include Rkatsiteli and the local Mtsvane, producing whites that can be zesty, fresh, and peachy, but are more often flat, dull, and oxidized.

Like Moldova, Georgia has struggled to find alternative markets for its wines in the wake of the politically motivated ban imposed by Russia in 2006 on wine imports from the country. While the Georgian wine industry has a good and improving reputation in the West, it still suffers from infrastructure problems. With an estimated 150,000 owners sharing 60,000ha, managing fruit quality and consistency is a huge problem. However, the potential for exciting wines is starting to show in the output from wineries owning vineyards, such as Chandrebi Estate, Telavi, Teliani Valley, Vinoterra, and Tbilvino.

Saperavi 🍇 Rkatsiteli, Mtsvane 🏔 Kakheti, Kartli, Imereti, Racha-Lechkhumi ⬛ Chandrebi Estate *(www.orovela.com)*; Telavi *(www.tewince!. com)*; Georgian Wines & Spirits *(www.gws.ge)*

Ukraine

UKRAINE'S VINEYARD AREA had fallen to 82,000ha in 2004, with about 80 per cent being wine grapes. Commercial viticulture is concentrated in the Crimea and Odessa regions and is mostly vinifera varieties, including Rkatsiteli, Aligoté, Cabernet Sauvignon, and Saperavi. There are also several local crosses, such as Bastardo and Magarach Ruby, developed at the world-famous research institute at Magarach. The climate is continental, with winter cold moderated by the Black Sea. The terrain is mostly flat, apart from the Carpathians in the southwest and the dramatic Crimean Mountains in the south, and vineyards are largely high-trained and widely spaced for mass production and mechanization. Yields today are often low due to the age of vines and lack of investment for replanting.

Sparkling wine remains important in Ukraine, both for export to Russia and for home consumption, and was first produced in the late 19th century at Novy Svet in Crimea. Tank fermentation is typical, based on Pinot Blanc, Aligoté, and Feteasca, though three producers make bottle-fermented wines. There's little foreign investment in Ukraine except from German Sekt giant Henkell & Co, which bought a majority shareholding in one of Ukraine's biggest producers in 2007.

The Crimea region has the most favourable climate for wine production, and the Massandra winery is its pride and joy. Built in the 1890s to supply the Tsar's summer palace, today the cellar is used for ageing and bottling wines. Its deep, cool cellars also house a collection of Crimea's best wines, largely sweet and fortified, with the oldest bottles being 'sherry-style' wines dating back to the 18th century. Massandra controls around 2,500ha of vines on sunny hillsides and a number of satellite wineries where primary winemaking takes place. It still sells wines dating back several decades, including port-style Ruby of Crimea, Surozh Kokour, Livadia Muscat, and sweet red Kagor made from Saperavi.

Cabernet Sauvignon, Saperavi, Bastardo 🍇 Rkatsiteli, Aligoté, Feteasca, Pinot Blanc 🏔 Crimea, Odessa

The Caucasus, Georgia's key wine-producing region

WINE BOTTLES

FOR MOST OF ITS HISTORY, wine has been stored in bulk – from earthen amphorae to wooden casks – and decanted into vessels as required. The wine bottle was developed for table service in England in the 1630s, and was globular or onion-shaped. By the 1720s, bottles had become taller with flatter sides – known as a mallet shape. By the 1820s, uniform cylindrical bottles became the standard.

**c.70 BC
Italy**

**Stoneware
pitcher**

Pitcher and jug
Stoneware, pewter, and even leather jugs were used for serving wine from the Middle Ages. Frailty and expense made early glass an impractical vessel.

Pewter jug 1660s

Onion-shaped 1670

EARLY BOTTLE LABELS

Wine bottles of the 18th and early 19th centuries were unlabelled. To identify their contents, 'bottle tickets' or labels of silver, porcelain, or mother-of-pearl were attached to the bottle neck with a thin chain or string.

**Bordeaux label
1850s**

CLARET

**Madeira label
1822**

MADEIRA

HOCK

**Rhein label
1809**

1

2

3

Variety
The capacities and styles of early bottles varied enormously from workshop to workshop, and according to customer requirements.

Colour
The olive or even blackish colour of early bottles stems from impurities in the raw materials or from the fumes of the kilns.

Mallet-shaped 1738

Mallet-shaped 1764

Mallet-shaped 1780

MODERN BOTTLE SHAPES

The shapes of wine bottles today offer clues about the nature and style of the wine they contain. A slender, elongated bottle (1, 2) is called a German or Alsatian 'flute', and commonly contains white wines made from Riesling, Gewürtztraminer, and similar varieties. A broad and sloping shape (3) is called a Burgundy bottle and is linked to the varieties of eastern France (including those of the Rhône Valley). Finally, a straight-sided, high-shouldered shape (4, 5, 6) is referred to as a Bordeaux bottle. The wine within it is frequently based on Bordeaux varieties such as Cabernet Sauvignon or Merlot. These correlations are not formal or inviolate, but an established tradition.

THE AMERICANS

DESPITE COMMON GRAPES AND PHILOSOPHIES *, there is little similarity between wine production in North and South America. Canada, in the far north, experiences Arctic winters and low temperatures throughout the growing season. In Chile (see p536), Argentina (see p544), Mexico, Brazil, Uruguay, and Peru in the south, the main challenge is an excess of heat.*

Vinicola Aurora, Brazil

Okanagan Valley, British Columbia, Canada

Canada

DESPITE ITS low profile, Canada is an increasingly important wine producer. At the start of the 1970s the industry was dominated by alcoholic, sweet wines. Since the innovative Inniskillin winery was founded in 1974 with its emphasis on quality, the industry has been transformed.

The Canadian climate is notable for its severe winters, spring frosts, and short growing season. The main vineyard areas are located near to large lakes to help moderate temperatures. The climate causes numerous problems, but also provides the perfect environment for ice wine. Based on the German *Eiswein*, Canadian ice wine is produced from grape varieties such as Vidal and Riesling, which are allowed to freeze on the vine. Harvested late in the year when the temperatures have dropped to at least -8°C, the grapes are pressed and the frozen water is separated from the remainder of the must. The liquid left behind is fermented into an extremely concentrated and lusciously sweet dessert wine. The low temperatures necessary for the production of ice wine occur here much more regularly than in Germany,

Inniskillen ice wine, Canada

making Canada the largest producer of this wine style in the world.

The principal wine regions are the Niagara Peninsula in Ontario and the Okanagan Valley in British Columbia. In addition to ice wine, these areas specialize in fragrant, dry, cool-climate whites from Riesling, Chardonnay, Gewürztraminer, and Pinot Blanc. Red wine production is more difficult in the Canadian climate, but an increasing number of wineries make promising reds from Pinot Noir, Cabernet Sauvignon, Merlot, and Syrah.

🍷 *Pinot Noir, Cabernet Sauvignon, Merlot, Syrah*
🍷 *Riesling, Chardonnay, Vidal* 🏠 *Niagara Peninsula, Okanagan Valley* ▣ Burrowing Owl Vineyards *(www.bovwine.com)*; Inniskillin *(www.inniskillin.com)*

Mexico

THE MEXICAN WINE INDUSTRY has recently been transformed by a combination of foreign investment and ambitious local producers. The majority of the vines planted are still used for table grapes or brandy, but the domestic market for quality wine is on the rise.

Lying below California, Baja California is Mexico's leading wine district. Guadalupe Valley is its most famous subregion, and is home to many of Mexico's finest estates, such as Monte Xanic, Casa Pedro Domecq, and Château Camou. Red wines are a speciality, and the best come from Cabernet Sauvignon, Merlot, Nebbiolo, Petite Sirah, or Zinfandel. Lying to the east of Baja California, Sonaro is another major grape growing district.

🍷 *Cabernet Sauvignon, Merlot, Petite Sirah, Zinfandel* 🍷 *Colombard, Chenin Blanc, Trebbiano* 🏠 *Baja California, Sonoro* ▣ La Cetto *(www. lacetto.com)*; Monte Xanic *(www.montexanic.com)*; Casa Pedro Domecq *(www.domecq.com.mx)*; Château Camou *(www.chateaucamou.com.mx)*

Brazil

BRAZIL IS South America's third largest wine producer by volume. Today just over half the country's 60,000ha of vineyards are dedicated to wine, the remainder for table grapes. Driven by foreign investment, classic European vines now account for 20 per cent of total production in Brazil. The majority of vineyards are concentrated in the south, around the hilly Serra Gaucha region. This high altitude area specializes in whites from Chardonnay, Sémillon, Gewürztraminer, and Welschriesling Frontera is a newer wine region on the border with Uruguay. It has been planted with European grape varieties, predominantly white.

🍷 *Cabernet Franc, Merlot, Cabernet Sauvignon* 🍇 *Chardonnay, Welschriesling, Sémillon, Gewürztraminer, Isabella* 🏚 *Serra Gaucha, Frontera* 🔖 Vinicola Aurora (www.vinicolaaurora.com.br)

Uruguay

SINCE THE VINE was first planted by Basque immigrants in the 1870s, the wine industry in Uruguay has made impressive progress. Although the bulk of the harvest still supplies the local population with cheap and basic wine, a number of estates are now focusing on more ambitious styles. Combining modern techniques with both local and international grape varieties, this new wave of producers points to an exciting future for Uruguayan wine.

The majority of the vineyards are situated in the cooler south around Montevideo, home to many of Uruguay's most important estates. The Pisano family planted its first vineyard here in 1914 and today exports its high quality wines to a number of international markets. Another important producer, Establecimiento Juanicó grows its grapes in neighbouring Canalones, where the influence of the ocean moderates temperatures and encourages a prolonged growing season. Further north, a number of provinces show considerable potential. On the border with the Frontera wine region of Brazil, Rivera province is home to winemaker Jean Carrau's *bodega* Cerro Chapeu. With vines grown at high altitudes on deep, sandy soils, the area is quickly developing an excellent reputation. Towards the centre of the country, the vineyards of Carpinteria and El

Tending grapes in Pisano's vineyards, Uruguay

Carmen also show promise. The Tannat grape, known locally as Harriague, is the most widely planted variety. Originally from the south of France, Tannat is responsible for some of the country's most distinctive wines, typically with deep colour, firm structure, and black berry fruits. Quality, however, can vary considerably. International grape varieties such as Cabernet Sauvignon, Merlot, Sauvignon Blanc, and Chardonnay are also gaining in popularity.

🍷 *Tannat, Cabernet Sauvignon, Cabernet Franc, Merlot* 🍇 *Pinot Blanc, Sauvignon Blanc, Chardonnay* 🏚 *Rivera, Carpinteria, El Carmen, Canalones* 🔖 Establecimiento Juanicó (www.juanico.com.uy); Cerrau Chapeau (www.castelpujol.com); Pisano (www.pisanowines.com)

Tacama's Vineyard, Peru

Peru

DESPITE A GENERALLY unfavourable climate, Peru is the oldest wine nation in South America. Winters are so warm in many parts of the country that vines actually yield two crops a year. The majority of this harvest is used for table grapes or *pisco*, the local brandy. Yet in certain locations, some remarkably promising wines can be made. Peru's wine regions are concentrated on the central coast around the city of Pisco. Here, sea breezes from the Pacific help to reduce the extremes of temperature. The country's finest winery, Tacama's Vineyard, is situated in nearby Ica, and produces a range of still and sparkling wines from Tannat, Malbec, Sauvignon Blanc, and Sémillon. The company has been assisted by French expertise and now exports internationally.

🍷 *Tannat, Petit Verdot, Malbec, Cabernet Sauvignon* 🍇 *Sauvignon Blanc, Sémillon, Albilla* 🏚 *Ica* 🔖 Tacama's Vineyard (www.tacama.com)

ASIA

ASIA'S CLIMATE *is generally unsuited to quality wine production. Vines have been grown on the continent for thousands of years, but the grapes have mainly been eaten at the table. As the populations of China, Japan, and India develop an interest in wine, however, the domestic industries have gradually come to the fore. With investment and expertise, a number of areas show surprising potential.*

Wines from Sula Vineyards, India

China

ALTHOUGH GRAPE seeds were introduced in the 2nd century BC, the wine industry in China is still in its infancy. Today, the majority of the country's 165,000ha of vineyards concentrate on table grape or dried grape production. Many of the best grape growing areas are found in the cooler coastal provinces of Shandong, Hebei, and Tianjin. Founded by a British wine merchant, Huadong winery in Shandong was the first to offer modern wines from European grape varieties such as Chardonnay, Riesling, and Cabernet Sauvignon. Huaxia Winery in Changli, Hebei, is another leading estate, responsible for Great Wall Red. State facilities such as Chang Yu and Qingdao in Shandong also show promise.

Huadong Winery, China

🍇 *Cabernet Sauvignon* 🍇 *Chardonnay, Riesling* 🏯 *Shandong, Hebei, Tianjin* ▤ *Huadong Winery (www.huadongwinery.com)*

Japan

JAPAN HAS CULTIVATED the vine since the 7th century, but has traditionally focused on table grape production. Just 10 per cent of the annual harvest finds its way to the wine industry, and many local producers bolster their brands with imported grape concentrate. The country's monsoonal climate makes life extremely difficult for growers. Fungal diseases are a constant menace in the wine regions of Yamanashi and Katsunuma. On the north island, low temperatures are the main concern for estates in central Hokkaido. Wine made from Japan's domestic varieties tends to be exceptionally light, but the white Koshu demonstrates some potential. European grapes also show promise – Cabernet Sauvignon in West Yamanashi and Chardonnay in Nagaro.

🍇 *Cabernet Sauvignon* 🍇 *Koshu, Chardonnay, Neo-Muscat, Ryugan (Senkoji)* 🏯 *Yamanashi, Katsunuma, central Hokkaido*

India

DESPITE ITS SEEMINGLY unfavourable climate, India is capable of producing world class wines. The country has grown vines since at least 300 BC, but today nearly 90 per cent of all vineyards are dedicated to table grapes or raisins. The neighbouring states of Maharashtra, Karnataka, and Andhra Pradesh are the most important viticultural regions. Large volumes of ordinary wine are still made in India, but several estates are leading the way forward. Château Indage in Maharashtra is most famous for sparkling wines such as Omar Khayyam, while Grover Vineyards near Bangalore makes a range of concentrated wines based on French grape varieties such as Cabernet Sauvignon. In Maharashtra, Sula Vineyards produces intense whites from Sauvignon Blanc and Chenin Blanc.

🍇 *Cabernet Sauvignon, Pinot Noir, Merlot* 🍇 *Sauvignon Blanc, Chenin Blanc, Chardonnay* 🏯 *Maharashtra, Karnataka, Andhra Pradesh* ▤ *Grover Vineyards (www.grover-vineyards.com); Sula Vineyards (www.sulawines.com; Château Indage (www.indagegroup.com)*

Display of barrels, Yamanashi region, Japan

AFRICA

THESE NORTH AFRICAN NATIONS *were responsible for two thirds of the entire international wine trade in the 1950s. The bulk of the wine was exported to France, the colonial power at the time. Following independence, much of this market dried up, sending vineyards and wineries spiralling into decline. A tentative recovery has begun, but is hampered by the importance of the Islamic religion in many of these countries, which forbids followers from the consumption of alcohol.*

Ploughing the vineyard, southern Tunisia

Morocco

SINCE MOROCCO'S independence from France in 1956, vineyard areas in the country have plummeted from 55,000ha to nearer 10,000ha. Today the industry is dominated by SODEA, a state-owned company, which is struggling to overcome years of neglect. The innovative Celliers de Meknès and a number of foreign investors offer hope for the future, but substantial progress still needs to be made.

Production in Morocco is dominated by red wines. The lacklustre Carignan is the most widely planted variety, with Cinsaut and Grenache also featuring. Cabernet Sauvignon, Merlot, and Syrah are increasing in importance and are responsible for many of the country's best wines. The high altitude vineyards Meknès-Fès and Berkane are considered to be the finest regions.

🍇 *Carignan, Cinsaut, Grenache, Cabernet Sauvignon, Merlot* 🍇 *Clairette, Muscat, Chenin Blanc, Chardonnay* 🗺 *Meknès-Fès, Berkane* 🗄 *Celliers de Meknès*

Tunisia

TUNISIA HAS PRODUCED wine ever since the Phoenicians founded Carthage around 800 BC. From 1883 to 1963 the country was a French protectorate, and the industry retains a strong Gallic flavour. Tunisia and France share a number of common grape varieties, such as Carignan, Grenache, Clairette, and Alicante.

Today, winemaking in Tunisia is hampered by a lack of investment. Three quarters of production lies in the hands of the state, which has generally been slow to embrace new technology. Several private companies have begun to take advantage of the country's mature vineyards, but much work remains to be done. Although light rosés currently dominate the industry, Tunisia's future probably lies in its full-flavoured reds.

🍇 *Carignan, Grenache, Cinsaut* 🍇 *Clairette, Muscat d'Alexandrie* 🗺 *Nabeul, Cap Bon, Bizerte*

Algeria

ALGERIA HAS AN unusually large wine industry for a Muslim country. Nearly 60,000ha of vineyards remain as a legacy of French sovereignty (1830–1962). Production has fallen dramatically since independence, with roughly 50 per cent of vines now used for table grapes, but wine is still an important export. The major regions in Algeria are on the northern coast. Here, a Mediterranean climate produces wines that are typically robust and high in alcohol. The main varieties are the red grapes Carignan, Alicante Bouschet, Cinsaut, and Grenache, many planted by the French in the 1950s. White grapes such as Ugni Blanc and Clairette are also grown. Better quality grapes such as Cabernet Sauvignon and Merlot are slowly appearing. Although there are over 70 wineries, the industry is almost completely dominated by the state-controlled ONCV.

🍇 *Carignan, Alicante, Cinsaut, Grenache* 🍇 *Ugni Blanc, Clairette* 🗺 *Coteaux de Tlemcen, Coteaux de Mascara, Dahra Hills*

Celliers de Meknès, Morocco

REFERENCE

READING A WINE LABEL

THERE ARE FEW PRODUCTS in the world today that reveal as much about their provenance as a bottle of wine. The average wine label is packed with information; some is required by law in the country where the wine is made or sold, while other details are provided voluntarily by the producer.

Understanding a wine label is often far from straightforward, and those from the traditional wine regions of Europe can be particularly difficult for the uninitiated. In some cases there is simply no substitute for knowledge:

Penèdes label, Spain

recognizing a producer (generally the most important piece of information on the label), understanding appellations and classifications, and possessing an appreciation of the major wine styles will all help significantly with the decision-making.

Wine labels broadly divide into two styles: geographical and varietal. Both share certain information, such as alcohol content. However, they differ mainly over the emphasis they place on two key factors: the origin of a wine and the grape variety or varieties from which it was made.

Geographical Wine Label

An Old World or geographical-style label is found mainly in European wine countries where the area of production is the most important element. The name of the region, village, or vineyard will appear prominently on the front of the bottle, along with a guarantee that the wine originates from the area quoted. In France this is governed by Appellation d'Origine Contrôlée (AOC), in Italy Denominazione di Origine Controllata (DOC), in Spain Denominación de Origen (DO), and in Germany Qualitätswein mit Prädikat (QmP).

The geographical labels of some Old World wines, such as French vins de pays (see p52) and most German wines, include the name of the main grape variety. The vast majority of geographical labels do not state the grapes, which means that a certain amount of knowledge is required. Each region has its own wine styles, so knowing more about the regional background will reveal the flavours, characteristics and grape varieties you can expect.

Region of origin is the most important information on the label, revealing the style of wine. Each region is only allowed to use certain grape varieties, which are rarely mentioned on the label. The *terroir* of each of these regions evokes its own particular characteristics. Here, the area of production is Corton-Charlemagne, a Côte de Beaune vineyard in Burgundy.

Appellation Contrôlée or Appellation d'Origine Contrôlée (AOC) confirms that the wine comes from the vineyard of Corton-Charlemagne and has been produced according to local regulations.

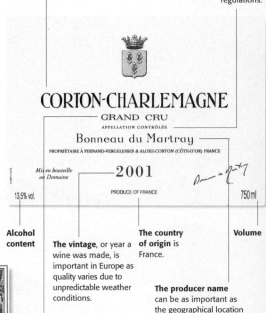

Alcohol content

The vintage, or year a wine was made, is important in Europe as quality varies due to unpredictable weather conditions.

The country of origin is France.

Volume

The producer name can be as important as the geographical location in determining the potential quality of the wine.

Classification of quality is indicated here by *grand cru*, meaning 'great growth'. This is the highest level in Burgundy.

Rheingau label, Germany

◁ **Display of wines from Leeuwin Estate, Western Australia**

Varietal Wine Label

The varietal-style label is found in less traditional wine countries such as Australia, USA, and South Africa, which are often referred to as the New World. A varietal label highlights grape variety – the most important ingredient in determining the taste of a wine – making life easier for the consumer. The flavour will change according to the producer and the region where the grapes are grown but the grape name gives an invaluable indication as to the individual character-istics of the wine. This is not to say that origin is unimportant on a varietal wine label. There are an in-creasing number of regions in the New World that have established a distinguished reputation for the quality of their varietal wines. Among these are Napa Valley in California for Cabernet Sauvignon, Oregon for Pinot Noir, South Africa's Cape Peninsula for Chenin Blanc and Pinotage, New Zealand's Marlborough for Sauvignon Blanc, and the Australian regions Barossa and Hunter valleys for Shiraz and Clare and Eden valleys for Riesling.

The producer name is just as important here as on a geographical label. Good producers will make quality wines across their range, but may specialize in certain grape varieties.

The name of the range a wine falls into is often shown. Art Series is Leeuwin Estate's top range.

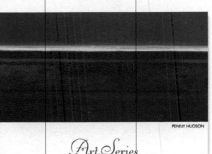

The vintage tends to be less important for New World wines than for those from the Old World. However, there can still be vintage variation, depending on the region.

PENNY HUDSON

Art Series

LEEUWIN ESTATE

2001

MARGARET RIVER
PINOT NOIR

13.5% vol   PRODUCE OF AUSTRALIA   750mL

Volume

Alcohol content

The country of origin is Australia.

The region gives a clue as to the style and weight of the wine. Certain regions have an excellent reputation and Margaret River is known to make rich, elegant Pinot Noir.

The grape name is normally the most visible piece of infor-mation. It gives an excellent indicator as to the style and character of the wine.

de Trafford
CHENIN BLANC
WINE OF ORIGIN STELLENBOSCH
2000
MONT FLEUR · PO BOX 495 · STELLENBOSCH · FAX 021 8801611

Chenin Blanc label, South Africa

Country Wine Law

For information on individual countries, see France pp52–3, Italy pp192–3, Spain pp290–91, Portugal p331, Germany pp348–9, South Africa p446.

READING THE BACK LABEL

Many wines now carry a back label. This can be an essential source of extra information, often revealing as much, if not more, than the front. The details on a back label can range from a brief history of the estate or region of production, through to climate (cool temperatures may make more complex, subtle wines), harvest procedures (handpicking is gentler), detailed winemaking techniques, and food recommendations. It is important to remember that the producer is in the business of selling the wine, so the contents may not be quite as stunning as their tasting notes suggest. European wines with geographical style labels would benefit most from a back label but unfortunately they are the least likely to have one.

Back label from South Africa

BUYING WINE

THERE HAS NEVER BEEN SO MUCH CHOICE *when it comes to purchasing wine. For many, it is simply a matter of supermarket convenience. However, there can be distinct advantages in buying from other sources: a wine merchant offers expert advice; using on-line merchants means you can easily shop around for the best prices and the choice is vast; and buying at auction can fulfil a sense of adventure, as well as make a potential investment.*

Supermarkets

Convenience is probably the main reason why most wine in the UK is bought in supermarkets, and they are a reliable, if not especially adventurous, source of wine. All the major chains in Britain now have good ranges, although they do not tend to stock wine from small producers and obscure styles. However, what they lack in breadth they more than make up for in special offers and value for money. Their own-brand ranges can be particularly good value. Tesco is the country's most popular wine retailer and has a strong and increasingly interesting selection. Sainsbury's, which is next in terms of sales, has a well-chosen and reliable range. Asda specializes in great-value, everyday wines, and Morrisons is the least adventurous of the big four. The award-winning range at Marks & Spencer has improved enormously in recent years. Unfortunately, two of the best supermarkets for wine are only found in certain areas of the country: Booths in the north, and Waitrose in the centre and south. Both sell quality wines and champion smaller producers.

Wine Merchants

These range from large off-licence chains such as Threshers and Wine Rack (owned by the same company: *www.thresher group.com*), through to national wine specialists such as Oddbins *(see right)*, and more local outfits, such as London-based Berry Brothers & Rudd *(see right)* and Philglas & Swiggot *(www.philglas-swiggot.co.uk)*, as well as Cambridge-based Noel Young *(www.nywines.co.uk)*.

Although the range and standards of UK off licences have been improving of late, their main advantage over supermarkets is still one of physical convenience rather than of expert advice or quality wines.

Specialist wine merchants remain a destination of choice for wine lovers *(see right)*. They have much to offer in terms of advice, range, and wines from small, high-quality producers. Owners and staff have often tasted most of the wines on sale and are happy to share their knowledge and recommendations. Take time to discuss your requirements and preferences: price, styles of wines you enjoy, food with which you plan to drink the wine, and the occasion on which you want to serve it.

Mail Order

A large volume of wine is bought through mail order companies or clubs, such as the The Sunday Times Wine Club *(www.sunday timeswineclub.co.uk)* and Laithwaites *(www.laithwaites.co.uk)*. These firms offer generous discounts and exclusive wines sourced directly from producers, as well as providing regular mailings and member tasting events. However, the quality of the wines can be variable, and the 'promotional' prices are not always the best value. Also available is the mail order service offered by many of the specialist wine merchants *(see right)* and The Wine Society *(www.the winesociety.com)*, which often includes free delivery subject to a minimum order.

Auctions & Exchanges

It is not without risk, but buying at an auction or internet exchange can be an excellent way of acquiring cases of wine, particularly older vintages which are not easily available. Major auction houses such as Christie's *(www.christies.com)* and Sotheby's *(www.sothebys.com)* hold regular wine sales, as do smaller, local houses. It is best to become familiar with the procedure of a live auction before bidding and to be aware of the charges on top of the hammer price (buyer's commission ranges from 10 to 15 per cent plus VAT). Also be sure to learn as much as possible about the condition and provenance of lots before bidding.

Wine exchanges are a much more recent phenomenon, where companies conduct their business over the internet. Sellers place an offer price for a wine on the site, and if a buyer accepts the price, the wine is traded. Wines are inspected for condition, and an additional fee (usually around 10 per cent), plus delivery and VAT, is charged for the service.

Investing in Wine

Until recently, wine was considered a sure-fire investment. Today, however, it is accepted that there are as many risks involved in buying wine as in any other form of investment. Seek proper advice and conduct personal research before investing in wine. Some basic guidelines are:
• Focus on estates with a proven record from the classic regions of France (Bordeaux, Burgundy, and Northern Rhône).
• Buy only the best vintages.
• Buy a broad portfolio of different wines.
• Buy wines that have been praised highly or given a high score by a renowned wine critic if possible.
• Be wary of heavily-hyped vintages (like 2000 Bordeaux) as their value may not increase further.
• Keep wine in perfect storage conditions to maintain its quality and assist its resale.
• Discover the optimum drinking times for the wine, as its value gradually declines once it has passed its peak.

Direct from Producers

Wine almost always tastes better at its source, thanks to a combination of the often beautiful surroundings and the chance to meet the people who created it. It is customary to buy at least a couple of bottles when you have enjoyed the hospitality of an estate. Be aware, however, that there will not necessarily be major savings to be made on the standard retail price.

Restaurants

The subject of wine in restaurants is not without controversy. Many restaurants make the bulk of their profits through wine sales, so mark-ups can be as high as 400 per cent. Many of the best restaurants have a dedicated wine waiter or sommelier. It is their job to cater for everything connected with wine during your meal, from advice on the best bottle to accompany your food, through to decanting and pouring the wine into your glass. State your budget and preferences, and a good sommelier should help find the perfect wine. For advice on choosing wine to match your meal when there is no sommelier at hand, see pp652–5.

After ordering, the waiter should bring the unopened bottle to your table, allowing you to check the name and vintage are correct. It will then be opened and a small measure poured for you to taste. This is to ensure the wine is not corked, or otherwise faulty. If there is a problem with a wine, return it.

To avoid ordering wine in a restaurant opt for a 'bring your own' (BYO) establishment. The website www.winepages.com/byoblist.html has a reasonable list of such venues (mainly UK but also some international). Some places, however, charge a hefty corkage fee. It is always worth calling the restaurant in advance to check.

On the Web

Most supermarkets, wine merchants, and mail order companies have a presence on the internet. However, there are also a number of web-only companies. Virgin Wines (www.virginwines.com) is one of the most successful, offering mixed cases and recommended wines, alongside à la carte selections for more experienced wine drinkers, and a delivery service. Everywine (www.everywine.co.uk) also has an extensive selection of wines, although the sheer choice can be bewildering and many are only available by the case.

UK WINE MERCHANTS: PICK OF THE CROP

Adnams
www.adnamswines.co.uk
Extensive selection of both Old and New World wines at attractive prices.

Berry Brothers & Rudd
www.bbr.com
Vast range of wines, especially good on older vintages and classic regions.

Corney & Barrow
www.corneyandbarrow.com
Chain of wine bars, as well as a national wholesale operation with an extensive range covering all budgets.

Justerini & Brooks
www.justeriniandbrooks.com
Very strong on classic regions like Bordeaux and Burgundy.

Lay & Wheeler
www.laywheeler.com
Dynamic merchant with outstanding website and mailings.

Majestic
www.majestic.co.uk
Great range plus one-off bin ends; there is a minimum purchase of one case (12 bottles of wine, which can be mixed).

Oddbins
www.oddbins.com
Knowledgeable and passionate staff and an excellent choice of widely sourced wines.

Tanners
www.tanners-wines.co.uk
Four outstanding stores and excellent mail order facilities.

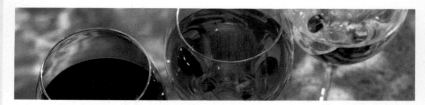

STORING & SERVING WINE

OVER THE YEARS *wine has become associated with a number of procedures, like cellaring, breathing, and decanting. While it is not strictly essential to know anything about these terms to enjoy wine, an understanding of these practices can maximize the pleasure gained from both buying and drinking it.*

STORING WINE

The majority of wines sold today are designed to be enjoyed young. Almost all mid-priced bottles will survive in a rack for around 12 months, but are likely to deteriorate if left for longer. Traditionally, most wines worth cellaring were from the Old World, but age-worthy bottles are now created by the finest producers elsewhere, too. If in any doubt, it is always better to drink a wine too young rather than too old.

Why Store Wine?

As wines sit in the bottle, a series of chemical reactions takes place that changes relatively simple fruity flavours to more developed, complex tastes. In reds, the colour becomes lighter, the tannins get softer, and the wine takes on aromas such as cedar, leather, or mushrooms. Whites, on the other hand, deepen in colour, and become less sweet and more intense. Typical aromas of a mature white wine include nuts, wax, and even diesel. The effect of oak barrels – hints of vanilla, coconut, and spice – lessen in all wines as they mature.

Cellars

A cellar can range from a humble, under-stair cupboard to a vast underground labyrinth, as long as conditions are right for maturation. The key features to think about when choosing the perfect

'cellar' are as follows:
• A constant temperature between 10 and 15°C is preferable. Slightly higher than this is not a major concern: the wine will mature more quickly, but slightly less favourably. It is temperature variation that causes most harm.
• Wine dislikes light, which is why many bottles are made of coloured glass. Dark rooms or sealed boxes are best.
• A lack of moisture can cause corks to dry out, contract, and let air into the bottle, which will oxidize the wine, eventually turning it into vinegar. Slightly damp cellars, on the other hand, will not harm the wine.
• Excess movement or vibration can damage wine so avoid storage next to large machinery, such as fridges and washing machines, and also avoid handling or unnecessary transport.
• Wine is best stored on its side, as constant contact between cork and liquid prevents the cork from drying out. Sparkling wines and wines with a screwcap can be stored upright due to the difference in closure material. If you want to cellar wine but lack the ideal conditions, there are alternative options: buying a wine fridge or cabinet which can hold bottles in perfect storage conditions; or paying for dedicated storage with a professional firm. Contact your local wine merchant for advice.

SERVING WINE

There are many rituals around the serving of wine. Most are based on sound logic, while a few are more a matter of tradition, with little scientific basis. The following guide will equip you with the essentials.

Serving Order

There are a number of generally accepted rules for serving wine:
• White before red – although a light-bodied red can be enjoyed before a full-bodied white.
• Dry before sweet whites – this avoids making the wine taste excessively acidic.
• Light before heavy reds – lighter wines tend to taste thin after a heavier example.
• Lower quality wines before more illustrious ones.
There is no clear consensus on whether young or old wines should be consumed first. Much depends on the individual wine.

Glasses

Using the correct wine glasses can influence the taste of a wine. Although you can buy individual glass designs for different wines, a good all-purpose wine glass will normally suffice. This should have a stem so that you do not have to handle the bowl; and the bowl should be large enough to hold a decent measure, yet still allow room for the wine to be swirled. The bowl should be narrower at the rim than at the base, directing the aromas towards your nose. Finally, clear glass – not cut, coloured, or patterned – allows the colour of the wine to show through. The only major styles that require a different shape of glass are champagne and sparkling wines. Their tall, straight, thin glasses are specifically designed to show off and retain the bubbles.

Temperatures

The correct temperature is extremely important to the taste of wine. White wines are often served too cold, and reds too warm. Some guidelines to follow:
• Sparkling wines: Cool temperatures of around 8°C.
• Light, aromatic whites: Quite cold – around 10°C or a few hours in the fridge. Chilling emphasizes the crisp, fresh taste and does not dull the aromas.
• White burgundy & other Chardonnays: These are less aromatic, so serve around 12°C.
• Light- and medium-bodied reds: Chill slightly to around 12 or 13°C (half an hour in the fridge), particularly in summer.
• Full-bodied reds: Low temperatures emphasize tannins, so serve these reasonably warm, around 15°C.

Decanting

Certain high quality wines (mostly reds), such as the 2000 Bordeaux, opened before their peak, can benefit greatly from exposure to oxygen in the air – or breathing – before drinking. Simply pulling the cork on a bottle and allowing it to stand open is unlikely to make much difference. Using a decanter, however, will. The shape of the vessel used makes little difference, as long as it is made of glass and open-topped.

Another reason to use a decanter is to separate a wine from its sediment or deposit, especially if it is unfiltered. Wines

that 'throw a sediment include vintage port, unfiltered or traditional LBV port, crusted port, older vintages of red bordeaux, red burgundy, Rhône reds, Barolo, Barbaresco, and other full-bodied reds.

To decant a wine, stand the bottle upright for at least 24 hours to allow the sediment to fall to the bottom. Then, pull the cork and with a source of light, either a lighted candle or a naked light bulb, behind the neck to allow you to see the contents, slowly pour the wine into the decanter. Stop when you see the sediment reach the neck of the bottle. Do not leave wine in a decanter for a lengthy period of time, as prolonged exposure to oxygen will ruin it.

Opening Fizz

The correct procedure for opening a sparkling wine or champagne is as follows:
• Hold the bottle at an angle of approximately 55 degrees.
• Point the neck of the bottle away from other people and from breakables.
• Carefully remove the foil

and wire muzzle.
• Holding the bottle in one hand and the cork in the other, gently twist the bottle (not the cork) until the cork eases with a satisfying pop.

How Much per Person?

Serving quantities depend on the occasion and, of course, the drinking capacities of your guests. At dinner parties estimate between half a bottle and a whole bottle of wine per person per evening. When ordering large amounts of wine for an event, remember that many retailers operate a sale or return policy, which allows customers to return unopened bottles. In this instance always err on the generous side when ordering.

Leftover Wine

Leftover wine should be poured into the smallest appropriate bottle size, sealed with the original cork if possible, and kept in the fridge. It should then be finished off within 24 to 48 hours, as deterioration will quickly set in.

RED & WHITE WINES TO KEEP

Keeping times depend on the quality of the producer, vineyard site, and vintage. Below are some broad storage recommendations. Bear in mind that only the finest wines can age for longer periods:

Whites
Chardonnay: 2 to 5 years for top quality wine from outside Burgundy.
Riesling: 2 years for low priced wines; 5 to 20 years for the best German examples; sweeter styles keep longer than drier.
Sémillon: 5 to 10 years for the best from Hunter Valley, Australia; 1 to 2 years for others.
Sweet wine: 5 to 20 years for the best examples from Sauternes, Germany, and Hungary.
White burgundy: 1 to 10 years for Chablis; 2 to 8 years for other good white burgundies.
White Rhône: 3 to 10 years for

wines made from Marsanne and Roussanne.

Reds
Barolo & Barbaresco: 5 to 20 years for the best examples; 2 to 5 years if unsure of quality.
Cabernet Sauvignon-based wines: 3 to 10 years.
Merlot: 3 to 15 years for good quality St-Émilion or Pomerol; less time if from elsewhere.
Pinot Noir: 2 to 5 years for the best examples from New Zealand, USA, and Australia.
Red bordeaux: 5 to 20 years.
Red burgundy: 2 to 10 years.
Rhône: 5 to 15 years for the best vintages; wine from Southern Rhône needs less time than the Northern Rhône.
Shiraz: 5 to 15 years for the best wines.
Vintage port: 10 to 40 years.

TASTING WINE

WINE CAN BE *simply consumed like any other beverage. However, the variety of styles and flavours on offer means that a lot can be missed by just guzzling it down. The process of tasting wine implies a more thoughtful and methodical approach, helping to maximize the pleasure you derive from every glass.*

PRACTICALITIES

It is best to taste wine in a naturally-lit, odourless room to allow its true colour to be examined and to avoid other aromas interfering with the sense of smell. Avoid perfume, mints, and smoke. The most important factor when tasting is the shape and size of glass, as this can have a major impact on the taste of a wine *(see p646)*.

Look

Looking at a wine can provide valuable clues to its character. Note the colour and check that the wine is clear – cloudiness can indicate a fault. For reds, tilt the glass away from you against a white background and inspect the rim of the liquid to see the true colour. As a red wine ages, it changes from bright purple to tawny and then to brown. So if a red wine looks brown, it may be past its best (although brown would be normal in wines such as sherry and tawny port). A deep golden colour in a white wine may indicate the wine has been aged in oak, but it can also indicate a sweet wine style or particularly ripe fruit.

Smell

This is, without question, the most important stage of tasting. Smelling wine will vastly improve your enjoyment and knowledge. Firstly, gently sniff the wine.

Make a note of any first impressions, as they are often the most revealing. Holding the glass by its stem, swirl the wine in order to help release its aromas. Then take another sniff. Note the fruit aromas you detect now. Are they intense or relatively subdued? Is there a range of suggested 'flavours'? If so, this might indicate complexity, a sign of quality. Does it smell of the fruity flavours often found in a young wine, or does it boast more mature, developed aromas such as mushrooms, leather, and diesel? Is any one smell dominant, and do you like it? *See pp650–51* for help identifying the aromas you detect.

Taste

This stage often merely confirms the impression received on the nose. Take a small sip and allow the wine to linger on your tongue and mouth. You can enhance the flavours by pursing your lips and sucking a small amount of air into your mouth. This takes practice, but it is something professional tasters encourage as the presence of oxygen amplifies the flavours experienced. If you are tasting a lot of wines in one session, it is normally sensible to spit out each wine after noting the flavours and neutralize the palate by eating a cracker or taking a sip of water. Here are some further guidelines:

• Note the sweetness of the wine, detected on the tip of the tongue: is it dry, medium, or sweet?
• Consider the acidity – the element of a wine that keeps it fresh – detected on the sides of the tongue. Is it in balance with the rest of the flavours?
• For red wines think about tannins – the drying, mouth-puckering elements picked up by your gums. Are they harsh and bitter, or in balance with the wine?
• How heavy does the wine feel in your mouth? Do you think it is light-, medium- or full-bodied?
• Assess the fruit qualities of the wine. Are they pure and fruity (as in a young wine), or mature and complex (as in an older one)?
• Can you recognize any individual flavours?
• Consider how long the flavours last in your mouth after you spit or swallow. This is known as the 'finish' and, in general, the longer it lasts, the better the wine.

MAKING TASTING NOTES

Compiling tasting notes is not necessary, but it does allow you to build up a record of wines you have enjoyed. This in turn will allow you to make more informed buying decisions in the future. Try to put at least one comment for each of the various stages in the process, as well as a conclusion. This might be a score or a summary of your general impressions of the wine.

DESCRIBING A WINE

It is virtually impossible to truly articulate the complexities and subtleties of even the most basic of wines. When it comes to identifying aromas and flavours, wine tasters borrow their vocabulary from all kinds of areas, including fruits, flowers, spices, nuts, and types of wood. Some of the flavour compounds actually exist in certain wines. For example, vanilla aromas come from vanillin, which occurs naturally in new oak barrels. However, others are mere impressions that wines create in the mind of the taster. Everyone's sense of smell and taste is, of course, different, as we all have our own memory bank of flavours. It is important to remember that no identification is right or wrong.

DESCRIPTIVE TERMS

There are a large number of commonly used words and phrases for discussing the style and character of a wine. Definitions are not water-tight and there is often a large margin of overlap between various terms.

Age-worthy: Will benefit from further maturation in the bottle. Typical examples of age-worthy wines are young with either powerful tannins, good acidity, or some sweetness (see pp646–7).
Aromatic: A wine with lots of perfumed, fruity aromas, which normally leap out of the glass. Aromatic grape varieties include Sauvignon Blanc, Riesling, Gewürztraminer, and Muscat.
Austere: A wine that lacks fruity flavours and displays harsh, bitter tannins and/or high acidity.
Acidic: All wines need acidity to keep them balanced, but too much is a fault. Acidity is detected on the sides of the tongue.
Balanced: A wine with all its components (mainly acidity, alcohol, fruit, tannins, sugar, and extract) in harmony, with no one element prominent.
Big: A full-bodied wine that leaves a major impression on the senses, typically containing high levels of fruit, tannins, and/or alcohol. Also used to mean plenty of flavour.
Bitter: Normally a negative term used to describe a wine with an excess of harsh tannins, which leaves a bitter taste in the mouth, detected at the back of the tongue. In many Italian reds, however, a certain amount of bitterness is a highly desirable characteristic.
Blockbuster: Used to describe wines which are exceptionally 'big'. Think large amounts of fruit, alcohol, tannins, or oaky flavours.
Body: The weight or feel of wine in the mouth, determined by its alcohol and extract. To work out whether a wine is light-, medium- or full-bodied, it is sometimes useful to compare it to the feel of water.
Clean: Lacking faults in terms of its aroma and flavour.
Complex: A wine with many layers of aroma and flavour – many different fruits, plus other characteristics such as spice and vanilla. Complexity is one of the elements that separates an average wine from a good or great one. The most complex wines have typically gone through a period of ageing, allowing more flavours to develop.
Concentrated: An intense taste, normally found in wines with high levels of tannin, sugar, and flavouring and colouring compounds.
Crisp: Noticeable acidity but in a positive, refreshing way. Usually used for white wines with clean, fresh flavours.
Dry: No obvious sugar or sweetness in the wine. Note that very ripe, fruity flavours and new oak flavours can sometimes give the impression of sweetness, although the wine itself can still be dry. 'Dried-out' is a term given to red wines which have spent too long in barrel or bottle and have lost their fruit flavour.
Easy-drinking: A relatively simple wine that can be enjoyed without much thought. It will be fruity and, if red, low in tannin.
Elegant: A subjective term used to describe a good quality, subtle, and balanced wine which is not too fruity, and is extremely pleasant to drink.
Extract: All the solid matter in a wine such as tannins, sugars, and colouring and flavouring compounds. Extract gives a wine its body.
Finesse: Displaying elegance.
Flabby: A negative term used for a wine which has low acidity and is therefore unbalanced. It can make for a slightly cloying taste.
Fleshy: A wine which feels almost solid in texture when in the mouth, thanks to high levels of fruit and extract.
Fresh: Like crisp, noticeably acidic in an attractive, refreshing way. Normally used for young white wines.
Fruity: A wine with plenty of attractive fruit flavours.
Harsh: Rough around the edges, lacking in subtlety.
Heavy: Normally refers to a full-bodied, tannic red wine, and means it is tough to drink or heavy going. It may indicate that the wine needs to spend further time in bottle.
Mature: Ready to drink. Generally used for quality wines that require time in bottle. Over-mature is a euphemism for past its best.
Oaky: Normally a negative term to describe when oak flavours dominate other flavours in a wine. If the wine is young and good quality, it may lose some of its oakiness with a few years in bottle. Oak flavours can be desirable but only if they are balanced by fruit.
Powerful: A 'big' wine with high levels of extract and/or alcohol. Can be used in a positive or negative sense.

Continued overleaf ▷

Racy: Similar to crisp and fresh, meaning noticeable levels of refreshing acidity. Especially associated with German Riesling.

Rich: Like concentrated, implying deep, intense flavours in the mouth. Can also be used to mean slightly sweet.

Ripe: Wine made from ripe grapes and showing flavours of richer, warmer-climate fruits, such as pineapples (rather than apples). Ripe wine might also suggest a certain sweetness, even though it may not contain sugar.

Simple: Lacking complexity, with one-dimensional flavours. This is a fault in expensive wine, but it may not be a problem for everyday drinking wine.

Soft: A red wine with gentle tannins. Also known as smooth.

Structured: Normally refers to the tannins in a red wine, which support the other elements. In a 'well-structured' wine the tannins are noticeable but still balanced. Sometimes used for acidity in white wines, for example a wine can be described as having a 'good acidic structure'.

Subtle: Normally linked to finesse, it means a wine contains a number of different nuances and tastes. It can also be a euphemism for a wine lacking in fruity flavours.

Sweet: A wine with noticeable levels of sugar, detected by the tip of the tongue. The phrase 'sweet fruit flavours' can also be used to describe an extremely ripe style of wine.

Tannic: An excess of tannins, the drying compounds that come from the skins, pips, and stalks of grapes. Some tannic wines simply require further maturation in bottle. Tannins are not neces-sarily a bad thing, they just need to be balanced by fruity flavours.

Up-front: Straightforward, fruity flavours. Normally made in an easy-drinking style.

Warm: A wine with an excess of alcohol leaves a 'warm' finish. Can be used to describe full-bodied, spicy red wines.

AROMAS & FLAVOURS

There are thousands of different identifiable aromas and flavours in wine, but here is a list of the most common ones. Certain flavours speak for themselves (such as blackcurrant), whereas others, such as mineral or vegetal, require slightly more explanation. Each entry includes examples of grape varieties or wines in which the flavour is usually encountered.

Apple: Often found in cooler-climate, dry white wines, such as Chablis, Muscadet, and Vouvray.

Apricot: Common in riper styles of white wine such as Viognier and oak-fermented Chardonnay.

Blackcurrant: Widely associated with Cabernet Sauvignon and some other red grape varieties such as Merlot, Syrah/Shiraz, and Cabernet Franc. Occasionally a certain underripe blackcurrant flavour can be detected in Sauvignon Blanc.

Buttery: A creamy texture reminiscent of butter (rather than a specific flavour) is commonly found in oak-fermented Chardonnay and other white wines. This is caused by malolactic fermentation in the barrel, particularly where lees stirring is used (see p39).

Cherry: Widely found in red wines, especially in Italy. Barbera, Sangiovese, and Corvina (from Valpolicella) are just a few of the Italian grape varieties that tend to show this flavour.

Citrus: A character widely found in white wines, particularly fresh, aromatic styles. Can be further narrowed down to lemon, lime, orange etc.

Coconut: A flavour commonly associated with both whites and reds when they have been fermented or matured in new American oak barrels. In excess it can indicate a fault.

Creamy: Used to indicate a smooth, quite full-bodied texture in a wine, or a smell of cream.

Diesel: Widely found in mature bottles of Riesling, particularly in older German examples. It tends to occur earlier in Australian Riesling.

Earthy: A soil-like aroma commonly identified in older bottles of red bordeaux.

Farmyard: A slightly dirty, earthy, manure-type aroma. In a young wine it may indicate poor (unclean) winemaking practices. In an older bottle of red burgundy it can be a desirable, developed character.

Floral: A number of cool-climate whites display aromas vaguely reminiscent of flowers. Some are easy to identify, such as elderflower (aromatic whites), violets (mature bordeaux), and roses (Gewürztraminer whites, and Nebbiolo-based reds such as Barolo and Barbaresco).

Game/gaminess: A decaying, fleshy aroma commonly associ-ated with older bottles of Pinot Noir (red burgundy), Syrah (Northern Rhône), and other mature red wines.

Gooseberry: A classic flavour of Sauvignon Blanc. Also in other aromatic, zesty white wines.

Grapey: A term meaning smelling of grapes: a vaguely 'sweet' fruity aroma. The only variety for which this is true is Muscat (and all its various names and clones).

Grass: Widely found in fresh, aromatic wines from cooler climates from grapes such as Sauvignon Blanc, Sémillon, and Chenin Blanc.

Honey: Normally found in sweeter styles of wine, particularly when the grapes have been affected by botrytis, such as Sauternes, German Rieslings (BA, TBA), Tokay Pinot Gris (also called Tokay d'Alsace), and sweet wines from the Loire.

Jammy: A slightly derogatory term for a red wine bursting with up-front flavours of blackcurrant, raspberry, and other fruits, but lacking in structure. It normally implies the wine lacks finesse.

Lemon: Widely found in white wines, particularly those from cooler climates.

Liquorice: Commonly associated with full-bodied red wines made from Syrah.

Lychee: An aroma widely found in wines made from Gewürztraminer.

Mineral: It is difficult to taste mineral but the term is usually used to describe a sharp, earthy character in cool-climate wines such as Chablis and Sauvignon Blanc from Sancerre and Pouilly Fumé.

Mint: Particularly associated with Cabernet Sauvignon grown in warm-climate countries.

Mushroom: An aroma displayed by Pinot Noir as it matures. Italian wines Barolo and Barbaresco are sometimes believed to smell of more exotic mushrooms such as wh te truffle.

Pepper (black): Commonly associated with the red wines of southern France (especially from the Rhône Valley and the Grenache grape variety).

Plum: Apparent in many red wines but particularly those made from Merlot.

Rose: Found in Gewürztraminer and wines made from the Nebbiolo grape variety such as Barolo and Barbaresco.

Rubber: Can indicate a wine fault caused by excessive sulphur, or is widely (and positively) associated with the Syrah grape variety.

Spice: Found in wines fermented and matured in new oak barrels. Also apparent in certain red grape varieties, such as Grenache (which often has a peppery flavour) and other southern French wines.

Summer fruits: Aromas such as strawberry, raspberry, and cherry.

Especially associated with young Pinot Noir.

Tangy: Similar to zesty, but perhaps with more orange fruits. Mostly applies to whites but can also be used to describe reds such as fruity, crisp Cabernet Franc from the Loire.

Tobacco: A mature, developed aroma found in older bottles of Cabernet Sauvignon, particularly red bordeaux.

Toast: It can be used to describe aromas from oak barrels, or is also found in mature champagne and Sémillons from Australia's Hunter Valley.

Tropical fruits: Ripe flavours such as pineapple, banana, and mango which are normally used to describe Australian Chardonnay.

Vanilla: An aroma derived directly from new oak barrels.

Vegetal: Rotting vegetable-type aromas found in older bottles of red and white wines, especially burgundy (of both colours). It might sound unpleasant, but it is a desirable attribute in these styles of wine.

Yeast: Bread-type aroma widely associated with champagne (and the secondary fermentation process used to create it).

Zesty: Aromas of lemon, lime and, sometimes, orange. Normally found in crisp, refreshing dry white wines.

COMMON FAULTS

Wine today is much more reliable than ever before. With the exception of a corked bottle, seriously flawed wine is relatively rare. There are, however, a number of problems you may encounter, which would warrant returning a bottle of wine to the place of purchase.

Corked: This is the most common wine fault, found in 2 to 5 per cent of all wines sold. It is caused by a mould found in some natural corks that can taint the wine, and has nothing to do with pieces of cork floating in your glass. Corked wine smells musty and lacks fruit flavours, but this may not become obvious until it has spent a few minutes in the glass. Plastic corks or screwcaps eliminate this problem.

Oxidized: Over-exposure to oxygen harms wine, eventually turning it into vinegar. A wine may become oxidized if its seal is insufficiently airtight, if left too long in bottle before opening, or if left too long once opened.

Sulphur: All wines are bottled with a dose of sulphur, which acts as a preservative. However, if too much sulphur is added, the wine acquires an astringent, rubbery smell. In large quantities, it can be dangerous for asthmatics.

Poor winemaking: If you taste a wine with excess acidity, tannins, or oak, or with an absence of fruity flavours, it may simply be the result of poor quality winemaking.

WINE & FOOD MATCHING

W INE HAS BEEN *complemented by food for thousands of years. While soft drinks may taste too artificial and spirits overpower the cuisine, wine comes into its own at the dinner table thanks to moderate alcohol, refreshing acidity, and the sheer range of flavours. It is possible to enjoy many combinations of food and wine and is worth knowing some successful pairings that have stood the test of time.*

GUIDELINES

Whether selecting a bottle to accompany a take-away, or choosing different wines for every course at a formal dinner party, there are a number of basic guidelines to follow:

• Decide on the dominant taste in the food and choose a wine to accompany it.

• Select a wine to match the weight and power of your food. Full-flavoured foods require full-flavoured, full-bodied wines. Delicate dishes are overpowered by heavily oaked or excessively tannic styles, so they require light wines. Note that full-bodied whites have a similar power and weight to lighter reds, so work equally well with dishes such as grilled tuna or roast turkey.

• Sweet food should be matched by a similarly sweet wine. Many Thai dishes, for example, contain a lot of sugar, which is why off-dry styles such as German Riesling or Gewürztraminer from Alsace work so well.

• Tannins in a red wine taste softer when they are served with red meat. This is why classic combinations like beef with red bordeaux and lamb with red Rioja are so effective.

• The more complicated the flavours in a dish, the more difficult it is to find a wine to pair with it. *See p655 (on wine and food matching in restaurants)*

for wines that work well with a range of different flavours.

• If serving top quality wine, match the food to the wine rather than vice versa. Simply prepared dishes using the finest ingredients generally work best, allowing the wine to take centre stage.

• Try to match regional dishes with the same region's wines.

Apéritifs

An apéritif should simply whet your appetite, leaving you ready to enjoy the food and wine to come, so never choose anything too heavy or overbearing.

• Dry, light, and refreshing white wine works well. Avoid oaked wine. Think Australian or New Zealand Riesling, unoaked Sémillon, unoaked South African Chenin Blanc, Muscadet, or Pinot Blanc from Alsace.

• A dry German Riesling can be good, with its appetizing acidity and fresh flavours.

• Champagne and sparkling wines are ideal, particularly for special occasions. Their dryness and relative acidity stimulates the tastebuds.

• A dry *fino* or *manzanilla* sherry is excellent, but its high alcohol content (around 15 per cent) means it is better if canapés, such as olives or salted almonds, are also being served.

• Do not serve the best wine of

the evening as an apéritif. A well-made, basic bottle will provide a benchmark, allowing true appreciation of the subtleties of the better wines to follow.

With Starters

Bear in mind the best order for serving wine when choosing your starter – white before red, dry before sweet, light- before fuller-bodied, and in ascending order of quality. If the choice of menu requires a full-bodied red for the starter, avoid serving a dish that needs a light white for the main.

Asparagus: Sauvignon Blanc.

Asparagus (with creamy sauce): Fuller wines such as Chablis or other unoaked Chardonnays.

Consommé: Dry sherry, such as a *fino, manzanilla,* or dry *amontillado.*

Foie gras: Sauternes, although serving a sweet wine this early in the meal could present problems later. Champagne and Gewürztraminer also work.

Gazpacho: Relatively neutral, dry whites.

Pâtés and terrines: A wine that works with the main ingredient in its cooked form *(see fish and meat sections).*

Salad (no dressing): Most dry white wines – Sauvignon Blanc, Riesling, and unoaked Chardonnay are good options.

Salad (with creamy dressing):

A richer wine, such as Chablis or Pinot Blanc.

Salad (with vinaigrette): A wine with high acidity like Vinho Verde, Sauvignon Blanc, or dry German Riesling.

Salad (with bacon): Sauvignon Blanc in all its guises.

Soup (chicken): Medium-bodied Chardonnay or Pinot Blanc.

Soup (chunky, meaty): Basic red wines, such as southern French reds (Côtes du Rhône or Vin de Pays d'Oc, for example), or inexpensive Italian wines.

Soup (creamy and fishy): Fuller-flavoured Chardonnay or wines like Muscadet, white bordeaux, or Pinot Grigio. Sparkling wines can also work well, as can light rosés.

With Fish & Seafood

The dominant flavour in seafood dishes will often be the sauce. Creamy dishes demand a full-bodied white, whereas tomato-based ones require a medium-bodied red. Also consider the intensity of the cooking method, and the quality of the ingredients.

Bouillabaisse: Inexpensive whites, reds, and rosés from the South of France.

Chowder (creamy): Basic Chardonnay.

Chowder (tomato-based): Medium-bodied Italian reds.

Cod (battered): Crisp, dry whites, such as Sauvignon Blanc or unoaked Chenin Blanc.

Cod and haddock (fresh): Unoaked Chardonnay or dry white bordeaux.

Crab: Sauvignon Blanc or dry Riesling.

Hake: Sauvignon Blanc, Pinot Blanc, Soave, or white Rioja.

Halibut: Muscadet or Chablis.

Herring: Muscadet.

Lobster: Good white burgundy.

Mackerel and sardines (fresh): Vinho Verde, Albariño, Sauvignon Blanc, Muscadet, or light rosés.

Mackerel (smoked): An oily white like Alsace Pinot Gris.

Mussels: Muscadet or Sauvignon Blanc.

Salmon (barbecued): Lighter reds such as Pinot Noir or Beaujolais.

Salmon (grilled): A reasonably delicate wine, such as unoaked Chardonnay or Alsace Pinot Blanc. White Rhône, white bordeaux, and dry Riesling are also decent matches.

Salmon (poached): A delicate white such as Chablis or dry white bordeaux.

Salmon (smoked): Anything from Chablis to Sauvignon Blanc or dry Riesling. Smoked salmon also works well with champagne and other sparkling wines.

Sea bass (with butter sauce): White burgundy.

Sea bass (with tomato sauce): Medium-bodied reds from Italy or southern France (such as Côtes du Rhône).

Trout (fresh): Pinot Blanc, Chablis, or unoaked Chardonnay.

Trout (smoked): A good white burgundy.

Tuna (fresh) Fuller-bodied, dry whites such as Sémillon or Australian Chardonnay. Alternatively, light to medium reds like Pinot Noir, basic Argentinian Malbec, or Beaujolais.

Turbot: Good quality white burgundy, Californian Chardonnay, or top, dry white bordeaux.

With White Meats

In general, white meat has a relatively neutral flavour, so concentrate on the recipes and preparation when selecting a wine to show it off.

Chicken (barbecued): Chardonnay, Sauvignon Blanc, or light red wines such as Beaujolais.

Chicken (with creamy sauce): White bordeaux, Riesling from Alsace or New Zealand, or oaked South African Chenin Blanc.

Chicken (roasted): Chardonnay, Pinot Noir, or soft Merlot.

Chicken casserole: Light Italian reds or inexpensive reds from southern France.

Coq au vin: Red burgundy, but inexpensive Côtes du Rhône can also be served.

Pork (roasted): A range of wines from white burgundy and Sauvignon Blanc through to lighter reds like basic Merlot, Pinot Noir, or Beaujolais.

Pork (spare ribs): Zinfandel or a fruity Shiraz from Australia, South Africa, or California.

Pork (with apple sauce): Off-dry styles like German Riesling, or New World Colombard, Verdelho, or Chenin Blanc.

Pork sausages: Inexpensive reds from southern France.

Turkey (plain roast): Oaked Chardonnay or red wine like soft Merlot and Pinot Noir.

Turkey (with cranberry sauce/stuffing): Red wine such as burgundy, Merlot-based bordeaux, Northern Rhône Syrah, or sparkling Shiraz from Australia.

Veal: Dry white wines such as unoaked Chardonnay and those from the Northern Rhône, or soft fruity reds like Chianti and Merlot.

With Red Meats, Barbecues & Game

These meats lend themselves to fuller-bodied styles of wine. Beef and lamb in particular tend to be complemented by tannic red wines. However, the sauces served also affect the choice.

Barbecues: Powerful wines, such as fruity New World Chardonnay, Shiraz, Zinfandel, or Merlot.

Beef (hamburgers, steak *au poivre*, or in pastry): Californian Zinfandel, French Syrah, or Australian Shiraz.

Beef (roast beef or steak): Full-bodied reds from Bordeaux and Northern and Southern Rhône, as well as Shiraz from Australia, and good quality Rioja.

Beef (with wine sauce): Red burgundy.

Continued overleaf ▷

Duck (roast): Traditional reds, such as red burgundy, Barolo, or Rioja.

Duck (with apple/orange sauce): Australian Sémillon, or Riesling from Germany or Alsace.

Duck (with cherry sauce): Fruity reds, such as New World Cabernet Sauvignon or Shiraz.

Game: Classic European reds such as bordeaux, burgundy, Rioja, or Barolo; or New World wines such as Californian, Australian, or New Zealand Cabernet Sauvignon and Pinot Noir.

Lamb (casseroles, hotpots and meat stews): Spicy French reds such as Vin de Pays d'Oc, Coteaux du Languedoc, or Côtes du Rhône.

Lamb (chops): Good quality reds from Rioja, Bordeaux, or Chianti, as well as New World Cabernet Sauvignon and Merlot. Alternatively, reds from the South of France, particularly if garlic has been used in the dish.

Lamb (roast): Top quality bordeaux and burgundy. Alternatively, Rioja, Chianti, and New World Cabernet Sauvignon or Merlot.

With Vegetarian Dishes

Vegetarians and vegans may find some wines unsuitable due to animal products used in them. Gelatin, isinglass (made from fish), and egg whites are sometimes used to fine (clarify) wines. Consult the back label or contact the retailer to pinpoint vegetarian or vegan friendly wine. It can be difficult to pair vegetarian food with top white burgundy or high quality, full-bodied reds, but dishes like mushroom or pumpkin risotto stand up to the challenge.

Lentil- and vegetable-based casseroles: Reds from the South of France or southern Italy.

Mushroom risotto: Full-bodied Italian styles (Barolo, Chianti Classico, and Brunello di Montalcino for example), but also good red burgundy.

Mushroom Wellington: Red bordeaux and New World Cabernet Sauvignon.

Pasta (with creamy sauce): A dry Italian white, or unoaked Chardonnay, Pinot Blanc, or Sémillon.

Pasta (with tomato-based sauce): Light Italian reds such as Valpolicella or Chianti.

Pumpkin or butternut squash-based risotto: Quality dry whites from Burgundy, or top-quality Chardonnay from elsewhere in the world.

Quiches and omelettes (egg-dominant): Unoaked Chardonnay, Pinot Blanc, or light reds like Beaujolais.

Quiches and omelettes (mushroom-dominant): Medium-bodied reds, such as Pinot Noir.

Quorn and tofu: Choose a wine according to the flavour of the ingredients with which they are cooked, as they tend to take on the same flavour.

Vegetarian chilli (with Quorn mince): Hearty reds from the South of France, or fruity wines like Merlot and Zinfandel.

Vegetarian lasagne (with tofu): A full-bodied white such as Chardonnay or Pinot Gris.

Vegetarian stir-fry (with tofu): Gewürztraminer, Sauvignon Blanc, or Riesling from Germany or the New World.

Vegetable tarts, pies and pasties: Spicy reds from southern France.

Vegetable tarts, pies and pasties (with creamy sauce): New World Viognier, Chenin Blanc, or Chardonnay.

Veggie burgers and nut roast: Reds like Shiraz, red bordeaux, and New World Cabernet Sauvignon, as these dishes can taste quite 'meaty'.

With Ethnic Dishes

Chinese (general): Riesling, Gewürztraminer, Pinot Gris, or Sauvignon Blanc.

Chinese (meatier, darker dishes): Fruity reds such as New World Merlot, Zinfandel, or Shiraz.

Chinese (sweet and sour): Riper, 'sweeter' styles, like Australian Sémillon, Californian Chardonnay, or Gewürztraminer from Alsace.

Indian (chicken tikka *masala*): Inexpensive Chardonnay.

Indian (korma): Inexpensive Chardonnay or German Riesling.

Indian (*rogan josh* and balti): Soft, fruity reds, such as Shiraz or New World Cabernet Sauvignon.

Indian (tandoori): Sauvignon Blanc.

Indian (hot & spicy): Avoid wine and choose lager, water, or *lassi* instead.

Japanese (sushi): A 'rice wine' such as saké is traditional.

Japanese (teriyaki sauces): Fruity reds such as Zinfandel from California.

Thai (curry): Inexpensive Sauvignon Blanc or Australian Sémillon.

Thai (general): Off-dry whites such as German Riesling or Gewürztraminer.

With Puddings

Always try to select a wine that is sweeter than your dessert. You can also choose a wine with a slightly higher alcohol content here as it is the end of the meal. Many intensely flavoured desserts are complemented beautifully by powerful, fortified styles.

Chocolate (milk): Moscato d'Asti.

Chocolate (plain/dark): A sweet red, such as *recioto* from Northeast Italy or LBV port.

Chocolate cake: Select your wine depending on the richness of the chocolate. The orange flavours in certain Muscats (Australia) can work sensationally with a range of different chocolates.

Christmas cake: Australian Liqueur Muscat, Moscato d'Asti, or fortified Muscat.

Crème brûlée: Sauternes is

classic but most sweet wines work successfully.

Fruit: A wide variety, such as sweeter styles of Riesling, Sémillon, or Chenin Blanc. Moscato d'Asti works particularly well with blackcurrants, fruit salad, and lemon mousse.

Fruit tarts and pies: Choose a wine based on the dominant flavour – normally the fruit itself.

Ice cream: Thick, sticky styles such as Marsala, Pedro-Ximénez (PX) sherry, or Australian Liqueur Muscat.

Pecan pie: *Recioto* from Northeast Italy, sweet *oloroso* sherry, or even a tawny port.

Tiramisu: Italian dessert wines like Moscato d'Asti or *passito* styles, or Australian Liqueur Muscat.

Trifles: Fortified wines like sweet *amontillado* sherry.

With Cheeses

Cheese and wine can be a wonderful combination, but pairing them is not as easy as many people think. The diverse flavours and textures of different cheeses mean that anything from a sweet white to a fortified red can be served successfully.

Blue cheeses: A sweet wine is generally required but tawny port can also work well. Roquefort and Sauternes is a classic combination.

Brie: Beaujolais, or other light and fruity reds.

Camembert: Beaujolais or other light and fruity reds, but can also be paired with fuller-flavoured wines from Chianti, as well as whites such as Chablis.

Goat's cheese: Sauvignon Blanc, particularly from the Loire Valley.

Gruyère and Emmenthal: Wines such as Shiraz, Northern Rhône reds, or Merlot. However, Riesling can work well, too.

Mature Cheddar: Good red bordeaux, Châteauneuf-du-Pape, or tawny port.

Mozzarella: Unoaked Chardonnay.

Parmesan: Italian reds, particularly those made from Sangiovese.

Pungent cheeses (such as Munster): Gewürztraminer.

Sheep's cheese: Sweeter styles of white wine like Riesling and Muscat, as well as spicy reds from southern France.

Traditional English hard cheeses: Cool-climate, dry whites such as Sauvignon Blanc or Chenin Blanc.

Social Occasions

Sometimes the occasion dictates the type of wine required. Bottles that work at an informal gathering will be quite different from wines at an engagement party, for example.

With food: The general rules of wine and food matching still apply. However, it is often wise to select bottles that are generally food-friendly *(see In Restaurants)*, as guests are then able to enjoy one wine with all canapés served, and with several different courses should they choose.

Without food: In general, wines that are better enjoyed on their own tend to be light, inexpensive, and unpretentious. For parties and social events where no food is on offer, steer clear of anything too full-bodied and avoid high acidity or excessive tannins. Also take the time of year and weather into account.

In summer: Choose crisp, refreshing wines like Riesling, Chenin Blanc, and other cool-climate, relatively low alcohol whites. Alternatively, opt for light, fruity reds suitable for a brief chilling. Beaujolais, basic Merlot, and Pinot Noir are good choices.

In winter: Opt for something medium-bodied, whether red or white, focusing on bright, fruity flavours and avoiding lots of oak. Good bets are Sémillon, unoaked Chardonnay, and Pinot Blanc, as well as whites from the Southern Rhône. Reds such as Cabernet-Shiraz blends from Australia, inexpensive Zinfandel, Chilean Merlot, and Argentinian Malbec are also highly enjoyable at this time of year.

At celebrations: Champagne and sparkling wines are the classic choices. Champagne tends to be more expensive, so is generally only an option for those with a bigger budget. Sparkling wines made elsewhere in the world can work very well, however, and are normally a better choice to use in cocktails such as buck's fizz.

In Restaurants

Many top restaurants have a sommelier to offer diners advice on wine. However, if no sommelier is on hand, there are a few types of wine that are good with most foods. And remember, if you are all ordering different dishes, half bottles can help everyone get something to complement their particular meal.

• Opt for medium-bodied styles, avoiding extremes. For whites, unoaked Chardonnay, Sémillon, or Sauvignon Blanc are the most versatile. For reds, Pinot Noir, inexpensive Merlot, or a fruity Cabernet-Merlot blend are an excellent choice.

• Italian reds and whites (especially reds) tend to complement many dishes.

• If the restaurant focuses on a particular nationality or style of cooking, try and choose wines of the same nationality.

GLOSSARY

Like any other *specialist subject, the world of wine has developed its own unique vocabulary. Here is a list of many of the most common terms used in this book along with their definitions.*

A

acid/acidity: All wines contain various acids, including tartaric, malic, and citric. Acidity is an essential element in wine, helping to maintain freshness and balance – too much and it can taste unduly sharp and acidic, too little and a 'flabby', cloying wine will result.

acidification: The addition of chemical acids to the must during winemaking to compensate for a lack of natural acidity in the grapes.

ageing: Most wines are designed to be enjoyed as soon as they are released. However, a proportion will improve in bottle if stored in a cool, dark place. Full-bodied reds, sweet whites, and fortified wines can all benefit from ageing – however, if in doubt, it is better to drink a wine too young than too old.

amarone (Italy): A DOC red wine made in Valpolicella (Northeast Italy) from dried (*passito*) grapes.

American oak: A type of wood originating from forests on the east side of the USA, which is used to make oak barrels. Popular in both North and South America, Spain, and Australia, American oak barrels tend to impart a more powerful vanilla flavour than their European counterparts.

amontillado (Spain): A full, nutty flavoured sherry, which can be dry or medium in style.

appellation: A legally defined area where grapes are grown and wine is produced. It is also sometimes used as a shortened version of AOC or AC.

Appellation d'Origine Contrôlée or AOC (France): Also known as Appellation Contrôlée (AC). The highest quality classification for wines produced in France. It guarantees that a bottle has been made in a specific region, according to local regulations. Not all AOC or AC wines are good quality, but on average they should be better (though not necessarily better value) than wines with a lower classification such as *vin de pays* or *vin de table*.

azienda (Italy): Estate.

B

barrel: Barrels or casks can be used at several stages of winemaking. Better quality whites may be fermented in barrel to produce subtle and complex wood flavours. Maturation in barrel helps to soften the wine and, if the oak is new, pick up aromas such as cedar or vanilla. 'Barrel select' may imply quality, but actually has no legal definition. *See also* American oak and French oak.

barrel-aged: The process of maturing wine in oak barrels, softening its taste and possibly adding oak flavours. *See* barrel.

barrel-fermented: This indicates a wine has been fermented in an oak barrel. Normally applicable to white wines, the process helps to better integrate oak flavours.

barrique (France): A small oak cask or barrel which holds 225 litres of wine.

base wine: The still wine used to create champagne and other sparkling wine.

bin: Originally a collection or stack of wine bottles. It is commonly found on wine labels, to signify different brands of wine.

biodynamism: An extreme form of organic viticulture which emphasizes the health of the soil. Some of its methods may sound bizarre, but a number of world-class wines are produced using this approach.

blanc de blancs (France): White wine made entirely from white grapes. Commonly used for champagne and other sparkling wines.

blanc de noirs (France): Wine made entirely from red grapes. Common term for champagne and other sparkling wines.

blend: A mixture of wines of different grape varieties, styles, origin, or age, contrived to improve the balance of the wine or maintain a constant style.

blush: A term widely used in the US for a pale pink wine.

bodega (Spain): Winery or cellar.

bordeaux: A wine from the Bordeaux region of France made using the grape varieties and/or techniques common in this area. Bordeaux is a famously full-bodied red wine made from a blend of Cabernet Sauvignon, Merlot, Cabernet Franc, Malbec, and Petit Verdot which is often matured in oak barrels. It can age for decades.

botrytis: A vine disease, also known as noble rot, responsible for some of the world's greatest dessert wines. In the correct conditions, the fungus *(Botrytis cinerea)* produces shrivelled, sugar-rich grapes which can be fermented into a naturally sweet and intensely flavoured wine.

bottle fermentation: The technique which gives champagne its 'fizz'. After a normal fermentation, still wine is placed into a bottle with sugar and yeast. A secondary fermentation begins, producing carbon dioxide gas inside the bottle and creating a sparkling wine. The term is normally used by sparkling wine producers outside the Champagne region.

Bourgogne: The French word for Burgundy.

brut: Means dry. Normally found on sparkling wines.

burgundy: A wine from the Burgundy region of France, made using the grape varieties and/or the techniques common in this region. The area is world famous for its dry whites made from Chardonnay and medium-bodied reds from Pinot Noir.

C

canopy: All parts of the vine that are visible above ground including the trunk, leaves, shoots, stems, and grapes.

canopy management: The practice of manipulating the vine and its canopy to ensure the grapes and leaves are correctly exposed to the sun. It also aims to ensure a good circulation of air through the vine, helping to prevent fungal diseases. Canopy management includes vine training and pruning.

cantina (Italy): Winery.

cantina sociale (Italy): Co-operative.

carbonic maceration: A winemaking technique associated with Beaujolais in France. The grapes are fermented as whole berries, producing a deep coloured, fruity wine which is light in tannin.

cava (Spain): A popular sparkling wine produced in Spain. Made predominantly in the northwest of the country using grape varieties such as Macabeo, Xarel-lo, Parellada, and, increasingly, Chardonnay.

chaptalization: The practice of increasing alcohol levels through the addition of sugar during winemaking. Common in cooler wine regions where the climate may struggle to produce sufficient natural sugar in the grapes.

château (France): Used to denote a French winegrowing/producing estate. The term is widely used in Bordeaux.

clairet (France): A dark pink style of wine halfway between a rosé and a light red.

WINE LAW

For more information on terminology used on wine labels see the following: France *pp52–3*; Italy *pp192–3*; Spain *pp290–91*; Portugal *p329*; Germany *pp348–9*.

claret: A uniquely English term for red bordeaux.

classico (Italy): The original zone of production within a DOC(G) region (generally with better vineyards).

clone: A group of vines all descended from a single parent vine using cuttings or buds. They are genetically identical to the parent plant and are usually selected for characteristics such as fine flavour or good colour.

cold fermentation: A slow fermentation at low temperatures to extract freshness and fruit flavour from the grapes.

colheita: A tawny style port made from a single harvest and aged in wood for a minimum of seven years.

co-operative: An organization which is collectively owned by its members. Typically wine co-operatives consist of a number of growers who join together for winemaking and marketing purposes. Quality can vary from good to extremely poor.

KEY CLIMATIC TERMS

continental climate: A climate characterized by extreme temperature variations across the year. Usually found in regions well away from the influence of water (sea or lakes). Cold winters and hot summers are the norm.

degree days: A unit devised to measure the suitability of climates for viticulture.

macroclimate: The overall climate within a region.

maritime climate: A climate which is influenced by a large body of water, typically a sea or lake. Temperatures will tend to remain relatively stable across the year with mild winters and warm summers.

marginal climate: A climate that is barely sufficient to permit viticulture. Normally applied to weather that is too cold rather than too warm. Expect regions with a marginal climate to have wide variations in quality between vintages.

mesoclimate: The climate in a small district or even an individual vineyard.

microclimate: A specific climate within a very small area.

moderate climate: A climate with only minimal temperature variation over the course of the year. Most commonly found near to a large body of water. *See* maritime climate.

corked: Wine which has been affected by a mouldy, musty taint from a defective natural cork. The wine may be stripped of its normal fruit flavours and can have a slightly bitter taste. It is believed that around six per cent of wines using natural corks are corked, and many producers and retailers have now changed over to screw-caps and synthetic closures.

côte(s)/coteaux (France): Hill or hillside.

crémant (France): Indicates a sparkling wine produced in France (but outside the appellation of Champagne) using the same methods as champagne.

crianza (Spain): A wine that has spent at least six months in oak and 18 months in bottle before release (for reds).

cru (France): Literally 'growth' or 'vineyard'. Hence *cru classé* means classified vineyard. The term *cru bourgeois* is a classification for estates in Bordeaux's Médoc appellation. *See also premier cru* and *grand cru*.

crusted port: A non-vintage port style bottled unfiltered like a vintage port.

cuvée (France): Normally used to mean blend. The use of the word on wine labels such as *cuvée de prestige* or *tête de cuvée* is no guarantee of excep-tional quality. In champagne, *cuvée* denotes the first and finest juice to come from the press.

cuvée de prestige: A term normally associated with champagne and referring to a top quality, luxury wine made from the best vineyards and matured for many years before release. Examples include Dom Pérignon from Moët & Chandon and La Grande Dame from Veuve Clicquot Ponsardin.

D

decanting: The process of pouring wine from its original bottle into another vessel or decanter. The technique is normally used for old or unfiltered wines to separate the liquid from the sediment deposited in the bottle. It can also be used for younger wines, to allow them to be exposed to air, or 'breathe'.

Denominação de Origem Controlada or DOC (Portugal): This is the highest category of wine in Portugal, equivalent to AOC in France.

Denominación de Origen or DO (Spain): The Spanish classification for quality wines, just below Denominacíon de Origen Calificada or DOCa. Equivalent to AOC in France.

Denominación de Origen Calificada or DOCa (Spain): The highest quality classification for wines produced in Spain.

Denominación de Origen de Pago or DO Pago (Spain): This category is for fine wines from single estates which have a proven track record for quality.

Denominazione di Origine Controllata or DOC (Italy): Italian classification for quality wines, just below Denomin-azione di Origine Controllata e Garantita or DOCG. Equivalent to AOC in France.

Denominazione di Origine Controllata e Garantita or DOCG (Italy): The highest quality classifi-cation for wines produced in Italy.

dessert/sweet wine: Wine con-taining large amounts of sugar. It tastes sweet and is traditionally used to accompany dessert.

disgorgement: The process by which sediment is removed from a champagne bottle following the second fermentation.

domaine (France): Estate.

dosage: This is the term given to the replenishment of the small amount of wine lost during disgorgement in the process of making champagne. Sugar is also normally added at this stage.

dry-farmed: Vines grown without the use of irrigation, thus relying entirely on natural rainfall.

E

Eiswein (Germany): Sweet wine made in Germany in tiny quantities from grapes which have naturally frozen on the vine. The berries are pressed immediately, leaving the moisture behind as ice and producing a luscious, intensely-flavoured liquid.

en primeur: Wine sold by a producer before it has been bottled. Typically customers pay for the wine six months after the harvest and must wait a further 18 months before they receive it. This is the best way to secure a wine limited in quantity, but is no guarantee of a cheaper price.

estate bottled/grown: Today, most quality producers bottle on site. It is no guarantee of quality, but is generally a good indicator. In the USA, estate bottled wine must also come from the producer's own vineyards or those on a long-term lease. The equivalent in France is *mise en bouteille à la propriété/au domaine/au château*; in Italy it is *imbottigliato all'origine*; in Spain *embotellado en la propiedad*.

F

fermentation: The process that turns the juice of crushed, pressed, or whole grapes into wine. The natural sugars contained within the berries are converted into alcohol and carbon dioxide using yeast. Fermentation generally takes place in stainless steel, lined concrete, or large wooden vats, or in oak barrels. *See also* malolactic fermentation.

filtration: A technique which removes the tiny solid particles from a wine before bottling, leaving it clear and bright. Some producers believe that filtration can strip a wine of its flavour and will avoid the technique – often including words such as unfiltered or *non-filtré* on their label. Wines which have not been filtered will generally require decanting.

finca (Spain): Estate.

fining: A process used to remove suspended deposits in wine. When a fining agent such as egg white or bentonite clay is added, it binds with the deposits and causes them to fall to the bottom of the cask.

fino: A pale, relatively light, dry style of sherry matured with the flor (yeast) growing on the surface.

first growth: *See premier cru.*

flor (Spain): A yeast which is encouraged to grow in certain styles of sherry. Flor covers the surface of the maturing wine, protecting it from oxidation and imparting a distinctive flavour.

flying winemaker: An individual who produces wine in a number of locations around the world. The term was originally coined when highly trained New World winemakers were brought in to revitalize old fashioned, traditional estates in Europe.

fortified: A wine which has been bolstered by the addition of a spirit, usually grape spirit. Examples include port, sherry, madeira, and Liqueur Muscat.

French oak: A type of wood originating from forests in France such as Allier and Vosges. French oak is widely considered to make the finest barrels for

fermenting and maturing wine.

fruit set: This is when the fertilized vine flowers become grape berries – not all flowers will actually turn into berries.

fungal diseases: A collective term for a number of diseases such as powdery mildew, downy mildew, and black rot. The fungi attack grapes or foliage and, without preventative measures, can cause considerable damage. The benevolent disease *Botrytis cinerea* is also included in this category.

futures: The American term for *en primeur.*

G

garage wine: A relatively recent term given to the tiny quantities of top quality (and often very expensive) wine made by small-scale producers. Equipment and facilities are generally extremely basic and production may even take place in a garage, hence the name.

grand cru (France): Meaning literally 'great vineyard'. In Burgundy the term *grand cru* is applied to the finest vineyards in the region. In the St-Émilion area of Bordeaux, the best châteaux are classified as *grand cru classé*, with the top tier known as *premier grand cru classé. See also premier cru.*

grand vin (France): Often seen on French AOC labels, this literally means 'great wine' and is often used to indicate that this is the top wine of a particular estate.

gran reserva (Spain): For reds this is a wine which has spent at least 18 months in oak and at least five years in oak and bottle before release.

green harvesting: The practice of removing and discarding grapes in the build-up to the (conventional) harvest. The idea is to allow the vine to concentrate its energies on ripening the grapes that remain.

H

hybrid: A plant created from parents which belong to different species of vine. An example is the Baco Noir grape variety, made by breeding Folle Blanche of the *Vitis vinifera* species with a variety of *Vitis riparia*, a native American species of vine. In the EU, quality wine can only be made entirely from *Vitis vinifera* plants.

I

Ice wine: The name given to *Eiswein* when it is produced outside Germany.

Indicazione Geografica Tipica or IGT (Italy): A relatively recent classification for Italian wines similar to *vin de pays* in France.

J K

jeroboam: A bottle size containing three litres or four conventional (75cl) bottles.

jóven (Spain): A young wine with little or no oak maturation, designed for early drinking.

L

Late Bottled Vintage or LBV (Portugal): A port from a specified vintage which has been matured for between four and six years in wood before bottling.

late harvest: *See vendange tardive.*

lees: Known as *lie* in France, lees are the remains of yeast, grape seeds and other sediment that settle in a wine after fermentation. Extended contact with the lees plays an important role in wines such as Muscadet and champagne. Lees stirring (*bâtonnage* in French) in cask helps to accentuate this process.

limited release: A term much favoured by marketing people on wine labels. It may indicate additional quality, but there is no guarantee.

long-lived: This term describes a wine able to develop and improve in bottle over years or decades. Only a small proportion of wines are capable of this. *See also* ageing.

M

maceration: The practice of soaking grape skins in their juice or must. This gives red wines their colour, tannins, and flavours.

madeira: A fortified wine produced on the Portuguese island of Madeira.

maderized: A wine which has been exposed to oxygen and/ or heated to make it taste like madeira. The term is also used occasionally to describe a wine which has been oxidized.

magnum: A 1.5 litre bottle (equivalent to two conventional bottles). Wine in a magnum tends to mature more slowly and elegantly than in 75cl bottles and this is believed to be the ideal size for champagne.

malolactic fermentation: A process which converts tart malic acids (as found in apples) into softer lactic acids (as found in milk). It occurs shortly after the first (conventional) fermentation. Most red wines undergo malolactic fermentation; in whites the decision largely depends on the style of wine the producer is trying to achieve.

Master of Wine or MW: An extremely demanding wine qualification developed by the Institute of Masters of Wine in London. It covers subjects such as winemaking, distribution, tasting, and commercial aspects. There are currently fewer than 250 MWs worldwide.

maturation: The process of ageing or maturing a wine in cask or bottle, normally at the winery. Once the wine is released it may be matured further by the purchaser, but this is more commonly referred to as cellaring or laying down.

Meritage: A wine made from the same blend of grape varieties as bordeaux (Cabernet Sauvignon, Merlot, Cabernet Franc, Malbec, and Petit Verdot for reds; Sauvignon Blanc and Sémillon for whites) but from an alternative origin, usually California or South Africa.

méthode traditionnelle/ classique (France): A sparkling wine made using the same techniques as champagne. In particular it indicates the wine has undergone a secondary fermentation in bottle.

monopoly or *monopole* (France): A term used for a vineyard completely owned by one individual or organization.

must: The mass of grape juice, skins, seeds, stems, and other matter before fermentation begins.

mutage: A French word to describe the process of halting fermentation before it has naturally finished, normally through the addition of a spirit. The technique is used to create port or *vin doux naturel*.

N

négociant (France): Literally merchant; a person or organization that buys grapes, must, or wine from growers to bottle under its own label. Particularly important in areas with large numbers of small vineyard holdings such as Burgundy. The quality of *négociant* wines can range from poor to excellent.

non-vintage (NV): A blend of wines from different years. Although the term 'vintage' is often used to imply high quality, there is nothing inherently wrong with non-vintage wine – indeed most champagnes are NV.

O

oak: The wood favoured by winemakers to ferment and mature their wines. In general the newer and smaller the oak barrel, the more of a woody, vanilla flavour it will impart. Many cheaper wines receive their oaky taste from oak chips or oak staves which are submerged directly into the tanks. *See also* American oak, French oak.

oaked: A wine made in a deliberately creamy, oaky style through the use of oak barrels, oak chips, or oak staves. *See also* unoaked.

oenology (or enology): The technical term for the study of wine. It tends to be primarily associated with winemaking.

old vines: As a vine matures it tends to produce smaller quantities of better quality grapes, so old vines or *vieilles vignes* on a label may indicate a more concentrated and complex wine. Unfortunately there are no regulations governing what exactly constitutes 'old'.

oloroso: A full-bodied, rich and nutty style of sherry which has been deliberately and carefully oxidized during maturation. It can range in style from dry to medium sweet.

organic: It is very difficult to produce a completely organic wine as certain chemicals are virtually essential during wine-making. Many wines advertised as such are simply grown without the use of chemical fertilizers, fungicides, and pesticides.

P

passito (Italy): A strong, powerful wine made from dried grapes; it can be sweet as in *recioto*, or dry as in *amarone*.

Pierce's Disease: A potentially devastating bacterial disease for which there is no known cure. The disease is spread by small insects known as sharpshooters and attacks the leaves of the vine. It is most common in the southern part of the USA and South America.

phylloxera: A vine disease which devastated the vineyards of Europe at the end of the 19th century. Phylloxera is a small insect or aphid that feeds on the roots of grapevines and ultimately kills the plant. Even today there is no cure for the pest – instead almost all European vines are grafted onto rootstocks from American species, which are phylloxera-resistant.

port: A sweet, fortified wine produced in the Douro Valley in northern Portugal.

premier cru (France): First growth or first vineyard. In the Médoc region of Bordeaux, the finest châteaux are classified as *premier cru*. In St-Émilion just across the river, the top producers are known as *premier grand cru classé*. Confusingly, in Burgundy *premier cru* vineyards lie just below *grand cru* in the overall classification hierarchy.

Prosecco: An easy-going sparkling wine made from the grape variety of the same name, which is grown largely in the Veneto region in Italy. Styles range from dry to medium sweet.

Q

Qualitätswein mit Prädikat or QmP (Germany): Meaning 'quality wine with special characteristics', this is Germany's top classification for wine.

quinta (Portugal): Estate.

KEY SOIL TERMS

albariza: Chalky soil typical of Jerez in Spain, where sherry is produced. It retains moisture and the white colour reflects sun onto the vines.

alluvial: Fine-grained soils composed of alluvium deposits – typically containing mud, sand, silt, and stones. Where the stone and sand content is high, this soil is valued for viticulture as in the Médoc region of Bordeaux.

calcareous: Chalky-type soil *(see below)* composed of calcium carbonate, calcium, or limestone (known as *calcaire* in France).

chalk: Soft, fine-grained, crumbly, and porous sedimentary rock, this soil is valued in viticulture for its good drainage. Champagne is an important wine region with chalky soil.

clay: Fine-grained but heavily textured, this soil is known for its capacity to hold water and nutrients.

duplex: A soil type with a porous topsoil on top of a non-porous layer, such as sand over clay.

galestro: A clay-like sediment that is in the process of becoming stone.

Typical of many of the best vineyards in Chianti, Tuscany.

gneiss: A crystalline rock similar to granite.

granite: A coarse grained rock composed of minerals.

gravelly: Soil containing a large proportion of pebbles, which may be alluvial in origin (known as *graves* in France). Typical soil of the Left Bank region of Bordeaux.

ironstone: A soil containing a proportion of iron.

limestone: Sedimentary rock made of calcium carbonate, it is typically hard and not easily penetrated by vine roots except via cracks. This soil sometimes overlies reservoirs of water that can be reached by longer roots of well-established vines.

loam: A rich soil made up of a number of elements such as clay, sand, and other organic matter.

loess: A soil consisting of fine grains of clay and silt that have been deposited by the wind. Common in vineyards in Austria and Germany.

marl: A crumbly soil made of limestone and clay, plus shells. Many vineyards of the Côte d'Or in Burgundy are on calcareous marl.

quartz: Consisting of silicon dioxide, this soil is typically infertile but has good drainage.

sandstone: Sedimentary rocks usually composed of grains of sand. This soil varies greatly in fertility and drainage.

schist: A group of medium- or coarse-grained metamorphic rocks that easily split into thin layers. Occurs in vineyards in Alsace and Côte Rôtie, Rhône Valley.

siliceous: Composed of silica (silicon dioxide) – which is found in quartz and sand.

silt: a multi-grained alluvial deposit, silt is a major component of the soils of the Napa Valley, California.

slate: A compact, fine-grained metamorphic rock. Many vineyards of Germany's Mosel-Saar-Ruwer are on slate, which holds moisture and heat.

terra rossa: Red-brown clay or loam over limestone renowned in the vineyards of Coonawarra, South Australia.

tuffeau: A calcareous soil, a soft form of limestone.

R

racking: The process of separating a wine from its sediment in the winery. The sediment is normally allowed or encouraged to fall to the bottom of the barrel. The liquid is then drained or pumped into a clean vessel.

raisining: The practice of drying grapes either on the vine or after picking. Raisined grapes are normally concentrated with sugar, making excellent sweet wines.

recioto (Italy): Red or white sweet wine made from dried *(passito)* grapes. Usually quite strong and a speciality of the Veneto.

reserva (Spain): Wine produced in a good vintage that has received special treatment in the winery. A red *reserva* must spend a minimum of 18 months in cask and the balance of five years in bottle before release. Whites require at least six months in cask and a total of two years before they leave the winery.

reserve: A term seen regularly on wine labels to denote a special bottling or release. Unless the wine comes from a reputable producer, however, it is no guarantee of special quality.

residual sugar: Sugar that remains in a wine after fermentation. High levels of residual sugar make a wine taste sweet.

riserva (Italy): A wine which is given extended ageing before it is released and has a higher alcoholic strength.

rootstock: The root system of a vine. Today almost all vines consist of an American rootstock grafted onto a fruiting European variety to protect against phylloxera.

rosé (France)/*rosado* (Spain): Wines with a pink colour, in effect a halfway house between a red and a white wine. The only region that is allowed to produce rosés by mixing red and white wines is Champagne; the vast majority of other rosés are made using red grapes and a short period of maceration.

ruby port: The youngest and fruitiest style of port.

S

sec (France): Dry.

sediment: Solid matter found in wine. This can come from yeasts, fragments of grape skin and pulp during winemaking, or it can form naturally in the wine. Certain wines 'throw' a sediment when they have been matured in bottle for long periods and will need decanting.

Sekt (Germany): The German word for sparkling wine.

Sélection de Grains Nobles (France): Classification in Alsace for wines made from extremely ripe grapes, which will normally have been affected by noble rot. SGN wines are only made in exceptional vintages and will be sweet.

sherry: A fortified wine from the Jerez region of Spain. There are two basic styles of sherry, *see fino* and *oloroso*.

single vineyard: Wine made using grapes from just one vineyard.

solera (Spain): A system of blending (or fractional blending) used in the sherry industry and for other wines.

spumante (Italy): Sparkling. Asti Spumante is an appellation for sparkling wines produced in the Asti region in Northwest Italy.

stabilization: The processes in the winery designed to ensure a wine undergoes no further fermentation or reaction once it is bottled. These include fining and filtration.

Strohwein (Austria): A classification in Austria for wine made from grapes which have been dried on beds of straw or reeds for at least three months.

structure: A tasting term used primarily for red wines to describe the weight of fruit and tannins on the palate. Full-bodied wines such as high quality red bordeaux should have a 'good structure'.

superiore (Italy): Usually applied to DOCG wines with a higher alcoholic strength, not an indicator of quality.

T

table wine: Theoretically the lowest wine classification in the European Union. In general, these wines are cheap and not so cheerful. However, some of Europe's finest wines are labelled table wine. Price is a good guide to quality here – finer wines in this category tend to cost significantly more than basic table wine.

tannins: The astringent, mouth-drying compounds found when a teabag is soaked in water too long. Tannins in grapes are found in the skins, seeds, and stalks, and are particularly important in the composition of a red wine. Not only do they provide the wine with its structure and weight, but they also act as a preservative, helping it to mature in bottle. A wine with excessive tannins is described as 'tannic'.

tawny port: A style of port characterized by its distinctive tawny colour. Better examples achieve their appearance and soft, mellow taste through extended maturation in cask. These may come with an indication of age – 10, 20, 30, or over 40 years.

tenuta (Italy): Estate.

terroir: A French word used to describe the overall growing environment of a vineyard, covering its climate, soil, slope, and exposure, among other factors. Advocates of *terroir* believe that a wine should not simply taste of fermented grape juice, but rather it should express a sense of the place where the grapes are grown.

traditional method: The process used to make champagne. The term is normally found on sparkling wine originating from outside the Champagne region, indicating it has been produced using the same quality-conscious techniques.

Trockenbeerenauslese or **TBA** (Germany): A German classification for the ripest grapes in the country. Made from grapes affected by noble rot, these wines are normally low in alcohol, lusciously sweet, rare, and extremely expensive.

U

unfiltered/*non-filtré*: *See* filtration.

unoaked: A wine deliberately made without oak barrels to emphasize its fresh fruit flavours.

V

varietal: A wine which has been labelled on the basis of its principal grape variety. It can also be used as another word for 'grape variety'.

vendange tardive (France): A French term meaning late harvest. Grapes which have been harvested later tend to be riper and more concentrated, producing sweeter styles of wine. In Alsace the term carries a legal definition, elsewhere it can be used simply at the discretion of the producer.

vieilles vignes (France): Literally 'old vines'. As a vine gets older it tends to produce fewer, but better quality grapes. It is no guarantee of a superior wine, as there is no legal definition of what constitutes old.

vin de pays (France)/*vino de la tierra* (Spain)/ *vinho regional* (Portugal): Often representing excellent value, 'country wines' sit between table wine and appellation controlled wine in the overall classification hierarchy.

vin de table (France)/*vino de mesa* (Spain)/*vino da tavola* (Italy)/*vinho de mesa* (Portugal): *See* table wine.

vin doux naturel (France): A sweet wine produced by adding spirit to the fermenting must before all the sugar has been converted to alcohol. *See also mutage.*

vine density: The number of vines planted in a specified area in a vineyard. High density planting (around 8,000 vines per hectare) is practised in many European vineyards, as the competition between plants is believed to help lower yields and produce better quality grapes.

vine pull: The removal of vines. In certain parts of Europe, where overproduction is a problem, governments pay growers to pull up their vines in vine pull schemes.

vinification: Essentially, 'wine-making', the process that converts grape juice into finished wine.

vin santo (Italy): A dessert wine made in Tuscany from grapes that have been dried on racks. The wine must be matured in casks for at least three years.

vintage: Can be used to mean either 'harvest' or the year in which the grapes were grown to produce a wine. A vintage wine must come from a single year. Vintage champagne is only produced in exceptional years and must be matured for at least three years on its lees. *See also* non-vintage.

vintage port: The very best port made from a single fine harvest and aged in wood for around two years. It is 'declared' or released by producers only in the best vintages, on average three times a decade.

viticulture: Essentially, 'grape growing', covering the skills, science and techniques required to produce commercial-quality grapes.

Vitis vinifera: The species of vine responsible for the vast majority of the world's wines.

W

Weingut (Germany): Wine estate.

wooded/unwooded: *See* oaked *and* unoaked.

XYZ

yeast: A single-cell fungus which is responsible for converting sugar into alcohol during fermentation. In many regions yeasts occur naturally on the skins of grapes and in the air – these so-called 'wild' strains are often preferred by local winemakers. Cultured yeasts, which are often more reliable, can also be used.

yield: The total amount of wine produced by a vine or vineyard in a particular vintage. In general lower yields produce better quality grapes and in European appellations maximum yields are prescribed by law. This ranges from around 38 hectolitres per hectare for *grand cru* red burgundy to over 100 hl/ha for less illustrious classifications.

FURTHER REFERENCE

THERE IS A WEALTH *of wine-related information available in books, magazines, and on the internet. Many producers now have their own websites, too. Attending tastings, joining a wine society, or logging on to internet wine forums are other ways to pursue a keen interest in wine, and get to know fellow wine lovers.*

GENERAL WEBSITES
The following websites are reliable sources of information.
www.wine-pages.com
UK site featuring outstanding tasting notes, recommended wines, news stories, and much more. Updated regularly.
www.wineanorak.com
Well-designed site including buying guide, tasting notes, and an entertaining web diary from UK-based wine lover Jamie Goode.
www.winedine.co.uk
UK website including entertaining articles on a range of wine-, food-, and travel-related subjects.
www.wineloverspage.com
Extremely popular American site with extensive tasting notes, expert columnists, weekly recipes to match recommended wines, book reviews, and plenty more.
www.marksquires.com
Highly entertaining (and fairly irreverent) site from an American lawyer-cum-wine lover. Excellent articles plus detailed tasting notes.
www.gangofpour.com
Vast, dynamic site compiled by a group of four wine-loving friends from Detroit, California, and Canada. Particularly strong on US and Canadian wines.

SUBSCRIPTION SITES
Some wine websites require a subscription fee for full access:
www.erobertparker.com
This website by the world's most influential wine critic consists

mainly of archived tasting notes and articles from his newsletters: *The Wine Advocate* and *The Hedonist's Gazette*.
www.jancisrobinson.com
Excellent website by one of the most knowledgeable and entertaining UK wine journalists. Several free articles are available.
www.burghound.com
The most comprehensive web-based source of information on Burgundy. Relatively expensive.

WINE FORUMS
A web forum is a virtual space where like-minded people can exchange views. Some also host off-line tasting events, so they are a good way of discovering wine groups in local areas. Some reputable ones are:
• **www.wine-pages.com/ forum**
A Europe-focused forum.
• **fora.erobertparker. com/cgi-bin/ultimatebb.cgi**
Part of Robert Parker's website.
• **www.wldg.com**
Informative and entertaining.
• **www.westcoastwine.net/ forum**
Good general forum.

REFERENCE
www.wine-searcher.com
An excellent way to discover the best prices and stockists of a particular wine. Searches, which are free of charge, can locate retailers all over the world.

www.epicurious.com/run/ winedictionary/home
Brilliant 3,500-entry wine dictionary which is free to use.

LEARNING ABOUT WINE
www.wset.co.uk
The Wine and Spirit Education Trust provides courses and qualifications recognized worldwide.
www.wineeducation.org
Contains the most basic knowledge through to very detailed information, all free of charge.

WINE DIRECTORIES
An excellent way of discovering new wine-related websites, as well as the web addresses of many leading producers:
www.vine2wine.com
www.wineweb.com

REGIONAL SITES
There are many useful websites on specific wine regions:
Argentina
www.argentinewines.com/ing
Basic general information on the country, its regions, and its wines. Some sections, however, are only available in Spanish.
Australia
www.winetitles.com.au/awol
Plenty of information for the interested wine drinker.
Chile
www.winesofchile.org
The official website of Chilean wine's promotional body.

France

www.terroir-france.com
Useful general information on the whole country, as well as links to details of specific regions and recommended books.

www.vinsdalsace.com
Official Alsace site, packed with interesting regional information.

www.medoc-wines.com
Good on the history of Bordeaux, its appellations, and details of individual châteaux.

www.bivb.com
The official site on Burgundy, with useful background information on the region and its wines.

www.burgundyreport.com
American wine enthusiast Bill Nanson's lively, informative tasting notes and reports from Burgundy.

www.champagne.fr
The official Champagne site, with basic information and links to producers.

www.languedoc-wines.com/english
Well-designed, official site on the Languedoc, with excellent links to individual producers in that area.

www.vins-centre-loire.com/en/actualites
Strong on the central Loire.

www.vins-rhone.com
Informative official site on the Rhône Valley with comprehensive details of the area's history and appellations, and links to its numerous producers.

Germany

www.winepage.de
Clear and entertaining site produced by a German wine lover. Excellent features, guides, and links.

www.germanwinesociety.org
Detailed information on Germany and its wines.

Italy

www.winenews.it
An excellent site if you read Italian.

www.italianmade.com
Equally good site on Italian wines.

New Zealand

www.winesofnz.com
Information is quite basic but contains a comprehensive list of New Zea land wineries.

Portugal

www.viniportugal.pt
A little trade-oriented, but there is information on producers and links to other worthwhile sites.

South Africa

www.wine.co.za
Includes useful news, information, and links.

Spain

www.jrnet.com/vino
Entertaining site, covering much more than simply Spanish wine.

USA

www.allamericanwineries.com
An extensive list of US wineries.

www.winecountry.com
The focus is on California, with extensive information on regional news and tourism.

www.oregonwines.com
Excellent on the producers and wines of this region. Also articles, reviews, and wine and food matching advice.

MAGAZINES

Decanter
The most comprehensive UK wine magazine comes out monthly. Excellent columnists, in-depth articles, and reliable buying guide. Not ideal for novices as it assumes a certain amount of reader knowledge. Also has a website (www.decanter.com) with archived articles, harvest reports, and a vintage section.

The World of Fine Wine
Describing itself as the first cultural journal of the wine world, this beautifully produced quarterly magazine from the UK is renowned for its intellectual, scholarly approach, with in-depth features, tastings, and essays by the best writers in the field.

Wine Spectator
The most authoritative wine magazine in the USA, with extensive wine rat ngs, in-depth regional reviews, and top quality columnists. Its 17 issues a year are widely available. Also offers a great website *(www.winespectator.com)*, featuring archived articles and reviews, plus a list of worldwide wineries. Full access requires a subscription but even the free section is excellent.

The Wine Advocate
Although it is a newsletter rather than a magazine, this American magazine is the mouthpiece of wine critic Robert Parker. There are six issues a year.

BOOKS

Hugh Johnson's Pocket Wine Book (Mitchell Beazley)
Incredibly compact considering the volume of information. Perfect to tuck in your pocket.

Parker's Wine Buyer's Guide, **Robert Parker** (Dorling Kindersley)
Comprehensive coverage of all major wine regions from one of the world's top wine critics.

The Sotheby's Wine Encyclopedia, **Tom Stevenson** (Dorling Kindersley)
A formidable work from one of the world's leading wine writers. Clear and well designed, this covers all the major wine regions in considerable detail.

The Oxford Companion to Wine (Oxford University Press)
No other book provides such encyclopedic information on such a wide range of subjects.

The World Atlas of Wine, **Jancis Robinson and Hugh Johnson** (Mitchell Beazley)
Two of the world's best wine writers combine forces in this beautifully illustrated atlas.

Wine Report, **Tom Stevenson** (Dorling Kindersley)
Compact, up-to-the-minute coverage on top wine regions, leading producers, and vintages.

Jancis Robinson's Wine Course (BBC Books)
An informative and highly entertaining read.

General Index

Page numbers in **bold** type refer to main entries.

Acknowledgments

DORLING KINDERSLEY, DEPARTURE LOUNGE, AND SANDS PUBLISHING SOLUTIONS would like to thank the following people, whose contributions and assistance have made the preparation of this book possible.

CONSULTANT
Susan Keevil
Susan Keevil swapped her desk job as editor of *Decanter* magazine for a writing career roving the world's wine regions in 2000, and the last few years have seen plenty of vinous adventure. Back home she writes about these excursions (and more) for *WINE*, *Decanter*, and *Food & Travel* magazines, and has a column in the American magazine *The Wine News*. She was winner of the Lanson Award for Annual Wine Guides, for the *Which? Wine Guide 2003* (awarded May 2003).

CONTRIBUTORS
Geoff Adams (Southeastern Europe)
Geoff Adams is an author, freelance journalist, wine columnist, and competition judge. His articles have been published in *Decanter*, *Harpers Wine & Spirit Weekly*, *Greece Magazine*, and *The Journal*, amongst others. He has also participated in judging at international wine competitions around the world.

Christine Austin (Chile & Argentina)
Christine Austin has been reporting on wine for 20 years through her regular column in the *Yorkshire Post* and through magazines, books, radio, and television. She has travelled extensively to wine regions around the world, and is passionate about the wines of South America.

Richard Baudains (Northeast Italy, Central Italy)
Richard Baudains is a specialist writer on Italian wine. He is a regular contributor to *Decanter* as well as a number of other publications in the USA and Italy. He lives in Gorizia, Italy.

Julie Besonen (New York State)
Julie Besonen is the food editor at *Paper Magazine* in New York City. She also contributes stories on wine, cocktails, and travel to several other publications.

Stephen Brook (Germany, Burgundy, California, pp472–3, pp476–7)
Stephen Brook began his career as an editor in book publishing, and has been writing books on wine, travel, and other subjects since 1982. He is a contributing editor to *Decanter*, and the author of numerous award-winning books on wine such as *The Wines of California* and *Bordeaux: People, Power & Politics*.

Kathleen Buckley (Alsace)
Kathleen Buckley's wine and travel articles have appeared in *Decanter*, *Harpers Wine & Spirit Weekly*, *The San Francisco Chronicle*, and *Wine Business Monthly* among other publications.

Giles Fallowfield (Champagne)
Giles Fallowfield has been writing about champagne for 20 years for a wide range of publications. He was the Lanson Award Champagne Writer of the Year in 2001 and 2003.

Dr Caroline Gilby MW (Central & Eastern Europe. Southeastern Europe)
Caroline Gilby started her wine career as senior buyer for a major UK retail chain, covering Eastern Europe. She is now a freelance writer, lecturer, and independent consultant and she regularly judges at international wine shows.

Richard Jones (Grape Varieties, Czech Republic, Slovakia, Croatia, Other Countries, Reference, Wine Law features pp34–41, pp166–7, pp190–91)
Richard Jones was first bitten by the wine bug in the mid-1990s when he became the Wine Communications

Co-ordinator at Oddbins. He now works as a freelance journalist, researcher, and copywriter specializing in wine and spirits.

Susan Keevil (General Introduction, History & Culture of Wine, Wine Styles) *See above.*

James Lawther MW (Bordeaux, The Rhône Valley, South of France, The Loire Valley, pp48–51, pp54–7)
James Lawther has lived and worked in France for the past 20 years. Based in Bordeaux since 1996, he is a contributing editor to *Decanter*, writes and lectures on wine, and acts as a guide to the vineyards of France.

Konstantinos Lazarakis MW (Greece)
Konstantinos Lazarakis became the first Greek Master of Wine in 2002 and is the holder of a Bollinger Foundation Medal for excellence in wine tasting. His organization Wine & Spirits Professional Consultants runs WSET courses throughout Greece. He is the author of *The Wines of Greece*, and he also writes for a number of trade and lifestyle magazines in Greece and abroad.

Angela Lloyd (South Africa)
Angela Lloyd, an independent wine writer since 1985, contributes to a wide range of South African magazines, newspapers, and journals, as well as recognized international publications. She has an 24-year association with the *John Platter South African Wine Guide* and experience on wine tasting panels.

Giles MacDonogh (Austria, Switzerland, Hungary)
Giles MacDonogh is a regular contributor to the food and drink pages of several UK publications. He has also written books on wine: *Syrah, Grenache & Mourvèdre*, *The Wine & Food of Austria*, *Austria: New Wines from the Old World*, and *Portuguese Table Wines*.

Richard Mayson (Portugal)
Richard Mayson has spent 25 years researching and writing about the wines of Portugal. His books include *Port and the Douro* and *The Wines and Vineyards of Portugal*. Richard contributes to a number of publications, including *Decanter* and the *The World of Fine Wine*, and he lectures at Leiths School of Food and Wine in London.

Michael Palij MW (Northwest Italy, South Italy & the Islands, pp186–93)
Michael Palij is an importer, journalist, and long-standing advocate of all things Italian. A Canadian, he moved to the UK in 1989 and qualified as a Master of Wine in 1995.

Stuart Peskett (Bordeaux, The Rhône Valley, South of France, The Loire Valley, Southeastern Europe, pp48–57)
Stuart Peskett is a freelance journalist who has been working in the wine and spirits trade since 2003. His previous roles include news editor at *Harpers Wine & Spirit Weekly* and acting assistant editor at *Decanter*. He has also written for *Wine & Spirit* and *Drinks International*.

Jeni Port (Australia, New Zealand)
Jeni Port is a Melbourne-based wine writer with *The Age* newspaper and *Winestate* magazine, among other publications. A past president of the Wine Press Club of Victoria, she is also the author of *Choosing Australian Wines* and *Crushed By Women: Women & Wine*.

John Radford (Spain)
John Radford is a freelance writer, broadcaster, lecturer, and wine enthusiast with a special interest in Spain. His book *The New Spain* won four international awards. He also contributes regularly to magazines such as *Decanter* and *Harpers Wine & Spirit Weekly*, and is a regular speaker at wine seminars.

Roger Voss (Alsace)
Roger Voss is the author of *Food & Wine of France*, *The Wines of the Loire, Alsace & the Rhône* and several wine pocketbooks. Based in Bordeaux, France, he is the European editor of the New York-based *Wine Enthusiast Magazine*, a columnist for *Harpers Wine & Spirit Weekly* and a regular contributor to *Decanter*.

Gary Werner (Southern Germany, Eastern Germany, Austria, Switzerland)
Gary Werner is a freelance wine writer and editor based in Britain. His work appears in *Decanter*, *Wine International*, *Harpers Wine & Spirit Weekly*, and *The Drinks Business*. He also contributes to the Wine Intelligence market research consultancy and to the wine website jancisrobinson.com.

Dr Paul White (Pacific Northwest)
Former Oregonian Paul White learned his analytical skills as captain of the Oxford University Blind Wine Tasting Team. Now based in Wellington, New Zealand, he judges wine competitions globally and writes for magazines such as *The World of Fine Wine*, *Decanter*, *Santé*, and *Slow Food*.

David Williams (Grape Varieties, New York State, Other Countries, Reference, pp34–41)
A former editor of *Wine & Spirit* magazine, David Williams is a freelance drinks author who has written for a variety of titles around the world, including *The World of Fine Wine*, *Harpers Wine & Spirit Weekly*, and *Time Out London* magazines, and *The Guardian* newspaper.

AT DORLING KINDERSLEY
Project Editor: Robert Sharman
Designer: Kathryn Wilding
Senior Editor: Gary Werner
Senior Art Editor: Sue Metcalfe-Megginson
Managing Art Editor: Karla Jennings
Senior Managing Cartographer: David Roberts
Managing Editors: Deirdre Headon, Adèle Hayward
Art Director: Peter Luff
DTP Designers: Louise Waller, Julian Dams, Traci Salter
Picture Research: Anna Bedewell
Picture Library: Richard Dabb
Production Controller: Mandy Inness

PROOFREADER
Fiona Wild

INDEXERS
Hilary Bird, Christine Bernstein

CARTOGRAPHY
Dominic Beddow, Simonetta Giori, Sibby Postgate at Draughtsman Ltd (www.magneticnorth.net)

DESIGN & EDITORIAL ASSISTANCE
Bernhard Wolf Koppneyer, Davin Kuntze, Amber Tokeley, Clare Tomlinson

PICTURE RESEARCH
Caroline Blake, Claire Gouldstone, Rita Selvaggio, Bridget Tily, Melanie Watson, Debbie Woska

CARTOGRAPHY
DORLING KINDERSLEY would like to thank the following for their assistance with mapping:
Australian Wine & Brandy Corporation; Berry Brothers & Rudd; Chianti Classico.com; CIVB Bordeaux; Deutsches Weininstitut GmbH; HEPC; Mary Pateras; Michael Cooper (author of *Wine Atlas of New Zealand*); National Vine & Wine Chamber; SAWIS (South Africa Wine Industry & Systems); Stellenbosch tourist office; Vinterra International SA; Wine Industry Association of Western Australia; WOSA (Wines of South Africa); www.winecountry.it. *Sotheby's Wine Encyclopedia* (published by Dorling Kindersley) was used as a reference source for maps of Eastern Europe.

Artworks
Stephen Conlin 29b, 38–9, 40-41; Lee Redmond 38tr, 40tr; Simon Roulstone 22-3, 24-5; Deborah Maizels

Studio Photography
Steve Gorton

SPECIAL ASSISTANCE
DORLING KINDERSLEY would like to thank producers for their assistance, especially in supplying images and labels for the guide. Particular thanks go to The Gay Hussar; Elizabeth Ferguson at Berkmann Wine Cellars; Catherine Borgmeister at Peretti Communications; Philglas & Swiggot, Battersea, London; Oddbins, Clapham, London; and especially Kate Hall at Berry Brothers & Rudd, London.

PICTURE CREDITS
Key: t = top; tl = top left; tlc = top left centre; tc = top centre; tr = top right; cla = centre left above; ca = centre above; cra = centre right above; cl = centre left; c = centre; cr = centre right; clb = centre left below; cb = centre below; crb = centre right below; bl = bottom left; b = bottom; bc = bottom centre; bcl = bottom centre left; br = bottom right.

Every effort has been made to trace the copyright holders and we apologize in advance for any unintentional omissions. We would be pleased to insert the appropriate acknowledgments in any subsequent edition of this publication.

DORLING KINDERSLEY would like to thank the following individuals, companies, and picture libraries for their kind permission to reproduce their photographs:

ADAGP: © Jean Cocteau, Paris and DACS, London 2004 71c; AKG-IMAGES: 14tl, 16tl, 16bl, 18tl, 19bl, Rabatti-Domingie 186b, Erich Lessing 14bl, 14/15c, 15tr, 17tr, 269c; ALAMY: 25, Nick Carding 413 cr, isifa Image Service s.r.o. 406cl, 407br, 408cb, 411, Martin Siepmann 412cl, Swerve 416; ALFRED GRATIEN: 168tl; ANTINORI: 265b, 265c; ANTIVAL: 540cra; ART ARCHIVE, THE: Biblioteque des Arts Decoratifs Gianni Dagli Orti 19cr, Museo Degli Argenti Pitti Palace, Florence Gianni Dagli Orti 16cl, Provinciaal Museum G M Kam Nijmegen Netherlands/Dagli Orti 634t; 635tc; AUSTRALIAN WINE EXPORT COUNCIL, AWEC, ADELAIDE, AUSTRALIA: 20bcl, 26cra, 27tr, 33cr, 35br, 36tr, 36br, 36br, 36bra, 556cb, 557c, 560, 561c, 562br, 564t, 574, 575b, 581bl, 588, 589c, 591tl, 602, 603c, 604b, 607bl, 656t, 662t, 664t.

BADIA DA COLTIBUONO: 258tl, 259bl; BEAULIEU VINEYARDS: 476cl; BELLAVISTA: 202tr; BERINGER BLASS: 558clb; BERINGER: 481tl, 490tc; BINDERER: 632–33; BISOL DESIDERIO & FIGLI: 226c; BIVB/DOMAINE A: 101clb; BOCCADIGABBIA: 239c; BODEGA COLOMÉ: 551br; BODEGAS SALENTEIN: 544t, 550tc; BOUCHARD FINLAYSON: 455tr; BRIDGEMAN ART LIBRARY: Biblioteca Marciana, Venice *The Natural History of Pliny the Elder* (AD 23–79) 15bcr, Museo della Civiltà Romana, Rome 186t,

Museo Diocesano de Solsona, Lerida, Spain Jaime Ferrer (1430–57) 15tcr, The Stapleton Collection after a portrait by Titian, Sarah Countess of Essex 18bl, Private Collection/ Lucien Herve 71br, BYRON: 507clb.

CA DEL BOSCO: 203br; CALITERRA: 542tr; CANOE RIDGE VINEYARD: 511cr; CASTELLO DI VOLPAIA: 259crb; CATENA ZAPATA: 530–31, 535bc; CAVALLERI: 204bl; CEPHAS: Gerry Akehurst 427bl, Jerry Alexander 476br, 478, Kevin Argue 35cr, 37c, Franck Auberson 37tl, Nigel Blythe 36ca, 78tl, 224t, 300t, 347br, 351tl, 352t, 354tr, 356bl, 357b, 391br, Emma Borg 457bl, Fernando Briones 32tl, 294c, Nick Carding 386-387, 410, Andy Christodolo 24, 37bc, 36cl, 215b, 371br, 384bl, 428tr, 536t, 539b, 539tr, 543b, 545bl, 546tl, 547bl, 577tl, 579br, 587bl, 603b, David Copeman 326c, Tony Dickinson 632tr, Jeffery Drewitz 586cla, J Juan Espi 456cl, Bruce Fleming 528–9, Dario Fusaro 190bl, 190cl, 195b, 195c, 206c 237c, Andrew Jefford 422b, Kevin Judd 33tl, 33c, 34br, 34bl, 35c, 35tc, 37bc, 41cr, 159cr, 176, 191cl, 470–71, 472bl, 481cr, 528br, 561b, 563tl, 590cra, 591br, 604cr, 616tr, 617bc, 618t, 628–9, 636cla, M J Kielty 394c, Herbert Lehmann 266clb, 373cr, 374t, 393bl, 396bl, 407tl, Mike Newton 191bl, Char Abu Mansoor 422tr, Diana Mewes 1c, 103bl, John Millwood 435br, R & K Muschenetz 37cr, 479b, 482t, 497cr, 500br, 505bl, Fred R Palmer 521b, Neil Phillips 4tr, 289c, 306bc, Alain Proust 449bl, 462br, 462cl 463bl, 463crb, 463tc, Mick Rock 5tl, 25 (1 & 5), 28c, 29tr, 29tc, 29cl, 32cl, 32tc, 33cl, 33tc, 33tr, 32br, 35cl, 35tr, 35tr, 38bl, 39tc, 39cl, 40tl, 40bl, 40cl, 41tl, 56tr, 56b, 63t, 66br, 75t, 77tr, 79br, 84t, 92t, 93b, 1001tr, 101b, 102t, 108c, 110t, 114t, 115b, 118, 119b, 121br, 121tl, 124bl, 127bl, 129t, 159r, 159 (background), 164, 165b, 170t, 179cr, 184–5, 190bc, 190c, 190tl, 191b, 191c, 191cr, 191tl, 194, 196tl, 197tl, 198t, 200tr, 206t, 207bl, 208tl, 214, 219b, 225bl, 231bl, 238bc, 240c, 240t, 241b, 242tr, 243b 244bl, 254t, 255tr, 256tr, 257bl, 258clb, 258cra, 258crb, 263tc, 269c, 270cb, 271b, 272t, 273bl, 274b, 274tl, 277tr, 230t, 294t, 295b, 302tr, 303br, 304bl, 304t, 307bl, 307cr, 315b, 315cr, 315tl, 317bl, 318tr, 322c, 323cb, 327tr, 328bl, 333br, 334bl, 335tl, 342br, 355b, 358b, 370br, 376tl 388tc, 388bl, 390, 392br, 393tl, 394t, 395bc, 397bc, 398cla, 399tl, 400tr, 403tl, 404t, 423cr, 425tl, 426t, 439bl, 499br, 503tr, 509b, 511tl, 513bl, 515b, 520, 522cla 524t, 528bl, 559br, 578t, 587cr, 630tr, Ian Shaw 34cl, 56c, 74br, 76t, 77bl, 91tl, 109c, 150, 156tl, Ted Stefanski 484b, Peter Stowell 370ca, Mike Taylor 638bl, 639tr, Peter Titmuss 443cr, Stephen Wolfenden 70c; CHAMPAGNE DRAPPIER: 168cr, 173t; CHATEAU ROTHSCHILD: bottle and labels courtesy of Chateau Mouton Rothschild, Pauillac, France, 70–71; CHAMPAGNE JACQUART: 171cr; CHÂTEAU BEAU-SÉJOUR BÉCOT: 80cr; CHÂTEAU DE LA MALTROYE: 91cra; CHÂTEAU DE PIBARNON: 149tl; CHÂTEAU DE STADTBREDIMUS: 630c; CHÂTEAU DE REIGNAC: 87br; CHÂTEAU DUCRU-BEAUCAILLOU: 72cla; CHÂTEAU HAUT BRION: 73tr; CHÂTEAU KSARA: 432cl, 434t; CHÂTEAU LAFITE-ROTHSCHILD: 64br, 68br; CHÂTEAU LA NERTHE: 133tr; CHÂTEAU MARGAUX: 19tl, 65cb; CHÂTEAU MOUTON-ROTHSCHILD: 69bl, CHÂTEAU PALMER: 65t, 73clb; CHÂTEAU PAPE CLÉMENT: 74tl; CHÂTEAU PAVIE MACQUIN: 76c; CHÂTEAU PENIN: 84bl; CHÂTEAU REYNON: 86tc; CHIANTI CLASSICO.COM: 254c; CHURCHILL'S: 338cr; CIVB, BORDEAUX: 59b, 63c, Ph. Roy 85tr; CIVA: 178tl; CLONAKILLA: 585tc; CLOS FOURTET: 81br; CLOUDY BAY: Kevin Judd 612–13, 614ca, 616clb; COLDSTREAM HILLS: 574t; COLTERENZIO: 189tr; CONCHA Y TORO: 543cl; CORBIS: Archivo Iconografico, S.A. *The Sick Bacchus* by Michelangelo Merisi da Caravaggio 10c, Gianni & Tiziana Baldizzone 109cr, 179bc, Morton Beebe 46–7, Bettmann 474–5, 475tl, Jonathan Blair 268, 330cla, Michael Busselle 12bl, 151c, 286–7, Chateaux Margaux/Mr Alfred Danflou 1867 19tl, Elio Col 231tl, 230t, 373tl, Jim Cornfield 323tl, Gianni Dagli Orti 15bl, 17tl, Robert Holmes

38cl, 58, 489br, 586br, Hulton-Deutsch Collection 475tr, Owen Franken 88, 140b, 188b, 199br, David J & Janice L Frent Collection 474tr, Farrell Grehan 378tr, K J Historical 474b, Mimmo Jodice 275cr, Bob Krist 187c, William Manning 34tr, Gail Mooney 128t, 418–19, Fabio Muzzi/Corbis Sygma 236, Pat O'Hara 633bl, Charles O'Rear 2–3, 39br, 108bc, 122t, 124t, 288bl, 472ca, 557br, 556tr, 577cr, Raymond Reuter/Corbis Sygma 21t, Maiman Rick/Corbis Sygma 488crb, Calen Rowell 476tr, Vittoriano Rastelli 253bc, Sylvain Saustier 22, Stapleton Collection 15b, Phil Schermeister 478cl, Vince Streano 252cl, Jim Sugar 485tr, Swim Ink 165c, Underwood & Underwood 474c, Patrick Ward 344–5; CSL (Crown Copyright) 529bl; CULLEN WINES: Frances Andrijich 608tc.

DAMIANITZA: 402tl, 403bc, 405c; D'AMBRA: 271tl; D'ARENBERG: 566br; DE BORTOLI WINES: 575c, 577bc; DELILLE CELLARS: 512t, 516tr; DE TRAFFORD WINES: 5tr; DEUTSCHES WEININSTITUT: Hartmann 359br, 364clb, 369tr, Kämper 359tc; DOMAINE ARMAND ROUSSEAU: 98t; DOMAINE DE LA RECTORIE: 143c; DOMAINE DE LA VOUGERAIE: 99tr; DOMAINE DES COMTES LAFON: 107b; DOMAINE DES LAMBRAYS: 96cb; DOMAINE DU CASTEL: 433br, 437br; DOMAINE DU CHÂTEAU DE CHOREY: 105b; DOMAINE HENRI BOURGEOIS: 163bl; DOMAINE JEAN-FRANÇOIS COCHE-DURY: 106t; DOMAINE MARCEL DEISS: 57cb, 82t; DOMAINE WARDY: 433cr; DOMENICO CLERICO: 207c; DORLING KINDERSLEY: 28tc, 28tl, 44cr, 59c, 66tc, 109bl, 113b, 321br, 323tr, 437ca, 141cr, Shaen Adey 458cb, Max Alexander 89b, 96t, 97b, 102c, 109t, 111tr, 137c, 138cla, 141b, 143b, 146cb, 147bl, 177b, 316t, Philip Enticknap 177c, 180t, 181br, Steve Gorton 175clb, 321br, 329clb, 329crb, 339bc, Paul Harris 336tr, Andrew McKinney 489tl, Ian O'Leary 13tr, 24c, 26bl, 27bl, 28bc, 29cr, 29tl, 30b, 30bl, 30tr, 32bc, 32bl, 32c, 32tr, 42bl, 42br, 42cl, 42tr, 43tl, 44tc, 44cr, 44tl, 45bl, 45tl, 43bl, 89c, 125ca, 402bc, 438cla, 473cb, 608bc, 650tc, 650tr, 651cra, 651tr, 652tcr, 652tl, 655bc, Neil Lukas 169t, Rob Reichenfeld 330tr, Kim Sayer 153tl, 157br, 188c, 307cr, 385tl, Clive Streeter 152bc, 155tc, 322tr, 323bl, 328tr, Linda Whitwam 318bl, 324–5, 326b, 329bl, 329tr, 331tl, 332c, 332t, 337br, 337c, 420c, Peter Wilson 374c, 375tr; DUCKHORN: 491tl; DURIUS ALTO DUERO: 292b.

EDI SIMCIC: courtesy of Edi Simcic 412b; ELLA MILROY: 140t, 142tr, 648tl, 648tlc, 648t, 648r, 648rc; EMILIO MORO: 297cr; ENGLISH WINES GROUP: 631b; ERNEST & JULIO GALLO: 506br; ERRÁZURIZ: 532bl, 540bl; ESTATE BIBLIA CHORA: 421br, 429bl; EVHARIS ESTATE: 430tr; EYRIE VINEYARDS: 515ca.

FABRE MONTMAYOU: 4tl, 35bl, 532tr, 535tl, 549br; FAIRVIEW: 445b, 457tl; FELTON ROAD, CENTRAL OTAGO: 615tl; FÉLIX SOLÍS: 318t; FETZER: 34ca, 35tl, 487bl, 494crb; FONSECA PORTO: 339tr; FORADORI: 223tc; FRANZ PROIDL: 378bl; FREIXENET: 288c, 305tr, 312t.

GETTY IMAGES: Wayne Walton 413tl; GAROFOLI GIOACCHINO: 247br; GIROLAMO DORIGO: 232cr; GIUSEPPE MASCARELLO: 212tl; GLEN CARLOU: 444cla, 446bc, 459tr; GLORIA FERRER: 480br, 493tr; GOLDWATER ESTATE: 622tr; GRGICH HILLS: courtesy of Grigich Hills 417c; GROOTE POST: 447c, 451br, 448t; GROSSET WINES: 559cl, 568tc; GUIGAL: 130br.

HARAS DE PIRQUE: 12tr, 532c, 534tl, 537br, 541tr; HARDY WINE COMPANY: 554bl, 558crb; HERITAGE IMAGE: The British Museum 14cl; HOLT STUDIOS: Nigel Cattlin 25 (3 & 4); HULTON ARCHIVE: 18cbl; HUMBERTO CANALE: 551cra.

ICEX (SPANISH INSTITUTE FOR FOREIGN TRADE): 293tl, 307tl; ILLUMINATI DINO: 251tc; INNISKILLEN: 636cb; INTERLOIRE/FIVAL: Monsieur Gilles d'Auzac, Monsieur Bouvais, Ephémère Tours,

Monsieur Frappier, Monsieur José Saudubois, Monsieur Christian Waiter, Zoom Studios: 28cr, 30tr, 151b,152cla, 154c, 155b, 154t; INTER RHÔNE: Philippe Médard 28br, 28tr, 28cl, Isabelle Desarzens 28bl, 119c, 126c, 127tr, 658tr, Alain Gas 122cr, 123br, 128bl, Alain Maigre 125bl.

JANSZ: 6ᵀ1tr; JEAN-MARC BROCARD: 55bc, 95tc; JIM BARRY WINES: 568bl; JORDAN WINES: 460bl; JOSKO GRAVNER: 232bc; © JUDITH MILLER/DK/CHRISTOPHER SYKES ANTIQUES: 474tl; 620 (clockwise from tr) Drewatt Neate, Donnington Priory Salesrooms, Below stairs of Hungerford, Donnington Priory Salesrooms, Christopher Sykes Antiques, Below stairs of Hungerford, Below stairs of Hungerford; 621 (clockwise from tr) Christopher Sykes Antiques, Christopher Sykes Antiques, Drewatt Neate, Donnington Priory Salesrooms, Christopher Sykes Antiques, Drewatt Neate, Donnington Priory Salesrooms, Christopher Sykes Antiques.

KANONKOP: 466tc; KANTE: 233tc; KAVAKLIDERE: 433tl; KENWOOD: 492ca; KLEIN CONSTANTIA ESTATE: 440–41, 456bc; KLOOVENBURG: 450tl; KUMEU RIVER WINES: 615br.

LA MONDOTTE: 62bl; LA RIOJA ALTA: 301b, 306cl; LA STOPPA: 201bl; LE DÔME: 83tc; LEEUWIN ESTATE: 652tcl, 652tcr; MARTIN FARQUHARSON: 640–41; LEÓN BEYER: 55tr; LE VIGNE DI ZAMÒ: 217ca; LIVIO FELLUGA: 231cr; LIVON: 234tl; LOUIS JADOT: 100tl; LUCIANO SANDRONE: 212bc.

MACULAN: 227tl; MARCHESI DE' FRESCOBALDI: 237b; MARJAN SIMCIC: courtesy of Marjan Simcic 415; MARQUÉS DE RISCAL: 297br, 302bc, 306tc; MARTÍN CÓDAX: 296tl; MARY EVANS PICTURE LIBRARY: 16–17, 19tr, 19ct, 19br, 20tr, 48c, 48bl (Explorer Archives), 475br; Douglas McCarthy 17br; MASCIARELLI: 239tl, 245t, 251br; MASI: 227br, 229b, 229cl; MATTEO CORREGGIA: 213tr; MCGUIGAN SIMEON WINES: 558c, 582crb, 587tl; MCWILLIAM'S MOUNT PLEASANT WINES: 576tl; MEERLUST ESTATE: 466crb; MGM: The Kobal Collection 71cl; MOLETTIERI: 279tr; MONTANA WINES: 614b; MORIS FARMS: 262cl; MOSS WOOD WINERY: 609bl; MOUNT LANGI GHIRAN WINES: 593bl; MOUTON CADET: 85bl.

NATIONAL ARCHIVES OF SOUTH AFRICA: 18–19c; NATIONAL LIBRARY OF AUSTRALIA: Wolfgang Sievers/DACS, London 2004 571b; NATIONAL MARITIME MUSEUM, LONDON: 554c; NAVARRO: 480cl, 484tl; NECTARIS: 220bc; NEIL ELLIS WINES: 467tr; New York Wine & Grape Foundation/Randall Tagg Photography: 522cb, 523cr, 525br; NEW ZEALAND WINEGROWERS: Gilbert Van Reenen 627tr; NEUDORF VINEYARDS: 619br; NONINO: 219tr; NYETIMBER VINEYARD: 631ca; OCHOA VIÑEDOS Y BODEGA – OLITE – NAVARRA – ESPAÑA: 310tl; NOVOSTI PHOTO LIBRARY: 632bc.

ORLANDO WYNDHAM: 558bl, 584tl, 598tl, 599ca.

PHOTOGRAPHERS DIRECT: Geophotos 406b, Ladi Kirn 414, Sovfoto 391t, 407c, Petrs Varc 409bl, David Wooton Photography 413b; PANTHER CREEK CELLARS: 35tl, 41br, 501tr, 10–11b, 508, 509c; PAPANTONIS WINERY: 426c; PATRICIA HARBOTTLE: 634bcl, 634bl; PAUL CLUVER: 447tl, 453crb; PONZI VINEYARDS: 514cb; PRAHOVA VALLEY: 400cb, 401br. PETER LEHMANN: 562c; PICARDY: 610tr; PHOTO SCALA, FLORENCE: 14b, Works of Mercy: Sheltering

Pilgrims detail, San Martino dei Buononimi, Ghirlandaio Domenico (school) 8–9; PHOTOS 12.COM: Keystone Pressdienst 20tl, 20b, Oasis, Bibliothèque de L'Arsenal/Snark Archives 17cr, ARJ/Musee de Cluny 16bl; PINOTAGE ASSOCIATION: 451tc; PIPER-HEIDSIECK: 168bl; PIPERS BROOK VINEYARD: 589b, 595tr, 601bl; PIQUERAS: 314cla, 320bl; PISANO: 637tr; PRODUTTORI COLTERENZIO: 221tr; PRODUTTORI SAN MICHELE APPIANO: 217tl.

QUADY WINERY: 478cla, 489tr; QUINTA DE AVALEDA – VINHO VERDE: 331cr, 338tc.

RECAS WINERY: 400c; REX FEATURES/ROGER VIOLLET: 70cl, 528tl, 528c; RIVERA: 277c; ROBERT MONDAVI: 483tr, 488bl; ROCCA DI MONTEGROSSI: 253tl; ROMANO DAL FORNO: 228tl; ROOTSTOCK: Hendrik Holler 20–21c, 21br, 50tl, 57tr, 90cl, 108cr, 179cb; ROYAL BOTANIC GARDEN, KEW: Le phylloxera, moyens propsoespuor le combattre, etat actuel de la question by P. Mouillefert, published Paris, G Masson, 1879 529t; RUINART: 54tr, 175br; RUPERT & ROTHSCHILD VIGNERONS: 464br.

SADIE FAMILY WINES: 451cl; SCIENCE PHOTO LIBRARY: Alfred Pasieka: 528tr; SCOTCHMANS HILL: 590bl; SEÑA: 536c; SHAW & SMITH: 21tl, 563bl, 566ca, 572tl; SIMONSIG: 459b; SOPEXA/CIVCP/FRANÇOIS MILLO: 49c, 136, 137b, 139tl, 139bl, 146t, 646t, 655br; 660tl: SOUTHCORP WINES: 13b, 567tl, 571clb, 573crb, 596cl, 28t; SPRINGFIELD ESTATE: 446tl, 452t, 454tr; STAG'S LEAP WINE CELLAR: 477br, 21tc; STEENBERG VINEYARDS: 461bl, 468bl; STERLING VINEYARDS: 488tl, 489clb; STIMSON LANE VINEYARDS & ESTATES: 516bc; STONIER WINES: 594bl; SULA: 638tr; SUNDAY TIMES, SOUTH AFRICA: Ruvan Boshoff 444cb.

TABLAS CREEK VINEYARD: 501ca; TAHBILK WINES: 597tr; TANNERS WINES: 603br; TEDESCHI: 228bl; TE MATA ESTATE: 624cr; TENUTA SAN LEONARDO: 215c, 217br, 218t; TENUTE SILVIO NARDI: 267clb; TORRES: 313b, 313c; TSANTALI: 423tr, 425cr, 429tc.

V&A IMAGES: 634c row, 634bc, 635tl, 635tr; VERBAND DEUTSCHER PRÄDIKATSWEINGÜTER: 348bc; VERGELEGEN: 442b, 445tr, 462tr, 469cl, 469b, 469clb; VIEUX CHÂTEAU CERTAN: 83br; VILLIERA WINES: 468tc; VINICOLA AURORA: 636tr; VINTNERS COMPANY, LONDON: 17bl; VOYAGER ESTATE (WA) PTY LTD: 11tr, 606t, 610clb.

W & J GRAHAM'S PORT & CO: 29c, 328cl, 335bc, 341tr; WEINGUT CHRISTMANN: 366tc; WEINGUT DR LOOSEN: Robin Head 360cra; WEIN AUS ÖSTERREICH: Südoststeiermark/Kapfenstein, © ÖWM, Faber 377b; WEINGUT ERICH & WALTER POLZ: 383br; WEINGUT FAMILIE NIGL: 379tr; WEINGUT GEHEMER RAT DR VON BASSERMANN-JORDAN: 346c; WEINGUT GEORG BREUER: 351br, 355c; WEINGUT MEYER-NÄKEL: 368br, 362tl; WEINGUT PETER JAKOB KÜHN: 364tr; WEINGUT PRIELER: 372ca; WEINGUT REICHSGRAF VON KESSELSTAFF: 346b; WEINGUT REICHSRAT VON BUHL: 367crb; WEINGUT REINHOLD HAART: 353bl; WEINGUT WIENINGER: 381tl; WEINGUT WITTMANN: 357ca; WEINLAUBENHOF KRACHER: 383tr; WELGEMEEND ESTATE: 465br, 458t; WOLF BLASS WINERY: 552–3.

YALUMBA: 559cr, 565br; YARRA YERING: 600cl.

All other images © Dorling Kindersley.
For further information see www.dkimages.com

VINTAGE CHART

VINTAGE CHARTS SHOULD BE used as a guide to the weather conditions in a particular region, in a given year. All vintages are rated out of 5, with '5' as outstanding and '1' as poor. In every vintage there will be good and bad wines made, but a '5' vintage will produce more successful bottles than a '1'. In regions associated with full-bodied reds, such as Bordeaux, the higher-rated vintages will normally require longer periods of maturation in bottle before they are ready to drink. Thus a youthful vintage graded '2' may be more enjoyable to open than a freshly bottled '4'. Also, it is worth remembering that great producers will generally make enjoyable wines whatever the weather conditions. *See also Storing Wine, p646.*

	VINTAGE	2008	2007	2006	2005	2004	2003	2002	2001	2000	19..
FRANCE	Bordeaux – Left Bank	2	3	4	5	4	3	4	4	5	4
	Bordeaux – Right Bank	3	3	4	5	4	3	3	4	5	4
	Bordeaux – Sauternes	3	5	3	5	3	5	4	5	3	4
	Burgundy – red	3	3	4	5	3	2	5	4	3	5
	Burgundy – white	4	4	4	4	3	2	5	3	4	4
	Northern Rhône	3	4	5	4	4	4	2	4	5	5
	Southern Rhône	3	5	4	5	4	4	1	4	5	5
	South of France	4	4	5	5	4	4	3	5	4	3
	Loire Valley	4	4	4	5	4	4	4	4	3	2
	Champagne	3	3	4	3	4	2	5	1	3	5
	Alsace	4	4	2	5	4	3	4	5	5	5
ITALY	Northern Italy	4	4	4	2	4	3	2	4	5	5
	Tuscany	4	4	5	2	4	3	2	4	4	5
	Spain – Rioja	4	3	3	4	4	4	4	4	5	2	4
	Portugal – Port	-	5	-	-	-	3	-	-	5	
	Germany	4	5	4	5	4	3	4	5	3	4
	South Africa	4	4	4	3	4	4	3	4	4	4
US	California	3	4	3	4	4	3	4	5	3	4
	Pacific Northwest	4	3	4	4	4	3	3	4	4	5
	New York State	4	4	3	4	4	3	5	5	2	4
	Australia	4	3	4	5	4	4	5	4	3	3
	New Zealand	3	4	5	4	3	3	4	4	4	4